LAROUSSE

DIZIONARIO TASCABILE

ITALIANO INGLESE

INGLESE ITALIANO

Realizzato da / Produced by

LAROUSSE

21, rue du Montparnasse
75283 Paris Cedex 06, France

ISBN 2-03-420715-7
Distribuzione/Sales : Larousse Kingfisher Chambers Inc., New York
Library of Congress Catalog Card Number
98-75563

LAROUSSE

POCKET DICTIONARY

ITALIAN ENGLISH

ENGLISH ITALIAN

TRADEMARKS

Words considered to be trademarks have been designated in this dictionary by the symbol ®. However, neither the presence nor the absence of such designation should be regarded as affecting the legal status of any trademark.

MARCHI REGISTRATI

Le parole considerate marchi registrati sono contrassegnate in questo dizionario con il simbolo ®. In ogni caso, né la presenza né l'assenza di tale simbolo implica alcuna valutazione del reale stato giuridico di un marchio.

AL LETTORE

Il dizionario POCKET Larousse è stato realizzato per rispondere alle esigenze di chi viaggia o comincia a studiare l'inglese.

Con più di 32 000 parole ed espressioni e oltre 45 000 traduzioni, questo nuovo dizionario comprende non solo la terminologia generale di base, ma anche molte espressioni che permettono di decifrare cartelli, segnali stradali e menu.

Le divisioni semantiche sono accuratamente indicate e la consultazione delle voci complesse di uso più frequente è facilitata dai numerosi esempi e dalla presentazione chiara ed efficace.

Completo e allo stesso tempo praticissimo, questo dizionario si rivelerà un indispensabile compagno di studio e di viaggio. "Good luck", e non esitate ad inviarci i vostri suggerimenti.

L'EDITORE

TO OUR READERS

The Larousse POCKET dictionary has been designed with beginners and travelers in mind.

With over 32,000 references and 45,000 translations, this new dictionary gives thorough coverage of general vocabulary plus extensive treatment of the language found on street signs and menus.

Clear sense markers are provided throughout, while special emphasis has been placed on basic words, with many examples of usage and a particularly user-friendly layout.

Easy to use and comprehensive, this handy book packs a lot of wordpower for users at school, at home and on the move. "Buona fortuna", and don't hesitate to send us your comments.

THE PUBLISHER

ABBREVIATIONS — ABBREVIAZIONI

abbreviation	*abbr*	abbreviazione
adjective	*adj*	aggettivo
adverb	*adv*	avverbio
adjective	*agg*	aggettivo
American English	*Am*	inglese americano
anatomy	ANAT	anatomia
article	*art*	articolo
auxiliary	*aus*	ausiliare
automobile, cars	AUT(O)	automobile
auxiliary	*aux*	ausiliare
adverb	*avv*	avverbio
British English	*Br*	inglese britannico
commerce, business	COMM	commercio
comparative	*compar*	comparativo
computers	COMPUT	informatica
conjunction	*conj/cong*	congiunzione
continuous	*cont*	forma progressiva
culinary, cooking	CULIN	cucina, culinaria
before – *dav s* indicates that the translation is always used directly before the noun which it modifies	*dav*	davanti a – *dav s* indica che la traduzione viene sempre usata davanti al sostantivo del quale è attributo.
juridical, legal	DIR	diritto
exclamation	*excl/esclam*	esclamazione
feminine	*f*	femminile
informal	*fam*	familiare
figurative	*fig*	figurato
finance, financial	FIN	finanza
formal	*fml/form*	formale
inseparable – shows that a phrasal verb is 'fused', i.e. inseparable, e.g. **look after** where the object cannot come between the verb and the particle, e.g. *I looked after him* but not **I looked him after*	*fus*	non separabile – indica che un 'phrasal verb' (verbo + preposizione o avverbio) non può essere separato dalla sua particella. Ad esempio, con **look after**, il complemento oggetto non può essere frapposto al verbo e alla preposizione; si dice cioè *I looked after him* ma non si può dire **I looked him after*
generally	*gen*	generalmente
geography	GEOG	geografia
gerund	*ger*	gerundio
grammar	GRAMM	grammatica
informal	*inf*	familiare
computers	INFORM	informatica
interrogative	*interr*	interrogativo
invariable	*inv*	invariabile

juridical, legal	JUR	diritto
masculine	*m*	maschile
mathematics	MAT(H)	matematica
medicine	MED	medicina
military	MIL	militare
music	MUS	musica
noun	*n*	sostantivo
nautical, maritime	NAUT	nautica
numeral	*num*	numerale
oneself	*o.s.*	
pejorative	*pej*	spregiativo
plural	*pl*	plurale
politics	POL	politica
past participle	*pp*	participio passato
preposition	*prep*	preposizione
pronoun	*pron*	pronome
past tense	*pt*	passato
	qc	qualcosa
	qn	qualcuno
registered trademark	®	marchio registrato
religion	RELIG	religione
noun	*s*	sostantivo
someone, somebody	*sb*	
school	SCH/SCOL	scuola
Scottish English	*Scot*	scozzese
separable	*sep*	separabile
– shows that a phrasal verb is separable, e.g. **let in**, **help out** where the object can come between the verb and the particle, e.g. *I let her in, he helped me out*		– indica che un 'phrasal verb' (verbo + preposizione o avverbio) può essere separato dalla sua particella. Ad esempio **let in**, **help out**, per i quali il complemento oggetto si situa tra il verbo e la particella: *I let her in, he helped me out*
singular	*sg*	singolare
subject	*sog*	soggetto
pejorative	*spreg*	spregiativo
something	*sthg*	
subject	*subj*	soggetto
superlative	*superl*	superlativo
technology	TECH/TECNOL	tecnica, tecnologia
verb	*v/vb*	verbo
intransitive verb	*vi*	verbo intransitivo
impersonal verb	*v impers*	verbo impersonale
vulgar	*volg*	volgare
reflexive verb	*vr*	verbo riflessivo
transitive verb	*vt*	verbo transitivo
vulgar	*vulg*	volgare
cultural equivalent	≃	equivalenza culturale

PHONETIC TRANSCRIPTION — TRASCRIZIONE FONETICA

English vowels

[ɪ]	pit, big, rid
[e]	pet, tend
[æ]	pat, bag, mad
[ʌ]	run, cut
[ɒ]	pot, log
[ʊ]	put, full
[ə]	mother, suppose
[iː]	bean, weed
[ɑː]	barn, car, laugh
[ɔː]	born, lawn
[uː]	loop, loose
[ɜː]	burn, learn, bird

Vocali italiane

[a]	pane, casa
[e]	verde, entrare
[ɛ]	letto, pezzo
[i]	vino, isola
[o]	monte, pozzo
[ɔ]	corpo, sciocco
[u]	una, cultura

English diphthongs

[eɪ]	bay, late, great
[aɪ]	buy, light, aisle
[ɔɪ]	boy, foil
[əʊ]	no, road, blow
[aʊ]	now, shout, town
[ɪə]	peer, fierce, idea
[eə]	pair, bear, share
[ʊə]	poor, sure, tour

Semi-vowels — Semivocali

Semi-vowels		Semivocali
you, spaniel	[j]	ieri, viola
wet, why, twin	[w]	fuori, guasto

Consonants — Consonanti

Consonants		Consonanti
pop, people	[p]	porta, sapore
bottle, bib	[b]	barca, libro
train, tip	[t]	torre, patata
dog, did	[d]	dare,odore
come, kitchen	[k]	cane, chiesa
gag, great	[g]	gara, ghiro
chain, wretched	[tʃ]	cena, ciao
jet, fridge	[dʒ]	gente, gioco
fib, physical	[f]	fine, afa
vine, livid	[v]	vero, ovvio
think, fifth	[θ]	
this, with	[ð]	
seal, peace	[s]	stella, casa
zip, his	[z]	sdraio, rosa
sheep, machine	[ʃ]	scimmia, ascia
usual, measure	[ʒ]	
how, perhaps	[h]	
metal, comb	[m]	mamma, amico
night, dinner	[n]	notte, anno
sung, parking	[ŋ]	
	[ɲ]	gnocchi, ogni
little, help	[l]	lana, pollo
	[ʎ]	gli, figlio
right, carry	[r]	re, dorato

The symbol [ˈ] precedes a syllable carrying primary stress and the symbol [ˌ] precedes a syllable carrying secondary stress.

I simboli [ˈ] e [ˌ] indicano rispettivamente un accento primario e uno secondario nella sillaba seguente.

The symbol [ʳ] in English phonetics indicates that the final "r" is pronounced only when followed by a word beginning with a vowel. Note that it is nearly always pronounced in American English.

Il simbolo [ʳ] nella trascrizione fonetica dell'inglese indica che la «r» in fine di parola viene pronunciata soltanto se seguita da una parola che comincia per vocale. Da notare che nell' inglese americano la «r» viene quasi sempre pronunciata.

The position of the tonic stress in Italian is indicated by a dot immediately beneath the accented vowel on Italian headwords (**cạmera, valịgia**). No dot is given on those words which end in an accented vowel, as Italian spelling allows for a written accent in these cases (**città, perché**). Full phonetics have been provided for words of foreign origin which do not follow Italian pronunciation rules (**cracker** [ˈkrɛker], **brioche** [briˈɔʃ]).

L'accento nelle voci italiane è segnalato da un punto sotto la vocale accentata (**cạmera, valịgia**), con l'eccezione delle parole con l'accento sull'ultima sillaba, per le quali l'ortografia italiana prevede l'accento grafico (**città, perché**). Le parole di origine straniera sono seguite dalla trascrizione fonetica nei casi in cui la pronuncia generalmente adottata non rispetta le regole fonetiche dell'italiano (**cracker** [ˈkrɛker], **brioche** [briˈɔʃ]).

English Compounds

A compound is a word or expression which has a single meaning but is made up of more than one word, e.g. **point of view, kiss of life, virtual reality** and **West Indies.** It is a feature of this dictionary that English compounds appear in the A–Z list in strict alphabetical order. The compound **blood test** will therefore come after **bloodshot** which itself follows **blood pressure**.

Composti Inglesi

In inglese si definiscono composti quelle espressioni che, pur essendo formate da più di una parola, costituiscono un'unica unità di significato, come ad es. **point of view, kiss of life, virtual reality** e **West Indies**. In questo dizionario i composti inglesi seguono l'ordine alfabetico generale. Il composto **blood test** figura perciò dopo **bloodshot** che, a sua volta, segue **blood pressure**.

ITALIAN VERBS

Key: *pr ind* = presente indicativo, *imperf* = imperfetto, *fut* = futuro, *cond* = condizionale, *pr cong* = presente congiuntivo, *imperat* = imperativo, *ger* = gerundio, *pp* = participio passato

AMARE: *pr ind* amo, ami, ama, amiamo, amate, amano, *imperf* amavo, amavi, amava, amavamo, amavate, amavano, *fut* amerò, amerai, amerà, ameremo, amerete, ameranno, *cond* amerei, ameresti, amerebbe, ameremmo, amereste, amerebbero, *pr cong* ami, ami, ami, amiamo, amiate, amino, *imperat* ama, ami, amate, *ger* amando, *pp* amato
andare: *pr ind* vado, vai, va, andiamo, andate, vanno, *fut* andrò, *cond* andrei, *pr cong* vada, vada, vada, andiamo, andiate, vadano, *imperat* va', vada, andate, *ger* andando, *pp* andato
aprire: *pr ind* apro, *pr cong* apra, *pp* aperto
avere: *pr ind* ho, hai, ha, abbiamo, avete, hanno, *imperf* avevo, *fut* avrò, *cond* avrei, *pr cong* abbia, *imperat* abbi, abbia, abbiate, *ger* avendo, *pp* avuto
bere: *pr ind* bevo, *imperf* bevevo, *fut* berrò, *cond* berrei, *pr cong* beva, *imperat* bevi, beva, bevete, *ger* bevendo, *pp* bevuto
cadere: *fut* cadrò
correre: *pp* corso
cuocere: *pr ind* cuocio, cuoci, cuoce, cuociamo, cuocete, cuociono, *pp* cotto
dare: *pr ind* do, dai, dà, diamo, date, danno, *fut* darò, *pr cong* dia, *imperat* da', dia, date
dire: *pr ind* dico, dici, dice, diciamo, dite, dicono, *imperf* dicevo, *fut* dirò, *pr cong* dica, dica, dica, diciamo, diciate, dicano, *imperat* di', dica, dite, *ger* dicendo, *pp* detto
dovere: *pr ind* devo, devi, deve, dobbiamo, dovete, devono, *fut* dovrò, *cond* dovrei, *pr cong* deva, deva, deva, dobbiamo, dobbiate, devano
essere: *pr ind* sono, sei, è, siamo, siete, sono, *imperf* ero, eri, era, eravamo, eravate, erano, *fut* sarò, *cond* sarei, *pr cong* sia, *imperat* sii, sia, siate, *ger* essendo, *pp* stato
fare: *pr ind* faccio, fai, fa, facciamo, fate, fanno, *imperf* facevo, *pr cong* faccia, *imperat* fai, faccia, fate, *ger* facendo, *pp* fatto
FINIRE: *pr ind* finisco, finisci, finisce, finiamo, finite, finiscono, *imperf* finivo, finivi, finiva, finivamo, finivate, finivano, *fut* finirò, finirai, finirà, finiremo, finirete, finiranno, *cond* finirei, finiresti, finirebbe, finiremmo, finireste, finirebbero, *pr cong* finisca, finisca, finisca, finiamo, finiate, finiscano, *imperat* finisci, finisca, finite, *ger* finendo, *pp* finito
giungere: *pp* giunto
leggere: *pp* letto
mettere: *pp* messo
morire: *pr ind* muoio, muori, muore, moriamo, morite, muoiono, *fut* morirò, *pr cong* muoia, *imperat* muori, muoia, morite, *pp* morto
muovere: *pp* mosso
nascere: *pp* nato
piacere: *pr ind* piaccio, piaci, piace, piacciamo, piacete, piacciono, *pr cong* piaccia, *pp* piaciuto

porre: *pr ind* pongo, poni, pone, poniamo, ponete, pongono, *imperf* ponevo, *fut* porrò, *cond* porrei, *pr cong* ponga, *imperat* poni, ponga, ponete, *ger* ponendo, *pp* posto
potere: *pr ind* posso, puoi, può, possiamo, potete, possono, *fut* potrò, *pr cong* possa
prendere: *pp* preso
ridurre: *pr ind* riduco, *imperf* riducevo, *fut* ridurrò, *pr cong* riduca, *ger* riducendo, *pp* ridotto
riempire: *pr ind* riempio, riempi, riempie, riempiamo, riempite, riempiono, *ger* riempiendo
rimanere: *pr ind* rimango, rimani, rimane, rimaniamo, rimanete, rimangono, *fut* rimarrò, *pr cong* rimanga, *pp* rimasto
rispondere: *pp* risposto
salire: *pr ind* salgo, sali, sale, saliamo, salite, salgono, *pr cong* salga
sapere: *pr ind* so, sai, sa, sappiamo, sapete, sanno, *fut* saprò, *pr cong* sappia, *imperat* sappi, sappia, sappiate
scegliere: *pr ind* scelgo, scegli, sceglie, scegliamo, scegliete, scelgono, *pr cong* scelga, *imperat* scegli, scelga, scegliete, *pp* scelto
sciogliere: *pr ind* sciolgo, sciogli, scioglie, sciogliamo, sciogliete, sciolgono, *pr cong* sciolga, *imperat* sciogli, sciolga, sciogliete, *pp* sciolto
scrivere: *pp* scritto
sedere: *pr ind* siedo, siedi, siede, sediamo, sedete, siedono, *pr cong* sieda
SERVIRE: *pr ind* servo, servi, serve, serviamo, servite, servono, *imperf* servivo, servivi, serviva, servivamo, servivate, servivano, *fut* servirò, servirai, servirà, serviremo, servirete, serviranno, *cond* servirei, serviresti, servirebbe, serviremmo, servireste, servirebbero, *pr cong* serva, serva, serva, serviamo, serviate, servano, *imperat* servi, serva, servite, *ger* servendo, *pp* servito
spegnere: *pr ind* spengo, spegni, spegne, spegniamo, spegnete, spengono, *pr cong* spenga, *pp* spento
stare: *pr ind* sto, stai, sta, stiamo, state, stanno, *fut* starò, *pr cong* stia, *imperat* sta, stia, state, *pp* stato
tacere: *pr ind* taccio, taci, tace, tacciamo, tacete, tacciono, *pr cong* taccia, *pp* taciuto
TEMERE: *pr ind* temo, temi, teme, temiamo, temete, temono, *imperf* temevo, temevi, temeva, temevamo, temevate, temevano, *fut* temerò, temerai, temerà, temeremo, temerete, temeranno, *cond* temerei, temeresti, temerebbe, temeremmo, temereste, temerebbero, *pr cong* tema, tema, tema, temiamo, temiate, temano, *imperat* temi, tema, temete, *ger* temendo, *pp* temuto
tenere: *pr ind* tengo, tieni, tiene, teniamo, tenete, tengono, *fut* terrò, *pr cong* tenga
togliere: *pr ind* tolgo, togli, toglie, togliamo, togliete, tolgono, *pr cong* tolga, *imperat* togli, tolga, togliete, *pp* tolto
trarre: *pr ind* traggo, trai, trae, traiamo, traete, traggono, *fut* trarrò, *pr cong* tragga, *imperat* trai, tragga, traete, *ger* traendo, *pp* tratto
uscire: *pr ind* esco, esci, esce, usciamo, uscite, escono, *pr cong* esca
vedere: *fut* vedrò, *pp* visto
venire: *pr ind* vengo, vieni, viene, veniamo, venite, vengono, *fut* verrò, *pr cong* venga, *pp* venuto
vivere: *pp* vissuto
volere: *pr ind* voglio, vuoi, vuole, vogliamo, volete, vogliono, *fut* vorrò, *cond* vorrei, *pr cong* voglia

Verbi Irregolari Inglesi

Infinitive	Past Tense	Past Participle
arise	arose	arisen
awake	awoke	awoken
be	was/ were	been
bear	bore	born(e)
beat	beat	beaten
begin	began	begun
bend	bent	bent
bet	bet /betted	bet /betted
bid	bid	bid
bind	bound	bound
bite	bit	bitten
bleed	bled	bled
blow	blew	blown
break	broke	broken
breed	bred	bred
bring	brought	brought
build	built	built
burn	burnt /burned	burnt /burned
burst	burst	burst
buy	bought	bought
can	could	–
cast	cast	cast
catch	caught	caught
choose	chose	chosen
come	came	come
cost	cost	cost
creep	crept	crept
cut	cut	cut
deal	dealt	dealt
dig	dug	dug
do	did	done
draw	drew	drawn
dream	dreamed /dreamt	dreamed /dreamt
drink	drank	drunk
drive	drove	driven
eat	ate	eaten
fall	fell	fallen
feed	fed	fed
feel	felt	felt
fight	fought	fought
find	found	found
fling	flung	flung
fly	flew	flown
forget	forgot	forgotten
freeze	froze	frozen
get	got	got (Am gotten)
give	gave	given
go	went	gone
grind	ground	ground
grow	grew	grown

Infinitive	Past Tense	Past Participle
hang	hung /hanged	hung /hanged
have	had	had
hear	heard	heard
hide	hid	hidden
hit	hit	hit
hold	held	held
hurt	hurt	hurt
keep	kept	kept
kneel	knelt /kneeled	knelt /kneeled
know	knew	known
lay	laid	laid
lead	led	led
lean	leant /leaned	leant /leaned
leap	leapt /leaped	leapt /leaped
learn	learnt /learned	learnt /learned
leave	left	left
lend	lent	lent
let	let	let
lie	lay	lain
light	lit /lighted	lit /lighted
lose	lost	lost
make	made	made
may	might	–
mean	meant	meant
meet	met	met
mow	mowed	mown /mowed
pay	paid	paid
put	put	put
quit	quit /quitted	quit /quitted
read	read	read
rid	rid	rid
ride	rode	ridden
ring	rang	rung
rise	rose	risen
run	ran	run
saw	sawed	sawn
say	said	said
see	saw	seen
seek	sought	sought
sell	sold	sold
send	sent	sent
set	set	set
shake	shook	shaken
shall	should	–
shed	shed	shed
shine	shone	shone
shoot	shot	shot
show	showed	shown
shrink	shrank	shrunk

Infinitive	Past Tense	Past Participle
shut	shut	shut
sing	sang	sung
sink	sank	sunk
sit	sat	sat
sleep	slept	slept
slide	slid	slid
sling	slung	slung
smell	smelt /smelled	smelt /smelled
sow	sowed	sown /sowed
speak	spoke	spoken
speed	sped /speeded	sped /speeded
spell	spelt /spelled	spelt /spelled
spend	spent	spent
spill	spilt /spilled	spilt /spilled
spin	spun	spun
spit	spat	spat
split	split	split
spoil	spoiled /spoilt	spoiled /spoilt
spread	spread	spread
spring	sprang	sprung
stand	stood	stood
steal	stole	stolen
stick	stuck	stuck
sting	stung	stung
stink	stank	stunk
strike	struck	struck /stricken
swear	swore	sworn
sweep	swept	swept
swell	swelled	swollen /swelled
swim	swam	swum
swing	swung	swung
take	took	taken
teach	taught	taught
tear	tore	torn
tell	told	told
think	thought	thought
throw	threw	thrown
tread	trod	trodden
wake	woke /waked	woken /waked
wear	wore	worn
weave	wove /weaved	woven /weaved
weep	wept	wept
win	won	won
wind	wound	wound
wring	wrung	wrung
write	wrote	written

ITALIANO-INGLESE
ITALIAN-ENGLISH

a (**ad** + *vocale*) *prep* **1.** *(complemento di termine)* to; **dare qc a qn** to give sthg to sb, to give sb sthg; **chiedere qc a qn** to ask sb sthg.
2. *(stato in luogo)* at; **abito a Torino** I live in Turin; **stiamo a casa** let's stay (at) home; **la piscina è a due chilometri da qui** the swimming pool is two kilometres from here.
3. *(moto a luogo)* to; **andiamo a letto** let's go to bed; **torno a Roma** I'm going back to Rome; **mi porti allo stadio?** can you take me to the stadium?
4. *(temporale)* at; **c'è un volo alle 8.30** there's a flight at 8.30; **a domani!** see you tomorrow!; **al mattino** in the morning; **alla sera** in the evening.
5. *(modo, mezzo)*: **alla milanese** in the Milanese style, the Milanese way; **riscaldamento a gas** gas heating; **a piedi** on foot; **vestire alla moda** to dress fashionably; **scrivere a matita** to write in pencil.
6. *(con prezzi)* at; **comprare qc a metà prezzo** to buy sthg half-price.
7. *(per caratteristica)*: **camicia a maniche corte** short-sleeved shirt; **finestra a doppi vetri** double-glazed window.
8. *(per rapporto)* per, a; **50 chilometri all'ora** 50 kilometres per o an hour; **pagato a ore** paid by the hour.

A *abbr* = **autostrada**.

abbacchio *sm* spring lamb; ~ **alla romana** *lamb cooked slowly with white wine or vinegar, rosemary, anchovies and garlic.*

abbaglianti *smpl*: **accendere gli ~** to put one's headlights on full beam *(Br)* o high beam *(Am)*.

abbagliare *vt (accecare)* to dazzle.

abbaiare *vi* to bark.

abbandonare *vt (persona, luogo)* to abandon; *(ricerche)* to abandon, to give up.

abbandono *sm (di persona, luogo)* neglect; *(rinuncia)* abandonment.

abbassare *vt* to lower; *(volume, radio, tv)* to turn down.
◆ **abbassarsi** *vr (persona)* to bend down; *(livello)* to drop; **abbassarsi a fare qc** to lower o.s. by doing sthg.

abbasso *esclam*: ~ **la scuola!** down with school!

abbastanza *avv (a sufficienza)* enough; *(piuttosto)* rather, quite; **averne ~ di** to have had enough of.

abbattere *vt (muro)* to knock down; *(albero)* to cut down; *(cavallo)* to destroy; *(aereo)* to shoot down; *(sconfiggere)* to defeat.
◆ **abbattersi** *vr* to lose heart.

abbattuto, -a *agg (depresso)* depressed.
abbazia *sf* abbey.
abbeverare *vt (animali)* to water.
◆ **abbeverarsi** *vr* to drink.
abbia → **avere**.
abbiente *agg* well-off.
abbigliamento *sm* clothes *(pl)*; ~ **donna** women's wear; ~ **sportivo** sportswear; ~ **uomo** menswear.
abbinare *vt*: ~ **qc (a qc)** to link sthg (to sthg).
abboccare *vi* to bite.
abboccato, -a *agg* sweetish.
abbonamento *sm (a giornale)* subscription; *(a autobus, teatro)* season ticket; **fare l'~ (a qc)** *(a giornale)* to take out a subscription (to sthg); *(a autobus, teatro)* to buy a season ticket (for sthg).
abbonarsi *vr*: ~ **(a qc)** *(a autobus, teatro)* to buy a season ticket (for sthg); *(a giornale)* to subscribe (to sthg).
abbonato, -a *sm, f (a giornale)* subscriber; *(a autobus, teatro)* season ticket holder; *(a telefono)* subscriber; (TV) licence holder.
abbondante *agg* abundant.
abbondanza *sf* abundance.
abbordabile *agg (prezzo)* reasonable.
abbottonare *vt* to button up.
◆ **abbottonarsi** *vr*: **abbottonarsi il cappotto** to button up one's coat.
abbottonatura *sf* buttons *(pl)*.
abbozzare *vt (disegno)* to sketch; ~ **un sorriso** to smile faintly.
abbozzo *sm* sketch.
abbracciare *vt* to embrace, to hug; *(fede)* to embrace; *(professione)* to take up.
◆ **abbracciarsi** *vr* to embrace, to hug one another.
abbraccio *sm* embrace, hug.
abbreviare *vt* to shorten.
abbreviazione *sf* abbreviation.
abbronzante ◇ *agg* suntan *(davs)* ◇ *sm* suntan cream.
abbronzare *vt* to tan.
◆ **abbronzarsi** *vr* to get a tan.
abbronzato, -a *agg* tanned.
abbronzatura *sf* suntan.
abbrustolire *vt (pane)* to toast; *(caffè)* to roast.
abdicare *vi* to abdicate.
abete *sm* fir tree.
abile *agg (bravo)* capable; *(mossa, manovra)* skilful; *(idoneo)*: ~ **(a qc)** fit (for sthg).
abilità *sf (bravura)* ability; *(astuzia)* cleverness.
abilmente *avv (con bravura)* skilfully; *(con astuzia)* cleverly.
abisso *sm* abyss.
abitacolo *sm (di auto)* inside; *(di aereo)* cockpit, cabin; *(di camion)* cab.
abitante *smf (di paese)* inhabitant; *(di casa)* occupant.
abitare ◇ *vi* to live ◇ *vt* to live in; **dove abita?** where do you live?; **abito a Roma** I live in Rome; **abito in Italia** I live in Italy.
abitato, -a ◇ *agg (casa)* occupied; *(paese)* inhabited ◇ *sm* built-up area.
abitazione *sf* house.
abito *sm (da donna)* dress; *(da uomo)* suit; ~ **da sera** evening dress.
◆ **abiti** *smpl* clothes.
abituale *agg* usual.
abitualmente *avv* usually.
abituare *vt* to accustom; ~ **qn a fare qc** to accustom sb to doing sthg.
◆ **abituarsi** *vr (adattarsi)*: **abituarsi a qc** to get used to sthg; **abituarsi a fare qc** to get used to doing sthg.
abitudine *sf* habit; **aver l'~ di fare qc** to be in the habit of doing sthg; **per ~** out of habit.
abolire *vt (tassa)* to abolish; *(legge)* to repeal; *(eliminare)* to eliminate.

aborigeno, -a *sm, f* aborigine.
abortire *vi (accidentalmente)* to miscarry; *(volontariamente)* to have an abortion.
aborto *sm (volontario)* abortion; ~ **(spontaneo)** miscarriage.
abrogare *vt (legge)* to repeal.
Abruzzo *sm*: **l'~** the Abruzzo *(region of central Italy)*.
abside *sf* apse.
abusare : abusare di *v + prep (posizione, potere)* to take advantage of; *(persona)* to rape; ~ **dell'alcool** to drink too much.
abusivo, -a *agg* unauthorized, unlawful.
abuso *sm (eccesso)* overindulgence; *(uso illecito)* abuse.
a.C. *(abbr di avanti Cristo)* BC.
accademia *sf* academy, school; ~ **di belle arti** fine arts academy.
accadere *vi* to happen.
accaduto *sm*: **raccontare l'~** to describe what happened.
accalcarsi *vr* to crowd.
accampamento *sm* camp.
accampare *vt (truppe)* to encamp; *(richieste)* to make; *(diritti)* to assert.
◆ **accamparsi** *vr (in tende)* to camp; *(fig: in alloggio)* to camp (out).
accanimento *sm (tenacia)* tenacity; *(odio)* fury.
accanito, -a *agg (odio)* fierce; *(lavoratore)* assiduous; **fumatore ~** chain smoker.
accanto ◇ *avv* nearby ◇ *agg inv* next door ◇ *prep*: ~ **a** beside.
accaparrare *vt (fare incetta)* to buy up; *(voti, favore)* to secure, to gain; **accaparrarsi qc** to secure sthg for o.s.
accappatoio *sm* bathrobe.
accarezzare *vt (persona, animale)* to caress, to stroke; *(fig: idea)* to toy with.
accattone, -a *sm, f* beggar.
accavallare *vt (gambe)* to cross.
◆ **accavallarsi** *vr (eventi)* to overlap.
accecare *vt (rendere cieco)* to blind; *(abbagliare)* to dazzle.
accedere *vi*: ~ **a qc** to gain access to sthg.
accelerare ◇ *vi* to accelerate ◇ *vt* to speed up.
accelerato, -a ◇ *agg* quick ◇ *sm* stopping train.
acceleratore *sm* accelerator.
accendere *vt (fuoco, sigaretta)* to light; *(radio, luce, fornello, motore)* to turn on; *(speranza, odio)* to arouse; **scusi, ha da ~?** excuse me, have you got a light?
◆ **accendersi** *vr (prendere fuoco)* to catch fire; *(entrare in funzione)* to start up.
accendigas *sm inv lighter for gas ring.*
accendino *sm* (cigarette) lighter.
accennare *vt (menzionare)* to mention; *(indicare)* to point to; ~ **un sorriso** to half-smile.
◆ **accennare a** *v + prep (menzionare)* to mention; *(alludere a)* to hint at; *(dare segno di)* to show signs of.
accensione *sf* ignition.
accentare *vt (parola, sillaba)* to stress.
accento *sm* accent; **mettere l'~ su qc** to stress sthg.
accentuare *vt (differenze, difetto, pregio)* to emphasize.
◆ **accentuarsi** *vr* to become more marked.
accerchiare *vt* to encircle, to surround.
accertamento *sm* check.
accertare *vt* to check.
◆ **accertarsi di** *vr + prep* to make sure of.
acceso, -a ◇ *pp* → **accendere** ◇ *agg (fuoco, sigaretta)* lighted; *(radio, luce, motore)* on; *(colore)* bright.

accessibile *agg (luogo)* accessible; *(prezzo)* affordable.
accesso *sm (entrata)* access; (MED) fit; *(fig: impeto)* outburst.
accessori *smpl* accessories.
accettare *vt* to accept; *(proposta)* to agree to; ~ **di fare qc** to agree to do sthg; **'si accettano carte di credito'** 'credit cards welcome'.
accettazione *sf (locale)* reception; **'~ bagagli'** 'check-in'.
acchiappare *vt* to catch.
acciacco, -chi *sm* ailment.
acciaio *sm* steel; ~ **inossidabile** stainless steel.
accidentale *agg* accidental.
accidentalmente *avv* accidentally.
accidentato, -a *agg* uneven.
accidenti *esclam (con rabbia)* blast!, damn!; *(con stupore)* good heavens!
acciuffare *vt* to catch.
acciuga, -ghe *sf* anchovy; **acciughe al limone** *fresh anchovies marinated in lemon juice and dressed with oil.*
acclamare *vt (applaudire)* to cheer, to applaud; *(eleggere)* to acclaim.
accludere *vt* to enclose.
accogliente *agg* cosy.
accoglienza *sf* welcome.
accogliere *vt* to receive; *(dare il benvenuto)* to welcome.
accoltellare *vt* to knife.
accomodare *vt* to repair.
◆ **accomodarsi** *vr (sedersi)* to sit down; *(venire avanti)* to come in; **s'accomodi!** *(si sieda)* take a seat!; *(venga avanti)* come in!
accompagnamento *sm* accompaniment.
accompagnare *vt (persona)* to go/come with, to accompany; *(piatto, abito)* to go with; *(con musica)* to accompany.
accompagnatore, -trice *sm, f* companion; ~ **turistico** tourist guide.
acconsentire *vi*: ~ **(a qc)** to agree (to sthg).
accontentare *vt* to satisfy.
◆ **accontentarsi**: **accontentarsi di** *vr + prep* to be satisfied with.
acconto *sm* down payment; **dare un ~** to pay a deposit; **in ~** on account.
accorciare *vt* to shorten.
accordare *vt (strumento)* to tune; *(concedere)* to grant; *(colori)* to match.
◆ **accordarsi** *vr (mettersi d'accordo)* to agree.
accordo *sm (patto)* agreement; *(armonia)* harmony; **d'~!** all right!; **andare d'~ con qn** to get on well with sb; **essere d'~ con** to agree with; **mettersi d'~ con qn** *(trovare un accordo)* to reach an agreement with sb; *(per appuntamento)* to make an arrangement with sb.
accorgersi : **accorgersi di** *v + prep* to notice.
accorrere *vi (in aiuto)* to rush up; *(verso un luogo)* to rush.
accorto, -a ◇ *pp* → **accorgersi** ◇ *agg* shrewd.
accostare ◇ *vt (persona)* to approach; *(porta)* to leave ajar; *(avvicinare)*: ~ **qc a qc** to move sthg near sthg ◇ *vi* to pull in; *(nave)* to come alongside; *(cambiare rotta)* to change course; *(in auto)* to draw up.
accreditare *vt (fatto, notizia)* to confirm; *(denaro)* to credit.
accrescere *vt* to increase.
◆ **accrescersi** *vr* to grow.
accucciarsi *vr (cane)* to lie down.
accudire *vt (malato, bambino)* to look after.
◆ **accudire a** *v + prep (casa, faccende)* to attend to.
accumulare *vt* to accumulate;

(denaro) to save; *(accatastare)* to pile up.
accurato, -a *agg (lavoro)* careful; *(persona)* thorough.
accusa *sf (di una colpa)* accusation; (DIR) charge.
accusare *vt*: ~ **qn (di qc)** *(incolpare)* to accuse sb of sthg; (DIR) to charge.
acerbo, -a *agg* unripe.
acero *sm* maple.
aceto *sm* vinegar.
acetone *sm (per unghie)* nail varnish remover.
ACI *sm (abbr di Automobile Club d'Italia)* = AA *(Br)*, = AAA *(Am)*.
acidità *sf*: ~ **di stomaco** heartburn.
acido, -a ◇ *agg (sapore)* sour; *(commento, persona)* sharp ◇ *sm* acid.
acino *sm* grape.
acne *sf* acne.
acqua *sf* water; **sott'~** underwater; ~ **corrente** running water; ~ **cotta** *Tuscan soup made from stale bread, onions and tomatoes*; ~ **dolce** fresh water; ~ **minerale (gassata/naturale)** (carbonated/still) mineral water; ~ **ossigenata** hydrogen peroxide; ~ **del rubinetto** tap water; ~ **salata** salt water; ~ **tonica** tonic water; **acque termali** hot springs; ~ **in bocca!** keep it to yourself!; **'~ non potabile'** 'not drinking water'.
acquaforte (*pl* **acqueforti**) *sf* etching.
acquaio *sm* sink.
acquamarina (*pl* **acquemarine**) *sf* aquamarine.
acquaragia *sf* turpentine.
acquario *sm* aquarium.
◆ **Acquario** *sm* Aquarius.
acquasanta *sf* holy water.
acquatico, -a, -ci, -che *agg (pianta, animale)* aquatic; (SPORT) water *(dav s)*.
acquavite *sf* brandy.
acquazzone *sm* cloudburst.
acquedotto *sm* aqueduct.
acqueo *agg m* → **vapore**.
acquerello *sm* watercolour.
acquirente *smf* buyer.
acquisire *vt (ottenere)* to acquire.
acquistare *vt (comperare)* to buy; *(ottenere)* to acquire. .
acquisto *sm* purchase; **fare acquisti** to shop.
acquolina *sf*: **far venire l'~ in bocca a qn** to make sb's mouth water.
acquoso, -a *agg* watery.
acrilico, -a, -ci, -che *agg & sm* acrylic.
acrobata, -i, -e *smf* acrobat.
acrobazia *sf (di acrobata)* acrobatic feat; *(di aereo)* stunt.
acropoli *sf inv* acropolis.
aculeo *sm (di vespa)* sting; *(di riccio)* spine; *(di pianta)* prickle.
acume *sm* acumen.
acustico, -a, -ci, -che *agg* acoustic.
acuto, -a *agg (voce, suono)* high-pitched; *(intenso)* intense; *(appuntito)* pointed; *(intelligente)* sharp; (MAT) acute.
ad → **a**.
adagio *avv* slowly; **'entrare/uscire ~'** *sign warning drivers to enter or leave side roads etc slowly*.
adattamento *sm (adeguamento, di opera)* adaptation; *(modifica)* adjustment.
adattare *vt* to adapt.
◆ **adattarsi** *vr*: **adattarsi (a qc)** *(adeguarsi)* to adapt (to sthg).
adatto, -a *agg*: ~ **(a)** suitable (for); ~ **a fare qc** suitable to do sthg.
addebitare *vt* to debit.
addestramento *sm* training.
addestrare *vt* to train.
addetto, -a ◇ *agg (persona)* responsible ◇ *sm, f* person respon-

sible; ~ **stampa** press attaché; **gli addetti ai lavori** *(fig)* the experts.

addio *esclam* goodbye!

addirittura ◇ *avv (perfino)* even; *(direttamente)* directly ◇ *esclam* really?

addirsi : addirsi a *vr + prep* to be suitable for.

additivo *sm* additive.

addizionale *agg* additional.

addizione *sf* addition.

addobbo *sm* decoration; **addobbi natalizi** Christmas decorations.

addolcire *vt* to sweeten.

addolorare *vt* to sadden.

◆ **addolorarsi** *vr* to upset o.s.

addome *sm* abdomen.

addomesticare *vt* to house-train.

addormentare *vt* to send to sleep.

◆ **addormentarsi** *vr* to fall asleep.

addossare *vt (al muro)* to lean; *(attribuire)* to lay.

addosso ◇ *avv (sulla persona)* on ◇ *prep*: ~ **a** *(su)* on; *(contro)* against; **mettersi qc** ~ to put sthg on; **dare** ~ **a** *(criticare)* to attack; **eravamo uno** ~ **all'altro** we were right next to each other.

adeguare *vt*: ~ **qc a qc** to adjust sthg to sthg.

◆ **adeguarsi** *vr*: **adeguarsi a qc** to adapt to sthg.

adeguato, -a *agg* adequate.

adempiere *vt (compiere)* to carry out; *(esaudire)* to grant.

adenoidi *sfpl* adenoids.

aderente *agg (attillato)* close-fitting; *(adesivo)* adhesive.

aderire *vi*: ~ **a qc** *(attaccarsi)* to stick to sthg; *(partito)* to join sthg; *(proposta)* to support sthg; *(richiesta)* to agree to sthg.

adesivo, -a ◇ *agg* adhesive ◇ *sm (etichetta)* sticky label.

adesso *avv (ora)* now; *(tra poco)* any moment now; *(poco fa)* just now.

adiacente *agg* adjacent.

adibire *vt*: ~ **qc a qc** to use sthg as sthg.

Adige *sm*: **l'**~ the River Adige.

adirarsi *vr* to get angry.

adocchiare *vt (scorgere)* to glimpse; *(guardare)* to eye.

adolescente *smf* adolescent.

adolescenza *sf* adolescence.

adoperare *vt* to use.

adorabile *agg* adorable.

adorare *vt (persona, cosa)* to adore; *(divinità)* to worship.

adottare *vt (bambino)* to adopt; *(misure, decisione)* to take.

adottivo, -a *agg (figlio, patria)* adopted; *(genitori)* adoptive.

adozione *sf* adoption.

adriatico, -a, -ci, -che *agg* Adriatic.

◆ **Adriatico** *sm*: **l'Adriatico** the Adriatic (Sea).

adulterio *sm* adultery.

adulto, -a *agg & sm, f (di età)* adult.

aerare *vt* to air.

aereo, -a ◇ *agg* air *(dav s)* ◇ *sm* (aero)plane, aircraft; ~ **da turismo** light aircraft.

aerobica *sf* aerobics *(sg)*.

aeronautica *sf (aviazione)* airforce.

aeroplano *sm* (aero)plane *(Br)*, airplane *(Am)*.

aeroporto *sm* airport.

aerosol *sm* aerosol.

A.F. *(abbr di alta frequenza)* HF.

afa *sf* closeness.

affabile *agg* affable.

affacciarsi *vr (mostrarsi)* to show o.s.

◆ **affacciarsi su** *vr + prep* to show o.s. at.

affamato, -a *agg* starving.

affannarsi *vr (stancarsi)* to tire o.s.; *(agitarsi)* to worry.

affanno *sm (di respiro)* breathlessness; *(ansia)* worry.
affare *sm* business; *(faccenda)* business, affair; *(occasione)* bargain; *(fam: cosa)* thing; **è un ~!** it's a bargain!; **affari** business *(sg)*; **per affari** on business; **fare affari con** to do business with; **Affari Esteri** Foreign Affairs.
affascinante *agg* charming.
affascinare *vt* to charm, to fascinate.
affaticarsi *vr* to get tired.
affatto *avv* completely; **non ... ~** not ... at all; **niente ~** not at all.
affermare *vt* to affirm.
♦ **affermarsi** *vr* to make a name for o.s.
affermativo, -a *agg* affirmative.
affermazione *sf (dichiarazione)* affirmation; *(successo)* success.
afferrare *vt (prendere)* to seize; *(capire)* to grasp.
♦ **afferrarsi a** *vr + prep* to grasp at.
affettare *vt* to slice.
affettato, -a ◇ *agg (a fette)* sliced; *(artificioso)* affected ◇ *sm* sliced cold meat.
affetto, -a ◇ *sm (attaccamento)* affection ◇ *agg*: **essere ~ da** *(malattia)* to suffer from.
affettuoso, -a *agg* affectionate.
affezionarsi *vr*: **~ a** to become fond of.
affezionato, -a *agg* fond.
affidamento *sm* (DIR) custody; *(fiducia)*: **fare ~ su** to rely on.
affidare *vt* to entrust; **~ qn/qc a qn** to entrust sb/sthg to sb.
affiggere *vt (cartello, poster)* to stick up.
affilare *vt* to sharpen.
affilato, -a *agg (lama, punta)* sharp.
affinché *cong* in order that, so that.
affinità *sf inv* affinity.
affissione *sf*: **'divieto di ~'** 'post no bills'.
affisso, -a ◇ *pp* → **affiggere** ◇ *sm* poster.
affittare *vt (dare in affitto)* to let, to rent (out); *(prendere in affitto)* to rent; **'affittasi'** 'to let'.
affitto *sm* rent; **dare in ~** to let, to rent (out); **prendere in ~** to rent.
affliggere *vt* to torment.
♦ **affliggersi** *vr* to torment o.s.
afflitto, -a ◇ *pp* → **affliggere** ◇ *agg* afflicted.
affluente *sm* tributary.
affluire *vi (fiume)* to flow; *(gente, merce)* to pour in.
affogare *vi & vt* to drown.
affogato *sm (gelato) ice cream or 'semifreddo' with coffee, whisky or a liqueur poured over it.*
affollato, -a *agg* crowded.
affondare *vi & vt* to sink.
affrancare *vt* to stamp.
affrancatura *sf* postage.
affresco, -schi *sm* fresco.
affrettare *vt* to hurry.
♦ **affrettarsi** *vr* to hurry.
affrontare *vt (nemico)* to confront; *(spesa)* to meet; *(argomento)* to tackle.
affronto *sm* insult.
affumicato, -a *agg (cibo)* smoked; *(vetro)* tinted; *(annerito)* blackened.
afoso, -a *agg* close.
Africa *sf*: l'~ Africa.
africano, -a *agg & sm, f* African.
afta *sf* mouth ulcer.
agenda *sf* diary.
agente *sm* agent; **~ di polizia** policeman (*f* policewoman); **gli agenti atmosferici** the elements.
agenzia *sf (impresa)* agency; *(succursale)* branch; **~ di cambio** bureau de change; **~ immobiliare** estate agent's *(Br)*, real-estate office *(Am)*; **~ di viaggi** travel agency.

agevolare *vt (facilitare)* to facilitate; *(aiutare)* to help.
agevolazione *sf*: **~ di pagamento** easy (payment) terms *(pl)*.
aggeggio *sm* thing.
aggettivo *sm* adjective.
agghiacciante *agg* terrible.
aggiornare *vt (persona, opera)* to bring up-to-date; *(seduta)* to postpone.
◆ **aggiornarsi** *vr* to bring o.s. up-to-date.
aggiornato, -a *agg* up-to-date.
aggirare *vt* to get round.
◆ **aggirarsi** *vr* to wander.
◆ **aggirarsi su** *vr + prep* to be about.
aggiudicare *vt* to award.
◆ **aggiudicarsi** *vr* to gain.
aggiungere *vt* to add.
aggiunta *sf*: **in ~** in addition.
aggiunto, -a *pp* → **aggiungere**.
aggiustare *vt* to mend.
◆ **aggiustarsi** *vr* to come to an agreement.
agglomerato *sm*: **~ urbano** built-up area.
aggrapparsi *vr* to cling on; **~ a** to cling to.
aggravare *vt* to make worse.
◆ **aggravarsi** *vr* to get worse.
aggredire *vt* to attack.
aggressione *sf* attack.
aggressivo, -a *agg* aggressive.
agguato *sm* ambush.
agiato, -a *agg (persona)* well-off; *(vita)* comfortable.
agile *agg* agile, nimble.
agio *sm*: **essere a proprio ~** to feel at ease; **mettersi a proprio ~** to make o.s. at home.
agire *vi (comportarsi)* to act; **~ da** *(fare da)* to act as.
agitare *vt* to shake; *(mano)* to wave; *(coda)* to wag; *(turbare)* to upset; **'~ prima dell'uso'** 'shake before use'.
◆ **agitarsi** *vr (turbarsi)* to get worked up; *(muoversi)* to writhe; *(mare)* to get rough; **agitarsi nel letto** to toss and turn in bed.
agitato, -a *agg (inquieto)* worried; *(mare)* rough.
agitazione *sf (inquietudine)* agitation; *(subbuglio)* turmoil.
agli = a + gli, → **a**.
aglio *sm* garlic.
agnello *sm* lamb; **~ alla norcina** *leg of lamb larded with ham, garlic, parsley and marjoram.*
agnolotti *smpl ravioli stuffed with pork, salami, Parmesan cheese and spinach.*
ago (*pl* **aghi**) *sm* needle.
agonia *sf* agony.
agopuntura *sf* acupuncture.
agosto *sm* August, → **settembre**.
agricolo, -a *agg* agricultural.
agricoltore *sm (contadino)* farm worker; *(imprenditore)* farmer.
agricoltura *sf* agriculture.
agriturismo *sm* farm holidays *(pl)*.
agrodolce *sm*: **in ~** in a sweet and sour sauce.
agrume *sm* citrus fruit.
aguzzare *vt* to sharpen; **~ le orecchie** to prick up one's ears.
aguzzo, -a *agg* sharp.
ahi *esclam* ouch!
ai = a + i, → **a**.
Aia *sf*: **l'~** The Hague.
AIDS *sm o sf* AIDS.
A.I.G. *(abbr di Associazione Italiana Alberghi per la Gioventù)* = YHA.
air-terminal ['ɜr 'tɛrminal] *sm inv* air terminal.
aiuola *sf* flower bed.
aiutante *smf* assistant.
aiutare *vt* to help; **~ qn (a fare qc)** to help sb (to do sthg).
aiuto *sm* help, assistance; *(assistente)* assistant; **~!** help!; **chiedere ~** to ask for help; **essere di ~ a qn**

to be of help to sb; **venire in ~ di qn** to come to sb's aid.
al = **a** + **il**, → **a**.
ala (*pl* **ali**) *sf* wing; *(giocatore)* winger.
alano *sm* Great Dane.
alba *sf* dawn; **all'~** at dawn.
albanese *agg & smf* Albanian.
Albania *sf*: **l'~** Albania.
albergatore, -trice *sm, f* hotelier.
albergo, -ghi *sm* hotel; **~ diurno** *public toilets where people can also wash, have a haircut, get their clothes ironed etc.*; **~ per la gioventù** youth hostel.
albero *sm* tree; *(di nave)* mast; *(di macchina)* shaft; **~ genealogico** family tree; **~ di Natale** Christmas tree.
albese *sf thin slices of raw beef served with oil, lemon and mushrooms or Parmesan cheese.*
albicocca, -che *sf* apricot.
albino, -a *agg & sm, f* albino.
album *sm inv* album; **~ da disegno** sketch book.
albume *sm* egg white.
alcol = **alcool**.
alcolico, -a, -ci, -che ◇ *agg* alcoholic ◇ *sm* alcoholic drink.
alcolizzato, -a *sm, f* alcoholic.
alcool *sm* alcohol.
alcuno, -a *agg s*: **non ... ~** *(nessuno)* no, not any.
◆ **alcuni, -e** ◇ *agg pl* some, a few ◇ *pron pl* some; **alcuni di** some of, a few of.
aldilà *sm*: **l'~** the next life.
alfabeto *sm* alphabet.
alfiere *sm (portabandiera)* standard bearer; *(negli scacchi)* bishop.
alga, -ghe *sf (di mare)* seaweed.
algebra *sf* algebra.
Algeria *sf*: **l'~** Algeria.
aliante *sm* glider.
alibi *sm inv* alibi.
alice *sf* anchovy; **alici areganate** *anchovies cooked in oil, vinegar, garlic, parsley and oregano.*
alienazione *sf (pazzia)* insanity; (DIR) transfer.
alieno, -a *sm, f* alien.
alimentare ◇ *agg* food *(dav s)* ◇ *vt (nutrire)* to feed; *(fig: rafforzare)* to strengthen; *(rifornire)* to supply.
◆ **alimentari** *smpl (cibi)* foodstuffs; **negozio di alimentari** grocer's.
alimentazione *sf (nutrimento)* nutrition; *(rifornimento)* supply.
alimento *sm* food.
◆ **alimenti** *smpl* alimony *(sg)*.
aliscafo *sm* hydrofoil.
alito *sm* breath.
all' = **a** + **l'**, → **a**.
alla = **a** + **la**, → **a**.
allacciare *vt (scarpe)* to tie up; *(cintura, vestito)* to fasten; *(telefono, gas)* to connect.
◆ **allacciarsi** *vr* to fasten.
allagare *vt* to flood.
◆ **allagarsi** *vr* to flood.
allargare *vt (ampliare)* to widen; *(aprire)* to open.
◆ **allargarsi** *vr* to widen.
allarmare *vt* to alarm.
allarme *sm* alarm; **~ d'incendio** fire alarm; **dare l'~** to give the alarm.
allattare *vt (al seno)* to breastfeed; *(artificialmente)* to bottle-feed.
alle = **a** + **le**, → **a**.
alleanza *sf* alliance.
allearsi *vr* to form an alliance.
allegare *vt* to enclose.
alleggerire *vt* to lighten.
allegria *sf* cheerfulness.
allegro, -a ◇ *agg (contento)* cheerful; *(colore)* bright; *(vivace)* lively ◇ *sm* (MUS) allegro.
allenamento *sm* training; **tenersi in ~** to keep in training.

allenare *vt* to train.
◆ **allenarsi** *vr* to train.
allenatore, -trice *sm, f* trainer, coach.
allentare *vt (vite, nodo)* to loosen; *(sorveglianza, disciplina)* to relax.
◆ **allentarsi** *vr* to work loose.
allergia *sf* allergy.
allergico, -a, -ci, -che *agg* allergic; **essere ~ a qc** to be allergic to sthg.
allestire *vt (mostra, spettacolo)* to get ready.
allevamento *sm (attività)* breeding, rearing; *(animali)* stock.
allevare *vt (animale)* to breed; *(bambino)* to bring up.
allibratore *sm* bookmaker.
allievo, -a *sm, f* pupil, student.
alligatore *sm* alligator.
allineare *vt* to align.
◆ **allinearsi** *vr (mettersi in fila)* to line up.
allo = **a** + **lo**, → **a**.
allodola *sf* skylark.
alloggiare *vi* to stay.
alloggio *sm* accommodation.
allontanare *vt (mandare via)* to send away; *(pericolo)* to avert.
◆ **allontanarsi** *vr* to go away.
allora ◇ *avv* then ◇ *cong (in tal caso)* then; *(ebbene)* well; **da ~** since then.
alloro *sm* laurel.
alluce *sm* big toe.
allucinante *agg (spaventoso)* terrifying; *(incredibile)* incredible.
allucinazione *sf* hallucination.
alludere : alludere a *v + prep* to allude to.
alluminio *sm* aluminium.
allungare *vt (accrescere)* to lengthen; *(gambe)* to stretch; *(diluire)* to water down.
◆ **allungarsi** *vr (accrescersi)* to lengthen; *(distendersi)* to stretch out.
allusione *sf* allusion; **fare allusioni** to drop hints.
alluso *pp* → **alludere**.
alluvione *sf* flood.
almeno *avv* at least.
Alpi *sfpl*: **le ~** the Alps.
alpinismo *sm* climbing.
alpinista, -i, -e *smf* climber.
alpino, -a *agg* alpine.
alquanto *avv* somewhat.
alt *esclam* halt!
altalena *sf (con funi)* swing; *(su asse)* see-saw *(Br)*, teeter-totter *(Am)*.
altare *sm* altar.
alterare *vt* to affect.
◆ **alterarsi** *vr (merce)* to be affected; *(irritarsi)* to get angry.
alternare *vt*: **~ qn/qc a** to alternate sb/sthg with.
◆ **alternarsi** *vr* to alternate.
alternativa *sf* alternative.
alternato, -a *agg* alternate; *(corrente)* alternating.
alterno, -a *agg* alternate.
altezza *sf (statura, di cosa)* height; *(di acqua)* depth; *(altitudine)* altitude.
altezzoso, -a *agg* haughty.
altipiano = **altopiano**.
altitudine *sf* altitude.
alto, -a ◇ *agg* high; *(persona, edificio, albero)* tall; *(profondo)* deep; *(suono, voce)* loud ◇ *sm* top ◇ *avv* high; *(parlare)* loud; **è ~ due metri** he's two metres tall; **ad alta voce** out loud, aloud; **alta moda** haute couture; **dall'~ in basso** from top to bottom; **alti e bassi** ups and downs; **in ~** upwards.
altoparlante *sm* loudspeaker.
altopiano (*pl* **altipiani**) *sm* plateau.
altrettanto, -a ◇ *agg (tempo, latte)* as much; *(persone, libri)* as many ◇ *pron* the same ◇ *avv* equally; **auguri! – grazie, ~!** all the best! – thank you, the same to you!

altrimẹnti *avv (se no)* otherwise; *(diversamente)* differently.

ạltro, -a ◇ *agg* **1.** *(diverso)* other; **ha un ~ modello?** have you got another o a different model?

2. *(supplementare)* other; **un ~ caffè?** another coffee?

3. *(rimanente)* other; **gli altri passeggeri sono pregati di restare al loro posto** would all remaining passengers please stay in their seats.

4. *(nel tempo)*: **l'~ giorno** the other day; **l'altr'anno** last year; **l'~ ieri** the day before yesterday; **domani l'~** the day after tomorrow.

5. *(in espressioni)*: **è tutt'~ che bello** it's far from being beautiful; **d'altra parte** on the other hand.

◇ *pron*: **l'~** the other (one); **un ~** another (one); **gli altri** *(il prossimo)* others, other people; **l'uno o l'~** one or the other; **se non ~** at least; **senz'~** of course; **tra l'~** among other things.

altroché *esclam* and how!

altrọnde : d'altronde *avv* on the other hand.

altrọve *avv* elsewhere.

altrụi *agg inv* other people's.

altruịsta, -i, -e *agg* altruistic.

altụra *sf* high ground.

alụnno, -a *sm, f* pupil.

alveạre *sm* beehive.

alzạre *vt (oggetto)* to lift; *(prezzi, volume, voce)* to raise.

◆ **alzarsi** *vr (dal letto, dalla sedia)* to get up; *(aumentare)* to rise; *(vento)* to get up.

amạca, -che *sf* hammock.

amalgamạre *vt* to combine.

◆ **amalgamarsi** *vr* to combine.

amạnte ◇ *smf* lover ◇ *agg*: **~ di qc** fond of sthg.

amạre *vt (persona)* to love; *(cosa)* to be fond of.

amareggiạto, -a *agg* embittered.

amarẹna *sf sour black cherry.*

amarẹtto *sm (biscotto)* macaroon; *(liquore) a liqueur made with almonds.*

amarẹzza *sf* bitterness.

amạro, -a *agg (sapore)* bitter; *(spiacevole)* nasty.

ambasciạta *sf* embassy.

ambasciatọre, -trịce *sm, f* ambassador.

ambedụe *agg inv & pron* both.

ambientạre *vt (film)* to set.

◆ **ambientarsi** *vr* to get used to a place.

ambiẹnte *sm (natura)* environment; *(cerchia)* surroundings *(pl)*.

ambịguo, -a *agg (parola, testo)* ambiguous; *(comportamento, persona)* dubious.

ambiziọne *sf* ambition.

ambiziọso, -a *agg* ambitious.

ạmbra *sf* amber.

ambulạnte *agg* itinerant.

ambulạnza *sf* ambulance.

ambulatọrio *sm* surgery.

Amẹrica *sf*: **l'~** America; **l'~ latina** Latin America.

americạno, -a *agg & sm, f* American.

amiạnto *sm* asbestos.

amichẹvole *agg* friendly.

amicịzia *sf* friendship; **fare ~ (con qn)** to make friends (with sb).

amịco, -a, -ci, -che *sm, f* friend; **~ del cuore** best friend.

ạmido *sm* starch.

ammaccạre *vt* to dent.

ammaccatụra *sf (su metallo)* dent; *(su gamba)* bruise.

ammaestrạre *vt* to train.

ammainạre *vt* to lower.

ammalạrsi *vr* to fall ill.

ammalạto, -a ◇ *agg* ill ◇ *sm, f* patient.

ammassạre *vt* to amass, to pile up.

ammazzare *vt* to kill.
◆ **ammazzarsi** *vr* to kill o.s.
ammenda *sf* fine.
ammesso, -a *pp* → **ammettere**.
ammettere *vt (riconoscere)* to admit; *(permettere)* to allow; *(a esame, scuola)* to accept; *(supporre)* to suppose, to assume.
amministrare *vt* to run, to manage.
amministratore *sm (di condominio)* manager; ~ **delegato** managing director.
ammirare *vt* to admire.
ammiratore, -trice *sm, f* admirer.
ammirazione *sf* admiration.
ammissione *sf (a esame)* admittance.
ammobiliato, -a *agg* furnished; **non** ~ unfurnished.
ammollo *sm* soaking; **lasciare qc in** ~ to leave sthg to soak.
ammoniaca *sf* ammonia.
ammonire *vt (rimproverare)* to warn; (SPORT) to book.
ammonizione *sf (rimprovero)* warning; (SPORT) booking.
ammontare : ammontare a *v + prep* to amount to.
ammorbidente *sm* fabric softener.
ammorbidire *vt (rendere morbido)* to soften.
ammortizzatore *sm* shock absorber.
ammucchiare *vt* to pile up.
ammuffito, -a *agg* mouldy.
ammutinamento *sm* mutiny.
amnistia *sf* amnesty.
amo *sm* bait.
amore *sm* love; **fare l'~ (con qn)** to make love (with sb); **amor proprio** self-esteem.
ampio, -a *agg (vasto)* wide; *(spazioso)* spacious; *(abbondante)* abundant.
ampliare *vt* to widen.
amplificatore *sm* amplifier.
amputare *vt* to amputate.
amuleto *sm* amulet.
anabbaglianti *smpl* dipped headlights *(Br)*, dimmed headlights *(Am)*.
anagrafe *sf (ufficio)* registry office *(Br)*, office of vital statistics *(Am)*.
analcolico, -a, -ci, -che ◇ *agg* non-alcoholic ◇ *sm* soft drink.
analfabeta, -i, -e *agg & smf* illiterate.
analisi *sf inv (studio)* analysis; (MED) test; ~ **del sangue** blood test.
analista, -i, -e *smf* analyst.
analizzare *vt* to analyse.
analogo, -a, -ghi, -ghe *agg* similar.
ananas *sm inv* pineapple.
anarchia *sf* anarchy.
ANAS *sf (abbr di Azienda Nazionale Autonoma delle Strade) national road board.*
anatomia *sf* anatomy.
anatomico, -a, -ci, -che *agg (sedile)* contoured.
anatra *sf* duck.
anca, -che *sf* hip.
anche *cong (pure)* too; *(persino)* even.
ancora[1] *sf* anchor.
ancora[2] *avv (tuttora)* still; *(persino)* even; *(di nuovo)* again; *(di più)* more, still; ~ **più bello** even more beautiful; ~ **un po'** a bit more; ~ **una volta** once more; **non** ~ not yet.
andare ◇ *vi* 1. *(muoversi)* to go; **scusi, per ~ alla stazione?** could you tell me the way to the station, please?; ~ **a Napoli** to go to Naples; ~ **avanti/indietro** to go forwards/backwards; ~ **in vacanza** to go on holiday *(Br)*, to go on vacation *(Am)*.
2. *(strada)* to go.
3. *(indica uno stato)*: **come va?** how are you?; ~ **bene/male** *(persona)* to

be well/unwell; *(situazione)* to go well/badly.
4. *(piacere)*: **il suo modo di fare non mi va** I don't like the way he behaves; **non mi va di mangiare** I don't feel like eating.
5. *(funzionare)* to work.
6. *(con participio passato)*: **dove va messa la chiave?** where does the key go?; ~ **perso** *(essere smarrito)* to get lost.
7. *(in espressioni)*: ~ **bene a qn** *(come misura)* to fit sb; **queste scarpe mi vanno bene** these shoes fit (me); **ti va bene andare al cinema?** do you feel like going to the cinema?; ~ **via** *(partire)* to leave; *(macchia)* to come out.
◇ *sm*: **a lungo** ~ in time.
◆ **andarsene** *vr* to go away.
andata *sf*: **all'**~ on the way there; ~ **e ritorno** return (ticket) *(Br)*, round-trip ticket *(Am)*.
andatura *sf* walk.
andirivieni *sm inv* coming and going.
anello *sm (da dito)* ring; *(di catena)* link; ~ **di fidanzamento** engagement ring.
anemia *sf* anaemia.
anestesia *sf* anaesthesia.
anestetico *sm* anaesthetic.
anfiteatro *sm* amphitheatre.
anfora *sf* amphora.
angelo *sm* angel.
angina *sf* tonsillitis; ~ **pectoris** angina.
anglicano, -a *agg* Anglican.
angolo *sm* corner; ~ **cottura** kitchen area; **all'**~ on the corner.
angora *sf*: **d'**~ angora *(dav s)*.
angoscia *sf* anguish.
anguilla *sf* eel.
anguria *sf* watermelon.
anice *sm* aniseed.
anidride *sf*: ~ **carbonica** carbon dioxide.
anima *sf* soul.
animale *agg & sm* animal; ~ **domestico** pet.
animatore, -trice *sm, f*: ~ **turistico** entertainment organizer *(in holiday village)*.
animo *sm (mente)* mind; *(cuore)* heart; *(coraggio)*: **perdersi d'**~ to lose heart.
anitra = **anatra**.
annaffiare *vt* to water.
annaffiatoio *sm* watering can.
annata *sf* year; *(di vino)* vintage.
annegare *vt & vi* to drown.
◆ **annegarsi** *vr* to drown o.s.
anniversario *sm* anniversary.
anno *sm* year; **buon** ~! Happy New Year!; **quanti anni hai?** how old are you?; **ho 21 anni** I'm 21; **un bambino di tre anni** a three-year-old; ~ **accademico** academic year; ~ **bisestile** leap year; ~ **scolastico** school year.
annodare *vt* to tie.
annoiare *vt* to bore.
◆ **annoiarsi** *vr* to get bored.
annotare *vt (prendere nota)* to note down; *(commentare)* to annotate.
annuale *agg* annual.
annuario *sm* yearbook.
annuire *vi (con la testa)* to nod.
annullare *vt (partita, riunione, francobollo)* to cancel; *(matrimonio)* to annul; *(rendere vano)* to destroy.
annunciare *vt* to announce; *(indicare)* to indicate.
annunciatore, -trice *sm, f* announcer.
Annunciazione *sf*: **l'**~ the Annunciation.
annuncio *sm* announcement; ~ **pubblicitario** advertisement; **annunci economici** classified ads.
annuo, -a *agg* annual, yearly.
annusare *vt* to smell.
annuvolamento *sm* clouding over.
ano *sm* anus.

anomalo, -a *agg* anomalous.
anonimo, -a *agg* anonymous.
anoressia *sf* anorexia.
anormale ◇ *agg* abnormal ◇ *smf* abnormal person.
ANSA *sf (abbr di Agenzia Nazionale Stampa Associata) national press agency.*
ansia *sf* anxiety.
ansimare *vi* to pant.
ansioso, -a *agg (inquieto)* anxious; *(impaziente)*: **~ di fare qc** eager to do sthg.
anta *sf (di finestra)* shutter; *(di armadio)* door.
antagonista, -i, -e *smf* rival.
antartico, -a, -ci, -che *agg* Antarctic.
Antartide *sf*: **l'~** Antarctica.
anteguerra *sm* prewar period.
antenato, -a *sm, f* ancestor.
antenna *sf* aerial.
anteprima *sf* preview; **presentare qc in ~** to preview sthg.
anteriore *agg (sedili, ruote)* front *(dav s)*; *(nel tempo)* previous.
antiabbaglianti = **anabbaglianti**.
antibiotico *sm* antibiotic.
anticamera *sf* anteroom.
antichità *sf inv (passato)* antiquity; *(oggetto)* antique.
anticipare *vt (partenza)* to bring forward; *(denaro)* to pay in advance.
anticipo *sm (di denaro)* advance; *(di tempo)*: **il treno ha 10 minuti d'~** the train is 10 minutes early; **essere/arrivare in ~** to be/arrive early.
antico, -a, -chi, -che *agg (mobilio)* antique; *(dell'antichità)* ancient.
anticoncezionale *agg & sm* contraceptive.
anticonformista, -i, -e *agg & smf* nonconformist.
anticorpo *sm* antibody.
antidoto *sm* antidote.
antifascista, -i, -e *agg & smf* antifascist.
antifurto ◇ *agg inv* antitheft *(dav s)* ◇ *sm* antitheft device.
antigelo *sm inv* antifreeze.
Antille *sfpl*: **le ~** the West Indies.
antimafia *agg inv* anti-Mafia.
antincendio *agg inv* fire *(dav s)*.
antinebbia ◇ *agg inv* fog *(dav s)* ◇ *sm inv* fog lamp.
antiorario *agg m* → **senso**.
antipasto *sm* hors d'œuvre; **~ di mare** *mixed seafood hors d'œuvre*; **~ a scelta** *hors d'œuvres chosen from a buffet of grilled or baked vegetables, pickled foods, cold meats etc.*
antipatia *sf* antipathy.
antipatico, -a, -ci, -che *agg* unpleasant.
antiquariato *sm (commercio)* antique trade; **oggetti d'~** antiques.
antiquario, -a *sm, f* antique dealer.
antiquato, -a *agg* old-fashioned.
antiruggine *agg inv* rustproof.
antirughe *agg inv* antiwrinkle *(dav s)*.
antisettico, -a, -ci, -che *agg & sm* antiseptic.
antitetanica *sf* antitetanus injection.
antivipera *sm inv* antiviper serum.
antologia *sf* anthology.
anulare ◇ *agg* ring *(dav s)* ◇ *sm* ring finger.
anzi *cong (al contrario)* on the contrary; *(o meglio)* or rather.
anziano, -a ◇ *agg (di età)* elderly; *(di carica)* senior ◇ *sm, f (vecchio)* senior citizen.
anziché *cong* rather than.
anzitutto *avv* first of all.
apatia *sf* apathy.
apatico, -a, -ci, -che *agg* apathetic.

ape *sf* bee.
aperitivo *sm* aperitif.
aperto, -a ◇ *pp* → **aprire** ◇ *agg* open ◇ *sm*: **all'~** in the open air.
apertura *sf* opening.
apice *sm* peak; **essere all'~ di qc** to be at the height of sthg.
apicoltura *sf* beekeeping.
apnea *sf*: **in ~** *(subacqueo)* without breathing apparatus.
apolide ◇ *agg* stateless ◇ *smf* stateless person.
apostolo *sm* apostle.
apostrofo *sm* apostrophe.
appagare *vt* to satisfy.
appannare *vt (vetro)* to mist; *(fig: mente)* to dim.
◆ **appannarsi** *vr (vetro)* to mist up; *(fig: vista, mente)* to grow dim.
apparato *sm* (ANAT) system; *(impianto)* apparatus.
apparecchiare *vt*: **~ la tavola** to lay the table.
apparecchio *sm (congegno)* device; *(aereo)* aircraft; *(per i denti)* brace; **~ acustico** hearing aid.
apparente *agg* apparent.
apparentemente *avv* apparently.
apparenza *sf*: **in** o **all'~** apparently.
apparire *vi (mostrarsi)* to appear; *(sembrare)* to seem.
appariscente *agg* striking.
apparso, -a *pp* → **apparire**.
appartamento *sm* flat *(Br)*, apartment *(Am)*.
appartenere : **appartenere a** *v + prep* to belong to.
appassionato, -a ◇ *agg* passionate ◇ *sm, f* fan; **essere ~ di qc** to be keen on sthg.
appello *sm (chiamata)* rollcall; (DIR) appeal; **fare ~ a** to appeal to; **fare l'~** to call the roll.
appena ◇ *avv (a fatica)* hardly; *(da poco)* just; *(solo)* only, just ◇ *cong* as soon as; **non ~** as soon as.
appendere *vt* to hang up.
appendice *sf* appendix.
appendicite *sf* appendicitis.
Appennini *smpl*: **gli ~** the Apennines.
appeso, -a *pp* → **appendere**.
appetito *sm* appetite; **buon ~!** enjoy your meal!
appetitoso, -a *agg* appetizing.
appezzamento *sm* plot.
appiattire *vt* to flatten.
◆ **appiattirsi** *vr (al suolo, contro il muro)* to flatten o.s.; *(diventare piatto)* to become flatter.
appiccare *vt*: **~ il fuoco a qc** to set fire to sthg.
appiccicare *vt* to stick.
◆ **appiccicarsi** *vr*: **appiccicarsi (a)** to stick (to); *(fig: persona)* to cling (to).
appieno *avv* fully.
appigliarsi : **appigliarsi a** *vr + prep (afferrarsi)* to hold on to; *(fig: pretesto)* to cling to.
appiglio *sm (appoggio)* hold; *(fig: pretesto)* pretext.
appisolarsi *vr* to doze off.
applaudire *vt* to applaud.
applauso *sm* applause; **fare un ~** to give a round of applause.
applicare *vt* to apply.
◆ **applicarsi** *vr* to apply o.s.
applicazione *sf (di cerotto, pomata)* application; *(attuazione)* enforcement.
appoggiare *vt (per terra, sul tavolo)* to put (down); *(sostenere)* to support; *(al muro)*: **~ qc a** o **contro qc** to lean sthg against sthg.
◆ **appoggiarsi a** *vr + prep* to lean against.
appoggiatesta *sm inv* headrest.
apporre *vt (form)* to add.
appositamente *avv* on purpose; **~ per te** specially for you.
apposito, -a *agg* appropriate.
apposta *avv* deliberately; **fare qc ~** to do sthg on purpose.

apposto, -a *pp* → **apporre**.
apprendere *vt* to learn.
apprendista, -i, -e *smf* apprentice.
apprensivo, -a *agg* apprehensive.
appreso, -a *pp* → **apprendere**.
appretto *sm* starch.
apprezzamento *sm* appreciation.
apprezzare *vt* to appreciate.
approccio *sm* approach.
approdare *vi* to land; **non ~ a niente** to come to nothing.
approdo *sm (atto)* landing; *(luogo)* landing-place.
approfittare : approfittare di *v + prep* to take advantage of.
approfondire *vt (accentuare)* to deepen; *(studiare)* to study in depth.
appropriarsi : appropriarsi di *vr + prep* to appropriate.
approssimativo, -a *agg (calcolo)* approximate; *(conoscenza)* superficial.
approvare *vt (legge, proposta)* to pass; *(comportamento)* to approve of.
approvazione *sf* approval.
appuntamento *sm* appointment; *(amoroso)* date; **dare (un) ~ a qn** to arrange to meet sb; **prendere un ~ con** o **da qn** to make an appointment with sb.
appuntare *vt (matita)* to sharpen; *(fissare)* to pin; *(annotare)* to note.
appunto ◇ *sm (annotazione)* note; *(rimprovero)* reprimand ◇ *avv* exactly.
apribottiglie *sm inv* bottle opener.
aprile *sm* April, → **settembre**.
aprire ◇ *vt* to open; *(gas, acqua)* to turn on ◇ *vi* to open; **vai tu ad ~?** can you answer the door?; **'non ~ prima che il treno sia fermo'** 'do not open before the train has stopped'.
◆ **aprirsi** *vr (porta)* to open; *(inchiesta)* to start up; *(confidarsi)*: **aprirsi con qc** to open one's heart to sb.
apriscatole *sm inv* can opener.
aquila *sf* eagle.
aquilone *sm* kite.
Arabia Saudita *sf*: **l'~** Saudi Arabia.
arabo, -a ◇ *agg & sm, f* Arab ◇ *sm (lingua)* Arabic.
arachide *sf* peanut.
aragosta *sf* lobster.
arancia, -ce *sf* orange.
aranciata *sf* orange juice.
arancini *smpl rice balls with a filling of tomatoes and mozzarella cheese (a Sicilian speciality)*.
arancio *sm* orange tree.
arancione *agg & sm* orange.
arare *vt* to plough.
aratro *sm* plough.
arazzo *sm* tapestry.
arbitrario, -a *agg* arbitrary.
arbitro *sm* referee.
arbusto *sm* shrub.
archeologia *sf* archaeology.
archeologico, -a, -ci, -che *agg* archaeological.
architetto *sm* architect.
architettura *sf* architecture.
archivio *sm (luogo)* archives *(pl)*; *(raccolta)* files *(pl)*; (INFORM) file.
arcipelago, -ghi *sm* archipelago.
arcivescovo *sm* archbishop.
arco, -chi *sm (volta)* arch; *(arma)* bow; *(durata)*: **nell'~ di due mesi** in the space of two months.
arcobaleno *sm* rainbow.
ardere *vt & vi* to burn.
ardesia *sf (pietra)* slate.
ardire ◇ *vi* to dare ◇ *sm* daring.
ardore *sm* ardour.
area *sf* area; **'~ pedonale'** 'pedestrian precinct'; **~ di servizio** services *(pl)*.

arena *sf* arena.
arenarsi *vr* to run aground.
argenteria *sf* silverware.
Argentina *sf*: l'~ Argentina.
argentino, -a *agg & sm, f* Argentinian.
argento *sm* silver; **d'~** silver.
argilla *sf* clay.
argine *sm* bank.
argomento *sm (tema)* subject; *(ragionamento)* argument.
arguto, -a *agg (persona)* quick-witted; *(discorso, battuta)* witty.
aria *sf* air; *(aspetto)* appearance; **ha l'~ familiare** he looks familiar; **mandare all'~ qc** to ruin sthg; **all'~ aperta** in the open air; **~ condizionata** air-conditioning; **darsi delle arie** to fancy o.s.
arido, -a *agg (secco)* arid; *(fig: persona, cuore)* cold.
ariete *sm (animale)* ram.
◆ **Ariete** *sm* Aries.
aringa, -ghe *sf* herring.
arista *sf* saddle of pork.
aristocratico, -a, -ci, -che ◇ *agg* aristocratic ◇ *sm, f* aristocrat.
aritmetica *sf* arithmetic.
Arlecchino *sm* Harlequin.
arma, -i *sf (strumento)* weapon; *(di esercito)* division; **~ da fuoco** firearm.
armadio *sm* cupboard; **~ a muro** built-in cupboard.
armato, -a *agg* armed.
armatura *sf* armour.
armonia *sf* harmony.
arnese *sm (attrezzo)* tool; *(fam: oggetto)* thing.
arnia *sf* beehive.
Arno *sm*: l'~ the Arno.
aroma, -i *sm (odore)* aroma; *(essenza)* flavouring.
◆ **aromi** *smpl* herbs.
arpa *sf* harp.
arpione *sm* harpoon.
arrabbiarsi *vr* to get angry.
arrabbiato, -a *agg* angry; **all'arrabbiata** → **penne**.
arrampicarsi *vr* to climb.
arrangiarsi *vr* to get by.
arredamento *sm* furnishings *(pl)*.
arredare *vt* to furnish.
arrendersi *vr* to surrender.
arrestare *vt (catturare)* to arrest; *(emorragia, flusso)* to stop.
arresto *sm (cattura)* arrest; *(fermata)* stop; **~ cardiaco** cardiac arrest.
arretrato, -a *agg (pagamento, giornale)* back *(dav s)*; *(sottosviluppato)* backward; *(sorpassato)* old-fashioned.
◆ **arretrati** *smpl* arrears.
arricchire *vt* to enrich.
◆ **arricchirsi** *vr* to get rich.
arricciacapelli *sm inv* curling tongs *(pl)*.
arricciare *vt (capelli, nastro)* to curl; **~ il naso** to wrinkle one's nose.
arrivare *vi* to arrive; **arriverò a Firenze alle due** I'll get to Florence at two.
◆ **arrivare a** *v + prep (grado, livello)* to reach; **~ a fare qc** *(riuscire)* to manage to do sthg; *(giungere al punto di, osare)* to go so far as to do sthg.
arrivederci *esclam* goodbye!
arrivederla *esclam* goodbye!
arrivista, -i, -e *smf* social climber.
arrivo *sm* arrival; *(nello sport)* finishing line; **essere in ~** to be arriving; '**arrivi (nazionali/internazionali)**' '(domestic/international) arrivals'.
arrogante *agg* arrogant.
arrossire *vi* to blush.
arrostire *vt* to roast.
arrosto *sm* roast.
arrotolare *vt* to roll up.
arrotondare *vt (render tondo)* to round; *(numero)* to round off;

(stipendio) to add to.
arrugginito, -a *agg* rusty.
arruolarsi *vr* to enlist.
arsenale *sm (di armi)* arsenal; *(cantiere)* dockyard.
arte *sf* art; *(abilità)* skill.
arteria *sf* artery.
artico, -a, -ci, -che *agg* Arctic.
articolazione *sf* joint.
articolo *sm* article; *(merce)* article, item; **articoli da regalo** gifts.
Artide *sf*: **l'~** the Arctic.
artificiale *agg* artificial.
artigianato *sm* craftsmanship; **di ~** handcrafted.
artigiano, -a ◇ *agg* craft *(dav s)* ◇ *sm, f* craftsman (*f* craftswoman).
artiglio *sm* claw.
artista, -i, -e *smf* artist.
artistico, -a, -ci, -che *agg* artistic.
arto *sm* limb.
artrite *sf* arthritis.
artrosi *sf* osteoarthritis.
ascella *sf* armpit.
ascendente *sm (influsso)* ascendancy; *(astrologico)* ascendant.
Ascensione *sf*: **l'~** the Ascension.
ascensore *sm* lift *(Br)*, elevator *(Am)*.
ascesso *sm* abscess.
ascia (*pl* **asce**) *sf* axe.
asciugacapelli *sm inv* hairdryer.
asciugamano *sm* towel.
asciugare *vt* to dry.
◆ **asciugarsi** *vr (persona)* to dry o.s.; *(tinta, vestiti)* to dry.
asciutto, -a *agg (secco)* dry; *(magro)* thin.
ascoltare *vt* to listen to.
ascoltatore, -trice *sm, f* listener.
ascolto *sm*: **dare** o **prestare ~ a** to pay attention to; **essere in ~** to be listening.
asfaltato, -a *agg* asphalt *(dav s)*.
asfalto *sm* asphalt.
asfissia *sf* asphyxia.
asfissiare *vt & vi* to suffocate.
Asia *sf*: **l'~** Asia.
asiatico, -a, -ci, -che *agg & sm, f* Asian.
asilo *sm (scuola)* nursery; **~ nido** crèche; **~ politico** political asylum.
asino *sm* donkey.
asma *sf* asthma.
asola *sf* buttonhole.
asparago *sm* asparagus.
aspettare *vt* to wait for; **mi aspetto una risposta** I expect an answer; **~ un bambino** to be expecting a child.
aspettativa *sf (previsione)* expectation; *(congedo)* leave.
aspetto *sm (apparenza)* appearance; *(punto di vista)* point of view; *(elemento)* aspect.
aspirapolvere *sm inv* vacuum cleaner.
aspirare *vt (inalare)* to breathe in; *(risucchiare)* to suck up.
◆ **aspirare a** *v + prep* to aspire to.
aspiratore *sm* extractor.
aspirina® *sf* aspirin.
aspro, -a *agg (sapore)* sour.
assaggiare *vt* to taste.
assai *avv (molto)* very; *(abbastanza)* enough.
assalire *vt* to attack.
assassinare *vt* to murder.
assassinio *sm* murder.
assassino, -a *sm, f* murderer.
asse ◇ *sf* board ◇ *sm (di auto)* axle; *(retta)* axis.
assedio *sm* siege.
assegnare *vt*: **~ qc (a qn)** *(casa, rendita)* to allocate sthg (to sb); *(incarico, compiti)* to assign sthg (to sb); *(premio)* to award sthg (to sb).
assegno *sm (bancario)* cheque; *(sussidio)* benefit; **~ a vuoto** bounced cheque; **~ circolare** bank draft; **~ di studio** study grant; **~ di**

viaggio o turistico traveller's cheque; contro ~ cash on delivery.
assemblẹa *sf* meeting.
assẹnte ◇ *agg (da luogo)* absent; *(distratto)* vacant ◇ *smf* absentee.
assẹnza *sf (lontananza)* absence; *(mancanza)* lack.
assetạto, -a *agg* thirsty.
assicurạre *vt (auto, casa)* to insure; *(garantire)* to ensure; *(fissare)* to secure.
◆ **assicurarsi** *vr* to insure o.s.; **assicurarsi di fare qc** to be sure to do sthg; **assicurarsi che** to make sure that.
assicurạta *sf* registered letter.
assicurạto, -a *agg* insured.
assicurazione *sf (contratto)* insurance; *(garanzia)* assurance; ~ **sulla vita** life assurance.
assillạre *vt (infastidire)* to pester; *(sog: pensiero)* to torment.
Assịsi *sf* Assisi.
assistẹnte *smf* assistant; ~ **sociale** social worker; ~ **di volo** steward (*f* stewardess).
assistẹnza *sf* aid.
assịstere ◇ *vt* to assist; *(malato)* to care for ◇ *vi*: ~ **(a qc)** *(a lezioni)* to attend (sthg); *(a scena)* to be present (at sthg).
assịstito, -a *pp* → **assistere**.
ạsso *sm* ace.
associạre *vt* to associate.
◆ **associarsi** *vr*: **associarsi (a o con)** *(ditta)* to enter into a partnership (with); **associarsi a qc** *(club)* to join sthg.
associaziọne *sf* association.
assọlto, -a *pp* → **assolvere**.
assolutamẹnte *avv* absolutely.
assolụto, -a *agg* absolute.
assoluziọne *sf (accusato)* acquittal; (RELIG) absolution.
assọlvere *vt (accusato)* to acquit; (RELIG) to absolve; *(compito)* to carry out.
assomigliạre : assomigliare a *v + prep* to resemble, to look like.
assonnạto, -a *agg* sleepy.
assorbẹnte ◇ *agg (tampone)* absorbent ◇ *sm*: ~ **(igienico)** (sanitary) towel; ~ **interno** tampon.
assorbịre *vt* to absorb.
assordạnte *agg* deafening.
assortimẹnto *sm* assortment.
assortịto, -a *agg (vario)* assorted; *(accordato)* matching.
assụmere *vt (personale)* to take on; *(impegno)* to accept; *(atteggiamento)* to assume.
assụnto, -a *pp* → **assumere**.
assurdità *sf inv* absurdity.
assụrdo, -a *agg* absurd.
ạsta *sf (bastone)* pole; *(vendita)* auction.
astẹmio, -a *agg* teetotal.
astenẹrsi : astenersi da *vr + prep* to abstain from.
asterịsco, -schi *sm* asterisk.
astigmạtico, -a, -ci, -che *agg* astigmatic.
astrạtto, -a *agg* abstract.
astrologịa *sf* astrology.
astronạuta, -i, -e *smf* astronaut.
astronomịa *sf* astronomy.
astụccio *sm* case.
astụto, -a *agg (persona)* cunning; *(idea, azione)* shrewd.
astụzia *sf (furbizia)* shrewdness; *(stratagemma)* trick.
A.T. *abbr* = **alta tensione**.
ạteo, -a *sm, f* atheist.
ẠTI *(abbr di Aerotrasporti Italiani) Italian domestic airline.*
atlạnte *sm (geografico)* atlas.
atlạntico, -a, -ci, -che *agg* Atlantic.
Atlạntico *sm*: **l'(Oceano)** ~ the Atlantic (Ocean).
atlẹta, -i, -e *smf* athlete.
atlẹtica *sf* athletics *(sg)*.
atlẹtico, -a, -ci, -che *agg* athletic.
atmosfẹra *sf* atmosphere.

atmosferico, -a, -ci, -che *agg* atmospheric.
atomico, -a, -ci, -che *agg* atomic.
atomo *sm* atom.
atroce *agg* atrocious.
attaccante *sm* forward.
attaccapanni *sm inv* clothes stand.
attaccare *vt (unire)* to attach; *(appendere)* to hang up; *(assalire)* to attack; *(trasmettere)* to give.
◆ **attaccarsi** *vr* to stick.
attacco, -chi *sm* attack; *(presa)* socket.
atteggiamento *sm* attitude.
attendere *vt* to wait for.
attentato *sm* attack.
attento, -a *agg (che presta attenzione)* attentive; *(prudente)* careful; **stai ~!** *(non distrarti)* pay attention!; *(stai in guardia)* be careful!; **'attenti al cane'** 'beware of the dog'; **'attenti al gradino'** 'mind the step'.
attenzione *sf* attention; **~!** be careful!; **fare ~** *(concentrarsi)* to pay attention; *(essere prudente)* to be careful.
atterraggio *sm* landing.
atterrare *vi* to land.
attesa *sf* wait; **essere in ~ di** to be waiting for.
atteso, -a *pp* → **attendere**.
attestato *sm* certificate.
attico *sm* penthouse.
attillato, -a *agg* close-fitting.
attimo *sm* moment.
attirare *vt* to attract.
attitudine *sf* aptitude.
attività *sf inv* activity; *(occupazione)* occupation; (COMM) assets *(pl)*.
attivo, -a ◇ *agg* active ◇ *sm* assets *(pl)*.
atto *sm (azione, gesto)* act, deed; *(documento)* document; *(di dramma)* act; **mettere in ~** to put into action.
attonito, -a *agg* astonished.
attorcigliare *vt* to twist.
attore, -trice *sm, f* actor (*f* actress).
attorno *avv* around.
attracco, -chi *sm (manovra)* docking; *(luogo)* mooring.
attraente *agg* attractive.
attrarre *vt (affascinare)* to attract; *(richiamare)* to draw.
attrattiva *sf (richiamo)* attraction; *(qualità)* attractiveness.
attratto, -a *pp* → **attrarre**.
attraversamento *sm* crossing; **~ pedonale** pedestrian crossing.
attraversare *vt (strada, città)* to cross; *(periodo)* to go through.
attraverso *prep (da parte a parte)* across; *(per mezzo di)* through.
attrazione *sf* attraction.
attrezzatura *sf* equipment.
attrezzo *sm* tool.
attribuire : attribuire a *v + prep (opera)* to attribute to; **~ il merito a qn** to give sb the credit.
attrice → **attore**.
attrito *sm* friction.
attuale *agg (presente)* present; *(moderno)* topical.
attualità *sf inv* current events *(pl)*; **d'~** topical.
attualmente *avv* at present.
attuare *vt* to carry out.
attutire *vt (colpo, rumore)* to reduce.
audace *agg* bold.
audacia *sf* audacity.
audiovisivo, -a *agg* audiovisual.
auditorio *sm* auditorium.
audizione *sf* audition.
augurare *vt*: **~ qc a qn** to wish sb sthg; **augurarsi di fare qc** to hope to do sthg; **mi auguro che tutto vada bene** I hope that all goes well.
augurio *sm* wish; **auguri** greetings; **(tanti) auguri!** all the best!;

(per compleanno) happy birthday!; **fare gli auguri a qn** to give sb one's best wishes.
aula *sf* classroom.
aumentare *vt & vi* to increase.
aumento *sm* increase.
aureola *sf* halo.
auricolare *sm* earphone.
aurora *sf* dawn.
ausiliare *agg & sm* auxiliary.
austero, -a *agg* austere.
Australia *sf*: **l'~** Australia.
australiano, -a *agg & sm, f* Australian.
Austria *sf*: **l'~** Austria.
austriaco, -a, -ci, -che *agg & sm, f* Austrian.
autenticare *vt* to authenticate.
autentico, -a, -ci, -che *agg (firma, quadro)* authentic; *(fatto)* true; **è un ~ cretino** he's a real cretin.
autista, -i, -e *smf* driver.
auto *sf inv* car.
autoabbronzante ◇ *agg* self-tanning ◇ *sm* fake tanning cream.
autoadesivo, -a ◇ *agg* self-adhesive ◇ *sm* sticker.
autoambulanza *sf* ambulance.
autobiografia *sf* autobiography.
autobus *sm inv* bus.
autocarro *sm* truck.
autocisterna *sf* tanker.
autocontrollo *sm* self-control.
autodidatta, -i, -e *smf* self-taught person.
autodromo *sm* racing track.
autogol *sm inv* own goal.
autografo *sm* autograph.
autogrill® *sm inv* motorway restaurant.
autolinea *sf* bus service.
automa, -i *sm* automaton.
automatico, -a, -ci, -che *agg* automatic.
automazione *sf* automation.
automezzo *sm* motor vehicle.
automobile *sf* car *(Br)*, automobile *(Am)*.
automobilismo *sm (sport)* motor racing; *(industria)* car industry *(Br)*, auto industry *(Am)*.
automobilista, -i, -e *smf* motorist.
autonoleggio *sm* car hire.
autonomia *sf (indipendenza)* autonomy; *(di veicolo)* range.
autonomo, -a *agg* independent, autonomous.
autopsia *sf* autopsy.
autoradio *sf inv* car radio.
autore, -trice *sm, f (di libro)* author; *(di quadro)* painter; **l'~ del delitto** the person who committed the crime.
autorevole *agg* authoritative.
autorimessa *sf* garage.
autorità *sf inv* authority.
autoritario, -a *agg* authoritarian.
autorizzare *vt* to authorize.
autorizzazione *sf* authorization.
autoscatto *sm* timer.
autoscontro *sm* Dodgem® car.
autoscuola *sf* driving school.
autoservizi *smpl* bus services.
autostop *sm* hitchhiking; **fare l'~** to hitchhike.
autostoppista, -i, -e *smf* hitchhiker.
autostrada *sf* motorway *(Br)*, freeway *(Am)*.
autostradale *agg* motorway *(Br) (dav s)*, freeway *(Am) (dav s)*.
autoveicolo *sm* motor vehicle.
autovettura *sf* motorcar.
autunno *sm* autumn *(Br)*, fall *(Am)*.
avambraccio *sm* forearm.
avanguardia *sf*: **d'~** avant-garde; **essere all'~** to be in the vanguard.
avanti ◇ *avv (stato in luogo)* in front; *(moto)* forward ◇ *prep*: **~ a** *(stato in luogo)* ahead of; *(moto)*

ahead of, in front of; ~! *(invito a entrare)* come in!; *(esortazione)* come on!; **'avanti!'** *(al semaforo)* 'cross now', 'walk' *(Am)*; *(in banca)* 'enter'; **~ e indietro** backwards and forwards; **andare ~** to go on; **essere ~** *(nel lavoro, studio)* to be well ahead; **essere ~ negli anni** to be getting on (in years); **farsi ~** to come forward; **passare ~ a qn** to go in front of sb.

avanzare ◇ *vt (spostare avanti)* to move forward; *(proposta)* to put forward ◇ *vi (procedere)* to advance; *(restare)* to be left (over).

avanzo *sm (di cibo)* leftovers *(pl)*; *(di stoffa)* remnant.

avaria *sf (meccanico)* breakdown.

avariato, -a *agg (cibo)* off.

avaro, -a ◇ *agg* mean ◇ *sm, f* miser.

avena *sf* oats *(pl)*.

avere ◇ *vt* 1. *(possedere)* to have; **ha due fratelli** he's got two brothers; **non ho più soldi** I haven't got any money left.

2. *(come caratteristica)* to have; **~ occhi e capelli scuri** to have dark eyes and hair; **~ molta immaginazione** to have a lot of imagination.

3. *(età)*: **quanti anni hai?** how old are you?; **ho 18 anni** I'm 18 (years old).

4. *(portare addosso)* to have on, to wear; **ha un cappotto grigio** she's wearing a grey coat, she's got a grey coat on.

5. *(sentire)*: **~ caldo/freddo** to be hot/cold; **~ sonno** to be sleepy; **~ fame** to be hungry; **ho mal di testa** I've got a headache.

6. *(ottenere, ricevere)* to get.

7. *(in espressioni)*: **non ha niente a che fare o vedere con lui** that's got nothing to do with him; **non ne ho per molto** it won't take me long; **~ da fare** to have things to do; **avercela con qn** to be angry with sb; **quanti ne abbiamo oggi?** what's the date today?

◇ *v aus* to have; **non ho finito** I haven't finished; **gli ho parlato ieri** I spoke to him yesterday.

◆ **averi** *smpl (beni)* wealth *(sg)*.

avi *smpl* ancestors.

aviazione *sf* aviation.

avido, -a *agg* greedy.

AVIS *sf (abbr di Associazione Volontari Italiani del Sangue)* blood donors' association.

avocado *sm inv* avocado.

avorio *sm* ivory.

avvallamento *sm* depression.

avvantaggiare *vt* to favour.

◆ **avvantaggiarsi** *vr*: **avvantaggiarsi negli studi** to get ahead with one's studies; **avvantaggiarsi sui concorrenti** to get ahead of one's competitors.

◆ **avvantaggiarsi di** *vr + prep* to take advantage of.

avvelenamento *sm* poisoning.

avvelenare *vt* to poison; *(aria)* to pollute.

avvenente *agg* attractive.

avvenimento *sm* event.

avvenire ◇ *sm* future ◇ *vi* to happen.

avventarsi *vr*: **~ su o contro** to rush at.

avventato, -a *agg* rash.

avventura *sf* adventure; *(amorosa)* affair.

avventurarsi *vr* to venture.

avventuroso, -a *agg* adventurous.

avvenuto, -a *pp* → **avvenire**.

avverarsi *vr* to come true.

avverbio *sm* adverb.

avversario, -a ◇ *agg* opposing ◇ *sm, f* opponent.

avvertenza *sf (avviso)* notice.

◆ **avvertenze** *sfpl* instructions.

avvertimento *sm* warning.

avvertire *vt (avvisare)* to warn;

(dolore, fastidio) to feel.

avviamento *sm (di motore)* starting; (COMM) goodwill.

avviare *vt (cominciare)* to start; *(indirizzare)* to introduce.

◆ **avviarsi** *vr* to set off.

avvicinare *vt* to move closer.

◆ **avvicinarsi** *vr*: **avvicinarsi (a)** to move close (to).

avvilirsi *vr* to lose heart.

avvincente *agg* enthralling.

avvisare *vt (informare)* to inform; *(ammonire)* to warn.

avviso *sm (scritto)* notice; *(annuncio)* announcement; *(avvertimento)* warning; **a mio ~** in my opinion.

avvistare *vt* to sight.

avvitare *vt (lampadina)* to screw in; *(con viti)* to screw.

avvizzire *vi* to wither.

avvocato *sm* lawyer.

avvolgere *vt (fascia)* to wrap round; *(tappeto)* to roll up; *(avviluppare)* to wrap up.

◆ **avvolgersi** *vr (aggrovigliarsi)* to become tangled; *(avvilupparsi)* to wrap o.s. up.

avvolgibile *sm* roller blind.

avvolto, -a *pp* → **avvolgere**.

avvoltoio *sm* vulture.

azalea *sf* azalea.

azienda *sf* business, firm; **~ agricola** farm.

azionare *vt* to operate.

azione *sf* action; (COMM) share.

azionista, -i, -e *smf* shareholder.

azoto *sm* nitrogen.

azzannare *vt* to sink one's teeth into.

azzardare *vt* to venture.

◆ **azzardarsi** *vr*: **azzardarsi a fare qc** to dare to do sthg.

azzardo *sm* risk; **giocare d'~** to gamble.

azzeccare *vt* to get right.

azzuffarsi *vr* to scuffle.

azzurro, -a *agg & sm* blue.

◆ **Azzurri** *smpl*: **gli Azzurri** the Italian national team.

B

babà *sm inv* rum baba.

babbo *sm (fam)* dad, daddy; **Babbo Natale** Father Christmas.

baby-sitter [bebi'sitter] *smf inv* babysitter.

bacca, -che *sf (frutto)* berry.

baccalà *sm inv* dried salt cod; ~ **alla fiorentina** *dried salt cod cooked with garlic and tomato sauce*; ~ **alla vicentina** *dried salt cod poached in milk with onions, anchovies and parsley.*

bacheca, -che *sf (pannello)* notice board; *(cassetta)* display case.

baciare *vt* to kiss.

◆ **baciarsi** *vr* to kiss (each other).

bacinella *sf* bowl.

bacino *sm (in geografia, catino)* basin; (ANAT) pelvis.

bacio *sm* kiss; **baci di dama** *sweet pastries sandwiched together with chocolate cream.*

badare *vi*: ~ **a** *(prendersi cura di)* to look after; *(fare attenzione a)* to pay attention to; ~ **a** O **di fare qc** to take care to do sthg; **mio fratello non bada a spese** money's no object where my brother's concerned.

badia *sf* abbey.

baffi *smpl* moustache *(sg)*.

bagagliaio *sm (di macchina)* boot *(Br)*, trunk *(Am)*; *(di treno)* luggage van *(Br)*, baggage car *(Am)*.

bagaglio *sm* luggage, baggage; ~ **a mano** hand luggage; **ho un solo** ~ I have only one piece of luggage.

◆ **bagagli** *smpl* luggage *(sg)*; **fare i bagagli** to pack.

bagliore *sm (di lampi)* flash; *(di fari)* glare.

bagna cauda *sf oil, garlic and anchovy dip from Piedmont kept warm at the table and served with vegetables.*

bagnare *vt* to wet; *(tovaglia, vestiti)* to get wet; *(annaffiare)* to water; *(sog: fiume)* to flow through; *(sog: mare)* to wash.

◆ **bagnarsi** *vr (in mare)* to bathe; *(di pioggia, spruzzi)* to get wet.

bagnato, -a *agg* wet; ~ **fradicio** soaked through.

bagnino, -a *sm, f* lifeguard.

bagno *sm (nella vasca)* bath; *(in piscina, mare)* swim; *(stanza)* bathroom; **fare il** ~ *(nella vasca)* to have a bath; *(in mare)* to have a swim; ~ **pubblico** public baths *(pl)*.

◆ **bagni** *smpl (stabilimento)* bathing establishment.

bagnomaria *sm*: **cuocere a** ~ to cook in a double saucepan.

bagnoschiuma *sm inv* bath foam.

baia *sf* bay.

baita *sf* chalet.

balaustra *sf* balustrade.
balbettare *vi* to stammer.
balcone *sm* balcony.
balena *sf* whale.
balla *sf (frottola)* fib; *(di merci)* bale.
ballare *vi & vt* to dance.
ballerina *sf (scarpa)* pump, → **ballerino**.
ballerino, -a *sm, f* dancer; *(classico)* ballet-dancer (*f* ballerina).
balletto *sm* ballet.
ballo *sm* dance; *(festa)* dance, ball; **essere in ~** to be at stake; **tirare in ~** *(coinvolgere)* to involve; *(menzionare)* to mention.
balneare *agg* bathing *(dav s)*.
balneazione *sf* bathing; **'divieto di balneazione'** 'no bathing'.
balsamo *sm (per capelli)* conditioner; *(pomata)* ointment.
Baltico *sm*: **il (Mar) ~** the Baltic (Sea).
balzare *vi* to leap.
bambinaia *sf* nanny.
bambino, -a *sm, f* child; *(neonato)* baby.
bambola *sf* doll.
banale *agg* banal.
banana *sf* banana.
banca, -che *sf* bank; **~ dati** data bank.
bancarella *sf* stall.
bancario, -a ◇ *agg* bank *(dav s)* ◇ *sm, f* bank employee.
bancarotta *sf* bankruptcy.
banchina *sf (di porto)* quay; *(di stazione)* platform; **'~ non transitabile'** 'soft verges'.
banco, -chi *sm (di scuola)* desk; *(di negozio, bar)* counter; *(di mercato)* stall; *(banca)* bank; **~ di corallo** coral reef; **~ di nebbia** fog bank.
bancomat® *sm inv (sportello)* cash dispenser; *(tessera)* cash card; *(sistema)* automated banking.
bancone *sm* counter.
banconota *sf* bank note.
banda *sf (musicale)* band; *(striscia)* band, strip; *(di malviventi)* gang; *(di amici)* group.
bandiera *sf* flag.
bandito *sm* bandit.
bando *sm* announcement; **~ alle chiacchiere!** that's enough talking!
bar *sm inv* bar; **~-tabacchi** *bar that also sells cigarettes and stamps.*
bara *sf* coffin.
baracca, -che *sf* hut; *(spreg: casa)* dump; **mandare avanti la ~** *(fam)* to keep things going.
baraccone *sm* booth.
baratro *sm* barter.
barattolo *sm* jar; *(di latta)* can.
barba *sf* beard; **farsi la ~** to shave; **che ~!** what a bore!
barbaro, -a ◇ *agg* barbaric ◇ *sm, f* barbarian.
barbecue ['ba:bikju:] *sm inv* barbecue.
barbiere *sm* barber.
barbone, -a *sm, f* tramp.
barca, -che *sf* boat; **~ a remi** rowing boat *(Br)*, rowboat *(Am)*; **~ a vela** sailing boat *(Br)*, sailboat *(Am)*.
barcollare *vi* to stagger.
barella *sf* stretcher.
barista, -i, -e *smf* barman (*f* barmaid).
barman *sm inv* barman.
Barolo *sm* Barolo *(full-bodied red wine from Piedmont)*.
barra *sf* rod, bar; *(lineetta)* stroke; *(di barca)* tiller.
barricare *vt* to barricade.
◆ **barricarsi** *vr*: **barricarsi in/dietro** to barricade o.s. in/behind.
barriera *sf* barrier.
basare *vt* to base.
◆ **basarsi su** *vr + prep (persona)* to base o.s. on.
base *sf* base; *(fondamento)* basis; **a ~ di whisky** whisky-based; **in ~ a qc** on the basis of sthg.
baseball ['beizbol] *sm* baseball.

basette *sfpl* sideboards.
basilica, -che *sf* basilica.
basilico *sm* basil.
basso, -a ◇ *agg* low; *(persona)* short; *(acqua)* shallow ◇ *sm (fondo)* bottom; *(strumento, cantante)* bass; **in ~** at the bottom.
basta *esclam* that's enough!
bastare *vi & v impers* to be enough; **~ a qn** to be enough for sb; **basta che** so long as; **basta così!** that's enough!
bastone *sm* stick; **~ da passeggio** walking stick.
battaglia *sf* battle.
battello *sm* boat.
battere ◇ *vt* to beat; *(testa)* to hit; *(ore)* to strike; *(zona)* to scour ◇ *vi (cuore)* to beat; *(sole, pioggia)* to beat down; *(urtare)*: **~ contro** o **in qc** to hit sthg; **si batteva i denti dal freddo** our teeth were chattering with the cold; **~ a macchina** to type; **~ le mani** to clap; **in un batter d'òcchio** in the twinkling of an eye.
◆ **battersi** *vr* to fight.
batteria *sf (elettrica)* battery; *(strumento)* drums *(pl)*.
battesimo *sm* baptism.
battezzare *vt* to baptize.
battigia *sf* water's edge.
battistrada *sm inv* tread.
battito *sm* beat, beating; *(di orologio)* ticking; **~ cardiaco** heartbeat.
battuta *sf (spiritosaggine)* witty remark; *(teatrale)* cue; *(di tennis)* service.
baule *sm (da viaggio)* trunk; *(di auto)* boot *(Br)*, trunk *(Am)*.
bavaglino *sm* bib.
bavaglio *sm* gag.
bavarese *sf (dolce) cold dessert made with eggs, milk and cream.*
bavero *sm* collar.
bazzecola *sf (cosa poco importante)* trifle; *(cosa facile)*: **è una ~** it's no problem.
beato, -a *agg (felice)* happy; (RELIG) blessed; **~ te!** lucky you!
beauty-case ['bju:ti 'keis] *sm inv* beauty case.
beccare *vt* to peck; *(fam: sorprendere)* to catch; **beccarsi qc** *(fam) (raffreddore)* to catch sthg; *(ceffone)* to get sthg.
becco, -chi *sm* beak.
Befana *sf (festa)* Epiphany; *(personaggio) legendary old woman who brings children their presents at the Epiphany.*
beffa *sf* joke.
beffarsi : beffarsi di *vr + prep* to make fun of.
begli → **bello**.
bei → **bello**.
beige [bɛʒ] *agg inv & sm inv* beige.
bel → **bello**.
belga, -gi, -ghe *agg & smf* Belgian.
Belgio *sm*: **il ~** Belgium.
bella *sf* (SPORT) decider.
bellezza *sf* beauty; **che ~!** fantastic!
bello, -a *(dav sm* **bel** *(pl* **bei***) + consonante;* **bello** *(pl* **begli***) + s+consonante, gn, ps, z;* **bell'** *(pl* **begli***) + vocale)* ◇ *agg* **1.** *(donna, cosa)* beautiful; *(uomo)* handsome; **farsi ~** to make o.s. beautiful; **le belle arti** fine arts.
2. *(piacevole)* pleasant, lovely.
3. *(tempo)* fine, beautiful; **la bella stagione** the summer months *(pl)*; **fa ~** it's lovely weather.
4. *(buono)* good.
5. *(lodevole)* good, kind.
6. *(grande)*: **un bel piatto di spaghetti** a nice big plate of spaghetti; **una bella dormita** a good sleep; **è una bella cifra** it's a considerable sum of money.
7. *(rafforzativo)*: **è bell'e (che) andato** he's already gone; **è una bugia bell'e buona** it's an absolute lie; **alla bell'e meglio** somehow or

other; **un bel niente** absolutely nothing.

◇ *sm* 1. *(bellezza)* beauty.

2. *(punto culminante)*: **sul più ~** at that very moment; **il ~ è che ...** the best bit is that ...

belva *sf* wild beast.

belvedere *sm inv* scenic viewpoint.

benché *cong* although, though.

benda *sf (fasciatura)* bandage; *(per occhi)* blindfold.

bendare *vt (ferita)* to bandage; *(occhi)* to blindfold.

bene ◇ *avv* (*compar & superl* **meglio**) 1. *(in modo soddisfacente)* well; **avete mangiato ~?** did you enjoy your meal?

2. *(nel modo giusto)* well; **hai fatto ~** you did the right thing.

3. *(in buona salute)*: **stare/sentirsi ~** to be/feel well.

4. *(a proprio agio)*: **stare ~** to be o feel comfortable.

5. *(esteticamente)*: **stare ~** to look good.

6. *(rafforzativo)*: **è ben difficile** it's very difficult; **è ben più difficile del previsto** it's much more difficult than we thought; **lo credo ~** I can well believe it; **spero ~ che** I very much hope that.

7. *(in espressioni)*: **è ~ che lo sappiate** it's as well that you know; **sarebbe ~ aspettare** it would be better to wait; **dire ~ di qn** to speak well of sb; **ti sta ~!** it serves you right!; **va ~** all right, OK.

◇ *esclam* fine!, OK!

◇ *sm* good; **è per il tuo ~** it's for your own good; **è un ~ per tutti** it is a good thing for everyone.

◆ **beni** *smpl (proprietà)* property *(sg)*.

benedire *vt* to bless.

benedizione *sf* blessing.

beneducato, -a *agg* well-mannered.

beneficenza *sf* charity.

benessere *sm* wellbeing.

benestante *agg* well-to-do.

benevolo, -a *agg* benevolent.

beninteso *avv* certainly, of course.

benvenuto, -a *agg & sm* welcome; **benvenuti a Roma!** welcome to Rome!; **dare il ~ a qn** to welcome sb.

benzina *sf* petrol *(Br)*, gas *(Am)*; **fare ~** to get petrol *(Br)*, to get gas *(Am)*.

benzinaio, -a *sm, f* forecourt attendant.

bere *vt* to drink; **bevi qualcosa?** would you like something to drink?; **offrire da ~ a qn** to offer sb a drink.

bermuda *smpl* bermuda shorts.

bernoccolo *sm* bump.

bersaglio *sm* target.

besciamella *sf* béchamel sauce.

bestemmiare *vi* to curse, to swear.

bestia *sf* animal; **andare in ~** to fly into a rage.

bestiame *sm* livestock.

bevanda *sf* drink.

bevuto, -a *pp* → **bere**.

biancheria *sf* linen; **~ intima** underwear.

bianchetto *sm* correcting fluid.

bianco, -a, -chi, -che ◇ *agg & sm* white ◇ *sm, f (persona)* white man (*f* white woman); **riso in ~** plain rice; **pesce in ~** boiled fish; **in ~ e nero** black and white.

biasimare *vt* to blame.

bibbia *sf* bible.

biberon *sm inv* baby's bottle.

bibita *sf* drink.

biblioteca, -che *sf* library.

bicarbonato *sm*: **~ (di sodio)** bicarbonate (of soda).

bicchiere *sm* glass.

bici *sf inv (fam)* bike.
bicicletta *sf* bicycle; **andare in ~** to cycle.
bidè *sm inv* bidet.
bidone *sm* bin; *(fam) (imbroglio)* swindle; **fare un ~ a qn** *(fam) (imbrogliare)* to cheat sb; *(mancare a un appuntamento)* to stand sb up.
biennale *agg (ogni due anni)* two-yearly; *(per due anni)* two-year *(dav s)*.
◆ **Biennale** *sf*: **la Biennale** the Venice Arts Festival.
biforcarsi *vr* to fork.
BIGE *sm reduced-price train ticket for people under 26.*
bigiotteria *sf* costume jewellery; *(negozio)* costume jeweller's.
biglia = **bilia**.
bigliardo = **biliardo**.
bigliettaio, -a *sm, f* ticket inspector.
biglietteria *sf* ticket office; *(al teatro)* box office; **~ automatica** ticket machine.
biglietto *sm (scontrino)* ticket; *(messaggio)* note; *(banconota)* (bank) note; **fare il ~** to buy one's ticket; **~ d'andata e ritorno** return (ticket); **~ di (sola) andata** single (ticket); **~ collettivo** party ticket; **~ cumulativo** group ticket; **~ gratuito** complimentary ticket; **~ intero** full-price ticket; **~ ridotto** reduced-price ticket; **~ d'auguri** greetings card; **~ da visita** visiting card.
bignè *sm inv choux bun filled with custard or chocolate.*
bigodino *sm* curler.
bigoli *smpl*: **~ coi rovinazzi** *large spaghetti from Veneto in a sauce made with chicken giblets.*
bikini® *sm inv* bikini.
bilancia, -ce *sf* scales *(pl)*.
◆ **Bilancia** *sf* Libra.
bilancio *sm* (COMM) balance sheet; **~ preventivo** budget.
bilia *sf (di vetro)* marble; *(da biliardo)* billiard ball.
biliardo *sm (gioco)* billiards *(sg)*; *(tavolo)* billiard table.
bilico : **in bilico** *avv* balanced.
bilingue *agg* bilingual.
bimbo, -a *sm, f* little boy (*f* little girl).
binario *sm (rotaie)* railway track; *(marciapiede)* platform; **'ai binari'** 'to the trains'.
binocolo *sm* binoculars *(pl)*.
biologia *sf* biology.
biondo, -a *agg* blond (*f* blonde).
birichino, -a ◇ *agg* cheeky ◇ *sm, f* little rascal.
birillo *sm* skittle.
biro® *sf inv* Biro®.
birra *sf* beer; **~ chiara** lager; **~ scura** stout; **~ alla spina** draught beer.
birreria *sf* pub.
bis *esclam* encore!
bisbigliare *vi & vt* to whisper.
biscotto *sm* biscuit.
bisessuale *agg* bisexual.
bisestile *agg* → **anno**.
bisnonno, -a *sm, f* great-grandfather (*f* great-grandmother).
bisognare *v impers*: **bisogna stare attenti** we/I must be careful; **bisogna che tu venga subito** you have to come at once.
bisogno *sm* need, necessity; **aver ~ di** to need.
bistecca, -che *sf* steak; **~ al sangue** rare steak; **~ alla fiorentina** *T-bone steak grilled or cooked over charcoal.*
bisticciare *vi* to bicker.
bitter *sm inv* bitters *(pl)*.
bivio *sm* fork, junction.
bizza *sf* tantrum.
bizzarro, -a *agg* odd, eccentric.
bloccare *vt* to block; *(città)* to cut off; *(meccanismo)* to jam; *(prezzi)* to freeze.
◆ **bloccarsi** *vr (ascensore)* to get stuck; *(porta)* to jam.

blocchẹtto *sm (quaderno)* notebook.

blọcco, -chi *sm* block; *(quaderno)* notebook; *(di meccanismo)* blockage; *(di attività)* stoppage; **~ stradale** roadblock; **in ~** en bloc.

blu *agg inv & sm inv* blue.

blue-jeans [blu'dʒins] *smpl* jeans.

blụsa *sf* blouse.

bọa ◇ *sm inv (serpente)* boa ◇ *sf (galleggiante)* buoy.

bobịna *sf (di auto)* coil; *(di pellicola)* reel.

bọcca, -che *sf* mouth; **in ~ al lupo!** good luck!

boccạccia, -ce *sf*: **fare le boccacce** to pull faces.

boccạle *sm* jug.

bọccia, -ce *sf* bowl.

bocciạre *vt (studente)* to fail; *(proposta, progetto)* to reject.

boccọne *sm* mouthful; **mangiare un ~** to have a bite to eat.

boccọni *avv* face downwards.

boicottạre *vt* to boycott.

bọlla *sf* bubble; *(vescica)* blister; (COMM) bill.

bollẹnte *agg* boiling.

bollẹtta *sf* bill; *(ricevuta)* receipt.

bollettịno *sm* bulletin; **~ meteorologico** weather forecast.

bollịre *vt & vi* to boil.

bollịto, -a ◇ *agg* boiled ◇ *sm beef, veal or chicken, served with a parsley sauce.*

bollitọre *sm* kettle.

bọllo *sm (marchio)* stamp.

Bolọgna *sf* Bologna.

bolognẹse *agg* of/from Bologna; **alla ~** with meat and tomato sauce.

bọmba *sf* bomb.

bombardạre *vt* to bomb.

bọmbola *sf* cylinder.

bombolọne *sm* doughnut.

bonạccia *sf* (dead) calm.

bonạrio, -a *agg* good-natured.

bonẹt *sm inv chocolate-flavoured egg custard.*

bontà *sf* goodness.

borbottạre ◇ *vi* to grumble ◇ *vt* to mutter.

bordeaux [bor'do] *agg inv* maroon.

bọrdo *sm (orlo)* edge; *(guarnizione)* trim, border; *(di nave)* (ship's) side; **a ~ di** *(nave, aereo)* on board; *(auto)* in; *(moto)* on.

borghẹse *agg* middle-class; **in ~** in plain clothes.

borghesịa *sf* middle classes *(pl)*.

bọrgo, -ghi *sm (paesino)* hamlet; *(quartiere)* district.

borotạlco® *sm* talcum powder.

borrạccia, -ce *sf* flask.

bọrsa *sf* bag; **~ dell'acqua calda** hot-water bottle; **~ del ghiaccio** ice bag; **~ della spesa** shopping bag; **~ di studio** grant.

◆ **Borsa** *sf* Stock Exchange.

borsaiọlo *sm* pickpocket.

borsellịno *sm* purse.

borsẹtta *sf* handbag.

bọsco, -schi *sm* wood.

botạnico, -a, -ci, -che ◇ *agg* botanic ◇ *sm, f* botanist.

bọtta *sf* blow; *(rumore)* bang; **fare a botte** to come to blows.

bọtte *sf* barrel.

bottẹga, -ghe *sf* shop; *(laboratorio)* workshop.

bottegạio, -a *sm, f* shopkeeper.

bottịglia *sf* bottle.

bottigliọne *sm* large bottle.

bottọne *sm* button; **attaccare un ~ a qn** to buttonhole sb.

boutique [bu'tik] *sf inv* boutique.

box *sm inv (garage)* lock-up (garage); *(per bambini)* playpen; *(per animali)* pen.

boxe [bɔks] *sf* boxing.

boy-scout [bɔi'skaut] *sm inv* boy scout.

braccẹtto : a braccetto *avv* arm in arm.

bracciale *sm* bracelet.
braccialetto *sm* bracelet.
braccio *sm (arto: pl f* **braccia***)* arm; *(di edificio: pl m* **bracci***)* wing; *(di gru, fiume: pl m* **bracci***)* arm; **~ di ferro** arm wrestling; **sotto ~** arm in arm.
bracciolo *sm* arm.
brace *sf* embers *(pl)*; **alla ~** charcoal-grilled.
braciola *sf* steak; *(con osso)* chop.
braille ['braj] *sm* braille.
branco, -chi *sm (di animali)* herd; *(spreg: di persone)* gang, bunch.
branda *sf* camp bed.
brasato *sm* braised beef.
Brasile *sm*: **il ~** Brazil.
bravo, -a *agg* good; **~!** well done!; **~ a fare qc** good at doing sthg; **~ in qc** good at sthg.
bresaola *sf dried salt beef served thinly sliced.*
bretelle *sfpl (per pantaloni)* braces; *(spalline)* straps.
breve *agg* short, brief; **in ~** briefly; **tra ~** shortly.
brevetto *sm (di invenzione)* patent; *(patente)* licence.
brezza *sf* breeze.
bricco, -chi *sm* jug.
briciola *sf* crumb.
briciolo *sm*: **un ~ di qc** a bit of sthg.
brillante ◇ *agg* brilliant; *(lucente)* bright ◇ *sm* diamond.
brillare *vi* to shine.
brillo, -a *agg* tipsy.
brindisi *sm inv* toast; **fare un ~ a** to toast.
brioche [bri'ɔʃ] *sf inv round, sweet bread roll made with butter and eaten for breakfast.*
britannico, -a, -ci, -che *agg* British.
brivido *sm* shiver, shudder.
brocca, -che *sf* jug.
brodo *sm* broth; **pasta in ~** noodle soup; **riso in ~** rice soup.
bronchite *sf* bronchitis.
brontolare *vi* to grumble; *(stomaco, tuono)* to rumble.
bronzo *sm* bronze.
bruciapelo : a bruciapelo *avv* point-blank.
bruciare ◇ *vt* to burn; *(distruggere)* to burn down ◇ *vi* to burn; *(produrre bruciore)* to sting.
◆ **bruciarsi** *vr (persona)* to burn o.s.; *(oggetto)* to burn.
bruciato, -a *agg* burnt.
bruciatura *sf* burn.
bruno, -a *agg* dark.
bruschetta *sf bread toasted with garlic and olive oil.*
brusio *sm* buzz.
brutale *agg* brutal.
brutto, -a *agg (di aspetto)* ugly; *(tempo, giornata, strada)* bad; *(situazione, sorpresa, malattia)* nasty; *(rafforzativo)*: **~ imbroglione!** you rotten cheat!; **brutti ma buoni** almond and hazelnut meringues.
Bruxelles [bru'ksɛl] *sf* Brussels.
buca, -che *sf* hole; **~ delle lettere** letterbox.
bucare *vt* to make a hole o holes in; **~ una gomma** to puncture a tyre.
◆ **bucarsi** *vr (forarsi)* to have a puncture; *(pungersi)* to prick o.s.; *(fam: drogarsi)* to mainline.
bucatini *smpl*: **~ all'amatriciana** *dish from Lazio consisting of long, thin pasta tubes in a sauce of tomatoes, bacon, chillies and pecorino cheese.*
bucato *sm* washing.
buccellato *sm light, ring-shaped sponge cake from Sarzana and Lucca.*
buccia, -ce *sf* skin.
buco, -chi *sm* hole.
budino *sm type of egg custard baked in a mould*; **~ di riso** *egg custard made with rice, sultanas and sometimes rum.*

bufera *sf* storm.
buffet [by'fɛ] *sm inv* buffet.
buffo, -a *agg* funny.
bugia *sf* lie; *(candeliere)* candleholder.
bugiardo, -a ◇ *agg* lying ◇ *sm, f* liar.
buio, -a ◇ *agg* dark ◇ *sm* darkness; **far ~** to get dark.
Bulgaria *sf*: **la ~** Bulgaria.
bulgaro, -a *agg* Bulgarian.
bullone *sm* bolt.
buonanotte *esclam* good night!
buonasera *esclam* good evening!
buongiorno *esclam (in mattinata)* good morning!; *(nel pomeriggio)* good afternoon!
buongustaio, -a *sm, f* gourmet.
buono, -a ◇ *agg* (*dav sm* **buon** + *consonante o vocale;* **buono** + *s* + *consonante, gn, ps, z*) 1. *(di qualità)* good.
2. *(gradevole)* good.
3. *(generoso)*: **~ (con)** good (to), kind (to).
4. *(bravo, efficiente)* good; **non essere ~ a nulla** to be no good at anything; **è ~ solo a criticare** all he can do is criticize.
5. *(valido: biglietto, passaporto)* valid.
6. *(temperamento)* good; **avere un buon carattere** to be good-natured; **essere di buon umore** to be in a good mood.
7. *(occasione, momento)* right.
8. *(negli auguri)*: **buon appetito!** enjoy your meal!; **buon compleanno!** Happy Birthday!; **buona fortuna!** good luck!; **fate buon viaggio!** have a good journey!
9. *(rafforzativo)*: **ci vuole un'ora buona** it takes a good hour.
10. *(in espressioni)*: **~ a sapersi** that's nice to know; **a buon mercato** cheap; **di buon'ora** early; **alla buona** *(cena)* simple; *(vestirsi)* simp-ly; **farai i compiti, con le buone o con le cattive** like it or not, you'll do your homework.
◇ *sm* 1. *(aspetto positivo)* good; **il ~ è che ...** the good thing is that ...
2. *(tagliando)* voucher; *(invece di rimborso)* credit note; **~ sconto** voucher; **~ del tesoro** treasury bill.
buonsenso *sm* common sense.
buonumore *sm* good humour.
burattino *sm* puppet.
burla *sf* prank, trick.
burocrazia *sf* bureaucracy.
burrasca, -sche *sf* storm.
burrida *sf Sardinian dish made from dogfish cooked with garlic, vinegar, pine kernels and walnuts and served cold.*
burro *sm* butter; **~ di cacao** cocoa butter.
burrone *sm* ravine.
bus [bʌs] *sm inv (abbr di autobus)* bus.
bussare *vi* to knock.
bussola *sf* compass.
busta *sf (per lettera)* envelope; *(di plastica, carta)* bag; **~ paga** pay packet.
busto *sm* bust; *(indumento)* corset.
butano *sm* butane.
buttafuori *sm inv* bouncer.
buttare *vt (gettare)* to throw; **~ all'aria qc** to turn sthg upside down; **~ fuori qn** to throw sb out; **~ giù** *(abbattere)* to knock down; *(inghiottire)* to gulp down; **~ (via)** *(gettare)* to throw away; *(sprecare)* to waste.
◆ **buttarsi** *vr (gettarsi)* to jump; *(fig: tentare)* to have a go.
by-pass [bai'pas] *sm inv* bypass.

C

cabina *sf (di nave)* cabin; *(in spiaggia)* beach hut; *(in piscina)* cubicle; *(di camion)* cab; ~ **telefonica** telephone box.

cacao *sm* cocoa.

cacca *sf (fam)* poo.

caccia, -ce *sf (di animali)* hunting; *(inseguimento)* chase; ~ **al tesoro** treasure hunt.

cacciare *vt (animale)* to hunt; *(mandar via)* to get rid of; ~ **fuori qc** to throw sb out.

♦ **cacciarsi** *vr*: **dove si sarà cacciato?** where has he got to?; **cacciarsi nei guai** to get into trouble.

cacciatora *sf* → **pollo**.

cacciavite *sm inv* screwdriver.

cacciucco, -chi *sm fish soup from Livorno, served with toast rubbed with garlic.*

cachemire [ˈkaʃmir] *sm* cashmere.

caciocavallo *sm hard pear-shaped cheese from southern Italy.*

cadavere *sm* corpse, dead body.

cadere *vi* to fall; *(capelli)* to fall out; *(abito)* to hang; **far** ~ to knock over.

caduta *sf* fall; **la ~ dei capelli** hair loss; '~ **massi**' 'beware falling rocks'.

caffè *sm inv* coffee; *(locale)* cafe; **prendere un** ~ to have a coffee; ~ **corretto** coffee with a dash of spirits; ~ **macchiato** coffee with a dash of milk.

caffeina *sf* caffeine.

caffellatte *sm inv* hot milk with coffee.

caffettiera *sf* coffeepot.

cagna *sf* bitch.

CAI *(abbr di Club Alpino Italiano) Italian mountaineering association.*

cala *sf* bay.

calabrone *sm* hornet.

calamaretti *smpl* squid *(sg)*.

calamaro *sm* squid; **calamari ripieni** *squid stuffed with anchovies, capers, breadcrumbs and parsley, and cooked in white wine.*

calamita *sf* magnet.

calare ◇ *vt* to lower ◇ *vi (prezzo, peso)* to go down; *(vento)* to drop; *(sole)* to set.

calca, -che *sf* throng.

calcagno *sm* heel.

calce *sf* lime.

calciatore, -trice *sm, f* footballer.

calcio *sm (pedata)* kick; *(sport)* football *(Br)*, soccer; *(elemento chimico)* calcium; *(di arma)* butt; **dare un ~ a** to kick; **prendere a calci** to kick.

calcolare *vt* to calculate; *(prevedere)* to reckon on, to take into account.

calcolatrice *sf* calculator.

calcolo *sm (conteggio)* calculation; (MED) stone; **fare i calcoli** to do one's calculations; **è andato tutto secondo i calcoli** everything went according to plan.
caldaia *sf* boiler.
caldo, -a ◇ *agg* warm; *(a temperatura elevata)* hot ◇ *sm (calore)* heat; **avere ~** to be hot; **è** o **fa ~** it's hot.
calendario *sm* calendar.
calma ◇ *sf* calm ◇ *esclam* calm down!
calmante *sm* tranquillizer.
calmare *vt* to calm; *(dolore)* to soothe.
◆ **calmarsi** *vr (persona)* to calm down; *(mare)* to become calm; *(vento)* to drop.
calmo, -a *agg (tranquillo)* peaceful, calm; *(mare)* calm.
calore *sm* warmth.
caloria *sf (di cibo)* calorie.
calorifero *sm* radiator.
caloroso, -a *agg* warm.
calpestare *vt* to tread on.
calunnia *sf* slander.
calvizie *sf* baldness.
calvo, -a *agg* bald.
calza *sf (da donna)* stocking; *(da uomo)* sock; **fare la ~** to knit.
calzagatto *sm dish from Emilia Romagna consisting of polenta with beans, onions and bacon.*
calzamaglia (*pl* **calzamaglie**) *sf* tights *(pl) (Br)*, panty hose *(pl) (Am)*.
calzante *sm* shoehorn.
calzare ◇ *vt* to put on ◇ *vi* to fit.
calzature *sfpl* footwear *(sg)*.
calzettone *sm* knee(-length) sock.
calzino *sm* (short) sock.
calzolaio *sm (riparatore)* cobbler; *(fabbricante)* shoemaker.
calzoleria *sf* shoe shop.
calzoncini *smpl* shorts.
calzone *sm (cibo) pasty made from pizza dough stuffed with cheese, tomato, ham and egg.*
◆ **calzoni** *smpl* trousers.
camaleonte *sm* chameleon.
cambiale *sf* bill.
cambiamento *sm* change.
cambiare *vt & vi* to change; **~ le lire in sterline** to change lire into sterling; **~ un biglietto da centomila** to change a hundred thousand lire note.
◆ **cambiarsi** *vr* to change (one's clothes).
cambio *sm (sostituzione)* change; *(di denaro)* exchange; *(di automobile)* gears *(pl)*; **dare il ~ a qn** to take over from sb; **fare a ~ (con qn)** to swap (with sb); **in ~ di qc** in exchange for sthg; **~ automatico** automatic gearbox.
camera *sf* room; **~ (da letto)** bedroom; **~ d'aria** inner tube; **~ con bagno** room with a bath; **~ blindata** vault; **Camera di Commercio** Chamber of Commerce; **Camera dei Deputati** = House of Commons *(Br)*, = House of Representatives *(Am)*; **~ con doccia** room with a shower; **~ doppia** double room; **~ a due letti** twin-bedded room; **~ matrimoniale** room with a double bed; **~ degli ospiti** guestroom, spare room; **~ singola** single room.
cameriere, -a *sm, f* waiter (*f* waitress).
camice *sm* white coat.
camicetta *sf* blouse.
camicia *sf (da uomo)* shirt; *(da donna)* blouse, shirt; **~ da notte** *(da donna)* nightdress; *(da uomo)* nightshirt.
caminetto *sm* fireplace, hearth.
camino *sm (focolare)* fireplace, hearth; *(comignolo)* chimney.
camion *sm inv* truck.
camioncino *sm* van.
cammello *sm* camel; *(tessuto)* camelhair.

cammeo *sm* cameo.
camminare *vi* to walk.
camminata *sf* walk.
cammino *sm* way; **mettersi in ~** to set off.
camomilla *sf* camomile.
camorra *sf* Camorra.
camoscio *sm* chamois; **giacca di ~** suede jacket.
campagna *sf* country; *(propaganda, guerra)* campaign; **in ~** in the country; **andare in ~** to go to the country.
campana *sf* bell; **a ~** bell-shaped.
campanello *sm* bell; **suonare il ~** to ring the bell.
campanile *sm* bell-tower.
campare *vi* to get by.
campato, -a *agg*: **~ in aria** unfounded.
campeggiare *vi* to camp.
campeggiatore, -trice *sm, f* camper.
campeggio *sm (luogo)* campsite; *(attività)* camping.
camper *sm inv* camper van.
Campidoglio *sm*: **il ~** the Capitol.
camping *sm inv* campsite.
campionario *sm* (collection of) samples *(pl)*.
campionato *sm* championship.
campione, -essa ◇ *sm, f* champion ◇ *sm (esemplare)* sample.
campo *sm* field; *(accampamento)* camp; **~ da tennis** tennis court; **~ di golf** golf course; **~ profughi** refugee camp.
camposanto (*pl* **campisanti**) *sm* cemetery.
Canada *sm*: **il ~** Canada.
canadese ◇ *agg & smf* Canadian ◇ *sf (tenda)* ridge tent.
canaglia *sf* rogue.
canale *sm* channel; *(artificiale)* canal; **~ navigabile** ship canal.
canapa *sf* hemp.
canarino *sm* canary.
canasta *sf* canasta.
cancellare *vt (con gomma)* to rub out; *(con penna)* to cross out; *(annullare)* to cancel.
cancelleria *sf (materiale)* stationery.
cancello *sm* gate.
cancerogeno, -a *agg* carcinogenic.
cancrena *sf* (MED) gangrene.
cancro *sm* cancer.
◆ **Cancro** *sm* Cancer.
candeggina *sf* bleach.
candela *sf* candle; **~ (di accensione)** spark plug.
candelabro *sm* candelabra.
candeliere *sm* candlestick.
candidato, -a *sm, f* candidate.
candido, -a *agg (bianco)* (pure) white; *(puro)* pure, innocent.
candito, -a ◇ *agg* candied ◇ *sm* candied fruit.
cane *sm* dog; **~ da guardia** guard dog; **~ guida** guide dog; **~ lupo** Alsatian; **~ poliziotto** police dog; **non c'era un ~** there wasn't a soul there; **solo come un ~** all alone; **tempo da cani** lousy weather; **una vita da cani** a dog's life; **'cani al guinzaglio'** 'dogs must be kept on a lead'.
canestro *sm* basket.
cangiante *agg* iridescent.
canguro *sm* kangaroo.
canicola *sf* heat.
canile *sm (cuccia)* kennel; *(allevamento)* kennels *(pl)*; **~ municipale** dog pound.
canino *sm* canine.
canna *sf (pianta)* reed; *(di bicicletta)* crossbar; *(di fucile)* barrel; **~ fumaria** chimney flue; **~ da pesca** fishing rod; **~ da zucchero** sugar cane.
cannariculi *smpl thin curved pastry covered in honey.*
cannella *sf (spezia)* cinnamon; *(rubinetto)* tap.

cannello *sm* blowlamp.
cannelloni *smpl* cannelloni *(sg)*.
cannibale *smf* cannibal.
cannocchiale *sm* telescope.
cannolo *sm*: ~ **alla crema** *pastry tube filled with custard*; ~ **siciliano** *'cannolo' filled with sweetened ricotta cheese, candied fruit and chocolate.*
cannone *sm* gun.
cannuccia, -ce *sf* straw.
canoa *sf* canoe.
canone *sm (quota)* rent; *(regola)* rule.
canottaggio *sm* rowing.
canottiera *sf (biancheria)* vest *(Br)*, undershirt *(Am)*; *(per esterno)* sleeveless T-shirt.
canotto *sm* rubber dinghy; ~ **di salvataggio** lifeboat.
cantante *smf* singer.
cantare *vt & vi* to sing.
cantautore, -trice *sm, f* singer-songwriter.
cantiere *sm (edile)* building site; *(navale)* shipyard.
cantina *sf (seminterrato)* cellar; *(per il vino)* wine cellar; *(negozio)* wine shop.
canto *sm* (ARTE) singing; *(canzone)* song; *(di uccello)* chirping; **d'altro ~** on the other hand.
cantonata *sf*: **prendere una ~** to make a blunder.
cantone *sm (in Svizzera)* canton.
Canton Ticino *sm*: **il ~** the canton of Ticino.
cantucci *smpl wedge-shaped almond biscuits.*
canzonare *vt* to tease.
canzone *sf* song.
caos *sm* chaos.
CAP *abbr* = **codice di avviamento postale**.
capace *agg (esperto)* able, capable; *(ampio)* capacious; **essere ~ di fare qc** to be able to do sthg; **essere ~ di tutto** to be capable of anything.
capacità *sf inv (abilità)* ability; *(capienza)* capacity.
capanna *sf* hut.
capannone *sm (industriale)* shed; *(agricolo)* barn.
caparbio, -a *agg* stubborn.
caparra *sf* deposit.
capello *sm* hair.
◆ **capelli** *smpl* hair *(sg)*; **averne fin sopra i capelli** to be fed up to the back teeth.
capezzolo *sm* nipple.
capillare *sm* capillary.
capire *vt & vi* to understand; **non capisco** I don't understand; **scusi, non ho capito** I'm sorry, I don't understand; **si capisce!** certainly!
◆ **capirsi** *vr* to understand each other.
capitale ◇ *sf & sm* capital ◇ *agg (pena, peccato)* capital; *(fondamentale)* fundamental.
capitaneria *sf*: ~ **di porto** port authorities *(pl)*.
capitano *sm* captain.
capitare ◇ *vi (accadere)* to happen; *(giungere)* to turn up ◇ *v impers* to happen; ~ **a qn** to happen to sb; ~ **a proposito** to come at the right time.
capitello *sm* capital.
capitolino, -a *agg* Capitoline.
capitolo *sm* chapter.
capitombolo *sm* tumble.
capo *sm (principale)* boss; *(testa, estremità)* head; *(di gruppo)* leader; *(di tribù)* chief; ~ **di vestiario** item of clothing; **andare a ~** to start a new paragraph; **venire a ~ di qc** to get through sthg; **da ~** over again; **da un ~ all'altro (di qc)** from end to end (of sthg); **in ~ a un mese** within a month.
Capodanno *sm* New Year.
capofitto : a capofitto *avv* headfirst.
capolavoro *sm* masterpiece.

capolinea (*pl* **capilinea**) *sm* terminus.
capolino *sm*: **fare ~** to peep in/out.
capoluogo, -ghi *sm*: **~ di provincia** provincial capital, = county town *(Br)*; **~ di regione** regional capital.
capostazione (*pl* **capistazione**) *smf* station master.
capotavola (*mpl* **capitavola**, *fpl inv*) *smf* head of the table; **a ~** at the head of the table.
capoufficio (*mpl* **capiufficio**, *fpl inv*) *smf* office manager (*f* manageress).
capoverso *sm* paragraph.
capovolgere *vt (barca, oggetto)* to overturn; *(fig: situazione)* to reverse.
♦ **capovolgersi** *vr (barca)* to capsize; *(macchina)* to overturn; *(fig: situazione)* to be reversed.
capovolto, -a *pp* → **capovolgere**.
cappa *sf (di camino)* hood; *(mantello)* cape.
cappella *sf* chapel.
cappello *sm* hat; **~ di paglia** straw hat.
cappero *sm* caper.
cappone *sm* capon; **~ ripieno al forno** *capon stuffed with beef, Parmesan cheese and breadcrumbs.*
cappotto *sm* coat.
cappuccino *sm* cappuccino.
cappuccio *sm* hood; *(di penna)* cap.
capra *sf* goat.
Capri *sf* Capri.
capriccio *sm* tantrum; *(voglia)* whim; **fare i capricci** to be naughty.
capriccioso, -a *agg* naughty.
Capricorno *sm* Capricorn.
capriola *sf* somersault.
capriolo *sm* roe deer.
capro *sm*: **~ espiatorio** scapegoat.
capsula *sf (di farmaco)* capsule; *(di bottiglia)* cap.
carabiniere *sm member of the Italian police force responsible for civil and military matters.*
caraffa *sf* carafe, jug.
Caraibi *smpl*: **i ~** the Caribbean.
caramella *sf* sweet.
carato *sm* carat.
carattere *sm* character.
caratteristica, -che *sf* characteristic.
caratteristico, -a, -ci, -che *agg* characteristic.
caratterizzare *vt* to characterize.
carboidrato *sm* carbohydrate.
carbone *sm* coal.
carburante *sm* fuel.
carburatore *sm* carburettor.
carcerato, -a *sm, f* prisoner.
carcere (*pl f* **carceri**) *sm* prison.
carciofo *sm* artichoke; **carciofi alla romana** *sautéed or baked artichokes with parsley, mint and garlic.*
cardiaco, -a, -ci, -che *agg* cardiac, heart *(dav s)*.
cardigan *sm inv* cardigan.
cardinale ◇ *agg* → **numero, punto** ◇ *sm* cardinal.
cardine *sm* hinge.
cardo *sm* thistle.
carenza *sf* lack, deficiency.
carestia *sf* famine.
carezza *sf* caress; *(a animale)* stroke.
carezzare *vt* to caress; *(animale)* to stroke.
carica, -che *sf (incarico)* position, office; *(elettrica, di arma)* charge; **in ~** in office.
caricare *vt (mettere su)* to load; *(sveglia)* to wind up; **~ qc di qc** to load sthg with sthg; **~ qn di qc** to weigh sb down with sthg.
carico, -a, -chi, -che ◇ *agg (arma, macchina fotografica)* loaded; *(batteria)* charged; *(orologio)* wound

up ◇ *sm* load; ~ **(di qc)** weighed down (with sthg); **a ~ di** *(spesa)* charged to.

carie *sf inv (dei denti)* decay.

carino, -a *agg (grazioso)* pretty, lovely; *(gentile)* nice.

carnagione *sf* complexion.

carne *sf* meat; (ANAT) flesh; **~ di maiale/vitello** pork/veal; **~ macinata** O **tritata** mince.

carneficina *sf* massacre.

carnevale *sm* carnival.

caro, -a *agg* expensive, dear; *(amato)* dear; **costare ~** to be expensive; **Caro Luca** Dear Luca.

carota *sf* carrot.

carovita *sm* high cost of living.

carpaccio *sm thin slices of raw beef served with oil, lemon and shavings of Parmesan cheese.*

carpire *vt*: **~ qc a qn** *(segreto)* to get sthg out of sb.

carponi *avv* on all fours.

carrabile *agg* → **passo**.

carraio *agg m* → **passo**.

carreggiata *sf* carriageway.

carrello *sm* trolley.

carriera *sf* career; **far ~** to get on.

carro *sm* cart, wagon; **~ armato** tank; **~ attrezzi** breakdown truck *(Br)*, tow truck *(Am)*.

carrozza *sf (cocchio)* coach, carriage; *(vagone)* carriage *(Br)*, car *(Am)*; **'~ letto'** sleeping car; **'~ ristorante'** restaurant car.

carrozzeria *sf* bodywork.

carrozziere *sm* coachbuilder.

carrozzina *sf* pram *(Br)*, baby carriage *(Am)*.

carta *sf* paper; *(tessera)* card; **alla ~** à la carte; **~ d'argento** *senior citizens' railcard*; **~ automobilistica** O **stradale** road map; **~ da bollo** *paper carrying a government duty stamp*; **~ di credito** credit card; **~ geografica** map; **~ d'identità** identity card; **~ igienica** toilet paper; **~ d'imbarco** boarding pass; **~ da lettere** notepaper; **~ da pacchi** brown paper, wrapping paper; **~ da parati** wallpaper; **~ stagnola** silver foil; **~ verde** green card; **~ dei vini** wine list; **carte da gioco** playing cards.

cartacarbone *sf* carbon paper.

cartaccia, -ce *sf* waste paper.

cartapesta *sf* papier-mâché.

cartella *sf (di scolaro)* schoolbag; *(di professionista)* briefcase; *(per fogli)* folder; *(scheda)* file; **~ clinica** case history.

cartello *sm (avviso)* notice; *(in dimostrazioni)* placard; **~ stradale** road sign.

cartellone *sm (teatrale)* playbill; **~ (pubblicitario)** poster.

cartina *sf*: **~ (geografica)** map.

cartoccio *sm* paper bag; **al ~** in tin foil.

cartoleria *sf* stationer's.

cartolibreria *sf* stationer's and bookseller's.

cartolina *sf (illustrata)* (picture) postcard; **~ postale** postcard.

cartone *sm* cardboard.

◆ **cartoni animati** *smpl* cartoons.

casa *sf (costruzione)* house; *(dimora)* house, home; *(ditta)* firm; **andare a ~** to go home; **essere a** O **in ~** to be at home; **fatto in ~** homemade; **~ di cura** nursing home.

casalinga, -ghe *sf* housewife.

casalingo, -a, -ghi, -ghe *agg* homemade; *(amante della casa)* home-loving.

◆ **casalinghi** *smpl* household articles.

cascare *vi* to fall down.

cascata *sf* waterfall.

cascina *sf* farmstead.

casco, -schi *sm (protettivo)* helmet; *(per capelli)* dryer; *(di banane)* bunch.

casella *sf (riquadro)* square; *(scomparto)* compartment; **~ postale** post office box.

casello *sm* tollbooth.
caserma *sf* barracks *(pl)*.
casino *sm (fam: confusione)* mess.
casinò *sm inv* casino.
caso *sm* chance; *(eventualità)* event; *(poliziesco, medico)* case; **fare ~ a** to pay attention to; **non è il ~ di offendersi** you shouldn't take offence; **a ~** at random; **in ~ contrario** otherwise; **in ogni ~** in any case; **nel ~ venisse** should he come; **per ~** by chance; **in tutti i casi** at any rate; **'in ~ d'emergenza rompere il vetro'** 'in case of emergency break glass'.
casomai *cong* if by any chance.
cassa *sf (contenitore)* case, box; *(di negozio)* cash register; *(di supermercato)* checkout; *(di banca)* counter; *(amplificatore)* speaker; *(di orologio)* case; **~ automatica prelievi** cash dispenser; **~ continua** night safe; **~ toracica** chest.
cassaforte (*pl* **casseforti**) *sf* safe.
cassata *sf ice cream dessert containing candied fruit, served in slices like a cake*; **~ siciliana** *Sicilian dessert made with sponge, ricotta cheese, candied fruit and liqueur*.
casseruola *sf* saucepan.
cassetta *sf (contenitore)* box; *(di musica, film)* tape; **~ delle lettere** letterbox *(Br)*, mailbox *(Am)*; **~ di sicurezza** strongbox.
cassetto *sm* drawer.
cassettone *sm* chest of drawers.
cassiere, -a *sm, f (di negozio)* cashier; *(di banca)* teller.
cassoela *sf pork ribs with salami and savoy cabbage (a speciality of Lombardy)*.
cassonetto *sm large dustbin on wheels*.
castagna *sf* chestnut.
castagnaccio *sm Tuscan cake made from chestnut flour, pine kernels and sometimes sultanas and rosemary*.
castagno *sm* chestnut.
castano, -a *agg* chestnut.
castello *sm* castle.
castigo, -ghi *sm* punishment; **mettere qn in ~** to punish sb.
castoro *sm* beaver.
castrare *vt* to castrate.
casual ['kɜʃwal] *agg inv* casual.
casuale *agg* chance *(dav s)*.
catacomba *sf* catacomb.
catalogare *vt* to catalogue.
catalogo, -ghi *sm* catalogue.
catamarano *sm* catamaran.
catarifrangente *sm* reflector.
catarro *sm* catarrh.
catasta *sf* stack.
catastrofe *sf* catastrophe.
categoria *sf (gruppo)* category; *(di albergo)* class.
catena *sf* chain; **~ di montaggio** assembly line; **a ~** chain *(dav s)*; **catene (da neve)** (snow) chains.
catinella *sf* basin; **piovere a catinelle** to pour down.
catino *sm* basin.
catrame *sm* tar.
cattedra *sf* teacher's desk.
cattedrale *sf* cathedral.
cattiveria *sf (qualità)* wickedness; *(commento)* spiteful remark; *(atto)* spiteful act.
cattività *sf* captivity.
cattivo, -a *agg* bad; *(bambino)* naughty; *(sapore, odore)* bad, nasty; *(incapace)* poor.
cattolico, -a, -ci, -che *agg & sm, f* Catholic.
cattura *sf* capture.
catturare *vt* to capture.
caucciù *sm* rubber.
causa *sf* cause; (DIR) case; **a** O **per ~ di** because of.
causare *vt* to cause.
cautela *sf* caution, prudence.
cautelare *vt* to protect.
◆ **cautelarsi da** *vr + prep* to take precautions against.

cauto, -a *agg* cautious, prudent.
cauzione *sf* security; (DIR) bail.
cava *sf* quarry.
cavalcare *vt* to ride.
cavalcavia *sm inv* flyover.
cavalcioni *avv*: **a ~ di** astride.
cavaliere *sm (chi cavalca)* rider; *(medioevale, titolo)* knight; *(in balli)* partner.
cavalleria *sf* (MIL) cavalry; *(cortesia)* chivalry.
cavallerizzo, -a *sm, f (istruttore)* riding instructor; *(di circo)* bareback rider.
cavalletta *sf* grasshopper.
cavalletto *sm* easel.
cavallo *sm* horse; *(di pantaloni)* crotch; *(negli scacchi)* knight; **andare a ~** to ride; **~ (vapore)** horsepower.
cavallone *sm (ondata)* breaker.
cavare *vt* to extract; **cavarsela** to manage, to cope.
cavatappi *sm inv* corkscrew.
cavatelli *smpl*: **~ alla foggiana** *flat 'gnocchi' in a vegetable, cheese or meat sauce.*
caverna *sf* cave.
cavia *sf* guinea pig; **fare da ~** to be a guinea pig.
caviale *sm* caviar.
caviglia *sf* ankle.
cavità *sf inv (buca)* hollow; (ANAT) chamber.
cavo, -a ◇ *agg* hollow ◇ *sm* cable; *(corda)* rope.
cavolfiore *sm* cauliflower.
cavolo *sm* cabbage; **che ~ vuole?** *(fam)* what the hell does he want?
cazzotto *sm (fam)* punch.
cc *(abbr di centimetro cubico)* cc.
c/c *(abbr di conto corrente)* a/c.
C.C. *abbr* = **Carabinieri**.
C.D. *sm inv* CD.
ce → **ci**.
cece *sm* chickpea.
Cecoslovacchia *sf*: la ~ Czechoslovakia.
cedere ◇ *vt*: **~ qc (a qn)** to give sthg up (to sb) ◇ *vi (soffitto, pavimento)* to give way; **~ (a qc)** *(fig: persona)* to give in (to sthg), to yield (to sthg).
cedola *sf* coupon.
cedro *sm* lime.
CEE *sf (abbr di Comunità Economica Europea)* EEC.
ceffone *sm* slap.
celebrare *vt* to celebrate.
celebre *agg* famous.
celebrità *sf inv* fame.
celeste *agg & sm* sky-blue.
celibe ◇ *agg* single ◇ *sm* bachelor.
cella *sf* cell.
cellophane® ['tʃɛlofan] *sm* Cellophane®.
cellula *sf* cell; **~ fotoelettrica** photoelectric cell.
cellulare *sm (telefono)* mobile phone; *(furgone)* Black Maria.
cemento *sm* cement; **~ armato** reinforced concrete.
cena *sf* dinner.
cenare *vi* to have dinner.
cencio *sm (straccio)* rag.
◆ **cenci** *smpl* (CULIN) *Tuscan speciality of deep-fried sticks of dough sprinkled with sugar.*
cenere *sf* ash.
cenno *sm (con la mano)* gesture; *(col capo)* nod; *(allusione)* hint; *(sintomo)* sign; **fare ~ a qn** to beckon to sb; **fare ~ di sì/no** to nod/shake one's head.
cenone *sm* New Year's Eve dinner.
censimento *sm* census.
censura *sf (controllo)* censorship.
centenario, -a ◇ *agg (di età)* hundred-year-old; *(ogni cento anni)* centenary *(dav s)* ◇ *sm* centenary.
centerbe *sm inv type of liqueur made from herbs.*

centesimo, -a *num* hundredth, → **sesto**.
centigrado *agg m* → **grado**.
centimetro *sm* centimetre.
centinaio (*pl f* **centinaia**) *sm*: **un ~ (di)** a hundred.
cento *num* a o one hundred; **~ per ~** 100 per cent, → **sei**.
centomila *num* a o one hundred thousand, → **sei**.
centotredici *sm (numero telefonico)* = 999 *(Br)*, = 911 *(Am)*; *(polizia)* police *(pl)*.
centrale ◇ *agg (nel centro)* central; *(principale)* main ◇ *sf* head office; **~ elettrica** electric power station.
centralinista, -i, -e *smf* operator.
centralino *sm* telephone exchange; *(di albergo, ditta)* switchboard.
centrare *vt* to hit the centre of.
centrifuga, -ghe *sf* spin-dryer.
centro *sm* centre; **fare ~** *(colpire)* to hit the bull's eye; *(fig: risolvere)* to hit the nail on the head; **~ abitato** built-up area; **~ commerciale** shopping centre; **~ storico** old town.
ceppo *sm (di albero)* stump; *(ciocco)* log.
cera *sf* wax.
ceramica *sf* pottery.
cerbiatto *sm* fawn.
cerca *sf*: **essere in ~ di qc** to be in search of sthg.
cercare *vt* to look for.
◆ **cercare di** *v + prep*: **~ di fare qc** to try to do sthg.
cerchio *sm* circle; **mettersi in ~ (intorno a)** to form a circle (around).
cereale *sm* cereal.
cerimonia *sf* ceremony.
cerino *sm* match.
cernia *sf* grouper.
cerniera *sf (di porte, finestre)* hinge; **~ (lampo)** zip.
cerotto *sm* plaster.
certamente *avv* certainly.
certezza *sf* certainty; **sapere qc con ~** to know sthg for sure.
certificato *sm* certificate; **~ medico** medical certificate; **~ di nascita** birth certificate.
certo, -a ◇ *agg* **1.** *(convinto)* certain; **essere ~ di qc** to be certain of sthg; **sono ~ di aver prenotato** I'm positive I booked; **siete certi che sia lui?** are you sure it's him?
2. *(assicurato, evidente)* certain; **la vittoria è data per certa** victory is certain.
3. *(non specificato)* certain; **un ~ signor Rossi** a (certain) Mr Rossi; **c'è un ~ Paolo al telefono** there's someone called Paolo on the phone; **ho certe cose da fare** I have some things I need to do; **in certi casi** in some o certain cases.
4. *(qualche)*: **certi(-e)** some.
5. *(limitativo)* some; **avere un ~ intuito** to have some insight.
6. *(rafforzativo)* some; **ha certe idee!** he has some strange ideas!; **ha certi occhi azzurri!** he's got really blue eyes!; **avere una certa età** to be getting on.
◇ *avv*: **vieni anche tu? – ~!** are you coming too? – of course!; **di ~** certainly.
◆ **certi, -e** *pron (persone)* some (people); **certi dicono che …** some people say that …
certosa *sf* charterhouse.
cervello *sm* brain.
Cervino *sm*: **il ~** the Cervino.
cervo *sm* deer; **~ volante** stag beetle.
cesoie *sfpl* shears.
cespuglio *sm* bush.
cessare *vt* to stop.
cesso *sm* loo.
cesta *sf* basket.
cestino *sm (cesto)* basket; *(per cartacce)* wastepaper basket; **~ da**

viaggio packed lunch.
cesto *sm* basket.
ceto *sm* class.
cetriolo *sm* cucumber.
champagne [ʃam'paɲ] *sm inv* champagne.
charter ['tʃarter] *sm inv* charter.
che ◇ *pron relativo* 1. *(soggetto: persona)* who, that; **il dottore ~ mi ha visitato** the doctor who examined me.
2. *(complemento oggetto: persona)* whom, that; **la ragazza ~ hai conosciuto** the girl (whom o that) you met.
3. *(cosa, animale)* that, which; **la macchina ~ è in garage** the car which o that is in the garage; **il treno ~ abbiamo perso** the train (which o that) we missed.
4. *(fam: in cui)*: **la sera ~ siamo usciti** the evening we went out.
◇ *pron interr & esclam* what; **~ ne pensi?** what do you think?; **~ ti succede?** what's the matter?; **non so ~ fare** I don't know what to do; **grazie! – non c'è di ~!** thank you! – don't mention it!; **ma ~ dici!** what are you saying!
◇ *agg interr* 1. *(tra molti)* what; *(tra pochi)* which; **~ libro vuoi, questo o quello?** which book do you want, this one or that one?; **~ tipo è il tuo amico?** what's your friend like?
2. *(in esclamazioni)*: **~ strana idea!** what a strange idea!; **~ bello!** how lovely!
◇ *cong* 1. *(introduce una subordinata)* that; **è difficile ~ venga** he's unlikely to come; **sai ~ non è vero** you know (that) it's not true; **sono così stanca ~ non mi reggo in piedi** I'm so tired (that) I can hardly stand up; **sono contenta ~ sia partito** I'm pleased (that) he left.
2. *(temporale)*: **è già un anno ~ è partito** it's already a year since he left; **è un po' ~ non lo vedo** I haven't seen him for a while.
3. *(comparativa)* than; **è più furbo ~ intelligente** he's cunning rather than intelligent; **è più bello ~ mai** he's more handsome than ever.
4. *(introduce alternativa)* whether; **~ tu venga o no, io ci vado** I'm going, whether you come or not.
check-in [tʃɛ'kin] *sm inv* check-in.
chewing-gum ['tʃwingam] *sm* chewing-gum.
chi ◇ *pron relativo* 1. *(colui che)* the person who.
2. *(qualcuno che)*: **c'è ancora ~ crede alle sue storie** there are still people who believe his tales.
3. *(chiunque)* whoever, anyone who; **entra ~ vuole** anyone can come in.
◇ *pron interr* 1. *(soggetto)* who; **~ è?** who is it?; **~ è stato?** who was it?
2. *(complemento diretto)* who; **non so ~** I don't know who; **~ si vede!** look who's here!
3. *(complemento indiretto)* who, whom; **a ~ devo chiedere?** who should I ask?; **con ~ parti?** who are you leaving with?; **di ~ è questo ombrello?** whose umbrella is this?; **a ~ lo dici!** you're telling me!
chiacchierare *vi (conversare)* to chat; *(spettegolare)* to gossip.
chiacchiere *sfpl (pettegolezzi)* rumours, gossip *(sg)*; **fare due o quattro ~** to have a chat.
chiacchierone, -a *agg (loquace)* talkative; *(pettegolo)* gossipy.
chiamare *vt* to call.
◆ **chiamarsi** *vr* to be called; **come ti chiami?** what's your name?; **mi chiamo ...** my name is ...
chiamata *sf* call.
Chianti *sm* Chianti.
chiarezza *sf* clarity.
chiarire *vt (mettere in chiaro)* to make clear; *(spiegare)* to clarify; *(problema)* to clear up.

◆ **chiarirsi** *vr* to be cleared up.
chiaro, -a *agg* clear; *(colore)* light.
chiasso *sm* noise.
chiassoso, -a *agg* noisy.
chiave *sf* key; **chiudere a ~** to lock; **~ d'accensione** ignition key; **~ inglese** monkey wrench.
chiavetta *sf (dell'acqua, del gas)* tap; *(d'accensione)* key.
chic [sik] *agg inv* chic.
chicco, -chi *sm (di grano)* grain; *(di caffè)* bean; **~ d'uva** grape.
chiedere *vt (per sapere)* to ask; *(per avere)* to ask for; **~ qc a qn** to ask sb sthg.
◆ **chiedere di** *v + prep (per notizie)* to ask after; *(al telefono)* to ask for.
chiesa *sf* church.
chiesto, -a *pp* → **chiedere**.
chiglia *sf* keel.
chilo *sm (chilogrammo)* kilo; **mezzo ~ di** half a kilo of.
chilogrammo *sm* kilogram.
chilometro *sm* kilometre.
chimica *sf (disciplina)* chemistry, → **chimico**.
chimico, -a, -ci, -che ◇ *agg* chemical ◇ *sm, f* chemist.
chinarsi *vr* to bend.
chinotto *sm (bibita) type of soft drink.*
chiocciola *sf* snail.
chiodo *sm* nail; **~ fisso** fixed idea; **chiodi di garofano** cloves.
chioma *sf (di albero)* foliage; *(capigliatura)* (head of) hair.
chiosco, -schi *sm* kiosk.
chiostro *sm* cloister.
chiromante *smf* fortune-teller.
chirurgia *sf* surgery; **~ estetica** plastic surgery.
chissà *avv* who knows?
chitarra *sf* guitar.
chiudere ◇ *vt* to close, to shut; *(acqua, gas)* to turn off; *(strada)* to close; *(definitivamente)* to close down, to shut down; *(concludere)* to end ◇ *vi* to close, to shut; *(definitivamente)* to close down, to shut down; **~ a chiave** to lock.
◆ **chiudersi** *vr* to close, to shut; **chiudersi in casa** to lock o.s. in; **'si chiude da sé'** 'automatic door'.
chiunque *pron (indefinito)* anyone; *(relativo)* whoever; **~ sia** whoever it may be.
chiuso, -a ◇ *pp* → **chiudere** ◇ *agg* closed; *(persona)* reserved; **'~ per ferie'** 'closed for holidays'; **'~ per riposo settimanale'** 'weekly closing day'.
chiusura *sf (di negozio, ufficio, scuole)* closing; *(definitiva)* closure; *(termine)* end; *(dispositivo)* fastener.
ci (*diventa* **ce** *se precede lo, la, li, le, ne*) ◇ *pron personale* **1.** *(complemento oggetto)* us; **~ vedono** they can see us; **ascoltaci** listen to us.
2. *(complemento di termine)* (to) us; **~ può fare un favore?** can you do us a favour?; **non ce lo ha detto** he didn't tell us.
3. *(riflessivo)* ourselves; **~ laviamo** we wash ourselves.
4. *(reciproco)* each other; **~ vediamo stasera** see you tonight.
◇ *pron dimostrativo (a ciò, in ciò, su ciò)*: **~ penso io** I'll take care of it; **mettici un po' d'impegno!** put a bit of effort into it!; **quella sedia è vuota: posso appoggiarci la borsa?** that seat is empty: can I put my bag on it?; **~ puoi scommettere** you can bet on it.
◇ *avv* **1.** *(stato in luogo: qui)* here; *(stato in luogo: lì)* there; **~ fermiamo una sola notte** we are staying (here/there) for just one night.
2. *(moto a luogo: qui)* here; *(moto a luogo: lì)* there; **~ si può andare a piedi** you can walk there; **~ vengono spesso** they come here often.
3. *(moto per luogo)*: **~ passa l'autostrada** the motorway runs through it; **non ~ passa mai nessuno** nobody ever goes this/that way.

4. *(in espressioni)*: **c'è** there is; **~ sono** there are; **~ vuole un po' (di tempo)** it takes a bit of time; **io ~ sto** I agree; **non ~ sento/vedo** I can't hear/see.
ciabatta *sf (pantofola)* slipper; *(pane) type of long, flat bread.*
cialda *sf* wafer.
ciambella *sf (dolce) ring-shaped cake; (salvagente)* rubber ring; **~ di salvataggio** life buoy, life belt.
ciao *esclam (all'incontro)* hello!; *(di commiato)* bye!
ciascuno, -a *agg & pron* each; **~ di noi** each of us.
cibo *sm* food.
cicala *sf* cicada.
cicatrice *sf* scar.
cicca, -che *sf* cigarette end.
ciccione, -a *sm, f (fam)* fatty.
cicerone *sm* guide.
ciclabile *agg* → **pista**.
ciclamino *sm* cyclamen.
ciclismo *sm* cycling.
ciclista, -i, -e *smf* cyclist.
ciclo *sm* cycle.
ciclomotore *sm* moped.
ciclone *sm* cyclone.
cicogna *sf* stork.
cieco, -a, -chi, -che ◇ *agg* blind ◇ *sm, f* blind man (*f* woman).
cielo *sm* sky; *(paradiso)* heaven.
cifra *sf (numero)* figure; *(di denaro)* sum, figure.
ciglio *sm* (*di palpebra: pl f* **ciglia**) eyelash; (*di strada: pl m* **cigli**) edge.
cigno *sm* swan.
cigolare *vi* to squeak, to creak.
Cile *sm*: **il ~** Chile.
cilecca *sf*: **fare ~** to fail.
ciliegia, -gie o **-ge** *sf* cherry.
cilindro *sm (di motore)* cylinder; *(cappello)* top hat.
cima *sf* top; *(estremità)* end; **in ~ (a qc)** at the top (of sthg); **da ~ a fondo** from top to bottom, from beginning to end; **~ alla genovese** *veal stuffed with bacon, sweetbreads, brains, mushrooms, peas and grated cheese, served cold in slices.*
cimice *sf (insetto)* bug; *(puntina)* drawing pin *(Br)*, thumbtack *(Am)*.
ciminiera *sf* chimney; *(di nave)* funnel.
cimitero *sm* cemetery.
Cina *sf*: **la ~** China.
cin cin *esclam* cheers!
Cinecittà *sf film studios in Rome.*
cinema *sm inv* cinema.
cinepresa *sf* cine-camera.
cinese ◇ *agg & sm* Chinese ◇ *smf* Chinese person.
cingere *vt* to surround.
cinghia *sf* belt.
cinghiale *sm* wild boar.
cinguettare *vi* to chirp.
cinico, -a, -ci, -che *agg* cynical.
ciniglia *sf* chenille.
cinquanta *num* fifty, → **sei**.
cinquantesimo, -a *agg* fiftieth, → **sesto**.
cinquantina *sf (di età)*: **essere sulla ~** to be about 50; **una ~ (di)** about 50.
cinque *num* five, → **sei**.
cinquecento *num* five hundred, → **sei**.
◆ **Cinquecento** *sm*: **il Cinquecento** the sixteenth century.
cinto, -a *pp* → **cingere**.
cintura *sf* belt; *(punto vita)* waist; **~ di sicurezza** safety o seat belt; **'allacciare le cinture di sicurezza'** 'fasten your seat belts'.
ciò *pron* this, that; **~ che** what; **~ nonostante** nevertheless.
cioccolata *sf* chocolate; *(bevanda)* hot chocolate.
cioccolatino *sm* chocolate.
cioccolato *sm* chocolate.
cioè ◇ *avv* that is ◇ *cong (vale a dire)* that is; *(anzi)* or rather.
ciondolo *sm* pendant.

ciotola *sf* bowl.
ciottolo *sm* pebble.
cipolla *sf* onion.
cipresso *sm* cypress.
cipria *sf* face powder.
circa *avv & prep* about.
circo, -chi *sm* circus.
circolare ◇ *agg & sf* circular ◇ *vi* to circulate; *(veicoli)* to drive; *(persone)* to move along; *(notizia)* to go round.
circolazione *sf (di merce, moneta, giornali)* circulation; **mettere in ~** *(notizia)* to spread; *(merce, moneta)* to put into circulation; **~ sanguigna** circulation; **~ stradale** traffic.
circolo *sm* circle.
circondare *vt* to surround.
circonferenza *sf* circumference.
circonvallazione *sf* ring road.
circoscrizione *sf* district.
circostante *agg* surrounding.
circostanza *sf* circumstance; **date le circostanze** in O under the circumstances.
circuito *sm* circuit.
ciste = **cisti**.
cisterna *sf* tank.
cisti *sf inv* cyst.
citare *vt* (DIR) to summon; *(menzionare)* to cite; *(opera, autore)* to quote.
citofono *sm* entry phone.
città *sf inv* town; *(importante)* city; **~ universitaria** (university) campus.
◆ **Città del Vaticano** *sf* Vatican City.
cittadinanza *sf* citizenship; *(abitanti)* citizens *(pl)*.
cittadino, -a ◇ *sm, f* citizen ◇ *agg* town, city *(dav s)*.
ciuco, -chi *sm* ass, donkey.
ciuffo *sm* tuft.
civetta *sf* owl; *(fig: donna)* flirt.
civico, -a, -ci, -che *agg* civic.
civile ◇ *agg* civil; *(civilizzato)* civilized ◇ *sm* civilian.
civiltà *sf inv* civilization.
clacson *sm inv* horn.
clamoroso, -a *agg* sensational.
clandestino, -a ◇ *agg (illegale)* illegal; *(segreto)* clandestine ◇ *sm, f* stowaway.
classe *sf* class; *(aula)* classroom; **~ turistica** tourist class; **prima/seconda ~** first/second class; **che ~ fai?** what year are you in?
classico, -a, -ci, -che *agg (letteratura, arte, musica)* classical; *(moda, esempio)* classic.
classifica, -che *sf (sportiva)* league table; *(d'esame)* results *(pl)*; *(musicale)* charts *(pl)*.
classificare *vt (ordinare)* to classify; *(valutare)* to mark.
◆ **classificarsi** *vr*: **classificarsi primo** to come first.
claudicante *agg (zoppicante)* limping.
clausola *sf* (DIR) clause.
clavicola *sf* clavicle.
claxon = **clacson**.
clero *sm* clergy.
cliente *smf (di negozio, bar)* customer; *(di professionista)* client.
clientela *sf (di negozio, bar)* clientele; *(di professionista)* clients *(pl)*.
clima, -i *sm* climate.
clinica, -che *sf* clinic.
cloro *sm* chlorine.
club [klab] *sm inv* club.
cm *(abbr di centimetro)* cm.
coagulare *vt (sangue)* to coagulate; *(latte)* to curdle.
◆ **coagularsi** *vr (sangue)* to clot; *(latte)* to curdle.
coca *sf (fam: bibita)* Coke®.
Coca-Cola® *sf* Coca-Cola®.
cocaina *sf* cocaine.
coccinella *sf* ladybird.
coccio *sm (terracotta)* earthenware; *(frammento)* shard.

cocciuto, -a *agg* stubborn.
cocco, -chi *sm (albero)* coconut palm; *(frutto)* coconut.
coccodrillo *sm* crocodile.
coccolare *vt* to cuddle.
cocomero *sm* watermelon.
coda *sf (fila)* queue *(Br)*, line *(Am)*; *(di animale)* tail; **fare la ~** to queue *(Br)*, to stand in line *(Am)*; **mettersi in ~** to join the queue *(Br)* o line *(Am)*; **~ (di cavallo)** ponytail.
codardo, -a *agg* cowardly.
codesto, -a *agg & pron* this.
codice *sm* code; **~ (di avviamento) postale** postcode; **~ fiscale** tax code; **~ della strada** highway code.
coerente *agg* consistent.
coetaneo, -a *agg*: **siamo coetanei** we are the same age.
cofano *sm* bonnet *(Br)*, hood *(Am)*.
cogliere *vt* to pick; *(fig: occasione, momento)* to seize; **~ qn sul fatto** to catch sb redhanded.
cognac *sm inv* cognac.
cognato, -a *sm, f* brother-in-law (*f* sister-in-law).
cognome *sm* surname.
coi = con + i, → con.
coincidenza *sf (caso)* coincidence; *(aereo, treno)* connection.
coincidere *vi*: **~ (con qc)** *(oggetti)* to coincide (with sthg); *(versione dei fatti)* to agree (with sthg); *(date, eventi)* to clash (with sthg).
coinciso, -a *pp* → **coincidere**.
coinvolgere *vt*: **~ qn (in qc)** to involve sb (in sthg).
coinvolto, -a *pp* → **coinvolgere**.
col = con + il, → con.
colapasta = scolapasta.
colare ◇ *vt (filtrare)* to filter; *(pasta)* to drain ◇ *vi (liquido)* to drip; *(contenitore)* to leak; *(cera, burro)* to melt; **~ a picco** to sink.
colazione *sf (pranzo)* lunch; **(prima) ~** breakfast; **fare ~** *(al mattino)* to have breakfast.
colera *sm* cholera.
colica, -che *sf* colic.
colino *sm* colander.
colla *sf* glue.
collaborare *vi* to cooperate.
collaboratore, -trice *sm, f* collaborator.
collana *sf* necklace; *(serie)* series.
collant [kol'lan] *smpl* tights.
collare *sm* collar.
collasso *sm* collapse.
collaudo *sm* test.
colle *sm* hill.
collega, -ghi, -ghe *smf* colleague.
collegare *vt* to connect.
◆ **collegarsi** *vr* to link up.
◆ **collegarsi con** *vr + prep (per telefono, radio, TV)* to link up with.
collegio *sm* boarding school.
collera *sf* anger; **essere in ~ (con qn)** to be angry (with sb).
colletta *sf* collection.
collettivo, -a *agg (comune)* common; *(di gruppo)* group *(dav s)*.
colletto *sm* collar.
collezionare *vt* to collect.
collezione *sf* collection; **fare la ~ di qc** to collect sthg.
collina *sf* hill.
collirio *sm* eyewash.
collisione *sf* impact.
collo *sm* neck; *(di abito)* collar, neck; *(pacco)* package.
collocamento *sm* employment.
collocare *vt (disporre)* to place.
colloquio *sm (conversazione)* talk; *(esame)* oral exam; **~ di lavoro** interview.
colmo, -a ◇ *agg* full ◇ *sm*: **è il ~!** it's the last straw!
colomba *sf* dove; *(dolce)* Easter cake.
Colombia *sf*: **la ~** Colombia.
colonia *sf* colony; *(per bambini)* summer camp; **(acqua di) ~** (eau de) cologne.

colonna *sf* column; ~ **vertebrale** spine, spinal column.
colorante *sm (per alimenti)* food colouring; *(per tessuti)* dye.
colorare *vt* to colour.
colore *sm* colour; **di che ~?** what colour?; **di ~** coloured; **a colori** colour *(dav s)*.
coloro *pron mpl*: ~ **che** ... those who ...
colosseo *sm*: **il Colosseo** the Colosseum.
colpa *sf (responsabilità)* fault; *(reato)* offence; **dare la ~ (di qc) a qn/qc** to blame sb/sthg (for sthg); **per ~ di** through, owing to.
colpire *vt* to hit; *(impressionare, sog: malattia)* to strike.
colpo *sm* blow; *(sparo)* shot; *(alla porta)* knock; *(fam: infarto)* stroke; *(fam: rapina)* raid; **di ~** suddenly; **fare ~** to make a strong impression; **un ~ di fulmine** love at first sight; **~ di sole** sunstroke; **~ di stato** coup (d'état); **~ di telefono** phone call; **~ di testa** impulse; **~ di vento** gust of wind.
coltello *sm* knife.
coltivare *vt* to cultivate.
colto, -a ◇ *pp* → **cogliere** ◇ *agg* cultured.
coma *sm inv* coma.
comandante *sm (di nave)* captain; *(di esercito)* commanding officer.
comandare *vi* to be in command.
comando *sm* command; *(congegno)* control.
combaciare *vi* to fit together.
combattere *vt & vi* to fight.
combinare *vt (accordare)* to combine; *(organizzare)* to arrange; *(fam: fare)* to do.
combinazione *sf* combination; *(caso)* coincidence; **per ~** by chance.
combustibile ◇ *agg* combustible ◇ *sm* fuel.
come ◇ *avv* **1.** *(comparativo)* like; **ho dormito ~ un ghiro** I slept like a log; **~ me** like me; **~ sempre** as always; **~ se niente fosse** as if nothing had happened.
2. *(interrogativo)* how; **non so ~ fare** I don't know what to do; **~ sarebbe?** what do you mean?; **~ stai?** how are you?; **~ mai?** how come?
3. *(in qualità di)* as; **viaggiare ~ turista** to travel as a tourist.
4. *(in esclamazioni)* how; **~ mi dispiace!** I'm so sorry!
5. *(per esempio)* like; **mi piacciono i colori accesi ~ il rosso** I like bright colours like red.
◇ *cong* **1.** *(nel modo in cui)* how; **mi ha spiegato ~ lo ha conosciuto** she told me how she met him; **fai ~ ti dico** do as I tell you; **~ vuole** as you like.
2. *(comparativa)* as; **non è caldo ~ pensavo** it's not as hot as I thought.
3. *(quanto)* how; **sai ~ mi piace il cioccolato** you know how much I like chocolate.
cometa *sf* comet.
comfort *sm inv* comfort; **l'hotel dispone di tutti i ~** the hotel offers a wide range of amenities.
comico, -a, -ci, -che ◇ *agg* funny; *(genere)* comic ◇ *sm (attore)* comedian.
cominciare *vt & vi* to begin, to start; **~ a fare qc** to begin to do sthg, to begin doing sthg; **~ col fare qc** to begin by doing sthg.
comitiva *sf* group.
comizio *sm* meeting.
commedia *sf* play.
commemorare *vt* to commemorate.
commentare *vt* to comment on.
commento *sm* comment; *(a un testo, programma)* commentary.

commerciale *agg* commercial.
commerciante *smf (mercante)* trader; *(negoziante)* shopkeeper.
commerciare : commerciare in *v + prep* to deal in.
commercio *sm (vendita)* trade; **essere fuori ~** not to be for sale; **essere in ~** to be on the market.
commesso, -a ◇ *pp* → **commettere** ◇ *sm, f* shop assistant.
commestibile *agg* edible.
◆ **commestibili** *smpl* foodstuffs.
commettere *vt (crimine)* to commit; *(errore)* to make.
commissario *sm (di polizia)* superintendent; *(d'esami)* member of an examining board; **~ tecnico** national coach.
commissione *sf* commission.
◆ **commissioni** *sfpl* errands.
commosso, -a ◇ *pp* → **commuovere** ◇ *agg* moved.
commovente *agg* touching.
commozione *sf (emozione)* emotion; **~ cerebrale** concussion.
commuovere *vt* to move, to touch.
◆ **commuoversi** *vr* to be moved, to be touched.
comò *sm inv* chest of drawers.
comodino *sm* bedside table.
comodità *sf inv* comfort.
comodo, -a ◇ *agg* comfortable; *(conveniente)* convenient; *(utile)* handy ◇ *sm*: **fare ~ a qn** to be handy for sb; **fare il proprio ~** to do as one pleases; **con ~** at one's convenience.
compact disc ['kɔmpat 'disk] *sm inv* compact disc.
compagnia *sf* company; *(di amici)* group; **fare ~ a qn** to keep sb company; **~ aerea** airline; **~ d'assicurazione** insurance company.
compagno, -a *sm, f* companion; *(convivente)* partner; **~ di scuola** school friend; **~ di squadra** team mate.
comparire *vi* to appear.
compartimento *sm (di locale, spazio)* section; *(di treno)* compartment.
compasso *sm* pair of compasses.
compatibile *agg* compatible; **un comportamento non ~** inexcusable behaviour.
compatire *vt (aver compassione di)* to feel sorry for; *(scusare)* to make allowances for.
compatto, -a *agg (ben unito)* compact; *(folla)* dense; *(fig: solidale)* united.
compensare *vt* to compensate; **~ qn di qc** to compensate sb for sthg.
compenso *sm (paga)* payment; *(risarcimento)* compensation; *(ricompensa)* recompense; **in ~** on the other hand.
comperare = **comprare**.
compere *sfpl*: **far ~** to do the shopping.
competente *agg* competent.
competere *vi* to compete.
◆ **competere a** *v + prep* to be due to.
competizione *sf* competition.
compiacere *vt* to please.
◆ **compiacersi** *vr*: **compiacersi di o per qc** to be delighted at sthg; **compiacersi con qn** to congratulate sb.
compiaciuto, -a *pp* → **compiacere**.
compiere *vt (eseguire)* to fulfil; *(concludere)* to complete; **quando compi gli anni?** when is your birthday?; **compie 15 anni a maggio** he'll be 15 in May.
compilare *vt* to fill in.
compito *sm (incarico)* task; *(dovere)* duty; *(in classe)* test.
◆ **compiti** *smpl* homework *(sg)*; **fare i compiti** to do one's homework.
compleanno *sm* birthday; **buon**

~! Happy Birthday!
complessivo, -a *agg* overall.
complesso, -a ◇ *agg* complex ◇ *sm* complex; *(musicale)* band, group; **in** o **nel ~** on the whole.
completamente *avv* completely.
completare *vt* to complete.
completo, -a ◇ *agg* complete; *(pieno)* full ◇ *sm (vestiario)* suit; *(di oggetti)* set; **al ~** *(hotel, aereo)* fully booked; **c'era la famiglia al ~** the whole family was there.
complicare *vt* to complicate.
◆ **complicarsi** *vr* to become complicated.
complicato, -a *agg* complicated.
complicazione *sf (difficoltà)* snag; *(di malattia)* complication.
complice *smf* accomplice.
complimentarsi *vr*: **~ con qn** to congratulate sb.
complimento *sm* compliment; **complimenti!** congratulations!; **non fare complimenti** don't stand on ceremony.
componente ◇ *smf (membro)* member ◇ *sf (aspetto)* element.
componibile *agg* fitted.
comporre *vt (musica, poesia)* to compose; *(parola)* to make up; *(numero di telefono)* to dial.
comportamento *sm* behaviour.
comportare *vt* to involve.
◆ **comportarsi** *vr* to behave.
compositore, -trice *sm, f* composer.
composizione *sf* composition; **'~ principali treni'** *board showing the position of compartments, restaurant car etc making up main line trains.*
composto, -a ◇ *pp* → **comporre** ◇ *agg (persona, contegno)* composed; *(sostanza, parola)* compound ◇ *sm* compound; **~ da** composed of.
comprare *vt* to buy.
comprendere *vt (includere)* to include; *(capire)* to understand.
comprensione *sf* understanding.
comprensivo, -a *agg (tollerante)* understanding; *(inclusivo)* inclusive.
compreso, -a ◇ *pp* → **comprendere** ◇ *agg* inclusive; **~ nel prezzo** included in the price.
compressa *sf* tablet.
compromesso *sm* compromise.
compromettere *vt* to compromise.
computer [kom'pjuter] *sm inv* computer.
comunale *agg* municipal.
comune ◇ *agg* common; *(a più persone)* shared; *(ordinario)* ordinary ◇ *sm (edificio)* town hall; *(ente)* town council; *(area)* = borough; **avere qc in ~ (con qn)** to have sthg in common (with sb); **mettere qc in ~** to share sthg; **fuori del ~** out of the ordinary.
comunicare ◇ *vt* to communicate ◇ *vi (parlare, corrispondere)* to communicate; *(porta)*: **~ con** to lead to.
comunicazione *sf (atto)* communication; *(annuncio)* announcement; *(telefonica)* call; **dare la ~ a qn** to put a call through to sb.
comunione *sf (eucaristia)* Communion; **~ dei beni** (DIR) joint ownership of property.
comunismo *sm* communism.
comunista, -i, -e *agg & smf* communist.
comunità *sf inv* community; **la Comunità (Economica) Europea** the European (Economic) Community.
comunque ◇ *avv* anyway ◇ *cong (tuttavia)* however; *(in qualsiasi modo)* no matter how.
con *prep* with; **~ piacere!** with pleasure!; **viaggiare ~ il treno/la macchina** to travel by train/car.

concavo, -a *agg* concave.

concedere *vt (dare, accordare)* to grant; *(ammettere)* to concede; **~ a qn di fare qc** to allow sb to do sthg; **concedersi qc** to treat o.s. to sthg.

concentrare *vt* to concentrate; *(riassumere)* to condense.

◆ **concentrarsi** *vr* to concentrate.

concentrato, -a ◇ *agg* concentrated, concentrating ◇ *sm* concentrate.

concentrazione *sf* concentration.

concepimento *sm* conception.

concepire *vt (figlio)* to conceive; *(idea)* to devise.

concerto *sm* concert.

concessionario *sm* agent.

concesso, -a *pp* → **concedere**.

concetto *sm* concept; *(opinione)* opinion.

conchiglia *sf* shell.

conciliare *vt (impegni, attività)* to reconcile; *(sonno)* to be conducive to; *(contravvenzione)* to settle on the spot.

concime *sm* fertilizer.

concludere *vt* to conclude.

◆ **concludersi** *vr* to conclude.

conclusione *sf* conclusion; **in ~** in conclusion.

concluso, -a *pp* → **concludere**.

concordare ◇ *vt (stabilire)* to agree on; (GRAMM) to make agree ◇ *vi* to agree.

concorde *agg* in agreement.

concorrente *smf (in gara, affari)* competitor; *(ad un concorso)* contestant.

concorrenza *sf* competition.

concorso *sm* competition; *(esame)* competitive examination; **~ di bellezza** beauty contest.

concreto, -a *agg* concrete.

condanna *sf (sentenza)* sentence; *(pena)* conviction; *(disapprovazione)* condemnation.

condannare *vt* (DIR) to sentence; *(disapprovare)* to condemn.

condimento *sm (per insalata)* dressing; *(per carne)* seasoning.

condire *vt (insalata)* to dress; *(carne)* to season.

condividere *vt* to share.

condizionale ◇ *agg & sm* conditional ◇ *sf* (DIR) suspended sentence.

condizionatore *sm* air-conditioner.

condizione *sf* condition; **a ~ che** on condition that.

condoglianze *sfpl* condolences.

condominio *sm (edificio)* block of flats *(jointly owned)*; *(persone)* joint owners *(pl)*.

condotta *sf* conduct.

condotto, -a ◇ *pp* → **condurre** ◇ *sm* conduit; (ANAT) duct.

conducente *sm* driver; **'non parlare al ~'** 'please do not speak to the driver whilst the vehicle is in motion'.

condurre *vt (affare, azienda)* to run; *(bambino, prigioniero)* to take; *(vita)* to lead; *(gas, acqua)* to carry.

conduttore, -trice ◇ *sm, f* driver ◇ *sm (di calore, elettricità)* conductor.

confarsi : confarsi a *vr + prep* to suit.

confederazione *sf* confederation.

conferenza *sf (riunione)* conference; *(discorso)* lecture; **~ stampa** press conference.

conferire *vt (form)*: **~ qc a qn** to confer sthg on sb.

conferma *sf* confirmation.

confermare *vt* to confirm.

confessare *vt* to confess.

◆ **confessarsi** *vr* (RELIG) to confess; *(dichiararsi)*: **confessarsi colpevole** to plead guilty.

confessione *sf* confession.

confetto *sm (dolciume)* sugared

almond; *(pastiglia)* pill.

confezionare *vt (merce)* to package; *(pacco)* to make up; *(vestiario)* to make.

confezione *sf (involucro)* packaging; *(di vestiario)* tailoring; ~ **regalo** gift pack.

confidare *vt*: ~ **qc a qn** to confide sthg to sb.

◆ **confidare in** *v + prep* to have confidence in.

◆ **confidarsi** *vr*: **confidarsi con qn** to open one's heart to sb.

confidenziale *agg* confidential.

confinare : **confinare con** *v + prep* to border on.

◆ **confinarsi in** *vr + prep* to shut o.s. away in.

confine *sm (frontiera)* border; *(limite)* boundary.

confiscare *vt* to confiscate.

conflitto *sm (guerra)* conflict; *(contrasto)* clash.

confondere *vt* to confuse, to mix up; ~ **le idee a qn** to confuse sb.

◆ **confondersi** *vr (mescolarsi)* to merge; *(sbagliarsi)* to get mixed up; *(turbarsi)* to become confused.

conformità *sf* conformity; **in ~ con** in accordance with.

confortare *vt* to comfort.

confortevole *agg* comfortable.

confrontare *vt* to compare.

confronto *sm* comparison; **in ~ (a)** in comparison (with); **nei miei confronti** towards me.

confusione *sf (caos)* confusion; *(disordine)* mess; *(chiasso)* racket, noise; **far ~** *(confondersi)* to get mixed up; *(far rumore)* to make a racket.

confuso, -a ◇ *pp* → **confondere** ◇ *agg* confused.

congedare *vt (lasciar andare)* to dismiss; (MIL) to demobilize.

◆ **congedarsi** *vr (andar via)* to take one's leave; (MIL) to be demobilized.

congedo *sm* leave; (MIL) discharge.

congegno *sm* device.

congelare *vt* to freeze.

◆ **congelarsi** *vr* to freeze; *(fig: persona, mani)* to be frozen.

congelato, -a *agg* frozen.

congelatore *sm* freezer.

congeniale *agg* congenial.

congenito, -a *agg* congenital.

congestione *sf* congestion.

congettura *sf* conjecture.

congiungere *vt* to join (together).

◆ **congiungersi** *vr (strade)* to meet.

congiuntivo *sm* subjunctive.

congiunto, -a ◇ *pp* → **congiungere** ◇ *sm, f* relative.

congiunzione *sf* conjunction.

congiura *sf* conspiracy.

congratularsi *vr*: ~ **con qn per qc** to congratulate sb on sthg.

congratulazioni *sfpl* congratulations.

congresso *sm* congress.

coniglio *sm* rabbit.

coniugato, -a *agg* married.

coniuge *smf* spouse.

connazionale *smf* fellow countryman (*f* fellow countrywoman).

connettere *vt* to connect.

connotati *smpl* description *(sg)*.

cono *sm* cone; ~ **gelato** ice-cream cone.

conoscente *smf* acquaintance.

conoscenza *sf* knowledge; *(persona)* acquaintance; **perdere ~** to lose consciousness.

conoscere *vt* to know; *(incontrare)* to meet.

conosciuto, -a ◇ *pp* → **conoscere** ◇ *agg* well-known.

conquista *sf (azione)* conquest; *(risultato, cosa ottenuta)* achievement.

conquistare *vt (impadronirsi di)* to conquer; *(ottenere)* to gain; *(persona)* to win over.

consanguineo, -a *sm, f* blood relation.

consapevole *agg*: **~ di qc** aware of sthg.

conscio, -a, -sci, -sce *agg*: **~ di qc** conscious of sthg.

consegna *sf (recapito)* delivery; *(custodia)*: **dare qc in ~ a qn** to entrust sb with sthg.

consegnare *vt (recapitare)* to deliver; *(affidare)* to entrust.

conseguenza *sf* consequence; **di ~** consequently.

conseguire ◇ *vt* to obtain ◇ *vi*: **ne consegue che ...** it follows that ...

consenso *sm* consent.

consentire *vt* to allow.

◆ **consentire a** *v + prep* to agree to.

conserva *sf* preserve; **~ di frutta** jam; **~ di pomodoro** tomato sauce.

conservante *sm* preservative.

conservare *vt (tenere)* to keep; *(monumento, resti)* to preserve; '**~ in frigo**' 'keep refrigerated'.

◆ **conservarsi** *vr (cibo)* to keep; *(monumento, resti)* to be preserved.

conservatore, -trice *sm, f* conservative.

considerare *vt* to consider.

◆ **considerarsi** *vr* to consider o.s.

considerazione *sf*: **prendere in ~** to take into consideration.

considerevole *agg* considerable.

consigliare *vt (persona)* to advise; *(locale, metodo)* to recommend; **~ a qn di fare qc** to advise sb to do sthg.

◆ **consigliarsi con** *vr + prep*: **consigliarsi con qn** to ask sb's advice.

consigliere *sm (funzionario)* adviser; *(politico)* councillor.

consiglio *sm (suggerimento)* piece of advice; *(riunione)* meeting; *(organo)* council; **dare un ~ a qn** to give sb some advice; **~ d'amministrazione** board; **il Consiglio dei Ministri** = the Cabinet.

consistere : **consistere di** *v + prep* to consist of; **consistere in** *v + prep* to consist in.

consistito, -a *pp* → **consistere**.

consolare *vt (confortare)* to console; *(sollevare)* to cheer up.

◆ **consolarsi** *vr* to console o.s.

consolato *sm* consulate.

console *sm* consul.

consonante *sf* consonant.

constatare *vt* to notice.

consueto, -a *agg* usual.

consulente *smf* consultant.

consultare *vt* to consult.

◆ **consultarsi** *vr* to confer.

◆ **consultarsi con** *vr + prep* to consult with.

consultorio *sm* advice bureau.

consumare *vt* to consume; *(logorare)* to wear out.

◆ **consumarsi** *vr* to wear out.

consumatore *sm* consumer.

consumazione *sf (bibita)* drink; *(spuntino)* snack; **la ~ al tavolo è più cara** it's more expensive to eat/drink sitting at a table; '**~ obbligatoria**' 'minimum charge'.

consumismo *sm* consumerism.

consumo *sm* consumption.

contabile *smf* accountant.

contabilità *sf inv (operazioni)* accountancy; *(libri)* accounts *(pl)*; *(ufficio)* accounts department.

contachilometri *sm inv* = mileometer.

contadino, -a *sm, f* farmer.

contagiare *vt* to infect.

contagocce *sm inv* dropper.

contante ◇ *agg* → **denaro** ◇ *sm* cash; **pagare in contanti** to pay in cash.

contare *vt & vi* to count; **avere i soldi contati** not to have a penny to spare.

◆ **contare di** *v + prep*: ~ **di fare qc** to intend to do sthg.

◆ **contare su** *vr + prep* to count on.

contatore *sm* meter.

contattare *vt* to contact.

contatto *sm* contact.

conte, -essa *sm, f* count (*f* countess).

contegno *sm* attitude.

contemporaneamente *avv* simultaneously.

contemporaneo, -a *agg (dello stesso tempo)* contemporaneous; *(attuale)* contemporary.

contendere *vt*: ~ **qc a qn** to compete with sb for sthg.

contenere *vt* to contain.

◆ **contenersi** *vr* to contain o.s.

contenitore *sm* container.

contento, -a *agg (lieto)* happy, glad; *(soddisfatto)*: ~ **(di)** pleased (with).

contenuto *sm (cosa racchiusa)* contents *(pl)*; *(argomento)* content.

contestare *vt* to object to.

contestazione *sf (obiezione)* objection; *(protesta)* protest.

contesto *sm* context.

contiguo, -a *agg*: ~ **(a qc)** adjacent (to sthg).

continentale *agg* continental.

continente *sm (geografico)* continent; *(terraferma)* mainland.

contingente *sm* contingent.

continuamente *avv (senza interruzioni)* continuously; *(di frequente)* continually.

continuare ◇ *vt & vi* to continue ◇ *v impers*: **continua a piovere** it's still raining; ~ **a fare qc** to continue doing sthg.

continuazione *sf* continuation.

continuo, -a *agg (incessante)* continuous; *(serie, fila)* continual; **di** ~ continually.

conto *sm (calcolo)* calculation; *(di ristorante, albergo)* bill; *(bancario)* account; **mi porta il ~, per favore?** could you bring me the bill, please?; **fare ~ su** to rely on; **rendersi ~ di qc** to realize sthg; **tenere ~ di qc** to take account of sthg; ~ **corrente** current account; ~ **alla rovescia** countdown; **per ~ di qn** on behalf of sb; **fare i conti con qn** *(fam)* to sort sb out; **in fin dei conti** all things considered.

contorno *sm (di pietanza)* vegetables *(pl)*; *(linea)* outline.

contrabbando *sm* smuggling.

contrabbasso *sm* double bass.

contraccambiare *vt* to return.

contraccolpo *sm* rebound.

contraddire *vt* to contradict.

◆ **contraddirsi** *vr* to contradict o.s.

contraddizione *sf* contradiction.

contraffare *vt* to falsify; *(firma)* to forge.

contrapporre *vt* to set against.

contrariamente *avv*: ~ **a** contrary to.

contrario, -a ◇ *agg (opposto)* opposite; *(sfavorevole)* unfavourable ◇ *sm* opposite; **essere ~ a qc** to be against sthg; **avere qualcosa in ~** to have an objection; **al ~** on the contrary.

contrarre *vt* to contract.

◆ **contrarsi** *vr (muscolo)* to contract.

contrassegno *sm (marchio)* mark; **spedire qc (in) ~** to send sthg cash on delivery.

contrastare ◇ *vt* to hinder ◇ *vi*: ~ **(con)** to clash (with).

contrasto *sm* contrast; **essere in ~ con qc** *(opinione, esigenza)* to be in contrast with sthg.

contrattare *vt* to negotiate.

contrattempo *sm* hitch.

contratto, -a ◇ *pp* → **contrarre** ◇ *sm* contract.

contravvenzione *sf* fine.

contribuire : **contribuire a** *v + prep* to contribute to.

contributo *sm (partecipazione)* contribution; *(tassa)* levy.

contro *prep* against; **~ di me** against me; **prendere qc ~ il mal di gola** to take sthg for one's sore throat.

controfigura *sf* stuntman (*f* stuntwoman).

controllare *vt* to control; *(verificare)* to check; '**~ il resto**' 'please check your change'.

♦ **controllarsi** *vr* to control o.s.

controllo *sm (verifica)* check; *(sorveglianza)* supervision; *(dominio)* control; **perdere il ~** to lose control; **~ doganale** customs inspection; '**~ elettronico della velocità**' 'speed checks'; '**~ passaporti**' 'passport control'.

controllore *sm (di autobus, treni)* (ticket) inspector; **~ di volo** air-traffic controller.

contromano *avv* in the wrong direction.

controproducente *agg* counter-productive.

controsenso *sm* contradiction in terms.

controvoglia *avv* reluctantly.

contusione *sf* bruise.

convalescenza *sf* convalescence.

convalidare *vt (biglietto)* to validate; *(dubbio, sospetto)* to confirm; '**~ all'inizio del viaggio**' 'stamp your ticket at the start of your journey'.

convegno *sm* conference.

convenevoli *smpl* civilities.

conveniente *agg* favourable; *(prezzo)* cheap; *(affare)* advantageous.

convenire ◇ *vi (riunirsi)* to gather; *(concordare)* to agree; *(tornare utile)* to be worthwhile ◇ *v impers (essere consigliabile)*: **conviene avvertirli** it is advisable to inform them; **ti conviene aspettare** you'd better wait.

convento *sm* convent.

convenuto *pp* → **convenire**.

convenzionale *agg* conventional.

convenzioni *sfpl* conventions.

conversazione *sf (chiacchierata)* conversation.

convertire *vt* to convert.

♦ **convertirsi** *vr*: **convertirsi (a qc)** to convert (to sthg).

convincere *vt*: **~ qn di qc** to convince sb of sthg; **~ qn a fare qc** to persuade sb to do sthg.

convinto, -a ◇ *pp* → **convincere** ◇ *agg* convinced.

convivere *vi* to live together.

convocare *vt* to convene.

convoglio *sm* convoy.

convulsioni *sfpl* convulsions.

cooperativa *sf* cooperative.

coordinare *vt* to coordinate.

coperchio *sm* lid.

coperta *sf (da letto)* blanket; *(di nave)* deck.

copertina *sf* cover.

coperto, -a ◇ *pp* → **coprire** ◇ *agg (piscina, campo)* indoor *(dav s)*; *(persona)* wrapped up; *(cielo)* overcast ◇ *sm (a tavola)* place; *(al ristorante)* cover charge; **~ di qc** covered with sthg; **al ~** under cover.

copertone *sm (pneumatico)* tyre.

copia *sf* copy; **bella ~** final draft; **brutta ~** rough draft.

copiare *vt* to copy.

copione *sm* script.

coppa *sf (bicchiere)* goblet; *(di gelato)* tub; *(ciotola)* bowl; *(di reggiseno, trofeo)* cup; **~ dell'olio** oil sump.

coppia *sf (paio)* pair; *(di sposi, amanti)* couple; **a coppie** in pairs.

copricostume *sm inv* beach robe.

coprifuoco, -chi *sm* curfew.

copriletto *sm inv* bedspread.
coprire *vt* to cover; ~ **qn di qc** to cover sb with sthg; *(insulti)* to shower sb with sthg.
◆ **coprirsi** *vr (con indumenti)* to cover o.s.; **coprirsi di qc** *(muffa, fango)* to be covered in sthg.
coraggio ◇ *sm (forza d'animo)* courage; *(faccia tosta)* cheek ◇ *esclam* cheer up!; *(forza)* come on!; **avere il ~ di fare qc** *(avere l'animo)* to have the nerve to do sthg; *(avere faccia tosta)* to have the cheek to do sthg.
coraggioso, -a *agg* courageous, brave.
corallo *sm* coral.
Corano *sm*: **il ~** the Koran.
corazzieri *smpl the President's guard.*
corda *sf (fune)* rope; *(spago, di strumento)* string; **tagliare la ~** *(fig)* to sneak off; **corde vocali** vocal cords.
cordiale *agg* warm.
cordone *sm* cord; *(di persone)* cordon; ~ **ombelicale** umbilical cord.
coreografia *sf* choreography.
coriandolo *sm (spezia, pianta)* coriander.
◆ **coriandoli** *smpl* confetti *(sg)*.
coricarsi *vr* to go to bed.
cornamusa *sf* bagpipes *(pl)*.
cornetta *sf* receiver.
cornetto *sm (pasta)* croissant; *(gelato)* cone.
cornice *sf* frame.
cornicione *sm* cornice.
corno *(pl f* **corna**) *sm* horn; **facciamo le corna!** *(fam)* = touch wood!; **fare** o **mettere le corna a qn** *(fam)* to cheat on sb.
Cornovaglia *sf*: **la ~** Cornwall.
coro *sm* chorus; *(di chiesa)* choir.
corona *sf (reale)* crown; *(di fiori)* wreath.
corpo *sm* body; *(militare)* corps *(sg)*; ~ **insegnante** teaching staff; **(a) ~ a ~** hand to hand.
corporatura *sf* build.
corporeo, -a *agg* bodily.
corredare *vt*: ~ **qc di qc** to equip sthg with sthg.
corredo *sm (da sposa)* trousseau; *(attrezzatura)* kit.
correggere *vt* to correct.
corrente ◇ *agg (moneta)* valid; *(mese, anno)* current; *(comune)* everyday ◇ *sf* current; *(tendenza)* trend ◇ *sm*: **essere al ~ (di qc)** to be informed (about sthg); **mettere qn al ~ (di qc)** to inform sb (about sthg); ~ **alternata** alternating current; ~ **continua** direct current.
correntemente *avv (speditamente)* fluently; *(comunemente)* commonly.
correre ◇ *vi* to run; *(affrettarsi)* to rush ◇ *vt* to run; ~ **dietro a qn** to run after sb.
corretto, -a ◇ *pp* → **correggere** ◇ *agg (esatto)* correct; *(onesto)* proper.
correzione *sf* correction; *(di compiti)* marking.
corridoio *sm* corridor.
corridore *sm (atleta)* runner; *(pilota)* racer.
corriera *sf* coach, bus.
corriere *sm* courier.
corrimano *sm* handrail.
corrispondente ◇ *agg* corresponding ◇ *smf* correspondent.
corrispondenza *sf* correspondence.
corrispondere *vt* to return.
◆ **corrispondere a** *v + prep* to correspond to.
corrisposto, -a *pp* → **corrispondere**.
corrodere *vt* to corrode.
corrompere *vt (comprare)* to bribe; *(traviare)* to corrupt.
corroso, -a *pp* → **corrodere**.
corrotto, -a ◇ *pp* → **corrompere** ◇ *agg (disonesto)* corrupt.

corruzione *sf (disonestà)* corruption; *(con denaro)* bribery.

corsa *sf (a piedi)* running; *(gara)* race; *(di mezzo pubblico)* journey; **fare una ~** *(correre)* to run; *(sbrigarsi)* to dash; **di ~** in a rush; **corse dei cavalli** horse races.

corsia *sf (di strada)* lane; *(di ospedale)* ward; **~ preferenziale** bus and taxi lane; **~ di sorpasso** overtaking lane; '**~ chiusa**' 'lane closed'.

Corsica *sf*: **la ~** Corsica.

corso, -a ◇ *pp* → **correre** ◇ *sm* course; *(strada)* main street; **fare un ~ (di qc)** to take a course (in sthg); **~ accelerato** crash course; **~ d'acqua** watercourse; **corsi estivi** summer courses; **corsi serali** evening classes; **in ~** *(denaro)* in circulation; *(riunione, lavori)* in progress; **fuori ~** out of circulation.

corte *sf (reale)* court; **fare la ~ a qn** to court sb.

corteccia, -ce *sf* bark.

corteggiare *vt* to court.

corteo *sm (manifestazione)* demonstration; *(processione)* procession.

cortese *agg* polite.

cortesia *sf (qualità)* politeness; *(atto)* favour; **per ~** please.

cortile *sm* courtyard.

corto, -a *agg* short; **essere a ~ di qc** to be short of sthg.

cortocircuito *sm* short circuit.

corvo *sm* raven.

cosa *sf* thing; *(faccenda)* matter; **è una ~ da niente** it's nothing; **~?** what?; **~ c'è?** what's the matter?; **per prima ~** firstly.

coscia, -sce *sf (di uomo)* thigh; *(di pollo, agnello)* leg.

cosciente *agg (sveglio)* conscious; *(consapevole)*: **~ di qc** aware O conscious of sthg.

coscienza *sf* conscience; **avere qc sulla ~** to have sthg on one's conscience.

coscio *sm* leg.

cosciotto *sm* leg.

così ◇ *avv* **1.** *(in questo modo)* like this/like that; **fai ~** do it this way; **~ ~** so-so; **per ~ dire** so to speak; **meglio ~** it's better like this; **proprio ~!** just like that!; **e ~ via** and so on.

2. *(per descrivere misure)* so; **una scatola larga ~ e lunga ~** a box so wide and so long.

3. *(talmente)* so; **è ancora ~ presto!** it's still so early!; **~ poco/tanto** so little/much; **una ragazza ~ bella** such a beautiful girl.

4. *(conclusivo)* so; **~, non hai ancora deciso** so you haven't decided yet.

◇ *cong* **1.** *(perciò)* so, therefore.

2. *(a tal punto)*: **~ ... che** so ... (that); **sono ~ stanco che non sto in piedi** I'm so tired I can hardly stand up; **~ ... da** enough ... to; **è ~ sciocco da dire di no** he's silly enough to say no.

◇ *agg inv*: **non ho mai visto una macchina ~** I've never seen a car like that.

◆ **così che** *cong*: *(affinché)* so (that).

cosicché *cong* so that.

cosiddetto, -a *agg* so-called.

cosmetici *smpl* cosmetics.

coso *sm (fam)* thing.

cospargere *vt*: **~ qc di qc** to sprinkle sthg with sthg.

cosparso, -a *pp* → **cospargere**.

cospicuo, -a *agg* sizeable.

cospirare *vi* to conspire.

costa *sf* coast.

costante *agg (stabile, durevole)* constant; *(persona)* steadfast.

costare *vi* to cost; **quanto costa?** how much does it cost?; **~ caro** to be expensive.

costata *sf* chop.

costatare = **constatare**.
costeggiare *vt (fiancheggiare)* to go alongside; *(navigare)* to hug the coast of.
costellazione *sf* constellation.
costernato, -a *agg* dismayed.
costì *avv* there.
costiero, -a *agg* coastal.
costituire *vt (formare)* to constitute; *(fondare)* to set up.
◆ **costituirsi** *vr* to give o.s. up.
costituzione *sf* constitution; *(formazione)* setting-up.
costo *sm* cost; **a tutti i costi** at all costs.
costola *sf* rib.
costoletta *sf* cutlet.
costoso, -a *agg* expensive.
costretto, -a *pp* → **costringere**.
costringere *vt*: ~ **qn (a fare qc)** to force sb (to do sthg).
costruire *vt (fabbricare)* to build.
costruzione *sf* construction.
costume *sm (uso)* custom; *(abito)* costume; ~ **da bagno** swimsuit.
cotechino *sm* pork sausage.
cotoletta *sf* chop; *(di vitello)* cutlet; ~ **alla milanese** *escalope of veal, coated in egg and breadcrumbs then fried.*
cotone *sm* cotton; ~ **idrofilo** cotton wool.
cotta *sf*: **prendersi una ~ per qn** *(fam)* to have a crush on sb.
cotto, -a ◇ *pp* → **cuocere** ◇ *agg* cooked; *(fam: innamorato)* head over heels in love; **ben** ~ well-done.
cottura *sf* cooking.
coupon [ku'pon] *sm inv* coupon.
cozza *sf* mussel.
C.P. *(abbr di casella postale)* P.O. Box.
cracker ['krɛker] *sm inv* cracker.
crampo *sm* cramp.
cranio *sm* skull.
cratere *sm* crater.
crauti *smpl sauerkraut flavoured with cumin and juniper, a speciality of Trento.*
cravatta *sf* tie.
creare *vt* to create.
creativo, -a *agg* creative.
creatore, -trice *sm, f* creator; **il Creatore** the Creator.
creatura *sf* creature.
credente *smf* believer.
credenza *sf (convinzione)* belief; *(mobile)* sideboard.
credere *vt* to believe; **credo di sì/no** I think/don't think so; **credo (che) sia vero** I think that's true; **credo di fare la cosa giusta** I think I'm doing the right thing.
◆ **credere a** *v + prep* to believe; **non ci credo!** I don't believe it!
◆ **credere in** *v + prep* to believe in.
◆ **credersi** *vr* to consider o.s.
credito *sm* (COMM) credit; *(fiducia)* trust.
crema *sf* cream; *(liquida)* custard; ~ **di asparagi** cream of asparagus soup; ~ **depilatoria** hair-removing cream; ~ **pasticcera** confectioner's custard; ~ **solare** suntan cream; **gelato alla** ~ vanilla ice-cream.
crematorio *sm* crematorium.
cremazione *sf* cremation.
crème caramel ['krem'karamɛl] *sm inv* o *sf inv* crème caramel.
cremisi *agg inv* crimson.
cremoso, -a *agg* creamy.
crepaccio *sm* crevice.
crepapelle : a crepapelle *avv*: **ridere a** ~ to split one's sides laughing.
crepare *vi (fam: morire)* to snuff it; ~ **dal ridere** to die laughing.
crêpe [krɛp] *sf inv* pancake.
crepuscolo *sm (tramonto)* twilight.
crescere ◇ *vi* to grow; *(diventare adulto)* to grow up ◇ *vt* to bring up.

crescita *sf* growth.
cresima *sf* confirmation.
crespo, -a *agg* frizzy.
cresta *sf* crest.
creta *sf* clay.
cretino, -a *agg* idiot.
cric *sm inv (attrezzo)* jack.
criminale *agg & smf (criminoso)* criminal.
crimine *sm* crime.
criniera *sf* mane.
cripta *sf* crypt.
crisi *sf inv (fase difficile)* crisis; *(attacco)* fit; **in ~** in a state of crisis.
cristallo *sm* crystal.
cristianesimo *sm* Christianity.
cristiano, -a *agg & sm, f* Christian.
Cristo *sm* Christ; **avanti ~** BC; **dopo ~** AD.
criterio *sm (regola)* criterion; *(buon senso)* common sense.
critica, -che *sf (biasimo)* criticism; *(i critici)* critics *(pl)*, → **critico**.
criticare *vt* to criticize.
critico, -a, -ci, -che ◇ *agg* critical ◇ *sm, f (persona)* critic.
croccante ◇ *agg* crisp ◇ *sm* almond crunch.
crocchetta *sf* croquette.
croce *sf* cross; **la Croce Rossa** the Red Cross.
crocevia *sm inv* crossroads *(sg)*.
crociera *sf* cruise.
crocifisso *sm* crucifix.
crollare *vi (edificio, ponte)* to collapse; *(fig: per stanchezza, dolore)* to break down.
crollo *sm (di edificio, ponte)* collapse; *(di prezzi)* slump.
cronaca, -che *sf (attualità)* news *(sg)*; *(di partita)* commentary; **~ nera** crime news *(sg)*.
cronico, -a, -ci, -che *agg* chronic.
cronista, -i, -e *smf* reporter.
cronologico, -a, -ci, -che *agg* chronological.
crosta *sf (di pane)* crust; *(di formaggio)* rind; *(di ferita)* scab.
crostacei *smpl* shellfish.
crostata *sf fruit or jam tart with a pastry lattice topping.*
crostino *sm (per minestra)* crouton; *(tartina)* canapé; **crostini di fegato** *small pieces of toast spread with chicken liver pâté.*
croupier [kru'pje] *sm inv* croupier.
cruciale *agg* crucial.
cruciverba *sm inv* crossword.
crudele *agg* cruel.
crudo, -a *agg* raw.
crusca *sf* bran.
cruscotto *sm* dashboard.
cubo *sm* cube.
cuccetta *sf (di treno)* couchette; *(di nave)* berth.
cucchiaiata *sf* spoonful.
cucchiaino *sm* teaspoon.
cucchiaio *sm* spoon.
cuccia, -ce *sf* dog's bed; **a ~!** down!
cucciolo *sm* cub; *(di cane)* puppy.
cucina *sf (stanza)* kitchen; *(attività, cibi)* cooking; *(elettrodomestico)* cooker; **~ casalinga** home cooking; **~ a gas** gas cooker.
cucinare *vt* to cook.
cucire *vt* to sew.
cucitura *sf* stitching.
cuculo *sm* cuckoo.
cuffia *sf* cap; *(per l'ascolto)* headphones *(pl)*; **'è obbligatorio l'uso della ~'** 'swimming caps must be worn'.
cugino, -a *sm, f* cousin.
cui *pron relativo* **1.** *(in complemento indiretto: persona)* who, whom; **l'amico a ~ ho prestato il libro** the friend I lent the book to, the friend to whom I lent the book; **l'amico di ~ ti ho parlato** the friend I told you about; **la ragazza con ~**

esco the girl I'm going out with.
2. *(in complemento indiretto: cosa)* which; **il film a ~ mi riferisco** the film (which) I'm referring to; **l'appartamento in ~ vivo** the flat (which) I live in; **il motivo per ~ ti chiamo** the reason (that) I'm calling you.
3. *(tra articolo e sostantivo)*: **la città il ~ nome mi sfugge** the town whose name escapes me; **la persona alla ~ domanda rispondo** the person whose question I'm answering.
♦ **per cui** *cong (perciò)* so; **sono stanco, per ~ vado a letto** I'm tired, so I'm going to bed.
culla *sf* cradle.
culmine *sm* peak.
culo *sm (volg)* arse *(Br)*, ass *(Am)*.
culto *sm* cult; *(adorazione)* worship.
cultura *sf* culture.
culturismo *sm* body-building.
cumulativo *agg m* → **biglietto**.
cumulo *sm (mucchio)* heap, pile.
cunetta *sf (avvallamento)* bump.
cuocere *vt & vi* to cook.
cuoco, -a, -chi, -che *sm, f* cook.
cuoio *sm* leather; **~ capelluto** scalp.
cuore *sm* heart; **avere a ~ qc** to care about sthg; **nel ~ della notte** in the middle of the night.
cupo, -a *agg (scuro)* dark; *(voce)* deep.
cupola *sf* dome.
cura *sf* care; *(trattamento, terapia)* treatment; **avere ~ di** to take care of; **prendersi ~ di** to look after; **~ dimagrante** diet.
curare *vt (trattare)* to treat; *(guarire)* to cure.
curiosare *vi* to look around.
curiosità *sf inv* curiosity.
curioso, -a *agg (insolito)* curious; *(indiscreto)* inquisitive.
curva *sf* bend; **in ~** on a bend; **'~ pericolosa'** 'dangerous bend'.
curvare ◇ *vi (veicolo, autista)* to turn; *(strada)* to bend ◇ *vt* to bend.
curvo, -a *agg (linea)* curved; *(persona, spalle)* bent.
cuscino *sm (da divano)* cushion; *(guanciale)* pillow.
custode *smf* attendant; *(di scuola)* janitor.
custodia *sf (cura, controllo)* custody; *(astuccio)* case.
custodire *vt (assistere)* to look after; *(conservare)* to keep.
cute *sf* skin.

D

da *prep* 1. *(con verbo passivo)* by; **il viaggio è pagato dalla ditta** the trip is paid for by the company.
2. *(stato in luogo)* at; **abito ~ una zia** I'm living at an aunt's.
3. *(moto a luogo)* to; **andare dal medico/dal parrucchiere** to go to the doctor's/the hairdresser's.
4. *(moto per luogo)* through; **è entrato dall'ingresso principale** he came in through the main entrance; **il treno passa ~ Roma** the train goes via Rome.
5. *(indica l'origine, la provenienza)* from; **venire ~ Roma** to come from Rome; **ricevere una lettera ~ un amico** to get a letter from a friend.
6. *(indica tempo)* for; **aspetto ~ ore** I've been waiting for hours; **lavoro dalle 9 alle 5** I work from 9 to 5; **non lo vedo ~ ieri** I haven't seen him since yesterday; **comincerò ~ domani** I'll start from tomorrow.
7. *(indica condizione, funzione)* as; **~ grande voglio fare il pompiere** when I grow up I want to be a fireman; **fare ~ guida** to act as a guide.
8. *(indica la causa)* with; **tremare dal freddo** to shiver; **piangere dalla felicità** to cry for joy.
9. *(indica una caratteristica)* with; **una ragazza dagli occhi verdi** a girl with green eyes, a green-eyed girl; **una stanza ~ 200 000 lire a notte** a 200,000 lira a night room; **una bottiglia ~ un litro** a litre bottle.
10. *(indica il fine)*: **occhiali ~ sole** sunglasses; **qualcosa ~ mangiare** something to eat.
11. *(indica separazione)* from; **vedere ~ lontano/vicino** to see from a distance/close up; **essere lontano ~ casa** to be far from home; **la piscina è a 3 chilometri ~ qui** the swimming pool is 3 kilometres from here; **isolarsi ~ tutti** to cut o.s. off from everyone; **mettere qc ~ parte** to save sthg.
12. *(indica modo)* like; **trattare qn ~ amico** to treat sb like o as a friend; **puoi farlo ~ te** you can do it (for) yourself; **non è cosa ~ te!** it's not like you!
13. *(indica la conseguenza)*: **essere stanco ~ morire** to be dead tired.

daccapo *avv* from the beginning.

dado *sm (per gioco)* dice; *(estratto)* stock cube; *(per vite)* nut.

dagli = **da + gli**, → **da**.

dai[1] = **da + i**, → **da**.

dai[2] *esclam* go on!

daino *sm (animale)* deer.

dal = **da + il**, → **da**.

dall' = **da + l'**, → **da**.

dalla = **da + la**, → **da**.

dalle = **da + le**, → **da**.

dallo = **da** + **lo**, → **da**.
daltonico, -a, -ci, -che *agg* colour-blind.
dama *sf (gioco)* draughts *(sg)*; *(nel ballo)* partner.
damigiana *sf* demijohn.
danaro = **denaro**.
dancing ['dɛnsiŋ] *sm inv* dance hall.
danese ◇ *agg & sm* Danish ◇ *smf* Dane.
Danimarca *sf*: **la** ~ Denmark.
danneggiare *vt (rovinare)* to damage; *(nuocere a)* to harm.
danno *sm (materiale)* damage; *(morale)* harm; **i danni** (DIR) damages.
dannoso, -a *agg* harmful.
danza *sf* dance.
dappertutto *avv* everywhere.
dappoco *agg inv (persona)* inept; *(questione)* insignificant.
dapprima *avv* at first.
dare *vt* to give; *(risultati)* to produce; *(film)*: **cosa danno all'Odeon?** what's on at the Odeon?; ~ **qc a qn** to give sthg to sb, to give sb sthg; ~ **la mano a qn** to shake hands with sb; ~ **la nausea a qn** to make sb feel sick; ~ **la buonanotte a qn** to say goodnight to sb; ~ **da bere a qn** to give sb something to drink; ~ **una festa** to throw a party; ~ **del lei a qn** to address sb as 'lei'; ~ **del tu a qn** to address sb as 'tu'; ~ **qn per morto** to give sb up for dead; ~ **qc per scontato** to take sthg for granted; **darsi il cambio** to take it in turns; ~ **alla testa a qn** *(sog: alcool, successo)* to go to sb's head.
◆ **dare su** *v + prep (finestra)* to look out onto; *(porta)* to lead to.
◆ **darsi a** *vr + prep (dedicarsi a)* to devote o.s. to; **darsi al bere** to take to drink.
data *sf* date; ~ **di nascita** date of birth.
dato, -a ◇ *pp* → **dare** ◇ *agg* particular ◇ *sm* datum; ~ **che** given that; **un** ~ **di fatto** a fact; **i dati** the data.
datore, -trice *sm, f*: ~ **di lavoro** employer.
dattero *sm* date.
dattilografo, -a *sm, f* typist.
davanti ◇ *avv* in front; *(avanti)* ahead; *(nella parte anteriore)* at the front ◇ *agg inv* front *(dav s)* ◇ *sm* front ◇ *prep*: ~ **a** in front of; *(dirimpetto)* opposite.
davanzale *sm* windowsill.
davvero *avv* really.
d.C. *(abbr di dopo Cristo)* A.D.
dea *sf* goddess.
debito *sm* debt.
debole ◇ *agg* weak ◇ *sm*: **avere un** ~ **per** to have a weakness for.
debolezza *sf* weakness.
debuttare *vi* to make one's debut.
decaffeinato, -a *agg* decaffeinated.
decapitare *vt* to decapitate.
decappottabile *agg & sf* convertible.
deceduto, -a *agg* deceased.
decennio *sm* decade.
decente *agg* decent.
decesso *sm (form)* death.
decidere ◇ *vt* to decide on ◇ *vi* to decide; ~ **di fare qc** to decide to do sthg.
◆ **decidersi** *vr*: **decidersi (a fare qc)** to make up one's mind (to do sthg).
decimale *agg* decimal.
decimo, -a *num* tenth, → **sesto**.
decina *sf* ten; *(circa dieci)* about ten; **decine di** dozens of.
decisione *sf* decision; **prendere una** ~ to make a decision.
deciso, -a ◇ *pp* → **decidere** ◇ *agg* decisive; ~ **a fare qc** determined to do sthg.
decollare *vi* to take off.

decọllo *sm* takeoff.
decorạre *vt* to decorate.
decọtto *sm* decoction.
decrẹto *sm* decree.
dẹdica, -che *sf* dedication.
dedicạre *vt*: ~ **qc a qn** *(poesia, canzone)* to dedicate sthg to sb; *(fig: consacrare)* to devote sthg to sb.
◆ **dedicarsi a** *vr + prep* to devote o.s. to.
dẹdito, -a *agg*: ~ **a qc** *(studio)* devoted to sthg; *(droga, alcool)* addicted to sthg.
dedọtto, -a *pp* → **dedurre**.
dedụrre *vt (concludere)* to deduce; *(detrarre)* to deduct.
deduziọne *sf* deduction.
deficiẹnte *agg (spreg)* idiotic.
dẹficit *sm inv* deficit.
definịre *vt* to define.
definitịvo, -a *agg* definitive.
definiziọne *sf* definition.
deformạre *vt* to deform; *(fig: travisare)* to distort.
◆ **deformarsi** *vr* to become deformed.
defụnto, -a *sm, f* deceased.
degenerạre *vi* to degenerate.
dẹgli = **di + gli**, → **di**.
degnạrsi *vr*: ~ **di fare qc** to condescend to do sthg.
dẹgno, -a *agg*: ~ **di** worthy of.
degradạre *vt (peggiorare)* to degrade; (MIL) to demote.
degustaziọne *sf (assaggio)* tasting; *(negozio) specialist shop where beverages, especially wine or coffee, are tasted.*
dẹi = **di + i**, → **di**.
delegạre *vt*: ~ **qn (a fare qc)** to delegate sb (to do sthg); ~ **qc a qn** to delegate sthg to sb.
delegaziọne *sf* delegation.
delfịno *sm* dolphin.
delicatẹzza *sf (l'essere delicato)* delicacy; *(gentilezza)* consideration; *(atto gentile)* considerate act.
delicạto, -a *agg* delicate; *(gentile)* considerate.
delineạre *vt* to outline.
◆ **delinearsi** *vr (essere visibile)* to be outlined; *(fig: presentarsi)* to take shape.
delinquẹnte *smf* delinquent.
delịrio *sm* (MED) delirium; *(esaltazione)* frenzy.
delịtto *sm* crime.
deliziọso, -a *agg (cibo)* delicious; *(gradevole)* delightful.
dell' = **di + l'**, → **di**.
dẹlla = **di + la**, → **di**.
dẹlle = **di + le**, → **di**.
dẹllo = **di + lo**, → **di**.
dẹlta *sm inv* delta.
deltaplạno *sm* hang glider.
delụdere *vt* to disappoint.
delusiọne *sf* disappointment.
delụso, -a ◇ *pp* → **deludere** ◇ *agg* disappointed.
democrạtico, -a, -ci, -che *agg* democratic.
democrazịa *sf* democracy.
demolịre *vt* to demolish.
demọnio *sm* devil.
demoralizzạre *vt* to demoralize.
◆ **demoralizzarsi** *vr* to become demoralized.
denạro *sm* money; ~ **contante** cash.
denigrạre *vt* to denigrate.
denominạre *vt* to name.
denominaziọne *sf* name, denomination; ~ **d'origine controllata** *a mark guaranteeing that the product, especially wine, is of a good quality.*
densità *sf* density.
dẹnso, -a *agg* thick.
dẹnte *sm* tooth; ~ **da latte** milk tooth; ~ **del giudizio** wisdom tooth; **al** ~ al dente *(cooked enough to be still firm when bitten)*; **mettere qc sotto i denti** to have a bite to eat; **armato fino ai denti** armed to the teeth.

dentiera *sf (denti finti)* dentures *(pl)*.
dentifricio *sm* toothpaste.
dentista, -i, -e *smf* dentist.
dentro *avv & prep* inside; **darci ~** *(fam)* to put one's back into it; **~ di sé** inwardly, inside; **qui/là ~** in here/there; **dal di ~** from the inside; **in ~** inwards.
denuncia, -ce o **-cie** *sf*: **fare la ~** to make a statement to the police; **~ dei redditi** income tax return.
denunciare *vt (sporgere denuncia contro)* to report; *(rendere noto)* to declare.
deodorante *sm (per il corpo)* deodorant; *(per ambiente)* air freshener.
deperibile *agg* perishable.
depilazione *sf* hair removal.
dépliant [depli'an] *sm inv* brochure.
deplorevole *agg* deplorable.
depositare *vt* to deposit; *(persona)* to leave.
♦ **depositarsi** *vr* to settle.
deposito *sm* deposit; *(per autobus)* depot; *(per merci)* warehouse; *(di liquido)* sediment; **~ bagagli** left luggage office.
depravato, -a *sm, f* degenerate.
depressione *sf* depression.
depresso, -a ◇ *pp* → **deprimere** ◇ *agg* depressed.
deprimente *agg* depressing.
deprimere *vt* to depress.
♦ **deprimersi** *vr* to become depressed.
deputato, -a *sm, f* = Member of Parliament *(Br)*, = Representative *(Am)*.
derattizzazione *sf* rodent control.
deriva *sf*: **andare alla ~** to drift.
derivare : derivare da *v + prep* to derive from.
dermatologo, -a, -gi o **-ghi, -ghe** *sm, f* dermatologist.
derubare *vt* to rob.
descritto, -a *pp* → **descrivere**.
descrivere *vt* to describe.
descrizione *sf* description.
deserto, -a ◇ *agg (disabitato)* deserted; *(senza vegetazione)* barren ◇ *sm* desert.
desiderare *vt* to want, to desire; *(sessualmente)* to desire; **desidera?** can I help you?; **~ fare qc** to wish to do sthg; **lasciare a ~** to leave much to be desired.
desiderio *sm* wish.
desideroso, -a *agg*: **~ di fare qc** eager to do sthg.
designare *vt* to designate.
desistere : desistere da *v + prep (form)* to give up.
desistito *pp* → **desistere**.
destinare *vt (assegnare, riservare)* to assign; *(indirizzare)* to address.
destinatario, -a *sm, f* addressee.
destinazione *sf* destination; **arrivare a ~** to reach one's destination.
destino *sm* destiny, fate.
destra *sf (mano)* right hand; *(lato)* right; **la ~** (POL) the right wing; **tenere la ~** to keep to the right; **a ~** *(stato in luogo)* on the right; *(moto a luogo)* right; **di ~** *(dal lato destro)* right-hand.
destreggiarsi *vr (nel traffico)* to manoeuvre; *(fig: tra difficoltà)* to manage.
destro, -a *agg (opposto a sinistra)* right.
detenuto, -a *sm, f* prisoner.
detenzione *sf* detention.
detergente ◇ *agg* cleansing ◇ *sm (cosmetico)* cleansing cream; *(detersivo)* detergent.
deteriorare *vt* to impair.
♦ **deteriorarsi** *vr* to deteriorate.
determinante *agg* decisive.
determinare *vt (stabilire)* to determine.
determinazione *sf* determination.

detersivo *sm* detergent.
detestare *vt* to detest.
detrarre *vt* to deduct.
detratto, -a *pp* → **detrarre**.
dettagliato, -a *agg* detailed.
dettaglio *sm* detail; **al ~** (COMM) retail.
dettare *vt* to dictate; **~ legge** to lay down the law.
dettato *sm* dictation.
detto, -a ◇ *pp* → **dire** ◇ *agg* *(soprannominato)* known as ◇ *sm* saying.
devastare *vt* to devastate.
deviare ◇ *vt* to divert ◇ *vi (di direzione)*: **~ da qc** to turn off sthg.
deviazione *sf (del traffico)* detour; *(di fiume)* deviation.
devoto, -a *agg* devoted.
di ◇ *prep* 1. *(indica appartenenza)* of; **il libro ~ Marco** Marco's book; **la porta della camera** the bedroom door.
2. *(indica l'autore)* by; **un quadro ~ Giotto** a painting by Giotto.
3. *(partitivo)* of; **alcuni ~ noi** some of us.
4. *(nei paragoni)*: **sono più alto ~ te** I'm taller than you; **il migliore ~ tutti** the best of all.
5. *(indica argomento)* about, of; **un libro ~ storia** a history book; **parlare ~** to talk about.
6. *(temporale)* in; **d'estate** in (the) summer; **~ mattina** in the morning; **~ notte** at/by night; **~ sabato** on Saturdays.
7. *(indica provenienza)* from; **~ dove sei?** where are you from?; **sono ~ Messina** I'm from Messina.
8. *(indica una caratteristica)*: **un bambino ~ due anni** a two-year-old child, a child of two; **una statua ~ marmo** a marble statue; **una torre ~ 40 metri** a 40-metre tower; **un film ~ due ore** a two-hour film.
9. *(indica la causa)*: **urlare ~ dolore** to scream with pain; **sto morendo ~ fame!** I'm starving!; **soffrire ~ mal di testa** to suffer from headaches; **morire ~ vecchiaia** to die of old age.
10. *(indica contenuto)* of; **una bottiglia ~ vino** a bottle of wine.
11. *(seguito da infinito)*: **mi ha detto ~ non aspettare** he told me not to wait; **pensavo ~ uscire** I was thinking of going out; **capita ~ sbagliare** anyone can make a mistake; **mi sembra ~ conoscerlo** I think I know him.
12. *(in espressioni)*: **a causa ~** because of; **~ modo che** so as to; **dare del bugiardo a qn** to call sb a liar.
◇ *art* some; *(in negative)* any; **vorrei del pane** I'd like some bread; **ha degli spiccioli?** have you got any change?
diabete *sm* diabetes.
diabetico, -a, -ci, -che *agg* diabetic.
diaframma, -i *sm* diaphragm.
diagnosi *sf inv* diagnosis.
diagonale *agg & sf* diagonal.
diagramma, -i *sm* diagram.
dialetto *sm* dialect.
dialisi *sf* (MED) dialysis.
dialogo, -ghi *sm* dialogue.
diamante *sm* diamond.
diametro *sm* diameter.
diamine *esclam (certo)* absolutely!; **che ~ stai facendo?** what on earth are you doing?
diapositiva *sf* slide.
diario *sm* diary; *(a scuola)* homework book; *(calendario)* timetable.
diarrea *sf* diarrhoea.
diavolo *sm* devil; **che ~ vuole?** *(fam)* what the hell does he want?; **va al ~!** *(fam)* go to hell!
dibattito *sm* debate.
dica → **dire**.
dicembre *sm* December, → **settembre**.

diceria *sf* piece of gossip, rumour.
dichiarare *vt* to declare.
dichiarazione *sf* declaration.
diciannove *num* nineteen, → **sei**.
diciannovesimo, -a *num* nineteenth, → **sesto**.
diciassette *num* seventeen, → **sei**.
diciassettesimo, -a *num* seventeenth, → **sesto**.
diciottesimo, -a *num* eighteenth, → **sesto**.
diciotto *num* eighteen, → **sei**.
dieci *num* ten, → **sei**.
diecina = **decina**.
diesel ['dizel] *agg inv & sm inv* diesel.
dieta *sf* diet; **essere a ~** to be on a diet.
dietetico, -a, -ci, -che *agg* diet *(dav s)*.
dietro ◇ *avv (nella parte posteriore)* at/in the back; *(indietro)* behind ◇ *sm* back ◇ *prep*: **~ (a)** *(dopo)* after; *(di là da)* behind; **~ di me** behind me; **di ~** back *(dav s)*; **qui/lì ~** behind here/there; **~ pagamento** on payment.
difatti *cong* in fact.
difendere *vt* to defend.
◆ **difendersi** *vr* to defend o.s.
difensore *sm* defender.
difesa *sf* defence.
difeso, -a *pp* → **difendere**.
difetto *sm* defect; *(morale)* fault; **~ di fabbricazione** manufacturing defect.
difettoso, -a *agg (meccanismo)* faulty; *(vista, abito)* defective.
diffamare *vt (a parole)* to slander; *(per iscritto)* to libel.
differente *agg* different.
differenza *sf* difference; **non fa ~** it doesn't make any difference; **a ~ di** unlike.
difficile *agg* difficult; **è ~ che esca** *(poco probabile)* it's unlikely that he'll go out.
difficoltà *sf inv* difficulty.
diffidare : **diffidare di** *v + prep* to mistrust.
diffidente *agg* mistrustful.
diffondere *vt* to spread.
◆ **diffondersi** *vr* to spread.
diffusione *sf* diffusion.
diffuso, -a ◇ *pp* → **diffondere** ◇ *agg* widespread.
diga, -ghe *sf* dam.
digeribile *agg* digestible.
digerire *vt* to digest.
digestione *sf* digestion.
digestivo, -a ◇ *agg* digestive ◇ *sm liqueur drunk to aid digestion, after meals.*
digitale *agg* digital.
digitare *vt* (INFORM) to key in.
digiunare *vi* to fast.
digiuno, -a ◇ *sm* fasting ◇ *agg*: **essere ~** not to have eaten; **a ~** on an empty stomach.
dignità *sf* dignity.
dilagante *agg (fenomeno)* rampant.
dilagare *vi* to be rampant.
dilaniare *vt* to tear to pieces.
dilapidare *vt* to squander.
dilatare *vt (pupille)* to dilate; *(gas, metallo, corpo)* to expand.
◆ **dilatarsi** *vr (pupille)* to dilate; *(gas, metallo, corpo)* to expand.
dilazionare *vt* to defer.
dilemma, -i *sm* dilemma.
dilettante *smf* amateur.
diligente *agg* diligent.
diluire *vt (allungare)* to dilute; *(sciogliere)* to dissolve.
dilungarsi *vr*: **~ su** *(argomento)* to dwell upon; **~ in spiegazioni** to give a longwinded explanation.
diluvio *sm* downpour.
dimagrire *vi* to lose weight.
dimenare *vt (fianchi)* to swing; *(corpo)* to shake; *(coda)* to wag.
◆ **dimenarsi** *vr* to fling o.s. about.

dimensione *sf* dimension.
dimenticanza *sf* oversight.
dimenticare *vt* to forget; *(lasciare)* to leave; **dimenticarsi qc** to leave sthg.
♦ **dimenticarsi di** *vr + prep* to forget about; **dimenticarsi di fare qc** to forget to do sthg.
dimesso, -a ◇ *pp* → **dimettere** ◇ *agg* humble.
dimestichezza *sf* familiarity.
dimettere *vt* to discharge.
♦ **dimettersi** *vr* to resign.
dimezzare *vt* to halve.
diminuire ◇ *vt* to reduce ◇ *vi* to decrease; *(prezzi)* to drop.
diminuzione *sf* fall; *(di prezzi)* drop.
dimissioni *sfpl* resignation *(sg)*; **dare le ~** to hand in one's resignation.
dimostrare *vt (manifestare)* to show; *(provare)* to prove; **dimostra meno di vent'anni** he doesn't look twenty.
♦ **dimostrarsi** *vr* to prove to be.
dimostrazione *sf (d'affetto, simpatia)* show; *(di teoria)* proof; *(protesta, per prodotto)* demonstration.
dinamico, -a, -ci, -che *agg* dynamic.
dinamite *sf* dynamite.
dinamo *sf inv* dynamo.
dinanzi *prep*: **~ a** *(davanti a)* in front of; *(alla presenza di)* before.
dinosauro *sm* dinosaur.
dintorni *smpl* outskirts; **nei ~ di** in the vicinity of.
dio *(pl* **dei**) *sm* god.
♦ **Dio** *sm* God; **mio Dio!** my God!
diocesi *sf inv* diocese.
dipartimento *sm* department.
dipendente ◇ *agg* subordinate ◇ *smf* employee.
dipendenza *sf (subordinazione)* dependence; *(assuefazione)* addiction; **essere alle dipendenze di qn** to be employed by sb.
dipendere *vi*: **~ da** to depend on; *(derivare)* to be due to; **dipende** it depends.
dipeso, -a *pp* → **dipendere**.
dipingere *vt* to paint.
dipinto, -a ◇ *pp* → **dipingere** ◇ *sm* painting.
diploma, -i *sm* diploma.
diplomarsi *vr* to obtain a diploma.
diplomatico, -a, -ci, -che ◇ *agg* diplomatic ◇ *sm (funzionario)* diplomat; *(pasta) pastry made of layers of liqueur-soaked sponge, puff pastry and confectioner's custard, topped with icing sugar.*
diplomazia *sf* diplomacy.
diradare *vt* to cut down on.
♦ **diradarsi** *vr (nebbia, nubi)* to clear; *(vegetazione)* to thin out.
dire ◇ *vt* 1. *(pronunciare)* to say; **~ di sì/no** to say yes/no.
2. *(esprimere, raccontare)* to say; **~ qc a qn** to tell sb sthg; **~ a qn che/perché** to tell sb that/why; **~ la verità** to tell the truth; **dimmi tutto** tell me everything; **dica pure** *(in un negozio)* can I help you?
3. *(ordinare)*: **~ a qn di fare qc** to tell sb to do sthg.
4. *(sostenere)* to say; **dice che non è vero** he says it isn't true.
5. *(tradurre)*: **come si dice 'scusi' in inglese?** what's the English for 'scusi'?
6. *(pensare)* to think; **che ne dite di ...?** how about ...?; **e ~ che ...!** to think that ...!
7. *(in espressioni)*: **diciamo che ...** let's say that ...; **a ~ il vero ...** to tell the truth ...; **vuol ~ che ...** it means (that) ...; **non c'è che ~** there's no doubt about it; **il nome non mi dice niente** the name doesn't mean much to me; **dico davvero** O **sul serio!** I'm serious!; **a dir poco** at least; **a dir tanto** at most; **volevo ben ~!** I thought so!

◇ *v impers*: **si dice che** ... they say (that) ...; **si direbbe che** ... it seems (that) ...

direttamente *avv (per via diretta)* straight; *(senza intermediari)* directly.

direttissimo *sm* express train.

diretto, -a ◇ *pp* → **dirigere** ◇ *agg* direct ◇ *sm (treno)* through train; **essere ~ a** *(aereo, passeggero)* to be bound for; *(indirizzato)* to be intended for.

direttore, -trice *sm, f* manager (*f* manageress); *(di scuola elementare)* head (teacher) *(Br)*, principal *(Am)*; **~ d'orchestra** conductor.

direzione *sf* direction; *(di azienda)* management.

dirigente *smf* executive.

dirigere *vt (attenzione, sguardo)* to direct; *(scuola, azienda)* to run; *(orchestra)* to conduct.

◆ **dirigersi** *vr* to head.

dirimpetto *avv* opposite.

diritto, -a ◇ *agg & avv* straight ◇ *sm* right; *(leggi)* law; *(di abito, stoffa)* right side; *(nel tennis)* forehand; *(nella maglia)* plain stitch; **andare ~** *(in linea retta)* to go straight on; **vai ~ a casa** go straight home; **sempre (a) ~** straight on; **avere ~ a qc** to be entitled to sthg.

dirittura *sf*: **~ d'arrivo** home straight.

diroccato, -a *agg* in ruins.

dirottare *vt* to hijack; *(traffico)* to divert.

dirotto, -a *agg*: **piovere a ~** to pour.

dirupo *sm* precipice.

disabitato, -a *agg* uninhabited.

disaccordo *sm* disagreement.

disadattato, -a *agg* maladjusted.

disagio *sm (scomodità)* discomfort; *(imbarazzo)* uneasiness; **essere a ~** to be ill at ease.

disapprovare *vt* to disapprove.

disarmare *vt* to disarm.

disarmo *sm* disarmament.

disastro *sm* disaster; *(danno)* damage.

disastroso, -a *agg* disastrous.

disattento, -a *agg* inattentive.

disavanzo *sm* deficit.

disavventura *sf* mishap.

discapito *sm*: **a ~ di** to the detriment of.

discarica, -che *sf* dump.

discendente *smf* descendant.

discepolo, -a *sm, f* disciple.

discesa *sf* slope; *(movimento)* descent; **in ~** downhill; **~ libera** downhill race; '**~ a mare**' 'this way down to the sea'.

dischetto *sm* diskette.

disciplina *sf (ubbidienza)* discipline; *(materia)* subject.

disciplinato, -a *agg* disciplined.

disc-jockey [disk 'dʒɔkei] *smf inv* disc jockey.

disco, -schi *sm (musicale)* record; *(per computer)* disk; **~ orario** parking disc; **~ volante** flying saucer.

discolpare *vt* to clear.

discorde *agg* conflicting.

discorrere : **discorrere di** *v + prep* to talk about.

discorso ◇ *pp* → **discorrere** ◇ *sm* speech; *(conversazione)* conversation, talk.

discoteca, -che *sf* disco.

discretamente *avv (abbastanza bene)* fairly well; *(con tatto)* discreetly.

discreto, -a *agg (persona)* discreet; *(abbastanza buono)* reasonably good.

discrezione *sf (tatto)* discretion; *(moderazione)* moderation.

discriminare *vt* to discriminate.

discussione *sf (dibattito)* discussion; *(litigio)* argument.

discusso, -a *pp* → **discutere**.

discutere ◇ *vt (parlare di)* to discuss; *(contestare)* to question ◇ *vi* to argue; ~ **di** o **su** *(dibattere)* to discuss.
disdetto, -a *pp* → **disdire**.
disdire *vt* to cancel.
disegnare ◇ *vt* to draw; *(progettare)* to design ◇ *vi* to draw.
disegno *sm* drawing; *(motivo)* design; *(progetto)* project; ~ **di legge** bill.
diseredare *vt* to disinherit.
disertare *vt & vi* to desert.
disertore *sm* deserter.
disfare *vt* to undo; *(valigia)* to unpack; *(maglia)* to unravel; *(sciogliere)* to melt.
disfatto, -a *pp* → **disfare**.
disgelo *sm* thaw.
disgrazia *sf (incidente)* accident.
disgraziato, -a ◇ *agg (persona)* wretched; *(viaggio)* ill-fated; *(anno)* unlucky ◇ *sm, f (sfortunato)* poor wretch; *(canaglia)* rogue.
disguido *sm* error.
disgustare *vt* to disgust.
disgusto *sm* disgust.
disgustoso, -a *agg* disgusting.
disidratare *vt* to dehydrate.
disinfestare *vt* to disinfest.
disinfettante *agg & sm* disinfectant.
disinfettare *vt* to disinfect.
disinibito, -a *agg* uninhibited.
disintegrare *vt* to cause to disintegrate.
disinteressarsi : **disinteressarsi di** *vr + prep* to take no interest in.
disinteresse *sm (indifferenza)* indifference; *(generosità)* unselfishness.
disintossicare *vt* to detoxify; ~ **l'organismo** to clear out one's system.
◆ **disintossicarsi** *vr (da droga)* to be treated for drug addiction.
disintossicazione *sf (da droga)* treatment for drug addiction.
disinvolto, -a *agg* free and easy.
disinvoltura *sf* ease.
dislivello *sm (di quota)* difference in height; *(fig: differenza)* gap.
disoccupato, -a ◇ *agg* unemployed ◇ *sm, f* unemployed person.
disoccupazione *sf* unemployment.
disonesto, -a *agg* dishonest.
disopra ◇ *avv* above; *(al piano superiore)* upstairs ◇ *agg inv* above.
disordinato, -a *agg* untidy; *(vita)* disorderly.
disordine *sm (materiale)* untidiness; *(mentale)* confusion; **in** ~ in a mess.
disorganizzazione *sf* disorganization.
disorientato, -a *agg* disorientated.
disossare *vt* to bone.
disotto ◇ *avv* below; *(al piano inferiore)* downstairs ◇ *agg inv* below.
dispari *agg inv* odd.
disparte *avv*: **tenersi** o **starsene in** ~ to keep to o.s.
dispendioso, -a *agg* expensive.
dispensa *sf (stanza)* larder; *(mobile)* sideboard; *(fascicolo)* instalment.
disperarsi *vr* to despair.
disperatamente *avv* desperately.
disperato, -a *agg* desperate.
disperazione *sf* desperation.
disperdere *vt* to disperse.
disperso, -a ◇ *pp* → **disperdere** ◇ *sm, f* missing person.
dispetto *sm (atto)* spiteful trick; *(stizza)* vexation; **fare un ~ a qn** to play a spiteful trick on sb; **fare qc per** ~ to do sthg out of spite; **a ~ di** despite.
dispiacere ◇ *sm (dolore)* grief; *(rammarico)* regret ◇ *v impers*: **le**

dispiace se aspetto qui? do you mind if I wait here?; **mi dispiace che sia andata così** I'm sorry it worked out that way; **mi dispiace di non potermi trattenere** I'm afraid I can't stop.
dispiaciuto, -a ◇ *pp* → **dispiacere** ◇ *agg* sorry.
disponibile *agg* available; *(persona)* willing to help.
disponibilità *sf (di posto, camere)* availability; *(di persona)* willingness to help; *(di denaro)* liquid assets *(pl)*.
disporre *vt* to arrange.
♦ **disporre di** *v + prep (poter usare)* to have at one's disposal; *(avere)* to have.
dispositivo *sm* device.
disposizione *sf (di mobili, oggetti)* arrangement; *(comando)* order; *(attitudine)* disposition; (DIR) provision; **essere a ~ di qn** to be at sb's disposal; **mettere qc a ~ di qn** to make sthg available to sb.
disposto, -a ◇ *pp* → **disporre** ◇ *agg*: **~ a fare qc** prepared to do sthg.
disprezzare *vt* to despise.
disprezzo *sm* contempt.
disputa *sf* argument.
dissanguare *vt (fig: persona)* to bleed white.
disseminare *vt* to spread.
dissenso *sm (disapprovazione)* dissent; *(contrasto)* disagreement.
dissenteria *sf* dysentery.
disservizio *sm* inefficiency.
dissestato, -a *agg* uneven.
dissidente *smf* dissident.
dissidio *sm* disagreement.
dissimulare *vt* to conceal.
dissoluto, -a ◇ *pp* → **dissolvere** ◇ *agg* dissolute.
dissolvere *vt (sciogliere)* to dissolve; *(nebbia, fumo)* to disperse.
dissuadere *vt*: **~ qn dal fare qc** to dissuade sb from doing sthg.
dissuaso, -a *pp* → **dissuadere**.
distaccare *vt (oggetti)* to remove; *(dipendente)* to transfer; (SPORT) to outdistance.
♦ **distaccarsi da** *vr + prep (fig: allontanarsi)* to withdraw from.
distacco, -chi *sm* separation; *(indifferenza)* detachment.
distante *agg & avv* far away; **~ da** far from.
distanza *sf* distance; *(temporale)*: **a ~ di due mesi** after two months; **tenere le distanze** to keep one's distance.
distanziare *vt (separare)* to space out; (SPORT) to outdistance.
distare *vi*: **quanto dista da qui?** how far is it from here?
distendere *vt (gamba, mano)* to stretch out; *(telo, coperta)* to spread; *(rilassare)* to relax.
♦ **distendersi** *vr (sdraiarsi)* to lie down; *(rilassarsi)* to relax.
distesa *sf* expanse.
disteso, -a *pp* → **distendere**.
distillare *vt* to distil.
distilleria *sf* distillery.
distinguere *vt* to distinguish.
distintivo, -a ◇ *agg* distinctive ◇ *sm* badge.
distinto, -a ◇ *pp* → **distinguere** ◇ *agg (diverso)* different; *(immagine)* distinct; *(persona)* distinguished; **Distinti saluti** *(in lettera)* Yours faithfully.
distinzione *sf* distinction.
distogliere *vt*: **~ qc da qn** to take sthg away from sb; **~ qn da qc** to deter sb from sthg.
distolto, -a *pp* → **distogliere**.
distorsione *sf* (MED) sprain; *(di suono, immagine)* distortion.
distrarre *vt* to distract; *(divertire)* to amuse.
♦ **distrarsi** *vr* to be distracted; *(divertirsi)* to amuse o.s.
distratto, -a ◇ *pp* → **distrarre** ◇ *agg (sbadato)* absent-minded; *(di-*

sattento) inattentive.

distrazione *sf* distraction; *(svago)* amusement.

distretto *sm* district.

distribuire *vt (assegnare compiti)* to allocate; *(posta, giornali)* to distribute.

distributore *sm*: ~ **automatico** vending machine; ~ **(di benzina)** petrol pump *(Br)*, gasoline pump *(Am)*.

distribuzione *sf* distribution; *(ripartizione)* allocation.

distruggere *vt* to destroy.

distrutto, -a ◇ *pp* → **distruggere** ◇ *agg* shattered.

distruzione *sf* destruction.

disturbare *vt* to disturb; **'non ~ il conducente'** 'do not distract the driver'.

◆ **disturbarsi** *vr* to bother.

disturbo *sm (fastidio)* bother; *(malessere)* disorder; *(di comunicazione)* interference.

disubbidiente *agg* disobedient.

disubbidire *vi*: ~ **(a qn)** to disobey (sb).

disumano, -a *agg* inhuman.

disuso *sm*: **in ~** obsolete.

ditale *sm* thimble.

dito (*pl f* **dita**) *sm* finger; *(misura)* drop; ~ **(del piede)** toe.

ditta *sf* company, firm.

dittatura *sf* dictatorship.

dittongo, -ghi *sm* diphthong.

diurno, -a *agg* daytime *(dav s)*.

diva → **divo**.

divampare *vi* to flare up.

divano *sm* sofa; ~ **letto** sofa-bed.

divaricare *vt* to open wide.

divenire *vi* to become.

diventare *vi* to become; ~ **rosso** *(persona)* to go red.

diversificare *vt* to diversify.

diversità *sf inv* diversity; *(l'esser diverso)* difference.

diversivo *sm* diversion.

diverso, -a *agg* different; ~ **da** different from.

◆ **diversi, -e** ◇ *agg pl* various, several ◇ *pron pl* several; *(varie persone)* several (people).

divertente *agg* amusing.

divertimento *sm* amusement.

divertire *vt* to amuse.

◆ **divertirsi** *vr* to enjoy o.s.

dividere *vt* to divide; *(spartire)* to share out; *(separare)* to separate; *(condividere)* to share.

◆ **dividersi** *vr (ripartirsi)* to split up; *(coppia)* to separate.

divieto *sm* prohibition; **'~ di sosta'** 'no waiting'; **'~ di transito'** 'no thoroughfare'.

divinità *sf inv* divinity.

divino, -a *agg* divine.

divisa *sf* uniform.

divisione *sf* division.

diviso, -a *pp* → **dividere**.

divisorio, -a *agg* dividing.

divo, -a *sm, f* star.

divorare *vt* to devour.

divorziare *vi* to divorce.

divorziato, -a ◇ *agg* divorced ◇ *sm, f* divorced person.

divorzio *sm* divorce.

divulgare *vt (notizia)* to divulge; *(scienza, dottrina)* to popularize.

◆ **divulgarsi** *vr* to spread.

dizionario *sm* dictionary.

D.J. [diːˈdʒeɪ] *smf (abbr di disc-jockey)* DJ.

D.N.A. *sm* DNA.

DOC *(abbr di Denominazione di Origine Controllata) label guaranteeing the quality of an Italian wine.*

doccia, -ce *sf* shower; **fare la ~** to take O to have a shower.

docente ◇ *agg* teaching ◇ *smf* teacher; *(di università)* lecturer.

docile *agg (animale)* docile.

documentare *vt* to document.

◆ **documentarsi** *vr* to gather information.

documentario *sm* documentary.
documento *sm* document.
◆ **documenti** *smpl* documents.
dodicesimo, -a *num* twelfth, → **sesto**.
dodici *num* twelve, → **sei**.
dogana *sf* customs *(pl)*; **passare la ~** to go through customs.
doganale *agg* customs *(dav s)*.
doganiere *sm* customs officer.
dolce ◇ *agg* sweet; *(persona, carattere)* gentle; *(suono, musica, voce)* soft ◇ *sm (torta)* cake; *(portata)* dessert.
dolcezza *sf* sweetness.
dolcificante *sm* sweetener.
dolciumi *smpl* confectionery *(sg)*.
dolere *vi* to hurt.
◆ **dolersi di** *vr + prep (essere spiacente di)* to regret; *(lamentarsi di)* to complain of.
dollaro *sm* dollar.
dolo *sm* (DIR) malice.
Dolomiti *sfpl*: **le ~** the Dolomites.
dolore *sm (fisico)* pain; *(morale)* sorrow.
doloroso, -a *agg (intervento)* painful; *(situazione)* distressing.
domanda *sf (per sapere)* question; *(per ottenere)* request; (COMM) demand; **fare una ~ a qn** to ask sb a question; **fare ~** to apply.
domandare *vt (per sapere)* to ask; *(per ottenere)* to ask for; **~ qc a qn** to ask sb sthg.
◆ **domandarsi** *vr* to wonder.
domani ◇ *avv* tomorrow ◇ *sm (giorno seguente)* tomorrow; **a ~!** see you tomorrow!; **~ l'altro** the day after tomorrow; **il ~** the future; **~ mattina** tomorrow morning; **~ sera** tomorrow evening.
domare *vt (animale)* to tame; *(rivolta)* to put down; *(incendio)* to control.
domattina *avv* tomorrow morning.
domenica, -che *sf* Sunday, → **sabato**.
domestico, -a, -ci, -che *agg & sm, f* domestic.
domicilio *sm* domicile; **a ~** home *(dav s)*.
dominante *agg* dominant.
dominare *vt* to dominate; *(paese, popolo)* to rule; *(situazione, impulso)* to control.
◆ **dominarsi** *vr* to control o.s.
dominio *sm (potere)* power; *(controllo)* control; *(territorio)* dominion; **essere di ~ pubblico** to be common knowledge.
domino *sm* dominoes *(pl)*.
donare ◇ *vt* to give ◇ *vi*: **questo colore ti dona** this colour suits you; **~ il sangue** to give blood.
donatore, -trice *sm, f* giver; *(di sangue, organi)* donor.
dondolare ◇ *vt* to rock ◇ *vi* to sway.
◆ **dondolarsi** *vr* to sway.
dondolo *sm* swing hammock; **cavallo/sedia a ~** rocking horse/chair.
donna *sf* woman; *(nelle carte)* queen; **~ di servizio** maid.
dono *sm* gift.
doping ['dɒpiŋ] *sm* drug use *(in sport)*.
dopo ◇ *avv* afterwards; *(più tardi)* later; *(nello spazio)* after ◇ *prep (di tempo)* after; *(di luogo)* past, after ◇ *agg inv* after ◇ *cong*: **~ aver fatto qc** after doing sthg; **il giorno ~** the following day; **un giorno ~** a day later; **a ~!** see you later!; **~ di me** after me.
dopobarba *sm inv* aftershave.
dopodiché *avv* after which.
dopodomani *avv* the day after tomorrow.
dopoguerra *sm* post-war period.

dopolavoro *sm workers' recreational club.*
dopopranzo *avv* in the early afternoon.
doposcì *sm inv* après-ski.
doposcuola *sm inv supervised after-school activities.*
dopotutto *avv* after all.
doppiaggio *sm* dubbing.
doppiare *vt (film)* to dub; (SPORT) to lap; (NAUT) to round.
doppiato, -a *agg* dubbed.
doppio, -a *agg & avv* double ◇ *sm* (SPORT) ◇ doubles; **ne ha il ~ di me** *(quantità)* he has twice as much as me; *(numero)* he has twice as many as me.
doppione *sm* duplicate.
doppiopetto *sm* double-breasted jacket.
dorato, -a *agg (di colore)* golden; *(ricoperto d'oro)* gilt.
dormiglione, -a *sm, f* sleepyhead.
dormire *vi* to sleep.
dormitorio *sm* dormitory.
dorso *sm* back; *(di libro)* spine.
dosaggio *sm* dosage.
dosare *vt* to measure out; (MED) to dose.
dose *sf* amount; (MED) dose.
dosso *sm* bump; **togliersi** o **levarsi qc di ~** to take sthg off.
dotare *vt*: **~ qc di qc** to equip sthg with sthg.
dotato, -a *agg* gifted.
dote *sf (qualità)* gift; *(di sposa)* dowry.
Dott. *(abbr di dottore)* Dr.
dottorato *sm* doctorate.
dottore, -essa *sm, f (medico)* doctor; *(laureato)* graduate.
dottrina *sf* doctrine.
Dott.ssa *(abbr di dottoressa)* Dr.
dove *avv* where; **da ~ vieni?** where do you come from?; **di ~ sei?** where are you from?; **dov'è?** where is it?; **~ vai?** where are you going?; **siediti ~ vuoi** sit wherever you like.
dovere ◇ *vt* 1. *(essere debitore di)*: **~ qc a qn** to owe sb sthg; **gli devo dei soldi/un favore** I owe him some money/a favour; **quanto le devo?** *(in negozio)* how much does it come to?
2. *(aver l'obbligo di)*: **~ fare qc** to have to do sthg; **comportarsi come si deve** to behave o.s. properly; **ora devo andare** I have to o must go now.
3. *(aver bisogno di)*: **~ fare qc** to have to do sthg; **devo dormire almeno otto ore** I need at least eight hours' sleep; **devi sapere che ...** you should know that ...
4. *(esprime un rimprovero)*: **avreste dovuto pensarci prima** you should have thought of it earlier; **avrei dovuto saperlo** I should have known.
5. *(per suggerire)*: **dovrebbe prendersi delle vacanze** he should o ought to take a holiday.
6. *(esprime probabilità)*: **devono essere già le sette** it must be seven o'clock already; **il tempo dovrebbe rimettersi** the weather should improve.
7. *(esprime intenzione)*: **dovevamo partire ieri, ma ...** we were due to leave yesterday, but ...
◇ *sm* duty; **avere dei doveri verso qn** to have a duty to sb.
dovunque *avv (in qualunque luogo)* wherever; *(dappertutto)* everywhere.
dovuto, -a *agg*: **~ a** due to.
dozzina *sf* dozen; **una ~ di rose** a dozen roses.
drago, -ghi *sm* dragon.
dramma, -i *sm* drama.
drammatico, -a, -ci, -che *agg* dramatic.
drastico, -a, -ci, -che *agg* drastic.
drenare *vt* to drain.

dritto, -a *agg & avv* = **diritto**.
drizzare *vt (raddrizzare)* to straighten; ~ **le orecchie** to prick up one's ears.
◆ **drizzarsi** *vr*: **drizzarsi (in piedi)** to stand up.
droga, -ghe *sf* drug.
drogare *vt* to drug.
◆ **drogarsi** *vr* to take drugs.
drogato, -a *sm, f* drug addict.
drogheria *sf* grocer's.
droghiere *sm* grocer.
dromedario *sm* dromedary.
dubbio, -a ◇ *agg (incerto)* doubtful; *(equivoco)* questionable ◇ *sm* doubt; **ho il ~ che menta** I suspect that he's lying; **essere in ~** to be in doubt; **mettere in ~ qc** to question sthg; **senza ~** without a doubt.
dubbioso, -a *agg* uncertain.
dubitare : **dubitare di** *v + prep* to doubt; *(mettere in discussione)* to question; **dubito che venga** I doubt whether he'll come.
duca, -chi *sm* duke.
duchessa *sf* duchess.
due *num* two, → **sei**.
duecento *num* two hundred, → **sei**.
◆ **Duecento** *sm*: **il Duecento** the thirteenth century.
duemila *num* two thousand.
◆ **il Duemila** *sm* the year two thousand, → **sei**.
duepezzi *sm inv (bikini)* bikini; *(abito)* two-piece suit.
duna *sf* dune.
dunque ◇ *cong (perciò)* so; *(allora)* well ◇ *sm*: **venire al ~** to get to the point.
duomo *sm* cathedral.
duplex *sm inv* party line.
duplicato *sm* duplicate.
duplice *agg* double; **in ~ copia** in duplicate.
durante *prep* during.
durare ◇ *vi* to last ◇ *vt*: **~ fatica (a fare qc)** to tire o.s. out (doing sthg).
durata *sf (periodo)* duration.
durezza *sf (di materiale)* hardness; *(insensibilità)* severity.
duro, -a ◇ *agg* hard; *(carne)* tough; *(ostinato)* stubborn; *(severo)* harsh ◇ *sm, f* tough person; **tieni ~!** don't give in!
durone *sm* callus.

E

e *(spesso* **ed** *+ vocale) cong* and; **~ io?** what about me?; **~ vacci!** well then, go!

E *(abbr di est)* E.

è → essere.

ẹbano *sm* ebony.

ebbẹne *cong (allora)* well.

ebbrẹzza *sf (ubriachezza)*: **in stato di ~** drunk.

ẹbete *agg* idiotic.

ebollizịone *sf* boiling.

ebrạico, -a, -ci, -che *agg & sm* Hebrew.

ebrẹo, -a ◇ *agg* Jewish ◇ *sm, f* Jew.

Ẹbridi *sfpl*: **le (isole) ~** the Hebrides.

ecc. *(abbr di eccetera)* etc.

eccedẹnza *sf* excess.

eccẹdere *vt* to exceed.

◆ **eccedere in** *v + prep*: **~ nel bere/mangiare** to drink/eat too much.

eccellẹnte *agg* excellent.

eccellẹnza *sf* excellence; *(titolo)* Excellency.

eccẹllere *vi*: **~ (in qc)** to excel (at sthg).

eccẹlso *pp* **→ eccellere**.

eccẹntrico, -a, -ci, -che *agg* eccentric.

eccessịvo, -a *agg* excessive.

eccẹsso *sm* excess; **~ di velocità** speeding; **all'~** excessively; **bagaglio in ~** excess baggage.

eccẹtera *avv* etcetera.

eccẹtto ◇ *prep* except ◇ *cong*: **~ che** unless.

eccettuạre *vt* to except.

eccezionạle *agg* exceptional.

eccezịone *sf* exception; **a ~ di** with the exception of; **d'~** exceptional; **senza ~** without exception.

eccịdio *sm* massacre.

eccitạnte *agg (stimolante)* stimulating; *(provocante)* exciting.

eccitạre *vt (curiosità)* to arouse.

◆ **eccitarsi** *vr* to get excited; *(sessualmente)* to become aroused.

eccitazịone *sf* excitement.

ecclesiạstico, -a, -ci, -che ◇ *agg* ecclesiastical ◇ *sm* ecclesiastic.

ẹcco *avv* here is; **~ a lei** here you are; **~ fatto!** there, that's that!; **eccolo!** there he is!; **eccone uno!** there's one!

eccọme *avv* you bet!

eclịssi *sf inv* eclipse.

ẹco *(pl m* **echi***) sf* echo.

ecologịa *sf* ecology.

ecolọgico, -a, -ci, -che *agg* ecological.

economịa *sf* economy; *(scienza)* economics *(sg)*; **fare ~** to economize.

econọmico, -a, -ci, -che *agg (dell'economia)* economic; *(poco costoso)* economical.

ecosistema, -i *sm* ecosystem.
ecoturismo *sm* ecotourism.
ECU *sm inv* ECU.
eczema *sm* eczema.
ed → **e**.
edera *sf* ivy.
edicola *sf* newsstand.
edificare *vt* to build.
edificio *sm* building.
edile *agg* building *(dav s)*.
Edimburgo *sf* Edinburgh.
editore, -trice ◇ *agg* publishing *(dav s)* ◇ *sm* publisher.
editoria *sf* publishing (industry).
edizione *sf* edition; ~ **speciale** special edition.
educare *vt (formare)* to educate; *(bambino)* to bring up.
educato, -a *agg* polite.
educazione *sf (maniere)* (good) manners *(pl)*; *(formazione)* training; ~ **fisica** physical education.
effervescente *agg* effervescent.
effettivamente *avv* in fact.
effettivo, -a *agg* actual, real.
effetto *sm* effect; **in effetti** in fact, actually.
effettuare *vt* to carry out.
efficace *agg* effective.
efficacia *sf* effectiveness.
efficiente *agg* efficient.
efficienza *sf* efficiency.
effimero, -a *agg (gioia, successo)* short-lived.
egemonia *sf (supremazia)* hegemony.
Egitto *sm*: **l'**~ Egypt.
egli *pron* he; ~ **stesso** he himself.
egocentrico, -a, -ci, -che *agg* egocentric.
egoismo *sm* selfishness.
egoista, -i, -e *agg* selfish.
egregio, -a, -gi, -gie *agg (nelle lettere)*: **Egregio Signore** Dear Sir.
eguagliare = **uguagliare**.
ehi *esclam* hey!
E.I. *abbr* = **Esercito Italiano**.
elaborare *vt (progetto, piano)* to work out; *(con computer)* to process.
elaborato, -a *agg* elaborate.
elaboratore *sm*: ~ **(elettronico)** computer.
elaborazione *sf*: ~ **dei dati** data processing.
elasticità *sf* elasticity; *(di mente)* flexibility.
elasticizzato, -a *agg* stretch *(dav s)*.
elastico, -a, -ci, -che ◇ *agg* elastic; *(mente)* flexible ◇ *sm (gommino)* rubber band; *(da cucito)* elastic.
Elba *sf*: **l'(isola d')**~ Elba.
elefante *sm* elephant.
elegante *agg* elegant.
eleganza *sf* elegance.
eleggere *vt* to elect.
elementare *agg* elementary.
◆ **elementari** *sfpl*: **le (scuole) elementari** primary school *(sg) (Br)*, grade school *(sg) (Am)*.
elemento *sm (fattore)* element; *(di cucina)* unit; *(persona)* individual.
elemosina *sf* alms *(pl)*; **chiedere l'**~ to beg.
elencare *vt* to list.
elenco, -chi *sm* list; ~ **telefonico** telephone directory.
eletto, -a *pp* → **eleggere**.
elettorale *agg* electoral.
elettore, -trice *sm, f* voter.
elettrauto *sm inv (officina) workshop for electrical repairs on cars*; *(persona)* car electrician.
elettricista, -i *sm* electrician.
elettricità *sf* electricity.
elettrico, -a, -ci, -che *agg* electric.
elettrodomestico, -ci *sm* electrical household appliance.
elettronico, -a, -ci, -che *agg* electronic.
elezione *sf* election.

elica, -che *sf* propeller.
elicottero *sm* helicopter.
eliminare *vt* to eliminate.
eliminatoria *sf* qualifying round.
ella *pron* she.
elmetto *sm* helmet.
elogio *sm* praise.
eloquente *agg* eloquent.
eludere *vt* to evade.
elusivo, -a *agg* elusive.
elvetico, -a, -ci, -che *agg* Swiss.
emaciato, -a *agg* emaciated.
emanare *vt (luce)* to send out; *(calore)* to give off; *(legge)* to issue.
emancipato, -a *agg* emancipated.
emarginato, -a *sm, f* social outcast.
ematoma, -i *sm* haematoma.
embrione *sm* embryo.
emergenza *sf* emergency.
emergere *vi* to emerge.
emerso, -a *pp* → **emergere**.
emicrania *sf* migraine.
emigrante *smf* emigrant.
emigrare *vi (persona)* to emigrate; *(animale)* to migrate.
Emilia Romagna *sf*: **l'~** Emilia Romagna *(region in eastern central Italy)*.
emisfero *sm* hemisphere.
emittente *sf* broadcasting station.
emorragia *sf* hemorrhage.
emozionante *agg* thrilling.
emozione *sf* emotion.
emulsione *sf* emulsion.
enciclopedia *sf* encyclopedia.
ENEL *abbr Italian national electricity company*.
energia *sf* energy; **~ elettrica** electrical energy.
energico, -a, -ci, -che *agg* energetic.
enfasi *sf inv* emphasis.
enigma, -i *sm* enigma.
ennesimo, -a *agg* umpteenth.
enorme *agg* enormous.
enoteca, -che *sf (negozio)* vintage wine store; *(bar)* wine bar.
ente *sm* body, organization.
entrambi, -e ◇ *pron pl* both (of them) ◇ *agg pl*: **entrambe le città** both towns.
entrare *vi* to enter, to go in; **~ in qc** *(trovar posto)* to fit into sthg; *(essere ammesso)* to join sthg; **entra!** come in!; **questo non c'entra niente** that has nothing to do with it; **~ in una stanza** to enter a room; **~ in guerra** to go to war; **far ~ qn** to let sb in.
entrata *sf* entrance; '**~ libera**' *(in museo)* 'admission free'; *(in negozio)* 'browsers welcome'.
◆ **entrate** *sfpl (incasso)* takings; *(guadagno)* income *(sg)*.
entro *prep (periodo)* in, within; *(scadenza)* by.
entusiasmare *vt* to enthral.
◆ **entusiasmarsi** *vr*: **entusiasmarsi (per)** to get excited (about).
entusiasmo *sm* enthusiasm.
entusiasta, -i, -e *agg* enthusiastic.
enunciare *vt* to enunciate.
Eolie *sfpl*: **le (isole) ~** the Aeolian Islands.
epatite *sf* hepatitis.
epidemia *sf* epidemic.
epidermide *sf* epidermis.
Epifania *sf*: **l'~** the Epiphany.
epilessia *sf* epilepsy.
episodio *sm* episode.
epoca, -che *sf (era, età)* age; *(tempo)* time; **d'~** *(mobile, costume)* period *(dav s)*.
eppure *cong* and yet, nevertheless.
equatore *sm* equator.
equazione *sf* equation.
equestre *agg* equestrian.
equilibrare *vt* to balance.
equilibrato, -a *agg (propor-*

zionato) balanced; *(persona)* well-balanced.

equilibrio *sm (stabilità)* balance; *(posizione, stato)* equilibrium; **perdere l'~** to lose one's balance.

equino, -a *agg* equine, horse *(dav s)*.

equipaggiamento *sm (di nave, aereo)* fitting out; *(sportivo)* equipment.

equipaggio *sm* crew.

equitazione *sf* horse riding.

equivalente *agg & sm* equivalent.

equivalere : equivalere a *v + prep* to be equivalent to.

equivalso, -a *pp* → **equivalere**.

equivoco, -a, -ci, -che ◇ *agg (ambiguo)* equivocal; *(poco onesto)* dubious ◇ *sm* misunderstanding.

era *sf* age.

erba *sf (prato)* grass; *(pianta)* herb; **erbe aromatiche** herbs.

erbazzone *sm spinach and Parmesan cheese tart topped with bacon and parsley (a speciality of Emilia Romagna)*.

erboristeria *sf* herbalist's.

erede *smf* heir (*f* heiress).

eredità *sf inv* inheritance; *(biologica)* heredity; **lasciare qc in ~ (a qn)** to bequeath sthg (to sb).

ereditare *vt* to inherit.

ereditario, -a *agg* hereditary.

eresia *sf* heresy.

eretico, -a, -ci, -che *sm, f* heretic.

eretto, -a ◇ *pp* → **erigere** ◇ *agg* erect.

ergastolo *sm* life imprisonment.

erigere *vt* to erect.

ernia *sf* hernia.

ero → **essere**.

eroe, eroina *sm, f* hero (*f* heroine).

erogare *vt* to supply.

eroico, -a, -ci, -che *agg* heroic.

eroina *sf (droga)* heroin, → **eroe**.

erosione *sf* erosion.

erotico, -a, -ci, -che *agg* erotic.

errare *vi (vagare)* to wander; *(sbagliare)* to be mistaken.

errore *sm (di ortografia, calcolo)* mistake; *(colpa)* error; **per ~** by mistake.

erta *sf*: **stare all'~** to be on the alert.

eruzione *sf (di vulcano)* eruption; (MED) rash.

esagerare *vt & vi* to exaggerate.

esagerato, -a *agg* excessive.

esalazione *sf* exhalation.

esaltare *vt (lodare)* to extol; *(entusiasmare)* to excite.

esame *sm* examination; **fare** O **dare un ~** to take an exam; **~ del sangue** blood test.

esaminare *vt (analizzare)* to examine; *(candidato)* to interview.

esattamente *avv & esclam* exactly.

esattezza *sf* accuracy.

esatto, -a ◇ *agg (giusto)* correct; *(preciso)* exact ◇ *esclam* exactly!

esattore *sm* collector.

esauriente *agg* exhaustive.

esaurimento *sm* exhaustion; **~ (nervoso)** nervous breakdown.

esaurire *vt* to exhaust.

◆ **esaurirsi** *vr (merce)* to run out; *(persona)* to wear o.s. out.

esaurito, -a *agg (provviste, pozzo)* exhausted; *(merce)* sold out; *(persona)* worn out; **'tutto ~'** 'sold out'.

esausto, -a *agg* worn out.

esca (*pl* **esche**) *sf* bait.

escandescenza *sf*: **dare in escandescenze** to lose one's temper.

eschimese *smf* Eskimo.

esclamare *vi* to exclaim.

esclamazione *sf* exclamation.

escludere *vt* to exclude.

esclusiva *sf (di notizia)* scoop; (DIR) exclusive rights *(pl)*.

esclusivo, -a *agg* exclusive.
escluso, -a *pp* → **escludere**.
esco → **uscire**.
escogitare *vt* to come up with.
escursione *sf* excursion; ~ **termica** temperature range.
esecutivo, -a *agg & sm* executive.
esecuzione *sf* execution; *(di concerto)* performance.
eseguire *vt* to carry out; *(in musica)* to perform.
esempio *sm* example; **ad** o **per** ~ for example; **fare un** ~ to give an example.
esentare *vt*: ~ **qn/qc da qc** to exempt sb/sthg from sthg.
esente *agg*: ~ **da** *(esonerato da)* exempt from; *(libero da)* free from.
esequie *sfpl* funeral rites.
esercitare *vt* to exercise; *(professione)* to practise.
♦ **esercitarsi** *vr* to practise.
esercito *sm* army.
esercizio *sm* exercise; *(di professione)* practice; *(azienda, negozio)* business; **essere fuori** ~ to be out of practice.
esibire *vt* to show.
♦ **esibirsi** *vr* to perform.
esigente *agg* demanding.
esigenza *sf (bisogno)* requirement; *(pretesa)* demand.
esigere *vt (pretendere)* to demand; *(richiedere)* to require; *(riscuotere)* to collect.
esile *agg (sottile)* thin; *(persona)* slim.
esilio *sm* exile.
esistente *agg* existing.
esistenza *sf* existence.
esistere *vi* to exist.
esitare *vi* to hesitate.
esitazione *sf* hesitation.
esito *sm* outcome.
esorbitante *agg* exorbitant.
esordio *sm* debut.
esortare *vt*: ~ **qn a fare qc** to urge sb to do sthg.
esotico, -a, -ci, -che *agg* exotic.
espandere *vt* to expand.
♦ **espandersi** *vr (ingrandirsi)* to expand; *(odori, liquidi)* to spread.
espansione *sf (allargamento)* expansion; *(di attività)* growth.
espansivo, -a *agg* expansive.
espanso, -a *pp* → **espandere**.
espediente *sm* expedient.
espellere *vt (da scuola)* to expel; (MED) to excrete.
esperienza *sf* experience.
esperimento *sm (prova)* test; *(scientifico)* experiment.
esperto, -a ◇ *agg (con esperienza)* experienced; *(bravo)* skilful ◇ *sm* expert.
espiare *vt* to expiate.
esplicito, -a *agg* explicit.
esplodere ◇ *vi* to explode ◇ *vt* to fire.
esplorare *vt* to explore.
esploratore, -trice *sm, f* explorer.
esplosione *sf* explosion; *(di gioia, ira)* outburst.
esplosivo, -a *agg & sm* explosive.
esploso, -a *pp* → **esplodere**.
esporre *vt (merce)* to display; *(opera d'arte)* to show; *(pellicola)* to expose; *(idea, fatto)* to explain.
esportare *vt* to export.
esportazione *sf (spedizione)* exportation; *(merce)* exports *(pl)*.
esposizione *sf (di merce)* display; *(mostra)* exhibition; *(di pellicola)* exposure; *(resoconto)* account.
esposto, -a ◇ *pp* → **esporre** ◇ *sm* petition ◇ *agg*: ~ **a sud** facing south.
espressione *sf* expression.
espressivo, -a *agg* expressive.
espresso, -a ◇ *pp* → **esprimere** ◇ *sm (treno)* express; *(caffè)* espres-

so; *(lettera)* express letter.

esprimere *vt (pensiero, sentimento)* to express.

◆ **esprimersi** *vr (spiegarsi)* to express o.s.; *(parlare)* to speak.

espulso, -a *pp* → **espellere**.

essenziale *agg* essential.

essere ◇ *vi* 1. *(per descrivere)* to be; **sono italiano** I'm Italian; **sei solo?** are you alone?; **siamo di Torino** we're from Turin; **Franco è (un) medico** Franco is a doctor.

2. *(trovarsi)* to be; **dove siete?** where are you?; **il museo è in centro** the museum is in the town centre; **sono a casa** I'm at home; **sono stato in Scozia tre volte** I've been to Scotland three times.

3. *(esistere)*: **c'è** there is; **c'è un'altra possibilità** there's another possibility; **ci sono** there are; **ci sono vari alberghi** there are various hotels.

4. *(con data, ora)* to be; **oggi è martedì** today is Tuesday; **è l'una** it's one o'clock; **sono le due** it's two o'clock.

5. *(con prezzo, peso)*: **quant'è? – (sono) 10 000 lire** how much is it? – (that's) 10,000 lira; **sono due chili e mezzo** that's two and a half kilos.

6. *(indica appartenenza)*: ~ **di qn** to belong to sb; **questa macchina è di Paolo** this car is Paolo's.

7. *(indica bisogno, obbligo)*: **è da fare** it's still to be done; **la camera è da prenotare** the room is to be booked.

◇ *v impers* to be; **è tardi** it's late; **è vero che** ... it's true that ...; **oggi è freddo** it's cold today; **è meglio telefonare** it's better to phone.

◇ *v aus* 1. *(in tempi passati)* to have, to be; **sono tornato ieri** I came back yesterday; **erano già usciti** they'd already gone out; **sono nata a Roma** I was born in Rome; **ti sei lavato?** did you wash yourself?

2. *(in passivi)* to be; **questo oggetto è fatto a mano** this object is handmade; **sono stato pagato ieri** I was paid yesterday.

◇ *sm (creatura)* being; ~ **umano** human being; **gli esseri viventi** the living.

essi, -e → **esso**.

esso, -a *pron* it.

◆ **essi, -e** *pron pl (soggetto)* they; *(con preposizione)* them.

est *sm* east; **a ~ di Milano** east of Milan.

estate *sf* summer.

estendere *vt* to extend.

esteriore *agg (esterno)* external, outward; *(apparente)* superficial.

esterno, -a ◇ *agg* exterior; *(muro)* outer; *(pericolo)* external ◇ *sm* outside; **all'~** on the outside.

estero, -a ◇ *agg* foreign ◇ *sm*: **l'~** foreign countries *(pl)*; **all'~** abroad.

esteso, -a ◇ *pp* → **estendere** ◇ *agg* extensive.

estetista, -i, -e *smf* beautician.

estinguere *vt (fuoco)* to extinguish; *(debito)* to settle.

◆ **estinguersi** *vr (fuoco)* to go out; *(specie)* to become extinct.

estinto, -a *pp* → **estinguere**.

estintore *sm* (fire) extinguisher.

estivo, -a *agg* summer *(dav s)*.

estorcere *vt* to extort.

estraneo, -a ◇ *agg* unconnected ◇ *sm, f* stranger.

estrarre *vt* to extract; *(sorteggiare)* to draw.

estratto, -a ◇ *pp* → **estrarre** ◇ *sm (di sostanza)* essence; *(di libro)* extract; ~ **conto** bank statement.

estrazione *sf* extraction; ~ **a sorte** draw; ~ **sociale** social class.

estremità ◇ *sf inv* end ◇ *sfpl* extremities.

estremo, -a ◇ *agg (grande)* extreme; *(drastico)* drastic; *(ultimo)*

final, last ◇ *sm (punto)* extreme; *(fig: limite)* limit.
◆ **estremi** *smpl* details.
estroverso, -a *agg* extrovert.
estuario *sm* estuary.
esuberante *agg* exuberant.
età *sf inv* age; **abbiamo la stessa ~** we are the same age; **la maggiore ~** the legal age; **di mezza ~** middle-aged; **la terza ~** old age.
etere *sm* ether.
eternità *sf* eternity.
eterno, -a *agg* eternal.
eterogeneo, -a *agg* heterogeneous.
eterosessuale *agg & smf* heterosexual.
etica *sf* ethics.
etichetta *sf (di prodotto)* label; *(cerimoniale)* etiquette.
Etna *sm*: **l'~** Mount Etna.
etrusco, -a, -schi, -sche *agg* Etruscan.
◆ **Etruschi** *smpl*: **gli Etruschi** the Etruscans.
ettaro *sm* hectare.
etto *sm* = 100 grams.
ettogrammo *sm* hectogram.
eucaristia *sf*: **l'~** the Eucharist.
euforia *sf* euphoria.
EUR *sm residential area of Rome built on the site of the Rome Exhibition.*
Europa *sf*: **l'~** Europe.
europeo, -a *agg & sm, f* European.
eurovisione *sf*: **in ~** Eurovision *(dav s)*.
eutanasia *sf* euthanasia.
evacuare *vt* to evacuate.
evacuazione *sf* evacuation.
evadere ◇ *vt (tasse, fisco)* to evade; *(corrispondenza)* to deal with ◇ *vi*: **~ (da qc)** to escape (from sthg).
evaporare *vi* to evaporate.
evasione *sf* escape; **~ fiscale** tax evasion; **d'~** escapist.
evasivo, -a *agg* evasive.
evaso, -a ◇ *pp* → **evadere** ◇ *sm, f* escapee.
evenienza *sf*: **in ogni ~** should the need arise.
evento *sm* event.
eventuale *agg* possible.
eventualità *sf inv* possibility.
eventualmente *avv* if necessary.
evidente *agg (chiaro)* clear; *(ovvio)* obvious.
evidenza *sf* evidence; **mettere in ~** to highlight.
evitare *vt* to avoid; **~ di fare qc** to avoid doing sthg; **~ qc a qn** to spare sb sthg.
evocare *vt (ricordare)* to recall; *(spiriti)* to evoke.
evoluto, -a *agg (tecnica, paese)* advanced; *(persona)* broadminded.
evoluzione *sf (biologica)* evolution; *(progresso)* progress.
evviva *esclam* hurrah!
ex *prep*: **l'~ presidente** the former president; **la sua ~ moglie** his ex-wife.
extra *agg inv & sm inv* extra.
extracomunitario, -a ◇ *agg* from outside the EU ◇ *sm, f immigrant from a non-EU country.*
extraconiugale *agg* extramarital.
extraterrestre *smf* alien.

fa[1] → **fare**.

fa[2] *avv:* **un anno ~** a year ago; **tempo ~** some time ago.

fabbisogno *sm* needs *(pl)*.

fabbrica, -che *sf* factory.

fabbricare *vt (costruire)* to build; *(produrre)* to make.

faccenda *sf (questione)* affair, matter.

◆ **faccende** *sfpl*: **faccende (domestiche)** housework *(sg)*.

facchino *sm* porter.

faccia, -ce *sf* face; **di ~ a** opposite; **~ a ~** face to face; **che ~ tosta!** what a nerve!

facciata *sf (di edificio)* facade; *(di pagina)* side.

faccio → **fare**.

facile *agg* easy; **è ~ che il treno sia in ritardo** the train is likely to be late.

facilità *sf (caratteristica)* easiness; *(attitudine)* ease.

facilitare *vt* to make easier.

facoltà *sf inv* faculty; *(potere)* power.

facoltativo, -a *agg* optional.

facsimile *sm inv* facsimile.

fagiano *sm* pheasant.

fagiolino *sm* French bean *(Br)*, string bean *(Am)*.

fagiolo *sm* bean; **fagioli all'uccelletto** *white beans cooked with tomatoes and pepper (a Tuscan speciality)*.

fagotto *sm* bundle; *(strumento)* bassoon; **far ~** to pack one's bags and leave.

fai da te *sm inv* do-it-yourself.

falange *sf* finger bone.

falciare *vt* to mow.

falda *sf (di cappello)* brim; *(d'acqua)* water table; *(di monte)* slope.

falegname *sm* carpenter.

falla *sf* leak.

fallimento *sm* failure; (DIR) bankruptcy.

fallire ◇ *vi* (DIR) to go bankrupt; *(non riuscire)*: **~ (in qc)** to fail (in sthg) ◇ *vt* to miss.

fallo *sm* foul.

falò *sm inv* bonfire.

falsificare *vt* to forge.

falso, -a ◇ *agg* false; *(gioiello)* fake; *(banconota, quadro)* forged ◇ *sm* forgery.

fama *sf* fame; *(reputazione)* reputation.

fame *sf* hunger; **aver ~** to be hungry.

famiglia *sf* family.

familiare *agg (della famiglia)* family *(dav s)*; *(noto)* familiar; *(atmosfera)* friendly; *(informale)* informal.

◆ **familiari** *smpl* relations.

famoso, -a *agg* famous.

fanale *sm* light.

fanatico, -a, -ci, -che *agg* fanatical.
fango, -ghi *sm* mud.
fanno → **fare**.
fannullone, -a *sm, f* loafer.
fantascienza *sf* science fiction.
fantasia ◇ *sf (immaginazione)* imagination ◇ *agg inv* patterned.
fantasma, -i *sm* ghost.
fantastico, -a, -ci, -che *agg* fantastic; *(immaginario)* fantasy *(dav s)*.
fantino *sm* jockey.
fantoccio *sm* puppet.
farabutto *sm* crook.
faraglione *sm* stack.
faraona *sf* guinea fowl.
farcito, -a *agg (pollo)* stuffed; *(torta)* filled.
fard *sm inv* blusher.
fare ◇ *vt* 1. *(fabbricare, preparare)* to make; ~ **progetti** to make plans; ~ **da mangiare** to cook.
2. *(attuare)* to make; ~ **un viaggio** to go on a trip; ~ **un sogno** to dream.
3. *(essere occupato in)* to do; **cosa fai stasera?** what are you doing tonight?; **fa il meccanico** he's a mechanic; ~ **l'università** to go to university; **faccio tennis** I play tennis.
4. *(percorrere)* to do; **che percorso facciamo per rientrare?** which route shall we take to go back?
5. *(suscitare)* to make; **mi fa pena** I feel sorry for him; **farsi male** to hurt o.s.; ~ **paura** to be frightening; ~ **chiasso** to be noisy.
6. *(atteggiarsi a)* to play, to act; ~ **lo scemo** to behave like an idiot.
7. *(indica il risultato)*: **2 più 2 fa 4** 2 and 2 makes 4; **quanto fa?** what's the total?
8. *(credere)*: **ti facevo più furbo** I thought you were smarter than that.
9. *(acquisire)*: **farsi degli amici** to make friends; **farsi la macchina nuova** *(fam)* to get a new car.
10. *(con infinito)* to make; **far credere qc a qn** to make sb believe sthg; **far vedere qc a qn** to show sb sthg; **far costruire qc** to have sthg built.
11. *(in espressioni)*: **non ~ caso a** not to pay attention to; **non fa niente** *(non importa)* it doesn't matter; **farcela** to manage; **non ce la faccio più** I can't go on; **far bene/male (a qn)** to be good/bad (for sb).
◇ *vi* 1. *(agire)* to do; **come si fa a uscire?** how do you get out?; **fai come ti pare** do as you like; **non fa che ripetere le stesse cose** all he does is repeat the same things; **darsi da ~** to get busy.
2. *(fam: dire)* to say.
◇ *v impers* to be; **fa bello/brutto** it's lovely/awful weather; **fa caldo/freddo** it's hot/cold.
◆ **farsi** *vr (diventare)*: **farsi grande** to grow up; **farsi furbo** *(fam)* to get smart; **farsi vivo** to get in touch; **farsi avanti/indietro** *(spostarsi)* to move forward/back.
farfalla *sf* butterfly; **cravatta a ~** bow tie.
farina *sf* flour; ~ **gialla** maize flour.
farinata *sf type of bread similar to a very thin 'focaccia' but made from chickpea flour (a speciality of Liguria)*.
faringite *sf* pharyngitis.
farmacia *sf (negozio)* chemist's *(Br)*, drugstore *(Am)*; *(scienza)* pharmacy; **'farmacie di turno'** 'duty chemists'.
farmacista, -i, -e *smf* pharmacist.
farmaco, -ci *sm* medicine.
faro *sm (per navi)* lighthouse; *(di veicoli)* headlight; *(per aerei)* beacon.
farsa *sf* farce.
farsumagru *sm inv beef roll*

stuffed with mince, pecorino cheese, sausage and boiled eggs, cooked in Marsala and tomato puree (a Sicilian speciality).

fascia, -sce *sf (striscia)* strip, band; *(medica)* bandage; *(di territorio)* strip; *(di popolazione)* band; **~ elastica** elastic bandage; **~ oraria** time band.

fasciare *vt* to bandage.

fasciatura *sf* bandage.

fascicolo *sm (di rivista)* issue; *(di documenti)* file.

fascino *sm* charm.

fascio *sm (d'erba, di fibri)* bunch; *(di legna)* bundle; *(di luce)* beam.

fascismo *sm* Fascism.

fascista, -i, -e *agg & smf* Fascist.

fase *sf* phase; *(di motore)* stroke.

fast food [fast'fud] *sm inv* fast-food restaurant.

fastidio *sm* bother, trouble; **dare ~ a qn** to annoy sb; **le dà ~ se fumo?** do you mind if I smoke?

fastidioso, -a *agg* inconvenient.

fastoso, -a *agg* sumptuous.

fasullo, -a *agg (falso)* fake.

fata *sf* fairy.

fatale *agg (mortale)* fatal; *(inevitabile)* inevitable; *(sguardo)* irresistible.

fatalità *sf inv (inevitabilità)* inevitability; *(destino)* fate; *(disgrazia)* misfortune.

fatica *sf* hard work; *(stanchezza)* fatigue; **fare ~ a fare qc** to have difficulty doing sthg; **a ~** hardly.

faticoso, -a *agg (stancante)* exhausting; *(difficile)* hard.

fatidico, -a, -ci, -che *agg* fateful.

fato *sm* fate.

fatto, -a ◇ *pp* → **fare** ◇ *sm (cosa concreta)* fact; *(avvenimento)* event ◇ *agg*: **~ a mano** hand-made; **~ in casa** home-made; **il ~ è che ...** the fact is that ...; **cogliere qn sul ~** to catch sb in the act; **in ~ di vini ...** when it comes to wine ...; **sono fatti miei** that's my business.

fattoria *sf* farm.

fattorino *sm (per consegne)* delivery man; *(d'albergo)* messenger.

fattura *sf* invoice; *(magia)* spell.

fauna *sf* fauna.

favola *sf* fairy tale; *(cosa bella)* dream.

favoloso, -a *agg* fabulous.

favore *sm* favour; **per ~** please.

favorevole *agg* favourable; *(voto)* in favour.

favorire *vt (promuovere)* to promote; *(aiutare)* to favour; **vuoi ~?** would you like some?

favorito, -a *agg* favourite.

fazzoletto *sm (da naso)* handkerchief; *(per la testa)* headscarf.

febbraio *sm* February, → **settembre**.

febbre *sf* fever; **avere la ~** to have a temperature.

feci *sfpl* excrement *(sg)*.

fecondazione *sf* fertilization.

fede *sf* faith; *(anello)* wedding ring; **aver ~ in** to have faith in; **essere in buona/cattiva ~** to act in good/bad faith.

fedele ◇ *agg* faithful; *(cliente)* loyal; *(preciso)* accurate ◇ *smf* believer.

fedeltà *sf (lealtà)* faithfulness, loyalty; *(precisione)* accuracy.

federa *sf* pillowcase.

federazione *sf* federation.

fegato *sm* liver; *(fig: coraggio)* guts *(pl)*; **~ alla veneziana** *thinly sliced calves' liver and onions.*

felice *agg* happy.

felicità *sf* happiness.

felicitarsi *vr*: **~ con qn per qc** to congratulate sb on sthg.

felino, -a *agg & sm* feline.

felpa *sf (maglia)* sweatshirt; *(tessuto)* plush.

femmina *sf (animale)* female; *(figlia, ragazza)* girl.

femminile ◇ *agg* female; *(rivista, modi)* women's *(dav s)*; (GRAMM) feminine ◇ *sm* feminine.
femminismo *sm* feminism.
fenomenale *agg* phenomenal.
fenomeno *sm* phenomenon.
feriale *agg* working *(dav s)*.
ferie *sfpl* holidays *(Br)*, vacation *(sg) (Am)*; **andare in ~** to go on holiday *(Br)*, to go on vacation *(Am)*; **essere in ~** to be on holiday *(Br)*, to be on vacation *(Am)*.
ferire *vt (colpire)* to injure; *(addolorare)* to hurt.
◆ **ferirsi** *vr* to injure o.s.
ferita *sf* wound.
ferito, -a ◇ *agg* injured ◇ *sm, f* injured person.
fermaglio *sm* clip.
fermare ◇ *vt* to stop; *(bottone)* to fasten; *(sospetto)* to detain ◇ *vi* to stop.
◆ **fermarsi** *vr* to stop; *(sostare)* to stay; **fermarsi a fare qc** to stop to do sthg.
fermata *sf* stop; **~ dell'autobus** bus stop; '**~ prenotata**' 'bus stopping'; '**~ a richiesta**' 'request stop'.
fermento *sm* ferment.
fermo, -a *agg (persona)* still; *(veicolo)* stationary; *(mano, voce)* steady; *(orologio)* stopped; *(saldo)* firm; **stare ~** to keep still.
fermo posta *avv & sm inv* poste restante *(Br)*, general delivery *(Am)*.
feroce *agg (animale)* ferocious; *(dolore)* terrible.
ferragosto *sm (giorno) Italian public holiday which falls on 15 August*; *(periodo)* August holidays *(pl)*.
ferramenta *sf* ironmonger's *(Br)*, hardware store *(Am)*.
ferro *sm* iron; **toccare ~** to touch wood; **~ battuto** wrought iron; **~ da calza** knitting needle; **~ da stiro** iron; **carne ai ferri** grilled meat.
ferrovia *sf* railway *(Br)*, railroad *(Am)*; **Ferrovie dello Stato** *Italian railway system*, = British Rail *(Br)*, = Amtrak *(Am)*.
ferroviario, -a *agg* railway *(Br) (dav s)*, railroad *(Am) (dav s)*.
fertile *agg* fertile.
fervido, -a *agg* fervent, ardent.
fesso, -a *agg (fam)* stupid.
fessura *sf* crack; *(per gettone, moneta)* slot.
festa *sf (religiosa)* feast; *(giorno festivo)* holiday; *(ricevimento)* party; *(ricorrenza)*: **la ~ della mamma** Mother's Day; **far ~** to have a holiday; **far ~ a qn** to give sb a warm welcome; **buone feste!** *(a Natale)* Merry Christmas!
festeggiare *vt (ricorrenza)* to celebrate; *(persona)* to throw a party for.
festival *sm inv* festival.
festivo, -a *agg* festive; **giorno ~** holiday; **orario ~** *timetable for Sundays and public holidays*.
festone *sm* festoon.
festoso, -a *agg* merry.
feto *sm* foetus.
fetta *sf* slice.
fettuccine *sfpl ribbons of egg pasta*.
fettunta *sf toast flavoured with garlic and olive oil (a Tuscan speciality)*.
FF.SS. *abbr* = BR *(Br)*, = Amtrak *(Am)*.
fiaba *sf* fairy tale.
fiaccola *sf* torch.
fiamma *sf* flame; **dare alle fiamme** to set on fire.
fiammifero *sm* match.
fiancheggiare *vt* to border.
fianco, -chi *sm (di persona)* hip; *(di edificio, collina)* side; **di ~ a** next to.
fiasco, -schi *sm* flask; **fare ~** to flop.
fiato *sm (respiro)* breath; *(resisten-*

za) stamina; **avere il ~ grosso** to be out of breath.
fibbia *sf* buckle.
fibra *sf* fibre.
ficcanaso (*pl m* **ficcanasi**, *pl f inv*) *smf* busybody.
ficcare *vt* to put.
◆ **ficcarsi** *vr*: **dove ti eri ficcato?** where did you get to?
fico, -chi *sm* fig; ~ **d'India** prickly pear.
fidanzamento *sm* engagement.
fidanzarsi *vr* to get engaged.
fidanzato, -a ◇ *agg* engaged ◇ *sm, f* fiancé (*f* fiancée).
fidarsi *vr*: ~ **di** to trust.
fidato, -a *agg* trustworthy.
fiducia *sf* confidence.
fiducioso, -a *agg* confident.
fieno *sm* hay.
fiera *sf* fair.
fiero, -a *agg* proud.
fifa *sf (fam)* fright.
figlio, -a *sm, f* son (*f* daughter), child; ~ **unico** only child.
figura *sf* figure; *(illustrazione)* illustration, picture; **fare bella/brutta** ~ to create a good/bad impression.
figurare ◇ *vi* to appear ◇ *vt*: **figurarsi qc** to imagine sthg.
◆ **figurarsi** *vr*: **figurati!** of course not!
figurina *sf* picture card.
fila *sf (coda)* queue *(Br)*, line *(Am)*; *(di macchine)* line; *(di posti)* row; *(serie)* series; **fare la** ~ to queue *(Br)*, to stand in line *(Am)*; **di** ~ in succession.
filare ◇ *vt (lana)* to spin ◇ *vi (ragno, baco)* to spin; *(formaggio)* to go stringy; *(discorso)* to be coherent; *(fam: andarsene)* to split; **fila!** off you go!; ~ **diritto** to toe the line.
filastrocca, -che *sf* nursery rhyme.
filatelia *sf* philately, stamp-collecting.
filatelli *smpl thin strips of egg pasta served with a sauce made from pork, tomatoes, chillis and pecorino cheese (a speciality of Calabria).*
filatieddi = **filatelli**.
filetto *sm* fillet; ~ **al pepe verde** fillet steak with green peppercorns.
film *sm inv* film *(Br)*, movie *(Am)*.
filo *sm* thread; *(cavo)* wire; *(di lama, rasoio)* edge; *(di pane)* stick; ~ **d'erba** blade of grass; ~ **spinato** barbed wire; **fil di ferro** wire; **per ~ e per segno** word for word.
filobus *sm inv* trolleybus.
filosofia *sf* philosophy.
filtrare *vt & vi* to filter.
filtro *sm (apparecchio)* filter; *(di sigarette)* filter tip.
fin → **fino**.
finale ◇ *agg & sf* final ◇ *sm* end, ending.
finalmente *avv* at (long) last.
finanza *sf* finance; *(di frontiera)* = Customs and Excise.
◆ **finanze** *sfpl* finances.
finanziere *sm (banchiere)* financier; *(di frontiera)* customs officer; *(per tasse)* = Inland Revenue officer *(Br)*, = Internal Revenue officer *(Am)*.
finché *cong (per tutto il tempo)* as long as; *(fino a quando)* until.
fine ◇ *agg (sottile)* thin; *(polvere)* fine; *(elegante)* refined; *(vista, udito)* keen, sharp ◇ *sf (conclusione)* end ◇ *sm (scopo)* aim; **lieto** ~ happy ending; ~ **settimana** weekend; **alla** ~ in the end.
finestra *sf* window.
finestrino *sm* window.
fingere *vt (simulare)* to feign; ~ **di fare qc** to pretend to do sthg.
◆ **fingersi** *vr*: **fingersi malato** to pretend to be ill.
finimondo *sm* pandemonium.
finire ◇ *vt* to finish ◇ *vi* to finish;

(avere esito) to end; *(cacciarsi)* to get to; ~ **col fare qc** to end up doing sthg; ~ **di fare qc** to finish doing sthg.

finlandese ◇ *agg & sm* Finnish ◇ *smf* Finn.

Finlandia *sf*: **la** ~ Finland.

fino, -a ◇ *agg (sottile)* thin; *(oro, argento)* pure; *(udito, vista)* keen, sharp ◇ *avv* even ◇ *prep*: ~ **a** *(di tempo)* until; *(di luogo)* as far as; ~ **da** *(luogo)* as far as; **fin da domani** from tomorrow; **fin da ieri** since yesterday; ~ **qui/lì** as far as here/there.

finocchio *sm* fennel.

finora *avv* so far.

finta *sf (finzione)* pretence; *(nel pugilato)* feint; *(nel calcio)* dummy; **fare** ~ **di fare qc** to pretend to do sthg.

finto, -a ◇ *pp* → **fingere** ◇ *agg* false.

fiocco, -chi *sm (di nastro)* bow; *(di neve)* flake; **coi fiocchi** *(ottimo)* excellent, first-rate.

fiocina *sf* harpoon.

fioco, -a, -chi, -che *agg (voce)* faint; *(luce)* dim.

fioraio, -a *sm, f* florist.

fiore *sm* flower; **a fior d'acqua** on the surface of the water; **a fiori** *(stoffa)* with a floral pattern; **fiori di zucca ripieni** *fried courgette flowers stuffed with breadcrumbs, parsley and anchovies.*

◆ **fiori** *smpl (nelle carte)* clubs.

fiorentino, -a *agg & sm, f* Florentine.

fiorire *vi (albero)* to blossom; *(fiore)* to bloom.

Firenze *sf* Florence.

firma *sf (sottoscrizione)* signature; *(marca)* designer brand.

firmare *vt* to sign.

fiscale *agg* tax *(dav s)*.

fischiare ◇ *vi* to whistle ◇ *vt* to whistle; *(disapprovare)* to boo.

fischio *sm* whistle.

fisco *sm* = Inland Revenue *(Br)*, = Internal Revenue *(Am)*.

fisica *sf (materia)* physics *(sg)*, → **fisico**.

fisico, -a, -ci, -che ◇ *agg* physical ◇ *sm (corpo)* physique ◇ *sm, f* physicist.

fisionomia *sf* face.

fissare *vt (guardare)* to stare at; *(rendere fisso)* to fix; *(appuntamento)* to arrange; *(camera, volo)* to book.

◆ **fissarsi** *vr*: **fissarsi di fare qc** to set one's heart on doing sthg.

fisso, -a ◇ *agg (fissato)* fixed; *(impiego)* permanent; *(reddito)* regular ◇ *avv*: **guardare** ~ to stare.

fitta *sf* sharp pain.

fitto, -a ◇ *agg* thick ◇ *sm (affitto)* rent.

fiume *sm* river.

fiutare *vt (sog: cane)* to smell; *(fig: accorgersi di)* to get wind of.

flacone *sm* bottle.

flagrante *agg*: **cogliere qc in** ~ to catch sb in the act.

flash [flɛʃ] *sm inv* flash.

flessibile *agg* flexible.

flessione *sf (sulle gambe)* knee-bend; *(a terra)* sit-up; *(calo)* dip.

flesso, -a *pp* → **flettere**.

flettere *vt* to bend.

flipper *sm inv* pinball machine.

F.lli *abbr* Bros.

flora *sf* flora.

flotta *sf* fleet.

fluido, -a *agg & sm* fluid.

fluire *vi* to flow.

flusso *sm* flow; *(in fisica)* flux.

fluttuare *vi (ondeggiare)* to rise and fall; (FIN) to fluctuate.

F.M. *(abbr di Modulazione di frequenza)* FM.

focaccia, -ce *sf (dolce)* bun; *(pane) type of flat salted bread made with olive oil*; ~ **alla valdostana** *'focaccia' filled with fontina cheese.*

foce *sf* mouth.
focolare *sm* hearth.
fodera *sf (interna)* lining; *(esterna)* cover.
foglia *sf* leaf.
foglio *sm (di carta, di metallo)* sheet; *(documento)* document; *(banconota)* note; ~ **rosa** provisional driving licence; ~ **di via** expulsion order.
fogna *sf* sewer.
fognature *sfpl* sewers.
föhn [fɔn] = **fon.**
folclore *sm* folklore.
folcloristico, -a, -ci, -che *agg* folk *(dav s)*.
folgorare *vt (sog: fulmine)* to strike; *(sog: alta tensione)* to electrocute.
folla *sf* crowd.
folle *agg (pazzo)* mad; (TECNOL) idle; **in** ~ *(di auto)* in neutral.
follia *sf (pazzia)* madness; *(atto)* act of madness.
folto, -a *agg* thick.
fon *sm inv* hairdryer.
fondale *sm* bottom (of the sea).
fondamentale *agg* fundamental, basic.
fondamento *sm* foundation.
◆ **fondamenta** *sfpl* foundations.
fondare *vt* to found; *(basare)*: ~ **qc su qc** to base sthg on sthg.
◆ **fondarsi su** *vr + prep* to be based on.
fondazione *sf* foundation.
fondere ◇ *vt* to melt; *(aziende)* to merge ◇ *vi* to melt.
◆ **fondersi** *vr* to melt.
fondo, -a ◇ *agg (profondo)* deep ◇ *sm* bottom; *(di strada)* surface; *(di liquido)* dregs *(pl)*; *(sfondo)* background; (SPORT) long distance race; *(proprietà)* property; **andare a** ~ *(affondare)* to sink; **conoscere a** ~ to know very well; **in** ~ *(fig: tutto sommato)* after all; **andare fino in** ~ **a qc** *(approfondire)* to get to the bottom of sthg; **in** ~ **(a qc)** at the bottom (of sthg); *(stanza)* at the back (of sthg); *(libro, mese)* at the end (of sthg).
◆ **fondi** *smpl (denaro)* funds.
fonduta *sf* fondue.
fonetica *sf* phonetics *(sg)*.
fontana *sf* fountain.
fonte ◇ *sf (sorgente)* spring; *(origine)* source ◇ *sm*: ~ **battesimale** font.
fontina *sf a hard cheese made from cow's milk (a speciality of the Valle d'Aosta)*.
foraggio *sm* fodder.
forare *vt (praticare un foro in)* to pierce; *(gomma)* to puncture; *(biglietto)* to punch; *(pallone)* to burst.
forbici *sfpl* scissors.
forca, -che *sf (attrezzo)* pitchfork; *(patibolo)* gallows *(pl)*.
forchetta *sf* fork.
forcina *sf* hairpin.
foresta *sf* forest.
forestiero, -a ◇ *agg* foreign ◇ *sm, f* foreigner.
forfora *sf* dandruff.
forma *sf* shape; *(tipo)* form; *(stampo)* mould; **essere in** ~ to be fit; **a** ~ **di** in the shape of.
◆ **forme** *sfpl (del corpo)* figure *(sg)*.
formaggino *sm* processed cheese.
formaggio *sm* cheese.
formale *agg* formal.
formalità *sf inv* formality.
formare *vt* to form; *(comporre)* to make up; *(persona)* to train.
◆ **formarsi** *vr* to form.
formato *sm* size.
formazione *sf* formation; *(istruzione)* education; ~ **professionale** professional training.
formica®[1] *sf* Formica®.
formica[2]**, -che** *sf* ant.
formicolio *sm (intorpidimento)* pins and needles *(pl)*.

formidabile *agg* fantastic, amazing.
formula *sf (chimica)* formula; *(frase rituale)* set phrase; ~ **uno** formula one.
fornaio, -a *sm, f* baker.
fornello *sm (di elettrodomestico)* ring; ~ **elettrico** hotplate.
fornire *vt*: ~ **qc a qn** to supply sb with sthg; ~ **qn/qc di qc** to supply sb/sthg with sthg.
fornitore, -trice *sm, f* supplier.
forno *sm* oven; ~ **a legna** wood-burning stove; ~ **a microonde** microwave (oven).
foro *sm (buco)* hole; *(romano)* forum.
forse *avv* perhaps, maybe; *(circa)* about.
forte ◇ *agg* strong; *(suono)* loud; *(luce, colore)* bright ◇ *avv (vigorosamente)* hard; *(ad alta voce)* loudly; *(velocemente)* fast ◇ *sm (fortezza)* fort; *(specialità)* strong point.
fortezza *sf* fortress.
fortuito, -a *agg* chance *(dav s)*, fortuitous.
fortuna *sf* luck; *(patrimonio)* fortune; **buona** ~! good luck!; **portare** ~ to bring luck; **per** ~ luckily, fortunately.
fortunatamente *avv* luckily, fortunately.
fortunato, -a *agg (persona)* lucky; *(evento)* successful.
forviare = **fuorviare**.
forza *sf* strength; *(in fisica, violenza)* force; **a** ~ **di** by dint of; **per** ~ *(naturalmente)* of course; *(contro la volontà)* against one's will; **le forze armate** the armed forces.
forzare *vt (porta, finestra)* to force open; *(obbligare)*: ~ **qn a fare qc** to force sb to do sthg.
foschia *sf* haze.
fossa *sf (buca)* pit, hole; *(tomba)* grave.
fossato *sm* ditch; *(di castello)* moat.
fossile *sm* fossil.
fosso *sm* ditch.
foto *sf inv* photo.
fotocopia *sf* photocopy.
fotocopiare *vt* to photocopy.
fotogenico, -a, -ci, -che *agg* photogenic.
fotografare *vt* to photograph.
fotografia *sf* (ARTE) photography; *(immagine)* photograph; ~ **a colori** colour photograph; ~ **in bianco e nero** black and white photograph.
fotografo, -a *sm, f* photographer.
fototessera *sf* passport-size photograph.
fra = **tra**.
fracassare *vt* to smash.
fracasso *sm* crash.
fradicio, -a, -ci, -ce *agg* soaked.
fragile *agg* fragile; *(persona)* delicate.
fragola *sf* strawberry.
fragore *sm* loud noise.
fraintendere *vt* to misunderstand.
frammento *sm* fragment.
frana *sf* landslide; *(fig: persona)*: **essere una** ~ to be useless.
francese ◇ *agg & sm* French ◇ *smf (abitante)* Frenchman (*f* Frenchwoman); **i francesi** the French.
Francia *sf*: **la** ~ France.
franco, -a, -chi, -che ◇ *agg (sincero)* frank; (COMM) free ◇ *sm* franc; **farla franca** to get away with it.
francobollo *sm* stamp.
frangia, -ge *sf* fringe.
frantumare *vt* to smash.
◆ **frantumarsi** *vr* to smash.
frantumi *smpl*: **andare in** ~ to smash; *(sogno)* to be shattered.
frappé *sm inv* (milk) shake.

frase *sf* (GRAMM) sentence; *(espressione)* expression.
frastuono *sm* din.
frate *sm (monaco)* friar; *(pasta)* ring doughnut.
fratellastro *sm* stepbrother.
fratello *sm* brother.
frattempo *sm*: **nel ~** in the meantime, meanwhile.
frattura *sf* fracture.
frazione *sf (parte)* fraction; *(di comune)* village.
freccia, -ce *sf* arrow; **~ di direzione** indicator; **mettere la ~** to put the indicator on.
freddo, -a *agg & sm* cold; **aver ~** to be cold; **è** O **fa ~** it's cold.
freddoloso, -a *agg*: **essere ~** to feel the cold.
freezer ['fridzer] *sm inv* freezer.
fregare *vt (strofinare)* to rub; *(fam: imbrogliare)* to trick; **~ qc a qn** *(fam: rubare)* to nick sthg from sb; **fregarsene (di qc)** *(volg)* not to give a damn (about sthg).
frenare ◇ *vi* to brake ◇ *vt (rabbia, entusiasmo)* to curb; *(lacrime)* to hold back; *(avanzata, progresso)* to hold up.
frenata *sf* braking; **fare una ~** to brake.
frenetico, -a, -ci, -che *agg* hectic.
freno *sm (di veicolo)* brake; *(per cavallo)* bit; **~ a mano** handbrake.
frequentare *vt (corso, scuola)* to attend; *(locale)* to go to; *(persona)* to mix with.
frequente *agg* frequent.
fresco, -a, -schi, -sche ◇ *agg* fresh; *(temperatura)* cool; *(notizie)* recent ◇ *sm (temperatura)* cool; **è** O **fa ~** it's cool; **mettere al ~** to put in a cool place; **stare ~** to be way out.
fretta *sf (urgenza)* hurry; *(rapidità)* haste; **avere ~** to be in a hurry; **in ~ e furia** in a hurry.
fricassea *sf stewed meat and vegetables in an egg and lemon sauce.*
friggere ◇ *vt* to fry ◇ *vi* to sizzle.
frigo *sm inv* fridge.
frigobar *sm inv* minibar.
frigorifero *sm* refrigerator.
frittata *sf* omelette.
frittella *sf* fritter; **frittelle di mele** apple fritters.
fritto, -a ◇ *pp* → **friggere** ◇ *agg* fried ◇ *sm*: **~ misto** *mixed deep-fried fish and seafood.*
frittura *sf*: **~ di pesce** *deep-fried fish and seafood.*
frivolo, -a *agg* frivolous.
frizione *sf (di auto)* clutch; *(massaggio)* massage.
frizzante *agg* fizzy; *(vino)* sparkling.
frode *sf* fraud.
frontale *agg* frontal; *(scontro)* head-on.
fronte ◇ *sf* forehead ◇ *sm* front; **di ~** opposite; **di ~ a** *(faccia a faccia)* opposite; *(in una fila)* in front of; *(in confronto a)* compared with.
frontiera *sf* frontier.
frottola *sf (bugia)* lie.
frugare *vi & vt* to search.
frullare *vt* to whisk.
frullato *sm* milk shake.
frullatore *sm* blender, liquidizer.
frullino *sm* whisker.
frusta *sf (per animali)* whip.
frustino *sm* (riding) crop.
frutta *sf* fruit; **~ secca** dried fruit and nuts.
fruttivendolo *sm (negozio)* greengrocer's.
frutto *sm* fruit; *(profitto)* profit; **frutti di mare** seafood *(sg)*.
F.S. = **FF.SS.**
fucile *sm* rifle.
fuga, -ghe *sf* escape; **~ di gas** gas leak.
fuggire *vi (allontanarsi)* to escape; *(rifugiarsi)* to run away.

fulmine *sm* bolt of lightning.
fumare ◇ *vt* to smoke ◇ *vi* to smoke; *(emettere vapore)* to steam; '**vietato ~**' 'no smoking'.
fumatore, -trice *sm, f* smoker; **fumatori o non fumatori?** smoking or non-smoking?
fumetti *smpl (vignette)* cartoon strip *(sg)*; *(giornalino)* comics.
fumo *sm* smoke; *(vapore)* steam.
fune *sf* rope.
funebre *agg* funeral *(dav s)*; *(lugubre)* funereal.
funerale *sm* funeral.
fungo, -ghi *sm* mushroom; (MED) fungus; **~ mangereccio** edible mushroom.
funicolare *sf* funicular railway.
funivia *sf* cable way.
funzionamento *sm* functioning.
funzionare *vi* to work.
◆ **funzionare da** *v + prep* to act as.
funzione *sf* function; *(compito)* duty; *(religiosa)* service; **essere in ~** to be working; **in ~ di** *(secondo)* according to.
fuoco, -chi *sm* fire; *(fornello)* ring; *(in ottica)* focus; **al ~!** fire!; **dar ~ a qc** to set fire to sthg; **fare ~** to fire; **prender ~** to catch fire; **fuochi d'artificio** fireworks.
fuorché *cong* except.
fuori ◇ *avv* out, outside; *(fuori di casa)* out; *(all'aperto)* outdoors, outside ◇ *prep*: **~ (di)** out of, outside; **far ~ qn** *(fam)* to kill sb; **essere ~ di sé** to be beside oneself; **lasciare ~** to leave out; **tirare ~** to get out; **~ luogo** uncalled for; **~ mano** out of the way; **andare ~ strada** to leave the road; '**~ servizio**' 'out of order'.
fuoribordo *sm inv* outboard.
fuorilegge *smf inv* outlaw.
fuoristrada ◇ *sm inv* Jeep® ◇ *agg inv*: **moto ~** trail bike.
fuorviare *vt* to mislead.
furbo, -a *agg* clever, smart; *(spreg)* cunning.
furgone *sm* van.
furia *sf (ira)* fury; *(impeto)* violence; **a ~ di fare qc** by (means of) doing sthg; **andare su tutte le furie** to get into a towering rage.
furioso, -a *agg* furious.
furore *sm* fury; **far ~** to be all the rage.
furto *sm* theft; **~ con scasso** burglary.
fusa *sfpl*: **fare le ~** to purr.
fusione *sf (di cera, metallo)* melting; *(unione)* fusion.
fuso, -a ◇ *pp* → **fondere** ◇ *sm*: **~ orario** time zone.
fustino *sm* tub.
fusto *sm (di pianta)* stem; *(contenitore)* drum; *(fam: ragazzo)* hunk.
futile *agg* futile.
futuro, -a *agg & sm* future.

G

gabbia *sf* cage.
gabbiano *sm* seagull.
gabinetto *sm (bagno)* toilet; *(ministero)* cabinet; *(di dentista)* surgery.
gaffe [gaf] *sf inv* blunder.
gala *sf (sfarzo)* pomp; *(festa)* gala.
galassia *sf* galaxy.
galateo *sm* etiquette.
galera *sf* prison.
galla *sf*: **stare a ~** to float; **venire a ~** *(fig)* to come out.
galleggiante ◇ *agg* floating ◇ *sm (boa)* buoy; *(per la pesca)* float.
galleria *sf (traforo)* tunnel; *(museo)* gallery; *(di teatro)* circle; *(di cinema)* balcony; *(strada coperta)* arcade.
galletta *sf* cracker.
gallina *sf* hen.
gallo *sm* cock.
gamba *sf* leg; **essere in ~** to be smart.
gamberetto *sm* shrimp.
gambero *sm* prawn.
gamberoni *smpl*: **~ alla griglia** grilled crayfish.
gambo *sm* stem.
gancio *sm* hook.
gangheri *smpl*: **essere fuori dai ~** to fly off the handle.
gara *sf (nello sport)* race; *(concorso)* competitive bidding; **fare a ~** to compete.
garage [ga'raʒ] *sm inv* garage.
garantire *vt* to guarantee.
garanzia *sf (di merce)* guarantee; *(di debito)* guarantee, security.
gareggiare *vi* to compete.
gargarismo *sm*: **fare i gargarismi** to gargle.
garza *sf* gauze.
garzone *sm* boy.
gas *sm inv* gas; **dare ~** to step on the gas; **~ lacrimogeno** tear gas.
gasato, -a = **gassato**.
gasolio *sm* diesel (oil).
gassato, -a *agg (bevanda)* fizzy.
gassosa *sf* fizzy drink.
gastronomia *sf* gastronomy; *(negozio)* delicatessen.
gastronomico, -a, -ci, -che *agg* gastronomic.
gattino, -a *sm, f* kitten.
gatto, -a *sm, f* cat; **~ delle nevi** snow cat; **eravamo in quattro gatti** there were only a few of us.
gazzetta *sf* gazette.
G.d.F. *abbr* = **Guardia di Finanza**.
gel *sm inv* gel.
gelare *vi, vt & v impers* to freeze.
gelateria *sf* ice-cream shop *(Br)*, ice-cream parlour *(Am)*.
gelatina *sf* gelatine; **~ di frutta** fruit jelly.
gelato, -a ◇ *agg* frozen ◇ *sm* ice cream.
gelido, -a *agg* freezing, icy.
gelo *sm (freddo)* intense cold;

(ghiaccio) ice.

gelosia *sf* jealousy.

geloso, -a *agg* jealous.

gemello, -a *agg* twin.

◆ **gemelli** *smpl* *(di camicia)* cuff links.

◆ **Gemelli** *smpl* Gemini *(sg)*.

gemere *vi* to moan.

gemma *sf* *(pietra)* gem; *(di pianta)* bud.

generale *agg & sm* general; **in ~** in general.

generalità *sfpl* particulars.

generalmente *avv* generally.

generare *vt* *(produrre)* to generate, to produce.

generatore *sm* generator.

generazione *sf* generation.

genere *sm* *(tipo)* kind, type; *(di arte)* genre; (GRAMM) gender; *(di animali, vegetali)* genus; **il ~ umano** mankind; **in ~** generally.

◆ **generi** *smpl*: **generi alimentari** foodstuffs.

generico, -a, -ci, -che *agg* *(generale)* generic; *(vago)* vague; **medico ~** general practitioner.

genero *sm* son-in-law.

generoso, -a *agg* generous.

gengiva *sf* gum.

geniale *agg* brilliant.

genio *sm* genius; **andare a ~ a qn** to be liked by sb.

genitali *smpl* genitals.

genitore *sm* parent; **i nostri genitori** our parents.

gennaio *sm* January, → **settembre**.

Genova *sf* Genoa.

gente *sf* people *(pl)*.

gentile *agg* kind, nice; **Gentile Signore** Dear Sir; **Gentile Signor G. Paoli** Mr G. Paoli.

gentilezza *sf* kindness; **per ~** please.

gentiluomo (*pl* **gentiluomini**) *sm* gentleman.

genuino, -a *agg* genuine.

geografia *sf* geography.

geologia *sf* geology.

geometria *sf* geometry.

geranio *sm* geranium.

gerarchia *sf* hierarchy.

gergo, -ghi *sm* *(di giovani)* slang; *(specialistico)* jargon.

Germania *sf*: **la ~** Germany.

germe *sm* germ.

gerundio *sm* gerund.

gesso *sm* chalk; *(per frattura)* plaster.

gestione *sf* management.

gestire *vt* to run.

gesto *sm* gesture.

gestore *sm* manager.

Gesù *sm* Jesus.

gettare *vt* *(lanciare)* to throw; *(buttar via)* to throw away; *(grido)* to utter; *(acqua)* to spout; *(scultura)* to cast; **'non ~ alcun oggetto dal finestrino'** 'do not throw objects out of the window'.

◆ **gettarsi** *vr*: **gettarsi da/in** to throw o.s. from/into; **gettarsi in** *(fiume)* to flow into.

getto *sm* *(d'acqua, gas)* jet; *(vapore)* puff; **di ~** *(scrivere)* in one go.

gettone *sm* token; **~ telefonico** telephone token.

ghiacciaio *sm* glacier.

ghiacciato, -a *agg* frozen; *(freddo)* ice-cold.

ghiaccio *sm* ice.

ghiacciolo *sm* *(gelato)* ice lolly *(Br)*, Popsicle® *(Am)*; *(di fontana)* icicle.

ghiaia *sf* gravel.

ghiandola *sf* gland.

ghiotto, -a *agg* *(persona)* greedy; *(cibo)* appetizing.

già ◇ *avv* already; *(precedentemente)* already, before ◇ *esclam* of course!, yes!; **di ~?** already?

giacca, -che *sf* jacket; **~ a vento** windcheater.

giacché *cong* as, since.
giaccone *sm* heavy jacket.
giacere *vi* to lie.
giallo, -a ◇ *agg (colore)* yellow; *(carnagione)* sallow ◇ *sm (colore)* yellow; *(romanzo)* detective story; **film** ~ thriller; ~ **dell'uovo** yolk.
gianduiotto *sm* hazelnut chocolate.
Giappone *sm*: **il** ~ Japan.
giapponese ◇ *agg & sm* Japanese ◇ *smf* Japanese person.
giardinaggio *sm* gardening.
giardiniera *sf (verdure) starter of mixed pickled vegetables,* → **giardiniere**.
giardiniere, -a *sm, f* gardener.
giardino *sm* garden; ~ **botanico** botanical gardens *(pl)*; ~ **d'infanzia** nursery, kindergarten; ~ **pubblico** park; ~ **zoologico** zoo.
gigante ◇ *agg (enorme)* gigantic ◇ *sm* giant.
gigantesco, -a, -schi, -sche *agg* gigantic.
gilè *sm inv* waistcoat.
gin [dʒin] *sm inv* gin.
ginecologo, -a, -gi, -ghe *sm, f* gynaecologist.
ginestra *sf* broom.
Ginevra *sf* Geneva.
ginnastica *sf* gymnastics *(sg)*; **fare** ~ to do exercises.
ginocchio (*pl m* **ginocchi** o *pl f* **ginocchia**) *sm* knee; **stare in** ~ to be on one's knees, to kneel.
giocare ◇ *vi* to play; *(scommettere)* to gamble ◇ *vt* to play; *(scommettere)* to gamble; *(ingannare)* to take in; **sai ~ a tennis?** can you play tennis?; **giocarsi il posto** to lose one's job.
giocatore, -trice *sm, f* player; ~ **d'azzardo** gambler.
giocattolo *sm* toy.
gioco, -chi *sm* game; *(divertimento)* play; **mettere in ~ qc** to risk sthg; ~ **d'azzardo** game of chance; ~ **di parole** pun; **per** ~ as a joke.
giocoliere *sm* juggler.
gioia *sf* joy; *(gioiello)* jewel; **darsi alla pazza** ~ to live it up.
gioielleria *sf* jeweller's shop.
gioiello *sm* jewel, piece of jewellery.
giornalaio, -a *sm, f* newsagent *(Br)*, newsdealer *(Am)*.
giornale *sm (quotidiano)* newspaper; *(rivista)* magazine; ~ **radio** news bulletin.
giornaliero, -a *agg* daily.
giornalista, -i, -e *smf* journalist.
giornata *sf* day; **oggi è una bella** ~ it's lovely today; ~ **lavorativa** working day; **vivere alla** ~ to live for the day.
giorno *sm (ventiquattro ore)* day; *(opposto alla notte)* day, daytime; *(periodo di luce)* daylight; **a giorni alterni** on alternate days; **l'altro** ~ the other day; ~ **feriale** working day; ~ **festivo** holiday; ~ **libero** day off; **al** ~ by the day, per day; **di** ~ by day, during the day.
giostra *sf* merry-go-round.
giovane *agg* young; **da** ~ as a young man/woman; **i giovani** young people.
giovanile *agg* youthful.
giovanotto *sm* young man.
giovare : **giovare a** *v + prep* to be good for.
◆ **giovarsi di** *vr + prep* to make use of.
giovedì *sm inv* Thursday; ~ **grasso** *last Thursday of Carnival, before Lent,* → **sabato**.
gioventù *sf (età)* youth; *(giovani)* young people *(pl)*.
giovinezza *sf* youth.
giradischi *sm inv* record player.
giraffa *sf* giraffe.

giramento *sm*: ~ **di testa** dizziness.

girare ◇ *vt* to turn; *(visitare)* to go round; *(filmare)* to shoot; *(assegno, cambiale)* to endorse ◇ *vi* to turn; *(velocemente)* to spin; *(terra)* to revolve; *(andare in giro)* to go around.

◆ **girarsi** *vr* to turn around.

girarrosto *sm* spit.

girasole *sm* sunflower.

girata *sf (passeggiata)* stroll; *(in macchina)* drive; (FIN) endorsement.

girello *sm (di carne)* topside; *(per bambini)* baby-walker.

girevole *agg* turning, revolving.

giro *sm (viaggio)* tour; *(rotazione)* turn; *(di amici, colleghi)* circle; *(di pista)* lap; **fare un** ~ *(a piedi)* to go for a walk; *(in macchina)* to go for a drive; *(in bicicletta)* to go for a ride; **fare il** ~ **di** *(città, negozi)* to go round; ~ **d'affari** turnover; ~ **di parole** circumlocution; ~ **di prova** test diive; **in** ~ around; **nel** ~ **di un anno** in the space of a year; **prendere in** ~ **qn** to tease sb, to pull sb's leg; **essere su di giri** to be excited.

girotondo *sm* ring-a-ring-o'-roses.

gita *sf* trip; **andare in** ~ **a Roma** to go on a trip to Rome.

giù *avv* down; *(al piano di sotto)* downstairs; **in** ~ down, downwards; ~ **di lì** thereabouts; ~ **per le scale** down the stairs; **essere** ~ *(fig: essere depresso)* to be low.

giubbotto *sm* jacket.

giudicare ◇ *vt (valutare)* to judge; *(reputare)* to consider; (DIR) to find ◇ *vi* to judge.

giudice *sm* judge; *(nello sport)* umpire.

giudizio *sm* judgment; *(opinione)* opinion; *(a scuola)* report; **a mio** ~ in my opinion.

giugno *sm* June, → **settembre**.

giungere *vi*: ~ **a/in** to reach.

giungla *sf* jungle.

giunta *sf* committee; **per** ~ in addition.

giunto, -a *pp* → **giungere**.

giuramento *sm* oath.

giurare ◇ *vt* to swear ◇ *vi* to take an oath.

giuria *sf (di gare, concorsi)* judges *(pl)*; *(di tribunale)* jury.

giustificare *vt* to justify.

giustificazione *sf (scusa)* excuse; (SCOL) note (of absence).

giustizia *sf* justice.

giusto, -a ◇ *agg (equo)* fair, just; *(vero, adeguato)* right; *(esatto)* correct ◇ *avv (esattamente)* correctly; *(proprio)* just; **cercavo** ~ **te!** you're just the person I was looking for!

gli ◇ *art mpl (dav s + consonante, gn, ps, z, vocale e h)* the, → **il** ◇ *pron (a lui)* (to) him; *(a esso)* (to) it; *(a loro)* (to) them; **glielo hai detto?** have you told him/her?; **gliene devo due** I owe him/her two (of them).

gliela → **gli**.

gliele → **gli**.

glieli → **gli**.

glielo → **gli**.

gliene → **gli**.

globale *agg* global.

globo *sm* globe.

globulo *sm*: ~ **rosso/bianco** red/white corpuscle.

gloria *sf* glory.

gnocchi *smpl* gnocchi *(small dumplings made from potatoes and flour or from semolina)*.

goal [gɔl] *sm inv* goal.

gobba *sf (su schiena)* hump; *(rigonfiamento)* bump.

gobbo, -a ◇ *agg* hunchbacked; *(curvo)* round-shouldered ◇ *sm* hunchback.

goccia, -ce *sf* drop.

gocciolare *vi & vt* to drip.

godere *vt*: **godersi qc** to enjoy sthg.
◆ **godere di** *v + prep (avere)* to enjoy; ~ **di una riduzione** to benefit from a reduction.
goffo, -a *agg* clumsy.
gola *sf* throat; *(golosità)* greed; *(di monte)* gorge.
golf *sm inv (maglia)* sweater, jumper; *(sport)* golf.
golfo *sm* gulf.
goloso, -a *agg* greedy.
gomito *sm* elbow.
gomma *sf* rubber; *(per cancellare)* rubber *(Br)*, eraser *(Am)*; *(pneumatico)* tyre; **bucare** o **forare una** ~ to have a puncture; ~ **a terra** flat tyre; ~ **(da masticare)** chewing gum.
gommapiuma® *sf* foam rubber.
gommone *sm* rubber dinghy.
gondola *sf* gondola.
gondoliere *sm* gondolier.
gonfiare *vt (pallone, gomme)* to inflate; *(dilatare, ingrossare)* to swell; *(notizia, impresa)* to exaggerate.
◆ **gonfiarsi** *vr* to swell; *(fiume)* to rise.
gonfio, -a *agg (piede, occhi)* swollen; *(stomaco)* bloated.
gonna *sf* skirt; ~ **a pieghe** pleated skirt; ~ **pantalone** culottes *(pl)*.
gorgogliare *vi* to gurgle.
gorgonzola *sm* Gorgonzola *(a strong green-veined cheese made from cow's milk)*.
gorilla *sm inv (animale)* gorilla; *(guardia del corpo)* bodyguard.
goulash ['gulaʃ] *sm* goulash.
governante *sf (per bambini)* governess; *(di casa)* housekeeper.
governare *vt* to govern; *(animale)* to look after.
governatore *sm* governor.
governo *sm* government.
gracile *agg* delicate.
gradazione *sf (di colori)* scale; *(sfumatura)* shade; ~ **alcolica** alcoholic strength.
gradevole *agg* pleasant.
gradinata *sf (scalinata)* (flight of) steps; *(in stadi, teatri)* tiers *(pl)*.
gradino *sm* step.
gradire *vt (regalo)* to like, to appreciate; *(desiderare)* to like; **gradisce un caffè?** would you like a coffee?
grado *sm* degree; *(sociale)* level; (MIL) rank; **quanti gradi ha questo vino?** how strong is this wine?; **essere in** ~ **di fare qc** to be able to do sthg; ~ **centigrado** centigrade.
graduale *agg* gradual.
graduatoria *sf* (ranked) list.
graffetta *sf (fermaglio)* clip; *(di pinzatrice)* staple.
graffiare *vt* to scratch.
graffio *sm* scratch.
grafica *sf* graphics *(pl)*.
grafico, -a, -ci, -che ◇ *agg (rappresentazione, arti)* graphic ◇ *sm, f (pubblicitario)* designer ◇ *sm* graph.
grammatica, -che *sf (disciplina)* grammar; *(libro)* grammar book.
grammo *sm* gram.
grana ◇ *sf (fam) (seccatura)* trouble; *(soldi)* cash ◇ *sm inv a hard cheese similar to Parmesan*.
granaio *sm* granary, barn.
Gran Bretagna *sf*: **la** ~ Great Britain.
granché *pron*: **non ne so (un)** ~ I don't know much about it; **non è (un)** ~ it's nothing special.
granchio *sm* crab; **prendere un** ~ *(fig)* to blunder.
grande ◇ *(a volte* **gran***) agg (gen)* big; *(albero)* tall; *(rumore)* loud; *(scrittore, affetto, capacità)* great ◇ *sm (adulto)* grown-up, adult; ~ **magazzino** department store; **cosa farai da** ~? what will you do when you grow up?; **fare le cose**

in ~ to do things on a grand scale; **è un gran bugiardo** he's such a liar; **fa un gran caldo** it's very hot.

grandezza *sf (dimensioni)* size; *(eccellenza)* greatness.

grandinare *v impers* to hail.

grandine *sf* hail.

granello *sm (di sale, sabbia, polvere)* grain.

granita *sf* granita *(crushed ice with syrup, fruit juice or coffee poured over)*.

grano *sm* wheat.

granturco *sm* maize.

grappa *sf (acquavite)* grappa *(spirit distilled from grape marc)*.

grappolo *sm* bunch.

grasso, -a ◇ *agg (persona)* fat; *(cibo)* fatty; *(pelle, capelli)* greasy ◇ *sm* fat; *(unto)* grease.

grassoccio, -a, -ci, -ce *agg* plump.

grata *sf* grating.

gratis *avv* free.

gratitudine *sf* gratitude.

grato, -a *agg* grateful.

grattacielo *sm* skyscraper.

grattare *vt* to scratch; *(formaggio)* to grate; *(fam: rubare)* to pinch; **grattarsi il naso/la gamba** to scratch one's nose/leg.

◆ **grattarsi** *vr* to scratch o.s.

grattugia *sf* grater.

grattugiare *vt* to grate.

gratuito, -a *agg* free.

grave *agg (malattia, ferita)* serious; *(danno, perdite)* serious, great; *(responsabilità)* heavy; *(sacrificio)* great; *(voce, suono)* deep; *(contegno)* solemn.

gravemente *avv* seriously.

gravidanza *sf* pregnancy.

gravità *sf (in fisica)* gravity; *(serietà)* seriousness.

grazia *sf* grace; (DIR) pardon.

grazie *esclam* thank you!; **~ tante** O **mille!** thank you so much!; **~ dei fiori** O **per i fiori** thank you for the flowers; **~ a** thanks to.

grazioso, -a *agg* pretty, charming.

Grecia *sf*: **la ~** Greece.

greco, -a, -ci, -che *agg & sm, f* Greek.

gregge (*pl f* **greggi**) *sm* flock.

greggio, -a, -gi, -ge ◇ *agg* raw, unrefined; *(tessuto)* unbleached; *(diamante)* rough, uncut ◇ *sm* crude oil.

grembiule *sm (da cucina)* apron; *(per bambini)* smock.

grezzo = **greggio**.

gridare ◇ *vi* to shout; *(di dolore)* to yell, to cry out ◇ *vt* to shout.

grido (*pl f* **grida**) *sm (di persona)* shout, cry; **di ~** famous.

grigio, -a, -gi, -gie *agg & sm* grey.

griglia *sf* grill; **alla ~** grilled.

grigliata *sf* mixed grill *(of meat or fish)*.

grill *sm* = **griglia**.

grilletto *sm* trigger.

grillo *sm* cricket.

grinta *sf* determination.

grinzoso, -a *agg (tessuto)* creased; *(pelle)* wrinkled.

grissini *smpl* bread-sticks.

grolla *sf wooden goblet or bowl, typical of the Valle d'Aosta.*

grondare *vi* to stream.

◆ **grondare di** *v + prep* to drip with.

groppa *sf* rump.

groppo *sm* tangle; **avere un ~ alla gola** to have a lump in one's throat.

grossista, -i, -e *smf* wholesaler.

grosso, -a ◇ *agg* big, large; *(spesso)* thick; *(importante)* important; *(grave)* great ◇ *sm* majority; **dirla grossa** to tell a whopping lie; **questa volta l'hai fatta**

grossa! you've really done it this time!; **sbagliarsi di ~** to make a big mistake; **mare ~** rough sea; **pezzo ~** big shot; **sale ~** coarse salt.
grossolano, -a *agg (persona)* coarse; *(lavoro)* crude; *(errore)* gross.
grossomodo *avv* roughly, approximately.
grotta *sf* cave.
grottesco, -a, -schi, -sche *agg* grotesque.
groviera *sm o sf* Gruyère cheese.
groviglio *sm* tangle.
gru *sf inv (macchina)* crane.
gruccia, -ce *sf (stampella)* crutch; *(per abiti)* coat hanger.
grugnire *vi* to grunt.
grumo *sm (di sangue)* clot; *(di farina)* lump.
gruppo *sm* group; **~ sanguigno** blood group.
gruviera = **groviera**.
guadagnare *vt (soldi)* to earn; *(ottenere)* to gain; **guadagnarsi da vivere** to earn one's living.
guadagno *sm (denaro)* earnings *(pl)*; *(tornaconto)* profit.
guado *sm* ford.
guai *esclam*: **~ a te!** you'll be for it!
guaio *sm (pasticcio)* trouble; *(inconveniente)* problem; **essere nei guai** to be in trouble; **mettere qn nei guai** to get sb into trouble.
guancia, -ce *sf* cheek.
guanciale *sm* pillow.
guanto *sm* glove.
guardaboschi *sm inv* forest ranger.
guardacoste *sm inv (persona)* coastguard; *(nave)* (coastguard's) patrol boat.
guardalinee *sm inv* linesman.
guardamacchine *sm inv* car park attendant.
guardare ◇ *vt (osservare)* to look at, to watch; *(televisione, film)* to watch; *(bambini, borsa)* to look after ◇ *vi (edificio)* to look, to face; *(badare)*: **non ~ a spese** to spare no expense; **guarda!** look!
◆ **guardarsi** *vr* to look at o.s.
◆ **guardarsi da** *vr + prep* to be wary of; **guardarsi dal fare qc** to be careful not to do sthg.
guardaroba *sm inv* wardrobe; *(di locale)* cloakroom.
guardia *sf* guard; *(attività)* watch, guard duty; **fare la ~ a** to guard; **mettere qn in ~ contro qc** to warn sb about sthg; **~ del corpo** bodyguard; **Guardia di Finanza** *military body responsible for customs and fiscal matters*; **~ forestale** forest ranger; **~ medica** first-aid station; **di ~** on duty.
guardiano *sm* caretaker; **~ notturno** night watchman.
guardrail [gar'dreil] *sm inv* crash barrier.
guarire ◇ *vi* to recover; *(ferita)* to heal ◇ *vt* to cure; *(ferita)* to heal.
guarnizione *sf (ornamento)* trim; *(contorno)* accompaniment, garnish; *(per recipienti)* seal; *(di auto)* gasket.
guastafeste *smf inv* spoilsport.
guastare *vt* to spoil.
◆ **guastarsi** *vr (meccanismo)* to break down; *(cibo)* to go bad; *(tempo)* to change for the worse.
guasto, -a ◇ *agg (radio)* broken; *(ascensore, telefono)* out of order; *(cibo)* bad ◇ *sm* breakdown; **un ~ al motore** engine trouble.
guerra *sf* war; **essere in ~** to be at war; **~ mondiale** World War.
guerriglia *sf* guerrilla warfare.
gufo *sm* owl.
guglia *sf* spire.
guida *sf* guide; *(di veicolo)* driving; **~ a destra** right-hand drive; **~ a sinistra** left-hand drive.
guidare *vt (veicolo)* to drive; *(accompagnare)* to guide; **sai ~?**

can you drive?
guidatore, -trice *sm, f* driver.
guinzaglio *sm* lead.
guscio *sm* shell.
gustare *vt (cibo)* to taste; *(godersi)* to enjoy.
gusto *sm* taste; **al ~ di banana** banana-flavoured; **mangiare di ~** to enjoy one's food; **ridere di ~** to laugh heartily; **ci ha preso ~** he's come to like it.
gustoso, -a *agg* tasty.

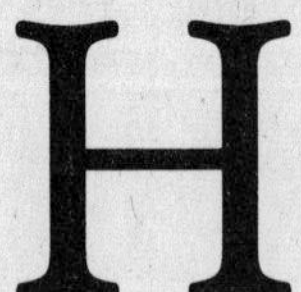

ha → **avere**.
habitat *sm inv* habitat.
hai → **avere**.
hall [ol] *sf inv* hall, foyer.
hamburger [am'burger] *sm inv* hamburger.
handicap ['ɛndikap] *sm inv* handicap.
handicappato, -a ◇ *agg* handicapped ◇ *sm, f* handicapped person, disabled person.
hanno → **avere**.
henné *sm inv* henna.
hg *(abbr di ettogrammo)* hg.
hi-fi [ai'fai] *sm inv* hi-fi.
hippy *agg inv & smf inv* hippy.
ho → **avere**.
hobby *sm inv* hobby.
hockey *sm* hockey *(Br)*, field hockey *(Am)*; ~ **su ghiaccio** ice hockey.
hostess *sf inv (di volo)* airhostess.
hotel *sm inv* hotel.

I

i *art mpl* the, → **il**.
iceberg ['aizbɛrg] *sm inv* iceberg.
Iddio *sm* God.
idea *sf* idea; *(opinione, impressione)* impression; *(progetto)*: **avere ~ di fare qc** to think of doing sthg; **neanche per ~!** don't even think about it!; **non avere la più pallida ~ di qc** not to have the slightest idea about sthg; **non ne ho ~** I've no idea; **cambiare ~** to change one's mind.
ideale *agg & sm* ideal.
ideare *vt (metodo, sistema)* to devise; *(viaggio)* to plan.
idem *avv (fam: lo stesso)* the same.
identico, -a, -ci, -che *agg* identical.
identità *sf inv* identity.
ideologia, -gie *sf* ideology.
idiota, -i, -e ◇ *agg* idiotic, stupid ◇ *smf* idiot.
idolo *sm* idol.
idoneo, -a *agg (adatto)*: **~ a** suitable for; (MIL) fit for.
idrante *sm* hydrant.
idratante *agg* moisturizing.
idratare *vt* to moisturize.
idraulico, -a, -ci, -che ◇ *agg* hydraulic ◇ *sm* plumber; **impianto ~** plumbing.
idrofilo *agg m* → **cotone**.
idrogeno *sm* hydrogen.
idroscalo *sm* seaplane base.
idrosolubile *agg* soluble (in water).
iella *sf (fam)* bad luck.
ieri *avv* yesterday; **~ mattina** yesterday morning; **~ notte** last night; **l'altro ~, ~ l'altro** the day before yesterday; **la posta di ~** yesterday's mail.
igiene *sf* hygiene.
igienico, -a, -ci, -che *agg* hygienic.
ignorante *agg* ignorant.
ignorare *vt (non sapere)* not to know; *(trascurare)* to ignore.
ignoto, -a *agg* unknown.
il (*mpl* **i**; *dav sm* **lo** (*pl* **gli**) + *s+consonante, gn, ps, z; f* **la**, *fpl* **le**; *dav sm o sf* **l'** + *vocale e h*) *art* **1.** *(gen)* the.
2. *(con nome comune)* the; **~ lago** the lake; **la finestra** the window; **lo studente** the student; **l'isola** the island.
3. *(con nome astratto)*: **~ tempo** time; **la vita** life.
4. *(con titolo)*: **~ Signor Pollini** Mr Pollini; **la regina Elisabetta** Queen Elizabeth.
5. *(con nomi geografici)*: **~ Po** the Po; **le Dolomiti** the Dolomites.
6. *(indica possesso)*: **si è rotto ~ naso** he broke his nose; **ha i capelli biondi** she has fair hair.
7. *(indica il tempo)*: **~ sabato** *(tutti i*

sabati) on Saturdays; *(quel sabato)* on Saturday; **la sera** in the evening; **è ~ 29 dicembre** it's the 29th of December; **dopo le tre** after three o'clock.

8. *(ciascuno)*: **5 000 lire l'uno** 5,000 lira each.

illazione *sf* inference.

illecito, -a *agg* illicit.

illegale *agg* illegal.

illegittimo, -a *agg* illegitimate.

illeso, -a *agg* unhurt.

illimitato, -a *agg (spazio, tempo)* unlimited; *(fiducia)* absolute.

illudere *vt* to deceive.

◆ **illudersi** *vr* to deceive o.s.

illuminare *vt* to light up, to illuminate.

illuminazione *sf* lighting; *(fig: intuizione)* enlightenment.

illusione *sf (falsa apparenza)* illusion; *(falsa speranza)* delusion.

illusionista, -i, -e *smf* conjurer.

illuso, -a ◇ *pp* → **illudere** ◇ *sm, f*: **essere un ~** to be fooling o.s.

illustrare *vt* to illustrate.

illustrazione *sf* illustration, picture.

imballaggio *sm* packaging.

imballare *vt* to pack (up).

imbalsamare *vt* to embalm.

imbarazzante *agg* embarrassing.

imbarazzare *vt* to embarrass.

imbarazzato, -a *agg* embarrassed.

imbarcadero *sm* landing stage.

imbarcare *vt (passeggero)* to board; *(merce)* to load.

◆ **imbarcarsi** *vr* to board.

imbarcazione *sf* boat; **imbarcazioni da diporto** pleasure boats.

imbarco, -chi *sm (salita a bordo)* boarding; *(carico)* loading; *(luogo)* point of departure.

imbattersi : imbattersi in *vr + prep* to run into.

imbecille ◇ *agg* stupid, idiotic ◇ *smf* imbecile, idiot.

imbellire ◇ *vt* to embellish ◇ *vi* to become more beautiful.

imbiancare ◇ *vt* to whitewash ◇ *vi (diventare bianco)* to turn white.

imbianchino *sm* decorator.

imboccare *vt (bambino)* to feed; *(strada)* to turn into.

imboccatura *sf (di condotto)* mouth; *(di strada)* entrance; *(di strumento musicale)* mouthpiece.

imbocco, -chi *sm* entrance.

imbottigliare *vt (liquido)* to bottle; *(nave)* to blockade; **è rimasto imbottigliato** he got stuck in a traffic jam.

imbottire *vt (cuscino)* to stuff; *(giacca)* to pad.

imbottito, -a *agg* stuffed; *(indumento)* padded, quilted; **panino ~** filled roll.

imbranato, -a *agg (fam)* clumsy.

imbrattare *vt* to dirty.

imbrogliare *vt (ingannare)* to deceive; *(ingarbugliare)* to entangle.

imbroglio *sm* swindle.

imbroglione, -a *sm, f* swindler.

imbronciato, -a *agg* sulky.

imbucare *vt* to post *(Br)*, to mail *(Am)*.

imburrare *vt* to butter.

imbuto *sm* funnel.

imitare *vt* to imitate.

imitazione *sf* imitation.

immacolato, -a *agg (bianco)* pure white; *(puro)* immaculate, pure.

immaginare *vt (rappresentarsi)* to imagine; *(supporre)* to suppose; **si immagini!** don't mention it!; **~ di fare qc** to imagine doing sthg.

immaginazione *sf* imagination.

immagine *sf* image.

immatricolare *vt (auto)* to register; *(studente)* to enrol.
immaturo, -a *agg* immature.
immedesimarsi : **immedesimarsi in** *vr + prep* to identify with.
immediatamente *avv* immediately.
immediato, -a *agg* immediate.
immenso, -a *agg* immense, enormous.
immergere *vt* to immerse.
◆ **immergersi** *vr* to dive.
◆ **immergersi in** *vr + prep (dedicarsi a)* to immerse o.s. in.
immersione *sf* dive.
immerso, -a *pp* → **immergere**.
immesso, -a *pp* → **immettere**.
immettere *vt* to introduce.
immigrante *smf* immigrant.
immigrato, -a *sm, f* immigrant.
imminente *agg* imminent.
immobile ◇ *agg* immobile ◇ *sm* property *(Br)*, real estate *(Am)*.
immobiliare *agg* property *(dav s) (Br)*, real estate *(dav s) (Am)*.
immodesto, -a *agg* immodest.
immondizia *sf* rubbish.
immorale *agg* immoral.
immortale *agg* immortal.
immunità *sf* immunity.
immunizzare *vt* to immunize.
impacchettare *vt* to wrap.
impacciato, -a *agg (goffo)* awkward; *(imbarazzato)* embarrassed.
impacco, -chi *sm* compress.
impadronirsi : **impadronirsi di** *vr + prep (città, beni)* to take possession of; *(lingua)* to master.
impalcatura *sf* scaffolding.
impallidire *vi* to go pale.
impalpabile *agg* impalpable.
impappinarsi *vr* to stumble.
imparare *vt* to learn; ~ **a fare qc** to learn to do sthg.
imparziale *agg* impartial, unbiased.
impassibile *agg* impassive.
impastare *vt (pane)* to knead; *(mescolare)* to mix.
impasto *sm (di farina)* dough; *(amalgama)* mixture.
impatto *sm* impact.
impaurire *vt* to frighten.
◆ **impaurirsi** *vr* to get frightened.
impaziente *agg* impatient; **essere ~ di fare qc** to be impatient to do sthg.
impazzire *vi* to go mad.
impedimento *sm* obstacle.
impedire *vt (ostacolare)* to obstruct; *(vietare)*: ~ **a qn di fare qc** to prevent sb from doing sthg.
impegnare *vt (occupare)* to keep busy; *(dare in pegno)* to pawn.
◆ **impegnarsi** *vr* to commit o.s.; **impegnarsi a fare qc** to undertake to do sthg; **impegnarsi in qc** to commit o.s. to sthg.
impegnativo, -a *agg (lavoro)* demanding, exacting; *(promessa)* binding.
impegnato, -a *agg (occupato)* busy; *(militante)* committed.
impegno *sm* commitment; *(incombenza)* engagement, appointment.
impellente *agg* pressing, urgent.
impenetrabile *agg* impenetrable.
impennarsi *vr (cavallo)* to rear (up); *(moto)* to do a wheelie; *(aereo)* to climb.
impennata *sf (di cavallo)* rearing; *(di moto)* wheelie; *(di aereo)* climb.
impensabile *agg* unthinkable, inconceivable.
impepata *sf*: ~ **di cozze** *mussels cooked with lots of pepper or chilli (a speciality of Naples).*
imperativo *sm* imperative.
imperatore, -trice *sm, f* emperor (*f* empress).
imperfezione *sf* imperfection.
impermeabile ◇ *agg* water-

proof ◇ *sm* raincoat.
impero *sm* empire.
impersonale *agg* impersonal.
impersonare *vt* to play.
impertinente *agg* impertinent.
imperturbabile *agg* imperturbable.
imperversare *vi (calamità)* to rage; *(fam: moda)* to be all the rage.
impervio, -a *agg* passable with difficulty.
impeto *sm (forza)* force; *(slancio)* surge.
impianto *sm (installazione)* installation; *(elettrico, del gas, antifurto)* system; *(macchinario)* plant; ~ **di riscaldamento** heating system; ~ **sportivo** sports complex; **impianti di risalita** ski lifts.
impiccare *vt* to hang.
◆ **impiccarsi** *vr* to hang o.s.
impiccione, -a *sm, f* busybody.
impiegare *vt (tempo)* to take; *(utilizzare)* to use; *(assumere)* to employ.
◆ **impiegarsi** *vr* to get a job.
impiegato, -a *sm, f* employee; ~ **di banca** bank clerk.
impiego, -ghi *sm (lavoro)* work, employment; *(uso)* use.
impigliare *vt* to entangle.
◆ **impigliarsi** *vr*: **impigliarsi in qc** to get entangled in sthg.
impigrire ◇ *vt* to make lazy ◇ *vi* to become lazy.
◆ **impigrirsi** *vr* to become lazy.
implacabile *agg* implacable, relentless.
implicare *vt (comportare)* to imply, to entail; *(coinvolgere)* to involve.
implicato, -a *agg*: **essere ~ in qc** to be implicated in sthg.
implicazione *sf* implication.
implicito, -a *agg* implicit.
implorare *vt* to implore.
impolverare *vt* to cover with dust.
◆ **impolverarsi** *vr* to get dusty.
imponente *agg* imposing.
impopolare *agg* unpopular.
imporre *vt (volontà, silenzio)* to impose; *(costringere)*: ~ **a qn di fare qc** to make sb do sthg.
◆ **imporsi** *vr (farsi ubbidire)* to impose o.s., to assert o.s.; *(avere successo)* to be successful; **imporsi di fare qc** to make o.s. do sthg.
importante *agg* important.
importanza *sf* importance; **avere ~** to be important, to matter; **dare ~ a qc** to give weight to sthg.
importare ◇ *vt* to import ◇ *vi* to matter, to be important ◇ *v impers* to matter; **non importa!** it doesn't matter!; **non mi importa** I don't care.
importato, -a *agg* imported.
importazione *sf* importation; *(prodotto)* import.
importo *sm* amount.
importunare *vt* to bother.
impossessarsi : **impossessarsi di** *vr + prep* to take possession of.
impossibile ◇ *agg* impossible ◇ *sm*: **fare l'~** to do all one can.
imposto, -a ◇ *pp* → **imporre** ◇ *sf (tassa)* tax, duty; *(di finestra)* shutter.
impostare *vt (lettera)* to post *(Br)*, to mail *(Am)*; *(lavoro)* to plan; *(domanda)* to formulate.
imposto, -a *pp* → **imporre**.
impostore, -a *sm, f* impostor.
impotente *agg* powerless; (MED) impotent.
impraticabile *agg* impassable.
imprecare *vi* to curse.
imprecazione *sf* curse.
impregnare *vt*: ~ **qc (di qc)** *(inzuppare)* to soak sthg (with sthg); *(di fumo, odore)* to impregnate sthg (with sthg).
imprenditore, -trice *sm, f*

(industriale) entrepreneur; *(appaltatore)* contractor.

impreparato, -a *agg* unprepared.

impresa *sf (azione)* undertaking; *(ditta)* business.

impresario, -a *sm, f (teatrale)* impresario; ~ **edile** building constructor.

impressionante *agg* impressive.

impressionare *vt (turbare)* to disturb; *(colpire)* to impress.

♦ **impressionarsi** *vr* to get upset.

impressione *sf* impression; *(sensazione)* impression, feeling; **ho l'~ di conoscerlo** I have the impression o feeling I know him; **fare ~** *(colpire)* to impress; *(turbare)* to upset; **fare buona/cattiva ~** to make a good/bad impression.

impresso, -a *pp* → **imprimere**.

imprestare *vt*: ~ **qc a qn** to lend sthg to sb.

imprevisto, -a ◇ *agg* unexpected ◇ *sm* unexpected event; **salvo imprevisti** circumstances permitting.

imprigionare *vt (incarcerare)* to imprison; *(tenere chiuso)* to confine.

imprimere *vt* to print; *(movimento)* to transmit.

improbabile *agg* improbable, unlikely.

impronta *sf (di piede, mano, zampa)* print; ~ **digitale** fingerprint.

improvvisamente *avv* suddenly, unexpectedly.

improvvisare *vt* to improvise.

♦ **improvvisarsi** *vr*: **si è improvvisato cuoco** he acted as cook.

improvvisata *sf* surprise.

improvviso, -a *agg (inatteso)* sudden, unexpected; *(istantaneo)* sudden; **all'~** suddenly.

imprudente *agg (persona)* unwise, imprudent; *(azione)* rash.

imprudenza *sf* rash action.

impudente *agg* impudent.

impugnare *vt (stringere)* to grasp; (DIR) to contest.

impugnatura *sf* handle.

impulsivo, -a *agg* impulsive.

impulso *sm* impulse; **d'~** on impulse.

impuntarsi *vr (bambino)* to stop dead; *(cavallo)* to jib; *(ostinarsi)* to dig one's heels in.

imputare *vt*: ~ **qc a qn** to attribute sthg to sb; ~ **qn di qc** to accuse sb of sthg.

imputato, -a *sm, f* defendant.

in *prep* 1. *(stato in luogo)* in; **abitare ~ campagna** to live in the country; **essere ~ casa** to be at home; **l'ho lasciato ~ macchina/nella borsa** I left it in the car/in the bag; **vivo ~ Italia** I live in Italy; **avere qc ~ mente** to have sthg in mind.

2. *(moto a luogo)* to; **andare ~ Italia** to go to Italy; **andare ~ montagna** to go to the mountains; **mettersi qc ~ testa** to get sthg into one's head; **entrare ~ macchina** to get into the car; **entrare nella stanza** to go into the room.

3. *(indica un momento)* in; ~ **primavera** in spring; **nel 1995** in 1995.

4. *(indica durata)* in; **l'ho fatto ~ cinque minuti** I did it in five minutes; ~ **giornata** within the day.

5. *(indica modo)*: **parlare ~ italiano** to speak in Italian; ~ **silenzio** in silence; **sono ancora in pigiama** I'm still in my pyjamas; **quant'è ~ lire?** how much is that in lira?; ~ **vacanza** on holiday *(Br)*, on vacation *(Am)*.

6. *(indica mezzo)* by; **pagare ~ contanti** to pay cash; **viaggiare ~ macchina** to travel by car.

7. *(indica materia)* made of; **statua ~ bronzo** bronze statue.

8. *(indica fine)*: **ha speso un capitale in libri** he spent a fortune on books; **dare ~ omaggio** to give as a free gift; **~ onore di** in honour of.

9. *(con valore distributivo)*: **siamo partiti ~ tre** three of us left; **~ tutto sono 10 000 lire** it's 10,000 lira in total.

inabile *agg*: **~ (a qc)** unfit (for sthg).

inaccessibile *agg (luogo)* inaccessible; *(persona)* unapproachable.

inaccettabile *agg* unacceptable.

inadatto, -a *agg* unsuitable.

inadeguato, -a *agg (insufficiente)* inadequate; *(non idoneo)* unsuitable.

inagibile *agg* unfit for use.

inalare *vt* to inhale.

inalberarsi *vr* to get angry.

inalterato, -a *agg* unchanged.

inamidare *vt* to starch.

inammissibile *agg* inadmissible.

inappetenza *sf* lack of appetite.

inappuntabile *agg (persona)* faultless, irreproachable; *(lavoro, vestito)* impeccable.

inarcare *vt (schiena)* to arch; **~ le sopracciglia** to raise one's eyebrows.

◆ **inarcarsi** *vr* to arch.

inaridire *vt* to dry (up).

◆ **inaridirsi** *vr* to dry up.

inaspettato, -a *agg* unexpected.

inasprire *vt* to make worse.

◆ **inasprirsi** *vr* to become bitter.

inattendibile *agg* unbelievable, unreliable.

inatteso, -a *agg* unexpected.

inattività *sf* inactivity.

inattuabile *agg* impractical, unfeasible.

inaudito, -a *agg* unheard-of, unprecedented.

inaugurare *vt (luogo, mostra)* to open; *(monumento)* to unveil.

inavvertenza *sf* carelessness.

inavvertitamente *avv* inadvertently.

incagliarsi *vr (nave)* to run aground; *(fig: trattative)* to break down.

incalcolabile *agg* incalculable.

incallito, -a *agg (mani, piedi)* calloused; *(fig: fumatore, giocatore)* inveterate.

incalzare ◇ *vt (inseguire)* to pursue; *(fig: premere)* to press ◇ *vi* to be imminent.

incamminarsi *vr* to set out.

incantevole *agg* enchanting.

incanto *sm (incantesimo)* enchantment; *(asta)* auction; **come per ~** as if by magic.

incapace *agg* incapable.

incapacità *sf (inettitudine)* incapacity; (DIR) incompetence.

incappare : **incappare in** *v + prep* to run into.

incaricare *vt* to entrust; **~ qn di qc** to entrust sb with sthg; **~ qn di fare qc** to ask sb to do sthg.

◆ **incaricarsi di** *vr + prep* to undertake to.

incaricato, -a ◇ *agg*: **~ di qc** entrusted with sthg ◇ *sm, f* representative.

incarico, -chi *sm* task.

incarnare *vt* to embody.

incarnirsi *vr* to become ingrown.

incartare *vt* to wrap up; **me lo può ~?** can you wrap it up for me?

incassare *vt (denaro)* to receive; *(assegno)* to cash; *(colpo, offesa)* to take; *(mobile)* to build in.

incasso *sm* takings *(pl)*.

incastrare *vt (connettere)* to join; *(fam: intrappolare)* to catch.

◆ **incastrarsi** *vr (rimanere bloccato)* to get stuck; *(combaciare)* to fit together.

incastro *sm* joint; **a ~** interlocking.

incatenare *vt (legare)* to chain.
incauto, -a *agg* imprudent, rash.
incavato, -a *agg* hollow; *(occhi)* sunken.
incavo *sm* hollow.
incavolarsi *vr (fam)* to lose one's temper.
incendiare *vt (dare fuoco a)* to set fire to.
◆ **incendiarsi** *vr* to catch fire.
incendio *sm* fire.
incenerire *vt* to incinerate.
incenso *sm* incense.
incensurato, -a *agg*: **essere ~** to have no previous convictions.
incentivo *sm* incentive.
inceppare *vt* to block, to obstruct.
◆ **incepparsi** *vr* to jam.
incerata *sf (tela)* oilcloth; *(giaccone)* oilskin.
incertezza *sf* uncertainty.
incerto, -a *agg* uncertain; *(tempo)* variable.
incetta *sf*: **fare ~ di qc** to buy sthg up.
inchiesta *sf* enquiry.
inchinarsi *vr (uomo)* to bow; *(donna)* to curtsy.
inchino *sm (di uomo)* bow; *(di donna)* curtsy.
inchiodare *vt* to nail.
inchiostro *sm* ink.
inciampare *vi* to trip; **~ in qc** to trip over sthg.
incidente *sm* accident; **~ stradale** road accident.
incidere *vt (intagliare)* to engrave; *(canzone)* to record; *(ascesso)* to lance.
◆ **incidere su** *v + prep* to affect.
incinta *agg f* pregnant.
incirca *avv*: **all'~** approximately, about.
incisione *sf (taglio)* cut; *(in arte)* engraving; *(di disco, canzone)* recording; (MED) incision.
incisivo, -a ◇ *agg* incisive ◇ *sm* incisor.
inciso, -a ◇ *pp* → **incidere** ◇ *sm*: **per ~** incidentally.
incitare *vt* to incite.
incivile *agg (non civilizzato)* uncivilized; *(maleducato)* rude.
inclinazione *sf* inclination.
includere *vt (accludere)* to enclose; *(comprendere)* to include.
incluso, -a ◇ *pp* → **includere** ◇ *agg (accluso)* enclosed; *(compreso)* included; **~ nel prezzo** included in the price.
incognito *sm*: **in ~** incognito.
incollare *vt (sovrapporre)* to stick; *(unire)* to stick, to glue.
◆ **incollarsi** *vr (stare vicino)*: **incollarsi a qn** to stick close to sb.
incolpare *vt*: **~ qn (di qc)** to blame sb (for sthg).
incolume *agg* unhurt.
incominciare *vt & vi* to begin, to start; **~ a fare qc** to begin to do sthg o doing sthg, to start to do sthg o doing sthg.
incompatibile *agg* incompatible.
incompetente *agg* incompetent.
incompiuto, -a *agg* unfinished, incomplete.
incompleto, -a *agg* incomplete.
incomprensibile *agg* incomprehensible.
inconcepibile *agg* inconceivable.
inconcludente *agg (persona)* ineffectual; *(discorsi)* inconclusive.
incondizionato, -a *agg* unconditional.
inconfondibile *agg* unmistakable.
inconsapevole *agg* unaware.
inconscio, -a, -sci, -sce *agg* unconscious.
incontaminato, -a *agg* un-

contaminated.

incontentabile *agg* impossible to please.

incontinenza *sf* incontinence.

incontrare *vt* to meet; *(difficoltà, favore)* to meet with.

♦ **incontrarsi** *vr* to meet.

incontrario : **all'incontrario** *avv (fam) (alla rovescia)* back to front; *(all'indietro)* backwards.

incontro ◇ *sm* meeting; *(casuale)* encounter; *(sportivo)* match ◇ *avv* towards; **andare/venire ~ a qn** *(avanzare verso)* to go/to come towards sb; *(incontrare)* to go/to come to meet sb; *(fig: con compromesso)* to meet sb halfway; **andare ~ a qc** *(spese)* to incur; *(difficoltà)* to encounter.

inconveniente *sm* setback, problem.

incoraggiare *vt* to encourage.

incosciente *agg (privo di coscienza)* unconscious; *(irresponsabile)* irresponsible.

incredibile *agg* incredible.

incrementare *vt* to increase.

incremento *sm* increase.

incrociare *vt* to cross; *(persona, veicolo)* to pass; **~ le gambe/braccia** to cross one's legs/arms; **~ le dita** to cross one's fingers.

♦ **incrociarsi** *vr (strade, linee)* to cross; *(persone, veicoli)* to pass each other.

incrocio *sm (crocevia)* crossroads *(sg)*; *(combinazione)* cross-breed.

incubatrice *sf* incubator.

incubo *sm* nightmare.

incurabile *agg* incurable.

incurante *agg*: **~ di** careless of, indifferent to.

incuriosire *vt* to make curious.

♦ **incuriosirsi** *vr* to become curious.

incustodito, -a *agg* unattended.

indaco *sm* indigo.

indaffarato, -a *agg* busy.

indagine *sf (di polizia)* investigation; *(studio)* research.

indebolire *vt* to weaken.

♦ **indebolirsi** *vr* to weaken, to become weak.

indecente *agg* indecent.

indecifrabile *agg* indecipherable.

indeciso, -a *agg* uncertain.

indefinito, -a *agg* indefinite.

indegno, -a *agg* disgraceful.

indelebile *agg* indelible.

indenne *agg* unhurt.

indennità *sf inv (rimborso)* payment; *(risarcimento)* compensation.

indescrivibile *agg* indescribable.

indeterminativo, -a *agg* indefinite.

indeterminato, -a *agg* indeterminate, vague.

India *sf*: **l'~** India.

indiano, -a *agg & sm, f* Indian.

indicare *vt (mostrare)* to show; *(col dito)* to point to; *(suggerire)* to recommend.

indicatore *sm* (TECNOL) gauge; **~ della benzina** petrol gauge; **~ di direzione** indicator; **~ di velocità** speedometer.

indicazione *sf (segnalazione)* indication; *(informazione)* piece of information; *(prescrizione)* direction.

indice *sm (dito)* index finger; *(di libro)* index; *(lancetta)* needle; *(indizio)* rating.

indietro *avv* back; *(moto a luogo)* backwards; **essere ~** *(col lavoro)* to be behind; *(orologio)* to be slow; **rimandare ~** to send back; **tornare ~** to go back; **all'~** backwards.

indifeso, -a *agg* defenceless.

indifferente *agg (insensibile)* indifferent; *(irrilevante)* insignificant; **mi è ~** it's all the same to me.

indigeno, -a *sm, f* native.

indigente *agg* destitute.

indigestione *sf* indigestion.

indigesto, -a *agg* indigestible.

indimenticabile *agg* unforgettable.

indipendente *agg* independent.

indipendenza *sf* independence.

indire *vt (concorso)* to announce; *(elezioni)* to call.

indiretto, -a *agg* indirect.

indirizzare *vt (lettera, discorso)* to address; *(mandare)* to refer.

indirizzo *sm* address; **scuola a ~ tecnico** = technical college.

indisciplinato, -a *agg* undisciplined.

indiscreto, -a *agg* indiscreet.

indiscrezione *sf (invadenza)* indiscretion; *(notizia)* unconfirmed report.

indiscusso, -a *agg* undisputed.

indiscutibile *agg* unquestionable.

indispensabile *agg* indispensable.

indispettire *vt* to annoy.

◆ **indispettirsi** *vr* to become annoyed.

indisponente *agg* annoying.

indistruttibile *agg* indestructible.

individuale *agg* individual.

individuare *vt* to identify.

individuo *sm* individual.

indiziato, -a ◇ *agg* suspected ◇ *sm, f* suspect.

indizio *sm (segno)* sign; *(per polizia)* clue; (DIR) piece of evidence.

indole *sf* nature.

indolenzito, -a *agg* aching, stiff.

indolore *agg* painless.

indomani *sm*: **l'~** the next day.

indossare *vt (mettere addosso)* to put on; *(avere addosso)* to wear.

indossatore, -trice *sm, f* model.

indotto, -a *pp* → **indurre**.

indovinare *vt* to guess; *(prevedere)* to predict; *(azzeccare)* to get right.

indovinello *sm* riddle.

indovino, -a *sm, f* fortuneteller.

indubbiamente *avv* undoubtedly.

indugiare *vi (temporeggiare)* to take one's time.

indugio *sm* delay; **senza ~** without delay.

indulgente *agg* indulgent.

indumento *sm* garment; **indumenti** *(abiti)* clothes.

indurire *vt* to harden.

◆ **indurirsi** *vr* to harden.

indurre *vt*: **~ qn a fare qc** to induce sb to do sthg.

industria *sf* industry; *(stabilimento)* industrial plant.

industriale ◇ *agg* industrial ◇ *sm* industrialist.

inebetito, -a *agg* stunned.

inebriante *agg* intoxicating.

ineccepibile *agg* unexceptionable.

inedito, -a *agg* unpublished.

inefficiente *agg* inefficient.

ineluttabile *agg* inescapable.

inerente *agg*: **~ a** concerning.

inerme *agg* unarmed, defenceless.

inerzia *sf* inactivity.

inesatto, -a *agg* inaccurate.

inesauribile *agg* inexhaustible.

inesistente *agg* nonexistent.

inesperienza *sf* inexperience.

inesperto, -a *agg* inexperienced.

inestimabile *agg* inestimable.

inevaso, -a *agg* outstanding.

inevitabile *agg* inevitable.

inevitabilmente *avv* inevitably.
in extremis *avv* in extremis.
infallibile *agg* infallible.
infantile *agg (di, per bambini)* child *(dav s)*; *(immaturo)* infantile.
infanzia *sf (periodo)* childhood; *(bambini)* children *(pl)*; **prima ~** infancy.
infarinare *vt (di farina)* to cover with flour; *(cospargere)* to sprinkle.
infarto *sm* heart attack.
infastidire *vt* to annoy.
♦ **infastidirsi** *vr* to get annoyed.
infatti *cong* in fact.
infatuarsi : **infatuarsi di** *vr + prep* to become infatuated with.
infatuazione *sf* infatuation.
infedele *agg* unfaithful.
infedeltà *sf inv* infidelity.
infelice *agg* unhappy; *(sfavorevole)* unsuccessful; *(mal riuscito)* poor; *(inopportuno)* unfortunate.
infelicità *sf* unhappiness.
inferiore ◇ *agg (sottostante)* lower; *(per qualità)* inferior ◇ *smf* inferior; **~ a** *(minore)* below; *(peggiore)* inferior to.
infermeria *sf* infirmary; *(di scuola)* sickbay.
infermiere, -a *sm, f* nurse.
infermo, -a *agg* infirm.
infernale *agg (fam: terribile)* terrible; *(diabolico)* diabolical.
inferno *sm* hell.
inferriata *sf* grating.
infestare *vt* to infest.
infettare *vt* to infect.
♦ **infettarsi** *vr* to become infected.
infettivo, -a *agg* infectious; **malattie infettive** infectious diseases.
infezione *sf* infection.
infiammabile *agg* flammable.
infiammare *vt (incendiare)* to set alight; (MED) to inflame.
♦ **infiammarsi** *vr (incendiarsi)* to catch fire; (MED) to become inflamed.
infiammazione *sf* inflammation.
infilare *vt (introdurre)* to insert; *(ago)* to thread; *(anello, vestito)* to slip on.
♦ **infilarsi in** *vr + prep* to slip into.
infine *avv (alla fine)* finally; *(insomma)* in short.
infinità *sf* infinity; **un'~ di** countless.
infinito, -a ◇ *agg (illimitato)* infinite; *(enorme, innumerevole)* countless ◇ *sm (spazio, tempo)* infinite; (GRAMM) infinitive.
infischiarsi : **infischiarsene di** *vr + prep* not to care about.
inflazione *sf* inflation.
inflessibile *agg* inflexible.
infliggere *vt* to inflict.
inflitto, -a *pp* → **infliggere**.
influente *agg* influential.
influenza *sf* influence; *(malattia)* flu; **avere ~ su** to have an influence on; **avere l'~** to have flu.
influenzare *vt* to influence.
influire : **influire su** *v + prep* to have an effect on.
influsso *sm* influence.
infondato, -a *agg* unfounded.
infondere *vt* to instil.
inforcare *vt (fieno)* to fork up; *(bicicletta, moto)* to get onto; *(occhiali)* to put on.
informale *agg* informal.
informare *vt*: **~ qn (di qc)** to inform sb (of sthg).
♦ **informarsi** *vr*: **informarsi di** o **su** to find out about.
informatica *sf* information technology.
informativo, -a *agg* informative.
informatore *sm* informer.
informazione *sf* piece of information; **chiedere informazioni (a qn)** to ask (sb) for information;

'informazioni' 'information'.
informicolirsi *vr*: **mi si è informicolita una gamba** I've got pins and needles in my leg.
infortunio *sm* accident.
infossarsi *vr (terreno)* to sink; *(guance)* to become hollow.
infradito *sm inv o sf inv* flip-flop.
infrangere *vt* to break.
◆ **infrangersi** *vr* to break.
infrangibile *agg* unbreakable.
infranto, -a ◇ *pp* → **infrangere** ◇ *agg* broken.
infrazione *sf* infringement.
infreddolito, -a *agg* chilled.
infuori *avv*: **all'~** outwards; **all'~ di** apart from.
infusione *sf* infusion.
infuso, -a ◇ *pp* → **infondere** ◇ *sm* herb tea.
ingannare *vt (imbrogliare)* to deceive; *(tempo)* to while away.
◆ **ingannarsi** *vr* to be mistaken.
inganno *sm* deception.
ingarbugliare *vt* to tangle; *(situazione, conti)* to muddle.
◆ **ingarbugliarsi** *vr* to become tangled; *(situazione)* to become muddled; *(impappinarsi)* to falter.
ingegnere *sm* engineer.
ingegneria *sf* engineering.
ingegno *sm (intelligenza)* intelligence; *(creatività)* ingenuity.
ingegnoso, -a *agg* ingenious.
ingelosire *vt* to make jealous.
◆ **ingelosirsi** *vr* to become jealous.
ingente *agg* huge.
ingenuo, -a *agg* naive.
ingerire *vt* to ingest.
ingessare *vt* to put in plaster.
Inghilterra *sf*: **l'~** England.
inghiottire *vt* to swallow; *(sopportare)* to put up with.
ingiallire *vi* to yellow.
ingigantire *vt (foto)* to enlarge; *(fig: problema)* to exaggerate.
inginocchiarsi *vr* to kneel down.
ingiù *avv*: **(all')~** downwards.
ingiustizia *sf (qualità)* injustice; *(atto)* unjust act.
ingiusto, -a *agg* unfair.
inglese ◇ *agg* English ◇ *smf* Englishman (*f* Englishwoman) ◇ *sm (lingua)* English.
ingoiare *vt (inghiottire)* to swallow; *(fig: sopportare)* to put up with.
ingolfare *vt* to flood.
◆ **ingolfarsi** *vr* to flood.
ingombrante *agg* cumbersome.
ingombrare *vt (passaggio, strada)* to obstruct; *(tavolo, stanza)* to clutter up.
ingombro, -a ◇ *agg* obstructed ◇ *sm*: **essere d'~** to be in the way.
ingordo, -a *agg* greedy.
ingorgo, -ghi *sm* traffic jam.
ingranaggio *sm (meccanismo)* gear; *(fig: operazioni, attività)* machinery.
ingranare ◇ *vt* to engage ◇ *vi (ingranaggio)* to engage; *(fam: prendere avvio)* to get going.
ingrandimento *sm* enlargement; *(ottico)* magnification.
ingrandire *vt* to enlarge; *(con microscopio, lente)* to magnify.
◆ **ingrandirsi** *vr (di misura)* to get bigger; *(d'importanza)* to become more important.
ingrassare ◇ *vi* to put on weight ◇ *vt (animali)* to fatten up; *(motore)* to grease.
ingrediente *sm* ingredient.
ingresso *sm (porta)* entrance; *(stanza)* hall; *(permesso di entrare)* admission; '**~ gratuito**' 'admission free'; '**~ libero**' 'admission free'.
ingrossare *vt (gambe, fegato)* to cause to swell.
◆ **ingrossarsi** *vr (gambe, fegato)* to swell.
ingrosso *avv*: **all'~** *(vendita)*

wholesale; *(grossomodo)* about, roughly.
inguine *sm* groin.
inibire *vt* to inhibit.
iniettare *vt* to inject.
iniezione *sf* injection.
inimicare *vt*: **inimicarsi qn** to make an enemy of sb.
inimitabile *agg* inimitable.
ininterrottamente *avv* non-stop.
ininterrotto, -a *agg* continuous, unbroken.
iniziale *agg & sf* initial.
inizialmente *avv* initially.
iniziare *vt & vi* to begin, to start; ~ **qn a qc** to introduce sb to sthg; ~ **a fare qc** to begin O start to do sthg.
iniziativa *sf* initiative; **prendere l'~** to take the initiative.
inizio *sm* start, beginning; **all'~** at the start, at the beginning; **dare ~ a qc** to start O begin sthg; **avere ~** to start, to begin.
innaffiare = **annaffiare**.
innalzare *vt* to erect.
innamorarsi *vr*: ~ **(di qn)** to fall in love (with sb).
innamorato, -a *agg*: ~ **(di qn)** in love (with sb).
innanzi ◇ *avv* in front ◇ *prep (davanti a)* in front of; *(prima di)* before.
innanzitutto *avv* first of all.
innato, -a *agg* innate.
innervosire *vt* to make nervous.
◆ **innervosirsi** *vr* to get nervous.
innescare *vt (bomba)* to prime; *(fig: fenomeno, meccanismo)* to trigger.
innestare *vt (pianta)* to graft; *(meccanismo, marcia)* to engage.
inno *sm* hymn; ~ **nazionale** national anthem.
innocente *agg* innocent.
innocuo, -a *agg* harmless.
innovazione *sf* innovation.
innumerevole *agg* countless.
inodore *agg* odourless.
inoffensivo, -a *agg* inoffensive.
inoltrare *vt* to forward.
◆ **inoltrarsi** *vr* to advance.
inoltrato, -a *agg* late.
inoltre *avv* besides.
inondazione *sf* flood.
inopportuno, -a *agg* inappropriate.
inorridire ◇ *vt* to horrify ◇ *vi* to be horrified.
inosservato, -a *agg*: **passare ~** to go unnoticed.
inquadrare *vt (personaggio, avvenimento)* to place; *(con telecamera)*: ~ **qn/qc** to get sb/sthg in the shot.
inquadratura *sf* shot.
inqualificabile *agg* contemptible.
inquietante *agg* disturbing.
inquilino, -a *sm, f* tenant.
inquinamento *sm* pollution.
inquinare *vt (contaminare)* to pollute; *(fig: prove)* to corrupt.
inquinato, -a *agg* polluted.
insabbiare *vt* to shelve.
◆ **insabbiarsi** *vr (nave)* to run aground; *(pratica, progetto)* to be shelved.
insaccato *sm* sausage.
insalata *sf (di verdure)* salad; *(lattuga)* lettuce; ~ **mista** mixed salad; ~ **di mare** seafood salad; ~ **di riso** rice salad; ~ **russa** Russian salad *(cold diced cooked vegetables mixed with mayonnaise)*.
insalatiera *sf* salad bowl.
insaponare *vt* to soap.
◆ **insaponarsi** *vr* to soap o.s.
insapore *agg* tasteless.
insaporire *vt* to flavour.
insaputa *sf*: **all'~ di qn** without sb's knowledge.
inscenare *vt* to stage.
insegna *sf* sign.

insegnamento *sm* teaching.
insegnante *smf* teacher.
insegnare *vt & vi* to teach; ~ **qc a qn** to teach sb sthg; ~ **a qn a fare qc** to teach sb to do sthg.
inseguire *vt* to pursue.
insenatura *sf* inlet, creek.
insensato, -a *agg (persona)* foolish; *(discorso, idea)* senseless.
insensibile *agg* insensitive.
inseparabile *agg* inseparable.
inserire *vt (introdurre)* to insert; *(includere)* to put in.
◆ **inserirsi** *vr*: **inserirsi in qc** *(entrare a far parte di)* to become part of sthg.
inserto *sm* insert.
inserviente *smf* attendant.
inserzione *sf* advertisement.
insetticida, -i *sm* insecticide.
insetto *sm* insect.
insicurezza *sf* insecurity.
insicuro, -a *agg* insecure.
insidia *sf* hidden danger.
insieme ◇ *avv* together ◇ *sm (totalità)* whole; (MAT) set ◇ *prep*: ~ **a** O **con** with; **mettere** ~ *(raccogliere)* to put together; **tutto** ~ all together; **tutti** ~ all together; **nell'**~ taken as a whole.
insignificante *agg* insignificant.
insinuare *vt* to insinuate.
insinuazione *sf* insinuation.
insipido, -a *agg* insipid.
insistente *agg (persona, richieste)* insistent; *(pioggia, dolore)* persistent.
insistere *vi* to insist; ~ **a** O **col fare qc** to persist in doing sthg.
insoddisfacente *agg* unsatisfactory.
insoddisfatto, -a *agg*: ~ **di** dissatisfied with.
insolazione *sf* sunstroke.
insolente *agg* insolent.
insolito, -a *agg* unusual.
insoluto, -a *agg (non risolto)* unsolved; *(non pagato)* outstanding.
insomma ◇ *avv* well ◇ *esclam* for Heaven's sake!
insonne *agg (persona)* unable to sleep; *(notte)* sleepless.
insonnia *sf* insomnia.
insonnolito, -a *agg* sleepy.
insopportabile *agg* unbearable.
insorgere *vi (popolo)* to rise up; *(difficoltà)* to arise.
insospettire *vt* to arouse suspicions in.
◆ **insospettirsi** *vr* to become suspicious.
insozzare *vt* to dirty.
insperato, -a *agg* unhoped-for.
inspiegabile *agg* inexplicable.
inspirare *vt* to breathe in.
installare *vt* to install.
instaurare *vt* to establish.
insù *avv*: **(all')**~ upwards.
insuccesso *sm* failure.
insudiciare *vt* to dirty.
◆ **insudiciarsi** *vr* to get dirty.
insufficiente *agg* insufficient.
insulina *sf* insulin.
insultare *vt* to insult.
insulto *sm* insult.
intaccare *vt* to attack; *(fare tacche in)* to cut into; *(risparmi)* to break into.
intanto *avv (nel frattempo)* meanwhile.
intarsio *sm* inlay.
intasare *vt* to block.
◆ **intasarsi** *vr* to become blocked.
intatto, -a *agg (intero)* intact; *(mai toccato)* untouched.
integrale *agg (totale)* complete; *(pane, farina)* wholemeal.
integrare *vt* to integrate.
◆ **integrarsi** *vr* to integrate.
integrità *sf* integrity.
integro, -a *agg (intero)* intact; *(onesto)* honest.
intelaiatura *sf* framework.

intelletto *sm* intellect.
intellettuale *agg & smf* intellectual.
intelligente *agg* intelligent.
intelligenza *sf* intelligence.
intemperie *sfpl* bad weather *(sg)*.
intendere *vt (capire)* to understand; *(udire)* to hear; *(avere intenzione di)*: ~ **fare qc** to intend to do sthg; **non intende ragioni** he won't listen to reason; **intendersela con qn** to have an affair with sb.
◆ **intendersi di** *vr + prep* to know about.
intenditore, -trice *sm, f* expert.
intensificare *vt* to intensify.
◆ **intensificarsi** *vr* to intensify.
intensità *sf* intensity.
intensivo, -a *agg* intensive.
intenso, -a *agg* intense.
intento, -a ◇ *sm* intention ◇ *agg*: ~ **(a fare qc)** intent (on doing sthg).
intenzione *sf* intention; **aver ~ di fare qc** to intend to do sthg.
interamente *avv* completely.
intercalare ◇ *sm* catchphrase ◇ *vt* to insert.
intercettare *vt* to intercept.
intercity [inter'siti] *sm inv fast train connecting major Italian cities.*
interdetto, -a *agg* taken aback.
interessamento *sm (interesse)* interest; *(intervento)* intervention.
interessante *agg* interesting; **in stato ~** *(incinta)* expecting.
interessare ◇ *vt (destare l'interesse di)* to interest; *(riguardare)* to concern ◇ *vi*: ~ **a qn** to interest sb; **ciò non mi interessa** I'm not interested in it.
◆ **interessarsi a** *vr + prep* to be interested in.
◆ **interessarsi di** *vr + prep (per informazioni)* to find out about; *(per lavoro, hobby)* to be interested in.
interessato, -a *agg (partecipe)* interested; *(calcolatore)* self-interested.
interesse *sm* interest; *(tornaconto)* self-interest.
◆ **interessi** *smpl* interests.
interferire *vi* to interfere.
interiezione *sf* interjection.
interiora *sfpl* entrails.
interiore *agg (lato, parte)* interior.
interlocutore, -trice *sm, f* interlocutor.
intermezzo *sm* interval.
interminabile *agg* endless.
intermittente *agg* intermittent.
internazionale *agg* international.
Internet *sm* the Internet; **navigare in ~** to surf the Net.
interno, -a ◇ *agg (di dentro)* interior, internal; *(nazionale)* domestic ◇ *sm* interior; *(telefono)* extension; *(in indirizzo)*: ~ **20** flat 20; **all'~** inside.
◆ **interni** *smpl*: **ministero degli Interni** = Home Office *(Br)*, Department of the Interior *(Am)*.
intero, -a *agg* whole; *(prezzo)* full; *(latte)* full-cream; **per ~** in full.
interpretare *vt* to interpret; *(recitare)* to perform.
interprete *smf (traduttore)* interpreter; *(attore, musicista)* performer.
interrogare *vt (studente)* to examine; *(sospetto)* to question.
interrogativo, -a ◇ *agg (sguardo)* enquiring; (GRAMM) interrogative ◇ *sm* question.
interrogazione *sf* oral examination.
interrompere *vt* to interrupt; *(linea telefonica, strada)* to cut off.
◆ **interrompersi** *vr* to stop.
interrotto, -a ◇ *pp* → **interrompere** ◇ *agg* cut off.
interruttore *sm* switch.
intersecare *vt* to intersect.
interurbana *sf* long-distance call.

interurbano, -a *agg (trasporti)* intercity; *(chiamata)* long-distance.
intervallo *sm* interval.
intervenire *vi* to intervene; *(partecipare)* to take part; (MED) to operate.
intervento *sm (intromissione)* intervention; *(partecipazione)* participation; *(discorso)* speech; (MED) operation.
intervenuto, -a *pp* → **intervenire**.
intervista *sf* interview.
intesa *sf (tra persone)* understanding; *(tra stati)* agreement.
inteso, -a ◇ *pp* → **intendere** ◇ *agg*: **resta ~ che** it is understood that; **siamo intesi?** are we agreed?
intestare *vt (lettera)* to address; **~ qc a qn** *(casa, auto)* to register sthg in sb's name; *(assegno)* to make sthg out to sb.
intestino *sm* intestine.
intimare *vt* to order.
intimidire *vt* to intimidate.
intimità *sf (spazio privato)* privacy; *(familiarità)* intimacy.
intimo, -a ◇ *agg* intimate; *(cerimonia, parti)* private; *(interiore)* innermost; *(igiene)* personal ◇ *sm (persona)* close friend.
intimorire *vt* to frighten.
intingolo *sm* sauce.
intitolare *vt (libro, film)* to entitle; *(via, piazza)*: **~ a** to name after.
◆ **intitolarsi** *vr* to be entitled.
intollerabile *agg* unbearable.
intollerante *agg* intolerant.
intolleranza *sf* intolerance.
intonaco, -ci o **-chi** *sm* plaster.
intonare *vt (canto)* to intone; *(vestiti)*: **~ qc a qc** to match sthg with sthg.
◆ **intonarsi** *vr* to go together.
intontire *vt* to stun.
intorno ◇ *avv* around, round ◇ *prep*: **~ a** around.
intossicare *vt* to poison.
intossicato, -a *agg* poisoned.
intossicazione *sf* poisoning.
intraducibile *agg* untranslatable.
intralciare *vt* to hamper.
intramontabile *agg* timeless.
intramuscolare *agg* → **iniezione**.
intransigente *agg* intransigent.
intransitivo, -a *agg* intransitive.
intraprendente *agg* enterprising.
intraprendere *vt* to undertake.
intrapreso, -a *pp* → **intraprendere**.
intrattabile *agg (persona)* intractable; *(prezzo)* non-negotiable.
intrattenere *vt (persona)* to entertain; *(relazioni, rapporti)* to maintain.
◆ **intrattenersi** *vr*: **intrattenersi su qc** to dwell on sthg.
intrecciare *vt (capelli)* to plait, to braid; *(nastri)* to intertwine.
◆ **intrecciarsi** *vr (fili)* to intertwine.
intrigante *agg* scheming.
intrigo, -ghi *sm (macchinazione)* intrigue.
introdurre *vt* to introduce; *(moneta)* to insert; **'vietato ~ cani'** 'dogs not allowed'.
◆ **introdursi** *vr (uso, tecnica)* to be introduced; *(entrare)* to enter.
introduzione *sf* introduction.
introito *sm (incasso)* income.
intromettersi *vr (immischiarsi)* to interfere; *(interporsi)* to intervene.
introvabile *agg* not to be found.
introverso, -a *agg* introverted.
intruso, -a *sm, f* intruder.
intuire *vt (cogliere)* to grasp; *(accorgersi)* to realize.
intuito *sm* intuition.
intuizione *sf* intuition.
inumidire *vt* to dampen.
◆ **inumidirsi** *vr* to become damp.

inutile *agg* useless; *(superfluo)* pointless.
inutilmente *avv* in vain.
invadente *agg* intrusive.
invadere *vt* to invade.
invaghirsi : **invaghirsi di** *vr + prep* to take a fancy to.
invalido, -a ◇ *agg* disabled ◇ *sm, f* disabled person.
invano *avv* in vain.
invasione *sf* invasion.
invasore *sm* invader.
invecchiare ◇ *vi (persona)* to grow old; *(vino)* to age ◇ *vt (vino, formaggio)* to age; *(persona)* to make look older.
invece ◇ *avv* but ◇ *prep*: **~ di** instead of.
inveire *vi*: **~ (contro)** to rail (against).
inventare *vt* to invent; **si è inventato tutto** he made it all up.
inventario *sm (registrazione)* stocktaking; *(lista)* inventory.
inventore, -trice *sm, f* inventor.
invenzione *sf* invention.
invernale *agg* winter *(dav s)*.
inverno *sm* winter; **in** O **d'~** in (the) winter.
inverosimile *agg* unbelievable.
inversione *sf (di ordine, tendenza)* inversion; *(di marcia)* U-turn.
inverso, -a *agg & sm* opposite; **fare qc all'~** to do sthg the wrong way round.
invertire *vt (ordine)* to invert; **~ la marcia** to do a U-turn.
investimento *sm* investment.
investire *vt (denaro)* to invest; *(persona, animale)* to knock down.
inviare *vt* to send.
inviato, -a *sm, f (incaricato)* envoy; *(giornalista)* correspondent.
invidia *sf* envy.
invidiare *vt* to envy; **~ qc a qn** to envy sb sthg.
invidioso, -a *agg* envious.
invincibile *agg (imbattibile)* invincible.
invio *sm (spedizione)* dispatching; *(merci)* consignment.
inviperito, -a *agg* furious.
invischiarsi : **invischiarsi in** *vr + prep* to get involved in.
invisibile *agg* invisible.
invitare *vt* to invite; **~ qn a fare qc** *(proporre di)* to invite sb to do sthg; *(sollecitare)* to request sb to do sthg.
invitato, -a *sm, f* guest.
invito *sm* invitation.
invocare *vt (Dio)* to invoke; *(chiedere)* to beg for; *(legge, diritto)* to cite.
invogliare *vt* to tempt.
involontario, -a *agg* involuntary.
involtino *sm thin slice of meat, rolled up and sometimes stuffed*; **~ primavera** spring roll.
involucro *sm* covering.
inzaccherare *vt* to splash with mud.
inzuppare *vt* to soak; *(biscotto)* to dip.
io *pron* I; **sono ~** it's me; **~ stesso** I myself.
iodio *sm* iodine.
iogurt = **yogurt**.
Ionio *sm*: **lo ~, il mar ~** the Ionian (Sea).
ipertensione *sf* hypertension.
ipnosi *sf* hypnosis.
ipnotizzare *vt* to hypnotize.
ipocrisia *sf* hypocrisy.
ipocrita, -i, -e ◇ *agg* hypocritical ◇ *smf* hypocrite.
ipoteca, -che *sf* mortgage.
ipotesi *sf inv* hypothesis.
ippica *sf* horse racing.
ippico, -a, -ci, -che *agg* horse *(dav s)*.
ippodromo *sm* racecourse.
ippopotamo *sm* hippopotamus.

Iran *sm*: l'~ Iran.
Iraq *sm*: l'~ Iraq.
iride *sf (di occhio)* iris; *(arcobaleno)* rainbow.
iris *sf inv* iris.
Irlanda *sf*: l'~ Ireland; **l'~ del Nord** Northern Ireland.
irlandese ◇ *agg* Irish ◇ *smf* Irishman (*f* Irishwoman).
ironia *sf* irony.
ironico, -a, -ci, -che *agg* ironic.
irradiare ◇ *vt* to light up ◇ *vi* to radiate.
irraggiungibile *agg* unreachable.
irragionevole *agg* unreasonable.
irrazionale *agg* irrational.
irreale *agg* unreal.
irrecuperabile *agg (oggetto)* irretrievable; *(fig: persona)* irredeemable.
irregolare *agg* irregular; *(discontinuo)* uneven.
irregolarità *sf inv* irregularity; *(discontinuità)* unevenness.
irremovibile *agg* inflexible.
irreparabile *agg* irreparable.
irrequieto, -a *agg* restless.
irresponsabile *agg* irresponsible.
irreversibile *agg* irreversible.
irriducibile *agg* unyielding.
irrigare *vt* to irrigate.
irrigidirsi *vr* to stiffen.
irrilevante *agg* insignificant.
irrisorio, -a *agg* ridiculous.
irritabile *agg* irritable.
irritante *agg* irritating.
irritare *vt* to irritate.
◆ **irritarsi** *vr* to become irritated.
irrompere : **irrompere in** *v + prep* to burst into.
irrotto, -a *pp* → **irrompere**.
irruente *agg* impetuous.
irruzione *sf* raid.

iscritto, -a ◇ *pp* → **iscrivere** ◇ *agg*: **essere ~ a qc** *(ad un circolo, partito)* to be a member of sthg; *(all'università)* to be enrolled in sthg; *(ad un esame)* to be entered for sthg; **per ~** in writing.
iscrivere *vt*: **~ qn (a qc)** *(scuola)* to register sb (at sthg), to enrol sb (at sthg); *(corso)* to register sb (for sthg), to enrol sb (for sthg).
◆ **iscriversi** *vr*: **iscriversi (a)** *(circolo, partito)* to become a member (of); *(università)* to enrol (in); *(esame)* to enter.
iscrizione *sf (a università)* enrolment; *(a esame)* entry; *(a partito)* membership; *(funeraria)* inscription.
Islanda *sf*: l'~ Iceland.
islandese ◇ *agg* Icelandic ◇ *smf* Icelander.
isola *sf* island; **~ pedonale** pedestrian precinct.
isolamento *sm (solitudine)* isolation; *(elettrico, termico)* insulation; *(acustico)* soundproofing.
isolante ◇ *agg* insulating ◇ *sm* insulator.
isolare *vt (tenere lontano)* to isolate; *(da freddo, corrente elettrica)* to insulate; *(da rumore)* to soundproof.
◆ **isolarsi** *vr* to cut o.s. off.
isolato, -a ◇ *agg* isolated ◇ *sm* block.
ispettore *sm* inspector.
ispezionare *vt* to inspect.
ispezione *sf* inspection.
ispirare *vt* to inspire.
◆ **ispirarsi a** *vr + prep* to draw one's inspiration from.
Israele *sm* Israel.
issare *vt* to hoist.
istantanea *sf* snapshot.
istantaneo, -a *agg* instantaneous, instant.
istante *sm* instant; **all'~** instantly, at once.

isterico, -a, -ci, -che *agg* hysterical.
istigare *vt*: ~ **qn a fare qc** to incite sb to do sthg.
istinto *sm* instinct.
istituire *vt* to institute.
istituto *sm (organismo)* institute; *(universitario)* department; ~ **di bellezza** beauty salon.
istituzione *sf* institution; **le istituzioni** *(le autorità)* the Establishment.
istmo *sm* (GEOG) isthmus.
istrice *sm (animale)* porcupine.
istruire *vt (insegnare a)* to teach; *(informare)* to instruct.
istruito, -a *agg* educated.
istruttore, -trice *sm, f* instructor.
istruzione *sf (insegnamento)* education; *(cultura)* learning.
♦ **istruzioni** *sfpl*: **istruzioni (per l'uso)** instructions (for use).
Italia *sf*: **l'~** Italy.
italiano, -a *agg & sm, f* Italian.
itinerario *sm (percorso)* route; *(descrizione)* itinerary; ~ **turistico** *(percorso)* tourist route.
Iugoslavia *sf*: **la ~** Yugoslavia.
IVA *sf (abbr di imposta sul valore aggiunto)* VAT.

J

jazz [dʒɛts] *sm* jazz.

jeans [dʒins] ◊ *smpl* jeans ◊ *sm* *(tessuto)* denim.

jeep® [dʒip] *sf inv* Jeep®.

jolly [ˈdʒɔlli] *sm inv* joker.

Jọnio = **Ionio**.

jọta *sf bean soup with onions and turnips marinated in wine (a speciality of Friuli).*

Jugoslạvia = **Iugoslavia**.

juke-box [dʒuːkˈbɔks] *sm inv* jukebox.

K

karaọke *sm inv (gioco)* karaoke; *(locale)* karaoke bar.

karatè *sm* karate.

Kẹnia *sm*: **il ~** Kenya.

kg *(abbr di chilogrammo)* kg.

kịller *smf inv* killer.

kitsch [kitʃ] *agg inv* kitsch.

kiwi [ˈkiwi] *sm inv* kiwi fruit.

km *(abbr di chilometro)* km.

k.o. *avv*: **mettere qn ~** to knock sb out.

koạla *sm inv* koala.

K-way® [kiˈwei] *sm inv* cagoule.

L

l' → **la, lo**.

la (l' *dav vocale e h*) ◇ *art f* the, → **il** ◇ *pron (persona)* her; *(animale, cosa)* it; *(forma di cortesia)* you.

là *avv* there; **di ~** *(nella stanza accanto)* in there; *(moto da luogo)* from there; *(nei paraggi)* over there; **al di ~ di** beyond.

labbro (*pl f* **labbra**) *sm* (ANAT) lip.

labirinto *sm (di strade, corridoi)* labyrinth; *(giardino)* maze.

laboratorio *sm (scientifico)* laboratory; *(artigianale)* workshop; **~ linguistico** language laboratory.

lacca, -che *sf (per capelli)* lacquer, hair spray; *(vernice)* lacquer.

laccio *sm* lace.

lacerare *vt* to tear, to rip.

◆ **lacerarsi** *vr* to tear.

lacero, -a *agg* torn.

lacrima *sf* tear; **in lacrime** in tears.

lacrimogeno *agg m* → **gas**.

lacuna *sf* gap.

ladro, -a *sm, f* thief.

laggiù *avv (in basso)* down there; *(lontano)* over there.

lagnarsi *vr (piagnucolare)* to moan, to groan; *(protestare)*: **~ (di)** to complain (about).

lago, -ghi *sm* lake.

laguna *sf* lagoon.

laico, -a, -ci, -che *agg* lay *(dav s)*.

lama *sf* blade.

lamentarsi *vr (emettere lamenti)* to groan, to moan; **~ (di)** *(dimostrarsi insoddisfatto)* to complain (about).

lamentela *sf* complaint, complaining *(sg)*.

lametta *sf* razor blade.

lamiera *sf* sheet metal.

lampada *sf* lamp; **fare la ~** to use a sunlamp; **~ da tavolo** table lamp.

lampadario *sm* chandelier.

lampadina *sf* light bulb; **~ tascabile** torch *(Br)*, flashlight *(Am)*.

lampeggiare *vi* to flash.

lampeggiatore *sm (freccia)* indicator; *(di ambulanza)* flashing light.

lampione *sm* streetlight.

lampo ◇ *sm (fulmine)* flash of lightning; *(bagliore)* flash ◇ *sf inv (cerniera)* zip *(Br)*, zipper *(Am)*.

lampone *sm* raspberry.

lana *sf* wool; **pura ~ vergine** pure new wool.

lancetta *sf* hand.

lancia, -ce *sf (arma)* lance; *(imbarcazione)* launch.

lanciare *vt (pietra, palla)* to throw; *(missile)* to launch; *(grido)* to give; *(insulto)* to hurl; *(fig: appello, moda, prodotto)* to launch.

◆ **lanciarsi** *vr* to throw o.s.; **lanciarsi in qc** *(mare)* to throw o.s. into sthg; *(impresa)* to embark on sthg.

lancinante *agg* piercing, shooting.
lancio *sm (tiro)* throw; *(di prodotti, missile)* launch.
languido, -a *agg* languid.
languore *sm (di stomaco)* hunger pangs *(pl)*.
lapide *sf (funeraria)* tombstone; *(commemorativa)* plaque.
lapis *sm inv* pencil.
lapsus *sm inv* slip.
lardo *sm* lard, bacon fat.
larghezza *sf (dimensione)* width, breadth; *(abbondanza)* generosity.
largo, -a, -ghi, -ghe ◇ *agg* wide, broad; *(indumento)* loose; *(percentuale, parte)* large ◇ *sm* width; *(piazza)* square; *(alto mare)*: **andare al ~** to take to the open sea; **è ~ 10 metri** it's 10 metres wide; **stare** o **tenersi alla larga (da)** to keep one's distance (from); **farsi ~** to push one's way.
larva *sf (insetto)* larva.
lasagne *sfpl* lasagne *(sg)*.
lasciare ◇ *vt* to leave; *(cessare di tenere)* to let go of; **posso ~ i bagagli in camera?** can I leave the luggage in the room?; **~ la porta aperta** to leave the door open; **~ qn in pace** to leave sb in peace; **lasciar detto a qn che ...** to leave sb word that ...; **~ a desiderare** to leave a lot to be desired; **prendere o ~** take it or leave it; **~ la presa** to let go ◇ *v aus*: **lasciami vedere** let me see; **lascia che faccia come vuole** let him do as he wants; **lascia perdere!** forget it!; **lasciar credere qc a qn** to let sb believe sthg; **lascialo stare!** leave him alone!
◆ **lasciarsi** *vr (separarsi)* to leave each other; **lasciarsi andare** to let o.s. go; **lasciarsi convincere** to allow o.s. to be persuaded.
laser *sm inv & agg inv* laser.
lassativo *sm* laxative.
lassù *avv* up there.
lastra *sf (di ghiaccio, vetro)* sheet; *(di pietra)* slab; *(radiografia)* plate.
laterale *agg* lateral, side *(dav s)*.
latino, -a *agg & sm* Latin.
latino-americano, -a *agg* Latin-American.
latitudine *sf* latitude.
lato *sm* side; **a ~ (di qc)** beside (sthg); **da un ~ ... dall'altro ...** on the one hand ... on the other hand ...
latta *sf* tin.
lattaio, -a *sm, f* milkman (*f* milkwoman).
lattante *smf* baby.
latte *sm* milk; **~ detergente** cleansing milk; **~ intero** full cream milk; **~ magro** o **scremato** skimmed milk; **~ in polvere** powdered milk; **~ di soia** soya milk.
latteria *sf* dairy.
latticini *smpl* dairy products.
lattina *sf* can.
lattuga, -ghe *sf* lettuce.
laurea *sf* degree.
laurearsi *vr* to graduate; **~ in qc** to graduate in sthg.
laureato, -a *agg & sm, f* graduate; **è ~ in legge** he has a law degree.
lava *sf* lava.
lavaggio *sm* washing; **~ automatico** *(per auto)* car wash.
lavagna *sf* blackboard.
lavanda *sf* lavender; **fare una ~ gastrica a qn** to pump sb's stomach.
lavanderia *sf* laundry; **~ automatica** launderette; **~ a secco** dry cleaner's.
lavandino *sm* sink.
lavapiatti *sf inv* dishwasher.
lavare *vt* to wash; **~ a secco qc** to dry-clean sthg; **lavarsi le mani** to wash one's hands; **lavarsi i denti** to clean one's teeth.
◆ **lavarsi** *vr* to wash o.s.

lavasecco *sm inv o sf inv* dry cleaner's.
lavastoviglie *sf inv* dishwasher.
lavatrice *sf* washing machine.
lavorare *vi & vt* to work; ~ **a maglia** to knit.
lavorativo, -a *agg* working *(dav s)*.
lavorato, -a *agg (mobile, tessuto)* elaborate; *(terreno)* cultivated.
lavoratore, -trice *sm, f* worker.
lavorazione *sf (di legno)* carving; *(di cotone)* manufacture.
lavoro *sm* work; *(occupazione)* work, job; **'lavori in corso'** 'men at work'; **lavori stradali** road works.
le ◇ *art fpl* the, → **il** ◇ *pron (complemento oggetto)* them; *(a lei)* (to) her; *(forma di cortesia)* (to) you.
leader ['lider] *smf inv* leader.
leale *agg* loyal.
lecca lecca *sm inv* lollipop.
leccare *vt* to lick.
lecito, -a *agg* permitted.
lega, -ghe *sf (associazione)* league; *(alleanza politica)* alliance; *(di metalli)* alloy.
legale ◇ *agg* legal ◇ *smf (avvocato)* lawyer.
legalizzare *vt* to legalize.
legame *sm (sentimentale)* tie; *(nesso)* link.
legare *vt (con catena, laccio)* to tie (up); *(sog: sentimento, interesse)* to bind.
legge *sf* law.
leggenda *sf (favola)* legend; *(didascalia)* key.
leggendario, -a *agg* legendary.
leggere *vt & vi* to read.
leggerezza *sf (di materiale, corpo)* lightness; *(fig: sconsideratezza)* thoughtlessness.
leggero, -a *agg* light; *(caffè, tè)* weak; *(di poca importanza)* slight.
legittimo, -a *agg* legitimate; **legittima difesa** self-defence.
legna *sf* firewood.
legname *sm* wood.
legno *sm (materia)* wood; *(pezzo)* piece of wood, stick.
legumi *smpl* pulses.
lei *pron (soggetto)* she; *(complemento oggetto, con preposizione)* her; *(forma di cortesia)* you; **è** ~ it's her; **io sto bene, e** ~? I'm fine, and you?; ~ **stessa** she herself/you yourself.
lentamente *avv* slowly.
lente *sf* lens; ~ **di ingrandimento** magnifying glass; **lenti a contatto** contact lenses.
lentezza *sf* slowness.
lenticchie *sfpl* lentils.
lento, -a ◇ *agg* slow; *(allentato)* loose ◇ *sm* slow dance.
lenza *sf* fishing line.
lenzuolo (*pl f* **lenzuola**) *sm* sheet.
leone *sm* lion.
◆ **Leone** *sm* Leo.
leopardo *sm* leopard.
lepre *sf* hare; ~ **in salmì** *marinated hare in a sauce made from its offal.*
lesbica, -che *sf* lesbian.
lesione *sf* lesion.
lesso, -a ◇ *agg* boiled ◇ *sm* boiled beef.
letale *agg* lethal.
letame *sm* manure.
lettera *sf* letter; **alla** ~ literally.
◆ **lettere** *sfpl (facoltà)* = arts.
letteratura *sf* literature.
lettino *sm (del medico)* couch; *(per bambini)* cot.
letto, -a ◇ *pp* → **leggere** ◇ *sm* bed; **andare a** ~ to go to bed; ~ **matrimoniale** o **a due piazze** double bed; ~ **a una piazza** single bed; **letti a castello** bunk beds; **letti gemelli** twin beds.
lettore, -trice ◇ *sm, f (di libro, giornale)* reader; *(di università)* foreign language assistant ◇ *sm*: ~ **di compact** CD player.
lettura *sf* reading.
leva *sf* lever; *(militare)* conscription; **fare** ~ **su qc** *(fig)* to play on

sthg; ~ **del cambio** gear lever *(Br)*, gear shift *(Am)*.

levante *sm* east.

levare *vt (togliere)* to remove; *(alzare)* to raise.

◆ **levarsi** *vr (vento)* to get up, to rise.

levata *sf* collection.

levatoio *agg m* → **ponte**.

levigare *vt* to smooth.

lezione *sf* lesson; *(all'università)* lecture.

lezioso, -a *agg* affected.

lezzo *sm* stink.

li *pron mpl* them.

lì *avv* there; **essere ~ (~) per fare qc** to be on the point of doing sthg; **da ~ in poi** *(tempo)* from then on; *(spazio)* from that point onwards.

Libano *sm*: **il ~** Lebanon.

libeccio *sm* southwest wind.

libellula *sf* dragonfly.

liberale *agg* liberal.

liberamente *avv* freely.

liberare *vt (prigioniero)* to free, to release; *(camera, posto)* to vacate.

◆ **liberarsi** *vr (annullare un impegno)* to free o.s.; **liberarsi di** to get rid of.

libero, -a *agg* free; **essere ~ di fare qc** to be free to do sthg; **~ professionista** self-employed professional; **'libero'** *(su taxi)* 'for hire'; *(in toilette)* 'vacant'.

libertà *sf inv* freedom; *(permesso)* liberty; **mettere in ~ qn** to free sb.

Libia *sf*: **la ~** Libya.

libreria *sf (negozio)* bookshop; *(mobile)* bookcase.

libretto *sm* (MUS) libretto; **~ degli assegni** cheque book; **~ di circolazione** log book; **~ di risparmio** savings book; **~ universitario** university report card.

libro *sm* book; **~ giallo** thriller.

licenza *sf (autorizzazione)* licence; *(militare)* leave; **~ media** school-leaving certificate.

licenziamento *sm* dismissal.

licenziare *vt* to dismiss.

◆ **licenziarsi** *vr* to resign.

liceo *sm* secondary school *(Br)*, high school *(Am)*.

lido *sm* beach; **il Lido di Venezia** the Venice Lido.

lieto, -a *agg (contento)*: **~ di conoscerla!** pleased to meet you!; **molto ~!** pleased to meet you!

lievitare *vi* to rise.

lievito *sm* yeast; **~ di birra** brewer's yeast.

Liguria *sf*: **la ~** Liguria.

lillà *agg inv & sm inv* lilac.

lima *sf* file.

limetta *sf*: **~ per unghie** nail file.

limitare *vt* to limit, to restrict.

◆ **limitarsi** *vr*: **limitarsi a fare qc** to limit o.s. to do sthg; **limitarsi nel bere** to restrict one's drinking.

limitato, -a *agg* limited.

limite *sm (confine)* border; *(punto estremo)* limit; **~ di velocità** speed limit; **entro certi limiti** within certain limits; **al ~** if the worst comes to the worst.

limitrofo, -a *agg* neighbouring.

limonata *sf* lemonade.

limone *sm* lemon.

limpido, -a *agg* clear.

linea *sf* line; *(itinerario)* route; **mantenere la ~** to look after one's figure; **avere qualche ~ di febbre** to have a slight temperature; **linee urbane** local buses; **in ~ d'aria** as the crow flies; **in ~ di massima** as a general rule; **a grandi linee** in broad outline; **è caduta la ~** we have been cut off.

lineare *agg* linear.

lineetta *sf* dash.

lingua *sf* (ANAT & CULIN) tongue; *(linguaggio)* language; **~ madre** mother tongue; **~ straniera** foreign language.

linguaggio *sm* language; **~ dei segni** sign language.

linguetta *sf* tongue.
linguistico, -a, -ci, -che *agg* linguistic.
lino *sm* linen.
linoleum *sm* linoleum.
liofilizzato, -a *agg* freeze-dried.
liquefare *vt* to melt.
◆ **liquefarsi** *vr* to melt.
liquefatto, -a *pp* → **liquefare**.
liquidare *vt (società, beni)* to liquidate; *(merce)* to sell off; *(sbarazzarsi di)* to get rid of; *(fig: questione, problema)* to solve.
liquidazione *sf (di merci)* selling off, clearance; *(indennità)* severance pay.
liquido, -a ◇ *agg* liquid ◇ *sm* liquid; *(denaro)* cash.
liquirizia *sf* liquorice.
liquore *sm* liqueur.
lira *sf* lira; **non avere una ~** not to have a penny *(Br)*, not to have a dime *(Am)*.
lirica *sf* opera.
lirico, -a, -ci, -che *agg (musica)* lyric.
lisca, -sche *sf* fishbone.
liscio, -a, -sci, -sce ◇ *agg (pietra, pelle)* smooth; *(capelli)* straight; *(whisky)* neat ◇ *sm (ballo)* ballroom dance; **andar ~** to go smoothly.
lista *sf* list; **essere in ~ d'attesa** to be on a waiting list; **~ dei vini** wine list.
listino *sm*: **~ (dei) prezzi** price list; **~ dei cambi** exchange rate.
Lit *abbr* = **lira**.
lite *sf* quarrel.
litigare *vi* to quarrel.
litigio *sm* quarrel.
litorale *sm* coast.
litoraneo, -a *agg* coastal.
litro *sm* litre.
livello *sm (altezza, piano)* level; **~ del mare** sea level.
livido, -a ◇ *agg (per percosse)* black and blue ◇ *sm* bruise; **~ per il freddo** blue with cold.
lo ◇ *art* the, → **il** ◇ *pron (persona)* him; *(animale, cosa)* it; **~ so** I know.
locale ◇ *agg* local ◇ *sm (stanza)* room; *(luogo pubblico)* premises *(pl)*; **~ notturno** night club.
località *sf inv* locality.
locanda *sf* inn.
locandina *sf* theatre poster.
locomotiva *sf* locomotive.
lodare *vt* to praise.
lode *sf (elogio)* praise; **laurearsi con 110 e ~** to graduate with first-class honours *(Br)*, to graduate summa cum laude *(Am)*.
loggia, -ge *sf* loggia.
loggione *sm*: **il ~** the gods *(pl)*.
logica *sf* logic.
logico, -a, -ci, -che *agg* logical.
logorare *vt* to wear out.
◆ **logorarsi** *vr* to wear out.
logorio *sm* wear and tear.
Lombardia *sf*: **la ~** Lombardy.
lombardo, -a *agg* Lombard.
lombata *sf* loin.
lombrico, -chi *sm* earthworm.
Londra *sf* London.
longitudine *sf* longitude.
lontananza *sf (distanza)* distance; *(di persona)* absence; **in ~** in the distance.
lontano, -a ◇ *agg (luogo)* distant, faraway; *(nel tempo)* far off; *(assente)* absent; *(parente)* distant ◇ *avv* far; **è ~?** is it far?; **è ~ 3 chilometri** it's 3 kilometres from here; **~ da** far (away) from; **da ~** from far away; **più ~** farther.
loquace *agg* talkative.
lordo, -a *agg* gross.
loro *pron (soggetto)* they; *(complemento oggetto, con preposizione)* them; *(form: complemento di termine)* (to) them; **~ stessi** they themselves.
◆ **il loro** *(f* **la loro**, *mpl* **i loro**, *fpl* **le loro***)* ◇ *agg* their ◇ *pron* theirs.
losco, -a, -schi, -sche *agg* suspicious, shady.

lotta *sf* struggle, fight.
lottare *vi* to fight.
lotteria *sf* lottery.
lotto *sm (gioco)* lottery; *(di terreno)* lot.
lozione *sf* lotion.
L.P. *sm inv* LP.
lubrificante *sm* lubricant.
lucchetto *sm* padlock.
luccicare *vi* to sparkle.
lucciola *sf* glow-worm, firefly.
luce *sf* light; *(elettricità)* electricity; **dare alla ~** to give birth to; **mettere in ~ qc** to highlight sthg; **~ del sole** sunlight; **luci d'arresto** brake lights; **luci di direzione** indicators; **luci di posizione** parking lights; **film a luci rosse** porno film.
lucernario *sm* skylight.
lucertola *sf* lizard.
lucidare *vt* to polish.
lucidatrice *sf* floor polisher.
lucido, -a ◇ *agg (pavimento, tessuto)* shiny; *(fig: mente, persona)* lucid ◇ *sm (da proiettore)* acetate; **~ da scarpe** shoe polish.
lucro *sm* profit.
luganega, -ghe *sf type of sausage (a speciality of Veneto and Lombardy).*
luglio *sm* July, → **settembre**.
lugubre *agg* gloomy.
lui *pron (soggetto)* he; *(complemento oggetto, con preposizione)* him; **è ~** it's him; **~ stesso** he himself.
lumaca, -che *sf* snail.
lume *sm* lamp; **a ~ di candela** by candlelight.
luminaria *sf* illuminations *(pl)*.
luminoso, -a *agg* luminous, bright.
luna *sf* moon; **~ di miele** honeymoon; **~ park** funfair; **~ piena** full moon.
lunario *sm*: **sbarcare il ~** to make ends meet.
lunedì *sm inv* Monday, → **sabato**.
lunghezza *sf* length; **~ d'onda** wavelength.
lungo, -a, -ghi, -ghe *agg* long; *(caffè)* weak; **è ~ 3 metri** it's 3 metres long; **saperla lunga** to know what's what; **a ~** for a long time; **di gran lunga** by far; **in ~ e in largo** far and wide; **andare per le lunghe** to drag on.
lungofiume *sm* embankment.
lungolago, -ghi *sm road around a lake.*
lungomare *sm* promenade.
lunotto *sm* rear window.
luogo, -ghi *sm* place; *(di delitto, incidente)* scene; **aver ~** to take place; **dare ~ a qc** to give rise to sthg; **~ comune** commonplace; **~ di culto** place of worship; **~ di nascita** place of birth; **del ~** local; **in primo ~** in the first place.
lupini *smpl* lupins.
lupo *sm* wolf.
lurido, -a *agg* filthy.
lusinga, -ghe *sf* flattery.
lusingare *vt* to flatter.
lussare *vt* to dislocate.
Lussemburgo *sm*: **il ~** Luxembourg.
lusso *sm* luxury; **di ~** de luxe, luxury.
lussuoso, -a *agg* luxurious.
lussureggiante *agg* luxuriant.
lussuria *sf* lust.
lustrare *vt* to polish.
lustrino *sm* sequin.
lustro, -a *agg* shiny.
lutto *sm* mourning; **essere in ~** to be in mourning.

ma *cong* but.
macabro, -a *agg* macabre.
macché *esclam* of course not!
maccheroni *smpl* macaroni *(sg)*; ~ **alla chitarra** *flat ribbons of egg pasta in a sauce of either tomatoes and chillis, or lamb (a speciality of Abruzzo)*.
macchia *sf (chiazza)* spot, stain; *(di colore)* spot; *(bosco)* scrub.
macchiare *vt* to stain, to mark.
◆ **macchiarsi** *vr (persona)* to get stains o marks on one's clothes; *(abiti, tappeto)* to become stained o marked.
macchiato, -a *agg* stained.
macchina *sf (automobile)* car; *(apparecchio)* machine; **andare in** ~ to go by car, to drive; ~ **fotografica** camera; ~ **da scrivere** typewriter.
macchinario *sm* machinery.
macchinetta *sf (caffettiera)* percolator; ~ **mangiasoldi** slot machine.
macchinista, -i *sm (di treno)* driver; *(di nave)* engineer.
macedonia *sf* fruit salad.
macellaio, -a *sm, f* butcher.
macelleria *sf* butcher's.
macerie *sfpl* rubble *(sg)*.
macigno *sm* rock, boulder.
macinacaffè *sm inv* coffee grinder.
macinapepe *sm inv* pepper grinder.
macinare *vt (grano)* to mill, to grind; *(caffè, pepe)* to grind; *(carne)* to mince *(Br)*, to grind *(Am)*.
macinato, -a ◇ *agg* minced *(Br)*, ground *(Am)* ◇ *sm* mince *(Br)*, ground beef *(Am)*.
macrobiotica *sf* health foods *(pl)*.
Madonna *sf* Madonna.
madre *sf* mother.
madrelingua ◇ *agg inv* mother tongue *(dav s)* ◇ *sf* mother tongue.
madreperla *sf* mother-of-pearl.
madrina *sf* godmother.
maestrale *sm* northwest wind.
maestro, -a ◇ *sm, f* teacher ◇ *sm* (MUS) maestro; *(artigiano, artista)* master; ~ **di tennis** tennis coach.
mafia *sf* Mafia.
mafioso, -a ◇ *agg* of the Mafia, Mafia *(dav s)* ◇ *sm, f* member of the Mafia.
magari ◇ *esclam* if only! ◇ *avv* maybe.
magazzino *sm* warehouse.
maggio *sm* May; **il primo** ~ May Day, → **settembre**.
maggioranza *sf* majority; **nella** ~ **dei casi** in the majority of cases.
maggiore ◇ *agg (comparativo: più grande, più numeroso)* larger, bigger; *(di quantità)* greater; *(più*

importante) major, more important; *(più vecchio)* elder, older; *(superlativo: più grande, più numeroso)* largest, biggest; *(di quantità)* greatest *(più importante)* most important; *(più vecchio)* eldest, oldest ◇ *sm* (MIL) major; **andare per la ~** to be very popular; **la ~ età** the age of majority; **la maggior parte (di)** the majority (of).

maggiorenne ◇ *agg* of age ◇ *smf* person who has come of age.

maggiormente *avv* much more.

magia *sf* magic.

magico, -a, -ci, -che *agg* magic.

magistratura *sf* magistracy.

maglia *sf (indumento)* sweater, jersey; *(di sportivo, tessuto)* jersey; *(di catena)* link; **lavorare a ~** to knit.

maglieria *sf* knitwear.

maglietta *sf* T-shirt; *(canottiera)* vest *(Br)*, undershirt *(Am)*.

maglione *sm* sweater, jumper.

magnate *sm* magnate.

magnetico, -a, -ci, -che *agg* magnetic.

magnifico, -a, -ci, -che *agg* magnificent.

mago, -a, -ghi, -ghe *sm, f (stregone)* sorcerer (*f* sorceress); *(illusionista)* magician.

magro, -a *agg (persona)* thin; *(formaggio, yogurt)* low-fat; *(carne)* lean; *(fig: scarso)* meagre.

mai *avv* never; *(qualche volta)*: **l'hai ~ visto?** have you ever seen him?; **non ... ~** never; **~ più** never again.

maiale *sm (animale)* pig; *(carne)* pork; **~ alle mele** *pork with brandy-flavoured apple sauce.*

maiolica *sf* majolica.

maionese *sf* mayonnaise.

mais *sm* maize.

maiuscola *sf* capital letter.

maiuscolo, -a *agg* capital.

mal = **male**.

malafede *sf* bad faith.

malaga *sm*: **gelato al ~** *rum and raisin ice cream.*

malandato, -a *agg (persona)* in poor shape; *(oggetto)* shabby.

malanno *sm* ailment.

malapena : a malapena *avv* hardly, scarcely.

malato, -a ◇ *agg* ill, sick ◇ *sm, f* sick person, patient; **essere ~ di cuore** to have a bad heart.

malattia *sf* illness, disease; **essere in ~** to be on sick leave.

malavita *sf* underworld.

malconcio, -a, -ci, -ce *agg* in a sorry state.

maldestro, -a *agg (poco abile)* inept; *(impacciato, goffo)* clumsy.

maldicenza *sf* malicious gossip.

male ◇ *sm (ingiustizia)* evil; *(dolore)* pain; *(malattia)* complaint ◇ *avv* badly; **ti fa ~?** does it hurt?; **mi fanno ~ i piedi** my feet hurt; **fare del ~ a qn** to hurt sb; **non c'è ~!** not bad!; **mal d'aereo** airsickness; **mal d'auto** carsickness; **mal di gola** sore throat; **mal di mare** seasickness; **mal di stomaco** stomachache; **mal di testa** headache; **andare a ~** to go off; **restarci** o **rimanerci ~** to be disappointed; **sentirsi ~** to feel ill; **di ~ in peggio** from bad to worse.

maledetto, -a ◇ *pp* → **maledire** ◇ *agg* damned.

maledire *vt* to curse.

maledizione *sf* curse.

maleducato, -a *agg* rude.

maleducazione *sf* rudeness.

maleodorante *agg* smelly.

malessere *sm (fisico)* ailment; *(mentale)* uneasiness.

malfamato, -a *agg* notorious.

malfattore, -trice *sm, f* wrongdoer.

malfermo, -a *agg* unsteady.

malformazione *sf* malformation, deformity.

malgrado ◇ *prep* in spite of ◇ *cong* although; **mio ~** against my will.

malignità *sf inv (d'animo)* malice; *(insinuazione)* spiteful remark.

maligno, -a *agg (persona, commento)* malicious; (MED) malignant.

malinconia *sf* melancholy.

malinconico, -a, -ci, -che *agg* gloomy.

malincuore : a malincuore *avv* reluctantly.

malintenzionato, -a *agg* ill-intentioned.

malinteso *sm* misunderstanding.

malizia *sf* cunning, malice.

malizioso, -a *agg* malicious.

malleabile *agg* malleable.

malmenare *vt* to beat up.

malnutrizione *sf* malnutrition.

malore *sm*: **ho avuto un ~** I suddenly felt ill.

malridotto, -a *agg* in a bad state.

malsano, -a *agg* unhealthy.

Malta *sf* Malta.

maltagliati *smpl soup pasta, cut into irregular shapes.*

maltempo *sm* bad weather.

malto *sm* malt.

maltrattare *vt* to ill-treat.

malumore *sm* bad temper; **essere di ~** to be in a bad mood.

malvagio, -a, -gi, -gie *agg* wicked.

malvolentieri *avv* unwillingly.

mamma *sf* mum *(Br)*, mom *(Am)*; **~ mia!** my goodness!

mammella *sf (di donna)* breast; *(di animale)* udder.

mammifero *sm* mammal.

manager ['mɛnadʒer] *smf inv* manager (*f* manageress).

manata *sf* slap.

mancanza *sf (scarsità, assenza)* lack; *(colpa)* fault; **sentire la ~ di qn** to miss sb; **in ~ di** for lack of.

mancare ◇ *vi (non esserci)* to be missing; *(essere lontano)* to be away; *(form: morire)* to pass away ◇ *vt (colpo, bersaglio)* to miss; **è mancata la luce per due ore** the electricity was off for two hours; **mi manchi molto** I miss you a lot; **manca il latte** there's no milk; **mi manca il tempo** I haven't got the time; **mi mancano mille lire** I still need a thousand lire; **ci è mancato poco che cadesse** it nearly fell; **manca un quarto alle quattro** it's quarter to four.

◆ **mancare a** *v + prep (promessa)* to fail to keep.

◆ **mancare di** *v + prep* to lack.

mancia, -ce *sf* tip; **dare la ~ (a qn)** to tip (sb).

manciata *sf* handful.

mancino, -a *agg* left-handed.

manco *avv (fam)* not even; **~ per sogno** O **per idea** I wouldn't dream of it.

mandarancio *sm* clementine.

mandare *vt* to send; *(grido)* to give; **~ a chiamare qn** to send for sb; **~ via qn** to send sb away; **~ avanti qn** to send sb on ahead; **~ avanti qc** to provide for sthg; **~ giù** to swallow.

mandarino *sm* mandarin (orange), tangerine.

mandata *sf (di chiave)* turn; **chiudere a doppia ~** to double-lock.

mandato *sm* (DIR) warrant; **~ d'arresto** arrest warrant.

mandibola *sf* jaw.

mandolino *sm* mandolin.

mandorla *sf* almond.

maneggiare *vt (strumenti, attrezzi)* to handle; *(denaro)* to manage, to deal with.

maneggio *sm* riding school.

manetta *sf* handle.

◆ **manette** *sfpl* handcuffs.

mangereccio *agg m* → **fungo**.

mangiare ◇ *vt (cibo)* to eat; *(fig: patrimonio)* to squander; *(negli scacchi)* to take ◇ *vi* to eat; **far da ~** to do the cooking; **mangiarsi le parole** to mumble.

mangiasoldi *agg inv* → **macchinetta**.

mangime *sm* fodder.

mangione, -a *sm, f* glutton.

mania *sf (fissazione)* obsession; **avere la ~ di fare qc** to have a habit of doing sthg.

maniaco, -a, -ci, -che ◇ *agg* manic ◇ *sm, f* maniac.

manica, -che *sf* sleeve; **a maniche corte** O **a mezze maniche** short-sleeved.

◆ **Manica** *sf*: **la Manica, il Canale della Manica** the (English) Channel.

manicaretto *sm* delicacy.

manichino *sm (di negozio)* dummy; *(per artisti)* model.

manico, -ci *sm* handle.

manicomio *sm (ospedale)* mental hospital; *(fig: confusione)* madhouse.

manicure *sf inv (persona)* manicurist; *(trattamento)* manicure.

maniera *sf* way; **in ~ che** so that; **in ~ da fare qc** so as to do sthg; **in tutte le maniere** at all costs.

manifestare ◇ *vt* to show ◇ *vi* to demonstrate.

◆ **manifestarsi** *vr* to appear.

manifestazione *sf (corteo)* demonstration; *(di sentimento)* show; *(di malattia)* symptom; *(spettacolo)* event.

manifesto *sm (cartellone)* poster.

maniglia *sf (di porta)* handle; *(di autobus)* strap.

manipolare *vt (con le mani)* to handle; *(fig: alterare)* to manipulate.

mano, -i *sf* hand; *(di vernice)* coat; **dare una ~ a qn** to give sb a hand; **darsi la ~** to shake hands; **fatto a ~** handmade; **di seconda ~** second-hand; **man ~** gradually; **andare contro ~** to drive on the wrong side of the road; **essere alla ~** to be easygoing; **fare man bassa** to take everything; **fuori ~** out of the way; **stare con le mani in ~** to twiddle one's thumbs.

manodopera *sf (lavoratori)* workforce; *(costo)* labour.

manomesso, -a *pp* → **manomettere**.

manomettere *vt (serratura)* to force.

manopola *sf* knob, control.

manovale *sm* labourer.

manovella *sf* handle.

manovra *sf* manoeuvre.

manovrare ◇ *vt (congegno)* to operate; *(fig: persona)* to manipulate ◇ *vi* (MIL) to manoeuvre; *(fig: tramare)* to plot.

manrovescio *sm* slap.

mansarda *sf* attic.

mansione *sf* task, job.

mantella *sf* cape.

mantello *sm (di animale)* coat; *(indumento)* cloak.

mantenere *vt* to keep; *(sostentare)* to support.

◆ **mantenersi** *vr (pagarsi da vivere)* to support o.s.; *(conservarsi)* to stay, to keep.

mantenimento *sm* maintenance.

manuale *agg & sm* manual.

manubrio *sm (di bicicletta, moto)* handlebars *(pl)*; *(di congegno)* handle.

manutenzione *sf* maintenance.

manzo *sm (carne)* beef.

mappa *sf* map.

mappamondo *sm (globo)* globe; *(su carta)* map of the world.

maraschino *sm* maraschino *(cherry liqueur)*.

maratona *sf* marathon.

marca, -che *sf (di prodotto)* brand; *(scontrino)* ticket; ~ **da bollo** revenue stamp; **prodotto di ~** quality product.
marcare *vt* to mark; *(goal)* to score.
marchio *sm* mark; *(di bestiame)* brand; ~ **di fabbrica** trademark; ~ **registrato** registered trademark.
marcia, -ce *sf* march; *(di auto)* gear; (SPORT) walking; **fare ~ indietro** to reverse; **mettersi in ~** to start off.
marciapiede *sm* pavement *(Br)*, sidewalk *(Am)*; *(di stazione)* platform.
marciare *vi* to march.
marcio, -a, -ci, -ce *agg* rotten.
marcire *vi (cibo)* to rot; *(ferita)* to fester.
marco, -chi *sm* mark.
mare *sm* sea; **andare al ~** to go to the seaside; **il Mare del Nord** the North Sea.
marea *sf* tide; **alta ~** high tide; **bassa ~** low tide.
mareggiata *sf* stormy sea.
maresciallo *sm* = warrant officer.
margarina *sf* margarine.
margherita *sf* daisy.
margine *sm (di pagina)* margin; *(di strada, bosco)* edge.
marina *sf* navy.
marinaio *sm* sailor.
marinare *vt* to marinate; ~ **la scuola** to play truant.
marinaro, -a *agg (popoli, tradizioni)* seafaring; **alla marinara** cooked with seafood.
marinata *sf* marinade.
marino, -a *agg* sea *(dav s)*.
marionetta *sf* marionette.
marito *sm* husband.
maritozzo *sm type of sweet bread containing sultanas, pine kernels and candied peel (a speciality of Lazio)*.
marittimo, -a *agg (clima)* maritime; *(scalo)* coastal; **località marittima** seaside resort.
marmellata *sf* jam; *(di arance)* marmalade.
marmitta *sf (di auto, moto)* silencer; *(pentola)* large cooking pot.
marmo *sm* marble.
marocchino, -a *agg & sm, f* Moroccan.
Marocco *sm*: **il ~** Morocco.
marrone ◇ *agg inv* brown ◇ *sm (colore)* brown; *(frutto)* chestnut.
marron glacé [mar'ron gla'se] *sm inv* marron glacé *(crystallized chestnut)*.
marsala *sm inv* Marsala *(sweet fortified wine)*.
marsupio *sm (borsello)* bum bag *(Br)*, fanny pack *(Am)*; *(di animale)* pouch.
martedì *sm inv* Tuesday, → **sabato**.
martellare ◇ *vt* to hammer ◇ *vi* to throb.
martello *sm* hammer.
martini® *sm inv (vermut)* Martini; *(cocktail)* Martini cocktail.
martire *smf* martyr.
marzapane *sm* marzipan.
marziale *agg* martial.
marziano, -a *sm, f* Martian.
marzo *sm* March, → **settembre**.
mascalzone *sm* scoundrel.
mascara *sm inv* mascara.
mascarpone *sm* mascarpone *(type of cream cheese)*.
mascella *sf* jaw.
maschera *sf* mask; *(costume)* fancy dress; *(di bellezza)* face pack; *(di cinema, teatro)* usher (*f* usherette).
mascherare *vt (volto)* to mask; *(emozioni)* to conceal.
◆ **mascherarsi** *vr*: **mascherarsi (da)** to dress up (as).
maschile *agg* (GRAMM) masculine; *(sesso, anatomia)* male; *(abiti)*

men's *(dav s)*; *(per ragazzi)* boy's *(dav s)*.

maschio, -a ◇ *agg* male ◇ *sm (animale, individuo)* male; *(ragazzo, figlio, neonato)* boy; **figlio ~** son.

mascolino, -a *agg* masculine.

mascotte [ma'skɔt] *sf inv* mascot.

masochista, -i, -e *smf* masochist.

massa *sf* mass; **una ~ di** *(errori, gente)* loads of; *(mattoni, legna)* a pile of; **la ~** the masses *(pl)*; **di ~** mass *(dav s)*; **in ~** en masse.

massacro *sm* massacre.

massaggiare *vt* to massage.

massaggiatore, -trice *sm, f* masseur (*f* masseuse).

massaggio *sm* massage.

massaia *sf* housewife.

massiccio, -a, -ci, -ce ◇ *agg (corporatura)* stout, big; *(edificio)* solid; **oro ~** solid gold ◇ *sm* massif.

massima *sf (detto)* maxim; *(temperatura)* maximum temperature; **in linea di ~** generally speaking.

massimo, -a *agg & sm* maximum; **al ~** at most.

mass media *smpl* mass media.

masso *sm* rock.

masticare *vt* to chew.

mastice *sm* putty.

mastino *sm* mastiff.

matassa *sf* skein.

matematica *sf* mathematics *(sg)*.

matematico, -a, -ci, -che *agg* mathematical; *(sicuro)* certain.

materassino *sm* air bed; *(da ginnastica)* mat.

materasso *sm* mattress.

materia *sf (in fisica)* matter; *(materiale)* material; *(disciplina, argomento)* subject; **materie prime** raw materials.

materiale ◇ *agg* material ◇ *sm* material; *(attrezzatura)* equipment; **beni ~** worldly goods; **~ sintetico** man-made material.

maternità *sf inv (condizione)* motherhood; *(di ospedale)* maternity ward; **essere in ~** to be on maternity leave.

materno, -a *agg* maternal; *(paese, lingua)* mother *(dav s)*.

matita *sf* pencil.

matrigna *sf* stepmother.

matrimoniale *agg* matrimonial.

matrimonio *sm* marriage; *(cerimonia)* wedding.

mattatoio *sm* slaughterhouse.

mattina *sf* morning; **di ~** in the morning.

mattinata *sf* morning.

mattiniero, -a *agg*: **essere ~** to be an early riser.

mattino *sm* morning.

matto, -a ◇ *agg* mad ◇ *sm, f* madman (*f* madwoman); **andare ~ per** to be crazy about.

mattone *sm* brick.

mattonella *sf* tile.

maturare *vi & vt (frutta, grano)* to ripen; *(persona)* to mature.

maturità *sf (diploma, esame)* = A levels *(pl) (Br)*, = SATs *(pl) (Am)*.

maturo, -a *agg (frutto)* ripe; *(persona)* mature.

mazza *sf (bastone)* club; *(da baseball, cricket)* bat; **~ da golf** golf club.

mazzo *sm (di fiori, chiavi)* bunch; *(di carte)* pack.

me *pron* me, → **mi**.

MEC *abbr* = **Mercato Comune Europeo**.

meccanica *sf (scienza)* mechanics *(sg)*, → **meccanico**.

meccanico, -a, -ci, -che ◇ *agg* mechanical ◇ *sm* mechanic.

meccanismo *sm* mechanism.

mèche [mɛʃ] *sfpl* streaks.

medaglia *sf* medal.

medaglione *sm (gioiello)* locket; **~ di vitello** veal medallion.

medesimo, -a *agg* same.

media *sf (valore intermedio)* average; *(di voti)* average mark *(Br)*,

average grade *(Am)*; **in ~** on average; **le (scuole) medie** = secondary school *(sg) (Br)*, junior high school *(sg) (Am)*.
mediante *prep* by means of.
mediatore, -trice *sm, f* mediator; (COMM) middleman.
medicare *vt* to dress.
medicina *sf* medicine.
medicinale *sm* medicine, drug.
medico, -a, -ci, -che ◇ *agg* medical ◇ *sm* doctor; **~ di guardia** doctor on call.
medievale *agg* medieval.
medio, -a ◇ *agg* average; *(di mezzo)* middle ◇ *sm*: **(dito) ~** middle finger.
mediocre *agg* mediocre.
medioevale = **medievale**.
medioevo *sm* Middle Ages *(pl)*.
meditare ◇ *vt* to plan ◇ *vi* to meditate.
mediterraneo, -a *agg* Mediterranean.
◆ **Mediterraneo** *sm*: **il (mar) Mediterraneo** the Mediterranean (Sea).
medusa *sf* jellyfish.
megafono *sm* megaphone.
meglio ◇ *avv* 1. *(comparativo)* better; **mi sento ~ di ieri** I feel better than I did yesterday; **andare ~** to get better; **così va ~** that's better; **per ~ dire** or rather.
2. *(superlativo)* best; **è la cosa che mi riesce ~** it's the thing I do best; **le persone ~ vestite** the best-dressed people.
◇ *agg inv* 1. *(migliore)* better; **la tua macchina è ~ della mia** your car is better than mine.
2. *(in costruzioni impersonali)* better; **è ~ rimanere qui** it would be better to stay here; **è ~ che te lo dica** I'd better tell you.
◇ *sm*: **fare del proprio ~** to do one's best; **agire per il ~** to do the right thing.
◇ *sf*: **avere la ~ su qn** to get the better of sb.
mela *sf* apple.
melagrana *sf* pomegranate.
melanzana *sf* aubergine *(Br)*, eggplant *(Am)*; **melanzane alla parmigiana** *fried aubergine slices covered in tomato and Parmesan cheese.*
melenso, -a *agg* dull.
melma *sf* mud.
melo *sm* apple tree.
melodia *sf* melody.
melodramma, -i *sm* melodrama.
melone *sm* melon.
membro, -i *sm (di club, associazione)* member.
memorabile *agg* memorable.
memoria *sf* memory; **sapere qc a ~** to know sthg by heart.
mendicante *smf* beggar.
meno ◇ *avv* 1. *(in comparativi)* less; **~ di** less than; **~ vecchio (di)** younger (than); **camminate ~ in fretta** don't walk so fast; **ne voglio (di) ~** I want less; **~ lo vedo meglio sto** the less I see him, the better I feel.
2. *(in superlativi)* least; **la camera ~ cara** the cheapest room; **il ~ interessante** the least interesting; **fare il ~ possibile** to do as little as possible; **la macchina che costa ~ (di tutte)** the least expensive car (of all); **è Luca che mi preoccupa ~** Luca worries me the least.
3. *(no)*: **non so se accettare o ~** I don't know whether to accept or not.
4. *(nelle ore)*: **le nove ~ un quarto** a quarter to nine *(Br)*, a quarter of nine *(Am)*.
5. *(nelle sottrazioni, nelle temperature)* minus.
6. *(in espressioni)*: **non essere da ~ (di qn)** to be just as good (as sb); **fare a ~ di** to do without; **~ male**

(che) c'eri tu! thank goodness you were there!; **venir ~ a** *(promessa)* to break; *(impegno)* not to fulfil; **non poteva fare a ~ di urlare** he couldn't help screaming.
◇ *prep* except (for); **c'erano tutti ~ (che) lei** they were all there except (for) her; **pensa a tutto ~ che a divertirsi** enjoying himself is the last thing on his mind.
◇ *agg inv* less; **oggi c'è ~ gente** there are fewer people today.
♦ **a meno che** *cong* unless; **vengo a ~ che non piova** I'm coming unless it rains.
menopausa *sf* menopause.
mensa *sf* canteen.
mensile *agg & sm* monthly.
mensola *sf* shelf.
menta *sf* mint; *(bibita)* peppermint cordial.
mentale *agg* mental.
mentalmente *avv* mentally.
mente *sf* mind; **avere in ~ di fare qc** to be thinking of doing sthg; **imparare/sapere qc a ~** to learn/know sthg by heart; **sfuggire** o **passare di ~ a qn** to slip sb's mind; **tenere a ~ qc** to bear sthg in mind.
mentire *vi* to lie.
mento *sm* chin.
mentre *cong (temporale)* while; *(avversativa)* while, whereas.
menu *sm inv* menu.
menzionare *vt* to mention.
menzogna *sf* lie.
meraviglia *sf (stupore)* amazement; *(cosa, persona)* marvel; **a ~** perfectly.
meravigliare *vt* to amaze.
♦ **meravigliarsi di** *vr + prep* to be amazed at.
meraviglioso, -a *agg* wonderful.
mercante *sm* trader.
mercantile ◇ *agg* merchant *(dav s)* ◇ *sm (nave)* merchant ship.
mercanzia *sf* goods *(pl)*, merchandise.
mercatino *sm* local market.
mercato *sm* market; **~ dei cambi** foreign exchange market; **~ nero** black market; **a buon ~** cheap; **Mercato Comune Europeo** Common Market.
merce *sf* goods *(pl)*, merchandise.
merceria *sf* haberdasher's *(Br)*, notions store *(Am)*.
mercoledì *sm inv* Wednesday, → **sabato**.
mercurio *sm* mercury.
merda *sf & esclam (volg)* shit.
merenda *sf* afternoon snack.
meridionale ◇ *agg* southern ◇ *smf* southerner.
Meridione *sm*: **il ~** the South of Italy.
meringa, -ghe *sf* meringue.
meritare ◇ *vt* to deserve ◇ *vi* to be good; **meritarsi qc** to deserve sthg.
merito *sm (qualità)* merit; *(riconoscimento)* credit; **per ~ di qn** thanks to sb; **finire a pari ~** to tie.
merlo *sm (uccello)* blackbird; *(di mura)* battlement.
merluzzo *sm* cod.
meschino, -a *agg (spregevole)* mean.
mescolare *vt (mischiare)* to mix; *(insalata)* to toss; *(caffé)* to stir; *(mettere in disordine)* to mix up.
♦ **mescolarsi** *vr (confondersi)* to mingle.
mese *sm* month.
messa *sf* mass.
messaggio *sm* message.
Messico *sm*: **il ~** Mexico.
messinscena *sf (teatrale)* production; *(finzione)* act.
messo, -a *pp* → **mettere**.
mestiere *sm (professione)* job; *(artigianale)* craft; *(manuale)* trade.
mestolo *sm* ladle.
mestruazioni *sfpl* period *(sg)*.

meta *sf (destinazione)* destination; *(scopo)* aim, goal.

metà *sf inv (parte)* half; *(punto di mezzo)* middle; **dividere qc a ~** to divide sthg in half; **essere a ~ strada** to be halfway; **fare a ~ (con qn)** to go halves (with sb).

metabolismo *sm* metabolism.

metafora *sf* metaphor.

metallico, -a, -ci, -che *agg (di metallo)* metal *(dav s)*; *(rumore, voce)* metallic.

metallo *sm* metal.

metano *sm* methane.

meteorologico, -a, -ci, -che *agg* meteorological, weather *(dav s)*.

meticoloso, -a *agg* meticulous.

metodico, -a, -ci, -che *agg* methodical.

metodo *sm* method.

metrico, -a, -ci, -che *agg* metric.

metro *sm (unità di misura)* metre; *(nastro)* tape measure; *(a stecche)* rule; **~ cubo** cubic metre; **~ quadrato** square metre.

metronotte *sm inv* night security guard.

metropoli *sf inv* metropolis.

metropolitana *sf* underground *(Br)*, subway *(Am)*.

mettere *vt* 1. *(collocare)* to put; **~ un annuncio** to place an advert; **~ i piatti in tavola** to set the table; **~ qn alla prova** to put sb to the test; **~ i libri in ordine** to tidy (up) the books; **~ l'antenna dritta** to put the aerial straight.

2. *(indossare)*: **mettersi qc** to put sthg on; **mettersi una sciarpa** to put a scarf on, to wear a scarf; **cosa mi metto oggi?** what shall I wear today?

3. *(tempo)*: **metterci**: **ci si mette un'ora per andare** it takes an hour to get there.

4. *(dedicare)*: **~ attenzione in qc** to do sthg with care; **mettercela tutta** to do one's best.

5. *(far funzionare)* to put on; **~ gli abbaglianti** to put one's headlights on full beam.

6. *(suscitare)*: **~ appetito a qn** to make sb hungry; **~ paura a qn** to scare sb.

7. *(supporre)*: **mettiamo che non venga** let's suppose he doesn't come.

8. *(in espressioni)*: **~ avanti/indietro l'orologio** to put the clock forward/back; **~ in chiaro qc** to clear sthg up; **~ in dubbio qc** to cast doubt on sthg; **mettersi in testa di fare qc** to get it into one's head to do sthg; **~ insieme** to put together.

◆ **mettersi** *vr* 1. *(porsi)*: **mettiti a sedere qui** sit here; **mettersi a tavola** to sit down to eat; **mettersi nei guai** to get into trouble.

2. *(vestirsi)*: **mettersi in pigiama** to put one's pyjamas on.

3. *(cominciare)*: **mettersi a fare qc** to start doing sthg; **s'è messo a gridare** he started screaming; **mettersi in viaggio** to set off.

4. *(in espressioni)*: **mettersi d'accordo** to agree; **mettersi bene/male** to turn out well/badly; **mettersi con qn** *(in società)* to go into partnership with sb; *(in coppia)* to go out with sb.

mezza *sf*: **la ~** *(mezzogiorno e mezzo)* half-past twelve.

mezzaluna (*pl* **mezzelune**) *sf (parte di luna)* half moon; *(coltello)* chopping blade; *(islamica)* crescent.

mezzanino *sm* mezzanine floor.

mezzanotte *sf* midnight.

mezzo, -a ◇ *agg* half ◇ *sm (metà)* half; *(parte centrale)* middle; *(strumento, procedimento)* means; *(veicolo)* vehicle ◇ *avv*: **~ pieno** half-full; **~ chilo** half a kilo; **~ litro** half a litre; **mezza pensione** half board; **abiti di mezza stagione**

spring/autumn clothes; **a mezze maniche** short-sleeved; **di mezza età** middle-aged; **quello di ~** the one in the middle, the middle one; **per ~ di** by means of; **le cinque e mezza** o **~** half-past five; **non vuole andarci di ~** he doesn't want to get involved; **fare a ~ (con qn)** to share (with sb); **levarsi** o **togliersi di ~** to get out of the way; **mezzi di comunicazione (di massa)** (mass) media; **mezzi pubblici** public transport *(sg)*; **mezzi di trasporto** means of transport.

◆ **mezzi** *smpl (economici)* means.

mezzogiorno *sm (ora)* midday, noon.

◆ **Mezzogiorno** *sm*: **il Mezzogiorno** Southern Italy.

mezzora *sf* half an hour.

mi (*diventa* **me** *se precede lo, la, li, le, ne*) *pron (complemento oggetto)* me; *(complemento di termine)* (to) me; *(riflessivo)* myself; **me li dai?** will you give them to me?

miagolare *vi* to miaow.

mica *avv (fam)*: **non ci avrai ~ creduto?** you didn't believe it, did you?; **non sono ~ scemo!** I'm not stupid, am I!; **~ male** not bad (at all).

miccia, -ce *sf* fuse.

micidiale *agg (mortale)* deadly; *(dannoso)* murderous; *(insopportabile)* unbearable.

micosi *sf inv* (MED) fungus.

microfono *sm* microphone.

microscopio *sm* microscope.

midolla *sf (mollica)* crumb.

midollo (*pl f* **midolla**) *sm* marrow.

mie → **mio**.

miei → **mio**.

miele *sm* honey.

migliaio (*pl f* **migliaia**) *sm* thousand; **un ~ (di persone)** about a thousand (people); **a migliaia** by the thousand.

miglio *sm (unità di misura: pl f* **miglia***)* mile; *(pianta)* millet.

miglioramento *sm* improvement.

migliorare ◇ *vt* to improve ◇ *vi (tempo, situazione)* to improve; *(malato)* to get better.

migliore *agg (comparativo)* better; **il/la ~** *(superlativo)* the best.

mignolo *sm* little finger *(Br)*, pinkie *(Am)*; *(del piede)* little toe.

mila *pl* → **mille**.

milanese ◇ *agg* Milanese ◇ *smf* person from Milan.

Milano *sf* Milan.

miliardo *sm* thousand million *(Br)*, billion *(Am)*.

milione *sm* million.

militare ◇ *agg* military ◇ *sm* serviceman; **fare il ~** to do one's military service.

mille (*pl* **mila**) *num* a o one thousand, → **sei**.

millefoglie *sm inv* millefeuille *(Br)*, napoleon *(Am)*.

millennio *sm* millennium.

millepiedi *sm inv* millipede.

millesimo, -a *num* thousandth, → **sesto**.

millimetro *sm* millimetre.

milza *sf* spleen.

mimare *vt* to mime.

mimetizzare *vt* to camouflage.

◆ **mimetizzarsi** *vr (animali, piante)* to camouflage o.s.

mimo *sm* mime.

mimosa *sf* mimosa.

min. *(abbr di minimo, di minuto)* min.

mina *sf (esplosiva)* mine; *(di matita)* lead.

minaccia, -ce *sf* threat.

minacciare *vt* to threaten; **~ di fare qc** to threaten to do sthg.

minaccioso, -a *agg* threatening, menacing.

minatore *sm* miner.

minerale *agg & sm* mineral.
minestra *sf* soup; ~ **in brodo** noodle broth; ~ **di verdure** vegetable soup.
minestrone *sm* minestrone.
miniatura *sf* miniature.
miniera *sf* mine.
minigolf *sm* minigolf.
minigonna *sf* miniskirt.
minima *sf* minimum temperature.
minimizzare *vt* to minimize.
minimo, -a ◇ *agg (il più piccolo)* slightest, least; *(il più basso)* lowest; *(molto piccolo)* very small, slight ◇ *sm (parte più piccola)* minimum; *(di motore)* idling speed; **come** ~ at the very least.
ministero *sm (settore amministrativo)* ministry.
ministro *sm* minister; ~ **degli Esteri** Foreign Secretary *(Br)*, Secretary of State *(Am)*.
minoranza *sf* minority; **essere in** ~ to be in a minority.
minore ◇ *agg (comparativo: di età)* younger; *(di grandezza)* smaller; *(di importanza)* minor; *(numero)* lower; *(grado)* lesser; *(superlativo: di età)* youngest; *(di grandezza)* smallest; *(di importanza)* least important; *(di numero)* lowest ◇ *smf (minorenne)* minor.
minorenne *smf* minor.
minuscola *sf* small letter.
minuscolo, -a *agg (scrittura)* small; *(molto piccolo)* tiny.
minuto, -a ◇ *agg (persona, corpo)* small; *(piccolo)* tiny, minute; *(fine)* fine ◇ *sm (unità)* minute.
mio (*f* **mia**, *mpl* **miei**, *fpl* **mie**) ◇ *agg*: **il** ~ **(la mia)** my ◇ *pron*: **il** ~ **(la mia)** mine; ~ **padre** my father; **un** ~ **amico** a friend of mine; **questa bici è mia** this bike is mine.
miope *agg* short-sighted.
mira *sf* aim; **prendere la** ~ to take aim; **prendere di** ~ **qc** *(fig)* to pick on sb.
miracolo *sm* miracle.
miraggio *sm* mirage.
mirare *vi*: ~ **a** to aim at.
miriade *sf* multitude; **una** ~ **di** a multitude of.
mirtillo *sm* blueberry.
miscela *sf (miscuglio)* mixture; *(di caffè)* blend; *(benzina)* petrol and oil mixture.
mischia *sf* brawl; *(nel rugby)* scrum.
mischiare *vt* to mix; ~ **le carte** to shuffle the cards.
◆ **mischiarsi** *vr* to mix.
miseria *sf* (extreme) poverty; *(quantità insufficiente)*: **è costato una** ~ it cost next to nothing; **porca** ~! *(volg: accidenti)* damn!, bloody hell!
misericordia *sf* mercy.
misero, -a *agg (povero)* poor, poverty-stricken; *(infelice)* wretched, miserable; *(insufficiente)* miserable.
missile *sm* missile.
missionario, -a *sm, f* missionary.
missione *sf* mission.
misterioso, -a *agg* mysterious.
mistero *sm* mystery.
misto, -a ◇ *agg* mixed ◇ *sm* mixture; **insalata mista** mixed salad; ~ **lana** woollen blend; ~ **cotone** cotton blend.
misura *sf (unità, provvedimento)* measure; *(dimensione)* measurement; *(taglia)* size; *(moderazione)* moderation; **prendere le misure di qc** to measure sthg; **su** ~ made-to-measure.
misurare ◇ *vt* to measure; *(abito)* to try on; *(vista)* to test ◇ *vi* to measure.
◆ **misurarsi con** *vr + prep* to compete with.
misurino *sm* measure.
mite *agg* mild.
mito *sm* myth.

mitra *sm inv* submachine gun.
mitragliatrice *sf* machine gun.
mittente *smf* sender.
mobile ◇ *agg* movable ◇ *sm* piece of furniture; **mobili** *(mobilia)* furniture *(sg)*.
mobilia *sf* furniture.
mobilitare *vt* to mobilize.
moca *sf inv* coffee machine.
mocassino *sm* mocassin.
moda *sf* fashion; **essere** O **andare di ~** to be in fashion; **passare di ~** to go out of fashion; **alla ~** fashionable; **di ~** fashionable.
modellare *vt* to model.
modellino *sm* model.
modello, -a ◇ *sm, f* model ◇ *sm* model; *(per sarta)* pattern; *(modulo)* form.
modem *sm inv* modem.
moderare *vt* to moderate.
moderato, -a *agg* moderate.
moderno, -a *agg* modern.
modestia *sf* modesty.
modesto, -a *agg* modest.
modico, -a, -ci, -che *agg* low.
modifica, -che *sf* alteration.
modo *sm* way; *(opportunità)* chance; *(GRAMM: verbale)* mood; **a ~ mio** in my way; **in ~ da fare qc** so as to do sthg; **~ di dire** expression; **di ~ che** so that; **in nessun ~** in no way; **in ogni ~** anyway; **in qualche ~** in some way; **in tutti i modi** in every way.
modulazione *sf*: **~ di frequenza** frequency modulation.
modulo *sm* form.
moglie, -gli *sf* wife.
mole *sf (dimensione)* massive shape; *(quantità)*: **una ~ di lavoro** masses of work.
molestare *vt* to annoy.
molesto, -a *agg* annoying.
molla *sf (meccanica)* spring.
◆ **molle** *sfpl (per camino, ghiaccio)* tongs.
mollare ◇ *vt (allentare)* to slacken; *(lasciar andare)* to let go; *(fam: fidanzato)* to ditch ◇ *vi (desistere)* to give in; **~ un ceffone a qn** *(fam: dare uno schiaffo)* to slap sb.
molle *agg (morbido)* soft; *(fig: persona)* weak.
molletta *sf (per capelli)* hair grip; *(per panni)* clothes peg.
mollica, -che *sf* crumb.
molo *sm (di porto)* jetty.
molteplice *agg (complesso)* complex.
◆ **molteplici** *agg pl (numerosi)* numerous, various.
moltiplicare *vt* to multiply.
moltiplicazione *sf* (MAT) multiplication; *(accrescimento)* increase.
moltitudine *sf* multitude.
molto, -a ◇ *agg* **1.** *(in grande quantità)* a lot of, much; **non ho ~ tempo** I don't have (very) much time; **hai molta fame?** are you very hungry? **2.** *(di numero elevato)*: **molti(-e)** a lot of, many; **ci sono molti turisti** there are a lot of tourists.
◇ *pron* a lot, much; **molti** *(molta gente)* many (people); **molti di noi** many of us.
◇ *avv* **1.** *(con verbi)* a lot, (very) much; **mi piace ~** I like it a lot O very much.
2. *(con aggettivi, avverbi)* very; *(con participio passato)* much; **è ~ simpatica** she's very nice; **è ~ meglio così** it's much better like this; **è ~ presto/tardi** it's very early/late; **~ volentieri!** certainly!
momentaneamente *avv* at the moment.
momentaneo, -a *agg* momentary.
momento *sm* moment; *(circostanza)* time; **all'ultimo ~** at the last moment; **da un ~ all'altro** *(tra poco)* (at) any moment; **dal ~ che** since; **per il ~** for the time being; **a momenti** *(tra poco)* soon; *(quasi)* nearly.

monaca, -che *sf* nun.
monaco, -ci *sm* monk.
monarchia *sf* monarchy.
monastero *sm (di monaci)* monastery; *(di monache)* convent.
mondano, -a *agg (di società)* society *(dav s)*; *(terreno)* earthly.
mondiale *agg* world *(dav s)*.
mondo *sm* world.
moneta *sf (di metallo)* coin; *(valuta)* currency; ~ **spicciola** change.
monetario, -a *agg* monetary.
monolocale *sm* studio flat *(Br)*, studio apartment *(Am)*.
monopattino *sm* scooter.
monopolio *sm* monopoly.
monoscì *sm inv* monoski.
monotono, -a *agg (ripetitivo)* monotonous; *(noioso)* dull.
montacarichi *sm inv* goods lift.
montagna *sf* mountain; *(zona)* the mountains *(pl)*; **andare in ~** to go to the mountains; **montagne russe** roller coaster *(sg)*.
montanaro, -a *sm, f* mountain dweller.
montano, -a *agg* mountain *(dav s)*.
montare ◇ *vi (salire)* to go up; *(cavalcare)* to ride ◇ *vt (congegno)* to assemble; *(cavallo, pietra preziosa)* to mount; *(panna)* to whip; *(albumi)* to whisk; *(fecondare)* to cover; ~ **in macchina** to get into a car; ~ **in treno** to get on a train; **montarsi la testa** to become bigheaded.
montatura *sf (di occhiali)* frames *(pl)*; *(di gioiello)* setting.
monte *sm* mountain; **andare a ~** to come to nothing; **mandare a ~ qc** to upset sthg; ~ **premi** prize money; **il Monte Bianco** Mont Blanc.
montone *sm (animale)* ram; *(carne)* mutton; *(giaccone)* sheepskin jacket.
montuoso, -a *agg* mountainous.
monumento *sm* monument.
mora *sf (commestibile)* blackberry; *(del gelso)* mulberry; (DIR) default.
morale ◇ *agg* moral ◇ *sf* morals *(pl)*; *(insegnamento)* moral ◇ *sm* morale; **essere giù di ~** to be feeling down.
morbido, -a *agg* soft.
morbillo *sm* measles *(sg)*.
morbo *sm* disease.
morboso, -a *agg* morbid.
mordere *vt* to bite.
morfina *sf* morphine.
moribondo, -a *agg* dying.
morire *vi* to die; *(estinguersi)* to die out; ~ **di fame** to die of hunger; ~ **di noia** to die of boredom; ~ **dal ridere** to kill o.s. laughing; **bello da ~** stunning.
mormorare ◇ *vi (bisbigliare)* to whisper; *(sparlare)* to gossip ◇ *vt* to murmur.
moro, -a *agg* dark.
morso, -a ◇ *pp* → **mordere** ◇ *sm* bite; *(di briglia)* bit.
mortadella *sf* Mortadella *(large pork sausage served cold in thin slices)*.
mortale ◇ *agg* mortal; *(letale)* deadly ◇ *sm* mortal.
mortalità *sf* mortality.
morte *sf* death; **avercela a ~ con qn** to have it in for sb.
mortificare *vt* to mortify.
morto, -a ◇ *pp* → **morire** ◇ *agg* dead ◇ *sm, f* dead man (*f* dead woman); **fare il ~** *(nell'acqua)* to float on one's back.
mosaico, -ci *sm* mosaic.
mosca, -sche *sf* fly; ~ **cieca** blind man's buff.
Mosca *sf* Moscow.
moscato *sm* muscatel *(sweet wine)*.
moscerino *sm* gnat.
moschettone *sm* spring clip.
moscone *sm (insetto)* bluebottle; *(imbarcazione)* pedalo.

mossa *sf* movement; *(negli scacchi)* move.

mosso, -a ◇ *pp* → **muovere** ◇ *agg (mare)* rough; *(capelli)* wavy; *(fotografia)* blurred.

mostarda *sf* mustard.

mostra *sf* exhibition; **mettersi in ~** to draw attention to o.s.; **in ~** on show; **la Mostra del cinema di Venezia** Venice Film Festival.

mostrare *vt* to show.

◆ **mostrarsi** *vr* to look; **mostrarsi in pubblico** to appear in public.

mostro *sm* monster.

mostruoso, -a *agg (orrendo)* monstrous; *(feroce)* ferocious; *(smisurato)* incredible.

motel *sm inv* motel.

motivo *sm (causa)* reason; *(di stoffa)* pattern; *(musicale)* tune; **per quale ~?** for what reason?; **senza ~** without a reason.

moto ◇ *sm (in fisica)* motion; *(movimento)* movement; *(esercizio fisico)* exercise ◇ *sf inv* motorbike; **mettere in ~** (AUTO) to start.

motocicletta *sf* motorcycle.

motocross *sm* motocross.

motore *sm* motor, engine; **a ~** motor *(dav s)*.

motorino *sm* moped; **~ d'avviamento** starter.

motoscafo *sm* motorboat.

motto *sm* maxim.

mousse [mus] *sf inv* mousse.

movimentare *vt* to liven up.

movimento *sm (attività)* activity.

mozzafiato *agg inv* breathtaking.

mozzare *vt* to cut off; **~ il fiato a qn** to take sb's breath away.

mozzarella *sf* mozzarella *(a round fresh cheese from Naples made from cow's or buffalo's milk)*; **~ in carrozza** *mozzarella sandwiched between two slices of bread, then dipped in egg and fried.*

mozzicone *sm* stub.

mozzo, -a ◇ *agg* cut off ◇ *sm* ship's boy.

mucca, -che *sf* cow.

mucchio *sm (cumulo)* heap; **un ~ di** *(fig: grande quantità)* loads of.

muffa *sf* mould.

muffole *sfpl* mittens.

mugolare *vi* to whine.

mulattiera *sf* mule track.

mulatto, -a *agg & sm, f* mulatto.

mulinello *sm (vortice)* whirl; *(da pesca)* reel.

mulino *sm* mill; **~ a vento** windmill.

mulo *sm* mule.

multa *sf* fine.

multare *vt* to fine.

multiplo, -a *agg & sm* multiple.

multiproprietà *sf inv* timeshare.

mungere *vt* to milk.

municipale *agg* municipal.

municipio *sm* town hall.

munire *vt*: **~ qn/qc di qc** to equip sb/sthg with sthg.

◆ **munirsi di** *vr + prep* to equip o.s. with.

muovere *vt* to move; *(critica, accusa)* to make.

◆ **muoversi** *vr* to move; *(fam: sbrigarsi)* to hurry up, to get a move on.

mura *sfpl* walls.

murare *vt* to wall up.

muratore *sm* bricklayer.

murena *sf* moray eel.

muro *sm* wall.

muscolare *agg* muscular, muscle *(dav s)*.

muscolo *sm* muscle; **muscoli** *(forza)* brawn *(sg)*.

muscoloso, -a *agg* muscular.

museo *sm* museum.

museruola *sf* muzzle.

musica *sf* music; **~ classica** classical music; **~ leggera** light music.

musicale *agg* musical.
musicista, -i, -e *smf* musician.
muso *sm (di animale)* muzzle; *(fam & spreg: di persona)* mug; *(di auto)* front end; *(aereo)* nose; **tenere il ~** to sulk.
muta *sf (da sub)* wet suit; *(di cani)* pack.
mutamento *sm* change.
mutande *sfpl* pants.
mutandine *sfpl* knickers.
mutare *vt & vi* to change.
mutazione *sf* change; *(genetica)* mutation.
mutilato, -a *sm, f person who has lost a limb*; **~ di guerra** disabled ex-serviceman *(Br)*, disabled war veteran *(Am)*.
muto, -a *agg* dumb; *(silenzioso)* silent; *(cinema, consonante)* silent.
mutua *sf* = National Health Service.
mutuo, -a ◇ *agg* mutual ◇ *sm* loan; *(per casa)* mortgage.

N *(abbr di nord)* N.
nafta *sf (olio combustibile)* fuel oil; *(gasolio)* diesel oil.
naftalina *sf* mothballs *(pl)*.
nailon® *sm* nylon.
nanna *sf (fam)*: **andare a ~** to go to beddy-byes.
nano, -a *agg & sm, f* dwarf.
napoletana *sf a type of coffee percolator.*
napoletano, -a *agg & sm, f* Neapolitan.
Napoli *sf* Naples.
narice *sf* nostril.
narrare *vt* to tell.
narrativa *sf* fiction.
nasale *agg* nasal.
nascere *vi* to be born; *(pianta)* to come up; *(sole)* to rise; *(fiume)* to have its source; *(dente)* to come through; *(attività, impresa)* to start up; **sono nata il 31 luglio del 1965** I was born on the 31st of July 1965.
◆ **nascere da** *v + prep* to arise from.
nascita *sf (di bambino, animale)* birth; *(di attività, movimento)* start; **data di ~** date of birth; **luogo di ~** place of birth.
nascondere *vt* to hide; *(dissimulare)* to hide, to conceal.
◆ **nascondersi** *vr* to hide.
nascondino *sm* hide and seek.
nascosto, -a ◇ *pp* → **nascondere** ◇ *agg* hidden; **di ~** secretly.
naso *sm* nose; **ficcare il ~ in qc** to poke one's nose into sthg.
nastro *sm* ribbon; **~ adesivo** adhesive tape; **~ trasportatore** conveyor belt.
Natale *sm* Christmas.
natalità *sf* birth rate.
natante *sm* craft.
nato, -a ◇ *pp* → **nascere** ◇ *agg (fig: per natura)* born; **nata Mattei** *(da nubile)* née Mattei.
NATO *sf* NATO.
natura *sf* nature; **~ morta** still life.
naturale *agg* natural.
naturalmente *avv* naturally; *(certamente sì)* naturally, of course.
naufragare *vi (nave)* to be wrecked; *(persona)* to be shipwrecked.
naufragio *sm* shipwreck.
naufrago, -a, -ghi, -ghe *sm, f* shipwrecked person.
nausea *sf* nausea.
nauseante *agg* nauseating.
nauseare *vt* to make sick.
nautico, -a, -ci, -che *agg* nautical.
navale *agg* naval.
navata *sf* nave.
nave *sf* ship; **~ passeggeri** passenger ship; **~ traghetto** ferry.

navetta *sf* shuttle; ~ **(spaziale)** space shuttle.
navigabile *agg* navigable.
navigare *vi (nave)* to sail; *(persona)* to navigate.
navigazione *sf* navigation.
naviglio *sm (nave)* vessel; *(canale)* canal.
nazionale ◇ *agg* national ◇ *sf (squadra)* national team.
nazionalità *sf inv* nationality.
nazione *sf* nation.
ne ◇ *pron* 1. *(di lui)* of/about him; *(di lei)* of/about her; *(di loro)* of/about them; ~ **apprezzo l'onestà** I value his honesty.
2. *(di un insieme)* of it, of them; **ha dei panini? – ~ vorrei due** have you got any rolls? – I'd like two (of them).
3. *(di ciò)* about it; **non parliamone più** let's not talk about it any more; **non ~ ho idea** I've no idea.
4. *(da ciò)*: ~ **deriva che ...** it follows that ...
◇ *avv (di là)* from there; ~ **veniamo proprio ora** we've just come from there.
né *cong*: **né ... né** neither ... nor; ~ **l'uno ~ l'altro sono italiani** neither of them are Italian; **non si è fatto ~ sentire ~ vedere** I haven't heard from him or seen him; **non voglio ~ il primo ~ il secondo** I don't want either the first one or the second.
neanche *cong & avv* not even; **non ... ~** not even ...; ~ **io lo conosco** I don't know him either; **non ho mangiato – ~ io** I haven't eaten – neither have I O I haven't either; ~ **per sogno** O **per idea!** not on your life!
nebbia *sf* fog.
nebulizzatore *sm* spray.
necessariamente *avv* necessarily.
necessario, -a ◇ *agg* necessary ◇ *sm* necessities *(pl)*; **è ~ farlo** it must be done; ~ **per toeletta** toiletries *(pl)*.
necessità *sf inv (bisogno)* necessity.
necessitare : necessitare di *v + prep* to need, to require.
necrologio *sm (annuncio)* obituary.
negare *vt* to deny; *(rifiutare)*: ~ **qc (a qn)** to refuse (sb) sthg; ~ **di aver fatto qc** to deny having done sthg.
negativo, -a *agg & sm* negative.
negato, -a *agg*: **essere ~ per qc** to be hopeless at sthg.
negli = **in + gli**, → **in**.
negligente *agg* negligent.
negoziante *smf* shopkeeper.
negozio *sm* shop; ~ **di giocattoli** toy shop.
negro, -a *agg & sm, f* black.
nei = **in + i**, → **in**.
nel = **in + il**, → **in**.
nell' = **in + l'**, → **in**.
nella = **in + la**, → **in**.
nelle = **in + le**, → **in**.
nello = **in + lo**, → **in**.
nemico, -a, -ci, -che ◇ *agg (esercito, stato)* enemy *(dav s)*; *(ostile)* hostile ◇ *sm, f* enemy.
nemmeno = **neanche**.
neo *sm* mole.
neofascismo *sm* neofascism.
neon *sm* neon.
neonato, -a *sm, f* newborn baby.
neozelandese ◇ *agg* New Zealand *(dav s)* ◇ *smf* New Zealander.
neppure = **neanche**.
nero, -a ◇ *agg (colore)* black; *(scuro)* dark; *(pane)* wholemeal ◇ *sm* black.
nervo *sm* nerve; **dare ai** O **sui nervi a qc** to get on sb's nerves.
nervosismo *sm* nervousness.
nervoso, -a ◇ *agg* nervous ◇ *sm*: **avere il ~** to be on edge.
nespola *sf* medlar.

nessuno, -a ◇ *agg* no ◇ *pron (non una persona)* nobody, no one; *(non una cosa)* none; *(qualcuno)*: **c'è ~?** is anybody in?; **nessuna città è bella quanto Roma** there's no city more beautiful than Rome; **non c'è nessun posto libero** there aren't any free seats; **da nessuna parte** nowhere; **~ lo sa** nobody knows; **non ho visto ~** I didn't see anybody; **~ di noi** none of us; **~ dei due** neither of them; **non me ne piace ~** I don't like any of them.

nettezza *sf*: **~ urbana** refuse department.

netto, -a *agg (preciso)* clear; *(deciso)* definite; *(peso, stipendio)* net.

netturbino *sm* dustman.

neutrale *agg* neutral.

neutralizzare *vt* to neutralize.

neutro, -a ◇ *agg* neutral; **essere ~** *(imparziale)* to be neutral ◇ *sm (in linguistica)* neuter.

neve *sf* snow.

nevicare *v impers* to snow; **nevica** it's snowing.

nevicata *sf* snowfall.

nevischio *sm* sleet.

nevralgia *sf* neuralgia.

nevrotico, -a, -ci, -che *agg* neurotic.

nicchia *sf* niche.

nicotina *sf* nicotine.

nido *sm* nest.

niente ◇ *pron* 1. *(nessuna cosa)* nothing; **non ... ~** nothing; **non faccio ~ la domenica** I do nothing on Sundays, I don't do anything on Sundays; **~ di ~** nothing at all; **grazie! – di ~!** thank you – not at all.

2. *(qualcosa)* anything; **le serve ~?** do you need anything?; **non per ~, ma ...** not that it matters, but ...

3. *(poco)*: **da ~** *(cosa)* not important; *(persona)* worthless.

◇ *agg inv (fam: nessuno)*: **non ha ~ buon senso** he has no common sense; **~ paura!** never fear!

◇ *avv*: **non ... ~** not ... at all; **non me ne importa ~** I couldn't care less; **questo non c'entra ~** this doesn't come into it at all; **non fa ~** it doesn't matter; **ti piace? – per ~!** do you like it? – not at all!

◇ *sm*: **basta un ~ per farlo contento** the slightest thing makes him happy; **un bel ~** nothing at all.

nientemeno ◇ *avv* no less, actually ◇ *esclam* you don't say!

night(-club) ['nait(-'klab)] *sm inv* nightclub.

Nilo *sm*: **il ~** the Nile.

ninnananna *sf* lullaby.

ninnolo *sm* knick-knack.

nipote *smf (di zii)* nephew (*f* niece); *(di nonni)* grandson (*f* granddaughter).

nitido, -a *agg* well-defined.

nitrire *vi* to neigh.

no *avv* no; **c'eri anche tu, ~?** you were there too, weren't you?; **lo sai, ~, com'è fatto** you know, don't you, what he's like?; **lo vuoi o ~?** do you want it or not?; **~ di certo** certainly not; **perché ~?** why not?

nobile *agg & smf* noble.

nobiltà *sf (aristocrazia)* nobility; *(di animo, azione)* nobleness.

nocciola ◇ *sf* hazelnut ◇ *agg inv* hazel.

nocciolina *sf*: **~ (americana)** peanut.

nocciolo[1] *sm (di frutto)* stone.

nocciolo[2] *sm (albero)* hazel.

noce *sf & sm* walnut; **~ di cocco** coconut; **~ moscata** nutmeg.

nocivo, -a *agg* harmful.

nodo *sm* knot; **avere un ~ alla gola** to have a lump in one's throat.

noi *pron (soggetto)* we; *(complemento oggetto, con preposizione)* us; **da ~** *(nel nostro paese)* in our country; **~**

stessi we ourselves.

noia *sf (tedio)* boredom; *(fastidio)* nuisance; **gli è venuto a ~** he's tired of it; **dar ~ a qn** to annoy sb; **avere delle noie con** to have trouble with.

noioso, -a *agg (monotono)* boring; *(fastidioso)* annoying.

noleggiare *vt (prendere a nolo)* to hire; *(dare a nolo)* to hire out.

noleggio *sm* hire *(Br)*, rental; **prendere qc a ~** to hire sthg.

nolo = **noleggio**.

nome *sm* name; (GRAMM) noun; **conoscere qn di ~** to know sb by name; **a ~ di qn** on behalf of sb; **~ di battesimo** Christian name; **~ da ragazza** maiden name.

nominare *vt (menzionare)* to mention; *(eleggere)* to appoint.

non *avv* not, → **affatto, ancora** *ecc.*

nonché *cong (e anche)* as well as; *(tanto meno)* let alone.

noncurante *agg*: **~ (di)** indifferent (to).

nondimeno *cong* nevertheless, however.

nonno, -a *sm, f* grandfather (*f* grandmother).

nonnulla *sm inv*: **un ~** a trifle.

nono, -a *num* ninth, → **sesto**.

nonostante ◇ *prep* in spite of ◇ *cong* although.

non vedente *smf* blind person.

nord ◇ *sm* north ◇ *agg inv* north, northern; **a ~ (di)** north (of); **nel ~** in the north.

nordest *sm* northeast.

nordico, -a, -ci, -che *agg* Nordic.

nordovest *sm* northwest.

norma *sf* rule; **di ~** as a rule; **a ~ di legge** according to the law.

normale *agg* normal.

normalità *sf* normality.

normanno, -a *agg* Norman.

norvegese *agg, smf & sm* Norwegian.

Norvegia *sf*: **la ~** Norway.

nostalgia *sf* nostalgia; **avere ~ di casa** O **di paese** to be homesick.

nostro, -a ◇ *agg*: **il ~ (la nostra)** our ◇ *pron*: **il ~ (la nostra)** ours; **~ padre** our father; **un ~ amico** a friend of ours; **questa casa è nostra** it's our house.

nota *sf* note; *(conto)* bill; *(elenco)* list; **prendere ~ (di qc)** to make a note (of sthg).

notaio *sm* notary public.

notare *vt (osservare, accorgersi di)* to notice; *(annotare)* to note down; **farsi ~** to get o.s. noticed.

notevole *agg (differenza, prezzo)* considerable; *(persona)* remarkable.

notificare *vt (form)* to notify.

notizia *sf (informazione)* news *(sg)*, piece of news; **le ultime notizie** the latest news; **avere notizie di qn** to hear from sb.

notiziario *sm* news *(sg)*.

noto, -a *agg* well-known; **rendere ~ qc a qn** to make sthg known to sb.

nottambulo, -a *sm, f* night bird.

notte *sf* night; **di ~** at night; **una ~ in bianco** a sleepless night.

notturno, -a *agg* night *(dav s)*; **animale ~** nocturnal animal.

novanta *num* ninety, → **sei**.

novantesimo, -a *num* ninetieth, → **sesto**.

nove *num* nine, → **sei**.

novecento *num* nine hundred, → **sei**.

◆ **Novecento** *sm*: **il Novecento** the twentieth century.

novella *sf* short story.

novembre *sm* November, → **settembre**.

novità *sf inv (cosa nuova)* something new; *(fatto, notizia recente)* (piece of) news *(sg)*; **le ~ musicali** the latest releases.

nozione *sf* notion, idea; **nozioni** *(di matematica, francese)* rudiments.

nozze *sfpl* wedding *(sg)*; ~ **d'oro** golden wedding.

nube *sf* cloud.

nubifragio *sm* rainstorm.

nubile *agg* single.

nuca, -che *sf* nape of the neck.

nucleare *agg* nuclear.

nucleo *sm (di cellula, atomo)* nucleus; *(di persone)* group; *(di soldati, polizia)* squad; ~ **familiare** family unit.

nudismo *sm* nudism.

nudista, -i, -e *smf* nudist.

nudo, -a ◇ *agg (persona)* naked; *(parete)* bare; **mettere a ~ qc** to lay sthg bare ◇ *sm* (ARTE) nude.

nugolo *sm*: **un ~ di** a host of.

nulla = **niente**.

nullità *sf inv (di ragionamento, documento)* nullity; *(persona)* nobody.

nullo, -a *agg (non valido)* (null and) void; (SPORT) drawn.

numerale *agg & sm* numeral.

numerare *vt* to number.

numero *sm* (MAT: *quantità)* number; *(segno, cifra)* numeral; *(di scarpe)* size; *(di rivista)* issue; ~ **civico** house number; ~ **chiuso** selective entry system; ~ **di conto** account number; ~ **di targa** numberplate; ~ **di telefono** telephone number; ~ **verde** = freefone number *(Br)*, = toll-free number *(Am)*; **dare i numeri** *(fig)* to be off one's head.

numeroso, -a *agg (molteplice)* numerous; *(grande)* large.

numismatica *sf* numismatics *(sg)*.

nuocere : nuocere a *v + prep* to harm.

nuora *sf* daughter-in-law.

nuotare *vi* to swim.

nuoto *sm* swimming.

nuovamente *avv* again.

Nuova Zelanda *sf*: **la ~** New Zealand.

nuovo, -a *agg* new; **di ~** again; ~ **di zecca** brand-new.

nuraghe, -ghi *sm prehistoric stone monument in Sardinia.*

nutriente *agg* nutritious.

nutrimento *sm* nourishment.

nutrire *vt (con cibo)* to feed; *(fig: sentimento)* to feel.

◆ **nutrirsi di** *vr + prep* to feed on.

nuvola *sf* cloud; **cascare dalle nuvole** to be flabbergasted.

nuvoloso, -a *agg* cloudy.

O

o *cong* or; ~ ... ~ either ... or.
O *(abbr di ovest)* W.
oasi *sf inv* oasis.
obbediente = **ubbidiente**.
obbedire = **ubbidire**.
obbligare *vt*: ~ **qn a fare qc** to force sb to do sthg.
obbligato, -a *agg (percorso, passaggio)* fixed; *(costretto)*: ~ **a fare qc** obliged to do sthg.
obbligatorio, -a *agg* compulsory.
obbligo, -ghi *sm* obligation; **avere l'~ di fare qc** to be obliged to do sthg.
obelisco, -schi *sm* obelisk.
obeso, -a *agg* obese.
obiettare *vt* to object.
obiettivo, -a ◇ *agg* objective ◇ *sm (fotografico)* lens; *(bersaglio, scopo)* objective.
obiettore *sm* objector; ~ **di coscienza** conscientious objector.
obiezione *sf* objection.
obitorio *sm* mortuary.
obliquo, -a *agg* slanting.
obliterare *vt* to stamp.
oblò *sm inv* porthole.
obsoleto, -a *agg* obsolete.
oca (*pl* **oche**) *sf* goose.
occasione *sf (momento favorevole)* opportunity; *(affare)* bargain; *(causa, circostanza)* occasion; **avere ~ di fare qc** to have the chance to do sthg; **cogliere l'~ per fare qc** to take the opportunity to do sthg; **d'~** second-hand.
occhiaie *sfpl* bags, rings.
occhiali *smpl*: ~ **(da vista)** glasses; ~ **da sole** sunglasses.
occhiata *sf*: **dare un'~ a** to have a look at.
occhiello *sm* buttonhole.
occhio *sm* eye; **a ~ nudo** with the naked eye; **tenere** O **non perdere d'~ qn/qc** to keep an eye on sb/sthg; **a ~ e croce** roughly; **costare un ~ della testa** to cost a fortune; **saltare** O **balzare all'~** to be obvious; **a quattr'occhi** in private; **sognare a occhi aperti** to daydream.
occhiolino *sm*: **fare l'~ (a qn)** to wink (at sb).
occidentale *agg (zona)* west, western; *(cultura, società)* Western.
occidente *sm* west.
◆ **Occidente** *sm*: **l'Occidente** the West.
occorrente *sm* everything necessary.
occorrenza *sf*: **all'~** if need be.
occorrere *vi* to be necessary; **occorre aspettare** you/we have to wait; **mi occorre tempo** I need time.
occorso, -a *pp* → **occorrere**.
occulto, -a *agg* occult.

occupare *vt (ingombrare)* to take up; *(paese, università)* to occupy; *(impegnare)* to keep busy.
◆ **occuparsi di** *vr + prep (prendersi cura di)* to take care of, to look after; *(impicciarsi in)* to interfere in; *(interessarsi di)*: **si occupa di politica** he's in politics; **occupati dei fatti tuoi!** mind your own business!
occupato, -a *agg (sedia, posto)* taken; *(telefono, bagno)* engaged; *(impegnato)* busy.
occupazione *sf (impiego)* occupation; *(in economia)* employment.
Oceania *sf*: **l'~** Oceania.
oceano *sm* ocean.
oculista, -i, -e *smf* eye specialist.
odiare *vt* to hate.
odio *sm* hatred.
odioso, -a *agg* hateful, odious.
odorare *vt* to smell.
◆ **odorare di** *v + prep* to smell of.
odorato *sm* (sense of) smell.
odore *sm* smell.
◆ **odori** *(da cucina) smpl* herbs.
offendere *vt* to offend.
◆ **offendersi** *vr* to take offence.
offensivo, -a *agg* offensive.
offerto, -a ◇ *pp* → **offrire** ◇ *sf (proposta)* offer; *(donazione)* donation; (FIN) supply; **~ speciale** special offer.
offesa *sf* offence.
offeso, -a ◇ *pp* → **offendere** ◇ *agg* offended.
officina *sf (di fabbrica)* workshop; *(per auto)* garage.
offrire *vt* to offer; *(cena, caffè)* to pay for; **~ da bere a qn** to buy sb a drink.
◆ **offrirsi di** *vr + prep*: **offrirsi di fare qc** to offer to do sthg.
offuscare *vt (luce)* to darken; *(vista, mente, memoria)* to dim.
◆ **offuscarsi** *vr (vista)* to dim.
oggettivo, -a *agg* objective.
oggetto *sm* object; **(ufficio) oggetti smarriti** lost property (office) *(Br)*, lost-and-found office *(Am)*.
oggi *avv* today; *(attualmente)* nowadays; **~ pomeriggio** this afternoon; **il giornale di ~** today's newspaper; **dall'~ al domani** from one day to the next.
oggigiorno *avv* nowadays.
ogni *agg inv (tutti)* every, each; *(distributivo)* every; **gente di ~ tipo** all sorts of people; **~ giorno/mese/anno** every day/month/year; **~ tre giorni** every three days; **in ~ caso** in any case; **ad ~ modo** anyway; **~ tanto** every so often; **~ volta che** whenever.
Ognissanti *sm* All Saints' Day.
ognuno, -a *pron* everyone, everybody; **~ di voi** each of you.
Olanda *sf*: **l'~** Holland.
olandese ◇ *agg & sm* Dutch ◇ *smf* Dutchman (*f* Dutchwoman); **gli olandesi** the Dutch.
oleoso, -a *agg* oily.
olfatto *sm* sense of smell.
oliare *vt* to oil.
oliera *sf* oil and vinegar cruet.
olimpiadi *sfpl*: **le ~** the Olympic Games.
olio *sm* oil; **~ (extra-vergine) d'oliva** (extra-virgin) olive oil; **~ di semi** vegetable oil; **sott'~** in oil.
oliva *sf* olive; **olive farcite all'anconetana** *olives stuffed with meat and vegetables, then covered in breadcrumbs and fried.*
olivastro, -a *agg (carnagione)* sallow.
olivo *sm* olive tree.
olmo *sm* elm.
oltraggio *sm* (DIR) offence.
oltralpe : d'oltralpe *agg* on the other side of the Alps.
oltranza : a oltranza *avv* to the (bitter) end.

oltre ◇ *prep (di là da)* beyond; *(più di)* over, more than; *(in aggiunta a)* as well as, besides ◇ *avv (più in là)* further; ~ **a** *(all'infuori di)* apart from; *(in aggiunta a)* as well as; **non ~ le cinque** no later than five o'clock.

oltrepassare *vt* to go beyond.

omaggio *sm (tributo)* homage; *(regalo)* gift; **in ~** *(con prodotto)* free.

ombelico, -chi *sm* navel.

ombra *sf (zona)* shade; *(figura)* shadow; **all'~** in the shade.

ombrello *sm* umbrella.

ombrellone *sm* beach umbrella.

ombretto *sm* eye shadow.

omeopatia *sf* homeopathy.

omesso, -a *pp* → **omettere**.

omettere *vt* to omit; **~ di fare qc** to omit to do sthg.

omicidio *sm* murder.

omissione *sf* omission.

omogeneizzato *sm* baby food.

omogeneo, -a *agg (uniforme)* homogeneous; *(armonico)* harmonious.

omonimo, -a *sm, f (persona)* namesake.

omosessuale *smf* homosexual.

On. *(abbr di onorevole)* Hon.

onda *sf* wave; **andare in ~** to go on the air; **mandare in ~ qc** to broadcast sthg; **onde lunghe/medie/corte** long/medium/short wave *(sg)*; **'onde pericolose'** *sign warning swimmers to take care.*

ondata *sf* wave; **a ondate** in waves.

ondulato, -a *agg (terreno)* undulating; *(capelli)* wavy; *(lamiera, carta)* corrugated.

onere *sm (form)* burden; **oneri fiscali** (DIR) taxes.

onestà *sf* honesty.

onesto, -a *agg* honest.

onnipotente *agg* omnipotent.

onomastico *sm* name day.

onorare *vt (celebrare)* to honour; *(fare onore a)* to do credit to.

onorario, -a ◇ *agg (cittadinanza, console)* honorary ◇ *sm* fee.

onore *sm* honour; **fare ~ a qc** *(pranzo)* to do justice to sthg; *(scuola, famiglia)* to be a credit to sthg; **in ~ di** in honour of; **fare gli onori di casa** to be the host (*f* hostess); **farsi ~** to distinguish o.s.

onorevole ◇ *agg (parlamentare)* Honourable ◇ *smf* = Member of Parliament *(Br)*, = Congressman (*f* Congresswoman) *(Am)*.

ONU *(abbr di Organizzazione delle Nazioni Unite)* UN.

opaco, -a, -chi, -che *agg (vetro)* opaque; *(colore, metallo)* dull.

opera *sf* work; *(in musica)* opera; **è tutta ~ sua!** it's all his doing!; **mettersi all'~** to get down to work; **~ d'arte** work of art; **opere pubbliche** public works.

operaio, -a ◇ *agg* working-class ◇ *sm, f* worker.

operare ◇ *vt (realizzare)* to carry out; (MED) to operate on ◇ *vi (agire)* to act.

◆ **operarsi** *vr (compiersi)* to take place; *(subire un'operazione)* to have an operation.

operatore, -trice *sm, f (di televisione, cinema)* cameraman (*f* camerawoman); **~ turistico** tour operator.

operazione *sf* operation; (FIN) transaction.

opinione *sf* opinion; **l'~ pubblica** public opinion.

opporre *vt (argomenti, ragioni)* to put forward; **~ resistenza** to put up some resistance; **~ un rifiuto** to refuse.

◆ **opporsi** *vr*: **opporsi (a)** to oppose.

opportunità *sf inv* opportunity.

opportuno, -a *agg* opportune.

opposizione *sf* opposition.

opposto, -a ◇ *pp* → **opporre** ◇ *agg (lato, senso)* opposite; *(idee)* opposing ◇ *sm* opposite.

oppressione *sf* oppression.

oppresso, -a *pp* → **opprimere**.

opprimente *agg* oppressive.

opprimere *vt (popolo)* to oppress; *(angosciare)* to weigh down.

oppure *cong (o invece)* or; *(se no)* or else, otherwise.

optare : **optare per** *v + prep* to opt for.

opuscolo *sm* brochure.

ora ◇ *sf* hour; *(momento)* time ◇ *avv* now; **a che ~ parte il treno?** what time does the train leave?; **è ~ di partire** it's time to leave; **che ~ è?, che ore sono?** what's the time?; **e ~?** now what?; **~ come ~** right now; **~ legale** summertime; **~ locale** local time; **~ di punta** rush hour; **50 km all'~** 50 km an hour; **di buon'~** early; **d'~ in poi** O **in avanti** from now on; **fare le ore piccole** to stay up till the small hours.

orale *agg & sm* oral.

oramai → **ormai**.

orario, -a ◇ *agg (segnale)* time *(dav s)*; *(velocità)* per hour; *(tariffa)* hourly ◇ *sm (di lavoro, visite)* hours *(pl)*; *(tabella)* timetable; **fuori ~** after hours; **in ~** on time; **~ di arrivo** arrival time; **~ di partenza** departure time; **~ di apertura** opening hours *(pl)*; **~ di chiusura** closing time; **~ d'ufficio** office hours *(pl)*.

orata *sf* sea bream.

orbita *sf (di satellite)* orbit; *(di occhio)* eye socket.

orchestra *sf* orchestra.

ordigno *sm* device.

ordinare *vt (al ristorante, bar)* to order; *(disporre in ordine)* to put in order; *(comandare)*: **~ a qn di fare qc** to order sb to do sthg.

ordinario, -a *agg (normale)* ordinary; *(mediocre, scadente)* poor.

ordinato, -a *agg* tidy.

ordinazione *sf* order.

ordine *sm* order; **essere in ~** *(stanza)* to be tidy; *(documenti)* to be in order; **mettere in ~ qc** *(stanza)* to tidy sthg; *(documenti)* to put sthg in order; **~ pubblico** public order.

orecchiabile *agg* catchy.

orecchiette *sfpl tiny ear-shaped pasta from Puglia.*

orecchino *sm* earring.

orecchio (*pl f* **orecchie**) *sm* ear; **avere ~** to have a good ear (for music).

orecchioni *smpl* mumps *(sg)*.

oreficeria *sf (negozio)* jeweller's.

orfano, -a *agg & sm, f* orphan.

organico, -a, -ci, -che ◇ *agg* organic ◇ *sm* staff.

organismo *sm (essere vivente)* organism; *(ente)* body.

organizzare *vt* to organize.

◆ **organizzarsi** *vr* to organize o.s.

organizzato, -a *agg* organized.

organizzatore, -trice *sm, f* organizer.

organizzazione *sf* organization.

organo *sm* organ.

orgasmo *sm* orgasm.

orgoglio *sm* pride.

orgoglioso, -a *agg* proud.

orientale ◇ *agg (paese, prodotto)* eastern; *(persona)* oriental ◇ *smf* Oriental.

orientamento *sm (posizione)* orientation; *(fig: indirizzo)* leanings *(pl)*; **perdere l'~** to lose one's bearings; **~ professionale** careers guidance.

orientare *vt (carta)* to orientate.

◆ **orientarsi** *vr* to find one's bearings.

oriente *sm* east.

◆ **Oriente** *sm*: **l'Oriente** the East.

origano *sm* oregano.

originale ◇ *agg* original; *(stravagante)* eccentric ◇ *sm* original.
originario, -a *agg (iniziale)* original; *(paese, lingua)* native.
origine *sf* origin; *(causa)* origin, cause; **avere ~ da qc** to originate from sthg; **dare ~ a qc** to cause sthg; **di ~ italiana** of Italian origin.
origliare *vi* to eavesdrop.
orina = **urina**.
oriundo, -a *sm, f*: **essere ~ italiano** to be of Italian extraction.
orizzontale *agg* horizontal.
orizzonte *sm* horizon.
orlo *sm (di fosso)* edge; *(di bicchiere)* rim; *(di gonna, pantaloni)* hem.
orma *sf* footprint.
ormai *avv (a questo punto)* by now; *(a quel punto)* by then; *(quasi)* almost; **~ è tardi** it's too late now.
ormeggiare *vt & vi* to moor.
ormeggio *sm* mooring.
ormone *sm* hormone.
ornamento *sm* ornament.
ornare *vt* to decorate.
oro *sm* gold; **d'~** gold.
orologio *sm* clock; *(da polso)* watch.
oroscopo *sm* horoscope.
orrendo, -a *agg (spaventoso, atroce)* horrendous; *(brutto)* horrible, awful.
orribile *agg* horrible.
orrore *sm* horror.
orsacchiotto *sm* teddy bear.
orso *sm* bear.
ortaggio *sm* vegetable.
ortica, -che *sf* nettle.
orticaria *sf* hives *(pl)*.
orto *sm* vegetable garden.
ortodosso, -a *agg* orthodox.
ortografia *sf* spelling.
orzaiolo *sm* stye.
orzo *sm* barley.
osare *vt*: **~ (fare qc)** to dare (to do sthg).
osceno, -a *agg* obscene.
oscillare *vi (dondolare)* to swing; *(fig: variare)* to vary.
oscillazione *sf (di pendolo)* swing; *(di prezzi)* fluctuation; *(di temperatura)* variation.
oscurità *sf* darkness.
oscuro, -a ◇ *agg* dark ◇ *sm*: **essere all'~ di qc** to be in the dark about sthg.
ospedale *sm* hospital.
ospitale *agg (persona)* hospitable; *(paese)* friendly.
ospitalità *sf* hospitality; **mi ha dato ~ per una notte** he put me up for a night.
ospitare *vt* to put up.
ospite *smf (chi ospita)* host (*f* hostess); *(ospitato)* guest.
ospizio *sm* old people's home.
ossa *pl* → **osso**.
osseo, -a *agg* bone *(dav s)*.
osservare *vt (guardare)* to observe, to watch; *(rilevare)* to notice; *(rispettare, mantenere)* to observe; **far ~ qc a qn** to point sthg out to sb.
osservatorio *sm* observatory.
osservazione *sf (esame)* observation; *(commento)* observation, remark; *(rimprovero)* criticism.
ossessionare *vt* to obsess.
ossessione *sf* obsession.
ossia *cong* that is.
ossidare *vt* to oxidize.
◆ **ossidarsi** *vr* to oxidize.
ossido *sm* oxide; **~ di carbonio** carbon monoxide.
ossigenare *vt* to oxygenate; *(capelli)* to bleach.
ossigeno *sm* oxygen.
osso *sm (umano: pl f* **ossa***)* bone; *(di carne: pl m* **ossi***)* bone.
ossobuco (*pl* **ossibuchi**) *sm veal knuckle cooked on the bone in tomatoes and white wine (a speciality of Milan)*.
ostacolare *vt* to obstruct.

ostacolo *sm* obstacle; *(in atletica)* hurdle; *(in equitazione)* fence.
ostaggio *sm* hostage.
ostello *sm*: ~ **(della gioventù)** (youth) hostel.
ostentare *vt* to flaunt.
osteria *sf* inn.
ostetrica, -che *sf* midwife.
ostia *sf* (RELIG) host.
ostile *agg* hostile.
ostilità ◇ *sf* hostility ◇ *sfpl* (MIL) hostilities.
ostinarsi *vr*: ~ **a fare qc** to persist in doing sthg.
ostinato, -a *agg* obstinate.
ostinazione *sf* persistence.
ostrica, -che *sf* oyster.
ostruire *vt* to obstruct, to block.
ottanta *num* eighty, → **sei**.
ottantesimo, -a *num* eightieth, → **sesto**.
ottantina *sf*: **una** ~ **(di)** about eighty; **essere sull'**~ to be in one's eighties.
ottavo, -a *num* eighth, → **sesto**.
ottenere *vt* to get.
ottico, -a, -ci, -che ◇ *agg* *(nervo)* optic; *(strumento)* optical ◇ *sm* optician.
ottimale *agg* optimum.
ottimismo *sm* optimism.
ottimista, -i, -e *smf* optimist.
ottimo, -a *agg* excellent, very good.
otto ◇ *num* eight, → **sei** ◇ *sm*: ~ **volante** roller coaster.
ottobre *sm* October, → **settembre**.
ottocento *num* eight hundred, → **sei**.
◆ **Ottocento** *sm*: **l'Ottocento** the nineteenth century.
ottone *sm* brass.
otturare *vt* to fill.
otturazione *sf* filling.
ottuso, -a *agg* obtuse.
ovale *agg* oval.
ovatta *sf* cotton wool.
overdose *sf inv* overdose.
ovest *sm & agg inv* west; **a** ~ **(di qc)** west (of sthg).
ovile *sm* sheepfold.
ovino, -a *agg* sheep *(dav s)*.
ovovia *sf* ski lift *(with oval cabins)*.
ovunque = **dovunque**.
ovvero *cong* or, in other words.
ovviare *vi*: ~ **a qc** to avoid sthg.
ovvio, -a *agg* obvious.
ozio *sm* idleness.
ozono *sm* ozone.

P

pacato, -a *agg* calm.

pacca, -che *sf* pat.

pacchetto *sm (di sigarette, caramelle)* packet; *(pacco)* parcel.

pacchiano, -a *agg* garish.

pacco, -chi *sm* parcel.

pace *sf* peace; **in ~** in peace; **fare (la) ~** to make it up.

pacemaker [pei'smɛker] *sm inv* pacemaker.

pacifico, -a, -ci, -che *agg* peaceful.

◆ **Pacifico** *sm*: **il Pacifico** the Pacific.

pacifista, -i, -e *agg & smf* pacifist.

padella *sf (da cucina)* frying pan; *(per malati)* bedpan.

padiglione *sm (di ospedale, fiera)* pavilion; *(di giardino)* marquee.

Padova *sf* Padua.

padre *sm* father.

padrino *sm* godfather.

padrone, -a *sm, f* owner; **essere ~ di fare qc** to be free to do sthg; **~ di casa** landlord (*f* landlady).

paesaggio *sm* landscape; *(panorama)* scenery.

paese *sm (nazione)* country; *(villaggio)* village; **~ di provenienza** country of origin; **mandare qn a quel ~** *(volg)* to tell sb to get lost.

◆ **Paesi Bassi** *smpl*: **i Paesi Bassi** the Netherlands.

paffuto, -a *agg* plump, chubby.

paga, -ghe *sf* pay.

pagamento *sm* payment; '**~ pedaggio**' 'toll to be paid here'.

pagano, -a *agg & sm, f* pagan.

pagare *vt* to pay; *(offrire)* to buy; **quanto l'hai pagato?** how much did you pay for it?; **~ con assegno** to pay by cheque; **~ con carta di credito** to pay by credit card; **~ in contanti** to pay cash.

pagella *sf* (school) report.

pagina *sf* page.

paglia *sf* straw.

pagliaccio *sm* clown.

pagnotta *sf* round loaf.

paio (*pl f* **paia**) *sm* pair; **un ~ di** *(alcuni)* a couple of; **un ~ di scarpe** a pair of shoes.

Pakistan *sm*: **il ~** Pakistan.

pala *sf (vanga)* shovel; *(di mulino, elica)* blade.

palato *sm* palate.

palazzo *sm (signorile)* palace; *(edificio)* building; *(condominio)* block of flats *(Br)*, apartment building *(Am)*; **~ di giustizia** law courts *(pl)*; **~ dello sport** indoor stadium.

palco, -chi *sm (palcoscenico)* stage; *(pedana)* stand; *(a teatro)* box.

palcoscenico, -ci *sm* stage.

Palermo *sf* Palermo.

Palestina *sf*: **la ~** Palestine.

palestra *sf* gymnasium.

paletta *sf (giocattolo, per giardiniere)* spade; *(per lo sporco)* dustpan; *(di polizia, capostazione)* signalling disc.
paletto *sm* stake.
palio *sm*: **mettere qc in ~** to offer sthg as a prize.
◆ **Palio** *sm*: **il Palio (di Siena)** the Palio *(traditional horse race held in the centre of Siena)*.
palla *sf* ball; **che palle!** *(volg)* what a drag!
pallacanestro *sf* basketball.
pallanuoto *sf* water polo.
pallavolo *sf* volleyball.
pallido, -a *agg* pale.
palloncino *sm* balloon.
pallone *sm (palla)* ball; *(da calcio)* football; **~ aerostatico** hot air balloon.
pallottola *sf* bullet.
palma *sf* palm tree.
palmo *sm* palm.
palo *sm (di legno)* post; *(di telefono)* pole; **~ della luce** lamppost.
palombaro *sm* (deep sea) diver.
palpebra *sf* eyelid.
palude *sf* marsh, swamp.
panca, -che *sf* bench.
pancarrè *sm* sliced bread.
pancetta *sf* bacon.
panchina *sf (di parco)* bench; *(di giardino)* garden seat.
pancia, -ce *sf (fam)* belly.
panciotto *sm* waistcoat.
panda *sm inv* panda.
pandoro *sm conical sponge cake eaten at Christmas.*
pane *sm* bread; *(pagnotta)* loaf; *(di burro)* block; **~ a** O **in cassetta** sliced bread; **~ integrale** wholemeal bread; **~ tostato** toast; **pan dolce** *Christmas cake with candied fruit (a speciality of Genoa)*; **pan di Spagna** sponge cake.
panetteria *sf* bakery.
panettone *sm traditional dome-shaped Christmas cake containing raisins and candied fruit.*
panforte *sm very rich round, flat cake made with almonds, hazelnuts, candied fruits and spices (a speciality of Siena).*
pangrattato *sm* breadcrumbs *(pl)*.
panico *sm* panic.
panificio *sm* baker's.
panino *sm* roll; **~ imbottito** O **ripieno** filled roll; **~ al prosciutto** ham roll.
paninoteca, -che *sf* sandwich bar.
panna *sf*: **~ (montata)** whipped cream; **~ cotta** *cold dessert made from cream and sugar, eaten with chocolate or fruit sauce*; **~ da cucina** cream.
panne : **in panne** *agg inv*: **ho l'auto in ~** my car has broken down.
pannello *sm* panel.
panno *sm* cloth; **mettersi nei panni di qn** to put o.s. in sb's shoes.
pannocchia *sf* cob.
pannolino *sm* nappy *(Br)*, diaper *(Am)*.
panorama, -i *sm* panorama.
panoramico, -a, -ci, -che *agg* panoramic.
panpepato *sm* = gingerbread.
pantaloni *smpl* trousers *(Br)*, pants *(Am)*.
pantera *sf* panther.
pantofole *sfpl* slippers.
panzanella *sf Tuscan salad of tomatoes, anchovies, tuna, onion and herbs, whose special ingredient is moistened bread.*
panzerotti *smpl large ravioli stuffed with cheese and tomato, and fried in oil.*
paonazzo, -a *agg* purple.
papa, -i *sm*: **il ~** the Pope.
papà *sm inv (fam)* daddy, dad.
papavero *sm* poppy.
papera *sf (errore)*: **fare una ~** to

make a slip of the tongue, → **papero**.

papero, -a *sm, f* gosling.

papillon [papi'jɔn] *sm inv* bow tie.

pappa *sf (fam)* baby food.

pappagallo *sm (animale)* parrot; *(per malati)* bedpan.

pappardelle *sfpl* large noodles; ~ **alla lepre** *'pappardelle' served with hare sauce.*

paprica *sf* paprika.

para *sf* crepe rubber.

parabola *sf* (MAT) parabola; (RELIG) parable.

parabrezza *sm inv* windscreen.

paracadute *sm inv* parachute.

paracarro *sm* post.

paradiso *sm* (RELIG) paradise, heaven.

paradossale *agg* paradoxical.

paradosso *sm* paradox.

parafango, -ghi *sm* mudguard.

parafulmine *sm* lightning conductor.

paraggi *smpl*: **nei** ~ in the neighbourhood.

paragonare *vt*: ~ **con** to compare with.

paragone *sm* comparison.

paragrafo *sm* paragraph.

paralisi *sf inv* paralysis.

paralizzare *vt* to paralyse.

parallela *sf* parallel.

◆ **parallele** *sfpl (attrezzo)* parallel bars.

parallelo, -a *agg & sm* parallel.

paralume *sm* lampshade.

parapetto *sm* parapet.

parare *vt (colpi)* to parry; *(occhi)* to shield; *(nel calcio)* to save.

parassita, -i *sm* parasite.

parata *sf (militare)* parade; *(nel calcio)* save.

paraurti *sm inv* bumper.

paravento *sm* screen.

parcella *sf* fee.

parcheggiare *vt* to park.

parcheggio *sm (area)* car park *(Br)*, parking lot *(Am)*; *(manovra)* parking; ~ **a pagamento** *car park where drivers must pay to park*; ~ **riservato** private car park.

parchimetro *sm* parking meter.

parco, -chi *sm* park; ~ **giochi** o **dei divertimenti** swing park.

parecchio, -a ◇ *agg* quite a lot of ◇ *pron* quite a lot ◇ *avv (con agg)* quite; *(con verbo)* quite a lot; **è ~ (tempo) che aspetto** I've been waiting for quite a while.

pareggiare ◇ *vt (capelli, orlo)* to make even; *(terreno)* to level; *(bilancio, conti)* to balance ◇ *vi* to draw.

pareggio *sm (in partite)* draw; *(del bilancio)* balance.

parente *smf* relative.

parentela *sf (vincolo)* relationship; *(famiglia)* relatives *(pl)*.

parentesi *sf inv (segno)* bracket; *(commento)* digression; **tra** ~ in brackets.

pareo *sm* pareo.

parere ◇ *sm (opinione)* opinion ◇ *vi (sembrare)* to seem; *(apparire)* to look ◇ *v impers*: **pare che** it seems that; **che te ne pare?** what do you think?; **fate come vi pare** do as you like; **mi pare di no** I don't think so; **mi pare di sì** I think so; **mi pare (che) vada bene** it seems (to be) all right; **pare (che) sia vero** it seems (to be) true.

parete *sf (di stanza)* wall; *(di montagna)* face.

pari ◇ *agg inv (in partite, giochi, superficie)* level; *(numero)* even ◇ *sm inv* equal; **alla** ~ *(ragazza)* au pair; **ora siamo** ~ now we're even; **essere ~ a** *(uguale)* to be the same as, to be equal to; **essere alla** ~ to be even; **mettersi in ~ con qc** to catch up with sthg; ~ ~ word for word.

Parigi *sf* Paris.

parlamentare ◇ *agg* parliamentary ◇ *smf* = Member of Parliament *(Br)*, = Congressman (*f* Congresswoman) *(Am)*.

parlamento *sm* parliament.

parlantina *sf (fam)*: **avere una buona ~** to have the gift of the gab.

parlare ◇ *vi* to talk, to speak ◇ *vt (lingua)* to speak; **~ (a qn) di** to talk o to speak (to sb) about; **parla italiano?** do you speak Italian?

Parma *sf* Parma.

parmigiano *sm* Parmesan (cheese).

parola *sf* word; **prendere la ~** to (begin to) speak; **rivolgere la ~ a qn** to talk to sb; **rimangiarsi la ~** to go back on one's word; **~ d'onore** word of honour; **~ d'ordine** password; **parole crociate** crossword (puzzle) *(sg)*; **è una ~!** it's not easy!

parolaccia, -ce *sf* swearword.

parrocchia *sf (chiesa)* parish church; *(zona)* parish.

parroco, -ci *sm* parish priest.

parrucca, -che *sf* wig.

parrucchiere, -a *sm, f (per signora)* hairdresser.

parso, -a *pp* → **parere**.

parte *sf* part; *(lato)* side; *(direzione)* way; *(quota)* share; (DIR) party; **fare ~ di qc** to be part of sthg; **mettere da ~ qc** *(risparmiare)* to put sthg aside; **prendere ~ a qc** to take part in sthg; **stare dalla ~ di** to be on the side of; **la maggior ~ di** most of; **la maggior ~ degli italiani** most Italians; **a ~ questo** apart from that; **a ~** *(spese, pacco)* separate; *(pagare, incartare)* separately; **da ~ di qn** from; *(ringraziare)* on sb's behalf; **d'altra ~** on the other hand; **dall'altra ~** the other way; **da nessuna ~** nowhere; **da ogni ~** everywhere; **da qualche ~** somewhere; **da questa ~** this way; **in ~** partly.

partecipare : partecipare a *v + prep (intervenire)* to take part in; *(spese)* to contribute to; *(gioia, dolore)* to share in.

partenza *sf* departure; *(nello sport)* start; **essere in ~ (per Roma)** to be about to leave (for Rome); **'partenze nazionali/internazionali'** 'domestic/international departures'.

participio *sm* participle.

particolare ◇ *agg* particular; *(caratteristico)* distinctive ◇ *sm* detail; **niente di ~** nothing special; **in ~** in particular.

particolareggiato, -a *agg* detailed.

partigiano, -a *sm, f* partisan.

partire *vi (persona)* to leave; *(treno, aereo)* to depart; *(nello sport)* to start; *(colpo)* to go off; **a ~ da** from; **parto da Milano alle cinque** I leave Milan at five.

partita *sf (competizione)* match; *(a carte, a tennis)* game; *(di merce)* consignment; **~ IVA** VAT registration number.

partito *sm* party.

parto *sm* birth.

partorire *vt* to give birth to.

parziale *agg (limitato)* partial; *(ingiusto)* biased.

pascolo *sm* pasture.

Pasqua *sf* Easter.

pasquale *agg* Easter *(dav s)*.

Pasquetta *sf* Easter Monday.

passabile *agg* passable.

passaggio *sm (transito)* passage; *(varco)* thoroughfare; *(in macchina)* lift; *(cambiamento)* change; **essere di ~** to be passing through; **~ a livello** level crossing *(Br)*, grade crossing *(Am)*; **~ pedonale** pedestrian crossing.

passamontagna *sm inv* balaclava.

passante ◇ *smf (persona)* passer-by ◇ *sm (per cintura)* loop.

passaporto *sm* passport.

passare ◇ *vi* to go by; *(da*

un'apertura) to go through; *(fare una visita)* to call in; *(cessare)* to go away; *(proposta)* to be passed ◇ *vt (attraversare)* to cross; *(trascorrere)* to spend; *(cera, vernice)* to apply; *(esame)* to pass; *(oltrepassare)* to go beyond; *(verdure)* to puree; *(porgere)* to pass; **mi è passato di mente!** it slipped my mind!; **ti passo Matteo** *(al telefono)* here's Matteo; **il treno passa da Firenze** the train goes via Florence; ~ **l'aspirapolvere** to vacuum; ~ **qc a qn** to pass o to give sb sthg; ~ **avanti a qn** to push in front of sb; ~ **da** o **per scemo** to be taken for a fool; ~ **sopra qc** *(fig: tollerare)* to overlook; **passarsela bene** to get on well; **come te la passi?** how are you getting on?

passatempo *sm* pastime.

passato, -a ◇ *agg (trascorso)* over ◇ *sm* past; ~ **di verdure** thin vegetable soup.

passaverdura *sm inv* vegetable mill.

passeggero, -a ◇ *agg* passing ◇ *sm, f* passenger.

passeggiare *vi* to walk.

passeggiata *sf (camminata)* walk; *(strada)* promenade; **fare una** ~ to take a walk.

passeggino *sm* pushchair.

passeggio *sm*: **andare a** ~ to go for a walk.

passerella *sf (passaggio)* footbridge; *(di aereo, nave)* gangway; *(di sfilata)* catwalk.

passerotto *sm* sparrow.

passione *sf* passion.

passivo, -a ◇ *agg* passive ◇ *sm* (GRAMM) passive; (COMM) liabilities *(pl)*.

passo *sm (movimento)* step; *(andatura)* pace; *(rumore)* footstep; *(valico)* pass; **allungare il** ~ to quicken one's pace; **fare il primo** ~ *(fig)* to make the first move; **a** ~ **d'uomo** dead slow; **'~ carraio** o **carrabile'** 'keep clear'; **fare due** o **quattro passi** to go for a short walk; **a due passi** a stone's throw away; **di questo** ~ at this rate.

pasta *sf* pasta; *(impasto)* dough; *(pasticcino)* pastry; *(di colla)* paste; ~ **in brodo** *soup with pasta in it*; ~ **frolla** shortcrust pastry; ~ **sfoglia** puff pastry.

pastasciutta *sf* pasta.

pastella *sf* batter.

pasticca, -che = **pastiglia**.

pasticceria *sf* ≃ cake shop.

pasticcino *sm* pastry.

pasticcio *sm (vivanda)* pie; *(disordine)* mess; *(guaio)* trouble; **essere nei pasticci** to be in trouble.

pasticcione, -a *sm, f* bungler.

pastiera *sf Neapolitan Easter tart with a filling of ricotta cheese and candied fruit.*

pastiglia *sf* pastille.

pastizzada *sf horse meat or beef and vegetables marinated in wine, generally served with polenta (a speciality of Veneto).*

pasto *sm* meal.

pastore *sm (di greggi)* shepherd; *(sacerdote)* minister; ~ **tedesco** German shepherd, Alsatian *(Br)*.

pastorizzato, -a *agg* pasteurized.

patata *sf* potato; **patate fritte** chips *(Br)*, French fries *(Am)*.

patatine *sfpl* crisps *(Br)*, chips *(Am)*.

pâté *sm inv* pâté.

patente *sf* licence; ~ **(di guida)** driving licence *(Br)*, driver's license *(Am)*.

paternità *sf* paternity.

paterno, -a *agg* paternal.

patetico, -a, -ci, -che *agg* pathetic.

patire *vt & vi* to suffer.

patria *sf* homeland.

patrigno *sm* stepfather.

patrimonio *sm (beni)* property;

(culturale, spirituale) heritage.

patrono *sm* patron saint.

pattinaggio *sm* skating; **~ su ghiaccio** ice skating.

pattinare *vi* to skate; **~ su ghiaccio** to ice-skate.

pattini *smpl*: **~ a rotelle** roller skates; **~ da ghiaccio** ice skates.

pattino *sm pedalo with oars.*

patto *sm (accordo)* pact; **a ~ che** on condition that.

pattuglia *sf* patrol.

pattumiera *sf* dustbin.

paura *sf* fear; **avere ~ (di)** to be afraid (of); **avere ~ di fare qc** to be afraid of doing sthg; **fare ~ a qn** to frighten sb; **per ~ di fare qc** for fear of doing sthg; **per ~ che** for fear that.

pauroso, -a *agg (spaventoso)* frightening; *(timoroso)* fearful.

pausa *sf (intervallo)* break; (MUS) pause; **fare una ~** to take a break.

pavimento *sm* floor.

pavone *sm* peacock.

paziente *agg & smf* patient.

pazienza *sf* patience; **perdere la ~** to lose one's patience; **~!** never mind!

pazzamente *avv* madly.

pazzesco, -a, -schi, -sche *agg* crazy.

pazzia *sf* madness; *(azione)* crazy thing.

pazzo, -a ◇ *agg (malato)* mad ◇ *sm, f* madman (*f* madwoman); **andare ~ per qc** to be crazy about sthg; **essere ~ di qn** to be crazy about sb; **darsi alla pazza gioia** to live it up.

peccare *vi* to sin; **~ di qc** to be guilty of sthg.

peccato *sm* sin; **è un ~ che** ... it's a pity that ...; **(che) ~!** what a pity!

peccatore, -trice *sm, f* sinner.

pecora *sf* sheep.

pecorino *sm a cheese made from ewe's milk.*

pedaggio *sm* toll.

pedalare *vi* to pedal.

pedale *sm* pedal; **a pedali** pedal *(dav s)*.

pedana *sf (poggiapiedi)* footboard; *(in atletica)* springboard; *(nella scherma)* piste.

pedata *sf (impronta)* footmark; *(calcio)* kick.

pediatra, -i, -e *smf* pediatrician.

pedicure *sm* pedicure.

pedina *sf* piece.

pedonale *agg* pedestrian *(dav s)*.

pedone *sm* pedestrian; *(negli scacchi)* pawn.

peggio ◇ *avv & agg inv* worse ◇ *smf*: **il/la ~** the worst; **~ per te!** so much the worse for you!; **temere il ~** to fear the worst; **alla ~** if the worst comes to the worst; **~ che mai** worse than ever.

peggioramento *sm* deterioration.

peggiorare *vt & vi* to worsen.

peggiore ◇ *agg (comparativo)* worse; *(superlativo)* worst ◇ *smf*: **il/la ~** the worst.

pelare *vt* to peel.

pelato, -a *agg* bald.

◆ **pelati** *smpl* peeled tomatoes.

pelle *sf* skin; *(conciata)* leather; **avere la ~ d'oca** to have goose pimples.

pellegrinaggio *sm* pilgrimage.

pelletteria *sf (prodotti)* leather goods *(pl)*; *(negozio)* leather goods shop.

pelliccia, -ce *sf (di animale)* fur; *(indumento)* fur coat.

pellicola *sf* film; **~ a colori** colour film.

pelo *sm (del corpo, di tessuto)* hair; *(di animale)* fur; **ce l'ho fatta per un ~** I made it by the skin of my teeth; **c'è mancato un ~ che lo investissero** they narrowly missed hitting him.

peloso, -a *agg* hairy.

peltro *sm* pewter.

peluche [pe'luʃ] *sm inv (tessuto)* plush; *(pupazzo)* cuddly toy.

pena *sf (condanna)* sentence; *(cruccio)* anxiety; *(pietà)* pity; (RELIG) torment; **mi fanno ~** I feel sorry for them; **(non) vale la ~ di andarci** it's (not) worth going; **~ di morte** death penalty; **a mala ~** hardly.

penalità *sf inv* penalty.

pendente ◇ *agg (appeso)* hanging; *(conto)* pending ◇ *sm (ciondolo)* pendant; *(orecchino)* drop earring.

pendenza *sf (inclinazione)* slope; *(di conto)* outstanding account.

pendere *vi (essere appeso)* to hang; *(essere inclinato)* to slope.

pendici *sfpl* slopes.

pendio *sm* slope.

pendola *sf* pendulum clock.

pendolare *smf* commuter.

pene *sm* penis.

penetrare *vi*: **~ in qc** *(entrare in)* to enter sthg; *(sog: chiodo, liquido)* to penetrate sthg.

penicillina *sf* penicillin.

penisola *sf* peninsula.

penitenza *sf (religiosa)* penitence; *(nei giochi)* forfeit.

penitenziario *sm* prison.

penna *sf* pen; *(di uccello)* feather; **~ a sfera** ballpoint pen; **~ stilografica** fountain pen;.

◆ **penne** *sfpl* pasta quills; **penne all'arrabbiata** *'penne' in a spicy sauce of tomatoes and chillies.*

pennarello *sm* felt-tip pen.

pennello *sm (da pittore)* brush; *(per vernici, tinte)* paintbrush; **~ da barba** shaving brush; **a ~** like a glove.

penombra *sf* half-light.

penoso, -a *agg* painful.

pensare ◇ *vi* to think ◇ *vt (immaginare)* to think; *(escogitare)* to think up; **cosa ne pensi?** what do you think (of it)?; **~ a** *(riflettere su, ricordare)* to think about; *(occuparsi di)* to see to; **pensa a un numero** think of a number; **~ di fare qc** to be thinking of doing sthg; **penso di no** I don't think so; **penso di sì** I think so; **pensarci su** to think it over.

pensiero *sm* thought; *(preoccupazione)* worry; **stare in ~ per qn** to be worried about sb.

pensile ◇ *agg* hanging ◇ *sm* wall cupboard.

pensilina *sf (di stazione)* platform roof; *(per autobus)* bus shelter.

pensionante *smf* lodger.

pensionato, -a ◇ *sm, f (persona)* pensioner ◇ *sm (per studenti)* hostel.

pensione *sf (somma)* pension; *(albergo)* boardinghouse; *(vitto e alloggio)* board and lodging; **andare in ~** to retire; **essere in ~** to be retired; **~ completa** full board; **mezza ~** half board.

Pentecoste *sf* Whitsun.

pentirsi *vr*: **~ di qc** to regret sthg; **~ di aver fatto qc** to regret doing sthg.

pentola *sf* pot; **~ a pressione** pressure cooker.

penultimo, -a *agg* penultimate.

pepare *vt* to pepper.

pepato, -a *agg* peppery.

pepe *sm* pepper.

peperonata *sf stewed sliced peppers, tomatoes and onions.*

peperoncino *sm* chilli pepper; **~ rosso** red chilli pepper.

peperone *sm* (capsicum) pepper.

per *prep* 1. *(indica lo scopo, la destinazione)* for; **è ~ te** it's for you; **fare qc ~ i soldi** to do sthg for money; **equipaggiarsi ~ la montagna** to kit o.s. out for the mountains; **~ fare qc** (in order) to do sthg; **sono venuto ~ vederti** I've come to see you; **è abbastanza grande ~ capire certe cose** he's old enough to understand these things.

2. *(attraverso)* through; **ti ho cercato ~ tutta la città** I've been looking for you all over town.
3. *(moto a luogo)* for, to; **il treno ~ Genova** the Genoa train; **partire ~ Napoli** to leave for Naples.
4. *(indica una durata, una scadenza)* for; **~ tutta la vita** for one's whole life; **sarò di ritorno ~ le cinque** I'll be back by five; **l'ho vista ~ Pasqua** I saw her at Easter; **fare qc ~ tempo** to do sthg in time; **~ sempre** forever.
5. *(indica il mezzo, il modo)* by; **gli ho parlato ~ telefono** I talked to him over the phone; **viaggiare ~ mare** to travel by sea; **fare qc ~ scherzo** to do sthg for a joke; **~ caso** by chance.
6. *(indica la causa)* for; **piangere ~ la rabbia** to cry with rage; **viaggiare ~ lavoro** to travel on business; **~ aver fatto qc** for doing sthg.
7. *(con valore distributivo)* per; **entrare uno ~ volta** to go in one at a time; **uno ~ uno** one by one.
8. *(come)* as; **tenere qc ~ certo** to take sthg for granted.
9. *(indica il prezzo)*: **lo ha venduto ~ un milione** he sold it for a million lira.
10. (MAT): **2 ~ 3 fa 6** 2 times 3 makes 6.
11. *(indica la conseguenza)*: **è troppo bello ~ essere vero** it's too good to be true.
12. *(indica limitazione)* for; **~ me, vi sbagliate** as far as I'm concerned, you are wrong; **~ questa volta** this time.

pẹra *sf* pear.

peraltro *avv* what is more.

perbẹne ◇ *agg inv* decent ◇ *avv* properly.

percentuale *sf* percentage.

percepire *vt (sentire)* to perceive; *(ricevere)* to receive.

perché ◇ *avv* why; **~ corri?** why are you running?; **~ non ci andiamo?** why don't we go?; **spiegami ~ lo hai fatto** tell me why you did it; **~ no?** why not?; **chissà ~** who knows why; **ecco ~** that's why.
◇ *cong* 1. *(per il fatto che)* because; **vado ~ ho fretta** I'm going because I'm in a hurry; **~ sì/no!** (just) because!
2. *(affinché)* so that; **telefona ~ non stiano in pensiero** phone so that (they) don't worry.
3. *(cosicché)*: **è troppo complicato ~ si possa capire** it's too complicated for anyone to understand.
◇ *sm inv (ragione)* reason; **senza un ~** for no reason.

perciò *cong* therefore.

percọrrere *vt (regione)* to travel over; *(distanza)* to cover.

percọrso, -a ◇ *pp* → **percorrere** ◇ *sm* journey.

percọsse *sfpl* blows.

percọsso, -a *pp* → **percuotere**.

percuọtere *vt (form)* to beat.

pẹrdere *vt* to lose; *(treno, lezione, film)* to miss; *(tempo, denaro)* to waste; *(liquido, gas)* to leak; **~ sangue** to lose blood; **lasciare ~** not to bother; **non avere nulla da ~** to have nothing to lose; **~ la testa** to lose one's head.
◆ **perdersi** *vr* to get lost.

pẹrdita *sf* loss; *(di acqua, gas)* leak; **una ~ di tempo** a waste of time; **a ~ d'occhio** as far as the eye can see.

perdonare *vt* to forgive.

perdọno *sm (di colpa, peccato)* pardon; *(scusa)* forgiveness.

perdutamẹnte *avv* desperately.

perfettamẹnte *avv* perfectly.

perfẹtto, -a *agg* perfect.

perfezionare *vt* to perfect.

perfeziọne *sf* perfection; **alla ~** perfectly.

pẹrfido, -a *agg* treacherous.

perfino *avv* even.
perforare *vt* to pierce.
pergola *sf* pergola.
pericolante *agg* unsafe.
pericolo *sm* danger; **essere fuori ~** to be out of danger; **essere in ~** to be in danger; '**~ (di morte)**' 'danger of death'.
pericoloso, -a *agg* dangerous.
periferia *sf* outskirts *(pl)*.
perimetro *sm* perimeter.
periodico, -a, -ci, -che ◇ *agg* periodic ◇ *sm* periodical.
periodo *sm* period.
perito *sm (esperto)* expert; **~ chimico** qualified chemist.
perla *sf* pearl.
perlustrare *vt* to patrol.
permaloso, -a *agg* touchy.
permanente ◇ *agg* permanent ◇ *sf* perm; '**permanente**' 'at all times'.
permanenza *sf* continued stay.
permesso, -a ◇ *pp* → **permettere** ◇ *sm (autorizzazione)* permission; *(congedo)* leave; *(documento)* permit; **(è) ~?** *(per entrare)* may I come in?; **~!** *(per passare)* excuse me!; **~ di soggiorno** residence permit.
permettere *vt* to allow; **~ a qn di fare qc** to allow sb to do sthg; **potersi ~ qc** *(spesa, acquisto)* to be able to afford sthg; **permettersi di fare qc** *(prendersi la libertà)* to take the liberty of doing sthg; **potersi ~ di fare qc** *(finanziariamente)* to be able to afford to do sthg.
perno *sm* hinge.
pernottamento *sm* overnight stay.
però *cong (ma)* but; *(tuttavia)* however.
perpendicolare *agg* perpendicular.
perplesso, -a *agg* puzzled.
perquisire *vt* to search.
perquisizione *sf* search.
perseguitare *vt* to persecute.
perseverare *vi* to persevere.
persiana *sf* shutter.
persiano, -a ◇ *agg* Persian ◇ *sm (pelliccia)* Persian lamb.
persino = **perfino**.
persistente *agg* persistent.
perso, -a *pp* → **perdere**.
persona *sf* person; **c'è una ~ che ti aspetta** there's somebody waiting for you; **conoscere qn di ~** to know sb personally; **in ~** in person.
personaggio *sm (di libro, film)* character; *(pubblico, politico)* figure.
personale ◇ *agg* personal ◇ *sm (dipendenti)* personnel, staff; *(fisico)* build.
personalità *sf inv* personality.
personalmente *avv* personally.
persuadere *vt* to persuade; **~ qn a fare qc** to persuade sb to do sthg; **~ qn di qc** to convince sb of sthg.
persuaso, -a *pp* → **persuadere**.
pertanto *cong (perciò)* therefore.
perturbare *vt* to upset.
perturbazione *sf* disturbance.
Perugia *sf* Perugia.
pesante *agg* heavy; *(fig: persona, film)* boring; *(scherzo)* in bad taste.
pesare ◇ *vt* to weigh ◇ *vi* to weigh; *(essere pesante)* to be heavy; *(essere spiacevole)* to be hard.
◆ **pesarsi** *vr* to weigh o.s.
pesca, -sche *sf (frutto)* peach; *(attività)* fishing; **pesche ripiene** *peaches stuffed with macaroons and baked in white wine*; **andare a ~** to go fishing; **~ di beneficenza** lucky dip; **~ subacquea** underwater fishing.
pescare *vt (pesce)* to catch; *(carta)* to draw; *(trovare)* to find out; **mi piace ~** I like fishing.
pescatore *sm* fisherman.
pesce *sm* fish; **~ d'aprile!** April Fool!

◆ **Pesci** *smpl* Pisces *(sg)*.
pescheria *sf* fishmonger's.
pescivendolo, -a *sm, f* fishmonger.
peso *sm* weight; **lancio del ~** shotput; **~ lordo** gross weight; **~ netto** net weight; **essere di ~ a qn** to be a burden on sb.
pessimismo *sm* pessimism.
pessimista, -i, -e *smf* pessimist.
pessimo, -a *agg* dreadful.
pestare *vt (calpestare)* to tread on; *(uva, aglio)* to crush; *(picchiare)* to beat up.
pesto, -a ◇ *agg*: **buio ~** pitch-black; **occhio ~** black eye ◇ *sm*: **~ (alla genovese)** pesto *(sauce made from basil, pine kernels, garlic, olive oil and cheese; a speciality of Genoa)*.
petalo *sm* petal.
petardo *sm* firecracker.
petroliera *sf* oil tanker.
petrolio *sm* oil.
pettegolezzi *smpl* gossip *(sg)*.
pettinare *vt* to comb.
◆ **pettinarsi** *vr* to comb one's hair.
pettine *sm* comb.
petto *sm (torace)* chest; *(seno)* breast; **~ di pollo** chicken breast; **a doppio ~** double-breasted.
pezzo *sm* piece; *(di spazio, tempo)* bit; **è un bel ~ che ti cerco** I've been looking for you for quite a while; **andare in (mille) pezzi** to be smashed (to smithereens); **cadere a pezzi** to fall to pieces; **~ di ricambio** spare part; **~ grosso** *(fig)* big shot.
piacere ◇ *sm* pleasure; *(favore)* favour ◇ *vi*: **mi piace** I like it; **mi piacciono i tulipani** I like tulips; **mi ha fatto molto ~ vederla** I was delighted to see her; **per ~** please; **~ (di conoscerla)!** pleased to meet you!; **~ mio!** the pleasure is mine!
piacevole *agg* pleasant.
piaga, -ghe *sf (lesione)* sore; *(fig: flagello)* plague.
pianerottolo *sm* landing.
pianeta, -i *sm* planet.
piangere *vi* to cry, to weep.
pianista, -i, -e *smf* pianist.
piano, -a ◇ *agg (piatto)* flat; (MAT) plane ◇ *avv (lentamente)* slowly; *(a bassa voce)* softly ◇ *sm (di edificio)* floor, storey; (GEOG & MAT) plane; *(livello)* level; *(programma, disegno)* plan; *(pianoforte)* piano; **andarci ~** to act with caution; **piano piano** *(poco a poco)* little by little; *(lentamente)* very slowly; **abitano al primo ~** they live on the first floor *(Br)*, they live on the second floor *(Am)*; **il ~ di sopra/di sotto** the floor above/below; **in primo ~** in the foreground.
piano-bar *sm inv bar with music provided by pianist.*
pianoforte *sm* piano.
pianoterra = **pianterreno**.
pianta *sf* plant; *(di piede)* sole; *(di città)* map; *(di casa)* plan; **~ grassa** succulent.
piantare *vt (semi)* to plant; *(conficcare)* to knock in; *(fam: abbandonare)* to leave; **piantala!** stop it!
pianterreno *sm* ground floor *(Br)*, first floor *(Am)*; **al ~** on the ground floor *(Br)*, on the first floor *(Am)*.
pianto ◇ *pp* → **piangere** ◇ *sm* crying, weeping.
pianura *sf* plain; **la ~ padana** the Paduan Plain.
piastrella *sf* tile.
piattaforma *sf (superficie piana)* platform; *(galleggiante)* rig.
piattino *sm* saucer.
piatto, -a ◇ *agg (piano)* flat; *(monotono)* dreary ◇ *sm (recipiente)* plate, dish; *(vivanda)* dish; *(portata)* course; **~ freddo** cold dish; **~ del giorno** today's special; **~ tipico** typical dish; **primo ~** first course; **secondo ~** second course; **lavare i**

piatti to wash the dishes; **piatti pronti** ready meals.

piazza *sf* square; **fare ~ pulita di** to make a clean sweep of.

piazzale *sm* large square.

piazzare *vt (collocare)* to place; *(vendere)* to sell.

♦ **piazzarsi** *vr (in gara)* to be placed.

piccante *agg* spicy.

picchetto *sm (di tenda)* peg; *(di scioperanti, soldati)* picket.

picchiare ◇ *vt (dar botte)* to beat (up); *(testa, pugni)* to bang ◇ *vi (alla porta, sul tavolo)* to thump; *(sole)* to beat down; **~ contro il muro** *(urtare)* to hit the wall.

♦ **picchiarsi** *vr* to fight.

piccino, -a *agg* small.

piccione *sm* pigeon.

picco, -chi *sm (vetta)* peak; **a ~** vertically; **colare a ~** to sink.

piccolo, -a *agg* small; *(breve)* short; *(di poco conto)* slight.

piccozza *sf* ice-axe.

picnic [pik'nik] *sm inv* picnic.

pidocchio *sm* louse.

piede *sm* foot; *(di mobile)* leg; **andare a piedi** to go on foot; **essere a piedi** to be on foot; **in piedi** standing; **prendere ~** to gain ground.

piedistallo *sm* pedestal.

piega, -ghe *sf* fold; *(di gonna)* pleat; *(di pantaloni, grinza)* crease; **prendere una brutta ~** to take a turn for the worse.

piegare *vt* to bend; *(foglio, tovaglia)* to fold; *(letto, sedia)* to fold up.

♦ **piegarsi** *vr (curvarsi)* to bend; *(letto, sedia)* to fold up.

♦ **piegarsi a** *vr + prep* to give in to.

pieghevole *agg (flessibile)* pliable; *(sedia, tavolo)* folding.

Piemonte *sm*: **il ~** Piedmont.

piena *sf* flood.

pieno, -a ◇ *agg* full ◇ *sm (di carburante)* full tank; *(culmine)* peak; **~ di** full of; **~ di sé** full of oneself; **a stomaco ~** on a full stomach; **in ~ inverno** in the middle of winter; **il ~, per favore** fill her up, please.

pietà *sf (compassione)* pity; **avere ~ di qn** to take pity on sb; **come attore fa ~** as an actor he's useless.

pietanza *sf* dish, course.

pietoso, -a *agg (che sente pietà)* compassionate; *(che ispira pietà)* pitiful.

pietra *sf* stone; **~ dura** semi-precious stone; **~ preziosa** precious stone.

pigiama, -i *sm* pyjamas *(pl)*.

pigiare *vt* to press.

pigliare *vt (prendere)* to take; *(afferrare)* to grab.

pigna *sf* pine cone.

pignolo, -a *agg* fussy, meticulous.

pignorare *vt* (DIR) to distrain.

pigrizia *sf* laziness.

pigro, -a *agg* lazy.

pila *sf (cumulo)* pile; *(batteria)* battery.

pilastro *sm* pillar.

pillola *sf* pill.

pilone *sm* pylon; *(di ponte)* pier.

pilota, -i, -e *smf (di aereo, nave)* pilot; *(di auto)* driver.

pinacoteca, -che *sf* art gallery.

pineta *sf* pinewood.

ping-pong *sm* table tennis.

pinguino *sm (animale)* penguin; *(gelato) chocolate-coated ice cream on a stick.*

pinna *sf (di pesce)* fin; *(per nuotare)* flipper.

pino *sm (albero)* pine tree; *(legno)* pine.

pinoccate *sfpl*: **~ alla perugina** *almond and pine kernel sweets.*

pinolo *sm* pine kernel.

pinzare *vt (con graffette)* to staple; *(sog: granchio)* to nip.

pinze *sfpl (utensile)* pliers.
pinzette *sfpl* tweezers.
pinzimonio *sm dip of seasoned oil.*
pioggia, -ge *sf* rain.
piolo *sm* rung.
piombare *vi (giungere)* to arrive unexpectedly; *(fig: nella disperazione)* to plunge; *(gettarsi)*: ~ **su** to fall upon.
piombino *sm (per pacchi)* lead seal; *(da pesca)* sinker.
piombo *sm* lead; **senza** ~ unleaded.
piovere ◇ *v impers* to rain ◇ *vi (pietre, proiettili, insulti)* to rain down; *(proteste)* to pour in; **piove** it's raining.
piovigginare *v impers* to drizzle.
piovoso, -a *agg* rainy.
pipa *sf* pipe.
pipì *sf (fam)*: **fare (la)** ~ to have a wee.
pipistrello *sm* bat.
pirata, -i *agg & sm* pirate; ~ **della strada** road hog.
Pirenei *smpl*: **i** ~ the Pyrenees.
pirofila *sf* Pyrex® dish.
piromane *smf* pyromaniac.
piroscafo *sm* steamer.
Pisa *sf* Pisa.
pisarei *smpl*: ~ **e fasò piacentini** *'gnocchi' in a sauce of beans, tomatoes and other vegetables.*
pisciare *vi (volg)* to piss.
piscina *sf* swimming pool.
pisello *sm* pea.
pisolino *sm*: **fare un** ~ to take a nap.
pista *sf (traccia)* trail; *(per corse)* track; *(da sci)* run; *(di aeroporto)* runway; ~ **da ballo** dance floor; ~ **ciclabile** cycle lane.
pistacchio *sm* pistachio.
pistola *sf* pistol, gun.
pitta *sf tart made with a yeasted dough and filled with tomatoes, anchovies, tuna and capers or ricotta cheese and boiled eggs.*
pittore, -trice *sm, f* painter.
pittoresco, -a, -schi, -sche *agg* picturesque.
pittura *sf* painting; '~ **fresca**' 'wet paint'.
pitturare *vt* to paint.
più ◇ *avv* 1. *(in comparativi)*: ~ **(di)** more (than); **ho fatto ~ tardi del solito** I was later than usual; ~ **triste che mai** sadder than ever; **poco ~ di** just over; **di** ~ *(in maggior quantità)* more; **l'ho pagato di** ~ I paid more for it.
2. *(in superlativi)*: **la ~ bella città** the most beautiful city; **la collina ~ alta** the highest hill; **il ~ grande** the biggest; **il ~ velocemente possibile** as quickly as possible.
3. *(oltre)* any more; **non parlo** ~ I'm not saying any more; **mai** ~ never again.
4. *(in espressioni)*: ~ **o meno** more or less; **per di** ~ what's more; **tre di** O **in** ~ three more; ~ **ci pensi, peggio è** the more you think about it, the worse it seems.
◇ *prep* 1. *(con l'aggiunta di)* plus; **siamo in sei ~ gli ospiti** there are six of us plus guests.
2. (MAT): **3 ~ 3 fa 6** 3 plus 3 makes 6.
◇ *agg inv* 1. *(in quantità, numero maggiore)* more; **ho ~ lavoro del solito** I've got more work than usual; **ho fatto ~ punti di te** I got more points than you; ~ **siamo, meglio è** the more of us there are, the better.
2. *(diversi)* several; **l'ho ripetuto ~ volte** I repeated it several times.
◇ *sm inv* 1. *(la maggior parte)* most; **il ~ delle volte** more often than not; **parlare del ~ e del meno** to talk about this and that.
2. *(la maggioranza)*: **i** ~ the majority.
piuma *sf* feather.
piumino *sm (trapunta)* duvet; *(giaccone)* quilted jacket.

piumone® *sm (trapunta)* duvet.
piuttosto *avv* rather; ~ **che** rather than.
pizza *sf* pizza; ~ **capricciosa** *pizza with cheese, tomato, artichokes and capers*; ~ **margherita** *pizza with cheese and tomato*; ~ **napoletana** *pizza with cheese, tomato, anchovies and capers*; ~ **quattro stagioni** *pizza with a different topping on each quarter.*
pizzaiola *sf*: **alla** ~ *in a tomato, garlic and oregano sauce.*
pizzeria *sf* pizzeria, pizza restaurant.
pizzetta *sf small pizza eaten as a snack.*
pizzicagnolo, -a *sm, f* delicatessen owner.
pizzicare ◇ *vt (con le dita)* to pinch; *(pungere)* to sting ◇ *vi (prudere)* to itch; *(cibo)* to be spicy.
pizzicheria *sf* delicatessen.
pizzico, -chi *sm* dash; **un ~ di sale** a pinch of salt.
pizzicotto *sm* pinch.
pizzo *sm (merletto)* lace; *(barba)* goatee.
placare *vt (ira)* to pacify; *(fame, sete)* to satisfy.
◆ **placarsi** *vr (vento)* to die down; *(mare)* to become calmer.
placca, -che *sf (targa)* plate; *(dentaria)* plaque.
placcare *vt (rivestire)* to plate; **placcato d'oro** gold-plated.
plagiare *vt (libro, canzone)* to plagiarize; *(persona)* to coerce.
plagio *sm (imitazione)* plagiarism; *(di persona)* coercion.
plancia, -ce *sf* bridge.
planetario, -a ◇ *agg* planetary ◇ *sm* planetarium.
plasmare *vt* to mould.
plastica, -che *sf (sostanza)* plastic; (MED) plastic surgery.
plastico, -a, -ci, -che ◇ *agg* plastic ◇ *sm (modello)* model; *(esplosivo)* plastic explosive.
plastilina® *sf* Plasticine®.
platano *sm* plane tree.
platea *sf (settore)* stalls *(pl)*; *(pubblico)* audience.
plausibile *agg* plausible.
plico, -chi *sm* parcel.
plurale *agg & sm* plural.
pneumatico, -ci *sm* tyre.
po' = **poco**.
Po *sm*: **il** ~ the Po.
poco, -a, -chi, -che ◇ *agg* **1.** *(in piccola quantità)* little, not much; **ha poca fantasia** he doesn't have much imagination; **a ~ prezzo** cheap.
2. *(in piccolo numero)*: **pochi** few, not many; **in poche parole** in few words.
◇ *sm* little.
◇ *pron* **1.** *(una piccola quantità)* (a) little; *(un piccolo numero)* few, not many; **pochi** *(non molta gente)* few (people); **pochi di noi** few of us.
2. *(in espressioni)*: **aver ~ da fare** to have little to do; **ci vuole ~ a capire che ...** it doesn't take much to understand that ...; **siamo tornati da ~** we've just got back; **è una cosa da ~** it's nothing; **per ~** nearly; **tra ~** soon, shortly; **(a) ~ a poco** little by little.
◇ *avv* **1.** *(con verbo)* little, not much; **mangia ~** he doesn't eat much.
2. *(con aggettivo, avverbio)* not very; **~ lontano da qui** not very far from here; **è ~ simpatica** she's not very nice; **sta poco bene** he's not very well.
3. *(indica tempo)*: **durare ~** not to last long; **~ dopo/prima** shortly afterwards/before.
◆ **un po'** *avv* a bit, a little; **restiamo ancora un po'** we'll stay a bit longer; **un po' di** a bit of, a little; **compra un po' di pane** buy some bread.

podere *sm* farm.
poderoso, -a *agg* powerful.
podio *sm* podium.
poesia *sf* (ARTE) poetry; *(componimento)* poem.
poeta, -essa, -i, -esse *sm, f* poet.
poetico, -a, -ci, -che *agg* poetic.
poggiare ◇ *vt* to rest ◇ *vi*: ~ **su qc** to rest on sthg.
poggiatesta *sm inv* headrest.
poi *avv* then; *(dopo)* later.
poiché *cong* as, since.
polare *agg* polar.
polaroid® *sf inv* Polaroid®.
polemica, -che *sf* controversy.
polemico, -a, -ci, -che *agg (persona, tono)* argumentative; *(discorso)* controversial.
polenta *sf* polenta *(type of savoury porridge made with maize flour)*; ~ **concia valdostana** *'polenta' cooked with soft cheeses and served with Parmesan cheese*; ~ **e osei** *'polenta' served with small birds wrapped in pork loin and flavoured with sage (a speciality of Lombardy)*; ~ **pasticciata alla veneta** *'polenta' baked in a meat, tomato and sausage sauce.*
poliambulatorio *sm* = health centre.
poliestere *sm* polyester.
polistirolo *sm* polystyrene.
politica, -che *sf (scienza)* politics *(sg)*; *(linea di condotta)* policy, → **politico**.
politico, -a, -ci, -che ◇ *agg* political ◇ *sm, f* politician.
polizia *sf* police; ~ **stradale** traffic police.
poliziesco, -a, -schi, -sche *agg* police *(dav s)*; *(romanzo, film)* detective *(dav s)*.
poliziotto, -a *sm, f* policeman (*f* policewoman).
polizza *sf* policy; ~ **di assicurazione** insurance policy.
pollaio *sm* hen house.
pollame *sm* poultry.
pollice *sm* thumb; *(unità di misura)* inch.
polline *sm* pollen.
pollo *sm* chicken; ~ **arrosto** roast chicken; ~ **alla cacciatora** *chicken in a sauce of mushrooms, tomatoes, olives, herbs and wine*; ~ **alla diavola** *chicken cut open and flattened out, marinated in lemon juice.*
polmone *sm* lung.
polmonite *sf* pneumonia.
polo ◇ *sm* pole ◇ *sf inv* polo shirt; **il ~ Nord/Sud** the North/South Pole.
Polonia *sf*: **la ~** Poland.
polpaccio *sm* calf.
polpastrello *sm* fingertip.
polpetta *sf* meatball.
polpettone *sm* meat loaf.
polpo *sm* octopus.
polsino *sm* cuff.
polso *sm* wrist; (MED) pulse.
poltiglia *sf* paste.
poltrona *sf* armchair; *(di teatro)* seat in the stalls.
poltrone, -a *sm, f* lazy person.
polvere *sf* dust; **latte in ~** powdered milk; **sapone in ~** soap powder.
polveroso, -a *agg* dusty.
pomata *sf* ointment.
pomeridiano, -a *agg* afternoon *(dav s)*.
pomeriggio *sm* afternoon; **di ~** in the afternoon.
pomice *sf* pumice.
pomo *sm* knob; ~ **d'Adamo** Adam's apple.
pomodoro *sm* tomato; **pomodori ripieni** *tomatoes stuffed with breadcrumbs, parsley, garlic and egg.*
pompa *sf* pump; *(sfarzo)* pomp; **pompe funebri** undertaker's *(sg)*.
pompare *vt* to pump.
Pompei *n* Pompei.

pompelmo *sm* grapefruit.
pompiere *sm* fireman.
pomposo, -a *agg (sfarzoso)* full of pomp; *(ostentato)* pompous.
ponderare *vt & vi* to ponder.
ponente *sm* west.
ponte *sm* bridge; *(di nave)* deck; *(impalcatura)* scaffolding; ~ **levatoio** drawbridge; **fare il** ~ *to have the day off between a national holiday and a weekend*; **il Ponte Vecchio** the Ponte Vecchio.
pontefice *sm* pontiff.
pony *sm inv* pony; ~ **express** express courier service.
popcorn *sm* popcorn.
popolare ◇ *agg* popular; *(popolano)* working-class *(dav s)* ◇ *vt* to populate.
popolarità *sf* popularity.
popolazione *sf* population.
popolo *sm* people *(pl)*.
popone *sm* melon.
poppa *sf* (NAUT) stern.
poppare *vt* to suck (from the breast).
porcellana *sf* porcelain.
porcellino *sm (maialino)* piglet; ~ **d'India** guinea pig.
porcino *sm* cep *(edible brown mushroom with nutty flavour)*.
porco, -ci *sm (animale)* pig; *(carne)* pork.
porcospino *sm* porcupine.
porgere *vt (tendere)* to hold out; *(dare)* to give; **porgo distinti saluti** *(in lettera)* yours sincerely.
pornografico, -a, -ci, -che *agg* pornographic.
poro *sm* pore.
porpora *agg inv* crimson.
porre *vt* to put; *(condizioni, limiti)* to set; *(riporre)* to place; *(supporre)*: **poniamo che** ... let us suppose that ...; ~ **una domanda** to ask a question; ~ **fine a qc** to put an end to sthg.
porro *sm (verdura)* leek; (MED) wart.
porta *sf* door; *(di città)* gate; *(nel calcio)* goal.
portabagagli *sm inv (bagagliaio)* boot *(Br)*, trunk *(Am)*; *(sul tetto)* roof rack.
portacenere *sm inv* ashtray.
portachiavi *sm inv* key ring.
portacipria *sm inv* compact.
portaerei *sf inv* aircraft carrier.
portafinestra (*pl* **portefinestre**) *sf* French window.
portafoglio *sm (per denaro)* wallet; (FIN & POL) portfolio.
portafortuna *sm inv* lucky charm.
portagioie *sm inv* jewel box.
portalettere = **postino**.
portamento *sm* bearing.
portamonete *sm inv* purse.
portapacchi *sm inv* luggage rack.
portare *vt (trasportare)* to carry; *(condurre, prendere)* to take; *(abiti, occhiali)* to wear; *(barba, capelli lunghi)* to have; *(fig: spingere)* to drive; ~ **qc a qn** *(consegnare)* to take sthg to sb; **portar via** to take; ~ **avanti** to carry on; ~ **fortuna** to bring luck.
portasapone *sm inv* soap dish.
portasigarette *sm inv* cigarette case.
portata *sf (piatto)* course; *(di veicolo)* capacity; *(di fiume)* flow; *(importanza)* importance; **essere a** ~ **di mano** to be within reach; **alla** ~ **di tutti** within everybody's grasp.
portatile *agg* portable; ~ **di handicap** disabled.
portatore, -trice *sm, f (di assegno)* bearer.
portatovagliolo *sm* napkin ring.
portauovo *sm inv* eggcup.
portico *sm* portico.
portiera *sf* door.
portiere, -a *sm, f (portinaio)* concierge, caretaker; *(di albergo)*

porter; *(nel calcio)* goalkeeper.

portineria *sf (di palazzo)* caretaker's lodge; *(di albergo)* reception.

porto, -a ◇ *pp* → **porgere** ◇ *sm* port; ~ **d'armi** licence to carry firearms.

Portogallo *sm*: **il** ~ Portugal.

portoghese *agg, sm & sf* Portuguese.

portone *sm* main entrance.

porzione *sf* portion; *(di cibo)* helping.

posa *sf* pose; **mettersi in** ~ to pose.

posacenere *sm inv* ashtray.

posare ◇ *vt* to put down ◇ *vi* to pose.

◆ **posarsi** *vr (uccello)* to perch.

posate *sfpl* cutlery *(sg)*.

positivo, -a *agg* positive.

posizione *sf* position.

posologia *sf* dosage.

possedere *vt (cose)* to own, to possess; *(qualità)* to have, to possess.

possessivo, -a *agg* possessive.

possesso *sm* possession, ownership; **essere in** ~ **di qc** to be in possession of sthg.

possibile ◇ *agg* possible ◇ *sm*: **fare (tutto) il** ~ **(per fare qc)** to do everything possible (to do sthg); **ma non è** ~! it can't be true!; **il più presto** ~ as soon as possible; **se** ~ if possible; **il più** ~ *(quantità)* as much as possible; *(numero)* as many as possible.

possibilità *sf inv (eventualità)* possibility; *(occasione)* chance; *(capacità)*: **avere la** ~ **di fare qc** to be able to do sthg.

posta *sf (negozio)* post office; *(lettere, servizio)* post, mail; **per** ~ by post O mail; ~ **aerea** air mail; ~ **elettronica** e-mail.

postale *agg* postal, post *(dav s)*.

posteggiare *vt* to park.

posteggiatore, -trice *sm, f* car park attendant *(Br)*, parking lot attendant *(Am)*.

posteggio *sm* car park *(Br)*, parking lot *(Am)*; ~ **a pagamento** *car park where drivers must pay to park*.

poster *sm inv* poster.

posteriore *agg (nello spazio)* rear, back; *(nel tempo)* later.

posticipare *vt* to postpone.

postino, -a *sm, f* postman (*f* postwoman).

posto, -a ◇ *pp* → **porre** ◇ *sm* place; *(spazio)* room; *(per persona)* place, seat; *(impiego)* job; **mettere a** ~ to tidy (up); ~ **di blocco** roadblock; ~ **letto** bed; ~ **di polizia** police station; **al** ~ **di** in (the) place of.

potabile *agg* → **acqua**.

potare *vt* to prune.

potente *agg* powerful.

potere ◇ *vi* **1.** *(essere in grado di)* can, to be able; **non ci posso andare** I can't go, I'm not able to go; **puoi farmi un favore?** can you do me a favour?; **non posso farci niente** I can't do anything about it.

2. *(avere il permesso di)* can, to be able; **non potete parcheggiare qui** you can't park here; **posso entrare?** can O may I come in?

3. *(esprime eventualità)*: **può far freddo** it can get cold; **possono aver perso il treno** they might O could have missed the train; **potrei sbagliarmi** I could be wrong; **può darsi** perhaps; **può darsi che sia partito** he may O might have left.

4. *(esprime suggerimento)*: **puoi provare** you can try.

5. *(in espressioni)*: **non ne posso più!** *(sono stufo)* I can't take any more!; *(sono stanco)* I'm exhausted!; **a più non posso** *(correre)* really fast; *(lavorare)* really hard; **si può fare** it can be done.

◇ *sm* **1.** *(comando)* power; **essere al** ~ to be in power.

2. *(facoltà)* power, ability.

povero, -a ◇ *agg* poor ◇ *sm, f* poor man (*f* woman); **i poveri** the poor; ~ **di qc** lacking in sthg.

pozza *sf* pool.

pozzanghera *sf* puddle.

pozzo *sm* well; ~ **petrolifero** oil well.

pranzare *vi* to have lunch.

pranzo *sm (di mezzogiorno)* lunch; *(banchetto)* dinner.

prassi *sf* usual procedure.

pratica, -che *sf* practice; *(esperienza)* practical experience; *(documenti)* paperwork; **mettere in ~ qc** to put sthg into practice; **in ~** in practice.

praticamente *avv (quasi)* practically; *(concretamente)* in a practical way.

pratico, -a, -ci, -che *agg* practical.

prato *sm (distesa d'erba)* meadow; *(di giardino)* lawn.

preavviso *sm* notice.

precario, -a *agg* precarious.

precauzione *sf* precaution.

precedente ◇ *agg* preceding, previous ◇ *sm* precedent; **senza precedenti** unprecedented; **precedenti penali** criminal record *(sg)*.

precedenza *sf (in auto)* right of way; *(priorità)* priority; **dare la ~ (a)** *(in auto)* to give way (to).

precedere *vt (nello spazio)* to be ahead of; *(nel tempo)* to precede.

precipitare *vi (cadere)* to fall; *(fig: situazione)* to come to a head.

◆ **precipitarsi** *vr* to rush.

precipitazione *sf (atmosferica)* precipitation; *(fretta)* haste.

precipizio *sm* precipice.

precisare *vt* to specify.

precisione *sf (esattezza)* precision; *(accuratezza)* accuracy.

preciso, -a *agg* precise; **sono le due precise** it's exactly two o'clock.

precoce *agg (bambino)* precocious; *(vecchiaia)* premature.

preda *sf* prey; **essere in ~ a qc** to be prey to sthg.

predetto, -a *pp* → **predire**.

predica, -che *sf* (RELIG) sermon; *(fam: ramanzina)* telling-off.

predire *vt* to foretell.

predisporre *vt* to prepare; ~ **qn/qc a qc** to predispose sb/sthg to sthg.

predisposizione *sf* tendency.

predominare *vi* to predominate.

prefabbricato, -a *agg* prefabricated.

preferenza *sf* preference.

preferire *vt* to prefer; ~ **qn/qc a** to prefer sb/sthg to.

preferito, -a *agg* favourite.

prefiggersi *vr*: ~ **uno scopo** to set o.s. a goal.

prefisso, -a ◇ *pp* → **prefiggersi** ◇ *sm* code.

pregare ◇ *vi* to pray ◇ *vt (Dio)* to pray to; ~ **qn di fare qc** *(supplicare)* to beg sb to do sthg; *(chiedere a)* to ask sb to do sthg; **i passeggeri sono gentilmente pregati di non fumare** passengers are kindly requested not to smoke.

preghiera *sf* prayer.

pregiato, -a *agg* precious.

pregio *sm (qualità)* good quality; *(valore)* value.

pregiudicare *vt* to prejudice.

pregiudicato, -a *sm, f* previous offender.

pregiudizio *sm* prejudice.

prego *esclam (risposta a ringraziamento)* don't mention it!; *(invito a sedersi)* take a seat!; *(invito ad entrare prima)* after you!

preistorico, -a, -ci, -che *agg* prehistoric.

prelavaggio *sm* prewash.

prelevare *vt (soldi)* to withdraw; *(campione, sangue)* to take.

prelievo *sm (in banca)* withdrawal; (MED) sample.

preliminare *agg & sm* preliminary.

pre-maman *agg inv* maternity *(dav s)*.

prematuro, -a *agg* premature.

premere ◇ *vt* to press ◇ *vi*: **~ su** to press on.

◆ **premere a** *v + prep*: **~ a qn** to matter to sb.

premiare *vt (dare un premio)* to give a prize to; *(merito, onestà)* to reward.

premiazione *sf* prize-giving.

premio *sm (vincita)* prize; *(ricompensa)* reward; **~ (di assicurazione)** (insurance) premium.

premunirsi *vr*: **~ contro qc** to protect o.s. against sthg.

premuroso, -a *agg* thoughtful.

prendere ◇ *vt* **1.** *(afferrare)* to take.
2. *(portare con sé)* to take; **prendi l'ombrello** take the umbrella.
3. *(mezzi di trasporto, strada)* to take; **~ il treno** to take the train; **prenda la prima a destra** take the first on the right.
4. *(mangiare, bere)* to have; **andiamo a ~ un caffè** let's go for a coffee; **~ qualcosa da bere** to have something to drink; **che cosa prendete?** *(da bere)* what would you like to drink?
5. *(lezioni, voto, stipendio)* to get; **~ qc in affitto** to rent sthg.
6. *(interpretare)* to take; **prenderla bene/male** to take it well/badly.
7. *(catturare, sorprendere)* to catch; **quanti pesci hai preso?** how many fish have you caught?; **~ qn con le mani nel sacco** to catch sb red-handed.
8. *(malattia, stato fisico)*: **~ freddo** to catch cold; **~ il sole** to sunbathe; **prendersi un raffreddore** to catch a cold.
9. *(sottrarre)*: **~ qc a qn** to take sthg (away) from sb.
10. *(scambiare)*: **~ qn per** to take sb for.
11. *(in espressioni)*: **andare a ~** *(persona)* to meet; *(cosa)* to go to get; **prendersi cura di** to look after; **~ fuoco** to catch fire; **~ un impegno** to take on a commitment; **~ le misure di** *(oggetto, persona)* to measure; **che ti prende?** what's the matter with you?; **prendersela** *(offendersi)* to get annoyed; *(preoccupare)* to worry; **prendersela con qn** *(arrabbiarsi)* to get angry with sb.
◇ *vi* **1.** *(colla, cemento)* to set; *(fuoco)* to catch.
2. *(cominciare)*: **~ a fare qc** to start doing sthg.

prendisole *sm inv* sundress.

prenotare *vt* to book; **ho prenotato una camera** I've booked a room.

prenotazione *sf* booking.

preoccupare *vt* to worry.

◆ **preoccuparsi** *vr*: **preoccuparsi (per)** to worry (about).

◆ **preoccuparsi di** *vr + prep (occuparsi di)* to think about.

preoccupato, -a *agg* worried.

preoccupazione *sf* worry.

preparare *vt* to prepare; *(documenti, cose)* to get ready; *(esame, concorso)* to prepare for; **~ da mangiare** to cook.

◆ **prepararsi** *vr (vestirsi)* to get ready; **~ a fare qc** to get ready to do sthg.

preparativi *smpl* preparations.

preposizione *sf* preposition.

prepotente ◇ *agg* domineering ◇ *smf* bully.

presa *sf (il prendere)* grip; *(nello sport, appiglio)* hold; *(di acqua, gas)* supply point; *(di sale, pepe)* pinch; *(di colla, cemento)* setting; *(di città)* capture; *(per spina)*: **~ (di corrente)** socket; **far ~** to set; **far ~ su qn** to captivate sb; **~ d'aria** air intake; **essere alle prese con** to be up against.

presbite *agg* longsighted.

prescindere : prescindere da *v + prep* to leave aside; **a ~ da** apart from.

prescritto, -a *pp* → **prescrivere**.

prescrivere *vt* to prescribe.

presentare *vt* to present; *(domanda, dimissioni)* to submit; *(persona)*: **~ qn a qn** to introduce sb to sb; **le presento mia moglie** this is my wife.

◆ **presentarsi** *vr (farsi conoscere)* to introduce o.s.; *(recarsi)* to present o.s.; *(capitare)* to arise; *(mostrarsi)* to look.

presentatore, -trice *sm, f* presenter.

presentazione *sf* presentation; **fare le presentazioni** to make the introductions.

presente ◇ *agg* present ◇ *smf*: **i presenti** those present; **tener ~ che** to bear in mind that; **aver ~** to remember.

presentimento *sm* presentiment.

presenza *sf* presence; **in ~ di tutti** in front of everybody.

presepe = **presepio**.

presepio *sm* Nativity scene, crib.

preservativo *sm* condom.

preside *smf* headteacher *(Br)*, principal *(Am)*.

presidente *smf* president; **~ del Consiglio** Prime Minister; **il ~ della Repubblica** the Italian President.

preso, -a *pp* → **prendere**.

pressappoco *avv* more or less.

pressare *vt* to press.

pressione *sf* pressure; **far ~ su qn** to put pressure on sb; **essere sotto ~** to be under pressure.

presso *prep (sulle lettere)* c/o; *(vicino a)* near; *(alle dipendenze di)* for, with; **~ qn** *(a casa di)* at sb's home.

◆ **pressi** *smpl*: **nei pressi di Siena** in the vicinity of Siena.

prestare *vt* to lend; **~ qc (a qn)** *(denaro, oggetti)* to lend (sb) sthg, to lend sthg (to sb); **~ aiuto a qn** to lend sb a hand; **~ attenzione a** to pay attention to.

◆ **prestarsi a** *vr + prep*: **prestarsi a fare qc** to offer to do sthg.

prestazione *sf* performance.

◆ **prestazioni** *sfpl* services.

prestigiatore, -trice *sm, f* conjurer.

prestito *sm* loan; **dare in ~ qc (a qn)** to lend sthg (to sb); **prendere qc in ~ (da qn)** to borrow sthg (from sb).

presto *avv (fra poco)* soon; *(in fretta)* quickly; *(nella giornata, nel tempo)* early; **fai ~!** hurry up!; **a ~!** see you soon!; **al più ~** as soon as possible.

presumere *vt* to presume.

presunto, -a *pp* → **presumere**.

presuntuoso, -a *agg* conceited.

prete *sm* priest.

pretendere *vt* to claim; *(a torto)* to pretend; **pretende che tutti lo ascoltino** he expects everyone to listen to him; **pretende di essere il migliore** he thinks he's the best.

preteso, -a *pp* → **pretendere**.

pretesto *sm (scusa)* excuse, pretext; *(occasione)* opportunity.

prevalente *agg* prevalent.

prevalere *vi* to prevail.

prevedere *vt* to foresee.

◆ **prevedere di** *v + prep* to expect.

prevenire *vt (anticipare)* to forestall; *(evitare)* to prevent.

preventivo, -a ◇ *agg* preventive ◇ *sm* estimate.

prevenzione *sf* prevention.

previdenza *sf* foresight; **~ sociale** social security *(Br)*, welfare *(Am)*.

previo, -a *agg*: **~ pagamento** upon payment.

previsione *sf (valutazione)* prediction; *(aspettativa)* expectation; **in ~ di** in anticipation of; **previsioni del tempo** o **meteorologiche** weather forecast.

previsto, -a ◇ *pp* → **prevedere** ◇ *agg* expected ◇ *sm*: **più/meno del ~** more/less than expected.

prezioso, -a *agg* precious, valuable.

prezzemolo *sm* parsley.

prezzo *sm* price; **~ comprensivo del servizio** price including service charge; **a buon ~** cheap.

prigione *sf* prison.

prigioniero, -a ◇ *agg (rinchiuso)* imprisoned; *(catturato)* captive ◇ *sm, f* prisoner.

prima ◇ *avv (in precedenza)* before; *(più presto)* earlier; *(per prima cosa, nello spazio)* first; *(un tempo)* once ◇ *sf (di teatro)* first night; *(marcia)* first gear; *(in treno, aereo)* first class ◇ *cong* before ◇ *prep*: **~ di** before; **fai ~ di qua** it's quicker this way; **~ che arrivi** before he arrives; **~ di fare qc** before doing sthg; **~ o poi** sooner or later; **~ d'ora** before now; **~ di tutto** first of all; **l'anno ~** the year before.

primario, -a ◇ *agg* primary ◇ *sm* (MED) chief physician.

primato *sm (supremazia)* primacy; (SPORT) record.

primavera *sf* spring.

primitivo, -a *agg (uomo, civiltà)* primitive; *(originario)* original.

primo, -a ◇ *agg* first; *(nel tempo)* early ◇ *sm (portata)* first course; *(giorno)* first; **il ~ (di) marzo** the first of March; **di prima qualità** first-class; **ai primi d'ottobre** in early October; **sulle prime** at first, in the beginning.

primogenito, -a *agg & sm, f* firstborn.

principale ◇ *agg* main, principal ◇ *smf* manager, boss.

principe *sm* prince.

principessa *sf* princess.

principiante *smf* beginner.

principio *sm (inizio, origine)* beginning; *(concetto, norma)* principle; **in** o **al ~** at first; **per ~** on principle.

priorità *sf inv (precedenza)* priority.

privare *vt*: **~ qn di qc** to deprive sb of sthg.

◆ **privarsi di** *vr + prep*: **privarsi di qc** to go without sthg.

privato, -a ◇ *agg* private ◇ *sm, f (cittadino)* private citizen ◇ *sm*: **in ~** in private.

privilegiare *vt* to favour.

privo, -a *agg*: **~ di qc** without sthg, lacking in sthg.

pro *sm inv*: **a che ~?** for what purpose?; **i ~ e i contro** the pros and cons.

probabile *agg* probable; **è ~ che piova** it will probably rain.

probabilità *sf inv* probability.

probabilmente *avv* probably.

problema, -i *sm* problem.

proboscide *sf* trunk.

procedere *vi (avanzare, progredire)* to proceed; *(agire)* to behave.

procedimento *sm* procedure.

processare *vt* to try.

processione *sf* procession.

processo *sm* (DIR) trial; *(operazione, metodo)* process.

procinto *sm*: **essere in ~ di fare qc** to be about to do sthg.

proclamare *vt* to proclaim.

procurare *vt*: **~ qc a qn** to obtain sthg for sb, to get sthg for sb; **procurarsi qc** to get sthg.

prodotto, -a ◇ *pp* → **produrre** ◇ *sm* product.

produrre *vt* to produce; *(provocare)* to cause.

produttore, -trice *sm, f* producer.

produzione *sf* production.
Prof. *(abbr di professore)* Prof.
profano, -a ◇ *agg* profane ◇ *sm* layman.
professionale *agg* professional.
professione *sf* profession.
professionista, -i, -e *smf (avvocato, medico)* professional person; *(non dilettante)* professional.
professore, -essa *sm, f* teacher; *(all'università)* professor.
profilo *sm* profile; **di ~** in profile.
profiterole [profite'rɔl] *sm inv* profiteroles *(pl)*.
profitto *sm* profit; **trarre ~ da qc** to take advantage of sthg.
profondità *sf inv* depth.
profondo, -a *agg* deep.
Prof.ssa *(abbr di professoressa)* Prof.
profugo, -a, -ghi, -ghe *sm, f* refugee.
profumare ◇ *vt* to perfume ◇ *vi* to smell good; **~ di** to smell of.
profumato, -a *agg* scented.
profumeria *sf* perfumery.
profumo *sm (odore)* scent, fragrance; *(cosmetico)* perfume.
progettare *vt* to plan.
progetto *sm* plan.
programma, -i *sm* programme; *(per vacanze, serata)* plan; (SCOL) syllabus; (INFORM) program.
programmare *vt (pianificare)* to plan; (INFORM) to program.
progredire *vi (avanzare)* to advance; *(migliorare)* to progress.
progressivo, -a *agg* progressive.
progresso *sm* progress; **fare progressi** to make progress.
proibire *vt* to forbid; **~ a qn di fare qc** to forbid sb to do sthg; **è proibito fumare** smoking is prohibited.
proiettare *vt (film)* to show; *(luce, ombra)* to cast.
proiettile *sm* bullet.
proiezione *sf (di film)* projection, showing.
proletariato *sm* proletariat.
prolunga, -ghe *sf* extension.
prolungare *vt* to prolong.
◆ **prolungarsi** *vr* to go on.
promessa *sf* promise; **mantenere una ~** to keep a promise.
promesso, -a *pp* → **promettere**.
promettere *vt*: **~ qc (a qn)** to promise (sb) sthg; **~ (a qn) di fare qc** to promise (sb) to do sthg; **promette bene!** that's a good start!
promontorio *sm* promontory.
promosso, -a *pp* → **promuovere**.
promotore, -trice *sm, f* promoter.
promozione *sf* promotion; (SCOL): **avere la ~** to go up a class.
promulgare *vt* to promulgate.
promuovere *vt* (SCOL) to pass; *(impiegato, iniziativa)* to promote.
pronome *sm* pronoun.
pronto, -a ◇ *agg* ready ◇ *esclam* hello! *(on the phone)*; **essere ~ a fare qc** to be ready to do sthg; **~ soccorso** first aid; **~, chi parla?** hello, who's speaking?
pronuncia, -ce *sf* pronunciation.
pronunciare *vt (parola, lettera)* to pronounce; *(dire)* to say.
◆ **pronunciarsi** *vr (parola, lettera)* to be pronounced; *(dichiararsi)* to declare o.s.
pronunzia = **pronuncia**.
proporre *vt*: **~ qc (a qn)** to propose sthg (to sb); **~ di fare qc** to suggest doing sthg.
◆ **proporsi di** *vr + prep*: **proporsi di fare qc** to decide to do sthg.
proporzionato, -a *agg* well proportioned.
proporzione *sf* (MAT) ratio; **in ~ a** in proportion to.
proposito *sm (progetto)* inten-

tion; **fare qc di ~** to do sthg on purpose; **a ~, ...** by the way, ...; **capitare a ~** *(avvenimento)* to happen at the right time.

proposta *sf* proposal.

proposto, -a *pp* → **proporre**.

proprietà *sf inv* property; **'~ privata'** 'private property'.

proprietario, -a *sm, f* owner.

proprio, -a ◇ *agg (possessivo)* own; *(senso)* literal, exact; *(tipico)* characteristic ◇ *avv (veramente)* really; *(precisamente)* just; *(affatto)* at all; **non ne ho ~ idea** I really have no idea; **~ così** that's just it; **non ~** not exactly; **mettersi in ~** to set up on one's own.

prora *sf (di nave)* prow; *(di aereo)* nose.

prosa *sf* prose.

prosciutto *sm* ham; **~ cotto** (cooked) ham; **~ crudo** Parma ham.

proseguire ◇ *vt* to carry on with, to continue ◇ *vi* to carry on, to continue.

prospettiva *sf (di disegno, punto di vista)* perspective; *(possibilità)* prospect.

prossimità *sf*: **in ~ di qc** near sthg.

prossimo, -a ◇ *agg* next ◇ *sm* neighbour.

prostituta *sf* prostitute.

protagonista, -i, -e *smf* protagonist.

proteggere *vt*: **~ qn/qc (da)** to protect sb/sthg (from).

protesta *sf* protest.

protestante *agg & smf* Protestant.

protestare *vi & vt* to protest.

protetto, -a *pp* → **proteggere**.

protezione *sf* protection.

prototipo *sm* prototype.

prova *sf (dimostrazione, conferma)* proof; *(esperimento)* test, trial; (DIR) proof, evidence; *(di spettacolo)* rehearsal; *(esame)* exam; **dar ~ di abilità** to prove to be skilful; **mettere qn alla ~** to put sb to the test; **fino a ~ contraria** until (it's) proved otherwise; **in ~** on trial; **fare le prove** to rehearse.

provare *vt (cibo)* to try; *(vestito)* to try on; *(sentire)* to feel, to experience; *(dimostrare)* to show; *(tentare)*: **~ a fare qc** to try to do sthg; **provarsi qc** to try sthg on.

◆ **provarsi a** *vr + prep*: **provarsi a fare qc** to try to do sthg.

provenienza *sf* origin; **in ~ da** *(treno, aereo)* from.

provenire : provenire da *v + prep* to come from; **proveniente da** *(treno, aereo)* from.

provenuto, -a *pp* → **provenire**.

proverbio *sm* proverb.

provetta *sf* test tube.

provincia, -ce o **-cie** *sf (ente)* province; *(opposta a grandi città)* provinces *(pl)*.

provinciale ◇ *agg* provincial ◇ *sf* main road.

provino *sm (audizione)* audition; *(fotografico)* screen test.

provocante *agg* provocative.

provocare *vt (causare)* to cause; *(sfidare)* to provoke.

provocazione *sf* provocation.

provolone *sm a hard cheese made from cow's milk*.

provvedere *vi (prendere provvedimenti)* to take measures; *(occuparsi di)*: **~ (a qc)** to provide (for sthg).

provvedimento *sm* measure.

provvisorio, -a *agg* temporary, provisional.

provviste *sfpl* supplies.

prua *sf* prow.

prudente *agg* cautious, prudent.

prudenza *sf* caution, prudence; **'prudenza'** 'caution'.

prudere *vi* to itch; **mi prude una gamba** my leg is itchy.

prugna *sf* plum; **~ secca** prune.

pruno *sm* prickle, thorn.

prurito *sm* itch.
P.S. ◇ *(abbr di postscriptum)* PS ◇ *abbr* = **Pubblica Sicurezza**.
pseudonimo *sm* pseudonym.
psicanalisi *sf* psychoanalysis.
psiche *sf* psyche.
psichiatra, -i, -e *smf* psychiatrist.
psicologia *sf* psychology.
psicologo, -a, -gi, -ghe *sm, f* psychologist.
P.T. *(abbr di poste e telecomunicazioni)* PO.
P.T.P. *(abbr di posto telefonico pubblico)* payphone.
pubblicare *vt* to publish.
pubblicazione *sf* publication.
◆ **pubblicazioni** *sfpl*: ~ **(matrimoniali)** (marriage) banns.
pubblicità *sf inv (annuncio)* advertisement; *(divulgazione)* publicity; *(attività)* advertising.
pubblico, -a, -ci, -che ◇ *agg* public; *(statale)* state *(dav s)* ◇ *sm (utenti)* public; *(spettatori)* audience; **in ~** in public; **la Pubblica Sicurezza** the police.
pube *sm* pubis.
pudore *sm* modesty.
pugilato *sm* boxing.
pugile *sm* boxer.
Puglia *sf*: **la ~** Apulia.
pugnalare *vt* to stab.
pugno *sm (mano)* fist; *(colpo)* punch; *(quantità)* handful.
pulce *sf* flea.
Pulcinella *sm* Punch.
pulcino *sm* chick.
puledro, -a *sm, f* colt (*f* filly).
pulire *vt* to clean; **pulirsi il viso/le scarpe** to clean one's face/shoes.
pulita *sf*: **dare una ~** to clean up.
pulito, -a *agg* clean; *(coscienza)* clear.
pulizia *sf (stato)* cleanliness; *(atto)* cleaning; **fare le pulizie** to do the cleaning.
pullman *sm inv* coach.
pullover *sm inv* pullover.
pulmino *sm* minibus.
pulsante *sm* button.
pulsare *vi* to beat.
puma *sm inv* puma.
pungere *vt* to sting.
pungiglione *sm* sting.
punire *vt* to punish.
punizione *sf (castigo)* punishment; *(nel calcio)* free kick.
punta *sf (di matita, spillo, coltello)* point; *(di continente, dita)* tip; **in ~ dei piedi** *(camminare)* on tiptoe.
puntare *vt (arma)* to aim; *(scommettere)* to bet; **~ i piedi** to dig one's heels in.
puntata *sf (episodio)* episode; *(scommessa)* bet; **teleromanzo a puntate** serial.
punteggiatura *sf* punctuation.
punteggio *sm* score.
puntina *sf*: **~ (da disegno)** drawing pin.
puntino *sm* dot; **fare qc a ~** to do sthg properly; **puntini di sospensione** suspension points.
punto, -a ◇ *pp* → **pungere** ◇ *sm* point; *(segno grafico)* full stop *(Br)*, period *(Am)*; *(MED, di cucito)* stitch; **~ esclamativo** exclamation mark; **~ interrogativo** question mark; **~ di riferimento** point of reference, landmark; **~ di ritrovo** meeting point; **~ vendita** point of sale; **~ e virgola** semi-colon; **~ di vista** point of view; **due punti** colon; **punti cardinali** points of the compass; **essere sul ~ di fare qc** to be about to do sthg; **essere a buon ~** to be at a good point; **fare il ~ della situazione** to take stock; **mettere a ~ qc** to adjust sthg; **di ~ in bianco** all of a sudden; **a tal ~ che** to such an extent that; **le tre in ~** three o'clock sharp.
puntuale *agg* punctual.
puntualità *sf* punctuality.

puntura *sf (di insetto)* sting; *(di spillo)* prick; *(fam: iniezione)* injection.
punzecchiare *vt (pungere)* to prick; *(fig: infastidire)* to tease.
pupazzo *sm* puppet.
pupilla *sf* pupil.
purché *cong* provided that.
pure ◇ *avv (anche)* also, too ◇ *cong* even if; **pur di fare qc** just to do sthg; **faccia ~!** please do!, go ahead!
purè *sm (di patate) mashed potatoes with milk, butter and Parmesan cheese.*
purezza *sf* purity.
purga, -ghe *sf* laxative.
purgatorio *sm* Purgatory.
puro, -a *agg* pure; *(verità)* simple.
purosangue *agg inv* thoroughbred.
purtroppo *avv* unfortunately.
pustola *sf* pimple.
putiferio *sm* row.
putrefare *vi* to putrefy, to rot.
putrefatto, -a ◇ *pp* → **putrefare** ◇ *agg* rotten.
putrido, -a *agg* putrid.
puttana *sf (volg)* whore.
puzza *sf* = **puzzo**.
puzzare *vi* to stink.
puzzo *sm* stink.
puzzola *sf* polecat.
puzzolente *agg* stinking.

Q

qua *avv* here; **al di ~ di** on this side of; **di ~ e di là** here and there; **per di ~** this way.

quaderno *sm* exercise book.

quadrante *sm (di orologio)* face; *(di bussola)* quarter.

quadrare *vi (bilancia)* to balance; *(coincidere)* to correspond; **non mi quadra** *(fam)* there's something not quite right about it.

quadrato, -a *agg & sm* square; **2 al ~** 2 squared.

quadretto *sm*: **a quadretti** *(tessuto)* checked; *(foglio)* squared.

quadrifoglio *sm* four-leaf clover.

quadrimestre *sm* (SCOL) term; *(periodo)* period of four months.

quadro *sm (pittura)* painting; *(fig: situazione)* picture; (TECNOL) board, panel; *(in azienda)* executive.

◆ **quadri** *smpl (nelle carte)* diamonds.

quadruplo, -a *agg & sm* quadruple.

quaggiù *avv* down here.

quaglia *sf* quail.

qualche *agg* **1.** *(alcuni)* a few, some; **restiamo solo ~ giorno** we are only staying a few days; **~ volta** a few times; **c'è ~ novità?** is there any news?

2. *(indeterminato)* some; **l'ho letto in ~ articolo** I read it in some article; **hai ~ libro da prestarmi?** have you any books to lend me?; **in ~ modo** somehow; **da ~ parte** somewhere.

3. *(un certo)* some; **ci siamo frequentati per ~ tempo** we've been seeing each other for some time; **~ cosa** = **qualcosa**.

qualcheduno, -a = **qualcuno**.

qualcosa *pron* something; *(nelle interrogative)* anything; **~ di nuovo** something new; **~ da bere** something to drink; **qualcos'altro** something else.

qualcuno, -a *pron (uno)* someone, somebody; *(nelle interrogative)* anyone, anybody; *(alcuni)* some; *(alcuni: nelle interrogative)* any; **qualcun altro** *(persona)* someone else; **~ di voi** some of you; *(nelle interrogative)* any of you.

quale ◇ *agg interr* **1.** *(persona)* which; **qual è il tuo scrittore preferito?** who is your favourite writer?; **da ~ dentista sei stato?** which dentist have you been to?

2. *(cosa)* which, what; **non so ~ libro scegliere** I don't know which book to choose; **in ~ albergo hai prenotato?** which hotel have you booked?

◇ *agg relativo* such as, like; **alcuni animali quali il cane** some animals such as the dog.

◇ *pron interr* which (one); **~ vuole di questi cappelli?** which of these hats do you want?; **non so ~**

scegliere I don't know which (one) to choose.

◇ *pron relativo* 1. *(soggetto)*: **il/la ~** *(persona)* who; *(cosa)* which, that; **suo fratello, il ~ è un mio amico** his brother, who is a friend of mine.

2. *(con preposizioni: persona)* who(m); *(cosa)* which, that; **l'albergo nel ~ alloggio** the hotel (that) I'm staying in; **la persona con la ~ parlavo** the person (whom) I was talking to; **l'uomo del ~ conosco il figlio** the man whose son I know.

3. *(in qualità di)* as; **vengo ~ accompagnatore** I'm coming as a tour guide.

qualifica, -che *sf* qualification.

qualificare *vt* to describe, to define.

◆ **qualificarsi** *vr* to qualify.

qualificativo, -a *agg* qualifying.

qualità *sf inv* quality; *(varietà)* type; **in ~ di** in one's capacity as.

qualsiasi = **qualunque**.

qualunque *agg* any; *(quale che)* whatever; **~ cosa** anything; **~ cosa succeda** whatever happens; **~ persona** anyone; **prendine uno ~** take whichever you want.

quando *avv & cong* when; **da ~ sono qui** from when I got here; **da ~ sei qui?** how long have you been here?; **da ~ in qua** since when; **di ~ sono queste foto?** when were these photos taken?

quantità *sf inv* quantity, amount; **una ~ di** a lot o lots of.

quanto, -a ◇ *agg interr* 1. *(quantità)* how much; *(numero)* how many; **~ tempo ci vuole?** how long does it take?; **quanti anni hai?** how old are you?

2. *(in frasi esclamative)* what; **quanta fatica sprecata!** what a waste of energy!

◇ *agg relativo (quantità)* as much as; *(numero)* as many as; **puoi restare quanti giorni vuoi** you can stay for as many days as you like.

◇ *pron interr (quantità)* how much; *(numero)* how many; **prima di comprare il pane guarda ~ ce n'è** before buying the bread see how much there is; **quanti ne vuoi?** how many do you want?; **quanti ne abbiamo oggi?** what's the date today?

◇ *pron relativo (quello che: quantità)* as much as; *(numero)* as many as; **dammene ~ ti pare** give me as much as you want; **per ~ ne so** as far as I know.

◇ *avv* 1. *(interrogativo: quantità)* how much; *(numero)* how many; **quant'è?** how much is it? **~ ti fermi?** how long are you staying?; **~ è alta questa montagna?** how high is this mountain?; **~ mi dispiace!** I'm so sorry!; **~ costa/costano?** how much is it/are they?

2. *(relativo)* as much as; **mi sforzo ~ posso** I try as hard as I can; **~ prima** as soon as possible.

3. *(in espressioni)*: **in ~** *(perché)* as; **per ~** however.

quaranta *num* forty, → **sei**.

quarantena *sf* quarantine.

quarantesimo, -a *num* fortieth, → **sesto**.

quarantina *sf*: **una ~ (di)** about forty; **essere sulla ~** to be in one's forties.

quaresima *sf* (RELIG): **la ~** Lent.

quarta *sf (marcia)* fourth gear.

quartetto *sm* quartet.

quartiere *sm* area, district; **quartier generale** headquarters *(pl)*.

quarto, -a ◇ *num* fourth ◇ *sm (parte)* quarter; **un ~ d'ora** a quarter of an hour; **le tre e un ~** quarter past three *(Br)*, quarter after three *(Am)*; **le tre meno un ~** quarter to three *(Br)*, quarter of three *(Am)*; **un ~ di vino** a quarter litre of wine, → **sesto**.

quarzo *sm* quartz.

quasi ◇ *avv* nearly ◇ *cong* as if; **~ mai** hardly ever; **~ sempre** almost always; ~ ~ **vengo anch'io** I might just come too.

quassù *avv* up here.

quattordicesimo, -a *num* fourteenth, → **sesto**.

quattordici *num* fourteen, → **sei**.

quattrini *smpl (fam)* money *(sg)*.

quattro *num* four; **farsi in ~ (per fare qc)** to go out of one's way (to do sthg); **eravamo ~ gatti** *(fam)* there were only a few of us there; **in ~ e quattr'otto** in less than no time, → **sei**.

quattrocento *num* four hundred, → **sei**.

◆ **Quattrocento** *sm*: **il Quattrocento** the fifteenth century.

quei → **quello**.

quegli → **quello**.

quello, -a (*dav sm* **quel** (*pl* **quei**) + *consonante*; **quello** (*pl* **quegli**) + *s+consonante, gn, ps, x, z*; **quell'** (*pl* **quegli**) + *vocale)* ◇ *agg* **1.** *(indica lontananza)* that, those *(pl)*; **quella casa** that house; **quegli alberi** those trees; **quei bambini** those children.
2. *(per sottolineare)*: **spegni quella tv!** switch that TV off!
3. *(per cosa, persona già nota)* that, those *(pl)*; **non mi piace quella gente** I don't like those people.
◇ *pron* **1.** *(indica lontananza)* that (one), those (ones) *(pl)*; **quella è la mia macchina** that one's my car; **prendo ~ in offerta** I'll take the one on special offer; ~ **lì** that one (there).
2. *(con pronome relativo)*: **faccio ~ che posso** I'll do what I can; **quelli che potevano si sono fermati** those who could, stopped.

quercia, -ce *sf* oak.

querelare *vt* to bring a legal action against.

quesito *sm* query.

questionario *sm* questionnaire.

questione *sf* question; **è ~ di giorni** it's a matter of days; **in ~** in question.

questo, -a ◇ *agg* **1.** *(indica prossimità)* this, these *(pl)*; **questa finestra è aperta** this window is open; **partiamo ~ giovedì** we're leaving this Thursday.
2. *(simile)* such; **non uscire con questa pioggia** don't go out in rain like this.
3. *(il seguente/precedente)* this, these *(pl)*; **~ è il mio consiglio** this is my advice.
◇ *pron* **1.** *(indica prossimità)* this (one), these (ones) *(pl)*; **~ è Franco** this is Franco; **~ qui** o **qua** this one (here).
2. *(per riassumere)* that; **~ è tutto** that's all; **questa è bella!** that's rich!

questura *sf (organo)* police headquarters *(pl)*.

qui *avv* here; **da ~ in avanti** from now on; **di** o **da ~** from here; **di ~ a un anno** in a year's time; **di ~ a poco** in a little while.

quiete *sf* quiet.

quindi *cong* so, therefore.

quindicesimo, -a *num* fifteenth, → **sesto**.

quindici *num* fifteen; **~ giorni** a fortnight, → **sei**.

quindicina *sf* about fifteen; **una ~ di giorni** about a fortnight.

quinta *sf (marcia)* fifth gear.

◆ **quinte** *sfpl (di teatro)* wings.

quintale *sm* = 100 kilograms.

quinto, -a *num* fifth, → **sesto**.

quintuplo *sm*: **il ~ del prezzo normale** five times the normal price.

Quirinale *nm*: **il ~** *official residence of the President of Italy*.

quota *sf (altitudine)* altitude; *(di denaro, bene)* share; **perdere ~** to lose height; **prendere ~** to climb; **~ d'iscrizione** *(a circolo)* membership fee.

quotato, -a *agg* valued.

quotidianamente *avv* daily.

quotidiano, -a ◇ *agg* daily ◇ *sm* daily (newspaper).

quoziente *sm* quotient; **~ d'intelligenza** IQ.

R

rabarbaro *sm* rhubarb.
rabbia *sf (collera)* anger, rage; *(malattia)* rabies; **far ~ a qn** to drive sb mad.
rabbino *sm* rabbi.
rabbioso, -a *agg* angry; (MED) rabid.
rabbonire *vt* to calm down.
◆ **rabbonirsi** *vr* to calm down.
rabbrividire *vi (di freddo)* to shiver; *(di paura)* to shudder.
raccapezzarsi *vr*: **non mi ci raccapezzo** I can't make it out.
raccapricciante *agg* horrifying.
raccattapalle *smf inv* ball-boy (*f* ball-girl).
raccattare *vt* to pick up.
racchetta *sf (da tennis)* racket; *(da ping-pong)* bat *(Br)*, paddle *(Am)*; *(da sci)* ski pole.
raccogliere *vt (da terra)* to pick up; *(frutti, fiori)* to pick; *(mettere insieme)* to collect; *(voti)* to win.
◆ **raccogliersi** *vr (radunarsi)* to meet, to gather; *(in meditazione, preghiera)* to gather one's thoughts.
raccolta *sf* collection; *(agricola)* harvest; **fare la ~ di qc** to collect sthg.
raccolto, -a ◇ *pp* → **raccogliere** ◇ *sm* harvest, crop.
raccomandare *vt* to recommend; *(affidare)* to entrust; **~ a qn di fare qc** to urge sb to do sthg.
◆ **raccomandarsi** *vr*: **raccomandarsi a** to appeal to; **mi raccomando, non fare tardi!** don't be late now, will you!
raccomandata *sf* registered letter.
raccomandato, -a *agg (lettera)* registered; *(candidato)* recommended.
raccomandazione *sf (consiglio)* recommendation.
raccontare *vt* to tell.
racconto *sm (esposizione)* account; *(romanzo)* short story.
raccordo *sm* connection, link; *(di autostrada)* slip road *(Br)*, entrance/exit ramp *(Am)*; **~ anulare** ring road *(Br)*, beltway *(Am)*.
racimolare *vt* to scrape together.
rada *sf* harbour.
radar *sm inv* radar.
raddoppiare ◇ *vt (rendere doppio)* to double; *(aumentare)* to redouble ◇ *vi* to double.
radente *agg (tiro, volo)* very low.
radere *vt* to shave; **~ qc al suolo** to raze sthg to the ground.
◆ **radersi** *vr* to shave.
radiare *vt* to strike off.
radiatore *sm* radiator.
radiazione *sf* radiation.
radicale *agg* radical.

radicalmente *avv* radically, completely.
radicchio *sm* chicory.
radice *sf* root; ~ **quadrata** square root.
radio *sf inv* radio; *(stazione)* radio station; **alla** ~ on the radio.
radioamatore, -trice *sm, f* radio ham.
radioascoltatore, -trice *sm, f* listener.
radioattivo, -a *agg* radioactive.
radiocomandato, -a *agg* remote-controlled.
radiografia *sf* X-ray.
radioso, -a *agg* bright.
radiotaxi *sm inv* minicab.
rado, -a *agg* sparse; **di** ~ rarely.
radunare *vt (persone)* to gather; *(cose)* to assemble.
◆ **radunarsi** *vr* to gather.
raduno *sm* meeting.
rafano *sm* radish.
raffermo, -a *agg* stale.
raffica, -che *sf (di vento)* gust; *(di mitra)* burst.
raffigurare *vt* to portray.
raffinato, -a *agg* refined; *(stile)* sophisticated.
raffineria *sf* refinery.
rafforzare *vt* to strengthen.
raffreddare *vt* to cool; *(fig: rapporti, interesse)* to cool, to dampen.
◆ **raffreddarsi** *vr (bevanda, cibo)* to get cold; *(fig: persona, amicizia)* to cool down; *(ammalarsi)* to catch a cold.
raffreddato, -a *agg*: **essere** ~ to have a cold.
raffreddore *sm* cold.
rafia *sf* raffia.
ragazza *sf (giovane donna)* girl; *(fidanzata)* girlfriend; ~ **madre** single mother.
ragazzata *sf* childish trick.
ragazzo *sm (giovane)* boy; *(fidanzato)* boyfriend.
raggiante *agg* radiant, beaming.
raggio *sm (di sole, infrarosso)* ray; *(area)* range; (MAT) radius; *(di ruota)* spoke.
raggirare *vt* to trick, to cheat.
raggiungere *vt (persona)* to catch up; *(luogo)* to reach; *(fig: fine)* to achieve.
raggiunto, -a *pp* → **raggiungere**.
raggomitolarsi *vr* to curl up.
raggranellare *vt* to scrape together.
raggrinzire *vt & vi* to shrivel up.
◆ **raggrinzirsi** *vr* to shrivel.
raggruppare *vt (mettere insieme)* to assemble; *(a gruppi)* to group together.
◆ **raggrupparsi** *vr* to assemble.
ragguagli *smpl*: **dare** ~ to give details.
ragionamento *sm (riflessione)* reasoning; *(discorso)* argument.
ragionare *vi* to reason.
◆ **ragionare di** *v + prep (parlare di)* to argue about.
ragione *sf* reason; **avere** ~ to be right; **dare** ~ **a qn** to side with sb; **a maggior** ~ even more so.
ragioneria *sf (materia)* accountancy; *(scuola)* commercial school; *(reparto)* accounts *(pl)*.
ragionevole *agg* reasonable.
ragioniere, -a *sm, f* accountant.
ragliare *vi* to bray.
ragnatela *sf* cobweb, spider's web.
ragno *sm* spider.
ragù *sm inv sauce of minced beef, tomatoes and onions.*
RAI *sf Italian broadcasting corporation.*
rallegramenti *smpl* congratulations.
rallentare *vt* to slow down.
rally ['rɛlli] *sm inv* rally.
ramaiolo *sm* ladle.
ramanzina *sf* telling-off.

rame *sm* copper.
ramino *sm* rummy.
rammaricarsi : rammaricarsi di *vr + prep* to regret.
rammendare *vt (stoffa)* to mend; *(lana)* to darn.
rammentare *vt* to remember; ~ **qc a qn** to remind sb of sthg.
◆ **rammentarsi di** *vr + prep* to remember.
rammollito, -a *agg* soft.
ramo *sm* branch.
ramoscello *sm* twig.
rampa *sf* flight *(of stairs)*; ~ **di lancio** launch pad.
rampicante *agg* climbing.
rampone *sm (fiocina)* harpoon; *(in alpinismo)* crampon.
rana *sf* frog.
rancido, -a *agg* rancid.
rancore *sm* rancour.
randagio, -a, -gi, -gie o **-ge** *agg* stray.
randello *sm* club.
rango, -ghi *sm* rank.
rannicchiarsi *vr* to huddle up.
rannuvolarsi *vr* to cloud over.
ranocchio *sm* frog.
rantolo *sm* death rattle.
rapa *sf* turnip.
rapace ◇ *agg* predatory ◇ *sm* bird of prey.
rapare *vt* to crop.
rapida *sf* rapids *(pl)*.
rapidamente *avv* rapidly, fast.
rapidità *sf* rapidity.
rapido, -a ◇ *agg (svelto)* fast; *(breve)* quick, rapid ◇ *sm* express (train).
rapimento *sm* kidnapping.
rapina *sf* robbery; ~ **a mano armata** armed robbery.
rapinare *vt* to rob.
rapinatore, -trice *sm, f* robber.
rapire *vt* to kidnap.
rapitore, -trice *sm, f* kidnapper.
rapporto *sm (resoconto)* report; *(tra persone)* relationship; *(connessione)* connection, relation; (MAT) ratio; **rapporti sessuali** sexual intercourse *(sg)*.
rapprendersi *vr* to curdle.
rappresentante *smf* representative.
rappresentare *vt* to represent; *(raffigurare)* to depict; *(mettere in scena)* to stage, to perform.
rappresentazione *sf (spettacolo)* performance; *(raffigurazione)* representation.
rappreso, -a *pp* → **rapprendersi**.
raramente *avv* rarely.
rarità *sf inv (scarsità)* rarity; *(oggetto)* rare thing.
raro, -a *agg* rare.
rasare *vt* to shave.
◆ **rasarsi** *vr* to shave.
rasato, -a *agg* shaven.
raschiare *vt* to scrape.
rasentare *vt (sfiorare)* to graze; *(muro)* to hug, to keep close to; *(fig: avvicinarsi a)* to border on.
rasente *prep* close to.
raso, -a ◇ *pp* → **radere** ◇ *agg (cucchiaio)* level; ~ **terra** close to the ground.
rasoio *sm* razor; ~ **elettrico** electric razor.
rassegna *sf* review; *(cinematografica, teatrale)* season; **passare in** ~ (MIL) to review.
rassegnare *vt*: ~ **le dimissioni** to hand in one's resignation.
◆ **rassegnarsi** *vr* to resign o.s.
rasserenarsi *vr* to clear up.
rassettare *vt (stanza, capelli)* to tidy (up); *(vestito)* to mend.
rassicurare *vt* to reassure.
rassodare *vt (terreno)* to harden; *(muscoli)* to tone.
rassomigliare : rassomigliare a *v + prep* to resemble.
rastrellare *vt (foglie)* to rake; *(fig: zona)* to comb.
rastrello *sm* rake.

rata *sf* instalment; **pagare qc a rate** to pay for sthg in instalments.
rateale *agg* by o in instalments.
ratificare *vt* (DIR) to ratify.
ratto *sm* rat.
rattoppare *vt* to patch.
rattrappire *vt* to numb.
◆ **rattrappirsi** *vr* to go numb.
rattristare *vt* to make sad.
◆ **rattristarsi** *vr* to become sad.
rauco, -a, -chi, -che *agg* raucous.
ravanello *sm* radish.
ravioli *smpl* ravioli.
ravvicinare *vt* *(avvicinare)* to bring closer; *(rappacificare)* to reconcile.
◆ **ravvicinarsi** *vr* to be reconciled.
ravvivare *vt* to brighten up.
razionale *agg* rational.
razionalità *sf* rationality.
razionare *vt* to ration.
razione *sf* ration.
razza *sf* *(di persone)* race; *(di animali)* breed; *(pesce)* ray; **che ~ di domanda è questa?** *(fam)* what sort of question is that?
razzia *sf* raid.
razziale *agg* racial.
razzismo *sm* racism.
razzista, -i, -e *agg & smf* racist.
razzo *sm* rocket.
razzolare *vi* to scratch about.
re *sm inv* king.
reagire *vi*: **~ (a qc)** to react (to sthg).
reale *agg* *(vero)* real; *(di re)* royal.
realista, -i, -e *smf* realist.
realizzare *vt* *(progetto)* to carry out; *(sogno)* to fulfil; *(film)* to produce; *(rendersi conto di)* to realize; (COMM) to realize.
◆ **realizzarsi** *vr* *(persona)* to be fulfilled; *(progetto)* to be carried out; *(sogno)* to come true.
realizzazione *sf* *(attuazione)* carrying-out.
realmente *avv* really.
realtà *sf inv* reality; **in ~** in reality.
reato *sm* offence, crime.
reattore *sm* *(aereo)* jet; *(motore)* jet engine; *(in fisica)* reactor.
reazionario, -a *agg* reactionary.
reazione *sf* reaction.
rebus *sm inv* *game in which pictures represent the syllables of words.*
recapitare *vt* to deliver.
recapito *sm* *(luogo)* address; *(consegna)* delivery; **~ telefonico** (tele)phone number.
recare *vt*: **~ disturbo a qn** to disturb sb.
◆ **recarsi** *vr* to go.
recensione *sf* review.
recente *agg* recent; **di ~** recently.
recentemente *avv* recently.
recessione *sf* recession.
recidere *vt* to cut off.
recintare *vt* to fence in.
recinto *sm* *(spazio)* enclosure; *(recinzione)* fence.
recipiente *sm* container.
reciproco, -a, -ci, -che *agg* reciprocal.
reciso, -a *pp* → **recidere**.
recita *sf* play.
recitare ◇ *vt* *(poesia)* to recite; *(ruolo)* to play ◇ *vi* to act.
reclamare ◇ *vi* to complain ◇ *vt* to claim.
réclame [re'klam] *sf inv* advertising.
reclamo *sm* *(protesta)* complaint.
reclinabile *agg* reclining.
reclusione *sf* (DIR) imprisonment.
reclutare *vt* to recruit.
record *sm inv* record.
recuperare *vt* *(riprendere)* to recover, to get back; *(svantaggio, tempo)* to make up; *(rottami)* to salvage.
redatto, -a *pp* → **redigere**.
redattore, -trice *sm, f* editor.

redazione *sf (stesura)* writing; *(ufficio)* editorial department; *(personale)* editorial staff.
redditizio, -a *agg* profitable.
reddito *sm* income.
redigere *vt (articolo, lettera)* to write; *(documento, contratto)* to draw up.
redini *sfpl* reins.
referendum *sm inv* referendum.
referenze *sfpl* references.
referto *sm* medical report.
refettorio *sm* refectory, dining hall.
refrigerare *vt* to refrigerate.
refurtiva *sf* stolen goods *(pl)*.
regalare *vt (dono)* to give (as a present); *(dare gratis)* to give away.
regalo *sm (dono)* present, gift.
regata *sf* regatta.
reggere ◇ *vt (tenere)* to hold; *(sostenere)* to bear, to support; *(sopportare)* to bear; *(governare)* to govern; (GRAMM) to take, to be followed by ◇ *vi (durare)* to last; *(essere logico)* to stand up, to hold good; *(resistere)*: ~ **a qc** to withstand sthg.
◆ **reggersi** *vr*: **non mi reggo in piedi** I can't stand up.
reggia, -ge *sf* palace.
reggicalze *sm inv* suspender belt.
reggimento *sm* regiment.
reggipetto = **reggiseno**.
reggiseno *sm* bra.
regia *sf (di film)* direction; *(di dramma)* production.
regime *sm (politico)* regime; *(alimentare)* diet.
regina *sf* queen.
regionale *agg* regional.
regione *sf* region.
regista, -i, -e *smf* director.
registrare *vt* to register; *(su cassetta)* to record; (COMM) to enter.
registratore *sm* tape recorder; ~ **di cassa** cash register.
registrazione *sf (di nascita, morte)* registration; *(di musica, programma)* recording; (COMM) entry.
registro *sm* register; ~ **di classe** attendance register.
regnare *vi* to reign.
regno *sm* kingdom; *(fig: ambito)* realm.
◆ **Regno Unito** *sm*: **il Regno Unito** the United Kingdom.
regola *sf* rule; **essere in ~** to be (all) in order; **fare qc a ~ d'arte** to do sthg perfectly.
regolabile *agg* adjustable.
regolamento *sm* regulations *(pl)*.
regolare ◇ *agg* regular ◇ *vt* to regulate; *(apparecchio, macchina)* to adjust; *(questione, conto)* to settle
◆ **regolarsi** *vr (comportarsi)* to behave; *(moderarsi)* to control o.s.; **regolarsi nel bere/mangiare** to watch what one drinks/eats.
regolarmente *avv* regularly.
regolo *sm* ruler; ~ **calcolatore** slide rule.
regredire *vi* to regress.
reintegrare *vt* to reinstate.
relativamente *avv* relatively, comparatively; ~ **a** in relation to, as regards.
relativo, -a *agg* relative; ~ **a** relating to.
relax *sm* relaxation.
relazione *sf* relationship; *(amorosa)* affair; *(resoconto)* report.
relegare *vt* to relegate.
religione *sf* religion.
religioso, -a ◇ *agg* religious ◇ *sm, f* monk (*f* nun).
reliquia *sf* relic.
relitto *sm* wreck, piece of wreckage.
remare *vi* to row.
remo *sm* oar.
rendere ◇ *vt (restituire)* to give back, to return; *(far diventare)* to make; *(produrre)* to yield ◇ *vi (persona, azienda)* to do well; *(lavoro)*

to pay well; ~ **possibile qc** to make sthg possible; ~ **l'idea** *(persona)* to make o.s. clear.

◆ **rendersi** *vr (diventare)* to become; **rendersi utile** to make o.s. useful.

rendiconto *sm (relazione)* report; (COMM) statement of accounts.

rendimento *sm (efficienza)* efficiency; *(di scolaro, macchina)* performance.

rendita *sf* unearned income; **vivere di** ~ *(fig: studente)* to get by on one's past performance.

rene *sm* kidney.

renitente *agg* reluctant; **è** ~ **ai consigli** he won't listen to advice; **essere** ~ **alla leva** *to fail to report for military service.*

renna *sf* reindeer.

Reno *sm*: **il** ~ the Rhine.

reparto *sm (di negozio)* department; *(d'ospedale)* ward; (MIL) unit.

repentaglio *sm*: **mettere a** ~ **qc** to put sthg at risk.

reperibile *agg (merce, persona)* available; *(al lavoro)* on call.

reperto *sm (resto)* find; *(resoconto)* report.

repertorio *sm (teatrale)* repertoire; *(elenco)* index.

replica, -che *sf (in televisione)* repeat; *(a teatro)* repeat performance.

replicare *vt* to reply.

repressione *sf* repression.

represso, -a *pp* → **reprimere**.

reprimere *vt* to repress.

◆ **reprimersi** *vr* to restrain o.s.

repubblica, -che *sf* republic.

repubblicano, -a *agg* republican.

repulsione *sf* repulsion.

reputare *vt* to consider.

reputazione *sf* reputation.

requisire *vt* to requisition.

requisito *sm* requisite.

resa *sf (l'arrendersi)* surrender; *(restituzione)* return; *(rendimento)* yield; ~ **dei conti** *(fig)* day of reckoning.

residence ['rɛzidens] *sm inv* residential hotel.

residente *agg* resident.

residenza *sf* residence.

residenziale *agg* residential.

residuo, -a ◇ *agg* residual, remaining ◇ *sm (avanzo)* remainder; *(scoria)* waste.

resina *sf* resin.

resistente *agg (robusto)* strong; *(durevole)* durable; ~ **al calore** heat-proof, heat-resistant.

resistenza *sf* resistance; *(di materiale)* strength; *(a fatica, dolore)* endurance; ~ **(elettrica)** (electrical) resistance.

resistere *vi (tener duro)* to hold out.

◆ **resistere a** *v + prep (opporsi)* to resist; *(sopportare)* to withstand.

resistito, -a *pp* → **resistere**.

reso, -a *pp* → **rendere**.

resoconto *sm* account.

respingere *vt* to reject; *(attacco, aggressore)* to repel; (SCOL) to fail.

respinto, -a *pp* → **respingere**.

respirare *vi & vt* to breathe.

respiratore *sm (per immersione)* aqualung; (MED) respirator.

respirazione *sf* breathing; ~ **artificiale** artificial respiration.

respiro *sm (respirazione)* breathing; *(movimento)* breath; **tirare un** ~ **di sollievo** to heave a sigh of relief.

responsabile ◇ *agg* responsible ◇ *smf (in azienda, negozio)* person in charge; *(colpevole)* culprit; **essere** ~ **di qc** *(incaricato di)* to be in charge of sthg; *(colpevole di)* to be responsible for sthg.

responsabilità *sf inv* responsibility; *(colpa)* responsibility, liability.

ressa *sf* crowd.

restare *vi* to stay, to remain;

(avanzare) to be left, to remain; *(trovarsi)* to be; ~ **a piedi** to remain standing; **mi restano pochi giorni** I only have a few days left.

restaurare *vt* to restore.

restauro *sm* restoration.

restituire *vt* to give back, to return.

resto *sm* rest, remainder; *(di denaro)* change; (MAT) remainder; **del** ~ moreover, besides.

♦ **resti** *smpl (ruderi)* ruins; *(di cibo)* leftovers; *(di persona, animale)* remains.

restringere *vt (dimensioni)* to reduce; *(tessuto)* to shrink; *(limitare)* to limit, to restrict.

♦ **restringersi** *vr (strada)* to (become) narrow; *(stoffa)* to shrink; *(per numero, estensione)* to reduce.

resurrezione *sf* resurrection.

resuscitare = **risuscitare**.

rete *sf* net; *(recinzione)* wire fence; *(radiotelevisiva, stradale)* network; *(del letto)* bedsprings *(pl)*; *(nel calcio: punto)* goal.

♦ **Rete** *sf* (INFORM): **la Rete** the Net.

reticente *agg* reticent.

reticolato *sm (intreccio di linee)* network; *(recinzione)* fencing, wire netting.

retina *sf* (ANAT) retina.

retino *sm* net.

retorico, -a, -ci, -che *agg (spreg)* pompous.

retribuire *vt* to remunerate, to pay.

retribuzione *sf* remuneration, pay.

retro *sm inv* back; **sul** ~ at the back; **vedi** ~ see over.

retrocedere *vi* to recede; (SPORT) to be relegated.

retrocesso, -a *pp* → **retrocedere**.

retrogrado, -a *agg* retrograde.

retromarcia *sf* reverse.

retroscena *sm inv (antefatti)* background.

retrospettivo, -a *agg* retrospective.

retrovisore *sm* rear-view mirror.

retta *sf (linea)* straight line; *(di pensionato)* charge; **dar** ~ **a** to pay attention to.

rettangolare *agg* rectangular.

rettangolo *sm* rectangle.

rettificare *vt (form)* to rectify.

rettile *sm* reptile.

rettilineo, -a *agg & sm* straight.

retto, -a ◇ *pp* → **reggere** ◇ *agg (diritto)* straight; *(persona, comportamento)* honest; **angolo** ~ right angle.

rettore *sm* rector.

reumatismi *smpl* rheumatism *(sg)*.

reversibile *agg* reversible.

revisionare *vt (apparecchio, macchina)* to service, to overhaul; *(testo)* to revise.

revisione *sf (di apparecchio)* service; *(di conti)* audit(ing); *(di scritto)* revision.

revocare *vt* to revoke.

revolver *sm inv* revolver.

riabilitare *vt* to rehabilitate.

riacquistare *vt* to regain.

riaggiustare *vt* to readjust.

rialzare *vt* to raise.

♦ **rialzarsi** *vr* to get up.

rialzo *sm* rise.

rianimazione *sf (reparto)* intensive care.

riaperto, -a *pp* → **riaprire**.

riapertura *sf* reopening; ~ **delle scuole** beginning of the school term.

riaprire *vt & vi* to reopen.

♦ **riaprirsi** *vr* to reopen.

riarmo *sm* rearming.

riassetto *sm* reorganization.

riassumere *vt (ricapitolare)* to summarize; *(impiegato)* to reemploy; *(riprendere)* to resume.

riassunto, -a ◇ *pp* → **riassumere** ◇ *sm* summary.
riattaccare *vt (attaccare di nuovo)* to re-attach; *(bottone)* to sew back on; *(ricominciare)* to start again; *(al telefono)* to hang up.
riavere *vt (avere di nuovo)* to have again; *(avere indietro)* to get back; *(riacquistare)* to regain, to recover.
♦ **riaversi da** *vr + prep* to recover from.
ribadire *vt* to confirm.
ribaltabile *agg* folding.
ribaltare *vt* to overturn.
ribassare ◇ *vt* to lower ◇ *vi* to fall.
ribasso *sm* fall, reduction.
ribattere ◇ *vt (palla)* to return ◇ *vi (replicare)* to answer back.
ribellarsi *vr* to rebel; ~ **a qn** to rebel against sb.
ribelle *agg* rebellious.
ribellione *sf* rebellion.
ribes *sm inv*: ~ **nero** blackcurrant; ~ **rosso** redcurrant.
ribollire *vi (fig)* to seethe.
ribrezzo *sm* horror; **far ~ a qn** to revolt sb.
ricadere *vi (cadere di nuovo)* to fall again; *(in errore, vizio)* to relapse; *(capelli, vestiti)* to hang down.
♦ **ricadere su** *v + prep* to fall on.
ricalcare *vt* to trace.
ricamare *vt* to embroider.
ricambiare *vt (sentimento, favore)* to return; *(cambiare di nuovo)* to change again.
ricambio *sm (sostituzione)* exchange, replacement; **in ~** in return.
♦ **ricambi** *smpl* spare parts.
ricamo *sm* embroidery.
ricapitolare *vt* to summarize.
ricaricare *vt (macchina fotografica, arma)* to reload; *(batteria)* to recharge; *(orologio)* to wind up.
ricattare *vt* to blackmail.
ricatto *sm* blackmail.
ricavare *vt (estrarre)* to extract; *(ottenere)* to obtain.
ricavato *sm (guadagno)* proceeds *(pl)*.
ricchezza *sf* wealth.
♦ **ricchezze** *sfpl* wealth *(sg)*; ~ **naturali** natural resources.
ricciarelli *smpl diamond-shaped sweets made from marzipan (a speciality of Siena)*.
riccio, -a, -ci, -ce ◇ *agg* curly ◇ *sm (di capelli)* curl; *(animale)* hedgehog; ~ **di mare** sea urchin.
ricciolo *sm* curl.
ricciuto, -a *agg* curly.
ricco, -a, -chi, -che *agg* rich, wealthy; ~ **di qc** rich in sthg.
ricerca, -che *sf* research; *(di persona, di cosa)* search; **essere alla ~ di** to be in search of.
ricercare *vt (cercare di nuovo)* to look for (again); *(ladro)* to look for, to search for.
ricercatezza *sf* refinement.
ricercato, -a *agg (elegante)* refined; *(apprezzato)* in demand, sought-after; **essere ~ dalla polizia** to be wanted by the police.
ricercatore, -trice *sm, f* researcher.
ricetta *sf* recipe; ~ **medica** prescription.
ricettazione *sf* receiving (stolen goods).
ricevere *vt (lettera, regalo)* to receive, to get; *(schiaffo, palla)* to get; *(accogliere)* to welcome; *(ospite)* to entertain; *(cliente, paziente)* to receive.
ricevimento *sm* reception.
ricevitore *sm* receiver.
ricevuta *sf* receipt; **mi può fare una ~?** may I have a receipt?
ricezione *sf* reception.
richiamare *vt (ritelefonare, per far tornare)* to call back; *(attirare)* to attract; *(rimproverare)* to reprimand; ~ **alla mente qc a qn** to

remind sb of sthg.
richiamo *sm (per far tornare)* call; *(attrazione)* appeal, attraction; *(di vaccinazione)* booster.
richiedere *vt (ridomandare)* to ask again; *(aiuto, spiegazioni)* to ask for; *(necessitare di)* to require; **gli ho richiesto le chiavi** *(indietro)* I asked him for my keys back.
richiesta *sf (domanda)* request; *(esigenza)* demand; **a ~** on request.
richiesto, -a ◇ *pp* → **richiedere** ◇ *agg* in demand, sought-after.
richiudere *vt* to close again.
riciclare *vt* to recycle.
ricollegare *vt (centri isolati)* to reconnect; *(fatti, discorsi)* to connect, to relate.
◆ **ricollegarsi** *vr*: **ricollegarsi a** *(riferirsi)* to refer to; *(fatto)* to be connected with.
ricominciare *vt & vi* to begin again, to start again; **~ a fare qc** to begin again, to resume doing sthg.
ricompensa *sf* reward.
ricompensare *vt* to reward.
ricomporre *vt* to reconstruct.
◆ **ricomporsi** *vr* to regain one's composure.
ricomposto, -a *pp* → **ricomporre**.
riconciliare *vt* to reconcile.
◆ **riconciliarsi** *vr* to be reconciled.
ricondotto, -a *pp* → **ricondurre**.
ricondurre *vt (in luogo)* to take back, to bring back.
riconferma *sf (conferma ulteriore)* reconfirmation; *(dimostrazione)* proof.
riconfermare *vt* to reconfirm.
riconoscente *agg* grateful.
riconoscere *vt* to recognize; *(ammettere)* to admit.
riconquistare *vt (territorio)* to reconquer; *(stima, rispetto)* to regain.
riconsegnare *vt* to give back.
ricoperto, -a *pp* → **ricoprire**.
ricopiare *vt* to copy.
ricoprire *vt (poltrona, dolce)* to cover; *(carica)* to hold; **~ qn/qc di qc** to cover sb/sthg with sthg.
ricordare *vt* to remember, to recall; **~ qc a qn** to remind sb of sthg; **non mi ricordo l'indirizzo** I don't remember the address.
◆ **ricordarsi di** *vr + prep* to remember; **ricordarsi di aver fatto qc** to remember doing o having done sthg; **ricordarsi di fare qc** to remember to do sthg.
ricordo *sm (memoria)* memory; *(oggetto)* souvenir.
ricorrente *agg* recurrent.
ricorrenza *sf* anniversary.
ricorrere *vi (ripetersi)* to recur.
◆ **ricorrere a** *v + prep (rivolgersi a)* to turn to; *(utilizzare)* to resort to.
ricorso, -a ◇ *pp* → **ricorrere** ◇ *sm* (DIR) appeal; **far ~ a qc** *(utilizzare)* to resort to sthg.
ricostruire *vt (edificio)* to rebuild; *(fatto)* to reconstruct.
ricotta *sf* ricotta *(soft cheese made from milk whey)*.
ricoverare *vt*: **~ qn in ospedale** to admit sb to hospital.
ricreare *vt (creare di nuovo)* to recreate.
ricreazione *sf (a scuola)* break.
ricredersi *vr* to change one's mind.
ricucire *vt* to mend.
ricuperare = **recuperare**.
ridacchiare *vi* to snigger.
ridare *vt (dare di nuovo)* to give again; *(restituire)* to give back.
ridere *vi* to laugh; **morire dal ~** to die laughing.
◆ **ridere di** *v + prep* to laugh at.
ridetto, -a *pp* → **ridire**.
ridicolo, -a *agg* ridiculous.
ridimensionare *vt*: **~ un problema** to get a problem into perspective.

ridire *vt (ripetere)* to repeat; **avere qualcosa da ~** to find fault.
ridondante *agg* redundant.
ridosso *sm*: **a ~ (di qc)** behind (sthg).
ridotto, -a ◇ *pp* → **ridurre** ◇ *agg (prezzo)* reduced; *(formato)* smaller; **~ male** in a bad state.
ridurre *vt* to reduce.
◆ **ridursi** *vr (diminuire)* to shrink.
◆ **ridursi a** *vr + prep* to be reduced to.
riduzione *sf* reduction.
rielaborare *vt* to redesign.
riempire *vt* to fill; *(modulo)* to fill in; **~ di** to fill with.
◆ **riempirsi di** *vr + prep (stadio, cinema)* to fill with; *(fam: mangiare)* to stuff o.s. with.
rientrare *vi (entrare di nuovo)* to go/come back in; *(a casa, in patria)* to return; *(essere compreso)* to be included; *(avere una rientranza)* to curve inwards.
riepilogo, -ghi *sm* summary.
rievocare *vt (ricordare)* to recall; *(far ricordare)* to commemorate.
rifare *vt (fare di nuovo)* to do again; *(ricostruire)* to rebuild; **~ il letto** to make the bed.
◆ **rifarsi di** *vr + prep (perdita)* to recover; **rifarsi di qc su qn** to get one's own back on sb for sthg.
rifatto, -a *pp* → **rifare**.
riferimento *sm* reference; **fare ~ a** to refer to.
riferire *vt*: **~ qc (a qn)** to report sthg (to sb).
◆ **riferirsi a** *vr + prep* to refer to.
rifilare *vt*: **~ qc a qn** *(fam: merce)* to palm sthg off on sb; *(fam: compito)* to saddle sb with sthg.
rifiniture *sfpl* finishing touches.
rifiorire *vi* to flower again.
rifiutare *vt* to refuse; **~ di fare qc** to refuse to do sthg.
rifiuto *sm* refusal.
◆ **rifiuti** *smpl (spazzatura)* rubbish *(sg) (Br)*, trash *(sg) (Am)*.
riflessione *sf* reflection.
riflessivo, -a *agg* reflexive.
riflesso, -a ◇ *pp* → **riflettere** ◇ *sm (luce)* reflection; *(conseguenza)* repercussion; (MED) reflex.
riflettere *vt & vi* to reflect; **~ su** to reflect on, to think about.
◆ **riflettersi** *vr* to be reflected.
◆ **riflettersi su** *vr + prep (influire)* to influence, to have repercussions on.
riflettore *sm (di teatro)* spotlight; *(di stadio)* floodlight.
riflusso *sm (flusso contrario)* flow; *(di marea)* ebb.
riforma *sf* reform.
riformare *vt* to reform; (MIL) to invalid out.
rifornimento *sm*: **fare ~ di qc** to stock up with sthg.
◆ **rifornimenti** *smpl* supplies.
rifornire *vt*: **~ qn/qc di** to supply sb/sthg with.
◆ **rifornirsi di** *vr + prep* to stock up with.
rifrangere *vt* to refract.
rifratto, -a *pp* → **rifrangere**.
rifugiarsi *vr* to take refuge.
rifugiato, -a *sm, f* refugee.
rifugio *sm (riparo)* shelter, refuge; **~ alpino** mountain hut.
riga, -ghe *sf* line; *(di capelli)* parting; *(righello)* ruler; **mettersi in ~** to get into line; **a righe** *(tessuto)* striped; *(foglio)* lined.
rigare ◇ *vt* to scratch ◇ *vi*: **~ diritto** to toe the line.
rigattiere *sm* junk dealer.
rigettare *vt (gettare indietro)* to throw back; *(respingere)* to reject; *(fam: vomitare)* to throw up.
rigetto *sm* (MED) rejection.
rigidità *sf (di oggetto)* rigidity; *(del corpo)* stiffness; *(di clima)* harshness; *(di regolamento, persona)* strictness.

rigido, -a *agg (non elastico)* rigid; *(membra)* stiff; *(clima)* harsh; *(severo)* strict.

rigirare *vt (voltare)* to turn (round); ~ **il discorso** to change the subject.

◆ **rigirarsi** *vr (voltarsi)* to turn round; *(nel letto)* to turn over.

rigo, -ghi *sm* line.

rigoglioso, -a *agg* luxuriant.

rigore *sm* rigour; (SPORT) penalty; **essere di ~** to be compulsory.

rigoroso, -a *agg* rigorous.

rigovernare *vt* to wash up.

riguardare *vt (guardare di nuovo)* to look at again; *(controllare)* to check; *(concernere)* to concern.

◆ **riguardarsi** *vr* to look after o.s.; **riguardati!** look after yourself!, take care!; **questo non ti riguarda** this has nothing to do with you.

riguardo *sm (attenzione)* care; *(stima)* regard, respect; ~ **a** with regard to.

rilanciare *vt* to relaunch.

rilancio *sm* relaunch; *(economico)* recovery.

rilasciare *vt (intervista)* to give; *(ostaggio)* to release; *(documento, diploma)* to issue.

rilassare *vt* to relax.

◆ **rilassarsi** *vr* to relax.

rilegare *vt* to bind.

rilento *avv*: **a ~** slowly.

rilevante *agg* relevant.

rilevare *vt (notare)* to notice; *(mettere in evidenza)* to point out; *(dati)* to collect; (COMM) to take over.

rilievo *sm* relief; **mettere in ~ qc** to emphasize sthg.

riluttante *agg* reluctant.

rima *sf* rhyme.

rimandare *vt (mandare di nuovo)* to send again; *(mandare indietro)* to send back; *(riunione, esame)* to postpone; ~ **qn a qc** *(in testo)* to refer sb to sthg; ~ **qn in italiano** (SCOL) to make sb resit their Italian exam.

rimando *sm* cross-reference.

rimanente ◇ *agg* remaining ◇ *sm* remainder.

rimanenza *sf* remainder.

rimanere *vi (in luogo)* to stay, to remain; *(nel tempo)* to last, to remain; *(avanzare)* to be left; *(essere)* to be; **mi sono rimaste diecimila lire** I have ten thousand lire left; **siamo rimasti in due** there are (only) two of us left; **sono rimasto solo** I was left on my own; ~ **indietro** *(di luogo)* to be left behind; *(nel lavoro)* to fall behind.

rimarginare *vt* to heal.

◆ **rimarginarsi** *vr* to heal.

rimasto, -a *pp* → **rimanere**.

rimasuglio *sm* scrap.

rimbalzare *vi (palla)* bounce; *(proiettile)* to ricochet.

rimbalzo *sm (di palla)* bounce; *(di proiettile)* ricochet.

rimbambito, -a *agg* daft.

rimboccare *vt (lenzuola, coperta)* to tuck in; *(maniche, pantaloni)* to turn up; **rimboccarsi le maniche** to roll up one's sleeves.

rimbombare *vi* to rumble.

rimborsare *vt* to reimburse, to refund.

rimborso *sm* refund; ~ **spese** refund of expenses.

rimediare ◇ *vt (fam: procurarsi)* to find ◇ *vi*: ~ **a qc** *(sbaglio, danno)* to make amends for sthg.

rimedio *sm* remedy; **porre ~ a qc** to remedy sthg.

rimescolare *vt (liquido)* to mix well; *(carte)* to shuffle.

rimessa *sf (per veicoli)* garage; *(per aerei)* hangar; *(nel calcio)* throw-in.

rimesso, -a *pp* → **rimettere**.

rimettere *vt (mettere di nuovo)* to put back; *(indossare di nuovo)* to put back on; *(perdonare)* to forgive, to pardon; *(vomitare)* to vomit; ~ **a**

posto to tidy up; **rimetterci (qc)** to lose (sthg).

◆ **rimettersi** *vr* *(guarire)* to get better, to recover; *(tempo)* to clear up; **rimettersi a fare qc** to start doing sthg again.

rimmel® *sm inv* mascara.

rimodernare *vt* to modernize.

rimontare ◇ *vt* to reassemble ◇ *vi* to catch up.

rimorchiare *vt* *(veicolo)* to tow; *(fam: ragazza)* to pick up.

rimorchiatore *sm* tug.

rimorchio *sm* *(operazione)* towing; *(di veicolo)* trailer.

rimorso *sm* remorse.

rimosso, -a *pp* → **rimuovere**.

rimozione *sf* *(spostamento)* removal; *(da carica, impiego)* dismissal; '~ **forzata** o **coatta**' 'towaway zone'.

rimpatriare ◇ *vt* to repatriate ◇ *vi* to go home.

rimpiangere *vt*: ~ **di aver fatto qc** to regret doing sthg.

rimpianto, -a ◇ *pp* → **rimpiangere** ◇ *sm* regret.

rimpiattino *sm* hide-and-seek.

rimpiazzare *vt* to replace.

rimpicciolire ◇ *vt* to make smaller ◇ *vi* to become smaller.

rimpinzarsi : rimpinzarsi di *vr + prep* to stuff o.s. with.

rimproverare *vt* to scold.

rimprovero *sm* scolding.

rimuginare ◇ *vt* to brood over ◇ *vi*: ~ **(su qc)** to ponder (sthg).

rimuovere *vt* *(spostare)* to remove; *(da carica)* to dismiss.

Rinascimento *sm*: **il** ~ the Renaissance.

rinascita *sf* *(di foglie, capelli)* regrowth; *(economica, sociale)* revival.

rincalzare *vt* *(lenzuola)* to tuck in; *(muro, scala)* to prop up.

rincarare *vi* to increase in price.

rincasare *vi* to return home.

rinchiudere *vt* to confine.

◆ **rinchiudersi in** *vr + prep* to shut o.s. up in.

rinchiuso, -a *pp* → **rinchiudere**.

rincorrere *vt* to chase.

rincorsa *sf* run-up.

rincorso, -a *pp* → **rincorrere**.

rincrescere *vi*: **mi rincresce che tu parta** I'm sorry you're leaving; **mi rincresce di non poterti aiutare** I'm sorry I can't help you.

rinculo *sm* recoil.

rinfacciare *vt*: ~ **qc a qn** *(colpa, difetto)* to reproach sb with o for sthg; *(favore)* to throw sthg in sb's face.

rinforzare *vt* *(muscoli, capelli)* to strengthen; *(rendere più solido)* to reinforce.

rinforzo *sm* reinforcement.

rinfrescante *agg* refreshing.

rinfrescare ◇ *vt* *(atmosfera)* to cool ◇ *v impers*: **è rinfrescato** it's got cooler; ~ **la memoria a qn** to refresh sb's memory.

◆ **rinfrescarsi** *vr* *(ristorarsi)* to refresh o.s.; *(lavarsi)* to freshen up.

rinfresco, -schi *sm* reception.

rinfusa : alla rinfusa *avv* higgledy-piggledy.

ringhiare *vi* to snarl.

ringhiera *sf* *(di balcone)* railings *(pl)*; *(di scala)* banisters *(pl)*.

ringiovanire ◇ *vt*: ~ **qn** to make sb look younger ◇ *vi* to look young again, to be rejuvenated.

ringraziamento *sm* thanks *(pl)*.

ringraziare *vt* to thank; ~ **qn di qc** to thank sb for sthg.

rinnegare *vt* *(persona)* to disown; *(fede)* to renounce.

rinnovamento *sm* *(cambiamento)* updating; *(di impianti, locale)* renovation.

rinnovare *vt* to renew; *(locale)* to renovate.

rinnovo *sm* *(di contratto, guardaroba)* renewal; *(di casa)* renovation.

rinoceronte *sm* rhinoceros.
rinomato, -a *agg* famous.
rinsaldare *vt* to strengthen.
rintocco, -chi *sm (di campana)* toll; *(di orologio)* chime.
rintracciare *vt* to track down.
rintronare ◇ *vt* to deafen ◇ *vi* to boom.
rinuncia, -ce *sf* renunciation.
rinunciare : rinunciare a *v + prep (rifiutare)* to renounce; *(privarsi di)* to give up; ~ **a fare qc** to give up doing sthg.
rinunzia = **rinuncia**.
rinunziare = **rinunciare**.
rinvenire ◇ *vt (trovare)* to find; *(scoprire)* to find out ◇ *vi* to come round/to, to revive.
rinvenuto, -a *pp* → **rinvenire**.
rinviare *vt* to return; ~ **qc (a)** *(posporre)* to postpone sthg (until).
rinvio *sm (di lettera, palla)* return; *(di appuntamento, riunione)* postponement; *(a pagina, capitolo)* cross-reference.
rione *sm* quarter.
riordinare *vt (mettere in ordine)* to tidy up; *(cambiare ordine)* to reorganize.
riorganizzare *vt* to reorganize.
riparare *vt (aggiustare)* to repair; *(proteggere)* to protect; *(rimediare)* to make up for.
◆ **ripararsi** *vr* to shelter; **ripararsi da qc** to shelter/protect o.s. from sthg.
riparazione *sf* repair.
riparo *sm (protezione)* protection; *(rifugio)* shelter.
ripartire ◇ *vt (eredità, guadagno)* to share out; *(compiti, responsabilità)* to allocate ◇ *vi* to leave again.
ripassare ◇ *vt* to go over ◇ *vi* to go/come back.
ripensare : ripensare a *v + prep (riflettere su)* to think over; *(cambiare idea)* to change one's mind about; *(ricordare)* to recall.
ripercosso, -a *pp* → **ripercuotersi**.
ripercuotersi : ripercuotersi su *vr + prep* to influence.
ripercussione *sf* repercussion.
ripescare *vt (dall'acqua)* to fish out; *(ritrovare)* to find.
ripetere *vt* to repeat.
◆ **ripetersi** *vr (persona)* to repeat o.s.; *(avvenimento)* to happen again.
ripetitivo, -a *agg* repetitive.
ripetizione *sf (replica)* repetition.
◆ **ripetizioni** *sfpl* private lessons.
ripiano *sm* shelf.
ripicca, -che *sf*: **per** ~ out of spite.
ripido, -a *agg* steep.
ripiegare ◇ *vt (lenzuola)* to fold (up); *(piegare di nuovo)* to refold ◇ *vi (indietreggiare)* to retreat.
◆ **ripiegare su** *v + prep (rassegnarsi a)* to make do with.
ripiego, -ghi *sm* expedient; **per** ~ as a makeshift.
ripieno, -a ◇ *agg*: ~ **(di qc)** *(casa, cassetto)* full (of sthg); *(panino)* filled (with sthg); *(tacchino)* stuffed (with sthg) ◇ *sm (di panino)* filling.
riporre *vt (mettere al suo posto)* to put back; *(mettere via)* to put away; ~ **la propria fiducia in qn** to place one's trust in sb.
riportare *vt (restituire, ricondurre)* to take/bring back; *(riferire)* to report, to tell; *(ottenere)* to obtain.
riposare ◇ *vi (rilassarsi)* to rest; *(dormire)* to sleep ◇ *vt* to rest.
◆ **riposarsi** *vr (rilassarsi)* to rest; *(dormire)* to sleep.
riposo *sm* rest; *(sonno)* sleep; **a** ~ retired.
ripostiglio *sm* store room.
riposto, -a *pp* → **riporre**.
riprendere ◇ *vt (prendere di nuovo)* to take again; *(ritirare)* to take back; *(ricominciare)* to resume; *(rimproverare)* to reproach; *(filmare)*

to shoot, to film ◇ *vi*: ~ **a fare qc** to start doing sthg again.

♦ **riprendersi da** *vr* + *prep* to recover from.

ripresa *sf (di attività)* resumption; *(da malattia)* recovery; *(di motore)* acceleration; *(cinematografica)* shot; **a più riprese** several times.

ripreso, -a *pp* → **riprendere**.

riprodotto, -a *pp* → **riprodurre**.

riprodurre *vt* to reproduce.

♦ **riprodursi** *vr* to reproduce.

riproduzione *sf* reproduction.

riprova *sf* confirmation.

riprovevole *agg* reprehensible.

ripugnante *agg* disgusting.

ripugnare *vi*: ~ **a qn** *(disgustare qn)* to repel o disgust sb.

ripulire *vt (pulire)* to clean up; *(rubare)* to clean out.

riquadro *sm* square; *(di parete, soffitto)* panel.

risalire *vt* to go back up.

♦ **risalire a** *v* + *prep* to go back to.

risaltare *vi* to stand out.

risalto *sm* prominence; **mettere in ~ qc** to make sthg stand out.

risaputo, -a *agg*: **è ~ che ...** it is common knowledge that ...

risarcimento *sm* compensation.

risarcire *vt*: ~ **qn (di qc)** to compensate sb (for sthg).

risata *sf* laugh.

riscaldamento *sm* heating; ~ **centrale** central heating.

riscaldare *vt (stanza)* to heat; *(mani)* to warm; *(cibo)* to heat up.

♦ **riscaldarsi** *vr (persona)* to warm up; *(diventare caldo)* to get warmer.

riscatto *sm* ransom.

rischiarare *vt* to light up.

♦ **rischiararsi** *vr* to clear.

rischiare ◇ *vt* to risk ◇ *vi*: **rischio di arrivare in ritardo** I'm likely to be late; **ha rischiato di essere investito** he nearly got run over.

rischio *sm* risk; **correre il ~ di fare qc** to run the risk of doing sthg.

rischioso, -a *agg* risky.

risciacquare *vt* to rinse.

riscontrare *vt* to find.

riscontro *sm (conferma)* confirmation.

riscosso, -a *pp* → **riscuotere**.

riscuotere *vt (somma)* to collect; *(stipendio, pensione)* to receive; *(assegno)* to cash; *(successo, consenso)* to win, to earn.

risentire : **risentire di** *v* + *prep* to be affected by.

♦ **risentirsi** *vr*: **risentirsi di** o **per qc** to take offence at sthg.

riserva *sf (provvista, giocatore)* reserve; *(di caccia, pesca)* preserve; *(restrizione)* reservation; **essere in ~** (AUTO) to be low on petrol *(Br)* o gas *(Am)*; **di ~** in reserve.

riservare *vt* to save; *(prenotare)* to book, to reserve.

riservato, -a *agg (posto, carattere)* reserved; *(informazione, lettera)* confidential.

risi e bisi *smpl rice and pea soup (a speciality of Veneto)*.

risiedere *vi* to reside.

riso ◇ *pp* → **ridere** ◇ *sm (cereale)* rice; *(il ridere: pl f* **risa***)* laughter.

risolto, -a *pp* → **risolvere**.

risoluto, -a *agg (deciso)* determined.

risoluzione *sf (decisione)* resolution.

risolvere *vt (problema, caso)* to solve; *(questione)* to resolve.

♦ **risolversi** *vr (problema)* to resolve itself.

♦ **risolversi a** *vr* + *prep*: **risolversi a fare qc** to make up one's mind to do sthg.

♦ **risolversi in** *vr* + *prep (andare a finire)* to turn out.

risonanza *sf* resonance; **avere grande ~** *(fatto, notizia)* to arouse a great deal of interest.

risorgere *vi (risuscitare)* to revive; *(problema)* to recur.
risorsa *sf* resort.
◆ **risorse** *sfpl* resources.
risorto, -a *pp* → **risorgere**.
risotto *sm* risotto; ~ **alla boscaiola** *risotto with tomatoes, mushrooms and parsley*; ~ **di mare** seafood risotto; ~ **alla milanese** *risotto with saffron and lots of Parmesan cheese*; ~ **ai tartufi** *risotto with truffles*.
risparmiare ◇ *vi* to save ◇ *vt (non consumare)* to save; *(non uccidere)* to spare; *(evitare)*: ~ **qc a qn** to spare sb sthg.
risparmio *sm (somma)* savings *(pl)*; *(di tempo, soldi, fatica)* saving.
rispecchiare *vt* to reflect.
rispettabile *agg* respectable.
rispettare *vt* to respect; **farsi ~** to command respect.
rispettivamente *avv* respectively.
rispettivo, -a *agg* respective.
rispetto *sm* respect; **mancare di ~ (a qn)** to be disrespectful (to sb); ~ **a** *(a paragone di)* compared to; *(in relazione a)* as for.
rispettoso, -a *agg* respectful.
risplendere *vi* to shine.
rispondere *vi* to answer, to reply; *(freni)* to respond.
◆ **rispondere a** *v + prep (corrispondere)* to meet; ~ **a qn** to answer sb.
◆ **rispondere di** *v + prep* to be responsible for.
risposta *sf* answer; *(azione)* response; **in ~ a qc** in reply to sthg.
risposto *pp* → **rispondere**.
rissa *sf* brawl.
ristabilire *vt* to restore.
◆ **ristabilirsi** *vr* to recover.
ristagnare *vi (acqua)* to become stagnant; *(fig: industria)* to stagnate.
ristampa *sf (opera)* reprint.
ristorante *sm* restaurant.
ristoro *sm* refreshment.
ristretto, -a ◇ *pp* → **restringere** ◇ *agg (numero)* limited; *(brodo)* thick; *(uso)* restricted.
ristrutturare *vt (azienda)* to reorganize; *(casa)* to alter.
risucchiare *vt* to suck in.
risultare *vi* to turn out to be; **mi risulta che ...** I understand that ...; **non mi risulta** not as far as I know.
◆ **risultare da** *v + prep* to result from.
risultato *sm* result.
risuolare *vt* to resole.
risuscitare *vt* to resuscitate.
risvegliare *vt (dal sonno)* to wake up; *(memoria, appetito)* to awaken.
risvolto *sm (di pantaloni)* turn-up *(Br)*, cuff *(Am)*; *(di giacca)* lapel; *(fig: conseguenza)* implication.
ritagliare *vt* to cut out.
ritaglio *sm (di giornale)* cutting; *(di stoffa)* scrap; **nei ritagli di tempo** in one's spare time.
ritardare ◇ *vi* to be late ◇ *vt (rimandare)* to delay; *(rallentare)* to slow down.
ritardatario, -a *sm, f* latecomer.
ritardo *sm (di treno, pagamento)* delay; **in ~** late.
ritenere *vt (giudicare)* to believe; *(somma)* to deduct.
ritentare *vt* to try again.
ritirare *vt* to withdraw; *(pacco, da lavanderia)* to collect; *(insulto, promessa)* to take back.
◆ **ritirarsi** *vr (da attività)* to retire; *(restringersi)* to shrink.
ritirata *sf* retreat.
ritiro *sm (di pacco)* collection; *(di patente, passaporto)* confiscation; *(sportivo, spirituale)* retreat; *(da attività)* retirement.
ritmo *sm* (MUS) rhythm; *(di pulsazioni)* beat; *(di vita, lavoro)* pace.
rito *sm* rite.

ritornare *vi (andare, venire di nuovo)* to return, to go/come back; *(ricomparire)* to recur; *(ridiventare)*: ~ **pulito** to be clean again.
ritornello *sm* chorus.
ritorno *sm* return; **essere di ~** to be back.
ritrarre *vt (ritirare)* to withdraw; *(rappresentare)* to portray.
ritratto, -a ◇ *pp* → **ritrarre** ◇ *sm* portrait.
ritrovare *vt (cosa persa)* to find; *(riacquistare)* to regain.
◆ **ritrovarsi** *vr (incontrarsi)* to meet; *(in situazione)* to find o.s.
ritrovo *sm* meeting place.
ritto, -a *agg* upright.
riunione *sf (incontro)* meeting; *(riconciliazione)* reconciliation.
riunire *vt* to bring together.
◆ **riunirsi** *vr* to meet.
riuscire *vi (avere esito)* to turn out; *(aver successo)* to succeed; **~ a fare qc** to manage to do sthg; **~ in qc** to succeed in sthg.
riva *sf (di fiume)* bank; *(di lago, mare)* shore.
rivale *agg & smf* rival.
rivalutare *vt* to revalue.
rivedere *vt (vedere di nuovo)* to see again; *(riesaminare)* to review; *(ripassare)* to revise.
◆ **rivedersi** *vr* to meet again.
rivelare *vt* to reveal.
rivendicare *vt (diritto, bene)* to claim; *(attentato)* to claim responsibility for.
rivendita *sf (negozio)* dealer.
rivenditore, -trice *sm, f* retailer; **~ autorizzato** authorized dealer.
riversare *vt (fig: affetto)* to lavish; *(colpa)* to heap.
◆ **riversarsi** *vr* to pour.
rivestimento *sm* covering.
rivestire *vt (poltrona)* to cover; *(carica)* to hold; *(ruolo)* to play.
◆ **rivestirsi** *vr* to get dressed again.
riviera *sf* coast.
rivincita *sf (di partita)* return match; *(rivalsa)* revenge.
rivisto, -a ◇ *pp* → **rivedere** ◇ *sf (giornale)* magazine.
rivolgere *vt (parola)* to address; *(attenzione, occhiata)* to direct.
◆ **rivolgersi a** *vr + prep* to go and speak to.
rivoltante *agg* revolting.
rivoltare *vt (rigirare)* to turn over; *(disgustare)* to disgust.
◆ **rivoltarsi** *vr* to rebel.
rivoltella *sf* revolver.
rivolto, -a ◇ *pp* → **rivolgere** ◇ *sf* revolt.
rivoluzionario, -a *agg & sm, f* revolutionary.
rivoluzione *sf* revolution.
rizzare *vt* to stand on end.
◆ **rizzarsi** *vr* to stand up.
roastbeef ['rɔzbif] *sm inv joint of beef braised or grilled, then served sliced.*
roba *sf (cose)* stuff, things *(pl)*; **~ da mangiare** things to eat; **~ da matti!** (well I) never!
robiola *sf a type of soft rindless cheese.*
robot *sm inv (automa)* robot; *(da cucina)* food processor.
robusto, -a *agg* robust, sturdy.
rocca, -che *sf* fortress.
roccaforte *sf* stronghold.
rocchetto *sm* reel, spool.
roccia, -ce *sf* rock.
roccioso, -a *agg* rocky.
roco, -a, -chi, -che *agg* hoarse.
rodaggio *sm* running-in.
rodere *vt* to gnaw.
◆ **rodersi di** *vr + prep* to be consumed with.
rogna *sf (malattia)* scabies; *(fam: guaio)* nuisance.
rognone *sm* kidney; **rognoni alla romana** *kidneys fried with garlic, parsley and white wine.*

Roma *sf* Rome.
Romania *sf*: **la ~** Romania.
romanico, -a, -ci, -che *agg* Romanesque.
romano, -a *agg & sm, f* Roman.
romanticismo *sm* romanticism.
romantico, -a, -ci, -che *agg* romantic.
romanzo *sm (libro)* novel.
rombo *sm (rumore)* roar; *(pesce)* turbot; **a rombi** *(disegno)* diamond-patterned.
rompere ◇ *vt* to break; *(fidanzamento)* to break off; *(strappare)* to tear ◇ *vi (coppia)* to break up; **rompersi una gamba** to break one's leg; **smetti di ~!** *(fam)* lay off!
◆ **rompersi** *vr* to break.
rompicapo *sm* puzzle.
rompiscatole *smf inv (fam)* pest, pain in the neck.
rondine *sf* swallow.
ronzare *vi* to buzz.
ronzio *sm (di insetti)* buzzing; *(rumore)* drone.
rosa ◇ *agg inv (di colore)* pink; *(sentimentale)* sentimental ◇ *sf* rose ◇ *sm (colore)* pink.
rosé *sm inv* rosé.
rosicchiare *vt* to gnaw, to nibble.
rosmarino *sm* rosemary.
roso, -a *pp* → **rodere**.
rosolare *vt* to brown.
rosolia *sf* German measles *(sg)*.
rosone *sm (di soffitti)* ceiling rose; *(vetrata)* rose window.
rospo *sm* toad.
rossetto *sm* lipstick.
rosso, -a *agg & sm* red; **~ d'uovo** egg yolk.
rosticceria *sf shop selling cooked food such as roast chicken, lasagna etc.*
rosticciana *sf grilled or fried pork.*
rotaie *sfpl* rails.
rotazione *sf* rotation.
rotella *sf* cog.
rotolare *vi (palla, valanga)* to roll.
◆ **rotolarsi** *vr* to roll.
rotolo *sm* roll; **andare a rotoli** to go to rack and ruin.
rotonda *sf* circular terrace.
rotondo, -a *agg* round.
rotta *sf* route.
rottame *sm* scrap.
rotto, -a ◇ *pp* → **rompere** ◇ *agg (spezzato, guasto)* broken; *(strappato)* torn.
rottura *sf (azione)* breaking; *(interruzione)* breaking-off; *(fam: seccatura)* nuisance.
roulette [ru'lɛt] *sf* roulette.
roulotte [ru'lɔt] *sf inv* caravan.
routine [ru'tin] *sf inv* routine.
rovente *agg* red-hot.
rovescia *sf*: **alla ~** upside down; *(sottosopra)* inside out.
rovesciare *vt (liquido)* to spill; *(tavolo, sedia)* to overturn; *(situazione)* to turn upside down.
◆ **rovesciarsi** *vr (versarsi)* to spill; *(capovolgersi)* to overturn; *(barca)* to capsize.
rovescio *sm (di vestito, stoffa)* wrong side; *(pioggia)* downpour; *(nel tennis)* backhand; **al ~** *(con l'interno all'esterno)* inside out; *(con il davanti didietro)* back to front.
rovina *sf* ruin; **andare in ~** to collapse.
◆ **rovine** *sfpl* ruins.
rovinare *vt* to ruin.
◆ **rovinarsi** *vr (cosa)* to be ruined; *(persona)* to be ruined.
rovo *sm* bramble bush.
rozzo, -a *agg* rough.
ruba *sf*: **andare a ~** to sell like hot cakes.
rubare ◇ *vt* to steal ◇ *vi*: **hanno rubato in casa mia** my house has been burgled; **~ qc a qn** to steal sthg from sb.
rubinetto *sm* tap.

rubino *sm* ruby.
rubrica, -che *sf (di indirizzi)* address book; *(di giornale)* column.
ruderi *smpl* ruins.
rudimentale *agg* rudimentary, basic.
ruffiano, -a *sm, f* creep.
ruga, -ghe *sf* wrinkle.
rugby ['rɛgbi] *sm* rugby.
ruggine *sf* rust.
ruggire *vi* to roar.
rugiada *sf* dew.
rullino *sm* roll of film; **un ~ da 24** a 24-exposure film.
rullo *sm (rotolo, arnese)* roller; *(di tamburo)* roll.
rum *sm inv* rum.
rumore *sm* noise.
rumoroso, -a *agg* noisy.
ruolo *sm* role.
ruota *sf* wheel; **~ di scorta** spare wheel.
ruotare *vi & vt* to rotate.
rupe *sf* cliff.
ruscello *sm* stream.
ruspa *sf* excavator.
Russia *sf*: **la ~** Russia.
russo, -a *agg, sm & sf* Russian.
rustico, -a, -ci, -che *agg* rustic.
ruttare *vi* to belch.
ruvido, -a *agg* rough.
ruzzolare *vi* to tumble down.
ruzzolone *sm* tumble.

S

sabato *sm* Saturday; **torniamo ~** we'll be back on Saturday; **oggi è ~** it's Saturday today; **~ 6 maggio** Saturday 6 May; **~ pomeriggio** Saturday afternoon; **~ prossimo** next Saturday; **~ scorso** last Saturday; **di ~** on Saturdays; **a ~!** see you Saturday!
sabbia *sf* sand.
sabotare *vt* to sabotage.
sacca, -che *sf (borsa)* bag.
saccarina *sf* saccharin.
saccente *agg* conceited.
saccheggiare *vt (case, villaggi)* to loot; *(fig: con acquisti)* to buy up.
sacchetto *sm* bag.
sacco, -chi *sm (di carta, nylon®)* bag; *(di iuta)* sack; **un ~ di** a lot of; **~ a pelo** sleeping bag.
sacerdote *sm* priest.
sacrificare *vt* to sacrifice.
◆ **sacrificarsi** *vr* to make sacrifices.
sacrificio *sm* sacrifice.
sacro, -a *agg* sacred.
sadico, -a, -ci, -che ◇ *agg* sadistic ◇ *sm, f* sadist.
safari *sm inv* safari.
saggezza *sf* wisdom.
saggio, -a, -gi, -ge ◇ *agg* wise ◇ *sm (persona)* wise man, sage; *(campione)* sample; *(libro, ricerca)* essay.
Sagittario *sm* Sagittarius.
sagoma *sf (profilo, forma)* outline; *(fam: persona)* character.
sagra *sf* festival, feast.
sai → **sapere**.
saint-honoré [sɛtɔnɔ're] *sm inv* *dessert consisting of a puff pastry base topped with cream and surrounded by choux buns.*
sala *sf (salotto)* living room; *(di palazzo)* hall; **~ d'aspetto** o **d'attesa** waiting room; **~ da gioco** gaming room; **~ operatoria** operating theatre; **~ da pranzo** dining room.
salame *sm* salami.
salare *vt* to salt.
salario *sm* wage.
salatini *smpl* salted crackers.
salato, -a *agg (con sale)* salted; *(con troppo sale)* salty; *(fam: caro)* expensive.
saldare *vt (metalli)* to weld; *(debito, conto)* to settle.
saldo, -a ◇ *agg (resistente, stabile)* firm ◇ *sm* balance.
◆ **saldi** *mpl* sales.
sale *sm* salt; **~ grosso** cooking salt.
salice *sm* willow; **~ piangente** weeping willow.
saliente *agg* salient.
saliera *sf* saltcellar *(Br)*, salt shaker *(Am)*.
salire ◇ *vt (scale)* to go up ◇ *vi* to go up; *(aereo)* to climb; **~ in** o **su**

(treno, moto) to get onto; *(auto)* to get into; ~ **su** *(tetto, podio)* to climb onto; ~ **a bordo** to board.

salita *sf* climb; **in** ~ uphill.

saliva *sf* saliva.

salmì *sm* → **lepre**.

salmone *sm* salmon.

salone *sm* *(sala)* sitting room; *(mostra)* show.

salotto *sm* lounge.

salpare ◇ *vi (partire)* to set sail ◇ *vt*: ~ **l'ancora** to weigh anchor.

salsa *sf* sauce; ~ **di pomodoro** tomato sauce.

salsiccia, -ce *sf* sausage.

saltare ◇ *vt (scavalcare)* to jump (over); *(omettere)* to skip ◇ *vi* to jump; **fare** ~ **qc** to blow sthg up; ~ **fuori (da qc)** to jump out (from sthg); ~ **giù da qc** to jump down from sthg; ~ **su (qc)** to jump on (sthg).

saltimbocca *sm inv thin slices of veal rolled up with ham and sage.*

salto *sm (balzo)* jump; *(visita)*: **fare un** ~ **in città** to pop into town; ~ **in alto/lungo** high/long jump; ~ **con l'asta** pole vault.

salumeria *sf* delicatessen.

salumi *smpl* cold meats and salami.

salutare *vt (incontrandosi)* to greet, to say hello to; *(andando via)* to say goodbye to.

◆ **salutarsi** *vr (incontrandosi)* to say hello; *(andando via)* to say goodbye; **salutamelo!** say hello to him from me!

salute *sf* health; **bere alla** ~ **di qn** to drink to sb's health.

saluto *sm (incontrandosi)* greeting; *(andando via)* goodbye; *(col capo)* nod; *(con la mano)* wave.

salvadanaio *sm* moneybox.

salvagente *sm (giubbotto)* life jacket; *(ciambella)* life buoy; *(spartitraffico)* traffic island.

salvaguardare *vt* to safeguard.

salvare *vt (vita, persona)* to survive; *(onore)* to protect.

◆ **salvarsi** *vr* to save o.s.

salvataggio *sm* rescue.

salvavita® *sm inv* fuse box.

salve *esclam (fam)* hello!

salvezza *sf* safety.

salvia *sf* sage.

salvietta *sf* wet wipe.

salvo, -a ◇ *agg* safe ◇ *prep* except for; **essere in** ~ to be safe; ~ **imprevisti** barring accidents.

san → **santo**.

sandali *smpl* sandals.

sangue *sm* blood; **a** ~ **freddo** in cold blood.

sanguinare *vi* to bleed.

sanità *sf* health service.

sanitario, -a *agg (sistema, servizio)* health *(dav s)*; *(condizioni)* sanitary.

◆ **sanitari** *smpl* bathroom fittings.

San Marino *sf* San Marino.

sano, -a *agg* healthy; ~ **e salvo** safe and sound; ~ **come un pesce** as fit as a fiddle.

San Silvestro *sf*: **la notte di** ~ New Year's Eve.

santo, -a ◇ *agg* holy ◇ *sm, f* saint; **Santo Stefano** = Boxing Day; **tutto il** ~ **giorno** all day long.

santuario *sm* sanctuary.

sanzione *sf* sanction.

sapere *vt* to know; **mi sa che non viene** I don't think he's coming; ~ **fare qc** to know how to do sthg; **sai sciare?** can you ski?; **far** ~ **qc a qn** to let sb know sthg.

◆ **sapere di** *v + prep* to taste of.

sapone *sm* soap; ~ **da bucato** = household soap.

saponetta *sf* bar of soap.

sapore *sm* taste, flavour.

saporito, -a *agg* tasty.

saracinesca, -sche *sf* shutter.

sarcastico, -a, -ci, -che *agg* sarcastic.

sarde *sfpl*: ~ **e beccaficu** *fried sardines stuffed with breadcrumbs, pecorino cheese and tomatoes.*
Sardegna *sf*: **la** ~ Sardinia.
sardina *sf* sardine.
sardo, -a *agg & sm, f* Sardinian.
sarto, -a *sm, f* dressmaker; *(per azienda)* tailor.
sartù *sm inv*: ~ **di riso** *rice mould filled with liver, mushrooms, peas, meatballs, mozzarella cheese and boiled eggs (a speciality of Naples).*
sasso *sm* stone.
sassofono *sm* saxophone.
satellite *sm (naturale, artificiale)* satellite; (TV) satellite TV.
satira *sf* satire.
sauna *sf* sauna.
savoiardi *smpl* sponge fingers.
saziare *vt* to satisfy.
sazietà *sf*: **mangiare a** ~ to eat one's fill.
sazio, -a *agg* full.
sbadato, -a *agg* careless.
sbadigliare *vi* to yawn.
sbadiglio *sm* yawn.
sbafo *sm*: **a** ~ at somebody else's expense.
sbagliare ◇ *vt* to get wrong ◇ *vi (fare un errore)* to make a mistake; *(avere torto)* to be wrong; ~ **mira** to miss one's aim; ~ **strada** to take the wrong road; **ho sbagliato a contare** I counted wrong.
◆ **sbagliarsi** *vr (fare un errore)* to make a mistake; *(avere torto)* to be wrong; **sbagliarsi di grosso** to be completely wrong.
sbagliato, -a *agg* wrong.
sbaglio *sm* mistake; **fare uno** ~ to make a mistake; **fare qc per** ~ to do sthg by mistake.
sballottare *vt* to toss about.
sbalzare *vt* to throw.
sbalzo *sm (di temperatura)* sudden change.
sbandare *vi* to skid.
sbandata *sf* skid; **prendersi una** ~ **per qn** to fall for sb.
sbandierare *vt (sventolare)* to wave; *(ostentare)* to show off.
sbando *sm*: **allo** ~ adrift.
sbaraglio *sm*: **andare allo** ~ to risk everything.
sbarazzare *vt* to clear up.
◆ **sbarazzarsi di** *vr + prep* to get rid of.
sbarazzino, -a *agg* cheeky.
sbarcare ◇ *vt (merce)* to unload; *(passeggeri)* to disembark ◇ *vi (da nave)* to disembark.
sbarco *sm (di merci)* unloading; *(di passeggeri)* disembarkation.
sbarra *sf (spranga)* bar; *(segno grafico)* stroke; *(di passaggio a livello)* barrier.
sbarrare *vt (porta, finestra)* to bar; *(passaggio)* to block; ~ **gli occhi** to open one's eyes wide.
sbarrato, -a *agg (strada)* blocked; *(porta)* barred; *(casella)* crossed; *(parola)* crossed out; *(occhi)* wide open.
sbatacchiare *vt* to bang, to slam.
sbattere ◇ *vt* to beat; *(porta)* to bang, to slam ◇ *vi* to bang; ~ **contro** *(muro)* to bang against, to knock against; ~ **fuori qn** to throw sb out.
◆ **sbattersene** *vr (fam)* not to give a damn.
sbattuto, -a *agg* downcast.
sbavare *vi* to dribble.
sbellicarsi *vr*: ~ **dal ridere** to split one's sides laughing.
sbiadire *vt* to fade.
◆ **sbiadirsi** *vr* to fade.
sbiadito, -a *agg* faded.
sbiancare ◇ *vi* to grow pale ◇ *vt* to bleach.
sbieco, -a, -chi, -che *agg*: **di** ~ *(obliquamente)* at an angle.
sbigottire *vt* to dismay.
◆ **sbigottirsi** *vr* to be dismayed.
sbigottito, -a *agg* dismayed, aghast.

sbilanciare *vt* to unbalance.
◆ **sbilanciarsi** *vr (perdere l'equilibrio)* to lose one's balance; *(fig: compromettersi)* to compromise o.s.
sbirciare *vt (con curiosità)* to eye; *(di sfuggita)* to peep at.
sbizzarrirsi *vr* to satisfy one's whims.
sbloccare *vt* to unblock; ~ **la situazione** to get things moving.
◆ **sbloccarsi** *vr (meccanismo)* to become unblocked; *(situazione)* to return to normal.
sboccare : sboccare in *v + prep (fiume)* to flow into; *(strada)* to lead into; *(concludersi con)* to end in.
sboccato, -a *agg* foul-mouthed.
sbocciare *vi* to bloom.
sbocco, -chi *sm (di strada)* end; *(di fiume)* mouth; *(fig: esito)* way out.
sbornia *sf (fam)*: **prendersi una ~** to get plastered.
sborsare *vt (pagare)* to pay out.
sbottare *vi (in risata)* to burst out; *(di rabbia)* to explode.
sbottonare *vt* to unbutton; **sbottonarsi la giacca** to undo one's jacket.
◆ **sbottonarsi** *vr (fam: confidarsi)* to open up.
sbracciarsi *vr* to wave one's arms about.
sbracciato, -a *agg (vestito)* sleeveless; *(persona)* with bare arms.
sbraitare *vi* to shout.
sbranare *vt* to tear to pieces.
sbriciolare *vt* to crumble.
◆ **sbriciolarsi** *vr (pane, muro)* to crumble.
sbrigare *vt (faccenda)* to deal with.
◆ **sbrigarsi** *vr* to hurry; **sbrigarsi a fare qc** to hurry up and do sthg.
sbrodolare *vt* to stain.
sbronza *sf (fam)*: **prendersi una ~** to get plastered.
sbronzo, -a *agg (fam)* plastered.
sbucare *vi (uscire)* to come out; *(saltar fuori)* to spring out.
sbucciare *vt* to peel; **sbucciarsi un ginocchio** to graze one's knee.
sbuffare *vi (per fastidio, noia)* to snort; *(per caldo)* to pant.
scabroso, -a *agg* indecent.
scacchi *smpl* chess *(sg)*; **a ~** *(tessuto)* checked.
scacciare *vt (persona, animale)* to drive away; *(preoccupazioni)* to dispel.
scadente *agg (prodotto)* poor-quality; *(qualità)* poor.
scadenza *sf (di cibo)* sell-by date; *(di documento, contratto)* expiry date; *(di medicinali)* "use-by" date; *(per iscrizione, consegna)* deadline.
scadere *vi* to expire; *(cibo)* to pass its sell-by date.
scaffale *sm* shelf.
scafo *sm* hull.
scaglia *sf (frammento)* flake, chip; *(di pesce)* scale.
scagliare *vt* to throw.
◆ **scagliarsi contro** *vr + prep (assalire)* to hurl o.s. against; *(fig: insultare)* to hurl abuse at.
scaglione *sm* echelon; **a scaglioni** in groups.
scala *sf (gradini)* stairs *(pl)*, staircase; *(a pioli)* ladder; *(di valori)* scale; **su larga ~** on a large scale; **~ mobile** escalator; **le scale** the stairs.
scalare *vt (mura, montagna)* to climb; *(somma)* to knock off; *(capelli)* to layer.
scalata *sf* climb.
scalatore, -trice *sm, f* climber.
scalcinato, -a *agg (fig: casa)* shabby.
scaldabagno *sm* water heater.
scaldare *vt* to heat.
◆ **scaldarsi** *vr (al fuoco, al sole)* to warm o.s.; *(fig: accalorarsi)* to get excited.

scaleo *sm* stepladder.
scalfire *vt* to scratch.
scalinata *sf* flight of steps.
scalino *sm* step.
scalmanarsi *vr* to get worked up.
scalo *sm* call; **fare ~ a** *(in aereo)* to make a stopover at; *(in nave)* to call at; **~ merci** goods yard *(Br)*, freight yard *(Am)*.
scaloppina *sf* escalope.
scalpore *sm (risonanza)* stir; **fare** o **destare ~** to cause a stir.
scaltro, -a *agg* shrewd.
scalzo, -a *agg* barefooted.
scambiare *vt* to exchange, to swap; **~ qn/qc per** *(confondere)* to mistake sb/sthg for; **scambiarsi qc** to exchange sthg.
scambio *sm (di regali, opinioni)* exchange; *(confusione)* mistake; (COMM) trade; **fare a ~ con qn** to swap with sb.
scampagnata *sf* trip to the country.
scampare *vt* to escape; **scamparla (bella)** to have a narrow escape.
◆ **scampare a** *v + prep* to escape.
scampo *sm*: **non c'è (via di) ~** there is no way out; **trovare ~ in qc** to find safety in sthg.
◆ **scampi** *smpl* scampi *(sg)*.
scampolo *sm* remnant.
scandalizzare *vt* to make a spectacle of o.s..
◆ **scandalizzarsi** *vr* to be scandalized.
scandalo *sm* scandal; **dare ~** to make a spectacle of o.s.; **fare ~** to cause a scandal.
scandaloso, -a *agg* scandalous.
Scandinavia *sf*: **la ~** Scandinavia.
scandire *vt* to articulate.
scannare *vt (animale)* to butcher; *(persona)* to cut the throat of.
scansafatiche *smf inv* idler, waster.
scansare *vt (spostare)* to shift; *(colpo)* to ward off; *(difficoltà, fatica)* to avoid; *(persona)* to shun.
◆ **scansarsi** *vr* to step aside.
scanso *sm*: **a ~ di equivoci** (in order) to avoid any misunderstandings.
scantinato *sm* basement.
scanzonato, -a *agg* easygoing.
scapaccione *sm* slap.
scapestrato, -a *agg* dissolute.
scapito *sm*: **a ~ di** to the detriment of.
scapolo *sm* bachelor.
scappamento *sm* → **tubo**.
scappare *vi (fuggire)* to escape; *(da casa)* to run away; *(andare)* to rush; **mi è scappato detto** I let it slip; **mi è scappato di mano** it slipped out of my hands; **mi è scappato di mente** it slipped my mind; **mi è scappato da ridere** I couldn't help laughing; **lasciarsi ~ l'occasione** to miss an opportunity.
scappatella *sf* casual affair.
scappatoia *sf* way out.
scarabocchiare ◇ *vt* to scrawl ◇ *vi* to scribble.
scarafaggio *sm* cockroach.
scaramanzia *sf*: **per ~** for luck.
scaraventare *vt* to hurl.
◆ **scaraventarsi** *vr* to fling o.s.
scarcerare *vt* to release.
scarica, -che *sf (di pugni)* hail; *(di pistola)* volley; **~ elettrica** electrical discharge.
scaricare *vt (merci, camion, arma)* to unload; *(passeggeri)* to let off; *(batteria)* to run down; *(fig: colpa)* to shift.
◆ **scaricarsi** *vr (batteria)* to go flat; *(fig: rilassarsi)* to unwind.
scarico, -a, -chi, -che ◇ *agg (camion, arma)* unloaded; *(batteria)* flat ◇ *sm (di merci)* unloading; *(discarica)* dump; **'divieto di ~'** 'no dumping'.
scarlatto, -a *agg* scarlet.

scarpa *sf* shoe; **che numero di scarpe porta?** what size shoe do you take?; **scarpe da ginnastica** plimsolls *(Br)*, sneakers *(Am)*.
scarpata *sf* slope.
scarponi *smpl* boots; ~ **da sci** ski boots.
scarseggiare *vi* to be scarce.
◆ **scarseggiare di** *v + prep* to be short of.
scarsità *sf inv* scarcity, shortage.
scarso, -a *agg* scarce; **un chilo ~** just under a kilo.
scartare *vt (regalo)* to unwrap; *(eliminare)* to reject; *(nelle carte)* to discard.
scarto *sm (scelta)* discarding; *(cosa scartata)* reject; *(differenza)* gap, difference.
scassinare *vt* to break open.
scasso *sm* → **furto**.
scatenare *vt* to provoke, to stir up.
◆ **scatenarsi** *vr (temporale)* to break; *(persona)* to go wild.
scatenato, -a *agg (persona, ballo)* wild.
scatola *sf* box; *(di latta)* tin, can; **in ~** *(cibo)* tinned, canned; **rompere le scatole a qn** *(fam)* to get up sb's nose.
scattante *agg* agile.
scattare ◇ *vt (foto)* to take ◇ *vi (balzare)* to jump; *(molla, congegno)* to be released; *(allarme)* to go off; *(manifestare ira)* to fly into a rage; **far ~** *(molla, congegno)* to release; *(allarme)* to set off.
scatto *sm (di congegno)* release; *(rumore)* click; *(di foto)* shot; *(balzo)* fit; **di ~** suddenly.
scaturire : scaturire da *v + prep (sgorgare)* to gush from; *(fig: derivare)* to come from.
scavalcare *vt (muro, ostacolo)* to climb over; *(fig: concorrenti)* to overtake.
scavare *vt (fossa, terreno)* to dig; *(render cavo)* to hollow out.
scavo *sm* excavation.
scegliere *vt* to choose.
scelta *sf* choice; *(raccolta)* selection; **non avere ~** to have no choice; **'frutta o formaggio a ~'** 'choice of fruit or cheese'.
scelto, -a ◇ *pp* → **scegliere** ◇ *agg (gruppo)* select; *(frutta)* choice.
scemo, -a *agg (fam)* stupid, silly.
scena *sf* scene.
scenata *sf* row, scene.
scendere ◇ *vi (venir giù)* to go/come down; *(da treno)* to get off; *(diminuire)* to go down ◇ *vt* to go/come down; ~ **dal treno** to get off the train; ~ **dalla macchina** to get out of the car.
sceneggiato *sm* serial.
sceneggiatura *sf* screenplay.
scervellarsi *vr* to rack one's brains.
sceso, -a *pp* → **scendere**.
scettico, -a, -ci, -che *agg* sceptical.
scheda *sf (cartoncino)* card; *(modulo)* form; ~ **magnetica** magnetic card.
schedare *vt (libro)* to catalogue; **è stato schedato dalla polizia** he has a police record.
schedario *sm (raccolta)* file; *(mobile)* filing cabinet.
schedina *sf* = pools coupon.
scheggia, -ge *sf* splinter.
scheletro *sm* skeleton.
schema, -i *sm* plan.
scherma *sf* fencing.
schermo *sm* screen.
scherno *sm* derision.
scherzare *vi* to joke.
scherzo *sm (battuta, gesto)* joke; *(brutto tiro)* trick; **è uno ~** *(cosa facile)* it's child's play; **fare qc per ~** to do sthg for a laugh.
scherzoso, -a *agg* playful.
schiaccianoci *sm inv* nutcrackers *(pl)*.

schiacciare *vt (comprimere)* to crush; *(noce)* to crack; *(pulsante)* to press; *(fig: avversario)* to overwhelm; (SPORT) to smash.
◆ **schiacciarsi** *vr* to get squashed.

schiacciata *sf (focaccia) type of flat salted bread made with olive oil;* (SPORT) smash.

schiacciato, -a *agg (appiattito)* flat; *(deformato)* squashed.

schiaffo *sm* slap.

schiamazzi *smpl* screams.

schiantare *vt* to break.
◆ **schiantarsi** *vr* to break up.

schianto *sm (rumore)* crash; **è uno ~!** *(fam)* she's/it's a knockout!

schiarire *vt* to lighten.
◆ **schiarirsi** *vr (cielo)* to clear up; *(colore)* to become lighter; **schiarirsi la voce** to clear one's throat.

schiavitù *sf* slavery.

schiavo, -a ◇ *sm, f* slave ◇ *agg*: **~ di** a slave to.

schiena *sf* back.

schienale *sm* back.

schiera *sf* group.

schierare *vt (esercito, squadra)* to draw up; *(libri, oggetti)* to line up.
◆ **schierarsi** *vr (mettersi in fila)* to line up; **schierarsi con/contro qn** to side with/oppose sb.

schietto, -a *agg (persona)* frank; *(vino)* not watered-down.

schifezza *sf*: **essere una ~** *(cibo)* to be disgusting; *(film)* to be awful.

schifo *sm* disgust; **mi fa ~** it makes me sick; **fare ~** *(cibo, insetto)* to be disgusting; *(film)* to be awful.

schifoso, -a *agg (disgustoso)* disgusting; *(pessimo, brutto)* awful.

schioccare *vt (dita)* to snap; *(lingua)* to click.

schiuma *sf (marina)* foam; *(di sapone)* lather; **~ da barba** shaving foam.

schivare *vt* to dodge, to avoid.

schivo, -a *agg* reserved, shy.

schizzare ◇ *vt* to splash ◇ *vi (acqua, getto)* to spurt; *(fig: saltar via)* to dart away.

schizzo *sm (spruzzo)* stain, splash; *(disegno)* sketch.

sci *sm inv (attrezzo)* ski; *(attività)* skiing; **~ d'acqua** water skiing; **~ da fondo** cross-country skiing.

scia *sf (di nave)* wake; *(di profumo, fumo)* trail.

sciacquare *vt* to rinse; **sciacquarsi la bocca** to rinse out one's mouth.

sciacquone *sm* flush; **tirare lo ~** to flush the toilet.

sciagura *sf* disaster.

sciagurato, -a *agg (sfortunato)* unlucky; *(cattivo)* wicked.

scialacquare *vt* to squander.

scialbo, -a *agg (colore)* pale; *(sapore)* bland; *(persona)* dull.

scialle *sm* shawl.

scialuppa *sf* sloop; **~ di salvataggio** lifeboat.

sciame *sm* swarm.

sciangai *sm (gioco)* pick-up-sticks.

sciare *vi* to ski.

sciarpa *sf* scarf.

sciatore, -trice *sm, f* skier.

sciatto, -a *agg* untidy.

scientifico, -a, -ci, -che *agg* scientific.

scienza *sf (studio della realtà)* science; *(sapere)* knowledge.
◆ **scienze** *sfpl* science *(sg)*.

scienziato, -a *sm, f* scientist.

scimmia *sf* monkey.

scimmiottare *vt* to ape.

scindere *vt (dividere)* to divide.

scintilla *sf* spark.

scintillare *vi* to sparkle.

scioccare *vt* to shock.

sciocchezza *sf (cosa stupida)* silly thing; *(cosa poco importante)* trifle.

sciocco, -a, -chi, -che *agg* silly.

sciogliere *vt (nodo)* to untie; *(capelli)* to loosen; *(animale)* to let

loose; *(ghiaccio, burro)* to melt; *(pastiglia, società)* to dissolve; *(mistero)* to solve; *(assemblea)* to close.
◆ **sciogliersi** *vr (nodo)* to come untied; *(neve, burro)* to melt.
scioglilingua *sm inv* tongue twister.
sciolto, -a ◇ *pp* → **sciogliere** ◇ *agg (disinvolto)* easy; *(agile)* agile.
sciopero *sm* strike; **essere in ~** to be on strike.
sciovia *sf* ski lift.
scippare *vt*: **~ qn** to snatch sb's bag.
scippo *sm* bagsnatching.
sciroppo *sm (medicina)* cough mixture; *(di frutta)* syrup.
scissione *sf (separazione)* split.
scisso, -a *pp* → **scindere**.
sciupare *vt (vestito, libro)* to spoil, to ruin.
◆ **sciuparsi** *vr (rovinarsi)* to get spoiled; *(deperire)* to become run down.
scivolare *vi (scorrere)* to glide; *(perdere l'equilibrio)* to slip, to slide.
scivolo *sm (gioco)* slide.
scivoloso, -a *agg* slippery.
scoccare ◇ *vt (freccia)* to shoot ◇ *vi (ore)* to strike.
scocciare *vt (fam)* to annoy.
◆ **scocciarsi** *vr (fam)* to be annoyed.
scodella *sf* bowl.
scodinzolare *vi* to wag its tail.
scogliera *sf* rocks *(pl)*.
scoglio *sm (roccia)* rock; *(fig)* stumbling block.
scoiattolo *sm* squirrel.
scolapasta *sm inv* colander.
scolapiatti *sm inv* draining rack.
scolare *vt* to drain.
scolaro, -a *sm, f* schoolboy (*f* schoolgirl).
scolastico, -a, -ci, -che *agg* school *(dav s)*.
scollare *vt (staccare)* to unstick.
◆ **scollarsi** *vr* to come unstuck.
scollato, -a *agg (abito)* low-cut.
scollatura *sf* neckline.
scolorire *vt* to fade.
◆ **scolorirsi** *vr* to fade.
scolpire *vt* to sculpt; *(legno)* to carve; *(iscrizione)* to engrave.
scombussolare *vt* to upset.
scommessa *sf* bet.
scommesso, -a *pp* → **scommettere**.
scommettere *vt* to bet.
scomodare *vt* to bother.
◆ **scomodarsi** *vr* to put o.s. out; **scomodarsi a fare qc** to go to the bother of doing sthg.
scomodo, -a *agg (poltrona)* uncomfortable; *(orario)* inconvenient.
scompagnato, -a *agg (calzini)* odd.
scomparire *vi (sparire)* to disappear.
scomparso, -a *pp* → **scomparire**.
scompartimento *sm (di treno)* compartment.
scomparto *sm* compartment.
scompigliare *vt (capelli)* to ruffle, to mess up.
scompiglio *sm* confusion.
scomporre *vt (mobile, armadio)* to take to pieces.
◆ **scomporsi** *vr (perdere il controllo)* to lose one's composure.
scomposto, -a *pp* → **scomporre**.
sconcertare *vt* to disconcert.
sconcio, -a, -ci, -ce *agg (osceno)* obscene.
sconfiggere *vt* to defeat.
sconfinare *vi (uscire dai confini)* to cross the border; *(fig)*: **~ da** to stray from.
sconfinato, -a *agg* boundless.
sconfitta *sf* defeat.
sconfitto, -a *pp* → **sconfiggere**.

sconforto *sm* dejection.

scongelare *vt* to defrost.

scongiurare *vt (supplicare)* to implore; *(pericolo, minaccia)* to ward off.

sconnesso, -a *agg (ragionamento)* incoherent.

sconosciuto, -a ◇ *agg* unknown ◇ *sm, f* stranger.

sconsiderato, -a *agg* thoughtless.

sconsigliare *vt* to advise against; ~ **qc a qn** to advise sb against sthg; ~ **a qn di fare qc** to advise sb against doing sthg.

scontare *vt (detrarre)* to deduct; *(pena)* to serve; *(colpa, errore)* to pay for.

scontato, -a *agg (prezzo)* discounted; *(previsto)* taken for granted; **dare qc per** ~ to take sthg for granted.

scontento, -a *agg*: ~ **(di)** dissatisfied (with).

sconto *sm* discount; **fare uno** ~ to give a discount.

scontrarsi *vr (urtarsi)* to collide; *(combattere, discordare)* to clash.

scontrino *sm* receipt; **'munirsi dello scontrino alla cassa'** 'pay at the till and obtain a receipt'.

scontro *sm (urto)* collision; *(combattimento, fig)* clash.

scontroso, -a *agg* surly.

sconveniente *agg (indecente)* improper.

sconvolgente *agg* disturbing.

sconvolgere *vt (persona)* to disturb, to shake; *(ordine, piani)* to upset.

sconvolto, -a *pp* → **sconvolgere**.

scopa *sf (arnese)* broom.

scoperta *sf* discovery.

scoperto, -a ◇ *pp* → **scoprire** ◇ *agg* uncovered; *(capo, braccia)* bare.

scopo *sm* purpose, aim; **allo** ~ **di fare qc** in order to do sthg; **a che** ~? for what purpose?

scoppiare *vi (spaccarsi)* to burst; *(esplodere)* to explode; ~ **dal caldo** *(fam)* to be boiling (hot); ~ **a piangere** to burst into tears; ~ **a ridere** to burst out laughing.

scoppio *sm (rumore, di pneumatico)* bang; *(esplosione)* explosion; *(di risa)* burst; *(di guerra)* outbreak; **a** ~ **ritardato** delayed-action.

scoprire *vt* to discover; *(liberare da copertura)* to uncover.

◆ **scoprirsi** *vr (svestirsi)* to dress less warmly; *(rivelarsi)* to give o.s. away.

scoraggiare *vt* to discourage.

◆ **scoraggiarsi** *vr* to become discouraged.

scorbutico, -a, -ci, -che *agg (scontroso)* cantankerous.

scorciatoia *sf* short cut; **prendere una** ~ to take a short cut.

scordare *vt* to forget.

◆ **scordarsi di** *vr + prep* to forget; **scordarsi di fare qc** to forget to do sthg.

scorgere *vt* to see, to make out.

scorpacciata *sf*: **fare una** ~ **(di qc)** to stuff o.s. (with sthg).

scorpione *sm* scorpion.

◆ **Scorpione** *sm* Scorpio.

scorrazzare *vi* to run around.

scorrere ◇ *vi (liquido, fiume, traffico)* to flow; *(fune)* to run; *(tempo)* to pass ◇ *vt (giornale, libro)* to glance through.

scorretto, -a *agg (errato)* incorrect; *(sleale)* unfair.

scorrevole *agg (porta)* sliding; *(traffico, stile)* flowing.

scorrimento *sm (di traffico)* flow.

scorsa *sf*: **dare una** ~ **a qc** to glance through sthg.

scorso, -a ◇ *pp* → **scorrere** ◇ *agg* last.

scorta *sf*: **fare** ~ **di qc** to stock up with sthg; **di** ~ spare.

scortare *vt* to escort.

scortese *agg* impolite.
scorticare *vt (pelle)* to graze; *(animale)* to skin.
scorto, -a *pp* → **scorgere**.
scorza *sf (di albero)* bark; *(di frutto)* peel.
scorzanera *sf type of bitter-tasting root vegetable.*
scosceso, -a *agg* steep.
scossa *sf (movimento)* jolt; *(elettrica)* shock.
scosso, -a ◇ *pp* → **scuotere** ◇ *agg* shaken.
scossone *sm* jolt.
scostare *vt* to move aside.
◆ **scostarsi** *vr* to move aside.
scotch®[1] [skɔtʃ] *sm inv (nastro adesivo)* = Sellotape® *(Br)*, Scotch® tape *(Am)*.
scotch[2] [skɔtʃ] *sm inv (whisky)* Scotch.
scottadito : **a scottadito** *avv* piping hot.
scottare ◇ *vt (ustionare)* to burn; *(cuocere)* to scald ◇ *vi (bevanda, pietanza)* to be too hot.
◆ **scottarsi** *vr* to burn o.s.
scottatura *sf* burn.
scotto, -a *agg* overcooked.
scout ['skaut] *smf inv* scout.
scovare *vt (negozio, ristorante)* to discover.
Scozia *sf*: la ~ Scotland.
scozzese ◇ *agg* Scottish ◇ *smf* Scotsman (*f* Scotswoman); **gli scozzesi** the Scots.
screditare *vt* to discredit.
screpolare *vt* to crack.
◆ **screpolarsi** *vr* to crack.
screziato, -a *agg* streaked.
screzio *sm* disagreement.
scricchiolare *vi* to creak.
scricchiolio *sm* creaking.
scriminatura *sf* parting.
scritta *sf* inscription.
scritto, -a ◇ *pp* → **scrivere** ◇ *agg* written ◇ *sm (opera)* work; *(cosa scritta)* letter.
scrittore, -trice *sm, f* writer.
scrittura *sf* writing.
scrivania *sf* writing desk.
scrivere *vt & vi* to write; **~ a qn** to write to sb.
◆ **scriversi** *vr (parola)*: **come si scrive 'cuore'?** how do you write O spell 'cuore'?
scroccare *vt (fam)* to scrounge.
scrollare *vt (agitare)* to shake; *(spalle)* to shrug; **scrollarsi qc di dosso** to shake sthg off.
scrosciare *vi (pioggia)* to pelt down; *(applausi)* to thunder.
scroscio *sm (d'acqua)* pelting; *(d'applausi)* thunder.
scrostare *vt (intonaco)* to strip off.
◆ **scrostarsi** *vr (pareti, tegame)* to peel.
scrupolo *sm (timore)* scruple; *(diligenza)* conscientiousness; **senza scrupoli** unscrupulous.
scrupoloso, -a *agg (persona)* scrupulous; *(resoconto, lavoro)* meticulous.
scrutare *vt* to scrutinize; *(orizzonte)* to search.
scucire *vt (cucitura)* to unpick.
◆ **scucirsi** *vr* to come unstitched.
scuderia *sf* stable.
scudetto *sm* (SPORT) championship shield.
scudo *sm* shield.
sculacciare *vt* to spank.
scultore, -trice *sm, f* sculptor.
scultura *sf* sculpture.
scuola *sf* school; **andare a ~** to go to school; **~ elementare** = primary school *(Br)*, grade school *(Am)(for children aged from 6 to 11)*; **~ guida** driving school; **~ materna** nursery school *(for children aged from 3 to 5)*; **~ media** *first three years of secondary school for children aged from 11 to 14*; **~ dell'obbligo** compulsory education; **scuole tecniche**

schools which prepare their students for practical professions; **scuole serali** evening classes.

scuotere *vt* to shake; *(spalle)* to shrug.

◆ **scuotersi** *vr* to shake o.s.

scurire ◇ *vt* to darken ◇ *vi* to grow dark.

◆ **scurirsi** *vr* to grow dark.

scuro, -a ◇ *agg* dark ◇ *sm (buio)* darkness.

scusa *sf* excuse; **chiedere ~ (a qn)** to apologize (to sb).

scusare *vt (perdonare)* to forgive; *(giustificare)* to excuse.

◆ **scusarsi** *vr* to apologize; **(mi) scusi, dov'è la stazione?** excuse me, where is the station?; **scusi!** sorry!

sdebitarsi *vr*: **~ con qn di qc** to repay sb for sthg.

sdentato, -a *agg* toothless.

sdolcinato, -a *agg* oversentimental.

sdraia *sf* deckchair.

sdraiarsi *vr* to lie down.

sdraio *sm*: **(sedia a) ~** deckchair.

sdrammatizzare *vt* to play down.

sdrucciolare *vi* to slip.

se ◇ *cong* 1. *(nel caso in cui)* if; **rimani ~ vuoi** stay if you want; **~ è possibile** if it's possible; **~ fossi in te** if I were you; **~ non sbaglio ...** if I'm not wrong ...

2. *(dato che)* if; **~ lo dici, sarà vero** if you say so, it must be true.

3. *(con frasi dubitative & interrogative indirette)* whether, if; **vedi ~ puoi venire** see whether o if you can come; **chiedile ~ le piace** ask her if she likes it.

4. *(esprime un suggerimento)*: **e ~ andassimo al cinema?** how about going to the cinema?

5. *(esprime un augurio)* if; **~ solo potessi!** if only I could!

6. *(in espressioni)*: **anche ~** even if; **~ mai** if; **neanche ~** even if; **~ non altro** if nothing else; **~ no** otherwise.

◇ *pron* → **si**.

sé *pron (per cosa)* itself; *(per persona)* himself/herself/themselves; **tenere qc per ~** to keep sthg for oneself; **pensa solo a se stesso** he only thinks of himself.

sebbene *cong* although.

sec. *(abbr di secolo)* c.

secca, -che *sf (di mare, fiume)* shallows *(pl)*.

seccare *vt* to dry; *(prosciugare)* to dry up; *(infastidire)* to annoy.

◆ **seccarsi** *vr* to dry; *(prosciugarsi)* to dry up; *(infastidirsi)* to get annoyed.

seccato, -a *agg (infastidito)* annoyed.

seccatore, -trice *sm, f* nuisance.

seccatura *sf (fastidio)* nuisance.

secchiello *sm (contenitore)* bucket.

secchio *sm* bucket.

secchione, -a *sm, f (fam)* swot.

secco, -a, -chi, -che ◇ *agg* dry; *(funghi, prugne)* dried; *(brusco)* curt ◇ *sm*: **essere a ~ di qc** *(fig: non avere)* to be without sthg; **tirare in ~ una barca** to beach a boat; **lavare a ~** to dry-clean.

secolare *agg (vecchio di secoli)* age-old.

secolo *sm* century; *(periodo lungo)*: **non lo vedo da secoli** I haven't seen him for ages.

seconda *sf (marcia)* second gear; **viaggiare in ~** to travel second-class; **a ~ di** according to.

secondario, -a *agg* secondary; **scuola secondaria** secondary school.

secondo, -a ◇ *num* second ◇ *agg (altro)* second ◇ *sm (tempo)* second; *(portata)* main course ◇ *prep* according to; **~ me** in my opinion; **di seconda mano** second-hand, → **sesto**.

sedano *sm* celery.
sedativo *sm* sedative.
sede *sf (di organizzazione)* headquarters *(pl)*; *(di azienda)* head office.
sedentario, -a *agg* sedentary.
sedere ◇ *sm (parte del corpo)* bottom ◇ *vi*: **mettersi a ~** to sit down.
◆ **sedersi** *vr* to sit down.
sedia *sf* chair.
sedicesimo, -a *num* sixteenth, → **sesto**.
sedici *num* sixteen, → **sei**.
sedile *sm (di veicolo)* seat.
sedotto, -a *pp* → **sedurre**.
seducente *agg* seductive.
sedurre *vt (uomo, donna)* to seduce; *(sog: idea, proposta)* to appeal to.
seduta *sf* session.
sega, -ghe *sf* saw.
segale *sf* rye.
segare *vt* to saw.
seggio *sm* seat; **~ elettorale** polling station.
seggiola *sf* chair.
seggiolino *sm (sedia pieghevole)* folding chair.
seggiolone *sm (per bambini)* high chair.
seggiovia *sf* chair lift.
segnalare *vt (comunicare)* to point out; *(indicare)* to indicate.
segnalazione *sf (indicazione)* indication; *(raccomandazione)* recommendation.
segnale *sm (indicazione)* signal; *(stradale)* sign; **~ acustico** sound signal; **~ d'allarme** alarm; **~ orario** time signal.
segnaletica *sf (stradale)* road signs *(pl)*.
segnalibro *sm* bookmark.
segnaposto *sm* place card.
segnare *vt (mettere un segno)* to mark; *(indicare)* to indicate; (SPORT) to score; **segnarsi qc** to make a note of sthg.
segno *sm* sign; *(lettera, numero)* symbol; *(contrassegno, traccia)* mark; **fare ~ a qn di fare qc** to signal sb to do sthg; **fare ~ di no** to shake one's head; **fare ~ di sì** to nod one's head; **perdere il ~** to lose one's place; **cogliere** o **colpire nel ~** *(fig)* to hit the mark.
segretario, -a *sm, f* secretary.
segreteria *sf (di azienda, scuola)* secretary's office; *(di partito)* position of Secretary.
◆ **segreteria telefonica** *sf* answering machine.
segreto, -a *agg & sm* secret.
seguente *agg* following, next.
seguire ◇ *vt* to follow ◇ *vi* to follow; *(continuare)*: **segue a pag. 70** continued on page 70.
seguito *sm (proseguimento)* continuation; *(risultato)* result; *(scorta)* retinue; *(favore)* following; **in ~ a** following; **di ~** at a stretch, on end; **in ~** subsequently.
sei[1] → **essere**.
sei[2] *agg num* six; **ha ~ anni** he/she is six (years old); **sono le ~** it's six o'clock; **il ~ gennaio** the sixth of January; **pagina ~** page six; **il ~ di picche** the six of spades; **erano in ~** there were six of them.
seicento *num* six hundred, → **sei**.
◆ **Seicento** *sm*: **il Seicento** the seventeenth century.
selciato *sm* cobbles *(pl)*, cobbled surface.
selettivo, -a *agg* selective.
selezionare *vt* to select.
selezione *sf* selection.
self-service ['sɛl 'sɛrvis] *agg inv & sm inv* self-service.
sella *sf* saddle.
selvaggina *sf* game.
selvaggio, -a, -gi, -ge ◇ *agg* wild; *(tribù)* savage; *(delitto)* brutal ◇ *sm, f* savage.
selvatico, -a, -ci, -che *agg* wild.

semaforo *sm (apparecchio)* traffic lights *(pl)*.
sembrare ◇ *vi* to seem ◇ *v impers*: **sembra che** it seems that; **mi sembra di conoscerlo** I think I know him; **sembra che stia per piovere** it looks like it's going to rain.
seme *sm* seed; *(nocciolo)* stone; *(di carte da gioco)* suit.
semestre *sm* six-month period; (SCOL) semester.
semifinale *sf* semifinal.
semifreddo *sm dessert similar to ice cream*.
seminare *vt* to sow.
seminario *sm* seminar; (RELIG) seminary.
seminterrato *sm* basement.
semmai ◇ *cong* if (ever) ◇ *avv* if anything.
semolino *sm* semolina.
semplice *agg* simple; *(filo, consonante)* single; **è una ~ proposta** it's just a suggestion.
semplicemente *avv* simply.
semplicità *sf* simplicity.
semplificare *vt* to simplify.
sempre *avv* always; *(ancora)* still; **va ~ meglio/peggio** things are getting better and better/ worse and worse; **~ che ci riesca** provided he manages it; **da ~** always; **di ~** usual; **per ~** forever.
senape *sf* mustard.
senato *sm* senate.
senatore, -trice *sm, f* senator.
sennò *avv (altrimenti)* otherwise.
seno *sm (petto)* breast.
sensazionale *agg* sensational.
sensazione *sf* sensation, feeling; **fare ~** to cause a sensation.
sensibile *agg* sensitive; *(notevole)* noticeable; **~ a** *(caldo, freddo)* sensitive to; *(complimenti)* susceptible to.
sensibilità *sf* sensitivity.
senso *sm (facoltà, coscienza)* sense; *(sentimento, impressione)* feeling; *(significato)* meaning, sense; *(direzione)* direction; **non avere ~** to make no sense; **a ~ unico** one-way; **in ~ orario** clockwise; **perdere i sensi** to lose consciousness.
sentenza *sf (di processo)* sentence; *(massima)* maxim.
sentiero *sm* path.
sentimentale *agg* sentimental.
sentimento *sm* feeling.
sentire *vt (udire)* to hear; *(percepire, con il tatto)* to feel; *(odore)* to smell; *(sapore)* to taste; **senti!** listen!
◆ **sentirsi** *vr (bene, stanco, allegro)* to feel; **sentirsi di fare qc** to feel like doing sthg; **sentirsi bene/male** to feel well/ill; *(telefonarsi)*: **ci sentiamo domani** speak to you tomorrow.
senza *prep & cong* without; **~ di me** without me; **senz'altro** certainly, of course; **~ dubbio** undoubtedly; **~ che tu te ne accorga** without you noticing it.
senzatetto *smf inv* homeless person.
separare *vt* to separate.
◆ **separarsi** *vr (coniugi)* to separate; *(gruppo)* to split up; **separarsi da** *vr + prep (coniuge)* to separate from.
separato, -a *agg (disgiunto)* separate; *(coniuge)* separated.
separazione *sf* separation.
sepolto, -a *pp* → **seppellire**.
seppellire *vt* to bury.
seppia *sf* cuttlefish.
sequenza *sf* sequence.
sequestrare *vt* (DIR) to sequestrate; *(persona)* to kidnap.
sequestro *sm* (DIR) sequestration; *(rapimento)* kidnapping.
sera *sf* evening; **di ~** in the evening.

serale *agg* evening *(dav s)*.
serata *sf* evening; *(ricevimento)* party.
serbare *vt* to put aside, to keep; **~ rancore a qn** to bear sb a grudge.
serbatoio *sm (di veicolo)* tank.
serbo *sm*: **avere qc in ~** to have sthg in store; **tenere qc in ~** to put sthg aside.
serenata *sf* serenade.
sereno, -a ◇ *agg (tempo, cielo)* clear; *(persona)* calm ◇ *sm (bel tempo)* fine weather.
serie *sf inv (successione)* series *(inv)*; *(insieme)* set; (SPORT) division; **produzione in ~** mass production.
serietà *sf* seriousness; *(coscienziosità)* reliability.
serio, -a ◇ *agg* serious; *(coscienzioso)* reliable ◇ *sm*: **sul ~** *(davvero)* seriously; **prendere qn/qc sul ~** to take sb/sthg seriously.
serpente *sm* snake; *(pelle)* snakeskin.
serra *sf (per piante)* greenhouse.
serranda *sf* rolling shutter.
serrare *vt (chiudere)* to close; *(stringere)* to shut tightly.
serratura *sf* lock.
servire ◇ *vt* to serve ◇ *vi (in tennis, pallavolo)* to serve; *(essere utile)* to be of use; **~ a fare qc** to be used for doing sthg; **~ a qn** to be of use to sb; **mi serve un martello** I need a hammer; **~ da** to be used as.
◆ **servirsi** *vr (prendere da mangiare/bere)* to help o.s..
◆ **servirsi da** to shop at.
◆ **servirsi di** *vr + prep (utilizzare)* to use.
servitù *sf (condizione)* slavery; *(personale)* domestic staff.
servizio *sm* service; *(di piatti, bicchieri)* set; *(giornalistico)* report; **essere di ~** to be on duty; **'~ compreso'** 'service included'; **~ militare** military service.
◆ **servizi** *smpl (di abitazione)* kitchen and bathroom.
sessanta *num* sixty, → **sei**.
sessantesimo, -a *num* sixtieth, → **sesto**.
sessantina *sf*: **una ~ (di)** about sixty; **essere sulla ~** to be in one's sixties.
sesso *sm* sex.
sessuale *agg* sexual.
sesto, -a ◇ *agg num & pron num* sixth ◇ *sm (frazione)* sixth; **rimettersi in ~** to recover.
seta *sf* silk.
setacciare *vt (separare)* to sieve.
sete *sf* thirst; **avere ~** to be thirsty.
settanta *num* seventy, → **sei**.
settantesimo, -a *num* seventieth, → **sesto**.
settantina *sf*: **una ~ (di)** about seventy; **essere sulla ~** to be in one's seventies.
sette *num* seven, → **sei**.
settecento *num* seven hundred, → **sei**.
◆ **Settecento** *sm*: **il Settecento** the eighteenth century.
settembre *sm* September; **a** O **in ~** in September; **lo scorso ~** last September; **il prossimo ~** next September; **all'inizio di ~** at the beginning of September; **alla fine di ~** at the end of September; **il due ~** the second of September.
settentrionale *agg* northern.
settentrione *sm* north.
setter *sm inv* setter.
settimana *sf* week.
settimanale ◇ *agg* weekly ◇ *sm* weekly publication.
settimo, -a *num* seventh, → **sesto**.
settore *sm* sector.
severamente *avv*: **'è ~ vietato attraversare i binari'** 'crossing the track is strictly forbidden'.
severo, -a *agg* strict, severe.
sevizie *sfpl* torture *(sg)*.

sexy *agg inv* sexy.
sezione *sf* section; (MED) dissection.
sfaccendato, -a *agg* lazy.
sfacchinata *sf* hard work.
sfacciato, -a *agg (persona)* cheeky.
sfacelo *sm (rovina)* ruin.
sfamare *vt* to feed.
◆ **sfamarsi** *vr* to satisfy one's hunger.
sfare *vt* to undo.
sfarzo *sm* pomp, magnificence.
sfasciare *vt (sbendare)* to unbandage; *(rompere)* to smash.
◆ **sfasciarsi** *vr (rompersi)* to fall to pieces.
sfaticato, -a *agg* lazy.
sfatto, -a *pp* → **sfare**.
sfavorevole *agg* unfavourable.
sfera *sf* sphere.
sferrare *vt (attacco)* to launch; ~ **un colpo contro qn** to lash out at sb.
sfibrare *vt* to exhaust.
sfida *sf* challenge.
sfidare *vt* to challenge; *(pericolo, morte)* to defy; ~ **qn a fare qc** to challenge sb to do sthg.
sfiducia *sf* distrust.
sfigurare ◇ *vt* to disfigure ◇ *vi* to make a bad impression.
sfilare ◇ *vt (togliere)* to take off ◇ *vi (marciare)* to parade; **sfilarsi le scarpe** to slip off one's shoes.
◆ **sfilarsi** *vr (calze)* to ladder.
sfilata *sf (corteo)* march; *(di moda)* fashion show.
sfinire *vt* to exhaust.
sfiorare *vt* to skim (over).
sfiorire *vi* to wither.
sfitto, -a *agg* vacant.
sfizioso, -a *agg* enticing.
sfocato, -a = **sfuocato**.
sfociare : **sfociare in** *v + prep (fiume)* to flow into.
sfoderare *vt (giacca)* to remove the lining from; *(spada)* to draw; *(fig)* to show off.
sfoderato, -a *agg* unlined.
sfogare *vt* to give vent to.
◆ **sfogarsi** *vr (aprirsi)* to pour out one's feelings; **sfogarsi su qn** *(scaricare la collera)* to vent one's anger on sb.
sfoggiare *vt* to show off.
sfogliare *vt (giornale)* to leaf through.
sfogliatelle *sfpl puff pastries filled with spiced ricotta cheese and candied fruit.*
sfogo, -ghi *sm (passaggio)* outlet; *(di sentimenti)* outburst; *(eruzione cutanea)* rash; **dare ~ a qc** to give vent to sthg.
sfoltire *vt* to thin.
sfondare *vt (contenitore)* to break the bottom of; *(porta)* to break down.
◆ **sfondarsi** *vr (contenitore)* to burst at the bottom.
sfondo *sm* background.
sformato *sm savoury pudding made with vegetables and cheese or sometimes with meat, baked in a mould and then turned out.*
sfornare *vt (pane, dolci)* to take out of the oven.
sfortuna *sf* misfortune; **portare ~** to bring bad luck.
sfortunatamente *avv* unfortunately.
sfortunato, -a *agg* unlucky.
sforzare *vt* to force; *(occhi, voce, motore)* to strain.
◆ **sforzarsi** *vr* to make an effort.
sforzo *sm* effort; **fare uno ~** to make an effort.
sfottere *vt (fam)* to tease.
sfratto *sm* eviction.
sfrecciare *vi* to shoot past.
sfregare *vt (strofinare)* to rub.
sfregio *sm (taglio)* gash.
sfrenato, -a *agg* unrestrained.
sfrontato, -a *agg* impudent.

sfruttamento *sm* exploitation.
sfruttare *vt* to exploit.
sfuggire *vi (scappare)* to escape.
♦ **sfuggire a** *v + prep (sottrarsi a)* to escape from; ~ **di mano a qn** to slip out of sb's hands; ~ **di mente a qn** to slip sb's mind; **non gli sfugge nulla** he misses nothing.
sfuggita : di sfuggita *avv* in passing.
sfumare ◇ *vt (colore)* to shade off; *(capelli)* to taper ◇ *vi (colore)* to shade off; *(svanire)* to vanish.
sfumato, -a *agg (colore)* soft.
sfumatura *sf (tonalità)* shade; *(fig: piccola differenza)* touch, hint; *(di capelli)* tapering.
sfuocato, -a *agg* blurred, out of focus.
sfuriata *sf (sfogo violento)* outburst of anger; *(rimprovero)* telling off.
sgabello *sm* stool.
sgabuzzino *sm* storage room.
sgambetto *sm*: **fare lo ~ a qn** to trip sb up.
sganciare *vt (vestito, allacciatura)* to unfasten; *(rimorchio, vagone)* to uncouple; *(bombe)* to drop; *(fam: soldi)* to fork out.
♦ **sganciarsi** *vr (staccarsi)* to come undone.
sgarbato, -a *agg* impolite.
sghignazzare *vi* to laugh scornfully.
sgobbare *vi (fam)* to slog.
sgocciolare ◇ *vt (bottiglia)* to drain ◇ *vi* to drip.
sgolarsi *vr* to make o.s. hoarse.
sgomb(e)rare *vt (strada, soffitta)* to clear.
sgombero, -a = **sgombro**.
sgombro, -a ◇ *agg* clear ◇ *sm (evacuazione)* evacuation; *(pesce)* mackerel.
sgomentare *vt* to dismay.
♦ **sgomentarsi** *vr* to be dismayed.
sgominare *vt* to rout.
sgonfiare *vt* to deflate.
♦ **sgonfiarsi** *vr (canotto)* to deflate; *(caviglia)* to go down.
sgorbio *sm (scarabocchio)* scribble; *(fig: persona)* fright.
sgradevole *agg* unpleasant.
sgradito, -a *agg* unwelcome.
sgranare *vt (fagioli)* to shell.
sgranchirsi *vr*: ~ **le gambe** to stretch one's legs.
sgranocchiare *vt* to munch.
sgraziato, -a *agg* graceless.
sgretolare *vt (frantumare)* to cause to crumble.
♦ **sgretolarsi** *vr* to crumble.
sgridare *vt* to scold.
sguaiato, -a *agg* coarse.
sgualcire *vt* to crumple.
♦ **sgualcirsi** *vr* to become crumpled.
sguardo *sm (occhiata)* look; *(espressione)* expression.
sguinzagliare *vt (cane)* to take off the lead.
sgusciare ◇ *vt (fagioli)* to shell ◇ *vi (sfuggire)* to slip away.
shampoo [ˈʃampo] *sm inv* shampoo.
shock [ʃɔk] *sm inv* shock.
si (*diventa* **se** *quando precede lo, la, li, le, ne*) *pron* **1.** *(riflessivo: persona)* himself (*f* herself), themselves *(pl)*; *(impersonale)* oneself; *(cosa, animale)* itself, themselves *(pl)*; **lavarsi** to wash (oneself); ~ **stanno preparando** they are getting ready.
2. *(con verbo transitivo)*: **lavarsi i denti** to brush one's teeth; ~ **è comprato un vestito** he bought himself a suit.
3. *(reciproco)* each other, one another; ~ **sono conosciuti a Roma** they met in Rome.
4. *(impersonale)*: ~ **può sempre provare** one O you can always try; ~ **dice che** ... they say that ..., it is said that ...; ~ **vede che è stanco**

one ○ you can see he's tired; '~ **prega di non fumare**' 'please do not smoke'; **non ~ sa mai** you never know.

5. *(passivo)*: **questi prodotti ~ trovano dappertutto** these products are found everywhere.

sì *avv & sm inv* yes; **dire di ~** to say yes; **uno ~ e uno no** every other one.

sia[1] → **essere**.

sia[2] *cong*: **~ ... che, ~ ... ~** both ... and; **~ che ... ~ che** whether ... or; **~ che tu venga, ~ che tu non venga** whether you come or not.

siamo → **essere**.

sicché *cong (e quindi)* and so.

siccità *sf inv* drought.

siccome *cong* as, since.

Sicilia *sf*: **la ~** Sicily.

siciliano, -a *agg & sm, f* Sicilian.

sicura *sf (di auto)* safety lock; *(di arma)* safety catch.

sicurezza *sf (mancanza di pericolo)* safety, security; *(certezza)* certainty; **di ~** safety *(dav s)*, security *(dav s)*.

sicuro, -a ◇ *agg* safe; *(amico, informazione)* reliable; *(fiducioso)* confident; *(certo)* certain ◇ *avv* certainly; **di ~** certainly; **andare sul ~** to play safe; **essere ~ di sè** to be sure of o.s.; **al ~** in a safe place.

Siena *sf* Siena.

siepe *sf* hedge.

sieropositivo, -a *agg* HIV-positive.

siete → **essere**.

Sig. *(abbr di signor)* Mr.

Sig.a *(abbr di signora)* Ms.

sigaretta *sf* cigarette.

sigaro *sm* cigar.

Sigg. *abbr* Messrs.

sigla *sf (abbreviazione)* acronym; *(musicale)* signature tune; **~ automobilistica** *two-letter abbreviation of province on a vehicle's number plate.*

Sig.na *(abbr di signorina)* Miss.

significare *vt* to mean; **che cosa significa?** what does it mean?

significativo, -a *agg (discorso)* significant; *(sguardo)* meaningful.

significato *sm* meaning.

signor *sm* → **signore**.

signora *sf (donna)* lady; *(moglie)* wife; **buon giorno ~** good morning (Madam); **Gentile Signora** *(in una lettera)* Dear Madam; **la ~ Poli** Mrs Poli; **signore e signori** ladies and gentlemen.

signore *sm (uomo)* gentleman; **buon giorno ~** good morning (Sir); **il ~ desidera?** what can I do for you, sir?; **Gentile Signore** *(in una lettera)* Dear Sir; **i Signori Rossi** *(marito e moglie)* Mr and Mrs Rossi; **il Signor Martini** Mr Martini.

signorina *sf (ragazza)* young lady; **buon giorno ~** good morning (Madam); **la ~ Logi** Miss Logi.

Sig.ra *abbr* Mrs.

silenzio *sm* silence; **fare ~** to be quiet.

silenzioso, -a *agg* quiet, silent.

sillaba *sf* syllable.

simbolico, -a, -ci, -che *agg* symbolic.

simbolo *sm* symbol.

simile *agg (analogo)* similar; *(tale)*: **una persona ~** such a person; **~ a** similar to.

simmetrico, -a, -ci, -che *agg* symmetric(al).

simpatia *sf (inclinazione)* liking; *(qualità)* pleasantness.

simpatico, -a, -ci, -che *agg* nice.

simulare *vt (fingere)* to feign; *(imitare)* to simulate.

simultaneo, -a *agg* simultaneous.

sin = **sino**.

sinagoga, -ghe *sf* synagogue.

sincero, -a *agg (persona)* sincere; *(dolore, gioia)* genuine, heart-felt.

sindacalista, -i, -e *smf* trade unionist.

sindacato *sm (di lavoratori)* trade union.
sindaco, -ci *sm* mayor.
sinfonia *sf* symphony.
singhiozzo *sm* hiccups *(pl)*.
♦ **singhiozzi** *smpl* sobs; **a singhiozzi** *(fig)* by fits and starts.
singolare ◇ *agg (originale)* unusual; (GRAMM) singular ◇ *sm* (GRAMM) singular.
singolo, -a *agg* single.
sinistra *sf*: **la ~** the left; (POL) the left (wing); **scrivere con la ~** to write with one's left hand; **a ~** left; **a ~ di** to the left of.
sinistro, -a ◇ *agg* left; *(minaccioso)* sinister ◇ *sm* accident.
sino = **fino**.
sinonimo *sm* synonym.
sintesi *sf inv (riassunto)* summary.
sintetico, -a, -ci, -che *agg (artificiale)* synthetic; *(succinto)* brief.
sintetizzare *vt (riassumere)* to summarize.
sintomo *sm* symptom.
sintonizzare *vt* to tune in.
♦ **sintonizzarsi su** *vr + prep* to tune in to.
sipario *sm* curtain.
sirena *sf (apparecchio)* siren; *(nella mitologia)* mermaid.
siringa, -ghe *sf (per iniezioni)* syringe; *(da cucina)* = piping bag.
sistema, -i *sm* system.
sistemare *vt (ordinare)* to tidy up; *(risolvere)* to sort out, to settle; *(alloggiare)* to find accommodation *(Br)* o accommodations *(Am)* for; *(procurare un lavoro a)* to find a job for; *(maritare)* to marry off.
♦ **sistemarsi** *vr (risolversi)* to be settled; *(trovare alloggio)* to find accommodation *(Br)* o accommodations *(Am)*; *(trovare lavoro)* to find work; *(sposarsi)* to marry.
sistematico, -a, -ci, -che *agg* systematic.
sistemazione *sf (disposizione)* arrangement; *(alloggio)* accommodation *(Br)*, accommodations *(Am)*; *(lavoro)* employment.
sito *sm* (INFORM): **~ Web** Web site.
situare *vt* to situate, to locate.
situazione *sf* situation.
skate-board ['skεit 'bord] *sm inv* skateboard.
ski-lift [ski'lift] *sm inv* ski lift.
ski-pass [ski'pas] *sm inv* ski pass.
slacciare *vt* to undo.
slanciato, -a *agg* slender.
slancio *sm (balzo)* dash; *(fig)* burst.
slavina *sf* snowslide.
slavo, -a *agg* Slavonic, Slav.
sleale *agg (persona)* disloyal; *(azione)* treacherous.
slegare *vt* to untie.
slip *sm inv* briefs *(pl)*.
slitta *sf* sledge.
slittare *vi* to slide; *(automobile)* to skid.
slogan *sm inv* slogan.
slogare *vt* to dislocate.
slogatura *sf* dislocation.
smacchiatore *sm* stain remover.
smagliante *agg* dazzling.
smagliare *vt (collant, calze)* to ladder.
smagliatura *sf (di calze)* ladder; *(della pelle)* stretch mark.
smaltire *vt (merce)* to sell off; *(rifiuti)* to discharge; *(cibo)* to digest; **~ la sbornia** to get over one's hangover.
smalto *sm (per metalli, di denti)* enamel; *(per ceramica)* glaze; *(per unghie)* nail varnish.
smania *sf (agitazione)* restlessness; *(desiderio)* craving; **aver la ~ di qc** to have a craving for sthg.
smarrire *vt* to lose.
♦ **smarrirsi** *vr* to get lost.
smarrito, -a *agg* lost; *(sbigottito)* bewildered.
smascherare *vt* to unmask.

smemorato, -a *agg* absent-minded.

smentire *vt (notizia)* to deny; *(testimonianza)* to refute.

smentita *sf (di notizia)* denial.

smeraldo *sm* emerald.

smesso, -a *pp* → **smettere**.

smettere *vt* to stop; *(abito)* to stop wearing; **smettere di fare qc** to stop doing sthg; **smettila!** stop it!

smidollato, -a *agg* spineless.

sminuire *vt* to belittle.

sminuzzare *vt* to crumble.

smistamento *sm (di posta, pacchi)* sorting; *(di treni)* shunting.

smistare *vt (posta)* to sort; *(treni)* to shunt.

smisurato, -a *agg* enormous, huge.

smodato, -a *agg* excessive.

smog *sm inv* smog.

smoking *sm inv* dinner jacket *(Br)*, tuxedo *(Am)*.

smontabile *agg* that can be dismantled.

smontare ◇ *vt (macchina, libreria)* to take to pieces; *(fig: far perdere l'entusiasmo a)* to discourage ◇ *vi (da cavallo)* to dismount; *(da turno di lavoro)* to finish (work).

smorfia *sf* grimace.

smorfioso, -a *agg* simpering.

smorzare *vt (suoni)* to muffle; *(colore)* to tone down; *(entusiasmo)* to dampen.

smosso, -a *pp* → **smuovere**.

smottamento *sm* landslide.

smunto, -a *agg* pinched.

smuovere *vt (spostare)* to shift; *(da proposito, intenzione)* to deter.

smussare *vt (spigolo)* to round off.

snack-bar *sm inv* snack bar.

snaturato, -a *agg* inhuman.

snello, -a *agg* slim, slender.

snervante *agg* exhausting.

snidare *vt* to flush out.

snobismo *sm* snobbery.

snodare *vt (slegare)* to untie; *(arti)* to loosen up.

◆ **snodarsi** *vr (slegarsi)* to come loose.

sobbalzare *vi (balzare)* to jolt; *(trasalire)* to jump.

sobborgo, -ghi *sm* suburb.

sobrio, -a *agg* sober.

socchiudere *vt (porta)* to leave ajar; *(occhi)* to half-close.

socchiuso, -a *pp* → **socchiudere**.

soccorrere *vt* to help.

soccorso, -a ◇ *pp* → **soccorrere** ◇ *sm* help, aid; ~ **stradale** breakdown service.

sociale *agg* social.

socialista, -i, -e *agg* socialist.

socializzare *vi* to socialize.

società *sf inv (gruppo umano)* society; *(associazione)* association, club; (COMM) company; ~ **per azioni** limited company *(Br)*, incorporated company *(Am)*.

socievole *agg* sociable.

socio, -a, -ci, cie *sm, f (di circolo)* member; (COMM) partner.

soda®[1] *sf* soda.

soda[2] *sf (bevanda)* soda water.

soddisfacente *agg* satisfactory.

soddisfare *vt* to satisfy.

soddisfatto, -a *agg* satisfied; **essere ~ di** *(contento)* to be satisfied with.

soddisfazione *sf* satisfaction.

sodo, -a *agg* hard, firm.

sofà *sm inv* sofa.

sofferente *agg* suffering.

sofferto, -a *pp* → **soffrire**.

soffiare ◇ *vi* to blow ◇ *vt* to blow; ~ **qn/qc a qn** to pinch sb/sthg from sb; **soffiarsi il naso** to blow one's nose.

soffiata *sf (fam)* tip-off.

soffice *agg* soft.

soffio *sm (di fiato, vento)* breath; ~ **al cuore** heart murmur.

soffitta *sf* attic.
soffitto *sm* ceiling.
soffocante *agg* suffocating, stifling.
soffocare ◇ *vt* to suffocate ◇ *vi* to suffocate.
soffriggere *vt & vi* to fry lightly.
soffrire ◇ *vt (patire)* to suffer; *(sopportare)* to bear ◇ *vi* to suffer.
◆ **soffrire di** *v + prep* to suffer from.
soffritto *sm lightly fried onions and herbs.*
sofisticato, -a *agg* sophisticated.
software ['sɔftwɛr] *sm* software.
soggetto, -a ◇ *agg*: **essere ~ a** to be subject to ◇ *sm* subject.
soggezione *sf (sottomissione)* subjection; *(imbarazzo)* uneasiness; **dare ~ a qn** to make sb ill at ease.
soggiorno *sm (permanenza)* stay; *(stanza)* living room.
soglia *sf* threshold.
sogliola *sf* sole.
sognare ◇ *vt* to dream of o about ◇ *vi* to dream; **~ ad occhi aperti** to daydream.
sogno *sm* dream; **fare un brutto ~** to have a bad dream.
soia *sf* soya.
solaio *sm* attic.
solamente *avv* only, just.
solare *agg* solar, sun *(dav s)*.
solarium *sm inv* solarium.
solco, -chi *sm (in terreno)* furrow; *(incisione)* groove; *(scia)* wake.
soldato *sm* soldier; **~ semplice** private.
soldo *sm*: **non avere un ~** to be penniless.
◆ **soldi** *smpl (denaro)* money *(sg)*.
sole *sm* sun; **prendere il ~** to sunbathe.
soleggiato, -a *agg* sunny.
solenne *agg* solemn.
solere *v impers*: **come si suol dire** as they say.
soletta *sf (suola)* insole.
solfo = **zolfo**.
solidale *agg*: **essere ~ con qn** to be in agreement with sb.
solidarietà *sf* solidarity.
solido, -a *agg & sm* solid.
solista, -i, -e *smf* soloist.
solitario, -a ◇ *agg (persona)* lonely, solitary; *(luogo)* lonely ◇ *sm (di carte)* patience *(Br)*, solitaire *(Am)*; *(brillante)* solitaire.
solito, -a *agg* usual; **essere ~ fare qc** to be in the habit of doing sthg; **(come) al ~** as usual; **di ~** usually.
solitudine *sf* solitude.
sollecitare *vt (risposta, pagamento)* to press for.
solleone *sm (caldo)* summer heat; *(periodo)* dog days *(pl)*.
solletico *sm* tickling; **soffrire il ~** to be ticklish.
sollevamento *sm* lifting; **~ pesi** (SPORT) weight lifting.
sollevare *vt (tirare su)* to lift, to raise; *(problema, questione)* to raise; *(fare insorgere)* to stir up.
◆ **sollevarsi** *vr (da terra)* to get up; *(insorgere)* to rise up.
sollevato, -a *agg (confortato)* relieved.
sollievo *sm* relief.
solo, -a ◇ *agg (senza compagnia)* alone; *(isolato)* lonely; *(unico)* only ◇ *avv (soltanto)* only, just; **c'è un ~ posto a sedere** there's only one seat; **da ~** by oneself; **ho ~ 5 000 lire** I only have 5,000 lire; **non ~ ... ma anche** not only ... but also; **a ~** (MUS) solo.
soltanto *avv* only.
solubile *agg* soluble; **caffè ~** instant coffee.
soluzione *sf* solution.
Somalia *sf*: **la ~** Somalia.
somaro, -a *sm, f (asino)* donkey, ass; *(fig: a scuola)* dunce.
somiglianza *sf* resemblance.
somigliare : **somigliare a** *v* +

prep (nell'aspetto) to look like; *(nel modo di essere)* to be like.
◆ **somigliarsi** *vr* to be alike.
somma *sf* sum.
sommare *vt* (MAT) to add up.
sommario, -a ◇ *agg* brief ◇ *sm (di libro)* index.
sommergere *vt* to submerge; **~ di** *(fig)* to overwhelm with.
sommergibile *sm* submarine.
sommerso, -a ◇ *pp* → **sommergere** ◇ *agg (isola, città)* underwater.
somministrare *vt* to administer.
sommità *sf inv (cima)* summit.
sommo, -a *agg* highest; *(eccellente)* outstanding, excellent; **per sommi capi** in short, in brief.
sommossa *sf* uprising.
sommozzatore, -trice *sm, f* (deep-sea) diver.
sonda *sf (spaziale,* MED*)* probe.
sondaggio *sm (indagine)* survey.
sondare *vt (fondo marino)* to sound; *(intenzioni, opinioni)* to sound out.
sonnambulo, -a *agg*: **essere ~** to sleepwalk.
sonnellino *sm* nap.
sonnifero *sm* sleeping pill.
sonno *sm* sleep; **avere ~** to be sleepy; **prendere ~** to fall asleep.
sono → **essere**.
sonoro, -a ◇ *agg (onde, di film)* sound *(dav s)*; *(voce, risata, schiaffo)* ringing ◇ *sm (di film)* soundtrack.
sontuoso, -a *agg* sumptuous.
soppiatto : **di soppiatto** *avv* secretly.
sopportare *vt (peso)* to support, to bear; *(umiliazione, dolore)* to bear; *(tollerare)* to put up with.
soppresso, -a *pp* → **sopprimere**.
sopprimere *vt (legge)* to abolish; *(servizio, treno)* to withdraw, to do away with; *(parola)* to delete.
sopra ◇ *prep (su)* on; *(al di sopra di)* above; *(al di là di)* over; *(riguardo a)* about, on ◇ *avv (in alto)* above; *(in lettera, scritto)*: **come precisato ~** as detailed above; **al di ~ di** above; **di ~** upstairs.
soprabito *sm* overcoat.
sopracciglio (*pl f* **sopracciglia**) *sm* eyebrow.
sopraffare *vt* to overcome.
sopraffatto, -a *pp* → **sopraffare**.
sopraggiungere *vi (giungere all'improvviso)* to arrive (unexpectedly); *(accadere)* to occur (unexpectedly).
sopraggiunto, -a *pp* → **sopraggiungere**.
sopralluogo, -ghi *sm (di polizia)* on-the-spot investigation; *(visita)* inspection.
soprammobile *sm* ornament.
soprannaturale *agg* supernatural.
soprannome *sm* nickname.
soprano *sm* soprano.
soprassalto : **di soprassalto** *avv* with a start.
soprattutto *avv* above all, especially.
sopravvalutare *vt* to overestimate.
sopravvento *sm*: **avere il ~ su** to have the upper hand over.
sopravvissuto, -a ◇ *pp* → **sopravvivere** ◇ *sm, f* survivor.
sopravvivere *vi* to survive.
◆ **sopravvivere a** *v + prep* to survive.
soprelevata *sf* elevated section.
soprintendente *smf (a attività, lavoro)* superintendent, supervisor.
soprintendenza *sf (attività)* supervision; *(ufficio)* superintendency.
sopruso *sm* abuse of power.
soqquadro *sm*: **mettere qc a ~** to turn sthg upside down.
sorbetto *sm* sorbet.

sorbire *vt* to sip; **sorbirsi qn/qc** *(fig)* to put up with sb/sthg.
sorcio *sm* mouse.
sordido, -a *agg* sordid, squalid.
sordina *sf*: **in ~** softly.
sordo, -a ◇ *agg (non udente)* deaf; *(rumore, tonfo)* muffled, dull ◇ *sm, f* deaf person.
sordomuto, -a ◇ *agg* deaf and dumb ◇ *sm, f* deaf and dumb person.
sorella *sf* sister.
sorellastra *sf* stepsister.
sorgente *sf (d'acqua)* spring; *(di fiume, elettricità, calore)* source.
sorgere *vi* to rise; *(sospetto, dubbio)* to arise.
sorpassare *vt* (AUTO) to overtake; *(superare)* to exceed.
sorpassato, -a *agg* old-fashioned.
sorpasso *sm (di veicolo)* overtaking; **fare un ~** to overtake.
sorprendere *vt (cogliere)* to catch; *(stupire)* to surprise.
◆ **sorprendersi di** *vr + prep* to be surprised at.
sorpresa *sf* surprise; **fare una ~ a qn** to give sb a surprise; **di ~** by surprise.
sorpreso, -a *pp* → **sorprendere**.
sorreggere *vt* to support.
sorretto, -a *pp* → **sorreggere**.
sorridente *agg* smiling.
sorridere *vi* to smile.
sorriso, -a ◇ *pp* → **sorridere** ◇ *sm* smile.
sorsata *sf* gulp.
sorso *sm (sorsata)* gulp; *(piccola quantità)* sip.
sorta *sf* kind, sort.
sorte *sf* fate; **tirare a ~** to draw lots.
sorteggio *sm* draw.
sortilegio *sm* spell.
sorveglianza *sf* supervision; (POLIZIA) surveillance.
sorvegliare *vt* to watch.
sorvolare ◇ *vt (territorio)* to fly over ◇ *vi*: **~ su** *(territorio)* to fly over; *(fig)* to pass over.
S.O.S. *sm* SOS; **lanciare un ~** to send out an SOS.
sosia *smf inv* double.
sospendere *vt (attaccare)* to hang; *(attività, pagamenti, funzionario)* to suspend.
sospensione *sf* suspension.
sospeso, -a ◇ *pp* → **sospendere** ◇ *agg (interrotto)* suspended; **lasciare qc in ~** to leave sthg unfinished; **tenere qn in ~** to keep sb in suspense.
sospettare ◇ *vt* to suspect ◇ *vi*: **~ di qn** *(avere sospetti su)* to suspect sb; *(diffidare di)* to be suspicious of sb.
sospetto, -a ◇ *agg* suspicious ◇ *sm, f* suspect ◇ *sm* suspicion.
sospirare *vi* to sigh; **farsi ~** to keep sb waiting.
sospiro *sm* sigh; **tirare un ~ di sollievo** to heave a sigh of relief.
sosta *sf (in luogo)* stop; *(pausa)* break; **fare ~ a/in** to make a stop at/in; **'divieto di ~'** 'no waiting'; **senza ~** nonstop; **'~ consentita solo per carico e scarico'** 'no waiting except for loading and unloading'.
sostantivo *sm* noun.
sostanza *sf* substance.
sostanzioso, -a *agg (cibo)* nourishing; *(notevole)* substantial.
sostare *vi (fermarsi)* to stop.
sostegno *sm* support.
sostenere *vt* to support; **~ che** to maintain (that); **~ gli esami** to sit exams.
◆ **sostenersi** *vr (tenersi dritto)* to hold o.s. up.
sostenitore, -trice *sm, f* supporter.
sostentamento *sm* maintenance.

sostenuto, -a *agg (tono, stile)* elevated; *(ritmo, passo)* sustained.

sostituire *vt (rimpiazzare)* to replace; *(prendere il posto di)* to take over from; ~ **qn/qc con** to substitute sb/sthg with; ~ **qn/qc a** to substitute sb/sthg for.

sostituto, -a *sm, f* substitute.

sostituzione *sf* substitution.

sottaceti *smpl* pickles.

sottana *sf (gonna)* skirt; *(di prete)* cassock.

sotterfugio *sm* subterfuge.

sotterraneo, -a ◇ *agg* underground; *(fig)* clandestine, secret ◇ *sm* cellar.

sottigliezza *sf (di spessore)* thinness; *(fig)* subtlety; *(dettaglio)* quibble.

sottile *agg (non spesso)* thin; *(capelli)* fine; *(slanciato)* slim; *(vista, odorato, ingegno)* sharp, keen; **non andare per il** ~ not to mince matters.

sottintendere *vt* to imply.

sottinteso, -a ◇ *pp* → **sottintendere** ◇ *sm* allusion.

sotto ◇ *prep* under; *(più in basso di)* below ◇ *avv (in posizione inferiore)* underneath; *(più in basso, in scritto)* below; **al di ~ di** under, below; **sott'olio** in oil; **di ~** *(al piano inferiore)* downstairs.

sottobanco *avv (comprare)* under the counter.

sottobicchiere *sm* coaster.

sottobosco *sm* undergrowth.

sottobraccio *avv (prendere)* by the arm; *(camminare)* arm in arm.

sottofondo *sm* (MUS) background music.

sottolineare *vt* to underline; *(dare risalto a)* to emphasize.

sottolio → **sotto**.

sottomarino, -a ◇ *agg* underwater *(dav s)* ◇ *sm* submarine.

sottomesso, -a ◇ *pp* → **sottomettere** ◇ *agg* submissive.

sottomettere *vt (al proprio dominio)* to subdue.

◆ **sottomettersi a** *vr + prep* to submit to.

sottopassaggio *sm (per auto)* underpass; *(per pedoni, in stazione)* subway, underpass; **'servirsi del ~'** 'please use the subway'.

sottoporre *vt*: ~ **qn a qc** to subject sb to sthg; ~ **qc a qn** to submit sthg to sb.

◆ **sottoporsi a** *vr + prep (subire)* to undergo.

sottoposto, -a *pp* → **sottoporre**.

sottoscala *sm inv* cupboard under the stairs.

sottoscritto, -a ◇ *pp* → **sottoscrivere** ◇ *sm, f* undersigned.

sottoscrivere *vt* to sign.

◆ **sottoscrivere a** *v + prep* to subscribe to.

sottosopra *avv* upside down.

sottostante *agg* lower.

sottosuolo *sm (di terreno)* subsoil; *(locale)* basement.

sottosviluppato, -a *agg* underdeveloped.

sottoterra *avv* underground.

sottotitoli *smpl* subtitles.

sottovalutare *vt* to underestimate.

sottoveste *sf* underskirt.

sottovoce *avv* in a low voice.

sottovuoto *avv* vacuum-packed.

sottrarre *vt* (MAT) to subtract; *(fondi)* to take away, to remove; ~ **qc a qn** *(rubare)* to steal sthg from sb.

◆ **sottrarsi a** *vr + prep* to escape, to avoid.

sottratto, -a *pp* → **sottrarre**.

sottrazione *sf* (MAT) subtraction; *(furto)* removal.

souvenir [suve'nir] *sm inv* souvenir.

sovietico, -a, -ci, -che *agg* soviet.

sovraccaricare *vt* to overload.
sovrano, -a *agg & sm, f* sovereign.
sovrapporre *vt* to put on top of.
sovrapposto, -a *pp* → **sovrapporre**.
sovrastare *vt (valle, paese)* to overhang.
sovrumano, -a *agg* superhuman.
sovvenzionare *vt* to subsidize.
sovversivo, -a *agg* subversive.
sozzo, -a *agg* filthy.
S.p.A. *(abbr di società per azioni)* = Ltd *(Br)*, = Inc. *(Am)*.
spaccare *vt* to break, to split.
♦ **spaccarsi** *vr* to break, to split.
spaccatura *sf* split.
spacciare *vt (droga)* to push.
♦ **spacciarsi per** *vr + prep* to pass o.s. off as.
spacciatore, -trice *sm, f (di droga)* pusher.
spacco, -chi *sm* split; *(di gonna)* slit.
spaccone, -a *sm, f* boaster.
spada *sf* sword.
spaesato, -a *agg* disorientated.
spaghetteria *sf restaurant specializing in pasta dishes.*
spaghetti *smpl* spaghetti *(sg)*; ~ **aglio, olio e peperoncino** *spaghetti with garlic, chilli and olive oil*; ~ **alla carbonara** *spaghetti in an egg, bacon and cheese sauce*; ~ **pomodoro e basilico** *spaghetti in a fresh tomato and basil sauce*; ~ **alla puttanesca** *spaghetti in a sauce of tomatoes, anchovies, olives and capers*; ~ **alle vongole** *spaghetti in a clam sauce.*
Spagna *sf*: **la** ~ Spain.
spagnolo, -a ◇ *agg* Spanish ◇ *sm, f* Spaniard ◇ *sm (lingua)* Spanish.
spago, -ghi *sm* string.
spaiato, -a *agg* odd.
spalancare *vt* to open wide.
spalla *sf* shoulder; **voltare le spalle a qn** to turn one's back on sb; **di spalle** from behind.
spalliera *sf (di letto)* head; (SPORT) wall bars *(pl)*.
spallina *sf (di reggiseno, sottoveste)* strap; *(imbottitura)* shoulder pad.
spalmare *vt* to spread.
spalti *smpl (di stadio)* terraces.
spandere *vt (versare)* to pour; *(spargere)* to spread.
♦ **spandersi** *vr* to spread.
spappolare *vt* to pulp.
♦ **spappolarsi** *vr* to get mushy.
sparare ◇ *vi* to fire ◇ *vt (colpo, fucilata)* to fire.
sparecchiare ◇ *vi* to clear the table ◇ *vt*: ~ **la tavola** to clear the table.
spareggio *sm* (SPORT) play-off.
spargere *vt (sparpagliare)* to scatter; *(versare)* to spill; *(divulgare)* to spread.
♦ **spargersi** *vr (sparpagliarsi)* to scatter; *(divulgarsi)* to spread.
sparire *vi* to disappear.
sparlare : **sparlare di** *v + prep* to run down.
sparo *sm* shot.
sparpagliare *vt* to scatter.
♦ **sparpagliarsi** *vr* to scatter.
sparso, -a ◇ *pp* → **spargere** ◇ *agg* scattered.
spartire *vt (dividere)* to share out.
spartitraffico *sm inv* central reservation *(Br)*, median strip *(Am)*.
spasmo *sm* spasm.
spassarsela *vr* to have a good time.
spasso *sm (film, scena)* amusement, fun; *(persona)* laugh, scream; *(passeggiata)*: **andare a** ~ to go for a walk; **essere a** ~ *(fig)* to be out of work.
spauracchio *sm* scarecrow.
spaventapasseri *sm inv* scarecrow.
spaventare *vt* to frighten.

◆ **spaventarsi** *vr* to become frightened.
spavento *sm (paura)* fear, fright; **far ~ a qn** to give sb a fright.
spaventoso, -a *agg* frightening.
spazientirsi *vr* to lose one's patience.
spazio *sm* space.
spazioso, -a *agg* spacious.
spazzaneve *sm inv* snowplough.
spazzare *vt (pavimento)* to sweep; *(sporco, foglie)* to sweep up.
spazzatura *sf (rifiuti)* rubbish.
spazzino, -a *sm, f* road sweeper.
spazzola *sf (per capelli)* hairbrush; *(per abiti)* clothes brush; **~ da scarpe** shoe brush.
spazzolare *vt* to brush.
spazzolino *sm*: **~ (da denti)** toothbrush.
spazzolone *sm* scrubbing brush.
specchiarsi *vr* to look at o.s. (in a mirror).
specchietto *sm (da borsetta)* pocket mirror; *(prospetto)* scheme, table; **~ (retrovisore)** rear-view mirror.
specchio *sm* mirror.
speciale *agg* special.
specialista, -i, -e *sm, f* specialist.
specialità *sf inv* speciality; **~ della casa** speciality of the house.
specialmente *avv* especially.
specie ◇ *sf inv (di piante, animali)* species *(inv)*; *(sorta)* kind ◇ *avv* especially; **una ~ di** a kind of.
specificare *vt* to specify.
specifico, -a, -ci, -che *agg* specific.
speculare *vi* to speculate.
speculazione *sf* speculation.
spedire *vt* to send.
spedizione *sf (di lettera, merci)* sending; *(viaggio)* expedition.
spegnere *vt (fuoco, sigaretta)* to put out; *(luce, TV, gas)* to turn off.
spellare *vt (coniglio)* to skin.
◆ **spellarsi** *vr* to peel.
spendere *vt & vi* to spend.
spensierato, -a *agg* carefree.
spento, -a ◇ *pp* → **spegnere** ◇ *agg (colore)* dull; *(sguardo)* lifeless.
speranza *sf* hope.
sperare *vt* to hope for; **spero che venga** I hope he'll come; **spero di sì** I hope so; **~ di fare qc** to hope to do sthg.
◆ **sperare in** *v + prep* to trust in.
sperduto, -a *agg (luogo)* out-of-the-way; *(persona)* lost.
spericolato, -a *agg* fearless.
sperimentale *agg* experimental.
sperimentare *vt (sottoporre a esperimento, fig)* to test; *(fare esperienza di)* to experience.
sperma, -i *sm* sperm.
sperperare *vt* to squander.
spesa *sf (somma)* expense; *(acquisti)* shopping; **fare la ~** to do the shopping; **fare spese** *(acquisti)* to go shopping.
◆ **spese** *sfpl (uscite)* expenses; **spese postali** postage *(sg)*; **spese di viaggio** travel expenses; **a spese di** at the expense of.
spesso, -a ◇ *agg* thick ◇ *avv* often.
spessore *sm* thickness.
Spett. *abbr* = **spettabile**.
spettabile *agg (nelle lettere)*: **~ ditta** Messrs ... & Co.
spettacolo *sm (rappresentazione)* show; *(vista)* sight.
spettare : spettare a *v + prep* to be up to; **spetta a te dirglielo** it's up to you to tell him.
spettatore, -trice *sm, f (di spettacolo)* member of the audience; *(di avvenimento)* onlooker.
spettinare *vt*: **~ qn** to ruffle sb's hair.
◆ **spettinarsi** *vr* to get one's hair messed up.
spettro *sm (fantasma)* spectre.

spezia *sf* spice.
spezzare *vt (rompere)* to break; *(viaggio, giornata)* to break (up).
◆ **spezzarsi** *vr* to break.
spezzatino *sm* stew.
spezzato, -a ◇ *agg (diviso)* broken ◇ *sm (vestito)* jacket and trousers.
spezzettare *vt* to break into small pieces.
spia *sf (di polizia)* informer; *(agente)* spy; *(luminosa)* warning light; *(indizio)* indication, sign; **fare la ~** to be a sneak.
spiacente *agg*: **essere ~ (di fare qc)** to be sorry (for doing sthg).
spiacevole *agg* unpleasant.
spiaggia, -ge *sf* beach; **~ privata** private beach.
spianare *vt (terreno)* to level; *(pasta)* to roll out; **~ il terreno** *(fig)* to prepare the ground.
spiare *vt* to spy on.
spiazzo *sm* open space.
spiccare ◇ *vi (risaltare)* to stand out ◇ *vt*: **~ un balzo** to jump; **~ il volo** to fly off.
spiccato, -a *agg* marked, strong.
spicchio *sm (d'arancia)* segment; *(di mela, pera)* slice; **~ d'aglio** clove of garlic.
spicciarsi *vr* to hurry up.
spicciolo, -a *agg*: **moneta spicciola** small change.
◆ **spiccioli** *smpl* small change.
spiedino *sm (pietanza)* kebab.
spiedo *sm* spit; **allo ~** spit-roasted.
spiegare *vt (far capire)* to explain; *(vele)* to unfurl; *(lenzuola)* to unfold; **~ qc a qn** to explain sthg to sb.
◆ **spiegarsi** *vr (farsi capire)* to make o.s. clear; *(diventare chiaro)* to become clear; **spieghiamoci!** let's get things straight!
spiegazione *sf* explanation.
spietato, -a *agg* ruthless.
spiga, -ghe *sf (di grano)* ear.
spigolo *sm (di mobile, muro)* corner.
spilla *sf* brooch; **~ da balia** safety pin.
spillare *vt (soldi)*: **~ qc a qn** to tap sb for sthg.
spillo *sm (da sarto)* pin.
spilorcio, -a, -ci, -ce *agg* mean, stingy.
spina *sf (di pianta)* thorn; *(di riccio)* spine; *(lisca)* bone; *(elettrica)* plug; **birra alla ~** draught beer; **~ dorsale** backbone.
spinaci *smpl* spinach *(sg)*.
spinello *sm (fam: sigaretta)* joint.
spingere *vt & vi* to push; **~ qn a fare qc** to press sb to do sthg.
◆ **spingersi** *vr* to push on.
spinoso, -a *agg* prickly, thorny.
spinta *sf (pressione, urto)* push; *(incoraggiamento)* incentive, spur; *(raccomandazione)*: **dare una ~ a qn** to pull strings for sb.
spinto, -a ◇ *pp* → **spingere** ◇ *agg (scabroso)* risqué.
spintone *sm* push, shove.
spionaggio *sm* espionage.
spioncino *sm* peephole, spy hole.
spiraglio *sm (fessura)* chink; *(di luce)* gleam, glimmer.
spirale *sf* spiral; *(anticoncezionale)* coil.
spirito *sm (intelletto)* mind; *(fantasma, disposizione d'animo,* RELIG*)* spirit; *(vivacità d'ingegno)* wit; *(senso dell'umorismo)* humour; *(alcol)*: **ciliegie sotto ~** cherries preserved in alcohol.
spiritoso, -a *agg* witty.
spirituale *agg* spiritual.
splendente *agg* shining.
splendere *vi* to shine.
splendido, -a *agg (bellissimo)* magnificent.
splendore *sm* splendour; *(luce)* brilliance.

spogliare *vt (svestire)* to undress; ~ **qn di qc** *(derubare, privare)* to strip sb of sthg.
◆ **spogliarsi** *vr* to undress.
spogliarello *sm* striptease.
spogliatoio *sm (di palestra, piscina)* changing room; *(di abitazione)* dressing room.
spoglio *sm (di schede elettorali)* counting.
spola *sf (bobina)* spool; **fare la ~ (tra)** to go to and fro (between).
spolpare *vt* to strip the flesh off.
spolverare *vt & vi* to dust.
sponda *sf (di fiume)* bank; *(di lago)* shore; *(di letto)* edge; *(di biliardo)* cushion.
sponsorizzare *vt* sponsor.
spontaneo, -a *agg* spontaneous; *(non artificioso)* natural.
spopolare ◇ *vt* to depopulate ◇ *vi* to draw the crowds.
◆ **spopolarsi** *vr* to become depopulated.
sporadico, -a, -ci, -che *agg* sporadic.
sporcare *vt* to dirty; **sporcarsi le mani** to get one's hands dirty.
◆ **sporcarsi** *vr* to get dirty.
sporcizia *sf (l'esser sporco)* dirtiness; *(cosa sporca)* dirt.
sporco, -a, -chi, -che ◇ *agg* dirty ◇ *sm* dirt.
sporgente *agg* protruding; *(occhi)* bulging.
sporgere ◇ *vt* to put out ◇ *vi* to stick out.
◆ **sporgersi** *vr* to lean out.
sport *sm inv* sport.
sporta *sf* shopping bag.
sportello *sm (di mobile, treno)* door; *(di banca, posta)* window, counter; ~ **automatico** cash dispenser.
sportivo, -a ◇ *agg (programma, campo)* sports *(dav s)*; *(persona)* sporty; *(abbigliamento)* casual; *(comportamento, spirito)* sporting ◇ *sm, f* sportsman (*f* sportswoman).
sporto, -a *pp* → **sporgere**.
sposare *vt* to marry.
◆ **sposarsi** *vr* to get married.
◆ **sposarsi con** *vr + prep* to marry.
sposato, -a *agg* married.
sposo, -a *sm, f* bridegroom (*f* bride); **gli sposi** the newlyweds.
spossante *agg* exhausting.
spostare *vt* to move; *(cambiare)* to change.
◆ **spostarsi** *vr* to move.
spot *sm inv (faretto)* spotlight; *(pubblicità)* advert.
spranga, -ghe *sf* bar.
spray *sm inv* spray.
sprecare *vt* to waste.
spreco, -chi *sm* waste.
spregiudicato, -a *agg (senza scrupoli)* unscrupulous.
spremere *vt (arancia, limone)* to squeeze.
spremiagrumi *sm inv* lemon squeezer.
spremuta *sf* fresh fruit juice; ~ **di arancia** freshly-squeezed orange juice.
sprezzante *agg* scornful.
sprigionare *vt* to emit.
◆ **sprigionarsi** *vr* to emanate.
sprizzare *vi* to spurt.
sprofondare *vi (crollare)* to collapse; *(affondare)* to sink.
sproporzionato, -a *agg* out of all proportion.
sproposito *sm* blunder; *(somma esagerata)*: **costa uno ~** it costs a fortune; **parlare a ~** to talk out of turn.
sprovveduto, -a *agg* inexperienced.
sprovvisto, -a *agg*: ~ **di** lacking in; **cogliere qn alla sprovvista** to catch sb unawares.
spruzzare *vt (profumo)* to spray; *(acqua)* to sprinkle; *(persona)* to splash.

spruzzatore *sm* spray.
spruzzo *sm* spray.
spugna *sf (da bagno)* sponge; *(tessuto)* towelling.
spuma *sf (schiuma)* foam, froth.
spumante *sm* sparkling wine.
spumone *sm (dolce) a foamy dessert made from whisked egg white, milk and sugar.*
spuntare ◇ *vi (apparire)* to appear ◇ *vt (tagliare la punta di)* to break the point of; **spuntarsi i capelli** to trim one's hair; **spuntarla** *(fig)* to make it.
spuntino *sm* snack.
spunto *sm (punto di partenza)* starting point.
sputare ◇ *vt* to spit out ◇ *vi* to spit.
sputo *sm* spit.
squadra *sf (di operai,* SPORT*)* squad, team; *(strumento)* set square.
squadrare *vt (scrutare)* to look at closely; *(foglio, blocco)* to square.
squagliare *vt* to melt; **squagliarsela** *(fam)* to clear off.
◆ **squagliarsi** *vr* to melt.
squalificare *vt* to disqualify.
squallido, -a *agg* wretched, miserable.
squallore *sm* wretchedness, misery.
squalo *sm* shark.
squama *sf* scale.
squamarsi *vr* to flake off.
squarciagola : a squarciagola *avv* at the top of one's voice.
squarciare *vt* to rip.
squartare *vt* to quarter.
squattrinato, -a *agg* penniless.
squilibrato, -a *agg* unbalanced.
squilibrio *sm (fisico)* disequilibrium; *(psichico)* derangement; *(disparità)* imbalance.
squillo *sm (di telefono, campanello)* ring; *(di tromba)* blare.
squisito, -a *agg (cibo)* delicious; *(raffinato)* exquisite; *(persona)* delightful.
sradicare *vt (albero)* to uproot.
srotolare *vt* to unroll.
stabile ◇ *agg* stable; *(lavoro, occupazione)* steady ◇ *sm (edificio)* building.
stabilimento *sm (complesso)* factory, plant; ~ **balneare** bathing establishment.
stabilire *vt* to establish; *(fissare)* to fix; ~ **che** *(decidere)* to decide (that).
◆ **stabilirsi** *vr* to settle.
stabilità *sf* stability.
staccare ◇ *vt (separare)* to detach, to separate; (SPORT) to leave behind ◇ *vi (risaltare)* to stand out; *(fam: finire il lavoro)* to knock off.
◆ **staccarsi** *vr (bottone, cerotto)* to come off; **staccarsi da** *(venir via da)* to come off; *(fig: allontanarsi)* to move away from.
staccionata *sf (recinzione)* fence; (SPORT) hurdle.
stadio *sm* (SPORT) stadium; *(fase)* stage.
staffa *sf (di sella, pantaloni)* stirrup; **perdere le staffe** *(fig)* to fly off the handle.
staffetta *sf* (SPORT) relay race.
stagionale ◇ *agg* seasonal ◇ *smf* seasonal worker.
stagionato, -a *agg* seasoned.
stagione *sf* season; **alta/bassa ~** high/low season; **vestiti di mezza ~** clothes for spring and autumn.
stagno, -a ◇ *agg (a tenuta d'acqua)* watertight; *(a tenuta d'aria)* airtight ◇ *sm (laghetto)* pond; *(metallo)* tin.
stagnola *sf* tinfoil.
stalla *sf (per cavalli)* stable; *(per bovini)* cowshed.
stamattina *avv* this morning.
stambecco, -chi *sm* ibex.
stampa *sf (tecnica)* printing; *(con*

stampante, opera) print; *(giornalisti)*: **la ~** the press; **'stampe'** 'printed matter'.

stampante *sf* (INFORM) printer.

stampare *vt* to print; *(pubblicare)* to publish; *(nella memoria)* to impress.

stampatello *sm* block letters *(pl)*.

stampella *sf* crutch.

stampo *sm* mould; *(fig: sorta)* type.

stancare *vt (affaticare)* to tire; *(stufare)* to bore.

◆ **stancarsi** *vr* to get tired; **stancarsi di** *(stufarsi di)* to grow tired of.

stanchezza *sf* tiredness.

stanco, -a, -chi, -che *agg* tired; *(stufo)*: **~ di** fed up with; **~ morto** dead tired.

stanghetta *sf (di occhiali)* leg.

stanotte *avv* tonight; *(nella notte appena passata)* last night.

stante *agg*: **a sé ~** separate, independent.

stantio, -a *agg (cibo)* stale.

stanza *sf (camera)* room; **~ da bagno** bathroom; **~ da letto** bedroom.

stanziare *vt* to allocate.

stare *vi (rimanere)* to stay; *(abitare)* to live; *(con gerundio)*: **sto leggendo** I'm reading; **come sta?** how are you?; **ti sta bene!** (it) serves you right!; **ci stai?** is that OK with you?; **sta a voi decidere** it's up to you to decide; **queste scarpe mi stanno strette** these shoes are tight; **~ per fare qc** to be about to do sthg; **~ bene/male** to be well/not very well; **~ a guardare** to watch; **~ in piedi** to stand (up); **~ seduto** to sit, to be sitting; **~ simpatico a qn** to like sb; **~ zitto** to shut up; **starci** to fit.

starnutire *vi* to sneeze.

starnuto *sm* sneeze.

stasera *avv* this evening, tonight.

statale ◇ *agg* state *(dav s)*, government *(dav s)* ◇ *smf* civil servant ◇ *sf* main road.

statistica, -che *sf (disciplina)* statistics *(pl)*; *(dati)* statistic.

stato ◇ *pp* → **essere, stare** ◇ *sm (condizione)* state, condition; *(nazione)* state; **essere in ~ interessante** to be pregnant; **~ d'animo** state of mind; **~ civile** marital status; **gli Stati Uniti (d'America)** the United States (of America).

statua *sf* statue.

statunitense *agg* United States *(dav s)*, of the United States.

statura *sf (fisica)* height.

statuto *sm* statute.

stazionario, -a *agg (immutato)* unchanged.

stazione *sf* station; **~ degli autobus** bus station; **~ balneare** seaside resort; **~ centrale** central station; **~ ferroviaria** railway station *(Br)*, railroad station *(Am)*; **~ di polizia** police station; **~ sciistica** ski resort; **~ di servizio** petrol station *(Br)*, gas station *(Am)*; **~ termale** spa.

stecca, -che *sf (asticella)* stick; *(di sigarette)* carton; *(da biliardo)* cue.

steccato *sm* fence.

stella *sf* star; **stelle filanti** shooting stars; **albergo a tre stelle** three-star hotel.

stellato, -a *agg* starry.

stelo *sm (di fiore)* stem.

stemma, -i *sm* coat of arms.

stendere *vt (allungare)* to stretch (out); *(panni, vele)* to spread (out); *(bucato)* to hang out.

◆ **stendersi** *vr (sdraiarsi)* to lie down.

stenografare *vt* to take down in shorthand.

stentare *vi*: **~ a fare qc** to find it hard to do sthg.

stento *sm*: **a ~** with difficulty.

◆ **stenti** *smpl (privazioni)* hardship *(sg)*.

sterco, -chi *sm* dung.
stereo *sm inv* stereo.
stereotipo *sm* stereotype.
sterile *agg (uomo, donna)* sterile.
sterilizzare *vt* to sterilize.
sterlina *sf* pound (sterling).
sterminare *vt* to exterminate.
sterminato, -a *agg* immense.
sterminio *sm* extermination.
sterzare *vi* to steer.
sterzo *sm* steering.
steso, -a *pp* → **stendere**.
stesso, -a ◇ *agg* same; *(in persona, proprio)*: **il presidente ~** the president himself o in person ◇ *pron*: **lo ~/la stessa** the same (one); **io ~** I myself; **lei stessa** she herself; **lo faccio per me ~** I'm doing it for myself; **fare qc lo ~** to do sthg just the same; **fa** o **è lo ~** it doesn't matter; **per me è lo ~** it's all the same to me.
stesura *sf (atto)* drafting; *(documento)* draft.
stile *sm* style; **~ libero** freestyle.
stilista, -i, -e *smf* designer.
stilografica, -che *sf* fountain pen.
stima *sf (valutazione)* valuation; *(apprezzamento)* esteem; **fare la ~ di qc** to estimate the value of sthg; **avere ~ di qn** to have a high opinion of sb.
stimare *vt (valutare)* to value; *(ritenere)* to consider; *(apprezzare)* to respect.
stimolare *vt* to stimulate; **~ qn a fare qc** to spur sb on to do sthg.
stimolo *sm* stimulus.
stingere *vi* to fade.
◆ **stingersi** *vr* to fade.
stinto, -a *pp* → **stingere**.
stipendio *sm* salary.
stipite *sm (di porta, finestra)* jamb.
stipulare *vt* to draw up.
stirare *vt (con il ferro)* to iron.
stiro *sm* → **asse, ferro**.
stirpe *sf* stock, birth.
stitichezza *sf* constipation.
stivale *sm* boot.
stivaletto *sm* ankle boot.
stizza *sf* anger.
stizzirsi *vr* to get irritated.
stoccafisso *sm* wind-dried cod, stockfish.
stoffa *sf* material, fabric; **avere la ~ di** to have the makings of.
stola *sf* stole.
stolto, -a *agg* stupid.
stomaco, -chi o **-ci** *sm* stomach.
stonato, -a *agg* (MUS) off key.
stop ◇ *sm inv* (AUTO: *segnale)* stop sign; (AUTO: *luce)* brake light *(Br)*, stoplight ◇ *esclam* stop!; **'stop con segnale rosso'** 'stop when light is on red'.
storcere *vt* to twist; **~ il naso** to turn up one's nose; **storcersi una caviglia** to twist one's ankle.
◆ **storcersi** *vr* to twist.
stordire *vt* to stun.
stordito, -a *agg* stunned.
storia *sf (avvenimenti umani, materia, opera)* history; *(vicenda, invenzione)* story; *(faccenda)* business *(no pl)*; *(scusa)* excuse.
storico, -a, -ci, -che ◇ *agg* historic(al) ◇ *sm, f* historian.
stormo *sm (di uccelli)* flock.
storpiare *vt (rendere storpio)* to cripple; *(parola)* to mangle; *(concetto)* to twist.
storta *sf*: **prendere una ~ al piede** to sprain one's foot.
storto, -a ◇ *pp* → **storcere** ◇ *agg (chiodo)* twisted, bent; *(gambe, quadro)* crooked; **andare ~** to go wrong.
stoviglie *sfpl* dishes.
strabico, -a, -ci, -che *agg (persona)* squint-eyed; *(occhi)* squint.
straccadenti *smpl type of very hard biscuit.*

stracchino *sm a creamy cow's milk cheese from Lombardy.*
stracciare *vt (vestito, foglio)* to tear.
stracciatella *sf (gelato) chocolate-chip ice cream; (minestra) broth enriched with eggs, semolina and Parmesan cheese.*
straccio *sm* rag; *(per pulizie)* duster, cloth.
straccione, -a *sm, f* ragamuffin.
strada *sf* road; *(urbana)* street; *(percorso)* way; ~ **facendo** on the way; **tagliare la ~ a qn** to cut across sb; ~ **panoramica** scenic route; ~ **senza uscita** dead end; '~ **deformata**' 'uneven road surface'; '~ **privata**' 'private road'; '~ **transitabile con catene**' 'road negotiable with chains'.
stradale ◇ *agg* road *(dav s)* ◇ *sf* traffic police.
strafalcione *sm (sproposito)* howler.
straforo : di straforo *avv* on the sly.
strafottente *agg* arrogant.
strage *sf* massacre.
stralunato, -a *agg (occhi)* rolling; *(persona)* dazed.
stramazzare *vi* to fall heavily.
strangolare *vt* to strangle.
straniero, -a ◇ *agg* foreign ◇ *sm, f* foreigner.
strano, -a *agg* strange.
straordinario, -a ◇ *agg* extraordinary; *(treno)* special ◇ *sm (lavoro)* overtime.
strapazzare *vt* to ill-treat.
◆ **strapazzarsi** *vr* to tire o.s. out.
strappo *sm (in tessuto,* MED*)* tear; *(fam: passaggio)* lift *(Br)*, ride *(Am)*; **fare uno ~ alla regola** to make an exception to the rule.
straripare *vi* to overflow.
strascico, -chi *sm (di abito)* train; *(fig: conseguenza)* aftereffect.
strascinati *smpl squares of pasta in a tomato and minced meat sauce (a speciality of Calabria).*
stratagemma, -i *sm* stratagem.
strategia *sf* strategy.
strato *sm (di polvere, di crema)* layer; *(di vernice, smalto)* coat.
stravagante *agg* eccentric.
stravedere : stravedere per *v + prep* to be crazy about.
stravisto *pp* → **stravedere**.
stravolgere *vt* to distort.
stravolto, -a *pp* → **stravolgere**.
strazio *sm*: **essere uno ~** *(libro, film)* to be awful; *(persona)* to be a pain.
strega, -ghe *sf* witch.
stregone *sm (mago)* sorcerer; *(di tribù)* witchdoctor.
stremare *vt* to exhaust.
stremo *sm*: **essere allo ~ delle forze** to be at the end of one's tether.
strepitoso, -a *agg* resounding.
stress *sm* stress.
stressante *agg* stressful.
stretta *sf* grip; ~ **di mano** handshake; **mettere alle strette qn** to put sb in a tight corner.
strettamente *avv (serratamente)* tightly; *(rigorosamente)* strictly.
stretto, -a ◇ *pp* → **stringere** ◇ *agg (strada, stanza)* narrow; *(vestito, scarpe)* tight; *(rigoroso, preciso)* strict ◇ *sm* strait; **parenti stretti** close family (sg).
strettoia *sf* bottleneck.
striato, -a *agg* streaked.
stridere *vi (freni)* to creak; *(cicale, grilli)* to chirr; *(colori)* to clash.
strillare *vi & vt* to scream.
strillo *sm* scream.
striminzito, -a *agg (vestito)* shabby; *(persona)* skinny.
stringa, -ghe *sf* lace.
stringato, -a *agg* concise.
stringere ◇ *vt (vite, nodo)* to tighten; *(denti, pugno)* to clench; *(labbra)* to press; *(tenere stretto)* to

grip; *(abito)* to take in; *(patto, accordo)* to conclude ◇ *vi* to be tight; ~ **qn tra le braccia** to hug sb; ~ **la mano a qn** to shake hands with sb; ~ **i tempi** to get a move on; **il tempo stringe** time is short.
◆ **stringersi** *vr* to squeeze up.
striscia, -sce *sf (nastro)* strip; *(riga)* stripe; **strisce (pedonali)** zebra crossing (sg).
strisciare ◇ *vi (serpente)* to slither; *(passare rasente)* to scrape ◇ *vt (macchina)* to scrape; *(piedi)* to drag.
striscione *sm* banner.
stritolare *vt* to crush.
strizzare *vt* to wring out; ~ **l'occhio** to wink.
strofinaccio *sm* cloth.
strofinare *vt* to rub.
stroncare *vt* to break off; *(rivolta)* to put down; *(libro, film)* to pan.
stropicciare *vt (braccio, occhi)* to rub; *(vestito)* to crease.
strozzapreti *smpl 'gnocchi' either in a meat sauce, or made with eggs and spinach and served with butter and cheese.*
strozzare *vt (strangolare)* to strangle; *(sog: cibo)* to choke.
◆ **strozzarsi** *vr* to choke.
strudel *sm inv* apple strudel.
strumento *sm (musicale, di precisione)* instrument; *(di fabbro, meccanico)* tool.
strusciare *vt* to rub.
◆ **strusciarsi** *vr* to rub o.s.
strutto *sm* lard.
struttura *sf* structure.
struzzo *sm* ostrich.
stuccare *vt (buco)* to plaster; *(vetro)* to putty.
stucco, -chi *sm (malta)* plaster; *(decorazione)* stucco; **rimanere di ~** to be dumbfounded.
studente, -essa *sm, f* student; *(di liceo)* pupil.
studentesco, -a, -schi, -sche *agg* student *(dav s)*.
studentessa → **studente**.
studiare *vt & vi* to study.
studio *sm (attività)* studying; *(ricerca, stanza)* study; *(di professionista)* office; *(di televisione, radio)* studio; ~ **medico** surgery *(Br)*, office *(Am)*; **gli studi** *(scuola, università)* studies.
studioso, -a ◇ *agg* studious ◇ *sm, f* scholar.
stufa *sf* stove; ~ **elettrica** heater.
stufare *vt (seccare)*: **mi hai stufato con le tue chiacchiere!** I'm sick and tired of you talking!
◆ **stufarsi** *vr*: **stufarsi (di)** *(fam)* to get fed up (with).
stufato *sm* stew.
stufo, -a *agg (fam)*: **essere ~ (di)** to be fed up (with).
stuoia *sf* straw mat.
stupefacente ◇ *agg* amazing ◇ *sm* drug.
stupendo, -a *agg* marvellous.
stupidaggine *sf* stupid thing.
stupido, -a *agg* stupid.
stupire *vt* to amaze.
◆ **stupirsi di** *vr + prep* to be amazed by.
stupore *sm* astonishment.
stupro *sm* rape.
sturare *vt* to unblock.
stuzzicadenti *sm inv* toothpick.
stuzzicare *vt (irritare)* to tease; ~ **l'appetito** to whet one's appetite.
su ◇ *prep* **1.** *(stato in luogo)* on; **le chiavi sono sul tavolo** the keys are on the desk; **a 2 000 metri sul livello del mare** at 2,000 metres above sea level; **una casa sul mare** a house by the sea.
2. *(moto a luogo)* on, onto; **venite sulla terrazza** come onto the terrace.
3. *(argomento)* about, on; **un libro sulla vita di Napoleone** a book about Napoleon's life.

4. *(tempo)* around; **vengo sul tardo pomeriggio** I'll come in the late afternoon; **sul momento** at that moment; **sul presto** fairly early.

5. *(prezzo e misura)* about; **costerà sulle 200 000 lire** it will cost about 200,000 lira; **peserà sui tre chili** he weighs about three kilos; **un uomo sulla quarantina** a man about forty years old.

6. *(modo)*: **facciamo dolci solo ~ ordinazione** we only make cakes to order; **~ appuntamento** by appointment; **vestito ~ misura** made-to-measure suit; **parlare sul serio** to be serious; **nove volte ~ dieci** nine times out of ten.

◇ *avv* 1. *(in alto)* up; *(al piano di sopra)* upstairs; **in ~** *(verso l'alto)* up(wards); *(in poi)* onwards; **dai 18 anni in ~** from the age of 18 onwards.

2. *(per esortare)* come on; **~, sbrigatevi!** come on, hurry up!; **~ con la vita!** cheer up!

sub *smf inv* diver.

subacqueo, -a ◇ *agg* underwater ◇ *sm, f* diver.

subbuglio *sm* turmoil; **essere in ~** to be in a turmoil.

subdolo, -a *agg* sly.

subentrare *vi*: **~ a qn** to take sb's place.

subire *vt (ingiustizia, conseguenze)* to suffer; *(operazione)* to undergo; **~ un torto** to be wronged.

subissare *vt*: **~ qn di qc** to shower sb with sthg.

subito *avv (immediatamente)* straightaway, immediately, at once; **torno ~** I'll be right back.

sublime *agg* sublime.

subordinato, -a *agg*: **~ a** *(dipendente da)* dependent on.

suburbano, -a *agg* suburban.

succedere *vi (accadere)* to happen; **~ a qn** *(subentrare)* to succeed sb; **che cos'è successo?** what happened?

◆ **succedersi** *vr* to follow one another.

successivamente *avv* afterwards.

successivo, -a *agg* following.

successo, -a ◇ *pp* → **succedere** ◇ *sm* success; **di ~** successful.

successore *sm* successor.

succhiare *vt* to suck.

succhiotto *sm* dummy.

succinto, -a *agg (conciso)* succinct; *(abito)* scanty.

succo, -chi *sm* juice; **~ di frutta** fruit juice; **~ di pomodoro** tomato juice.

sud ◇ *sm* south ◇ *agg inv* south; **a ~ (di qc)** south (of sthg); **nel ~** in the south.

Sudafrica *sm*: **il ~** South Africa.

Sudamerica *sm*: **il ~** South America.

sudare *vi* to sweat.

suddetto, -a *agg* above-mentioned.

suddividere *vt* to subdivide.

sudest *sm* southeast.

sudicio, -a, -ci, -ce o **-cie** *agg* dirty.

sudore *sm* sweat.

sudovest *sm* southwest.

sue → **suo**.

sufficiente ◇ *agg (che basta)* enough, sufficient; *(tono, atteggiamento)* arrogant ◇ *sm* (SCOL) pass.

sufficienza *sf*: **a ~** enough.

suffragio *sm (voto)* vote; **~ universale** universal suffrage.

suggerimento *sm* suggestion.

suggerire *vt (consigliare)* to suggest; *(risposta)* to tell.

suggestionare *vt* to influence.

suggestivo, -a *agg* evocative.

sughero *sm* cork.

sugli = **su + gli**, → **su**.

sugo, -ghi *sm (condimento)* sauce; *(di arrosto)* juices *(pl)*; *(succo)* juice; **~ di pomodoro** tomato sauce.

sui = **su + i**, → **su**.
suicidarsi *vr* to commit suicide.
suicidio *sm* suicide.
suino, -a ◇ *agg* pork *(dav s)* ◇ *sm* pig.
sul = **su + il**, → **su**.
sull' = **su + l'**, → **su**.
sulla = **su + la**, → **su**.
sulle = **su + le**, → **su**.
sullo = **su + lo**, → **su**.
suo (*f* **sua**, *mpl* **suoi**, *fpl* **sue**) ◇ *agg (di lui)* his; *(di lei)* her; *(di esso, essa)* its; *(forma di cortesia)* your; *(proprio)* one's ◇ *pron (di lui)* his; *(di lei)* hers; *(di esso, essa)* its; *(forma di cortesia)* yours; *(proprio)* one's; **i suoi** *(di lui)* his family; *(di lei)* her family.
suocero, -a *sm, f* father-in-law (*f* mother-in-law).
◆ **suoceri** *smpl* in-laws.
suoi → **suo**.
suola *sf* sole.
suolo *sm (terra)* ground; *(terreno)* soil.
suonare ◇ *vt (strumento)* to play; *(campanello)* to ring; *(clacson)* to sound; *(allarme)* to set off; *(ore)* to strike ◇ *vi (musicista)* to play; *(telefono, campana)* to ring; *(allarme, sveglia)* to go off; *(fig: parole)* to sound.
suono *sm* sound.
suora *sf* nun.
super *sf inv* four-star (petrol) *(Br)*, premium *(Am)*.
superare *vt (confine, traguardo, fiume)* to cross; *(limite)* to exceed; *(veicolo)* to overtake; *(esame, concorso, prova)* to pass; *(ostacolo)* to overcome; *(essere migliore di)* to beat; **ha superato la trentina** he is over 30.
superbo, -a *agg (arrogante)* haughty; *(grandioso)* superb.
superficiale *agg* superficial.
superficie, -ci *sf* surface; (MAT) area.
superfluo, -a *agg* superfluous.
superiore ◇ *sm, f* superior ◇ *agg (di sopra)* upper; *(quantità, numero)* larger, greater; *(prezzo)* higher; *(qualità)* superior; **di età ~ ai 26 anni** above 26.
superlativo *sm* superlative.
supermercato *sm* supermarket.
superstrada *sf* = (toll-free) motorway *(Br)*, = (toll-free) expressway *(Am)*.
suppergiù *avv* more or less.
supplementare *agg* extra.
supplemento *sm* supplement; *(di prezzo)* extra charge; **~ rapido** additional charge for fast train.
supplente *smf* (SCOL) supply teacher.
supporre *vt* to suppose.
supposta *sf* suppository.
supposto, -a *pp* → **supporre**.
surriscaldare *vt* to overheat.
suscitare *vt* to arouse.
susina *sf* plum.
susseguire *vt* to follow.
◆ **susseguirsi** *vr* to follow one another.
sussidio *sm* subsidy.
sussulto *sm (sobbalzo)* start.
sussurrare *vt* to whisper.
svagarsi *vr (divertirsi)* to enjoy o.s.; *(distrarsi)* to take one's mind off things.
svago, -ghi *sm (divertimento)* fun; *(passatempo)* pastime.
svaligiare *vt* to burgle.
svalutare *vt* to devalue.
svanire *vi* to disappear, to vanish.
svantaggio *sm (aspetto negativo)* disadvantage; **essere in ~** (SPORT) to be behind.
svariato, -a *agg (vario)* varied; *(numeroso)* various.
svedese ◇ *agg & sm* Swedish ◇ *smf* Swede.
sveglia *sf (orologio)* alarm clock; **la ~ è alle sei** we have to get up at six.

svegliare *vt* to wake (up).
◆ **svegliarsi** *vr* to wake up.
sveglio, -a *agg (desto)* awake; *(intelligente)* smart.
svelare *vt* to reveal.
svelto, -a *agg* quick; **alla svelta** quickly.
svendita *sf* sale.
svenire *vi* to faint.
sventare *vt* to foil.
sventolare ◇ *vt* to wave ◇ *vi* to flutter.
sventura *sf (sfortuna)* bad luck, misfortune; *(disgrazia)* disaster.
svenuto, -a *pp* → **svenire**.
svestire *vt* to undress.
◆ **svestirsi** *vr* to get undressed.
Svezia *sf*: **la ~** Sweden.
sviare *vt* to distract; **~ il discorso** to change the subject.
svignarsela *vr (fam)* to sneak off.
sviluppare *vt* to develop.
◆ **svilupparsi** *vr (ragazzo)* to grow; *(industria, attività)* to expand, to grow; *(incendio, infezione)* to spread.
sviluppo *sm* development; **età dello ~** puberty.
svincolo *sm (stradale)* motorway junction.
svitare *vt* to unscrew.
Svizzera *sf*: **la ~** Switzerland.
svizzero, -a *agg & sm, f* Swiss.
svogliato, -a *agg* listless.
svolgere *vt (attività, lavoro)* to carry out; *(srotolare)* to unroll, to unwind; *(tema)* to write.
◆ **svolgersi** *vr (fatto, film)* to take place; *(srotolarsi)* to unwind.
svolta *sf* turn; *(mutamento)* turning point.
svoltare *vi* to turn; **~ a sinistra** to turn left.
svolto, -a *pp* → **svolgere**.
svuotare *vt* to empty.

T

tabaccaio, -a *sm, f* tobacconist.
tabaccheria *sf* tobacconist's.
tabacco, -chi *sm* tobacco.
tabella *sf* *(cartellone)* board; *(prospetto)* table; ~ **oraria** timetable.
tabellone *sm* *(con orari)* timetable (board); *(per affissioni)* billboard.
tabù *sm inv* taboo.
tacca, -che *sf* notch.
taccagno, -a *agg* mean.
tacchino *sm* turkey.
tacciare *vt*: ~ **qn di qc** to accuse sb of sthg.
tacco, -chi *sm* heel; **tacchi a spillo** stilettos.
taccuino *sm* notebook.
tacere ◇ *vi* to be quiet ◇ *vt* to keep quiet about.
taciturno, -a *agg* taciturn.
tafano *sm* horsefly.
tafferuglio *sm* brawl.
taglia *sf* *(misura)* size; *(corporatura)* build; ~ **unica** one size.
tagliacarte *sm inv* paper knife.
taglialegna *sm inv* woodcutter.
tagliando *sm* coupon.
tagliare *vt* to cut; *(affettare)* to slice; *(carne)* to carve; *(legna)* to chop; *(recidere)* to cut off; *(ritagliare)* to cut out; *(intersecare)* to cut across; *(vino)* to mix; ~ **corto** to cut short; ~ **la strada a qn** to cut in front of sb; **tagliarsi i capelli** to have one's hair cut.
◆ **tagliarsi** *vr* to cut o.s.
tagliatelle *sfpl* tagliatelle *(sg)*.
tagliaunghie *sm inv* nail clippers *(pl)*.
tagliente *agg* sharp.
tagliere *sm* chopping board.
taglio *sm* cut; *(di stoffa)* length; *(parte tagliente)* edge; ~ **cesareo** (MED) caesarean section; **banconote di piccolo/grosso** ~ small/large denomination bank notes.
tagliuzzare *vt* to cut into small pieces.
tailleur [ta'jœr] *sm inv* suit *(for women)*.
Taiwan *sm*: **il** ~ Taiwan.
talco *sm* talcum powder.
tale ◇ *agg dimostrativo* **1.** *(di questo tipo)* such; **non ammetto tali atteggiamenti** I won't allow such behaviour.
2. *(così grande)*: **mi hai fatto una** ~ **paura!** you gave me such a fright!; **è un** ~ **disordinato!** he's so untidy!; **fa un** ~ **freddo!** it's so cold!; **è di una gentilezza** ~ **che non si può dirgli di no** he's so nice (that) you can't say no to him; **fa un rumore** ~ **da farti venire il mal di testa** it makes so much noise (that) it gives you a headache.
3. *(in paragoni)*: ~ ... ~ like ... like; ~ **madre** ~ **figlia** like mother like

daughter; ~ **quale** just like; **è ~ quale lo ricordavo** he's just like I remembered.

◇ *agg indefinito (non precisato)*: **ti cerca un tal signor Marchi** someone called Mr Marchi is looking for you; **il giorno ~ all'ora ~** on such and such a day at such and such a time.

◇ *pron indefinito (persona non precisata)*: **un ~ mi ha chiesto di te** some man asked me about you; **quel ~** that person.

taleggio *sm a type of soft cheese from Lombardy.*

talento *sm* talent.

talloncino *sm* counterfoil.

tallone *sm* heel.

talmente *avv* so.

talora *avv* sometimes.

talpa *sf* mole.

talvolta *avv* sometimes.

tamburellare *vi* to drum.

tamburello *sm (strumento)* tambourine; *(gioco) ball game played with a round bat.*

tamburo *sm* drum.

Tamigi *sm*: **il ~** the Thames.

tamponamento *sm* collision; **~ a catena** pileup.

tamponare *vt* (AUTO) to bump into; *(ferita)* to plug.

tampone *sm* (MED) wad; *(assorbente interno)* tampon.

tana *sf* den.

tandem *sm inv* tandem.

tanfo *sm* stench.

tanga *sm inv* tanga.

tangente *sf* (MAT) tangent; *(quota)* share.

tangenziale *sf* bypass.

tango, -ghi *sm* tango.

tanica, -che *sf (recipiente)* (jerry) can.

tantino : un tantino *avv* a little, a bit.

tanto, -a ◇ *agg* **1.** *(in grande quantità)* a lot of, much; *(così tanto)* such a lot of, so much; **abbiamo ancora ~ tempo** we've still got a lot of time; **lo conosco da ~ tempo** I've known him for a long time.

2. *(in numero elevato)*: **tanti(-e)** a lot of, many; *(così tanti)* such a lot of, so many; **ho tanti amici** I've got a lot of o many friends; **tanti auguri!** all the best!; *(di compleanno)* happy birthday!

3. *(in paragoni)*: **~ ... quanto** *(quantità)* as much ... as; *(numero)* as many ... as; **non ho tanta immaginazione quanta ne hai tu** I haven't got as much imagination as you; **ha tanti fratelli quante sorelle** he's got as many brothers as sisters.

◇ *pron* **1.** *(una grande quantità)* a lot, much; *(così tanto)* such a lot, so much; **mi piace il cioccolato e ne mangio ~** I like chocolate and eat a lot of it; **c'è ~ da fare** there's a lot o plenty to do.

2. *(un grande numero)*: **tanti(-e)** many, a lot; *(così tanti)* so many, such a lot; **è una ragazza come tante** she's just an ordinary girl; **l'hanno visto in tanti** many people saw it.

3. *(una quantità indeterminata)*: **di questi soldi tanti sono per la casa, tanti per le tue spese** so much of this money is for the house and so much for your expenses; **pago un ~ al mese** I pay so much per month.

4. *(in paragoni)*: **~ quanto** as much as; **tanti quanti** as many as.

5. *(in espressioni)*: **~ vale che tu stia a casa** you may as well stay at home; **di ~ in ~** from time to time.

◇ *avv* **1.** *(molto)* very; **ti ringrazio ~** thank you very much; **non ~** *(poco)* not much; **~ meglio!** so much the better!

2. *(così)* so; **è ~ sciocco da crederci** he's silly enough to believe it; **è ~ grasso che non ci passa** he's so fat that he can't get through; **non**

pensavo piovesse ~ I didn't think it rained so much.

3. *(in paragoni)*: ~ ... **quanto** as ... as; **non studia ~ quanto potrebbe** he doesn't study as much as he could.

4. *(soltanto)*: ~ **per divertirsi/parlare** just for enjoyment/for the sake of talking; ~ **per cambiare** just for a change; **una volta** ~ for once.

◇ *cong* after all.

tappa *sf (fermata)* stop; *(parte di tragitto, nel ciclismo)* stage.

tappare *vt (buco, falla)* to plug; *(bottiglia)* to cork; **tapparsi le orecchie** to turn a deaf ear.

tapparella *sf* store.

tappeto *sm (da pavimento)* carpet; *(più piccolo)* rug; **mandare qn al** ~ (SPORT) to floor sb.

tappezzare *vt (pareti)* to paper; *(poltrona)* to cover.

tappezzeria *sf (tessuto)* soft furnishings *(pl)*; *(carta da parati)* wallpaper.

tappo *sm (di plastica, metallo)* top; *(di sughero)* cork; *(fam: spreg: persona bassa)* shorty.

taralli *smpl ring-shaped biscuits flavoured with aniseed and pepper (a speciality of southern Italy).*

tarantella *sf* tarantella *(a folk dance from the South of Italy).*

tarantola *sf* tarantula.

tarchiato, -a *agg* stocky.

tardare ◇ *vi (arrivare tardi)* to be late ◇ *vt (ritardare)* to delay; ~ **a fare qc** to be late in doing sthg.

tardi *avv* late; **fare** ~ to be late; **più** ~ later; **al più** ~ at the latest; **sul** ~ late in the day.

targa, -ghe *sf (di auto)* numberplate; *(con indicazione)* plate.

targhetta *sf (su campanello)* nameplate; *(piccola targa)* tag.

tariffa *sf* rate; *(di trasporti)* fare; ~ **ridotta** reduced fare; ~ **unica** flat rate.

tarlo *sm* woodworm.

tarma *sf* moth.

tarocchi *smpl* tarot cards.

tartagliare *vi* to stammer, to stutter.

tartaro *sm* tartar.

tartaruga, -ghe *sf (di terra)* tortoise; *(di mare)* turtle; *(materiale)* tortoiseshell.

tartina *sf* canapé.

tartufo *sm (fungo)* truffle; *(gelato) type of chocolate ice cream.*

tasca, -sche *sf (di giacca, pantaloni)* pocket.

tascabile ◇ *agg* pocket *(dav s)* ◇ *sm* paperback.

taschino *sm* breast pocket.

tassa *sf (imposta)* tax; *(per servizio)* fee; ~ **di iscrizione** membership fee.

tassametro *sm* taximeter.

tassare *vt* to tax.

tassativo, -a *agg* peremptory.

tassello *sm* plug.

tassì = **taxi**.

tassista, -i, -e *smf* taxi driver.

tasso *sm (indice)* rate; *(percentuale)* percentage; *(animale)* badger; ~ **di cambio** exchange rate.

tastare *vt (polso)* to take; ~ **il terreno** *(fig)* to see how the land lies.

tastiera *sf* keyboard.

tasto *sm (di pianoforte, computer)* key; *(di* TV, *radio)* button.

tastoni *avv*: **procedere (a)** ~ to feel one's way.

tattico, -a, -ci, -che *agg* tactical.

tatto *sm (senso)* touch; *(fig: accortezza)* tact.

tatuaggio *sm* tattoo.

tatuare *vt* to tattoo.

tavola *sf* (MAT, *mobile)* table; *(asse)* plank; **mettersi** O **andare a** ~ to sit down to eat; ~ **calda** snack bar.

tavoletta *sf* bar.

tavolino *sm* *(da salotto)* small table; *(di bar)* table; *(scrivania)* writing desk.

tavolo *sm* table.

taxi *sm inv* taxi.

tazza *sf* cup; *(del water)* toilet bowl; **una ~ di caffè** a cup of coffee.

tazzina *sf* coffee cup.

T.C.I. *(abbr di Touring Club Italiano)* ≈ AA, ≈ RAC.

te *pron* you, → **ti**.

tè *sm inv* tea.

teatrale *agg* theatrical.

teatrino *sm* puppet theatre.

teatro *sm* theatre; **~ tenda** *marquee used for public performances.*

tecnica, -che *sf* technique; *(tecnologia)* technology, → **tecnico**.

tecnico, -a, -ci, -che ◇ *agg* technical ◇ *sm, f* technician.

tecnologia *sf* technology.

tecnologico, -a, -ci, -che *agg* technological.

tedesco, -a, -schi, -sche *agg, sm & sf* German.

tegame *sm* pan.

teglia *sf* baking tin.

tegola *sf* tile.

teiera *sf* teapot.

tel. *(abbr di telefono)* tel.

tela *sf (tessuto)* cloth; *(quadro)* canvas; **~ cerata** oilcloth.

telaio *sm (per tessere)* loom; *(di macchina)* chassis; *(di finestra, letto)* frame.

telecamera *sf* television camera.

telecomando *sm* remote control.

telecronaca, -che *sf* television report.

teleferica, -che *sf* cableway.

telefilm *sm inv* TV film *(Br)*, TV movie *(Am)*.

telefonare *vi & vt* to (tele)phone; **~ a qn** to (tele)phone sb.

telefonata *sf* (tele)phone call; **~ a carico (del destinatario)** reverse charge call.

telefonico, -a, -ci, -che *agg* (tele)phone *(dav s)*.

telefonino *sm* mobile phone.

telefonista, -i, -e *smf* switchboard operator.

telefono *sm* telephone; **~ cellulare** mobile phone; **~ a gettoni** payphone; **~ pubblico** public phone; *(cabina)* call box; **~ a scatti** metered phone; **~ a scheda (magnetica)** cardphone; **al ~** on the phone; **per ~** by phone.

telegiornale *sm* television news *(sg)*.

telegrafare *vt & vi* to cable, to telegraph.

telegramma, -i *sm* telegram.

teleobiettivo *sm* telephoto lens.

Telepass® *sm inv* motorway toll card.

teleromanzo *sm* serial.

teleschermo *sm* television screen.

telescopio *sm* telescope.

teleselezione *sf* direct dialling.

televisione *sf* television; **alla ~** on television.

televisivo, -a *agg* television *(dav s)*.

televisore *sm* television (set); **~ in bianco e nero** black-and-white television; **~ a colori** colour television.

telex *sm inv* telex.

telo *sm* cloth.

tema, -i *sm (argomento, soggetto)* topic, subject; (SCOL) essay; (MUS) theme.

temere ◇ *vt* to fear, to be afraid of ◇ *vi* to be afraid; **temo che non venga** I'm afraid he won't come; **temo di no** I'm afraid not; **temo di sì** I'm afraid so; **temo di non farcela** I'm afraid I can't make it.

◆ **temere per** *v + prep* to fear for.

tempera *sf* tempera.
temperamatite *sm inv* pencil sharpener.
temperamento *sm (carattere)* temperament; *(carattere forte)* strong character.
temperato, -a *agg (clima, stagione)* temperate.
temperatura *sf* temperature.
temperino *sm (coltello)* penknife; *(temperamatite)* pencil sharpener.
tempesta *sf* storm; ~ **di neve** blizzard.
tempestare *vt*: ~ **qn di domande** to bombard sb with questions.
tempestivo, -a *agg* timely.
tempestoso, -a *agg* stormy.
tempia *sf* temple (ANAT).
tempio *sm* temple *(building)*.
tempo *sm (cronologico, ritmo)* time; *(meteorologico)* weather; (GRAMM) tense; *(di partita)* half; *(di film)* part; **quanto ~ ci vuole?** how long does it take?; **avere il ~ di** o **per fare qc** to have the time to do sthg; **fare qc per ~** to do sthg in time; **perdere ~** to waste time; **~ di cottura** cooking time; **~ libero** free time; **~ fa** some time ago; **in ~** in time; **allo stesso ~** at the same time.
temporale ◇ *agg* (GRAMM) of time ◇ *sm* (thunder)storm.
temporaneo, -a *agg* temporary.
temporeggiare *vi* to play for time.
tenace *agg (persona, carattere)* tenacious.
tenacia *sf* tenacity.
tenaglie *sfpl* pliers.
tenda *sf (di finestra)* curtain; *(da campeggio)* tent; ~ **canadese** ridge tent.
tendenza *sf* tendency.
tendere *vt (elastico, muscoli)* to stretch; *(corda)* to tighten; *(mano)* to hold out.
◆ **tendere a** *v + prep*: ~ **a qc** *(propendere per)* to be inclined to sthg; *(essere simile a)* to verge on sthg; ~ **a fare qc** to tend to do sthg.
tendine *sm* tendon.
tenebre *sfpl* darkness *(sg)*.
tenente *sm* lieutenant.
tenere ◇ *vt* 1. *(reggere)* to hold; ~ **qc in mano** to hold sthg (in one's hand); ~ **qn per mano** to hold sb by the hand.
2. *(mantenere)* to keep; ~ **la finestra aperta** to keep the window open; ~ **le mani in tasca** to keep one's hands in one's pockets; ~ **qc a mente** to remember sthg; ~ **il posto a qn** to keep a seat for sb; ~ **qn occupato** to keep sb busy; **tenga pure il resto** keep the change.
3. *(promessa, segreto)* to keep.
4. *(conferenza, riunione)* to hold; ~ **un discorso** to make a speech.
5. *(non allontanarsi da)*: ~ **la destra/sinistra** to keep right/left; ~ **la strada** to hold the road.
6. *(in espressioni)*: **tieni!** *(dando qc)* here!; **la lana tiene caldo** wool is warm; ~ **compagnia a qn** to keep sb company; ~ **conto di qc** to take sthg into account; ~ **d'occhio qn** to keep an eye on sb.
◇ *vi (corda, diga)* to hold; **questa colla non tiene** this glue isn't sticking; ~ **duro** to hold out.
◆ **tenere a** *v + prep (dare importanza a)* to care about; ~ **a fare qc** to be keen to do sthg.
◆ **tenere per** *v + prep (fare il tifo per)* to support; **per che squadra tieni?** which team do you support?
◆ **tenersi** *vr* 1. *(reggersi)*: **tenersi (a)** to hold on (to); **tienti forte!** hold on!
2. *(restare)*: **tienti pronto** be ready; **tenersi in disparte** to stand apart; **tenersi a disposizione di qn** to be at sb's disposal; **tenersi a distanza** to keep one's distance.

3. *(aver luogo)* to be held.
tenerezza *sf* tenderness.
tenero, -a *agg (cibo)* tender; *(materia)* soft.
tenia *sf* tapeworm.
tennis *sm* tennis; ~ **da tavolo** table tennis.
tennista, -i, -e *smf* tennis player.
tenore *sm (tono)* tone; (MUS) tenor; ~ **di vita** standard of living.
tensione *sf* tension; **alta** ~ high voltage.
tentacolo *sm* tentacle.
tentare *vt (sperimentare)* to try; *(allettare)* to tempt; ~ **di fare qc** to try o to attempt to do sthg.
tentativo *sm* attempt.
tentazione *sf* temptation.
tentennare *vi (oscillare)* to wobble; *(esitare)* to hesitate.
tentoni *avv*: **andare (a)** ~ to feel one's way.
tenuta *sf (abbigliamento)* clothes *(pl)*; *(di liquidi, gas)* capacity; *(podere)* estate; **a** ~ **d'aria** airtight; ~ **di strada** roadholding.
teoria *sf* theory; **in** ~ in theory.
teoricamente *avv* theoretically.
teorico, -a, -ci, -che *agg* theoretical.
tepore *sm* warmth.
teppista, -i, -e *smf* hooligan.
tequila [te'kila] *sf inv* tequila.
terapeutico, -a, -ci, -che *agg* therapeutic.
terapia *sf* therapy.
tergicristallo *sm* windscreen wiper.
tergiversare *vi* to avoid the issue.
tergo *sm*: **a** ~ overleaf.
terital® *sm* Terylene®.
termale *agg* thermal.
terme *sfpl (stabilimento)* spa *(sg)*; *(nell'antica Roma)* baths.
termico, -a, -ci, -che *agg (di temperatura)* thermal.
terminal *sm inv* (air) terminal.
terminale ◇ *agg* final ◇ *sm* terminal.
terminare ◇ *vt* to finish ◇ *vi* to end.
termine *sm (fine)* end; *(scadenza)* deadline; *(parola)* term; **portare** o **condurre a** ~ **qc** to bring sthg to a conclusion; **a breve/lungo** ~ short-/long-term; **senza mezzi termini** without beating about the bush.
♦ **termini** *smpl* terms.
termite *sf* termite.
termometro *sm* thermometer.
termos = **thermos**.
termosifone *sm* radiator.
termostato *sm* thermostat.
terra *sf (pianeta)* Earth; *(terraferma, territorio)* land; *(suolo)* ground; *(sostanza)* soil; ~ **battuta** (SPORT) clay; **a** o **per** ~ *(sedere)* on the ground; *(cadere)* to the ground; **essere a** ~ to feel low; **essere** ~ ~ to be down to earth.
terracotta *sf* terracotta.
terraferma *sf* dry land.
terrapieno *sm* embankment.
terrazza *sf* terrace.
terrazzo *sm (balcone)* balcony; *(di terreno)* terrace.
terremoto *sm* earthquake.
terreno, -a ◇ *agg (vita)* earthly; *(beni)* worldly ◇ *sm (suolo)* land; *(appezzamento)* plot of land.
terreo, -a *agg* wan.
terrestre *agg (del pianeta)* of the Earth; *(di terraferma)* land *(dav s)*.
terribile *agg* terrible; *(irrequieto)* wild.
terrificante *agg* terrifying.
terrina *sf* tureen.
territoriale *agg* territorial.
territorio *sm (nazionale, straniero)* territory; *(montuoso, desertico)* region.
terrore *sm* terror.
terrorismo *sm* terrorism.

terrorista, -i, -e *smf* terrorist.
terrorizzare *vt* to terrorize.
terso, -a *agg* clear.
terza *sf (marcia)* third gear.
terzetto *sm* trio.
terzino *sm* fullback.
terzo, -a *num* third; **la terza età** old age.
♦ **terzi** *smpl (altri)* others, → **sesto**.
terzultimo, -a *sm, f* third from last.
tesa *sf* brim.
teschio *sm* skull.
tesi *sf inv* theory; ~ **(di laurea)** thesis.
teso, -a ◇ *pp* → **tendere** ◇ *agg (corda)* taut; *(faccia, situazione)* tense; *(rapporti)* strained.
tesoreria *sf* treasury.
tesoro *sm (oggetti preziosi, denaro)* treasure; *(naturale)* resources *(pl)*; *(fam: appellativo)* darling; **ministro del Tesoro** Chancellor of the Exchequer *(Br)*, Secretary of the Treasury *(Am)*.
tessera *sf* membership card; ~ **magnetica** magnetic card.
tessere *vt* to weave.
tessile *agg* textile *(dav s)*.
tessitura *sf* weaving.
tessuto *sm (stoffa)* material; *(muscolare, osseo)* tissue.
test *sm inv* test; ~ **di gravidanza** pregnancy test.
testa *sf* head; **di** ~ *(vagone)* front; **mettersi in** ~ **di fare qc** to set one's mind on doing sthg; **dalla** ~ **ai piedi** from head to foot; **essere in** ~ **(a qc)** to be in the lead (in sthg); **fare qc di** ~ **propria** to do sthg off one's own bat; **montarsi la** ~ to become bigheaded; **perdere la** ~ to lose one's head; **dare alla** ~ **a qn** to go to sb's head; **essere fuori di** ~ to be out of one's mind; **fare a** ~ **o croce** to toss up; **a** ~ each.
testamento *sm* will.
testardo, -a *agg* stubborn.
testaroli *smpl broad pasta in a 'pesto' sauce (a speciality of La Spezia).*
teste *smf* witness.
testicolo *sm* testicle.
testimone *smf* witness.
testimoniare ◇ *vt (il vero, falso)* to testify; *(provare)* to prove ◇ *vi* to testify.
testina *sf* head.
testo *sm* text.
testone, -a *sm, f* stubborn person.
testuggine *sf* tortoise.
tetano *sm* tetanus.
tetro, -a *agg* gloomy.
tettarella *sf* teat.
tette *sfpl (fam)* boobs.
tetto *sm* roof; **i senza** ~ the homeless.
tettoia *sf* canopy.
Tevere *sm*: **il** ~ the Tiber.
TG *sm inv* TV news *(sg)*.
thermos *sm inv* Thermos flask®.
thriller *sm inv* thriller.
ti *(diventa* **te** *se precede lo, la, li, le, ne) pron (complemento oggetto)* you; *(complemento di termine)* (to) you; *(riflessivo)* yourself; **te li do** I'll give them to you.
tibia *sf* tibia.
tic *sm inv (nervoso)* tic; *(rumore)* tick.
ticchettio *sm* ticking.
ticket *sm inv* (MED) prescription charge.
tiepido, -a *agg* lukewarm.
tifare : tifare per *v + prep* to support.
tifo *sm* (SPORT): **fare il** ~ **per** to be a fan of.
tifone *sm* typhoon.
tifoso, -a *sm, f* supporter, fan.
tiglio *sm* lime.
tigrato, -a *agg* striped.
tigre *sm o f* tiger.

tilt *sm*: **andare in ~** to stop functioning.
timballo *sm* pie.
timbrare *vt* to stamp.
timbro *sm (arnese, marchio)* stamp; *(di voce)* timbre.
timer ['taimer] *sm inv* timer.
timidezza *sf* shyness.
timido, -a *agg (persona, sguardo)* shy, timid; *(tentativo, accenno)* bashful.
timo *sm* thyme.
timone *sm* rudder.
timore *sm* fear.
timpano *sm* eardrum.
tinello *sm* small dining room.
tingere *vt* to dye; **tingersi i capelli** to dye one's hair.
tinozza *sf* tub.
tinta *sf (materiale)* paint; *(colore)* colour; **farsi la ~** *(dal parrucchiere)* to have one's hair dyed; **in ~ unita** in one colour.
tintarella *sf (fam)* suntan.
tintinnare *vi* to tinkle.
tinto, -a ◇ *pp* → **tingere** ◇ *agg* dyed.
tintoria *sf* dry cleaner's.
tintura *sf*: **~ di iodio** iodine.
tipa *sf (fam) (donna)* woman; *(ragazza)* girl.
tipico, -a, -ci, -che *agg* typical.
tipo *sm (specie)* type, kind; *(modello)* type; *(fam: individuo)* bloke *(Br)*, guy *(Am)*.
tipografia *sf (stabilimento)* printing works *(sg)*.
tipografo, -a *sm, f* printer.
TIR *sm inv (abbr di Transports Internationaux Routiers)* HGV.
tiramisù *sm inv dessert made from sponge soaked in coffee and covered with sweetened cream cheese and cocoa.*
tiranno, -a *sm, f* tyrant.
tirare ◇ *vt* to pull; *(lanciare)* to throw; *(riga, tende)* to draw; *(sparare)* to fire ◇ *vi* to be tight; **tira vento** it's windy; **~ calci contro qc** to kick sthg; **~ diritto** to go straight on; **~ fuori** to pull out; **~ a indovinare** to guess; **~ a sorte** to draw lots; **~ su** to lift; **tirarsi indietro** *(rinunciare)* to draw back; **'tirare'** *(su porta)* 'pull'.
tiratore *sm* shot.
tiratura *sf (di giornale)* circulation.
tirchio, -a *agg (fam)* mean.
tiro *sm (d'arma)* shooting; (SPORT) shot; *(traino)* draught; **~ con l'arco** archery; **giocare un brutto ~ a qn** to play a nasty trick on sb.
tirocinio *sm* apprenticeship.
tiroide *sf* thyroid.
tirrenico, -a, -ci, -che *agg* Tyrrhenian.
Tirreno *sm*: **il (mar) ~** the Tyrrhenian Sea.
tisana *sf* herb tea.
titolare *smf* owner.
titolo *sm* title; **~ di studio** academic qualification; **titoli di credito** instruments of credit.
titubante *agg* hesitant.
tivù *sf inv (fam)* TV, telly *(Br)*.
tizio, -a *sm, f* person.
tizzone *sm* ember.
toast [tɔst] *sm inv* toasted sandwich.
toccare ◇ *vt* to touch; *(tastare)* to feel; *(argomento)* to touch on; *(riguardare)* to concern ◇ *vi* to touch the bottom; **'vietato ~'** 'do not touch'.
◆ **toccare a** *v + prep (spettare)* to be up to; *(capitare)* to happen to; **a chi tocca?** whose turn is it?; **mi tocca ricomprarlo** I have to buy it back.
tocco, -chi *sm* touch.
toga, -ghe *sf (di magistrato)* robe.
togliere *vt (rimuovere)* to take off; *(privare di)* to take away; *(liberare)* to get out; **~ qc a qn** to take sthg (away) from sb; **ciò non toglie che ...** this doesn't mean that ...;

togliersi gli occhiali to take one's glasses off; **~ l'appetito a qn** to put sb off his food.
toilette [twa'lɛt] *sf inv* toilet.
tollerabile *agg* tolerable.
tollerante *agg* tolerant.
tollerare *vt* to tolerate.
tolto, -a *pp* → **togliere**.
tomba *sf* grave.
tombino *sm* manhole.
tombola *sf* = bingo.
tonaca, -che *sf* habit.
tonalità *sf inv (di colore)* shade; (MUS) key.
tondo, -a *agg (circolare)* round.
tonfo *sm (rumore)* thud; *(caduta)* fall.
tonico, -a, -ci, -che *agg & sm* tonic.
tonificare *vt* to tone up.
tonnellata *sf* ton.
tonno *sm* tuna fish; **~ in scatola** tinned tuna fish.
tono *sm* tone; **essere giù di ~** to be under the weather.
tonsille *sfpl* tonsils.
tonto, -a *agg* stupid; **fare il finto ~** to pretend not to understand.
top *sm inv* top.
topaia *sf* dump.
topazio *sm* topaz.
topless *sm inv*: **essere in ~** to be topless.
topo *sm* mouse.
toppa *sf (di stoffa)* patch; *(di serratura)* keyhole.
torace, -ci *sm* thorax, chest.
torbido, -a *agg* cloudy.
torcere *vt (panni)* to wring; *(piegare)* to twist.
◆ **torcersi** *vr* to double up.
torchio *sm* press.
torcia, -ce *sf* torch.
torcicollo *sm* stiff neck.
torero *sm* bullfighter.
Torino *sf* Turin.
tormenta *sf* blizzard.
tormentare *vt (procurare fastidio)* to annoy.
◆ **tormentarsi** *vr* to fret.
tormento *sm (angoscia)* torment; *(fastidio)* nuisance.
tornaconto *sm* advantage.
tornante *sm* hairpin bend.
tornare *vi* to go/come back; *(ridiventare)* to become again; *(riuscire giusto)* to be correct; **~ utile** to come in handy; **~ a casa** to go/come home.
torneo *sm* tournament.
toro *sm* bull.
◆ **Toro** *sm* Taurus.
torre *sf (edificio)* tower; *(negli scacchi)* rook; **~ di controllo** control tower; **la ~ di Pisa** the Leaning Tower of Pisa.
torrefazione *sf (negozio) shop where coffee is roasted and sold.*
torrente *sm* torrent.
torrido, -a *agg* torrid.
torrione *sm* keep.
torrone *sm* nougat.
torsione *sf* twisting.
torso *sm* torso; **a ~ nudo** bare-chested.
torsolo *sm* core.
torta *sf (dolce)* cake; **~ gelato** ice-cream gâteau; **~ di mele** apple tart; **~ pasqualina** *puff-pastry tart filled with spinach, ricotta cheese, Parmesan cheese and eggs (a speciality of Genoa)*; **~ salata** flan.
tortellini *smpl* tortellini; **~ all'emiliana** *'tortellini' filled with pork, ham, Parmesan cheese and spices, generally served in broth.*
tortiera *sf* cake tin.
tortino *sm* pie.
torto, -a ◇ *pp* → **torcere** ◇ *sm (ingiustizia)* wrong; *(colpa)*: **avere ~** to be wrong; **a ~** wrongly.
tortora *sf* turtledove.
tortuoso, -a *agg* winding.
tortura *sf* torture.
torturare *vt* to torture.

tosaerba *sm inv o sf inv* lawnmower.
tosare *vt (pecora)* to shear; *(siepe)* to clip.
Toscana *sf*: **la ~** Tuscany.
toscano, -a *agg* Tuscan.
tosse *sf* cough.
tossico, -a, -ci, -che *agg* toxic.
tossicomane *smf* drug addict.
tossire *vi* to cough.
tosta *agg f* → **faccia**.
tostapane *sm inv* toaster.
tostare *vt* to toast.
tot *agg inv & pron inv (quantità)* so much; *(numero)* so many *(pl)*.
totale *agg & sm* total; **in ~** in total.
totalità *sf*: **la ~ di** all of.
totalizzare *vt* to score.
totano *sm* squid.
totip *sm betting game based on horse racing similar to the pools.*
totocalcio *sm* pools *(pl)*.
toupet [tu'pe] *sm inv* toupee.
tournée [tur'ne] *sf inv* tour.
tovaglia *sf* tablecloth.
tovagliolo *sm* napkin.
tozzo, -a ◇ *agg* squat ◇ *sm*: **un ~ di pane** a crust of bread.
tra *prep (in mezzo a due)* between; *(in mezzo a molti)* among(st); *(di tempo, distanza)* in; **tenere qn ~ le braccia** to hold sb in one's arms; **quale preferisci ~ questi?** which one of these do you like best?; **detto ~ (di) noi** between me and you; **~ sé e sé** to oneself.
traballare *vi* to stagger.
trabiccolo *sm (fam)* car.
traboccare *vi* to overflow.
trabocchetto *sm* trap.
tracannare *vt* to gulp down.
traccia, -ce *sf (segno)* mark; *(indizio)* trace.
tracciare *vt (solco)* to trace; *(disegnare)* to draw.
tracciato *sm (percorso)* route; *(grafico)* graph.
trachea *sf* windpipe.
tracolla *sf* shoulder bag; **a ~** over one's shoulder.
tradimento *sm (slealtà)* treachery; *(adulterio)* infidelity; **a ~** by surprise.
tradire *vt* to betray; *(coniuge)* to be unfaithful to.
◆ **tradirsi** *vr* to give o.s. away.
traditore, -trice *sm, f* traitor.
tradizionale *agg* traditional.
tradizione *sf* tradition.
tradotto, -a *pp* → **tradurre**.
tradurre *vt* to translate.
traduttore, -trice *sm, f* translator.
traduzione *sf* translation.
trafelato, -a *agg* breathless.
trafficare ◇ *vt* to deal in ◇ *vi* to busy o.s.
traffico, -ci *sm (di veicoli)* traffic; *(di droga, armi)* dealing.
trafiggere *vt* to pierce.
trafiletto *sm* short article.
trafitto, -a *pp* → **trafiggere**.
traforo *sm* tunnel.
tragedia *sf* tragedy.
traghetto *sm* ferry.
tragico, -a, -ci, -che *agg* tragic.
tragitto *sm* journey.
traguardo *sm* finishing line.
traiettoria *sf* trajectory.
trainare *vt (tirare)* to tow.
traino *sm (operazione)* pulling; *(di auto)* towing.
tralasciare *vt* to leave out.
traliccio *sm (per elettricità)* pylon.
tram *sm inv* tram.
trama *sf* plot.
tramandare *vt* to pass on.
trambusto *sm* turmoil.
tramezzino *sm* sandwich.
tramite *prep* through.
tramontana *sf* north wind.
tramonto *sm* sunset.
tramortire *vt* to stun.

trampolino *sm (per tuffi)* springboard, divingboard; *(sci)* ski jump.
tramutare *vt*: ~ **qn/qc in** to change sb/sthg into.
◆ **tramutarsi in** *vr + prep* to turn into.
trancio *sm* slice.
tranello *sm* trap.
trangugiare *vt* to gulp down.
tranne *prep* except (for); ~ **che** unless.
tranquillante *sm* tranquillizer.
tranquillità *sf (stato d'animo)* calm; *(di luogo)* peacefulness; *(sicurezza)* peace of mind.
tranquillizzare *vt* to reassure.
◆ **tranquillizzarsi** *vr* to calm down.
tranquillo, -a *agg* quiet; *(non preoccupato)* calm; **stai ~** don't worry.
transalpino, -a *agg* transalpine.
transatlantico, -a, -ci, -che ◇ *agg* transatlantic ◇ *sm* ocean liner.
transatto *pp* → **transigere**.
transazione *sf* transaction.
transenna *sf* barrier.
transigere *vi*: **in fatto di puntualità non transige** she won't stand for people being late.
transistor *sm inv* transistor.
transitabile *agg* passable.
transitare *vi* to pass.
transitivo, -a *agg* (GRAMM) transitive.
transito *sm* transit; **'divieto di ~'** 'no entry'.
transizione *sf* transition.
trapano *sm* drill.
trapassare *vt* to pierce.
trapelare *vi* to leak out.
trapezio *sm (di circo)* trapeze.
trapezista, -i, -e *smf* trapeze artist.
trapiantare *vt* to transplant.
trapianto *sm* transplant.
trappola *sf* trap.
trapunta *sf* quilt.
trarre *vt*: ~ **in inganno qn** to deceive sb; ~ **origine da qc** to come from sthg; ~ **in salvo qn** to rescue sb; ~ **vantaggio da qc** to benefit from sthg.
trasalire *vi* to jump.
trasandato, -a *agg* shabby.
trasbordare ◇ *vt* to transfer ◇ *vi* to change ship/plane/train.
trascinare *vt* to drag.
◆ **trascinarsi** *vr (strisciare)* to drag o.s. along; *(nel tempo)* to drag on.
trascorrere ◇ *vt* to spend ◇ *vi* to pass.
trascorso, -a *pp* → **trascorrere**.
trascritto, -a *pp* → **trascrivere**.
trascrivere *vt* to transcribe.
trascurabile *agg* negligible.
trascurare *vt (lavoro, persona)* to neglect; *(dettagli)* to disregard.
trascurato, -a *agg* neglected.
trasferibile ◇ *agg (biglietto)* transferable ◇ *sm* transfer.
trasferimento *sm* transfer.
trasferire *vt (impiegato)* to transfer; *(negozio, sede)* to move.
◆ **trasferirsi** *vr* to move.
trasferta *sf (viaggio)* transfer; *(indennità)* travelling expenses *(pl)*; (SPORT) away game.
trasformare *vt* to transform; ~ **qc in qc** to turn sthg into sthg; *(edificio, stanza)* to convert sthg into sthg.
◆ **trasformarsi** *vr* to change completely; **trasformarsi in** to turn into.
trasformatore *sm* transformer.
trasformazione *sf* transformation.
trasfusione *sf* transfusion.
trasgredire *vt* to disobey.
traslocare *vi* to move.
trasloco, -chi *sm (di mobili)* removal; *(trasferimento)* move.
trasmesso, -a *pp* → **trasmettere**.

trasmettere *vt* (RADIO, TV) to broadcast; *(malattia)* to pass on; *(far pervenire)* to send.

trasmissione *sf (programma)* programme; (TECNOL) transmission.

trasparente *agg (acqua)* transparent; *(vestito)* see-through.

trasparenza *sf* transparency.

traspirazione *sf* perspiration.

trasportare *vt* to transport.

trasporto *sm* transport.

trastullarsi *vr (divertirsi)* to amuse o.s.; *(perdere tempo)* to waste time.

trasversale *agg (obliquo)* cross *(dav s)*; *(via)* side *(dav s)*.

trattamento *sm* treatment.

trattare *vt (persona)* to treat; *(argomento)* to discuss; *(negoziare)* to negotiate; *(commerciare)* to deal in.

◆ **trattare di** *v + prep* to deal with.

◆ **trattarsi** *vr*: **di cosa si tratta?** what is it about?

trattative *sfpl* negotiations.

trattato *sm (patto)* treaty; *(testo)* treatise.

trattenere *vt (far rimanere)* to detain; *(lacrime, risa)* to hold back; *(somma)* to deduct; ~ **qn dal fare qc** to stop sb doing sthg.

◆ **trattenersi** *vr* to stay; **quanto si trattiene?** how long are you staying?; **trattenersi dal fare qc** to stop o.s. doing sthg.

trattenuta *sf* deduction.

trattino *sm (tra parole)* hyphen; *(per discorso diretto)* dash.

tratto, -a ◇ *pp* → **trarre** ◇ *sm (di penna)* stroke; *(di strada, mare)* stretch; **ad un ~, d'un ~** suddenly.

◆ **tratti** *smpl* features.

trattore *sm* tractor.

trattoria *sf restaurant specializing in local cuisine.*

trauma, -i *sm (shock)* shock; (MED) trauma.

travagliato, -a *agg* troubled.

travaglio *sm* labour.

travasare *vt* to decant.

trave *sf* beam.

traveggole *sfpl*: **avere le ~** to be seeing things.

traveller's cheque ['traveler 'tʃɛk] *sm inv* traveller's cheque.

traversa *sf (via)* side street; (SPORT) crossbar.

traversare *vt* to cross.

traversata *sf (marittima)* crossing; *(aerea)* flight.

traverso, -a ◇ *agg* side *(dav s)* ◇ *avv*: **di ~** crosswise.

travestimento *sm* disguise.

travestire *vt* to dress up.

◆ **travestirsi da** *vr + prep* to dress up as.

travisare *vt* to misinterpret.

travolgere *vt* to sweep away.

travolto, -a *pp* → **travolgere**.

tre *num* three, → **sei**.

treccia, -ce *sf* plait.

trecento *num* three hundred, → **sei**.

◆ **Trecento** *sm*: **il ~** the fourteenth century.

tredicesima *sf* Christmas bonus.

tredicesimo, -a *num* thirteenth, → **sesto**.

tredici *num* thirteen, → **sei**.

tregua *sf (armistizio)* truce; *(sosta)* rest.

trekking *sm* trekking.

tremare *vi*: ~ **(di)** *(paura)* to shake O tremble (with); *(freddo)* to shiver O tremble (with).

tremarella *sf (fam)* shivers *(pl)*.

tremendo, -a *agg* terrible, awful.

trementina *sf* turpentine.

tremila *num* three thousand, → **sei**.

Tremiti *sfpl*: **le (isole) ~** the Tremiti Islands.

tremito *sm* shudder.

trenino *sm* toy train.
treno *sm* train; ~ **diretto** fast train; ~ **espresso** express train; ~ **intercity** Intercity train®; ~ **interregionale** long-distance train; ~ **merci** goods train *(Br)*, freight train *(Am)*; ~ **regionale** local train; **'treni in arrivo'** 'arrivals'; **'treni in partenza'** 'departures'.
trenta *num* thirty, → **sei**.
trentesimo, -a *num* thirtieth, → **sesto**.
trentina *sf*: **una ~ (di)** about thirty; **essere sulla ~** to be in one's thirties.
Trentino *sm*: **il ~-Alto Adige** Trentino-Alto Adige.
tresca, -sche *sf* intrigue.
triangolare *agg* triangular.
triangolo *sm* triangle.
tribolare *vi* to suffer.
tribù *sf inv* tribe.
tribuna *sf* stand.
tribunale *sm* court.
tributo *sm* tax.
tricheco, -chi *sm* walrus.
triciclo *sm* tricycle.
tricolore *agg* three-coloured.
tridimensionale *agg* three-dimensional.
triennio *sm* three-year period.
Trieste *sf* Trieste.
trifoglio *sm* clover.
trifolato, -a *agg (verdura, carne) cooked in oil, garlic and parsley*.
triglia *sf* red mullet.
trimestre *sm (tre mesi)* quarter; (SCOL) term.
trincea *sf* trench.
trinciapollo *sm inv* poultry shears *(pl)*.
trio *sm* trio.
trionfale *agg* triumphal.
trionfare *vi (vincere)* to triumph.
trionfo *sm* triumph.
triplicare *vt* to triple.
triplice *agg* triple.
triplo, -a ◇ *agg* triple ◇ *sm*: **il ~** three times as much.
trippa *sf* tripe.
triste *agg* sad; *(luogo)* gloomy.
tristezza *sf (afflizione)* sadness; *(squallore)* dreariness.
tritacarne *sm inv* mincer *(Br)*, grinder *(Am)*.
tritaghiaccio *sm inv* ice crusher.
tritare *vt* to chop; *(carne)* to mince *(Br)*, to grind *(Am)*.
trito, -a ◇ *agg* chopped ◇ *sm* chopped ingredients *(pl)*; **~ e ritrito** *(fig)* trite.
triturare *vt* to mince *(Br)*, to grind *(Am)*.
trivellare *vt* to drill.
triviale *agg* crude.
trofeo *sm* trophy.
tromba *sf* trumpet; **~ d'aria** whirlwind; **~ delle scale** stairwell.
trombone *sm* trombone.
troncare *vt* to cut off.
tronco, -chi *sm* trunk.
trono *sm* throne.
tropicale *agg* tropical.
tropico *sm* tropic; **i tropici** the tropics.
troppo, -a ◇ *agg* **1.** *(in quantità eccessiva)* too much; **c'è troppa acqua** there's too much water.
2. *(in numero eccessivo)*: **troppi(-e)** too many; **ho mangiato troppi biscotti** I've eaten too many biscuits.
◇ *pron* **1.** *(una quantità eccessiva)* too much; **ho poco tempo libero, tu ~** I have little free time, you have too much.
2. *(un numero eccessivo)*: **troppi(-e)** too many; **non voglio altri problemi, ne ho fin troppi** I don't want any more problems, I've got too many already; **lo sanno in troppi** too many people know.
◇ *avv* **1.** *(in misura eccessiva)* too; **sei ~ stanco** you are too tired; **parla ~ velocemente** he speaks too

quickly; **spendo ~** I spend too much; **ho bevuto un bicchiere di ~** I've had one drink too many; **essere di ~** to be in the way.
2. *(molto)*: **non mi sento ~ bene** I'm not feeling too good.
trota *sf* trout.
trottare *vi* to trot.
trotto *sm* trot.
trottola *sf* spinning top.
troupe [trup] *sf inv* troupe.
trovare *vt* to find; *(per caso)* to come across; **andare a ~ qn** to go and see sb.
◆ **trovarsi** *vr (essere, stare)* to be; *(incontrarsi)* to meet.
trovata *sf* good idea.
truccare *vt (attore)* to make up; *(motore)* to soup up; *(risultato, partita)* to fix.
◆ **truccarsi** *vr* to make o.s. up.
trucco, -chi *sm (artificio, inganno)* trick; *(cosmetico)* make-up; *(operazione)* making-up.
truce *agg* fierce.
trucidare *vt* to slaughter.
truciolo *sm* shaving.
truffa *sf* fraud.
truffare *vt* to swindle.
truffatore, -trice *sm, f* swindler.
truppa *sf* troop.
tu ◇ *pron* you ◇ *sm*: **a ~ per ~** face to face; **~ stesso** you yourself; **se lo dici ~!** if you say so!
tubare *vi* to coo.
tubatura *sf* piping, pipes *(pl)*.
tubercolosi *sf* tuberculosis.
tubero *sm* tuber.
tubetto *sm* tube.
tubo *sm* pipe; **~ di scappamento** exhaust (pipe).
tue → **tuo**.
tuffarsi *vr (in acqua)* to dive.
tuffo *sm* dive.
tulipano *sm* tulip.
tumbada *sf baked egg custard with crushed macaroons.*
tumore *sm* tumour.
tunica, -che *sf* tunic.
Tunisia *sf*: **la ~** Tunisia.
tunnel *sm inv* tunnel.
tuo (*f* **tua**, *mpl* **tuoi**, *fpl* **tue**) ◇ *agg*: **il ~ (la tua)** your ◇ *pron*: **il ~ (la tua)** yours; **~ padre** your father; **un ~ amico** a friend of yours; **questi soldi sono tuoi** this is your money.
tuoi → **tuo**.
tuonare *v impers*: **tuona** it's thundering.
tuono *sm (di lampo)* thunder.
tuorlo *sm*: **~ (d'uovo)** yolk.
turacciolo *sm (di sughero)* cork; *(di plastica)* top.
turare *vt (buco)* to plug; *(orecchie, naso)* to block.
◆ **turarsi** *vr*: **~ il naso** to hold one's nose.
turbamento *sm (sconcerto)* anxiety.
turbante *sm (copricapo)* turban.
turbare *vt (sconcertare)* to trouble.
turbolento, -a *agg (persona)* boisterous.
turchese *agg & sm* turquoise.
Turchia *sf*: **la ~** Turkey.
turismo *sm* tourism.
turista, -i, -e *smf* tourist.
turistico, -a, -ci, -che *agg* tourist *(dav s)*.
turno *sm (di lavoro)* shift; *(di gioco)* turn; **è il tuo ~** it's your turn; **fare a ~ (a fare qc)** to take turns (to do sthg); **essere di ~** to be on duty.
tuta *sf (da lavoro)* overalls *(pl)*; *(sportiva)* tracksuit.
tutela *sf* protection.
tutelare *vt* to protect.
◆ **tutelarsi** *vr* to protect o.s.
tutina *sf* romper suit.
tuttavia *cong* yet, nevertheless.
tutto, -a ◇ *agg* **1.** *(la totalità di)* all (of), the whole (of); **~ il vino** all the wine; **~ il giorno** all day, the whole day; **in tutta Europa** all

over Europe; **tutti i presenti** everyone present; **tutte le piante** all the plants; **tutti e cinque** all five of us/you/them; **tutti e due** both of us/you/them; **tutta una pizza** a whole pizza.

2. *(ogni)*: **tutti(-e)** every; **telefona tutti i giorni** he phones every day; **in tutti i casi** in every case; **tutte le volte che** every time (that).

3. *(esclusivamente)* all; **è tutta colpa tua** it's all your fault; **è ~ casa e chiesa** he's a family man and a regular churchgoer.

4. *(molto)* very; **è tutta contenta** she's very happy; **sei ~ sporco** you're all dirty.

◇ *pron* **1.** *(la totalità)* all; **bevilo ~** drink all of it; **li ho visti tutti** I've seen all of them; **in ~** *(nel complesso)* in all; **in ~ fanno 300 000 lire** that's 300,000 lira in all.

2. *(la totalità della gente)*: **tutti** everyone, all; **verremo tutti (quanti)** we will all come, everybody will come; **tutti voi** all of you.

3. *(ogni cosa)* everything; **mi ha raccontato ~** he told me everything; **non è ~** that's not everything; **vende di ~** it sells all sorts of things; **mangio un po' di ~** I eat a bit of everything; **in ~ e per ~** completely; **~ compreso** all in; **~ esaurito** sold out; **~ sommatò** all things considered.

4. *(qualunque cosa)* anything; **è capace di ~** he's capable of anything.

◇ *avv (interamente)* completely; **tutt'altro** anything but; **~ il contrario** quite the opposite; **del ~** completely; **tutt'al più** at the most.

◇ *sm*: **il ~** the lot; **il ~ per ~** everything.

tuttọra *avv* still.

tutù *sm inv* tutu.

T.V. *sf inv* TV.

tweed [twid] *sm* tweed.

U

ubbidiente *agg* obedient.
ubbidire *vi* to obey.
ubriacare *vt*: ~ **qn** to get sb drunk.
◆ **ubriacarsi** *vr* to get drunk.
ubriaco, -a, -chi, -che *agg & sm, f* drunk.
uccello *sm* bird.
uccidere *vt* to kill.
◆ **uccidersi** *vr* to kill o.s.
udienza *sf (colloquio)* audience; (DIR) hearing.
udire *vt* to hear.
udito *sm* hearing.
uffa *esclam* tut!
ufficiale ◇ *agg* official ◇ *sm* (MIL) officer; *(funzionario)*: ~ **giudiziario** clerk of the court.
ufficialmente *avv* officially.
ufficio *sm* office; ~ **cambi** bureau de change; ~ **di collocamento** employment office; ~ **informazioni** information bureau; ~ **oggetti smarriti** lost property office *(Br)*, lost-and-found office *(Am)*; ~ **postale** post office; ~ **turistico** tourist office.
Uffizi *mpl*: **gli** ~ the Uffizi *(art gallery in Florence)*.
Ufo *sm inv* UFO.
uggioso, -a *agg* dull.
uguaglianza *sf* equality.
uguagliare *vt* to equal.
uguale ◇ *agg (identico)* the same; *(pari)* equal ◇ *avv*: **costano** ~ they cost the same; **essere** ~ **a** *(identico)* to be the same as; *(pari)* to be equal to; (MAT) to equal.
ugualmente *avv (in modo uguale)* equally; *(lo stesso)* all the same.
ulcera *sf* ulcer.
uliva = **oliva**.
ulivo = **olivo**.
ulteriore *agg* further.
ultimare *vt* to finish.
ultimatum *sm inv* ultimatum.
ultimo, -a ◇ *agg* last; *(più recente)* latest ◇ *sm, f* last (one); **da** ~ in the end; **fino all'**~ till the end; **per** ~ last; **l'**~ **piano** the top floor.
ultravioletto, -a *agg* ultraviolet.
umanità *sf* humanity.
umano, -a *agg* human; *(benevolo)* humane.
umidità *sf (di clima)* humidity; *(di stanza, muro)* dampness.
umido, -a ◇ *agg (bagnato)* damp; *(clima)* humid ◇ *sm*: **in** ~ stewed.
umile *agg* humble.
umiliante *agg* humiliating.
umiliare *vt* to humiliate.
◆ **umiliarsi** *vr* to humble o.s.
umiliazione *sf* humiliation.
umore *sm* mood; **essere di buon/cattivo** ~ to be in a good/bad mood.
umorismo *sm* humour.

umoristico, -a, -ci, -che *agg* humorous.
un → **uno**.
un' → **uno**.
unanime *agg* unanimous.
unanimità *sf* unanimity; **all'~** unanimously.
uncinetto *sm* crochet hook.
undicesimo, -a *num* eleventh, → **sesto**.
undici *num* eleven, → **sei**.
ungere *vt (padella, teglia)* to grease; *(macchiare)* to get greasy.
◆ **ungersi** *vr (macchiarsi)* to get covered in grease; **ungersi di crema solare** to put suntan lotion on.
Ungheria *sf*: l'~ Hungary.
unghia *sf* nail.
unicamente *avv* only.
unico, -a, -ci, -che *agg (singolo)* only; *(incomparabile)* unique.
unifamiliare *agg* one-family *(dav s)*.
uniformare *vt (adeguare)* to adapt; *(superficie)* to level.
◆ **uniformarsi a** *vr + prep* to comply with.
uniforme *agg & sf* uniform.
unione *sf* union; **l'Unione Sovietica** the Soviet Union.
unire *vt (mettere insieme)* to join; *(persone)* to unite; *(collegare)* to link; *(mescolare)* to combine.
◆ **unirsi** *vr (associarsi)* to join together; *(strade)* to meet.
unità *sf inv* unit; *(unione)* unity; **~ di misura** unit of measurement.
unito, -a *agg (amici, parenti)* close; *(da uno scopo)* united; *(oggetti)* joined.
universale *agg* universal.
università *sf inv* university.
universitario, -a *agg* university *(dav s)*.
universo *sm* universe.
uno, -a (*dav sm* **un** + *consonante* o *vocale,* **uno** + *s+consonante, gn, ps, x, z; dav sf* **un'** + *vocale,* **una** + *consonante)* ◇ *art indeterminativo* a, an; **~ studente** a student; **una donna** a woman; **un albero** a tree; **un'arancia** an orange; **un giorno ci andrò** one day I'll go; **ho avuto una fortuna!** it was such a stroke of luck!
◇ *pron* **1.** *(uno qualunque)* one; **me ne dai ~?** can you give me one (of them)?; **~ dei miei libri/dei migliori** one of my books/of the best; **l'un l'altro** each other, one another; **sanno tutto l'~ dell'altro** they know everything about each other; **l'~ o l'altro** either (of you/them/us); **né l'~ né l'altro** neither (of you/them/us); **l'~ e l'altro** both (of you/them/us).
2. *(un tale)* someone, somebody; **sta parlando con una** he's talking to some woman.
3. *(uso impersonale)* one, you; **se ~ può** if one o you can.
◇ *num* one, → **sei**.
unto, -a ◇ *pp* → **ungere** ◇ *sm* grease.
untuoso, -a *agg* greasy.
uomo (*pl* **uomini**) *sm* man; **~ d'affari** businessman; **da ~** men's.
uovo (*pl f* **uova**) *sm* egg; **~ in camicia** poached egg; **~ alla coque** boiled egg; **~ di Pasqua** Easter egg; **~ sodo** hard-boiled egg; **~ al tegamino** fried egg; **uova strapazzate** scrambled eggs.
uragano *sm* hurricane.
urbano, -a *agg* urban.
urgente *agg* urgent.
urgenza *sf (necessità)* urgency; (MED) emergency; **essere operato d'~** to have emergency surgery.
urgere *vi* to be needed urgently.
urina *sf* urine.
urlare ◇ *vi (persona)* to scream; *(animale)* to howl ◇ *vt* to yell.
urlo *sm (di persona: pl f* **urla***)* scream; *(di animale: pl m* **urli***)* howl.
urna *sf*: **andare alle urne** to go to the polls.

urrà *esclam* hurrah!

URSS *sf*: **l'(ex) ~** the former USSR.

urtare ◇ *vt (scontrare)* to bump into; *(irritare)* to annoy ◇ *vi*: **~ contro** o **in qc** to bump into sthg. ♦ **urtarsi** *vr (scontrarsi)* to collide; *(irritarsi)* to get annoyed.

urto *sm* crash.

USA *smpl*: **gli ~** the USA *(sg)*.

usanza *sf* custom.

usare *vt* to use; **~ fare qc** to be in the habit of doing sthg; **qui usa così** it's the custom here.

usato, -a ◇ *agg (consumato)* worn; *(di seconda mano)* used ◇ *sm* second-hand goods *(pl)*.

usciere, -a *sm, f* usher.

uscio *sm* door.

uscire *vi* to go out; *(libro, numero)* to come out; **~ di strada** to go off the road.

uscita *sf (porta)* exit, way out; *(al cinema, ristorante)* evening out; *(di autostrada)* junction; *(di libro)* publication; *(di film)* release; (COMM) expenditure; **ci vediamo all'~ da scuola** I'll meet you after school; **~ di sicurezza** o **emergenza** emergency exit.

usignolo *sm* nightingale.

uso *sm (impiego)* use; *(abitudine)* custom; **fuori ~** out of use; **'per ~ esterno'** 'for external use'.

USSL *(abbr di Unità Socio-Sanitaria Locale) local health and social centre.*

ustionare *vt* to burn; **ustionarsi un braccio** to burn one's arm.

ustione *sf* burn.

usuale *agg* common.

usufruire : usufruire di *v + prep* to make use of.

usuraio, -a *sm, f* moneylender.

utensile *sm* tool; **utensili da cucina** kitchen utensils.

utente *smf* user.

utero *sm* uterus.

utile ◇ *agg* useful ◇ *sm* (COMM) profit; **rendersi ~** to be helpful; **posso esserle ~?** can I help you?

utilità *sf* usefulness; **essere di grande ~** to be of great use.

utilitaria *sf* economy car.

utilizzare *vt* to use, to make use of.

uva *sf* grapes *(pl)*.

uvetta *sf* raisins *(pl)*.

V

va → **andare**.
vacanza *sf* holiday *(Br)*, vacation *(Am)*; **andare/essere in ~** to go/be on holiday *(Br)*, to go/be on vacation *(Am)*.
vacca, -che *sf* cow.
vaccinare *vt* to vaccinate.
vaccinazione *sf* vaccination.
vacillare *vi (barcollare)* to sway; *(fig: memoria, coraggio)* to be failing.
vado → **andare**.
vagabondo, -a *sm, f (senza dimora fissa)* tramp; *(fannullone)* loafer.
vagare *vi* to wander.
vagina *sf* vagina.
vagito *sm* wailing.
vaglia *sm inv* money order; **~ postale** postal order.
vagliare *vt (valutare)* to weigh up.
vago, -a, -ghi, -ghe *agg* vague.
vagone *sm* carriage *(Br)*, car *(Am)*; **~ letto** sleeper; **~ ristorante** restaurant car.
vai → **andare**.
valanga, -ghe *sf* avalanche.
Val d'Aosta = **Valle d'Aosta**.
valere ◇ *vi (biglietto)* to be valid; *(regola)* to apply; *(avere valore)* to be worth ◇ *vt (avere un valore di)* to be worth; *(equivalere a)* to be equal to; **~ la pena di fare qc** to be worth doing sthg; **far ~ qc** to assert sthg; **vale a dire** that is to say.
◆ **valersi di** *vr + prep* to take advantage of.
valevole *agg* valid.
valico, -chi *sm* pass.
validità *sf* validity.
valido, -a *agg (valevole)* valid; *(efficace)* effective; *(abile)* capable.
valigia, -gie ○ **-ge** *sf* suitcase; **fare le valigie** to pack.
vallata *sf* valley.
valle *sf* valley.
◆ **Valle d'Aosta** *sf*: **la Valle d'Aosta** Valle d'Aosta.
valore *sm* value; *(validità)* validity; *(talento)* merit.
◆ **valori** *smpl (gioielli)* valuables; *(ideali)* values.
valorizzare *vt* to bring out.
valoroso, -a *agg* courageous.
valso, -a *pp* → **valere**.
valuta *sf* currency.
valutare *vt (quadro, persona)* to value; *(valore, peso)* to estimate.
valutazione *sf (di un bene)* valuation; *(calcolo sommario)* estimate; (SCOL) assessment.
valvola *sf (in meccanica)* valve; *(in elettrotecnica)* fuse.
vampata *sf* blaze.
vampiro *sm* vampire.
vandalismo *sm* vandalism.
vandalo, -a *sm, f* vandal.
vanga, -ghe *sf* spade.
vangelo *sm* gospel.

vanificare *vt* to nullify.
vaniglia *sf* vanilla.
vanità *sf* vanity.
vanitoso, -a *agg* vain.
vanno → **andare**.
vano, -a ◇ *agg* vain ◇ *sm (stanza)* room; *(apertura)* opening.
vantaggio *sm* advantage; *(in competizioni)* lead; **trarre ~ da qc** to benefit from sthg; **essere in ~** to be in the lead.
vantaggioso, -a *agg* favourable.
vantarsi *vr* to boast; **~ di fare qc** to boast about doing sthg.
vanvera *sf*: **parlare a ~** to talk nonsense.
vapore *sm*: **~ (acqueo)** steam; **cuocere a ~** to steam.
vaporetto *sm* steamer.
vaporizzatore *sm* spray.
vaporoso, -a *agg (abito)* floaty.
varare *vt (legge)* to pass; *(nave)* to launch.
varcare *vt* to cross.
varco, -chi *sm* passage.
variabile *agg* variable.
variante *sf* variation.
variare ◇ *vt* to vary ◇ *vi (modificarsi)* to vary; *(essere diverso)* to fluctuate.
variazione *sf* variation.
varice *sf* varicose vein.
varicella *sf* chickenpox.
variegato, -a *agg* variegated.
varietà ◇ *sf inv* variety ◇ *sm inv* variety show.
vario, -a *agg (svariato)* varied; *(numeroso, diverso)* various.
variopinto, -a *agg* multicoloured.
vasca, -sche *sf (contenitore)* tank; *(di fontana)* basin; *(nel nuoto)* length; **~ (da bagno)** bath.
vaschetta *sf* basin.
vasellame *sm* crockery.
vasetto *sm (di yogurt)* pot; *(di marmellata)* jar.
vaso *sm* vase; *(per piante)* pot.
vassoio *sm* tray.
vasto, -a *agg (superficie)* vast.
Vaticano *sm*: **il ~** the Vatican.
ve → **vi**.
vecchiaia *sf* old age.
vecchio, -a ◇ *agg* old; *(sorpassato)* old-fashioned ◇ *sm, f* old man (*f* old woman).
vece *sf*: **fare le veci di qn** to take sb's place.
vedere *vt & vi* to see; **vedrò di fare qualcosa** I'll see what I can do; **questo non ha niente a che ~ con me** this has nothing to do with me; **non la posso ~** *(fig)* I can't stand her; **non vedo l'ora di arrivare** I can't wait to get there; **farsi ~ da uno specialista** to see a specialist; **da qui si vede il mare** you can see the sea from there.
◆ **vedersi** *vr (guardarsi)* to see o.s.; *(incontrarsi)* to meet; **ci vediamo!** see you!
vedovo, -a *sm, f* widower (*f* widow).
veduta *sf* view.
vegetale ◇ *agg* vegetable *(dav s)* ◇ *sm* plant.
vegetariano, -a *agg* vegetarian.
vegetazione *sf* vegetation.
veglia *sf* wakefulness.
veglione *sm* ball.
veicolo *sm* vehicle; **'veicoli lenti'** 'slow lane'.
vela *sf (tela)* sail; *(sport)* sailing.
velare *vt* to veil.
veleno *sm* poison.
velenoso, -a *agg (sostanza)* poisonous.
velina *sf* tissue paper.
vellutato, -a *agg* velvety.
velluto *sm* velvet; **~ a coste** cord.
velo *sm (indumento)* veil.
veloce *agg* fast.
velocemente *avv* quickly.
velocità *sf* speed; **'~ max 15 kmh'** = 'maximum speed 10 mph'.

vena *sf* vein; **non essere in ~ di qc** not to be in the mood for sthg.
vendemmia *sf* grape harvest.
vendemmiare *vi* to harvest the grapes.
vendere *vt* to sell; **'vendesi'** 'for sale'.
vendetta *sf* revenge.
vendicare *vt* to avenge.
◆ **vendicarsi** *vr* to avenge o.s.; **vendicarsi di** to take one's revenge for; **vendicarsi su qn** to take one's revenge on sb.
vendita *sf* sale; **essere in ~** to be on sale; **'in ~ qui'** 'on sale here'.
venditore, -trice *sm, f* seller; **~ ambulante** pedlar.
venerdì *sm inv* Friday, → **sabato**.
Venezia *sf* Venice.
veneziana *sf* venetian blind, → **veneziano**.
veneziano, -a *agg & sm, f* Venetian.
venire *vi* to come; **mi viene da piangere** I feel like crying; **quanto vengono le mele?** how much are the apples?; **~ bene/male** to turn out well/badly; **~ giù** to come down; **~ via** *(persona)* to leave; *(macchia)* to come out; *(etichetta)* to come off; **~ a sapere qc** to learn sthg.
ventata *sf* gust.
ventesimo, -a *num* twentieth, → **sesto**.
venti *num* twenty, → **sei**.
ventilare *vt* to ventilate.
ventilatore *sm (apparecchio)* fan; *(nel muro)* ventilator.
ventina *sf*: **una ~ (di)** about twenty; **essere sulla ~** to be in one's twenties.
vento *sm* wind; **'forte ~ laterale'** 'strong side wind'.
ventosa *sf (di gomma)* suction pad.
ventoso, -a *agg* windy.
ventre *sm* stomach.
venturo, -a *agg* next.
venuto, -a → **venire**.
veramente *avv* really.
veranda *sf* veranda.
verbale *sm* minutes *(pl)*.
verbo *sm* verb.
verde ◇ *agg* green ◇ *sm (colore)* green; *(vegetazione)* greenery.
verdetto *sm* verdict.
verdura *sf* vegetables *(pl)*.
verduraio, -a *sm, f* greengrocer.
vergine *agg* virgin; *(cassetta)* blank.
◆ **Vergine** *sf* Virgo.
vergogna *sf (pentimento, scandalo)* shame; *(timidezza)* shyness; *(imbarazzo)* embarrassment.
vergognarsi *vr*: **~ (di)** *(per disonore)* to be ashamed (of); *(per timidezza)* to be embarrassed (about).
vergognoso, -a *agg (scandaloso)* shameful; *(timido)* shy.
verifica, -che *sf* check.
verificare *vt* to check.
◆ **verificarsi** *vr* to happen.
verità *sf* truth; **dire la ~** to tell the truth.
verme *sm* worm.
vermicelli *smpl* vermicelli *(sg)*.
vermut *sm inv* vermouth.
vernice *sf (sostanza)* paint; *(pelle)* patent leather; **'~ fresca'** 'wet paint'.
verniciare *vt* to paint.
vero, -a ◇ *agg (reale)* true; *(autentico)* real, genuine ◇ *sm* truth.
verosimile *agg* likely, probable.
verruca, -che *sf* wart.
versamento *sm* deposit.
versante *sm* slopes *(pl)*.
versare *vt (in recipiente)* to pour; *(rovesciare)* to spill; *(pagare)* to pay; *(depositare)* to deposit.
◆ **versarsi** *vr* to spill.
versatile *agg* versatile.
versione *sf* version; *(traduzione)* translation.

verso ◇ *sm (di poesia)* line; *(di animale)* cry; *(direzione)* direction ◇ *prep (in direzione di, nei confronti di)* towards; *(in prossimità di)* near; *(di tempo, età)* around, about; **non c'è ~ di convincerlo** there's no way of convincing him; **fare il ~ a qn** to mimic sb.
vertebra *sf* vertebra.
verticale *agg & sf* vertical.
vertice *sm* peak; (MAT) vertex.
vertigine *sf* dizziness; **soffrire di vertigini** to be afraid of heights.
vescovo *sm* bishop.
vespa *sf* wasp.
vestaglia *sf* dressing gown.
veste *sf*: **in ~ di** as.
vestiario *sm* wardrobe, clothes *(pl)*.
vestire *vt & vi* to dress.
◆ **vestirsi** *vr* to get dressed.
vestito *sm (da uomo)* suit; *(da donna)* dress.
◆ **vestiti** *smpl (indumenti)* clothes.
Vesuvio *sm*: **il ~** Vesuvius.
veterinario, -a *sm, f* vet(erinary surgeon) *(Br)*, veterinarian *(Am)*.
vetrata *sf (di casa)* glass door/window; *(di chiesa)* stained glass window.
vetrina *sf (di negozio)* shop window.
vetro *sm (materiale)* glass; *(frammento)* piece of glass; *(di finestra)* windowpane; *(di auto)* window.
vetta *sf* top.
vettovaglie *sfpl* supplies.
vettura *sf (automobile)* car; *(di treno)* carriage *(Br)*, car *(Am)*.
vezzeggiativo *sm* term of endearment.
vezzo *sm* habit.
vi ◇ *(diventa* **ve** *se precede lo, la, li, le, ne) pron (complemento oggetto)* you; *(complemento di termine)* (to) you; *(riflessivo)* yourselves; *(reciproco)* each other ◇ *avv* = **ci**; **ve li do** I'll give them to you.
via ◇ *sf* way; *(strada)* street, road ◇ *avv* away ◇ *prep* via ◇ *esclam (per scacciare)* go away!; *(in gara, gioco)* go! ◇ *sm inv*: **dare il ~** (SPORT) to give the starting signal; **dare il ~ a qc** *(progetto)* to give the green light to sthg; **~ aerea** *(posta)* by airmail; **~ mare** by sea; **~ terra** overland; **in ~ eccezionale** as an exception; **per ~ di** *(a causa di)* because of; **in ~ di guarigione** on the road to recovery; **una ~ di mezzo** a middle course; **e così ~** and so on.
viabilità *sf* practicability.
Viacard® *sf inv credit card for motorway tolls.*
viaggiare *vi* to travel.
viaggiatore, -trice *sm, f* passenger.
viaggio *sm* travel; *(tragitto)* journey; *(gita)* trip; **buon ~!** have a good trip!; **essere in ~** to be away; **fare un ~** to go on a trip; **~ d'affari** business trip; **~ di nozze** honeymoon; **~ organizzato** package tour.
viale *sm (corso)* avenue; *(in un parco)* path.
viavai *sm* coming and going.
vibrare *vi* to vibrate.
vibrazione *sf* vibration.
vice *smf inv* deputy.
vicenda *sf* event.
◆ **a vicenda** *avv* in turn.
viceversa *avv* vice versa.
vicinanza *sf* proximity; **nelle vicinanze (di qc)** in the vicinity (of sthg).
vicinato *sm (zona)* neighbourhood; *(vicini)* neighbours *(pl)*.
vicino, -a ◇ *agg (nello spazio)* near, nearby; *(nel tempo)* close at hand ◇ *sm, f* neighbour ◇ *avv* nearby ◇ *prep*: **~ a** *(accanto a)* next to; *(nei pressi di)* near; **~ di casa** neighbour; **da ~** close up.
vicolo *sm* alley; **~ cieco** blind alley.

video *sm inv (musicale)* video; *(schermo)* screen.
videocassetta *sf* video(cassette).
videocitofono *sm entryphone with closed circuit TV.*
videogame ['videogeim] = **videogioco**.
videogioco, -chi *sm* video game.
videoregistratore *sm* video(recorder) *(Br)*, VCR *(Am)*.
Videotel® *sm* = Viewdata®.
vietare *vt* to forbid; ~ **a qn di fare qc** to forbid sb to do sthg; ~ **qc a qn** to forbid sthg to sb.
vietato, -a *agg* forbidden; '~ **l'accesso**' 'no entry'; '~ **l'accesso ai mezzi non autorizzati**' 'no entry for unauthorized vehicles'; '**è ~ fare il bagno nelle ore notturne**' 'no swimming at night'; '~ **fumare**' 'no smoking'; '~ **ai minori**' 'adults only'.
Vietnam *sm*: **il** ~ Vietnam.
vigilare *vt* to watch over.
vigile ◇ *agg* watchful ◇ *smf*: ~ **(urbano)** *local police officer who deals mainly with traffic offences*; **i vigili del fuoco** the fire brigade.
vigilia *sf* eve; ~ **di Natale** Christmas Eve.
vigliacco, -a, -chi, -che ◇ *agg* cowardly ◇ *sm, f* coward.
vigna *sf* vines *(pl)*.
vigore *sm* vigour; **in** ~ (DIR) in force.
vile *agg* cowardly.
villa *sf* villa.
villaggio *sm* village; ~ **turistico** holiday village.
villano, -a ◇ *agg* rude ◇ *sm, f* boor.
villeggiatura *sf* holiday *(Br)*, vacation *(Am)*.
villetta *sf* cottage.
vimini *smpl* wicker *(sg)*.
vinavil® *sm* glue.
vincere ◇ *vt (gioco, partita, battaglia)* to win; *(avversario)* to beat ◇ *vi* to win.
vincita *sf (vittoria)* win; *(premio)* winnings *(pl)*.
vincitore, -trice *sm, f* winner.
vincolo *sm (legame)* tie; *(obbligo)* obligation.
vino *sm* wine; ~ **bianco** white wine; ~ **rosso** red wine.
vinto, -a ◇ *pp* → **vincere** ◇ *agg (partita)* won; *(concorrente)* beaten; **darla vinta a qn** to let sb have their way; **non darsi per** ~ not to give up.
viola ◇ *agg inv & sm inv* purple ◇ *sf (fiore)* violet.
violare *vt* to violate.
violentare *vt* to rape.
violento, -a *agg* violent.
violenza *sf* violence.
violino *sm* violin.
viottolo *sm* track.
vipera *sf* viper.
virare *vi* (NAUT) to come about; *(aereo)* to turn.
virgola *sf* (GRAMM) comma; (MAT) point.
virgolette *sfpl* quotation marks.
virile *agg* manly.
virtù *sf inv* virtue.
virus *sm inv* virus.
viscere *sfpl* entrails.
viscido, -a *agg* slimy.
viscosa *sf* viscose.
visibile *agg (che si vede)* visible; *(chiaro)* evident.
visibilità *sf* visibility.
visiera *sf* peak.
visionare *vt* to examine.
visione *sf (vista)* sight; *(modo di vedere)* view; *(apparizione)* vision; **prendere ~ di qc** to look over sthg; **prima** ~ TV premiere.
visita *sf (di amico)* visit; *(di medico)* examination; **fare ~ a qn** to pay sb a visit; ~ **medica** medical examination.

visitare *vt* to visit; *(sog: medico)* to examine.
viso *sm* face.
vispo, -a *agg* lively.
vissuto, -a *pp* → **vivere**.
vista *sf (facoltà)* (eye)sight; *(possibilità di vedere)* sight; *(panorama)* view; **conoscere qn di ~** to know sb by sight; **a prima ~** at first sight.
visto, -a ◇ *pp* → **vedere** ◇ *sm* visa.
vistoso, -a *agg* gaudy.
vita *sf* life; (ANAT) waist.
vitale *agg* vital.
vitamina *sf* vitamin.
vite *sf (pianta)* vine; *(utensile)* screw.
vitello *sm (animale)* calf; *(carne)* veal; *(pelle)* calfskin; **~ tonnato** *boiled veal served cold with tuna mayonnaise*.
vittima *sf* victim.
vitto *sm* food; **~ e alloggio** board and lodging.
vittoria *sf* victory.
viva *esclam*: **~ le vacanze!** hurray for the holidays!
vivace *agg (persona)* lively; *(colore)* bright.
vivacità *sf* vivacity.
vivaio *sm (di piante)* nursery; *(di pesci)* hatchery.
vivanda *sf* food.
vivente *agg* → **essere**.
vivere ◇ *vi* to live ◇ *vt (vita)* to live; *(passare)* to live through.
viveri *smpl* food *(sg)*.
vivo, -a *agg (vivente)* alive, living; *(persona)* lively; *(colore)* bright; **dal ~** from life; **farsi ~ (con qn)** to get in touch (with sb).
viziare *vt* to spoil.
viziato, -a *agg (bambino)* spoilt; *(aria)* stale.
vizio *sm (cattiva abitudine)* bad habit; *(morale)* vice; *(difetto)* defect.
V.le *(abbr di viale)* Ave.
vocabolario *sm (dizionario)* dictionary; *(lessico)* vocabulary.
vocabolo *sm* word.
vocale ◇ *agg* vocal ◇ *sf* vowel.
vocazione *sf (inclinazione)* natural bent.
voce *sf (suono)* voice; *(diceria)* rumour; *(di elenco)* entry; **a bassa/alta ~** in a low/loud voice; **sotto ~** in a whisper.
voga *sf*: **essere in ~** to be in fashion.
vogatore, -trice ◇ *sm, f* oarsman (*f* oarswoman) ◇ *sm* rowing machine.
voglia *sf (desiderio)* desire; *(sulla pelle)* birthmark; **avere ~ di fare qc** to feel like doing sthg; **avere ~ di qc** to feel like sthg; **levarsi la ~ di qc** to satisfy one's desire for sthg; **contro ~** unwillingly.
voi *pron* you; **~ stessi** you yourselves.
volano *sm* shuttlecock.
volante ◇ *agg* flying ◇ *sm (di veicolo)* steering wheel ◇ *sf (polizia)* flying squad.
volantino *sm* leaflet.
volare *vi* to fly.
volatile *sm* bird.
vol-au-vent [volo'van] *sm inv* vol-au-vent.
volenteroso, -a *agg* willing.
volentieri *avv (con piacere)* willingly; *(come risposta)* with pleasure.
volere ◇ *vt* 1. *(desiderare, esigere)* to want; **cosa vuoi?** what do you want?; **voglio delle spiegazioni** I want some explanations; **~ fare qc** to want to do sthg; **voglio che tu venga** I want you to come; **cosa volete fare stasera?** what do you want to do tonight?; **ti vogliono al telefono** you're wanted on the phone; **come vuoi** as you like; **vorrei un cappuccino** I'd like a cappuccino; **vorrei andare** I'd like to go; **senza volerlo** unintentionally; **se si vuole accomodare?** if you would care to take a seat?
2. *(consentire a)*: **se tua madre**

vuole, ti porto al cinema if your mother agrees, I'll take you to the cinema; **vogliamo andare?** shall we go?
3. *(soldi)*: **quanto vuole per questo orologio?** how much do you want for this watch?
4. *(credere)* to think; **la leggenda vuole che** ... legend has it that ...
5. *(decidersi a)*: **la macchina non vuole partire** the car won't start.
6. *(necessitare di)* to need; **volerci** *(coraggio, materiale)* to need; *(tempo)* to take; **ci vuole pazienza** you must be patient; **ci vogliono ancora dieci minuti per finire** it'll take another ten minutes to finish.
7. *(in espressioni)*: **voler bene a qn** *(affetto)* to be fond of sb; *(amare)* to love sb; **voler dire** to mean; **volerne a qn** to have a grudge against sb.
◇ *sm* will, wish; **contro il ~ di qn** against sb's wishes.

volgare *agg* vulgar.

volgere *vt* to turn; **il tempo volge al bello** the weather's getting better; **~ al termine** to draw to an end.

volo *sm* flight; **~ charter** charter flight; **~ di linea** scheduled flight; **capire qc al ~** to understand sthg straightaway.

volontà *sf inv* will; **buona ~** goodwill; **a ~** as much as one likes.

volontario, -a ◇ *agg* voluntary ◇ *sm, f* volunteer.

volpe *sf* fox.

volt *sm inv* volt.

volta *sf (circostanza)* time; *(di edificio)* vault; **a sua ~** in his/her turn; **di ~ in ~** from time to time; **una ~** once; **due volte** twice; **tre volte** three times; **una ~ che** once; **una ~ tanto** just for once; **uno per** o **alla ~** one at a time; **a volte** sometimes.

voltafaccia *sm inv* about-turn.

voltare *vt & vi* to turn; **~ l'angolo** to turn the corner; **~ pagina** to turn over a new leaf.
◆ **voltarsi** *vr* to turn.

voltastomaco *sm* nausea; **dare il ~ a qn** to make sb feel sick.

volto, -a ◇ *pp* → **volgere** ◇ *sm* face.

volubile *agg* fickle.

volume *sm* volume.

voluminoso, -a *agg* voluminous, bulky.

vomitare *vt & vi* to vomit, to throw up.

vomito *sm* vomit.

vongola *sf* clam.

vorace *agg (animale)* voracious; *(persona)* greedy.

voragine *sf* abyss.

vortice *sm* whirl.

vostro, -a ◇ *agg*: **il ~ (la vostra)** your ◇ *pron*: **il ~ (la vostra)** yours; **~ padre** your father; **un ~ amico** a friend of yours; **sono vostri questi bagagli?** is this your luggage?

votare ◇ *vt* to vote on ◇ *vi* to vote.

votazione *sf (procedimento)* vote; (SCOL) marks *(pl)*.

voto *sm* (DIR) vote; (SCOL) marks *(pl)*.

vulcanico, -a, -ci, -che *agg* volcanic.

vulcano *sm* volcano.

vulnerabile *agg* vulnerable.

vuotare *vt* to empty.
◆ **vuotarsi** *vr* to empty.

vuoto, -a ◇ *agg* empty; *(pagina)* blank ◇ *sm (spazio vuoto)* empty space; *(bottiglia)* empty (bottle); *(in fisica)* vacuum; **andare a ~** to fail; **parlare a ~** to waste one's breath.

W-Z

wafer ['vafer] *sm inv* wafer.
Walkman® *sm inv* Walkman®, personal stereo.
water (closet) ['vater ('kloz)] *sm inv* toilet.
watt [vat] *sm inv* watt.
wc *(abbr di water closet)* WC.
week-end [wi'kɛnd] *sm inv* weekend.
western ['wɛstern] *agg inv*: **film ~** western.
whisky ['wiski] *sm inv* whisky.
windsurf ['windsərf] *sm inv (tavola)* windsurf board; *(sport)* windsurfing.
würstel ['vurstel] *sm inv* frankfurter.

xenofobia *sf* xenophobia.
xilofono *sm* xylophone.

yacht [jɔt] *sm inv* yacht.
yoga *sm* yoga.
yogurt *sm inv* yoghurt.

zabaione *sm cream dessert made from egg yolks whipped with sugar and Marsala.*
zafferano *sm* saffron.
zaino *sm* rucksack.
zampa *sf* paw; **a quattro zampe** on all fours.
zampillo *sm* spurt.
zampirone *sm* mosquito repellent.
zampone *sm boiled pig's trotter stuffed with minced meat and spices.*
zanna *sf (di elefante)* tusk; *(di carnivori)* fang.
zanzara *sf* mosquito.
zanzariera *sf* mosquito net.
zappa *sf* hoe.
zappare *vt* to hoe.
zattera *sf* raft.
zavorra *sf* ballast.
zazzera *sf* fringe.
zebra *sf* zebra.
◆ **zebre** *sfpl (fam)* zebra crossing *(sg) (Br)*, crosswalk *(sg) (Am)*.
zecca, -che *sf (insetto)* tick; *(officina di monete)* mint.
zelante *agg* zealous.
zelo *sm* zeal.
zenzero *sm* ginger.
zeppo, -a *agg* crammed.
zeppole *sfpl type of ring doughnut eaten at carnival time in the south of Italy.*
zerbino *sm* doormat.
zero *sm* zero; (SPORT) nil; **sotto ~** subzero.
zigomo *sm* cheekbone.
zigzag *sm inv* zigzag.
zimbello *sm* laughingstock.
zingaro, -a *sm, f* gipsy.
zio, -a *sm, f* uncle (*f* aunt).

zip *sm inv* zip.
zitella *sf (spreg)* spinster.
zitto, -a *agg* silent; **state zitti!** be quiet!
zoccolo *sm (calzatura)* clog; *(di cavallo)* hoof.
zodiaco *sm* zodiac.
zolfo *sm* sulphur.
zolla *sf* clod.
zolletta *sf* lump.
zona *sf* area; ~ **blu** o **verde** *zone where traffic is restricted*; ~ **disco** parking meter zone; ~ **industriale** industrial estate; '~ **militare**' 'army property'; ~ **pedonale** pedestrian precinct *(Br)*, pedestrian zone *(Am)*.
zonzo : a zonzo *avv*: **andare a ~** to wander about.
zoo *sm inv* zoo.
zoom [dzum] *sm inv* zoom.
zoppicare *vi* to limp.
zoppo, -a *agg* lame.
zucca, -che *sf* pumpkin.
zuccherato, -a *agg* sweetened.
zuccheriera *sf* sugar bowl.
zucchero *sm* sugar; ~ **filato** candyfloss; ~ **vanigliato** vanilla sugar; ~ **a velo** icing sugar *(Br)*, confectioner's sugar *(Am)*.
zuccheroso, -a *agg* sugary.
zucchina *sf* courgette; **zucchine ripiene** *courgettes stuffed with minced meat, breadcrumbs, eggs and spices.*
zucchino = **zucchina**.
zuccone, -a *sm, f (sciocco)* blockhead; *(testardo)* stubborn person.
zuccotto *sm* ice-cream sponge.
zuffa *sf* brawl.
zuppa *sf* soup; ~ **inglese** = trifle *(Br)*, *dessert made from sponge soaked in liqueur, with custard and chocolate.*
zuppiera *sf* tureen.
zuppo, -a *agg*: ~ **(di)** soaked (with).
Zurigo *sf* Zurich.

ENGLISH-ITALIAN
INGLESE-ITALIANO

a [*stressed* eɪ, *unstressed* ə] (**an** *before vowel or silent 'h'*) *indefinite article* 1. un/uno (una/un'); **a restaurant** un ristorante; **a brush** uno spazzolino; **a chair** una sedia; **an island** un'isola; **a friend** un amico (un'amica); **to be a doctor** essere medico, fare il medico.

2. *(instead of the number one)* un/uno (una/un'); **a month ago** un mese fa; **a hundred and twenty pounds** centoventi sterline; **a thousand** mille; **four and a half** quattro e mezzo.

3. *(in prices, ratios)* a; **£2 a kilo** 2 sterline al chilo; **three times a week** tre volte alla settimana.

AA *n (Br: abbr of Automobile Association)* = ACI *m*.

aback [ə'bæk] *adv*: **to be taken ~** restare sbalordito(-a).

abandon [ə'bændən] *vt* abbandonare.

abattoir ['æbətwɑːʳ] *n* mattatoio *m*.

abbey ['æbɪ] *n* abbazia *f*.

abbreviation [əˌbriːvɪ'eɪʃn] *n* abbreviazione *f*.

abdomen ['æbdəmən] *n* addome *m*.

abide [ə'baɪd] *vt*: **I can't ~ him** non lo sopporto.

◆ **abide by** *vt fus* rispettare.

ability [ə'bɪlətɪ] *n* capacità *f inv*.

able ['eɪbl] *adj* capace; **to be ~ to do sthg** essere capace di fare qc, poter fare qc.

abnormal [æb'nɔːml] *adj* anormale.

aboard [ə'bɔːd] ◇ *adv* a bordo ◇ *prep* a bordo di, su.

abolish [ə'bɒlɪʃ] *vt* abolire.

aborigine [ˌæbə'rɪdʒənɪ] *n* aborigeno *m* (-a *f*).

abort [ə'bɔːt] *vt (call off)* sospendere.

abortion [ə'bɔːʃn] *n* aborto *m*; **to have an ~** abortire.

about [ə'baʊt] ◇ *adv* 1. *(approximately)* circa, più o meno; **~ 50 people** una cinquantina di persone; **~ a thousand** un migliaio; **at ~ six o'clock** verso le sei.

2. *(referring to place)* qua e là; **to walk ~** camminare.

3. *(on the point of)*: **to be ~ to do sthg** stare per fare qc.

◇ *prep* 1. *(concerning)* su, a proposito di; **a book ~ Scotland** un libro sulla Scozia; **what's it ~?** di che cosa si tratta?; **I'll talk to you ~ it** te ne parlerò; **what ~ a coffee?** cosa ne diresti di un caffè?

2. *(referring to place)* per, in giro per; **there are lots of hotels ~ the town** ci sono molti alberghi nella città.

above [ə'bʌv] ◇ *prep* sopra ◇ *adv*

(higher) (di) sopra; *(more)* oltre; ~ **all** soprattutto.
abroad [ə'brɔːd] *adv* all'estero.
abrupt [ə'brʌpt] *adj (sudden)* improvviso(-a).
abscess ['æbses] *n* ascesso *m*.
absence ['æbsəns] *n* assenza *f*.
absent ['æbsənt] *adj* assente.
absent-minded [-'maɪndɪd] *adj* distratto(-a).
absolute ['æbsəluːt] *adj* assoluto(-a).
absolutely [*adv* 'æbsəluːtlɪ, *excl* ˌæbsə'luːtlɪ] ◇ *adv (completely)* assolutamente ◇ *excl* assolutamente!
absorb [əb'sɔːb] *vt* assorbire.
absorbed [əb'sɔːbd] *adj*: **to be ~ in sthg** essere assorto(-a) in qc.
absorbent [əb'sɔːbənt] *adj* assorbente.
abstain [əb'steɪn] *vi*: **to ~ (from)** astenersi (da).
absurd [əb'sɜːd] *adj* assurdo(-a).
ABTA ['æbtə] *n associazione delle agenzie di viaggio britanniche.*
abuse [*n* ə'bjuːs, *vb* ə'bjuːz] ◇ *n (insults)* insulti *mpl*; *(wrong use)* abuso *m*; *(maltreatment)* maltrattamento *m* ◇ *vt (insult)* insultare; *(use wrongly)* abusare di; *(maltreat)* maltrattare.
abusive [ə'bjuːsɪv] *adj* offensivo(-a).
AC *(abbr of alternating current)* c.a.
academic [ˌækə'demɪk] ◇ *adj (educational)* accademico(-a) ◇ *n* professore *m* universitario (professoressa *f* universitaria).
academy [ə'kædəmɪ] *n* accademia *f*.
accelerate [ək'seləreɪt] *vi* accelerare.
accelerator [ək'seləreɪtə^r] *n* acceleratore *m*.
accent ['æksent] *n* accento *m*.
accept [ək'sept] *vt* accettare.
acceptable [ək'septəbl] *adj* accettabile.
access ['ækses] *n* accesso *m*.
accessible [ək'sesəbl] *adj (place)* accessibile.
accessories [ək'sesərɪz] *npl* accessori *mpl*.
access road *n* strada *f* d'accesso.
accident ['æksɪdənt] *n* incidente *m*; **by ~** per caso.
accidental [ˌæksɪ'dentl] *adj* accidentale.
accident insurance *n* assicurazione *f* contro gli infortuni.
accident-prone *adj* soggetto(-a) a frequenti infortuni.
acclimatize [ə'klaɪmətaɪz] *vi* acclimatarsi.
accommodate [ə'kɒmədeɪt] *vt* alloggiare.
accommodation [əˌkɒmə'deɪʃn] *n* alloggio *m*.
accommodations [əˌkɒmə'deɪʃnz] *npl (Am)* = **accommodation**.
accompany [ə'kʌmpənɪ] *vt* accompagnare.
accomplish [ə'kʌmplɪʃ] *vt* realizzare.
accord [ə'kɔːd] *n*: **of one's own ~** di propria iniziativa.
accordance [ə'kɔːdəns] *n*: **in ~ with** in conformità a.
according [ə'kɔːdɪŋ]: **according to** *prep* secondo.
accordion [ə'kɔːdɪən] *n* fisarmonica *f*.
account [ə'kaʊnt] *n (at bank, shop)* conto *m*; *(report)* resoconto *m*; **to take into ~** tener conto di; **on no ~** in nessun caso; **on ~ of** a causa di.
◆ **account for** *vt fus (explain)* spiegare; *(constitute)* rappresentare.
accountant [ə'kaʊntənt] *n* ragioniere *m* (-a *f*).
account number *n* numero *m* di conto.
accumulate [ə'kjuːmjʊleɪt] *vt*

accumulare.

accurate ['ækjʊrət] *adj* preciso(-a).

accuse [ə'kju:z] *vt*: **to ~ sb of sthg** accusare qn di qc.

accused [ə'kju:zd] *n*: **the ~** l'imputato *m* (-a *f*).

ace [eɪs] *n (card)* asso *m*.

ache [eɪk] ◇ *n* dolore *m* ◇ *vi*: **my head ~s** mi fa male la testa.

achieve [ə'tʃi:v] *vt* ottenere.

acid ['æsɪd] ◇ *adj* acido(-a) ◇ *n* acido *m*.

acid rain *n* pioggia *f* acida.

acknowledge [ək'nɒlɪdʒ] *vt (accept)* riconoscere; *(letter)* accusare ricevuta di.

acne ['æknɪ] *n* acne *f*.

acorn ['eɪkɔ:n] *n* ghianda *f*.

acoustic [ə'ku:stɪk] *adj* acustico(-a).

acquaintance [ə'kweɪntəns] *n (person)* conoscente *mf*.

acquire [ə'kwaɪə^r] *vt* acquisire.

acre ['eɪkə^r] *n* = 4 046,9 m^2, acro *m*.

acrobat ['ækrəbæt] *n* acrobata *mf*.

across [ə'krɒs] ◇ *prep (to, on other side of)* dall'altra parte di; *(from one side to the other of)* attraverso, da una parte all'altra di ◇ *adv (to other side)* dall'altra parte; **to walk ~ sthg** attraversare qc (a piedi); **to drive ~ sthg** attraversare qc (in macchina); **10 miles ~** largo 10 miglia; **~ from** di fronte a.

acrylic [ə'krɪlɪk] *n* acrilico *m*.

act [ækt] ◇ *vi* agire; *(behave)* comportarsi; *(in play, film)* recitare ◇ *n* atto *m*; (POL) legge *f*; *(performance)* numero *m*; **to ~ as** *(serve as)* fare da.

action ['ækʃn] *n* azione *f*; **to take ~** agire; **to put sthg into ~** mettere in pratica qc; **out of ~** *(machine)* fuori uso; *(person)* fuori combattimento.

active ['æktɪv] *adj (busy)* attivo(-a).

activity [æk'tɪvətɪ] *n* attività *f inv*.

activity holiday *n vacanza organizzata per ragazzi con attività ricreative di vario genere.*

act of God *n* causa *f* di forza maggiore.

actor ['æktə^r] *n* attore *m*.

actress ['æktrɪs] *n* attrice *f*.

actual ['æktʃʊəl] *adj (real)* effettivo(-a), reale; *(itself)* in sé.

actually ['æktʃʊəlɪ] *adv (really)* veramente; *(in fact)* in effetti.

acupuncture ['ækjʊpʌŋktʃə^r] *n* agopuntura *f*.

acute [ə'kju:t] *adj* acuto(-a).

ad [æd] *n (inf) (for product)* pubblicità *f inv*; *(for job)* annuncio *m*.

AD *(abbr of Anno Domini)* d.C.

adapt [ə'dæpt] ◇ *vt* adattare ◇ *vi* adattarsi.

adapter [ə'dæptə^r] *n (for foreign plug)* adattatore *m*; *(for several plugs)* presa *f* multipla.

add [æd] *vt (put, say in addition)* aggiungere; *(numbers, prices)* sommare.

◆ **add up** *vt sep* sommare.

◆ **add up to** *vt fus (total)* ammontare a.

adder ['ædə^r] *n* vipera *f*.

addict ['ædɪkt] *n* tossicodipendente *mf*.

addicted [ə'dɪktɪd] *adj*: **to be ~ to sthg** essere assuefatto(-a) a qc.

addiction [ə'dɪkʃn] *n* dipendenza *f*.

addition [ə'dɪʃn] *n (added thing)* aggiunta *f*; *(in maths)* addizione *f*; **in ~** inoltre; **in ~ to** oltre a.

additional [ə'dɪʃənl] *adj* supplementare.

additive ['ædɪtɪv] *n* additivo *m*.

address [ə'dres] ◇ *n (on letter)* indirizzo *m* ◇ *vt (speak to)* rivolgersi a; *(letter)* indirizzare.

address book *n* rubrica *f*.

addressee [,ædre'si:] *n* destinatario *m* (-a *f*).

adequate ['ædɪkwət] *adj* adeguato(-a).

adhere [əd'hɪə^r] *vi*: **to ~ to** *(stick to)* aderire a; *(obey)* rispettare.

adhesive [əd'hi:sɪv] ◇ *adj* adesivo(-a) ◇ *n* adesivo *m*.

adjacent [ə'dʒeɪsənt] *adj* adiacente.

adjective ['ædʒɪktɪv] *n* aggettivo *m*.

adjoining [ə'dʒɔɪnɪŋ] *adj* contiguo(-a).

adjust [ə'dʒʌst] ◇ *vt* aggiustare ◇ *vi*: **to ~ to** adattarsi a.

adjustable [ə'dʒʌstəbl] *adj* regolabile.

adjustment [ə'dʒʌstmənt] *n* *(of machine)* regolazione *f*; *(of plan)* modifica *f*.

administration [əd,mɪnɪ'streɪʃn] *n* amministrazione *f*.

administrator [əd'mɪnɪstreɪtə^r] *n* amministratore *m* (-trice *f*).

admiral ['ædmərəl] *n* ammiraglio *m*.

admire [əd'maɪə^r] *vt* ammirare.

admission [əd'mɪʃn] *n* *(permission to enter, entrance cost)* ingresso *m*.

admission charge *n* ingresso *m*.

admit [əd'mɪt] *vt* *(confess)* ammettere; *(allow to enter)* far entrare; **to ~ to sthg** ammette-re qc; **'~s one'** *(on ticket)* 'valido per una sola persona'.

adolescent [,ædə'lesnt] *n* adolescente *mf*.

adopt [ə'dɒpt] *vt* adottare.

adopted [ə'dɒptɪd] *adj* adottivo(-a).

adorable [ə'dɔ:rəbl] *adj* adorabile.

adore [ə'dɔ:^{r}] *vt* adorare.

Adriatic [eɪdrɪ'ætɪk] *n*: **the ~ (Sea)** l'Adriatico *m*, il mar Adriatico.

adult ['ædʌlt] ◇ *n* adulto *m* (-a *f*) ◇ *adj* *(entertainment, films)* per adulti; *(animal)* adulto(-a).

adult education *n* = educazione *f* permanente.

adultery [ə'dʌltərɪ] *n* adulterio *m*.

advance [əd'vɑ:ns] ◇ *n* *(money)* anticipo *m*; *(movement)* avanzamento *m* ◇ *adj* *(payment)* anticipato(-a) ◇ *vt* anticipare ◇ *vi* *(move forward)* avanzare; *(improve)* fare progressi; **~ warning** preavviso *m*.

advance booking *n* prenotazione *f* anticipata.

advanced [əd'vɑ:nst] *adj* *(student)* di livello avanzato; *(level)* avanzato(-a).

advantage [əd'vɑ:ntɪdʒ] *n* vantaggio *m*; **to take ~ of** approfittare di.

adventure [əd'ventʃə^r] *n* avventura *f*.

adventurous [əd'ventʃərəs] *adj* avventuroso(-a).

adverb ['ædvɜ:b] *n* avverbio *m*.

adverse ['ædvɜ:s] *adj* avverso(-a).

advert ['ædvɜ:t] = **advertisement**.

advertise ['ædvətaɪz] *vt* *(product, event)* fare pubblicità a.

advertisement [əd'vɜ:tɪsmənt] *n* *(for product)* pubblicità *f inv*; *(for job)* annuncio *m*.

advice [əd'vaɪs] *n* consigli *mpl*; **a piece of ~** un consiglio; **to ask for sb's ~** chiedere consiglio a qn.

advisable [əd'vaɪzəbl] *adj* consigliabile.

advise [əd'vaɪz] *vt* consigliare; **to ~ sb to do sthg** consigliare a qn di fare qc; **to ~ sb against doing sthg** sconsigliare a qn di fare qc.

advocate [*n* 'ædvəkət, *vb* 'ædvəkeɪt] ◇ *n* (JUR) avvocato *m* (difensore) ◇ *vt* sostenere.

aerial ['eərɪəl] *n* antenna *f*.

aerobics [eə'rəʊbɪks] *n* aerobica *f*.

aerodynamic [,eərəʊdaɪ'næmɪk] *adj* aerodinamico(-a).

aeroplane ['eərəpleɪn] *n* aeroplano *m*.

aerosol ['eərəsɒl] *n* aerosol *m*.

affair [ə'feə^r] *n* *(event)* affare *m*;

(love affair) relazione *f*.

affect [ə'fekt] *vt (influence)* incidere su.

affection [ə'fekʃn] *n* affetto *m*.

affectionate [ə'fekʃnət] *adj* affettuoso(-a).

affluent ['æfluənt] *adj* ricco(-a).

afford [ə'fɔːd] *vt*: **to be able to ~ sthg** potersi permettere qc; **I can't ~ it** non me lo posso permettere; **I can't ~ the time** non ho tempo.

affordable [ə'fɔːdəbl] *adj* accessibile.

afloat [ə'fləʊt] *adj* a galla.

afraid [ə'freɪd] *adj* spaventato(-a); **to be ~ of** aver paura di; **I'm ~ so/not** temo di sì/di no.

Africa ['æfrɪkə] *n* l'Africa *f*.

African ['æfrɪkən] ◇ *adj* africano(-a) ◇ *n* africano *m* (-a *f*).

after ['ɑːftəʳ] ◇ *prep & adv* dopo ◇ *conj* dopo che; **he arrived ~ me** arrivò dopo di me; **a quarter ~ ten** *(Am)* le dieci e un quarto; **to be ~ sb/sthg** *(in search of)* cercare qn/qc; **~ all** dopo tutto.

◆ **afters** *npl* dessert *m*.

aftercare ['ɑːftəkeəʳ] *n* assistenza *f* postospedaliera.

aftereffects ['ɑːftərɪˌfekts] *npl* conseguenze *fpl*; *(of illness)* postumi *mpl*.

afternoon [ˌɑːftə'nuːn] *n* pomeriggio *m*; **good ~!** buon giorno! *(il pomeriggio)*.

afternoon tea *n spuntino pomeridiano a base di tramezzini, dolci, tè o caffè.*

aftershave ['ɑːftəʃeɪv] *n* dopobarba *m*.

aftersun ['ɑːftəsʌn] *n* doposole *m*.

afterwards ['ɑːftəwədz] *adv* dopo.

again [ə'gen] *adv* ancora, di nuovo; **~ and ~** più volte; **never ... ~** non ... mai più.

against [ə'genst] *prep* contro; **to lean ~ sthg** appoggiarsi a qc; **~ the law** contro la legge.

age [eɪdʒ] *n* età *f*; **under ~** minorenne; **I haven't seen him for ~s** *(inf)* non lo vedo da secoli.

aged [eɪdʒd] *adj*: **~ eight** di otto anni.

age group *n* fascia *f* d'età.

age limit *n* limite *m* d'età.

agency ['eɪdʒənsɪ] *n* agenzia *f*.

agenda [ə'dʒendə] *n* ordine *m* del giorno.

agent ['eɪdʒənt] *n* agente *mf*.

aggression [ə'greʃn] *n* aggressività *f*; **act of ~** aggressione *f*.

aggressive [ə'gresɪv] *adj* aggressivo(-a).

agile [*Br* 'ædʒaɪl, *Am* 'ædʒəl] *adj* agile.

agility [ə'dʒɪlətɪ] *n* agilità *f*.

agitated ['ædʒɪteɪtɪd] *adj* agitato(-a).

ago [ə'gəʊ] *adv*: **a month ~** un mese fa; **how long ~?** quanto tempo fa?

agonizing ['ægənaɪzɪŋ] *adj (pain)* atroce; *(decision)* straziante.

agony ['ægənɪ] *n (physical)* dolore *m* atroce; *(mental)* agonia *f*.

agree [ə'griː] *vi (be in agreement)* essere d'accordo; *(consent)* acconsentire; *(correspond)* concordare; **it doesn't ~ with me** *(food)* mi fa male; **to ~ to sthg** accettare qc; **to ~ to do sthg** accettare di fare qc.

◆ **agree on** *vt fus (time, price)* concordare, mettersi d'accordo su.

agreed [ə'griːd] *adj* stabilito(-a); **to be ~** *(person)* essere d'accordo.

agreement [ə'griːmənt] *n* accordo *m*; **in ~ with** d'accordo con.

agriculture ['ægrɪkʌltʃəʳ] *n* agricoltura *f*.

ahead [ə'hed] *adv (in front)* davanti; *(forwards)* avanti; **the months ~** i prossimi mesi; **to be ~** *(winning)* condurre; **~ of** *(in front of)* davanti a; *(in better position than)* in vantaggio su; *(in time)* in anticipo su.

aid [eɪd] ◇ *n* aiuto *m* ◇ *vt* aiutare; **in ~ of** a favore di; **with the ~ of** con l'aiuto di.
AIDS [eɪdz] *n* AIDS *m*.
ailment ['eɪlmənt] *n (fml)* acciacco *m*.
aim [eɪm] ◇ *n (purpose)* scopo *m* ◇ *vt (gun, camera, hose)* puntare ◇ *vi*: **to ~ (at)** mirare (a); **to ~ to do sthg** avere l'intenzione di fare qc.
air [eəʳ] ◇ *n* aria *f* ◇ *vt (room)* arieggiare ◇ *adj* aereo(-a); *(travel)* in aereo; **by ~** *(travel)* in aereo; *(send)* via aerea.
airbed ['eəbed] *n* materassino *m*.
airborne ['eəbɔːn] *adj* in volo.
air-conditioned [-kən'dɪʃnd] *adj* con aria condizionata.
air-conditioning [-kən'dɪʃnɪŋ] *n* aria *f* condizionata.
aircraft ['eəkrɑːft] *(pl inv) n* aeromobile *m*.
aircraft carrier [-ˌkærɪəʳ] *n* portaerei *f inv*.
airfield ['eəfiːld] *n* campo *m* d'aviazione.
airforce ['eəfɔːs] *n* aeronautica *f* militare.
air freshener [-ˌfreʃnəʳ] *n* deodorante *m* per ambienti.
airhostess ['eəˌhəustɪs] *n* hostess *f inv*.
airing cupboard ['eərɪŋ-] *n sgabuzzino della caldaia dove viene riposta la biancheria ad asciugare*.
airletter ['eəˌletəʳ] *n* aerogramma *m*.
airline ['eəlaɪn] *n* compagnia *f* aerea.
airliner ['eəˌlaɪnəʳ] *n* aereo *m* di linea.
airmail ['eəmeɪl] *n* posta *f* aerea; **by ~** per via aerea.
airplane ['eərpleɪn] *n (Am)* aeroplano *m*.
airport ['eəpɔːt] *n* aeroporto *m*.
air raid *n* incursione *f* aerea.
airsick ['eəsɪk] *adj*: **to be ~** soffrire di mal d'aria.
air steward *n* assistente *m* di volo.
air stewardess *n* assistente *f* di volo.
air traffic control *n (people)* controllori *mpl* di volo.
airy ['eərɪ] *adj* arioso(-a).
aisle [aɪl] *n (in church)* navata *f*; *(in plane, cinema)* corridoio *m*; *(in supermarket)* corsia *f*.
aisle seat *n* posto *m* corridoio.
ajar [ə'dʒɑːʳ] *adj* socchiuso(-a).
alarm [ə'lɑːm] ◇ *n* allarme *m* ◇ *vt* allarmare.
alarm clock *n* sveglia *f*.
alarmed [ə'lɑːmd] *adj (door, car)* dotato(-a) di allarme.
alarming [ə'lɑːmɪŋ] *adj* allarmante.
Albert Hall ['ælbət-] *n*: **the ~** l'Albert Hall *f (sala concerti di Londra)*.
album ['ælbəm] *n* album *m inv*.
alcohol ['ælkəhɒl] *n* alcool *m*.
alcohol-free *adj* analcolico(-a).
alcoholic [ˌælkə'hɒlɪk] ◇ *adj* alcolico(-a) ◇ *n* alcolizzato *m* (-a *f*).
alcoholism ['ælkəhɒlɪzm] *n* alcolismo *m*.
alcove ['ælkəuv] *n* rientranza *f*.
ale [eɪl] *n* birra *f*.
alert [ə'lɜːt] ◇ *adj* vigile ◇ *vt* allertare.
A levels *npl* = esami *mpl* di maturità.
algebra ['ældʒɪbrə] *n* algebra *f*.
alias ['eɪlɪəs] *adv* alias.
alibi ['ælɪbaɪ] *n* alibi *m inv*.
alien ['eɪlɪən] *n (foreigner)* straniero *m* (-a *f*); *(from outer space)* alieno *m* (-a *f*).
alight [ə'laɪt] ◇ *adj* in fiamme ◇ *vi (fml: from train, bus)*: **to ~ (from)** scendere (da).
align [ə'laɪn] *vt* allineare.

alike [ə'laɪk] ◇ *adj* simile ◇ *adv* allo stesso modo; **to look ~** assomigliarsi.

alive [ə'laɪv] *adj (living)* vivo(-a).

all [ɔːl] ◇ *adj* tutto(-a); **~ the food** tutto il cibo; **~ the money** tutti i soldi; **~ the houses** tutte le case; **~ trains stop at Tonbridge** tutti i treni fermano a Tonbridge; **~ the time** sempre; **~ day** tutto il giorno.

◇ *adv* **1.** *(completely)* completamente, interamente; **~ alone** tutto solo (tutta sola).

2. *(in scores)*: **it's two ~** sono due pari.

3. *(in phrases)*: **~ but empty** quasi vuoto; **~ over** *(finished)* finito.

◇ *pron* **1.** *(the whole amount)* tutto(-a); **~ of the work** tutto il lavoro; **is that ~?** *(in shop)* basta così?

2. *(everybody, everything)* tutti(-e); **~ of the girls/rooms** tutte le ragazze/camere; **~ of us went** ci siamo andati tutti.

3. *(with superlative)*: **the best of ~** il migliore di tutti.

4. *(in phrases)*: **in ~** *(in total)* in tutto; *(in summary)* nel complesso; **can I help you at ~?** posso esserle di aiuto?

Allah ['ælə] *n* Allah *m*.

allege [ə'ledʒ] *vt* asserire.

allergic [ə'lɜːdʒɪk] *adj*: **to be ~ to** essere allergico(-a) a.

allergy ['ælədʒɪ] *n* allergia *f*.

alleviate [ə'liːvɪeɪt] *vt* alleviare.

alley ['ælɪ] *n (narrow street)* vicolo *m*.

alligator ['ælɪgeɪtə^r] *n* alligatore *m*.

all-in *adj (Br: inclusive)* tutto compreso *(inv)*.

all-night *adj (bar, petrol station)* aperto(-a) tutta la notte.

allocate ['æləkeɪt] *vt (money, task)* assegnare.

allotment [ə'lɒtmənt] *n (Br: for vegetables)* piccolo lotto di terra preso in affitto per coltivarvi ortaggi.

allow [ə'laʊ] *vt (permit)* permettere; *(time, money)* calcolare; **to ~ sb to do sthg** permettere a qn di fare qc; **to be ~ed to do sthg** avere il permesso di fare qc, poter fare qc.

♦ **allow for** *vt fus* tener conto di.

allowance [ə'laʊəns] *n (state benefit)* assegno *m*; *(for expenses)* indennità *f inv*; *(Am: pocket money)* paghetta *f*.

all right ◇ *adv (satisfactorily)* bene; *(yes, okay)* va bene ◇ *adj*: **is everything ~?** va tutto bene?; **is it ~ if I smoke?** Le dispiace se fumo?; **are you ~?** ti senti bene?; **how was the film? – it was ~** com'era il film? – niente di speciale; **how are you? – I'm ~** come stai? – non c'è male.

ally ['ælaɪ] *n* alleato *m* (-a *f*).

almond ['ɑːmənd] *n* mandorla *f*.

almost ['ɔːlməʊst] *adv* quasi.

alone [ə'ləʊn] ◇ *adj* solo(-a) ◇ *adv* da solo(-a); **to leave sb ~** lasciare qn in pace; **to leave sthg ~** lasciar stare qc.

along [ə'lɒŋ] ◇ *prep* lungo ◇ *adv*: **to walk ~** camminare; **to bring sthg ~** portare qc; **all ~** sempre; **~ with** insieme a.

alongside [əˌlɒŋ'saɪd] ◇ *prep* accanto a ◇ *adv*: **to come ~** accostare.

aloof [ə'luːf] *adj* distaccato(-a).

aloud [ə'laʊd] *adv* a voce alta.

alphabet ['ælfəbet] *n* alfabeto *m*.

Alps [ælps] *npl*: **the ~** le Alpi.

already [ɔːl'redɪ] *adv* già.

also ['ɔːlsəʊ] *adv* anche.

altar ['ɔːltə^r] *n* altare *m*.

alter ['ɔːltə^r] *vt* cambiare.

alteration [ˌɔːltə'reɪʃn] *n* modifica *f*.

alternate [*Br* ɔːl'tɜːnət, *Am* 'ɔːltərnət] *adj* alterni(-e).

alternating current ['ɔːltəneɪtɪŋ-] *n* corrente *f* alternata.

alternative [ɔːlˈtɜːnətɪv] ◇ *adj* alternativo(-a) ◇ *n* alternativa *f*.
alternatively [ɔːlˈtɜːnətɪvlɪ] *adv* in alternativa.
alternator [ˈɔːltəneɪtəʳ] *n* alternatore *m*.
although [ɔːlˈðəʊ] *conj* sebbene, benché.
altitude [ˈæltɪtjuːd] *n* altitudine *f*.
altogether [ˌɔːltəˈgeðəʳ] *adv (completely)* del tutto; *(in total)* in tutto.
aluminium [ˌæljʊˈmɪnɪəm] *n (Br)* alluminio *m*.
aluminum [əˈluːmɪnəm] *(Am)* = **aluminium**.
always [ˈɔːlweɪz] *adv* sempre.
am [æm] → **be**.
a.m. *(abbr of ante meridiem)*: **at two ~** alle due di notte; **at ten ~** alle dieci di mattina.
amateur [ˈæmətəʳ] *n* dilettante *mf*.
amazed [əˈmeɪzd] *adj* stupito(-a).
amazing [əˈmeɪzɪŋ] *adj* incredibile.
Amazon [ˈæməzn] *n (river)*: **the ~** il Rio delle Amazzoni.
ambassador [æmˈbæsədəʳ] *n* ambasciatore *m* (-trice *f*).
amber [ˈæmbəʳ] *adj (traffic lights)* giallo(-a); *(jewellery)* d'ambra.
ambiguous [æmˈbɪgjʊəs] *adj* ambiguo(-a).
ambition [æmˈbɪʃn] *n* ambizione *f*.
ambitious [æmˈbɪʃəs] *adj* ambizioso(-a).
ambulance [ˈæmbjʊləns] *n* ambulanza *f*.
ambush [ˈæmbʊʃ] *n* imboscata *f*.
amenities [əˈmiːnətɪz] *npl (in hotel)* comfort *m inv*; *(in town)* strutture *fpl (sportive, ricreative ecc.)*.
America [əˈmerɪkə] *n* l'America *f*.
American [əˈmerɪkən] ◇ *adj* americano(-a) ◇ *n (person)* americano *m* (-a *f*).
amiable [ˈeɪmɪəbl] *adj* amabile.
ammunition [ˌæmjʊˈnɪʃn] *n* munizioni *fpl*.
amnesia [æmˈniːzɪə] *n* amnesia *f*.
among(st) [əˈmʌŋ(st)] *prep* tra, fra.
amount [əˈmaʊnt] *n (quantity)* quantità *f inv*; *(sum)* somma *f*.
◆ **amount to** *vt fus (total)* ammontare a.
amp [æmp] *n* ampere *m inv*; **a 13-~ plug** una spina con fusibile da 13 ampere.
ample [ˈæmpl] *adj* più che sufficiente.
amplifier [ˈæmplɪfaɪəʳ] *n* amplificatore *m*.
amputate [ˈæmpjʊteɪt] *vt* amputare.
Amtrak [ˈæmtræk] *n compagnia ferroviaria statunitense*.
amuse [əˈmjuːz] *vt* divertire.
amusement arcade [əˈmjuːzmənt-] *n* sala *f* giochi.
amusement park *n* luna park *m inv*.
amusements [əˈmjuːzmənts] *npl giostre e giochi al luna park*.
amusing [əˈmjuːzɪŋ] *adj* divertente.
an [*stressed* æn, *unstressed* ən] → **a**.
anaemic [əˈniːmɪk] *adj (Br: person)* anemico(-a).
anaesthetic [ˌænɪsˈθetɪk] *n (Br)* anestetico *m*.
analgesic [ˌænælˈdʒiːzɪk] *n* analgesico *m*.
analyse [ˈænəlaɪz] *vt* analizzare.
analyst [ˈænəlɪst] *n* analista *mf*.
analyze [ˈænəlaɪz] *(Am)* = **analyse**.
anarchy [ˈænəkɪ] *n* anarchia *f*.
anatomy [əˈnætəmɪ] *n (science)* anatomia *f*; *(of animal)* struttura *f*; *(of person)* corpo *m*.

ancestor ['ænsestəʳ] *n* antenato *m* (-a *f*).

anchor ['æŋkəʳ] *n* àncora *f*.

anchovy ['æntʃəvɪ] *n* acciuga *f*.

ancient ['eɪnʃənt] *adj (customs, monument)* antico(-a).

and [*strong form* ænd, *weak form* ənd, ən] *conj* e, ed *(before, vowel)*; **more ~ more** sempre più; **~ you?** e tu?; **a hundred ~ one** centouno; **to try ~ do sthg** cercare di fare qc; **to go ~ see** andare a vedere.

Andes ['ændi:z] *npl*: **the ~** le Ande.

anecdote ['ænɪkdəʊt] *n* aneddoto *m*.

anemic [ə'ni:mɪk] *(Am)* = **anaemic**.

anesthetic [,ænɪs'θetɪk] *(Am)* = **anaesthetic**.

angel ['eɪndʒl] *n* angelo *m*.

anger ['æŋgəʳ] *n* rabbia *f*.

angina [æn'dʒaɪnə] *n* angina *f* pectoris.

angle ['æŋgl] *n* angolo *m*; **at an ~** storto(-a).

angler ['æŋgləʳ] *n* pescatore *m* (-trice *f*).

angling ['æŋglɪŋ] *n* pesca *f*.

angry ['æŋgrɪ] *adj (person)* arrabbiato(-a); *(words)* pieno(-a) di rabbia; **to get ~ (with sb)** arrabbiarsi (con qn).

animal ['ænɪml] *n* animale *m*.

aniseed ['ænɪsi:d] *n* semi *mpl* d'anice.

ankle ['æŋkl] *n* caviglia *f*.

annex ['æneks] *n (building)* edificio *m* annesso.

annihilate [ə'naɪəleɪt] *vt* annientare.

anniversary [,ænɪ'vɜ:sərɪ] *n* anniversario *m*.

announce [ə'naʊns] *vt* annunciare.

announcement [ə'naʊnsmənt] *n* annuncio *m*.

announcer [ə'naʊnsəʳ] *n* annunciatore *m* (-trice *f*).

annoy [ə'nɔɪ] *vt* dare fastidio a.

annoyed [ə'nɔɪd] *adj* seccato(-a); **to get ~ (with sb)** arrabbiarsi (con qn).

annoying [ə'nɔɪɪŋ] *adj* seccante, irritante.

annual ['ænjʊəl] *adj* annuale.

anonymous [ə'nɒnɪməs] *adj* anonimo(-a).

anorak ['ænəræk] *n* giacca *f* a vento.

another [ə'nʌðəʳ] ◇ *adj* un altro (un'altra) ◇ *pron* un'altro (un'altra *f*); **can I have ~ (one)?** posso prenderne un altro?; **in ~ two weeks** fra altre due settimane; **one ~** l'un l'altro (l'un l'altra); **to help one ~** aiutarsi (l'un l'altro); **to talk to one ~** parlarsi; **one after ~** uno dopo l'altro (una dopo l'altra).

answer ['ɑ:nsəʳ] ◇ *n* risposta *f* ◇ *vt* rispondere a ◇ *vi* rispondere; **to ~ the door** andare ad aprire (la porta); **to ~ the phone** rispondere al telefono.

◆ **answer back** *vi* rispondere male.

answering machine ['ɑ:nsərɪŋ-] = **answerphone**.

answerphone ['ɑ:nsəfəʊn] *n* segreteria *f* telefonica.

ant [ænt] *n* formica *f*.

Antarctic [æn'tɑ:ktɪk] *n*: **the ~** l'Antartide *f*.

antenna [æn'tenə] *n (Am: aerial)* antenna *f*.

anthem ['ænθəm] *n* inno *m*.

antibiotics [,æntɪbaɪ'ɒtɪks] *npl* antibiotici *mpl*.

anticipate [æn'tɪsɪpeɪt] *vt (expect)* aspettarsi; *(guess correctly)* prevedere.

anticlimax [æntɪ'klaɪmæks] *n* delusione *f*.

anticlockwise [,æntɪ'klɒkwaɪz] *adv (Br)* in senso antiorario.

antidote ['æntɪdəʊt] *n* antidoto *m*.

antifreeze ['æntɪfri:z] *n* antigelo *m*.

antihistamine [,æntɪ'hɪstəmɪn] *n* antistaminico *m*.

antiperspirant [,æntɪ'pɜ:spərənt] *n* deodorante *m* (ad azione antitraspirante).

antiquarian bookshop [,æntɪ'kweərɪən-] *n* libreria *f* antiquaria.

antique [æn'ti:k] *n* pezzo *m* d'antiquariato.

antique shop *n* negozio *m* d'antiquariato.

antiseptic [,æntɪ'septɪk] *n* antisettico *m*.

antisocial [,æntɪ'səʊʃl] *adj (person)* asociale; *(behaviour)* incivile.

antlers ['æntləz] *npl* palchi *mpl*.

anxiety [æŋ'zaɪətɪ] *n* ansia *f*.

anxious ['æŋkʃəs] *adj (worried)* preoccupato(-a); *(eager)* ansioso(-a).

any ['enɪ] *adj* ◇ 1. *(in questions)*: **have you got ~ money?** hai (dei) soldi?; **have you got ~ postcards?** ha delle cartoline?; **is there ~ coffee left?** c'è ancora del caffè?

2. *(in negatives)*: **I haven't got ~ money** non ho soldi; **I haven't got ~ Italian stamps** non ho nessun francobollo italiano; **we don't have ~ rooms** non abbiamo camere libere.

3. *(no matter which)* qualunque, qualsiasi; **take ~ one you like** prendi quello che preferisci.

◇ *pron* 1. *(in questions)* ne; **I'm looking for a hotel – are there ~ nearby?** sto cercando un albergo – ce ne sono da queste parti?

2. *(in negatives)* ne; **I don't want ~ (of them)** non ne voglio.

3. *(no matter which one)*: **you can sit at ~ of the tables** potete sedere a qualsiasi tavolo.

◇ *adv* 1. *(in questions)*: **is that ~ better?** così va un po' meglio?; **is there ~ more ice cream?** c'è ancora un po' di gelato?; **~ other questions?** altre domande?

2. *(in negatives)*: **he's not ~ better** non c'è nessun miglioramento; **we can't wait ~ longer** non ossiamo più aspettare.

anybody ['enɪ,bɒdɪ] = **anyone**.

anyhow ['enɪhaʊ] *adv* comunque; *(carelessly)* alla rinfusa.

anyone ['enɪwʌn] *pron (someone)* qualcuno; *(any person)* chiunque; **is ~ there?** c'è nessuno?; **there wasn't ~ in** non c'era nessuno.

anything ['enɪθɪŋ] *pron (something)* qualcosa; *(no matter what)* qualunque cosa, qualsiasi cosa; **have you ~ bigger?** ha niente di più grande?; **I don't want ~ to eat** non voglio mangiare niente.

anyway ['enɪweɪ] *adv* comunque.

anywhere ['enɪweə^r] *adv (in questions)* da qualche parte; *(with negative)* da nessuna parte; *(any place)* dovunque, da qualunque OR qualsiasi parte; **did you go ~ else?** siete andati da qualche altra parte?; **~ you like** dove vuoi.

apart [ə'pɑ:t] *adv (separated)*: **the towns are 5 miles ~** le due città distano 8 km l'una dall'altra; **we live ~** non viviamo insieme; **to come ~** andare in pezzi; **~ from** *(except for)* a parte; *(as well as)* oltre a.

apartheid [ə'pɑ:theɪt] *n* apartheid *f*.

apartment [ə'pɑ:tmənt] *n (Am)* appartamento *m*.

apathetic [,æpə'θetɪk] *adj* apatico(-a).

ape [eɪp] *n* scimmia *f*.

aperitif [ə,perə'ti:f] *n* aperitivo *m*.

aperture ['æpətʃə^r] *n (of camera)* apertura *f*.

APEX ['eɪpeks] *n (plane ticket)* biglietto *m* APEX; *(Br: train ticket) biglietto ferroviario con data prefissata e dal prezzo ridotto comprato due* *settimane prima della partenza.*

apiece [ə'pi:s] *adv (for each item)* l'uno (l'una); *(to, for each person)* ciascuno(-a).

apologetic [ə,pɒlə'dʒetɪk] *adj*: **to be ~** scusarsi.

apologize [ə'pɒlədʒaɪz] *vi*: **to ~ (to sb for sthg)** scusarsi (con qn per qc).

apology [ə'pɒlədʒɪ] *n* scuse *fpl*.

apostrophe [ə'pɒstrəfɪ] *n* apostrofo *m*.

appal [ə'pɔ:l] *vt (Br)* sconvolgere.

appall [ə'pɔ:l] *(Am)* = **appal**.

appalling [ə'pɔ:lɪŋ] *adj* spaventoso(-a).

apparatus [,æpə'reɪtəs] *n (device)* apparecchio *m*; *(in gym)* attrezzatura *f*.

apparently [ə'pærəntlɪ] *adv (it seems)* a quanto pare; *(evidently)* evidentemente.

appeal [ə'pi:l] ◇ *n* (JUR) appello *m*; *(fundraising campaign)* raccolta *f* di fondi ◇ *vi* (JUR) fare appello; **to ~ to sb for help** chiedere aiuto a qn; **it doesn't ~ to me** non mi attira.

appear [ə'pɪə^r] *vi* apparire; *(seem)* sembrare; *(before court)* comparire; **it ~s that** sembra che.

appearance [ə'pɪərəns] *n (arrival)* comparsa *f*; *(look)* aspetto *m*.

appendices [ə'pendɪsi:z] *pl* → **appendix**.

appendicitis [ə,pendɪ'saɪtɪs] *n* appendicite *f*.

appendix [ə'pendɪks] (*pl* **-dices**) *n* appendice *f*.

appetite ['æpɪtaɪt] *n* appetito *m*.

appetizer ['æpɪtaɪzə^r] *n* stuzzichino *m*.

appetizing ['æpɪtaɪzɪŋ] *adj* appetitoso(-a).

applaud [ə'plɔ:d] *vt & vi* applaudire.

applause [ə'plɔ:z] *n* applauso *m*.

apple ['æpl] *n* mela *f*.

apple charlotte [-'ʃɑ:lət] *n dolce di pane o pan di Spagna, ripieno di mele e pane sbriciolato e cotto in forno.*

apple crumble *n mele cotte ricoperte da uno strato di pasta frolla sbriciolata.*

apple juice *n* succo *m* di mela.

apple pie *n* torta *f* di mele ricoperta di pasta.

apple sauce *n* mele *fpl* grattugiate.

apple tart *n* crostata *f* di mele.

apple turnover [-'tɜ:n,əʊvə^r] *n* sfogliatella *f* di mele.

appliance [ə'plaɪəns] *n* apparecchio *m*; **electrical/domestic ~** elettrodomestico *m*.

applicable [ə'plɪkəbl] *adj*: **to be ~ (to)** essere applicabile (a); **if ~** se pertinente.

applicant ['æplɪkənt] *n* candidato *m* (-a *f*).

application [,æplɪ'keɪʃn] *n (for job, membership)* domanda *f*.

application form *n* modulo *m* di domanda.

apply [ə'plaɪ] ◇ *vt (lotion, paint)* dare; *(brakes)* azionare ◇ *vi*: **to ~ (to sb for sthg)** *(make request)* fare domanda (per qc presso qn); **to ~ (to sb)** *(be applicable)* essere valido (per qn); **to ~ for a job** fare domanda di lavoro.

appointment [ə'pɔɪntmənt] *n (with doctor, hairdresser, businessman)* appuntamento *m*; **to have/make an ~ (with)** avere/prendere un appuntamento (con); **by ~** per OR su appuntamento.

appreciable [ə'pri:ʃəbl] *adj* apprezzabile.

appreciate [ə'pri:ʃɪeɪt] *vt* apprezzare; *(understand)* rendersi conto di.

apprehensive [,æprɪ'hensɪv] *adj* preoccupato(-a).

apprentice [ə'prentɪs] *n* apprendista *mf*.

apprenticeship [ə'prentɪsʃɪp] *n* apprendistato *m*.

approach [ə'prəʊtʃ] ◇ *n (road)* accesso *m*; *(to problem, situation)* approccio *m* ◇ *vt (come nearer to)* avvicinare; *(problem, situation)* affrontare ◇ *vi* avvicinarsi.

appropriate [ə'prəʊprɪət] *adj* adatto(-a).

approval [ə'pru:vl] *n* approvazione *f*.

approve [ə'pru:v] *vi*: **to ~ (of sb/sthg)** approvare (qn/qc).

approximate [ə'prɒksɪmət] *adj* approssimativo(-a).

approximately [ə'prɒksɪmətlɪ] *adv* circa.

Apr. *(abbr of April)* apr.

apricot ['eɪprɪkɒt] *n* albicocca *f*.

April ['eɪprəl] *n* aprile *m*, → **September**.

April Fools' Day *n* il primo aprile, giorno in cui si fanno i 'pesci d'aprile'.

apron ['eɪprən] *n* grembiule *m* (da cucina).

apt [æpt] *adj (appropriate)* appropriato(-a); **to be ~ to do sthg** avere tendenza a fare qc.

aquarium [ə'kweərɪəm] (*pl* **-ria** [-rɪə]) *n* acquario *m*.

Aquarius [ə'kweərɪəs] *n* Acquario *m*.

aqueduct ['ækwɪdʌkt] *n* acquedotto *m*.

Arab ['ærəb] ◇ *adj* arabo(-a) ◇ *n (person)* arabo *m* (-a *f*).

Arabic ['ærəbɪk] ◇ *adj* arabo(-a) ◇ *n (language)* arabo *m*.

arbitrary ['ɑ:bɪtrərɪ] *adj* arbitrario(-a).

arc [ɑ:k] *n* arco *m*.

arcade [ɑ:'keɪd] *n (for shopping)* galleria *f*; *(of video games)* sala *f* giochi.

arch [ɑ:tʃ] *n* arco *m*.

archaeology [ˌɑ:kɪ'ɒlədʒɪ] *n* archeologia *f*.

archbishop [ˌɑ:tʃ'bɪʃəp] *n* arcivescovo *m*.

archery ['ɑ:tʃərɪ] *n* tiro *m* con l'arco.

archipelago [ˌɑ:kɪ'peləgəʊ] *n* arcipelago *m*.

architect ['ɑ:kɪtekt] *n* architetto *mf*.

architecture ['ɑ:kɪtektʃə^r] *n* architettura *f*.

archives ['ɑ:kaɪvz] *npl* archivi *mpl*.

Arctic ['ɑ:ktɪk] *n*: **the ~** l'Artide *f*.

are [*weak form* ə^r, *strong form* ɑ:^r] → **be**.

area ['eərɪə] *n (region)* zona *f*; *(space, zone)* area *f*; *(surface size)* superficie *f*; **dining ~** zona pranzo.

area code *n (Am)* prefisso *m*.

arena [ə'ri:nə] *n (at circus)* pista *f*; *(sports ground)* campo *m*.

aren't = **are not**.

Argentina [ˌɑ:dʒən'ti:nə] *n* l'Argentina *f*.

argue ['ɑ:gju:] ◇ *vi (quarrel)*: **to ~ (with sb about sthg)** litigare (con qn per qc) ◇ *vt*: **to ~ (that)** ... sostenere (che) ...

argument ['ɑ:gjʊmənt] *n (quarrel)* discussione *f*; *(reason)* argomento *m*.

arid ['ærɪd] *adj* arido(-a).

Aries ['eəri:z] *n* Ariete *m*.

arise [ə'raɪz] (*pt* **arose**, *pp* **arisen** [ə'rɪzn]) *vi (problem, opportunity)* presentarsi; **to ~ from** derivare da.

aristocracy [ˌærɪ'stɒkrəsɪ] *n* aristocrazia *f*.

arithmetic [ə'rɪθmətɪk] *n* aritmetica *f*.

arm [ɑ:m] *n (of person)* braccio *m*; *(of chair)* bracciolo *m*; *(of garment)* manica *f*.

armbands ['ɑ:mbændz] *npl (for swimming)* braccioli *mpl*.

armchair ['ɑːmtʃeəʳ] *n* poltrona *f*.

armed [ɑːmd] *adj* armato(-a).

armed forces *npl*: **the ~** le forze armate.

armor *(Am)* = **armour**.

armour ['ɑːməʳ] *n (Br)* armatura *f*.

armpit ['ɑːmpɪt] *n* ascella *f*.

arms [ɑːmz] *npl (weapons)* armi *fpl*.

army ['ɑːmɪ] *n* esercito *m*.

A road *n (Br)* strada *f* statale.

aroma [ə'rəʊmə] *n* aroma *m*.

aromatic [,ærə'mætɪk] *adj* aromatico(-a).

arose [ə'rəʊz] *pt* → **arise**.

around [ə'raʊnd] ◇ *adv* in giro ◇ *prep (surrounding)* intorno a; *(to the other side of)* dall'altra parte di; *(near)* vicino a; *(all over)* per; *(approximately)* circa; **~ here** *(in the area)* da queste parti; **~ the corner** dietro l'angolo; **to turn ~** girarsi; **to look ~** *(turn head)* guardarsi intorno; *(in shop, city)* dare un'occhiata in giro; **at ~ two o'clock** verso le due; **is Paul ~?** c'è Paul?

arouse [ə'raʊz] *vt* destare.

arrange [ə'reɪndʒ] *vt (flowers, books)* sistemare; *(meeting, event)* organizzare; **to ~ to do sthg (with sb)** mettersi d'accordo (con qn) per fare qc.

arrangement [ə'reɪndʒmənt] *n (agreement)* accordo *m*; *(layout)* disposizione *f*; **by ~** su richiesta; **to make ~s (to do sthg)** fare il necessario (per fare qc).

arrest [ə'rest] ◇ *n* arresto *m* ◇ *vt* arrestare; **under ~** in arresto.

arrival [ə'raɪvl] *n* arrivo *m*; **on ~** all'arrivo; **new ~** *(person)* nuovo arrivato *m* (nuova arrivata *f*).

arrive [ə'raɪv] *vi* arrivare; **to ~ at** *(place)* arrivare in/a.

arrogant ['ærəgənt] *adj* arrogante.

arrow ['ærəʊ] *n* freccia *f*.

arson ['ɑːsn] *n* incendio *m* doloso.

art [ɑːt] *n* arte *f*.

◆ **arts** *npl (humanities)* discipline *fpl* umanistiche; **the ~s** *(fine arts)* l'arte *f*.

artefact ['ɑːtɪfækt] *n* manufatto *m*.

artery ['ɑːtərɪ] *n* arteria *f*.

art gallery *n* galleria *f* d'arte.

arthritis [ɑː'θraɪtɪs] *n* artrite *f*.

artichoke ['ɑːtɪtʃəʊk] *n* carciofo *m*.

article ['ɑːtɪkl] *n* articolo *m*.

articulate [ɑː'tɪkjʊlət] *adj* chiaro(-a).

artificial [,ɑːtɪ'fɪʃl] *adj* artificiale.

artist ['ɑːtɪst] *n* artista *mf*.

artistic [ɑː'tɪstɪk] *adj (design)* artistico(-a); *(person)* dotato(-a) di senso artistico.

arts centre *n* centro *m* artistico.

as [*unstressed* əz, *stressed* æz] ◇ *adv (in comparisons)*: **~ … ~** (così) … come; **~ white ~ snow** bianco come la neve; **he's ~ tall ~ I am** è alto quanto me; **~ many ~** tanti … quanti (tante … quante); **~ much ~** tanto … quanto (tanta … quanta); **twice ~ big** due volte più grande.

◇ *conj* **1.** *(referring to time)* mentre, nel momento in cui; **~ the plane was coming in to land** nel momento in cui l'aereo si preparava ad atterrare.

2. *(referring to manner)* come; **~ expected …** come previsto … ; **do ~ you like** fa' come vuoi.

3. *(introducing a statement)* come; **~ you know …** come sai …

4. *(because)* poiché, dato che.

5. *(in phrases)*: **~ for** quanto a; **~ from** (a partire) da; **~ if** come se; **it looks ~ if it will rain** sembra che stia per piovere.

◇ *prep (referring to function, job)* come; **to work ~ a teacher** fare l'insegnante.

asap *(abbr of as soon as possible)* il più presto possibile.

ascent [ə'sent] *n (climb)* scalata *f*.

ascribe [ə'skraıb] *vt*: **to ~ sthg to** attribuire qc a.

ash [æʃ] *n (from cigarette, fire)* cenere *f*; *(tree)* frassino *m*.

ashore [ə'ʃɔːʳ] *adv* a riva.

ashtray ['æʃtreı] *n* portacenere *m inv*.

Asia [*Br* 'eıʃə, *Am* 'eıʒə] *n* l'Asia *f*.

Asian [*Br* 'eıʃn, *Am* 'eıʒn] ◇ *adj* asiatico(-a) ◇ *n* asiatico *m* (-a *f*).

aside [ə'saıd] *adv (to one side)* di lato; **to move ~** spostarsi.

ask [ɑːsk] ◇ *vt (person)* chiedere a; *(request)* chiedere; *(invite)* invitare ◇ *vi*: **to ~ about sthg** chiedere informazioni su qc; **to ~ sb sthg** chiedere qc a qn; **to ~ sb about sthg** chiedere a qn di qc; **to ~ sb to do sthg** chiedere a qn di fare qc; **to ~ sb for sthg** chiedere qc a qn; **to ~ a question** fare una domanda; **can I ~ you about this translation?** posso farti qualche domanda su questa traduzione?

◆ **ask for** *vt fus (ask to talk to)* chiedere di; *(request)* chiedere.

asleep [ə'sliːp] *adj* addormentato(-a); **to be ~** dormire; **to fall ~** addormentarsi.

asparagus [ə'spærəgəs] *n* asparagi *mpl*.

asparagus tips *npl* punte *fpl* d'asparagi.

aspect ['æspekt] *n* aspetto *m*.

aspirin ['æsprın] *n* aspirina® *f*.

ass [æs] *n (animal)* asino *m*.

assassinate [ə'sæsıneıt] *vt* assassinare.

assault [ə'sɔːlt] ◇ *n* aggressione *f* ◇ *vt* aggredire.

assemble [ə'sembl] ◇ *vt (bookcase, model)* montare ◇ *vi* riunirsi.

assembly [ə'semblı] *n (at school) riunione quotidiana di alunni e professori.*

assembly hall *n (at school) locale di una scuola dove alunni e professori si riuniscono ogni giorno prima delle lezioni.*

assembly point *n punto di raduno in caso di emergenza.*

assert [ə'sɜːt] *vt (fact, innocence)* sostenere; *(authority)* far valere; **to ~ o.s.** farsi valere.

assess [ə'ses] *vt (person, situation, effect)* valutare; *(value, damage, cost)* stimare.

assessment [ə'sesmənt] *n (of person, situation, effect)* valutazione *f*; *(of value, damage, cost)* stima *f*.

asset ['æset] *n (valuable person, thing)* punto *m* di forza.

assign [ə'saın] *vt*: **to ~ sthg to sb** *(give)* assegnare qc a qn; **to ~ sb to do sthg** *(designate)* incaricare qn di fare qc.

assignment [ə'saınmənt] *n (task)* incarico *m*; (SCH) ricerca *f*.

assist [ə'sıst] *vt* aiutare.

assistance [ə'sıstəns] *n* aiuto *m*; **to be of ~ (to sb)** essere d'aiuto (a qn).

assistant [ə'sıstənt] *n* assistente *mf*.

associate [*n* ə'səʊʃıət, *vb* ə'səʊʃıeıt] ◇ *n (partner)* socio *m* (-a *f*); *(colleague)* collega *mf* ◇ *vt*: **to ~ sb/sthg with** associare qn/qc a; **to be ~d with** venire associato a.

association [ə,səʊsı'eıʃn] *n* associazione *f*.

assorted [ə'sɔːtıd] *adj* assortito(-a).

assortment [ə'sɔːtmənt] *n* assortimento *m*.

assume [ə'sjuːm] *vt (suppose)* supporre; *(control)* assumere; *(responsibility)* assumersi.

assurance [ə'ʃʊərəns] *n (promise)* promessa *f*; *(insurance)* assicurazione *f*.

assure [ə'ʃʊəʳ] *vt* assicurare; **to ~ sb (that) ...** assicurare a qn che ...

asterisk ['æstərısk] *n* asterisco *m*.

asthma ['æsmə] *n* asma *f*.

asthmatic [æs'mætɪk] *adj* asmatico(-a).

astonished [ə'stɒnɪʃt] *adj* stupito(-a).

astonishing [ə'stɒnɪʃɪŋ] *adj* incredibile.

astound [ə'staʊnd] *vt* sbalordire.

astray [ə'streɪ] *adv*: **to go ~** smarrirsi.

astrology [ə'strɒlədʒɪ] *n* astrologia *f*.

astronomy [ə'strɒnəmɪ] *n* astronomia *f*.

asylum [ə'saɪləm] *n (mental hospital)* manicomio *m*.

at [*unstressed* ət, *stressed* æt] *prep* **1.** *(indicating place, position)* a; **~ school** a scuola; **~ the hotel** in OR all'albergo; **~ home** a casa; **~ my mother's** da mia madre.
2. *(indicating direction)*: **to throw sthg ~** tirare qc contro; **to look ~ sb/sthg** guardare qn/qc; **to smile ~ sb** sorridere a qn.
3. *(indicating time)* a; **~ nine o'clock** alle nove; **~ night** di notte.
4. *(indicating rate, level, speed)* a; **it works out ~ £5 each** viene 5 sterline a testa; **~ 60 km/h** a 60km/h.
5. *(indicating activity)*: **she's ~ lunch** sta pranzando; **to be good/bad ~ sthg** essere/non essere bravo in qc.
6. *(indicating cause)*: **shocked ~ sthg** scioccato da qc; **angry ~ sb** arrabbiato con qn; **delighted ~ sthg** contentissimo di qc.

ate [*Br* et, *Am* eɪt] *pt* → **eat**.

atheist ['eɪθɪɪst] *n* ateo *m* (-a *f*).

athlete ['æθli:t] *n* atleta *mf*.

athletics [æθ'letɪks] *n* atletica *f*.

Atlantic [ət'læntɪk] *n*: **the ~ (Ocean)** l'Atlantico *m*, l'Oceano *m* Atlantico.

atlas ['ætləs] *n* atlante *m*.

atmosphere ['ætməsfɪəʳ] *n* atmosfera *f*; *(air in room)* aria *f*.

atom ['ætəm] *n* atomo *m*.

A to Z *n (map)* stradario *m*.

atrocious [ə'trəʊʃəs] *adj (very bad)* orrendo(-a).

attach [ə'tætʃ] *vt* attaccare; **to ~ sthg to sthg** attaccare qc a qc.

attachment [ə'tætʃmənt] *n (device)* accessorio *m*.

attack [ə'tæk] ◇ *n* attacco *m* ◇ *vt* aggredire.

attacker [ə'tækəʳ] *n* aggressore *m*.

attain [ə'teɪn] *vt (fml)* conseguire.

attempt [ə'tempt] ◇ *n* tentativo *m* ◇ *vt* tentare; **to ~ to do sthg** tentare di fare qc.

attend [ə'tend] *vt (meeting)* partecipare a; *(school)* frequentare; *(mass)* ascoltare.

◆ **attend to** *vt fus (deal with)* occuparsi di.

attendance [ə'tendəns] *n (people at concert, match)* affluenza *f*; *(at school)* frequenza *f*.

attendant [ə'tendənt] *n (at public toilets, cloakroom)* addetto *m* (-a *f*); *(at museum)* custode *mf*.

attention [ə'tenʃn] *n* attenzione *f*; **to pay ~ (to)** fare attenzione (a).

attic ['ætɪk] *n* soffitta *f*.

attitude ['ætɪtju:d] *n* atteggiamento *m*.

attorney [ə'tɜ:nɪ] *n (Am)* avvocato *m*.

attract [ə'trækt] *vt* attirare.

attraction [ə'trækʃn] *n (liking)* attrazione *f*; *(attractive feature)* attrattiva *f*.

attractive [ə'træktɪv] *adj* attraente.

attribute [ə'trɪbju:t] *vt*: **to ~ sthg to** attribuire qc a.

aubergine ['əʊbəʒi:n] *n (Br)* melanzana *f*.

auburn ['ɔ:bən] *adj* castano ramato *(inv)*.

auction ['ɔ:kʃn] *n* asta *f*.

audience ['ɔ:dɪəns] *n (of play, concert, film)* pubblico *m*; *(of TV)* tele-

spettatori *mpl*; *(of radio)* ascoltatori *mpl*.
audio [ˈɔːdɪəʊ] *adj* audio *(inv)*.
audio-visual [-ˈvɪʒʊəl] *adj* audiovisivo(-a).
auditorium [ˌɔːdɪˈtɔːrɪəm] *n* sala *f*.
Aug. *(abbr of August)* ago.
August [ˈɔːgəst] *n* agosto *m*, → **September**.
aunt [ɑːnt] *n* zia *f*.
au pair [ˌəʊˈpeəʳ] *n* ragazza *f* alla pari.
aural [ˈɔːrəl] *adj* uditivo(-a).
Australia [ɒˈstreɪlɪə] *n* l'Australia *f*.
Australian [ɒˈstreɪlɪən] ◇ *adj* australiano(-a) ◇ *n* australiano *m* (-a *f*).
Austria [ˈɒstrɪə] *n* l'Austria *f*.
Austrian [ˈɒstrɪən] ◇ *adj* austriaco(-a) ◇ *n* austriaco *m* (-a *f*).
authentic [ɔːˈθentɪk] *adj* autentico(-a).
author [ˈɔːθəʳ] *n (of book, article)* autore *m* (-trice *f*); *(by profession)* scrittore *m* (-trice *f*).
authority [ɔːˈθɒrətɪ] *n* autorità *f inv*; **the authorities** le autorità.
authorization [ˌɔːθəraɪˈzeɪʃn] *n* autorizzazione *f*.
authorize [ˈɔːθəraɪz] *vt* autorizzare; **to ~ sb to do sthg** autorizzare qn a fare qc.
autobiography [ˌɔːtəbaɪˈɒgrəfɪ] *n* autobiografia *f*.
autograph [ˈɔːtəgrɑːf] *n* autografo *m*.
automatic [ˌɔːtəˈmætɪk] ◇ *adj* automatico(-a) ◇ *n (car)* automobile *f* con cambio automatico.
automatically [ˌɔːtəˈmætɪklɪ] *adv* automaticamente.
automobile [ˈɔːtəməbiːl] *n (Am)* automobile *f*.
autumn [ˈɔːtəm] *n* autunno *m*; **in (the) ~** in autunno.
auxiliary (verb) [ɔːgˈzɪljərɪ-] *n* ausiliare *m*.
available [əˈveɪləbl] *adj* disponibile.
avalanche [ˈævəlɑːnʃ] *n* valanga *f*.
Ave. *(abbr of avenue)* V.le.
avenue [ˈævənjuː] *n* viale *m*.
average [ˈævərɪdʒ] ◇ *adj* medio(-a); *(not very good)* mediocre ◇ *n* media *f*; **on ~** in media.
aversion [əˈvɜːʃn] *n* avversione *f*.
aviation [ˌeɪvɪˈeɪʃn] *n* aviazione *f*.
avid [ˈævɪd] *adj* avido(-a).
avocado [ˌævəˈkɑːdəʊ] (*pl* **-s** OR **-es**) *n*: **~ (pear)** avocado *m inv*.
avoid [əˈvɔɪd] *vt* evitare; **to ~ doing sthg** evitare di fare qc.
await [əˈweɪt] *vt* attendere.
awake [əˈweɪk] (*pt* **awoke**, *pp* **awoken**) ◇ *adj* sveglio(-a) ◇ *vi* svegliarsi.
award [əˈwɔːd] ◇ *n* premio *m* ◇ *vt*: **to ~ sb sthg** *(prize)* assegnare qc a qn; *(damages, compensation)* accordare qc a qn.
aware [əˈweəʳ] *adj* consapevole; **to be ~ of** rendersi conto di.
away [əˈweɪ] *adv* via; *(look, turn)* da un'altra parte; **to drive ~** allontanarsi; **to walk ~** allontanarsi; **to go ~ on holiday** partire per le vacanze; **to put sthg ~** mettere via qc, mettere a posto qc; **to take sthg ~ (from sb)** portare via qc (a qn), prendere qc (a qn); **far ~** molto lontano; **it's 10 miles ~ (from here)** è a 10 miglia (da qui); **the festival is two weeks ~** mancano due settimane al festival.
awesome [ˈɔːsəm] *adj (impressive)* imponente; *(inf: excellent)* fantastico(-a).
awful [ˈɔːfəl] *adj* orribile; **I feel ~** sto malissimo; **an ~ lot of** un mucchio di.
awfully [ˈɔːflɪ] *adv (very)* molto, terribilmente.

awkward ['ɔːkwəd] *adj (movement)* sgraziato(-a); *(position)* goffo(-a); *(shape, size)* poco funzionale; *(situation, question)* imbarazzante; *(task, time)* difficile.

awning ['ɔːnɪŋ] *n* tenda *f*.

awoke [ə'wəʊk] *pt* → **awake**.

awoken [ə'wəʊkən] *pp* → **awake**.

axe [æks] *n* scure *f*.

axle ['æksl] *n* asse *m*.

B

BA *(abbr of Bachelor of Arts)* *(degree)* laurea *f* in materie umanistiche; *(person)* laureato *m* (-a *f*) in materie umanistiche.

babble ['bæbl] *vi* balbettare.

baby ['beɪbɪ] *n* bambino *m* (-a *f*); **to have a ~** avere un bambino; **~ sweetcorn** piccole spighe di mais.

baby carriage *n (Am)* carrozzina *f*.

baby food *n* alimenti *mpl* per l'infanzia.

baby-sit *vi* fare da baby-sitter.

baby wipe *n* salvietta *f* umidificata (per bambini).

back [bæk] ◇ *adv* indietro ◇ *n (of person)* schiena *f*; *(of chair)* schienale *m*; *(of car, book, bank note)* retro *m*; *(of room)* fondo *m*; *(of hand)* dorso *m* ◇ *adj (seat, wheels)* posteriore ◇ *vi (car, driver)* fare retromarcia ◇ *vt (support)* appoggiare; **to put sthg ~** rimettere qc (a posto); **to arrive ~** ritornare; **to give sthg ~** restituire OR dare indietro qc; **to write ~ to sb** rispondere a qn; **at the ~ of** sul retro di, dietro; **in ~ of** *(Am)* sul retro di, dietro; **~ to front** davanti di dietro.

◆ **back up** ◇ *vt sep (support)* appoggiare ◇ *vi (car, driver)* fare retromarcia.

backache ['bækeɪk] *n* mal *m* di schiena.

backbone ['bækbəʊn] *n* spina *f* dorsale.

back door *n* porta *f* posteriore.

backfire [ˌbæk'faɪə^r] *vi (car)* fare un'autoaccensione.

background ['bækgraʊnd] *n* sfondo *m*; *(of person)* background *m inv*.

backlog ['bæklɒg] *n* cumulo *m*; **a ~ of work** del lavoro arretrato.

backpack ['bækpæk] *n* zaino *m*.

backpacker ['bækpækə^r] *n persona che viaggia con zaino e sacco a pelo*.

back seat *n* sedile *m* posteriore.

backside [ˌbæk'saɪd] *n (inf)* sedere *m*.

back street *n* viuzza *f*.

backstroke ['bækstrəʊk] *n* dorso *m (nel nuoto)*.

backwards ['bækwədz] *adv (look)* indietro; *(fall, move)* all'indietro; *(wrong way round)* al contrario.

bacon ['beɪkən] *n* pancetta *f*, bacon *m*; **~ and eggs** uova *fpl* e pancetta.

bacteria [bæk'tɪərɪə] *npl* batteri *mpl*.

bad [bæd] (*compar* **worse**, *superl* **worst**) *adj* cattivo(-a); *(harmful)* dannoso(-a); *(accident, wound)* brutto(-a); *(eyesight, heart)* debole; *(arm, leg)* malandato(-a); **drinking is ~ for you** bere ti fa male; **to go ~** *(milk, yoghurt)* andare a male; **not ~**

(film, food, journey) niente male; **how are you? – not ~** come stai? – non c'è male.
badge [bædʒ] *n* distintivo *m*.
badger ['bædʒəʳ] *n* tasso *m*.
badly ['bædlɪ] (*compar* **worse**, *superl* **worst**) *adv* male; *(injured)* gravemente; *(affected)* profondamente; *(very much)* tanto.
badly paid [-peɪd] *adj* mal pagato(-a).
badminton ['bædmɪntən] *n* badminton *m*.
bad-tempered [-'tempəd] *adj* irascibile.
bag [bæg] *n* sacchetto *m*; *(handbag)* borsa *f*; *(piece of luggage)* borsone *m*; **a ~ of crisps** un sacchetto di patatine.
bagel ['beɪgəl] *n* *panino a forma di ciambella*.
baggage ['bægɪdʒ] *n* bagagli *mpl*.
baggage allowance *n* franchigia *f* bagaglio.
baggage reclaim *n* ritiro *m* bagagli.
baggy ['bægɪ] *adj* largo(-a).
bagpipes ['bægpaɪps] *npl* cornamusa *f*.
bail [beɪl] *n* cauzione *f*.
bait [beɪt] *n* esca *f*.
bake [beɪk] ◇ *vt* cuocere (al forno) ◇ *n*: **vegetable ~** verdure *fpl* al forno.
baked [beɪkt] *adj* cotto(-a) al forno.
baked Alaska [-ə'læskə] *n* meringata *f*.
baked beans *npl* fagioli *mpl* al sugo di pomodoro.
baked potato *n* patata *f* cotta al forno con la buccia.
baker ['beɪkəʳ] *n* fornaio *m* (-a *f*); **~'s** *(shop)* panificio *m*, panetteria *f*.
Bakewell tart ['beɪkwel-] *n* *torta con una base di pasta frolla, uno strato di marmellata e uno di pan di Spagna alle mandorle, ricoperta da una glassa dal caratteristico aspetto a onde*.
balance ['bæləns] ◇ *n* *(of person)* equilibrio *m*; *(of bank account, remainder)* saldo *m* ◇ *vt* *(object)* tenere in equilibrio.
balcony ['bælkənɪ] *n* balcone *m*.
bald [bɔːld] *adj* calvo(-a).
bale [beɪl] *n* balla *f*.
ball [bɔːl] *n* (SPORT) palla *f*; *(in football, rugby)* pallone *m*; *(in golf, table tennis)* pallina *f*; *(of wool, string)* gomitolo *m*; *(dance)* ballo *m*; **on the ~** *(fig)* in gamba.
ballad ['bæləd] *n* ballata *f*.
ballerina [ˌbælə'riːnə] *n* ballerina *f*.
ballet ['bæleɪ] *n* balletto *m*.
ballet dancer *n* ballerino *m* classico (ballerina classica *f*).
balloon [bə'luːn] *n* *(at party etc)* palloncino *m*.
ballot ['bælət] *n* *(vote)* votazione *f* a scrutinio segreto.
ballpoint pen ['bɔːlpɔɪnt-] *n* penna *f* a sfera.
ballroom ['bɔːlrʊm] *n* sala *f* da ballo.
ballroom dancing *n* ballo *m* liscio.
bamboo [bæm'buː] *n* bambù *m*.
bamboo shoots *npl* germogli *mpl* di bambù.
ban [bæn] ◇ *n* divieto *m* ◇ *vt* vietare; **to ~ sb from doing sthg** vietare a qn di fare qc.
banana [bə'nɑːnə] *n* banana *f*.
banana split *n* banana split *f inv*.
band [bænd] *n* *(musical group)* banda *f*; *(for rock, jazz)* complesso *m*, gruppo *m*; *(strip of paper, rubber)* striscia *f*.
bandage ['bændɪdʒ] ◇ *n* benda *f* ◇ *vt* fasciare.
B and B *abbr* = **bed and breakfast**.
bandstand ['bændstænd] *n* palco

m dell'orchestra.

bang [bæŋ] ◇ *n (of gun, explosion)* scoppio *m* ◇ *vt* sbattere.

banger ['bæŋəʳ] *n (Br: inf: sausage)* salsiccia *f*; **~s and mash** salsicce e purè di patate.

bangle ['bæŋgl] *n* braccialetto *m*.

bangs [bæŋz] *npl (Am)* frangia *f*.

banister ['bænɪstəʳ] *n* ringhiera *f*.

banjo ['bændʒəʊ] (*pl* **-s** OR **-es**) *n* banjo *m inv*.

bank [bæŋk] *n (for money)* banca *f*; *(of river, lake)* riva *f*; *(slope)* scarpata *f*.

bank account *n* conto *m* bancario.

bank book *n* libretto *m* di banca.

bank charges *npl* commissioni *fpl* bancarie.

bank clerk *n* impiegato *m* (-a *f*) di banca.

bank draft *n* assegno *m* circolare.

banker ['bæŋkəʳ] *n* banchiere *m*.

banker's card *n* carta *f* assegni.

bank holiday *n (Br)* giorno *m* festivo.

bank manager *n* direttore *m* (-trice *f*) di banca.

bank note *n* banconota *f*.

bankrupt ['bæŋkrʌpt] *adj* fallito(-a).

bank statement *n* estratto *m* conto.

banner ['bænəʳ] *n* striscione *m*.

bannister ['bænɪstəʳ] = **banister**.

banquet ['bæŋkwɪt] *n (formal dinner)* banchetto *m*; *(at Indian restaurant etc) menu per più persone*.

bap [bæp] *n (Br)* panino *m*.

baptize [*Br* bæp'taɪz, *Am* 'bæptaɪz] *vt* battezzare.

bar [bɑːʳ] ◇ *n (pub, in hotel)* bar *m inv*; *(counter in pub)* banco *m*; *(of metal, wood)* sbarra *f*; *(of chocolate)* tavoletta *f* ◇ *vt (obstruct)* sbarrare; **a ~ of soap** una saponetta.

barbecue ['bɑːbɪkjuː] ◇ *n* barbecue *m inv* ◇ *vt* arrostire alla griglia.

barbecue sauce *n salsa piccante usata per condire carne o pesce alla griglia*.

barbed wire [bɑːbd-] *n* filo *m* spinato.

barber ['bɑːbəʳ] *n* barbiere *m*; **~'s** *(shop)* barbiere *m*.

bar code *n* codice *m* a barre.

bare [beəʳ] *adj (feet, arms)* nudo(-a); *(head)* scoperto(-a); *(room, cupboard)* vuoto(-a); **the ~ minimum** il minimo indispensabile.

barefoot [,beə'fʊt] *adv* a piedi nudi.

barely ['beəlɪ] *adv (hardly)* appena; *(with difficulty)* a malapena.

bargain ['bɑːgɪn] ◇ *n (agreement)* accordo *m*; *(cheap buy)* occasione *f* ◇ *vi (haggle)* contrattare sul prezzo.

◆ **bargain for** *vt fus* aspettarsi.

bargain basement *n* reparto *m* occasioni.

barge [bɑːdʒ] *n* chiatta *f*.

◆ **barge in** *vi* fare irruzione; **to ~ in on sb** interrompere qn.

bark [bɑːk] ◇ *n (of tree)* corteccia *f* ◇ *vi* abbaiare.

barley ['bɑːlɪ] *n* orzo *m*.

barmaid ['bɑːmeɪd] *n* barista *f*.

barman ['bɑːmən] (*pl* **-men** [-mən]) *n* barista *m*.

bar meal *n pasto leggero servito in un bar o un pub*.

barn [bɑːn] *n* granaio *m*.

barometer [bə'rɒmɪtəʳ] *n* barometro *m*.

baron ['bærən] *n* barone *m*.

baroque [bə'rɒk] *adj* barocco(-a).

barracks ['bærəks] *npl* caserma *f*.

barrage ['bærɑːʒ] *n (of questions)* raffica *f*; *(of criticism)* ondata *f*.

barrel ['bærəl] *n (of beer, wine, oil)* barile *m*; *(of gun)* canna *f*.

barren [ˈbærən] *adj (land, soil)* sterile.
barricade [ˌbærɪˈkeɪd] *n* barricata *f*.
barrier [ˈbærɪəʳ] *n* barriera *f*.
barrister [ˈbærɪstəʳ] *n (Br)* avvocato *m*.
bartender [ˈbɑːtendəʳ] *n (Am)* barista *m*.
barter [ˈbɑːtəʳ] *vi* barattare.
base [beɪs] ◇ *n* base *f* ◇ *vt*: **to ~ sthg on** basare qc su; **I'm ~d in London** ho base a Londra.
baseball [ˈbeɪsbɔːl] *n* baseball *m*.
baseball cap *n* cappellino *m* da baseball.
basement [ˈbeɪsmənt] *n* seminterrato *m*.
bases [ˈbeɪsiːz] *pl* → **basis**.
bash [bæʃ] *vt (inf)* sbattere.
basic [ˈbeɪsɪk] *adj (fundamental)* fondamentale; *(accommodation, meal)* semplice.
◆ **basics** *npl*: **the ~s** i rudimenti.
basically [ˈbeɪsɪklɪ] *adv (in conversation)* in sostanza; *(fundamentally)* fondamentalmente.
basil [ˈbæzl] *n* basilico *m*.
basin [ˈbeɪsn] *n (washbasin)* lavabo *m*; *(bowl)* terrina *f*.
basis [ˈbeɪsɪs] (*pl* **-ses**) *n* base *f*; **on a weekly ~** settimanalmente; **on the ~ of** sulla base di.
basket [ˈbɑːskɪt] *n* cesto *m*.
basketball [ˈbɑːskɪtbɔːl] *n (game)* pallacanestro *f*.
basmati rice [bəzˈmæti-] *n tipo di riso aromatico utilizzato nella cucina indiana*.
bass[1] [beɪs] ◇ *n (singer)* basso *m* ◇ *adj*: **~ guitar** basso *m*.
bass[2] [bæs] *n (freshwater fish)* pesce *m* persico; *(sea fish)* spigola *f*, branzino *m*.
bassoon [bəˈsuːn] *n* fagotto *m*.
bastard [ˈbɑːstəd] *n (vulg)* stronzo *m* (-a *f*).
bat [bæt] *n (in cricket, baseball)* mazza *f*; *(in table tennis)* racchetta *f*; *(animal)* pipistrello *m*.
batch [bætʃ] *n (of goods)* lotto *m*; *(of people)* scaglione *m*.
bath [bɑːθ] ◇ *n* bagno *m*; *(tub)* vasca *f* (da bagno) ◇ *vt* fare il bagno a; **to have a ~** fare il OR un bagno.
◆ **baths** *npl (Br: public swimming pool)* piscina *f*.
bathe [beɪð] *vi* fare il bagno.
bathing [ˈbeɪðɪŋ] *n (Br)* balneazione *f*.
bathrobe [ˈbɑːθrəʊb] *n (for bathroom, swimming pool)* accappatoio *m*; *(dressing gown)* vestaglia *f*.
bathroom [ˈbɑːθrʊm] *n* bagno *m*.
bathroom cabinet *n* armadietto *m* del bagno.
bathtub [ˈbɑːθtʌb] *n* vasca *f* da bagno.
baton [ˈbætən] *n (of conductor)* bacchetta *f*; *(truncheon)* manganello *m*.
batter [ˈbætəʳ] ◇ *n* (CULIN) pastella *f* ◇ *vt (wife, child)* picchiare.
battered [ˈbætəd] *adj* (CULIN) *ricoperto di pastella e fritto*.
battery [ˈbætərɪ] *n (for radio)* pila *f*; *(for car)* batteria *f*.
battery charger [-ˌtʃɑːdʒəʳ] *n* caricabatteria *m inv*.
battle [ˈbætl] *n* battaglia *f*.
battlefield [ˈbætlfiːld] *n* campo *m* di battaglia.
battlements [ˈbætlmənts] *npl* parapetto *m*.
battleship [ˈbætlʃɪp] *n* corazzata *f*.
bay [beɪ] *n (on coast)* baia *f*; *(for parking)* posto *m* macchina.
bay leaf *n* foglia *f* d'alloro.
bay window *n* bow-window *m inv*.
B & B *abbr* = **bed and breakfast**.
BC *(abbr of before Christ)* a.C.

be [biː] (*pt* **was, were,** *pp* **been**) ◇ *vi* **1.** *(exist)* essere; **there is** c'è; **there are** ci sono; **are there any shops near here?** ci sono dei negozi qui vicino?
2. *(referring to location)* essere; **the hotel is near the airport** l'albergo è OR si trova vicino all'aeroporto.
3. *(referring to movement)*: **has the postman been?** è venuto il postino?; **have you ever been to Ireland?** sei mai stato in Irlanda?; **I'll ~ there in ten minutes** sarò lì tra dieci minuti.
4. *(occur)* essere; **my birthday is in November** il mio compleanno è in novembre.
5. *(identifying, describing)* essere; **he's a doctor** è medico; **I'm Italian** sono italiano; **I'm hot/cold** ho caldo/freddo.
6. *(referring to health)* stare; **how are you?** come sta?; **I'm fine** sto bene; **she's ill** è malata.
7. *(referring to age)*: **how old are you?** quanti anni hai?; **I'm 14 (years old)** ho 14 anni.
8. *(referring to cost)* costare; **how much is it?** *(item)* quanto costa?; *(meal, shopping)* quant'è?; **it's £10** *(item)* costa 10 sterline; *(meal, shopping)* sono 10 sterline.
9. *(referring to time, dates)* essere; **what time is it?** che ore sono?; **it's ten o'clock** sono le dieci; **it's the 9th of April** è il 9 aprile.
10. *(referring to measurement)* essere; **it's 2 m wide/long** è largo/lungo 2 m; **I'm 6 feet tall** sono alto 1 metro e 80; **I'm 8 stone** peso 50 chili.
11. *(referring to weather)* fare; **it's hot/cold** fa caldo/freddo; **it's sunny** c'è il sole; **it's windy** c'è vento; **it's going to be nice today** oggi farà bello.
◇ *aux vb* **1.** *(forming continuous tense)*: **I'm learning Italian** sto imparando l'italiano; **what are you reading?** cosa stai leggendo?, cosa leggi?; **he's arriving tomorrow** arriva domani, arriverà domani; **we've been visiting the museum** abbiamo visitato il museo.
2. *(forming passive)* essere; **the flight was delayed** il volo è stato ritardato.
3. *(with infinitive to express order)*: **all rooms are to ~ vacated by 10 a.m.** tutte le camere devono essere lasciate libere per le 10.
4. *(with infinitive to express future tense)*: **the race is to start at noon** la corsa è prevista per mezzogiorno.
5. *(in tag questions)*: **it's cold, isn't it?** fa freddo, (non è) vero?

beach [biːtʃ] *n* spiaggia *f*.

bead [biːd] *n (of glass, wood etc)* grano *m*.

beak [biːk] *n* becco *m*.

beaker ['biːkəʳ] *n* bicchiere *m*.

beam [biːm] ◇ *n (of light)* raggio *m*; *(of wood, concrete)* trave *f* ◇ *vi (smile)* sorridere.

bean [biːn] *n* fagiolo *m*; *(of coffee)* chicco *m*.

bean curd [-kɜːd] *n* tofu *m*.

beansprouts ['biːnspraʊts] *npl* germogli *mpl* di soia.

bear [beəʳ] (*pt* **bore,** *pp* **borne**) ◇ *n (animal)* orso *m* ◇ *vt (support)* reggere; *(endure)* sopportare; **to ~ left/right** tenersi sulla sinistra/destra.

bearable ['beərəbl] *adj* sopportabile.

beard [bɪəd] *n* barba *f*.

bearer ['beərəʳ] *n (of cheque)* portatore *m*; *(of passport)* titolare *mf*.

bearing ['beərɪŋ] *n (relevance)* attinenza *f*; **to get one's ~s** orizzontarsi.

beast [biːst] *n* bestia *f*.

beat [biːt] (*pt* **beat,** *pp* **beaten**

[biːtn]) ◇ *n (of heart, pulse)* battito *m*; (MUS) tempo *m* ◇ *vt* battere; *(eggs, cream)* sbattere.

◆ **beat down** ◇ *vi (sun, rain)* battere ◇ *vt sep*: **I ~ him down to £20** gli ho fatto abbassare il prezzo a 20 sterline.

◆ **beat up** *vt sep* pestare.

beautiful [ˈbjuːtɪfʊl] *adj* bello(-a).

beauty [ˈbjuːtɪ] *n* bellezza *f*.

beauty parlour *n* istituto *m* di bellezza.

beauty spot *n (place)* bellezza *f* naturale.

beaver [ˈbiːvəʳ] *n* castoro *m*.

became [bɪˈkeɪm] *pt* → **become**.

because [bɪˈkɒz] *conj* perché; **~ of** a causa di.

beckon [ˈbekən] *vi*: **to ~ (to)** fare cenno (a).

become [bɪˈkʌm] (*pt* **became**, *pp* **become**) *vi* diventare; **what became of him?** cosa ne è stato di lui?

bed [bed] *n* letto *m*; *(of sea)* fondo *m*; (CULIN) strato *m*; **in ~** a letto; **to get out of ~** alzarsi; **to go to ~** andare a letto; **to go to ~ with sb** andare a letto con qn; **to make the ~** fare il letto.

bed and breakfast *n (Br)* = pensione *f*.

bedclothes [ˈbedkləʊðz] *npl* lenzuola *fpl* e coperte *fpl*.

bedding [ˈbedɪŋ] *n* biancheria *f* da letto.

bed linen *n* lenzuola *fpl* (e federe *fpl*).

bedroom [ˈbedrʊm] *n* camera *f* da letto.

bedside table [ˈbedsaɪd-] *n* comodino *m*.

bedsit [ˈbedˌsɪt] *n (Br)* camera *f* ammobiliata.

bedspread [ˈbedspred] *n* copriletto *m inv*.

bedtime [ˈbedtaɪm] *n* ora *f* di andare a letto.

bee [biː] *n* ape *f*.

beech [biːtʃ] *n* faggio *m*.

beef [biːf] *n* manzo *m*; **~ Wellington** pasticcio *m* di manzo.

beefburger [ˈbiːfˌbɜːgəʳ] *n* hamburger *m inv*.

beehive [ˈbiːhaɪv] *n* alveare *m*.

been [biːn] *pp* → **be**.

beer [bɪəʳ] *n* birra *f*.

beer garden *n giardino per i clienti di un pub*.

beer mat *n* sottobicchiere *m*.

beetle [ˈbiːtl] *n* scarabeo *m*.

beetroot [ˈbiːtruːt] *n* barbabietola *f*.

before [bɪˈfɔːʳ] ◇ *adv* prima ◇ *prep* prima di; *(fml: in front of)* davanti a ◇ *conj*: **~ it gets too late** prima che sia troppo tardi; **I've been there ~** ci sono già stato; **~ doing sthg** prima di fare qc; **~ you leave** prima di partire; **the day ~** il giorno prima; **the week ~ last** due settimane fa.

beforehand [bɪˈfɔːhænd] *adv* in anticipo.

befriend [bɪˈfrend] *vt* trattare da amico.

beg [beg] ◇ *vi* elemosinare ◇ *vt*: **to ~ sb to do sthg** supplicare qn di fare qc; **to ~ for sthg** elemosinare qc.

began [bɪˈgæn] *pt* → **begin**.

beggar [ˈbegəʳ] *n* mendicante *mf*.

begin [bɪˈgɪn] (*pt* **began**, *pp* **begun**) *vt & vi* cominciare, iniziare; **to ~ doing** OR **to do sthg** cominciare a fare qc; **to ~ by doing sthg** cominciare col fare qc; **to ~ with** *(at the start)* all'inizio; *(firstly)* per prima cosa.

beginner [bɪˈgɪnəʳ] *n* principiante *mf*.

beginning [bɪˈgɪnɪŋ] *n* inizio *m*.

begun [bɪˈgʌn] *pp* → **begin**.

behalf [bɪˈhɑːf] *n*: **on ~ of** a nome di.

behave [bɪˈheɪv] *vi* comportarsi; **to ~ (o.s.)** *(be good)* comportarsi bene.

behavior [bɪ'heɪvjəʳ] *(Am)* = **behaviour**.

behaviour [bɪ'heɪvjəʳ] *n* comportamento *m*.

behind [bɪ'haɪnd] ◇ *adv (at the back)* dietro; *(late)* indietro ◇ *prep (at the back of)* dietro ◇ *n (inf)* didietro *m*; **to leave sthg ~** dimenticare qc; **to stay ~** restare indietro; **we're all ~ you** *(supporting)* siamo tutti con te.

beige [beɪʒ] *adj* beige *(inv)*.

being ['biːɪŋ] *n* essere *m*; **to come into ~** nascere.

belated [bɪ'leɪtɪd] *adj* tardivo(-a).

belch [beltʃ] *vi* ruttare.

Belgian ['beldʒən] ◇ *adj* belga ◇ *n* belga *mf*.

Belgian waffle *n (Am) cialda dalla caratteristica superficie a quadretti che si mangia con sciroppo d'acero, panna o frutta.*

Belgium ['beldʒəm] *n* il Belgio.

belief [bɪ'liːf] *n (faith)* fede *f*; *(opinion)* convinzione *f*.

believe [bɪ'liːv] ◇ *vt* credere ◇ *vi*: **to ~ in** *(God)* credere in; **to ~ in doing sthg** credere che sia giusto fare qc.

believer [bɪ'liːvəʳ] *n* credente *mf*.

bell [bel] *n (of church)* campana *f*; *(of phone)* suoneria *f*; *(of door)* campanello *m*.

bellboy ['belbɔɪ] *n* fattorino *m* d'albergo.

bellow ['beləʊ] *vi* muggire.

belly ['belɪ] *n (inf)* pancia *f*.

belly button *n (inf)* ombelico *m*.

belong [bɪ'lɒŋ] *vi (be in right place)* essere al suo posto; **to ~ to** *(property)* appartenere a; *(to club, party)* far parte di; **where does this ~?** dove sta questo?

belongings [bɪ'lɒŋɪŋz] *npl* effetti *mpl* personali.

below [bɪ'ləʊ] ◇ *adv* sotto; *(downstairs)* di sotto; *(in text)* qui sotto ◇ *prep* sotto.

belt [belt] *n (for clothes)* cintura *f*; (TECH) cinghia *f*.

beltway ['beltweɪ] *n (Am)* raccordo *m* anulare.

bench [bentʃ] *n* panchina *f*.

bend [bend] (*pt & pp* **bent**) ◇ *n (in road)* curva *f*; *(in river)* ansa *f*; *(in pipe)* gomito *m* ◇ *vt* piegare ◇ *vi (road, river, pipe)* fare una curva.

◆ **bend down** *vi* abbassarsi.

◆ **bend over** *vi* chinarsi.

beneath [bɪ'niːθ] *adv & prep* sotto.

beneficial [ˌbenɪ'fɪʃl] *adj* benefico(-a).

benefit ['benɪfɪt] ◇ *n (advantage)* beneficio *m*; *(money)* indennità *f inv* ◇ *vt* giovare a ◇ *vi*: **to ~ (from)** beneficiare (di); **for the ~ of** per.

benign [bɪ'naɪn] *adj* (MED) benigno(-a).

bent [bent] *pt & pp* → **bend**.

bereaved [bɪ'riːvd] *adj (family)* del defunto.

beret ['bereɪ] *n* basco *m*.

Bermuda shorts [bə'mjuːdə-] *npl* bermuda *mpl*.

berry ['berɪ] *n* bacca *f*.

berserk [bə'zɜːk] *adj*: **to go ~** andare su tutte le furie.

berth [bɜːθ] *n (for ship)* ormeggio *m*; *(in ship, train)* cuccetta *f*.

beside [bɪ'saɪd] *prep (next to)* accanto a; **that's ~ the point** questo non c'entra.

besides [bɪ'saɪdz] ◇ *adv* inoltre ◇ *prep* oltre a.

best [best] ◇ *adj* migliore ◇ *adv* meglio ◇ *n*: **the ~** il migliore (la migliore); **a pint of ~** *(beer)* = un boccale di birra scura; **I like this one ~** questo mi piace più di tutti; **she played ~** ha giocato meglio di tutti; **the ~ thing to do is ...** la miglior cosa da fare è ...; **to make the ~ of sthg** accontentarsi di qc; **to do one's ~** fare del proprio meglio; '**~ before ...**' 'da consumarsi preferibilmente entro ...'; **at ~** per bene che vada; **all the ~!** auguri!

best man *n* testimone *m* (di nozze).

best-seller [-'seləʳ] *n (book)* best seller *m inv*.

bet [bet] (*pt & pp* **bet**) ◇ *n* scommessa *f* ◇ *vt* scommettere ◇ *vi*: **to ~ (on)** scommettere (su); **I ~ (that) you can't do it** scommetto che non sei capace di farlo.

betray [bɪ'treɪ] *vt* tradire.

better ['betəʳ] ◇ *adj* migliore ◇ *adv* meglio; **she's ~ at tennis than me** è più brava di me a tennis; **are you ~ now?** stai meglio adesso?; **you had ~ ...** faresti meglio a ...; **to get ~** migliorare.

betting ['betɪŋ] *n* scommesse *fpl*.

betting shop *n (Br)* = sala *f* scommesse.

between [bɪ'twiːn] ◇ *prep* tra, fra ◇ *adv (in time)* nel frattempo; **in ~** *(in space)* in mezzo; *(in time)* nel frattempo.

beverage ['bevərɪdʒ] *n (fml)* bevanda *f*.

beware [bɪ'weəʳ] *vi*: **to ~ of** stare attento a; **'~ of the dog'** 'attenti al cane'.

bewildered [bɪ'wɪldəd] *adj* sconcertato(-a).

beyond [bɪ'jɒnd] ◇ *prep* oltre ◇ *adv* più avanti; **~ doubt** senza dubbio; **~ reach** irraggiungibile.

biased ['baɪəst] *adj* di parte.

bib [bɪb] *n (for baby)* bavaglino *m*.

bible ['baɪbl] *n* bibbia *f*.

biceps ['baɪseps] *n* bicipite *m*.

bicycle ['baɪsɪkl] *n* bicicletta *f*.

bicycle path *n* pista *f* ciclabile.

bicycle pump *n* pompa *f* per la bicicletta.

bid [bɪd] (*pt & pp* **bid**) ◇ *n (at auction)* offerta *f*; *(attempt)* tentativo *m* ◇ *vt (money)* fare un'offerta di ◇ *vi*: **to ~ (for)** fare un'offerta (per).

bidet ['biːdeɪ] *n* bidè *m inv*.

big [bɪg] *adj* grande; *(problem, mistake, risk)* grosso(-a); **my ~ brother** mio fratello maggiore; **how ~ is it?** quanto è grande?

bike [baɪk] *n (inf) (bicycle)* bici *f inv*; *(motorcycle)* moto *f inv*.

biking ['baɪkɪŋ] *n*: **to go ~** *(on bicycle)* andare in bicicletta; *(on motorcycle)* andare in moto.

bikini [bɪ'kiːnɪ] *n* bikini® *m inv*.

bikini bottom *n* pezzo *m* di sotto del bikini®.

bikini top *n* pezzo *m* di sopra del bikini®.

bilingual [baɪ'lɪŋgwəl] *adj* bilingue.

bill [bɪl] *n (for meal, hotel room)* conto *m*; *(for electricity etc)* bolletta *f*; *(Am: bank note)* banconota *f*; *(at cinema, theatre)* programma *m*; (POL) proposta *f* di legge; **can I have the ~, please?** il conto, per favore.

billboard ['bɪlbɔːd] *n* tabellone *m*.

billfold ['bɪlfəʊld] *n (Am)* portafoglio *m*.

billiards ['bɪljədz] *n* biliardo *m*.

billion ['bɪljən] *n (thousand million)* miliardo *m*; *(Br: million million)* mille miliardi.

bin [bɪn] *n (rubbish bin)* pattumiera *f*; *(wastepaper bin)* cestino *m*; *(for flour)* barattolo *m*; *(on plane)* armadietto *m* in alto; **bread ~** portapane *m inv*.

bind [baɪnd] (*pt & pp* **bound**) *vt (tie up)* legare.

binding ['baɪndɪŋ] *n (of book)* rilegatura *f*; *(for ski)* attacco *m*.

bingo ['bɪŋgəʊ] *n* = tombola *f*.

binoculars [bɪ'nɒkjʊləz] *npl* binocolo *m*.

biodegradable [ˌbaɪəʊdɪ'greɪdəbl] *adj* biodegradabile.

biography [baɪ'ɒgrəfɪ] *n* biografia *f*.

biological [ˌbaɪə'lɒdʒɪkl] *adj* biologico(-a).

biology [baɪ'ɒlədʒɪ] *n* biologia *f*.

birch [bɜːtʃ] *n* betulla *f*.

bird [bɜːd] *n* uccello *m*; *(Br: inf: woman)* pollastrella *f*.

bird-watching [-ˌwɒtʃɪŋ] *n* osservazione *f* degli uccelli.

Biro® ['baɪərəʊ] (*pl* **-s**) *n* biro® *f inv*.

birth [bɜːθ] *n* nascita *f*; **by ~** di nascita; **to give ~ to** dare alla luce, partorire.

birth certificate *n* certificato *m* di nascita.

birth control *n* controllo *m* delle nascite.

birthday ['bɜːθdeɪ] *n* compleanno *m*; **happy ~!** buon compleanno!

birthday card *n* biglietto *m* d'auguri di compleanno.

birthday party *n* festa *f* di compleanno.

birthplace ['bɜːθpleɪs] *n* luogo *m* di nascita.

biscuit ['bɪskɪt] *n (Br)* biscotto *m*; *(Am: scone) focaccina di pasta non lievitata da mangiare con burro e marmellata o insieme a piatti salati.*

bishop ['bɪʃəp] *n* (RELIG) vescovo *m*; *(in chess)* alfiere *m*.

bistro ['biːstrəʊ] (*pl* **-s**) *n* ristorantino *m*.

bit [bɪt] ◇ *pt* → **bite** ◇ *n (piece)* pezzetto *m*; *(of drill)* punta *f*; *(of bridle)* morso *m*; *(amount)*: **a ~** un po'; **a ~ of money** un po' di soldi; **to do a ~ of reading** leggere un po'; **not a ~** per niente; **~ by ~** a poco a poco.

bitch [bɪtʃ] *n (vulg: woman)* stronza *f*; *(dog)* cagna *f*.

bite [baɪt] (*pt* **bit**, *pp* **bitten**) ◇ *n* morso *m*; *(from insect)* puntura *f* ◇ *vt* mordere; *(subj: insect)* pungere; **to have a ~ to eat** mangiare un boccone.

bitter ['bɪtəʳ] ◇ *adj (taste, food)* amaro(-a); *(weather, wind)* pungente; *(person)* amareggiato(-a); *(argument, conflict)* aspro(-a) ◇ *n (Br: beer) tipo di birra amarognola.*

bitter lemon *n* limonata *f* amara.

bizarre [bɪ'zɑːʳ] *adj* bizzarro(-a).

black [blæk] ◇ *adj* nero(-a) ◇ *n (colour)* nero *m*; *(person)* negro *m* (-a *f*).

◆ **black out** *vi* perdere conoscenza.

black and white *adj* in bianco e nero.

blackberry ['blækbrɪ] *n* mora *f*.

blackbird ['blækbɜːd] *n* merlo *m*.

blackboard ['blækbɔːd] *n* lavagna *f*.

black cherry *n* ciliegia *f* nera.

blackcurrant [ˌblæk'kʌrənt] *n* ribes *m inv* nero.

black eye *n* occhio *m* nero.

Black Forest gâteau *n* torta *f* di cioccolato e panna.

black ice *n* strato *m* di ghiaccio invisibile.

blackmail ['blækmeɪl] ◇ *n* ricatto *m* ◇ *vt* ricattare.

blackout ['blækaʊt] *n (power cut)* black-out *m inv*.

black pepper *n* pepe *m* nero.

black pudding *n (Br)* sanguinaccio *m*.

blacksmith ['blæksmɪθ] *n* fabbro *m*.

bladder ['blædəʳ] *n* vescica *f*.

blade [bleɪd] *n (of knife, saw)* lama *f*; *(of propeller, oar)* pala *f*; *(of grass)* filo *m*.

blame [bleɪm] ◇ *n* colpa *f* ◇ *vt* incolpare; **to ~ sb for sthg** incolpare qn di qc; **to ~ sthg on sb** dare a qn la colpa di qc.

bland [blænd] *adj (food)* insipido(-a).

blank [blæŋk] ◇ *adj (space, cassette)* vuoto(-a); *(page)* bianco(-a);

(expression) assente ◇ *n (empty space)* spazio *m* (in) bianco.

blank cheque *n* assegno *m* in bianco.

blanket ['blæŋkɪt] *n* coperta *f*.

blast [blɑ:st] ◇ *n (explosion)* esplosione *f*; *(of wind)* raffica *f*; *(of air)* folata *f* ◇ *excl (inf)* maledizione!; **at full ~** a tutto volume.

blaze [bleɪz] ◇ *n (fire)* incendio *m* ◇ *vi (fire)* ardere; *(sun, light)* risplendere.

blazer ['bleɪzəʳ] *n* blazer *m inv*.

bleach [bli:tʃ] ◇ *n* candeggina *f* ◇ *vt (clothes)* candeggiare; *(hair)* decolorare.

bleak [bli:k] *adj* triste.

bleed [bli:d] (*pt & pp* **bled** [bled]) *vi* sanguinare.

blend [blend] ◇ *n (of coffee, whisky)* miscela *f* ◇ *vt* mescolare.

blender ['blendəʳ] *n* frullatore *m*.

bless [bles] *vt* benedire; **~ you!** *(said after sneeze)* salute!

blessing ['blesɪŋ] *n* benedizione *f*.

blew [blu:] *pt* → **blow**.

blind [blaɪnd] ◇ *adj* cieco(-a) ◇ *n (for window)* tendina *f* avvolgibile ◇ *npl*: **the ~** i non vedenti.

blind corner *n* svolta *f* senza visibilità.

blindfold ['blaɪndfəʊld] ◇ *n* benda *f* ◇ *vt* bendare.

blind spot *n* (AUT) punto *m* senza visibilità.

blink [blɪŋk] *vi* battere le palpebre.

blinkers ['blɪŋkəz] *npl (Br)* paraocchi *mpl*.

bliss [blɪs] *n* estasi *f*.

blister ['blɪstəʳ] *n* vescica *f*.

blizzard ['blɪzəd] *n* bufera *f* di neve.

bloated ['bləʊtɪd] *adj (after eating)* strapieno(-a).

blob [blɒb] *n (of paint)* chiazza *f*.

block [blɒk] ◇ *n (of stone, wood, ice)* blocco *m*; *(building)* palazzo *m*; *(Am: in town, city)* isolato *m* ◇ *vt (obstruct)* bloccare; **to have a ~ed (up) nose** avere il naso chiuso.

◆ **block up** *vt sep* ostruire.

blockage ['blɒkɪdʒ] *n* ostruzione *f*.

block capitals *npl* stampatello *m* maiuscolo.

block of flats *n* condominio *m*.

bloke [bləʊk] *n (Br: inf)* tipo *m*, tizio *m*.

blond [blɒnd] ◇ *adj* biondo(-a) ◇ *n* biondo *m*.

blonde [blɒnd] ◇ *adj* biondo(-a) ◇ *n* bionda *f*.

blood [blʌd] *n* sangue *m*.

blood donor *n* donatore *m* (-trice *f*) di sangue.

blood group *n* gruppo *m* sanguigno.

blood poisoning *n* setticemia *f*.

blood pressure *n* pressione *f* sanguigna; **to have high ~** avere la pressione alta; **to have low ~** avere la pressione bassa.

bloodshot ['blʌdʃɒt] *adj* arrossato(-a).

blood test *n* analisi *f inv* del sangue.

blood transfusion *n* trasfusione *f* di sangue.

bloody ['blʌdɪ] ◇ *adj (hands, handkerchief)* insanguinato(-a); *(Br: vulg: damn)* maledetto(-a) ◇ *adv (Br: vulg)* veramente.

bloody mary [-'meərɪ] *n* Bloody Mary *m inv*.

bloom [blu:m] ◇ *n* fiore *m* ◇ *vi* fiorire; **in ~** in fiore.

blossom ['blɒsəm] *n* fiori *mpl*.

blot [blɒt] *n* macchia *f*.

blotch [blɒtʃ] *n* chiazza *f*.

blotting paper ['blɒtɪŋ-] *n* carta *f* assorbente.

blouse [blaʊz] *n* camicetta *f*.

blow [bləʊ] (*pt* **blew**, *pp* **blown**) ◇

vt (subj: wind) soffiare; *(whistle, trumpet)* suonare; *(bubbles)* fare ◇ *vi* soffiare; *(fuse)* saltare ◇ *n* colpo *m*; **to ~ one's nose** soffiarsi il naso.
◆ **blow up** ◇ *vt sep (cause to explode)* far saltare in aria; *(inflate)* gonfiare ◇ *vi (explode)* saltare in aria.
blow-dry ◇ *n* piega *f* föhn ◇ *vt* fonare.
blown [bləʊn] *pp* → **blow**.
BLT *n panino imbottito con pancetta, lattuga e pomodoro.*
blue [blu:] ◇ *adj* azzurro(-a); *(film)* spinto(-a) ◇ *n* azzurro *m*.
◆ **blues** *n* (MUS) blues *m*.
bluebell ['blu:bel] *n* campanula *f*.
blueberry ['blu:bərɪ] *n* mirtillo *m*.
bluebottle ['blu:ˌbɒtl] *n* moscone *m*.
blue cheese *n formaggio con muffa di stagionatura.*
bluff [blʌf] ◇ *n (cliff)* promontorio *m* ◇ *vi* bleffare.
blunder ['blʌndər] *n* cantonata *f*.
blunt [blʌnt] *adj (pencil)* spuntato(-a); *(knife)* non affilato(-a); *(fig: person)* brusco(-a).
blurred [blɜ:d] *adj (photo)* sfocato(-a); *(vision)* offuscato(-a).
blush [blʌʃ] *vi* arrossire.
blusher ['blʌʃər] *n* fard *m inv*.
blustery ['blʌstərɪ] *adj* burrascoso(-a).
board [bɔ:d] ◇ *n (plank)* tavola *f*; *(notice board, for games)* tabellone *m*; *(for chess)* scacchiera *f*; *(blackboard)* lavagna *f*; *(of company)* consiglio *m* d'amministrazione ◇ *vt (plane, ship)* imbarcarsi su; *(bus)* salire su; **~ and lodging** vitto e alloggio; **full ~** pensione *f* completa; **half ~** mezza pensione; **on ~** *adv* a bordo ◇ *prep* su.
board game *n* gioco *m* di società.
boarding ['bɔ:dɪŋ] *n* imbarco *m*.
boarding card *n* carta *f* d'imbarco.
boardinghouse ['bɔ:dɪŋhaʊs, *pl* -haʊzɪz] *n* pensione *f*.
boarding school *n* collegio *m*.
board of directors *n* consiglio *m* d'amministrazione.
boast [bəʊst] *vi*: **to ~ (about sthg)** vantarsi (di qc).
boat [bəʊt] *n (small)* barca *f*; *(large)* nave *f*; **by ~** in barca.
bob [bɒb] *n (hairstyle)* carré *m inv*.
bobby pin ['bɒbɪ-] *n (Am)* forcina *f*.
bodice ['bɒdɪs] *n* corpino *m*.
body ['bɒdɪ] *n* corpo *m*; *(of car)* carrozzeria *f*; *(organization)* organismo *m*.
bodyguard ['bɒdɪgɑ:d] *n (person)* guardia *f* del corpo.
bodywork ['bɒdɪwɜ:k] *n* carrozzeria *f*.
bog [bɒg] *n* pantano *m*.
bogus ['bəʊgəs] *adj* falso(-a).
boil [bɔɪl] ◇ *vt (water)* bollire, far bollire; *(kettle)* mettere a bollire; *(food)* lessare ◇ *vi* bollire ◇ *n (on skin)* foruncolo *m*.
boiled egg [bɔɪld-] *n* uovo *m* alla coque.
boiled potatoes [bɔɪld-] *npl* patate *fpl* lesse.
boiler ['bɔɪlər] *n* caldaia *f*.
boiling (hot) ['bɔɪlɪŋ-] *adj (inf) (water)* bollente; **I'm ~** sto morendo di caldo; **it's ~** si scoppia dal caldo.
bold [bəʊld] *adj (brave)* audace.
bollard ['bɒlɑ:d] *n (Br: on road)* colonnina *f* spartitraffico.
bolt [bəʊlt] ◇ *n (on door, window)* chiavistello *m*; *(screw)* bullone *m* ◇ *vt (door, window)* sprangare.
bomb [bɒm] ◇ *n* bomba *f* ◇ *vt* bombardare.
bombard [bɒm'bɑ:d] *vt* bombardare.
bomb scare *n allarme causato dalla presunta presenza di una bomba.*

bomb shelter *n* rifugio *m* antiaereo.

bond [bɒnd] *n (tie, connection)* legame *m*.

bone [bəʊn] *n (of person, animal)* osso *m*; *(of fish)* lisca *f*.

boned [bəʊnd] *adj (chicken)* disossato(-a); *(fish)* senza lische.

boneless ['bəʊnləs] *adj (chicken, pork)* disossato(-a).

bonfire ['bɒn,faɪəʳ] *n* falò *m inv*.

bonnet ['bɒnɪt] *n (Br: of car)* cofano *m*.

bonus ['bəʊnəs] (*pl* **-es**) *n (extra money)* gratifica *f*; *(additional advantage)* extra *m inv*.

bony ['bəʊnɪ] *adj (fish)* pieno(-a) di spine; *(chicken)* pieno di ossi.

boo [buː] *vi* fischiare.

boogie ['buːgɪ] *vi (inf)* ballare.

book [bʊk] ◇ *n* libro *m*; *(for writing in)* quaderno *m*; *(of tickets, stamps)* blocchetto *m*; *(of matches)* pacchetto *m* ◇ *vt (reserve)* prenotare.

◆ **book in** *vi (at hotel)* registrarsi.

bookable ['bʊkəbl] *adj (seats, flight)* prenotabile.

bookcase ['bʊkkeɪs] *n* libreria *f*.

booking ['bʊkɪŋ] *n (reservation)* prenotazione *f*.

booking office *n (at theatre)* botteghino *m*; *(at station)* ufficio *m* prenotazioni.

bookkeeping ['bʊk,kiːpɪŋ] *n* contabilità *f*.

booklet ['bʊklɪt] *n* opuscolo *m*.

bookmaker's ['bʊk,meɪkəz] *n* = sala *f* scommesse.

bookmark ['bʊkmɑːk] *n* segnalibro *m*.

bookshelf ['bʊkʃelf] (*pl* **-shelves** [-ʃelvz]) *n* scaffale *m*.

bookshop ['bʊkʃɒp] *n* libreria *f*.

bookstall ['bʊkstɔːl] *n* bancarella *f* di libri.

bookstore ['bʊkstɔːʳ] = **bookshop**.

book token *n* buono *m* libri.

boom [buːm] ◇ *n (sudden growth)* boom *m inv* ◇ *vi (voice, guns)* tuonare.

boost [buːst] *vt (profits, production)* incrementare; *(confidence)* aumentare; *(spirits)* sollevare.

booster ['buːstəʳ] *n (injection)* richiamo *m*.

boot [buːt] *n (shoe)* stivale *m*; *(for walking)* scarpone *m*; *(for football)* scarpetta *f*; *(Br: of car)* bagagliaio *m*.

booth [buːð] *n (for telephone)* cabina *f*; *(at fairground)* baraccone *m*.

booze [buːz] ◇ *n (inf)* alcool *m* ◇ *vi (inf)* sbevazzare.

bop [bɒp] *n (inf: dance)*: **to have a ~** ballare.

border ['bɔːdəʳ] *n (of country)* frontiera *f*; *(edge)* orlo *m*; **the Borders** *zona di confine fra Inghilterra e Scozia*.

bore [bɔːʳ] ◇ *pt* → **bear** ◇ *n (inf)* noia *f* ◇ *vt (person)* annoiare; *(hole)* praticare.

bored [bɔːd] *adj* annoiato(-a).

boredom ['bɔːdəm] *n* noia *f*.

boring ['bɔːrɪŋ] *adj* noioso(-a).

born [bɔːn] *adj*: **to be ~** nascere.

borne [bɔːn] *pp* → **bear**.

borough ['bʌrə] *n* = comune *m*.

borrow ['bɒrəʊ] *vt*: **to ~ sthg (from sb)** prendere in prestito qc (da qn).

bosom ['bʊzəm] *n* seno *m*.

boss [bɒs] *n* capo *m*.

◆ **boss around** *vt sep* dare ordini a.

bossy ['bɒsɪ] *adj* autoritario(-a).

botanical garden [bə'tænɪkl-] *n* giardino *m* botanico.

both [bəʊθ] ◇ *adj & pron* tutti(-e) e due, entrambi(-e) ◇ *adv*: **~ ... and** sia ... sia, sia ... che; **it is ~ stupid and dangerous** è stupido e pericoloso insieme; **~ of them**

entrambi, tutti e due; ~ **of us** entrambi, tutti e due.
bother ['bɒðəʳ] ◇ *vt (worry)* preoccupare; *(annoy, pester)* disturbare ◇ *vi* preoccuparsi ◇ *n (trouble)* fatica *f*; **I can't be ~ed** non ne ho voglia; **don't ~, I'll go!** non ti scomodare, vado io!; **it's no ~!** non c'è problema!
bottle ['bɒtl] *n* bottiglia *f*; *(for baby)* biberon *m inv*.
bottle bank *n* campana *f* per la raccolta del vetro.
bottled ['bɒtld] *adj* imbottigliato(-a); ~ **beer** birra in bottiglia; ~ **water** acqua minerale.
bottle opener [-,əʊpnəʳ] *n* apribottiglie *m inv*.
bottom ['bɒtəm] ◇ *adj (lowest, last)* ultimo(-a); *(worst)* più basso(-a) ◇ *n* fondo *m*; *(of hill)* piedi *mpl*; *(buttocks)* sedere *m*; **the ~ shelf** l'ultimo scaffale in basso; ~ **gear** prima *f*.
bought [bɔːt] *pt & pp* → **buy**.
boulder ['bəʊldəʳ] *n* masso *m*.
bounce [baʊns] *vi (rebound)* rimbalzare; *(jump)* saltare; *(cheque)* essere scoperto.
bouncer ['baʊnsəʳ] *n (inf)* buttafuori *m inv*.
bouncy ['baʊnsɪ] *adj (person)* pimpante.
bound [baʊnd] ◇ *pt & pp* → **bind** ◇ *vi* saltellare ◇ *adj*: **it's ~ to rain** pioverà di sicuro; **to be ~ for** essere diretto(-a) a; **it's out of ~s** l'accesso è vietato.
boundary ['baʊndrɪ] *n* confine *m*.
bouquet [bʊ'keɪ] *n* bouquet *m inv*; *(big bunch of flowers)* mazzo *m* di fiori.
bourbon ['bɜːbən] *n* bourbon *m inv*.
bout [baʊt] *n (of illness)* attacco *m*; *(of activity)* periodo *m*.
boutique [buː'tiːk] *n* boutique *f inv*.
bow[1] [baʊ] ◇ *n (of head)* inchino *m*; *(of ship)* prua *f* ◇ *vi* inchinarsi.
bow[2] [bəʊ] *n (knot)* fiocco *m*; *(weapon)* arco *m*; (MUS) archetto *m*.
bowels ['baʊəlz] *npl* (ANAT) intestino *m*.
bowl [bəʊl] *n* ciotola *f*; *(for washing)* bacinella *f*; *(of toilet)* tazza *f*; **fruit ~** fruttiera *f*; **salad ~** insalatiera *f*; **sugar ~** zuccheriera *f*.
◆ **bowls** *npl* bocce *fpl*.
bowling alley ['bəʊlɪŋ-] *n (building)* bowling *m inv*.
bowling green ['bəʊlɪŋ-] *n* campo *m* di bocce.
bow tie [,bəʊ-] *n* farfalla *f*.
box [bɒks] ◇ *n* scatola *f*; *(on form)* casella *f*; *(in theatre)* palco *m* ◇ *vi* fare del pugilato; **a ~ of chocolates** una scatola di cioccolatini; **jewellery ~** portagioie *m inv*; **tool ~** cassetta *f* degli attrezzi.
boxer ['bɒksəʳ] *n (fighter)* pugile *m*.
boxer shorts *npl* boxer *mpl*.
boxing ['bɒksɪŋ] *n* pugilato *m*.
Boxing Day *n* Santo Stefano *m*.
boxing gloves *npl* guantoni *mpl*.
boxing ring *n* ring *m inv*.
box office *n* botteghino *m*.
boy [bɔɪ] ◇ *n* ragazzo *m*; *(son)* figlio *m* ◇ *excl (inf)*: **(oh) ~!** accidenti!
boycott ['bɔɪkɒt] *vt* boicottare.
boyfriend ['bɔɪfrend] *n* ragazzo *m*.
boy scout *n* boy-scout *m inv*.
BR *abbr* = **British Rail**.
bra [brɑː] *n* reggiseno *m*.
brace [breɪs] *n (for teeth)* apparecchio *m* (per i denti).
◆ **braces** *npl (Br)* bretelle *fpl*.
bracelet ['breɪslɪt] *n* braccialetto *m*.
bracken ['brækn] *n* felce *f*.
bracket ['brækɪt] *n (written symbol)* parentesi *f inv*; *(support)* reggimensola *m inv*.
brag [bræg] *vi* vantarsi.

braid [breɪd] *n (hairstyle)* treccia *f*; *(on clothes)* passamano *m*.
brain [breɪn] *n* cervello *m*.
brainy ['breɪnɪ] *adj (inf)* sveglio(-a).
braised [breɪzd] *adj* brasato(-a).
brake [breɪk] ◇ *n* freno *m* ◇ *vi* frenare.
brake block *n* freno *m*.
brake fluid *n* fluido *m* dei freni.
brake light *n* stop *m inv*.
brake pad *n* pastiglia *f* (del freno).
brake pedal *n* (pedale *m* del) freno *m*.
bran [bræn] *n* crusca *f*.
branch [brɑːntʃ] *n* ramo *m*; *(of bank, company)* filiale *f*.
◆ **branch off** *vi* diramarsi.
branch line *n* diramazione *f*.
brand [brænd] ◇ *n* marca *f* ◇ *vt*: **to ~ sb (as)** bollare qn (come).
brand-new *adj* nuovo(-a) di zecca.
brandy ['brændɪ] *n* brandy *m inv*.
brash [bræʃ] *adj (pej)* sfrontato(-a).
brass [brɑːs] *n* ottone *m*.
brass band *n* fanfara *f*.
brasserie ['bræsərɪ] *n* = trattoria *f*.
brassiere [*Br* 'bræsɪə^r, *Am* brə'zɪr] *n* reggiseno *m*.
brat [bræt] *n (inf)* discolo *m* (-a *f*).
brave [breɪv] *adj* coraggioso(-a).
bravery ['breɪvərɪ] *n* coraggio *m*.
bravo [ˌbrɑː'vəʊ] *excl* bravo(-a)!
brawl [brɔːl] *n* rissa *f*.
Brazil [brə'zɪl] *n* il Brasile.
brazil nut *n* noce *f* del Brasile.
breach [briːtʃ] *vt (contract)* rompere; *(confidence)* tradire.
bread [bred] *n* pane *m*; **~ and butter** pane *m* imburrato.
bread bin *n (Br)* portapane *m inv*.
breadboard ['bredbɔːd] *n* tagliere *m* (per il pane).
bread box *(Am)* = **bread bin**.
breadcrumbs ['bredkrʌmz] *npl* pangrattato *m*.
breaded ['bredɪd] *adj* impanato(-a).
bread knife *n* coltello *m* da pane.
bread roll *n* panino *m*.
breadth [bretθ] *n* larghezza *f*, ampiezza *f*.
break [breɪk] (*pt* **broke**, *pp* **broken**) ◇ *n (interruption)* interruzione *f*; *(rest, pause)* pausa *f*; (SCH) ricreazione *f* ◇ *vt* rompere; *(law, rule)* infrangere; *(promise, contract)* non rispettare; *(a record)* battere ◇ *vi* rompersi; *(dawn)* spuntare; *(voice)* cambiare; **without a ~** senza sosta; **a lucky ~** un colpo di fortuna; **to ~ one's leg** rompersi la gamba; **to ~ the news to sb** dare una notizia a qn; **to ~ one's journey** fare una sosta.
◆ **break down** ◇ *vi (car, machine)* guastarsi ◇ *vt sep (door, barrier)* abbattere.
◆ **break in** *vi (enter by force)* fare irruzione.
◆ **break off** ◇ *vt (detach)* staccare; *(holiday)* interrompere ◇ *vi (stop suddenly)* interrompersi.
◆ **break out** *vi (fire, war, panic)* scoppiare; **he broke out in a rash** gli è venuto uno sfogo.
◆ **break up** *vi (with spouse, partner)* lasciarsi; *(meeting, marriage, school)* finire.
breakage ['breɪkɪdʒ] *n* danni *mpl*.
breakdown ['breɪkdaʊn] *n (of car)* guasto *m*; *(in communications, negotiation)* interruzione *f*; *(mental)* esaurimento *m* nervoso.
breakdown truck *n* carro *m* attrezzi.
breakfast ['brekfəst] *n* colazione *f*; **to have ~** fare colazione; **to have sthg for ~** mangiare qc a colazione.

breakfast cereal *n* cereali *mpl.*
break-in *n* scasso *m.*
breakwater ['breɪk,wɔːtəʳ] *n* frangiflutti *m inv.*
breast [brest] *n (of woman)* seno *m; (of chicken, duck)* petto *m.*
breastbone ['brestbəʊn] *n* sterno *m.*
breast-feed *vt* allattare (al seno).
breaststroke ['breststrəʊk] *n* nuoto *m* a rana.
breath [breθ] *n (of person)* alito *m; (air inhaled)* respiro *m;* **out of ~** senza fiato; **to go for a ~ of fresh air** andare a prendere una boccata d'aria.
Breathalyser® ['breθəlaɪzəʳ] *n (Br)* etilometro *m.*
Breathalyzer® ['breθəlaɪzər] *(Am)* = **Breathalyser®**.
breathe [briːð] *vi* respirare.
◆ **breathe in** *vi* inspirare.
◆ **breathe out** *vi* espirare.
breathtaking ['breθ,teɪkɪŋ] *adj* mozzafiato *(inv).*
breed [briːd] (*pt & pp* **bred** [bred]) ◇ *n (of animal)* razza *f; (of plant)* varietà *f inv* ◇ *vt (animals)* allevare ◇ *vi* riprodursi.
breeze [briːz] *n* brezza *f.*
breezy ['briːzɪ] *adj (weather, day)* ventilato(-a).
brew [bruː] ◇ *vt (tea)* fare ◇ *vi*: **the tea/coffee is ~ed** il tè/caffè è pronto.
brewery ['brʊərɪ] *n* fabbrica *f* di birra.
bribe [braɪb] ◇ *n* bustarella *f,* tangente *f* ◇ *vt* corrompere.
bric-a-brac ['brɪkəbræk] *n* cianfrusaglie *fpl.*
brick [brɪk] *n* mattone *m.*
bricklayer ['brɪk,leɪəʳ] *n* muratore *m.*
brickwork ['brɪkwɜːk] *n* muratura *f* di mattoni.
bride [braɪd] *n* sposa *f.*
bridegroom ['braɪdgrʊm] *n* sposo *m.*
bridesmaid ['braɪdzmeɪd] *n* damigella *f* d'onore.
bridge [brɪdʒ] *n* ponte *m; (card game)* bridge *m.*
bridle ['braɪdl] *n* briglia *f.*
bridle path *n* sentiero *m (per cavalli).*
brief [briːf] ◇ *adj* breve ◇ *vt* mettere al corrente; **in ~** in breve.
◆ **briefs** *npl* mutande *fpl.*
briefcase ['briːfkeɪs] *n (hard)* ventiquattr'ore *f inv; (soft)* cartella *f.*
briefly ['briːflɪ] *adv* brevemente.
brigade [brɪ'geɪd] *n* brigata *f.*
bright [braɪt] *adj (light, sun)* vivido(-a); *(weather, room, idea)* luminoso(-a); *(clever)* sveglio(-a); *(lively, cheerful, in colour)* vivace.
brilliant ['brɪljənt] *adj* brillante; *(inf: wonderful)* stupendo(-a).
brim [brɪm] *n (of hat)* tesa *f;* **it's full to the ~** è pieno fino all'orlo.
brine [braɪn] *n* salamoia *f.*
bring [brɪŋ] (*pt & pp* **brought**) *vt* portare.
◆ **bring along** *vt sep* portare.
◆ **bring back** *vt sep* riportare.
◆ **bring in** *vt sep (introduce)* introdurre; *(earn)* rendere.
◆ **bring out** *vt sep (new product)* far uscire.
◆ **bring up** *vt sep (child)* allevare; *(subject)* sollevare; *(food)* vomitare.
brink [brɪŋk] *n*: **on the ~ of sthg** sull'orlo di qc; **on the ~ of doing sthg** sul punto di fare qc.
brisk [brɪsk] *adj (quick)* rapido(-a); *(efficient)* energico(-a); *(wind)* pungente.
bristle ['brɪsl] *n (of brush)* setola *f; (on chin)* pelo *m* ispido.
Britain ['brɪtn] *n* la Gran Bretagna.
British ['brɪtɪʃ] ◇ *adj* britanni-

co(-a) ◇ *npl*: the ~ i Britannici.
British Rail *n* = le Ferrovie dello Stato.
British Telecom [-'telɪkɒm] *n* = la Telecom Italia.
Briton ['brɪtn] *n* britannico *m* (-a *f*).
brittle ['brɪtl] *adj* friabile.
broad [brɔːd] *adj* ampio(-a); *(accent)* marcato(-a).
B road *n (Br)* = strada *f* provinciale.
broad bean *n* fava *f*.
broadcast ['brɔːdkɑːst] (*pt & pp* **broadcast**) ◇ *n* trasmissione *f* ◇ *vt* trasmettere.
broadly ['brɔːdlɪ] *adv (in general)* grossomodo; ~ **speaking** in linea di massima.
broccoli ['brɒkəlɪ] *n* broccoli *mpl*.
brochure ['brəʊʃəʳ] *n* opuscolo *m*.
broiled [brɔɪld] *adj (Am)* alla griglia.
broke [brəʊk] ◇ *pt* → **break** ◇ *adj (inf)* al verde.
broken ['brəʊkn] ◇ *pp* → **break** ◇ *adj* rotto(-a); *(English, Italian)* stentato(-a).
bronchitis [brɒŋ'kaɪtɪs] *n* bronchite *f*.
bronze [brɒnz] *n* bronzo *m*.
brooch [brəʊtʃ] *n* spilla *f*.
brook [brʊk] *n* ruscello *m*.
broom [bruːm] *n* scopa *f*.
broomstick ['bruːmstɪk] *n* manico *m* di scopa.
broth [brɒθ] *n* brodo *m*.
brother ['brʌðəʳ] *n* fratello *m*.
brother-in-law *n* cognato *m*.
brought [brɔːt] *pt & pp* → **bring**.
brow [braʊ] *n (forehead)* fronte *f*; *(eyebrow)* sopracciglio *m*.
brown [braʊn] ◇ *adj (tanned)* abbronzato(-a); *(eyes, hair)* castano(-a) ◇ *n* marrone *m*.
brown bread *n* pane *m* integrale.
brownie ['braʊnɪ] *n* (CULIN) *biscotto con noci e cioccolato.*
Brownie ['braʊnɪ] *n* giovane esploratrice *f*, coccinella *f*.
brown rice *n* riso *m* integrale.
brown sauce *n (Br) salsa piccante, usata con la carne e i salumi.*
brown sugar *n* zucchero *m* di canna.
browse [braʊz] *vi (in shop)* dare un'occhiata; **to ~ through** *(book, paper)* sfogliare.
browser ['braʊzəʳ] *n*: **'~s welcome'** 'entrata libera'.
bruise [bruːz] *n* livido *m*.
brunch [brʌntʃ] *n* brunch *m inv*.
brunette [bruː'net] *n* bruna *f*.
brush [brʌʃ] ◇ *n (for hair)* spazzola *f*; *(for teeth)* spazzolino *m*; *(for painting)* pennello *m* ◇ *vt* spazzolare; *(clean, tidy)* spazzare; *(move with hand)* scostare; **to ~ one's hair** spazzolarsi i capelli; **to ~ one's teeth** lavarsi i denti.
Brussels ['brʌslz] *n* Bruxelles *f*.
brussels sprouts *npl* cavoletti *mpl* di Bruxelles.
brutal ['bruːtl] *adj* brutale.
BSc *n (abbr of Bachelor of Science) (titolare di una) laurea in discipline scientifiche.*
BT *abbr* = **British Telecom**.
bubble ['bʌbl] *n* bolla *f*.
bubble bath *n* bagnoschiuma *m inv*.
bubble gum *n* gomma *f* da masticare *(con cui si può fare le bolle)*.
bubbly ['bʌblɪ] *n (inf)* spumante *m*.
buck [bʌk] *n (Am: inf: dollar)* dollaro *m*; *(male animal)* maschio *m*.
bucket ['bʌkɪt] *n* secchio *m*.
Buckingham Palace ['bʌkɪŋəm-] *n* il Palazzo di Buckingham *(residenza della famiglia reale britannica)*.
buckle ['bʌkl] ◇ *n* fibbia *f* ◇ *vt*

(fasten) allacciare ◇ *vi (warp)* piegarsi.

buck's fizz [ˌbʌksˈfɪz] *n bibita a base di champagne e succo d'arancia.*

bud [bʌd] ◇ *n* germoglio *m* ◇ *vi* germogliare.

Buddhist [ˈbʊdɪst] *n* buddista *mf*.

buddy [ˈbʌdɪ] *n (inf)* amico *m*.

budge [bʌdʒ] *vi* spostarsi.

budgerigar [ˈbʌdʒərɪgɑːʳ] *n* pappagallino *m*.

budget [ˈbʌdʒɪt] ◇ *adj (holiday, travel)* a basso prezzo ◇ *n* bilancio *m* preventivo; **the Budget** *(Br)* la Legge finanziaria.

◆ **budget for** *vt fus*: **to ~ for sthg** preventivare la spesa di qc.

budgie [ˈbʌdʒɪ] *n (inf)* pappagallino *m*.

buff [bʌf] *n (inf)* patito *m* (-a *f*).

buffalo [ˈbʌfələʊ] (*pl* **-s** OR **-es**) *n* bufalo *m*.

buffalo wings *npl (Am)* ali *fpl* di pollo fritte.

buffer [ˈbʌfəʳ] *n (on train)* respingente *m*.

buffet [*Br* ˈbʊfeɪ, *Am* bəˈfeɪ] *n* buffet *m inv*.

buffet car *n* vagone *m* ristorante.

bug [bʌg] ◇ *n (insect)* insetto *m*; *(inf: mild illness)* virus *m inv* ◇ *vt (inf: annoy)* dare fastidio a.

buggy [ˈbʌgɪ] *n (pushchair)* passeggino *m*; *(Am: pram)* carrozzina *f*.

bugle [ˈbjuːgl] *n* tromba *f*.

build [bɪld] (*pt & pp* **built**) ◇ *n* corporatura *f* ◇ *vt* costruire.

◆ **build up** ◇ *vt sep* aumentare ◇ *vi* accumularsi.

builder [ˈbɪldəʳ] *n* costruttore *m* (-trice *f*).

building [ˈbɪldɪŋ] *n* edificio *m*.

building site *n* cantiere *m* edile.

building society *n (Br)* = istituto *m* di credito edilizio.

built [bɪlt] *pt & pp* → **build**.

built-in *adj* incorporato(-a).

built-up area *n* agglomerato *m* urbano.

bulb [bʌlb] *n (for lamp)* lampadina *f*; *(of plant)* bulbo *m*.

Bulgaria [bʌlˈgeərɪə] *n* la Bulgaria.

bulge [bʌldʒ] *vi* essere rigonfio(-a).

bulk [bʌlk] *n*: **the ~ of** la maggior parte di; **in ~** all'ingrosso.

bulky [ˈbʌlkɪ] *adj* ingombrante.

bull [bʊl] *n* toro *m*.

bulldog [ˈbʊldɒg] *n* bulldog *m inv*.

bulldozer [ˈbʊldəʊzəʳ] *n* bulldozer *m inv*.

bullet [ˈbʊlɪt] *n* proiettile *m*, pallottola *f*.

bulletin [ˈbʊlətɪn] *n (on radio, TV)* notiziario *m*; *(publication)* bollettino *m*.

bullfight [ˈbʊlfaɪt] *n* corrida *f*.

bull's-eye *n* centro *m* (del bersaglio).

bully [ˈbʊlɪ] ◇ *n* prepotente *mf* ◇ *vt* fare il prepotente con.

bum [bʌm] *n (inf: bottom)* sedere *m*; *(Am: inf: tramp)* barbone *m* (-a *f*).

bum bag *n (Br)* marsupio *m*.

bumblebee [ˈbʌmblbiː] *n* bombo *m*.

bump [bʌmp] ◇ *n (on knee, leg)* rigonfiamento *m*; *(on head)* bernoccolo *m*; *(on road)* cunetta *f*; *(sound)* tonfo *m*; *(minor accident)* scontro *m* leggero ◇ *vt (head, leg)* sbattere.

◆ **bump into** *vt fus (hit)* sbattere contro; *(meet)* imbattersi in.

bumper [ˈbʌmpəʳ] *n (on car)* paraurti *m inv*; *(Am: on train)* respingente *m*.

bumpy [ˈbʌmpɪ] *adj (road)* dissestato(-a); **the flight was ~** c'è stata un po' di turbolenza durante il volo.

bun [bʌn] *n (cake)* focaccina *f*; *(bread roll)* panino *m*; *(hairstyle)* crocchia *f*.

bunch [bʌntʃ] *n (of people)* gruppo *m*; *(of flowers, keys)* mazzo *m*; *(of grapes)* grappolo *m*; *(of bananas)* casco *m*.

bundle [ˈbʌndl] *n* fascio *m*.

bung [bʌŋ] *n* tappo *m*.

bungalow [ˈbʌŋgələʊ] *n casa a un solo piano*.

bunion [ˈbʌnjən] *n* rigonfiamento *m* dell'alluce.

bunk [bʌŋk] *n (bed)* cuccetta *f*.

bunk bed *n* letto *m* a castello.

bunker [ˈbʌŋkəʳ] *n* bunker *m inv*; *(for coal)* carbonaia *f*.

bunny [ˈbʌnɪ] *n* coniglietto *m*.

buoy [*Br* bɔɪ, *Am* ˈbuːɪ] *n* boa *f*.

buoyant [ˈbɔɪənt] *adj* galleggiante.

BUPA [ˈbuːpə] *n compagnia d'assicurazione britannica per assistenza medica privata*.

burden [ˈbɜːdn] *n (load)* carico *m*; *(responsibility)* peso *m*.

bureaucracy [bjʊəˈrɒkrəsɪ] *n* burocrazia *f*.

bureau de change [ˌbjʊərəʊdəˈʃɒndʒ] *n* agenzia *f* di cambio.

burger [ˈbɜːgəʳ] *n* hamburger *m inv*; *(made with nuts, vegetables etc)* hamburger vegetariano.

burglar [ˈbɜːgləʳ] *n* scassinatore *m* (-trice *f*).

burglar alarm *n* allarme *m* antifurto.

burglarize [ˈbɜːgləraɪz] *(Am)* = **burgle**.

burglary [ˈbɜːglərɪ] *n* furto *m* con scasso.

burgle [ˈbɜːgl] *vt* scassinare.

burial [ˈberɪəl] *n* sepoltura *f*.

burn [bɜːn] (*pt & pp* **burnt** OR **burned**) ◇ *n* bruciatura *f* ◇ *vt & vi* bruciare.

◆ **burn down** ◇ *vt sep* incendiare ◇ *vi*: **the building was ~ed down** l'edificio è stato interamente distrutto dalle fiamme.

burning (hot) [ˈbɜːnɪŋ-] *adj* rovente.

Burns' Night [bɜːnz-] *n festa celebrata in onore del poeta scozzese Robert Burns il 25 gennaio*.

burnt [bɜːnt] *pt & pp* → **burn**.

burp [bɜːp] *vi (inf)* ruttare.

burrow [ˈbʌrəʊ] *n* tana *f*.

burst [bɜːst] (*pt & pp* **burst**) ◇ *n* scoppio *m* ◇ *vt* far scoppiare ◇ *vi* scoppiare; **he ~ into the room** irruppe nella stanza; **to ~ into tears** scoppiare in lacrime; **to ~ open** *(door)* spalancarsi.

bury [ˈberɪ] *vt* seppellire.

bus [bʌs] *n* autobus *m inv*; **by ~** in autobus.

bus conductor [-ˌkənˈdʌktəʳ] *n* bigliettaio *m* (-a *f*).

bus driver *n* conducente *mf*.

bush [bʊʃ] *n* cespuglio *m*.

business [ˈbɪznɪs] *n* affari *mpl*; *(shop, firm)* impresa *f*; *(affair)* faccenda *f*; **mind your own ~!** fatti gli affari tuoi!; '**~ as usual**' 'aperto (regolarmente)'.

business card *n* biglietto *f* da visita.

business class *n* business class *f inv*.

business hours *npl* orario *m* di apertura.

businessman [ˈbɪznɪsmæn] (*pl* **-men** [-men]) *n* uomo *m* d'affari.

business studies *npl* ≈ amministrazione *f* aziendale.

businesswoman [ˈbɪznɪsˌwʊmən] (*pl* **-women** [-wɪmɪn]) *n* donna *f* d'affari.

busker [ˈbʌskəʳ] *n (Br)* musicista *mf* ambulante.

bus lane *n* corsia *f* preferenziale (per autobus).

bus pass *n* abbonamento *m* all'autobus.

bus shelter *n* pensilina *f*.

bus station *n* stazione *f* degli autobus.

bus stop *n* fermata *f* dell'autobus.
bust [bʌst] ◇ *n (of woman)* seno *m* ◇ *adj*: **to go ~** *(inf)* fallire.
bustle ['bʌsl] *n (activity)* trambusto *m*.
bus tour *n* gita *f* in autobus.
busy ['bɪzɪ] *adj* occupato(-a); *(day, schedule)* pieno(-a); *(street, office)* affollato(-a); **to be ~ doing sthg** essere occupato a fare qc.
busy signal *n (Am)* segnale *m* di occupato.
but [bʌt] ◇ *conj* ma, però ◇ *prep* tranne; **the last ~ one** il penultimo (la penultima); **~ for** a parte.
butcher ['bʊtʃə^r^] *n* macellaio *m* (-a *f*); **~'s** *(shop)* macelleria *f*.
butt [bʌt] *n (of rifle)* calcio *m*; *(of cigarette, cigar)* mozzicone *m*.
butter ['bʌtə^r^] ◇ *n* burro *m* ◇ *vt* imburrare.
butter bean *n* fagiolo *m* bianco.
buttercup ['bʌtəkʌp] *n* ranunculo *m*.
butterfly ['bʌtəflaɪ] *n* farfalla *f*.
butterscotch ['bʌtəskɒtʃ] *n caramella dura di zucchero e burro*.
buttocks ['bʌtəks] *npl* natiche *fpl*.
button ['bʌtn] *n* bottone *m*; *(Am: badge)* distintivo *m*.
buttonhole ['bʌtnhəʊl] *n (hole)* occhiello *m*.
button mushroom *n* champignon *m inv*.
buttress ['bʌtrɪs] *n* contrafforte *m*.
buy [baɪ] (*pt & pp* **bought**) ◇ *vt* comprare ◇ *n*: **a good ~** un buon acquisto; **to ~ sthg for sb, to ~ sb sthg** comprare qc per qn, comprare qc a qn.
buzz [bʌz] ◇ *vi* ronzare ◇ *n (inf: phone call)*: **to give sb a ~** dare un colpo di telefono a qn.
buzzer ['bʌzə^r^] *n* cicalino *m*.
by [baɪ] ◇ *prep* **1.** *(expressing cause, agent)* da; **he was hit ~ a car** è stato investito da un'automobile; **funded ~ the government** finanziato dal governo; **a book ~ Joyce** un libro di Joyce.
2. *(expressing method, means)*: **~ car/train/plane** in macchina/treno/aereo; **~ post/phone** per posta/telefono; **to pay ~ credit card** pagare con la carta di credito; **to win ~ cheating** vincere con l'imbroglio.
3. *(near to, beside)* vicino a, accanto a; **~ the sea** *(holiday)* al mare; *(town)* sul mare.
4. *(past)* davanti a; **a car went ~ the house** un'automobile è passata davanti alla casa.
5. *(via)* da; **go out ~ the door on the left** uscite dalla porta sulla sinistra.
6. *(with time)*: **be there ~ nine** trovati lì per le nove; **~ day/night** di giorno/notte; **~ now** ormai.
7. *(expressing quantity)* a; **sold ~ the dozen/thousand** venduti a dozzine/migliaia; **prices fell ~ 20%** i prezzi sono diminuiti del 20%; **we charge ~ the hour** facciamo pagare a ore.
8. *(expressing meaning)*: **what do you mean ~ that?** cosa intendi dire con questo?
9. *(in sums, measurements)* per; **two metres ~ five** due metri per cinque.
10. *(according to)* per, secondo; **~ law** per legge; **it's fine ~ me** per me va bene.
11. *(expressing gradual process)*: **bit ~ bit** (a) poco a poco; **one ~ one** uno per uno; **year ~ year** di anno in anno.
12. *(in phrases)*: **~ mistake** per errore; **~ oneself** *(alone)* (da) solo; *(unaided)* da solo; **he's a lawyer ~ profession** è avvocato di professione.
◇ *adv (past)*: **to go ~** passare.
bye(-bye) [baɪ(baɪ)] *excl (inf)* ciao!
bypass ['baɪpɑːs] *n (road)* circonvallazione *f*.

C

C *(abbr of Celsius, centigrade)* C.
cab [kæb] *n (taxi)* taxi *m inv*; *(of lorry)* cabina *f*.
cabaret [ˈkæbəreɪ] *n* spettacolo *m* di cabaret.
cabbage [ˈkæbɪdʒ] *n* cavolo *m*.
cabin [ˈkæbɪn] *n* cabina *f*; *(wooden house)* capanna *f*.
cabin crew *n* personale *m* di bordo.
cabinet [ˈkæbɪnɪt] *n (cupboard)* armadietto *m*; (POL) consiglio *m* di gabinetto.
cable [ˈkeɪbl] *n* cavo *m*.
cable car *n* funivia *f*.
cable television *n* televisione *f* via cavo.
cactus [ˈkæktəs] (*pl* **-tuses** OR **-ti** [-taɪ]) *n* cactus *m inv*.
Caesar salad [ˌsiːzə-] *n insalata di lattuga, acciughe, olive, crostini e parmigiano.*
cafe [ˈkæfeɪ] *n* caffè *m*.
cafeteria [ˌkæfɪˈtɪərɪə] *n* ristorante *m* self-service.
cafetière [kæfˈtjeəʳ] *n tipo di caffettiera con pressa che separa la polvere dal caffè ottenuto.*
caffeine [ˈkæfiːn] *n* caffeina *f*.
cage [keɪdʒ] *n* gabbia *f*.
cagoule [kəˈguːl] *n (Br)* K-way® *m inv*.
Cajun [ˈkeɪdʒən] *adj tipico della popolazione di origine francese della Louisiana.*
cake [keɪk] *n (large)* torta *f*; *(small)* pasta *f*; *(of soap)* pezzo *m*.
calculate [ˈkælkjʊleɪt] *vt* calcolare.
calculator [ˈkælkjʊleɪtəʳ] *n* calcolatrice *f*.
calendar [ˈkælɪndəʳ] *n* calendario *m*.
calf [kɑːf] (*pl* **calves**) *n (of cow)* vitello *m*; *(part of leg)* polpaccio *m*.
call [kɔːl] ◇ *n (visit)* visita *f*; *(phone call)* telefonata *f*; *(of bird)* richiamo *m*; *(at airport)* chiamata *f*; *(at hotel)* sveglia *f* ◇ *vt* chiamare; *(meeting)* convocare; *(elections, strike)* indire ◇ *vi (visit)* passare; *(phone)* chiamare; **on ~** *(nurse, doctor)* reperibile; **to pay sb a ~** fare una visita a qn; **to be ~ed** chiamarsi; **what is he ~ed?** come si chiama?; **to ~ sb a liar** dare del bugiardo a qn; **to ~ sb's name** chiamare qn; **this train ~s at ...** questo treno ferma a ...; **who's ~ing?** chi parla?
◆ **call back** ◇ *vt sep* richiamare ◇ *vi (phone again)* richiamare; *(visit again)* ripassare.
◆ **call for** *vt fus (come to fetch)* passare a prendere; *(demand)* chiedere; *(require)* richiedere.
◆ **call on** *vt fus (visit)* fare visita a; **to ~ on sb to do sthg** chiedere a qn di fare qc.

◆ **call out** ◇ *vt sep (name, winner)* annunciare; *(doctor, fire brigade)* chiamare ◇ *vi* gridare.

◆ **call up** *vt sep* (MIL) chiamare alle armi; *(telephone)* chiamare.

call box *n* cabina *f* telefonica.

caller ['kɔːlə^r] *n (visitor)* visitatore *m* (-trice *f*); *(on phone) persona che chiama.*

calm [kɑːm] ◇ *adj* calmo(-a) ◇ *vt* calmare.

◆ **calm down** ◇ *vt sep* calmare ◇ *vi* calmarsi.

Calor gas® ['kælə-] *n* butano *m*.

calorie ['kælərɪ] *n* caloria *f*.

calves [kɑːvz] *pl* → **calf**.

camcorder ['kæm,kɔːdə^r] *n* videocamera *f*.

came [keɪm] *pt* → **come**.

camel ['kæml] *n* cammello *m*.

camembert ['kæməmbeə^r] *n* camembert *m inv*.

camera ['kæmərə] *n (for photographs)* macchina *f* fotografica; *(for filming)* macchina da presa.

cameraman ['kæmərəmæn] (*pl* **-men** [-men]) *n* cameraman *m inv*.

camera shop *n* fotografo *m*.

camisole ['kæmɪsəʊl] *n* canottiera *f*.

camp [kæmp] ◇ *n (for holidaymakers)* campeggio *m*, camping *m inv*; *(for soldiers, prisoners)* campo *m* ◇ *vi* accamparsi.

campaign [kæm'peɪn] ◇ *n* campagna *f* ◇ *vi*: **to ~ (for/against)** fare una campagna (per/contro).

camp bed *n* branda *f*.

camper ['kæmpə^r] *n (person)* campeggiatore *m* (-trice *f*); *(van)* camper *m inv*.

camping ['kæmpɪŋ] *n*: **to go ~** andare in campeggio.

camping stove *n* fornello *m* da campeggio.

campsite ['kæmpsaɪt] *n* campeggio *m*, camping *m inv*.

campus ['kæmpəs] (*pl* **-es**) *n* campus *m inv*.

can[1] [kæn] *n (of food)* scatola *f*; *(of drink)* lattina *f*; *(of paint)* barattolo *m*; *(of oil)* latta *f*.

can[2] [*weak form* kən, *strong form* kæn] (*pt & conditional* **could**) *aux vb*

1. *(be able to)* potere; **~ you help me?** puoi aiutarmi?; **I ~ see you** ti vedo.

2. *(know how to)* sapere; **~ you drive?** sai guidare?; **I ~ speak Italian** parlo (l')italiano.

3. *(be allowed to)* potere; **you can't smoke here** è proibito fumare qui.

4. *(in polite requests)* potere; **~ you tell me the time?** mi può dire l'ora?, mi sa dire l'ora?; **~ I speak to the manager?** posso parlare al direttore?

5. *(expressing occasional occurrence)*: **it ~ get cold at night** può fare freddo la notte.

6. *(expressing possibility)* potere; **they could be lost** si potrebbero essere persi.

Canada ['kænədə] *n* il Canada.

Canadian [kə'neɪdɪən] ◇ *adj* canadese ◇ *n* canadese *mf*.

canal [kə'næl] *n* canale *m*.

canapé ['kænəpeɪ] *n* tartina *f*.

cancel ['kænsl] *vt* annullare.

cancellation [,kænsə'leɪʃn] *n* annullamento *m*.

cancer ['kænsə^r] *n* cancro *m*.

Cancer ['kænsə^r] *n* Cancro *m*.

candidate ['kændɪdət] *n* candidato *m* (-a *f*).

candle ['kændl] *n* candela *f*.

candlelit dinner ['kændllɪt-] *n* cena *f* a lume di candela.

candy ['kændɪ] *n (Am) (confectionery)* dolciumi *mpl*; *(sweet)* caramella *f*.

candyfloss ['kændɪflɒs] *n (Br)* zucchero *m* filato.

cane [keɪn] *n (for walking)* bastone *m*; *(for punishment)* bacchetta *f*; *(for*

furniture, baskets) vimini *mpl.*
canister ['kænɪstəʳ] *n (for tea)* barattolo *m*; *(for gas)* bombola *f.*
cannabis ['kænəbɪs] *n* cannabis *f.*
canned [kænd] *adj (food)* in scatola; *(drink)* in lattina.
cannon ['kænən] *n* cannone *m.*
cannot ['kænɒt] = **can not**.
canoe [kə'nuː] *n* canoa *f.*
canoeing [kə'nuːɪŋ] *n* canottaggio *m.*
canopy ['kænəpɪ] *n (over bed etc)* baldacchino *m.*
can't [kɑːnt] = **cannot**.
cantaloup(e) ['kæntəluːp] *n* melone *m* (cantalupo).
canteen [kæn'tiːn] *n* mensa *f.*
canvas ['kænvəs] *n (for tent, bag)* tela *f.*
cap [kæp] *n (hat)* berretto *m*; *(of pen, bottle)* tappo *m*; *(contraceptive)* diaframma *m.*
capable ['keɪpəbl] *adj (competent)* capace; **to be ~ of doing sthg** essere capace di fare qc.
capacity [kə'pæsɪtɪ] *n (ability)* capacità *f inv*; *(of stadium, theatre)* capienza *f.*
cape [keɪp] *n (of land)* capo *m*; *(cloak)* cappa *f.*
capers ['keɪpəz] *npl* capperi *mpl.*
capital ['kæpɪtl] *n (of country)* capitale *f*; *(money)* capitale *m*; *(letter)* maiuscola *f.*
capital punishment *n* pena *f* capitale.
cappuccino [,kæpʊ'tʃiːnəʊ] (*pl* **-s**) *n* cappuccino *m.*
Capricorn *n* Capricorno *m.*
capsicum ['kæpsɪkəm] *n* peperone *m.*
capsize [kæp'saɪz] *vi* rovesciarsi.
capsule ['kæpsjuːl] *n (for medicine)* capsula *f.*
captain ['kæptɪn] *n* capitano *m.*
caption ['kæpʃn] *n* didascalia *f.*
capture ['kæptʃəʳ] *vt (person, animal)* catturare; *(town, castle)* conquistare.
car [kɑːʳ] *n (motorcar)* automobile *f*, macchina *f*; *(railway wagon)* vagone *m.*
carafe [kə'ræf] *n* caraffa *f.*
caramel ['kærəmel] *n (sweet)* caramella *f* mou®; *(burnt sugar)* caramello *m.*
carat ['kærət] *n* carato *m*; **24-~ gold** oro a 24 carati.
caravan ['kærəvæn] *n (Br)* roulotte *f inv.*
caravanning ['kærəvænɪŋ] *n (Br)*: **to go ~** andare in vacanza in roulotte.
caravan site *n (Br)* campeggio *m* per roulotte.
carbohydrate [,kɑːbəʊ'haɪdreɪt] *n (in foods)* carboidrato *m.*
carbon ['kɑːbən] *n* carbone *m.*
carbon copy *n* copia *f* fatta con carta carbone.
carbon dioxide [-daɪ'ɒksaɪd] *n* anidride *f* carbonica.
carbon monoxide [-mɒ'nɒksaɪd] *n* monossido *m* di carbonio.
car boot sale *n (Br) mercatino di oggetti usati esposti nei bagagliai aperti delle automobili dei venditori.*
carburetor [,kɑːbə'retəʳ] *(Am)* = **carburettor**.
carburettor [,kɑːbə'retəʳ] *n (Br)* carburatore *m.*
car crash *n* incidente *m* automobilistico.
card [kɑːd] *n (for filing, notes)* scheda *f*; *(for greetings)* biglietto *m*; *(showing membership)* tessera *f*; *(of businessperson)* biglietto da visita; *(postcard)* cartolina *f*; *(playing card)* carta *f*; *(cardboard)* cartoncino *m*; **~s** *(game)* carte *fpl.*
cardboard ['kɑːdbɔːd] *n* cartone *m.*
car deck *n* ponte *m* auto.
cardiac arrest [,kɑːdɪæk-] *n* arresto *m* cardiaco.

cardigan ['kɑ:dɪgən] *n* cardigan *m inv*.

care [keəʳ] ◇ *n* cura *f* ◇ *vi*: **I don't ~** non me ne importa; **to take ~ of** *(look after)* prendersi cura di; *(deal with)* occuparsi di; **would you ~ to ...?** *(fml)* se vuole ...; **to take ~ to do sthg** stare attento a fare qc; **take ~!** *(goodbye)* stammi bene!; **with ~** con cura; **to ~ about** *(think important)* avere a cuore; *(person)* voler bene a.

career [kə'rɪəʳ] *n* carriera *f*.

carefree ['keəfri:] *adj* spensierato(-a).

careful ['keəfʊl] *adj* *(cautious)* attento(-a); *(driver)* prudente; *(thorough)* accurato(-a); **be ~!** attento(-a)!

carefully ['keəflɪ] *adv* *(cautiously)* con cautela; *(thoroughly)* attentamente.

careless ['keələs] *adj* *(inattentive)* sbadato(-a); *(unconcerned)* spensierato(-a).

caretaker ['keəˌteɪkəʳ] *n* *(Br)* custode *mf*.

car ferry *n* traghetto *m*.

cargo ['kɑ:gəʊ] (*pl* **-es** OR **-s**) *n* carico *m*.

car hire *n* *(Br)* autonoleggio *m*.

Caribbean [*Br* ˌkærɪ'bi:ən, *Am* kə'rɪbɪən] *n*: **the ~** *(area)* i Caraibi.

caring ['keərɪŋ] *adj* premuroso(-a).

carnation [kɑ:'neɪʃn] *n* garofano *m*.

carnival ['kɑ:nɪvl] *n* carnevale *m*.

carousel [ˌkærə'sel] *n* *(for luggage)* nastro *m* trasportatore; *(Am: merry-go-round)* giostra *f*.

carp [kɑ:p] *n* carpa *f*.

car park *n* *(Br)* parcheggio *m*.

carpenter ['kɑ:pəntəʳ] *n* falegname *m*.

carpentry ['kɑ:pəntrɪ] *n* falegnameria *f*.

carpet ['kɑ:pɪt] *n* *(rug)* tappeto *m*; *(wall-to-wall)* moquette *f inv*.

car rental *n* *(Am)* autonoleggio *m*.

carriage ['kærɪdʒ] *n* carrozza *f*.

carriageway ['kærɪdʒweɪ] *n* *(Br)* carreggiata *f*.

carrier (bag) ['kærɪəʳ-] *n* sacchetto *m*.

carrot ['kærət] *n* carota *f*.

carrot cake *n* torta *f* di carote.

carry ['kærɪ] ◇ *vt* portare; *(disease)* essere portatore di ◇ *vi* *(voice, sound)* arrivare.

◆ **carry on** ◇ *vi* continuare ◇ *vt fus* *(continue)* continuare; *(conduct)* compiere; **to ~ on doing sthg** continuare a fare qc.

◆ **carry out** *vt sep* *(work, repairs, investigation)* effettuare; *(plan)* portare a compimento; *(order)* eseguire; *(promise)* adempiere.

carrycot ['kærɪkɒt] *n* *(Br)* culla *f* portatile.

carryout ['kærɪaʊt] *n* *(Am & Scot: meal)* cibo *m* da asporto.

carsick ['kɑ:ˌsɪk] *adj*: **to be ~** soffrire il mal d'auto.

cart [kɑ:t] *n* *(for transport)* carro *m*; *(inf: video game cartridge)* cartuccia *f*; *(Am: in supermarket)* carrello *m*.

carton ['kɑ:tn] *n* *(of milk, juice)* cartone *m*; *(box)* scatola *f*.

cartoon [kɑ:'tu:n] *n* *(drawing)* vignetta *f*; *(comic strip)* fumetto *m*; *(film)* cartone *m* animato.

cartridge ['kɑ:trɪdʒ] *n* cartuccia *f*.

carve [kɑ:v] *vt* *(wood, stone)* intagliare; *(meat)* tagliare.

carvery ['kɑ:vərɪ] *n* *ristorante dove si mangia carne arrosto, tagliata appositamente al banco per il cliente.*

car wash *n* autolavaggio *m*.

case [keɪs] *n* *(Br: suitcase)* valigia *f*; *(container)* custodia *f*; *(instance, patient)* caso *m*; *(*JUR*: trial)* causa *f*; **in any ~** in ogni caso; **in ~ it rains** nel caso che piova; **in ~ of** in caso di; **(just) in ~** in caso di necessità;

in that ~ allora.

cash [kæʃ] ◇ *n (coins, notes)* contanti *mpl*; *(money in general)* soldi *mpl* ◇ *vt*: **to ~ a cheque** incassare un assegno; **to pay ~** pagare in contanti.

cash desk *n* cassa *f*.

cash dispenser [-ˌdɪˈspensəʳ] *n* cassa *f* automatica.

cashew (nut) [ˈkæʃuː-] *n* noce *f* di acagiù.

cashier [kæˈʃɪəʳ] *n* cassiere *m* (-a *f*).

cashmere [kæʃˈmɪəʳ] *n* cachemire *m*.

cashpoint [ˈkæʃpɔɪnt] *n (Br)* cassa *f* automatica.

cash register *n* registratore *m* di cassa.

casino [kəˈsiːnəʊ] (*pl* **-s**) *n* casinò *m inv*.

cask [kɑːsk] *n* barile *m*.

cask-conditioned [-ˌkənˈdɪʃnd] *adj* fermentato(-a) in barili.

casserole [ˈkæsərəʊl] *n (stew)* stufato *m*; **~ (dish)** casseruola *f*.

cassette [kæˈset] *n* cassetta *f*.

cassette recorder *n* registratore *m* (a cassette).

cast [kɑːst] (*pt & pp* **cast**) ◇ *n (actors)* cast *m inv*; *(for broken bone)* ingessatura *f* ◇ *vt (shadow, light, look)* gettare; **to ~ doubt on** mettere in dubbio; **to ~ one's vote** votare.

◆ **cast off** *vi (boat, ship)* salpare.

caster [ˈkɑːstəʳ] *n* rotella *f*.

caster sugar *n (Br)* zucchero *m* semolato.

castle [ˈkɑːsl] *n (building)* castello *m*; *(in chess)* torre *f*.

casual [ˈkæʒʊəl] *adj (relaxed)* disinvolto(-a); *(offhand)* noncurante; *(clothes)* casual *(inv)*; **~ work** lavoro occasionale.

casualty [ˈkæʒjʊəltɪ] *n (injured person)* ferito *m* (-a *f*); *(dead person)* morto *m* (-a *f*); **~ (ward)** pronto soccorso *m*.

cat [kæt] *n* gatto *m*.

catalog [ˈkætəlɒg] *(Am)* = **catalogue**.

catalogue [ˈkætəlɒg] *n* catalogo *m*.

catapult [ˈkætəpʌlt] *n* fionda *f*.

cataract [ˈkætərækt] *n (in eye)* cateratta *f*.

catarrh [kəˈtɑːʳ] *n* catarro *m*.

catastrophe [kəˈtæstrəfɪ] *n* catastrofe *f*.

catch [kætʃ] (*pt & pp* **caught**) ◇ *vt* prendere; *(surprise, hear)* cogliere; *(attention)* attirare ◇ *vi (become hooked)* impigliarsi ◇ *n (of window, door)* fermo *m*; *(snag)* intoppo *m*.

◆ **catch up** ◇ *vt sep* raggiungere ◇ *vi*: **to ~ up (with sthg)** *(sleep, work)* recuperare (qc); **to ~ up with sb** raggiungere qn.

catching [ˈkætʃɪŋ] *adj (inf)* contagioso(-a).

category [ˈkætəgərɪ] *n* categoria *f*.

cater [ˈkeɪtəʳ]: **cater for** *vt fus (Br) (needs)* provvedere a; *(anticipate)* tenere conto di; *(tastes)* soddisfare.

caterpillar [ˈkætəpɪləʳ] *n* bruco *m*.

cathedral [kəˈθiːdrəl] *n* cattedrale *f*, duomo *m*.

Catholic [ˈkæθlɪk] ◇ *adj* cattolico(-a) ◇ *n* cattolico *m* (-a *f*).

Catseyes® [ˈkætsaɪz] *npl (Br)* catarifrangenti *mpl*.

cattle [ˈkætl] *npl* bestiame *m*.

cattle grid *n griglia metallica posta sul suolo stradale per impedire il passaggio di pecore, mucche etc.*

caught [kɔːt] *pt & pp* → **catch**.

cauliflower [ˈkɒlɪˌflaʊəʳ] *n* cavolfiore *m*.

cauliflower cheese *n cavolfiore gratinato con besciamella.*

cause [kɔːz] ◇ *n* causa *f*; *(justification)* ragione *f* ◇ *vt* causare; **to ~ sb to make a mistake** far fare un errore a qn.

causeway ['kɔːzweɪ] *n* strada *f* rialzata.
caustic soda [ˌkɔːstɪk-] *n* soda *f* caustica.
caution ['kɔːʃn] *n (care)* cautela *f*; *(warning)* avvertimento *m*.
cautious ['kɔːʃəs] *adj* cauto(-a).
cave [keɪv] *n* grotta *f*.
◆ **cave in** *vi* crollare.
caviar(e) ['kævɪɑːʳ] *n* caviale *m*.
cavity ['kævətɪ] *n (in tooth)* carie *f inv*.
CD *n (abbr of compact disc)* CD *m inv*.
CDI *n (abbr of compact disc interactive)* CDI *m inv*.
CD player *n* lettore *m* di compact disc.
CDW *n (abbr of collision damage waiver)* franchigia *f*.
cease [siːs] *vt & vi (fml)* cessare.
ceasefire ['siːsˌfaɪəʳ] *n* cessate il fuoco *m inv*.
ceilidh ['keɪlɪ] *n festa scozzese o irlandese con danze folcloristiche*.
ceiling ['siːlɪŋ] *n* soffitto *m*.
celebrate ['selɪbreɪt] ◇ *vt (win, birthday)* festeggiare; *(Mass)* celebrare ◇ *vi* festeggiare.
celebration [ˌselɪ'breɪʃn] *n (event)* festa *f*.
◆ **celebrations** *npl (festivities)* festeggiamenti *mpl*.
celebrity [sɪ'lebrətɪ] *n (person)* celebrità *f inv*.
celeriac [sɪ'lerɪæk] *n* sedano *m* rapa.
celery ['selərɪ] *n* sedano *m*.
cell [sel] *n (of plant, body)* cellula *f*; *(in prison)* cella *f*.
cellar ['seləʳ] *n* cantina *f*.
cello ['tʃeləʊ] (*pl* **-s**) *n* violoncello *m*.
Cellophane® ['seləfeɪn] *n* cellophane® *m*.
Celsius ['selsɪəs] *adj* Celsius *(inv)*.
cement [sɪ'ment] *n* cemento *m*.
cement mixer *n* betoniera *f*.
cemetery ['semɪtrɪ] *n* cimitero *m*.
cent [sent] *n (Am)* cent *m inv*.
center ['sentər] *(Am)* = **centre**.
centigrade ['sentɪgreɪd] *adj* centigrado(-a).
centimetre ['sentɪˌmiːtəʳ] *n* centimetro *m*.
centipede ['sentɪpiːd] *n* centopiedi *m inv*.
central ['sentrəl] *adj* centrale.
central heating *n* riscaldamento *m* autonomo.
central locking [-'lɒkɪŋ] *n* chiusura *f* delle porte centralizzata.
central reservation *n (Br)* zona *f* spartitraffico.
centre ['sentəʳ] ◇ *n (Br)* centro *m* ◇ *adj (Br)* centrale; **the ~ of attention** il centro dell'attenzione.
century ['sentʃʊrɪ] *n* secolo *m*.
ceramic [sɪ'ræmɪk] *adj* di ceramica.
◆ **ceramics** *npl* oggetti *mpl* di ceramica.
cereal ['sɪərɪəl] *n (breakfast food)* cereali *mpl*.
ceremony ['serɪmənɪ] *n* cerimonia *f*.
certain ['sɜːtn] *adj* certo(-a); **she's ~ to be late** farà tardi di sicuro; **to be ~ of sthg** essere certo di qc; **to make ~ (that)** assicurarsi che.
certainly ['sɜːtnlɪ] *adv* certamente, certo.
certificate [sə'tɪfɪkət] *n* certificato *m*.
certify ['sɜːtɪfaɪ] *vt (declare true)* attestare.
chain [tʃeɪn] ◇ *n* catena *f*; *(of islands)* arcipelago *m* ◇ *vt*: **to ~ sthg to sthg** incatenare qc a qc.
chain store *n negozio che fa parte di una catena*.
chair [tʃeəʳ] *n* sedia *f*.
chair lift *n* seggiovia *f*.
chairman ['tʃeəmən] (*pl* **-men**

[-mən]) *n* presidente *m*.

chairperson ['tʃeə,pɜːsn] (*pl* **-s**) *n* presidente *m* (-essa *f*).

chairwoman ['tʃeə,wʊmən] (*pl* **-women** [-,wɪmɪn]) *n* presidentessa *f*.

chalet ['ʃæleɪ] *n* chalet *m inv*; *(at holiday camp)* bungalow *m inv*.

chalk [tʃɔːk] *n* gesso *m*; **a piece of ~** un gesso.

chalkboard ['tʃɔːkbɔːd] *n (Am)* lavagna *f*.

challenge ['tʃælɪndʒ] ◇ *n* sfida *f* ◇ *vt (question)* mettere in discussione; **to ~ sb (to sthg)** sfidare qn (a qc).

chamber ['tʃeɪmbə^r^] *n (room)* sala *f*.

chambermaid ['tʃeɪmbəmeɪd] *n* cameriera *f* (d'albergo).

champagne [,ʃæm'peɪn] *n* champagne *m inv*.

champion ['tʃæmpjən] *n* campione *m* (-essa *f*).

championship ['tʃæmpjənʃɪp] *n* campionato *m*.

chance [tʃɑːns] ◇ *n (luck)* caso *m*; *(possibility)* probabilità *f inv*; *(opportunity)* possibilità *f inv*, occasione *f* ◇ *vt*: **to ~ it** *(inf)* provarci; **to take a ~** rischiare; **by ~** per caso; **I came on the off ~ you'd be here** sono venuto per vedere se per caso ci fossi.

Chancellor of the Exchequer [,tʃɑːnsələrəvðəɪks'tʃekə^r^] *n (Br)* = ministro *m* del Tesoro.

chandelier [,ʃændə'lɪə^r^] *n* lampadario *m*.

change [tʃeɪndʒ] ◇ *n (alteration)* cambiamento *m*; *(money received back)* resto *m*; *(coins)* spiccioli *mpl* ◇ *vt* cambiare ◇ *vi* cambiare; *(change clothes)* cambiarsi; **a ~ of clothes** vestiti *mpl* di ricambio; **do you have ~ for a pound?** mi può cambiare una sterlina?; **for a ~** per cambiare; **to get ~d** cambiarsi; **to ~ money** cambiare i soldi; **to ~ a nappy** cambiare un pannolino; **to ~ a wheel** cambiare una ruota; **to ~ trains/planes** cambiare treno/aereo; **all ~!** *(on train)* per tutte le altre stazioni si cambia!

changeable ['tʃeɪndʒəbl] *adj (weather)* variabile.

change machine *n distributore automatico di monete.*

changing room ['tʃeɪndʒɪŋ-] *n (for sport)* spogliatoio *m*; *(in shop)* camerino *m*.

channel ['tʃænl] *n* canale *m*; **the (English) Channel** la Manica.

Channel Islands *npl*: **the ~** le Isole della Manica.

Channel Tunnel *n*: **the ~** il tunnel sotto la Manica.

chant [tʃɑːnt] *vt* (RELIG) cantare; *(words, slogan)* scandire.

chaos ['keɪɒs] *n* caos *m*.

chaotic [keɪ'ɒtɪk] *adj* caotico(-a).

chap [tʃæp] *n (Br: inf)* tipo *m*.

chapatti [tʃə'pætɪ] *n* pane *m* azzimo indiano.

chapel ['tʃæpl] *n* cappella *f*.

chapped [tʃæpt] *adj* screpolato(-a).

chapter ['tʃæptə^r^] *n* capitolo *m*.

character ['kærəktə^r^] *n* carattere *m*; *(in film, book, play)* personaggio *m*; *(inf: person, individual)* tipo *m*.

characteristic [,kærəktə'rɪstɪk] ◇ *adj* caratteristico(-a) ◇ *n* caratteristica *f*.

charcoal ['tʃɑːkəʊl] *n (for barbecue)* carbone *m* di legna.

charge [tʃɑːdʒ] ◇ *n (price)* spesa *f*; (JUR) accusa *f* ◇ *vt (customer)* far pagare; *(money)* chiedere; (JUR) accusare; *(battery)* ricaricare ◇ *vi (ask money)* far pagare; *(rush)* precipitarsi; **to be in ~ (of)** essere responsabile (di); **to take ~ (of)** assumere la responsabilità (di); **free of ~** gratis; **extra ~** supplemento *m*; **there is no ~ for service** il servizio è gratuito.

char-grilled ['tʃɑːgrɪld] *adj* alla brace.
charity ['tʃærətɪ] *n (organization)* ente *m* di beneficenza; **to give to ~** dare soldi in beneficenza.
charity shop *n negozio che vende articoli vari, il cui ricavato è destinato ad un ente di beneficenza.*
charm [tʃɑːm] ◇ *n (attractiveness)* fascino *m* ◇ *vt* affascinare.
charming ['tʃɑːmɪŋ] *adj* affascinante.
chart [tʃɑːt] *n (diagram)* grafico *m*; *(map)* carta *f*; **the ~s** l'hit-parade *f inv*.
chartered accountant [ˌtʃɑːtəd-] *n* esperto *m* (-a *f*) contabile.
charter flight ['tʃɑːtə-] *n* volo *m* charter.
chase [tʃeɪs] ◇ *n* inseguimento *m* ◇ *vt* inseguire.
chat [tʃæt] ◇ *n* chiacchierata *f* ◇ *vi* chiacchierare; **to have a ~ (with)** fare quattro chiacchiere (con).
◆ **chat up** *vt sep (Br: inf)* agganciare.
château ['ʃætəʊ] *n* castello *m*.
chat show *n (Br)* talk show *m inv*.
chatty ['tʃætɪ] *adj (person)* chiacchierone(-a); *(letter)* pieno di pettegolezzi.
chauffeur ['ʃəʊfə^r] *n* autista *m*.
cheap [tʃiːp] *adj* a buon mercato; *(pej: low-quality)* dozzinale.
cheap day return *n biglietto di andata e ritorno a prezzo ridotto, valido per un solo giorno e soggetto a restrizioni di orario.*
cheaply ['tʃiːplɪ] *adv* a basso prezzo.
cheat [tʃiːt] ◇ *n* imbroglione *m* (-a *f*) ◇ *vi* imbrogliare ◇ *vt*: **to ~ sb out of sthg** sottrarre qc a qn con l'inganno.
check [tʃek] ◇ *n (inspection)* controllo *m*; *(Am: bill)* conto *m*; *(Am: tick)* segno *m*; *(Am)* = **cheque** ◇ *vt* controllare; *(Am: tick)* spuntare ◇ *vi* verificare; **to ~ for sthg** controllare qc; **to ~ on sthg** controllare qc.
◆ **check in** ◇ *vt sep (luggage)* far passare al check-in ◇ *vi (at hotel)* farsi registrare; *(at airport)* fare il check-in.
◆ **check off** *vt sep* spuntare.
◆ **check out** *vi* saldare il conto e andarsene.
◆ **check up** *vi*: **to ~ up (on)** fare delle indagini (su).
checked [tʃekt] *adj* a quadri.
checkers ['tʃekəz] *n (Am)* dama *f*.
check-in desk *n* banco *m* dell'accettazione bagagli OR del check-in.
checkout ['tʃekaʊt] *n* cassa *f*.
checkpoint ['tʃekpɔɪnt] *n* posto *m* di blocco.
checkroom ['tʃekrʊm] *n (Am)* deposito *m* bagagli.
checkup ['tʃekʌp] *n* check-up *m inv*.
cheddar (cheese) ['tʃedə^r-] *n tipo di formaggio semi-stagionato.*
cheek [tʃiːk] *n* guancia *f*; **what a ~!** che faccia tosta!
cheeky ['tʃiːkɪ] *adj* sfacciato(-a).
cheer [tʃɪə^r] ◇ *n* acclamazione *f* ◇ *vi* acclamare.
cheerful ['tʃɪəfʊl] *adj* allegro(-a); *(colour)* vivace.
cheerio [ˌtʃɪərɪ'əʊ] *excl (Br: inf)* ciao!
cheers [tʃɪəz] *excl (when drinking)* cincin!; *(Br: inf: thank you)* grazie!
cheese [tʃiːz] *n* formaggio *m*.
cheeseboard ['tʃiːzbɔːd] *n (cheese and biscuits)* piatto *m* di formaggi.
cheeseburger ['tʃiːzˌbɜːgə^r] *n* cheeseburger *m inv (panino con hamburger e formaggio fuso)*.
cheesecake ['tʃiːzkeɪk] *n dolce a base di biscotti, formaggio fresco e panna.*

chef [ʃef] *n* chef *m inv*.
chef's special *n* specialità *f inv* della casa.
chemical [ˈkemɪkl] ◇ *adj* chimico(-a) ◇ *n* sostanza *f* chimica.
chemist [ˈkemɪst] *n* *(Br: pharmacist)* farmacista *mf*; *(scientist)* chimico *m* (-a *f*); **~'s** *(Br: shop)* farmacia *f*.
chemistry [ˈkemɪstrɪ] *n* chimica *f*.
cheque [tʃek] *n (Br)* assegno *m*; **to pay by ~** pagare con un assegno.
chequebook [ˈtʃekbʊk] *n* libretto *m* degli assegni.
cheque card *n* carta *f* assegni.
cherry [ˈtʃerɪ] *n* ciliegia *f*.
chess [tʃes] *n* scacchi *mpl*.
chest [tʃest] *n (of body)* torace *m*; *(box)* cassa *f*.
chestnut [ˈtʃesnʌt] ◇ *n* castagna *f* ◇ *adj (colour)* castano(-a).
chest of drawers *n* cassettone *m*.
chew [tʃuː] ◇ *vt* masticare ◇ *n* *(sweet)* caramella *f* (morbida).
chewing gum [ˈtʃuːɪŋ-] *n* gomma *f* da masticare.
chic [ʃiːk] *adj* alla moda, chic *(inv)*.
chicken [ˈtʃɪkɪn] *n (bird)* gallina *f*; *(meat)* pollo *m*.
chicken breast *n* petto *m* di pollo.
chicken Kiev [-ˈkiːev] *n filetto di pollo farcito con burro all'aglio, impanato e fritto.*
chicken pox [-pɒks] *n* varicella *f*.
chickpea [ˈtʃɪkpiː] *n* cece *m*.
chicory [ˈtʃɪkərɪ] *n* cicoria *f*.
chief [tʃiːf] ◇ *adj (highest-ranking)* capo *(inv)*; *(main)* principale ◇ *n* capo *m*.
chiefly [ˈtʃiːflɪ] *adv (mainly)* principalmente; *(especially)* soprattutto.
child [tʃaɪld] (*pl* **children**) *n* *(young boy, girl)* bambino *m* (-a *f*); *(son, daughter)* figlio *m* (-a *f*).
child abuse *n* maltrattamento *m* di minori.
child benefit *n (Br)* = assegno *m* di famiglia.
childhood [ˈtʃaɪldhʊd] *n* infanzia *f*.
childish [ˈtʃaɪldɪʃ] *adj (pej)* infantile.
childminder [ˈtʃaɪldˌmaɪndəʳ] *n* *(Br)* bambinaia *f*.
children [ˈtʃɪldrən] *pl* → **child**.
childrenswear [ˈtʃɪldrənzweəʳ] *n* abbigliamento *m* per bambini.
child seat *n (in car)* seggiolino *m* per bambini.
Chile [ˈtʃɪlɪ] *n* il Cile.
chill [tʃɪl] ◇ *n (illness)* infreddatura *f* ◇ *vt* raffreddare; **there's a ~ in the air** l'aria è fredda.
chilled [tʃɪld] *adj* freddo(-a); **'serve ~'** 'servire fresco'.
chilli [ˈtʃɪlɪ] (*pl* **-ies**) *n (vegetable)* peperoncino *m* piccante; *(dish)* = **chilli con carne**.
chilli con carne [ˈtʃɪlɪkɒnˈkɑːnɪ] *n piatto messicano a base di carne e fagioli rossi cotti in spezie e salsa piccante.*
chilly [ˈtʃɪlɪ] *adj* freddo(-a).
chimney [ˈtʃɪmnɪ] *n* camino *m*.
chimneypot [ˈtʃɪmnɪpɒt] *n* comignolo *m*.
chimpanzee [ˌtʃɪmpənˈziː] *n* scimpanzé *m inv*.
chin [tʃɪn] *n* mento *m*.
china [ˈtʃaɪnə] *n (material)* porcellana *f*.
China [ˈtʃaɪnə] *n* la Cina.
Chinese [ˌtʃaɪˈniːz] ◇ *adj* cinese ◇ *n (language)* cinese *m* ◇ *npl*: **the ~** i cinesi; **a ~ restaurant** un ristorante cinese.
chip [tʃɪp] ◇ *n (small piece)* scheggia *f*; *(mark)* scheggiatura *f*; *(counter)* fiche *f inv*; (COMPUT) chip *m inv* ◇ *vt* scheggiare.
◆ **chips** *npl (Br: French fries)* patate *fpl* fritte; *(Am: crisps)* patatine *fpl*.

chiropodist [kɪ'rɒpədɪst] *n* callista *mf*.
chisel ['tʃɪzl] *n* cesello *m*.
chives [tʃaɪvz] *npl* erba *f* cipollina.
chlorine ['klɔːriːn] *n* cloro *m*.
choc-ice ['tʃɒkaɪs] *n (Br) blocco di gelato ricoperto di cioccolato.*
chocolate ['tʃɒkələt] ◇ *n (food)* cioccolato *m*, cioccolata *f*; *(sweet)* cioccolatino *m*; *(drink)* cioccolata ◇ *adj* al cioccolato.
chocolate biscuit *n* biscotto *m* al cioccolato.
choice [tʃɔɪs] ◇ *n* scelta *f* ◇ *adj (meat, ingredients)* di prima qualità; **the dressing of your ~** il condimento di vostra scelta.
choir ['kwaɪəʳ] *n* coro *m*.
choke [tʃəʊk] ◇ *n* (AUT) (valvola *f* dell')aria *f inv* ◇ *vt* soffocare ◇ *vi (on fishbone etc)* strozzarsi; *(to death)* soffocare.
cholera ['kɒlərə] *n* colera *m*.
choose [tʃuːz] (*pt* **chose**, *pp* **chosen**) *vt & vi* scegliere; **to ~ to do sthg** scegliere di fare qc.
chop [tʃɒp] ◇ *n (of meat)* braciola *f* ◇ *vt* tagliare.
◆ **chop down** *vt sep* abbattere.
◆ **chop up** *vt sep* tagliare a pezzetti.
chopper ['tʃɒpəʳ] *n (inf: helicopter)* elicottero *m*.
chopping board ['tʃɒpɪŋ-] *n* tagliere *m*.
choppy ['tʃɒpɪ] *adj* increspato(-a).
chopsticks ['tʃɒpstɪks] *npl* bastoncini *mpl* cinesi.
chop suey [ˌtʃɒp'suːɪ] *n piatto cinese a base di riso, striscioline di maiale o pollo, verdura e germogli di soia.*
chord [kɔːd] *n* accordo *m*.
chore [tʃɔːʳ] *n* faccenda *f*.
chorus ['kɔːrəs] *n (part of song)* ritornello *m*; *(group of singers, dancers)* coro *m*.
chose [tʃəʊz] *pt* → **choose**.
chosen ['tʃəʊzn] *pp* → **choose**.
choux pastry [ʃuː-] *n* pasta *f* per bignè.
chowder ['tʃaʊdəʳ] *n zuppa di pesce o frutti di mare.*
chow mein [ˌtʃaʊ'meɪn] *n piatto cinese di tagliolini fritti con verdure, carne o frutti di mare.*
Christ [kraɪst] *n* Cristo *m*.
christen ['krɪsn] *vt (baby)* battezzare.
Christian ['krɪstʃən] ◇ *adj* cristiano(-a) ◇ *n* cristiano *m* (-a *f*).
Christian name *n* nome *m* di battesimo.
Christmas ['krɪsməs] *n* Natale *m*; **Happy ~!** Buon Natale!
Christmas card *n* biglietto *m* d'auguri di Natale.
Christmas carol [-'kærəl] *n* canto *m* di Natale.
Christmas Day *n* il giorno di Natale.
Christmas Eve *n* la vigilia di Natale.
Christmas pudding *n dolce tradizionale natalizio a base di uva passa e frutta candita.*
Christmas tree *n* albero *m* di Natale.
chrome [krəʊm] *n* cromo *m*.
chuck [tʃʌk] *vt (inf) (throw)* buttare; *(boyfriend, girlfriend)* mollare.
◆ **chuck away** *vt sep* buttare via.
chunk [tʃʌŋk] *n* pezzo *m*.
church [tʃɜːtʃ] *n* chiesa *f*; **to go to ~** andare in chiesa.
churchyard ['tʃɜːtʃjɑːd] *n* cimitero *m*.
chute [ʃuːt] *n* scivolo *m*.
chutney ['tʃʌtnɪ] *n salsa piccante agrodolce a base di frutta e spezie.*
cider ['saɪdəʳ] *n* sidro *m*.
cigar [sɪ'gɑːʳ] *n* sigaro *m*.
cigarette [ˌsɪgə'ret] *n* sigaretta *f*.
cigarette lighter *n* accendino *m*.

cinema [ˈsɪnəmə] *n* cinema *m inv*.

cinnamon [ˈsɪnəmən] *n* cannella *f*.

circle [ˈsɜːkl] ◇ *n (shape, ring)* cerchio *m*; *(in theatre)* galleria *f* ◇ *vt (draw circle around)* cerchiare; *(move round)* girare intorno a ◇ *vi (plane)* girare in circolo.

circuit [ˈsɜːkɪt] *n (track)* circuito *m*; *(lap)* giro *m*.

circular [ˈsɜːkjʊlə^r] ◇ *adj* circolare ◇ *n* circolare *f*.

circulation [ˌsɜːkjʊˈleɪʃn] *n (of blood)* circolazione *f*; *(of newspaper, magazine)* tiratura *f*.

circumstances [ˈsɜːkəmstənsɪz] *npl* circostanze *fpl*; **in** OR **under the ~** date le circostanze.

circus [ˈsɜːkəs] *n* circo *m*.

cistern [ˈsɪstən] *n (of toilet)* serbatoio *m* dell'acqua.

citizen [ˈsɪtɪzn] *n* cittadino *m* (-a *f*).

city [ˈsɪtɪ] *n* città *f inv*; **the City** la City *(il centro finanziario di Londra)*.

city centre *n* centro *m* (della) città.

city hall *n (Am)* municipio *m*.

civilian [sɪˈvɪljən] *n* civile *m*.

civilized [ˈsɪvɪlaɪzd] *adj (society)* civilizzato(-a); *(person, evening)* cortese.

civil rights [ˌsɪvl-] *npl* diritti *mpl* civili.

civil servant [ˌsɪvl-] *n* impiegato *m* (-a *f*) statale.

civil service [ˌsɪvl-] *n* amministrazione *f* pubblica.

civil war [ˌsɪvl-] *n* guerra *f* civile.

cl *(abbr of centilitre)* cl.

claim [kleɪm] ◇ *n (assertion)* affermazione *f*; *(demand)* richiesta *f*, domanda *f*; *(for insurance)* domanda di indennizzo ◇ *vt (allege)* affermare, sostenere; *(demand)* richiedere; *(credit, responsibility)* rivendicare ◇ *vi (on insurance)* richiedere l'indennizzo.

claimant [ˈkleɪmənt] *n (of benefit)* richiedente *mf*.

claim form *n* modulo *m* per il rimborso.

clam [klæm] *n* vongola *f*.

clamp [klæmp] ◇ *n (for car)* ganascia *f* (bloccaruota) ◇ *vt (car)* bloccare con ganasce.

clap [klæp] *vi* applaudire.

claret [ˈklærət] *n vino rosso di Bordeaux*.

clarinet [ˌklærəˈnet] *n* clarinetto *m*.

clash [klæʃ] ◇ *n (noise)* rumore *m* metallico; *(confrontation)* scontro *m* ◇ *vi (colours)* stonare; *(event, date)* coincidere.

clasp [klɑːsp] ◇ *n (fastener)* fermaglio *m* ◇ *vt* stringere.

class [klɑːs] ◇ *n* classe *f*; *(teaching period)* lezione *f* ◇ *vt*: **to ~ sb/sthg (as)** classificare qn/qc (come).

classic [ˈklæsɪk] ◇ *adj* classico(-a) ◇ *n* classico *m*.

classical [ˈklæsɪkl] *adj* classico(-a).

classical music *n* musica *f* classica.

classification [ˌklæsɪfɪˈkeɪʃn] *n* classificazione *f*.

classified ads [ˌklæsɪfaɪd-] *npl* piccoli annunci *mpl*.

classroom [ˈklɑːsrʊm] *n* aula *f*.

claustrophobic [ˌklɔːstrəˈfəʊbɪk] *adj (person)* claustrofobo(-a); *(place, situation)* claustrofobico(-a).

claw [klɔː] *n (of bird, cat, dog)* artiglio *m*; *(of crab, lobster)* pinza *f*.

clay [kleɪ] *n* argilla *f*.

clean [kliːn] ◇ *vt* pulire ◇ *adj* pulito(-a); **to ~ one's teeth** lavarsi i denti; **I have a ~ driving licence** non sono mai stato multato per infrazioni gravi.

cleaner [ˈkliːnə^r] *n (person)* addetto *m* (-a *f*) alle pulizie; *(substance)* detergente *m*.

cleanse [klenz] *vt* pulire.

cleanser [ˈklenzə^r] *n* detergente *m*.

clear [klɪəʳ] ◇ *adj* chiaro(-a); *(transparent)* trasparente; *(unobstructed)* libero(-a); *(view)* sgombro(-a); *(day, sky)* sereno(-a) ◇ *vt (road, path)* sgombrare; *(pond)* ripulire; *(jump over)* saltare; *(declare not guilty)* scagionare; *(authorize)* autorizzare; *(cheque)* autorizzare l'accreditamento di ◇ *vi (weather)* schiarirsi; *(fog)* levarsi; **to be ~ (about sthg)** avere capito esattamente (qc); **to be ~ of sthg** *(not touching)* essere staccato da qc; **to ~ one's throat** schiarirsi la voce; **to ~ the table** sparecchiare.

◆ **clear up** ◇ *vt sep (room, toys)* mettere a posto; *(problem, confusion)* chiarire ◇ *vi (weather)* schiarirsi; *(tidy up)* mettere a posto.

clearance ['klɪərəns] *n (authorization)* autorizzazione *f*; *(free distance)* distanza *f*; *(for takeoff)* autorizzazione (al decollo).

clearance sale *n* liquidazione *f* totale della merce.

clearing ['klɪərɪŋ] *n* radura *f*.

clearly ['klɪəlɪ] *adv* chiaramente.

clearway ['klɪəweɪ] *n (Br)* strada *f* con divieto di fermata.

clementine ['kleməntaɪn] *n* mandarancio *m*.

clerk [*Br* klɑːk, *Am* klɜːrk] *n (in office)* impiegato *m* (-a *f*); *(Am: in shop)* commesso *m* (-a *f*).

clever ['klevəʳ] *adj (person)* intelligente; *(idea, device)* ingegnoso(-a).

click [klɪk] ◇ *n* scatto *m* ◇ *vi (make sound)* schioccare.

client ['klaɪənt] *n* cliente *mf*.

cliff [klɪf] *n (by the sea)* scoglio *m*; *(inland)* rupe *f*.

climate ['klaɪmɪt] *n* clima *m*.

climax ['klaɪmæks] *n* culmine *m*.

climb [klaɪm] ◇ *vt* salire su; *(tree)* arrampicarsi su; *(mountain)* scalare ◇ *vi* salire; *(plane)* prendere quota.

◆ **climb down** ◇ *vt fus* scendere da ◇ *vi* scendere.

◆ **climb up** *vt fus* salire su.

climber ['klaɪməʳ] *n (person)* scalatore *m* (-trice *f*).

climbing ['klaɪmɪŋ] *n* alpinismo *m*; **to go ~** fare alpinismo.

climbing frame *n (Br)* castello *m (gioco per bambini)*.

clingfilm ['klɪŋfɪlm] *n (Br)* pellicola *f* (per alimenti).

clinic ['klɪnɪk] *n* clinica *f*.

clip [klɪp] ◇ *n (fastener)* fermaglio *m*; *(for paper)* graffetta *f*; *(of film, programme)* sequenza *f* ◇ *vt (fasten)* fermare insieme; *(cut)* tagliare; *(tickets)* forare.

cloak [kləʊk] *n* mantello *m*.

cloakroom ['kləʊkrʊm] *n (for coats)* guardaroba *m inv*; *(Br: toilet)* toilettes *fpl*.

clock [klɒk] *n* orologio *m*; *(mileometer)* contachilometri *m inv*; **round the ~** 24 ore su 24.

clockwise ['klɒkwaɪz] *adv* in senso orario.

clog [klɒg] ◇ *n* zoccolo *m* ◇ *vt* intasare.

close[1] [kləʊs] ◇ *adj* vicino(-a); *(relation, contact, resemblance)* stretto(-a); *(friend)* intimo(-a); *(examination)* attento(-a); *(race, contest)* combattuto(-a) ◇ *adv* vicino; **~ by** vicino; **~ to** *(near)* vicino a; *(on the verge of)* sull'orlo di.

close[2] [kləʊz] ◇ *vt* chiudere ◇ *vi (door, jar, eyes)* chiudersi; *(shop, office)* chiudere; *(deadline, offer, meeting)* finire.

◆ **close down** *vt sep & vi* chiudere (definitivamente).

closed [kləʊzd] *adj* chiuso(-a).

closely ['kləʊslɪ] *adv (related, involved)* strettamente; *(follow, examine)* da vicino, attentamente.

closet ['klɒzɪt] *n (Am)* armadio *m*.

close-up ['kləʊs-] *n* primo piano *m*.

closing time ['kləʊzɪŋ-] *n* orario *m* di chiusura.

clot [klɒt] *n (of blood)* grumo *m*.
cloth [klɒθ] *n (fabric)* stoffa *f*, tessuto *m*; *(piece of cloth)* strofinaccio *m*, panno *m*.
clothes [kləʊðz] *npl* vestiti *mpl*, abiti *mpl*.
clothesline ['kləʊðzlaɪn] *n* filo *m* della biancheria.
clothes peg *n (Br)* molletta *f*.
clothespin ['kləʊðzpɪn] *(Am)* = **clothes peg**.
clothes shop *n* negozio *m* di abbigliamento.
clothing ['kləʊðɪŋ] *n* abbigliamento *m*.
clotted cream [ˌklɒtɪd-] *n panna molto densa tipica della Cornovaglia.*
cloud [klaʊd] *n* nuvola *f*.
cloudy ['klaʊdɪ] *adj (sky, day)* nuvoloso(-a); *(liquid)* torbido(-a).
clove [kləʊv] *n (of garlic)* spicchio *m*.
◆ **cloves** *npl (spice)* chiodi *mpl* di garofano.
clown [klaʊn] *n* pagliaccio *m*.
club [klʌb] *n (organization)* club *m inv*, circolo *m*; *(nightclub)* locale *m* notturno; *(stick)* mazza *f*.
◆ **clubs** *npl (in cards)* fiori *mpl*.
clubbing ['klʌbɪŋ] *n*: **to go ~** *(inf)* andare in discoteca.
club class *n* club class *f inv*.
club sandwich *n (Am) sandwich a due o più strati.*
club soda *n (Am)* acqua *f* di seltz.
clue [klu:] *n (information)* indizio *m*; *(in crossword)* definizione *f*; **I haven't got a ~** non ho la minima idea.
clumsy ['klʌmzɪ] *adj (person)* goffo(-a).
clutch [klʌtʃ] ◇ *n* frizione *f* ◇ *vt* tenere stretto, afferrare.
cm *(abbr of centimetre)* cm.
c/o *(abbr of care of)* c/o.
Co. *(abbr of company)* C.ia.
coach [kəʊtʃ] *n (bus)* pullman *m inv*, autobus *m inv*; *(of train)* carrozza *f*; (SPORT) allenatore *m* (-trice *f*).
coach party *n (Br) gruppo in viaggio organizzato in pullman.*
coach station *n* stazione *f* dei pullman.
coach trip *n (Br)* escursione *f* in pullman.
coal [kəʊl] *n* carbone *m*.
coal mine *n* miniera *f* di carbone.
coarse [kɔ:s] *adj (rough)* ruvido(-a); *(vulgar)* rozzo(-a).
coast [kəʊst] *n* costa *f*.
coaster ['kəʊstə^r] *n (for glass)* sottobicchiere *m*.
coastguard ['kəʊstgɑ:d] *n* guardia *f* costiera.
coastline ['kəʊstlaɪn] *n* costa *f*.
coat [kəʊt] ◇ *n* cappotto *m*; *(of animal)* pelo *m* ◇ *vt*: **to ~ sthg (with)** ricoprire qc (con OR di).
coat hanger *n* gruccia *f* (per abiti).
coating ['kəʊtɪŋ] *n* rivestimento *m*.
cobbled street ['kɒbld-] *n* strada *f* in acciottolato.
cobbles ['kɒblz] *npl* ciottoli *mpl*.
cobweb ['kɒbweb] *n* ragnatela *f*.
Coca-Cola® [ˌkəʊkə'kəʊlə] *n* Coca-Cola® *f*.
cocaine [kəʊ'keɪn] *n* cocaina *f*.
cock [kɒk] *n (male chicken)* gallo *m*.
cock-a-leekie [ˌkɒkə'li:kɪ] *n* zuppa *f* di porri e pollo.
cockerel ['kɒkrəl] *n* galletto *m*.
cockles ['kɒklz] *npl* cardii *mpl*.
cockpit ['kɒkpɪt] *n* cabina *f* di pilotaggio.
cockroach ['kɒkrəʊtʃ] *n* scarafaggio *m*.
cocktail ['kɒkteɪl] *n* cocktail *m inv*.
cocktail party *n* cocktail *m inv*.
cock-up *n (Br: vulg)* casino *m*.
cocoa ['kəʊkəʊ] *n (drink)* cacao *m*.

coconut ['kəʊkənʌt] *n* noce *f* di cocco.

cod [kɒd] *(pl inv) n* merluzzo *m*.

code [kəʊd] *n* codice *m*; *(dialling code)* prefisso *m*.

cod-liver oil *n* olio *m* di fegato di merluzzo.

coeducational [ˌkəʊedjuːˈkeɪʃənl] *adj* misto(-a).

coffee ['kɒfɪ] *n* caffè *m inv*; **black/white ~** caffè nero/macchiato; **ground/instant ~** caffè macinato/istantaneo.

coffee bar *n (Br)* caffè *m inv*.

coffee break *n* pausa *f* per il caffè.

coffeepot ['kɒfɪpɒt] *n* caffettiera *f*.

coffee shop *n (cafe)* caffè *m inv*, bar *m inv*; *(in store etc)* caffetteria *f*.

coffee table *n* tavolino *m* (basso).

coffin ['kɒfɪn] *n* bara *f*.

cog(wheel) ['kɒg(wiːl)] *n* ingranaggio *m*.

coil [kɔɪl] ◇ *n (of rope)* rotolo *m*; *(Br: contraceptive)* spirale *f* ◇ *vt* avvolgere, arrotolare.

coin [kɔɪn] *n* moneta *f*.

coinbox ['kɔɪnbɒks] *n (Br)* telefono *m* a monete.

coincide [ˌkəʊɪn'saɪd] *vi*: **to ~ (with)** coincidere (con).

coincidence [kəʊ'ɪnsɪdəns] *n* coincidenza *f*.

Coke® [kəʊk] *n* coca® *f*.

colander ['kʌləndəʳ] *n* colino *m*.

cold [kəʊld] ◇ *adj* freddo(-a) ◇ *n (illness)* raffreddore *m*; *(low temperature)* freddo *m*; **I'm ~** ho freddo; **it's ~** fa freddo; **to get ~** *(food, drink)* raffreddarsi; *(person)* avere freddo; *(weather)* venire freddo; **to catch ~** prendere freddo; **to catch a ~** prendere il raffreddore.

cold cuts *(Am)* = **cold meats**.

cold meats *npl* affettati *mpl*.

coleslaw ['kəʊlslɔː] *n insalata di cavolo, carote, cipolle e maionese.*

colic ['kɒlɪk] *n* colica *f*.

collaborate [kə'læbəreɪt] *vi* collaborare.

collapse [kə'læps] *vi (building, tent)* crollare; *(person)* avere un collasso.

collar ['kɒləʳ] *n (of shirt, coat)* colletto *m*; *(of dog, cat)* collare *m*.

collarbone ['kɒləbəʊn] *n* clavicola *f*.

colleague ['kɒliːg] *n* collega *mf*.

collect [kə'lekt] ◇ *vt* raccogliere; *(as a hobby)* collezionare; *(go and get)* andare a prendere ◇ *vi (dust, leaves, crowd)* raccogliersi ◇ *adv (Am)*: **to call ~** fare una telefonata a carico del destinatario.

collection [kə'lekʃn] *n (of stamps, coins etc)* collezione *f*, raccolta *f*; *(of stories, poems)* raccolta; *(of money)* colletta *f*; *(of mail)* levata *f*.

collector [kə'lektəʳ] *n (as a hobby)* collezionista *mf*.

college ['kɒlɪdʒ] *n (school)* istituto *m* superiore; *(Br: of university) tipo di organizzazione indipendente di studenti e professori in cui si dividono certe università*; *(Am: university)* università *f inv*.

collide [kə'laɪd] *vi*: **to ~ (with)** scontrarsi (con).

collision [kə'lɪʒn] *n* collisione *f*.

cologne [kə'ləʊn] *n* (acqua *f* di) colonia *f*.

colon ['kəʊlən] *n* (GRAMM) due punti *mpl*.

colonel ['kɜːnl] *n* colonnello *m*.

colony ['kɒlənɪ] *n* colonia *f*.

color ['kʌlər] *(Am)* = **colour**.

colour ['kʌləʳ] ◇ *n* colore *m* ◇ *adj (photograph, film)* a colori ◇ *vt (hair)* tingere; *(food)* colorare.

◆ **colour in** *vt sep* colorare.

colour-blind *adj* daltonico(-a).

colourful ['kʌləfʊl] *adj* vivace.

colouring ['kʌlərɪŋ] *n (of food)*

colorante *m*; *(complexion)* colorito *m*.

colouring book *n* album *m inv* da colorare.

colour supplement *n* supplemento *m* a colori.

colour television *n* televisione *f* a colori.

column ['kɒləm] *n* colonna *f*; *(newspaper article)* rubrica *f*.

coma ['kəumə] *n* coma *m*.

comb [kəum] ◇ *n* pettine *m* ◇ *vt*: **to ~ one's hair** pettinarsi.

combination [ˌkɒmbɪ'neɪʃn] *n* combinazione *f*.

combine [kəm'baɪn] *vt*: **to ~ sthg (with)** combinare qc (con).

combine harvester ['kɒmbaɪn-'hɑːvɪstə^r] *n* mietitrebbia *f*.

come [kʌm] (*pt* **came**, *pp* **come**) *vi* 1. *(move)* venire; **we came by taxi** siamo venuti in taxi; **~ and see!** vieni a vedere!; **~ here!** vieni qui! 2. *(arrive)* arrivare; **they still haven't ~** non sono ancora arrivati; **to ~ home** tornare a casa; **'coming soon'** 'prossimamente'. 3. *(in order)*: **to ~ first** *(in sequence)* venire per primo; *(in competition)* arrivare primo; **to ~ last** *(in sequence)* venire per ultimo; *(in competition)* arrivare ultimo. 4. *(reach)*: **to ~ up/down to** arrivare a. 5. *(become)*: **to ~ undone** slacciarsi; **to ~ true** realizzarsi. 6. *(be sold)*: **they ~ in packs of six** si vendono in confezioni da sei.

◆ **come across** *vt fus (person)* imbattersi in; *(thing)* trovare (per caso).

◆ **come along** *vi (progress)* procedere; *(arrive)* arrivare; **~ along!** *(as encouragement)* forza!; *(hurry up)* sbrigati!

◆ **come apart** *vi* cadere a pezzi.

◆ **come back** *vi* tornare.

◆ **come down** *vi (price)* calare.

◆ **come down with** *vt fus (illness)* buscarsi.

◆ **come from** *vt fus* venire da.

◆ **come in** *vi (enter)* entrare; *(arrive)* arrivare; *(tide)* salire; **~ in!** avanti!

◆ **come off** *vi (become detached)* staccarsi, venir via; *(succeed)* riuscire.

◆ **come on** *vi (project)* procedere; *(student)* fare progressi; **~ on!** *(as encouragement)* forza!; *(hurry up)* sbrigati!

◆ **come out** *vi* uscire; *(photo)* venire, riuscire; *(stain)* scomparire; *(sun, moon)* apparire.

◆ **come over** *vi (visit)* venire.

◆ **come round** *vi (visit)* venire; *(regain consciousness)* riprendere conoscenza.

◆ **come to** *vt fus (subj: bill)*: **it ~s to £10** viene 10 sterline.

◆ **come up** *vi (go upstairs)* salire; *(be mentioned)* essere sollevato(-a); *(happen, arise)* presentarsi; *(sun, moon)* sorgere.

◆ **come up with** *vt fus (idea)* proporre.

comedian [kə'miːdjən] *n* comico *m* (-a *f*).

comedy ['kɒmədɪ] *n* commedia *f*; *(humour)* humour *m*.

comfort ['kʌmfət] ◇ *n (ease)* benessere *m*; *(luxury)* comfort *m inv*, comodità *f inv*; *(consolation)* conforto *m* ◇ *vt* confortare, consolare.

comfortable ['kʌmftəbl] *adj* comodo(-a); *(after operation)* in condizioni stazionarie; *(financially)* agiato(-a); **I don't feel ~ here** non mi sento a mio agio qui.

comic ['kɒmɪk] ◇ *adj* comico(-a) ◇ *n (person)* comico *m* (-a *f*); *(magazine)* giornalino *m*.

comical ['kɒmɪkl] *adj* comico(-a).

comic strip *n* fumetto *m*.

comma ['kɒmə] *n* virgola *f*.

command [kəˈmɑːnd] ◇ *n (order)* comando *m*, ordine *m*; *(mastery)* padronanza *f* ◇ *vt (order)* ordinare a; *(be in charge of)* comandare.

commander [kəˈmɑːndəʳ] *n* comandante *m*.

commemorate [kəˈmeməreɪt] *vt* commemorare.

commence [kəˈmens] *vi (fml)* cominciare.

comment [ˈkɒment] ◇ *n* commento *m* ◇ *vi* commentare.

commentary [ˈkɒməntrɪ] *n (on TV)* telecronaca *f*; *(on radio)* radiocronaca *f*.

commentator [ˈkɒmənteɪtəʳ] *n (on TV)* telecronista *mf*; *(on radio)* radiocronista *mf*.

commerce [ˈkɒmɜːs] *n* commercio *m*.

commercial [kəˈmɜːʃl] ◇ *adj* commerciale ◇ *n* pubblicità *f inv*.

commercial break *n* intervallo *m* pubblicitario.

commission [kəˈmɪʃn] *n* commissione *f*.

commit [kəˈmɪt] *vt (crime, sin)* commettere; **to ~ o.s. (to doing sthg)** impegnarsi (a fare qc); **to ~ suicide** suicidarsi.

committee [kəˈmɪtɪ] *n* comitato *m*.

commodity [kəˈmɒdətɪ] *n* merce *f*, articolo *m*.

common [ˈkɒmən] ◇ *adj* comune; *(pej: vulgar)* volgare ◇ *n (Br: land)* prato *m* pubblico; **in ~** *(shared)* in comune.

commonly [ˈkɒmənlɪ] *adv (generally)* comunemente.

Common Market *n* Mercato *m* comune.

common room *n (for teachers)* sala *f* professori; *(for students)* sala di ritrovo.

common sense *n* buon senso *m*.

Commonwealth [ˈkɒmənwelθ] *n*: **the ~** il Commonwealth.

communal [ˈkɒmjʊnl] *adj (bathroom, kitchen)* in comune.

communicate [kəˈmjuːnɪkeɪt] *vi*: **to ~ (with)** comunicare (con).

communication [kəˌmjuːnɪˈkeɪʃn] *n* comunicazione *f*.

communication cord *n (Br)* freno *m* di emergenza.

communist [ˈkɒmjʊnɪst] *n* comunista *mf*.

community [kəˈmjuːnətɪ] *n* comunità *f inv*.

community centre *n* centro *m* sociale.

commute [kəˈmjuːt] *vi* fare il pendolare.

commuter [kəˈmjuːtəʳ] *n* pendolare *mf*.

compact [*adj* kəmˈpækt, *n* ˈkɒmpækt] ◇ *adj* compatto(-a) ◇ *n (for make-up)* portacipria *m inv*; *(Am: car)* utilitaria *f*.

compact disc [ˌkɒmpækt-] *n* compact disc *m inv*.

compact disc player *n* lettore *m* di compact disc.

company [ˈkʌmpənɪ] *n (business)* società *f inv*, compagnia *f*; *(companionship, guests)* compagnia; **to keep sb ~** fare OR tenere compagnia a qn.

company car *n* auto *f* della ditta.

comparatively [kəmˈpærətɪvlɪ] *adv* relativamente.

compare [kəmˈpeəʳ] *vt*: **to ~ sthg (with)** confrontare qc (con); **~d with** paragonato a.

comparison [kəmˈpærɪsn] *n* confronto *m*, paragone *m*; **in ~ with** in confronto a.

compartment [kəmˈpɑːtmənt] *n (of train)* scompartimento *m*; *(section)* compartimento *m*.

compass [ˈkʌmpəs] *n (magnetic)* bussola *f*; **(a pair of) ~es** un compasso.

compatible [kəmˈpætəbl] *adj* compatibile.

compensate ['kɒmpenseɪt] ◇ *vt* risarcire ◇ *vi*: **to ~ (for sthg)** compensare (qc); **to ~ sb for sthg** compensare qn di OR per qc.

compensation [,kɒmpen'seɪʃn] *n (money)* risarcimento *m*.

compete [kəm'pi:t] *vi (take part)* gareggiare, concorrere; **to ~ with sb for sthg** competere con qn per qc.

competent ['kɒmpɪtənt] *adj* competente.

competition [,kɒmpɪ'tɪʃn] *n (race, contest)* gara *f*, competizione *f*; *(rivalry)* concorrenza *f*; **the ~** *(rivals)* la concorrenza.

competitive [kəm'petətɪv] *adj (price)* competitivo(-a); *(person)* che ha spirito di competizione.

competitor [kəm'petɪtə^r] *n* concorrente *mf*.

complain [kəm'pleɪn] *vi*: **to ~ (about)** lamentarsi (di).

complaint [kəm'pleɪnt] *n (statement)* lamentela *f*, reclamo *m*; *(illness)* malattia *f*.

complement ['kɒmplɪ,ment] *vt* completare.

complete [kəm'pli:t] ◇ *adj* completo(-a) ◇ *vt* completare; *(a form)* riempire; **~ with** completo di.

completely [kəm'pli:tlɪ] *adv* completamente.

complex ['kɒmpleks] ◇ *adj* complesso(-a) ◇ *n* complesso *m*.

complexion [kəm'plekʃn] *n (of skin)* carnagione *f*.

complicated ['kɒmplɪkeɪtɪd] *adj* complicato(-a).

compliment [*n* 'kɒmplɪmənt, *vb* 'kɒmplɪment] ◇ *n* complimento *m* ◇ *vt* fare i complimenti a.

complimentary [,kɒmplɪ'mentərɪ] *adj (seat, ticket)* (in) omaggio *(inv)*; *(words, person)* lusinghiero(-a).

compose [kəm'pəʊz] *vt* comporre; **to be ~d of** essere composto da OR di.

composed [kəm'pəʊzd] *adj* composto(-a), calmo(-a).

composer [kəm'pəʊzə^r] *n* compositore *m* (-trice *f*).

composition [,kɒmpə'zɪʃn] *n (essay)* composizione *f*.

compound ['kɒmpaʊnd] *n (substance)* composto *m*; *(word)* parola *f* composta.

comprehensive [,kɒmprɪ'hensɪv] *adj* esauriente, completo(-a).

comprehensive (school) *n (Br) scuola secondaria ad ammissione non selettiva.*

compressed air [kəm'prest-] *n* aria *f* compressa.

comprise [kəm'praɪz] *vt* comprendere.

compromise ['kɒmprəmaɪz] *n* compromesso *m*.

compulsory [kəm'pʌlsərɪ] *adj* obbligatorio(-a).

computer [kəm'pju:tə^r] *n* computer *m inv*.

computer game *n* gioco *m* su computer.

computerized [kəm'pju:təraɪzd] *adj* computerizzato(-a).

computer operator *n* operatore *m* (-trice *f*) di computer.

computer programmer [-'prəʊgræmə^r] *n* programmatore *m* (-trice *f*).

computing [kəm'pju:tɪŋ] *n* informatica *f*.

con [kɒn] *n (inf: trick)* truffa *f*; **all mod ~s** tutti i comfort.

conceal [kən'si:l] *vt* nascondere.

conceited [kən'si:tɪd] *adj (pej)* presuntuoso(-a).

concentrate ['kɒnsəntreɪt] ◇ *vi* concentrarsi ◇ *vt*: **to be ~d** *(in one place)* essere concentrato; **to ~ on sthg** concentrarsi su qc.

concentrated ['kɒnsəntreɪtɪd] *adj (juice, soup, baby food)* concentrato(-a).

concentration [,kɒnsən'treɪʃn] *n*

concentrazione *f*.

concern [kən'sɜ:n] ◇ *n (worry)* preoccupazione *f*; *(matter of interest)* affare *m*; (COMM) azienda *f* ◇ *vt (be about)* trattare di; *(worry)* preoccupare; *(involve)* riguardare; **to be ~ed about** essere preoccupato per; **to be ~ed with** riguardare; **to ~ o.s. with sthg** preoccuparsi di qc; **as far as I'm ~ed** per quanto mi riguarda.

concerned [kən'sɜ:nd] *adj (worried)* preoccupato(-a).

concerning [kən'sɜ:nɪŋ] *prep* riguardo a, circa.

concert ['kɒnsət] *n* concerto *m*.

concession [kən'seʃn] *n (reduced price)* riduzione *f*.

concise [kən'saɪs] *adj* conciso(-a).

conclude [kən'klu:d] ◇ *vt* concludere ◇ *vi (fml: end)* concludersi.

conclusion [kən'klu:ʒn] *n* conclusione *f*.

concrete ['kɒŋkri:t] ◇ *adj (building, path)* di cemento; *(idea, plan)* concreto(-a) ◇ *n* calcestruzzo *m*, cemento *m* armato.

concussion [kən'kʌʃn] *n* commozione *f* cerebrale.

condensation [,kɒnden'seɪʃn] *n* condensazione *f*.

condensed milk [kən'denst-] *n* latte *m* condensato.

condition [kən'dɪʃn] *n* condizione *f*; *(illness)* malattia *f*; **to be out of ~** non essere in forma; **on ~ that** a condizione che *(+ subjunctive)*.

conditioner [kən'dɪʃnər] *n (for hair)* balsamo *m*; *(for clothes)* ammorbidente *m*.

condo ['kɒndəʊ] *(Am: inf)* = **condominium**.

condom ['kɒndəm] *n* preservativo *m*.

condominium [,kɒndə'mɪnɪəm] *n (Am) (block of flats)* condominio *m*; *(flat)* appartamento *m* in un condominio.

conduct [*vb* kən'dʌkt, *n* 'kɒndʌkt] ◇ *vt (investigation, business)* dirigere, condurre; (MUS) dirigere ◇ *n (fml: behaviour)* condotta *f*; **to ~ o.s.** *(fml)* comportarsi.

conductor [kən'dʌktər] *n* (MUS) direttore *m* (-trice *f*) d'orchestra; *(on bus)* bigliettaio *m* (-a *f*); *(Am: on train)* capotreno *mf*.

cone [kəʊn] *n* cono *m*; *(on roads)* cono spartitraffico.

confectioner's [kən'fekʃnəz] *n (shop)* negozio *m* di dolciumi.

confectionery [kən'fekʃnərɪ] *n* dolciumi *mpl*.

conference ['kɒnfərəns] *n* conferenza *f*.

confess [kən'fes] *vi*: **to ~ (to sthg)** confessare (qc).

confession [kən'feʃn] *n* confessione *f*.

confidence ['kɒnfɪdəns] *n (self-assurance)* sicurezza *f* di sé; *(trust)* fiducia *f*; **to have ~ in** avere fiducia in.

confident ['kɒnfɪdənt] *adj (self-assured)* sicuro(-a) di sé; *(certain)* sicuro.

confined [kən'faɪnd] *adj* ristretto(-a).

confirm [kən'fɜ:m] *vt* confermare.

confirmation [,kɒnfə'meɪʃn] *n* conferma *f*; (RELIG) cresima *f*.

conflict [*n* 'kɒnflɪkt, *vb* kən'flɪkt] ◇ *n* conflitto *m* ◇ *vi*: **to ~ (with)** essere in conflitto (con).

conform [kən'fɔ:m] *vi*: **to ~ (to)** conformarsi (a).

confuse [kən'fju:z] *vt* confondere; **to ~ sthg with sthg** confondere qc con qc.

confused [kən'fju:zd] *adj* confuso(-a).

confusing [kən'fju:zɪŋ] *adj (explanation, plot)* confuso(-a).

confusion [kən'fju:ʒn] *n* confusione *f*.

congested [kən'dʒestɪd] *adj (street)* congestionato(-a).
congestion [kən'dʒestʃn] *n (traffic)* congestione *f*.
congratulate [kən'grætʃʊleɪt] *vt*: **to ~ sb (on sthg)** congratularsi con qn (per OR di qc).
congratulations [kən,grætʃʊ'leɪʃənz] *excl* congratulazioni!
congregate ['kɒŋgrɪgeɪt] *vi* riunirsi.
Congress ['kɒŋgres] *n (Am)* il Congresso.
conifer ['kɒnɪfəʳ] *n* conifera *f*.
conjunction [kən'dʒʌŋkʃn] *n* (GRAMM) congiunzione *f*.
conjurer ['kʌndʒərəʳ] *n* prestigiatore *m* (-trice *f*).
connect [kə'nekt] ◇ *vt* collegare, connettere; *(telephone, machine)* collegare; *(caller on phone)* dare la linea a ◇ *vi*: **to ~ with** *(train, plane)* avere la coincidenza con; **to ~ sthg with sthg** *(associate)* collegare qc con OR a qc.
connecting flight [kə'nektɪŋ-] *n* volo *m* di coincidenza.
connection [kə'nekʃn] *n (link)* collegamento *m*; *(train, plane)* coincidenza *f*; **it's a bad ~** *(on phone)* la linea è disturbata; **a loose ~** *(in machine)* un contatto difettoso; **in ~ with** riguardo a, a proposito di.
conquer ['kɒŋkəʳ] *vt (country)* conquistare.
conscience ['kɒnʃəns] *n* coscienza *f*.
conscientious [,kɒnʃɪ'enʃəs] *adj* coscienzioso(-a).
conscious ['kɒnʃəs] *adj (awake)* cosciente; *(deliberate)* consapevole; **to be ~ of** *(aware)* essere consapevole di.
consent [kən'sent] *n* consenso *m*.
consequence ['kɒnsɪkwəns] *n (result)* conseguenza *f*.
consequently ['kɒnsɪkwəntlɪ] *adv* di conseguenza.
conservation [,kɒnsə'veɪʃn] *n* tutela *f* dell'ambiente.
conservative [kən'sɜːvətɪv] *adj* conservatore(-trice).
◆ **Conservative** ◇ *adj* conservatore(-trice) ◇ *n* conservatore *m* (-trice *f*).
conservatory [kən'sɜːvətrɪ] *n* veranda *f* vetrata.
consider [kən'sɪdəʳ] *vt* considerare; **to ~ doing sthg** pensare di fare qc.
considerable [kən'sɪdrəbl] *adj* considerevole.
consideration [kən,sɪdə'reɪʃn] *n* considerazione *f*; **to take sthg into ~** prendere qc in considerazione.
considering [kən'sɪdərɪŋ] *prep* considerando.
consist [kən'sɪst] : **consist in** *vt fus* consistere in; **to ~ in doing sthg** consistere nel fare qc.
◆ **consist of** *vt fus* essere composto di OR da.
consistent [kən'sɪstənt] *adj (coherent)* coerente; *(worker, performance)* costante.
consolation [,kɒnsə'leɪʃn] *n* consolazione *f*.
console ['kɒnsəʊl] *n* console *f inv*.
consonant ['kɒnsənənt] *n* consonante *f*.
conspicuous [kən'spɪkjʊəs] *adj* cospicuo(-a).
constable ['kʌnstəbl] *n (Br)* agente *m* di polizia.
constant ['kɒnstənt] *adj (unchanging)* costante; *(continuous)* continuo(-a).
constantly ['kɒnstəntlɪ] *adv (all the time)* continuamente.
constipated ['kɒnstɪpeɪtɪd] *adj* stitico(-a).
constitution [,kɒnstɪ'tjuːʃn] *n* costituzione *f*.
construct [kən'strʌkt] *vt* costruire.

construction [kən'strʌkʃn] *n* costruzione *f*; **under ~** in costruzione.

consul ['kɒnsəl] *n* console *m*.

consulate ['kɒnsjʊlət] *n* consolato *m*.

consult [kən'sʌlt] *vt* consultare.

consultant [kən'sʌltənt] *n (Br: doctor)* specialista *mf*.

consume [kən'sju:m] *vt* consumare.

consumer [kən'sju:mə^r] *n* consumatore *m* (-trice *f*).

contact ['kɒntækt] ◇ *n (communication)* contatto *m*; *(person)* conoscenza *f* ◇ *vt* mettersi in contatto con; **in ~ with** *(in communication with)* in contatto con; *(touching)* a contatto con.

contact lens *n* lente *f* a contatto.

contagious [kən'teɪdʒəs] *adj* contagioso(-a).

contain [kən'teɪn] *vt* contenere.

container [kən'teɪnə^r] *n (box etc)* contenitore *m*, recipiente *m*.

contaminate [kən'tæmɪneɪt] *vt* contaminare.

contemporary [kən'tempərərɪ] ◇ *adj* contemporaneo(-a) ◇ *n* contemporaneo *m* (-a *f*).

contend [kən'tend]: **contend with** *vt fus* affrontare.

content [*adj* kən'tent, *n* 'kɒntent] ◇ *adj* contento(-a) ◇ *n (of vitamins, fibre etc)* contenuto *m*.

◆ **contents** *npl (things inside)* contenuto *m*; *(at beginning of book)* indice *m*.

contest [*n* 'kɒntest, *vb* kən'test] ◇ *n (competition)* gara *f*, concorso *m*; *(struggle)* lotta *f* ◇ *vt (election, seat)* candidarsi per; *(decision, will)* contestare.

context ['kɒntekst] *n* contesto *m*.

continent ['kɒntɪnənt] *n* continente *m*; **the Continent** *(Br)* l'Europa *f* continentale.

continental [,kɒntɪ'nentl] *adj (Br: European)* (dell'Europa) continentale.

continental breakfast *n* colazione *f* continentale.

continental quilt *n (Br)* piumone® *m*.

continual [kən'tɪnjʊəl] *adj* continuo(-a).

continually [kən'tɪnjʊəlɪ] *adv* continuamente, di continuo.

continue [kən'tɪnju:] *vt & vi* continuare; **to ~ doing sthg** continuare a fare qc; **to ~ with sthg** continuare con qc.

continuous [kən'tɪnjʊəs] *adj* continuo(-a).

continuously [kən'tɪnjʊəslɪ] *adv* continuamente, senza interruzione.

contraception [,kɒntrə'sepʃn] *n* contraccezione *f*.

contraceptive [,kɒntrə'septɪv] *n* contraccettivo *m*.

contract [*n* 'kɒntrækt, *vb* kən'trækt] ◇ *n* contratto *m* ◇ *vt (fml: illness)* contrarre.

contradict [,kɒntrə'dɪkt] *vt* contraddire.

contraflow ['kɒntrəfləʊ] *n (Br) sistema che permette il traffico nei due sensi su una stessa carreggiata dell'autostrada per lavori in corso o per un incidente.*

contrary ['kɒntrərɪ] *n*: **on the ~** al contrario.

contrast [*n* 'kɒntrɑ:st, *vb* kən'trɑ:st] ◇ *n* contrasto *m* ◇ *vt* mettere in contrasto; **in ~ to** contrariamente a.

contribute [kən'trɪbju:t] ◇ *vt (help, money)* dare (come contributo) ◇ *vi*: **to ~ to** contribuire a.

contribution [,kɒntrɪ'bju:ʃn] *n* contributo *m*.

control [kən'trəʊl] ◇ *n* controllo *m*; *(operating device)* comando *m* ◇ *vt* controllare; *(machine)* regolare; **to be in ~** avere la situazione sotto controllo; **to get out of ~** *(situation)* sfuggire di mano; **to go out of ~** *(car, plane)* non rispondere ai comandi; **under ~** sotto controllo.

◆ **controls** *npl* comandi *mpl*.

control tower *n* torre *f* di controllo.

controversial [ˌkɒntrəˈvɜːʃl] *adj* controverso(-a); *(person)* polemico(-a).

convenience [kənˈviːnjəns] *n* comodità *f inv*; **at your ~** quando Le è più comodo.

convenient [kənˈviːnjənt] *adj* comodo(-a); **would tomorrow be ~?** domani andrebbe bene?

convent [ˈkɒnvənt] *n* convento *m*.

conventional [kənˈvenʃənl] *adj* convenzionale.

conversation [ˌkɒnvəˈseɪʃn] *n* conversazione *f*.

conversion [kənˈvɜːʃn] *n (change)* trasformazione *f*; *(of currency)* conversione *f*; *(to building)* ristrutturazione *f*.

convert [kənˈvɜːt] *vt (change)* trasformare; *(currency, person)* convertire; **to ~ sthg into** trasformare qc in.

converted [kənˈvɜːtɪd] *adj (barn, loft)* ristrutturato(-a).

convertible [kənˈvɜːtəbl] *n* cabriolet *m inv*.

convey [kənˈveɪ] *vt (fml: transport)* trasportare; *(idea, impression)* dare.

convict [*n* ˈkɒnvɪkt, *vb* kənˈvɪkt] ◇ *n* carcerato *m* (-a *f*) ◇ *vt*: **to ~ sb (of)** giudicare qn colpevole (di).

convince [kənˈvɪns] *vt*: **to ~ sb (of sthg)** convincere qn (di qc); **to ~ sb to do sthg** convincere qn a fare qc.

convoy [ˈkɒnvɔɪ] *n* convoglio *m*.

cook [kʊk] ◇ *n* cuoco *m* (-a *f*) ◇ *vt (meal)* cucinare; *(food)* cuocere ◇ *vi (person)* cucinare; *(food)* cuocere.

cookbook [ˈkʊkˌbʊk] = **cookery book**.

cooker [ˈkʊkə^r] *n* cucina *f (elettrodomestico)*.

cookery [ˈkʊkərɪ] *n* cucina *f*.

cookery book *n* libro *m* di cucina.

cookie [ˈkʊkɪ] *n (Am)* biscotto *m*.

cooking [ˈkʊkɪŋ] *n* cucina *f*.

cooking apple *n* mela *f* da cuocere.

cooking oil *n* olio *m* per cucinare.

cool [kuːl] ◇ *adj (temperature)* fresco(-a); *(calm)* calmo(-a); *(unfriendly)* freddo(-a); *(inf: great)* fantastico(-a) ◇ *vt* raffreddare.

◆ **cool down** *vi (become colder)* raffreddarsi; *(become calmer)* calmarsi.

cooperate [kəʊˈɒpəreɪt] *vi* collaborare, cooperare.

cooperation [kəʊˌɒpəˈreɪʃn] *n* collaborazione *f*.

cooperative [kəʊˈɒpərətɪv] *adj (helpful)* disposto(-a) a collaborare.

coordinates [kəʊˈɔːdɪnəts] *npl (clothes)* coordinati *mpl*.

cope [kəʊp] *vi*: **to ~ with** far fronte a; **I can't ~!** non ce la faccio!

copilot [ˈkəʊˌpaɪlət] *n* secondo pilota *m*.

copper [ˈkɒpə^r] *n (metal)* rame *m*; *(Br: inf: coin) moneta in rame da uno o due penny*.

copy [ˈkɒpɪ] ◇ *n* copia *f* ◇ *vt* copiare.

cord(uroy) [ˈkɔːd(ərɔɪ)] *n* velluto *m* a coste.

core [kɔː^r] *n (of fruit)* torsolo *m*.

coriander [ˌkɒrɪˈændə^r] *n* coriandolo *m (spezia)*.

cork [kɔːk] *n (in bottle)* tappo *m* (di sughero).

corkscrew [ˈkɔːkskruː] *n* cavatappi *m inv*.

corn [kɔːn] *n (Br: crop)* cereali *mpl*; *(Am: maize)* granturco *m*; *(on foot)* callo *m*.

corned beef [ˌkɔːnd-] *n* carne *f* di manzo in scatola.

corner ['kɔ:nəʳ] *n* angolo *m*; *(bend in road)* curva *f*; *(in football)* calcio *m* d'angolo; **it's just around the ~** è qui dietro l'angolo.

corner shop *n (Br)* negozietto *m (di alimentari e prodotti per la casa)*.

cornet ['kɔ:nɪt] *n (Br: ice-cream cone)* cornetto *m*.

cornflakes ['kɔ:nfleɪks] *npl* cornflakes *mpl*.

corn-on-the-cob *n* pannocchia *f* bollita.

Cornwall ['kɔ:nwɔ:l] *n* la Cornovaglia.

corporal ['kɔ:pərəl] *n* caporale *m*.

corpse [kɔ:ps] *n* cadavere *m*.

correct [kə'rekt] ◇ *adj* giusto(-a) ◇ *vt* correggere.

correction [kə'rekʃn] *n* correzione *f*.

correspond [ˌkɒrɪ'spɒnd] *vi*: **to ~ (to)** *(match)* corrispondere (a); **to ~ (with)** *(exchange letters)* essere in corrispondenza (con).

corresponding [ˌkɒrɪ'spɒndɪŋ] *adj* corrispondente.

corridor ['kɒrɪdɔ:ʳ] *n* corridoio *m*.

corrugated iron ['kɒrəgeɪtɪd-] *n* lamiera *f* ondulata.

corrupt [kə'rʌpt] *adj* corrotto(-a).

cosmetics [kɒz'metɪks] *npl* cosmetici *mpl*.

cost [kɒst] (*pt & pp* **cost**) ◇ *n* costo *m*; *(fig: loss)* prezzo *m* ◇ *vt* costare; **how much does it ~?** quanto costa?

costly ['kɒstlɪ] *adj (expensive)* costoso(-a).

costume ['kɒstju:m] *n* costume *m*.

cosy ['kəʊzɪ] *adj (Br: room, house)* accogliente.

cot [kɒt] *n (Br: for baby)* lettino *m* (per bambini); *(Am: camp bed)* brandina *f*.

cottage ['kɒtɪdʒ] *n* cottage *m inv*.

cottage cheese *n* formaggio *m* magro in fiocchi.

cottage pie *n (Br) pasticcio a base di carne macinata e purè di patate.*

cotton ['kɒtn] ◇ *adj* di cotone ◇ *n* cotone *m*.

cotton candy *n (Am)* zucchero *m* filato.

cotton wool *n* cotone *m* idrofilo.

couch [kaʊtʃ] *n* divano *m*; *(at doctor's)* lettino *m*.

couchette [ku:'ʃet] *n* cuccetta *f*.

cough [kɒf] ◇ *n* tosse *f* ◇ *vi* tossire; **to have a ~** avere la tosse.

cough mixture *n* sciroppo *m* per la tosse.

could [kʊd] *pt* → **can**.

couldn't ['kʊdnt] = **could not**.

could've ['kʊdəv] = **could have**.

council ['kaʊnsl] *n (Br: of town)* comune *m*; *(Br: of county)* = regione *f*; *(organization)* consiglio *m*.

council house *n (Br)* casa *f* popolare.

councillor ['kaʊnsələʳ] *n (Br: of town, county)* consigliere *m* (-a *f*).

council tax *n (Br)* ≃ tassa *f* comunale.

count [kaʊnt] ◇ *vt & vi* contare ◇ *n (nobleman)* conte *m*.

◆ **count on** *vt fus* contare su.

counter ['kaʊntəʳ] *n (in shop)* banco *m*; *(in bank)* sportello *m*; *(in board game)* fiche *f inv*.

counterclockwise [ˌkaʊntə'klɒkwaɪz] *adv (Am)* in senso antiorario.

counterfoil ['kaʊntəfɔɪl] *n* matrice *f*.

countess ['kaʊntɪs] *n* contessa *f*.

country ['kʌntrɪ] ◇ *n* paese *m*; *(countryside)* campagna *f* ◇ *adj* di campagna.

country and western *n* (musica *f*) country *m*.

country house *n* villa *f* di campagna.

country road *n* strada *f* di campagna.

countryside [ˈkʌntrɪsaɪd] *n* campagna *f*.

county [ˈkaʊntɪ] *n* contea *f*.

couple [ˈkʌpl] *n* coppia *f*; **a ~ (of)** un paio (di).

coupon [ˈkuːpɒn] *n (for discount etc)* buono *m*; *(for orders, enquiries)* tagliando *m*.

courage [ˈkʌrɪdʒ] *n* coraggio *m*.

courgette [kɔːˈʒet] *n (Br)* zucchino *m*.

courier [ˈkʊrɪəʳ] *n (for holidaymakers)* accompagnatore *m* (-trice *f*); *(for delivering letters)* corriere *m*.

course [kɔːs] *n* corso *m*; *(of meal)* portata *f*; *(of treatment, injections)* ciclo *m*; *(of ship, plane)* rotta *f*; *(for golf)* campo *m*; **of ~** *(certainly)* certo; *(evidently)* naturalmente; **of ~ not** certo che no; **in the ~ of** nel corso di, durante.

court [kɔːt] *n* (JUR*: building, room*) tribunale *m*; (SPORT) campo *m*; *(of king, queen)* corte *f*.

courtesy coach [ˈkɜːtɪsɪ-] *n* pullman *m inv* gratuito *(di hotel, aeroporto ecc.)*.

court shoes *npl* scarpe *fpl* décolleté.

courtyard [ˈkɔːtjɑːd] *n* cortile *m*.

cousin [ˈkʌzn] *n* cugino *m* (-a *f*).

cover [ˈkʌvəʳ] ◇ *n (covering)* fodera *f*; *(lid)* coperchio *m*; *(of book, magazine)* copertina *f*; *(blanket)* coperta *f*; *(insurance)* copertura *f* ◇ *vt* coprire; *(apply to)* comprendere; *(discuss)* trattare; *(report)* fare un servizio su; **to be ~ed in** essere ricoperto di OR da; **to ~ sthg with sthg** coprire qc con qc; **to take ~** mettersi al riparo.

◆ **cover up** *vt sep (put cover on)* coprire; *(facts, truth)* nascondere.

cover charge *n* coperto *m*.

cover note *n (Br)* polizza *f* di assicurazione provvisoria.

cow [kaʊ] *n* vacca *f*.

coward [ˈkaʊəd] *n* vigliacco *m* (-a *f*).

cowboy [ˈkaʊbɔɪ] *n* cow-boy *m inv*.

crab [kræb] *n* granchio *m*.

crack [kræk] ◇ *n (in cup, glass)* incrinatura *f*, crepa *f*; *(gap)* fessura *f* ◇ *vt (cup, glass, wood)* incrinare; *(nut)* schiacciare; *(egg)* rompere; *(whip)* schioccare ◇ *vi (cup, glass, wood)* incrinarsi; **to ~ a joke** *(inf)* fare una battuta.

cracker [ˈkrækəʳ] *n (biscuit)* cracker *m inv*; *(for Christmas) tubo di cartone rivestito di carta da regalo che quando viene aperto produce uno scoppio e fa uscire una sorpresa. Tipico delle feste natalizie.*

cradle [ˈkreɪdl] *n* culla *f*.

craft [krɑːft] *n (skill)* arte *f*; *(trade)* artigianato *m*; *(boat: pl inv)* imbarcazione *f*.

craftsman [ˈkrɑːftsmən] (*pl* **-men** [-mən]) *n* artigiano *m*.

cram [kræm] *vt*: **to ~ sthg into** stipare qc in; **to be crammed with** essere stipato di.

cramp [kræmp] *n* crampo *m*; **stomach ~s** crampi allo stomaco.

cranberry [ˈkrænbərɪ] *n* mirtillo *m*.

cranberry sauce *n* salsa *f* di mirtilli.

crane [kreɪn] *n (machine)* gru *f inv*.

crap [kræp] ◇ *adj (vulg)* di merda ◇ *n (vulg)* merda *f*.

crash [kræʃ] ◇ *n (accident)* incidente *m*; *(noise)* schianto *m* ◇ *vt (car)* sfasciare ◇ *vi (car, train)* schiantarsi; *(plane)* precipitare.

◆ **crash into** *vt fus* schiantarsi contro.

crash helmet *n* casco *m*.

crash landing *n* atterraggio *m* di fortuna.

crate [kreɪt] *n* cassa *f*.

crawl [krɔːl] ◇ *vi (baby)* andare carponi; *(person)* strisciare; *(insect)*

muoversi lentamente; *(traffic)* andare a passo d'uomo ◇ *n (swimming stroke)* stile *m* libero.
crawler lane ['krɔːləʳ-] *n (Br)* corsia *f* per veicoli lenti.
crayfish ['kreɪfɪʃ] *(pl inv) n* gambero *m* di fiume.
crayon ['kreɪɒn] *n* matita *f* colorata.
craze [kreɪz] *n* mania *f*.
crazy ['kreɪzɪ] *adj* matto(-a), pazzo(-a); **to be ~ about** andare matto per.
crazy golf *n* minigolf *m*.
cream [kriːm] ◇ *n* crema *f*; *(fresh)* panna *f* ◇ *adj (in colour)* color crema *(inv)*.
cream cake *n (Br)* torta *f* alla panna.
cream cheese *n* formaggio *m* cremoso.
cream sherry *n* sherry *m inv* dolce.
cream tea *n (Br) merenda a base di tè e 'scones', serviti con marmellata e panna.*
creamy ['kriːmɪ] *adj (food)* alla panna; *(texture)* cremoso(-a).
crease [kriːs] *n* grinza *f*.
creased [kriːst] *adj* sgualcito(-a).
create [kriː'eɪt] *vt* creare.
creative [kriː'eɪtɪv] *adj* creativo(-a).
creature ['kriːtʃəʳ] *n* creatura *f*.
crèche [kreʃ] *n (Br)* nursery *f inv*.
credit ['kredɪt] *n (praise)* merito *m*; *(money)* credito *m*; *(part of school, university course) sezione completata di un corso di studio*; **to be in ~** essere in attivo.
◆ **credits** *npl (of film)* titoli *mpl*.
credit card *n* carta *f* di credito; **to pay by ~** pagare con la carta di credito; **'all major ~s accepted'** 'si accettano tutte le maggiori carte di credito'.
creek [kriːk] *n (inlet)* insenatura *f*; *(Am: river)* ruscello *m*.
creep [kriːp] (*pt & pp* **crept**) ◇ *vi (crawl)* strisciare; *(walk)* muoversi furtivamente ◇ *n (inf: groveller)* leccapiedi *mf inv*.
cremate [krɪ'meɪt] *vt* cremare.
crematorium [ˌkremə'tɔːrɪəm] *n* crematorio *m*.
crepe [kreɪp] *n (thin pancake)* crêpe *f inv*.
crept [krept] *pt & pp* → **creep**.
cress [kres] *n* crescione *m*.
crest [krest] *n* cresta *f*; *(emblem)* stemma *m*.
crew [kruː] *n (of ship, plane)* equipaggio *m*.
crew neck *n* girocollo *m*.
crib [krɪb] *n (Am: cot)* lettino *m* (per bambini).
cricket ['krɪkɪt] *n (game)* cricket *m*; *(insect)* grillo *m*.
crime [kraɪm] *n* crimine *m*.
criminal ['krɪmɪnl] ◇ *adj* criminale ◇ *n* criminale *mf*.
cripple ['krɪpl] ◇ *n* storpio *m* (-a *f*) ◇ *vt (subj: disease, accident)* storpiare.
crisis ['kraɪsɪs] (*pl* **crises** ['kraɪsiːz]) *n* crisi *f inv*.
crisp [krɪsp] *adj (bacon, pastry)* croccante; *(fruit, vegetable)* sodo (-a).
◆ **crisps** *npl (Br)* patatine *fpl*.
crispy ['krɪspɪ] *adj* croccante.
critic ['krɪtɪk] *n* critico *m* (-a *f*).
critical ['krɪtɪkl] *adj* critico(-a).
criticize ['krɪtɪsaɪz] *vt* criticare.
crockery ['krɒkərɪ] *n* stoviglie *fpl*.
crocodile ['krɒkədaɪl] *n* coccodrillo *m*.
crocus ['krəʊkəs] (*pl* **-es**) *n* croco *m*.
crooked ['krʊkɪd] *adj (bent, twisted)* storto(-a).
crop [krɒp] *n (kind of plant)* coltivazione *f*; *(harvest)* raccolto *m*.
◆ **crop up** *vi* saltare fuori.
cross [krɒs] ◇ *adj* arrabbiato(-a) ◇ *n* croce *f*; *(mixture)* incrocio *m* ◇

vt (road, river, ocean) attraversare; *(arms, legs)* incrociare; *(Br: cheque)* sbarrare ◇ *vi (intersect)* incrociarsi.
◆ **cross out** *vt sep* sbarrare.
◆ **cross over** *vt fus (road)* attraversare.
crossbar ['krɒsbɑːʳ] *n (of goal)* traversa *f*; *(of bicycle)* canna *f*.
cross-Channel ferry *n* traghetto *m* di servizio sulla Manica.
cross-country (running) *n* corsa *f* campestre.
crossing ['krɒsɪŋ] *n (on road)* attraversamento *m*; *(sea journey)* traversata *f*.
crossroads ['krɒsrəʊdz] *(pl inv) n* incrocio *m*.
crosswalk ['krɒswɔːk] *n (Am)* passaggio *m* pedonale.
crossword (puzzle) ['krɒswɜːd-] *n* cruciverba *m inv*.
crotch [krɒtʃ] *n (of person)* inforcatura *f*.
crouton ['kruːtɒn] *n* crostino *m*.
crow [krəʊ] *n* cornacchia *f*.
crowbar ['krəʊbɑːʳ] *n* piede *m* di porco.
crowd [kraʊd] *n* folla *f*; *(at match)* spettatori *mpl*.
crowded ['kraʊdɪd] *adj* affollato(-a).
crown [kraʊn] *n (of king, queen, on tooth)* corona *f*; *(of head)* sommità *f inv*.
Crown Jewels *npl*: **the ~** i gioielli della Corona.
crucial ['kruːʃl] *adj* cruciale.
crude [kruːd] *adj (drawing)* abbozzato(-a); *(estimate)* approssimativo(-a); *(rude)* rozzo(-a).
cruel [krʊəl] *adj* crudele.
cruelty ['krʊəltɪ] *n* crudeltà *f*.
cruet (set) ['kruːɪt-] *n* ampolliera *f*.
cruise [kruːz] ◇ *n* crociera *f* ◇ *vi (car, plane, ship)* andare a velocità di crociera.
cruiser ['kruːzəʳ] *n (pleasure boat)* cabinato *m*.
crumb [krʌm] *n* briciola *f*.
crumble ['krʌmbl] ◇ *n frutta cotta ricoperta da uno strato di pasta frolla sbriciolata* ◇ *vi (building, cliff)* sgretolarsi; *(pastry, cake, cheese)* sbriciolarsi.
crumpet ['krʌmpɪt] *n tipo di focaccina da mangiarsi calda con burro, marmellata ecc.*
crunchy ['krʌntʃɪ] *adj* croccante.
crush [krʌʃ] ◇ *n (drink)* spremuta *f* ◇ *vt* schiacciare; *(ice)* frantumare.
crust [krʌst] *n* crosta *f*.
crusty ['krʌstɪ] *adj* croccante.
crutch [krʌtʃ] *n (stick)* stampella *f*; *(between legs)* = **crotch**.
cry [kraɪ] ◇ *n* urlo *m*, grido *m*; *(of bird)* verso *m* ◇ *vi (weep)* piangere; *(shout)* urlare, gridare.
◆ **cry out** *vi* urlare, gridare.
crystal ['krɪstl] *n (in jewellery etc)* cristallo *m*; *(glass)* cristallo *m*.
cub [kʌb] *n (animal)* cucciolo *m*.
Cub [kʌb] *n* lupetto *m*.
cube [kjuːb] *n* cubo *m*; *(of sugar, ice)* cubetto *m*.
cubicle ['kjuːbɪkl] *n* cabina *f*.
Cub Scout = **Cub**.
cuckoo ['kʊkuː] *n* cuculo *m*.
cucumber ['kjuːkʌmbəʳ] *n* cetriolo *m*.
cuddle ['kʌdl] *n* coccola *f*.
cuddly toy ['kʌdlɪ-] *n* pupazzo *m* di peluche.
cue [kjuː] *n (in snooker, pool)* stecca *f*.
cuff [kʌf] *n (of sleeve)* polsino *m*; *(Am: of trousers)* risvolto *m*.
cuff links *npl* gemelli *mpl*.
cuisine [kwɪ'ziːn] *n* cucina *f*.
cul-de-sac ['kʌldəsæk] *n* vicolo *m* cieco.
cult [kʌlt] ◇ *n* (RELIG) culto *m* ◇ *adj* di culto.
cultivate ['kʌltɪveɪt] *vt (grow)* coltivare.

cultivated ['kʌltɪveɪtɪd] *adj (person)* raffinato(-a).
cultural ['kʌltʃərəl] *adj* culturale.
culture ['kʌltʃə^r] *n* cultura *f*.
cumbersome ['kʌmbəsəm] *adj* ingombrante.
cumin ['kju:mɪn] *n* cumino *m*.
cunning ['kʌnɪŋ] *adj* furbo(-a).
cup [kʌp] *n* tazza *f*; *(trophy, competition, of bra)* coppa *f*.
cupboard ['kʌbəd] *n (for food, dishes)* credenza *f*; *(for clothes)* armadio *m*.
curator [ˌkjʊə'reɪtə^r] *n* conservatore *m* (*di museo*).
curb [kɜ:b] *(Am)* = **kerb**.
curd cheese [ˌkɜ:d-] *n* cagliata *f*.
cure [kjʊə^r] ◇ *n (for illness)* cura *f* ◇ *vt (illness, person)* curare; *(food)* trattare.
curious ['kjʊərɪəs] *adj* curioso(-a).
curl [kɜ:l] ◇ *n (of hair)* riccio *m* ◇ *vt (hair)* arricciare.
curler ['kɜ:lə^r] *n* bigodino *m*.
curly ['kɜ:lɪ] *adj* riccio(-a).
currant ['kʌrənt] *n* uvetta *f*.
currency ['kʌrənsɪ] *n (money)* moneta *f*.
current ['kʌrənt] ◇ *adj* attuale ◇ *n* corrente *f*.
current account *n (Br)* conto *m* corrente.
current affairs *npl* attualità *f*.
currently ['kʌrəntlɪ] *adv* attualmente.
curriculum [kə'rɪkjələm] *n* curricolo *m*.
curriculum vitae [-'vi:taɪ] *n (Br)* curriculum vitae *m inv*.
curried ['kʌrɪd] *adj* al curry.
curry ['kʌrɪ] *n* piatto *m* al curry.
curse [kɜ:s] *vi* bestemmiare.
cursor ['kɜ:sə^r] *n* cursore *m*.
curtain ['kɜ:tn] *n (in house)* tenda *f*; *(in theatre)* sipario *m*.
curve [kɜ:v] ◇ *n* curva *f* ◇ *vi* curvare.
curved [kɜ:vd] *adj* curvo(-a).
cushion ['kʊʃn] *n (for sitting on)* cuscino *m*.
custard ['kʌstəd] *n* crema *f* gialla.
custom ['kʌstəm] *n (tradition)* usanza *f*; **'thank you for your ~'** 'arrivederci e grazie'.
customary ['kʌstəmrɪ] *adj* abituale.
customer ['kʌstəmə^r] *n (of shop)* cliente *mf*.
customer services *n (department)* servizio *m* clienti.
customs ['kʌstəmz] *n* dogana *f*; **to go through ~** passare la dogana.
customs duty *n* dazio *m* doganale.
customs officer *n* doganiere *m*.
cut [kʌt] (*pt & pp* **cut**) ◇ *n* taglio *m*; *(in taxes)* riduzione *f* ◇ *vt & vi* tagliare; **~ and blow-dry** taglio e piega föhn; **to ~ o.s.** tagliarsi; **to ~ one's finger** tagliarsi un dito; **to have one's hair ~** tagliarsi i capelli; **to ~ the grass** tagliare l'erba; **to ~ sthg open** aprire qc.
◆ **cut back** *vi*: **to ~ back on sthg** ridurre qc.
◆ **cut down** *vt sep (tree)* tagliare.
◆ **cut down on** *vt fus* ridurre.
◆ **cut off** *vt sep* tagliare; *(supply)* sospendere; **I've been ~ off** *(on phone)* è caduta la linea; **to be ~ off** *(isolated)* rimanere isolato.
◆ **cut out** ◇ *vt sep (newspaper article, photo)* ritagliare ◇ *vi (engine)* spegnersi; **to ~ out smoking** smettere di fumare; **~ it out!** *(inf)* dacci un taglio!
◆ **cut up** *vt sep* tagliare a pezzetti.
cute [kju:t] *adj* carino(-a).
cut-glass *adj* in vetro intagliato.
cutlery ['kʌtlərɪ] *n* posate *fpl*.
cutlet ['kʌtlɪt] *n (of meat)* costoletta *f*; *(of nuts, vegetables)* crocchetta *f*.
cut-price *adj* a prezzo scontato.

cutting ['kʌtɪŋ] *n (from newspaper)* ritaglio *m*.

CV *n (Br: abbr of curriculum vitae)* curriculum *m inv*.

cwt *abbr* = **hundredweight**.

cycle ['saɪkl] ◇ *n (bicycle)* bicicletta *f*; *(series)* ciclo *m* ◇ *vi* andare in bicicletta.

cycle hire *n* noleggio *m* biciclette.

cycle lane *n* pista *f* ciclabile.

cycle path *n* pista *f* ciclabile.

cycling ['saɪklɪŋ] *n* ciclismo *m*; **to go ~** andare in bicicletta.

cycling shorts *npl* pantaloncini *mpl* da ciclista.

cyclist ['saɪklɪst] *n* ciclista *mf*.

cylinder ['sɪlɪndəʳ] *n (of gas)* bombola *f*; *(in engine)* cilindro *m*.

cynical ['sɪnɪkl] *adj* cinico(-a).

Czech [tʃek] ◇ *adj* ceco(-a) ◇ *n (person)* ceco *m* (-a *f*); *(language)* ceco *m*.

Czechoslovakia [ˌtʃekəslə-'vækɪə] *n* la Cecoslovacchia.

Czech Republic *n*: **the ~** la Repubblica Ceca.

D

dab [dæb] *vt (wound)* tamponare.

dad [dæd] *n (inf)* papà *m inv*, babbo *m*.

daddy [ˈdædɪ] *n (inf)* papà *m inv*, babbo *m*.

daddy longlegs [-ˈlɒŋlegz] *(pl inv) n* tipula *f*.

daffodil [ˈdæfədɪl] *n* giunchiglia *f*.

daft [dɑːft] *adj (Br: inf)* stupido(-a).

daily [ˈdeɪlɪ] ◇ *adj* quotidiano(-a) ◇ *adv* quotidianamente ◇ *n*: **a ~ (newspaper)** un quotidiano.

dairy [ˈdeərɪ] *n (on farm)* caseificio *m*; *(shop)* latteria *f*.

dairy product *n* latticino *m*.

daisy [ˈdeɪzɪ] *n* margherita *f*.

dam [dæm] *n* diga *f*.

damage [ˈdæmɪdʒ] ◇ *n* danno *m* ◇ *vt* danneggiare; *(back, leg)* lesionare.

damn [dæm] ◇ *excl (inf)* accidenti! ◇ *adj (inf)* maledetto(-a); **I don't give a ~** non me ne importa un accidente.

damp [dæmp] ◇ *adj* umido(-a) ◇ *n* umidità *f*.

damson [ˈdæmzn] *n* susina *f* damaschina.

dance [dɑːns] ◇ *n* danza *f*; *(social event)* ballo *m* ◇ *vi* ballare; **to have a ~** ballare.

dance floor *n (in club)* pista *f* da ballo.

dancer [ˈdɑːnsə^r] *n* ballerino *m* (-a *f*).

dancing [ˈdɑːnsɪŋ] *n* danza *f*; **to go ~** andare a ballare.

dandelion [ˈdændɪlaɪən] *n* dente *m* di leone.

dandruff [ˈdændrʌf] *n* forfora *f*.

Dane [deɪn] *n* danese *mf*.

danger [ˈdeɪndʒə^r] *n* pericolo *m*; **in ~** in pericolo.

dangerous [ˈdeɪndʒərəs] *adj* pericoloso(-a).

Danish [ˈdeɪnɪʃ] ◇ *adj* danese ◇ *n (language)* danese *m*.

Danish pastry *n* sfoglia *f* alla frutta.

dare [deə^r] *vt*: **to ~ to do sthg** osare fare qc; **to ~ sb to do sthg** sfidare qn a fare qc; **how ~ you!** come ti permetti!

daring [ˈdeərɪŋ] *adj* audace.

dark [dɑːk] ◇ *adj (room, night)* buio(-a); *(colour, skin)* scuro(-a); *(person)* bruno(-a) ◇ *n*: **after ~** col buio; **the ~** il buio.

dark chocolate *n* cioccolata *f* fondente.

dark glasses *npl* occhiali *mpl* scuri.

darkness [ˈdɑːknɪs] *n* oscurità *f*.

darling [ˈdɑːlɪŋ] *n (term of affection)* caro *m* (-a *f*).

dart [dɑːt] *n* freccia *f*.

◆ **darts** *n (game)* freccette *fpl*.

dartboard [ˈdɑːtbɔːd] *n* bersaglio

m per freccette.

dash [dæʃ] ◇ *n (of liquid)* goccio *m*; *(in writing)* trattino *m* ◇ *vi* precipitarsi.

dashboard ['dæʃbɔːd] *n* cruscotto *m*.

data ['deɪtə] *n* dati *mpl*.

database ['deɪtəbeɪs] *n* data base *m inv*.

date [deɪt] ◇ *n (day)* data *f*; *(meeting)* appuntamento *m*; *(Am: person)* ragazzo *m* (-a *f*); *(fruit)* dattero *m* ◇ *vt (cheque, letter)* datare; *(person)* uscire con ◇ *vi (become unfashionable)* passare di moda; **what's the ~?** quanti ne abbiamo oggi?; **to have a ~ with sb** avere (un) appuntamento con qn.

date of birth *n* data *f* di nascita.

daughter ['dɔːtəʳ] *n* figlia *f*.

daughter-in-law *n* nuora *f*.

dawn [dɔːn] *n* alba *f*.

day [deɪ] *n (of week)* giorno *m*; *(period, working day)* giornata *f*; **what ~ is it today?** che giorno è oggi?; **what a lovely ~!** che bella giornata!; **to have a ~ off** avere un giorno libero; **to have a ~ out** trascorrere una giornata fuori; **by ~** *(travel)* di giorno; **the ~ after tomorrow** dopodomani; **the ~ before** il giorno prima; **the ~ before yesterday** l'altro ieri, ieri l'altro; **the following ~** il giorno dopo; **have a nice ~!** buona giornata!

daylight ['deɪlaɪt] *n (light)* luce *f* (del giorno); *(dawn)* alba *f*.

day return *n (Br: railway ticket) biglietto di andata e ritorno valido per un giorno*.

dayshift ['deɪʃɪft] *n* turno *m* di giorno.

daytime ['deɪtaɪm] *n* giorno *m*.

day-to-day *adj (everyday)* quotidiano(-a).

day trip *n* gita *f (di un giorno)*.

dazzle ['dæzl] *vt* abbagliare.

DC *(abbr of direct current)* c.c.

dead [ded] ◇ *adj* morto(-a); *(battery)* scarico(-a) ◇ *adv* proprio; **the line has gone ~** è caduta la linea; **~ on time** in perfetto orario; **it's ~ ahead** è proprio a diritto; **'~ slow'** 'a passo d'uomo'.

dead end *n (street)* strada *f* senza uscita.

deadline ['dedlaɪn] *n* termine *m* ultimo, scadenza *f*.

deaf [def] ◇ *adj* sordo(-a) ◇ *npl*: **the ~** i non udenti.

deal [diːl] (*pt & pp* **dealt**) ◇ *n (agreement)* accordo *m* ◇ *vt (cards)* dare; **a good/bad ~** un buon/cattivo affare; **a great ~ of** una gran quantità di; **it's a ~!** affare fatto!

◆ **deal in** *vt fus* commerciare in.

◆ **deal with** *vt fus (handle)* affrontare; *(be about)* trattare di.

dealer ['diːləʳ] *n* (COMM) commerciante *mf*; *(in drugs)* spacciatore *m* (-trice *f*).

dealt [delt] *pt & pp* → **deal**.

dear [dɪəʳ] ◇ *adj* caro(-a) ◇ *n*: **my ~** mio caro (mia cara); **Dear Sir** Gentile Signore; **Dear Madam** Gentile Signora; **Dear John** Caro John; **oh ~!** oh Dio!

death [deθ] *n* morte *f*.

debate [dɪ'beɪt] ◇ *n* dibattito *m* ◇ *vt (wonder)* riflettere su.

debit ['debɪt] ◇ *n* debito *m* ◇ *vt (account)* addebitare su.

debt [det] *n (money owed)* debito *m*; **to be in ~** essere indebitato.

Dec. *(abbr of December)* dic.

decaff ['diːkæf] *n (inf)* caffè *m inv* decaffeinato.

decaffeinated [dɪ'kæfɪneɪtɪd] *adj* decaffeinato(-a).

decanter [dɪ'kæntəʳ] *n* bottiglia *f* da liquore.

decay [dɪ'keɪ] ◇ *n (of wood)* disfacimento *m*; *(of building)* rovina *f*; *(of tooth)* carie *f* ◇ *vi (rot)* putrefarsi.

deceive [dɪ'si:v] *vt* ingannare.
decelerate [ˌdi:'seləreɪt] *vi* decelerare.
December [dɪ'sembəʳ] *n* dicembre *m*, → **September**.
decent ['di:snt] *adj (adequate, respectable)* decente; *(kind)* carino(-a); *(people)* perbene *inv*.
decide [dɪ'saɪd] *vt & vi* decidere; **to ~ to do sthg** decidere di fare qc.
◆ **decide on** *vt fus* scegliere.
decimal ['desɪml] *adj* decimale.
decimal point *n* = virgola *f*.
decision [dɪ'sɪʒn] *n* decisione *f*; **to make a ~** prendere una decisione.
decisive [dɪ'saɪsɪv] *adj (person)* deciso(-a); *(event, factor)* decisivo(-a).
deck [dek] *n (level of ship)* ponte *m*; *(exposed part of ship)* coperta *f*; *(of bus)* piano *m*; *(of cards)* mazzo *m*.
deckchair ['dektʃeəʳ] *n* sedia *f* a sdraio.
declare [dɪ'kleəʳ] *vt* dichiarare; **to ~ (that)** dichiarare che; **'goods to ~'** 'articoli da dichiarare'; **'nothing to ~'** 'nulla da dichiarare'.
decline [dɪ'klaɪn] ◇ *n* calo *m*; *(of country)* declino *m* ◇ *vi (get worse)* peggiorare; *(refuse)* declinare.
decorate ['dekəreɪt] *vt (with wallpaper)* tappezzare; *(with paint)* pitturare; *(make attractive)* decorare.
decoration [ˌdekə'reɪʃn] *n (decorative object)* decorazione *f*.
decorator ['dekəreɪtəʳ] *n* imbianchino *m*.
decrease [*n* 'di:kri:s, *vb* di:'kri:s] ◇ *n* diminuzione *f* ◇ *vi* diminuire.
dedicated ['dedɪkeɪtɪd] *adj (committed)* devoto(-a).
deduce [dɪ'dju:s] *vt* dedurre.
deduct [dɪ'dʌkt] *vt* dedurre.
deduction [dɪ'dʌkʃn] *n* deduzione *f*.
deep [di:p] ◇ *adj* profondo(-a); *(colour)* intenso(-a) ◇ *adv* in profondità; **the pool is 2 metres ~** la piscina è profonda 2 metri.
deep end *n (of swimming pool)* *parte dove l'acqua è più alta.*
deep freeze *n* congelatore *m*.
deep-fried [-'fraɪd] *adj* fritto(-a).
deep-pan *adj*: **~ pizza** *pizza a pasta alta e soffice.*
deer [dɪəʳ] *(pl inv) n* cervo *m*.
defeat [dɪ'fi:t] ◇ *n* sconfitta *f* ◇ *vt (team, army, government)* sconfiggere.
defect ['di:fekt] *n* difetto *m*.
defective [dɪ'fektɪv] *adj* difettoso(-a).
defence [dɪ'fens] *n* difesa *f*.
defend [dɪ'fend] *vt* difendere.
defense [dɪ'fens] *(Am)* = **defence**.
deficiency [dɪ'fɪʃnsɪ] *n (lack)* carenza *f*.
deficit ['defɪsɪt] *n* deficit *m inv*.
define [dɪ'faɪn] *vt* definire.
definite ['defɪnɪt] *adj (clear)* preciso(-a); *(certain)* sicuro(-a); *(improvement)* deciso(-a).
definite article *n* articolo *m* determinativo.
definitely ['defɪnɪtlɪ] *adv (certainly)* senz'altro.
definition [ˌdefɪ'nɪʃn] *n (of word)* definizione *f*.
deflate [dɪ'fleɪt] *vt (tyre)* sgonfiare.
deflect [dɪ'flekt] *vt (ball)* deviare.
defogger [ˌdi:'fɒgər] *n (Am)* deumidificatore *m*.
deformed [dɪ'fɔ:md] *adj* deformato(-a).
defrost [ˌdi:'frɒst] *vt (food)* scongelare; *(fridge)* sbrinare; *(Am: demist)* disappannare.
degree [dɪ'gri:] *n (unit of measurement, amount)* grado *m*; *(qualification)* = laurea *f*; **to have a ~ in sthg** avere una laurea in qc.
dehydrated [ˌdi:haɪ'dreɪtɪd] *adj (food)* liofilizzato(-a); *(person)* disidratato(-a).

de-ice [diːˈaɪs] *vt* togliere il ghiaccio da.
de-icer [diːˈaɪsəʳ] *n* antighiaccio *m*.
dejected [dɪˈdʒektɪd] *adj* sconsolato(-a).
delay [dɪˈleɪ] ◇ *n* ritardo *m* ◇ *vt* *(flight, departure)* ritardare; *(person)* trattenere ◇ *vi* indugiare; **without ~** senza indugio.
delayed [dɪˈleɪd] *adj (train, flight)* in ritardo.
delegate [*n* ˈdelɪgət, *vb* ˈdelɪgeɪt] ◇ *n* delegato *m* (-a *f*) ◇ *vt (person)* delegare.
delete [dɪˈliːt] *vt* cancellare.
deli [ˈdelɪ] *n (inf: abbr of delicatessen)* negozio *m* di specialità gastronomiche.
deliberate [dɪˈlɪbərət] *adj (intentional)* intenzionale.
deliberately [dɪˈlɪbərətlɪ] *adv (intentionally)* deliberatamente.
delicacy [ˈdelɪkəsɪ] *n (food)* leccornia *f*.
delicate [ˈdelɪkət] *adj* delicato(-a).
delicatessen [ˌdelɪkəˈtesn] *n* negozio *m* di specialità gastronomiche.
delicious [dɪˈlɪʃəs] *adj* squisito(-a).
delight [dɪˈlaɪt] ◇ *n (feeling)* gioia *f* ◇ *vt* deliziare; **to take (a) ~ in doing sthg** provare piacere a fare qc.
delighted [dɪˈlaɪtɪd] *adj* felicissimo(-a).
delightful [dɪˈlaɪtfʊl] *adj* delizioso(-a).
deliver [dɪˈlɪvəʳ] *vt (goods, letters, newspaper)* consegnare; *(speech, lecture)* tenere; *(baby)* far nascere.
delivery [dɪˈlɪvərɪ] *n (of goods, letters)* consegna *f*; *(birth)* parto *m*.
delude [dɪˈluːd] *vt* illudere.
de luxe [dəˈlʌks] *adj* di lusso.
demand [dɪˈmɑːnd] ◇ *n (request)* richiesta *f*; *(claim)* rivendicazione *f*; (COMM) domanda *f*; *(requirement)* esigenza *f* ◇ *vt (request forcefully)* pretendere; *(require)* richiedere; **to ~ to do sthg** esigere di fare qc; **in ~** richiesto.
demanding [dɪˈmɑːndɪŋ] *adj* esigente.
demerara sugar [deməˈreərə-] *n* zucchero *m* di canna.
demist [ˌdiːˈmɪst] *vt (Br)* disappannare.
demister [ˌdiːˈmɪstəʳ] *n (Br)* deumidificatore *m*.
democracy [dɪˈmɒkrəsɪ] *n* democrazia *f*.
Democrat [ˈdeməkræt] *n (Am)* democratico *m* (-a *f*).
democratic [deməˈkrætɪk] *adj* democratico(-a).
demolish [dɪˈmɒlɪʃ] *vt (building)* demolire.
demonstrate [ˈdemənstreɪt] ◇ *vt (prove)* dimostrare; *(machine, appliance)* mostrare il funzionamento di ◇ *vi* dimostrare.
demonstration [demənˈstreɪʃn] *n* dimostrazione *f*.
denial [dɪˈnaɪəl] *n (refusal)* rifiuto *m*; *(statement)* smentita *f*.
denim [ˈdenɪm] *n* denim *m*.
◆ **denims** *npl* jeans *mpl*.
denim jacket *n* giubbotto *m* di jeans.
Denmark [ˈdenmɑːk] *n* la Danimarca.
dense [dens] *adj (crowd, forest)* fitto(-a); *(smoke)* denso(-a).
dent [dent] *n* ammaccatura *f*.
dental [ˈdentl] *adj* dentale.
dental floss [-flɒs] *n* filo *m* interdentale.
dental surgeon *n* dentista *mf*.
dental surgery *n (place)* studio *m* dentistico.
dentist [ˈdentɪst] *n* dentista *mf*; **to go to the ~'s** andare dal dentista.
dentures [ˈdentʃəz] *npl* dentiera *f*.

deny [dɪˈnaɪ] *vt* negare.
deodorant [diːˈəʊdərənt] *n* deodorante *m*.
depart [dɪˈpɑːt] *vi* partire.
department [dɪˈpɑːtmənt] *n* *(of business, shop)* reparto *m*; *(of government)* ministero *m*; *(of school, university)* dipartimento *m*.
department store *n* grandi magazzini *mpl*.
departure [dɪˈpɑːtʃəʳ] *n* partenza *f*; **'~s'** *(at airport)* 'partenze'.
departure lounge *n* sala *f* partenze.
depend [dɪˈpend] *vi*: **it ~s** dipende.
◆ **depend on** *vt fus* dipendere da; **~ing on** a seconda di.
dependable [dɪˈpendəbl] *adj* affidabile.
deplorable [dɪˈplɔːrəbl] *adj* deplorevole.
deport [dɪˈpɔːt] *vt* espellere.
deposit [dɪˈpɒzɪt] ◇ *n* deposito *m* ◇ *vt* depositare.
deposit account *n (Br)* conto *m* vincolato.
depot [ˈdiːpəʊ] *n (Am: for buses, trains)* stazione *f*.
depressed [dɪˈprest] *adj* depresso(-a).
depressing [dɪˈpresɪŋ] *adj* deprimente.
depression [dɪˈpreʃn] *n* depressione *f*.
deprive [dɪˈpraɪv] *vt*: **to ~ sb of sthg** privare qn di qc.
depth [depθ] *n (distance down)* profondità *f inv*; **out of one's ~** *(when swimming)* dove non si tocca; *(fig: unable to cope)* non all'altezza; **~ of field** *(in photography)* profondità di campo.
deputy [ˈdepjʊtɪ] *adj* vice *(inv)*.
derailleur [dəˈreɪljəʳ] *n* deragliatore *m*.
derailment [dɪˈreɪlmənt] *n* deragliamento *m*.
derelict [ˈderəlɪkt] *adj* abbandonato(-a).
derv [dɜːv] *n (Br)* benzina *f* diesel.
descend [dɪˈsend] *vt & vi* scendere.
descendant [dɪˈsendənt] *n* discendente *mf*.
descent [dɪˈsent] *n* discesa *f*.
describe [dɪˈskraɪb] *vt* descrivere.
description [dɪˈskrɪpʃn] *n* descrizione *f*.
desert [*n* ˈdezət, *vb* dɪˈzɜːt] ◇ *n* deserto *m* ◇ *vt* abbandonare.
deserted [dɪˈzɜːtɪd] *adj* deserto(-a).
deserve [dɪˈzɜːv] *vt* meritare.
design [dɪˈzaɪn] ◇ *n (pattern)* disegno *m*; *(art)* design *m*; *(of machine, building)* progetto *m* ◇ *vt (dress)* disegnare; *(machine, building)* progettare; **to be ~ed for** essere concepito per.
designer [dɪˈzaɪnəʳ] ◇ *n (of clothes)* stilista *mf*; *(of building)* architetto *m*; *(of product)* designer *mf inv* ◇ *adj (clothes, sunglasses)* firmato(-a).
desirable [dɪˈzaɪərəbl] *adj* desiderabile.
desire [dɪˈzaɪəʳ] ◇ *n* desiderio *m* ◇ *vt* desiderare; **it leaves a lot to be ~d** lascia molto a desiderare.
desk [desk] *n (in home, office)* scrivania *f*; *(at airport, station, of pupil)* banco *m*; *(at hotel)* portineria *f*.
desktop publishing [ˈdeskˌtɒp-] *n* desktop publishing *m*.
despair [dɪˈspeəʳ] *n* disperazione *f*.
despatch [dɪˈspætʃ] = **dispatch**.
desperate [ˈdesprət] *adj* disperato(-a); **to be ~ for sthg** avere un disperato bisogno di qc.
despicable [dɪˈspɪkəbl] *adj* spregevole.
despise [dɪˈspaɪz] *vt* disprezzare.
despite [dɪˈspaɪt] *prep* nonostante.
dessert [dɪˈzɜːt] *n* dessert *m inv*.
dessertspoon [dɪˈzɜːtspuːn] *n*

cucchiaino *m*.

destination [ˌdestɪˈneɪʃn] *n* destinazione *f*.

destroy [dɪˈstrɔɪ] *vt* distruggere.

destruction [dɪˈstrʌkʃn] *n* distruzione *f*.

detach [dɪˈtætʃ] *vt* staccare.

detached house [dɪˈtætʃt-] *n* villetta *f* unifamiliare.

detail [ˈdiːteɪl] *n* dettaglio *m*; **in ~** dettagliatamente.

◆ **details** *npl (facts)* informazioni *fpl*.

detailed [ˈdiːteɪld] *adj* dettagliato(-a).

detect [dɪˈtekt] *vt (sense)* avvertire; *(find)* scoprire.

detective [dɪˈtektɪv] *n* detective *mf inv*; **a ~ story** un racconto poliziesco.

detention [dɪˈtenʃn] *n* (SCH) *punizione che consiste nel trattenere un alunno a scuola oltre l'orario scolastico.*

detergent [dɪˈtɜːdʒənt] *n* detersivo *m*.

deteriorate [dɪˈtɪərɪəreɪt] *vi* deteriorarsi.

determination [dɪˌtɜːmɪˈneɪʃn] *n* determinazione *f*.

determine [dɪˈtɜːmɪn] *vt (control)* determinare; *(find out)* accertare.

determined [dɪˈtɜːmɪnd] *adj* risoluto(-a); **to be ~ to do sthg** essere determinato a fare qc.

deterrent [dɪˈterənt] *n* deterrente *m*.

detest [dɪˈtest] *vt* detestare.

detour [ˈdiːˌtʊəʳ] *n* deviazione *f*.

detrain [ˌdiːˈtreɪn] *vi (fml)* scendere dal treno.

deuce [djuːs] *n (in tennis)* parità *f*.

devastate [ˈdevəsteɪt] *vt* devastare.

develop [dɪˈveləp] ◇ *vt* sviluppare; *(machine, method)* perfezionare; *(illness, habit)* contrarre ◇ *vi (evolve)* svilupparsi.

developing country [dɪˈveləpɪŋ-] *n* paese *m* in via di sviluppo.

development [dɪˈveləpmənt] *n* sviluppo *m*; **a housing ~** un complesso residenziale.

device [dɪˈvaɪs] *n* congegno *m*.

devil [ˈdevl] *n* diavolo *m*; **what the ~ ...?** *(inf)* che diavolo ...?

devise [dɪˈvaɪz] *vt* escogitare.

devoted [dɪˈvəʊtɪd] *adj (person)* affezionato(-a).

dew [djuː] *n* rugiada *f*.

diabetes [ˌdaɪəˈbiːtiːz] *n* diabete *m*.

diabetic [ˌdaɪəˈbetɪk] ◇ *adj (person)* diabetico(-a); *(chocolate)* per diabetici ◇ *n* diabetico *m* (-a *f*).

diagnosis [ˌdaɪəgˈnəʊsɪs] (*pl* **-oses** [-əʊsiːz]) *n* diagnosi *f inv*.

diagonal [daɪˈægənl] *adj* diagonale.

diagram [ˈdaɪəgræm] *n* diagramma *m*.

dial [ˈdaɪəl] ◇ *n (of telephone)* disco *m* combinatore; *(of clock)* quadrante *m*; *(of radio)* scala *f* ◇ *vt (number)* comporre.

dialling code [ˈdaɪəlɪŋ-] *n (Br)* prefisso *m* telefonico.

dialling tone [ˈdaɪəlɪŋ-] *n (Br)* segnale *m* di libero.

dial tone *(Am)* = **dialling tone**.

diameter [daɪˈæmɪtəʳ] *n* diametro *m*.

diamond [ˈdaɪəmənd] *n (gem)* diamante *m*.

◆ **diamonds** *npl (in cards)* quadri *mpl*.

diaper [ˈdaɪpəʳ] *n (Am)* pannolino *m*.

diarrhoea [ˌdaɪəˈrɪə] *n* diarrea *f*.

diary [ˈdaɪərɪ] *n (for appointments)* agenda *f*; *(journal)* diario *m*.

dice [daɪs] *(pl inv) n* dado *m*.

diced [daɪst] *adj* a dadini.

dictate [dɪk'teɪt] *vt* dettare.
dictation [dɪk'teɪʃn] *n* dettato *m*.
dictator [dɪk'teɪtəʳ] *n* dittatore *m* (-trice *f*).
dictionary ['dɪkʃənrɪ] *n* dizionario *m*.
did [dɪd] *pt* → **do**.
die [daɪ] (*pt & pp* **died**, *cont* **dying** ['daɪɪŋ]) *vi* morire; **to be dying for sthg** *(inf)* morire dalla voglia di qc; **to be dying to do sthg** *(inf)* morire dalla voglia di fare qc.
◆ **die away** *vi* spegnersi.
◆ **die out** *vi* scomparire.
diesel ['di:zl] *n (fuel)* gasolio *m*; *(car)* diesel *m inv*.
diet ['daɪət] ◇ *n (for slimming, health)* dieta *f*; *(food eaten)* alimentazione *f* ◇ *vi* essere a dieta ◇ *adj* dietetico(-a).
diet Coke® *n* coca *f* light®.
differ ['dɪfəʳ] *vi*: **to ~ (from)** *(disagree)* non essere d'accordo (con); *(be dissimilar)* essere diverso (da).
difference ['dɪfrəns] *n* differenza *f*; **it makes no ~** è lo stesso; **a ~ of opinion** una divergenza di opinioni.
different ['dɪfrənt] *adj* diverso(-a); **to be ~ (from)** essere diverso (da); **a ~ route** un'altra strada.
differently ['dɪfrəntlɪ] *adv* in modo diverso.
difficult ['dɪfɪkəlt] *adj* difficile.
difficulty ['dɪfɪkəltɪ] *n* difficoltà *f inv*.
dig [dɪg] (*pt & pp* **dug**) *vt & vi* scavare.
◆ **dig out** *vt sep (rescue)* estrarre; *(find)* scovare.
◆ **dig up** *vt sep (from ground)* dissotterrare.
digest [dɪ'dʒest] *vt* digerire.
digestion [dɪ'dʒestʃn] *n* digestione *f*.
digestive (biscuit) [dɪ'dʒestɪv-] *n (Br) biscotto di frumento con farina integrale*.
digit ['dɪdʒɪt] *n (figure)* cifra *f*; *(finger, toe)* dito *m*.
digital ['dɪdʒɪtl] *adj* digitale.
dill [dɪl] *n* aneto *m*.
dilute [daɪ'lu:t] *vt (liquid)* diluire.
dim [dɪm] ◇ *adj (light)* debole; *(room)* buio(-a); *(inf: stupid)* ottuso(-a) ◇ *vt (light)* abbassare.
dime [daɪm] *n (Am)* moneta *f* da dieci centesimi di dollaro.
dimensions [dɪ'menʃnz] *npl* dimensioni *fpl*.
din [dɪn] *n* baccano *m*.
dine [daɪn] *vi* cenare.
◆ **dine out** *vi* cenare fuori.
diner ['daɪnəʳ] *n (Am: restaurant)* = tavola *f* calda; *(person)* cliente *mf*.
dinghy ['dɪŋgɪ] *n (with sail, oars)* barca *f*; *(for racing)* dinghy *m inv*; *(made of rubber)* canotto *m*.
dingy ['dɪndʒɪ] *adj (clothes)* sporco(-a); *(town, hotel)* squallido(-a).
dining car ['daɪnɪŋ-] *n* carrozza *f* ristorante.
dining hall ['daɪnɪŋ-] *n* refettorio *m*.
dining room ['daɪnɪŋ-] *n* sala *f* da pranzo.
dinner ['dɪnəʳ] *n (at lunchtime)* pranzo *m*; *(in evening)* cena *f*; **to have ~** *(at lunchtime)* pranzare; *(in evening)* cenare.
dinner jacket *n* giacca *f* dello smoking.
dinner party *n* cena *f*.
dinner set *n* servizio *m* da tavola.
dinner suit *n* smoking *m inv*.
dinnertime ['dɪnətaɪm] *n (at lunchtime)* ora *f* di pranzo; *(in evening)* ora di cena.
dinosaur ['daɪnəsɔ:ʳ] *n* dinosauro *m*.
dip [dɪp] ◇ *n (in road, land)* avvallamento *m*; *(food) salsetta cremosa in cui intingere patatine o verdure crude* ◇ *vt (into liquid)* immergere ◇ *vi (road, land)* digradare; **to have a**

~ *(swim)* fare una nuotatina; **to ~ one's headlights** *(Br)* spegnere gli abbaglianti.

diploma [dɪˈpləʊmə] *n* diploma *m*.

dipstick [ˈdɪpstɪk] *n* asta *f* di livello.

direct [dɪˈrekt] ◇ *adj* diretto(-a) ◇ *adv (go)* direttamente; *(travel)* senza fermarsi ◇ *vt*: **can you ~ me to the railway station?** mi può indicare la strada per la stazione?

direct current *n* corrente *f* continua.

direction [dɪˈrekʃn] *n (of movement)* direzione *f*; **to ask for ~s** chiedere indicazioni.

◆ **directions** *npl (instructions)* istruzioni *fpl*.

directly [dɪˈrektlɪ] *adv (exactly)* proprio; *(soon)* subito.

director [dɪˈrektəʳ] *n (of company)* amministratore *m* (-trice *f*); *(of film, play, TV programme)* regista *mf*; *(organizer)* direttore *m* (-trice *f*).

directory [dɪˈrektərɪ] *n* elenco *m*.

directory enquiries *n (Br)* informazioni *fpl* elenco abbonati.

dirt [dɜːt] *n* sporcizia *f*; *(earth)* terra *f*.

dirty [ˈdɜːtɪ] *adj* sporco(-a).

disability [ˌdɪsəˈbɪlətɪ] *n* handicap *m inv*; *(through old age, illness)* invalidità *f inv*.

disabled [dɪsˈeɪbld] ◇ *adj* disabile ◇ *npl*: **the ~** i portatori di handicap; '**~ toilet**' 'toilette per portatori di handicap'.

disadvantage [ˌdɪsədˈvɑːntɪdʒ] *n* svantaggio *m*.

disagree [ˌdɪsəˈgriː] *vi* non essere d'accordo; **to ~ with sb (about)** non essere d'accordo con qn (su); **those mussels ~d with me** quelle cozze mi hanno fatto male.

disagreement [ˌdɪsəˈgriːmənt] *n (argument)* discussione *f*; *(dissimilarity)* disaccordo *m*.

disappear [ˌdɪsəˈpɪəʳ] *vi* sparire.

disappearance [ˌdɪsəˈpɪərəns] *n* scomparsa *f*.

disappoint [ˌdɪsəˈpɔɪnt] *vt* deludere.

disappointed [ˌdɪsəˈpɔɪntɪd] *adj* deluso(-a).

disappointing [ˌdɪsəˈpɔɪntɪŋ] *adj* deludente.

disappointment [ˌdɪsəˈpɔɪntmənt] *n* delusione *f*.

disapprove [ˌdɪsəˈpruːv] *vi*: **to ~ of** disapprovare.

disarmament [dɪsˈɑːməmənt] *n* disarmo *m*.

disaster [dɪˈzɑːstəʳ] *n* disastro *m*.

disastrous [dɪˈzɑːstrəs] *adj* disastroso(-a).

disc [dɪsk] *n (Br)* disco *m*; *(Br: CD)* compact disc *m inv*; **I slipped a ~** mi è venuta l'ernia al disco.

discard [dɪˈskɑːd] *vt* scartare.

discharge [dɪsˈtʃɑːdʒ] *vt (prisoner)* rilasciare; *(patient)* dimettere; *(soldier)* congedare; *(smoke, gas)* emettere; *(liquid)* scaricare.

discipline [ˈdɪsɪplɪn] *n* disciplina *f*.

disc jockey *n* disc-jockey *mf inv*.

disco [ˈdɪskəʊ] (*pl* **-s**) *n (place)* discoteca *f*; *(event)* festa *f*.

discoloured [dɪsˈkʌləd] *adj* scolorito(-a).

discomfort [dɪsˈkʌmfət] *n* fastidio *m*.

disconnect [ˌdɪskəˈnekt] *vt* staccare; *(gas supply)* chiudere; *(pipe)* scollegare.

discontinued [ˌdɪskənˈtɪnjuːd] *adj (product)* di fine serie.

discotheque [ˈdɪskəʊtek] *n (place)* discoteca *f*; *(event)* festa *f*.

discount [ˈdɪskaʊnt] *n* sconto *m*.

discover [dɪˈskʌvəʳ] *vt* scoprire.

discovery [dɪˈskʌvərɪ] *n* scoperta *f*.

discreet [dɪ'skri:t] *adj* discreto(-a).
discrepancy [dɪ'skrepənsɪ] *n* discrepanza *f*.
discriminate [dɪ'skrɪmɪneɪt] *vi*: **to ~ against sb** discriminare contro qn.
discrimination [dɪ,skrɪmɪ'neɪʃn] *n (unfair treatment)* discriminazione *f*.
discuss [dɪ'skʌs] *vt* discutere.
discussion [dɪ'skʌʃn] *n* discussione *f*.
disease [dɪ'zi:z] *n* malattia *f*.
disembark [,dɪsɪm'bɑ:k] *vi* sbarcare.
disgrace [dɪs'greɪs] *n (shame)* vergogna *f*; **it's a ~!** è una vergogna!
disgraceful [dɪs'greɪsfʊl] *adj* vergognoso(-a).
disguise [dɪs'gaɪz] ◇ *n* travestimento *m* ◇ *vt* travestire; **in ~** travestito.
disgust [dɪs'gʌst] ◇ *n* disgusto *m* ◇ *vt* disgustare.
disgusting [dɪs'gʌstɪŋ] *adj* disgustoso(-a).
dish [dɪʃ] *n* piatto *m*; **to do the ~es** fare i piatti; '**~ of the day**' 'piatto del giorno'.
◆ **dish up** *vt sep* servire.
dishcloth ['dɪʃklɒθ] *n* strofinaccio *m*.
disheveled [dɪ'ʃevəld] *(Am)* = **dishevelled**.
dishevelled [dɪ'ʃevəld] *adj (Br) (hair)* arruffato(-a); *(appearance)* trasandato(-a).
dishonest [dɪs'ɒnɪst] *adj* disonesto(-a).
dish towel *n (Am)* strofinaccio *m*.
dishwasher ['dɪʃ,wɒʃər] *n (machine)* lavastoviglie *f inv*.
disinfectant [,dɪsɪn'fektənt] *n* disinfettante *m*.
disintegrate [dɪs'ɪntɪgreɪt] *vi* disintegrarsi.
disk [dɪsk] *n (Am)* = **disc**; (COMPUT) dischetto *m*.
disk drive *n* drive *m inv*.
dislike [dɪs'laɪk] ◇ *n (poor opinion)* antipatia *f* ◇ *vt*: **I ~ them** non mi piacciono; **to take a ~ to** prendere in antipatia.
dislocate ['dɪsləkeɪt] *vt*: **to ~ one's shoulder** slogarsi la spalla.
dismal ['dɪzml] *adj (weather, place)* deprimente; *(terrible)* pessimo(-a).
dismantle [dɪs'mæntl] *vt* smontare.
dismay [dɪs'meɪ] *n* sgomento *m*.
dismiss [dɪs'mɪs] *vt (not consider)* ignorare; *(from job)* licenziare; *(from classroom)* congedare.
disobedient [,dɪsə'bi:djənt] *adj* disubbidiente.
disobey [,dɪsə'beɪ] *vt* disubbidire.
disorder [dɪs'ɔ:dər] *n (confusion)* disordine *m*; *(illness)* disturbo *m*.
disorganized [dɪs'ɔ:gənaɪzd] *adj* disorganizzato(-a).
dispatch [dɪ'spætʃ] *vt* inviare.
dispense [dɪ'spens]: **dispense with** *vt fus* fare a meno di.
dispenser [dɪ'spensər] *n (device)* distributore *m*.
dispensing chemist [dɪ'spensɪŋ-] *n (Br: shop)* farmacia *f*.
disperse [dɪ'spɜ:s] ◇ *vt* disperdere ◇ *vi* disperdersi.
display [dɪ'spleɪ] ◇ *n (of goods)* esposizione *f*; *(public event)* spettacolo *m*; *(readout)* schermo *m* ◇ *vt (goods, information)* esporre; *(feeling, quality)* manifestare; **on ~** in mostra.
displeased [dɪs'pli:zd] *adj* contrariato(-a).
disposable [dɪ'spəʊzəbl] *adj* usa e getta *(inv)*.
dispute [dɪ'spju:t] ◇ *n (argument)* controversia *f*; *(industrial)* vertenza *f* ◇ *vt* mettere in discussione.
disqualify [,dɪs'kwɒlɪfaɪ] *vt* squalificare; **he is disqualified from driv-**

ing *(Br)* gli hanno ritirato la patente.

disregard [ˌdɪsrɪˈgɑːd] *vt* ignorare.

disrupt [dɪsˈrʌpt] *vt* disturbare.

disruption [dɪsˈrʌpʃn] *n* disordine *m*.

dissatisfied [ˌdɪsˈsætɪsfaɪd] *adj* insoddisfatto(-a).

dissolve [dɪˈzɒlv] ◇ *vt* sciogliere ◇ *vi* sciogliersi.

dissuade [dɪˈsweɪd] *vt*: **to ~ sb from doing sthg** dissuadere qn dal fare qc.

distance [ˈdɪstəns] *n* distanza *f*; **from a ~** da lontano; **in the ~** in lontananza.

distant [ˈdɪstənt] *adj* distante; *(in time)* lontano(-a).

distilled water [dɪˈstɪld-] *n* acqua *f* distillata.

distillery [dɪˈstɪlərɪ] *n* distilleria *f*.

distinct [dɪˈstɪŋkt] *adj (separate)* distinto(-a); *(noticeable)* chiaro(-a).

distinction [dɪˈstɪŋkʃn] *n (difference)* distinzione *f*; *(mark in exam)* lode *f*.

distinctive [dɪˈstɪŋktɪv] *adj* inconfondibile.

distinguish [dɪˈstɪŋgwɪʃ] *vt (perceive)* distinguere; **to ~ sthg from sthg** distinguere qc da qc.

distorted [dɪˈstɔːtɪd] *adj* distorto(-a).

distract [dɪˈstrækt] *vt* distrarre.

distraction [dɪˈstrækʃn] *n* distrazione *f*.

distress [dɪˈstres] *n (pain)* sofferenza *f*; *(anxiety)* angoscia *f*.

distressing [dɪˈstresɪŋ] *adj* doloroso(-a).

distribute [dɪˈstrɪbjuːt] *vt* distribuire.

distributor [dɪˈstrɪbjʊtəʳ] *n* (COMM) distributore *m*; (AUT) spinterogeno *m*.

district [ˈdɪstrɪkt] *n* regione *f*; *(of town)* quartiere *m*.

district attorney *n (Am)* = procuratore *m* della Repubblica.

disturb [dɪˈstɜːb] *vt (interrupt)* disturbare; *(worry)* turbare; *(move)* muovere; **'do not ~'** 'non disturbare'.

disturbance [dɪˈstɜːbəns] *n (violence)* disordini *mpl*.

ditch [dɪtʃ] *n* fossato *m*.

ditto [ˈdɪtəʊ] *adv* idem.

divan [dɪˈvæn] *n* divano *m*.

dive [daɪv] (*pt Am* **-d** OR **dove**, *pt Br* **-d**) ◇ *n (of swimmer)* tuffo *m* ◇ *vi* tuffarsi; *(under sea)* immergersi.

diver [ˈdaɪvəʳ] *n (from divingboard, rock)* tuffatore *m* (-trice *f*); *(under sea)* sommozzatore *m* (-trice *f*).

diversion [daɪˈvɜːʃn] *n (of traffic)* deviazione *f*; *(amusement)* diversivo *m*.

divert [daɪˈvɜːt] *vt (traffic, river)* deviare; *(attention)* distrarre.

divide [dɪˈvaɪd] *vt* dividere.

◆ **divide up** *vt sep* dividere.

diving [ˈdaɪvɪŋ] *n (from divingboard, rock)* tuffi *mpl*; *(under sea)* immersioni *fpl*; **to go ~** fare sub.

divingboard [ˈdaɪvɪŋbɔːd] *n* trampolino *m*.

division [dɪˈvɪʒn] *n* divisione *f*; *(in football league)* serie *f*.

divorce [dɪˈvɔːs] ◇ *n* divorzio *m* ◇ *vt* divorziare da.

divorced [dɪˈvɔːst] *adj* divorziato(-a).

DIY *n (abbr of do-it-yourself)* il fai da te.

dizzy [ˈdɪzɪ] *adj*: **I feel ~** mi gira la testa.

DJ *n (abbr of disc jockey)* discjockey *mf inv*.

do [duː] (*pt* **did**, *pp* **done**, *pl* **dos**) ◇ *aux vb* 1. *(in negatives)*: **don't ~ that!** non farlo!; **she didn't listen** non ha ascoltato.

2. *(in questions)*: **~ you like it?** ti piace?; **how ~ you do it?** come si fa?

3. *(referring to previous verb)*: **I eat more than you ~** io mangio più di te; **you made a mistake – no I didn't!** ti sei sbagliato – non è vero!; **so ~ I** anch'io.

4. *(in question tags)* vero?, non è vero?; **so, you like Scotland, ~ you?** e così ti piace la Scozia, non è vero?

5. *(for emphasis)*: **I ~ like this bedroom** questa camera mi piace proprio; **~ come in!** si accomodi!

◇ *vt* **1.** *(perform)* fare; **to ~ one's homework** fare i compiti; **what is she doing?** cosa sta facendo?; **what can I ~ for you?** in cosa posso esserle utile?

2. *(attend to)*: **to ~ one's hair** pettinarsi; **to ~ one's make-up** truccarsi; **to ~ one's teeth** lavarsi i denti.

3. *(cause)* fare; **to ~ damage** danneggiare; **to ~ sb good** fare bene a qn.

4. *(have as job)*: **what do you ~?** che lavoro fai?

5. *(provide, offer)* fare; **we ~ pizzas for under £4** facciamo pizze a meno di 4 sterline.

6. *(study)* fare.

7. *(subj: vehicle)* fare; **the car was doing 50 mph** la macchina andava a 80 all'ora.

8. *(inf: visit)* fare; **we're doing Scotland next week** la settimana prossima facciamo la Scozia.

◇ *vi* **1.** *(behave, act)* fare; **~ as I say** fai come ti dico.

2. *(progress, get on)* andare; **to ~ badly** andare male; **to ~ well** andare bene.

3. *(be sufficient)* bastare; **will £5 ~?** bastano 5 sterline?

4. *(in phrases)*: **how do you ~?** piacere!; **what has that got to ~ with it?** e questo che c'entra?

◇ *n (party)* festa *f*; **the ~s and don'ts** le cose da fare e da non fare.

◆ **do out of** *vt sep (inf)*: **to ~ sb out of sthg** fregare qc a qn.

◆ **do up** *vt sep (fasten)* allacciare; *(decorate)* rinnovare; *(wrap up)* impacchettare.

◆ **do with** *vt fus (need)*: **I could ~ with a drink** mi ci vuole proprio un bicchierino.

◆ **do without** *vt fus* fare a meno di.

dock [dɒk] ◇ *n (for ships)* molo *m*; (JUR) banco *m* degli imputati ◇ *vi* attraccare.

doctor [ˈdɒktəʳ] *n* dottore *m* (-essa *f*); **to go to the ~'s** andare dal dottore.

document [ˈdɒkjʊmənt] *n* documento *m*.

documentary [ˌdɒkjʊˈmentərɪ] *n* documentario *m*.

Dodgems® [ˈdɒdʒəmz] *npl (Br)* autoscontri *mpl*.

dodgy [ˈdɒdʒɪ] *adj (Br: inf: plan)* rischioso(-a); *(car)* poco sicuro(-a).

does [*weak form* dəz, *strong form* dʌz] → **do**.

doesn't [ˈdʌznt] = **does not**.

dog [dɒg] *n* cane *m*.

dog food *n* cibo *m* per cani.

doggy bag [ˈdɒgɪ-] *n sacchetto per portar via gli avanzi di un pasto consumato al ristorante.*

do-it-yourself *n* il fai da te.

dole [dəʊl] *n*: **to be on the ~** *(Br)* prendere il sussidio di disoccupazione.

doll [dɒl] *n* bambola *f*.

dollar [ˈdɒləʳ] *n* dollaro *m*.

Dolomites [ˈdɒləmaɪts] *npl*: **the ~** le Dolomiti.

dolphin [ˈdɒlfɪn] *n* delfino *m*.

dome [dəʊm] *n* cupola *f*.

domestic [dəˈmestɪk] *adj (of house, family)* domestico(-a); *(of country)* nazionale, interno(-a).

domestic appliance *n* elettrodomestico *m*.

domestic flight *n* volo *m* nazionale.

domestic science *n* economia *f* domestica.

dominate ['dɒmɪneɪt] *vt* dominare.

dominoes ['dɒmɪnəʊz] *n* domino *m*.

donate [də'neɪt] *vt* donare.

donation [də'neɪʃn] *n* donazione *f*.

done [dʌn] ◇ *pp* → **do** ◇ *adj (finished)* finito(-a); *(cooked)* cotto (-a).

donkey ['dɒŋkɪ] *n* asino *m*.

don't [dəʊnt] = **do not**.

door [dɔːʳ] *n (of building)* porta *f*; *(of vehicle, cupboard)* sportello *m*.

doorbell ['dɔːbel] *n* campanello *m*.

doorknob ['dɔːnɒb] *n* pomello *m*.

doorman ['dɔːmən] (*pl* **-men**) *n* portiere *m*.

doormat ['dɔːmæt] *n* zerbino *m*.

doormen ['dɔːmən] *pl* → **doorman**.

doorstep ['dɔːstep] *n* gradino *m* della porta; *(Br: inf: piece of bread)* grossa fetta *f* di pane.

doorway ['dɔːweɪ] *n* porta *f*.

dope [dəʊp] *n (inf: any illegal drug)* roba *f*; *(marijuana)* erba *f*.

dormitory ['dɔːmətrɪ] *n* dormitorio *m*.

Dormobile® ['dɔːmə,biːl] *n* camper *m inv*.

dosage ['dəʊsɪdʒ] *n* dosaggio *m*.

dose [dəʊs] *n (amount)* dose *f*; *(of illness)* attacco *m*.

dot [dɒt] *n* punto *m*; **on the ~** *(fig)* in punto.

dotted line ['dɒtɪd-] *n* linea *f* punteggiata.

double ['dʌbl] ◇ *adj* doppio(-a) ◇ *adv (twice)* due volte ◇ *n (twice the amount)* doppio *m*; *(alcohol)* dose *f* doppia ◇ *vt & vi* raddoppiare; **~ three, two, eight** trentatrè, ventotto; **a ~ whisky** un doppio whisky; **to bend sthg ~** piegare qc in due.

◆ **doubles** *n (in tennis)* doppio *m*.

double bed *n* letto *m* matrimoniale.

double-breasted [-'brestɪd] *adj* a doppio petto.

double cream *n (Br) panna molto densa ad alto contenuto di grassi.*

double-decker (bus) [-'dekəʳ-] *n* autobus *m inv* a due piani.

double doors *npl* porte *fpl* a due battenti.

double-glazing [-'gleɪzɪŋ] *n* doppi vetri *mpl*.

double room *n* camera *f* per due.

doubt [daʊt] ◇ *n* dubbio *m* ◇ *vt* dubitare di; **I ~ it** ne dubito; **I ~ she'll be there** dubito che ci sarà; **in ~** in dubbio; **no ~** *(almost certainly)* senza dubbio.

doubtful ['daʊtfʊl] *adj (uncertain)* incerto(-a); **it's ~ that ...** è improbabile che ... *(+ subjunctive)*.

dough [dəʊ] *n* pasta *f*, impasto *m (per pane, dolci)*.

doughnut ['dəʊnʌt] *n* bombolone *m*.

dove[1] [dʌv] *n (bird)* colomba *f*.

dove[2] [dəʊv] *pt (Am)* → **dive**.

Dover ['dəʊvəʳ] *n* Dover.

Dover sole *n* sogliola *f* di Dover.

down [daʊn] ◇ *adv* **1.** *(towards the bottom)* giù; **~ here** quaggiù; **~ there** laggiù; **to fall ~** cadere.

2. *(along)*: **I'm going ~ to the shops** vado ai negozi.

3. *(downstairs)*: **I'll come ~ later** scenderò più tardi.

4. *(southwards)*: **we're going ~ to London** andiamo a Londra.

5. *(in writing)*: **to write sthg ~** scrivere qc.

◇ *prep* **1.** *(towards the bottom of)*:

they ran ~ the hill corsero giù per la collina.
2. *(along)* lungo; **I was walking ~ the street** camminavo lungo la strada.
◇ *adj (inf: depressed)* giù *(inv)*.
◇ *n (feathers)* piumino *m*.
◆ **downs** *npl (Br)* colline *fpl*.

downhill [ˌdaʊnˈhɪl] *adv* in discesa.

Downing Street [ˈdaʊnɪŋ-] *n* Downing Street *f (strada di Londra dove si trova la residenza del primo ministro)*.

downpour [ˈdaʊnpɔːʳ] *n* acquazzone *m*.

downstairs [ˌdaʊnˈsteəz] ◇ *adj* di sotto ◇ *adv* al piano di sotto; **to go ~** scendere giù.

downtown [ˌdaʊnˈtaʊn] ◇ *adj (hotel)* del centro; *(train)* per il centro ◇ *adv* in centro; **~ New York** il centro di New York.

down under *adv (Br: inf: in Australia)* in Australia.

downwards [ˈdaʊnwədz] *adv* verso il basso.

doz. *abbr* = **dozen**.

doze [dəʊz] *vi* fare un pisolino.

dozen [ˈdʌzn] *n* dozzina *f*; **a ~ eggs** una dozzina di uova.

Dr *(abbr of doctor)* Dott. *m* (Dott.ssa *f*)

drab [dræb] *adj* grigio(-a).

draft [drɑːft] *n (early version)* bozza *f*; *(money order)* tratta *f*; *(Am)* = **draught**.

drag [dræg] ◇ *vt (pull along)* trascinare ◇ *vi (along ground)* strascicare; **what a ~!** *(inf)* che seccatura!
◆ **drag on** *vi* trascinarsi.

dragonfly [ˈdrægnflaɪ] *n* libellula *f*.

drain [dreɪn] ◇ *n (sewer)* fogna *f*; *(grating in street)* tombino *m* ◇ *vt (tank, radiator)* svuotare ◇ *vi (vegetables, washing-up)* scolare.

draining board [ˈdreɪnɪŋ-] *n* scolatoio *m*.

drainpipe [ˈdreɪnpaɪp] *n* tubo *m* di scarico.

drama [ˈdrɑːmə] *n (play, exciting event)* dramma *m*; *(art)* teatro *m*; *(excitement)* emozioni *fpl*.

dramatic [drəˈmætɪk] *adj (impressive)* sensazionale.

drank [dræŋk] *pt* → **drink**.

drapes [dreɪps] *npl (Am)* tende *fpl*.

drastic [ˈdræstɪk] *adj* drastico(-a); *(improvement)* netto(-a).

drastically [ˈdræstɪklɪ] *adv* sensibilmente.

draught [drɑːft] *n (Br: of air)* corrente *f* d'aria.

draught beer *n* birra *f* alla spina.

draughts [drɑːfts] *n (Br)* dama *f*.

draughty [ˈdrɑːftɪ] *adj* pieno(-a) di correnti d'aria.

draw [drɔː] (*pt* **drew**, *pp* **drawn**) ◇ *vt (with pen, pencil)* disegnare; *(line)* tracciare; *(pull)* tirare; *(attract)* attirare; *(conclusion)* trarre; *(comparison)* fare ◇ *vi (with pen, pencil)* disegnare; (SPORT) pareggiare ◇ *n* (SPORT*: result*) pareggio *m*; *(lottery)* estrazione *f*; **to ~ the curtains** tirare le tende.
◆ **draw out** *vt sep (money)* prelevare.
◆ **draw up** ◇ *vt sep (list, plan)* stendere ◇ *vi (car, bus)* accostarsi.

drawback [ˈdrɔːbæk] *n* inconveniente *m*.

drawer [drɔːʳ] *n* cassetto *m*.

drawing [ˈdrɔːɪŋ] *n* disegno *m*.

drawing pin *n (Br)* puntina *f* da disegno.

drawing room *n* salotto *m*.

drawn [drɔːn] *pp* → **draw**.

dreadful [ˈdredfʊl] *adj* terribile.

dream [driːm] ◇ *n* sogno *m* ◇ *vt* sognare ◇ *vi*: **to ~ (of)** sognare (di); **a ~ house** una casa di sogno.

dress [dres] ◇ *n* vestito *m*; *(clothes)* abbigliamento *m* ◇ *vt* vestire; *(wound)* fasciare; *(salad)* condire ◇ *vi (get dressed)* vestirsi; *(in particular* *way)* vestire; **to be ~ed in** essere vestito di; **to get ~ed** vestirsi.

◆ **dress up** *vi* mettersi in ghingheri.

dress circle *n* prima galleria *f*.

dresser [ˈdresəʳ] *n (Br: for crockery)* credenza *f*; *(Am: chest of drawers)* comò *m inv*.

dressing [ˈdresɪŋ] *n (for salad)* condimento *m*; *(for wound)* fasciatura *f*.

dressing gown *n* vestaglia *f*.

dressing room *n* camerino *m*.

dressing table *n* toilette *f inv*.

dressmaker [ˈdresˌmeɪkəʳ] *n* sarta *f*.

dress rehearsal *n* prova *f* generale.

drew [druː] *pt* → **draw**.

dribble [ˈdrɪbl] *vi (liquid)* gocciolare; *(baby)* sbavare.

drier [ˈdraɪəʳ] = **dryer**.

drift [drɪft] ◇ *n (of snow)* cumulo *m* ◇ *vi (in wind)* essere spinto dal vento; *(in water)* essere spinto dalla corrente.

drill [drɪl] ◇ *n* trapano *m* ◇ *vt (hole)* fare.

drink [drɪŋk] (*pt* **drank**, *pp* **drunk**) ◇ *n* bevanda *f*; *(alcoholic)* bicchierino *m* ◇ *vt & vi* bere; **would you like a ~?** vuoi qualcosa da bere?; **to have a ~** *(alcoholic)* bere un bicchierino.

drinkable [ˈdrɪŋkəbl] *adj (safe to drink)* potabile; *(wine)* bevibile.

drinking water [ˈdrɪŋkɪŋ-] *n* acqua *f* potabile.

drip [drɪp] ◇ *n (drop)* goccia *f*; (MED) flebo *f inv* ◇ *vi* gocciolare.

drip-dry *adj* che non si stira.

dripping (wet) [ˈdrɪpɪŋ-] *adj* fradicio(-a).

drive [draɪv] (*pt* **drove**, *pp* **driven**) ◇ *n (journey)* viaggio *m* (in macchina); *(in front of house)* viale *m* d'accesso ◇ *vi (drive car)* guidare; *(travel in car)* andare in macchina ◇ *vt (car, bus, train)* guidare; *(take in car)* portare (in macchina); *(operate, power)*: **it's driven by electricity** funziona a elettricità; **it's two hours' ~ from here** è a due ore di macchina da qui; **to go for a ~** andare a fare un giro in macchina; **to ~ sb to do sthg** spingere qn a fare qc; **to ~ sb mad** far diventare matto qn; **can you ~ me to the station?** mi accompagni alla stazione?

drivel [ˈdrɪvl] *n* scemenze *fpl*.

driven [ˈdrɪvn] *pp* → **drive**.

driver [ˈdraɪvəʳ] *n (of car, bus)* conducente *mf*; *(of train)* macchinista *mf*; *(of taxi)* tassista *mf*.

driver's license *(Am)* = **driving licence**.

driveshaft [ˈdraɪvʃɑːft] *n* albero *m* motore.

driveway [ˈdraɪvweɪ] *n* vialetto *m* d'accesso.

driving lesson [ˈdraɪvɪŋ-] *n* lezione *f* di guida.

driving licence [ˈdraɪvɪŋ-] *n (Br)* patente *f* di guida.

driving test [ˈdraɪvɪŋ-] *n* esame *m* di guida.

drizzle [ˈdrɪzl] *n* pioggerellina *f*.

drop [drɒp] ◇ *n (drip)* goccia *f*; *(small amount)* goccio *m*; *(distance down)* salto *m*; *(decrease)* calo *m*; *(in wages)* riduzione *f* ◇ *vt* lasciar cadere; *(reduce)* ridurre; *(from vehicle)* far scendere; *(omit)* saltare ◇ *vi (fall)* cadere; *(decrease)* diminuire; **to ~ a hint that** far capire che; **to ~ sb a line** scrivere due righe a qn.

◆ **drop in** *vi (inf)* fare un salto.

◆ **drop off** ◇ *vt sep (from vehicle)* far scendere ◇ *vi (fall asleep)* addormentarsi; *(fall off)* staccarsi.

◆ **drop out** *vi (of college, race)* ritirarsi.

drought [draʊt] *n* siccità *f inv*.

drove [drəʊv] *pt* → **drive**.

drown [draʊn] *vi* annegare.

drug [drʌg] ◇ *n* (MED) farmaco *m*; *(stimulant)* droga *f* ◇ *vt* drogare.
drug addict *n* tossicodipendente *mf*.
druggist [ˈdrʌgɪst] *n (Am)* farmacista *mf*.
drum [drʌm] *n* (MUS) tamburo *m*; *(container)* fusto *m*.
◆ **drums** *npl* batteria *f*.
drummer [ˈdrʌməʳ] *n* batterista *mf*.
drumstick [ˈdrʌmstɪk] *n (of chicken)* coscia *f* (di pollo).
drunk [drʌŋk] ◇ *pp* → **drink** ◇ *adj* ubriaco(-a) ◇ *n* ubriaco *m* (-a *f*); **to get ~** ubriacarsi.
dry [draɪ] ◇ *adj* secco(-a); *(weather, day)* asciutto(-a) ◇ *vt* asciugare ◇ *vi* asciugarsi; **to ~ o.s.** asciugarsi; **to ~ one's hair** asciugarsi i capelli.
◆ **dry up** *vi (become dry)* seccarsi; *(dry the dishes)* asciugare i piatti.
dry-clean *vt* pulire a secco.
dry cleaner's *n* lavanderia *f* (a secco).
dryer [ˈdraɪəʳ] *n (for clothes)* asciugabiancheria *m inv*; *(for hair)* asciugacapelli *m inv*.
dry-roasted peanuts [-ˈrəʊstɪd-] *npl* arachidi *fpl* tostate.
DSS *n (Br) ministero britannico per la previdenza sociale.*
DTP *n (abbr of desktop publishing)* desktop publishing *m*.
dual carriageway [ˈdjuːəl-] *n (Br)* strada *f* a doppia carreggiata.
dubbed [dʌbd] *adj (film)* doppiato(-a).
dubious [ˈdjuːbjəs] *adj (suspect)* dubbio(-a).
duchess [ˈdʌtʃɪs] *n* duchessa *f*.
duck [dʌk] ◇ *n* anatra *f* ◇ *vi* abbassarsi.
due [djuː] *adj (expected)* atteso(-a); *(owed)* dovuto(-a); **to be ~** *(bill, rent)* scadere; **in ~ course** a tempo debito; **~ to** a causa di.
duet [djuːˈet] *n* duetto *m*.
duffel bag [ˈdʌfl-] *n* sacca *f* da viaggio.
duffel coat [ˈdʌfl-] *n* montgomery *m inv*.
dug [dʌg] *pt & pp* → **dig**.
duke [djuːk] *n* duca *m*.
dull [dʌl] *adj (boring)* noioso(-a); *(not bright)* spento(-a); *(weather)* coperto(-a); *(pain)* sordo(-a).
dumb [dʌm] *adj (inf: stupid)* stupido(-a); *(unable to speak)* muto(-a).
dummy [ˈdʌmɪ] *n (Br: for baby)* ciuccio *m*; *(for clothes)* manichino *m*.
dump [dʌmp] ◇ *n (for rubbish)* discarica *f*; *(inf: place)* porcile *m* ◇ *vt (drop carelessly)* gettare; *(get rid of)* scaricare.
dumpling [ˈdʌmplɪŋ] *n gnocco di pasta cotto al vapore e servito insieme agli stufati.*
dune [djuːn] *n* duna *f*.
dungarees [ˌdʌŋgəˈriːz] *npl (for work)* tuta *f*; *(Br: fashion item)* salopette *f inv*.
dungeon [ˈdʌndʒən] *n* segreta *f*.
duplicate [ˈdjuːplɪkət] *n* duplicato *m*.
during [ˈdjʊərɪŋ] *prep* durante.
dusk [dʌsk] *n* crepuscolo *m*.
dust [dʌst] ◇ *n* polvere *f* ◇ *vt* spolverare.
dustbin [ˈdʌstbɪn] *n (Br)* pattumiera *f*.
dustcart [ˈdʌstkɑːt] *n (Br)* camion *m inv* delle immondizie.
duster [ˈdʌstəʳ] *n* straccio *m* (per spolverare).
dustman [ˈdʌstmən] (*pl* **-men** [-mən]) *n (Br)* netturbino *m*.
dustpan [ˈdʌstpæn] *n* paletta *f* (*per la spazzatura)*.
dusty [ˈdʌstɪ] *adj* polveroso(-a).
Dutch [dʌtʃ] ◇ *adj* olandese ◇ *n (language)* olandese *m* ◇ *npl*: **the ~** gli olandesi.

Dutchman [ˈdʌtʃmən] (*pl* **-men** [-mən]) *n* olandese *m*.

Dutchwoman [ˈdʌtʃˌwʊmən] (*pl* **-women** [-ˌwɪmɪn]) *n* olandese *f*.

duty [ˈdjuːtɪ] *n* *(moral obligation)* dovere *m*; *(tax)* dazio *m*, tassa *f*; **to be on ~** essere in OR di servizio; **to be off ~** essere fuori servizio, essere libero.

◆ **duties** *npl (job)* mansioni *fpl*.

duty chemist's *n* farmacia *f* di turno.

duty-free ◇ *adj* esente da dazio ◇ *n* duty free *m inv*.

duty-free shop *n* duty free shop *m inv*.

duvet [ˈduːveɪ] *n* piumone® *m*.

dwarf [dwɔːf] (*pl* **dwarves** [dwɔːvz]) *n* nano *m* (-a *f*).

dwelling [ˈdwelɪŋ] *n* *(fml)* abitazione *f*.

dye [daɪ] ◇ *n* tinta *f* ◇ *vt* tingere.

dynamite [ˈdaɪnəmaɪt] *n* dinamite *f*.

dynamo [ˈdaɪnəməʊ] (*pl* **-s**) *n* *(on bike)* dinamo *f inv*.

dyslexic [dɪsˈleksɪk] *adj* dislessico(-a).

E

E *(abbr of east)* E.

E111 *n* E111 *m*.

each [iːtʃ] ◇ *adj* ogni *(inv)*, ciascuno(-a) ◇ *pron* ciascuno *m* (-a *f*), ognuno *m* (-a *f*); ~ **one** ognuno; ~ **of them** ognuno di loro; **one** ~ uno ciascuno; **one of** ~ uno di ognuno; **they know** ~ **other** si conoscono.

eager [ˈiːgəʳ] *adj (pupil, expression)* entusiasta; **to be** ~ **to do sthg** essere impaziente di fare qc.

eagle [ˈiːgl] *n (bird)* aquila *f*.

ear [ɪəʳ] *n* orecchio *m*; *(of corn)* spiga *f*.

earache [ˈɪəreɪk] *n*: **to have** ~ avere mal *m* d'orecchi.

earl [ɜːl] *n* conte *m*.

early [ˈɜːlɪ] ◇ *adj (childhood)* primo(-a); *(train)* di buon'ora; *(before usual or arranged time)* anticipato(-a), precoce ◇ *adv* presto; **in the** ~ **morning** di primo mattino; **in the** ~ **20th century** all'inizio del XX secolo; **at the earliest** al più presto; ~ **on** presto; **to have an** ~ **night** andare a letto presto.

earn [ɜːn] *vt (money)* guadagnare; *(praise, success)* guadagnarsi; **to** ~ **a living** guadagnarsi da vivere.

earnings [ˈɜːnɪŋz] *npl* guadagni *mpl*.

earphones [ˈɪəfəʊnz] *npl* cuffie *fpl*.

earplugs [ˈɪəplʌgz] *npl* tappi *mpl* per le orecchie.

earrings [ˈɪərɪŋz] *npl* orecchini *mpl*.

earth [ɜːθ] ◇ *n* terra *f* ◇ *vt (Br: appliance)* mettere a terra; **how on** ~ ...? come diavolo ...?

earthenware [ˈɜːθnweəʳ] *adj* di terracotta.

earthquake [ˈɜːθkweɪk] *n* terremoto *m*.

ease [iːz] ◇ *n (lack of difficulty)* facilità *f* ◇ *vt (pain, problem)* alleviare; **at** ~ a proprio agio; **with** ~ con facilità.

◆ **ease off** *vi (pain, rain)* attenuarsi.

easily [ˈiːzɪlɪ] *adv* facilmente; *(by far)* senza dubbio.

east [iːst] ◇ *n* est *m* ◇ *adj* dell'est ◇ *adv* a est; **in the** ~ **of England** nell'Inghilterra orientale; **the East** *(Asia)* l'Oriente *m*.

eastbound [ˈiːstbaʊnd] *adj* diretto(-a) a est.

Easter [ˈiːstəʳ] *n* Pasqua *f*.

eastern [ˈiːstən] *adj* orientale, dell'est.

◆ **Eastern** *adj (Asian)* orientale.

Eastern Europe *n* l'Europa *f* dell'Est.

eastwards [ˈiːstwədz] *adv* verso est.

easy [ˈiːzɪ] *adj* facile; *(without problems)* tranquillo(-a); **to take it** ~

prendersela con calma.
easygoing [ˌiːzɪˈɡəʊɪŋ] *adj* rilassato(-a).
eat [iːt] (*pt* **ate**, *pp* **eaten** [ˈiːtn]) *vt & vi* mangiare.
◆ **eat out** *vi* mangiare fuori.
eating apple [ˈiːtɪŋ-] *n* mela *f* (da mangiare cruda).
ebony [ˈebənɪ] *n* ebano *m*.
EC *n (abbr of European Community)* CE *f*.
eccentric [ɪkˈsentrɪk] *adj* eccentrico(-a).
echo [ˈekəʊ] (*pl* **-es**) ◇ *n* eco *f* ◇ *vi* fare eco.
ecology [ɪˈkɒlədʒɪ] *n* ecologia *f*.
economic [ˌiːkəˈnɒmɪk] *adj* economico(-a).
◆ **economics** *n* economia *f*.
economical [ˌiːkəˈnɒmɪkl] *adj (car, system)* economico(-a); *(person)* parsimonioso(-a).
economize [ɪˈkɒnəmaɪz] *vi* economizzare, risparmiare.
economy [ɪˈkɒnəmɪ] *n* economia *f*.
economy class *n* classe *f* economica.
economy size *adj* in confezione economica.
ecotourism [iːkəʊˈtʊərɪzm] *n* ecoturismo *m*.
ecstasy [ˈekstəsɪ] *n* estasi *f inv*.
ECU [ˈekjuː] *n* ECU *m inv*.
eczema [ˈeksɪmə] *n* eczema *m*.
edge [edʒ] *n* bordo *m*; *(of knife)* taglio *m*.
edible [ˈedɪbl] *adj* commestibile.
Edinburgh [ˈedɪnbrə] *n* Edimburgo *f*.
Edinburgh Festival *n*: **the ~** il festival di Edimburgo.
edition [ɪˈdɪʃn] *n* edizione *f*; *(of TV programme)* puntata *f*.
editor [ˈedɪtə^r] *n (of newspaper, magazine)* direttore *m* (-trice *f*); *(of book)* curatore *m* (-trice *f*); *(of film, TV programme)* tecnico *m* (-a *f*) del montaggio.
editorial [ˌedɪˈtɔːrɪəl] *n* editoriale *m*.
educate [ˈedʒʊkeɪt] *vt* istruire.
education [ˌedʒʊˈkeɪʃn] *n* istruzione *f*.
EEC *n* C.E.E. *f*.
eel [iːl] *n* anguilla *f*.
effect [ɪˈfekt] *n* effetto *m*; **to put sthg into ~** mettere qc in atto; **to take ~** *(drug)* fare effetto; *(law)* entrare in vigore.
effective [ɪˈfektɪv] *adj (successful)* efficace; *(law, system)* effettivo(-a).
effectively [ɪˈfektɪvlɪ] *adv (successfully)* efficacemente; *(in fact)* effettivamente.
efficient [ɪˈfɪʃənt] *adj* efficiente.
effort [ˈefət] *n* sforzo *m*; **to make an ~ to do sthg** fare uno sforzo per fare qc; **it's not worth the ~** non ne vale la pena.
e.g. *adv* ad es.
egg [eg] *n* uovo *m*.
egg cup *n* portauovo *m inv*.
egg mayonnaise *n* uova *fpl* sode in maionese.
eggplant [ˈegplɑːnt] *n (Am)* melanzana *f*.
egg white *n* albume *m*.
egg yolk *n* tuorlo *m*.
Egypt [ˈiːdʒɪpt] *n* l'Egitto *m*.
eiderdown [ˈaɪdədaʊn] *n* piumone® *m*.
eight [eɪt] *num* otto, → **six**.
eighteen [ˌeɪˈtiːn] *num* diciotto, → **six**.
eighteenth [ˌeɪˈtiːnθ] *num* diciottesimo(-a), → **sixth**.
eighth [eɪtθ] *num* ottavo(-a), → **sixth**.
eightieth [ˈeɪtɪɪθ] *num* ottantesimo(-a), → **sixth**.
eighty [ˈeɪtɪ] *num* ottanta, → **six**.
Eire [ˈeərə] *n* la Repubblica d'Irlanda.
Eisteddfod [aɪˈstedfəd] *n festival culturale gallese*.

either [ˈaɪðəʳ, ˈiːðəʳ] ◇ *adj*: **~ book will do** va bene sia l'uno che l'altro libro ◇ *pron*: **I'll take ~ (of them)** prendo o l'uno(-a) o l'altro (-a); **I don't like ~ (of them)** non mi piace né l'uno(-a) né l'altro(-a). ◇ *adv*: **I can't ~** non posso neanch'io; **~ ... or** o ... o; **on ~ side** su entrambi i lati.

eject [ɪˈdʒekt] *vt (cassette)* espellere.

elaborate [ɪˈlæbrət] *adj (needlework, design)* elaborato(-a).

elastic [ɪˈlæstɪk] *n* elastico *m*.

elastic band *n (Br)* elastico *m*.

elbow [ˈelbəʊ] *n (of person)* gomito *m*.

elder [ˈeldəʳ] *adj* più vecchio(-a), maggiore.

elderly [ˈeldəlɪ] ◇ *adj* anziano(-a) ◇ *npl*: **the ~** gli anziani.

eldest [ˈeldɪst] *adj*: **the ~ son/daughter** il figlio/la figlia maggiore.

elect [ɪˈlekt] *vt* eleggere; **to ~ to do sthg** *(fml: choose)* scegliere di fare qc.

election [ɪˈlekʃn] *n* elezione *f*.

electric [ɪˈlektrɪk] *adj* elettrico(-a).

electrical goods [ɪˈlektrɪkl-] *npl* apparecchi *mpl* elettrici.

electric blanket *n* coperta *f* elettrica.

electric drill *n* trapano *m* elettrico.

electric fence *n* recinto *m* elettrificato.

electrician [ˌɪlekˈtrɪʃn] *n* elettricista *mf*.

electricity [ˌɪlekˈtrɪsətɪ] *n* elettricità *f*.

electric shock *n* scossa *f* elettrica.

electrocute [ɪˈlektrəkjuːt] *vt* fulminare.

electronic [ˌɪlekˈtrɒnɪk] *adj* elettronico(-a).

elegant [ˈelɪgənt] *adj* elegante.

element [ˈelɪmənt] *n* elemento *m*; *(of fire, kettle)* resistenza *f*; **the ~s** *(weather)* gli elementi.

elementary [ˌelɪˈmentərɪ] *adj* elementare.

elephant [ˈelɪfənt] *n* elefante *m*.

elevator [ˈelɪveɪtəʳ] *n (Am)* ascensore *m*.

eleven [ɪˈlevn] *num* undici, → **six**.

eleventh [ɪˈlevnθ] *num* undicesimo(-a), → **sixth**.

eligible [ˈelɪdʒəbl] *adj* che ha i requisiti.

eliminate [ɪˈlɪmɪneɪt] *vt* eliminare.

Elizabethan [ɪˌlɪzəˈbiːθn] *adj* elisabettiano(-a) *(seconda metà del* XVI *sec.)*.

elm [elm] *n* olmo *m*.

else [els] *adv*: **I don't want anything ~** non voglio nient'altro; **anything ~?** altro?; **everyone ~** tutti gli altri; **nobody ~** nessun altro; **nothing ~** nient'altro; **somebody ~** qualcun altro; **something ~** qualcos'altro; **somewhere ~** da qualche altra parte; **what ~?** che altro?; **who ~?** chi altri?; **or ~** altrimenti.

elsewhere [elsˈweəʳ] *adv* altrove.

e-mail [ˈiːmeɪl] *n (abbr of electronic mail)* posta *f* elettronica.

embankment [ɪmˈbæŋkmənt] *n (next to river)* argine *m*; *(next to road, railway)* terrapieno *m*.

embark [ɪmˈbɑːk] *vi (board ship)* imbarcarsi.

embarkation card [ˌembɑːˈkeɪʃn-] *n* carta *f* d'imbarco

embarrass [ɪmˈbærəs] *vt* imbarazzare.

embarrassed [ɪmˈbærəst] *adj* imbarazzato(-a).

embarrassing [ɪmˈbærəsɪŋ] *adj* imbarazzante.

embarrassment [ɪmˈbærəsmənt] *n* imbarazzo *m*.

embassy [ˈembəsɪ] *n* ambasciata *f*.

emblem [ˈembləm] *n* emblema *m*.

embrace [ɪmˈbreɪs] *vt* abbracciare.

embroidered [ɪm'brɔɪdəd] *adj* ricamato(-a).

embroidery [ɪm'brɔɪdərɪ] *n* ricamo *m*.

emerald ['emərəld] *n* smeraldo *m*.

emerge [ɪ'mɜːdʒ] *vi* emergere.

emergency [ɪ'mɜːdʒənsɪ] ◇ *n* emergenza *f* ◇ *adj* di emergenza; **in an ~** in caso di emergenza.

emergency exit *n* uscita *f* di sicurezza.

emergency landing *n* atterraggio *m* di emergenza.

emergency services *npl* servizi *mpl* di pronto intervento.

emigrate ['emɪgreɪt] *vi* emigrare.

emit [ɪ'mɪt] *vt* emettere.

emotion [ɪ'məʊʃn] *n* emozione *f*.

emotional [ɪ'məʊʃənl] *adj* emotivo(-a).

emphasis ['emfəsɪs] (*pl* **-ases** [-əsiːz]) *n* enfasi *f*; **to put the ~ on sthg** dare importanza a qc.

emphasize ['emfəsaɪz] *vt* sottolineare.

empire ['empaɪər] *n* impero *m*.

employ [ɪm'plɔɪ] *vt* impiegare.

employed [ɪm'plɔɪd] *adj* impiegato(-a).

employee [ɪm'plɔɪiː] *n* dipendente *mf*.

employer [ɪm'plɔɪər] *n* datore *m* (-trice *f*) di lavoro.

employment [ɪm'plɔɪmənt] *n* impiego *m*.

employment agency *n* agenzia *f* di collocamento.

empty ['emptɪ] ◇ *adj* vuoto(-a); *(threat, promise)* vano(-a) ◇ *vt* vuotare.

EMU *n (abbr of Economic Monetary Union)* unione *f* economica e monetaria.

emulsion (paint) [ɪ'mʌlʃn-] *n* pittura *f* a emulsione.

enable [ɪ'neɪbl] *vt*: **to ~ sb to do sthg** permettere a qn di fare qc.

enamel [ɪ'næml] *n* smalto *m*.

enclose [ɪn'kləʊz] *vt (surround)* cingere, circondare; *(with letter)* allegare.

enclosed [ɪn'kləʊzd] *adj (space)* contenuto(-a), limitato(-a).

encounter [ɪn'kaʊntər] *vt* incontrare.

encourage [ɪn'kʌrɪdʒ] *vt* incoraggiare; **to ~ sb to do sthg** incoraggiare qn a fare qc.

encouragement [ɪn'kʌrɪdʒmənt] *n* incoraggiamento *m*.

encyclopedia [ɪn,saɪklə'piːdjə] *n* enciclopedia *f*.

end [end] ◇ *n* fine *f*; *(purpose)* fine *m* ◇ *vt (story, evening, holiday)* finire; *(war, practice)* finire, mettere fine a ◇ *vi* finire; **to come to an ~** finire, giungere alla fine; **to put an ~ to sthg** mettere fine a qc; **for days on ~** per giorni e giorni; **in the ~** alla fine; **to make ~s meet** sbarcare il lunario.

♦ **end up** *vi* finire; **to ~ up doing sthg** finire con il fare qc.

endangered species [ɪn'deɪndʒəd-] *n* specie *f inv* in via d'estinzione.

ending ['endɪŋ] *n (of story, film, book)* fine *f*; (GRAMM) desinenza *f*.

endive ['endaɪv] *n (curly)* indivia *f* (riccia); *(chicory)* cicoria *f*.

endless ['endlɪs] *adj* interminabile, senza fine.

endorsement [ɪn'dɔːsmənt] *n (of driving licence) infrazione registrata sulla patente*.

endurance [ɪn'djʊərəns] *n* resistenza *f*, sopportazione *f*.

endure [ɪn'djʊər] *vt* sopportare.

enemy ['enɪmɪ] *n* nemico *m* (-a *f*).

energy ['enədʒɪ] *n* energia *f*.

enforce [ɪn'fɔːs] *vt (law)* applicare, far rispettare.

engaged [ɪn'geɪdʒd] *adj (to be married)* fidanzato(-a); *(Br: phone)* occupato(-a); *(toilet)* occupato(-a);

to get ~ fidanzarsi.
engaged tone *n (Br)* segnale *m* di occupato.
engagement [ɪnˈgeɪdʒmənt] *n (to marry)* fidanzamento *m*; *(appointment)* appuntamento *m*.
engagement ring *n* anello *m* di fidanzamento.
engine [ˈendʒɪn] *n (of vehicle)* motore *m*; *(of train)* locomotiva *f*.
engineer [ˌendʒɪˈnɪəʳ] *n (of roads, machinery)* ingegnere *m*; *(to do repairs)* tecnico *m* (-a *f*).
engineering [ˌendʒɪˈnɪərɪŋ] *n* ingegneria *f*.
engineering works *npl (on railway line)* lavori *mpl* in corso.
England [ˈɪŋglənd] *n* l'Inghilterra *f*.
English [ˈɪŋglɪʃ] ◇ *adj* inglese ◇ *n (language)* inglese *m* ◇ *npl*: **the ~** gli inglesi.
English breakfast *n* colazione *f* all'inglese.
English Channel *n*: **the ~** la Manica.
Englishman [ˈɪŋglɪʃmən] (*pl* **-men** [-mən]) *n* inglese *m*.
Englishwoman [ˈɪŋglɪʃˌwʊmən] (*pl* **-women** [-ˌwɪmɪn]) *n* inglese *f*.
engrave [ɪnˈgreɪv] *vt* incidere.
engraving [ɪnˈgreɪvɪŋ] *n* incisione *f*.
enjoy [ɪnˈdʒɔɪ] *vt* godersi; **to ~ doing sthg** divertirsi a fare qc; **I ~ swimming** mi piace nuotare; **to ~ o.s.** divertirsi; **~ your meal!** buon appetito!
enjoyable [ɪnˈdʒɔɪəbl] *adj* piacevole.
enjoyment [ɪnˈdʒɔɪmənt] *n* piacere *m*.
enlargement [ɪnˈlɑːdʒmənt] *n (of photo)* ingrandimento *m*.
enormous [ɪˈnɔːməs] *adj* enorme.
enough [ɪˈnʌf] ◇ *adj* abbastanza *(inv)*, sufficiente ◇ *pron & adv* abbastanza; **~ time** abbastanza tempo; **is that ~?** è abbastanza?, basta?; **it's not big ~** non è abbastanza grande; **to have had ~ (of)** averne abbastanza (di).
enquire [ɪnˈkwaɪəʳ] *vi* informarsi.
enquiry [ɪnˈkwaɪərɪ] *n (question)* domanda *f*; *(investigation)* indagine *f*, inchiesta *f*; **'Enquiries'** 'Informazioni'.
enquiry desk *n* banco *m* informazioni.
enrol [ɪnˈrəʊl] *vi (Br)* iscriversi.
enroll [ɪnˈrəʊl] *(Am)* = **enrol**.
en suite bathroom [ɒnˈswiːt] *n* bagno *m* privato.
ensure [ɪnˈʃʊəʳ] *vt* garantire, assicurare.
entail [ɪnˈteɪl] *vt* comportare.
enter [ˈentəʳ] ◇ *vt* entrare in; *(college, competition)* iscriversi a; *(on form)* scrivere ◇ *vi* entrare; *(in competition)* iscriversi.
enterprise [ˈentəpraɪz] *n (company)* impresa *f*; *(plan)* iniziativa *f*.
entertain [ˌentəˈteɪn] *vt (amuse)* divertire.
entertainer [ˌentəˈteɪnəʳ] *n* intrattenitore *m* (-trice *f*).
entertaining [ˌentəˈteɪnɪŋ] *adj* divertente.
entertainment [ˌentəˈteɪnmənt] *n (amusement)* divertimento *m*; *(show)* spettacolo *m*.
enthusiasm [ɪnˈθjuːzɪæzm] *n* entusiasmo *m*.
enthusiast [ɪnˈθjuːzɪæst] *n* appassionato *m* (-a *f*).
enthusiastic [ɪnˌθjuːzɪˈæstɪk] *adj* entusiasta.
entire [ɪnˈtaɪəʳ] *adj* intero(-a).
entirely [ɪnˈtaɪəlɪ] *adv* completamente.
entitle [ɪnˈtaɪtl] *vt*: **to ~ sb to sthg** dare a qn diritto a qc; **to ~ sb to do sthg** dare diritto a qn di fare qc.
entrance [ˈentrəns] *n* entrata *f*, ingresso *m*.

entrance fee *n* biglietto *m* d'ingresso.

entry ['entrɪ] *n (door, gate, admission)* entrata *f*, ingresso *m*; *(in dictionary)* voce *f*; *(piece in competition)* cosa *f* presentata; **'no ~'** *(sign on door)* 'ingresso vietato'; *(road sign)* 'divieto d'accesso'.

envelope ['envələup] *n* busta *f*.

envious ['envɪəs] *adj* invidioso(-a).

environment [ɪn'vaɪərənmənt] *n* ambiente *m*; **the ~** l'ambiente (naturale).

environmental [ɪn,vaɪərən'mentl] *adj* ambientale.

environmentally friendly [ɪn,vaɪərən'mentəlɪ-] *adj* che rispetta l'ambiente, ecologico(-a).

envy ['envɪ] *vt* invidiare.

epic ['epɪk] *n* epopea *f*.

epidemic [,epɪ'demɪk] *n* epidemia *f*.

epileptic [,epɪ'leptɪk] *adj* epilettico(-a).

episode ['epɪsəud] *n* episodio *m*.

equal ['i:kwəl] ◇ *adj (of same amount)* uguale; *(with equal rights)* uguale, pari *(inv)* ◇ *vt (number)* fare; **to be ~ to** *(number)* essere uguale a.

equality [ɪ'kwɒlətɪ] *n* uguaglianza *f*.

equalize ['i:kwəlaɪz] *vi* pareggiare.

equally ['i:kwəlɪ] *adv (bad, good, matched)* ugualmente; *(pay, treat, share)* equamente; *(at the same time)* allo stesso modo.

equation [ɪ'kweɪʒn] *n* equazione *f*.

equator [ɪ'kweɪtə^r] *n*: **the ~** l'equatore *m*.

equip [ɪ'kwɪp] *vt*: **to ~ sb/sthg with** fornire qn/qc di.

equipment [ɪ'kwɪpmənt] *n* attrezzatura *f*.

equipped [ɪ'kwɪpt] *adj*: **to be ~ with** essere fornito(-a) di.

equivalent [ɪ'kwɪvələnt] ◇ *adj* equivalente ◇ *n* equivalente *m*.

erase [ɪ'reɪz] *vt (letter, word)* cancellare.

eraser [ɪ'reɪzə^r] *n* gomma *f*.

erect [ɪ'rekt] ◇ *adj (person, posture)* eretto(-a) ◇ *vt (tent)* montare; *(monument)* erigere.

ERM *n* meccanismo *m* di cambio (dello SME).

erotic [ɪ'rɒtɪk] *adj* erotico(-a).

errand ['erənd] *n* commissione *f*.

erratic [ɪ'rætɪk] *adj* irregolare, incostante.

error ['erə^r] *n* errore *m*.

escalator ['eskəleɪtə^r] *n* scala *f* mobile.

escalope ['eskəlɒp] *n* cotoletta *f* alla milanese.

escape [ɪ'skeɪp] ◇ *n* fuga *f* ◇ *vi*: **to ~ (from)** *(from prison)* evadere (da); *(from danger)* fuggire (da); *(leak)* fuoriuscire (da).

escort [*n* 'eskɔ:t, *vb* ɪ'skɔ:t] ◇ *n (guard)* scorta *f* ◇ *vt* accompagnare.

espadrilles ['espə,drɪlz] *npl* espadrilles *fpl*.

especially [ɪ'speʃəlɪ] *adv (in particular)* specialmente, soprattutto; *(on purpose)* apposta; *(very)* particolarmente.

esplanade [,esplə'neɪd] *n* passeggiata *f* (a mare).

essay ['eseɪ] *n (at school, university)* composizione *f*, tema *m*.

essential [ɪ'senʃl] *adj (indispensable)* essenziale.

◆ **essentials** *npl*: **the ~s** l'essenziale *m*; **the bare ~s** il minimo indispensabile.

essentially [ɪ'senʃəlɪ] *adv* essenzialmente.

establish [ɪ'stæblɪʃ] *vt (set up, create)* fondare; *(fact, truth)* stabilire.

establishment [ɪ'stæblɪʃmənt] *n (business)* azienda *f*.

estate [ɪ'steɪt] *n (land in country)* proprietà *f inv*; *(for housing)* complesso *m* residenziale; *(Br: car)* = **estate car**.

estate agent *n (Br)* agente *mf* immobiliare.

estate car *n (Br)* station wagon *f inv*.

estimate [*n* 'estɪmət, *vb* 'estɪmeɪt] ◇ *n (guess)* stima *f*; *(from builder, plumber)* preventivo *m* ◇ *vt* stimare, valutare.

estuary ['estjʊərɪ] *n* estuario *m*.

ethnic minority ['eθnɪk-] *n* minoranza *f* etnica.

EU *n (abbr of European Union)* U.E. *f*.

Eurocheque ['jʊərəʊ,tʃek] *n* eurochèque *m inv*.

Europe ['jʊərəp] *n* l'Europa *f*.

European [,jʊərə'pɪən] ◇ *adj* europeo(-a) ◇ *n* europeo *m* (-a *f*).

European Community *n* Comunità *f* Europea.

evacuate [ɪ'vækjʊeɪt] *vt* evacuare.

evade [ɪ'veɪd] *vt (person, issue)* evitare; *(responsibility)* sottrarsi a.

evaporated milk [ɪ'væpəreɪtɪd-] *n* latte *m* concentrato.

eve [i:v] *n*: **on the ~ of** alla vigilia di.

even ['i:vn] ◇ *adj (uniform, equal)* regolare, uniforme; *(level, flat)* liscio(-a), piano(-a); *(contest)* alla pari; *(number)* pari *(inv)* ◇ *adv* perfino, anche; **to break ~** fare pari; **not ~** nemmeno; **~ so** ciò nonostante; **~ though** anche se.

evening ['i:vnɪŋ] *n* sera *f*; *(event, period)* serata *f*; **good ~!** buona sera!; **in the ~** di OR la sera.

evening classes *npl* corsi *mpl* serali.

evening dress *n (formal clothes)* abito *m* da sera; *(woman's garment)* vestito *m* da sera.

evening meal *n* cena *f*.

event [ɪ'vent] *n (occurrence)* evento *m*, avvenimento *m*; (SPORT) prova *f*; **in the ~ of** *(fml)* in caso di.

eventual [ɪ'ventʃʊəl] *adj* finale.

eventually [ɪ'ventʃʊəlɪ] *adv* alla fine.

ever ['evə^r] *adv* mai; **it's the worst ~** è il peggiore che sia mai esistito; **he was ~ so angry** era veramente arrabbiato; **for ~** *(eternally)* per sempre; **we've been waiting for ~** aspettiamo da tantissimo; **hardly ~** quasi mai.

◆ **ever since** ◇ *adv* fin da allora ◇ *prep* da ... in poi ◇ *conj* fin da quando.

every ['evrɪ] *adj* ogni *(inv)*; **~ day** ogni giorno, tutti i giorni; **~ other day** ogni due giorni; **one in ~ ten** uno su dieci; **we make ~ effort ...** facciamo ogni sforzo ...; **~ so often** ogni tanto.

everybody ['evrɪ,bɒdɪ] = **everyone**.

everyday ['evrɪdeɪ] *adj* di ogni giorno, quotidiano(-a).

everyone ['evrɪwʌn] *pron* ognuno *m* (-a *f*), tutti *mpl* (-e *fpl*).

everyplace ['evrɪ,pleɪs] *(Am)* = **everywhere**.

everything ['evrɪθɪŋ] *pron* tutto, ogni cosa.

everywhere ['evrɪweə^r] *adv* dappertutto; *(wherever)* dovunque.

evidence ['evɪdəns] *n (proof)* prova *f*; *(legal statement)* testimonianza *f*.

evident ['evɪdənt] *adj* evidente.

evidently ['evɪdəntlɪ] *adv* evidentemente.

evil ['i:vl] ◇ *adj* cattivo(-a), malvagio(-a) ◇ *n* male *m*.

ex [eks] *n (inf: wife, husband, partner)* ex *mf*.

exact [ɪg'zækt] *adj* esatto(-a); **'~ fare ready please'** 'si prega di munirsi dell'esatta somma per il biglietto'.

exactly [ɪgˈzæktli] *adv & excl* esattamente.

exaggerate [ɪgˈzædʒəreɪt] *vt & vi* esagerare.

exaggeration [ɪgˌzædʒəˈreɪʃn] *n* esagerazione *f*.

exam [ɪgˈzæm] *n* esame *m*; **to take an ~** fare un esame.

examination [ɪgˌzæmɪˈneɪʃn] *n* esame *m*; (MED) visita *f*.

examine [ɪgˈzæmɪn] *vt* esaminare; (MED) visitare.

example [ɪgˈzɑːmpl] *n* esempio *m*; **for ~** per esempio.

exceed [ɪkˈsiːd] *vt (be greater than)* superare; *(go beyond)* oltrepassare.

excellent [ˈeksələnt] *adj* eccellente.

except [ɪkˈsept] *prep & conj* eccetto, tranne; **~ for** a parte, all'infuori di; '**~ for access**' 'escluso residenti'; '**~ for loading**' 'escluso (per le operazioni di) carico'.

exception [ɪkˈsepʃn] *n (thing excepted)* eccezione *f*.

exceptional [ɪkˈsepʃnəl] *adj* eccezionale.

excerpt [ˈeksɜːpt] *n* estratto *m*.

excess [ɪkˈses, *before nouns* ˈekses] ◇ *adj* in eccesso ◇ *n* eccesso *m*.

excess baggage *n* bagaglio *m* in eccedenza.

excess fare *n (Br)* supplemento *m*.

excessive [ɪkˈsesɪv] *adj* eccessivo(-a).

exchange [ɪksˈtʃeɪndʒ] ◇ *n (of telephones)* centralino *m*; *(of students)* scambio *m* ◇ *vt* scambiare; **to ~ sthg for sthg** scambiare qc con qc; **we're here on an ~** siamo qui con uno scambio.

exchange rate *n* tasso *m* di cambio.

excited [ɪkˈsaɪtɪd] *adj* eccitato(-a).

excitement [ɪkˈsaɪtmənt] *n* eccitazione *f*; *(exciting thing)* cosa *f* eccitante.

exciting [ɪkˈsaɪtɪŋ] *adj* eccitante, emozionante.

exclamation mark [ˌekskləˈmeɪʃn-] *n (Br)* punto *m* esclamativo.

exclamation point [ˌekskləˈmeɪʃn-] *(Am)* = **exclamation mark**.

exclude [ɪkˈskluːd] *vt* escludere.

excluding [ɪkˈskluːdɪŋ] *prep* escluso(-a).

exclusive [ɪkˈskluːsɪv] ◇ *adj* esclusivo(-a) ◇ *n* esclusiva *f*; **~ of** escluso(-a).

excursion [ɪkˈskɜːʃn] *n* escursione *f*.

excuse [*n* ɪkˈskjuːs, *vb* ɪkˈskjuːz] ◇ *n* scusa *f* ◇ *vt (forgive)* scusare; *(let off)* dispensare; **~ me!** mi scusi!

ex-directory *adj (Br)* fuori elenco.

execute [ˈeksɪkjuːt] *vt (kill)* giustiziare.

executive [ɪgˈzekjʊtɪv] ◇ *adj (room)* per dirigenti ◇ *n (person)* dirigente *mf*.

exempt [ɪgˈzempt] *adj*: **~ (from)** esente (da).

exemption [ɪgˈzempʃn] *n* esenzione *f*.

exercise [ˈeksəsaɪz] ◇ *n* esercizio *m* ◇ *vi* fare esercizio OR del moto; **to do ~s** fare degli esercizi.

exercise book *n* quaderno *m*.

exert [ɪgˈzɜːt] *vt* esercitare.

exhaust [ɪgˈzɔːst] ◇ *vt* esaurire ◇ *n*: **~ (pipe)** tubo *m* di scappamento.

exhausted [ɪgˈzɔːstɪd] *adj* esausto(-a).

exhibit [ɪgˈzɪbɪt] ◇ *n (in museum, gallery)* oggetto *m* esposto ◇ *vt (in exhibition)* esporre.

exhibition [ˌeksɪˈbɪʃn] *n (of art)* esposizione *f*, mostra *f*.

exist [ɪgˈzɪst] *vi* esistere.

existence [ɪgˈzɪstəns] *n* esistenza *f*; **to be in ~** esistere.

existing [ɪgˈzɪstɪŋ] *adj* esistente.

exit ['eksɪt] ◇ *n* uscita *f* ◇ *vi* uscire.
exotic [ɪg'zɒtɪk] *adj* esotico(-a).
expand [ɪk'spænd] *vi (in size)* espandersi; *(in number)* aumentare.
expect [ɪk'spekt] *vt (believe likely)* aspettarsi, prevedere; *(await)* aspettare; **to ~ to do sthg** prevedere di fare qc; **to ~ sb to do sthg** *(require)* aspettarsi che qn faccia qc; **to be ~ing** *(be pregnant)* aspettare un bambino.
expedition [,ekspɪ'dɪʃn] *n* spedizione *f*; *(short outing)* gita *f*.
expel [ɪk'spel] *vt (from school)* espellere.
expense [ɪk'spens] *n* spesa *f*, costo *m*; **at the ~ of** *(fig)* a spese di. ◆ **expenses** *npl (of business trip)* spese *fpl*.
expensive [ɪk'spensɪv] *adj* costoso(-a), caro(-a).
experience [ɪk'spɪərɪəns] ◇ *n* esperienza *f* ◇ *vt* provare.
experienced [ɪk'spɪərɪənst] *adj* esperto(-a).
experiment [ɪk'sperɪmənt] ◇ *n* esperimento *m* ◇ *vi* fare esperimenti.
expert ['ekspɜːt] ◇ *adj (advice)* esperto(-a); *(treatment)* apposito(-a) ◇ *n* esperto *m* (-a *f*).
expire [ɪk'spaɪəʳ] *vi* scadere.
expiry date [ɪk'spaɪərɪ-] *n* data *f* di scadenza.
explain [ɪk'spleɪn] *vt* spiegare.
explanation [,eksplə'neɪʃn] *n* spiegazione *f*.
explode [ɪk'spləʊd] *vi (bomb)* esplodere.
exploit [ɪk'splɔɪt] *vt (person)* sfruttare.
explore [ɪk'splɔːʳ] *vt (place)* esplorare.
explosion [ɪk'spləʊʒn] *n (of bomb etc)* esplosione *f*.
explosive [ɪk'spləʊsɪv] *n* esplosivo *m*.
export [*n* 'ekspɔːt, *vb* ɪk'spɔːt] ◇ *n (of goods)* esportazione *f*; *(goods themselves)* merce *f* d'esportazione ◇ *vt* esportare.
exposed [ɪk'spəʊzd] *adj (place)* non riparato(-a).
exposure [ɪk'spəʊʒəʳ] *n (photograph)* foto *f inv*; (MED) assideramento *m*; *(to heat, radiation)* esposizione *f*.
express [ɪk'spres] ◇ *adj (letter, delivery, train)* espresso(-a) ◇ *n (train)* espresso *m* ◇ *vt* esprimere ◇ *adv* per espresso.
expression [ɪk'spreʃn] *n* espressione *f*.
expresso [ɪk'spresəʊ] (*pl* **-s**) *n* espresso *m*.
expressway [ɪk'spresweɪ] *n (Am)* autostrada *f* (urbana).
extend [ɪk'stend] ◇ *vt* prolungare; *(hand)* offrire ◇ *vi* estendersi.
extension [ɪk'stenʃn] *n (of building)* sala *f* annessa; *(for phone at work)* interno *m*; *(for phone in private house)* apparecchio *m* supplementare; *(for permit, essay)* proroga *f*.
extension lead *n* prolunga *f*.
extensive [ɪk'stensɪv] *adj (area)* esteso(-a), ampio(-a); *(damage)* grave; *(selection)* ampio.
extent [ɪk'stent] *n (of damage, knowledge)* estensione *f*; **to a certain ~** fino ad un certo punto; **to what ~ ...?** fino a che punto ...?
exterior [ɪk'stɪərɪəʳ] ◇ *adj* esterno(-a) ◇ *n (of car, building)* esterno *m*.
external [ɪk'stɜːnl] *adj* esterno(-a).
extinct [ɪk'stɪŋkt] *adj* estinto(-a).
extinction [ɪk'stɪŋkʃn] *n* estinzione *f*.
extinguish [ɪk'stɪŋgwɪʃ] *vt (fire, cigarette)* spegnere.
extinguisher [ɪk'stɪŋgwɪʃəʳ] *n* estintore *m*.

extortionate [ɪk'stɔːʃnət] *adj* esorbitante.

extra ['ekstrə] ◇ *adj (additional)* extra *(inv)*, supplementare; *(spare)* altro(-a), in più ◇ *n* extra *m inv* ◇ *adv (especially)* eccezionalmente; *(more)* di più; ~ **charge** supplemento *m*; ~ **large** extra-large *(inv)*.

◆ **extras** *npl (in price)* spese *fpl* supplementari.

extract [*n* 'ekstrækt, *vb* ɪk'strækt] ◇ *n (of yeast, malt etc)* estratto *m*; *(from book, opera)* brano *m* ◇ *vt (tooth)* estrarre.

extractor fan [ɪk'stræktə-] *n (Br)* aspiratore *m*.

extraordinary [ɪk'strɔːdnrɪ] *adj* straordinario(-a).

extravagant [ɪk'strævəgənt] *adj* dispendioso(-a).

extreme [ɪk'striːm] ◇ *adj* estremo(-a) ◇ *n* estremo *m*.

extremely [ɪk'striːmlɪ] *adv* estremamente.

extrovert ['ekstrəvɜːt] *n* estroverso *m* (-a *f*).

eye [aɪ] ◇ *n* occhio *m*; *(of needle)* cruna *f* ◇ *vt* osservare attentamente; **to keep an ~ on** tenere d'occhio.

eyebrow ['aɪbraʊ] *n* sopracciglio *m*.

eye drops *npl* collirio *m*, gocce *fpl* per gli occhi.

eyeglasses ['aɪglɑːsɪz] *npl (Am)* occhiali *mpl*.

eyelash ['aɪlæʃ] *n* ciglio *m*.

eyelid ['aɪlɪd] *n* palpebra *f*.

eyeliner ['aɪˌlaɪnə^r] *n* eye-liner *m inv*.

eye shadow *n* ombretto *m*.

eyesight ['aɪsaɪt] *n* vista *f*.

eye test *n* esame *m* oculistico.

eyewitness [ˌaɪ'wɪtnɪs] *n* testimone *mf* oculare.

F *(abbr of Fahrenheit)* F.

fabric ['fæbrɪk] *n (cloth)* stoffa *f*, tessuto *m*.

fabulous ['fæbjʊləs] *adj* favoloso(-a).

facade [fə'sɑːd] *n* facciata *f*.

face [feɪs] ◇ *n* faccia *f*; *(of cliff, mountain)* parete *f*; *(of clock, watch)* quadrante *m* ◇ *vt* essere di fronte a; *(accept, cope with)* affrontare; **to be ~d with** avere di fronte.

◆ **face up to** *vt fus* affrontare.

facecloth ['feɪsklɒθ] *n (Br)* panno *m* di spugna.

facial ['feɪʃl] *n* trattamento *m* del viso.

facilitate [fə'sɪlɪteɪt] *vt (fml)* facilitare.

facilities [fə'sɪlɪtiːz] *npl* attrezzature *fpl*.

facsimile [fæk'sɪmɪlɪ] *n* facsimile *m inv*.

fact [fækt] *n* fatto *m*; **in ~** in effetti.

factor ['fæktəʳ] *n* fattore *m*; **~ ten suntan lotion** crema *f* abbronzante a fattore di protezione dieci.

factory ['fæktərɪ] *n* fabbrica *f*.

faculty ['fækltɪ] *n* facoltà *f inv*.

FA Cup *n* = coppa *f* Italia *(di calcio)*.

fade [feɪd] *vi (light, sound)* affievolirsi; *(flower)* appassire; *(jeans, wallpaper)* sbiadire, sbiadirsi.

faded ['feɪdɪd] *adj (jeans)* sbiadito(-a).

fag [fæg] *n (Br: inf: cigarette)* sigaretta *f*.

Fahrenheit ['færənhaɪt] *adj* Fahrenheit *(inv)*.

fail [feɪl] ◇ *vt (exam)* non superare ◇ *vi* fallire; *(in exam)* essere bocciato; *(engine)* guastarsi; **to ~ to do sthg** *(not do)* non fare qc.

failing ['feɪlɪŋ] ◇ *n* difetto *m* ◇ *prep*: **~ that** se no.

failure ['feɪljəʳ] *n* fallimento *m*; *(unsuccessful person)* fallito *m* (-a *f*); *(act of neglecting)* mancanza *f*.

faint [feɪnt] ◇ *vi* svenire ◇ *adj* debole; *(outline)* indistinto(-a); **I haven't the ~est idea** non ho la più pallida idea.

fair [feəʳ] ◇ *adj (just)* giusto(-a), equo(-a); *(quite large, quite good)* discreto(-a); *(hair, person)* biondo(-a); *(skin)* chiaro(-a); *(weather)* bello(-a) ◇ *n (funfair)* luna park *m inv*; *(trade fair)* fiera *f*; **~ enough!** mi sembra giusto!

fairground ['feəgraʊnd] *n* luna park *m inv*.

fair-haired [-'heəd] *adj* biondo(-a).

fairly ['feəlɪ] *adv (quite)* abbastanza.

fairy ['feərɪ] *n* fata *f*.

fairy tale *n* fiaba *f*.

faith [feɪθ] *n* fede *f*.

faithfully [ˈfeɪθfʊlɪ] *adv*: **Yours ~** Distinti saluti.

fake [feɪk] ◇ *n (painting etc)* falso *m* ◇ *vt (signature, painting)* falsificare.

fall [fɔːl] (*pt* **fell**, *pp* **fallen** [ˈfɔːln]) ◇ *vi* cadere; *(number, pound, night)* scendere ◇ *n* caduta *f*; *(decrease)* abbassamento *m*; *(Am: autumn)* autunno *m*; **to ~ asleep** addormentarsi; **to ~ ill** ammalarsi; **to ~ in love** innamorarsi.

◆ **falls** *npl (waterfall)* cascate *fpl*.

◆ **fall behind** *vi (with work, rent)* rimanere indietro.

◆ **fall down** *vi (lose balance)* cadere.

◆ **fall off** *vi* cadere.

◆ **fall out** *vi (hair, teeth)* cadere; *(argue)* litigare.

◆ **fall over** *vi* cadere per terra.

◆ **fall through** *vi* fallire.

false [fɔːls] *adj* falso(-a).

false alarm *n* falso allarme *m*.

false teeth *npl* dentiera *f*.

fame [feɪm] *n* fama *f*.

familiar [fəˈmɪljəʳ] *adj (known)* familiare; *(informal)* (troppo) confidenziale; **to be ~ with** *(know)* conoscere.

family [ˈfæmlɪ] ◇ *n* famiglia *f* ◇ *adj (size)* familiare, da famiglia; *(film, holiday)* per famiglie.

family planning clinic [-ˈplænɪŋ-] *n* = consultorio *m* familiare.

family room *n (at hotel)* camera *f* familiare; *(at pub, airport)* sala *f* per famiglie con bambini.

famine [ˈfæmɪn] *n* carestia *f*.

famished [ˈfæmɪʃt] *adj (inf)* molto affamato(-a).

famous [ˈfeɪməs] *adj* famoso(-a).

fan [fæn] *n (held in hand)* ventaglio *m*; *(electric)* ventilatore *m*; *(enthusiast)* ammiratore *m* (-trice *f*); *(supporter)* tifoso *m* (-a *f*).

fan belt *n* cinghia *f* del ventilatore.

fancy [ˈfænsɪ] ◇ *vt (inf: feel like)* avere voglia di ◇ *adj (elaborate)* ricercato(-a); **I ~ her** *(inf)* mi piace; **~ (that)!** pensa un po'!

fancy dress *n* costume *m* (per maschera).

fan heater *n* stufa *f* elettrica con ventilatore.

fanlight [ˈfænlaɪt] *n (Br)* lunetta *f*.

fantastic [fænˈtæstɪk] *adj* fantastico(-a).

fantasy [ˈfæntəsɪ] *n (imagined thing)* fantasia *f*.

far [fɑːʳ] (*compar* **further** OR **farther**, *superl* **furthest** OR **farthest**) ◇ *adv* lontano; *(in degree)* molto, assai ◇ *adj* **at the ~ end (of)** in fondo (a); **how ~ is it (to London)?** quanto è lontano (da Londra)?; **as ~ as** *(place)* fino a; **as ~ as I'm concerned** per quanto mi riguarda; **as ~ as I know** per quel che ne so; **~ better** assai migliore; **by ~** di gran lunga; **so ~** *(until now)* finora; **to go too ~** *(behave unacceptably)* oltrepassare i limiti.

farce [fɑːs] *n (ridiculous situation)* farsa *f*.

fare [feəʳ] ◇ *n (on bus, train etc)* tariffa *f*; *(fml: food)* cibo *m* ◇ *vi* passarsela.

Far East *n*: **the ~** l'Estremo Oriente *m*.

fare stage *n (Br) fermata di autobus dove il prezzo del biglietto cambia.*

farm [fɑːm] *n* fattoria *f*.

farmer [ˈfɑːməʳ] *n* agricoltore *m*.

farmhouse [ˈfɑːmhaʊs, *pl* -haʊzɪz] *n* casa *f* colonica.

farming [ˈfɑːmɪŋ] *n* agricoltura *f*; *(of animals)* allevamento *m*.

farmland [ˈfɑːmlænd] *n* terreno *m* coltivabile.

farmyard [ˈfɑːmjɑːd] *n* aia *f*.

farther [ˈfɑːðəʳ] → **far**.

farthest [ˈfɑːðəst] → **far**.
fascinating [ˈfæsɪneɪtɪŋ] *adj* affascinante.
fascination [ˌfæsɪˈneɪʃn] *n* fascino *m*.
fashion [ˈfæʃn] *n* moda *f*; *(manner)* modo *m*, maniera *f*; **to be in ~** essere di moda; **to be out of ~** essere fuori moda.
fashionable [ˈfæʃnəbl] *adj* di moda, alla moda.
fashion show *n* sfilata *f* di moda.
fast [fɑːst] ◇ *adv (quickly)* velocemente, rapidamente; *(securely)* saldamente ◇ *adj* veloce, rapido(-a); **to be ~** *(clock)* andare avanti; **~ asleep** profondamente addormentato; **a ~ train** un treno diretto.
fasten [ˈfɑːsn] *vt (belt)* allacciare; *(coat)* abbottonare; *(two things)* fissare.
fastener [ˈfɑːsnəʳ] *n* chiusura *f*, fermaglio *m*.
fast food *n*: **~ outlet** fast food *m inv*.
fat [fæt] ◇ *adj* grasso(-a) ◇ *n* grasso *m*.
fatal [ˈfeɪtl] *adj (accident, disease)* mortale.
father [ˈfɑːðəʳ] *n* padre *m*.
Father Christmas *n (Br)* Babbo *m* Natale.
father-in-law *n* suocero *m*.
fattening [ˈfætnɪŋ] *adj* che fa ingrassare.
fatty [ˈfætɪ] *adj* grasso(-a).
faucet [ˈfɔːsɪt] *n (Am)* rubinetto *m*.
fault [ˈfɔːlt] *n (responsibility)* colpa *f*; *(flaw)* difetto *m*; *(in machine)* guasto *m*; **it's your ~** è colpa tua.
faulty [ˈfɔːltɪ] *adj* difettoso(-a).
favor [ˈfeɪvər] *(Am)* = **favour**.
favour [ˈfeɪvəʳ] ◇ *n (Br) (kind act)* favore *m* ◇ *vt (prefer)* preferire; **to be in ~ of** essere in favore di; **to do sb a ~** fare un favore a qn.
favourable [ˈfeɪvrəbl] *adj* favorevole.
favourite [ˈfeɪvrɪt] ◇ *adj* favorito(-a) ◇ *n* favorito *m* (-a *f*).
fawn [fɔːn] *adj* fulvo chiaro *(inv)*.
fax [fæks] ◇ *n* fax *m inv* ◇ *vt (document)* inviare per fax, faxare; *(person)* inviare un fax a.
fear [fɪəʳ] ◇ *n* paura *f* ◇ *vt (be afraid of)* avere paura di, temere; **for ~ of** per paura di.
feast [fiːst] *n (meal)* banchetto *m*.
feather [ˈfeðəʳ] *n* penna *f*, piuma *f*.
feature [ˈfiːtʃəʳ] ◇ *n (characteristic)* caratteristica *f*; *(in newspaper, on radio, TV)* servizio *m* (speciale) ◇ *vt (subj: film)* avere come protagonista; **~s** *(of face)* lineamenti *mpl*.
feature film *n* lungometraggio *m*.
Feb. *(abbr of February)* feb.
February [ˈfebrʊərɪ] *n* febbraio *m*, → **September**.
fed [fed] *pp* → **feed**.
fed up *adj* stufo(-a); **to be ~ with** essere stufo di.
fee [fiː] *n* pagamento *m*; *(of doctor, lawyer)* onorario *m*.
feeble [ˈfiːbəl] *adj* debole.
feed [fiːd] (*pt & pp* **fed**) *vt (person, animal)* dare da mangiare a; *(baby)* allattare; *(insert)* immettere.
feel [fiːl] (*pt & pp* **felt**) ◇ *vt (touch)* tastare, toccare; *(experience)* sentire; *(think)* credere, pensare ◇ *vi* sentirsi; *(seem)* essere ◇ *n (of material)*: **I like the ~ of it** è piacevole al tatto; **to ~ cold/hungry** avere freddo/fame; **to ~ like** *(fancy)* avere voglia di; **to ~ up to doing sthg** sentirsela di fare qc.
feeling [ˈfiːlɪŋ] *n (emotion)* sentimento *m*; *(sensation)* sensazione *f*; *(belief)* opinione *f*; **to hurt sb's ~s** ferire i sentimenti di qn.
feet [fiːt] → **foot**.
fell [fel] ◇ *pt* → **fall** ◇ *vt (tree)* abbattere.
fellow [ˈfeləʊ] ◇ *n (man)* tipo *m*,

individuo *m* ◇ *adj*: **my ~ students** i miei compagni di classe.

felt [felt] ◇ *pt & pp* → **feel** ◇ *n* feltro *m*.

felt-tip pen *n* pennarello *m*.

female ['fi:meɪl] ◇ *adj* femminile; *(child, animal)* femmina ◇ *n (animal)* femmina *f*.

feminine ['femɪnɪn] *adj* femminile.

feminist ['femɪnɪst] *n* femminista *mf*.

fence [fens] *n* recinto *m*.

fencing ['fensɪŋ] *n* (SPORT) scherma *f*.

fend [fend] *vi*: **to ~ for o.s.** provvedere a se stesso.

fender ['fendəʳ] *n (for fireplace)* parafuoco *m*; *(Am: on car)* parafango *m*.

fennel ['fenl] *n* finocchio *m*.

fern [fɜ:n] *n* felce *f*.

ferocious [fə'rəʊʃəs] *adj* feroce.

ferry ['ferɪ] *n* traghetto *m*.

fertile ['fɜ:taɪl] *adj (land)* fertile.

fertilizer ['fɜ:tɪlaɪzəʳ] *n* fertilizzante *m*.

festival ['festəvl] *n (of music, arts etc)* festival *m inv*; *(holiday)* festa *f*.

feta cheese ['fetə-] *n formaggio bianco di latte di pecora di origine greca*.

fetch [fetʃ] *vt* andare a prendere; *(be sold for)* essere venduto per.

fete [feɪt] *n* festa *f* all'aperto *(a scopo di beneficenza)*.

fever ['fi:vəʳ] *n* (MED) febbre *f*; **to have a ~** avere la febbre.

feverish ['fi:vərɪʃ] *adj (having a fever)* febbricitante.

few [fju:] ◇ *adj* pochi(-e); ◇ *pron* pochi *mpl* (-e *fpl*).

◆ **a few** ◇ *adj* qualche *(inv)* ◇ *pron* alcuni *mpl* (-e *fpl*); **quite a ~** parecchi.

fewer ['fju:əʳ] *adj & pron* meno *(inv)*.

fiancé [fɪ'ɒnseɪ] *n* fidanzato *m*.

fiancée [fɪ'ɒnseɪ] *n* fidanzata *f*.

fib [fɪb] *n (inf)* (piccola) bugia *f*.

fiber ['faɪbər] *(Am)* = **fibre**.

fibre ['faɪbəʳ] *n* fibra *f*.

fibreglass ['faɪbəglɑ:s] *n* fibra *f* di vetro.

fickle ['fɪkl] *adj* incostante, volubile.

fiction ['fɪkʃn] *n* narrativa *f*.

fiddle ['fɪdl] ◇ *n (violin)* violino *m* ◇ *vi*: **to ~ with sthg** giocherellare con qc.

fidget ['fɪdʒɪt] *vi* agitarsi.

field [fi:ld] *n* campo *m*.

field glasses *npl* binocolo *m*.

fierce [fɪəs] *adj* feroce; *(storm, heat)* violento(-a).

fifteen [fɪf'ti:n] *num* quindici, → **six**.

fifteenth [ˌfɪf'ti:nθ] *num* quindicesimo(-a), → **sixth**.

fifth [fɪfθ] *num* quinto(-a), → **sixth**.

fiftieth ['fɪftɪəθ] *num* cinquantesimo(-a), → **sixth**.

fifty ['fɪftɪ] *num* cinquanta, → **six**.

fig [fɪg] *n* fico *m*.

fight [faɪt] (*pt & pp* **fought**) ◇ *n* rissa *f*; *(argument)* lite *f*; *(struggle)* lotta *f* ◇ *vt* combattere; *(person)* azzuffarsi con ◇ *vi (physically)* combattere; *(quarrel)* litigare; *(struggle)* lottare; **to have a ~ with sb** fare a pugni con qn.

◆ **fight back** *vi* difendersi.

◆ **fight off** *vt sep (attacker)* respingere; *(illness)* vincere.

fighting ['faɪtɪŋ] *n* combattimento *m*.

figure [*Br* 'fɪgəʳ, *Am* 'fɪgjər] *n* figura *f*; *(number, statistic)* cifra *f*.

◆ **figure out** *vt sep* riuscire a capire.

file [faɪl] ◇ *n (folder)* cartella *f*; *(box)* schedario *m*; *(information on*

person) scheda *f*; (COMPUT) file *m inv*; *(tool)* lima *f* ◇ *vt (complaint, petition)* presentare; *(nails)* limare; **in single ~** in fila indiana.
filing cabinet ['faılıŋ-] *n* schedario *m*.
fill [fıl] *vt* riempire; *(role)* ricoprire; *(tooth)* otturare.
◆ **fill in** *vt sep (form)* riempire.
◆ **fill out** = **fill in**.
◆ **fill up** *vt sep* riempire; **~ her up!** *(with petrol)* il pieno, per favore!
filled roll ['fıld-] *n* panino *m* imbottito.
fillet ['fılıt] *n* filetto *m*.
fillet steak *n* bistecca *f* di filetto.
filling ['fılıŋ] ◇ *n (of cake, sandwich)* ripieno *m*; *(in tooth)* otturazione *f* ◇ *adj*: **it's very ~** sazia molto.
filling station *n* stazione *f* di servizio.
film [fılm] ◇ *n (at cinema)* film *m inv*; *(for camera)* pellicola *f* ◇ *vt* filmare.
film star *n* divo *m* (-a *f*) del cinema.
filter ['fıltə^r] *n* filtro *m*.
filthy ['fılθı] *adj* sudicio(-a).
fin [fın] *n* pinna *f*.
final ['faınl] ◇ *adj* ultimo(-a); *(decision)* definitivo(-a) ◇ *n* finale *f*.
finalist ['faınəlıst] *n* finalista *mf*.
finally ['faınəlı] *adv (at last)* finalmente; *(lastly)* infine.
finance [*n* 'faınæns, *vb* faı'næns] ◇ *n (money)* finanziamento *m*; *(profession)* finanza *f* ◇ *vt* finanziare.
◆ **finances** *npl* finanze *fpl*.
financial [fı'nænʃl] *adj* finanziario(-a).
find [faınd] (*pt & pp* **found**) ◇ *vt* trovare; *(find out)* scoprire ◇ *n* scoperta *f*; **to ~ the time to do sthg** trovare il tempo di fare qc.
◆ **find out** ◇ *vt sep (fact, truth)* scoprire ◇ *vi*: **to ~ out (about sthg)** *(learn)* scoprire (qc); *(get information)* informarsi (su qc).
fine [faın] ◇ *adv (thinly)* finemente; *(well)* bene ◇ *n* multa *f* ◇ *vt* multare ◇ *adj (good)* buono(-a); *(weather, day)* bello(-a); *(thin)* sottile; **it's ~** *(satisfactory)* va bene; **I'm ~** *(in health)* sto bene.
fine art *n* belle arti *fpl*.
finger ['fıŋgə^r] *n* dito *m*.
fingernail ['fıŋgəneıl] *n* unghia *f*.
fingertip ['fıŋgətıp] *n* polpastrello *m*.
finish ['fınıʃ] ◇ *n* fine *f*; *(on furniture)* finitura *f* ◇ *vt & vi* finire; **to ~ doing sthg** finire di fare qc.
◆ **finish off** *vt sep* finire; **finish up** *vi* finire; **to ~ up doing sthg** finire a fare qc.
Finland ['fınlənd] *n* la Finlandia.
Finn [fın] *n* finlandese *mf*.
Finnan haddock ['fınən-] *n (Scot)* eglefino *m* affumicato *(tipico della Scozia)*.
Finnish ['fınıʃ] ◇ *adj* finlandese ◇ *n (language)* finlandese *m*.
fir [fɜː^r] *n* abete *m*.
fire ['faıə^r] ◇ *n* fuoco *m*; *(uncontrolled)* incendio *m*; *(device)* stufa *f* ◇ *vt (from job)* licenziare; **to ~ a gun** sparare; **on ~** in fiamme; **to catch ~** prendere fuoco; **to make a ~** accendere un fuoco.
fire alarm *n* allarme *m* antincendio.
fire brigade *n (Br)* vigili *mpl* del fuoco.
fire department *(Am)* = **fire brigade**.
fire engine *n* autopompa *f*.
fire escape *n* scala *f* antincendio.
fire exit *n* uscita *f* di sicurezza.
fire extinguisher *n* estintore *m*.
fire hazard *n*: **it's a ~** rappresenta un pericolo di incendio.
fireman ['faıəmən] (*pl* **-men** [-mən]) *n* vigile *m* del fuoco.

fireplace ['faɪəpleɪs] *n* caminetto *m*.

fire regulations *npl* norme *fpl* antincendio.

fire station *n* caserma *f* dei vigili del fuoco.

firewood ['faɪəwud] *n* legna *f* da ardere.

firework display ['faɪəwɜːk-] *n* fuochi *mpl* d'artificio.

fireworks ['faɪəwɜːks] *npl (rockets)* fuochi *mpl* d'artificio.

firm [fɜːm] ◇ *adj (fruit)* sodo(-a); *(mattress)* duro(-a); *(structure)* solido(-a); *(grip)* saldo(-a); *(decision, belief)* fermo(-a) ◇ *n* ditta *f*.

first [fɜːst] ◇ *adj* primo(-a) ◇ *adv* prima; *(for the first time)* per la prima volta ◇ *n (event)* novità *f inv* ◇ *pron:* **the ~** il primo (la prima); **~ (gear)** prima *f*; **~ thing (in the morning)** per prima cosa; **for the ~ time** per la prima volta; **the ~ of January** il primo gennaio; **at ~** dapprima; **~ of all** prima di tutto.

first aid *n* pronto soccorso *m*.

first-aid kit *n* cassetta *f* del pronto soccorso.

first class *n (mail) posta celere, di solito consegnata entro uno o due giorni*; *(on train, plane, ship)* prima classe *f*.

first-class *adj (stamp) per consegna celere*; *(ticket)* di prima (classe); *(very good)* di prima qualità.

first floor *n (Br: floor above ground floor)* primo piano *m*; *(Am: ground floor)* pianterreno *m*.

firstly ['fɜːstlɪ] *adv* in primo luogo.

First World War *n*: **the ~** la prima guerra mondiale.

fish [fɪʃ] ◇ *(pl inv) n* pesce *m* ◇ *vi* pescare.

fish and chips *n* pesce *m* e patate fritti.

fishcake ['fɪʃkeɪk] *n* crocchetta *f* di pesce.

fisherman ['fɪʃəmən] (*pl* **-men** [-mən]) *n* pescatore *m*.

fish farm *n* vivaio *m*.

fish fingers *npl (Br)* bastoncini *mpl* di pesce.

fishing ['fɪʃɪŋ] *n* pesca *f*; **to go ~** andare a pesca.

fishing boat *n* barca *f* da pesca.

fishing rod *n* canna *f* da pesca.

fishmonger's ['fɪʃˌmʌŋgəz] *n (shop)* pescheria *f*.

fish sticks *(Am)* = **fish fingers**.

fish supper *n (Scot)* pesce *m* e patate fritti.

fist [fɪst] *n* pugno *m*.

fit [fɪt] ◇ *adj (healthy)* in forma ◇ *vt (be right size for)* andare (bene) a; *(kitchen, bath)* installare; *(a lock)* mettere; *(insert)* inserire ◇ *vi (be right size)* andare bene ◇ *n (of coughing, anger)* attacco *m*; *(epileptic)* crisi *f inv* epilettica; **they're a good ~** *(clothes, shoes)* sono della misura giusta; **to be ~ for sthg** *(suitable)* essere adatto(-a) a qc; **~ to eat** buono(-a) da mangiare; **it doesn't ~** *(object)* non c'entra; **it doesn't ~ me** *(jacket, skirt)* non mi sta OR va; **to get ~** rimettersi in forma; **to keep ~** tenersi in forma.

◆ **fit in** ◇ *vt sep (find time to do)* trovare il tempo per ◇ *vi (belong)* inserirsi.

fitness ['fɪtnɪs] *n (health)* forma *f*.

fitted carpet [ˌfɪtəd-] *n* moquette *f inv*.

fitted sheet [ˌfɪtəd-] *n* lenzuolo *m* con gli angoli.

fitting room ['fɪtɪŋ-] *n* camerino *m*.

five [faɪv] *num* cinque, → **six**.

fiver ['faɪvəʳ] *n (Br: inf)* cinque sterline *fpl*; *(note)* banconota *f* da cinque sterline.

fix [fɪks] *vt (attach, decide on)* fissare; *(mend)* riparare; *(drink, food)* preparare; *(arrange)* organizzare.

◆ **fix up** *vt sep*: **to ~ sb up with**

sthg procurare qc a qn.

fixture ['fɪkstʃəʳ] *n* (SPORT) incontro *m*; **~s and fittings** installazioni *fpl*.

fizzy ['fɪzɪ] *adj* frizzante.

flag [flæg] *n* bandiera *f*.

flake [fleɪk] ◇ *n (of snow)* fiocco *m* ◇ *vi* sfaldarsi.

flame [fleɪm] *n* fiamma *f*.

flammable ['flæməbl] *adj* infiammabile.

flan [flæn] *n* flan *m inv*.

flannel ['flænl] *n (material)* flanella *f*; *(Br: for washing face)* panno *m* di spugna.

◆ **flannels** *npl* pantaloni *mpl* di flanella.

flap [flæp] ◇ *n (of envelope)* linguetta *f*; *(of pocket)* risvolto *m* ◇ *vt (wings)* battere.

flapjack ['flæpdʒæk] *n (Br)* biscotto *m* di avena.

flare [fleəʳ] *n (signal)* razzo *m*.

flared [fleəd] *adj (trousers)* a zampa d'elefante; *(skirt)* scampanato(-a).

flash [flæʃ] ◇ *n (of light)* lampo *m*; *(for camera)* flash *m inv* ◇ *vi (light)* lampeggiare; **a ~ of lightning** un lampo; **to ~ one's headlights** lampeggiare.

flashlight ['flæʃlaɪt] *n* torcia *f* elettrica.

flask [flɑːsk] *n (Thermos)* thermos® *m inv*; *(hip flask)* borraccia *f*.

flat [flæt] ◇ *adj* piatto(-a); *(battery)* scarico(-a); *(drink)* sgasato(-a); *(rate, fee)* unico(-a) ◇ *adv (level)* in piano ◇ *n (Br: apartment)* appartamento *m*; **a ~ (tyre)** una gomma a terra; **~ out** a più non posso.

flatter ['flætəʳ] *vt* adulare.

flavor ['fleɪvər] *(Am)* = **flavour**.

flavour ['fleɪvəʳ] *n (Br: taste)* sapore *m*; *(of ice cream)* gusto *m*.

flavoured ['fleɪvəd] *adj*: **lemon-~** al gusto di limone.

flavouring ['fleɪvərɪŋ] *n* aroma *m*.

flaw [flɔː] *n* difetto *m*.

flea [fliː] *n* pulce *f*.

flea market *n* mercato *m* delle pulci.

fleece [fliːs] *n (downy material)* vello *m*.

fleet [fliːt] *n (of ships)* flotta *f*.

Flemish ['flemɪʃ] ◇ *adj* fiammingo(-a) ◇ *n (language)* fiammingo *m*.

flesh [fleʃ] *n (of person, animal)* carne *f*; *(of fruit, vegetable)* polpa *f*.

flew [fluː] *pt* → **fly**.

flex [fleks] *n* cavetto *m*.

flexible ['fleksəbl] *adj* flessibile.

flick [flɪk] *vt (a switch)* premere; *(with finger)* colpire con il dito.

◆ **flick through** *vt fus* sfogliare.

flies [flaɪz] *npl (of trousers)* patta *f*.

flight [flaɪt] *n* volo *m*; **a ~ (of stairs)** una rampa (di scale).

flight attendant *n* assistente *mf* di volo.

flimsy ['flɪmzɪ] *adj (object)* poco consistente; *(clothes)* leggero(-a).

fling [flɪŋ] (*pt & pp* **flung**) *vt* lanciare.

flint [flɪnt] *n (of lighter)* pietrina *f*.

flip-flop [flɪp-] *n (Br: shoe)* infradito *m inv or f inv*.

flipper ['flɪpəʳ] *n (Br: of swimmer)* pinna *f*.

flirt [flɜːt] *vi*: **to ~ (with sb)** flirtare (con qn).

float [fləʊt] ◇ *n (for swimming)* tavoletta *f*; *(for fishing)* galleggiante *m*; *(in procession)* carro *m*; *(drink)* *bevanda con del gelato aggiunto* ◇ *vi* galleggiare.

flock [flɒk] ◇ *n (of birds)* stormo *m*; *(of sheep)* gregge *m* ◇ *vi (people)* accalcarsi.

flood [flʌd] ◇ *n* alluvione *f* ◇ *vt* inondare ◇ *vi* straripare.

floodlight ['flʌdlaɪt] *n* riflettore *m*.

floor [flɔːʳ] *n (of room)* pavimento *m*; *(storey)* piano *m*; *(of nightclub)* pista *f*.

floorboard ['flɔːbɔːd] *n* asse *f* del pavimento.

floor show *n* varietà *m inv*.

flop [flɒp] *n (inf)* fiasco *m*.

floppy disk ['flɒpɪ-] *n* floppy disk *m inv*.

floral ['flɔːrəl] *adj (pattern)* floreale.

Florence ['flɒrəns] *n* Firenze *f*.

Florida Keys ['flɒrɪdə-] *npl*: **the ~** l'arcipelago *m* Keys.

florist's ['flɒrɪsts] *n (shop)* fioraio *m*.

flour ['flaʊəʳ] *n* farina *f*.

flow [fləʊ] ◇ *n (of river, blood)* flusso *m* ◇ *vi (river, blood)* scorrere.

flower ['flaʊəʳ] *n* fiore *m*.

flowerbed ['flaʊəbed] *n* aiuola *f*.

flowerpot ['flaʊəpɒt] *n* vaso *m* da fiori.

flown [fləʊn] *pp* → **fly**.

fl oz *abbr* = **fluid ounce**.

flu [fluː] *n* influenza *f*.

fluent ['fluːənt] *adj*: **to be ~ in Italian, to speak ~ Italian** parlare italiano correntemente.

fluff [flʌf] *n (on clothes)* pelucchi *mpl*.

fluid ounce ['fluːɪd-] *n* = 0,03 l.

flume [fluːm] *n* canale *m*.

flung [flʌŋ] *pp* → **fling**.

flunk [flʌŋk] *vt (Am: inf: exam)* essere bocciato(-a) a.

fluorescent [flʊə'resənt] *adj* fluorescente.

flush [flʌʃ] ◇ *vi (toilet)* funzionare ◇ *vt*: **to ~ the toilet** tirare lo sciacquone.

flute [fluːt] *n* flauto *m* traverso.

fly [flaɪ] (*pt* **flew**, *pp* **flown**) ◇ *n (insect)* mosca *f*; *(of trousers)* patta *f* ◇ *vt (plane, helicopter)* pilotare; *(airline)* volare con; *(transport)* trasportare in aereo ◇ *vi* volare; *(passenger)* andare in aereo; *(pilot a plane)* pilotare un aereo; *(flag)* sventolare.

fly-drive *n* fly and drive *m inv*.

flying ['flaɪɪŋ] *n*: **I'm frightened of ~** ho paura di volare.

flyover ['flaɪ,əʊvəʳ] *n (Br)* cavalcavia *m inv*.

flypaper ['flaɪ,peɪpəʳ] *n* carta *f* moschicida.

flysheet ['flaɪʃiːt] *n* telo *m* protettivo.

FM *n* FM *f*.

foal [fəʊl] *n* puledro *m*.

foam [fəʊm] *n (bubbles)* schiuma *f*; *(foam rubber)* gommapiuma® *f*.

focus ['fəʊkəs] ◇ *n (of camera)* fuoco *m* ◇ *vi (with camera, binoculars)* mettere a fuoco; **in ~** a fuoco; **out of ~** sfocato.

fog [fɒg] *n* nebbia *f*.

fogbound ['fɒgbaʊnd] *adj* bloccato(-a) dalla nebbia.

foggy ['fɒgɪ] *adj* nebbioso(-a).

fog lamp *n* antinebbia *m inv*.

foil [fɔɪl] *n (thin metal)* carta *f* di alluminio.

fold [fəʊld] ◇ *n (in paper, material)* piega *f* ◇ *vt* piegare; *(wrap)* avvolgere; **to ~ one's arms** incrociare le braccia.

◆ **fold up** *vi (chair, bed, bicycle)* piegarsi.

folder ['fəʊldəʳ] *n* cartella *f*.

foliage ['fəʊlɪɪdʒ] *n* fogliame *m*.

folk [fəʊk] ◇ *npl (people)* gente *f* ◇ *n*: **~ (music)** folk *m*.

◆ **folks** *npl (inf: relatives)*: **my ~s** i miei.

follow ['fɒləʊ] ◇ *vt* seguire; *(in order, time)* seguire a ◇ *vi* seguire; **~ed by** *(in time)* seguito da; **as ~s** come segue.

◆ **follow on** *vi (come later)* seguire.

following ['fɒləʊɪŋ] ◇ *adj (next)* successivo(-a); *(mentioned below)* seguente ◇ *prep* dopo.

follow on call *n* chiamata *f* successiva.

fond [fɒnd] *adj*: **to be ~ of** amare.
fondue [ˈfɒndu:] *n* fonduta *f*.
food [fu:d] *n* cibo *m*.
food poisoning [-ˌpɔɪznɪŋ] *n* avvelenamento *m* da cibo.
food processor [-ˌprəʊsesəʳ] *n* tritatutto-frullatore *m inv* elettrico.
foodstuffs [ˈfu:dstʌfs] *npl* generi *mpl* alimentari.
fool [fu:l] ◇ *n (idiot)* stupido *m* (-a *f*); *(pudding)* mousse *f inv* di frutta ◇ *vt* ingannare.
foolish [ˈfu:lɪʃ] *adj* stupido(-a).
foot [fʊt] (*pl* **feet**) *n (of person)* piede *m*; *(of animal)* zampa *f*; *(measurement)* = 30,48 cm, piede; *(of hill, cliff, bed)* piedi *mpl*; *(of wardrobe, tripod, stairs)* base *f*; **by ~** a piedi; **on ~** a piedi.
football [ˈfʊtbɔ:l] *n (Br: soccer)* calcio *m*; *(Am: American football)* football *m* americano; *(ball)* pallone *m*.
footballer [ˈfʊtbɔ:ləʳ] *n (Br)* calciatore *m* (-trice *f*).
football pitch *n (Br)* campo *m* di calcio.
footbridge [ˈfʊtbrɪdʒ] *n* sovrappassaggio *m*.
footpath [ˈfʊtpɑ:θ, *pl* -pɑ:ðz] *n* sentiero *m*.
footprint [ˈfʊtprɪnt] *n* orma *f*.
footstep [ˈfʊtstep] *n* passo *m*.
footwear [ˈfʊtweəʳ] *n* calzature *fpl*.
for [fɔ:ʳ] *prep* 1. *(expressing intention, purpose, reason)* per; **this book is ~ you** questo libro è per te; **what did you do that ~?** perché l'hai fatto?; **what's it ~?** a cosa serve?; **a town famous ~ its wine** una città famosa per il suo vino; **~ this reason** per questo motivo; **to go ~ a walk** andare a fare una passeggiata; **'~ sale'** 'vendesi'.
2. *(during)*: **I've lived here ~ ten years** abito qui da dieci anni, sono dieci anni che abito qui; **we talked ~ hours** abbiamo chiacchierato per ore.
3. *(by, before)* per; **be there ~ eight p.m.** trovati lì per le otto di sera; **I'll do it ~ tomorrow** lo farò per domani.
4. *(on the occasion of)* per; **I got socks ~ Christmas** ho avuto dei calzini per Natale; **what's ~ dinner?** cosa c'è per cena?
5. *(on behalf of)* per; **to do sthg ~ sb** fare qc per qn.
6. *(with time and space)* per; **there's no room ~ your suitcase** non c'è posto per la tua valigia; **have you got time ~ a coffee?** hai tempo per un caffè?; **it's time ~ dinner** è ora di cena.
7. *(expressing distance)* per; **'road works ~ 20 miles'** 'lavori in corso per 32 chilometri'.
8. *(expressing destination)* per; **a ticket ~ Edinburgh** un biglietto per Edimburgo; **this train is ~ London only** questo treno ferma solo a Londra.
9. *(expressing price)*: **I bought it ~ £5** l'ho comprato per 5 sterline, l'ho pagato 5 sterline.
10. *(expressing meaning)* per; **what's the Italian ~ 'boy'?** come si dice 'boy' in italiano?
11. *(with regard to)* per; **it's warm ~ November** fa caldo per essere novembre; **it's easy ~ you** è facile per te; **it's too far ~ us to walk** è troppo lontano per andarci a piedi.
forbid [fəˈbɪd] (*pt* **-bade** [-ˈbeɪd], *pp* **-bidden**) *vt* proibire, vietare; **to ~ sb to do sthg** proibire OR vietare a qn di fare qc.
forbidden [fəˈbɪdn] *adj* proibito(-a).
force [fɔ:s] ◇ *n* forza *f* ◇ *vt* forzare; **to ~ sb to do sthg** costringere qn a fare qc; **to ~ one's way through** farsi strada con la forza; **the ~s** le forze armate.
ford [fɔ:d] *n* guado *m*.

forecast [ˈfɔːkɑːst] *n* previsione *f*.
forecourt [ˈfɔːkɔːt] *n* spiazzo *m*.
forefinger [ˈfɔːˌfɪŋgəʳ] *n* indice *m*.
foreground [ˈfɔːgraʊnd] *n* primo piano *m*.
forehead [ˈfɔːhed] *n* fronte *f*.
foreign [ˈfɒrən] *adj* straniero(-a); *(travel)* all'estero.
foreign currency *n* valuta *f* estera.
foreigner [ˈfɒrənəʳ] *n* straniero *m* (-a *f*).
foreign exchange *n* cambio *m*.
Foreign Secretary *n (Br)* ministro *m* degli Esteri.
foreman [ˈfɔːmən] (*pl* **-men** [-mən]) *n (of workers)* capo operaio *m*.
forename [ˈfɔːneɪm] *n (fml)* nome *m* (di battesimo).
foresee [fɔːˈsiː] (*pt* **-saw** [-ˈsɔː], *pp* **-seen** [-ˈsiːn]) *vt* prevedere.
forest [ˈfɒrɪst] *n* foresta *f*.
forever [fəˈrevəʳ] *adv (eternally)* per sempre; *(continually)* in continuazione.
forgave [fəˈgeɪv] *pt* → **forgive**.
forge [fɔːdʒ] *vt (copy)* falsificare.
forgery [ˈfɔːdʒərɪ] *n (copy)* falso *m*.
forget [fəˈget] (*pt* **-got**, *pp* **-gotten**) ◇ *vt* dimenticare; *(give up)* lasciar perdere ◇ *vi* dimenticarsi; **to ~ about sthg** dimenticarsi di qc; **to ~ how to do sthg** dimenticare come si fa qc; **to ~ to do sthg** dimenticare di fare qc; **~ it!** lascia perdere!
forgetful [fəˈgetfʊl] *adj* smemorato(-a).
forgive [fəˈgɪv] (*pt* **-gave**, *pp* **-given** [-ˈgɪvn]) *vt* perdonare.
forgot [fəˈgɒt] *pt* → **forget**.
forgotten [fəˈgɒtn] *pp* → **forget**.
fork [fɔːk] *n (for eating with)* forchetta *f*; *(for gardening)* forca *f*; *(of road, path)* bivio *m*.
◆ **forks** *npl (of bike, motorbike)* forcelle *fpl*.
form [fɔːm] ◇ *n (type, shape)* forma *f*; *(piece of paper)* modulo *m*; (SCH) classe *f* ◇ *vt* formare; *(constitute)* costituire; *(produce)* creare ◇ *vi* formarsi; **off ~** giù di forma; **on ~** in forma; **to ~ part of** fare parte di.
formal [ˈfɔːml] *adj* formale.
formality [fɔːˈmælətɪ] *n* formalità *f inv*; **it's just a ~** è solo una formalità.
format [ˈfɔːmæt] *n* formato *m*.
former [ˈfɔːməʳ] ◇ *adj (previous)* precedente; *(first)* primo(-a) ◇ *pron*: **the ~** il primo; **the ~ President** l'ex Presidente.
formerly [ˈfɔːməlɪ] *adv* precedentemente.
formula [ˈfɔːmjʊlə] (*pl* **-as** OR **-ae** [iː]) *n* formula *f*.
fort [fɔːt] *n* forte *m*.
forthcoming [fɔːθˈkʌmɪŋ] *adj (future)* prossimo(-a).
fortieth [ˈfɔːtɪɪθ] *num* quarantesimo(-a), → **sixth**.
fortnight [ˈfɔːtnaɪt] *n (Br)* quindici giorni *mpl*.
fortunate [ˈfɔːtʃnət] *adj* fortunato(-a).
fortunately [ˈfɔːtʃnətlɪ] *adv* fortunatamente.
fortune [ˈfɔːtʃuːn] *n* fortuna *f*; **it costs a ~** *(inf)* costa una fortuna.
forty [ˈfɔːtɪ] *num* quaranta, → **six**.
forward [ˈfɔːwəd] ◇ *adv (move, lean)* in avanti ◇ *n* (SPORT) attaccante *mf* ◇ *vt* spedire; **to look ~ to doing sthg** non vedere l'ora di fare qc.
forwarding address [ˈfɔːwədɪŋ-] *n* recapito *m* nuovo.
fought [fɔːt] *pp* → **fight**.
foul [faʊl] ◇ *adj (unpleasant)* disgustoso(-a) ◇ *n* fallo *m*.
found [faʊnd] ◇ *pp* → **find** ◇ *vt* fondare.

foundation (cream) [faʊnˈdeɪʃn-] *n* fondotinta *m inv*.
foundations [faʊnˈdeɪʃnz] *npl* fondamenta *fpl*.
fountain [ˈfaʊntɪn] *n* fontana *f*.
fountain pen *n* penna *f* stilografica.
four [fɔːʳ] *num* quattro, → **six**.
four-star (petrol) *n* super *f inv*.
fourteen [ˌfɔːˈtiːn] *num* quattordici, → **six**.
fourteenth [ˌfɔːˈtiːnθ] *num* quattordicesimo(-a), → **sixth**.
fourth [fɔːθ] *num* quarto(-a), → **sixth**.
four-wheel drive *n (car)* veicolo *m* a quattro ruote motrici.
fowl [faʊl] *(pl inv) n* volatile *m*.
fox [fɒks] *n* volpe *f*.
foyer [ˈfɔɪeɪ] *n (of hotel)* hall *f inv*; *(of theatre)* foyer *m inv*.
fraction [ˈfrækʃn] *n* frazione *f*.
fracture [ˈfræktʃəʳ] ◇ *n* frattura *f* ◇ *vt* fratturare.
fragile [ˈfrædʒaɪl] *adj* fragile.
fragment [ˈfrægmənt] *n* frammento *m*.
fragrance [ˈfreɪgrəns] *n* profumo *m*.
frail [freɪl] *adj* debole.
frame [freɪm] ◇ *n (of window, tent, bicycle)* telaio *m*; *(of picture, photo)* cornice *f*; *(of glasses)* montatura *f* ◇ *vt (photo, picture)* incorniciare.
France [frɑːns] *n* la Francia.
frank [fræŋk] *adj* franco(-a).
frankfurter [ˈfræŋkfɜːtəʳ] *n* würstel *m inv*.
frankly [ˈfræŋklɪ] *adv* francamente.
frantic [ˈfræntɪk] *adj* frenetico(-a).
fraud [frɔːd] *n (crime)* frode *f*.
freak [friːk] ◇ *adj* strano(-a) ◇ *n (inf: fanatic)* fanatico *m* (-a *f*).
freckles [ˈfreklz] *npl* lentiggini *fpl*.
free [friː] ◇ *adj* libero(-a); *(costing nothing)* gratuito(-a) ◇ *vt (prisoner)* liberare ◇ *adv* gratis; **for ~** gratis; **~ of charge** gratis; **to be ~ to do sthg** essere libero di fare qc.
freedom [ˈfriːdəm] *n* libertà *f*.
freefone [ˈfriːfəʊn] *n (Br)* = numero *m* verde.
free gift *n* omaggio *m*.
free house *n (Br)* pub *m inv (che può vendere qualsiasi birra, non appartenendo a nessuna ditta)*.
free kick *n* calcio *m* di punizione.
freelance [ˈfriːlɑːns] *adj* freelance *(inv)*.
freely [ˈfriːlɪ] *adv* liberamente; *(available)* facilmente.
free period *n* (SCH) ora *f* di buco.
freepost [ˈfriːpəʊst] *n* affrancatura *f* a carico del destinatario.
free-range *adj (chicken)* ruspante; *(eggs)* di galline ruspanti.
free time *n* tempo *m* libero.
freeway [ˈfriːweɪ] *n (Am)* superstrada *f*.
freeze [friːz] (*pt* **froze**, *pp* **frozen**) ◇ *vt* congelare ◇ *vi* gelare ◇ *v impers*: **it's freezing** fa un freddo polare.
freezer [ˈfriːzəʳ] *n (deep freeze)* congelatore *m*; *(part of fridge)* freezer *m inv*.
freezing [ˈfriːzɪŋ] *adj* gelato(-a); *(temperatures)* sotto zero.
freezing point *n* temperatura *f* di congelamento.
freight [freɪt] *n (goods)* carico *m*.
French [frentʃ] ◇ *adj* francese ◇ *n (language)* francese *m* ◇ *npl*: **the ~** i francesi.
French bean *n* fagiolino *m*.
French bread *n* baguette *f inv*.
French dressing *n (in UK) condimento per insalata a base di olio e aceto*; *(in US) condimento per insalata a base di maionese e ketchup*.
French fries *npl* patatine *fpl* fritte.
Frenchman [ˈfrentʃmən] (*pl* **-men**

[-mən]) *n* francese *m*.

French toast *n (fried bread) fetta di pane passata nell'uovo e fritta.*

French windows *npl* portafinestra *f*.

Frenchwoman [ˈfrentʃˌwʊmən] (*pl* **-women** [-ˌwɪmɪn]) *n* francese *f*.

frequency [ˈfriːkwənsɪ] *n* frequenza *f*.

frequent [ˈfriːkwənt] *adj* frequente.

frequently [ˈfriːkwəntlɪ] *adv* frequentemente.

fresh [freʃ] *adj* fresco(-a); *(water)* dolce; *(new)* nuovo(-a); **to get some ~ air** prendere un po' d'aria fresca.

fresh cream *n* panna *f* fresca.

freshen [ˈfreʃn]: **freshen up** *vi* rinfrescarsi.

freshly [ˈfreʃlɪ] *adv* appena.

fresh orange (juice) *n* spremuta *f* d'arancia.

Fri. *(abbr of Friday)* ven.

Friday [ˈfraɪdɪ] *n* venerdì *m inv*, → **Saturday**.

fridge [frɪdʒ] *n* frigorifero *m*.

fried egg [fraɪd-] *n* uovo *m* al tegame.

fried rice [fraɪd-] *n piatto cinese a base di riso fritto.*

friend [frend] *n* amico *m* (-a *f*); **to be ~s with sb** essere amico di qn; **to make ~s with sb** fare amicizia con qn.

friendly [ˈfrendlɪ] *adj* cordiale; **to be ~ with sb** essere amico di qn.

friendship [ˈfrendʃɪp] *n* amicizia *f*.

fries [fraɪz] = **French fries**.

fright [fraɪt] *n* spavento *m*, paura *f*; **to give sb a ~** fare paura a qn.

frighten [ˈfraɪtn] *vt* spaventare, far paura a.

frightened [ˈfraɪtnd] *adj (scared)* spaventato(-a); **to be ~ (that)** ... *(worried)* avere paura che ...; **to be ~ of** avere paura di.

frightening [ˈfraɪtnɪŋ] *adj* spaventoso(-a).

frightful [ˈfraɪtfʊl] *adj (very bad, unpleasant)* terribile.

frilly [ˈfrɪlɪ] *adj* arricciato(-a).

fringe [frɪndʒ] *n* frangia *f*.

frisk [frɪsk] *vt* perquisire.

fritter [ˈfrɪtəʳ] *n* frittella *f*.

fro [frəʊ] *adv* → **to**.

frog [frɒg] *n* rana *f*.

from [frɒm] *prep* **1.** *(expressing origin, source)* da; **I'm ~ England** sono inglese; **I bought it ~ a supermarket** l'ho comprato al supermercato; **the train ~ Manchester** il treno (proveniente) da Manchester.

2. *(expressing removal, deduction)* da; **away ~ home** lontano da casa; **to take sthg (away) ~ sb** prendere qc a qn; **10% will be deducted ~ the total** dal totale verrà dedotto il 10%.

3. *(expressing distance)* da; **5 miles ~ London** a 5 miglia da Londra; **it's not far ~ here** non è lontano (da qui).

4. *(expressing position)* da; **~ here you can see the valley** da qui si vede la valle.

5. *(expressing starting time)* da; **open ~ nine to five** aperto dalle nove alle cinque; **~ next year** dall'anno prossimo.

6. *(expressing change)* da; **the price has gone up ~ £1 to £2** il prezzo è salito da 1 a 2 sterline.

7. *(expressing range)* da; **tickets are ~ £10** i biglietti vanno dalle 10 sterline in su.

8. *(as a result of)*: **I'm tired ~ walking all day** sono stanco per aver camminato tutto il giorno.

9. *(expressing protection)* da; **sheltered ~ the wind** al riparo dal vento.

10. *(in comparisons)*: **different ~** diverso da.

fromage frais [ˌfrɒmɑːʒˈfreɪ] *n* *formaggio fresco cremoso.*

front [frʌnt] ◇ *adj* anteriore ◇ *n* parte *f* anteriore; *(of weather)* fronte *m*; *(by the sea)* lungomare *m*; **in ~** *(further forward)* avanti; *(in the lead)* d'avanti; **in ~ of** davanti a.

front door *n* porta *f* principale.

frontier [frʌnˈtɪəʳ] *n* frontiera *f*.

front page *n* prima pagina *f*.

front seat *n* sedile *m* anteriore.

frost [frɒst] *n* gelo *m*.

frosty [ˈfrɒstɪ] *adj (morning, weather)* gelato(-a).

froth [frɒθ] *n* spuma *f*.

frown [fraʊn] ◇ *n* fronte *f* aggrottata ◇ *vi* aggrottare la fronte.

froze [frəʊz] *pt* → **freeze**.

frozen [frəʊzn] ◇ *pp* → **freeze** ◇ *adj* gelato(-a); *(food)* congelato(-a).

fruit [fruːt] *n (food)* frutta *f*; *(variety, single fruit)* frutto *m*; **a piece of ~** un frutto; **~s of the forest** frutti di bosco.

fruit cake *n torta con frutta secca.*

fruiterer [ˈfruːtərəʳ] *n (Br)* fruttivendolo *m* (-a *f*).

fruit juice *n* succo *m* di frutta.

fruit machine *n (Br)* slot-machine *f inv*.

fruit salad *n* macedonia *f*.

frustrating [frʌˈstreɪtɪŋ] *adj* frustrante.

frustration [frʌˈstreɪʃn] *n* frustrazione *f*.

fry [fraɪ] *vt* soffriggere; *(deep-fry)* friggere.

frying pan [ˈfraɪɪŋ-] *n* padella *f*.

ft *abbr* = **foot, feet**.

fudge [fʌdʒ] *n dolciume gommoso fatto con burro, latte e zucchero.*

fuel [fjʊəl] *n (for engine)* carburante *m*; *(for heating)* combustibile *m*.

fuel pump *n* pompa *f* del carburante.

fulfil [fʊlˈfɪl] *vt (Br) (promise)* mantenere; *(duty, role, need)* adempiere; *(conditions, request)* soddisfare; *(instructions)* eseguire.

fulfill [fʊlˈfɪl] *(Am)* = **fulfil**.

full [fʊl] ◇ *adj* pieno(-a); *(extent, fare)* intero(-a); *(name)* completo(-a) ◇ *adv (directly)* in pieno; **I'm ~ (up)** sono pieno; **at ~ speed** a tutta velocità; **in ~** per esteso.

full board *n* pensione *f* completa.

full-cream milk *n* latte *m* intero.

full-length *adj (skirt, dress)* lungo(-a).

full moon *n* luna *f* piena.

full stop *n* punto *m*.

full-time *adj & adv* a tempo pieno.

fully [ˈfʊlɪ] *adv (completely)* completamente.

fully-licensed *adj autorizzato a vendere alcolici.*

fumble [ˈfʌmbl] *vi (search clumsily)* rovistare.

fun [fʌn] *n* divertimento *m*; **it's good ~** è divertente; **for ~** per divertimento; **to have ~** divertirsi; **to make ~ of** prendere in giro.

function [ˈfʌŋkʃn] ◇ *n (role)* funzione *f*; *(formal event)* ricevimento *m* ◇ *vi* funzionare.

fund [fʌnd] ◇ *n (of money)* fondo *m* ◇ *vt* finanziare.

◆ **funds** *npl* fondi *mpl*.

fundamental [ˌfʌndəˈmentl] *adj* fondamentale.

funeral [ˈfjuːnərəl] *n* funerale *m*.

funfair [ˈfʌnfeəʳ] *n* luna park *m inv*.

funky [ˈfʌŋkɪ] *adj (inf: music)* funky *(inv)*.

funnel [ˈfʌnl] *n (for pouring)* imbuto *m*; *(on ship)* fumaiolo *m*.

funny [ˈfʌnɪ] *adj (amusing)* divertente; *(strange)* strano(-a); **to feel ~** *(ill)* sentirsi strano.

fur [fɜːʳ] *n* pelliccia *f*.

fur coat *n* pelliccia *f*.
furious ['fjʊərɪəs] *adj (angry)* furioso(-a).
furnished ['fɜːnɪʃt] *adj* ammobiliato(-a).
furnishings ['fɜːnɪʃɪŋz] *npl* arredamento *m*.
furniture ['fɜːnɪtʃəʳ] *n* mobilia *f*; **a piece of ~** un mobile.
furry ['fɜːrɪ] *adj* peloso(-a).
further ['fɜːðəʳ] → **far** ◇ ◇ *adv (in distance)* più lontano; *(more)* di più ◇ *adj (additional)* ulteriore; **until ~ notice** fino a nuovo avviso.
furthermore [,fɜːðə'mɔːʳ] *adv* inoltre.
furthest ['fɜːðɪst] → **far** ◇ ◇ *adj (most distant)* il più lontano (la più lontana) ◇ *adv (in distance)* il più lontano (possibile).
fuse [fjuːz] ◇ *n (of plug)* fusibile *m*; *(on bomb)* detonatore *m* ◇ *vi (plug, device)* saltare.
fuse box *n* scatola *f* dei fusibili.
fuss [fʌs] *n (agitation)* confusione *f*; *(complaints)* storie *fpl*.
fussy ['fʌsɪ] *adj (person)* difficile.
future ['fjuːtʃəʳ] ◇ *n* futuro *m* ◇ *adj* futuro(-a); **in ~** in futuro.

G

g *(abbr of gram)* g.

gable [ˈgeɪbl] *n* timpano *m*.

gadget [ˈgædʒɪt] *n* aggeggio *m*.

Gaelic [ˈgeɪlɪk] *n* gaelico *m*.

gag [gæg] *n (inf: joke)* gag *f inv*.

gain [geɪn] ◇ *n (improvement)* avanzamento *m*; *(profit)* guadagno *m* ◇ *vt* guadagnare; *(weight)* aumentare di; *(confidence, speed, popularity)* acquistare; *(achieve)* ottenere; *(subj: clock, watch)* andare avanti di ◇ *vi (get benefit)*: **to ~ from sthg** trarre vantaggio da qc.

gale [geɪl] *n* burrasca *f*.

gallery [ˈgælərɪ] *n* galleria *f*.

gallon [ˈgælən] *n (Br)* = 4,546 l, gallone *m*; *(Am)* = 3,791 l, gallone.

gallop [ˈgæləp] *vi* galoppare.

gamble [ˈgæmbl] ◇ *n* azzardo *m* ◇ *vi (bet money)* giocare d'azzardo.

gambling [ˈgæmblɪŋ] *n* gioco *m* d'azzardo.

game [geɪm] *n (gen, in tennis)* gioco *m*; *(of football, squash, cards)* partita *f*; *(wild animals, meat)* cacciagione *f*.

◆ **games** ◇ *n* (SCH) = attività *fpl* sportive ◇ *npl (sporting event)* gare *fpl*.

gammon [ˈgæmən] *n coscia di maiale da cuocere*.

gang [gæŋ] *n (of criminals)* banda *f*; *(of friends)* gruppo *m*.

gangster [ˈgæŋstəʳ] *n* gangster *m inv*.

gangway [ˈgæŋweɪ] *n (for ship)* passerella *f*; *(Br: in bus, aeroplane, theatre)* corridoio *m*.

gaol [dʒeɪl] *(Br)* = **jail**.

gap [gæp] *n (space)* buco *m*; *(of time)* intervallo *m*; *(difference)* divario *m*.

garage [ˈgærɑːʒ, ˈgærɪdʒ] *n (for keeping car)* garage *m inv*; *(Br: for petrol)* stazione *f* di servizio; *(for repairs)* autofficina *f*; *(Br: for selling cars)* concessionaria *f*.

garbage [ˈgɑːbɪdʒ] *n (Am: refuse)* spazzatura *f*.

garbage can *n (Am)* pattumiera *f*.

garbage truck *n (Am)* camion *m inv* della nettezza urbana.

garden [ˈgɑːdn] ◇ *n* giardino *m* ◇ *vi* fare giardinaggio.

◆ **gardens** *npl (public park)* giardini *mpl* pubblici.

garden centre *n* vivaio *m*.

gardener [ˈgɑːdnəʳ] *n* giardiniere *m* (-a *f*).

gardening [ˈgɑːdnɪŋ] *n* giardinaggio *m*.

garden peas *npl* piselli *mpl*.

garlic [ˈgɑːlɪk] *n* aglio *m*.

garlic bread *n* = bruschetta *f*.

garlic butter *n* burro *m* all'aglio.

garment [ˈgɑːmənt] *n* indumento *m*.

garnish [ˈgɑːnɪʃ] ◇ *n* guarnizione *f* ◇ *vt* guarnire.

gas [gæs] *n* gas *m inv*; *(Am: petrol)* benzina *f*.

gas cooker *n (Br)* cucina *f* a gas.

gas cylinder *n* bombola *f* del gas.

gas fire *n (Br)* stufa *f* a gas.

gasket [ˈgæskɪt] *n* guarnizione *f*.

gas mask *n* maschera *f* antigas.

gasoline [ˈgæsəliːn] *n (Am)* benzina *f*.

gasp [gɑːsp] *vi (in shock)* rimanere senza fiato.

gas pedal *n (Am)* acceleratore *m*.

gas station *n (Am)* stazione *f* di servizio.

gas stove *(Br)* = **gas cooker**.

gas tank *n (Am)* serbatoio *m* della benzina.

gasworks [ˈgæswɜːks] *(pl inv) n* officina *f* del gas.

gate [geɪt] *n (to garden, field)* cancello *m*; *(at airport)* uscita *f*.

gâteau [ˈgætəʊ] (*pl* **-x** [-z]) *n (Br)* torta *f*.

gateway [ˈgeɪtweɪ] *n (entrance)* entrata *f*.

gather [ˈgæðəʳ] ◇ *vt (collect)* raccogliere; *(speed)* acquistare; *(understand)* dedurre ◇ *vi (come together)* riunirsi.

gaudy [ˈgɔːdɪ] *adj* vistoso(-a).

gauge [geɪdʒ] ◇ *n (for measuring)* indicatore *m*; *(of railway track)* scartamento *m* ◇ *vt (calculate)* misurare.

gauze [gɔːz] *n* garza *f*.

gave [geɪv] *pt* → **give**.

gay [geɪ] *adj (homosexual)* gay *(inv)*.

gaze [geɪz] *vi*: **to ~ at** fissare.

GB *(abbr of Great Britain)* GB.

GCSE *n esami sostenuti a conclusione della scuola dell'obbligo.*

gear [gɪəʳ] *n (wheel)* ingranaggio *m*; *(speed)* marcia *f*; *(belongings)* roba *f*; *(equipment, clothes)* attrezzatura *f*; **in ~** con la marcia inserita.

gearbox [ˈgɪəbɒks] *n* cambio *m*.

gear lever *n* leva *f* del cambio.

gear shift *(Am)* = **gear lever**.

gear stick *(Br)* = **gear lever**.

geese [giːs] *pl* → **goose**.

gel [dʒel] *n* gel *m inv*.

gelatine [ˌdʒeləˈtiːn] *n* gelatina *f*.

gem [dʒem] *n* gemma *f*.

Gemini [ˈdʒemɪnaɪ] *n* Gemelli *mpl*.

gender [ˈdʒendəʳ] *n* genere *m*.

general [ˈdʒenərəl] ◇ *adj* generale; *(idea, statement)* generico(-a) ◇ *n* generale *m*; **in ~** in generale; *(usually)* in genere.

general anaesthetic *n* anestesia *f* totale.

general election *n* elezioni *fpl* politiche.

generally [ˈdʒenərəlɪ] *adv* generalmente.

general practitioner [-prækˈtɪʃənəʳ] *n* medico *m* generico.

general store *n* drogheria *f*.

generate [ˈdʒenəreɪt] *vt* generare.

generation [ˌdʒenəˈreɪʃn] *n* generazione *f*.

generator [ˈdʒenəreɪtəʳ] *n* generatore *m*.

generosity [ˌdʒenəˈrɒsətɪ] *n* generosità *f*.

generous [ˈdʒenərəs] *adj* generoso(-a).

genitals [ˈdʒenɪtlz] *npl* genitali *mpl*.

genius [ˈdʒiːnjəs] *n* genio *m*.

gentle [ˈdʒentl] *adj (careful)* delicato(-a); *(kind)* gentile; *(movement, breeze)* leggero(-a).

gentleman [ˈdʒentlmən] (*pl* **-men** [-mən]) *n* signore *m*; *(with good manners)* gentiluomo *m*; **'gentlemen'** *(men's toilets)* 'uomini'.

gently [ˈdʒentlɪ] *adv (carefully)* delicatamente.

gents [dʒents] *n (Br)* toilette *f inv* degli uomini.

genuine [ˈdʒenjʊɪn] *adj (authentic)* autentico(-a); *(sincere)* sincero(-a).

geographical [dʒɪəˈgræfɪkl] *adj* geografico(-a).

geography [dʒɪˈɒgrəfɪ] *n* geografia *f*.

geology [dʒɪˈɒlədʒɪ] *n* geologia *f*.

geometry [dʒɪˈɒmətrɪ] *n* geometria *f*.

Georgian [ˈdʒɔːdʒən] *adj (architecture etc)* georgiano(-a) *(del periodo dei re Giorgio I–IV, 1714–1830)*.

geranium [dʒɪˈreɪnjəm] *n* geranio *m*.

German [ˈdʒɜːmən] ◇ *adj* tedesco(-a) ◇ *n (person)* tedesco *m* (-a *f*); *(language)* tedesco *m*.

German measles *n* rosolia *f*.

Germany [ˈdʒɜːmənɪ] *n* la Germania.

germs [dʒɜːmz] *npl* germi *mpl*.

gesture [ˈdʒestʃəʳ] *n (movement)* gesto *m*.

get [get] (*pt & pp* **got**, *Am pp* **gotten**) ◇ *vt* **1.** *(obtain)* ottenere; *(job, house)* trovare; **I got some crisps from the shop** ho comprato delle patatine al negozio; **she got a job** ha trovato lavoro.

2. *(receive)* ricevere; **I got a book for Christmas** mi hanno regalato un libro per Natale; **you ~ a lot of rain here in winter** qui piove molto in inverno.

3. *(means of transport)* prendere; **let's ~ a taxi** prendiamo un taxi.

4. *(fetch)* andare a prendere; **could you ~ me the manager?** *(in shop)* mi può chiamare il direttore?; *(on phone)* mi può passare il direttore?

5. *(illness)* avere, prendere; **I've got a headache** ho mal di testa.

6. *(cause to become, do)*: **to ~ sthg done** *(do)* fare qc; *(have done)* far fare qc; **to ~ sb to do sthg** far fare qc a qn; **I can't ~ it open** non riesco ad aprirlo; **can I ~ my car repaired here?** posso far riparare qui la mia macchina?

7. *(move)*: **to ~ sthg in/out** far entrare/uscire qc; **I can't ~ it through the door** non riesco a farlo passare dalla porta.

8. *(understand)* capire; **to ~ a joke** capire una barzelletta.

9. *(time, chance)* avere, trovare; **we didn't ~ the chance to see everything** non siamo riusciti a vedere tutto.

10. *(answer)*: **I'll ~ it!** *(phone)* rispondo io!; *(door)* vado io!, → **have**.

◇ *vi* **1.** *(become)* diventare; **it's getting late** si sta facendo tardi; **to ~ bored** annoiarsi; **to ~ ready** prepararsi; **to ~ lost** perdersi; **~ lost!** *(inf)* vattene!

2. *(arrive)* arrivare; **when does the train ~ here?** a che ora arriva il treno?

3. *(go)*: **to ~ to/from** andare a/da.

4. *(manage)*: **to ~ to do sthg** riuscire a fare qc.

◇ *aux vb*: **to ~ delayed** essere trattenuto; **to ~ killed** essere ucciso.

◆ **get back** *vi (return)* ritornare.

◆ **get in** *vi (arrive)* arrivare; *(enter)* entrare.

◆ **get into** *vt fus (enter)* entrare in; **to ~ into the car** salire in macchina; **to ~ into bed** mettersi a letto; **to ~ into trouble** mettersi nei guai.

◆ **get off** *vi (leave train, bus)* scendere; *(depart)* partire.

◆ **get on** *vi (enter train, bus)* salire; *(in relationship)* andare d'accordo; **how are you getting on?** come va la vita?

◆ **get out** *vi (of car, bus, train)* scendere.

◆ **get through** *vi (on phone)* ottenere la comunicazione.

◆ **get up** *vi* alzarsi.

get-together *n (inf)* riunione *f*.

ghastly [ˈgɑːstlɪ] *adj (inf)* terribile.
gherkin [ˈgɜːkɪn] *n* cetriolino *m*.
ghetto blaster [ˈgetəʊˌblɑːstəʳ] *n (inf)* stereo *m* portatile.
ghost [gəʊst] *n* fantasma *m*.
giant [ˈdʒaɪənt] ◇ *adj* gigantesco(-a) ◇ *n (in stories)* gigante *m*.
giblets [ˈdʒɪblɪts] *npl* rigaglie *fpl*.
giddy [ˈgɪdɪ] *adj (dizzy)*: **I feel ~** mi gira la testa.
gift [gɪft] *n* regalo *m*; *(talent)* talento *m*.
gifted [ˈgɪftɪd] *adj* dotato(-a).
gift shop *n* negozio *m* di articoli da regalo.
gift voucher *n (Br)* buono *m* acquisto.
gig [gɪg] *n (inf: concert)* concerto *m*.
gigantic [dʒaɪˈgæntɪk] *adj* gigantesco(-a).
giggle [ˈgɪgl] *vi* ridacchiare.
gill [dʒɪl] *n (measurement)* = 0,142 l.
gimmick [ˈgɪmɪk] *n* trovata *f*.
gin [dʒɪn] *n* gin *m inv*; **~ and tonic** gin tonic.
ginger [ˈdʒɪndʒəʳ] ◇ *n* zenzero *m* ◇ *adj (colour)* rosso(-a).
ginger ale *n bibita analcolica gassata allo zenzero.*
ginger beer *n bibita analcolica allo zenzero.*
gingerbread [ˈdʒɪndʒəbred] *n torta o biscotto allo zenzero.*
gipsy [ˈdʒɪpsɪ] *n* zingaro *m* (-a *f*).
giraffe [dʒɪˈrɑːf] *n* giraffa *f*.
girdle [ˈgɜːdl] *n* panciera *f*.
girl [gɜːl] *n (child)* bambina *f*; *(young woman)* ragazza *f*; *(daughter)* femmina *f*.
girlfriend [ˈgɜːlfrend] *n (of boy, man)* ragazza *f*; *(of girl, woman)* amica *f*.
girl guide *n (Br)* giovane *f* esploratrice.
girl scout *(Am)* = **girl guide**.
giro [ˈdʒaɪrəʊ] *n (system)* giroconto *m*.
give [gɪv] (*pt* **gave**, *pp* **given** [ˈgɪvn]) *vt* dare; *(a smile, speech)* fare; *(attention)* prestare; *(time)* dedicare; **to ~ sb sthg** dare qc a qn; *(as present)* regalare qc a qn; **to ~ sthg a push** dare una spinta a qc; **to ~ sb a kiss** dare un bacio a qn; **it took an hour, ~ or take a few minutes** c'è voluta un'ora, minuto più minuto meno; '**~ way**' 'dare la precedenza'.
◆ **give away** *vt sep (get rid of)* dare via; *(reveal)* rivelare.
◆ **give back** *vt sep* restituire.
◆ **give in** *vi* arrendersi.
◆ **give off** *vt fus* emettere.
◆ **give out** *vt sep (distribute)* distribuire.
◆ **give up** ◇ *vt sep (cigarettes, chocolate)* rinunciare a; *(seat)* cedere ◇ *vi (admit defeat)* arrendersi; **to ~ up smoking** smettere di fumare.
glacier [ˈglæsjəʳ] *n* ghiacciaio *m*.
glad [glæd] *adj* contento(-a); **to be ~ to do sthg** essere contento di fare qc.
gladly [ˈglædlɪ] *adv (willingly)* volentieri.
glamorous [ˈglæmərəs] *adj* affascinante.
glance [glɑːns] ◇ *n* sguardo *m* ◇ *vi*: **to ~ (at)** dare uno sguardo (a).
gland [glænd] *n* ghiandola *f*.
glandular fever [ˈglændjʊlə-] *n* mononucleosi *f*.
glare [gleəʳ] *vi (person)* lanciare sguardi truci; *(sun, light)* abbagliare.
glass [glɑːs] ◇ *n (material)* vetro *m*; *(container, glassful)* bicchiere *m* ◇ *adj* di vetro.
◆ **glasses** *npl* occhiali *mpl*.
glassware [ˈglɑːsweəʳ] *n* oggetti *mpl* in vetro.
glen [glen] *n (Scot)* valle *f*.
glider [ˈglaɪdəʳ] *n* aliante *m*.
glimpse [glɪmps] *vt* intravedere.

glitter [ˈglɪtəʳ] *vi* luccicare.
global warming [ˌgləʊblˈwɔːmɪŋ] *n* effetto *m* serra.
globe [gləʊb] *n* globo *m*; **the ~** *(Earth)* il globo.
gloomy [ˈgluːmɪ] *adj* cupo(-a).
glorious [ˈglɔːrɪəs] *adj (weather, sight)* magnifico(-a); *(victory, history)* glorioso(-a).
glory [ˈglɔːrɪ] *n* gloria *f*.
gloss [glɒs] *n (shine)* lucido *m*; **~ (paint)** vernice *f* lucida.
glossary [ˈglɒsərɪ] *n* glossario *m*.
glossy [ˈglɒsɪ] *adj (magazine)* patinato(-a); *(photo)* lucido(-a).
glove [glʌv] *n* guanto *m*.
glove compartment *n* vano *m* portaoggetti.
glow [gləʊ] ◇ *n* barlume *m* ◇ *vi* brillare.
glucose [ˈgluːkəʊs] *n* glucosio *m*.
glue [gluː] ◇ *n* colla *f* ◇ *vt* incollare.
gnat [næt] *n* pappataci *m inv*.
gnaw [nɔː] *vt* rosicchiare.
go [gəʊ] (*pt* **went**, *pp* **gone**, *pl* **goes**) ◇ *vi* 1. *(move, travel, attend)* andare; **to ~ home** andare a casa; **to ~ to Italy** andare in Italia; **to ~ by bus** andare con l'autobus; **to ~ to school** andare a scuola; **to ~ for a walk** andare a fare una passeggiata; **to ~ and do sthg** andare a fare qc; **to ~ shopping** andare a fare spesa.
2. *(leave)* andarsene; *(bus, train)* partire; **it's time to ~** è ora d'andare; **~ away!** vattene!
3. *(become)* diventare; **she went pale** è impallidita; **the milk has gone sour** il latte è inacidito.
4. *(expressing future tense)*: **to be going to do sthg** stare per fare qc; *(intend to do)* avere intenzione di fare qc; **I'm going to be sick** sto per vomitare; **I'm going to phone them tonight** ho intenzione di chiamarli stasera.
5. *(function)* funzionare; **the car won't ~** la macchina non parte.
6. *(stop working)* rompersi; **the fuse has gone** è saltato il fusibile.
7. *(time)* passare.
8. *(progress)* andare; **to ~ well** andar bene.
9. *(bell, alarm)* suonare.
10. *(match, be appropriate)*: **to ~ (with)** andare (con).
11. *(be sold)* essere venduto(-a); **'everything must ~'** 'svendita totale'.
12. *(fit)* entrare.
13. *(lead)* andare, portare; **where does this path ~?** dove porta questo sentiero?
14. *(belong)* andare.
15. *(in phrases)*: **to let ~ of sthg** *(drop)* lasciare (andare) qc; **to ~** *(Am: to take away)* da asportare; **there are only three weeks to ~** mancano solo tre settimane.
◇ *n* 1. *(turn)* turno *m*; **it's your ~** tocca a te.
2. *(attempt)* prova *f*, tentativo *m*; **to have a ~ at sthg** provare qc; **'50p a ~'** *(in game)* '50 pence a partita'.
◆ **go ahead** *vi (take place)* aver luogo; **~ ahead!** fai pure!
◆ **go back** *vi (return)* ritornare.
◆ **go down** *vi (decrease)* abbassarsi, scendere; *(sun)* tramontare; *(tyre)* sgonfiarsi.
◆ **go down with** *vt fus (inf: illness)* prendere.
◆ **go in** *vi (enter)* entrare.
◆ **go off** *vi (alarm, bell)* suonare; *(go bad)* andare a male; *(lights, heating)* spegnersi.
◆ **go on** *vi (happen)* succedere; *(lights, heating)* accendersi; *(continue)*: **to ~ on doing sthg** continuare a fare qc.
◆ **go out** *vi (leave house)* uscire; *(light, fire, cigarette)* spegnersi; *(have relationship)*: **to ~ out (with sb)** stare insieme (a qn); **to ~ out**

for a meal andare a mangiare fuori.

◆ **go over** *vt fus (check)* controllare.

◆ **go round** *vi (revolve)* girare; *(be enough)* bastare per tutti.

◆ **go through** *vt fus (experience)* passare; *(spend)* spendere; *(search)* esaminare.

◆ **go up** *vi (increase)* aumentare.

◆ **go without** *vt fus* fare a meno di.

goal [gəʊl] *n (posts)* porta *f*; *(point scored)* goal *m inv*; *(aim)* scopo *m*.

goalkeeper [ˈgəʊlˌkiːpəʳ] *n* portiere *m*.

goalpost [ˈgəʊlpəʊst] *n* palo *m*.

goat [gəʊt] *n* capra *f*.

gob [gɒb] *n (Br: inf: mouth)* bocca *f*.

god [gɒd] *n* dio *m*.

◆ **God** *n* Dio *m*.

goddaughter [ˈgɒdˌdɔːtəʳ] *n* figlioccia *f*.

godfather [ˈgɒdˌfɑːðəʳ] *n* padrino *m*.

godmother [ˈgɒdˌmʌðəʳ] *n* madrina *f*.

gods [gɒdz] *npl*: **the ~** *(Br: inf: in theatre)* il loggione.

godson [ˈgɒdsʌn] *n* figlioccio *m*.

goes [gəʊz] → **go**.

goggles [ˈgɒglz] *npl (for swimming)* occhialini *mpl*; *(for skiing)* occhiali *mpl* da neve.

going [ˈgəʊɪŋ] *adj (available)* disponibile; **the ~ rate** la tariffa corrente.

go-kart [-kɑːt] *n* go-kart *m inv*.

gold [gəʊld] ◇ *n* oro *m* ◇ *adj* d'oro.

goldfish [ˈgəʊldfɪʃ] *(pl inv) n* pesce *m* rosso.

gold-plated [-ˈpleɪtɪd] *adj* placcato(-a) d'oro.

golf [gɒlf] *n* golf *m*.

golf ball *n* pallina *f* da golf.

golf club *n (place)* circolo *m* del golf; *(piece of equipment)* mazza *f* da golf.

golf course *n* campo *m* di golf.

golfer [ˈgɒlfəʳ] *n* golfista *mf*.

gone [gɒn] ◇ *pp* → **go** ◇ *prep (Br: past)*: **it's ~ ten** sono le dieci passate.

good [gʊd] *(compar* **better**, *superl* **best**) ◇ *adj* buono(-a); *(enjoyable)* bello(-a); *(skilled, well-behaved)* bravo(-a); *(kind)* gentile ◇ *n* bene *m*; **the weather's ~** fa bel tempo; **to have a ~ time** divertirsi; **to be ~ at sthg** saper fare qc bene; **a ~ ten minutes** dieci minuti buoni; **in ~ time** in anticipo; **to make ~ sthg** compensare qc; **for ~** per sempre; **for the ~ of** per il bene di; **to do sb ~** far bene a qn; **it's no ~** *(there's no point)* è inutile; **~ afternoon!** buon giorno!; **~ evening!** buona sera!; **~ morning!** buon giorno!; **~ night!** buona notte!

◆ **goods** *npl* merce *f*.

goodbye [ˌgʊdˈbaɪ] *excl* arrivederci!

Good Friday *n* Venerdì *m* Santo.

good-looking [-ˈlʊkɪŋ] *adj* attraente.

goods train [gʊdz-] *n* treno *m* merci.

goose [guːs] *(pl* **geese**) *n* oca *f*.

gooseberry [ˈgʊzbərɪ] *n* uva *f* spina.

gorge [gɔːdʒ] *n* gola *f*.

gorgeous [ˈgɔːdʒəs] *adj* stupendo(-a).

gorilla [gəˈrɪlə] *n* gorilla *m inv*.

gossip [ˈgɒsɪp] ◇ *n (about someone)* pettegolezzi *mpl* ◇ *vi (about someone)* fare pettegolezzi; *(chat)* chiacchierare; **to have a ~** chiacchierare.

gossip column *n* cronaca *f* rosa.

got [gɒt] *pt & pp* → **get**.

gotten [ˈgɒtn] *pp (Am)* → **get**.

goujons [ˈguːdʒɒnz] *npl (of fish)* frittelle *fpl*.

goulash [ˈguːlæʃ] *n* gulasch *m inv*.

gourmet ['gʊəmeɪ] ◇ *n* buongustaio *m* (-a *f*) ◇ *adj* per intenditori.

govern ['gʌvən] *vt (country, city)* governare.

government ['gʌvnmənt] *n* governo *m*.

gown [gaʊn] *n (dress)* abito *m* lungo.

GP *abbr* = **general practitioner**.

grab [græb] *vt (take hold of)* afferrare.

graceful ['greɪsfʊl] *adj (elegant)* aggraziato(-a).

grade [greɪd] *n (quality)* categoria *f*; *(in exam)* voto *m*; *(Am: year at school)* classe *f*.

gradient ['greɪdjənt] *n* pendenza *f*.

gradual ['grædʒʊəl] *adj* graduale.

gradually ['grædʒʊəlɪ] *adv* gradualmente.

graduate [*n* 'grædʒʊət, *vb* 'grædʒʊeɪt] ◇ *n (from university)* laureato *m* (-a *f*); *(Am: from high school)* diplomato *m* (-a *f*) ◇ *vi (from university)* laurearsi; *(Am: from high school)* diplomarsi.

graduation [,grædʒʊ'eɪʃn] *n (ceremony at university)* consegna *f* delle lauree; *(Am: ceremony at school)* consegna dei diplomi.

graffiti [grə'fi:tɪ] *n* graffiti *mpl*.

grain [greɪn] *n (seed)* chicco *m*; *(crop)* cereali *mpl*; *(of sand, salt)* granello *m*.

gram [græm] *n* grammo *m*.

grammar ['græməʳ] *n* grammatica *f*.

grammar school *n (in UK) scuola secondaria più selettiva e tradizionale delle altre.*

gramme [græm] = **gram**.

gramophone ['græməfəʊn] *n* grammofono *m*.

gran [græn] *n (Br: inf)* nonna *f*.

grand [grænd] ◇ *adj (impressive)* grandioso(-a) ◇ *n (inf) (£1,000)* mille sterline *fpl*; *($1,000)* mille dollari *mpl*.

grandad ['grændæd] *n (inf)* nonno *m*.

grandchild ['græntʃaɪld] (*pl* **-children** [-,tʃɪldrən]) *n* nipote *mf*.

granddaughter ['græn,dɔ:təʳ] *n* nipote *f*.

grandfather ['grænd,fɑ:ðəʳ] *n* nonno *m*.

grandma ['grænmɑ:] *n (inf)* nonna *f*.

grandmother ['græn,mʌðəʳ] *n* nonna *f*.

grandpa ['grænpɑ:] *n (inf)* nonno *m*.

grandparents ['græn,peərənts] *npl* nonni *mpl*.

grandson ['grænsʌn] *n* nipote *m*.

granite ['grænɪt] *n* granito *m*.

granny ['grænɪ] *n (inf)* nonna *f*.

grant [grɑ:nt] ◇ *n* (POL) sovvenzione *f*; *(for university)* borsa *f* di studio ◇ *vt (fml: give)* concedere; **to take sthg for ~ed** dare qc per scontato; **to take sb for ~ed** pensare di poter sempre contare su qn.

grapefruit ['greɪpfru:t] *n* pompelmo *m*.

grapefruit juice *n* succo *m* di pompelmo.

grapes [greɪps] *npl* uva *f*.

graph [grɑ:f] *n* grafico *m*.

graph paper *n* carta *f* millimetrata.

grasp [grɑ:sp] *vt* afferrare.

grass [grɑ:s] *n (plant)* erba *f*; *(lawn)* prato *m*; **'keep off the ~'** 'non calpestare il prato'.

grasshopper ['grɑ:s,hɒpəʳ] *n* cavalletta *f*.

grate [greɪt] *n* grata *f*.

grated ['greɪtɪd] *adj* grattugiato(-a).

grateful ['greɪtfʊl] *adj (person)* grato(-a).

grater ['greɪtəʳ] *n* grattugia *f*.

gratitude ['grætɪtju:d] *n* gratitudine *f*.
gratuity [grə'tju:ɪtɪ] *n (fml)* mancia *f*.
grave[1] [greɪv] ◇ *adj (mistake, news, concern)* grave ◇ *n* tomba *f*.
grave[2] [grɑ:v] *adj (accent)* grave.
gravel ['grævl] *n* ghiaia *f*.
graveyard ['greɪvjɑ:d] *n* cimitero *m*.
gravity ['grævətɪ] *n* gravità *f*.
gravy ['greɪvɪ] *n salsa ottenuta dal sugo di carne arrosto e resa più densa con della farina.*
gray [greɪ] *(Am)* = **grey**.
graze [greɪz] *vt (injure)* scorticare, escoriare.
grease [gri:s] *n (for machine)* olio *m*, lubrificante *m*; *(animal fat)* grasso *m*.
greaseproof paper ['gri:spru:f-] *n (Br)* carta *f* oleata.
greasy ['gri:sɪ] *adj (food, skin, hair)* grasso(-a); *(tools, clothes)* unto(-a).
great [greɪt] *adj* grande; *(very good)* eccellente, fantastico(-a); **(that's) ~!** fantastico!
Great Britain *n* la Gran Bretagna.
great-grandfather *n* bisnonno *m*.
great-grandmother *n* bisnonna *f*.
greatly ['greɪtlɪ] *adv* molto.
Greece [gri:s] *n* la Grecia.
greed [gri:d] *n* avidità *f*.
greedy ['gri:dɪ] *adj* avido(-a).
Greek [gri:k] ◇ *adj* greco(-a) ◇ *n (person)* greco *m* (-a *f*); *(language)* greco *m*.
Greek salad *n* insalata *f* greca *(a base di pomodori, cetriolo, formaggio greco e olive nere)*.
green [gri:n] ◇ *adj* verde; *(environmentalist)* ambientalista; *(inf: inexperienced)* inesperto(-a) ◇ *n (colour)* verde *m*; *(in village)* prato *m* pubblico; *(on golf course)* green *m inv*.
◆ **greens** *npl (vegetables)* verdura *f*.
green beans *npl* fagiolini *mpl*.
green card *n (Br: for car)* carta *f* verde; *(Am: work permit)* permesso *m* di soggiorno.
green channel *n uscita di porto o aeroporto riservata ai passeggeri che non hanno niente da dichiarare.*
greengage ['gri:ngeɪdʒ] *n* susina *f* Regina Claudia.
greengrocer's ['gri:nˌgrəʊsəz] *n (shop)* negozio *m* di frutta e verdura.
greenhouse ['gri:nhaʊs, *pl* -haʊzɪz] *n* serra *f*.
greenhouse effect *n* effetto *m* serra.
green light *n (go-ahead)*: **to give sb the ~** dare il via libera a qn.
green pepper *n* peperone *m* verde.
Greens [gri:nz] *npl*: **the ~** i Verdi.
green salad *n* insalata *f* verde.
greet [gri:t] *vt (say hello to)* salutare.
greeting ['gri:tɪŋ] *n* saluto *m*.
grenade [grə'neɪd] *n* granata *f*.
grew [gru:] *pt* → **grow**.
grey [greɪ] ◇ *adj* grigio(-a) ◇ *n* grigio *m*; **to go ~** diventar grigio.
greyhound ['greɪhaʊnd] *n* levriero *m*.
grid [grɪd] *n (grating)* grata *f*; *(on map etc)* reticolato *m*.
grief [gri:f] *n* dolore *m*; **to come to ~** *(plan)* naufragare; *(person)* finire male.
grieve [gri:v] *vi* affliggersi.
grill [grɪl] ◇ *n (on cooker)* grill *m inv*; *(for open fire)* griglia *f*; *(part of restaurant) area di un ristorante dove si cucina alla griglia* ◇ *vt* cuocere ai ferri OR alla griglia.
grille [grɪl] *n* (AUT) griglia *f*.

grilled [grɪld] *adj* alla griglia, ai ferri.
grim [grɪm] *adj (expression)* severo(-a); *(place)* lugubre; *(news)* triste.
grimace [ˈgrɪməs] *n* smorfia *f*.
grimy [ˈgraɪmɪ] *adj* sudicio(-a).
grin [grɪn] ◇ *n* (gran) sorriso *m* ◇ *vi* fare un gran sorriso.
grind [graɪnd] (*pt & pp* **ground**) *vt (pepper, coffee)* macinare.
grip [grɪp] ◇ *n (hold)* presa *f*; *(of tyres)* tenuta *f* di strada; *(handle)* impugnatura *f*; *(bag)* borsa *f* da viaggio ◇ *vt (hold)* afferrare.
gristle [ˈgrɪsl] *n* cartilagine *f*.
groan [grəʊn] ◇ *n* lamento *m* ◇ *vi* lamentarsi.
groceries [ˈgrəʊsərɪz] *npl* generi *mpl* alimentari.
grocer's [ˈgrəʊsəz] *n (shop)* drogheria *f*.
grocery [ˈgrəʊsərɪ] *n (shop)* drogheria *f*.
groin [grɔɪn] *n* inguine *m*.
groove [gruːv] *n* solco *m*.
grope [grəʊp] *vi* andare a tastoni; **to ~ for sthg** cercare qc a tastoni.
gross [grəʊs] *adj (weight, income)* lordo(-a).
grossly [ˈgrəʊslɪ] *adv (extremely)* estremamente.
grotty [ˈgrɒtɪ] *adj (Br: inf)* squallido(-a).
ground [graʊnd] ◇ *pt & pp* → **grind** ◇ *n (surface of earth)* terra *f*; *(soil)* terreno *m*; (SPORT) campo *m* ◇ *adj (coffee)* macinato(-a) ◇ *vt (Am: electrical connection)* mettere a terra; **to be ~ed** *(plane)* essere trattenuto a terra; **on the ~** a OR per terra.
◆ **grounds** *npl (of building)* terreni *mpl*; *(of coffee)* fondi *mpl*; *(reason)* motivo *m*, ragione *f*.
ground floor *n* pianterreno *m*.
groundsheet [ˈgraʊndʃiːt] *n* telo *m* impermeabile.
group [gruːp] *n* gruppo *m*.
grouse [graʊs] *(pl inv) n (bird)* gallo *m* cedrone.
grovel [ˈgrɒvl] *vi (be humble)* umiliarsi.
grow [grəʊ] (*pt* **grew**, *pp* **grown**) ◇ *vi (person, animal, plant)* crescere; *(fears, traffic)* aumentare; *(company, city)* espandersi; *(become)* diventare ◇ *vt (plant, crop)* coltivare; *(beard)* farsi crescere; **to ~ old** invecchiare.
◆ **grow up** *vi* crescere, diventare grande.
growl [graʊl] *vi (dog)* ringhiare.
grown [grəʊn] *pp* → **grow**.
grown-up ◇ *adj* adulto(-a) ◇ *n* adulto *m* (-a *f*).
growth [grəʊθ] *n (increase)* crescita *f*; (MED) tumore *m*.
grub [grʌb] *n (inf: food)* cibo *m*.
grubby [ˈgrʌbɪ] *adj (inf)* sporco(-a).
grudge [grʌdʒ] ◇ *n* rancore *m* ◇ *vt*: **to ~ sb sthg** invidiare qc a qn.
grueling [ˈgrʊəlɪŋ] *(Am)* = **gruelling**.
gruelling [ˈgrʊəlɪŋ] *adj (Br)* estenuante.
gruesome [ˈgruːsəm] *adj* raccapricciante.
grumble [ˈgrʌmbl] *vi (complain)* lagnarsi.
grumpy [ˈgrʌmpɪ] *adj (inf)* scorbutico(-a).
grunt [grʌnt] *vi* grugnire.
guarantee [ˌgærənˈtiː] ◇ *n* garanzia *f* ◇ *vt* garantire.
guard [gɑːd] ◇ *n (of prisoner etc)* guardia *f*; *(Br: on train)* capotreno *mf*; *(protective cover)* schermo *m* di protezione ◇ *vt (watch over)* sorvegliare; **to be on one's ~** stare in guardia.
guess [ges] ◇ *n* supposizione *f* ◇ *vt & vi* indovinare; **I ~ (so)** penso di sì; **have a ~!** indovina!
guest [gest] *n (in home)* ospite *mf*; *(in hotel)* cliente *mf*.

guesthouse ['gesthaʊs, *pl* -haʊzɪz] *n* pensione *f*.

guestroom ['gestrʊm] *n* camera *f* degli ospiti.

guidance ['gaɪdəns] *n* guida *f*, direzione *f*.

guide [gaɪd] ◇ *n* guida *f* ◇ *vt* guidare.

◆ **Guide** *n (Br)* giovane esploratrice *f*.

guidebook ['gaɪdbʊk] *n* guida *f*.

guide dog *n* cane *m* guida.

guided tour ['gaɪdɪd-] *n* visita *f* guidata.

guidelines ['gaɪdlaɪnz] *npl* direttive *fpl*.

guilt [gɪlt] *n* colpa *f*.

guilty ['gɪltɪ] *adj* colpevole; **to feel ~** sentirsi in colpa.

guinea pig ['gɪnɪ-] *n* cavia *f*.

guitar [gɪ'tɑːʳ] *n* chitarra *f*.

guitarist [gɪ'tɑːrɪst] *n* chitarrista *mf*.

gulf [gʌlf] *n (of sea)* golfo *m*.

Gulf War *n*: **the ~** la guerra del Golfo.

gull [gʌl] *n* gabbiano *m*.

gullible ['gʌləbl] *adj* credulone(-a).

gulp [gʌlp] *n (of drink)* sorso *m*.

gum [gʌm] *n* gomma *f* da masticare; *(adhesive)* colla *f*.

◆ **gums** *npl* gengive *fpl*.

gun [gʌn] *n (pistol)* pistola *f*; *(rifle)* fucile *m*; *(cannon)* cannone *m*.

gunfire ['gʌnfaɪəʳ] *n* sparatoria *f*.

gunshot ['gʌnʃɒt] *n* sparo *m*.

gust [gʌst] *n (of wind)* raffica *f*.

gut [gʌt] *n (inf: stomach)* stomaco *m*.

◆ **guts** *npl (inf) (intestines)* budella *fpl*; *(courage)*: **to have ~s** avere fegato.

gutter ['gʌtəʳ] *n (beside road)* cunetta *f*; *(of house)* grondaia *f*.

guy [gaɪ] *n (inf: man)* tipo *m*.

◆ **guys** *npl (Am: inf: people)* gente *f*.

Guy Fawkes Night [-'fɔːks-] *n festa che si celebra il 5 novembre per ricordare il fallimento della Congiura delle polveri.*

guy rope *n* cavo *m*.

gym [dʒɪm] *n* palestra *f*; *(school lesson)* ginnastica *f*.

gymnast ['dʒɪmnæst] *n* ginnasta *mf*.

gymnastics [dʒɪm'næstɪks] *n* ginnastica *f*.

gym shoes *npl* scarpe *fpl* da ginnastica.

gynaecologist [ˌgaɪnə'kɒlədʒɪst] *n* ginecologo *m* (-a *f*).

gypsy ['dʒɪpsɪ] = **gipsy**.

H

H ◇ *(abbr of hospital)* H ◇ *abbr* = **hot**.
habit [ˈhæbɪt] *n (custom)* abitudine *f*.
hacksaw [ˈhæksɔː] *n* seghetto *m*.
had [hæd] *pt & pp* → **have**.
haddock [ˈhædək] *(pl inv) n* eglefino *m (pesce simile al merluzzo)*.
hadn't [ˈhædnt] = **had not**.
haggis [ˈhægɪs] *n piatto tipico scozzese a base di avena e frattaglie di pecora.*
haggle [ˈhægl] *vi* mercanteggiare.
hail [heɪl] ◇ *n* grandine *f* ◇ *v impers* grandinare.
hailstone [ˈheɪlstəʊn] *n* chicco *m* di grandine.
hair [heəʳ] *n (on head)* capelli *mpl*; *(on animal)* pelo *m*; *(on human skin)* peli *mpl*; *(individual hair on head)* capello *m*; *(individual hair on skin)* pelo *m*; **to have one's ~ cut** tagliarsi i capelli.
hairband [ˈheəbænd] *n* cerchietto *m* per capelli.
hairbrush [ˈheəbrʌʃ] *n* spazzola *f* per capelli.
hairclip [ˈheəklɪp] *n* fermaglio *m* per capelli.
haircut [ˈheəkʌt] *n (style)* taglio *m* di capelli; **to have a ~** farsi tagliare i capelli.
hairdo [ˈheəduː] *(pl* **-s**) *n* acconciatura *f*, pettinatura *f*.
hairdresser [ˈheəˌdresəʳ] *n* parrucchiere *m* (-a *f*); **~'s** *(salon)* negozio *m* di parrucchiere; **to go to the ~'s** andare dal parrucchiere.
hairdryer [ˈheəˌdraɪəʳ] *n* asciugacapelli *m inv*, föhn *m inv*.
hair gel *n* gel *m inv* per capelli, gommina *f*.
hairgrip [ˈheəgrɪp] *n (Br)* molletta *f* (per capelli).
hairnet [ˈheənet] *n* retina *f* (per capelli).
hairpin bend [ˈheəpɪn-] *n* tornante *m*.
hair remover [-rɪˌmuːvəʳ] *n* crema *f* depilatoria.
hair rollers [-ˈrəʊləz] *npl* bigodini *mpl*.
hair slide *n* fermacapelli *m inv*.
hairspray [ˈheəspreɪ] *n* lacca *f* per capelli.
hairstyle [ˈheəstaɪl] *n* acconciatura *f*, pettinatura *f*.
hairy [ˈheərɪ] *adj (person, chest, legs)* peloso(-a).
half [*Br* hɑːf, *Am* hæf] (*pl* **halves**) ◇ *n* metà *f inv*; *(of match)* tempo *m*; *(half pint)* mezza pinta *f*; *(child's ticket)* biglietto *m* ridotto ◇ *adj* mezzo(-a) ◇ *adv*: **~ cooked** cotto a metà; **~ full** mezzo pieno; **I'm ~ Scottish** per metà sono scozzese; **a day and a ~** un giorno e mezzo; **four and a ~** quattro e mezzo; **~**

past seven sette e mezza; ~ as big as la metà di; an hour and a ~ un'ora e mezza; ~ an hour mezz'ora; ~ a dozen mezza dozzina; ~ price a metà prezzo.

half board *n* mezza pensione *f*.

half-day *n* mezza giornata *f*.

half fare *n* mezza tariffa *f*.

half portion *n* mezza porzione *f*.

half-price *adj* a metà prezzo.

half term *n (Br) vacanza a metà trimestre.*

half time *n* intervallo *m*.

halfway [hɑːfˈweɪ] *adv (in space)* a metà strada; *(in time)* a metà.

halibut [ˈhælɪbət] *(pl inv) n* halibut *m inv*.

hall [hɔːl] *n (of house)* ingresso *m*; *(large room, building)* sala *f*, salone *m*; *(country house)* maniero *m*.

hallmark [ˈhɔːlmɑːk] *n (on silver, gold)* marchio *m*.

hallo [həˈləʊ] = **hello**.

hall of residence *n* casa *f* dello studente.

Halloween [ˌhæləʊˈiːn] *n vigilia d'Ognissanti.*

halt [hɔːlt] ◇ *vi* fermarsi ◇ *n*: **to come to a ~** fermarsi.

halve [*Br* hɑːv, *Am* hæv] *vt* dimezzare.

halves [*Br* hɑːvz, *Am* hævz] *pl* → **half**.

ham [hæm] *n (meat)* prosciutto *m* (cotto).

hamburger [ˈhæmbɜːgəʳ] *n (beefburger)* hamburger *m inv*; *(Am: mince)* carne *f* macinata.

hamlet [ˈhæmlɪt] *n* paesino *m*.

hammer [ˈhæməʳ] ◇ *n* martello *m* ◇ *vt (nail)* piantare.

hammock [ˈhæmək] *n* amaca *f*.

hamper [ˈhæmpəʳ] *n* cesta *f*.

hamster [ˈhæmstəʳ] *n* criceto *m*.

hamstring [ˈhæmstrɪŋ] *n* tendine *m* del ginocchio.

hand [hænd] *n* mano *f*; *(of clock, watch, dial)* lancetta *f*; **to give sb a ~** dare una mano a qn; **to get out of ~** sfuggire di mano; **by ~** a mano; **in ~** *(time)* a disposizione; **on the one ~** da una parte; **on the other ~** d'altra parte.

◆ **hand in** *vt sep* consegnare.

◆ **hand out** *vt sep* distribuire.

◆ **hand over** *vt sep (give)* consegnare.

handbag [ˈhændbæg] *n* borsetta *f*.

handbasin [ˈhændbeɪsn] *n* lavabo *m*.

handbook [ˈhændbʊk] *n* manuale *m*.

handbrake [ˈhændbreɪk] *n* freno *m* a mano.

hand cream *n* crema *f* per le mani.

handcuffs [ˈhændkʌfs] *npl* manette *fpl*.

handful [ˈhændfʊl] *n (amount)* manciata *f*.

handicap [ˈhændɪkæp] *n* handicap *m inv*.

handicapped [ˈhændɪkæpt] ◇ *adj* handicappato(-a) ◇ *npl*: **the ~** i portatori di handicap.

handkerchief [ˈhæŋkətʃɪf] (*pl* **-chiefs** OR **-chieves** [-tʃiːvz]) *n* fazzoletto *m*.

handle [ˈhændl] ◇ *n (of door, window)* maniglia *f*; *(of knife, pan, suitcase)* manico *m* ◇ *vt (touch)* toccare; *(deal with)* occuparsi di; **'~ with care'** 'fragile'.

handlebars [ˈhændlbɑːz] *npl* manubrio *m*.

hand luggage *n* bagaglio *m* a mano.

handmade [ˌhændˈmeɪd] *adj* fatto(-a) a mano.

handout [ˈhændaʊt] *n (leaflet)* volantino *m*.

handrail [ˈhændreɪl] *n* corrimano *m*.

handset [ˈhændset] *n* ricevitore *m*; **'please replace the ~'** 'si prega di riporre il ricevitore'.

handshake ['hændʃeɪk] *n* stretta *f* di mano.

handsome ['hænsəm] *adj (man)* bello(-a).

handstand ['hændstænd] *n* verticale *f*.

handwriting ['hænd,raɪtɪŋ] *n* calligrafia *f*.

handy ['hændɪ] *adj (useful)* utile; *(convenient)* comodo(-a); *(good with one's hands)* abile; *(near)* vicino(-a), a portata di mano; **to come in ~** *(inf)* tornare utile.

hang [hæŋ] (*pt & pp* **hung**) ◇ *vt* appendere; *(execute: pt & pp hanged)* impiccare ◇ *vi (be suspended)* penzolare, pendere ◇ *n*: **to get the ~ of sthg** fare la mano a qc.

◆ **hang about** *vi (Br: inf)* ciondolare.

◆ **hang around** *(inf)* = **hang about**.

◆ **hang down** *vi* penzolare.

◆ **hang on** *vi (inf: wait)* aspettare.

◆ **hang out** ◇ *vt sep (washing)* stendere ◇ *vi (inf)* stare.

◆ **hang up** *vi (on phone)* riagganciare.

hangar ['hæŋəʳ] *n* hangar *m inv*.

hanger ['hæŋəʳ] *n* gruccia *f*, stampella *f*.

hang gliding *n* deltaplano *m*.

hangover ['hæŋ,əʊvəʳ] *n* postumi *mpl* di sbornia.

hankie ['hæŋkɪ] *n (inf)* fazzoletto *m*.

happen ['hæpən] *vi* succedere, accadere; **I ~ed to catch sight of him** mi è capitato di vederlo.

happily ['hæpɪlɪ] *adv (luckily)* fortunatamente.

happiness ['hæpɪnɪs] *n* felicità *f*.

happy ['hæpɪ] *adj* felice; **to be ~ about sthg** essere contento(-a) di qc; **to be ~ to do sthg** *(willing)* fare qc volentieri; **to be ~ with sthg** essere soddisfatto di qc; **Happy Birthday!** buon compleanno!; **Happy Christmas!** buon Natale!; **Happy New Year!** buon anno!

happy hour *n (inf) momento della giornata, di solito nel tardo pomeriggio, in cui, nei bar, le bevande vengono vendute a prezzo ridotto.*

harassment ['hærəsmənt] *n* molestie *fpl*.

harbor ['hɑːbər] *(Am)* = **harbour**.

harbour ['hɑːbəʳ] *n (Br)* porto *m*.

hard [hɑːd] ◇ *adj* duro(-a); *(difficult)* difficile; *(strenuous)* faticoso(-a); *(forceful)* forte; *(winter, frost)* rigido(-a); *(drugs)* pesante ◇ *adv (work)* duro; *(listen)* attentamente; *(hit)* con forza; *(rain)* a dirotto.

hardback ['hɑːdbæk] *n* edizione *f* rilegata.

hardboard ['hɑːdbɔːd] *n* pannello *m* di legno compresso.

hard-boiled egg [-bɔɪld-] *n* uovo *m* sodo.

hard disk *n* hard disk *m inv*, disco *m* rigido.

hardly ['hɑːdlɪ] *adv* a malapena, appena; **~ ever** quasi mai.

hardship ['hɑːdʃɪp] *n (difficult conditions)* privazioni *fpl*; *(difficult circumstance)* avversità *fpl*.

hard shoulder *n (Br)* corsia *f* d'emergenza.

hard up *adj (inf)* in bolletta.

hardware ['hɑːdweəʳ] *n (tools, equipment)* ferramenta *fpl*; (COMPUT) hardware *m*.

hardwearing [,hɑːd'weərɪŋ] *adj (Br)* resistente.

hardworking [,hɑːd'wɜːkɪŋ] *adj* instancabile.

hare [heəʳ] *n* lepre *f*.

harm [hɑːm] ◇ *n (injury)* male *m*; *(damage)* danno *m* ◇ *vt (injure)* far male a; *(damage)* danneggiare.

harmful ['hɑːmfʊl] *adj* nocivo(-a).

harmless ['hɑːmlɪs] *adj* innocuo(-a).

harmonica [hɑːˈmɒnɪkə] *n* armonica *f*.

harmony [ˈhɑːmənɪ] *n* armonia *f*.

harness [ˈhɑːnɪs] *n (for horse)* finimenti *mpl*; *(for child)* briglie *fpl*.

harp [hɑːp] *n* arpa *f*.

harsh [hɑːʃ] *adj (weather)* rigido(-a); *(conditions)* duro(-a); *(cruel)* severo(-a); *(sound)* sgradevole.

harvest [ˈhɑːvɪst] *n (of corn, fruit)* raccolto *m*; *(of grapes)* vendemmia *f*.

has [*weak form* həz, *strong form* hæz] → **have**.

hash browns [hæʃ-] *npl (Am)* frittelle *fpl* di patate.

hasn't [ˈhæznt] = **has not**.

hassle [ˈhæsl] *n (inf: problem)* seccatura *f*.

hastily [ˈheɪstɪlɪ] *adv (rashly)* precipitosamente.

hasty [ˈheɪstɪ] *adj (hurried)* affrettato(-a); *(rash)* precipitoso(-a).

hat [hæt] *n* cappello *m*.

hatch [hætʃ] ◇ *n (for food)* passavivande *m inv* ◇ *vi (egg)* schiudersi.

hatchback [ˈhætʃˌbæk] *n (car)* tre OR cinque porte *f inv*.

hatchet [ˈhætʃɪt] *n* accetta *f*.

hate [heɪt] ◇ *n* odio *m* ◇ *vt* odiare, detestare; **to ~ doing sthg** detestare fare qc.

hatred [ˈheɪtrɪd] *n* odio *m*.

haul [hɔːl] ◇ *vt* trascinare ◇ *n*: **a long ~** un percorso lungo e faticoso.

haunted [ˈhɔːntɪd] *adj (house)* abitato(-a) da fantasmi.

have [hæv] (*pt & pp* **had**) ◇ *aux vb* **1.** *(to form perfect tenses: gen)* avere; *(with many intransitive verbs)* essere; **I ~ finished** ho finito; **~ you been there? – no, I haven't** ci sei stato? – no; **the train had already gone** il treno era già partito.

2. *(must)*: **to ~ (got) to do sthg** dover fare qc; **do you ~ to pay?** si deve pagare?

◇ *vt* **1.** *(possess)*: **to ~ (got)** avere; **do you ~** OR **~ you got a double room?** avete una camera doppia?; **she has (got) brown hair** ha i capelli castani.

2. *(experience)* avere; **to ~ a cold** avere il raffreddore; **we had a great time** ci siamo divertiti un mondo.

3. *(replacing other verbs)*: **to ~ breakfast** fare colazione; **to ~ dinner** cenare; **to ~ lunch** pranzare; **to ~ a drink** bere qualcosa; **to ~ a shower** fare una doccia; **to ~ a swim** fare una nuotata; **to ~ a walk** fare una passeggiata.

4. *(cause to be)*: **to ~ sthg done** far fare qc; **to ~ one's hair cut** farsi tagliare i capelli.

5. *(be treated in a certain way)*: **I've had my wallet stolen** mi hanno rubato il portafoglio.

haversack [ˈhævəsæk] *n* zaino *m*.

havoc [ˈhævək] *n* caos *m*.

hawk [hɔːk] *n* falco *m*.

hawker [ˈhɔːkə^r] *n* venditore *m* (-trice *f*) ambulante.

hay [heɪ] *n* fieno *m*.

hay fever *n* raffreddore *m* da fieno.

haystack [ˈheɪˌstæk] *n* pagliaio *m*.

hazard [ˈhæzəd] *n* rischio *m*, pericolo *m*.

hazardous [ˈhæzədəs] *adj* rischioso(-a), pericoloso(-a).

hazard warning lights *npl (Br)* luci *fpl* di emergenza.

haze [heɪz] *n* foschia *f*.

hazel [ˈheɪzl] *adj* nocciola *(inv)*.

hazelnut [ˈheɪzlˌnʌt] *n* nocciola *f*.

hazy [ˈheɪzɪ] *adj (misty)* offuscato(-a).

he [hiː] *pron* lui, egli; **~'s tall** è alto.

head [hed] ◇ *n (of body)* testa *f*, capo *m*; *(of queue, page, bed)* cima *f*; *(of company, department, table)* capo; *(head teacher of primary or lower secondary school)* direttore *m*

(-trice *f*) di scuola; *(head teacher of upper secondary school)* preside *mf*; *(of beer)* schiuma *f* ◇ *vt (list)* essere in testa a; *(organization)* dirigere, essere a capo di ◇ *vi* dirigersi; **£10 a ~** 10 sterline a testa; **~s or tails?** testa o croce?

◆ **head for** *vt fus* dirigersi verso OR a.

headache ['hedeɪk] *n (pain)* mal *m* di testa; **to have a ~** avere mal di testa.

heading ['hedɪŋ] *n* intestazione *f*.

headlamp ['hedlæmp] *(Br)* = **headlight**.

headlight ['hedlaɪt] *n* fanale *m* anteriore.

headline ['hedlaɪn] *n (in newspaper)* titolo *m*; *(on TV, radio)* notizie *fpl* principali.

headmaster [ˌhed'mɑːstəʳ] *n (of primary or lower secondary school)* direttore *m* di scuola; *(of upper secondary school)* preside *m*.

headmistress [ˌhed'mɪstrɪs] *n (of primary or lower secondary school)* direttrice *f* di scuola; *(of upper secondary school)* preside *f*.

head of state *n* capo *m* di Stato.

headphones ['hedfəʊnz] *npl* cuffie *fpl*.

headquarters [ˌhed'kwɔːtəz] *npl (of company, bank)* sede *f* centrale; *(of police, army)* quartiere *m* generale.

headrest ['hedrest] *n* poggiatesta *m inv*.

headroom ['hedrʊm] *n (under bridge)* altezza *f* massima.

headscarf ['hedskɑːf] (*pl* **-scarves** [-skɑːvz]) *n* foulard *m inv*.

head start *n* vantaggio *m*.

head teacher *n (of primary or lower secondary school)* direttore *m* (-trice *f*) di scuola; *(of upper secondary school)* preside *mf*.

head waiter *n* capocameriere *m*.

heal [hiːl] ◇ *vt* curare ◇ *vi* guarire.

health [helθ] *n* salute *f*; **to be in good ~** essere in buona salute; **to be in poor ~** essere in cattive condizioni di salute; **your (very) good ~!** alla tua salute!

health centre *n* centro *m* sanitario.

health food *n* cibo *m* naturale.

health food shop *n* negozio *m* di prodotti naturali.

health insurance *n* assicurazione *f* contro le malattie.

healthy ['helθɪ] *adj* sano(-a).

heap [hiːp] *n* mucchio *m*; **~s of** *(inf)* un mucchio di.

hear [hɪəʳ] (*pt & pp* **heard** [hɜːd]) ◇ *vt* sentire; *(case, evidence)* esaminare ◇ *vi* sentire; **to ~ about sthg** sapere OR sentire di qc; **to ~ from sb** ricevere notizie da qn; **to have heard of** aver sentito parlare di.

hearing ['hɪərɪŋ] *n (sense)* udito *m*; *(at court)* udienza *f*; **to be hard of ~** esser duro d'orecchi.

hearing aid *n* apparecchio *m* acustico.

heart [hɑːt] *n* cuore *m*; **to know sthg (off) by ~** sapere qc a memoria; **to lose ~** scoraggiarsi.

◆ **hearts** *npl (in cards)* cuori *mpl*.

heart attack *n* infarto *m*.

heartbeat ['hɑːtbiːt] *n (rhythm)* battito *m* cardiaco.

heartburn ['hɑːtbɜːn] *n* bruciore *m* di stomaco.

heart condition *n*: **to have a ~** avere un disturbo cardiaco.

hearth [hɑːθ] *n* focolare *m*.

hearty ['hɑːtɪ] *adj (meal)* abbondante, sostanzioso(-a).

heat [hiːt] *n (warmth)* calore *m*; *(warm weather)* caldo *m*; *(of oven)* temperatura *f*.

◆ **heat up** *vt sep* riscaldare.

heater ['hiːtəʳ] *n (for room)* stufa *f*; *(radiator)* radiatore *m*; *(in car)* riscaldamento *m*; *(for water)* scaldabagno *m*.

heath [hiːθ] *n* brughiera *f*.

heather ['heðəʳ] *n* erica *f*.

heating ['hiːtɪŋ] *n* riscaldamento *m*.

heat wave *n* ondata *f* di caldo.

heave [hiːv] *vt (push)* spingere (con forza); *(pull)* tirare (con forza); *(lift)* sollevare (con forza).

Heaven ['hevn] *n* paradiso *m*.

heavily ['hevɪlɪ] *adv (smoke, drink)* molto; *(rain)* a dirotto.

heavy ['hevɪ] *adj* pesante; *(rain, traffic)* intenso(-a); *(fighting)* violento(-a); *(losses, defeat)* grave; **how ~ is it?** quanto pesa?; **to be a ~ smoker** essere un fumatore accanito.

heavy cream *n (Am) panna molto densa ad alto contenuto di grassi.*

heavy goods vehicle *n (Br)* veicolo *m* per trasporti pesanti.

heavy industry *n* industria *f* pesante.

heavy metal *n* heavy metal *m*.

heckle ['hekl] *vt* interrompere di continuo.

hectic ['hektɪk] *adj* frenetico(-a).

hedge [hedʒ] *n* siepe *f*.

hedgehog ['hedʒhɒg] *n* riccio *m*.

heel [hiːl] *n (of person)* calcagno *m*; *(of shoe)* tacco *m*.

hefty ['heftɪ] *adj (person)* robusto(-a); *(fine)* salato(-a).

height [haɪt] *n* altezza *f*; *(peak period)* apice *m*; **what ~ is it?** quanto è alto?

heir [eəʳ] *n* erede *m*.

heiress ['eərɪs] *n* erede *f*.

held [held] *pt & pp* → **hold**.

helicopter ['helɪkɒptəʳ] *n* elicottero *m*.

he'll [hiːl] = **he will**, = **he shall**.

Hell [hel] *n* inferno *m*.

hello [hə'ləʊ] *excl (as greeting)* ciao!; *(more formal)* buongiorno!; *(on phone)* pronto!; *(to attract attention)* ehi!

helmet ['helmɪt] *n* casco *m*.

help [help] ◇ *n* aiuto *m* ◇ *vt* aiutare; *(contribute to)* contribuire a ◇ *vi* aiutare, essere d'aiuto ◇ *excl* aiuto!; **I can't ~ it** non ci posso fare niente; **to ~ sb (to) do sthg** aiutare qn a fare qc; **to ~ o.s. (to sthg)** servirsi (di qc); **can I ~ you?** *(in shop)* desidera?

◆ **help out** *vi* aiutare, dare una mano.

helper ['helpəʳ] *n (assistant)* aiutante *mf*; *(Am: cleaner)* uomo *m* (donna *f*) delle pulizie.

helpful ['helpfʊl] *adj (person)* di grande aiuto; *(useful)* utile.

helping ['helpɪŋ] *n* porzione *f*.

helpless ['helplɪs] *adj* impotente; *(child)* indifeso(-a).

hem [hem] *n* orlo *m*.

hemophiliac [ˌhiːmə'fɪlɪæk] *n* emofiliaco *m* (-a *f*).

hemorrhage ['hemərɪdʒ] *n* emorragia *f*.

hen [hen] *n* gallina *f*.

hepatitis [ˌhepə'taɪtɪs] *n* epatite *f*.

her [hɜːʳ] ◇ *adj* il suo (la sua), i suoi (le sue) *(pl)* ◇ *pron (direct)* la; *(indirect)* le; *(after prep, stressed)* lei; **~ brother** suo fratello; **I know ~** la conosco; **it's ~** è lei; **send it to ~** mandaglielo, mandalo a lei; **tell ~** diglielo; **tell ~ that ...** dille che ...; **he's worse than ~** lui è peggio di lei.

herb [hɜːb] *n* erba *f*.

herbal tea ['hɜːbl-] *n* tè *m inv* d'erbe.

herd [hɜːd] *n (of cattle)* mandria *f*.

here [hɪəʳ] *adv* qui, qua; **~'s your book** eccoti il libro; **~ you are** eccoti (qui OR qua).

heritage ['herɪtɪdʒ] *n* eredità *f*, patrimonio *m*.

heritage centre *n centro informazioni in luoghi di interesse storico.*

hernia ['hɜːnjə] *n* ernia *f*.

hero ['hɪərəʊ] (*pl* **-es**) *n* eroe *m*.

heroin ['herəʊɪn] *n* eroina *f (droga)*.
heroine ['herəʊɪn] *n* eroina *f*.
heron ['herən] *n* airone *m*.
herring ['herɪŋ] *n* aringa *f*.
hers [hɜːz] *pron* il suo (la sua), i suoi (le sue) *(pl)*; **a friend of ~** un suo amico.
herself [hɜː'self] *pron (reflexive)* si; *(after prep)* se stessa, sé; **she did it ~** l'ha fatto da sola.
hesitant ['hezɪtənt] *adj* esitante.
hesitate ['hezɪteɪt] *vi* esitare.
hesitation [ˌhezɪ'teɪʃn] *n* esitazione *f*.
heterosexual [ˌhetərəʊ'sekʃʊəl] ◇ *adj* eterosessuale ◇ *n* eterosessuale *mf*.
hey [heɪ] *excl (inf)* ehi!
HGV *abbr* = **heavy goods vehicle**.
hi [haɪ] *excl (inf)* ciao!
hiccup ['hɪkʌp] *n*: **to have (the) ~s** avere il singhiozzo.
hide [haɪd] (*pt* **hid** [hɪd], *pp* **hidden** [hɪdn]) ◇ *vt* nascondere ◇ *vi* nascondersi ◇ *n (of animal)* pelle *f*.
hideous ['hɪdɪəs] *adj* raccapricciante.
hi-fi ['haɪfaɪ] *n* hi-fi *m inv*.
high [haɪ] ◇ *adj* alto(-a); *(price, speed, temperature)* alto, elevato(-a); *(wind)* forte; *(sound, voice)* acuto(-a), alto; *(inf: from drugs)* fatto(-a) ◇ *n (weather front)* anticiclone *m* ◇ *adv* alto, in alto; **how ~ is it?** quanto è alto?; **it's 10 metres ~** è alto 10 metri.
high chair *n* seggiolone *m*.
high-class *adj* di lusso.
Higher ['haɪəʳ] *n (Scot) esame sostenuto alla fine di studi secondari.*
higher education *n* istruzione *f* universitaria.
high heels *npl* tacchi *mpl* alti.
high jump *n* salto *m* in alto.
Highland Games ['haɪlənd-] *npl*: **the ~** *gare sportive disputate all'aperto nelle Highlands scozzesi.*
Highlands ['haɪləndz] *npl*: **the ~** le Highlands *fpl (regione montuosa nel nord della Scozia)*.
highlight ['haɪlaɪt] ◇ *n (best part)* clou *m inv* ◇ *vt (emphasize)* evidenziare.
◆ **highlights** *npl (of football match etc)* sintesi *f inv*; *(in hair)* colpi *mpl* di sole.
highly ['haɪlɪ] *adv (extremely)* molto; *(very well)* molto bene; **to think ~ of sb** avere grande stima di qn.
high-pitched [-'pɪtʃt] *adj* acuto(-a).
high-rise *adj* con tanti piani.
high school *n (in UK)* = scuola *f* secondaria inferiore e superiore; *(in US)* = scuola secondaria superiore.
high season *n* alta stagione *f*.
high-speed train *n* treno *m* ad alta velocità.
high street *n (Br)* strada *f* principale.
high tide *n* alta marea *f*.
highway ['haɪweɪ] *n (Am: between towns)* superstrada *f*; *(Br: any main road)* strada *f* principale.
Highway Code *n (Br)* codice *m* stradale.
hijack ['haɪdʒæk] *vt* dirottare.
hijacker ['haɪdʒækəʳ] *n* dirottatore *m* (-trice *f*).
hike [haɪk] ◇ *n* lunga camminata *f* ◇ *vi* fare una lunga camminata.
hiking ['haɪkɪŋ] *n*: **to go ~** andare a fare lunghe camminate.
hilarious [hɪ'leərɪəs] *adj* spassoso(-a).
hill [hɪl] *n* collina *f*, colle *m*.
hillwalking ['hɪlwɔːkɪŋ] *n*: **to go ~** fare lunghe camminate.
hilly ['hɪlɪ] *adj* collinoso(-a).
him [hɪm] *pron (direct)* lo; *(indirect)* gli; *(after prep, stressed)* lui; **I know**

~ lo conosco; **it's ~** è lui; **send it to ~** mandaglielo, mandalo a lui; **tell ~** diglielo; **tell ~ that** ... digli che ...; **she's worse than ~** lei è peggio di lui.

himself [hɪm'self] *pron (reflexive)* si; *(after prep)* se stesso, sé; **he did it ~** l'ha fatto da solo.

hinder ['hɪndəʳ] *vt* ostacolare.

Hindu ['hɪndu:] (*pl* **-s**) ◇ *adj* indù *(inv)* ◇ *n (person)* indù *mf inv*.

hinge [hɪndʒ] *n* cardine *m*.

hint [hɪnt] ◇ *n (indirect suggestion)* accenno *m*, allusione *f*; *(piece of advice)* consiglio *m*; *(slight amount)* accenno, punta *f* ◇ *vi*: **to ~ at sthg** alludere a qc.

hip [hɪp] *n* fianco *m*.

hippopotamus [ˌhɪpə'pɒtəməs] *n* ippopotamo *m*.

hippy ['hɪpɪ] *n* hippy *mf inv*.

hire ['haɪəʳ] *vt (car, bicycle, television)* noleggiare; **'for ~'** *(boats)* 'a noleggio'; *(taxi)* 'libero'.

◆ **hire out** *vt sep (car, bicycle, television)* dare a noleggio.

hire car *n (Br)* vettura *f* a noleggio.

hire purchase *n (Br)* acquisto *m* rateale.

his [hɪz] ◇ *adj* il suo (la sua), i suoi (le sue) *(pl)* ◇ *pron* il suo (la sua), i suoi (le sue) *(pl)*; **~ brother** suo fratello; **a friend of ~** un suo amico.

historical [hɪ'stɒrɪkəl] *adj* storico(-a).

history ['hɪstərɪ] *n* storia *f*; *(record)* passato *m*.

hit [hɪt] (*pt & pp* **hit**) ◇ *vt* colpire; *(bang)* sbattere, picchiare ◇ *n (record, play, film)* successo *m*.

hit-and-run *adj*: **~ accident** *incidente in cui l'automobilista colpevole non si ferma a prestare soccorso.*

hitch [hɪtʃ] ◇ *n (problem)* contrattempo *m* ◇ *vt*: **to ~ a lift** farsi dare un passaggio ◇ *vi* fare l'autostop.

hitchhike ['hɪtʃhaɪk] *vi* fare l'autostop.

hitchhiker ['hɪtʃhaɪkəʳ] *n* autostoppista *mf*.

hive [haɪv] *n (of bees)* alveare *m*.

HIV-positive *adj* sieropositivo(-a).

hoarding ['hɔ:dɪŋ] *n (Br: for adverts)* tabellone *m* per pubblicità.

hoarse [hɔ:s] *adj* rauco(-a).

hoax [həʊks] *n* burla *f*.

hob [hɒb] *n* piano *m* di cottura.

hobby ['hɒbɪ] *n* hobby *m inv*, passatempo *m*.

hock [hɒk] *n (wine)* vino *m* bianco del Reno.

hockey ['hɒkɪ] *n (on grass)* hockey *m* su prato; *(Am: ice hockey)* hockey su ghiaccio.

hoe [həʊ] *n* zappa *f*.

Hogmanay ['hɒgmənei] *n (Scot)* l'ultimo *m* dell'anno.

hold [həʊld] (*pt & pp* **held**) ◇ *vt* tenere; *(contain)* contenere; *(possess)* avere, possedere ◇ *vi (weather)* mantenersi; *(luck, offer)* permanere; *(on telephone)* restare in linea ◇ *n (grip)* presa *f*; *(of ship)* stiva *f*; *(of aircraft)* bagagliaio *m*; **to ~ sb prisoner** tenere prigioniero qn; **~ the line, please** resti in linea, per favore.

◆ **hold back** *vt sep (restrain)* trattenere; *(keep secret)* tenere segreto.

◆ **hold on** *vi (wait)* aspettare, attendere; *(on telephone)* restare in linea; **to ~ on to sthg** *(grip)* tenersi (stretto) a qc.

◆ **hold out** *vt sep (hand)* porgere, tendere.

◆ **hold up** *vt sep (delay)* bloccare.

holdall ['həʊldɔ:l] *n (Br)* borsone *m* da viaggio.

holder ['həʊldəʳ] *n (of passport, licence)* titolare *mf*, proprietario *m* (-a *f*); *(container)* contenitore *m*.

holdup ['həʊldʌp] *n (delay)* ritardo *m*.

hole [həʊl] *n (in sock, wall)* buco *m*; *(in ground, golf)* buca *f*.

holiday [ˈhɒlɪdeɪ] ◇ *n (Br: period of time)* vacanze *fpl*; *(time off work)* ferie *fpl*; *(public holiday)* festa *f* ◇ *vi (Br)* trascorrere le vacanze; **to be on ~** essere in vacanza; **to go on ~** andare in vacanza.

holidaymaker [ˈhɒlɪdɪˌmeɪkəʳ] *n (Br)* villeggiante *mf*.

holiday pay *n (Br)* retribuzione *f* delle ferie.

Holland [ˈhɒlənd] *n* l'Olanda *f*.

hollow [ˈhɒləʊ] *adj* cavo(-a).

holly [ˈhɒlɪ] *n* agrifoglio *m*.

Hollywood [ˈhɒlɪwʊd] *n* Hollywood *f*.

holy [ˈhəʊlɪ] *adj* sacro(-a).

home [həʊm] ◇ *n* casa *f*; *(own country)* patria *f*; *(for old people)* istituto *m*, ricovero *m* ◇ *adv* a casa ◇ *adj (not foreign)* interno(-a), nazionale; *(cooking)* casereccio(-a); **at ~** *(in one's house)* a casa; **to make o.s. at ~** fare come se si fosse a casa propria; **to go ~** andare a casa; **to leave ~** *(for good)* andarsene di casa; **~ address** indirizzo *m* di casa; **~ number** numero *m* (telefonico) di casa.

home economics *n* economia *f* domestica.

home help *n (Br)* collaboratore *m* domestico (collaboratrice domestica *f*).

homeless [ˈhəʊmlɪs] *npl*: **the ~** i senzatetto.

homemade [ˌhəʊmˈmeɪd] *adj (food)* casereccio(-a).

homeopathic [ˌhəʊmɪəʊˈpæθɪk] *adj* omeopatico(-a).

home page *n* (COMPUT) home page *f inv*.

Home Secretary *n (Br)* ministro *m* degli Interni.

homesick [ˈhəʊmsɪk] *adj*: **to be ~** avere nostalgia di casa.

homework [ˈhəʊmwɜːk] *n* compiti *mpl* a casa.

homosexual [ˌhɒməˈsekʃʊəl] ◇ *adj* omosessuale ◇ *n* omosessuale *mf*.

honest [ˈɒnɪst] *adj (trustworthy)* onesto(-a); *(frank)* sincero(-a), franco(-a).

honestly [ˈɒnɪstlɪ] *adv (truthfully)* onestamente; *(frankly)* sinceramente, francamente.

honey [ˈhʌnɪ] *n* miele *m*.

honeymoon [ˈhʌnɪmuːn] *n* luna *f* di miele, viaggio *m* di nozze.

honor [ˈɒnər] *(Am)* = **honour**.

honour [ˈɒnəʳ] *n (Br)* onore *m*.

honourable [ˈɒnrəbl] *adj* onorevole.

hood [hʊd] *n (of jacket, coat)* cappuccio *m*; *(on convertible car)* capote *f inv*; *(Am: car bonnet)* cofano *m*.

hoof [huːf] *n* zoccolo *m*.

hook [hʊk] *n* gancio *m*; *(for fishing)* amo *m*; **off the ~** *(telephone)* staccato.

hooligan [ˈhuːlɪgən] *n* teppista *mf*, hooligan *mf inv*.

hoop [huːp] *n* cerchio *m*.

hoot [huːt] *vi (driver)* suonare il clacson.

Hoover® [ˈhuːvəʳ] *n (Br)* aspirapolvere *m inv*.

hop [hɒp] *vi (person)* saltellare su una gamba.

hope [həʊp] ◇ *n* speranza *f* ◇ *vt* sperare; **to ~ for sthg** sperare in qc; **to ~ to do sthg** sperare di fare qc; **I ~ so** spero di sì.

hopeful [ˈhəʊpfʊl] *adj (optimistic)* fiducioso(-a).

hopefully [ˈhəʊpfəlɪ] *adv (with luck)* se tutto va bene.

hopeless [ˈhəʊplɪs] *adj (without any hope)* disperato(-a); **he's ~!** *(inf)* è un disastro!

hops [hɒps] *npl* luppolo *m*.

horizon [həˈraɪzn] *n* orizzonte *m*.

horizontal [ˌhɒrɪˈzɒntl] *adj* orizzontale.

horn [hɔːn] *n (of car)* clacson *m inv; (on animal)* corno *m*.

horoscope [ˈhɒrəskəʊp] *n* oroscopo *m*.

horrible [ˈhɒrəbl] *adj* orribile.

horrid [ˈhɒrɪd] *adj (very bad)* orrendo(-a); *(unkind)* odioso(-a); *(food, drink)* pessimo(-a).

horrific [hɒˈrɪfɪk] *adj* orripilante, terrificante.

hors d'oeuvre [hɔːˈdɜːvrə] *n* antipasto *m*.

horse [hɔːs] *n* cavallo *m*.

horseback [ˈhɔːsbæk] *n*: **on ~** a cavallo.

horse chestnut *n* ippocastano *m*.

horse-drawn carriage *n* carrozza *f* a cavalli.

horsepower [ˈhɔːsˌpaʊə^r] *n* cavallo *m* vapore.

horse racing *n* ippica *f*.

horseradish (sauce) [ˈhɔːsˌrædɪʃ-] *n* salsa *f* di rafano.

horse riding *n* equitazione *f*.

horseshoe [ˈhɔːsʃuː] *n* ferro *m* di cavallo.

hose [həʊz] *n (hosepipe)* tubo *m* per annaffiare.

hosepipe [ˈhəʊzpaɪp] *n* tubo *m* per annaffiare.

hosiery [ˈhəʊzɪərɪ] *n* calzetteria *f*.

hospitable [hɒˈspɪtəbl] *adj* ospitale.

hospital [ˈhɒspɪtl] *n* ospedale *m*; **in ~** all'ospedale.

hospitality [ˌhɒspɪˈtælətɪ] *n* ospitalità *f*.

host [həʊst] *n (of party, event)* ospite *m*; *(of show, TV programme)* conduttore *m* (-trice *f*).

hostage [ˈhɒstɪdʒ] *n* ostaggio *m*.

hostel [ˈhɒstl] *n (youth hostel)* ostello *m*.

hostess [ˈhəʊstes] *n (on aeroplane)* hostess *f inv*; *(of party, event)* ospite *f*.

hostile [*Br* ˈhɒstaɪl, *Am* ˈhɒstl] *adj* ostile.

hostility [hɒˈstɪlətɪ] *n* ostilità *f*.

hot [hɒt] *adj* caldo(-a); *(spicy)* piccante; **to be ~** *(person)* aver caldo; **it's ~** fa caldo.

hot chocolate *n* cioccolata *f* calda.

hot-cross bun *n panino dolce con uvetta e spezie tipico del periodo pasquale.*

hot dog *n* hot dog *m inv (panino imbottito con würstel e senape).*

hotel [həʊˈtel] *n* hotel *m inv*, albergo *m*.

hot line *n* telefono *m* rosso.

hotplate [ˈhɒtpleɪt] *n* piastra *f*.

hotpot [ˈhɒtpɒt] *n spezzatino di carne con patate.*

hot-water bottle *n* borsa *f* dell'acqua calda.

hour [ˈaʊə^r] *n* ora *f*; **I've been waiting for ~s** è un secolo che aspetto.

hourly [ˈaʊəlɪ] ◇ *adj (per hour)* orario(-a); *(every hour)* ogni ora ◇ *adv (per hour)* a ore; *(every hour)* ogni ora.

house [*n* haʊs, *pl* ˈhaʊzɪz, *vb* haʊz] ◇ *n* casa *f*; (SCH) *uno dei gruppi in cui sono divisi gli alunni di una scuola media o superiore in occasione di competizioni sportive ecc.* ◇ *vt (person)* alloggiare.

household [ˈhaʊshəʊld] *n* famiglia *f*.

housekeeping [ˈhaʊsˌkiːpɪŋ] *n* amministrazione *f* della casa.

House of Commons *n (Br)* Camera *f* dei Comuni.

House of Lords *n (Br)* Camera *f* dei Lord.

Houses of Parliament *npl (Br: building)* palazzo *m* del Parlamento.

housewife [ˈhaʊswaɪf] (*pl* **-wives** [-waɪvz]) *n* casalinga *f*.

house wine *n* vino *m* della casa.

housewives *pl* → **housewife**.

housework [ˈhaʊswɜːk] *n* lavori *mpl* di casa.

housing ['haʊzɪŋ] *n* alloggi *mpl.*
housing estate *n (Br)* complesso *m* residenziale.
housing project *(Am)* = **housing estate**.
hovercraft ['hɒvəkrɑ:ft] *n* hovercraft *m inv*.
hoverport ['hɒvəpɔ:t] *n* porto *m* per hovercraft.
how [haʊ] *adv* **1.** *(asking about way or manner)* come; ~ **do you get there?** come ci si arriva?; ~ **does it work?** come funziona?; **tell me ~ to do it** dimmi come devo fare.
2. *(asking about health, quality)* come; ~ **are you?** come stai?; ~ **are you doing?** come va?; ~ **are things?** come vanno le cose?; ~ **do you do?** piacere!; ~ **is your room?** com'è la tua camera?
3. *(asking about degree, amount)*: ~ **tall is he?** quanto è alto?; ~ **far is it?** quanto dista?; ~ **long will it take?** quanto tempo ci vorrà?; ~ **many?** quanti(-e)?; ~ **much?** quanto(-a)?; ~ **much is it?** quant'è?; ~ **old are you?** quanti anni hai?
4. *(in phrases)*: ~ **about some coffee?** cosa ne diresti di un caffè?; ~ **lovely!** che bello!
however [haʊ'evəʳ] *adv (nevertheless)* tuttavia; ~ **difficult it is** per quanto sia difficile.
howl [haʊl] *vi* ululare.
HP *abbr* = **hire purchase**.
HQ *n (abbr of headquarters)* Q.G. *m.*
hub airport [hʌb-] *n* aeroporto *m* principale.
hubcap ['hʌbkæp] *n* coprimozzo *m.*
hug [hʌg] ◇ *vt* abbracciare ◇ *n*: **to give sb a ~** abbracciare qn.
huge [hju:dʒ] *adj* enorme.
hull [hʌl] *n* scafo *m.*
hum [hʌm] *vi (bee, machine)* ronzare; *(person)* canterellare.
human ['hju:mən] ◇ *adj* umano(-a) ◇ *n*: ~ **(being)** essere *m* umano.
humanities [hju:'mænətɪz] *npl* materie *fpl* umanistiche.
human rights *npl* diritti *mpl* dell'uomo.
humble ['hʌmbl] *adj* umile.
humid ['hju:mɪd] *adj* umido(-a).
humidity [hju:'mɪdətɪ] *n* umidità *f.*
humiliating [hju:'mɪlɪeɪtɪŋ] *adj* umiliante.
humiliation [hju:,mɪlɪ'eɪʃn] *n* umiliazione *f.*
hummus ['hʊməs] *n salsetta cremosa a base di ceci, aglio e pasta di sesamo.*
humor ['hju:mər] *(Am)* = **humour**.
humorous ['hju:mərəs] *adj (story)* umoristico(-a); *(person)* spiritoso(-a).
humour ['hju:məʳ] *n* umorismo *m*; **sense of ~** senso *m* dell'umorismo.
hump [hʌmp] *n (bump)* dosso *m*; *(of camel)* gobba *f.*
humpbacked bridge ['hʌmpbækt-] *n* ponte *m* a schiena d'asino.
hunch [hʌntʃ] *n* impressione *f.*
hundred ['hʌndrəd] *num* cento; **a ~** cento, → **six**.
hundredth ['hʌndrətθ] *num* centesimo(-a), → **sixth**.
hundredweight ['hʌndrədweɪt] *n (in UK)* = 50,8 kg; *(in US)* = 45,4 kg.
hung [hʌŋ] *pt & pp* → **hang**.
Hungarian [hʌŋ'geərɪən] ◇ *adj* ungherese ◇ *n (person)* ungherese *mf*; *(language)* ungherese *m.*
Hungary ['hʌŋgərɪ] *n* l'Ungheria *f.*
hunger ['hʌŋgəʳ] *n* fame *f.*
hungry ['hʌŋgrɪ] *adj* affamato(-a); **to be ~** avere fame.
hunt [hʌnt] ◇ *n (Br: for foxes)* cac-

cia *f* ◇ *vt & vi* cacciare; **to ~ (for sb/sthg)** *(search)* cercare (qn/qc).

hunting ['hʌntɪŋ] *n* caccia *f*.

hurdle ['hɜːdl] *n* (SPORT) ostacolo *m*.

hurl [hɜːl] *vt (throw)* scaraventare, scagliare.

hurricane ['hʌrɪkən] *n* uragano *m*.

hurry ['hʌrɪ] ◇ *vt (person)* mettere fretta a ◇ *vi* affrettarsi, sbrigarsi ◇ *n*: **to be in a ~** avere fretta; **to do sthg in a ~** fare qc in fretta.

◆ **hurry up** *vi* sbrigarsi.

hurt [hɜːt] (*pt & pp* **hurt**) ◇ *vt (injure)* fare male a; *(emotionally)* ferire ◇ *vi* far male; **my arm ~s** mi fa male il braccio; **I ~ my arm** mi sono fatto male al braccio; **to ~ o.s.** farsi male.

husband ['hʌzbənd] *n* marito *m*.

hustle ['hʌsl] *n*: **~ and bustle** attività *f* febbrile.

hut [hʌt] *n* capanna *f*.

hyacinth ['haɪəsɪnθ] *n* giacinto *m*.

hydrofoil ['haɪdrəfɔɪl] *n* aliscafo *m*.

hygiene ['haɪdʒiːn] *n* igiene *f*.

hygienic [haɪ'dʒiːnɪk] *adj* igienico(-a).

hymn [hɪm] *n* inno *m*.

hypermarket ['haɪpəˌmɑːkɪt] *n* ipermercato *m*.

hyphen ['haɪfn] *n* trattino *m*.

hypocrite ['hɪpəkrɪt] *n* ipocrita *mf*.

hypodermic needle [ˌhaɪpə'dɜːmɪk-] *n* ago *m* ipodermico.

hysterical [hɪs'terɪkl] *adj (person)* isterico(-a); *(inf: very funny)* esilarante.

I

I [aɪ] *pron* io; **I'm tall** sono alto.
ice [aɪs] *n* ghiaccio *m*; *(ice cream)* gelato *m*.
iceberg [ˈaɪsbɜːg] *n* iceberg *m inv*.
iceberg lettuce *n* lattuga *f* iceberg.
icebox [ˈaɪsbɒks] *n (Am: fridge)* frigorifero *m*.
ice-cold *adj* ghiacciato(-a).
ice cream *n* gelato *m*.
ice cube *n* cubetto *m* di ghiaccio.
ice hockey *n* hockey *m* su ghiaccio.
Iceland [ˈaɪslənd] *n* l'Islanda *f*.
ice lolly *n (Br)* ghiacciolo *m*.
ice rink *n* pista *f* di pattinaggio su ghiaccio.
ice skates *npl* pattini *mpl* da ghiaccio.
ice-skating *n* pattinaggio *m* su ghiaccio; **to go ~** andare a pattinare sul ghiaccio.
icicle [ˈaɪsɪkl] *n* ghiacciolo *m*.
icing [ˈaɪsɪŋ] *n* glassa *f*.
icing sugar *n* zucchero *m* a velo.
icy [ˈaɪsɪ] *adj (covered with ice)* ghiacciato(-a); *(very cold)* gelido(-a), gelato(-a).
I'd [aɪd] = **I would, I had**.
ID *n (abbr of identification)* documento *m* (d'identità).
ID card *n* carta *f* d'identità.
IDD code *n* prefisso *m* (teleselettivo) internazionale.
idea [aɪˈdɪə] *n* idea *f*; **I've no ~** non ne ho idea.
ideal [aɪˈdɪəl] ◇ *adj* ideale ◇ *n* ideale *m*.
ideally [aɪˈdɪəlɪ] *adv* idealmente; *(suited)* perfettamente.
identical [aɪˈdentɪkl] *adj* identico(-a).
identification [aɪˌdentɪfɪˈkeɪʃn] *n (document)* documento *m* d'identità.
identify [aɪˈdentɪfaɪ] *vt* identificare.
identity [aɪˈdentətɪ] *n* identità *f inv*.
idiom [ˈɪdɪəm] *n (phrase)* espressione *f* idiomatica.
idiot [ˈɪdɪət] *n* idiota *mf*.
idle [ˈaɪdl] ◇ *adj (lazy)* ozioso(-a); *(not working)* inattivo(-a); *(unemployed)* disoccupato(-a) ◇ *vi (engine)* girare al minimo.
idol [ˈaɪdl] *n (person)* idolo *m*.
idyllic [ɪˈdɪlɪk] *adj* idilliaco(-a).
i.e. *(abbr of id est)* cioè.
if [ɪf] *conj* se; **~ I were you** se fossi in te; **~ not** *(otherwise)* se no.
ignition [ɪgˈnɪʃn] *n* (AUT) accensione *f*.
ignorant [ˈɪgnərənt] *adj* ignorante.
ignore [ɪgˈnɔːʳ] *vt* ignorare.
ill [ɪl] *adj (in health)* malato(-a);

(bad) cattivo(-a).

I'll [aɪl] = **I will, I shall**.

illegal [ɪ'li:gl] *adj* illegale.

illegible [ɪ'ledʒəbl] *adj* illeggibile.

illegitimate [ˌɪlɪ'dʒɪtɪmət] *adj* illegittimo(-a).

illiterate [ɪ'lɪtərət] *adj* analfabeta.

illness ['ɪlnɪs] *n* malattia *f*.

illuminate [ɪ'lu:mɪneɪt] *vt* illuminare.

illusion [ɪ'lu:ʒn] *n* illusione *f*.

illustration [ˌɪlə'streɪʃn] *n* illustrazione *f*.

I'm [aɪm] = **I am**.

image ['ɪmɪdʒ] *n* immagine *f*.

imaginary [ɪ'mædʒɪnrɪ] *adj* immaginario(-a).

imagination [ɪˌmædʒɪ'neɪʃn] *n* immaginazione *f*.

imagine [ɪ'mædʒɪn] *vt* immaginare.

imitate ['ɪmɪteɪt] *vt* imitare.

imitation [ˌɪmɪ'teɪʃn] ◇ *n* imitazione *f* ◇ *adj* finto(-a).

immaculate [ɪ'mækjʊlət] *adj (very clean)* immacolato(-a), lindo(-a); *(perfect)* impeccabile.

immature [ˌɪmə'tjʊəʳ] *adj* immaturo(-a).

immediate [ɪ'mi:djət] *adj (without delay)* immediato(-a).

immediately [ɪ'mi:djətlɪ] ◇ *adv (at once)* immediatamente, subito ◇ *conj (Br)* non appena.

immense [ɪ'mens] *adj* immenso(-a).

immersion heater [ɪ'mɜ:ʃn-] *n* scaldabagno *m inv* elettrico.

immigrant ['ɪmɪgrənt] *n* immigrato *m* (-a *f*).

immigration [ˌɪmɪ'greɪʃn] *n (to country)* immigrazione *f*; *(section of airport, port)* dogana *f*.

imminent ['ɪmɪnənt] *adj* imminente.

immune [ɪ'mju:n] *adj*: **to be ~ to** (MED) essere immune da.

immunity [ɪ'mju:nətɪ] *n* (MED) immunità *f*.

immunize ['ɪmju:naɪz] *vt* immunizzare.

impact ['ɪmpækt] *n* impatto *m*.

impair [ɪm'peəʳ] *vt* danneggiare.

impatient [ɪm'peɪʃnt] *adj* impaziente; **to be ~ to do sthg** essere impaziente di fare qc.

imperative [ɪm'perətɪv] *n* (GRAMM) imperativo *m*.

imperfect [ɪm'pɜ:fɪkt] *n* (GRAMM) imperfetto *m*.

impersonate [ɪm'pɜ:səneɪt] *vt (for amusement)* imitare.

impertinent [ɪm'pɜ:tɪnənt] *adj* impertinente.

implement [*n* 'ɪmplɪmənt, *vb* 'ɪmplɪment] ◇ *n* attrezzo *m*; *(for cooking)* utensile *m* ◇ *vt* mettere in atto, realizzare.

implication [ˌɪmplɪ'keɪʃn] *n (consequence)* implicazione *f*.

imply [ɪm'plaɪ] *vt (suggest)* lasciar intendere, sottintendere.

impolite [ˌɪmpə'laɪt] *adj* scortese.

import [*n* 'ɪmpɔ:t, *vb* ɪm'pɔ:t] ◇ *n* merce *f* d'importazione ◇ *vt* importare.

importance [ɪm'pɔ:tns] *n* importanza *f*.

important [ɪm'pɔ:tnt] *adj* importante.

impose [ɪm'pəʊz] ◇ *vt* imporre ◇ *vi* approfittare; **to ~ sthg on** imporre qc a.

impossible [ɪm'pɒsəbl] *adj* impossibile.

impractical [ɪm'præktɪkl] *adj* non pratico(-a).

impress [ɪm'pres] *vt* fare una buona impressione a.

impression [ɪm'preʃn] *n* impressione *f*.

impressive [ɪm'presɪv] *adj* impressionante.

improbable [ɪm'prɒbəbl] *adj* *(event)* improbabile; *(story, excuse)* inverosimile.

improper [ɪm'prɒpəʳ] *adj (incorrect, illegal)* scorretto(-a); *(rude)* sconveniente.

improve [ɪm'pru:v] *vt & vi* migliorare.

◆ **improve on** *vt fus* migliorare.

improvement [ɪm'pru:vmənt] *n (in weather, health)* miglioramento *m*; *(to home)* miglioria *f*.

improvise ['ɪmprəvaɪz] *vi* improvvisare.

impulse ['ɪmpʌls] *n* impulso *m*; **on ~** d'impulso.

impulsive [ɪm'pʌlsɪv] *adj* impulsivo(-a).

in [ɪn] ◇ *prep* 1. *(expressing place, position)* in; **~ a box** in una scatola; **~ the bedroom** in camera da letto; **~ the street** per strada; **~ Scotland** in Scozia; **~ Sheffield** a Sheffield; **~ the United States** negli Stati Uniti; **~ here/there** qui/là dentro; **~ the sun** al sole; **~ the rain** sotto la pioggia; **~ the middle** al centro; **an article ~ the paper** un articolo sul giornale.

2. *(participating in)* in; **who's ~ the play?** chi recita nella commedia?

3. *(expressing arrangement)* in; **~ a row** in fila; **they come ~ packs of three** vengono venduti in pacchetti da tre.

4. *(with time)*: **~ April** in aprile; **~ the afternoon** di OR nel pomeriggio; **at ten o'clock ~ the morning** alle dieci del mattino; **~ 1994** nel 1994; **it'll be ready ~ an hour** sarà pronto fra un'ora; **they're arriving ~ two weeks** arriveranno fra due settimane.

5. *(expressing means)*: **to write ~ ink** scrivere a penna; **~ writing** per iscritto; **they were talking ~ English** parlavano in inglese.

6. *(wearing)*: **the man ~ the blue jacket** l'uomo con la giacca blu; **dressed ~ white** vestito di bianco.

7. *(expressing state)*: **~ a bad mood** di pessimo umore; **to be ~ a hurry** essere di fretta; **to cry ~ pain** gridare di dolore; **to be ~ pain** soffrire; **~ ruins** in rovina.

8. *(with regard to)*: **a rise ~ prices** un aumento dei prezzi; **to be 50 metres ~ length** essere lungo 50 metri.

9. *(with numbers, ratios)*: **one ~ ten** uno su dieci; **~ dozens** a dozzine.

10. *(expressing age)*: **she's ~ her thirties** è sulla trentina.

11. *(with colours)*: **it comes ~ green or blue** è disponibile in verde o in blu.

12. *(with superlatives)* di; **the best ~ the world** il migliore del mondo.

◇ *adv* 1. *(inside)* dentro; **you can go ~ now** ora può entrare; **come ~!** avanti!

2. *(at home, work)*: **she's not ~** non c'è; **to stay ~** stare a casa.

3. *(train, bus, plane)*: **the train's not ~ yet** il treno non è ancora arrivato.

4. *(tide)*: **the tide is ~** c'è alta marea.

◇ *adj (inf: fashionable)* alla moda.

inability [,ɪnə'bɪlətɪ] *n*: **~ (to do sthg)** incapacità *f* (di fare qc).

inaccessible [,ɪnək'sesəbl] *adj* inaccessibile.

inaccurate [ɪn'ækjʊrət] *adj* inesatto(-a), impreciso(-a).

inadequate [ɪn'ædɪkwət] *adj* inadeguato(-a).

inappropriate [ɪnə'prəʊprɪət] *adj* non adatto(-a).

inauguration [ɪ,nɔ:gjʊ'reɪʃn] *n* inaugurazione *f*; *(of president etc)* insediamento *m* in carica.

incapable [ɪn'keɪpəbl] *adj*: **to be ~ of doing sthg** essere incapace di fare qc.

incense ['ɪnsens] *n* incenso *m*.

incentive [ɪn'sentɪv] *n* incentivo *m*.

inch [ɪntʃ] *n* = 2,5 cm, pollice *m*.
incident [ˈɪnsɪdənt] *n* episodio *m*, caso *m*.
incidentally [ˌɪnsɪˈdentəlɪ] *adv* a proposito.
incline [ˈɪnklaɪn] *n* pendio *m*.
inclined [ɪnˈklaɪnd] *adj (sloping)* inclinato(-a); **to be ~ to do sthg** essere propenso(-a) a fare qc.
include [ɪnˈkluːd] *vt* includere, comprendere.
included [ɪnˈkluːdɪd] *adj (in price)* compreso(-a); **to be ~ in sthg** essere compreso in qc.
including [ɪnˈkluːdɪŋ] *prep* compreso(-a).
inclusive [ɪnˈkluːsɪv] *adj*: **from the 8th to the 16th ~** dall'8 al 16 compreso; **~ of VAT** IVA compresa.
income [ˈɪŋkʌm] *n* reddito *m*.
income support *n (Br)* = sussidio *m* di indigenza.
income tax *n* imposta *f* sul reddito.
incoming [ˈɪnˌkʌmɪŋ] *adj* in arrivo.
incompetent [ɪnˈkɒmpɪtənt] *adj* incompetente.
incomplete [ˌɪnkəmˈpliːt] *adj* incompleto(-a).
inconsiderate [ˌɪnkənˈsɪdərət] *adj* sconsiderato(-a).
inconsistent [ˌɪnkənˈsɪstənt] *adj* incoerente.
incontinent [ɪnˈkɒntɪnənt] *adj* incontinente.
inconvenient [ˌɪnkənˈviːnjənt] *adj* scomodo(-a).
incorporate [ɪnˈkɔːpəreɪt] *vt* incorporare.
incorrect [ˌɪnkəˈrekt] *adj (answer, number)* sbagliato(-a); *(information)* inesatto(-a).
increase [*n* ˈɪnkriːs, *vb* ɪnˈkriːs] ◇ *n* aumento *m* ◇ *vt & vi* aumentare; **an ~ in sthg** un aumento di qc.
increasingly [ɪnˈkriːsɪŋlɪ] *adv* sempre più.
incredible [ɪnˈkredəbl] *adj* incredibile.
incredibly [ɪnˈkredəblɪ] *adv (very)* incredibilmente.
incur [ɪnˈkɜːʳ] *vt* incorrere in.
indecisive [ˌɪndɪˈsaɪsɪv] *adj* indeciso(-a).
indeed [ɪnˈdiːd] *adv (for emphasis)* davvero; *(certainly)* certamente.
indefinite [ɪnˈdefɪnɪt] *adj (time, number)* indefinito(-a), indeterminato(-a); *(answer, opinion)* vago(-a).
indefinitely [ɪnˈdefɪnətlɪ] *adv (closed, delayed)* indefinitamente.
independence [ˌɪndɪˈpendəns] *n* indipendenza *f*.
independent [ˌɪndɪˈpendənt] *adj* indipendente.
independently [ˌɪndɪˈpendəntlɪ] *adv* indipendentemente.
independent school *n (Br)* scuola *f* privata.
index [ˈɪndeks] *n (of book)* indice *m*; *(in library)* catalogo *m*.
index finger *n* dito *m* indice.
India [ˈɪndjə] *n* l'India *f*.
Indian [ˈɪndjən] ◇ *adj* indiano(-a) ◇ *n* indiano *m* (-a *f*); **an ~ restaurant** un ristorante indiano.
Indian Ocean *n*: **the ~** l'oceano *m* Indiano.
indicate [ˈɪndɪkeɪt] ◇ *vi* (AUT) mettere la freccia ◇ *vt* indicare.
indicator [ˈɪndɪkeɪtəʳ] *n* (AUT) indicatore *m* di direzione, freccia *f*.
indifferent [ɪnˈdɪfrənt] *adj (uninterested)* indifferente; *(not very good)* mediocre.
indigestion [ˌɪndɪˈdʒestʃn] *n* indigestione *f*.
indigo [ˈɪndɪgəʊ] *adj* indaco *(inv)*.
indirect [ˌɪndɪˈrekt] *adj* non diretto(-a).
individual [ˌɪndɪˈvɪdʒʊəl] ◇ *adj* individuale ◇ *n* individuo *m*.
individually [ˌɪndɪˈvɪdʒʊəlɪ] *adv* individualmente.

Indonesia [ˌɪndəˈniːzjə] *n* l'Indonesia *f*.

indoor [ˈɪndɔːʳ] *adj (swimming pool)* coperto(-a); *(sports)* praticato(-a) al coperto.

indoors [ˌɪnˈdɔːz] *adv* dentro.

indulge [ɪnˈdʌldʒ] *vi*: **to ~ in sthg** concedersi qc.

industrial [ɪnˈdʌstrɪəl] *adj* industriale.

industrial estate *n (Br)* zona *f* industriale.

industry [ˈɪndəstrɪ] *n* industria *f*.

inedible [ɪnˈedɪbl] *adj (unpleasant)* immangiabile; *(unsafe)* non commestibile.

inefficient [ˌɪnɪˈfɪʃnt] *adj* inefficiente.

inequality [ˌɪnɪˈkwɒlətɪ] *n* disuguaglianza *f*.

inevitable [ɪnˈevɪtəbl] *adj* inevitabile.

inevitably [ɪnˈevɪtəblɪ] *adv* inevitabilmente.

inexpensive [ˌɪnɪkˈspensɪv] *adj* poco costoso(-a).

infamous [ˈɪnfəməs] *adj* infame.

infant [ˈɪnfənt] *n* bambino *m* (-a *f*).

infant school *n (Br)* scuola *f* elementare *(per bambini da 5 a 7 anni)*.

infatuated [ɪnˈfætjʊeɪtɪd] *adj*: **to be ~ with** essere infatuato(-a) di.

infected [ɪnˈfektɪd] *adj* infetto(-a).

infectious [ɪnˈfekʃəs] *adj* contagioso(-a).

inferior [ɪnˈfɪərɪəʳ] *adj (person)* inferiore; *(goods, quality)* scadente.

infinite [ˈɪnfɪnət] *adj* infinito(-a).

infinitely [ˈɪnfɪnətlɪ] *adv* infinitamente.

infinitive [ɪnˈfɪnɪtɪv] *n* infinito *m*.

infinity [ɪnˈfɪnətɪ] *n (in space,* MATH*)* infinito *m*.

infirmary [ɪnˈfɜːmərɪ] *n* ospedale *m*.

inflamed [ɪnˈfleɪmd] *adj* (MED) infiammato(-a).

inflammation [ˌɪnfləˈmeɪʃn] *n* (MED) infiammazione *f*.

inflatable [ɪnˈfleɪtəbl] *adj* gonfiabile.

inflate [ɪnˈfleɪt] *vt* gonfiare.

inflation [ɪnˈfleɪʃn] *n (of prices)* inflazione *f*.

inflict [ɪnˈflɪkt] *vt* infliggere.

in-flight *adj* durante il volo.

influence [ˈɪnflʊəns] ◇ *vt* influenzare ◇ *n*: **~ (on)** influenza *f* (su).

inform [ɪnˈfɔːm] *vt* informare.

informal [ɪnˈfɔːml] *adj (occasion, dress)* informale.

information [ˌɪnfəˈmeɪʃn] *n* informazioni *fpl*; **a piece of ~** un'informazione.

information desk *n* banco *m* informazioni.

information office *n* ufficio *m* informazioni.

informative [ɪnˈfɔːmətɪv] *adj* istruttivo(-a).

infuriating [ɪnˈfjʊərɪeɪtɪŋ] *adj* molto irritante.

ingenious [ɪnˈdʒiːnjəs] *adj* ingegnoso(-a).

ingredient [ɪnˈgriːdjənt] *n* ingrediente *m*.

inhabit [ɪnˈhæbɪt] *vt* abitare.

inhabitant [ɪnˈhæbɪtənt] *n* abitante *mf*.

inhale [ɪnˈheɪl] *vi* aspirare.

inhaler [ɪnˈheɪləʳ] *n* inalatore *m*.

inherit [ɪnˈherɪt] *vt* ereditare.

inhibition [ˌɪnhɪˈbɪʃn] *n* inibizione *f*.

initial [ɪˈnɪʃl] ◇ *adj* iziale ◇ *vt* siglare.

◆ **initials** *npl* iniziali *fpl*.

initially [ɪˈnɪʃəlɪ] *adv* inizialmente.

initiative [ɪˈnɪʃətɪv] *n* iniziativa *f*.

injection [ɪnˈdʒekʃn] *n* iniezione *f*.

injure [ˈɪndʒəʳ] *vt (physically)* feri-

re; **to ~ o.s.** ferirsi; **to ~ one's arm** ferirsi al braccio.
injured ['ɪndʒəd] *adj (physically)* ferito(-a).
injury ['ɪndʒərɪ] *n (physical)* ferita *f*.
ink [ɪŋk] *n* inchiostro *m*.
inland [*adj* 'ɪnlənd, *adv* ɪn'lænd] ◇ *adj* interno(-a) ◇ *adv* nell'interno.
Inland Revenue *n (Br)* = Fisco *m*.
inn [ɪn] *n* locanda *f*.
inner ['ɪnər] *adj* interno(-a), interiore.
inner city *n quartieri vicino al centro di una città, generalmente sinonimo di problemi sociali.*
inner tube *n* camera *f* d'aria.
innocence ['ɪnəsəns] *n* innocenza *f*.
innocent ['ɪnəsənt] *adj* innocente.
inoculate [ɪ'nɒkjʊleɪt] *vt*: **to ~ sb (against sthg)** vaccinare qn (contro qc).
inoculation [ɪ,nɒkjʊ'leɪʃn] *n* vaccinazione *f*.
input ['ɪnpʊt] (*pt & pp* **input** OR **-ted**) *vt* (COMPUT) immettere.
inquire [ɪn'kwaɪər] = **enquire**.
inquiry [ɪn'kwaɪərɪ] = **enquiry**.
insane [ɪn'seɪn] *adj* pazzo(-a), matto(-a).
insect ['ɪnsekt] *n* insetto *m*.
insect repellent [-rə'pelənt] *n* insettifugo *m*.
insensitive [ɪn'sensətɪv] *adj* insensibile.
insert [ɪn'sɜːt] *vt* inserire, introdurre.
inside [ɪn'saɪd] ◇ *prep* dentro, all'interno di ◇ *adv* dentro ◇ *adj (internal)* interno(-a) ◇ *n*: **the ~** *(interior)* l'interno *m*; (AUT: *in UK)* la sinistra; (AUT: *in Europe, US)* la destra; **~ out** *(clothes)* a rovescio.
inside lane *n* (AUT) *(in UK)* corsia *f* di sinistra; *(in Europe, US)* corsia di destra.
inside leg *n* interno *m* gamba.
insight ['ɪnsaɪt] *n (glimpse)* idea *f*.
insignificant [,ɪnsɪg'nɪfɪkənt] *adj* insignificante.
insinuate [ɪn'sɪnjʊeɪt] *vt* insinuare.
insist [ɪn'sɪst] *vi* insistere; **to ~ on doing sthg** insistere nel fare qc.
insole ['ɪnsəʊl] *n* soletta *f*.
insolent ['ɪnsələnt] *adj* insolente.
insomnia [ɪn'sɒmnɪə] *n* insonnia *f*.
inspect [ɪn'spekt] *vt (object)* ispezionare; *(ticket, passport)* controllare.
inspection [ɪn'spekʃn] *n (of object)* ispezione *f*; *(of ticket, passport)* controllo *m*.
inspector [ɪn'spektər] *n (on bus, train)* controllore *m*; *(in police force)* ispettore *m* (-trice *f*).
inspiration [,ɪnspə'reɪʃn] *n* ispirazione *f*.
instal [ɪn'stɔːl] *(Am)* = **install**.
install [ɪn'stɔːl] *vt (Br)* installare.
installment [ɪn'stɔːlmənt] *(Am)* = **instalment**.
instalment [ɪn'stɔːlmənt] *n (payment)* rata *f*; *(episode)* puntata *f*, parte *f*.
instance ['ɪnstəns] *n (example, case)* esempio *m*, caso *m*; **for ~** per OR ad esempio.
instant ['ɪnstənt] ◇ *adj (results, success)* immediato(-a); *(coffee)* solubile ◇ *n (moment)* istante *m*.
instant coffee *n* caffè *m inv* solubile.
instead [ɪn'sted] *adv* invece; **~ of** invece di.
instep ['ɪnstep] *n* collo *m* del piede.
instinct ['ɪnstɪŋkt] *n* istinto *m*.
institute ['ɪnstɪtjuːt] *n* istituto *m*.
institution [,ɪnstɪ'tjuːʃn] *n* istituzione *f*.
instructions [ɪn'strʌkʃnz] *npl*

istruzioni *fpl*.
instructor [ɪnˈstrʌktəʳ] *n* istruttore *m* (-trice *f*).
instrument [ˈɪnstrʊmənt] *n* strumento *m*.
insufficient [ˌɪnsəˈfɪʃnt] *adj* insufficiente.
insulating tape [ˈɪnsjʊleɪtɪŋ-] *n* nastro *m* isolante.
insulation [ˌɪnsjʊˈleɪʃn] *n* *(material)* isolante *m*.
insulin [ˈɪnsjʊlɪn] *n* insulina *f*.
insult [*n* ˈɪnsʌlt, *vb* ɪnˈsʌlt] ◇ *n* insulto *m* ◇ *vt* insultare.
insurance [ɪnˈʃʊərəns] *n* assicurazione *f*.
insurance certificate *n* certificato *m* di assicurazione.
insurance company *n* compagnia *f* di assicurazione.
insurance policy *n* polizza *f* di assicurazione.
insure [ɪnˈʃʊəʳ] *vt* assicurare.
insured [ɪnˈʃʊəd] *adj*: **to be ~** essere assicurato(-a).
intact [ɪnˈtækt] *adj* intatto(-a).
intellectual [ˌɪntəˈlektjʊəl] ◇ *adj* intellettuale ◇ *n* intellettuale *mf*.
intelligence [ɪnˈtelɪdʒəns] *n* *(cleverness)* intelligenza *f*.
intelligent [ɪnˈtelɪdʒənt] *adj* intelligente.
intend [ɪnˈtend] *vt* *(mean)*: **to ~ to do sthg** avere intenzione di fare qc; **you weren't ~ed to know** non dovevi saperlo.
intense [ɪnˈtens] *adj* intenso(-a).
intensity [ɪnˈtensətɪ] *n* intensità *f*.
intensive [ɪnˈtensɪv] *adj* intensivo(-a).
intensive care *n* terapia *f* intensiva.
intent [ɪnˈtent] *adj*: **to be ~ on doing sthg** essere deciso(-a) a fare qc.
intention [ɪnˈtenʃn] *n* intenzione *f*.
intentional [ɪnˈtenʃənl] *adj* intenzionale.
intentionally [ɪnˈtenʃənəlɪ] *adv* intenzionalmente, apposta.
interchange [ˈɪntətʃeɪndʒ] *n* *(on motorway)* svincolo *m*.
Intercity® [ˌɪntəˈsɪtɪ] *n* *(Br)* intercity *m inv*.
intercom [ˈɪntəkɒm] *n* interfono *m*.
interest [ˈɪntrəst] ◇ *n* interesse *m* ◇ *vt* interessare; **to take an ~ in sthg** interessarsi di OR a qc.
interested [ˈɪntrəstɪd] *adj* interessato(-a); **to be ~ in sthg** interessarsi di qc.
interesting [ˈɪntrəstɪŋ] *adj* interessante.
interest rate *n* tasso *m* d'interesse.
interfere [ˌɪntəˈfɪəʳ] *vi* *(meddle)* immischiarsi; **to ~ with sthg** *(damage)* interferire con qc.
interference [ˌɪntəˈfɪərəns] *n* *(on TV, radio)* interferenza *f*.
interior [ɪnˈtɪərɪəʳ] ◇ *adj* interno(-a) ◇ *n* interno *m*.
intermediate [ˌɪntəˈmiːdjət] *adj* intermedio(-a).
intermission [ˌɪntəˈmɪʃn] *n* *(at cinema, theatre)* intervallo *m*.
internal [ɪnˈtɜːnl] *adj* interno(-a).
internal flight *n* volo *m* interno.
international [ˌɪntəˈnæʃənl] *adj* internazionale.
international flight *n* volo *m* internazionale.
Internet [ˈɪntənet] *n*: **the ~** Internet *m*.
interpret [ɪnˈtɜːprɪt] *vi* fare da interprete.
interpreter [ɪnˈtɜːprɪtəʳ] *n* interprete *mf*.
interrogate [ɪnˈterəgeɪt] *vt* interrogare.
interrupt [ˌɪntəˈrʌpt] *vt* interrompere.

intersection [ˌɪntəˈsekʃn] *n (of roads)* incrocio *m*.
interval [ˈɪntəvl] *n* intervallo *m*.
intervene [ˌɪntəˈviːn] *vi (person, event)* intervenire.
interview [ˈɪntəvjuː] ◇ *n (on TV, in magazine)* intervista *f*; *(for job)* colloquio *m* ◇ *vt (on TV, in magazine)* intervistare; *(for job)* fare un colloquio a.
interviewer [ˈɪntəvjuːəʳ] *n (on TV, in magazine)* intervistatore *m* (-trice *f*).
intestine [ɪnˈtestɪn] *n* intestino *m*.
intimate [ˈɪntɪmət] *adj* intimo(-a).
intimidate [ɪnˈtɪmɪdeɪt] *vt* intimidire.
into [ˈɪntʊ] *prep (inside)* in, dentro; *(against)* contro, in; *(concerning)* su; **4 ~ 20 goes 5 (times)** il 4 nel 20 ci sta 5 volte; **to translate ~ Italian** tradurre in italiano; **to change ~ sthg** trasformarsi in qc; **to be ~ sthg** *(inf: like)* essere appassionato di qc.
intolerable [ɪnˈtɒlrəbl] *adj* intollerabile.
intransitive [ɪnˈtrænzətɪv] *adj* intransitivo(-a).
intricate [ˈɪntrɪkət] *adj* intricato(-a).
intriguing [ɪnˈtriːgɪŋ] *adj* affascinante.
introduce [ˌɪntrəˈdjuːs] *vt* presentare; **I'd like to ~ you to Fred** ti presento Fred.
introduction [ˌɪntrəˈdʌkʃn] *n (to book, programme)* introduzione *f*; *(to person)* presentazione *f*.
introverted [ˈɪntrəˌvɜːtɪd] *adj* introverso(-a).
intruder [ɪnˈtruːdəʳ] *n* intruso *m* (-a *f*).
intuition [ˌɪntjuːˈɪʃn] *n (feeling)* intuizione *f*; *(faculty)* intuito *m*.
invade [ɪnˈveɪd] *vt* invadere.
invalid [*adj* ɪnˈvælɪd, *n* ˈɪnvəlɪd] ◇ *adj (ticket, cheque)* non valido(-a) ◇ *n* invalido *m* (-a *f*).
invaluable [ɪnˈvæljʊəbl] *adj* inestimabile.
invariably [ɪnˈveərɪəblɪ] *adv* sempre, invariabilmente.
invasion [ɪnˈveɪʒn] *n* invasione *f*.
invent [ɪnˈvent] *vt* inventare.
invention [ɪnˈvenʃn] *n* invenzione *f*.
inventory [ˈɪnventrɪ] *n* inventario *m*.
inverted commas [ɪnˈvɜːtɪd-] *npl* virgolette *fpl*.
invest [ɪnˈvest] ◇ *vt* investire ◇ *vi*: **to ~ in sthg** investire in qc.
investigate [ɪnˈvestɪgeɪt] *vt* indagare.
investigation [ɪnˌvestɪˈgeɪʃn] *n* indagine *f*.
investment [ɪnˈvestmənt] *n* investimento *m*.
invisible [ɪnˈvɪzɪbl] *adj* invisibile.
invitation [ˌɪnvɪˈteɪʃn] *n* invito *m*.
invite [ɪnˈvaɪt] *vt* invitare; **to ~ sb to do sthg** *(ask)* invitare qn a fare qc; **to ~ sb round** invitare qn.
invoice [ˈɪnvɔɪs] *n* fattura *f*.
involve [ɪnˈvɒlv] *vt (entail)* richiedere, comportare; **what does it ~?** che cosa comporta?; **to be ~d in sthg** essere coinvolto in qc.
involved [ɪnˈvɒlvd] *adj (entailed)* richiesto(-a), necessario(-a).
inwards [ˈɪnwədz] *adv* verso l'interno.
IOU *n* pagherò *m inv*.
IQ *n* Q.I. *m*.
Iran [ɪˈrɑːn] *n* l'Iran *m*.
Iraq [ɪˈrɑːk] *n* l'Iraq *m*.
Ireland [ˈaɪələnd] *n* l'Irlanda *f*.
iris [ˈaɪərɪs] (*pl* **-es**) *n (flower)* giaggiolo *m*, iris *f inv*.
Irish [ˈaɪrɪʃ] ◇ *adj* irlandese ◇ *n (language)* irlandese *m* ◇ *npl*: **the ~** gli irlandesi.
Irish coffee *n* Irish coffee *m inv (caffè con whisky e panna)*.

Irishman ['aɪrɪʃmən] (*pl* **-men** [-mən]) *n* irlandese *m*.
Irish stew *n spezzatino di agnello con patate e cipolle.*
Irishwoman ['aɪrɪʃ,wʊmən] (*pl* **-women** [-,wɪmɪn]) *n* irlandese *f*.
iron ['aɪən] ◇ *n (metal)* ferro *m*; *(for clothes)* ferro da stiro; *(golf club)* mazza *f* da golf ◇ *vt* stirare.
ironic [aɪ'rɒnɪk] *adj* ironico(-a).
ironing board ['aɪənɪŋ-] *n* asse *f* da stiro.
ironmonger's ['aɪən,mʌŋgəz] *n (Br)* ferramenta *f*.
irrelevant [ɪ'reləvənt] *adj* non pertinente, irrilevante.
irresistible [,ɪrɪ'zɪstəbl] *adj* irresistibile.
irrespective [,ɪrɪ'spektɪv]: **irrespective of** *prep* a prescindere da.
irresponsible [,ɪrɪ'spɒnsəbl] *adj* irresponsabile.
irrigation [,ɪrɪ'geɪʃn] *n* irrigazione *f*.
irritable ['ɪrɪtəbl] *adj* irritabile.
irritate ['ɪrɪteɪt] *vt* irritare.
irritating ['ɪrɪteɪtɪŋ] *adj* irritante.
IRS *n (Am)* = Fisco *m*.
is [ɪz] → **be**.
Islam ['ɪzlɑːm] *n (religion)* islamismo *m*.
island ['aɪlənd] *n* isola *f*.
isle [aɪl] *n* isola *f*.
isolated ['aɪsəleɪtɪd] *adj* isolato(-a).
Israel ['ɪzreɪəl] *n* Israele *m*.
issue ['ɪʃuː] ◇ *n (problem, subject)* questione *f*, problema *m*; *(of newspaper, magazine)* numero *m* ◇ *vt (statement, passport, document)* rilasciare; *(stamps, bank notes)* emettere.
it [ɪt] *pron* **1.** *(referring to specific thing: subject, after prep)* esso(-a); *(direct object)* lo (la); *(indirect object)* gli (le); **~'s big** è grande; **she hit ~** l'ha colpito; **give ~ to me** dammelo; **tell me about ~** parlamene; **we went to ~** ci siamo andati.
2. *(nonspecific)*: **~'s nice here** si sta bene qui; **~'s me** sono io; **who is ~?** chi è?
3. *(used impersonally)*: **~'s hot** fa caldo; **~'s six o'clock** sono le sei; **~'s Sunday** è domenica.
Italian [ɪ'tæljən] ◇ *adj* italiano(-a) ◇ *n (person)* italiano *m* (-a *f*); *(language)* italiano *m*; **an ~ restaurant** un ristorante italiano.
Italian Riviera *n*: **the ~** la Riviera Ligure.
Italy ['ɪtəlɪ] *n* l'Italia *f*.
itch [ɪtʃ] *vi (arm, leg)* prudere; *(person)* avere prurito.
item ['aɪtəm] *n (object)* articolo *m*; *(on agenda)* punto *m*; **news ~** notizia *f*.
itemized bill ['aɪtəmaɪzd-] *n* bolletta *f* con lettura dettagliata.
its [ɪts] *adj* il suo (la sua), i suoi (le sue) *(pl)*.
it's [ɪts] = **it is, it has**.
itself [ɪt'self] *pron (reflexive)* si; *(after prep)*, se stesso(-a) sé; **the house ~ is fine** la casa in sé va bene.
I've [aɪv] = **I have**.
ivory ['aɪvərɪ] *n* avorio *m*.
ivy ['aɪvɪ] *n* edera *f*.

J

jab [dʒæb] *n (Br: inf: injection)* puntura *f*.

jack [dʒæk] *n (for car)* cric *m inv*; *(playing card)* fante *m*.

jacket [ˈdʒækɪt] *n (garment)* giacca *f*; *(of book)* sopraccoperta *f*; *(Am: of record)* copertina *f*; *(of potato)* buccia *f*.

jacket potato *n patata cotta al forno con la buccia*.

jack-knife *vi* piegarsi su se stesso *(camion)*.

Jacuzzi® [dʒəˈkuːzɪ] *n* vasca *f* con idromassaggio.

jade [dʒeɪd] *n* giada *f*.

jail [dʒeɪl] *n* prigione *f*.

jam [dʒæm] ◇ *n (food)* marmellata *f*; *(of traffic)* ingorgo *m*; *(inf: difficult situation)* pasticcio *m* ◇ *vt (pack tightly)* stipare ◇ *vi (get stuck)* bloccarsi; **the roads are jammed** le strade sono intasate.

jam-packed [-ˈpækt] *adj (inf)* stipato(-a).

Jan. [dʒæn] *(abbr of January)* gen.

janitor [ˈdʒænɪtəʳ] *n (Am & Scot)* bidello *m* (-a *f*).

January [ˈdʒænjʊərɪ] *n* gennaio *m*, → **September**.

Japan [dʒəˈpæn] *n* il Giappone.

Japanese [ˌdʒæpəˈniːz] ◇ *adj* giapponese ◇ *n (language)* giapponese *m* ◇ *npl*: **the ~** i giapponesi.

jar [dʒɑːʳ] *n* barattolo *m*, vasetto *m*.

javelin [ˈdʒævlɪn] *n* giavellotto *m*.

jaw [dʒɔː] *n* mascella *f*.

jazz [dʒæz] *n* jazz *m*.

jealous [ˈdʒeləs] *adj* geloso(-a).

jeans [dʒiːnz] *npl* jeans *mpl*.

Jeep® [dʒiːp] *n* jeep® *f inv*.

Jello® [ˈdʒeləʊ] *n (Am)* gelatina *f*.

jelly [ˈdʒelɪ] *n (dessert)* gelatina *f*; *(Am: jam)* marmellata *f*.

jellyfish [ˈdʒelɪfɪʃ] *(pl inv) n* medusa *f*.

jeopardize [ˈdʒepədaɪz] *vt* mettere a repentaglio.

jerk [dʒɜːk] *n (movement)* strattone *m*, scossa *f*; *(inf: idiot)* imbecille *mf*.

jersey [ˈdʒɜːzɪ] (*pl* **-s**) *n (garment)* maglia *f*.

jet [dʒet] *n (aircraft)* aviogetto *m*; *(of liquid, gas)* getto *m*; *(outlet)* ugello *m*.

jetfoil [ˈdʒetfɔɪl] *n* aliscafo *m*.

jet lag *n* jetleg *m*.

jet-ski *n* acqua-scooter *m inv*.

jetty [ˈdʒetɪ] *n* molo *m*.

Jew [dʒuː] *n* ebreo *m* (-a *f*).

jewel [ˈdʒuːəl] *n* gioiello *m*.

◆ **jewels** *npl (jewellery)* gioielli *mpl*.

jeweler's [ˈdʒuːələz] *(Am)* = **jeweller's**.

jeweller's [ˈdʒuːələz] *n (Br)* gioielleria *f*.

jewellery [ˈdʒuːəlrɪ] *n (Br)* gioielli *mpl*.

jewelry [ˈdʒuːəlrɪ] *(Am)* = **jewellery**.
Jewish [ˈdʒuːɪʃ] *adj* ebreo(-a).
jigsaw (puzzle) [ˈdʒɪgsɔː-] *n* puzzle *m inv*.
jingle [ˈdʒɪŋgl] *n (of advert)* motivo *m* musicale di pubblicità.
job [dʒɒb] *n* lavoro *m*; **to lose one's ~** perdere il lavoro.
job centre *n (Br)* ufficio *m* di collocamento.
jockey [ˈdʒɒkɪ] (*pl* **-s**) *n* fantino *m* (-a *f*).
jog [dʒɒg] ◇ *vt (bump)* urtare lievemente ◇ *vi* fare footing ◇ *n*: **to go for a ~** andare a fare del footing.
jogging [ˈdʒɒgɪŋ] *n* footing *m*; **to go ~** fare del footing.
join [dʒɔɪn] *vt (club, organization)* iscriversi a; *(fasten together)* unire; *(other people, celebrations)* unirsi a; *(road, river)* congiungersi con; *(connect)* collegare; **to ~ a queue** mettersi in fila.
◆ **join in** ◇ *vt fus* prendere parte a ◇ *vi* partecipare.
joint [dʒɔɪnt] ◇ *adj* comune ◇ *n (of body)* articolazione *f*; *(Br: of meat)* taglio *m* di carne per arrosto; *(in structure)* giuntura *f*.
joke [dʒəʊk] ◇ *n* scherzo *m*; *(story)* barzelletta *f* ◇ *vi* scherzare.
joker [ˈdʒəʊkəʳ] *n (playing card)* jolly *m inv*, matta *f*.
jolly [ˈdʒɒlɪ] ◇ *adj (cheerful)* allegro(-a) ◇ *adv (Br: inf: very)* molto.
jolt [dʒəʊlt] *n* scossa *f*, sobbalzo *m*.
jot [dʒɒt]: **jot down** *vt sep* annotare in fretta.
journal [ˈdʒɜːnl] *n (professional magazine)* rivista *f*; *(diary)* diario *m*.
journalist [ˈdʒɜːnəlɪst] *n* giornalista *mf*.
journey [ˈdʒɜːnɪ] (*pl* **-s**) *n* viaggio *m*.
joy [dʒɔɪ] *n* gioia *f*.
joypad [ˈdʒɔɪpæd] *n (of video game)* comandi *mpl*.
joyrider [ˈdʒɔɪraɪdəʳ] *n chi ruba un'auto per farci un giro e poi l'abbandona*.
joystick [ˈdʒɔɪstɪk] *n (of video game)* joystick *m inv*.
judge [dʒʌdʒ] ◇ *n* giudice *mf* ◇ *vt* giudicare.
judg(e)ment [ˈdʒʌdʒmənt] *n* giudizio *m*.
judo [ˈdʒuːdəʊ] *n* judo *m*.
jug [dʒʌg] *n* brocca *f*, caraffa *f*.
juggernaut [ˈdʒʌgənɔːt] *n (Br)* grosso autotreno *m*, bestione *m*.
juggle [ˈdʒʌgl] *vi* fare giochi di destrezza *(con palle, birilli ecc.)*.
juice [dʒuːs] *n* succo *m*; *(from meat)* sugo *m*.
juicy [ˈdʒuːsɪ] *adj (food)* succoso(-a).
jukebox [ˈdʒuːkbɒks] *n* juke-box *m inv*.
Jul. *(abbr of July)* lug.
July [dʒuːˈlaɪ] *n* luglio *m*, → **September**.
jumble sale [ˈdʒʌmbl-] *n (Br)* vendita *f* di cose usate *(a scopo di beneficenza)*.
jumbo [ˈdʒʌmbəʊ] *adj (inf: big)* gigante.
jumbo jet *n* jumbo-jet *m inv*.
jump [dʒʌmp] ◇ *n* salto *m*, balzo *m* ◇ *vi* saltare, balzare; *(with fright)* sussultare; *(increase)* salire ◇ *vt (Am)*: **to ~ the train/bus** viaggiare sul treno/sull'autobus senza pagare; **to ~ the queue** *(Br)* saltare la fila.
jumper [ˈdʒʌmpəʳ] *n (Br: pullover)* maglione *m*, pullover *m inv*; *(Am: dress)* scamiciato *m*.
jump leads *npl* cavi *mpl* per batteria.
Jun. *(abbr of June)* giu.
junction [ˈdʒʌŋkʃn] *n (of roads)* incrocio *m*; *(of railway lines)* nodo *m* ferroviario; *(on motorways)* uscita *f*.

June [dʒuːn] *n* giugno *m*, → **September**.

jungle [ˈdʒʌŋgl] *n* giungla *f*.

junior [ˈdʒuːnjəʳ] ◇ *adj (of lower rank)* di grado inferiore, subalterno(-a); *(Am: after name)* junior ◇ *n (younger person)*: **to be sb's ~** essere più giovane di qn.

junior school *n (Br)* scuola *f* elementare *(per bambini da 7 a 11 anni)*.

junk [dʒʌŋk] *n (inf: unwanted things)* cianfrusaglie *fpl*.

junk food *n (inf)* porcherie *fpl*.

junkie [ˈdʒʌŋkɪ] *n (inf)* drogato *m* (-a *f*).

junk shop *n* negozio *m* di rigattiere.

jury [ˈdʒʊərɪ] *n* giuria *f*.

just [dʒʌst] ◇ *adv (recently, slightly)* appena; *(in the next moment)* giusto; *(exactly)* proprio; *(only)* solo ◇ *adj* giusto(-a); **to be ~ about to do sthg** stare per fare qc; **to have ~ done sthg** avere appena fatto qc; **~ about** *(almost)* praticamente, quasi; **(only) ~** per un pelo; **I've (only) ~ arrived** sono arrivato (appena) adesso; **I'm ~ coming** vengo (subito); **~ a minute!** (solo) un minuto!

justice [ˈdʒʌstɪs] *n* giustizia *f*.

justify [ˈdʒʌstɪfaɪ] *vt* giustificare.

jut [dʒʌt]: **jut out** *vi* sporgersi.

juvenile [ˈdʒuːvənaɪl] *adj (young)* giovanile; *(childish)* puerile; *(crime)* minorile.

K

kangaroo [ˌkæŋgəˈruː] *n* canguro *m*.
karate [kəˈrɑːtɪ] *n* karate *m*.
kebab [kɪˈbæb] *n*: **(shish) ~** spiedino *m* di carne; **(doner) ~** *pane azzimo imbottito con carne di agnello, insalata e salsa piccante*.
keel [kiːl] *n* chiglia *f*.
keen [kiːn] *adj (enthusiastic)* entusiasta; *(eyesight, hearing)* acuto(-a); **to be ~ on sthg** essere appassionato(-a) di qc; **to be ~ to do sthg** avere voglia di fare qc.
keep [kiːp] (*pt & pp* **kept**) ◇ *vt* tenere; *(promise)* mantenere; *(appointment)* rispettare; *(delay)* trattenere ◇ *vi (food)* mantenersi; *(remain)* restare; **to ~ (on) doing sthg** *(continuously)* continuare a fare qc; *(repeatedly)* fare qc di continuo; **to ~ sb from doing sthg** impedire a qn di fare qc; **~ back!** state indietro!; **'~ in lane!'** 'restare in corsia'; **'~ left'** 'tenere la sinistra'; **'~ off the grass!'** 'vietato calpestare l'erba'; **'~ out!'** 'vietato l'accesso'; **'~ your distance!'** 'mantenere la distanza (di sicurezza)'; **to ~ clear (of)** stare lontano (da).
◆ **keep up** ◇ *vt sep* mantenere, continuare ◇ *vi*: **to ~ up (with)** tenersi al passo (con).
keep-fit *n (Br)* ginnastica *f*.
kennel [ˈkenl] *n* canile *m*.
kept [kept] *pt & pp* → **keep**.
kerb [kɜːb] *n (Br)* orlo *m* del marciapiede.
kerosene [ˈkerəsiːn] *n (Am)* cherosene *m*.
ketchup [ˈketʃəp] *n* ketchup *m*.
kettle [ˈketl] *n* bollitore *m*; **to put the ~ on** mettere l'acqua a bollire.
key [kiː] ◇ *n* chiave *f*; *(of piano, typewriter)* tasto *m*; *(of map)* leggenda *f* ◇ *adj* chiave *(inv)*.
keyboard [ˈkiːbɔːd] *n* tastiera *f*.
keyhole [ˈkiːhəʊl] *n* buco *m* della serratura.
keypad [ˈkiːpæd] *n* tastiera *f*.
key ring *n* portachiavi *m inv*.
kg *(abbr of kilogram)* kg.
kick [kɪk] ◇ *n (of foot)* calcio *m* ◇ *vt* dare calci a, prendere a calci.
kickoff [ˈkɪkɒf] *n* calcio *m* d'inizio.
kid [kɪd] ◇ *n (inf) (child)* bimbo *m* (-a *f*), bambino *m* (-a *f*); *(young person)* ragazzo *m* (-a *f*) ◇ *vi (joke)* scherzare.
kidnap [ˈkɪdnæp] *vt* rapire.
kidnaper [ˈkɪdnæpər] *(Am)* = **kidnapper**.
kidnapper [ˈkɪdnæpəʳ] *n (Br)* rapitore *m* (-trice *f*).
kidney [ˈkɪdnɪ] (*pl* **-s**) *n (organ)* rene *m*; *(food)* rognone *m*.
kidney bean *n* fagiolo *m* comune.

kill [kɪl] *vt (person)* uccidere, ammazzare; *(time)* ammazzare; **my feet are ~ing me!** i piedi mi fanno un male!
killer [ˈkɪləʳ] *n* assassino *m* (-a *f*).
kilo [ˈkiːləʊ] (*pl* **-s**) *n* chilo *m*.
kilogram *n* [ˈkɪləˌgræm] *n* chilogrammo *m*.
kilometre [ˈkɪləˌmiːtəʳ] *n* chilometro *m*.
kilt [kɪlt] *n* kilt *m inv*.
kind [kaɪnd] ◇ *adj* gentile, buono(-a) ◇ *n (sort, type)* genere *m*, tipo *m*; **~ of** *(Am: inf)* un po'.
kindergarten [ˈkɪndəˌgɑːtn] *n* asilo *m* infantile.
kindly [ˈkaɪndlɪ] *adv*: **would you ~ ...?** potrebbe ..., per favore?
kindness [ˈkaɪndnɪs] *n* gentilezza *f*, cortesia *f*.
king [kɪŋ] *n* re *m inv*.
kingfisher [ˈkɪŋˌfɪʃəʳ] *n* martin *m inv* pescatore.
king prawn *n* gambero *m*.
king-size bed *n letto largo 160 cm*.
kiosk [ˈkiːɒsk] *n (for newspapers etc)* chiosco *m*, edicola *f*; *(Br: phone box)* cabina *f* (telefonica).
kipper [ˈkɪpəʳ] *n* aringa *f* affumicata.
kiss [kɪs] ◇ *n* bacio *m* ◇ *vt* baciare.
kiss of life *n* respirazione *f* bocca a bocca.
kit [kɪt] *n (set)* attrezzatura *f*; *(clothes)* completo *m*; *(for assembly)* scatola *f* di montaggio.
kitchen [ˈkɪtʃɪn] *n* cucina *f*.
kitchen unit *n* mobile *m* componibile (da cucina).
kite [kaɪt] *n (toy)* aquilone *m*.
kitten [ˈkɪtn] *n* gattino *m* (-a *f*).
kitty [ˈkɪtɪ] *n (of money)* cassa *f* comune.
kiwi fruit [ˈkiːwiː-] *n* kiwi *m inv*.
Kleenex® [ˈkliːneks] *n* fazzoletto *m* di carta.
km *(abbr of kilometre)* km.
km/h *(abbr of kilometres per hour)* km/h.
knack [næk] *n*: **to have the ~ of doing sthg** avere l'abilità di fare qc.
knackered [ˈnækəd] *adj (Br: inf)* stanco morto (stanca morta).
knapsack [ˈnæpsæk] *n* zaino *m*.
knee [niː] *n* ginocchio *m*.
kneecap [ˈniːkæp] *n* rotula *f*.
kneel [niːl] (*pt & pp* **knelt** [nelt]) *vi* inginocchiarsi.
knew [njuː] *pt* → **know**.
knickers [ˈnɪkəz] *npl (Br: underwear)* mutandine *fpl*.
knife [naɪf] (*pl* **knives**) *n* coltello *m*.
knight [naɪt] *n (in history)* cavaliere *m*; *(in chess)* cavallo *m*.
knit [nɪt] *vt* fare a maglia.
knitted [ˈnɪtɪd] *adj* fatto(-a) a maglia.
knitting [ˈnɪtɪŋ] *n* lavoro *m* a maglia.
knitting needle *n* ferro *m* (da calza).
knitwear [ˈnɪtweəʳ] *n* maglieria *f*.
knives [naɪvz] *pl* → **knife**.
knob [nɒb] *n (on door etc)* pomello *m*; *(on machine)* manopola *f*.
knock [nɒk] ◇ *n (at door)* colpo *m* ◇ *vt (head, elbow)* battere; *(chair, table)* battere contro ◇ *vi (at door etc)* bussare.
◆ **knock down** *vt sep (pedestrian)* investire; *(building)* demolire; *(price)* ribassare.
◆ **knock out** *vt sep (make unconscious)* tramortire; *(of competition)* eliminare.
◆ **knock over** *vt sep (glass, vase)* rovesciare; *(pedestrian)* investire.
knocker [ˈnɒkəʳ] *n (on door)* battente *m*.
knot [nɒt] *n* nodo *m*.
know [nəʊ] (*pt* **knew**, *pp* **known**)

vt sapere; *(person, place)* conoscere; **to get to ~ sb** imparare a conoscere qc; **to ~ about sthg** *(understand)* saperne di qc; *(have heard)* sapere di qc; **to ~ how to do sthg** saper fare qc; **to ~ of** sapere di; **to be ~n as** essere noto come; **to let sb ~ sthg** far sapere qc a qn; **you ~** *(for emphasis)* sai.

knowledge [ˈnɒlɪdʒ] *n* conoscenza *f*; **to my ~** che io sappia.

known [nəʊn] *pp* → **know**.

knuckle [ˈnʌkl] *n (of hand)* nocca *f*; *(of pork)* garretto *m*.

Koran [kɒˈrɑːn] *n*: **the ~** il Corano.

L

l *(abbr of litre)* l.
L *(abbr of learner)* = P.
lab [læb] *n (inf)* laboratorio *m*.
label [ˈleɪbl] *n* cartellino *m*, etichetta *f*.
labor [ˈleɪbər] *(Am)* = **labour**.
laboratory [*Br* ləˈbɒrətrɪ, *Am* ˈlæbrəˌtɔːrɪ] *n* laboratorio *m*.
labour [ˈleɪbəʳ] *n (work)* lavoro *m*; **to be in ~** (MED) avere le doglie.
labourer [ˈleɪbərəʳ] *n* manovale *m*.
Labour Party *n (Br)* partito *m* laburista.
labour-saving *adj* che fa risparmiare fatica.
lace [leɪs] *n (material)* merletto *m*; *(for shoe)* laccio *m*.
lace-ups *npl* scarpe *fpl* con i lacci.
lack [læk] ◇ *n* carenza *f* ◇ *vt* non avere ◇ *vi*: **to be ~ing** mancare.
lacquer [ˈlækəʳ] *n (for hair)* lacca *f*; *(paint)* vernice *f*.
lad [læd] *n (inf)* ragazzo *m*.
ladder [ˈlædəʳ] *n (for climbing)* scala *f*; *(Br: in tights)* smagliatura *f*.
ladies [ˈleɪdɪz] *n (Br: toilet)* toilette *f inv* per signore.
ladies room *(Am)* = **ladies**.
ladieswear [ˈleɪdɪzˌweəʳ] *n* abbigliamento *m* da donna.
ladle [ˈleɪdl] *n* mestolo *m*.
lady [ˈleɪdɪ] *n* signora *f*.
ladybird [ˈleɪdɪbɜːd] *n* coccinella *f*.
ladybug [ˈleɪdɪbʌg] *n (Am)* = **ladybird**.
lag [læg] *vi (trade)* ristagnare; **to ~ behind** *(move more slowly)* restare indietro.
lager [ˈlɑːgəʳ] *n* birra *f* (chiara).
lagoon [ləˈguːn] *n* laguna *f*.
laid [leɪd] *pt & pp* → **lay**.
lain [leɪn] *pp* → **lie**.
lake [leɪk] *n* lago *m*.
Lake District *n*: **the ~** la regione dei laghi *(nel nordovest dell'Inghilterra)*.
lamb [læm] *n* agnello *m*.
lamb chop *n* braciola *f* OR costoletta *f* d'agnello.
lame [leɪm] *adj* zoppo(-a).
lamp [læmp] *n* lampada *f*; *(bicycle lamp)* fanale *m*; *(in street)* lampione *m*.
lamppost [ˈlæmppəʊst] *n* lampione *m*.
lampshade [ˈlæmpʃeɪd] *n* paralume *m*.
land [lænd] ◇ *n* terra *f* ◇ *vi (plane)* atterrare; *(passengers)* sbarcare; *(fall)* cadere.
landing [ˈlændɪŋ] *n (of plane)* atterraggio *m*; *(on stairs)* pianerottolo *m*.
landlady [ˈlændˌleɪdɪ] *n (of house)* padrona *f* di casa; *(of pub)* proprietaria *f*.

landlord [ˈlændlɔːd] *n (of house)* padrone *m* di casa; *(of pub)* proprietario *m*.
landmark [ˈlændmɑːk] *n* punto *m* di riferimento.
landscape [ˈlændskeɪp] *n* paesaggio *m*.
landslide [ˈlændslaɪd] *n (of earth, rocks)* frana *f*.
lane [leɪn] *n (narrow road)* stradina *f*; *(on road, motorway)* corsia *f*; **'get in ~'** 'disporsi su più file'.
language [ˈlæŋgwɪdʒ] *n (of a people, country)* lingua *f*; *(system, words)* linguaggio *m*.
lap [læp] *n (of person)* grembo *m*; *(of race)* giro *m*.
lapel [ləˈpel] *n* risvolto *m*.
lapse [læps] *vi (passport, membership)* scadere.
lard [lɑːd] *n* strutto *m*.
larder [ˈlɑːdəʳ] *n* dispensa *f*.
large [lɑːdʒ] *adj* grande; *(person, dog, sum)* grosso(-a).
largely [ˈlɑːdʒlɪ] *adv* in gran parte.
large-scale *adj* su vasta scala.
lark [lɑːk] *n* allodola *f*.
laryngitis [ˌlærɪnˈdʒaɪtɪs] *n* laringite *f*.
lasagne [ləˈzænjə] *n* lasagne *fpl*.
laser [ˈleɪzəʳ] *n* laser *m inv*.
lass [læs] *n (inf)* ragazza *f*.
last [lɑːst] ◇ *adj* ultimo(-a); *(week, year, month)* scorso(-a) ◇ *adv (most recently)* l'ultima volta; *(after everything else)* per ultimo ◇ *vi (continue)* durare ◇ *pron*: **the ~ to come** l'ultimo ad arrivare; **the ~ but one** il penultimo (la penultima); **the day before ~** l'altro ieri; **~ year** l'anno scorso; **the ~ year** l'ultimo anno; **at ~** finalmente; **to arrive ~** arrivare (per) ultimo; **it won't ~ till tomorrow** *(food)* non va fino a domani.
lastly [ˈlɑːstlɪ] *adv* infine.
last-minute *adj* dell'ultimo momento.
latch [lætʃ] *n* serratura *f* a scatto; **the door is on the ~** la porta non è chiusa a chiave.
late [leɪt] ◇ *adj (not on time)* in ritardo; *(after usual time)* tardi *(inv)*; *(dead)* defunto(-a); *(morning, afternoon)* tardo(-a) ◇ *adv (not on time)* in ritardo; *(after usual time)* tardi; **in ~ June, ~ in June** verso la fine di giugno; **the train is running two hours ~** il treno viaggia con due ore di ritardo.
lately [ˈleɪtlɪ] *adv* ultimamente.
late-night *adj* aperto(-a) fino a tardi; **~ opening** apertura prolungata *(di negozi)*.
later [ˈleɪtəʳ] ◇ *adj (train)* successivo(-a) ◇ *adv*: **~ (on)** più tardi; **at a ~ date** in futuro.
latest [ˈleɪtɪst] *adj*: **the ~ fashion** l'ultima moda; **the ~** l'ultimo(-a); **at the ~** al più tardi.
lather [ˈlɑːðəʳ] *n* schiuma *f*.
Latin [ˈlætɪn] *n* latino *m*.
Latin America *n* l'America *f* Latina.
Latin American ◇ *adj* latino-americano(-a) ◇ *n* latino-americano *m* (-a *f*).
latitude [ˈlætɪtjuːd] *n (distance from Equator)* latitudine *f*.
latter [ˈlætəʳ] *n*: **the ~** quest'ultimo(-a).
laugh [lɑːf] ◇ *n* risata *f* ◇ *vi* ridere; **to have a ~** *(Br: inf)* farsi due risate.
◆ **laugh at** *vt fus (mock)* ridere di.
laughter [ˈlɑːftəʳ] *n* riso *m*.
launch [lɔːntʃ] *vt (boat)* varare; *(new product)* lanciare.
laund(e)rette [lɔːnˈdret] *n* lavanderia *f* (automatica).
laundry [ˈlɔːndrɪ] *n (washing)* bucato *m*; *(place)* lavanderia *f*.
lavatory [ˈlævətrɪ] *n* gabinetto *m*.
lavender [ˈlævəndəʳ] *n* lavanda *f*.
lavish [ˈlævɪʃ] *adj (meal, decoration)* sontuoso(-a).

law [lɔː] *n* legge *f*; **to be against the ~** essere contro la legge.
lawn [lɔːn] *n* prato *m*.
lawnmower [ˈlɔːnˌməʊəʳ] *n* tagliaerba *m inv*.
lawyer [ˈlɔːjəʳ] *n (in court)* avvocato *m*; *(solicitor)* notaio *m*.
laxative [ˈlæksətɪv] *n* lassativo *m*.
lay [leɪ] (*pt & pp* **laid**) ◇ *pt* → **lie** ◇ *vt (place)* poggiare; *(egg)* fare; **to ~ the table** apparecchiare la tavola.
◆ **lay off** *vt sep (worker)* licenziare.
◆ **lay on** *vt sep (food, transport)* fornire; *(entertainment)* organizzare.
◆ **lay out** *vt sep (display)* disporre.
lay-by (*pl* **lay-bys**) *n* piazzola *f* di sosta.
layer [ˈleɪəʳ] *n* strato *m*.
layman [ˈleɪmən] (*pl* **-men** [-mən]) *n* profano *m* (-a *f*).
layout [ˈleɪaʊt] *n (of building)* struttura *f*; *(of streets)* tracciato *m*.
lazy [ˈleɪzɪ] *adj* pigro(-a).
lb *abbr* = **pound**.
lead[1] [liːd] (*pt & pp* **led**) ◇ *vt (take)* condurre; *(team, party, march)* guidare; *(procession)* aprire ◇ *vi (be winning)* condurre ◇ *n (for dog)* guinzaglio *m*; *(cable)* cavo *m*; **to ~ sb to do sthg** indurre qn a fare qc; **to ~ to** portare a; **to ~ the way** fare strada; **to be in the ~** essere in testa.
lead[2] [led] ◇ *n* piombo *m*; *(for pencil)* mina *f* ◇ *adj* di piombo.
leaded petrol [ˈledɪd-] *n* benzina *f* con piombo.
leader [ˈliːdəʳ] *n (of group)* capo *m*; *(of union, party)* leader *mf inv*; *(in race)* chi è in testa.
leadership [ˈliːdəʃɪp] *n (position)* direzione *f*.
lead-free [led-] *adj* senza piombo.
leading [ˈliːdɪŋ] *adj (most important)* principale.
lead singer [liːd-] *n* cantante *mf* (solista).
leaf [liːf] (*pl* **leaves**) *n (of tree)* foglia *f*.
leaflet [ˈliːflɪt] *n* dépliant *m inv*.
league [liːg] *n* (SPORT) campionato *m*; *(association)* lega *f*.
leak [liːk] ◇ *n (hole)* buco *m*; *(of gas, water)* perdita *f* ◇ *vi (tank)* perdere; *(roof)* gocciolare.
lean [liːn] (*pt & pp* **leant** [lent] OR **-ed**) ◇ *adj (meat)* magro(-a); *(person, animal)* asciutto(-a) ◇ *vi (bend)* piegarsi; *(building)* pendere ◇ *vt*: **to ~ sthg against sthg** appoggiare qc a qc; **to ~ on** appoggiarsi a.
◆ **lean forward** *vi* sporgersi (in avanti).
◆ **lean over** *vi* sporgersi.
leap [liːp] (*pt & pp* **leapt** [lept] OR **-ed**) *vi (jump)* balzare.
leap year *n* anno *m* bisestile.
learn [lɜːn] (*pt & pp* **learnt** OR **-ed**) *vt* imparare; **to ~ (how) to do sthg** imparare a fare qc; **to ~ about sthg** *(hear about)* venire a sapere di qc; *(study)* studiare qc.
learner (driver) [ˈlɜːnəʳ-] *n* guidatore *m* (-trice *f*) principiante.
learnt [lɜːnt] *pt & pp* → **learn**.
lease [liːs] ◇ *n* contratto *m* d'affitto ◇ *vt* affittare; **to ~ sthg from sb** affittare qc da qn; **to ~ sthg to sb** affittare qc a qn.
leash [liːʃ] *n* guinzaglio *m*.
least [liːst] ◇ *adv* meno (di tutti) ◇ *adj* meno ... di tutti ◇ *pron*: **(the) ~** meno di tutti; **at ~** almeno; **the ~ he could do** il minimo che potesse fare.
leather [ˈleðəʳ] *n* cuoio *m*, pelle *f*.
◆ **leathers** *npl (of motorcyclist)* tuta *f* in pelle da motociclista.
leave [liːv] (*pt & pp* **left**) ◇ *vt* lasciare; *(school)* finire ◇ *vi (go away)* andarsene; *(train, bus)* partire ◇ *n (time off work)* permesso *m*; **to ~ a message** lasciare un messaggio, → **left**.
◆ **leave behind** *vt sep (not take

away) lasciare.
◆ **leave out** *vt sep* tralasciare.
leaves [liːvz] *pl* → **leaf**.
Lebanon [ˈlebənən] *n* il Libano.
lecture [ˈlektʃəʳ] *n (at university)* lezione *f*; *(at conference)* conferenza *f*.
lecturer [ˈlektʃərəʳ] *n* docente *mf* (universitario).
lecture theatre *n* aula *f (ad anfiteatro)*.
led [led] *pt & pp* → **lead**[1].
ledge [ledʒ] *n (of window)* davanzale *m*.
leek [liːk] *n* porro *m*.
left [left] ◇ *pt & pp* → **leave** ◇ *adj (not right)* sinistro(-a) ◇ *adv* a sinistra ◇ *n* sinistra *f*; **on the ~** a sinistra; **there are none ~** sono finiti.
left-hand *adj (side)* sinistro(-a); *(lane)* di sinistra.
left-hand drive *n* guida *f* a sinistra.
left-handed [-ˈhændɪd] *adj (person)* mancino(-a); *(implement)* per mancini.
left-luggage locker *n (Br)* armadietto *m* per deposito bagagli.
left-luggage office *n (Br)* deposito *m* bagagli.
left-wing *adj* di sinistra.
leg [leg] *n* gamba *f*; *(of animal)* zampa *f*; **~ of lamb** coscia *f* d'agnello.
legal [ˈliːgl] *adj* legale.
legal aid *n* assistenza *f* legale gratuita.
legalize [ˈliːgəlaɪz] *vt* legalizzare.
legal system *n* sistema *f* legale.
legend [ˈledʒənd] *n* leggenda *f*.
leggings [ˈlegɪŋz] *npl* fuseaux *mpl*, pantacollant *mpl*.
legible [ˈledʒɪbl] *adj* leggibile.
legislation [ˌledʒɪsˈleɪʃn] *n* legislazione *f*.
legitimate [lɪˈdʒɪtɪmət] *adj* legittimo(-a).
leisure [*Br* ˈleʒəʳ, *Am* ˈliːʒər] *n* tempo *m* libero.
leisure centre *n* centro *m* sportivo.
leisure pool *n* piscina *f*.
lemon [ˈlemən] *n* limone *m*.
lemonade [ˌleməˈneɪd] *n* limonata *f*.
lemon curd [-kɜːd] *n (Br) sorta di marmellata a base di succo e scorza di limone, uova, burro e zucchero.*
lemon juice *n* succo *m* di limone.
lemon meringue pie *n dolce composto da una base di pasta frolla e uno strato di crema al limone rivestito di meringa.*
lemon sole *n* limanda *f (varietà di sogliola)*.
lemon tea *n* tè *m* al limone.
lend [lend] (*pt & pp* **lent**) *vt* prestare; **to ~ sb sthg** prestare qc a qn.
length [leŋθ] *n (in distance)* lunghezza *f*; *(in time)* durata *f*; *(of swimming pool)* vasca *f*.
lengthen [ˈleŋθən] *vt* allungare.
lens [lenz] *n* lente *f*.
lent [lent] *pt & pp* → **lend**.
Lent [lent] *n* la Quaresima.
lentils [ˈlentlz] *npl* lenticchie *fpl*.
Leo (*pl* **-s**) *n* Leone *m*.
leopard [ˈlepəd] *n* leopardo *m*.
leopard-skin *adj* a pelle di leopardo.
leotard [ˈliːətɑːd] *n* calzamaglia *f*.
leper [ˈlepəʳ] *n* lebbroso *m* (-a *f*).
lesbian [ˈlezbɪən] ◇ *adj* lesbico(-a) ◇ *n* lesbica *f*.
less [les] *adj, adv & pron* meno; **~ than 20** meno di 20.
lesson [ˈlesn] *n (class)* lezione *f*.
let [let] (*pt & pp* **let**) *vt (allow)* lasciare; *(rent out)* affittare; **to ~ sb do sthg** lasciar fare qc a qn; **to ~ go of sthg** mollare qc; **to ~ sb have sthg** *(give)* dare qc a qn; **to ~ sb know**

sthg far sapere qc a qn; **~'s go!** andiamo!; **'to ~'** 'affittasi'.

◆ **let in** *vt sep (allow to enter)* far entrare.

◆ **let off** *vt sep (excuse)*: **to ~ sb off doing sthg** dispensare qn dal fare qc; **can you ~ me off at the station?** mi fa scendere alla stazione?.

◆ **let out** *vt sep (allow to go out)* far uscire.

letdown ['letdaʊn] *n (inf)* delusione *f*.

lethargic [lə'θɑːdʒɪk] *adj* apatico(-a).

letter ['letər] *n* lettera *f*.

letterbox ['letəbɒks] *n (Br)* buca *f* delle lettere.

lettuce ['letɪs] *n* lattuga *f*.

leuk(a)emia [luː'kiːmɪə] *n* leucemia *f*.

level ['levl] ◇ *adj (flat)* piano(-a); *(horizontal)* orizzontale ◇ *n* livello *m*; *(storey)* piano *m*; **to be ~ with** essere allo stesso livello di.

level crossing *n (Br)* passaggio *m* a livello.

lever [*Br* 'liːvər, *Am* 'levər] *n* leva *f*.

liability [ˌlaɪə'bɪlətɪ] *n (responsibility)* responsabilità *f*.

liable ['laɪəbl] *adj*: **to be ~ to do sthg** avere la tendenza a fare qc; **to be ~ for sthg** rispondere di qc.

liaise [lɪ'eɪz] *vi*: **to ~ with** mantenere i contatti con.

liar ['laɪər] *n* bugiardo *m* (-a *f*).

liberal ['lɪbərəl] *adj (tolerant)* liberale; *(generous)* generoso(-a).

Liberal Democrat Party *n* Partito *m* Liberaldemocratico.

liberate ['lɪbəreɪt] *vt* liberare.

liberty ['lɪbətɪ] *n* libertà *f inv*.

Libra *n* Bilancia *f*.

librarian [laɪ'breərɪən] *n* bibliotecario *m* (-a *f*).

library ['laɪbrərɪ] *n* biblioteca *f*.

Libya ['lɪbɪə] *n* la Libia.

lice [laɪs] *npl* pidocchi *mpl*.

licence ['laɪsəns] ◇ *n (Br: official document)* licenza *f* ◇ *vt (Am)* = **license**; **driving ~** patente *f* (di guida); **TV ~** abbonamento *m* alla televisione.

license ['laɪsəns] ◇ *vt (Br)* autorizzare ◇ *n (Am)* = **licence**.

licensed ['laɪsənst] *adj (restaurant, bar) munito di licenza per la vendita di alcolici.*

licensing hours ['laɪsənsɪŋ-] *npl (Br) orario in cui è consentita la vendita di alcolici.*

lick [lɪk] *vt* leccare.

lid [lɪd] *n (cover)* coperchio *m*.

lie [laɪ] (*pt* **lay**, *pp* **lain**, *cont* **lying**) ◇ *n* bugia *f* ◇ *vi (tell lie: pt & pp* **lied***)* mentire; *(be horizontal)* essere disteso; *(lie down)* sdraiarsi; *(be situated)* trovarsi; **to tell ~s** dire bugie; **to ~ about sthg** mentire su qc.

◆ **lie down** *vi* sdraiarsi.

lieutenant [*Br* lef'tenənt, *Am* luː'tenənt] *n* tenente *m*.

life [laɪf] (*pl* **lives**) *n* vita *f*.

life assurance *n* assicurazione *f* sulla vita.

life belt *n* salvagente *m*.

lifeboat ['laɪfbəʊt] *n* scialuppa *f* di salvataggio.

lifeguard ['laɪfgɑːd] *n* bagnino *m* (-a *f*).

life jacket *n* giubbotto *m* di salvataggio.

lifelike ['laɪflaɪk] *adj* fedele.

life preserver [-prɪ'zɜːvər] *n (Am) (life belt)* salvagente *m*; *(life jacket)* giubbotto *m* di salvataggio.

life-size *adj* a grandezza naturale.

lifespan ['laɪfspæn] *n* vita *f*.

lifestyle ['laɪfstaɪl] *n* stile *m* di vita.

lift [lɪft] ◇ *n (Br: elevator)* ascensore *m* ◇ *vt (raise)* sollevare, alzare ◇ *vi (fog)* alzarsi; **to give sb a ~** dare un passaggio a qn.

◆ **lift up** *vt sep* sollevare, alzare.

light [laɪt] (*pt & pp* **lit** OR **-ed**) ◇ *adj* leggero(-a); *(not dark)* chiaro(-a); *(traffic)* scorrevole ◇ *n* luce *f*; *(of car, bike)* faro *m* ◇ *vt (fire, cigarette)* accendere; *(room, stage)* illuminare; **have you got a ~?** hai da accendere?; **to set ~ to sthg** dar fuoco a qc.

◆ **lights** *npl (traffic lights)* semaforo *m*.

◆ **light up** ◇ *vt sep (house, road)* illuminare ◇ *vi (inf: light a cigarette)* accendersi una sigaretta.

light bulb *n* lampadina *f*.

lighter [ˈlaɪtəʳ] *n* accendino *m*.

light-hearted [-ˈhɑːtɪd] *adj* gioviale.

lighthouse [ˈlaɪthaʊs, *pl* -haʊzɪz] *n* faro *m*.

lighting [ˈlaɪtɪŋ] *n* illuminazione *f*.

light meter *n* contatore *m* della luce.

lightning [ˈlaɪtnɪŋ] *n* lampi *mpl*, fulmini *mpl*.

lightweight [ˈlaɪtweɪt] *adj (clothes, object)* leggero(-a).

like [laɪk] ◇ *prep* come; *(typical of)* tipico di ◇ *vt (want)* volere; **I ~ it** mi piace; **I ~ them** mi piacciono; **I ~ going out** mi piace uscire; **I'd ~ to sit down** vorrei sedermi; **I'd ~ a drink** vorrei bere qualcosa; **what's it ~?** com'è?; **to look ~ sb** assomigliare a qn; **do it ~ this** fallo così; **it's not ~ him** non è da lui.

likelihood [ˈlaɪklɪhʊd] *n* probabilità *f*.

likely [ˈlaɪklɪ] *adj* probabile.

likeness [ˈlaɪknɪs] *n* somiglianza *f*.

likewise [ˈlaɪkwaɪz] *adv* allo stesso modo; **to do ~** fare lo stesso.

lilac [ˈlaɪlək] *adj* lilla *(inv)*.

Lilo® [ˈlaɪləʊ] (*pl* **-s**) *n (Br)* materassino *m* (pneumatico).

lily [ˈlɪlɪ] *n* giglio *m*.

lily of the valley *n* mughetto *m*.

limb [lɪm] *n* arto *m*.

lime [laɪm] *n (fruit)* limetta *f*; **~ (juice)** succo *m* di limetta.

limestone [ˈlaɪmstəʊn] *n* calcare *m*.

limit [ˈlɪmɪt] ◇ *n* limite *m* ◇ *vt* limitare; **the city ~s** i confini della città.

limited [ˈlɪmɪtɪd] *adj (restricted)* limitato(-a); *(in company name)* a responsabilità limitata.

limp [lɪmp] ◇ *adj* floscio(-a) ◇ *vi* zoppicare.

line [laɪn] ◇ *n* linea *f*; *(row)* fila *f*; *(Am: queue)* coda *f*, fila; *(of words on page)* riga *f*; *(of poem, song)* verso *m*; *(for fishing)* lenza *f*; *(rope, washing line)* corda *f*; *(of business, work)* settore *m*, ramo *m* ◇ *vt (coat, drawers)* foderare; **in ~** *(aligned)* allineato; **it's a bad ~** la linea è disturbata; **the ~ is engaged** la linea è occupata; **to drop sb a ~** *(inf)* mandare due righe a qn; **to stand in ~** *(Am)* stare in fila.

◆ **line up** ◇ *vt sep (arrange)* organizzare ◇ *vi* allinearsi.

lined [laɪnd] *adj (paper)* rigato(-a), a righe.

linen [ˈlɪnɪn] *n (cloth)* lino *m*; *(tablecloths, sheets)* biancheria *f*.

liner [ˈlaɪnəʳ] *n (ship)* nave *f* di linea.

linesman [ˈlaɪnzmən] (*pl* **-men** [-mən]) *n* guardalinee *m inv*.

linger [ˈlɪŋgəʳ] *vi (in place)* attardarsi.

lingerie [ˈlænʒərɪ] *n* biancheria *f* intima *(femminile)*.

lining [ˈlaɪnɪŋ] *n (of coat, jacket)* fodera *f*; *(of brake)* guarnizione *f*.

link [lɪŋk] ◇ *n (connection)* collegamento *m*; *(between countries, companies)* relazione *f* ◇ *vt (connect)* collegare; **rail ~** collegamento ferroviario; **road ~** collegamento stradale.

lino [ˈlaɪnəʊ] *n (Br)* linoleum *m*.

lion [ˈlaɪən] *n* leone *m*.

lioness [ˈlaɪənes] *n* leonessa *f*.
lip [lɪp] *n (of person)* labbro *m*.
lip salve [-sælv] *n* burro *m* di cacao.
lipstick [ˈlɪpstɪk] *n* rossetto *m*.
liqueur [lɪˈkjʊəʳ] *n* liquore *m* (dolce).
liquid [ˈlɪkwɪd] *n* liquido *m*.
liquor [ˈlɪkər] *n (Am)* superalcolico *m*.
liquorice [ˈlɪkərɪs] *n* liquirizia *f*.
lisp [lɪsp] *n* difetto *f* di pronuncia *(relativo alla lettera s)*.
list [lɪst] ◇ *n* lista *f*, elenco *m* ◇ *vt* elencare.
listen [ˈlɪsn] *vi*: **to ~ (to)** ascoltare.
listener [ˈlɪsnəʳ] *n (on radio)* ascoltatore *m* (-trice *f*).
lit [lɪt] *pt & pp* → **light**.
liter [ˈliːtər] *(Am)* = **litre**.
literally [ˈlɪtərəlɪ] *adv* letteralmente.
literary [ˈlɪtərərɪ] *adj* letterario(-a).
literature [ˈlɪtrətʃəʳ] *n* letteratura *f*; *(printed information)* materiale *m* illustrativo.
litre [ˈliːtəʳ] *n (Br)* litro *m*.
litter [ˈlɪtəʳ] *n (rubbish)* rifiuti *mpl*.
litterbin [ˈlɪtəbɪn] *n (Br)* cestino *m* dei rifiuti.
little [ˈlɪtl] ◇ *adj* piccolo(-a); *(not much)* poco(-a) ◇ *pron & adv* poco; **as ~ as possible** il meno possibile; **~ by ~** poco a poco.
◆ **a little** ◇ *pron & adv* un po' ◇ *adj* un po' di.
little finger *n* mignolo *m*.
live[1] [lɪv] *vi* vivere; *(have home)* vivere, abitare; **to ~ with sb** vivere con qn.
◆ **live together** *vi* vivere insieme.
live[2] [laɪv] ◇ *adj (alive)* vivo(-a); *(programme, performance)* dal vivo; *(wire)* sotto tensione ◇ *adv* in diretta.
lively [ˈlaɪvlɪ] *adj (person)* vivace; *(place, atmosphere)* animato(-a).
liver [ˈlɪvəʳ] *n* fegato *m*.
lives [laɪvz] *pl* → **life**.
living [ˈlɪvɪŋ] ◇ *adj* vivente ◇ *n*: **to earn a ~** guadagnarsi da vivere; **what do you do for a ~?** che lavoro fa?
living room *n* soggiorno *m*.
lizard [ˈlɪzəd] *n* lucertola *f*.
load [ləʊd] ◇ *n (thing carried)* carico *m* ◇ *vt* caricare; **~s of** *(inf)* un sacco di.
loaf [ləʊf] (*pl* **loaves**) *n*: **a ~ (of bread)** una pagnotta.
loan [ləʊn] ◇ *n* prestito *m* ◇ *vt* prestare.
loathe [ləʊð] *vt* detestare.
loaves [ləʊvz] *pl* → **loaf**.
lobby [ˈlɒbɪ] *n (hall)* atrio *m*.
lobster [ˈlɒbstəʳ] *n* aragosta *f*.
local [ˈləʊkl] ◇ *adj* locale; *(train)* regionale ◇ *n (inf: local person)* abitante *mf* del posto; *(Br: pub)* bar *m* vicino; *(Am: train)* regionale *m*; *(Am: bus)* autobus *m inv*.
local anaesthetic *n* anestesia *f* locale.
local call *n* chiamata *f* urbana.
local government *n* amministrazione *f* locale.
locate [*Br* ləʊˈkeɪt, *Am* ˈləʊkeɪt] *vt (find)* localizzare; **to be ~d** essere situato.
location [ləʊˈkeɪʃn] *n (place)* posizione *f*.
loch [lɒk] *n (Scot)* lago *m*.
lock [lɒk] ◇ *n (on door, drawer)* serratura *f*; *(for bike)* lucchetto *m*; *(on canal)* chiusa *f* ◇ *vt (door, drawer, car)* chiudere a chiave; *(keep safely)* chiudere ◇ *vi (become stuck)* bloccarsi.
◆ **lock in** *vt sep* chiudere dentro.
◆ **lock out** *vt sep* chiudere fuori.
◆ **lock up** ◇ *vt sep (imprison)* mettere dentro ◇ *vi* chiudere porte e finestre.

locker ['lɒkəʳ] *n* armadietto *m*.

locker room *n (Am)* spogliatoio *m*.

locket ['lɒkɪt] *n* medaglione *m*.

locomotive [ˌləʊkə'məʊtɪv] *n* locomotiva *f*.

locum ['ləʊkəm] *n (doctor)* medico *m* sostituto.

locust ['ləʊkəst] *n* locusta *f*.

lodge [lɒdʒ] ◇ *n (for skiers)* rifugio *m*; *(for hunters)* casino *m* di caccia ◇ *vi (stay)* alloggiare; *(get stuck)* conficcarsi.

lodger ['lɒdʒəʳ] *n* pensionante *mf*.

lodgings ['lɒdʒɪŋz] *npl* camera *f* ammobiliata.

loft [lɒft] *n* soffitta *f*.

log [lɒg] *n (piece of wood)* ceppo *m*.

logic ['lɒdʒɪk] *n* logica *f*.

logical ['lɒdʒɪkl] *adj* logico(-a).

logo ['ləʊgəʊ] (*pl* **-s**) *n* logo *m inv*.

loin [lɔɪn] *n* lombata *f*.

loiter ['lɔɪtəʳ] *vi (remain)* attardarsi; *(walk around)* bighellonare.

lollipop ['lɒlɪpɒp] *n* lecca lecca *m inv*.

lolly ['lɒlɪ] *n (inf: lollipop)* lecca lecca *m inv*; *(Br: ice lolly)* ghiacciolo *m*.

Lombardy *n* la Lombardia.

London ['lʌndən] *n* Londra *f*.

Londoner ['lʌndənəʳ] *n* londinese *mf*.

lonely ['ləʊnlɪ] *adj (person)* solo(-a); *(place)* isolato(-a).

long [lɒŋ] ◇ *adj* lungo(-a) ◇ *adv* molto; **it's 2 metres ~** è lungo 2 metri; **it's two hours ~** dura due ore; **how ~ is it?** *(in length)* quanto è lungo?; *(in time)* quanto dura?; **a ~ time** molto tempo; **all day ~** tutto il giorno; **as ~ as** *(provided that)* purché; **for ~** per molto tempo; **no ~er** non più; **so ~!** *(inf)* ciao!

◆ **long for** *vt fus* desiderare ardentemente.

long-distance *adj (phone call)* interurbano(-a).

long drink *n* long drink *m inv*.

long-haul *adj* su lunga distanza.

longitude ['lɒndʒɪtju:d] *n* longitudine *f*.

long jump *n* salto *m* in lungo.

long-life *adj (milk, fruit juice)* a lunga conservazione; *(battery)* a lunga durata.

longsighted [ˌlɒŋ'saɪtɪd] *adj* presbite.

long-term *adj* a lungo termine.

long wave *n* onde *fpl* lunghe.

longwearing [ˌlɒŋ'weərɪŋ] *adj (Am)* resistente.

loo [lu:] (*pl* **-s**) *n (Br: inf)* gabinetto *m*.

look [lʊk] ◇ *n (glance)* sguardo *m*, occhiata *f*; *(appearance)* aspetto *m* ◇ *vi* guardare; *(seem)* sembrare; **you don't ~ well** non hai una gran bella cera; **to ~ onto** *(building, room)* dare su; **to have a ~** dare un'occhiata; **(good) ~s** bellezza *f*; **I'm just ~ing** *(in shop)* sto solo guardando; **~ out!** attento!

◆ **look after** *vt fus* occuparsi di.

◆ **look at** *vt fus (observe)* guardare; *(examine)* vedere.

◆ **look for** *vt fus* cercare.

◆ **look forward to** *vt fus* non veder l'ora di.

◆ **look out for** *vt fus* cercare.

◆ **look round** ◇ *vt fus (city, museum)* visitare; *(shop)* fare un giro da ◇ *vi* girarsi.

◆ **look up** *vt sep (in dictionary, phone book)* cercare.

loony ['lu:nɪ] *n (inf)* pazzo *m* (-a *f*).

loop [lu:p] *n* cappio *m*.

loose [lu:s] *adj (not fixed firmly)* allentato(-a); *(sweets, sheets of paper)* sciolto(-a); *(clothes)* largo(-a); **to let sb/sthg ~** lasciar libero qn/qc.

loosen ['lu:sn] *vt* allentare.

lop-sided [-ˈsaɪdɪd] *adj* storto(-a).
lord [lɔːd] *n* lord *m inv*.
lorry [ˈlɒrɪ] *n (Br)* camion *m inv*.
lorry driver *n (Br)* camionista *mf*.
lose [luːz] (*pt & pp* **lost**) *vt & vi* perdere; **to ~ weight** dimagrire.
loser [ˈluːzəʳ] *n (in contest)* perdente *mf*.
loss [lɒs] *n* perdita *f*.
lost [lɒst] ◇ *pt & pp* → **lose** ◇ *adj (person)* perso(-a); **to get ~** *(lose way)* perdersi.
lost-and-found office *n (Am)* ufficio *m* oggetti smarriti.
lost property office *n (Br)* ufficio *m* oggetti smarriti.
lot [lɒt] *n (group of people)* gruppo *m*; *(at auction)* lotto *m*; *(Am: car park)* parcheggio *m*; **a ~** *(large amount)* molto(-a), molti(-e) *(pl)*; *(to a great extent, often)* molto; **a ~ of time** molto tempo; **a ~ of problems** molti problemi; **~s (of)** molto(-a), molti(-e) *(pl)*, un sacco (di); **the ~** *(everything)* tutto quanto (tutta quanta).
lotion [ˈləʊʃn] *n* lozione *f*.
lottery [ˈlɒtərɪ] *n* lotteria *f*.
loud [laʊd] *adj (music, noise)* forte; *(voice)* alto(-a); *(colour, clothes)* sgargiante.
loudspeaker [ˌlaʊdˈspiːkəʳ] *n* altoparlante *m*.
lounge [laʊndʒ] *n (in house)* salotto *m*, soggiorno *m*; *(at airport)* sala *f* partenze.
lounge bar *n (Br) sala di un pub più confortevole e più cara del 'public bar'*.
lousy [ˈlaʊzɪ] *adj (inf: poor-quality)* schifoso(-a).
lout [laʊt] *n* teppista *mf*.
love [lʌv] ◇ *n* amore *m*; *(in tennis)* zero *m* ◇ *vt* amare; **I ~ reading** mi piace molto leggere; **I'd ~ a coffee** mi andrebbe un caffè; **I'd ~ to help** vorrei tanto aiutare; **to be in ~ (with)** essere innamorato (di); **(with) ~ from** *(in letter)* con affetto.
love affair *n* relazione *f*.
lovely [ˈlʌvlɪ] *adj (very beautiful)* bello(-a); *(very nice)* delizioso(-a).
lover [ˈlʌvəʳ] *n (sexual partner)* amante *mf*; *(enthusiast)* appassionato *m* (-a *f*).
loving [ˈlʌvɪŋ] *adj* affettuoso(-a).
low [ləʊ] ◇ *adj* basso(-a); *(quantity)* piccolo(-a); *(supply)* scarso(-a); *(standard, quality, opinion)* scadente; *(depressed)* depresso(-a) ◇ *n (area of low pressure)* area *f* di bassa pressione; **we're ~ on petrol** abbiamo poca benzina.
low-alcohol *adj* a basso contenuto alcolico.
low-calorie *adj* ipocalorico(-a).
low-cut *adj* scollato(-a).
lower [ˈləʊəʳ] ◇ *adj* inferiore ◇ *vt* abbassare.
lower sixth *n (Br) primo anno di studi superiori per studenti di 17 anni che prepareranno gli 'A levels'*.
low-fat *adj* magro(-a).
low tide *n* bassa marea *f*.
loyal [ˈlɔɪəl] *adj* fedele.
loyalty [ˈlɔɪəltɪ] *n* fedeltà *f*.
lozenge [ˈlɒzɪndʒ] *n (sweet)* pasticca *f*, pastiglia *f*.
LP *n* LP *m inv*.
L-plate *n (Br) targa indicante che chi guida la vettura non ha ancora preso la patente*.
Ltd *(abbr of limited)* = Srl.
lubricate [ˈluːbrɪkeɪt] *vt* lubrificare.
luck [lʌk] *n* fortuna *f*; **bad ~** sfortuna *f*; **good ~!** buona fortuna!; **with ~** con un po' di fortuna.
luckily [ˈlʌkɪlɪ] *adv* fortunatamente.
lucky [ˈlʌkɪ] *adj* fortunato(-a); **to be ~** essere fortunato.
ludicrous [ˈluːdɪkrəs] *adj* ridicolo(-a).

lug [lʌg] *vt (inf)* trascinare.
luggage [ˈlʌgɪdʒ] *n* bagagli *mpl.*
luggage compartment *n* bagagliaio *m.*
luggage locker *n* armadietto *m* per deposito bagagli.
luggage rack *n (on train)* portabagagli *m.*
lukewarm [ˈluːkwɔːm] *adj* tiepido(-a).
lull [lʌl] *n* pausa *f.*
lullaby [ˈlʌləbaɪ] *n* ninnananna *f.*
lumbago [lʌmˈbeɪgəʊ] *n* lombaggine *f.*
lumber [ˈlʌmbər] *n (Am: timber)* legname *m.*
luminous [ˈluːmɪnəs] *adj* fosforescente.
lump [lʌmp] *n (of coal, mud, butter)* pezzo *m*; *(of sugar)* zolletta *f*; *(on body)* nodulo *m.*
lump sum *n* compenso *m* forfettario.
lumpy [ˈlʌmpɪ] *adj (sauce)* grumoso(-a); *(mattress)* pieno(-a) di bozzi.
lunatic [ˈluːnətɪk] *n* pazzo *m* (-a *f*).
lunch [lʌntʃ] *n* pranzo *m*; **to have ~** pranzare.
luncheon [ˈlʌntʃən] *n (fml)* pranzo *m.*
luncheon meat *n* = carne di maiale *f* in scatola.
lunch hour *n* pausa *f* pranzo.
lunchtime [ˈlʌntʃtaɪm] *n* ora *f* di pranzo.
lung [lʌŋ] *n* polmone *m.*
lunge [lʌndʒ] *vi*: **to ~ at** gettarsi su.
lurch [lɜːtʃ] *vi* barcollare.
lure [ljʊəʳ] *vt* attirare.
lurk [lɜːk] *vi (person)* stare in agguato.
lush [lʌʃ] *adj (grass, field)* rigoglioso(-a).
lust [lʌst] *n (sexual desire)* libidine *f.*
Luxembourg [ˈlʌksəmbɜːg] *n* il Lussemburgo.
luxurious [lʌgˈʒʊərɪəs] *adj* di lusso.
luxury [ˈlʌkʃərɪ] ◇ *adj* di lusso ◇ *n* lusso *m.*
lying [ˈlaɪɪŋ] *cont* → **lie**.
lyrics [ˈlɪrɪks] *npl* parole *fpl.*

m ◇ *(abbr of metre)* m ◇ *abbr* = **mile**.

M *(Br: abbr of motorway)* A; *(abbr of medium)* M.

MA *n (abbr of Master of Arts) (titolare di) master in materie umanistiche.*

mac [mæk] *n (Br: inf: coat)* impermeabile *m*.

macaroni [ˌmækəˈrəʊnɪ] *n* maccheroni *mpl*.

macaroni cheese *n* maccheroni *mpl* gratinati.

machine [məˈʃiːn] *n* macchina *f*.

machinegun [məˈʃiːngʌn] *n* mitragliatrice *f*.

machinery [məˈʃiːnərɪ] *n* macchine *fpl*.

machine-washable *adj* lavabile in lavatrice.

mackerel [ˈmækrəl] *(pl inv) n* sgombro *m*.

mackintosh [ˈmækɪntɒʃ] *n (Br)* impermeabile *m*.

mad [mæd] *adj* pazzo(-a), matto(-a); *(angry)* arrabbiato(-a); *(uncontrolled)* furioso(-a); **to be ~ about** *(inf: like a lot)* andare pazzo per; **like ~** come un matto.

Madam [ˈmædəm] *n (form of address)* signora *f*.

made [meɪd] *pt & pp* → **make**.

madeira [məˈdɪərə] *n* madera *m*.

made-to-measure *adj* fatto(-a) su misura.

madness [ˈmædnɪs] *n* pazzia *f*.

magazine [ˌmægəˈziːn] *n (journal)* rivista *f*.

maggot [ˈmægət] *n* verme *m*.

magic [ˈmædʒɪk] *n* magia *f*.

magician [məˈdʒɪʃn] *n (conjurer)* mago *m* (-a *f*).

magistrate [ˈmædʒɪstreɪt] *n* magistrato *m*.

magnet [ˈmægnɪt] *n* calamita *f*.

magnetic [mægˈnetɪk] *adj* magnetico(-a).

magnificent [mægˈnɪfɪsənt] *adj* magnifico(-a).

magnifying glass [ˈmægnɪfaɪɪŋ-] *n* lente *f* d'ingrandimento.

mahogany [məˈhɒgənɪ] *n* mogano *m*.

maid [meɪd] *n* cameriera *f*.

maiden name [ˈmeɪdn-] *n* nome *m* da nubile.

mail [meɪl] ◇ *n* posta *f* ◇ *vt (Am)* spedire.

mailbox [ˈmeɪlbɒks] *n (Am)* cassetta *f* delle lettere.

mailman [ˈmeɪlmən] (*pl* **-men** [-mən]) *n (Am)* postino *m*.

mail order *n* vendita *f* per corrispondenza.

main [meɪn] *adj* principale.

main course *n* portata *f* principale.

main deck *n* ponte *m* principale, coperta *f*.

mainland [ˈmeɪnlənd] *n*: **the ~** il continente.

main line *n* linea *f* principale.

mainly [ˈmeɪnlɪ] *adv* principalmente.

main road *n* strada *f* principale.

mains [meɪnz] *npl*: **the ~** le condutture.

main street *n (Am)* corso *m*.

maintain [meɪnˈteɪn] *vt (keep)* mantenere; *(in good condition)* provvedere alla manutenzione di.

maintenance [ˈmeɪntənəns] *n (of car, machine)* manutenzione *f*; *(money)* alimenti *mpl*.

maisonette [ˌmeɪzəˈnet] *n (Br)* appartamento *m* (su due piani).

maize [meɪz] *n* granturco *m*, mais *m*.

major [ˈmeɪdʒəʳ] ◇ *adj (important)* importante; *(most important)* principale ◇ *n* (MIL) maggiore *m* ◇ *vi (Am)*: **to ~ in** laurearsi in.

majority [məˈdʒɒrətɪ] *n* maggioranza *f*.

major road *n* strada *f* principale.

make [meɪk] (*pt & pp* **made**) ◇ *vt*

1. *(produce, manufacture)* fare; **to be made of** essere (fatto) di; **to ~ lunch/supper** preparare il pranzo/la cena; **made in Japan** fabbricato in Giappone.

2. *(perform, do)* fare; *(decision)* prendere; **to ~ a mistake** fare un errore; **to ~ a phone call** fare una telefonata.

3. *(cause to be)* rendere; **to ~ sthg better** migliorare qc; **to ~ sb happy** rendere felice qn.

4. *(cause to do, force)* fare; **to ~ sb do sthg** far fare qc a qn, costringere qn a fare qc; **it made her laugh** l'ha fatta ridere.

5. *(amount to, total)* fare; **that ~s £5** fanno 5 sterline.

6. *(calculate)*: **I ~ it £4** mi viene 4 sterline; **I ~ it seven o'clock** io faccio le sette.

7. *(earn)* fare; **to ~ a loss** registrare una perdita.

8. *(inf: arrive in time for)*: **I don't think we'll ~ the 10 o'clock train** non credo che ce la faremo per il treno delle 10.

9. *(friend, enemy)* farsi.

10. *(have qualities for)*: **this would ~ a lovely bedroom** sarebbe una camera (da letto) molto carina.

11. *(bed)* fare, rifare.

12. *(in phrases)*: **to ~ do (with)** arrangiarsi (con); **to ~ good** *(damage)* risarcire; **to ~ it** *(arrive on time, be able to go)* farcela.

◇ *n (of product)* marca *f*.

◆ **make out** *vt sep (cheque, receipt)* fare; *(form)* compilare; *(see, hear)* distinguere, capire.

◆ **make up** *vt sep (invent)* inventare; *(comprise)* costituire, comporre; *(difference)* coprire.

◆ **make up for** *vt fus* compensare.

makeshift [ˈmeɪkʃɪft] *adj* di fortuna.

make-up *n (cosmetics)* trucco *m*.

malaria [məˈleərɪə] *n* malaria *f*.

Malaysia [məˈleɪzɪə] *n* la Malesia.

male [meɪl] ◇ *adj* maschile; *(child, animal)* maschio ◇ *n (animal)* maschio *m*.

malfunction [mælˈfʌŋkʃn] *vi (fml)* funzionare male.

malignant [məˈlɪgnənt] *adj (tumour)* maligno(-a).

mall [mɔːl] *n (shopping centre)* centro *m* commerciale.

mallet [ˈmælɪt] *n* maglio *m*.

malt [mɔːlt] *n* malto *m*.

maltreat [ˌmælˈtriːt] *vt* maltrattare.

malt whisky *n* whisky *m inv* di malto.

mammal [ˈmæml] *n* mammifero *m*.

man [mæn] (*pl* **men**) ◇ *n* uomo *m*

◇ *vt (office)* dotare di personale; *(phones)* rispondere a.

manage [ˈmænɪdʒ] ◇ *vt (company, business)* dirigere; *(suitcase)* farcela a portare; *(job)* riuscire a fare; *(food)* farcela a mangiare ◇ *vi (cope)* farcela; **can you ~ Friday?** venerdì ti andrebbe bene?; **to ~ to do sthg** riuscire a fare qc.

management [ˈmænɪdʒmənt] *n* direzione *f*.

manager [ˈmænɪdʒəʳ] *n (of business, bank, shop)* direttore *m*; *(of sports team)* allenatore *m*.

manageress [ˌmænɪdʒəˈres] *n (of business, bank, shop)* direttrice *f*.

managing director [ˈmænɪdʒɪŋ-] *n* amministratore *m* delegato.

mandarin [ˈmændərɪn] *n* mandarino *m*.

mane [meɪn] *n* criniera *f*.

maneuver [məˈnuːvər] *(Am)* = **manoeuvre**.

mangetout [ˌmɒnʒˈtuː] *n* pisello *m* mangiatutto.

mangle [ˈmæŋgl] *vt (body)* straziare.

mango [ˈmæŋgəʊ] (*pl* **-es** OR **-s**) *n* mango *m*.

Manhattan [mænˈhætən] *n* Manhattan *f*.

manhole [ˈmænhəʊl] *n* pozzo *m* d'ispezione.

maniac [ˈmeɪnɪæk] *n (inf)* pazzo *m* (-a *f*).

manicure [ˈmænɪkjʊəʳ] *n* manicure *f inv*.

manifold [ˈmænɪfəʊld] *n* (AUT) collettore *m*.

manipulate [məˈnɪpjʊləɪt] *vt (person)* manipolare; *(machine, controls)* manovrare.

mankind [ˌmænˈkaɪnd] *n* l'umanità *f*.

manly [ˈmænlɪ] *adj* virile.

man-made *adj* artificiale.

manner [ˈmænəʳ] *n (way)* modo *m*. ◆ **manners** *npl* maniere *fpl*.

manoeuvre [məˈnuːvəʳ] ◇ *n (Br)* manovra *f* ◇ *vt (Br)* manovrare.

manor [ˈmænəʳ] *n* grande casa *f* di campagna.

mansion [ˈmænʃn] *n* casa *f* signorile.

manslaughter [ˈmænˌslɔːtəʳ] *n* omicidio *m* colposo.

mantelpiece [ˈmæntlpiːs] *n* mensola *f* del caminetto.

manual [ˈmænjʊəl] ◇ *adj* manuale ◇ *n* manuale *m*.

manufacture [ˌmænjʊˈfæktʃəʳ] ◇ *n* fabbricazione *f* ◇ *vt (produce)* fabbricare.

manufacturer [ˌmænjʊˈfæktʃərəʳ] *n* fabbricante *m*.

manure [məˈnjʊəʳ] *n* concime *m*.

many [ˈmenɪ] (*compar* **more**, *superl* **most**) ◇ *adj* molti(-e) ◇ *pron* molti *mpl* (-e *fpl*); **how ~?** quanti(-e)?; **so ~** così tanti(-e); **too ~** troppi(-e); **take as ~ as you like** prendine quanti ne vuoi; **twice as ~ as** il doppio di.

map [mæp] *n (of country)* carta *f* geografica; *(of town)* pianta *f*.

Mar. *(abbr of March)* mar.

marathon [ˈmærəθn] *n* maratona *f*.

marble [ˈmɑːbl] *n (stone)* marmo *m*; *(glass ball)* bilia *f*, pallina *f* (di vetro).

march [mɑːtʃ] ◇ *n (demonstration)* marcia *f* ◇ *vi (walk quickly)* avanzare con passo deciso.

March [mɑːtʃ] *n* marzo *m*, → **September**.

mare [meəʳ] *n* giumenta *f*.

margarine [ˌmɑːdʒəˈriːn] *n* margarina *f*.

margin [ˈmɑːdʒɪn] *n* margine *m*.

marina [məˈriːnə] *n* porto *m* turistico.

marinated [ˈmærɪneɪtɪd] *adj* marinato(-a).

marital status [ˈmærɪtl-] *n* stato *m* civile.

mark [mɑːk] ◇ *n (spot)* macchia *f*; *(cut, symbol)* segno *m*; (SCH) voto *m*; *(of gas oven) numero corrispondente a una certa temperatura* ◇ *vt (blemish)* macchiare; *(put symbol on)* segnare; *(correct)* correggere; *(show position of)* indicare.

marker pen [ˈmɑːkə-] *n* (grosso) pennarello *m*.

market [ˈmɑːkɪt] *n* mercato *m*.

marketing [ˈmɑːkɪtɪŋ] *n* marketing *m*.

marketplace [ˈmɑːkɪtpleɪs] *n (place)* piazza *f* del mercato.

markings [ˈmɑːkɪŋz] *npl (on road)* segnaletica *f* orizzontale.

marmalade [ˈmɑːməleɪd] *n* marmellata *f* di agrumi.

marquee [mɑːˈkiː] *n* padiglione *m*.

marriage [ˈmærɪdʒ] *n* matrimonio *m*.

married [ˈmærɪd] *adj* sposato(-a); **to get ~** sposarsi.

marrow [ˈmærəʊ] *n (vegetable)* zucca *f*.

marry [ˈmærɪ] ◇ *vt* sposare ◇ *vi* sposarsi.

marsh [mɑːʃ] *n* palude *f*.

martial arts [ˌmɑːʃl-] *npl* arti *fpl* marziali.

marvellous [ˈmɑːvələs] *adj (Br)* meraviglioso(-a).

marvelous [ˈmɑːvələs] *(Am)* = **marvellous**.

marzipan [ˈmɑːzɪpæn] *n* marzapane *m*.

mascara [mæsˈkɑːrə] *n* mascara *m inv*.

masculine [ˈmæskjʊlɪn] *adj* maschile; *(woman)* mascolino(-a).

mashed potatoes [mæʃt-] *npl* purè *m inv* di patate.

mask [mɑːsk] *n* maschera *f*.

masonry [ˈmeɪsnrɪ] *n* muratura *f*.

mass [mæs] *n (large amount)* massa *f*; (RELIG) messa *f*; **~es (of)** *(inf: lots)* un sacco (di).

massacre [ˈmæsəkəʳ] *n* massacro *m*.

massage [*Br* ˈmæsɑːʒ, *Am* məˈsɑːʒ] ◇ *n* massaggio *m* ◇ *vt* massaggiare.

masseur [mæˈsɜːʳ] *n* massaggiatore *m*.

masseuse [mæˈsɜːz] *n* massaggiatrice *f*.

massive [ˈmæsɪv] *adj* enorme.

mast [mɑːst] *n (on boat)* albero *m*.

master [ˈmɑːstəʳ] ◇ *n (at school)* insegnante *m*; *(of servant, dog)* padrone *m* ◇ *vt (learn)* imparare a fondo.

masterpiece [ˈmɑːstəpiːs] *n* capolavoro *m*.

mat [mæt] *n (small rug)* tappetino *m*; *(on table)* sottopiatto *m*.

match [mætʃ] ◇ *n (for lighting)* fiammifero *m*; *(game)* partita *f*, incontro *m* ◇ *vt (in colour, design)* intonarsi a OR con; *(be the same as)* corrispondere a; *(be as good as)* uguagliare ◇ *vi (in colour, design)* intonarsi.

matchbox [ˈmætʃbɒks] *n* scatola *f* di fiammiferi.

matching [ˈmætʃɪŋ] *adj* intonato(-a).

mate [meɪt] ◇ *n (inf: friend)* amico *m* (-a *f*) ◇ *vi* accoppiarsi.

material [məˈtɪərɪəl] *n* materiale *m*; *(cloth)* stoffa *f*.

◆ **materials** *npl (equipment)* occorrente *m*.

maternity leave [məˈtɜːnətɪ-] *n* congedo *m* di maternità.

maternity ward [məˈtɜːnətɪ-] *n* reparto *m* maternità.

math [mæθ] *(Am)* = **maths**.

mathematics [ˌmæθəˈmætɪks] *n* matematica *f*.

maths [mæθs] *n (Br)* matematica *f*.

matinée [ˈmætɪneɪ] *n* matinée *f inv*.

matt [mæt] *adj* opaco(-a).

matter ['mætəʳ] ◇ *n (issue, situation)* questione *f*; *(physical material)* materia *f* ◇ *vi* importare; **it doesn't ~** non importa; **no ~ what happens** qualsiasi cosa accada; **there's something the ~ with my car** c'è qualcosa che non va con la mia macchina; **what's the ~?** che cosa c'è (che non va)?; **as a ~ of course** come è naturale; **as a ~ of fact** in realtà.

mattress ['mætrɪs] *n* materasso *m*.

mature [mə'tjʊəʳ] *adj (person, behaviour)* maturo(-a); *(cheese, wine)* stagionato(-a).

mauve [məʊv] *adj* (color) malva *(inv)*.

max. [mæks] *(abbr of maximum)* max.

maximum ['mæksɪməm] ◇ *adj* massimo(-a) ◇ *n* massimo *m*.

may [meɪ] *aux vb* **1.** *(expressing possibility)*: **it ~ be done as follows** si può procedere come segue; **it ~ rain** può darsi che piova; **they ~ have got lost** può darsi che si siano persi.

2. *(expressing permission)*: **~ I smoke?** posso fumare?; **you ~ sit, if you wish** può sedersi, se vuole.

3. *(when conceding a point)*: **it ~ be a long walk, but it's worth it** sarà anche lontano a piedi, ma ne vale la pena.

May [meɪ] *n* maggio *m*, → **September**.

maybe ['meɪbiː] *adv* forse.

mayonnaise [,meɪə'neɪz] *n* maionese *f*.

mayor [meəʳ] *n* sindaco *m*.

mayoress ['meərɪs] *n* sindaco *m (donna)*.

maze [meɪz] *n* labirinto *m*.

me [miː] *pron* mi; *(after prep, stressed)* me; **she knows ~** (lei) mi conosce; **it's ~** sono io; **send it to ~** mandalo a me; **tell ~** dimmi; **he's worse than ~** lui è peggio di me.

meadow ['medəʊ] *n* prato *m*.

meal [miːl] *n* pasto *m*.

mealtime ['miːltaɪm] *n* ora *f* di mangiare.

mean [miːn] (*pt & pp* **meant**) ◇ *adj (miserly)* avaro(-a), gretto(-a); *(unkind)* scortese, villano(-a) ◇ *vt (signify, matter)* significare, voler dire; *(intend, be serious about)* intendere; *(be a sign of)* significare; **I didn't ~ it** non dicevo sul serio; **to ~ to do sthg** avere l'intenzione di fare qc; **the bus was meant to leave at 8.30** l'autobus sarebbe dovuto partire alle 8.30; **it's meant to be good** dovrebbe essere buono.

meaning ['miːnɪŋ] *n* significato *m*, senso *m*.

meaningless ['miːnɪŋlɪs] *adj (irrelevant)* insignificante.

means [miːnz] ◇ *(pl inv) n (method)* mezzo *m* ◇ *npl (money)* mezzi *mpl*; **by all ~!** ma certo!; **by ~ of** per mezzo di.

meant [ment] *pt & pp* → **mean**.

meantime ['miːn,taɪm]: **in the meantime** *adv* nel frattempo.

meanwhile ['miːn,waɪl] *adv* nel frattempo.

measles ['miːzlz] *n* morbillo *m*.

measure ['meʒəʳ] ◇ *vt* misurare ◇ *n (step, action)* misura *f*, provvedimento *m*; *(of alcohol)* dose *f*; **the room ~s 10 m²** la stanza misura 10 m².

measurement ['meʒəmənt] *n* misura *f*.

meat [miːt] *n* carne *f*; **red ~** carne rossa; **white ~** carne bianca.

meatball ['miːtbɔːl] *n* polpetta *f* (di carne).

mechanic [mɪ'kænɪk] *n* meccanico *m*.

mechanical [mɪ'kænɪkl] *adj (device)* meccanico(-a).

mechanism ['mekənɪzm] *n* meccanismo *m*.

medal ['medl] *n* medaglia *f*.

media ['mi:djə] *n or npl*: **the ~** i (mass) media.

medical ['medɪkl] ◇ *adj* medico(-a) ◇ *n* visita *f* medica.

medication [,medɪ'keɪʃn] *n* medicine *fpl*.

medicine ['medsɪn] *n* medicina *f*.

medicine cabinet *n* armadietto *m* dei medicinali.

medieval [,medɪ'i:vl] *adj* medievale.

mediocre [,mi:dɪ'əʊkə^r] *adj* mediocre.

Mediterranean [,medɪtə'reɪnjən] *n*: **the ~** *(region)* la regione del Mediterraneo; **the ~ (Sea)** il (Mare) Mediterraneo.

medium ['mi:djəm] *adj* medio(-a); *(sherry)* semisecco(-a).

medium-dry *adj* semisecco(-a).

medium-sized [-saɪzd] *adj* di misura media.

medley ['medlɪ] *n*: **a ~ of cold meats** affettati *mpl* misti.

meet [mi:t] (*pt & pp* **met**) ◇ *vt* incontrare; *(get to know)* fare la conoscenza di, conoscere; *(go to collect)* andare a prendere; *(need, requirement)* soddisfare; *(cost, expenses)* far fronte a ◇ *vi* incontrarsi; *(get to know each other)* conoscersi.

◆ **meet up** *vi* incontrarsi.

◆ **meet with** *vt fus* incontrare.

meeting ['mi:tɪŋ] *n (for business)* incontro *m*.

meeting point *n (at airport, station)* punto *m* d'incontro.

melody ['melədɪ] *n* melodia *f*.

melon ['melən] *n* melone *m*.

melt [melt] *vi* sciogliersi; *(metal)* fondersi.

member ['membə^r] *n* membro *m*.

Member of Congress [-'kɒŋgres] *n* membro *m* del Congresso (Americano).

Member of Parliament *n* = deputato *m* (-a *f*).

membership ['membəʃɪp] *n (state of being a member)* appartenenza *f*; *(members)* (numero dei) membri *mpl*.

memorial [mɪ'mɔ:rɪəl] *n* monumento *m*.

memorize ['meməraɪz] *vt* memorizzare.

memory ['memərɪ] *n* memoria *f*; *(thing remembered)* ricordo *m*.

men [men] *pl* → **man**.

menacing ['menəsɪŋ] *adj* minaccioso(-a).

mend [mend] *vt* accomodare, aggiustare; *(clothes)* rammendare.

menopause ['menəpɔ:z] *n* menopausa *f*.

men's room *n (Am)* gabinetto *m* degli uomini.

menstruate ['menstrʊeɪt] *vi* avere le mestruazioni.

menswear ['menzweə^r] *n* abbigliamento *m* da uomo.

mental ['mentl] *adj* mentale.

mental hospital *n* ospedale *m* psichiatrico.

mentally handicapped ['mentəlɪ-] ◇ *adj* mentalmente handicappato(-a) ◇ *npl*: **the ~** i portatori di handicap mentale.

mentally ill ['mentəlɪ-] *adj* malato(-a) di mente.

mention ['menʃn] *vt* accennare a; **don't ~ it!** non c'è di che!

menu ['menju:] *n* menu *m inv*; **children's ~** menu per bambini.

merchandise ['mɜ:tʃəndaɪz] *n* mercanzia *f*, merce *f*.

merchant marine [,mɜ:tʃəntmə'ri:n] *(Am)* = **merchant navy**.

merchant navy [,mɜ:tʃənt-] *n (Br)* marina *f* mercantile.

mercury ['mɜ:kjʊrɪ] *n* mercurio *m*.

mercy ['mɜ:sɪ] *n* pietà *f*.

mere [mɪəʳ] *adj* semplice; **a ~ £5** solo 5 sterline.

merely [ˈmɪəlɪ] *adv* soltanto.

merge [mɜːdʒ] *vi (combine)* fondersi, unirsi; **'merge'** *(Am:* AUT*) segnale che indica agli automobilisti che si immettono su un'autostrada di disporsi sulla corsia di destra.*

merger [ˈmɜːdʒəʳ] *n* fusione *f*.

meringue [məˈræŋ] *n (egg white)* meringa *f*; *(cake)* meringa alla panna.

merit [ˈmerɪt] *n* merito *m*.

merry [ˈmerɪ] *adj* allegro(-a); **Merry Christmas!** Buon Natale!

merry-go-round *n* giostra *f*.

mess [mes] *n (untidiness)* disordine *m*, confusione *f*; *(difficult situation)* pasticcio *m*; **in a ~** *(untidy)* in disordine.

◆ **mess about** *vi (inf) (have fun)* divertirsi; *(behave foolishly)* fare lo scemo; **to ~ about with sthg** *(interfere)* intromettersi in qc.

◆ **mess up** *vt sep (inf: ruin, spoil)* mandare a monte.

message [ˈmesɪdʒ] *n* messaggio *m*.

messenger [ˈmesɪndʒəʳ] *n* messaggero *m* (-a *f*).

messy [ˈmesɪ] *adj* disordinato(-a).

met [met] *pt & pp* → **meet**.

metal [ˈmetl] ◇ *adj* metallico(-a), di metallo ◇ *n* metallo *m*.

metalwork [ˈmetəlwɜːk] *n (craft)* lavorazione *f* dei metalli.

meter [ˈmiːtəʳ] *n (device)* contatore *m*; *(Am)* = **metre**.

method [ˈmeθəd] *n* metodo *m*.

methodical [mɪˈθɒdɪkl] *adj* metodico(-a).

meticulous [mɪˈtɪkjʊləs] *adj* meticoloso(-a).

metre [ˈmiːtəʳ] *n (Br)* metro *m*.

metric [ˈmetrɪk] *adj* metrico(-a).

mews [mjuːz] *(pl inv) n (Br) stradina o cortile di antiche scuderie trasformate in appartamenti.*

Mexican [ˈmeksɪkn] ◇ *adj* messicano(-a) ◇ *n* messicano *m* (-a *f*).

Mexico [ˈmeksɪkəʊ] *n* il Messico.

mg *(abbr of milligram)* mg.

miaow [miːˈaʊ] *vi (Br)* miagolare.

mice [maɪs] *pl* → **mouse**.

microchip [ˈmaɪkrəʊtʃɪp] *n* microcircuito *m* integrato, microchip *m inv*.

microphone [ˈmɪkrəfəʊn] *n* microfono *m*.

microscope [ˈmaɪkrəskəʊp] *n* microscopio *m*.

microwave (oven) [ˈmaɪkrəweɪv-] *n* forno *m* a microonde.

midday [ˌmɪdˈdeɪ] *n* mezzogiorno *m*.

middle [ˈmɪdl] ◇ *n* mezzo *m*, parte *f* centrale ◇ *adj (central)* di mezzo; **in the ~ of the road** in mezzo alla strada; **in the ~ of April** a metà aprile; **to be in the ~ of doing sthg** stare facendo qc.

middle-aged *adj* di mezza età.

middle-class *adj* borghese.

Middle East *n*: **the ~** il Medio Oriente.

middle name *n* secondo nome *m*.

middle school *n (in UK)* scuola *f* media *(per ragazzi dagli 8 ai 13 anni)*.

midge [mɪdʒ] *n* pappataci *m inv*.

midget [ˈmɪdʒɪt] *n* nano *m* (-a *f*).

Midlands [ˈmɪdləndz] *npl*: **the ~** *le contee dell'Inghilterra centrale.*

midnight [ˈmɪdnaɪt] *n* mezzanotte *f*.

midsummer [ˈmɪdˈsʌməʳ] *n* piena estate *f*.

midway [ˌmɪdˈweɪ] *adv (in space)* a metà strada; *(in time)* a metà.

midweek [*adj* ˈmɪdwiːk, *adv* mɪdˈwiːk] ◇ *adj* di metà settimana ◇ *adv* a metà settimana.

midwife [ˈmɪdwaɪf] (*pl* **-wives** [-waɪvz]) *n* levatrice *f*.

midwinter ['mɪd'wɪntəʳ] *n* pieno inverno *m*.

might [maɪt] ◇ *aux vb* 1. *(expressing possibility)*: **we ~ go to Wales this year** forse andremo in Galles quest'anno; **I suppose they ~ still come** può ancora darsi che arrivino; **they ~ have been killed** avrebbero potuto rimanere uccisi.
2. *(fml: expressing permission)*: **~ I have a few words?** posso parlarle un attimo?
3. *(when conceding a point)*: **it ~ be expensive, but it's good quality** sarà anche caro, ma è di buona qualità.
4. *(would)*: **I'd hoped you ~ come too** speravo che venissi anche tu.
◇ *n (physical strength)* forza *f*.

migraine ['mi:greɪn, 'maɪgreɪn] *n* emicrania *f*.

Milan [mɪ'læn] *n* Milano *f*.

mild [maɪld] ◇ *adj (cheese, person)* dolce; *(detergent, taste)* delicato(-a); *(effect, flu)* leggero(-a); *(weather, climate)* mite; *(curiosity, surprise)* lieve ◇ *n (Br: beer)* birra *f* leggera.

mile [maɪl] *n* miglio *m*; **it's ~s away** è lontanissimo.

mileage ['maɪlɪdʒ] *n* distanza *f* in miglia, = chilometraggio *m*.

mileometer [maɪ'lɒmɪtəʳ] *n* = contachilometri *m inv*.

military ['mɪlɪtrɪ] *adj* militare.

milk [mɪlk] ◇ *n* latte *m* ◇ *vt (cow)* mungere.

milk chocolate *n* cioccolato *m* al latte.

milkman ['mɪlkmən] (*pl* **-men** [-mən]) *n* lattaio *m*.

milk shake *n* frappé *m inv*.

milky ['mɪlkɪ] *adj (drink)* con tanto latte.

mill [mɪl] *n (flour-mill)* mulino *m*; *(for pepper, coffee)* macinino *m*; *(factory)* fabbrica *f*.

milligram ['mɪlɪgræm] *n* milligrammo *m*.

millilitre ['mɪlɪ,li:təʳ] *n* millilitro *m*..

millimetre ['mɪlɪ,mi:təʳ] *n* millimetro *m*.

million ['mɪljən] *n* milione *m*; **~s of** *(fig)* milioni di.

millionaire [,mɪljə'neəʳ] *n* = miliardario *m* (-a *f*).

mime [maɪm] *vi* mimare.

min. [mɪn] *(abbr of minute, minimum)* min.

mince [mɪns] *n (Br)* carne *f* macinata.

mincemeat ['mɪnsmi:t] *n (sweet filling) miscuglio a base di uvetta e spezie*; *(Am: mince)* carne *f* macinata.

mince pie *n pasticcino con ripieno a base di uvetta e spezie che si mangia durante il periodo natalizio.*

mind [maɪnd] ◇ *n* mente *f* ◇ *vt (be careful of)* fare attenzione a; *(look after)* badare a ◇ *vi*: **I don't ~** non m'importa; **do you ~ if ...?** le dispiace se ...?; **never ~!** *(don't worry)* non preoccuparti!, non importa!; **it slipped my ~** mi è sfuggito di mente; **to my ~** secondo me, a mio parere; **to bear sthg in ~** tenere presente qc; **to change one's ~** cambiare idea; **to have sthg in ~** avere in mente qc; **to have sthg on one's ~** essere preoccupato per qc; **to make one's ~ up** decidersi; **do you ~ the noise?** le dà fastidio il rumore?; **I wouldn't ~ a drink** non mi dispiacerebbe bere qualcosa; **'~ the gap!'** *(on underground) annuncio che avverte i viaggiatori sulla metropolitana di fare attenzione alla buca tra le carrozze e il marciapiede.*

mine[1] [maɪn] *pron* il mio (la mia), i miei (le mie) *(pl)*; **a friend of ~** un mio amico.

mine[2] [maɪn] *n (for coal etc)* miniera *f*; *(bomb)* mina *f*.

miner ['maɪnəʳ] *n* minatore *m*.

mineral ['mɪnərəl] *n* minerale *m*.

mineral water *n* acqua *f* minerale.
minestrone [ˌmɪnɪˈstrəʊnɪ] *n* minestrone *m*.
mingle [ˈmɪŋgl] *vi* mescolarsi.
miniature [ˈmɪnətʃəʳ] ◇ *adj* in miniatura ◇ *n (bottle)* bottiglia *f* mignon.
minibar [ˈmɪnɪbɑːʳ] *n* minibar *m inv*.
minibus [ˈmɪnɪbʌs] (*pl* **-es**) *n* minibus *m inv*.
minicab [ˈmɪnɪkæb] *n (Br)* radiotaxi *m inv*.
minimal [ˈmɪnɪml] *adj* minimo(-a).
minimum [ˈmɪnɪməm] ◇ *adj* minimo(-a) ◇ *n* minimo *m*.
miniskirt [ˈmɪnɪskɜːt] *n* minigonna *f*.
minister [ˈmɪnɪstəʳ] *n (in government)* ministro *m*; *(in church)* pastore *m*.
ministry [ˈmɪnɪstrɪ] *n (of government)* ministero *m*.
minor [ˈmaɪnəʳ] ◇ *adj* minore, di secondaria importanza ◇ *n (fml)* minorenne *mf*.
minority [maɪˈnɒrətɪ] *n* minoranza *f*.
minor road *n* strada *f* secondaria.
mint [mɪnt] *n (sweet)* caramella *f* alla menta; *(plant)* menta *f*.
minus [ˈmaɪnəs] *prep (in subtraction)* meno; **it's ~ 10 (degrees C)** è meno 10 (gradi).
minuscule [ˈmɪnəskjuːl] *adj* minuscolo(-a).
minute[1] [ˈmɪnɪt] *n* minuto *m*; **any ~** da un momento all'altro; **just a ~!** (solo) un minuto!
minute[2] [maɪˈnjuːt] *adj* minuscolo(-a).
minute steak [ˌmɪnɪt-] *n* fettina *f* (di carne).
miracle [ˈmɪrəkl] *n* miracolo *m*.
miraculous [mɪˈrækjʊləs] *adj* miracoloso(-a).
mirror [ˈmɪrəʳ] *n* specchio *m*; *(on car)* specchietto *m*.
misbehave [ˌmɪsbɪˈheɪv] *vi* comportarsi male.
miscarriage [ˌmɪsˈkærɪdʒ] *n* aborto *m* spontaneo.
miscellaneous [ˌmɪsəˈleɪnjəs] *adj (things)* vario(-a); *(collection)* misto(-a).
mischievous [ˈmɪstʃɪvəs] *adj* birichino(-a).
misconduct [ˌmɪsˈkɒndʌkt] *n* condotta *f* scorretta.
miser [ˈmaɪzəʳ] *n* avaro *m* (-a *f*).
miserable [ˈmɪzrəbl] *adj (unhappy)* infelice; *(place, news, weather)* deprimente; *(amount)* misero(-a).
misery [ˈmɪzərɪ] *n (unhappiness)* tristezza *f*; *(poor conditions)* miseria *f*.
misfire [ˌmɪsˈfaɪəʳ] *vi (car)* perdere colpi.
misfortune [mɪsˈfɔːtʃuːn] *n (bad luck)* sfortuna *f*.
mishap [ˈmɪshæp] *n* disavventura *f*.
misjudge [ˌmɪsˈdʒʌdʒ] *vt* giudicare male.
mislay [ˌmɪsˈleɪ] (*pt & pp* **-laid**) *vt* smarrire.
mislead [ˌmɪsˈliːd] (*pt & pp* **-led**) *vt* trarre in inganno.
miss [mɪs] ◇ *vt* perdere; *(not notice)* non vedere; *(fail to hit)* mancare ◇ *vi* sbagliare; **I ~ you** mi manchi.
♦ **miss out** ◇ *vt sep* saltare, omettere ◇ *vi*: **to ~ out on sthg** perdersi qc.
Miss [mɪs] *n* Signorina *f*.
missile [*Br* ˈmɪsaɪl, *Am* ˈmɪsl] *n (weapon)* missile *m*; *(thing thrown)* oggetto *m (scagliato)*.
missing [ˈmɪsɪŋ] *adj (lost)* scomparso(-a); *(after accident)* disperso(-a); **to be ~** *(not there)* mancare.
missing person *n* persona *f* scomparsa.

mission [ˈmɪʃn] *n* missione *f*.
missionary [ˈmɪʃənrɪ] *n* missionario *m* (-a *f*).
mist [mɪst] *n* foschia *f*.
mistake [mɪˈsteɪk] (*pt* **-took**, *pp* **-taken**) ◇ *n* sbaglio *m*, errore *m* ◇ *vt (misunderstand)* fraintendere; **by ~** per sbaglio; **to make a ~** fare uno sbaglio; **to ~ sb/sthg for** scambiare qn/qc per.
Mister [ˈmɪstəʳ] *n* Signor *m*.
mistook [mɪˈstʊk] *pt* → **mistake**.
mistress [ˈmɪstrɪs] *n (lover)* amante *f*; *(Br: teacher)* insegnante *f*.
mistrust [ˌmɪsˈtrʌst] *vt* diffidare di.
misty [ˈmɪstɪ] *adj* nebbioso(-a).
misunderstanding [ˌmɪsʌndəˈstændɪŋ] *n* malinteso *m*.
misuse [ˌmɪsˈjuːs] *n* cattivo uso *m*.
mitten [ˈmɪtn] *n* muffola *f*, manopola *f*.
mix [mɪks] ◇ *vt* mescolare ◇ *n (for cake, sauce)* (miscuglio) preparato *m* ◇ *vi (socially)*: **to ~ with people** veder gente; **to ~ sthg with sthg** mescolare qc a OR con qc.
◆ **mix up** *vt sep (confuse)* confondere; *(put into disorder)* mescolare.
mixed [mɪkst] *adj (school)* misto(-a).
mixed grill *n* grigliata *f* mista.
mixed salad *n* insalata *f* mista.
mixed vegetables *npl* verdure *fpl* miste.
mixer [ˈmɪksəʳ] *n (for food)* frullatore *m*; *(drink) bevanda analcolica usata nella preparazione di cocktail.*
mixture [ˈmɪkstʃəʳ] *n (combination)* mescolanza *f*.
mix-up *n (inf)* confusione *f*.
ml *(abbr of millilitre)* ml.
mm *(abbr of millimetre)* mm.
moan [məʊn] *vi (in pain, grief)* gemere; *(inf: complain)* lamentarsi.
moat [məʊt] *n* fossato *m*.
mobile [ˈməʊbaɪl] *adj* mobile.
mobile phone *n* telefono *m* cellulare, telefonino *m*.
mock [mɒk] ◇ *adj* finto(-a) ◇ *vt* deridere, prendersi gioco di ◇ *n (Br: exam)* esercitazione *f* d'esame.
mode [məʊd] *n* modo *m*.
model [ˈmɒdl] *n* modello *m*; *(fashion model)* modello *m* (-a *f*).
modem [ˈməʊdem] *n* modem *m inv*.
moderate [ˈmɒdərət] *adj* moderato(-a).
modern [ˈmɒdən] *adj* moderno(-a).
modernized [ˈmɒdənaɪzd] *adj* rimodernato(-a).
modern languages *npl* lingue *fpl* moderne.
modest [ˈmɒdɪst] *adj* modesto(-a).
modify [ˈmɒdɪfaɪ] *vt* modificare.
mohair [ˈməʊheəʳ] *n* mohair *m*.
moist [mɔɪst] *adj* umido(-a).
moisture [ˈmɔɪstʃəʳ] *n* umidità *f*.
moisturizer [ˈmɔɪstʃəraɪzəʳ] *n* idratante *m*.
molar [ˈməʊləʳ] *n* molare *m*.
mold [məʊld] *(Am)* = **mould**.
mole [məʊl] *n (animal)* talpa *f*; *(spot)* neo *m*.
molest [məˈlest] *vt* molestare.
mom [mɒm] *n (Am: inf)* mamma *f*.
moment [ˈməʊmənt] *n* momento *m*; **at the ~** al momento; **for the ~** per il momento.
Mon. *(abbr of Monday)* lun.
monarchy [ˈmɒnəkɪ] *n*: **the ~** la monarchia.
monastery [ˈmɒnəstrɪ] *n* monastero *m*.
Monday [ˈmʌndɪ] *n* lunedì *m inv*, → **Saturday**.
money [ˈmʌnɪ] *n* denaro *m*, soldi *mpl*.
money belt *n* marsupio *m*.
money order *n* vaglia *m inv* (postale).

mongrel ['mʌŋgrəl] *n* cane *m* bastardo.

monitor ['mɒnɪtəʳ] ◇ *n (computer screen)* monitor *m inv* ◇ *vt (check, observe)* controllare.

monk [mʌŋk] *n* monaco *m*.

monkey ['mʌŋkɪ] (*pl* **monkeys**) *n* scimmia *f*.

monkfish ['mʌŋkfɪʃ] *n* bottatrice *f*.

monopoly [mə'nɒpəlɪ] *n* monopolio *m*.

monorail ['mɒnəʊreɪl] *n* monorotaia *f*.

monotonous [mə'nɒtənəs] *adj* monotono(-a).

monsoon [mɒn'su:n] *n* monsone *m*.

monster ['mɒnstəʳ] *n* mostro *m*.

month [mʌnθ] *n* mese *m*; **every ~** ogni mese; **in a ~'s time** fra un mese.

monthly ['mʌnθlɪ] ◇ *adj* mensile ◇ *adv* mensilmente, ogni mese.

monument ['mɒnjʊmənt] *n* monumento *m*.

mood [mu:d] *n* umore *m*; **to be in a (bad) ~** essere di cattivo umore; **to be in a good ~** essere di buon umore.

moody ['mu:dɪ] *adj (in a bad mood)* di malumore; *(changeable)* lunatico(-a), volubile.

moon [mu:n] *n* luna *f*.

moonlight ['mu:nlaɪt] *n* chiaro *m* di luna.

moor [mɔ:ʳ] ◇ *n* brughiera *f* ◇ *vt* ormeggiare.

moose [mu:s] *(pl inv) n* alce *m*.

mop [mɒp] ◇ *n (for floor)* lavapavimenti *m inv* ◇ *vt (floor)* lavare con lo straccio.

◆ **mop up** *vt sep (clean up)* asciugare con uno straccio.

moped ['məʊped] *n* ciclomotore *m*.

moral ['mɒrəl] ◇ *adj* morale ◇ *n (lesson)* morale *f*.

morality [mə'rælɪtɪ] *n* moralità *f*.

more [mɔ:ʳ] ◇ *adj* **1.** *(a larger amount of)* più; **there are ~ tourists than usual** ci sono più turisti del solito.
2. *(additional)* altro(-a); **are there any ~ cakes?** ci sono altri OR ancora pasticcini?; **I'd like two ~ bottles** vorrei altre due bottiglie; **there's no ~ wine** non c'è più vino.
3. *(in phrases)*: **~ and more** sempre più.
◇ *adv* **1.** *(in comparatives)* più; **it's ~ difficult than before** è più difficile di prima; **speak ~ clearly** parla più chiaramente.
2. *(to a greater degree)* di più; **we ought to go to the cinema ~** dovremmo andare più spesso al cinema.
3. *(in phrases)*: **not ... any ~** non ... più; **I don't go there any ~** non ci vado più; **once ~** ancora una volta, un'altra volta; **~ or less** più o meno; **we'd be ~ than happy to help** saremmo più che lieti di dare una mano.
◇ *pron* **1.** *(a larger amount)* più; **I've got ~ than you** ne ho più di te; **~ than 20 types of pizza** oltre 20 tipi di pizza.
2. *(an additional amount)* ancora; **is there any ~?** ce n'è ancora?; **there's no ~** non ce n'è più.

moreover [mɔ:'rəʊvəʳ] *adv (fml)* inoltre.

morning ['mɔ:nɪŋ] *n* mattina *f*, mattino *m*; **two o'clock in the ~** le due di notte; **good ~!** buon giorno!; **in the ~** *(early in the day)* di mattina; *(tomorrow morning)* domattina.

morning-after pill *n* pillola *f* del giorno dopo.

morning sickness *n* nausea *f* mattutina.

Morocco [mə'rɒkəʊ] *n* il Marocco.

moron ['mɔːrɒn] *n (inf)* deficiente *mf*.

Morse (code) [mɔːs-] *n* alfabeto *m* Morse.

mortgage ['mɔːgɪdʒ] *n* mutuo *m* (ipotecario).

mosaic [mə'zeɪɪk] *n* mosaico *m*.

Moslem ['mɒzləm] = **Muslim**.

mosque [mɒsk] *n* moschea *f*.

mosquito [mə'skiːtəʊ] (*pl* **-es**) *n* zanzara *f*.

mosquito net *n* zanzariera *f*.

moss [mɒs] *n* muschio *m*.

most [məʊst] ◇ *adj* **1.** *(the majority of)* la maggior parte di; **~ people agree** la maggior parte della gente è d'accordo.

2. *(the largest amount of)*: **I drank (the) ~ beer** sono quello che ha bevuto più birra.

◇ *adv* **1.** *(in superlatives)* più; **the ~ expensive hotel in town** l'albergo più caro della città.

2. *(to the greatest degree)* di più, maggiormente; **I like this one ~** questo è quello che mi piace di più.

3. *(fml: very)* molto, estremamente; **they were ~ welcoming** sono stati estremamente accoglienti.

◇ *pron* **1.** *(the majority)* la maggior parte; **~ of the villages** la maggior parte dei paesi; **~ of the time** la maggior parte del tempo.

2. *(the largest amount)*: **she earns (the) ~** è quella che guadagna di più.

3. *(in phrases)*: **at ~** al massimo; **to make the ~ of sthg** sfruttare al massimo qc.

mostly ['məʊstlɪ] *adv* per lo più.

MOT *n (Br: test) revisione annuale obbligatoria degli autoveicoli di più di tre anni.*

motel [məʊ'tel] *n* motel *m inv*.

moth [mɒθ] *n* farfalla *f* notturna.

mother ['mʌðəʳ] *n* madre *f*.

mother-in-law *n* suocera *f*.

mother-of-pearl *n* madreperla *f*.

motif [məʊ'tiːf] *n* motivo *m*.

motion ['məʊʃn] ◇ *n (movement)* movimento *m*, moto *m* ◇ *vi*: **to ~ to sb** fare cenno a qn.

motionless ['məʊʃənlɪs] *adj* immobile.

motivate ['məʊtɪveɪt] *vt (encourage)* motivare, stimolare.

motive ['məʊtɪv] *n* motivo *m*.

motor ['məʊtəʳ] *n (engine)* motore *m*.

Motorail® ['məʊtəreɪl] *n* treno *m* auto-cuccette.

motorbike ['məʊtəbaɪk] *n* moto *f inv*.

motorboat ['məʊtəbəʊt] *n* motoscafo *m*.

motorcar ['məʊtəkɑːʳ] *n* automobile *f*.

motorcycle ['məʊtə,saɪkl] *n* motocicletta *f*.

motorcyclist ['məʊtə,saɪklɪst] *n* motociclista *mf*.

motorist ['məʊtərɪst] *n* automobilista *mf*.

motor racing *n* corse *fpl* automobilistiche.

motorway ['məʊtəweɪ] *n (Br)* autostrada *f*.

motto ['mɒtəʊ] (*pl* **-s**) *n* motto *m*.

mould [məʊld] ◇ *n (Br) (shape)* forma *f*, stampo *m*; *(substance)* muffa *f* ◇ *vt (Br)* formare, modellare.

mouldy ['məʊldɪ] *adj (Br)* ammuffito(-a).

mound [maʊnd] *n (hill)* monticello *m*, collinetta *f*; *(pile)* mucchio *m*.

mount [maʊnt] ◇ *n (for photo)* supporto *m*; *(mountain)* monte *m* ◇ *vt (horse)* montare a OR su; *(photo)* sistemare ◇ *vi (increase)* aumentare.

mountain ['maʊntɪn] *n* montagna *f*.

mountain bike *n* mountain bike *f inv*.

mountaineer [,maʊntɪ'nɪəʳ] *n* alpinista *mf*.
mountaineering [,maʊntɪ'nɪərɪŋ] *n*: **to go ~** fare alpinismo.
mountainous ['maʊntɪnəs] *adj* montagnoso(-a).
Mount Rushmore [-'rʌʃmɔːʳ] *n* il monte Rushmore.
mourning ['mɔːnɪŋ] *n*: **to be in ~** essere in lutto.
mouse [maʊs] (*pl* **mice**) *n (animal)* topo *m*; (COMPUT) mouse *m inv*.
moussaka [muː'sɑːkə] *n piatto tipico della cucina greca e turca, composto da strati di carne macinata, melanzane e besciamella.*
mousse [muːs] *n* mousse *f inv*.
moustache [mə'stɑːʃ] *n (Br)* baffi *mpl*.
mouth [maʊθ] *n* bocca *f*; *(of cave, tunnel)* entrata *f*, imboccatura *f*; *(of river)* foce *f*, bocca.
mouthful ['maʊθfʊl] *n (of food)* boccone *m*; *(of drink)* sorsata *f*.
mouthorgan ['maʊθ,ɔːgən] *n* armonica *f* (a bocca).
mouthpiece ['maʊθpiːs] *n (of telephone)* microfono *m*; *(of musical instrument)* bocchino *m*.
mouthwash ['maʊθwɒʃ] *n* collutorio *m*.
move [muːv] ◇ *n* mossa *f*; *(change of house)* trasloco *m* ◇ *vt (shift)* muovere, spostare; *(emotionally)* commuovere ◇ *vi (shift)* muoversi, spostarsi; **to ~ (house)** cambiare casa, traslocare; **to make a ~** *(leave)* andarsene.
◆ **move along** *vi* circolare, andare avanti.
◆ **move in** *vi (to house)* andare/venire ad abitare.
◆ **move off** *vi (train, car)* partire.
◆ **move on** *vi (after stopping)* ripartire.
◆ **move out** *vi (from house)* sgombrare.
◆ **move over** *vi* spostarsi.
◆ **move up** *vi (make room)* spostarsi.
movement ['muːvmənt] *n* movimento *m*.
movie ['muːvɪ] *n* film *m inv*.
movie theater *n (Am)* cinema *m inv*.
moving ['muːvɪŋ] *adj (emotionally)* commovente.
mow [məʊ] *vt*: **to ~ the lawn** tagliare l'erba (del prato).
mozzarella [,mɒtsə'relə] *n* mozzarella *f*.
MP *n (abbr of Member of Parliament)* = deputato *m* (-a *f*).
mph *(abbr of miles per hour) miglia all'ora.*
Mr ['mɪstəʳ] *abbr* Sig.
Mrs ['mɪsɪz] *abbr* Sig.ra.
Ms [mɪz] *abbr abbreviazione che comprende sia Mrs che Miss.*
MSc *n (abbr of Master of Science)* (degree) master *m inv* in materie scientifiche.
much [mʌtʃ] (*compar* **more**, *superl* **most**) ◇ *adj* molto(-a); **I haven't got ~ money** non ho molti soldi; **as ~ food as you can eat** tanto cibo quanto ne riesci a mangiare; **how ~ time is left?** quanto tempo resta?; **they have so ~ money** hanno tanti di quei soldi; **we have too ~ work** abbiamo troppo lavoro.
◇ *adv* **1.** *(to a great extent)* molto; **it's ~ better** è molto meglio; **I like it very ~** mi piace moltissimo; **it's not ~ good** *(inf)* non è un granché; **thank you very ~** grazie tante.
2. *(often)* spesso, molto; **we don't go there ~** non ci andiamo spesso.
◇ *pron* molto; **I haven't got ~** non ne ho molto; **as ~ as you like** quanto ne vuoi; **how ~ is it?** quant'è?, quanto costa?
muck [mʌk] *n (dirt)* sudiciume *m*.
◆ **muck about** *vi (Br) (inf) (have fun)* divertirsi; *(waste time)* gingillarsi.

◆ **muck up** *vt sep (Br: inf)* pasticciare.

mud [mʌd] *n* fango *m*.

muddle ['mʌdl] *n*: **to be in a ~** *(confused)* essere confuso; *(in a mess)* essere in disordine.

muddy ['mʌdı] *adj* fangoso(-a).

mudguard ['mʌdgɑ:d] *n* parafango *m*.

muesli ['mju:zlı] *n* muesli *m*.

muffin ['mʌfın] *n (roll)* panino *m* soffice *(mangiato caldo, con burro)*; *(cake)* pasticcino *m* soffice.

muffler ['mʌflə^r] *n (Am: silencer)* marmitta *f*.

mug [mʌg] ◇ *n (cup)* tazza *f* (cilindrica) ◇ *vt* aggredire e derubare.

mugging ['mʌgıŋ] *n* aggressione *f (a scopo di rapina)*.

muggy ['mʌgı] *adj* afoso(-a).

mule [mju:l] *n* mulo *m*.

multicoloured ['mʌltı,kʌləd] *adj* multicolore.

multiple ['mʌltıpl] *adj* multiplo(-a).

multiplex cinema ['mʌltıpleks-] *n* cinema *m inv* multisala.

multiplication [,mʌltıplı'keıʃn] *n* moltiplicazione *f*.

multiply ['mʌltıplaı] ◇ *vt* moltiplicare ◇ *vi* moltiplicarsi.

multistorey (car park) [,mʌltı-'stɔ:rı-] *n* parcheggio *m* multipiano.

mum [mʌm] *n (Br: inf)* mamma *f*.

mummy ['mʌmı] *n (Br: inf: mother)* mamma *f*.

mumps [mʌmps] *n* orecchioni *mpl*.

munch [mʌntʃ] *vt* sgranocchiare.

municipal [mju:'nısıpl] *adj* municipale.

mural ['mju:ərəl] *n* dipinto *m* murale.

murder ['mɜ:də^r] ◇ *n* assassinio *m*, omicidio *m* ◇ *vt* assassinare.

murderer ['mɜ:dərə^r] *n* assassino *m* (-a *f*), omicida *mf*.

muscle ['mʌsl] *n* muscolo *m*.

museum [mju:'zi:əm] *n* museo *m*.

mushroom ['mʌʃrʊm] *n* fungo *m*.

music ['mju:zık] *n* musica *f*.

musical ['mju:zıkl] ◇ *adj* musicale; *(person)* portato(-a) per la musica ◇ *n* musical *m inv*.

musical instrument *n* strumento *m* musicale.

musician [mju:'zıʃn] *n* musicista *mf*.

Muslim ['mʊzlım] ◇ *adj* musulmano(-a) ◇ *n* musulmano *m* (-a *f*).

mussels ['mʌslz] *npl* cozze *fpl*.

must [mʌst] ◇ *aux vb* dovere ◇ *n (inf)*: **it's a ~** è d'obbligo; **I ~ go** devo andare; **the room ~ be vacated by ten** la camera deve essere lasciata entro le dieci; **you ~ have seen it** devi averlo visto; **you ~ see that film** devi vedere quel film; **you ~ be joking!** stai scherzando!

mustache ['mʌstæʃ] *(Am)* = **moustache**.

mustard ['mʌstəd] *n* senape *f*, mostarda *f*.

mustn't ['mʌsənt] = **must not**.

mutter ['mʌtə^r] *vt* borbottare.

mutton ['mʌtn] *n* carne *f* di montone.

mutual ['mju:tʃʊəl] *adj (feeling)* reciproco(-a), mutuo(-a); *(friend, interest)* comune.

muzzle ['mʌzl] *n (for dog)* museruola *f*.

my [maı] *adj* il mio (la mia), i miei (le mie) *(pl)*; **~ brother** mio fratello.

myself [maı'self] *pron (reflexive)* mi; *(after prep)* me; **I did it ~** l'ho fatto da solo.

mysterious [mı'stıərıəs] *adj* misterioso(-a).

mystery ['mıstərı] *n* mistero *m*.

myth [mıθ] *n* mito *m*.

N *(abbr of North)* N.
nag [næg] *vt* tormentare.
nail [neɪl] ◇ *n (of finger, toe)* unghia *f*; *(metal)* chiodo *m* ◇ *vt (fasten)* inchiodare.
nailbrush ['neɪlbrʌʃ] *n* spazzolino *m* da unghie.
nail file *n* limetta *f* per unghie.
nail scissors *npl* forbicine *fpl* da unghie.
nail varnish *n* smalto *m* per unghie.
nail varnish remover [-rə'mu:vəʳ] *n* acetone *m*, solvente *m* per unghie.
naive [naɪ'i:v] *adj* ingenuo(-a).
naked ['neɪkɪd] *adj (person)* nudo(-a).
name [neɪm] ◇ *n* nome *m* ◇ *vt (baby, animal)* chiamare; *(place)* denominare; *(identify)* dire il nome di, nominare; *(date, price)* fissare; **first ~** nome di battesimo; **last ~** cognome *m*; **what's your ~?** come si chiama?; **my ~ is ...** mi chiamo ...
namely ['neɪmlɪ] *adv* cioè, vale a dire.
nan bread [næn-] *n pane indiano schiacciato e soffice.*
nanny ['nænɪ] *n (childminder)* bambinaia *f*; *(inf: grandmother)* nonna *f*.
nap [næp] *n*: **to have a ~** fare un pisolino.
napkin ['næpkɪn] *n* tovagliolo *m*.
Naples ['neɪplz] *n* Napoli *f*.
nappy ['næpɪ] *n* pannolino *m*.
nappy liner *n* pannolino *m*.
narcotic [nɑ:'kɒtɪk] *n* narcotico *m*.
narrow ['nærəʊ] ◇ *adj (road, gap)* stretto(-a) ◇ *vi (road, gap)* restringersi.
narrow-minded [-'maɪndɪd] *adj* di idee ristrette.
nasty ['nɑ:stɪ] *adj (person, comment, taste)* cattivo(-a); *(accident, moment, feeling)* brutto(-a).
nation ['neɪʃn] *n* nazione *f*.
national ['næʃənl] ◇ *adj* nazionale ◇ *n* cittadino *m* (-a *f*).
national anthem *n* inno *m* nazionale.
National Health Service *n* = Servizio *m* Sanitario Nazionale.
National Insurance *n (Br: contributions)* = Previdenza *f* Sociale.
nationality [ˌnæʃə'nælətɪ] *n* nazionalità *f inv*.
national park *n* parco *m* nazionale.
nationwide ['neɪʃənwaɪd] *adj* su scala nazionale.
native ['neɪtɪv] ◇ *adj (customs, population)* indigeno(-a); *(country)* d'origine ◇ *n* nativo *m* (-a *f*); **a ~ speaker of English** una persona di madrelingua inglese.
Native American ◇ *adj* india-

no(-a) (d'America) ◇ *n* indiano *m* (-a *f*) (d'America).
NATO ['neɪtəʊ] *n* NATO *f*.
natural ['nætʃrəl] *adj (charm)* naturale; *(ability)* innato(-a); *(swimmer, actor)* nato(-a).
natural gas *n* metano *m*, gas *m* naturale.
naturally ['nætʃrəlɪ] *adv (of course)* naturalmente.
natural yoghurt *n* yogurt *m inv* naturale.
nature ['neɪtʃə^r] *n* natura *f*.
nature reserve *n* riserva *f* naturale.
naughty ['nɔːtɪ] *adj (child)* birichino(-a).
nausea ['nɔːzɪə] *n* nausea *f*.
navigate ['nævɪgeɪt] *vi (in boat, plane)* calcolare la rotta; *(in car)* fare da navigatore.
navy ['neɪvɪ] ◇ *n (ships)* marina *f* (militare) ◇ *adj*: ~ **(blue)** blu scuro *(inv)*.
NB *(abbr of nota bene)* N.B.
near [nɪə^r] ◇ *adv* vicino ◇ *adj (place, object)* vicino(-a); *(relation)* prossimo(-a) ◇ *prep*: ~ **(to)** *(edge, object, place)* vicino a, presso; **in the ~ future** nel prossimo futuro.
nearby [nɪə'baɪ] ◇ *adv* vicino ◇ *adj* vicino(-a).
nearly ['nɪəlɪ] *adv* quasi.
near side *n (for right-hand drive)* destra *f*; *(for left-hand drive)* sinistra *f*.
neat [niːt] *adj (room)* ordinato(-a); *(writing)* chiaro(-a); *(work)* preciso(-a); *(whisky, vodka etc)* liscio(-a).
neatly ['niːtlɪ] *adv (placed, arranged)* in modo ordinato; *(written)* in modo chiaro.
necessarily [ˌnesə'serɪlɪ, *Br* 'nesəsrəlɪ] *adv*: **not ~** non necessariamente.
necessary ['nesəsrɪ] *adj* necessario(-a); **it is ~ to do it** è necessario farlo.
necessity [nɪ'sesətɪ] *n* necessità *f inv*.
◆ **necessities** *npl* necessità *fpl*.
neck [nek] *n* collo *m*.
necklace ['neklɪs] *n* collana *f*.
nectarine ['nektərɪn] *n* pescanoce *f*.
need [niːd] ◇ *n* bisogno *m* ◇ *vt* avere bisogno di; **to ~ to do sthg** dover fare qc; **you don't ~ to go** non c'è bisogno che tu ci vada.
needle ['niːdl] *n* ago *m*; *(for record player)* puntina *f*.
needlework ['niːdlwɜːk] *n* (SCH) cucito *m*.
needn't ['niːdənt] = **need not**.
needy ['niːdɪ] *adj* bisognoso(-a).
negative ['negətɪv] ◇ *adj* negativo(-a) ◇ *n (in photography)* negativo *m*; (GRAMM) negazione *f*.
neglect [nɪ'glekt] *vt* trascurare.
negligence ['neglɪdʒəns] *n* negligenza *f*.
negotiations [nɪˌgəʊʃɪ'eɪʃnz] *npl* negoziati *mpl*, trattative *fpl*.
negro ['niːgrəʊ] (*pl* **-es**) *n* negro *m* (-a *f*).
neighbour ['neɪbə^r] *n* vicino *m* (-a *f*).
neighbourhood ['neɪbəhʊd] *n* quartiere *m*, vicinato *m*.
neighbouring ['neɪbərɪŋ] *adj* vicino(-a), confinante.
neither ['naɪðə^r, niːðə^r] ◇ *adj*: ~ **bag is big enough** nessuna delle due borse è abbastanza grande ◇ *pron*: ~ **of us** nessuno(-a) di noi (due) ◇ *conj*: ~ **do I** neanch'io, nemmeno io; ~ **... nor ...** né ... né ...
neon light ['niːɒn-] *n* luce *f* al neon.
nephew ['nefjuː] *n* nipote *m*.
nerve [nɜːv] *n (in body)* nervo *m*; *(courage)* coraggio *m*; **what a ~!** che faccia tosta!
nervous ['nɜːvəs] *adj* nervoso(-a).
nervous breakdown *n* esauri-

mento *m* nervoso.
nest [nest] *n* nido *m*.
net [net] ◇ *n* rete *f* ◇ *adj* netto(-a).
Net [net] *n* (COMPUT): **the ~** la Rete; **to surf the ~** navigare in Internet.
netball ['netbɔːl] *n specie di pallacanestro femminile.*
Netherlands ['neðələndz] *npl*: **the ~** i Paesi Bassi.
nettle ['netl] *n* ortica *f*.
network ['netwɜːk] *n* rete *f*.
neurotic [ˌnjʊə'rɒtɪk] *adj* nevrotico(-a).
neutral ['njuːtrəl] ◇ *adj (country, person)* neutrale; *(in colour)* neutro(-a) ◇ *n* (AUT): **in ~** in folle.
never ['nevəʳ] *adv* (non ...) mai; **she's ~ late** non è mai in ritardo; **I ~ knew he was married** non sapevo che fosse sposato; **~ mind!** non preoccuparti!
nevertheless [ˌnevəðə'les] *adv* tuttavia, ciononostante.
new [njuː] *adj* nuovo(-a).
newly ['njuːlɪ] *adv* di recente.
new potatoes *npl* patate *fpl* novelle.
news [njuːz] *n (information)* notizie *fpl*; *(on TV)* telegiornale *m*; *(on radio)* giornale *m* radio; **a piece of ~** una notizia.
newsagent ['njuːzeɪdʒənt] *n (shop)* giornalaio *m*.
newspaper ['njuːzˌpeɪpəʳ] *n* giornale *m*.
New Year *n* anno *m* nuovo.
New Year's Day *n* Capodanno.
New Year's Eve *n* l'ultimo *m* dell'anno, San Silvestro *m*.
New Zealand [-'ziːlənd] *n* la Nuova Zelanda.
next [nekst] ◇ *adj* prossimo(-a); *(room, house)* accanto ◇ *adv (afterwards)* dopo; *(on next occasion)* di nuovo; **when does the ~ bus leave?** quando parte il prossimo autobus?; **~ to** *(by the side of)* accanto a; **the week after ~** la settimana dopo la prossima.
next door *adv* accanto.
next of kin [-kɪn] *n* parente *m* prossimo (parente prossima *f*).
NHS *n (abbr of National Health Service)* = S.S.N. *m*.
nib [nɪb] *n* pennino *m*.
nibble ['nɪbl] *vt (eat)* mangiucchiare; *(bite)* mordicchiare.
nice [naɪs] *adj (taste, meal)* buono(-a); *(day, clothes, house)* bello(-a); *(person, gesture)* simpatico(-a), gentile; *(feeling, job)* piacevole; **to have a ~ time** divertirsi; **~ to see you!** piacere di rivederti!
nickel ['nɪkl] *n (metal)* nichel *m*; *(Am: coin) moneta da cinque centesimi di dollaro.*
nickname ['nɪkneɪm] *n* soprannome *m*.
niece [niːs] *n* nipote *f*.
night [naɪt] *n* notte *f*; *(evening)* sera *f*; **at ~** *(not in daytime)* di notte; *(in evening)* di sera; **by ~** di notte; **last ~** *(yesterday evening)* ieri sera; *(very late)* ieri notte.
nightclub ['naɪtklʌb] *n* locale *m* notturno.
nightdress ['naɪtdres] *n* camicia *f* da notte.
nightie ['naɪtɪ] *n (inf)* camicia *f* da notte.
nightlife ['naɪtlaɪf] *n* vita *f* notturna.
nightly ['naɪtlɪ] *adv* ogni notte; *(every evening)* ogni sera.
nightmare ['naɪtmeəʳ] *n* incubo *m*.
night safe *n* cassa *f* continua.
night school *n* scuola *f* serale.
nightshift ['naɪtʃɪft] *n* turno *m* di notte.
nil [nɪl] *n* (SPORT) zero *m*.
Nile [naɪl] *n*: **the ~** il Nilo.
nine [naɪn] *num* nove, → **six**.
nineteen [ˌnaɪn'tiːn] *num* diciannove; **~ ninety-five** millenovecentonovantacinque, → **six**.

nineteenth [ˌnaɪnˈtiːnθ] *num* diciannovesimo(-a), → **sixth**.
ninetieth [ˈnaɪntɪəθ] *num* novantesimo(-a), → **sixth**.
ninety [ˈnaɪntɪ] *num* novanta, → **six**.
ninth [naɪnθ] *num* nono(-a), → **sixth**.
nip [nɪp] *vt (pinch)* pizzicare.
nipple [ˈnɪpl] *n (of breast)* capezzolo *m*; *(of bottle)* tettarella *f*.
nitrogen [ˈnaɪtrədʒən] *n* azoto *m*.
no [nəʊ] ◇ *adv* no ◇ *adj* nessuno(-a) ◇ *n* no *m inv*; **I've got ~ time** non ho tempo; **I've got ~ money left** non ho più soldi.
noble [ˈnəʊbl] *adj* nobile.
nobody [ˈnəʊbədɪ] *pron* nessuno.
nod [nɒd] *vi (in agreement)* annuire.
noise [nɔɪz] *n* rumore *m*.
noisy [ˈnɔɪzɪ] *adj* rumoroso(-a).
nominate [ˈnɒmɪneɪt] *vt (choose)* nominare; *(suggest)* proporre come candidato.
non-alcoholic *adj* analcolico(-a).
none [nʌn] *pron* nessuno *m* (-a *f*); **there's ~ left** non ce n'è più.
nonetheless [ˌnʌnðəˈles] *adv* tuttavia, nondimeno.
non-fiction *n* opere *fpl* non narrative *(saggistica ecc.)*.
non-iron *adj*: **'non-iron'** 'lava e indossa', 'non stiro'.
nonsense [ˈnɒnsəns] *n* sciocchezze *fpl*, fesserie *fpl*.
non-smoker *n* non fumatore *m* (-trice *f*).
non-stick *adj* antiaderente.
non-stop ◇ *adj (flight)* diretto(-a); *(talking, arguing)* continuo(-a) ◇ *adv (fly)* senza scalo; *(run, rain)* ininterrottamente, senza sosta.
noodles [ˈnuːdlz] *npl* taglierini *mpl*.
noon [nuːn] *n* mezzogiorno *m*.
no-one = **nobody**.
nor [nɔːʳ] *conj* neanche, nemmeno; **~ do I** neanch'io, nemmeno io, → **neither**.
normal [ˈnɔːml] *adj* normale.
normally [ˈnɔːməlɪ] *adv* normalmente.
north [nɔːθ] ◇ *n* nord *m*, settentrione *m* ◇ *adj* del nord ◇ *adv (fly, walk)* verso nord; *(be situated)* a nord; **in the ~ of England** nel nord dell'Inghilterra.
North America *n* l'America *f* del Nord.
northbound [ˈnɔːθbaʊnd] *adj* diretto(-a) a nord.
northeast [ˌnɔːθˈiːst] *n* nord-est *m*.
northern [ˈnɔːðən] *adj* settentrionale, del nord.
Northern Ireland *n* l'Irlanda *f* del Nord.
North Pole *n* Polo *m* Nord.
North Sea *n* Mare *m* del Nord.
northwards [ˈnɔːθwədz] *adv* verso nord.
northwest *n* nord-ovest *m*.
Norway [ˈnɔːweɪ] *n* la Norvegia.
Norwegian [nɔːˈwiːdʒən] ◇ *adj* norvegese ◇ *n (person)* norvegese *mf*; *(language)* norvegese *m*.
nose [nəʊz] *n (of person)* naso *m*; *(of animal, plane)* muso *m*; *(of rocket)* punta *f*.
nosebleed [ˈnəʊzbliːd] *n* emorragia *f* nasale.
no-smoking area *n* zona *f* non fumatori.
nostril [ˈnɒstrəl] *n* narice *f*.
nosy [ˈnəʊzɪ] *adj* curioso(-a).
not [nɒt] *adv* non; **she's ~ there** non c'è; **~ yet** non ancora; **~ at all** *(pleased, interested)* per niente; *(in reply to thanks)* di niente, prego.
notably [ˈnəʊtəblɪ] *adv (in particular)* in particolare.
note [nəʊt] ◇ *n* nota *f*; *(message, bank note)* biglietto *m* ◇ *vt (notice)* notare; *(write down)* annotare; **to take ~s** prendere appunti.

notebook ['nəʊtbʊk] *n* taccuino *m*.
noted ['nəʊtɪd] *adj* celebre.
notepaper ['nəʊtpeɪpəʳ] *n* carta *f* da lettere.
nothing ['nʌθɪŋ] *pron* niente, nulla; **he did ~** non ha fatto niente; **~ new/interesting** niente di nuovo/ interessante; **for ~** per niente.
notice ['nəʊtɪs] ◇ *vt* notare, accorgersi di ◇ *n (written announcement)* avviso *m*; *(warning)* preavviso *m*; **to take ~ of** fare caso a; **to hand in one's ~** dare il preavviso, licenziarsi.
noticeable ['nəʊtɪsəbl] *adj* evidente.
notice board *n* tabellone *m* per avvisi.
notion ['nəʊʃn] *n* idea *f*.
notorious [nəʊ'tɔːrɪəs] *adj* famigerato(-a).
nougat ['nuːgɑː] *n* torrone *m*.
nought [nɔːt] *n* zero *m*.
noun [naʊn] *n* nome *m*, sostantivo *m*.
nourishment ['nʌrɪʃmənt] *n* nutrimento *m*.
Nov. *(abbr of November)* nov.
novel ['nɒvl] ◇ *n* romanzo *m* ◇ *adj* nuovo(-a).
novelist ['nɒvəlɪst] *n* romanziere *m* (-a *f*).
November [nə'vembəʳ] *n* novembre *m*, → **September**.
now [naʊ] ◇ *adv* ora, adesso ◇ *conj*: **~ (that)** adesso che, ora che; **just ~** proprio ora; **right ~** *(at the moment)* in questo momento; *(immediately)* subito; **by ~** ormai; **from ~ on** d'ora in poi.
nowadays ['naʊədeɪz] *adv* oggigiorno.
nowhere ['nəʊweəʳ] *adv* da nessuna parte, in nessun posto.
nozzle ['nɒzl] *n* boccaglio *m*.
nuclear ['njuːklɪəʳ] *adj* nucleare.
nude [njuːd] *adj* nudo(-a).
nudge [nʌdʒ] *vt* dare un colpetto di gomito a.
nuisance ['njuːsns] *n*: **it's a real ~!** è una vera seccatura!; **he's such a ~!** è un tale scocciatore!
numb [nʌm] *adj* intorpidito(-a).
number ['nʌmbəʳ] ◇ *n* numero *m* ◇ *vt (give number to)* numerare.
numberplate ['nʌmbəpleɪt] *n* targa *f*.
numeral ['njuːmərəl] *n* numero *m*, cifra *f*.
numerous ['njuːmərəs] *adj* numeroso(-a).
nun [nʌn] *n* suora *f*.
nurse [nɜːs] ◇ *n* infermiera *f* ◇ *vt (look after)* avere cura di, curare; **male ~** infermiere *m*.
nursery ['nɜːsərɪ] *n (in house)* stanza *f* dei bambini; *(for plants)* vivaio *m*.
nursery (school) *n* scuola *f* materna.
nursery slope *n* pista *f* per sciatori principianti.
nursing ['nɜːsɪŋ] *n (profession)* professione *f* d'infermiera.
nut [nʌt] *n (to eat)* frutta *f* secca *(noci, nocciole, ecc.)*; *(of metal)* dado *m*.
nutcrackers ['nʌtˌkrækəz] *npl* schiaccianoci *m inv*.
nutmeg ['nʌtmeg] *n* noce *f* moscata.
nylon ['naɪlɒn] ◇ *n* nailon *m* ◇ *adj* di nailon.

o' [ə] *abbr* = **of**.

O *n (zero)* zero *m*.

oak [əʊk] ◇ *n* quercia *f* ◇ *adj* di quercia.

OAP *abbr* = **old age pensioner**.

oar [ɔːʳ] *n* remo *m*.

oatcake ['əʊtkeɪk] *n* biscotto *m* di farina d'avena.

oath [əʊθ] *n (promise)* giuramento *m*.

oatmeal ['əʊtmiːl] *n* farina *f* d'avena.

oats [əʊts] *npl* avena *f*.

obedient [ə'biːdjənt] *adj* ubbidiente.

obey [ə'beɪ] *vt (person, command)* ubbidire a; *(regulations)* osservare.

object [*n* 'ɒbdʒɪkt, *vb* ɒb'dʒekt] ◇ *n (thing)* oggetto *m*; *(purpose)* scopo *m*; (GRAMM) complemento *m* oggetto ◇ *vi*: **to ~ (to)** *(disapprove of)* disapprovare; *(oppose)* opporsi (a), protestare (contro).

objection [əb'dʒekʃn] *n* obiezione *f*.

objective [əb'dʒektɪv] *n* obiettivo *m*.

obligation [ˌɒblɪ'geɪʃn] *n* obbligo *m*, dovere *m*.

obligatory [ə'blɪgətrɪ] *adj* obbligatorio(-a).

oblige [ə'blaɪdʒ] *vt*: **to ~ sb to do sthg** obbligare qn a fare qc.

oblique [ə'bliːk] *adj* obliquo(-a).

oblong ['ɒblɒŋ] ◇ *adj* oblungo(-a), rettangolare ◇ *n* rettangolo *m*.

obnoxious [əb'nɒkʃəs] *adj* odioso(-a).

oboe ['əʊbəʊ] *n* oboe *m*.

obscene [əb'siːn] *adj* osceno(-a).

obscure [əb'skjʊəʳ] *adj* oscuro(-a).

observant [əb'zɜːvnt] *adj* dotato(-a) di spirito d'osservazione.

observation [ˌɒbzə'veɪʃn] *n* osservazione *f*.

observatory [əb'zɜːvətrɪ] *n* osservatorio *m*.

observe [əb'zɜːv] *vt (watch, see)* osservare.

obsessed [əb'sest] *adj* ossessionato(-a).

obsession [əb'seʃn] *n* ossessione *f*.

obsolete ['ɒbsəliːt] *adj* obsoleto(-a).

obstacle ['ɒbstəkl] *n* ostacolo *m*.

obstinate ['ɒbstənət] *adj* ostinato(-a).

obstruct [əb'strʌkt] *vt (road, path)* ostruire.

obstruction [əb'strʌkʃn] *n (in road, path)* ostruzione *f*.

obtain [əb'teɪn] *vt* ottenere.

obtainable [əb'teɪnəbl] *adj* ottenibile.

obvious ['ɒbvɪəs] *adj* ovvio(-a), evidente.

obviously ['ɒbvɪəslɪ] *adv* ovviamente.

occasion [ə'keɪʒn] *n* occasione *f*; *(important event)* avvenimento *m*.

occasional [ə'keɪʒənl] *adj* saltuario(-a), occasionale.

occasionally [ə'keɪʒnəlɪ] *adv* saltuariamente, di tanto in tanto.

occupant ['ɒkjʊpənt] *n* occupante *mf*.

occupation [,ɒkjʊ'peɪʃn] *n* lavoro *m*; *(on form)* occupazione *f*.

occupied ['ɒkjʊpaɪd] *adj (toilet)* occupato(-a).

occupy ['ɒkjʊpaɪ] *vt* occupare.

occur [ə'kɜːʳ] *vi (happen)* accadere, avvenire; *(exist)* trovarsi, essere presente.

occurrence [ə'kʌrəns] *n (event)* evento *m*, caso *m*.

ocean ['əʊʃn] *n* oceano *m*; **the ~** *(Am: sea)* il mare.

o'clock [ə'klɒk] *adv*: **it's one ~** è l'una; **it's seven ~** sono le sette; **at one ~** all'una; **at seven ~** alle sette.

Oct. *(abbr of October)* ott.

October [ɒk'təʊbəʳ] *n* ottobre *m*, → **September**.

octopus ['ɒktəpəs] *n* polpo *m*, piovra *f*.

odd [ɒd] *adj (strange)* strano(-a); *(number)* dispari *(inv)*; *(not matching)* spaiato(-a); *(occasional)* saltuario(-a), occasionale; **60 ~ miles** una sessantina di miglia; **some ~ bits of paper** vari pezzetti di carta; **~ jobs** lavori *mpl* occasionali.

odds [ɒdz] *npl (in betting)* quota *f*; *(chances)* probabilità *fpl*; **~ and ends** un po' di tutto.

odor ['əʊdər] *(Am)* = **odour**.

odour ['əʊdəʳ] *n (Br)* odore *m*.

of [ɒv] *prep* **1.** *(gen)* di; **the handle ~ the door** la maniglia della porta; **a group ~ schoolchildren** un gruppo di scolari; **a great love ~ art** un grande amore per l'arte.

2. *(expressing amount)* di; **a piece ~ cake** una fetta di torta; **a fall ~ 20%** un ribasso del 20%; **a town ~ 50,000 people** una città di 50 000 abitanti.

3. *(made from)* di, in; **a house ~ stone** una casa di pietra; **it's made ~ wood** è di OR in legno.

4. *(referring to time)* di; **the summer ~ 1969** l'estate del 1969; **the 26th ~ August** il 26 agosto.

5. *(indicating cause)* di; **he died ~ cancer** è morto di cancro.

6. *(on the part of)* da parte di; **that was very kind ~ you** è stato molto gentile da parte tua.

7. *(Am: in telling the time)*: **it's ten ~ four** sono le quattro meno dieci.

off [ɒf] ◇ *adv* **1.** *(away)*: **to drive ~** partire; **to get ~** *(from bus, train, plane, boat)* scendere; **we're ~ to Austria next week** partiamo per l'Austria la settimana prossima.

2. *(expressing removal)*: **to cut sthg ~** tagliare qc; **to take sthg ~** togliere qc.

3. *(so as to stop working)*: **to turn sthg ~** *(TV, radio, engine)* spegnere qc; *(tap)* chiudere qc.

4. *(expressing distance or time away)*: **it's 10 miles ~** è a 10 miglia (da qui); **it's two months ~** mancano due mesi; **it's a long way ~** è lontano.

5. *(not at work)*: **I'm ~ next Tuesday** martedì prossimo non lavoro; **I'm taking a week ~** prendo una settimana di ferie.

◇ *prep* **1.** *(away from)* da; **to get ~ sthg** scendere da qc; **~ the coast** al largo della costa; **just ~ the main road** poco lontano dalla strada principale.

2. *(indicating removal)* da; **take the lid ~ the jar** togli il tappo dal barattolo; **they've taken £20 ~ the price** mi hanno fatto uno sconto di 20 sterline.

3. *(absent from)*: **to be ~ work** essere assente dal lavoro.

4. *(inf: from)* da; **I bought it ~ her** l'ho comprato da lei.
5. *(inf: no longer liking)*: **I'm ~ my food** non ho appetito, non mi va di mangiare.
◇ *adj* 1. *(food)* andato(-a) a male.
2. *(TV, radio, engine)* spento(-a); *(tap)* chiuso(-a).
3. *(cancelled)* annullato(-a).
4. *(not available)* esaurito(-a).

offence [ə'fens] *n (Br) (minor crime)* infrazione *f*; *(serious crime)* reato *m*; **to take ~ (at)** offendersi (per).

offend [ə'fend] *vt (upset)* offendere.

offender [ə'fendəʳ] *n (criminal)* delinquente *mf*.

offense [ə'fens] *(Am)* = **offence**.

offensive [ə'fensıv] *adj (insulting)* offensivo(-a).

offer ['ɒfəʳ] ◇ *n* offerta *f* ◇ *vt* offrire; **on ~** *(at reduced price)* in offerta; **to ~ to do sthg** offrirsi di fare qc; **to ~ sb sthg** offrire qc a qn.

office ['ɒfıs] *n (room)* ufficio *m*.

office block *n* palazzo *m* di uffici.

officer ['ɒfısəʳ] *n* (MIL) ufficiale *m*; *(policeman)* agente *m* (di polizia).

official [ə'fıʃl] ◇ *adj* ufficiale ◇ *n* funzionario *m* (-a *f*).

officially [ə'fıʃəlı] *adv* ufficialmente.

off-licence *n (Br)* negozio *m* di bevande alcoliche.

off-peak *adj (train)* delle ore non di punta; *(ticket)* a tariffa ridotta.

off sales *npl (Br)* vendita *f* di bevande alcoliche da asporto.

off-season *n* bassa stagione *f*.

offshore ['ɒfʃɔːʳ] *adj (breeze)* di terra.

off side *n (for right-hand drive)* lato *m* destro; *(for left-hand drive)* lato sinistro.

off-the-peg *adj* confezionato(-a).

often ['ɒfn, 'ɒftn] *adv* spesso; **how ~ do the buses run?** ogni quanto passano gli autobus?; **every so ~** ogni tanto.

oh [əʊ] *excl* oh!

oil [ɔıl] *n* olio *m*; *(fuel)* petrolio *m*.

oilcan ['ɔılkæn] *n* oliatore *m*.

oil filter *n* filtro *m* dell'olio.

oil rig *n* piattaforma *f* petrolifera.

oily ['ɔılı] *adj* unto(-a).

ointment ['ɔıntmənt] *n* unguento *m*, pomata *f*.

OK [,əʊ'keı] ◇ *adv (inf) (expressing agreement)* va bene, d'accordo; *(satisfactorily, well)* bene ◇ *adj (of average quality)* non male; **is that ~?** va bene?; **are you ~?** tutto bene?

okay [,əʊ'keı] = **OK**.

old [əʊld] *adj* vecchio(-a); *(person)* vecchio, anziano(-a); **how ~ are you?** quanti anni hai?; **I'm 36 years ~** ho 36 anni; **to get ~** invecchiare.

old age *n* vecchiaia *f*.

old age pensioner *n* pensionato *m* (-a *f*).

O-level *n esame oggi sostituito dal 'GCSE'*.

olive ['ɒlıv] *n* oliva *f*.

olive oil *n* olio *m* d'oliva.

Olympic Games [ə'lımpık-] *npl* giochi *mpl* olimpici, Olimpiadi *fpl*.

omelette ['ɒmlıt] *n* frittata *f*, omelette *f inv*; **mushroom ~** frittata ai funghi.

ominous ['ɒmınəs] *adj* sinistro(-a).

omit [ə'mıt] *vt* omettere.

on [ɒn] ◇ *prep* 1. *(expressing position, location)* su; **it's ~ the table** è sul tavolo; **a picture ~ the wall** un quadro alla parete; **the exhaust ~ the car** il tubo di scappamento dell'automobile; **~ my right** alla mia destra; **~ the right** a OR sulla destra; **we stayed ~ a farm** ci siamo fermati in una fattoria; a

hotel ~ George Street un albergo in George Street.

2. *(with forms of transport)*: **~ the train/plane** in treno/aereo; **to get ~ a bus** salire su un autobus.

3. *(expressing means, method)*: **~ foot** a piedi; **~ the radio** alla radio; **~ TV** in TV, alla televisione; **~ the piano** al piano.

4. *(using)*: **it runs ~ unleaded petrol** va a benzina verde; **to be ~ medication** prendere medicine.

5. *(about)* su; **a book ~ Germany** un libro sulla Germania.

6. *(expressing time)*: **~ arrival** all'arrivo; **~ Tuesday** martedì; **~ 25th August** il 25 agosto.

7. *(with regard to)* su; **a tax ~ imports** una tassa sulle importazioni; **the effect ~ Britain** l'effetto sulla Gran Bretagna.

8. *(describing activity, state)* in; **~ holiday** in vacanza; **~ offer** in offerta; **~ sale** in vendita.

9. *(in phrases)*: **do you have any money ~ you?** *(inf)* hai un po' di soldi con te?; **the drinks are ~ me** offro io da bere.

◇ *adv* 1. *(in place, covering)*: **to have sthg ~** *(clothes)* indossare qc; **put the lid ~** mettici il coperchio; **to put one's clothes ~** vestirsi.

2. *(film, play, programme)*: **the news is ~** c'è il telegiornale; **what's ~ at the cinema?** cosa danno al cinema?

3. *(with transport)*: **to get ~** salire.

4. *(functioning)*: **to turn sthg ~** *(TV, radio, engine)* accendere qc; *(tap)* aprire qc.

5. *(taking place)*: **how long is the festival ~?** quanto (tempo) dura il festival?

6. *(further forward)*: **to drive ~** continuare a guidare.

7. *(in phrases)*: **do you have anything ~ tonight?** fai qualcosa stasera?

◇ *adj (TV, engine, light)* acceso(-a); *(tap)* aperto(-a).

once [wʌns] ◇ *adv* una volta ◇ *conj* una volta che, non appena; **at ~** *(immediately)* subito; *(at the same time)* insieme, contemporaneamente; **for ~** per una volta; **~ more** ancora una volta.

oncoming [ˈɒnˌkʌmɪŋ] *adj (traffic)* che procede in senso opposto.

one [wʌn] ◇ *num* uno(-a) ◇ *adj (only)* unico(-a) ◇ *pron* uno(-a); **thirty-~** trentuno; **~ fifth** un quinto; **that ~** quello(-a); **which ~?** quale?; **this ~** questo(-a); **I want ~** ne voglio uno; **the ~ I told you about** quello di cui ti ho detto; **~ of my friends** uno dei miei amici; **~ day** un giorno.

one-piece (swimsuit) *n* costume *m* intero.

oneself [wʌnˈself] *pron (reflexive)* si; *(after prep)* se stesso(-a), sé.

one-way *adj (street)* a senso unico; *(ticket)* di sola andata.

onion [ˈʌnjən] *n* cipolla *f*.

onion bhaji [-ˈbɑːdʒɪ] *n polpetta a base di cipolla e spezie varie, fritta e servita come antipasto nella cucina indiana.*

onion rings *npl* rondelle *fpl* di cipolle fritte.

only [ˈəʊnlɪ] ◇ *adj* solo(-a), unico(-a) ◇ *adv* solo, soltanto; **he's an ~ child** è figlio unico; **I ~ want one** ne voglio solo uno; **we've ~ just arrived** siamo appena arrivati; **there's ~ just enough** ce n'è appena a sufficienza; **'members ~'** 'riservato ai soci'; **not ~** non solo.

onto [ˈɒntuː] *prep (with verbs of movement)* su; **to get ~ sb** *(telephone)* chiamare qn.

onward [ˈɒnwəd] ◇ *adv* = **onwards** ◇ *adj*: **the ~ journey** il proseguimento.

onwards [ˈɒnwədz] *adv (forwards)*

in avanti; **from now ~** da ora in poi; **from October ~** da ottobre in poi.

opal ['əupl] *n* opale *m o f*.

opaque [əu'peɪk] *adj (not transparent)* opaco(-a).

open ['əupn] ◇ *adj* aperto(-a) ◇ *vt* aprire ◇ *vi (door, lock, meeting)* aprirsi; *(shop, office, bank)* aprire; *(play, film)* cominciare; **are you ~ at the weekend?** siete aperti il fine settimana?; **wide ~** spalancato(-a); **in the ~ (air)** all'aperto.

◆ **open onto** *vt fus* dare su.

◆ **open up** *vi* aprire.

open-air *adj* all'aperto.

opening ['əupnɪŋ] *n* apertura *f*; *(opportunity)* opportunità *f inv*.

opening hours *npl* orario *m* di apertura.

open-minded [-'maɪndɪd] *adj* aperto(-a).

open-plan *adj* senza pareti divisorie.

open sandwich *n* tartina *f*.

opera ['ɒpərə] *n* opera *f*.

opera house *n* teatro *m* dell'opera.

operate ['ɒpəreɪt] ◇ *vt (machine)* azionare, far funzionare ◇ *vi (work)* funzionare, agire; **to ~ on sb** operare qn.

operating room ['ɒpəreɪtɪŋ-] *n (Am)* = **operating theatre**.

operating theatre ['ɒpəreɪtɪŋ-] *n (Br)* sala *f* operatoria.

operation [ˌɒpə'reɪʃn] *n* operazione *f*; **to be in ~** *(law, system)* essere in vigore; **to have an ~** operarsi.

operator ['ɒpəreɪtə^r] *n (on phone)* centralinista *mf*.

opinion [ə'pɪnjən] *n* opinione *f*, parere *m*; **in my ~** a mio parere, secondo me.

opponent [ə'pəunənt] *n* avversario *m* (-a *f*).

opportunity [ˌɒpə'tjuːnətɪ] *n* opportunità *f inv*, occasione *f*.

oppose [ə'pəuz] *vt* opporsi a.

opposed [ə'pəuzd] *adj*: **to be ~ to** essere contrario(-a) a.

opposite ['ɒpəzɪt] ◇ *adj (facing)* di fronte; *(totally different)* opposto(-a), contrario(-a) ◇ *prep* di fronte a ◇ *n*: **the ~ (of)** il contrario (di).

opposition [ˌɒpə'zɪʃn] *n* opposizione *f*; (SPORT) avversari *mpl*.

opt [ɒpt] *vt*: **to ~ to do sthg** scegliere di fare qc.

optician's [ɒp'tɪʃns] *n (shop)* ottico *m*.

optimist ['ɒptɪmɪst] *n* ottimista *mf*.

optimistic [ˌɒptɪ'mɪstɪk] *adj* ottimistico(-a).

option ['ɒpʃn] *n (alternative)* scelta *f*, alternativa *f*; *(optional extra)* optional *m inv*.

optional ['ɒpʃənl] *adj* facoltativo(-a).

or [ɔː^r] *conj* o, oppure; *(otherwise)* se no, altrimenti; *(after negative)*: **I can't read ~ write** non so (né) leggere né scrivere.

oral ['ɔːrəl] ◇ *adj* orale ◇ *n* orale *m*.

orange ['ɒrɪndʒ] ◇ *adj* arancione ◇ *n (fruit)* arancia *f*; *(colour)* arancione *m*.

orange juice *n* succo *m* d'arancia.

orange squash *n (Br)* aranciata *f* non gassata.

orbit ['ɔːbɪt] *n* orbita *f*.

orbital (motorway) ['ɔːbɪtl-] *n (Br)* raccordo *m* anulare.

orchard ['ɔːtʃəd] *n* frutteto *m*.

orchestra ['ɔːkɪstrə] *n* orchestra *f*.

ordeal [ɔː'diːl] *n* (durissima) esperienza *f*, travaglio *m*.

order ['ɔːdə^r] ◇ *n* ordine *m*; *(in restaurant, for goods)* ordinazione *f* ◇ *vt & vi* ordinare; **in ~ to** allo scopo di, per; **out of ~** *(not working)* guasto; **in working ~** funzionante; **to ~ sb to do sthg** ordinare a qn di fare qc.

order form *n* modulo *m* d'ordinazione.

ordinary ['ɔːdənrɪ] *adj* ordinario(-a), comune.

ore [ɔːʳ] *n* minerale *m* (grezzo).

oregano [ˌɒrɪ'gɑːnəʊ] *n* origano *m*.

organ ['ɔːgən] *n* organo *m*.

organic [ɔː'gænɪk] *adj (food)* biologico(-a).

organization [ˌɔːgənaɪ'zeɪʃn] *n* organizzazione *f*.

organize ['ɔːgənaɪz] *vt* organizzare.

organizer ['ɔːgənaɪzəʳ] *n (person)* organizzatore *m* (-trice *f*); *(diary)* agenda *f*.

oriental [ˌɔːrɪ'entl] *adj* orientale.

orientate ['ɔːrɪenteɪt] *vt*: **to ~ o.s.** orientarsi.

origin ['ɒrɪdʒɪn] *n* origine *f*.

original [ə'rɪdʒənl] *adj (first)* originario(-a); *(novel)* originale.

originally [ə'rɪdʒənəlɪ] *adv (formerly)* originariamente.

originate [ə'rɪdʒəneɪt] *vi*: **to ~ (from)** avere origine (da).

ornament ['ɔːnəmənt] *n (object)* soprammobile *m*.

ornamental [ˌɔːnə'mentl] *adj* ornamentale.

ornate [ɔː'neɪt] *adj* molto ornato(-a).

orphan ['ɔːfn] *n* orfano *m* (-a *f*).

orthodox ['ɔːθədɒks] *adj* ortodosso(-a).

ostentatious [ˌɒstən'teɪʃəs] *adj* pretenzioso(-a); *(action, behaviour)* ostentato(-a).

ostrich ['ɒstrɪtʃ] *n* struzzo *m*.

other ['ʌðəʳ] ◇ *adj* altro(-a) ◇ *pron* altro(-a) ◇ *adv*: **~ than** a parte; **the ~ (one)** l'altro; **the ~ day** l'altro giorno; **one after the ~** uno dopo l'altro.

otherwise ['ʌðəwaɪz] *adv* altrimenti.

otter ['ɒtəʳ] *n* lontra *f*.

ought [ɔːt] *aux vb* dovere; **you ~ to have gone** avresti dovuto andarci; **you ~ to see a doctor** dovresti andare dal dottore; **the car ~ to be ready by Friday** la macchina dovrebbe essere pronta per venerdì.

ounce [aʊns] *n (unit of measurement)* = 28,35 g, oncia *f*.

our ['aʊəʳ] *adj* il nostro (la nostra), i nostri (le nostre) *(pl)*; **~ mother** nostra madre.

ours ['aʊəz] *pron* il nostro (la nostra), i nostri (le nostre) *(pl)*; **a friend of ~** un nostro amico.

ourselves [aʊə'selvz] *pron (reflexive)* ci; *(after prep)* noi stessi (-e), noi; **we did it ~** l'abbiamo fatto da soli.

out [aʊt] ◇ *adj* **1.** *(light, cigarette)* spento(-a).

2. *(wrong)* inesatto(-a); **the bill's £10 ~** c'è un errore di 10 sterline nel conto.

◇ *adv* **1.** *(outside)* fuori; **to get ~ (of)** *(car)* scendere (da); **to go ~ (of)** uscire (da); **it's cold ~** fa freddo fuori.

2. *(not at home, work)* fuori; **to go ~** uscire, andare fuori.

3. *(so as to be extinguished)*: **to turn sthg ~** spegnere qc; **put your cigarette ~** spegni la sigaretta.

4. *(expressing removal)*: **to pour sthg ~** versare qc; **to take sthg ~ (of)** tirar fuori qc (da); *(from bank)* ritirare qc (da).

5. *(outwards)*: **to stick ~** sporgere.

6. *(expressing distribution)*: **to hand sthg ~** distribuire qc.

7. *(in phrases)*: **to stay ~ of the sun** evitare il sole; **made ~ of wood** in OR di legno; **five ~ of ten women** cinque donne su dieci; **I'm ~ of cigarettes** ho finito le sigarette.

outback ['aʊtbæk] *n*: **the ~** l'outback *m*, l'entroterra *m* australiano.

outboard (motor) ['aʊtbɔːd-] *n* motore *m* fuoribordo.

outbreak ['aʊtbreɪk] *n (of fighting)* scoppio *m*; *(of disease)* epidemia *f*.

outburst ['aʊtbɜːst] *n* scoppio *m*.

outcome ['aʊtkʌm] *n* esito *m*, risultato *m*.

outcrop ['aʊtkrɒp] *n* affioramento *m*.

outdated [ˌaʊt'deɪtɪd] *adj* antiquato(-a).

outdo [ˌaʊt'duː] (*pt* **-did**, *pp* **-done**) *vt* fare meglio di, superare.

outdoor ['aʊtdɔːʳ] *adj* all'aperto.

outdoors [aʊt'dɔːz] *adv* all'aperto, fuori.

outer ['aʊtəʳ] *adj* esterno(-a).

outer space *n* spazio *m* cosmico.

outfit ['aʊtfɪt] *n (clothes)* completo *m*.

outing ['aʊtɪŋ] *n* gita *f*.

outlet ['aʊtlet] *n (pipe)* scarico *m*, sbocco *m*; **'no ~'** *(Am)* 'strada senza uscita'.

outline ['aʊtlaɪn] *n* profilo *m*.

outlook ['aʊtlʊk] *n (for future)* prospettiva *f*; *(of weather)* previsioni *fpl*; *(attitude)* modo *m* di vedere.

out-of-date *adj (old-fashioned)* superato(-a); *(passport, licence)* scaduto(-a).

outpatients' (department) ['aʊtˌpeɪʃnts-] *n* reparto *m* pazienti esterni.

output ['aʊtpʊt] *n (of factory)* produzione *f*; (COMPUT: *printout*) output *m inv*, tabulato *m*.

outrage ['aʊtreɪdʒ] *n (cruel act)* atrocità *f inv*.

outrageous [aʊt'reɪdʒəs] *adj (shocking)* scandaloso(-a).

outright [ˌaʊt'raɪt] *adv (tell, deny)* apertamente; *(own)* completamente.

outside [*adv* ˌaʊt'saɪd, *adj, prep & n* 'aʊtsaɪd] ◇ *adv* fuori, all'esterno ◇ *prep* fuori di ◇ *adj* esterno(-a) ◇ *n*: **the ~** *(of building, car, container)* l'esterno *m*; (AUT: *in UK*) la destra; (AUT: *in Europe, US*) la sinistra; **an ~ line** una linea esterna; **~ of** *(Am) (on the outside of)* fuori di; *(apart from)* all'infuori di.

outside lane *n* corsia *f* di sorpasso.

outsize ['aʊtsaɪz] *adj (clothes)* di taglia forte.

outskirts ['aʊtskɜːts] *npl* periferia *f*.

outstanding [ˌaʊt'stændɪŋ] *adj (remarkable)* eccellente; *(problem)* rilevante; *(debt)* da pagare, in sospeso.

outward ['aʊtwəd] *adj (journey)* di andata; *(external)* esteriore.

outwards ['aʊtwədz] *adv* verso l'esterno, in fuori.

oval ['əʊvl] *adj* ovale.

ovation [əʊ'veɪʃn] *n* ovazione *f*.

oven ['ʌvn] *n* forno *m*.

oven glove *n* guanto *m* da forno.

ovenproof ['ʌvnpruːf] *adj* da forno.

oven-ready *adj* pronto(-a) per mettere in forno.

over ['əʊvəʳ] ◇ *prep* **1.** *(above)* sopra, su; **a bridge ~ the river** un ponte sul fiume.

2. *(across)* oltre, al di là di; **with a view ~ the park** con vista sul parco; **to walk ~ sthg** attraversare qc a piedi; **it's just ~ the road** è proprio qui di fronte.

3. *(covering)* su; **put a plaster ~ the wound** mettere un cerotto sulla ferita.

4. *(more than)* più di; **it cost ~ £1,000** è costato più di 1 000 sterline.

5. *(during)* durante; **~ the past two years** negli ultimi due anni.

6. *(with regard to)* su; **an argument ~ the price** una discussione sul prezzo.

7. *(in phrases)*: **all ~ the world/**

country in tutto il mondo/paese.

◇ *adv* 1. *(downwards)*: **to fall ~** cadere; **to bend ~** piegarsi (in avanti).

2. *(referring to position, movement)*: **to fly ~ to Canada** andare in Canada in aereo; **~ here** qui; **~ there** là.

3. *(round to other side)*: **to turn sthg ~** rigirare qc.

4. *(more)*: **children aged 12 and ~** ragazzi dai 12 anni in su.

5. *(remaining)*: **to be (left) ~** restare.

6. *(to one's house)*: **to invite sb ~ for dinner** invitare qn a cena; **we have some friends coming ~** verranno da noi OR a trovarci degli amici.

◇ *adj (finished)*: **to be ~** essere finito(-a).

overall [*adv* ˌəʊvərˈɔːl, *n* ˈəʊvərɔːl] ◇ *(in general)* complessivamente, nell'insieme ◇ *n (Br: coat)* grembiule *m*; *(Am: boiler suit)* tuta *f* (da lavoro); **how much does it cost ~?** quanto costa in tutto?

◆ **overalls** *npl (Br: boiler suit)* tuta *f* (da lavoro); *(Am: dungarees)* salopette *f inv*.

overboard [ˈəʊvəbɔːd] *adv (from ship)* in mare.

overbooked [ˌəʊvəˈbʊkt] *adj*: **to be ~** avere più prenotazioni dei posti disponibili.

overcame [ˌəʊvəˈkeɪm] *pt* → **overcome**.

overcast [ˌəʊvəˈkɑːst] *adj* coperto(-a).

overcharge [ˌəʊvəˈtʃɑːdʒ] *vt* far pagare un prezzo eccessivo a.

overcoat [ˈəʊvəkəʊt] *n* cappotto *m*.

overcome [ˌəʊvəˈkʌm] (*pt* **-came**, *pp* **-come**) *vt (defeat)* sopraffare; *(problem)* superare.

overcooked [ˌəʊvəˈkʊkt] *adj* troppo cotto(-a).

overcrowded [ˌəʊvəˈkraʊdɪd] *adj* sovraffollato(-a).

overdo [ˌəʊvəˈduː] (*pt* **-did**, *pp* **-done**) *vt (exaggerate)* esagerare con; **to ~ it** esagerare.

overdone [ˌəʊvəˈdʌn] ◇ *pp* → **overdo** ◇ *adj (food)* troppo cotto(-a).

overdose [ˈəʊvədəʊs] *n* overdose *f inv*.

overdraft [ˈəʊvədrɑːft] *n* scoperto *m* (di conto).

overdue [ˌəʊvəˈdjuː] *adj (bus, flight)* in ritardo; *(rent, payment)* in arretrato.

over easy *adj (Am: egg)*: **eggs ~** *uova al tegamino fritte da entrambe le parti.*

overexposed [ˌəʊvərɪkˈspəʊzd] *adj (photograph)* sovraesposto(-a).

overflow [*vb* ˌəʊvəˈfləʊ, *n* ˈəʊvəfləʊ] ◇ *vi (container, bath)* traboccare; *(river)* straripare ◇ *n (pipe)* troppopieno *m*.

overgrown [ˌəʊvəˈgrəʊn] *adj (garden, path)* ricoperto(-a) di erbacce.

overhaul [ˌəʊvəˈhɔːl] *n (of machine, car)* revisione *f*.

overhead [*adj* ˈəʊvəhed, *adv* ˌəʊvəˈhed] ◇ *adj* aereo(-a) ◇ *adv* in alto, al di sopra.

overhead locker *n (on plane)* scomparto *m* in alto.

overhear [ˌəʊvəˈhɪəʳ] (*pt & pp* **-heard**) *vt* sentire (per caso).

overheat [ˌəʊvəˈhiːt] *vi* surriscaldarsi.

overland [ˈəʊvəlænd] *adv* via terra.

overlap [ˌəʊvəˈlæp] *vi* sovrapporsi.

overleaf [ˌəʊvəˈliːf] *adv* a tergo.

overload [ˌəʊvəˈləʊd] *vt* sovraccaricare.

overlook [*vb* ˌəʊvəˈlʊk, *n* ˈəʊvəlʊk] ◇ *vt (subj: building, room)* dare su; *(miss)* lasciarsi sfuggire, trascurare ◇ *n*: **(scenic) ~** *(Am)* punto *m* panoramico.

overnight [*adv* ˌəʊvəˈnaɪt *adj* ˈəʊvənaɪt] ◇ *adv (during the night)* durante la notte; *(until next day)* per la notte ◇ *adj (train, journey)* di notte.

overnight bag *n* piccola borsa *f* da viaggio.

overpass ['əʊvəpɑːs] *n* cavalcavia *m inv*.

overpowering [ˌəʊvə'paʊərɪŋ] *adj (heat, smell)* opprimente, soffocante.

oversaw [ˌəʊvə'sɔː] *pt* → **oversee**.

overseas [*adv* ˌəʊvə'siːz, *adj* 'əʊvəsiːz] ◇ *adv* all'estero *(oltremare)* ◇ *adj* straniero(-a); *(trade)* estero(-a).

oversee [ˌəʊvə'siː] (*pt* **-saw**, *pp* **-seen**) *vt* sovrintendere a.

overshoot [ˌəʊvə'ʃuːt] (*pt & pp* **-shot**) *vt (turning, motorway exit)* oltrepassare.

oversight ['əʊvəsaɪt] *n* svista *f*.

oversleep [ˌəʊvə'sliːp] (*pt & pp* **-slept**) *vi* non svegliarsi *(all'ora prevista)*.

overtake [ˌəʊvə'teɪk] (*pt* **-took**, *pp* **-taken**) *vt & vi* sorpassare; **'no overtaking'** 'divieto di sorpasso'.

overtime ['əʊvətaɪm] *n* straordinario *m*.

overtook [ˌəʊvə'tʊk] *pt* → **overtake**.

overture ['əʊvəˌtjʊə^r] *n* (MUS) ouverture *f inv*.

overturn [ˌəʊvə'tɜːn] *vi* rovesciarsi.

overweight [ˌəʊvə'weɪt] *adj* sovrappeso *(inv)*.

overwhelm [ˌəʊvə'welm] *vt* sopraffare.

owe [əʊ] *vt* dovere; **to ~ sb sthg** dovere qc a qn; **owing to** a causa di.

owl [aʊl] *n* gufo *m*.

own [əʊn] ◇ *adj* proprio(-a) ◇ *vt* possedere ◇ *pron*: **my ~** il mio (la mia), i miei (le mie) *(pl)*; **a room of my ~** una stanza (solo) per me; **on my ~** da solo; **to get one's ~ back** prendersi la rivincita.

◆ **own up** *vi*: **to ~ up to sthg** ammettere qc.

owner ['əʊnə^r] *n* proprietario *m* (-a *f*).

ownership ['əʊnəʃɪp] *n* proprietà *f*, possesso *m*.

ox [ɒks] (*pl* **oxen** ['ɒksən]) *n* bue *m*.

oxtail soup ['ɒksteɪl-] *n* minestra *f* di coda di bue.

oxygen ['ɒksɪdʒən] *n* ossigeno *m*.

oyster ['ɔɪstə^r] *n* ostrica *f*.

oz *abbr* = **ounce**.

ozone-friendly ['əʊzəʊn-] *adj* che non danneggia l'ozono.

P

p ◇ *(abbr of page)* p., pag. ◇ *abbr* = **penny, pence**.

pace [peɪs] *n* passo *m*.

pacemaker [ˈpeɪsˌmeɪkəʳ] *n (for heart)* pacemaker *m inv*.

Pacific [pəˈsɪfɪk] *n*: **the ~ (Ocean)** il Pacifico, l'Oceano *m* Pacifico.

pacifier [ˈpæsɪfaɪəʳ] *n (Am: for baby)* succhiotto *m*.

pacifist [ˈpæsɪfɪst] *n* pacifista *mf*.

pack [pæk] ◇ *n (of washing powder)* pacco *m*; *(of cigarettes, crisps)* pacchetto *m*; *(Br: of cards)* mazzo *m*; *(rucksack)* zaino *m* ◇ *vt (suitcase, bag)* preparare, fare; *(clothes, camera etc)* mettere in valigia; *(to package)* impacchettare, imballare ◇ *vi (for journey)* fare i bagagli OR le valigie; **a ~ of lies** un mucchio di bugie; **to ~ sthg into sthg** stipare qc in qc; **to ~ one's bags** fare i bagagli OR le valigie.

◆ **pack up** *vi (pack suitcase)* fare la valigia; *(tidy up)* riordinare; *(Br: inf: machine, car)* guastarsi.

package [ˈpækɪdʒ] ◇ *n* pacchetto *m* ◇ *vt* imballare.

package holiday *n* vacanza *f* organizzata.

package tour *n* viaggio *m* organizzato.

packaging [ˈpækɪdʒɪŋ] *n (material)* imballaggio *m*, confezione *f*.

packed [pækt] *adj (crowded)* stipato(-a).

packed lunch *n* pranzo *m* al sacco.

packet [ˈpækɪt] *n* pacchetto *m*; **it cost a ~** *(Br: inf)* è costato un mucchio di soldi.

packing [ˈpækɪŋ] *n (material)* imballaggio *m*; **to do one's ~** fare i bagagli OR le valigie.

pad [pæd] *n (of paper)* blocco *m*; *(of cloth, cotton wool)* tampone *m*; *(for protection)* imbottitura *f*.

padded [ˈpædɪd] *adj (jacket, seat)* imbottito(-a).

padded envelope *n* busta *f* imbottita.

paddle [ˈpædl] ◇ *n (pole)* pagaia *f* ◇ *vi (wade)* sguazzare; *(in canoe)* remare *(con la pagaia)*.

paddling pool [ˈpædlɪŋ-] *n* piscina *f* per bambini.

paddock [ˈpædək] *n (at racecourse)* paddock *m inv*.

padlock [ˈpædlɒk] *n* lucchetto *m*.

page [peɪdʒ] ◇ *n (of book, newspaper)* pagina *f* ◇ *vt* chiamare.

paid [peɪd] ◇ *pt & pp* → **pay** ◇ *adj (holiday, work)* pagato(-a).

pain [peɪn] *n* dolore *m*; **to be in ~** avere dolore, soffrire; **he's such a ~!** *(inf)* è un tale rompiscatole!

◆ **pains** *npl (trouble)* disturbo *m*.

painful [ˈpeɪnfʊl] *adj* doloroso (-a).

painkiller [ˈpeɪnˌkɪləʳ] *n* analgesico *m*, antidolorifico *m*.

paint [peɪnt] ◇ *n* vernice *f*, colore *m* ◇ *vt & vi* dipingere; **to ~ one's nails** dipingersi le unghie.

◆ **paints** *npl (tubes, pots etc)* colori *mpl*.

paintbrush ['peɪntbrʌʃ] *n* pennello *m*.

painter ['peɪntəʳ] *n (artist)* pittore *m* (-trice *f*); *(decorator)* imbianchino *m*.

painting ['peɪntɪŋ] *n (picture)* dipinto *m*, quadro *m*; *(artistic activity)* pittura *f*; *(by decorator)* tinteggiatura *f*.

pair [peəʳ] *n (of two things)* paio *m*; **in ~s** a coppie, a due a due; **a ~ of pliers** un paio di pinze; **a ~ of scissors** un paio di forbici; **a ~ of shorts** un paio di calzoncini; **a ~ of tights** un paio di collant; **a ~ of trousers** un paio di pantaloni.

pajamas [pə'dʒɑːməz] *(Am)* = **pyjamas**.

Pakistan [*Br* ˌpɑːkɪ'stɑːn, *Am* ˌpækɪ'stæn] *n* il Pakistan.

Pakistani [*Br* ˌpɑːkɪ'stɑːnɪ, *Am* ˌpækɪ'stænɪ] ◇ *adj* pakistano(-a) ◇ *n* pakistano *m* (-a *f*).

pakora [pə'kɔːrə] *npl frittelle piccanti a base di verdura e spezie varie servite come antipasto nella cucina indiana.*

pal [pæl] *n (inf)* amico *m* (-a *f*).

palace ['pælɪs] *n* palazzo *m*.

palatable ['pælətəbl] *adj (food, drink)* gustoso(-a).

palate ['pælət] *n* palato *m*.

pale [peɪl] *adj* pallido(-a).

pale ale *n* birra *f* chiara.

palm [pɑːm] *n (of hand)* palmo *m*; **~ (tree)** palma *f*.

palpitations [ˌpælpɪ'teɪʃnz] *npl* palpitazioni *fpl*.

pamphlet ['pæmflɪt] *n* opuscolo *m*.

pan [pæn] *n (saucepan)* pentola *f*; *(frying pan)* padella *f*.

pancake ['pænkeɪk] *n* crêpe *f inv*.

pancake roll *n* involtino *m* primavera.

panda ['pændə] *n* panda *m inv*.

panda car *n (Br)* auto *f inv* della polizia.

pane [peɪn] *n* vetro *m*.

panel ['pænl] *n (of wood)* pannello *m*; *(group of experts)* gruppo *m* di esperti; *(on TV, radio)* giuria *f*.

paneling ['pænəlɪŋ] *(Am)* = **panelling**.

panelling ['pænəlɪŋ] *n (Br)* rivestimento *m* a pannelli.

panic ['pænɪk] (*pt & pp* **-ked**, *cont* **-king**) ◇ *n* panico *m* ◇ *vi* farsi prendere dal panico.

panniers ['pænɪəz] *npl (for bicycle)* borse *fpl* da bicicletta.

panoramic [ˌpænə'ræmɪk] *adj* panoramico(-a).

pant [pænt] *vi* ansare.

panties ['pæntɪz] *npl (inf)* mutandine *fpl*.

pantomime ['pæntəmaɪm] *n (Br) spettacolo natalizio per bambini.*

pantry ['pæntrɪ] *n* dispensa *f*.

pants [pænts] *npl (Br: underwear)* mutande *fpl*; *(Am: trousers)* pantaloni *mpl*.

panty hose ['pæntɪ-] *npl (Am)* collant *m inv*.

papadum ['pæpədəm] = **poppadom**.

paper ['peɪpəʳ] ◇ *n (material)* carta *f*; *(newspaper)* giornale *m*; *(exam)* esame *m* (scritto) ◇ *adj* di carta ◇ *vt* tappezzare (con carta da parati); **a piece of ~** un pezzo di carta.

◆ **papers** *npl (documents)* documenti *mpl*.

paperback ['peɪpəbæk] *n* libro *m* in brossura.

paper bag *n* sacchetto *m* di carta.

paperboy ['peɪpəbɔɪ] *n ragazzo che recapita i giornali a domicilio.*

paper clip *n* graffetta *f*.

papergirl ['peɪpəgɜːl] *n ragazza che recapita i giornali a domicilio.*

paper handkerchief *n* fazzoletto *m* di carta.

paper shop *n* giornalaio *m*.

paperweight ['peɪpəweɪt] *n* fermacarte *m inv*.

paprika ['pæprɪkə] *n* paprica *f*.

par [pɑː[r]] *n (in golf)* norma *f*.

paracetamol [ˌpærə'siːtəmɒl] *n* paracetamolo *m*.

parachute ['pærəʃuːt] *n* paracadute *m inv*.

parade [pə'reɪd] *n (procession)* parata *f*; *(of shops)* fila *f* di negozi.

paradise ['pærədaɪs] *n* paradiso *m*.

paraffin ['pærəfɪn] *n* cherosene *m*.

paragraph ['pærəgrɑːf] *n* paragrafo *m*.

parallel ['pærəlel] *adj*: ~ **(to)** parallelo(-a) (a).

paralysed ['pærəlaɪzd] *adj (Br)* paralizzato(-a).

paralyzed ['pærəlaɪzd] *(Am)* = **paralysed**.

paramedic [ˌpærə'medɪk] *n* paramedico *m*.

paranoid ['pærənɔɪd] *adj* paranoico(-a).

parasite ['pærəsaɪt] *n* parassita *m*.

parasol ['pærəsɒl] *n* parasole *m inv*.

parcel ['pɑːsl] *n* pacco *m*, pacchetto *m*.

parcel post *n* servizio *m* pacchi postali.

pardon ['pɑːdn] *excl*: ~? prego?; ~ **(me)!** mi scusi!; **I beg your ~!** *(apologizing)* scusi!; **I beg your ~?** *(asking for repetition)* prego?

parent ['peərənt] *n* genitore *m*.

parish ['pærɪʃ] *n (of church)* parrocchia *f*; *(village area)* = comune *m*.

park [pɑːk] ◇ *n* parco *m* ◇ *vt & vi* parcheggiare.

park and ride *n parcheggio decentrato presso una stazione di mezzi pubblici locali.*

parking ['pɑːkɪŋ] *n* parcheggio *m*; **'no ~'** 'sosta vietata'.

parking brake *n (Am)* freno *m* a mano.

parking lot *n (Am)* parcheggio *m*, posteggio *m*.

parking meter *n* parchimetro *m*.

parking space *n* posto *m* per parcheggiare.

parking ticket *n* multa *f* per sosta vietata.

parkway ['pɑːkweɪ] *n (Am) viale con alberi o piante nella banchina spartitraffico.*

parliament ['pɑːləmənt] *n* parlamento *m*.

Parmesan (cheese) [pɑːmɪ'zæn] *n* parmigiano *m*, grana *m*.

parrot ['pærət] *n* pappagallo *m*.

parsley ['pɑːslɪ] *n* prezzemolo *m*.

parsnip ['pɑːsnɪp] *n* pastinaca *f*.

parson ['pɑːsn] *n* curato *m*, parroco *m*.

part [pɑːt] ◇ *n* parte *f*; *(of machine, car)* pezzo *m*; *(of serial)* puntata *f*; *(Am: in hair)* scriminatura *f* ◇ *adv* in parte ◇ *vi (couple)* separarsi; **in this ~ of Italy** in questa zona dell'Italia; **to form ~ of** costituire parte di; **to play a ~ in** avere un ruolo in; **to take ~ in** prendere parte a; **for my ~** da parte mia; **for the most ~** per lo più, in generale; **in these ~s** da queste parti.

partial ['pɑːʃl] *adj (not whole)* parziale; **to be ~ to sthg** avere un debole per qc.

participant [pɑː'tɪsɪpənt] *n* partecipante *mf*.

participate [pɑː'tɪsɪpeɪt] *vi*: **to ~ (in)** partecipare (a).

particular [pə'tɪkjʊlə[r]] *adj* particolare; *(fussy)* esigente; **in ~** in particolare, specialmente; **nothing in ~** niente di particolare.

◆ **particulars** *npl (details)* particolari *mpl.*

particularly [pəˈtɪkjʊləlɪ] *adv* particolarmente, soprattutto.

parting [ˈpɑːtɪŋ] *n (Br: in hair)* scriminatura *f.*

partition [pɑːˈtɪʃn] *n (wall)* tramezzo *m.*

partly [ˈpɑːtlɪ] *adv* parzialmente, in parte.

partner [ˈpɑːtnəʳ] *n (husband)* marito *m*; *(wife)* moglie *f*; *(lover, in game, dance)* compagno *m* (-a *f*); (COMM) socio *m* (-a *f*).

partnership [ˈpɑːtnəʃɪp] *n* associazione *f*; (COMM) società *f inv.*

partridge [ˈpɑːtrɪdʒ] *n* pernice *f.*

part-time *adj & adv* part time.

party [ˈpɑːtɪ] *n (for fun)* festa *f*; (POL) partito *m*; *(group of people)* gruppo *m*; **to have a ~** fare una festa.

pass [pɑːs] ◇ *vt* passare; *(move past)* oltrepassare, passare davanti a; *(test, exam)* passare, superare; *(overtake)* sorpassare; *(law)* approvare ◇ *vi* passare ◇ *n (document)* lasciapassare *m inv*, permesso *m*; *(in mountain)* passo *m*; *(in exam)* sufficienza *f*; (SPORT) passaggio *m*; **to ~ sb sthg** passare qc a qn.

◆ **pass by** ◇ *vt fus (building, window etc)* passare davanti a ◇ *vi* passare.

◆ **pass on** *vt sep (message)* passare.

◆ **pass out** *vi (faint)* svenire.

◆ **pass up** *vt sep (opportunity)* lasciarsi sfuggire.

passable [ˈpɑːsəbl] *adj (road)* transitabile; *(satisfactory)* passabile.

passage [ˈpæsɪdʒ] *n (corridor)* passaggio *m*, corridoio *m*; *(in book)* brano *m*, passo *m*; *(sea journey)* traversata *f.*

passageway [ˈpæsɪdʒweɪ] *n* corridoio *m.*

passenger [ˈpæsɪndʒəʳ] *n* passeggero *m* (-a *f*).

passerby [ˌpɑːsəˈbaɪ] *n* passante *mf.*

passing place [ˈpɑːsɪŋ-] *n (for cars)* piazzola *f.*

passion [ˈpæʃn] *n* passione *f.*

passionate [ˈpæʃənət] *adj (showing strong feeling)* appassionato(-a); *(sexually)* passionale.

passive [ˈpæsɪv] *n* passivo *m.*

passport [ˈpɑːspɔːt] *n* passaporto *m.*

passport control *n* controllo *m* passaporti.

passport photo *n* fototessera *f.*

password [ˈpɑːswɜːd] *n (for computer)* password *f inv*, parola *f* d'accesso.

past [pɑːst] ◇ *adj* passato(-a); *(last)* ultimo(-a); *(former)* ex *(inv)* ◇ *prep (in times)* dopo; *(further than)* oltre, al di là di; *(in front of)* davanti a ◇ *adv* oltre ◇ *n (former time)* passato *m*; **~ (tense)** (GRAMM) passato; **the ~ month** il mese scorso; **twenty ~ four** le quattro e venti; **to run ~** passare di corsa; **in the ~** in passato.

pasta [ˈpæstə] *n* pasta *f.*

paste [peɪst] *n (spread)* pasta *f*, crema *f* (da spalmare); *(glue)* colla *f.*

pastel [ˈpæstl] *n (for drawing)* pastello *m*; *(colour)* colore *m* pastello.

pasteurized [ˈpɑːstʃəraɪzd] *adj* pastorizzato(-a).

pastille [ˈpæstɪl] *n* pastiglia *f.*

pastime [ˈpɑːstaɪm] *n* passatempo *m.*

pastry [ˈpeɪstrɪ] *n* pasta *f.*

pasture [ˈpɑːstʃəʳ] *n* pascolo *m.*

pasty [ˈpæstɪ] *n (Br)* pasticcio *m.*

pat [pæt] *vt* dare un colpetto (affettuoso) a.

patch [pætʃ] *n (for clothes)* toppa *f*; *(of colour, cloud, damp)* macchia *f*; *(for skin)* cerotto *m*; *(for eye)* benda *f*; **a bad ~** *(fig)* un brutto periodo.

pâté [ˈpæteɪ] *n* pâté *m inv.*

patent [*Br* 'peɪtənt, *Am* 'pætənt] *n* brevetto *m*.
path [pɑːθ] *n (in park, country)* sentiero *m*, viottolo *m*; *(in garden)* vialetto *m*.
pathetic [pə'θetɪk] *adj (pej: useless)* penoso(-a).
patience ['peɪʃns] *n (quality)* pazienza *f*; *(Br: card game)* solitario *m*.
patient ['peɪʃnt] ◇ *adj* paziente ◇ *n* paziente *mf*, malato *m* (-a *f*).
patio ['pætɪəʊ] *n* terrazza *f*.
patriotic [*Br* ˌpætrɪ'ɒtɪk, *Am* ˌpeɪtrɪ'ɒtɪk] *adj* patriottico(-a).
patrol [pə'trəʊl] ◇ *vt* pattugliare ◇ *n (group)* pattuglia *f*.
patrol car *n* auto *f inv* di pattuglia.
patron ['peɪtrən] *n (fml: customer)* cliente *mf*; **'~s only'** 'riservato ai clienti'.
patronizing ['pætrənaɪzɪŋ] *adj (person)* che tratta con aria di superiorità.
pattern ['pætn] *n (of shapes, colours)* disegno *m*, motivo *m*; *(for sewing)* modello *m*.
patterned ['pætənd] *adj* fantasia *(inv)*.
pause [pɔːz] ◇ *n* pausa *f* ◇ *vi* fare una pausa, soffermarsi.
pavement ['peɪvmənt] *n (Br: beside road)* marciapiede *m*; *(Am: roadway)* pavimentazione *f*.
pavilion [pə'vɪljən] *n edificio annesso a campo sportivo, adibito a spogliatoio.*
paving stone ['peɪvɪŋ-] *n* lastra *f* di pietra.
pavlova *n dolce composto da due strati di meringa farciti di panna montata e frutta.*
paw [pɔː] *n* zampa *f*.
pawn [pɔːn] ◇ *vt* impegnare, dare in pegno ◇ *n (in chess)* pedone *m*.
pay [peɪ] (*pt & pp* **paid**) ◇ *vt* pagare ◇ *vi (give money)* pagare; *(be profitable)* rendere ◇ *n* paga *f*, stipendio *m*; **to ~ sb for sthg** pagare qn per qc; **to ~ money into an account** versare dei soldi su un conto; **to ~ attention (to)** fare attenzione (a); **to ~ sb a visit** fare visita a qn; **to ~ by credit card** pagare con la carta di credito.
◆ **pay back** *vt sep (money)* restituire; *(person)* rimborsare.
◆ **pay for** *vt fus (purchase)* pagare.
◆ **pay in** *vt sep (cheque, money)* versare.
◆ **pay out** *vt sep (money)* sborsare.
◆ **pay up** *vi* saldare il debito.
payable ['peɪəbl] *adj (bill)* pagabile; ~ **to** *(cheque)* pagabile a, intestato(-a) a.
payment ['peɪmənt] *n (of money, bill)* pagamento *m*; *(amount)* pagamento, versamento *m*.
payphone ['peɪfəʊn] *n* telefono *m* pubblico.
PC ◇ *n (abbr of personal computer)* PC *m inv* ◇ *abbr (Br)* = **police constable**.
PE *abbr* = **physical education**.
pea [piː] *n* pisello *m*.
peace [piːs] *n* pace *f*; **to leave sb in ~** lasciare qn in pace; **~ and quiet** pace e tranquillità.
peaceful ['piːsfʊl] *adj (place, day, feeling)* tranquillo(-a), calmo(-a); *(demonstration)* pacifico(-a).
peach [piːtʃ] *n* pesca *f*.
peach melba [-'melbə] *n* pesche *fpl* melba.
peacock ['piːkɒk] *n* pavone *m*.
peak [piːk] *n (of mountain)* cima *f*, vetta *f*; *(of hat)* visiera *f*; *(fig: highest point)* apice *m*, culmine *m*.
peak hours *npl* ore *fpl* di punta.
peak rate *n* tariffa *f* ore di punta.
peanut ['piːnʌt] *n* arachide *f*, nocciolina *f* americana.
peanut butter *n* burro *m* di arachidi.
pear [peəʳ] *n* pera *f*.

pearl [pɜːl] *n* perla *f*.

peasant ['peznt] *n* contadino *m* (-a *f*).

pebble ['pebl] *n* ciottolo *m*.

pecan pie ['piːkæn-] *n torta di noci pecan*.

peck [pek] *vi (bird)* beccare.

peculiar [pɪ'kjuːljəʳ] *adj (strange)* strano(-a), singolare; **to be ~ to** *(exclusive)* essere peculiare di.

peculiarity [pɪˌkjuːlɪ'ærətɪ] *n (special feature)* particolarità *f inv*.

pedal ['pedl] ◇ *n* pedale *m* ◇ *vi* pedalare.

pedal bin *n* pattumiera *f* a pedale.

pedalo ['pedələʊ] (*pl* **-s**) *n* moscone *m* a pedali, pedalò® *m inv*.

pedestrian [pɪ'destrɪən] *n* pedone *m* (-a *f*).

pedestrian crossing *n* passaggio *m* pedonale.

pedestrianized [pɪ'destrɪənaɪzd] *adj* riservato(-a) ai pedoni.

pedestrian precinct *n (Br)* zona *f* pedonale.

pedestrian zone *(Am)* = **pedestrian precinct**.

pee [piː] ◇ *vi (inf)* fare la pipì ◇ *n*: **to have a ~** *(inf)* fare la pipì.

peel [piːl] ◇ *n* buccia *f*; *(of orange, lemon)* scorza *f* ◇ *vt (fruit, vegetables)* sbucciare ◇ *vi (paint)* staccarsi; *(skin)* spellarsi.

peep [piːp] *n*: **to have a ~** dare una sbirciatina.

peer [pɪəʳ] *vi*: **to ~ at** fissare, scrutare.

peg [peg] *n (for tent)* picchetto *m*; *(hook)* attaccapanni *m inv*; *(for washing)* molletta *f*.

pelican crossing ['pelɪkən-] *n (Br) passaggio pedonale con semaforo a comando manuale*.

pelvis ['pelvɪs] *n* bacino *m*.

pen [pen] *n (for writing)* penna *f*; *(for animals)* recinto *m*.

penalty ['penltɪ] *n (fine)* multa *f*, sanzione *f*; *(in football)* rigore *m*.

pence [pens] *npl* penny *m inv*; **it costs 20 ~** costa 20 penny.

pencil ['pensl] *n* matita *f*.

pencil case *n* portamatite *m inv*.

pencil sharpener *n* temperamatite *m inv*.

pendant ['pendənt] *n* pendente *m*, ciondolo *m*.

pending ['pendɪŋ] *prep (fml)* in attesa di.

penetrate ['penɪtreɪt] *vt* penetrare.

penfriend ['penfrend] *n* amico *m* (-a *f*) per corrispondenza.

penguin ['peŋgwɪn] *n* pinguino *m*.

penicillin [ˌpenɪ'sɪlɪn] *n* penicillina *f*.

peninsula [pə'nɪnsjʊlə] *n* penisola *f*.

penis ['piːnɪs] *n* pene *m*.

penknife ['pennaɪf] (*pl* **-knives**) *n* temperino *m*.

penny ['penɪ] (*pl* **pennies**) *n (in UK)* penny *m inv*; *(in US)* centesimo *m*.

pension ['penʃn] *n* pensione *f*.

pensioner ['penʃənəʳ] *n* pensionato *m* (-a *f*).

penthouse ['penthaʊs, *pl* -haʊzɪz] *n* superattico *m*.

penultimate [pe'nʌltɪmət] *adj* penultimo(-a).

people ['piːpl] ◇ *npl (persons)* persone *fpl*; *(in general)* gente *f* ◇ *n (nation)* popolo *m*; **the ~** *(citizens)* il popolo.

pepper ['pepəʳ] *n (spice)* pepe *m*; *(vegetable)* peperone *m*.

peppercorn ['pepəkɔːn] *n* grano *m* di pepe.

peppermint ['pepəmɪnt] ◇ *adj* alla menta (piperita) ◇ *n (sweet)* caramella *f* di menta.

pepper pot *n* pepiera *f*.

pepper steak *n* bistecca *f* al pepe.

Pepsi® ['pepsɪ] *n* Pepsi® *f inv*.

per [pɜːʳ] *prep* per, a; ~ **person** a persona; ~ **week** alla settimana; **£20** ~ **night** 20 sterline a notte.

perceive [pə'siːv] *vt* percepire.

per cent *adv* per cento.

percentage [pə'sentɪdʒ] *n* percentuale *f*.

perch [pɜːtʃ] *n (for bird)* posatoio *m*, asticella *f*.

percolator ['pɜːkəleɪtəʳ] *n* caffettiera *f* a filtro.

perfect [*adj & n* 'pɜːfɪkt, *vb* pə'fekt] ◇ *adj* perfetto(-a) ◇ *vt* perfezionare ◇ *n*: **the ~ (tense)** il passato prossimo.

perfection [pə'fekʃn] *n*: **to do sthg to ~** fare qc alla perfezione.

perfectly ['pɜːfɪktlɪ] *adv (very well)* perfettamente, alla perfezione.

perform [pə'fɔːm] ◇ *vt (task, operation)* eseguire, fare; *(play)* rappresentare; *(concert)* eseguire ◇ *vi (actor)* recitare; *(singer)* cantare.

performance [pə'fɔːməns] *n (of play, concert, film)* spettacolo *m*; *(by actor)* interpretazione *f*; *(musician)* esecuzione *f*; *(of car)* prestazioni *fpl*.

performer [pə'fɔːməʳ] *n* artista *mf*.

perfume ['pɜːfjuːm] *n* profumo *m*.

perhaps [pə'hæps] *adv* forse.

perimeter [pərɪmɪtəʳ] *n* perimetro *m*.

period ['pɪərɪəd] ◇ *n* periodo *m*; (SCH) lezione *f*; *(menstruation)* mestruazioni *fpl*; *(Am: full stop)* punto *m* ◇ *adj (costume, furniture)* d'epoca.

periodic [,pɪərɪ'ɒdɪk] *adj* periodico(-a).

period pains *npl* dolori *mpl* mestruali.

periphery [pə'rɪfərɪ] *n* periferia *f*.

perishable ['perɪʃəbl] *adj* deperibile.

perk [pɜːk] *n* vantaggio *m*.

perm [pɜːm] ◇ *n* permanente *f* ◇ *vt*: **to have one's hair ~ed** farsi la permanente.

permanent ['pɜːmənənt] *adj* permanente.

permanent address *n* residenza *f*.

permanently ['pɜːmənəntlɪ] *adv* permanentemente.

permissible [pə'mɪsəbl] *adj (fml)* permissibile, ammissibile.

permission [pə'mɪʃn] *n* permesso *m*.

permit [*vb* pə'mɪt, *n* 'pɜːmɪt] ◇ *vt* permettere ◇ *n* permesso *m*; **to ~ sb to do sthg** permettere a qn di fare qc; '**~ holders only**' 'solo autorizzati'.

perpendicular [,pɜːpən'dɪkjʊləʳ] *adj* perpendicolare.

persevere [,pɜːsɪ'vɪəʳ] *vi* perseverare.

persist [pə'sɪst] *vi* persistere; **to ~ in doing sthg** ostinarsi a fare qc.

persistent [pə'sɪstənt] *adj* persistente; *(person)* ostinato(-a).

person ['pɜːsn] (*pl* **people**) *n* persona *f*; **in ~** di persona.

personal ['pɜːsənl] *adj* personale.

personal assistant *n* segretario *m* (-a *f*) personale.

personal belongings *npl* effetti *mpl* personali.

personal computer *n* personal computer *m inv*.

personality [,pɜːsə'nælətɪ] *n* personalità *f inv*.

personally ['pɜːsnəlɪ] *adv* personalmente.

personal property *n* beni *mpl* mobili.

personal stereo *n* walkman® *m inv*.

personnel [,pɜːsə'nel] *npl* personale *m*.

perspective [pəˈspektɪv] *n* prospettiva *f*.
Perspex® [ˈpɜːspeks] *n* *(Br)* = plexiglas® *m*.
perspiration [ˌpɜːspəˈreɪʃn] *n* traspirazione *f*, sudore *m*.
persuade [pəˈsweɪd] *vt*: **to ~ sb (to do sthg)** persuadere qn (a fare qc); **to ~ sb that ...** persuadere qn che ...
persuasive [pəˈsweɪsɪv] *adj* persuasivo(-a), convincente.
pervert [ˈpɜːvɜːt] *n* pervertito *m* (-a *f*).
pessimist [ˈpesɪmɪst] *n* pessimista *mf*.
pessimistic [ˌpesɪˈmɪstɪk] *adj* pessimistico(-a).
pest [pest] *n* *(insect)* insetto *m* nocivo; *(animal)* animale *m* nocivo; *(inf: person)* peste *f*.
pester [ˈpestəʳ] *vt* tormentare.
pesticide [ˈpestɪsaɪd] *n* pesticida *m*.
pet [pet] *n* animale *m* domestico; **the teacher's ~** il favorito dell'insegnante.
petal [ˈpetl] *n* petalo *m*.
pet food *n* cibo *m* per animali (domestici).
petition [pɪˈtɪʃn] *n* *(letter)* petizione *f*.
petits pois *npl* pisellini *mpl*.
petrified [ˈpetrɪfaɪd] *adj* *(frightened)* impietrito(-a) (dalla paura).
petrol [ˈpetrəl] *n* *(Br)* benzina *f*.
petrol can *n* *(Br)* tanica *f* per la benzina.
petrol cap *n* *(Br)* tappo *m* del serbatoio.
petrol gauge *n* *(Br)* indicatore *m* di livello della benzina.
petrol pump *n* *(Br)* pompa *f* di benzina.
petrol station *n* *(Br)* stazione *f* di rifornimento.
petrol tank *n* *(Br)* serbatoio *m* della benzina.
pet shop *n* negozio *m* di animali.
petticoat [ˈpetɪkəʊt] *n* sottoveste *f*.
petty [ˈpetɪ] *adj* *(pej: person, rule)* meschino(-a).
petty cash *n* piccola cassa *f*.
pew [pjuː] *n* panca *f* (di chiesa).
pewter [ˈpjuːtəʳ] *adj* di peltro.
PG *(abbr of parental guidance) sigla che contraddistingue i film non vietati ai minori, per i quali è però consigliato l'accompagnamento dei genitori.*
pharmacist [ˈfɑːməsɪst] *n* farmacista *mf*.
pharmacy [ˈfɑːməsɪ] *n* *(shop)* farmacia *f*.
phase [feɪz] *n* fase *f*.
PhD *n* *(degree)* = dottorato *m* di ricerca.
pheasant [ˈfeznt] *n* fagiano *m*.
phenomena [fɪˈnɒmɪnə] *pl* → **phenomenon**.
phenomenal [fɪˈnɒmɪnl] *adj* fenomenale.
phenomenon [fɪˈnɒmɪnən] (*pl* **-mena**) *n* fenomeno *m*.
Philippines [ˈfɪlɪpiːnz] *npl*: **the ~** le Filippine.
philosophy [fɪˈlɒsəfɪ] *n* filosofia *f*.
phlegm [flem] *n* *(in throat)* catarro *m*.
phone [fəʊn] ◇ *n* telefono *m* ◇ *vt* *(Br)* telefonare a ◇ *vi* *(Br)* telefonare; **to be on the ~** *(talking)* essere al telefono; *(connected)* avere il telefono.
◆ **phone up** ◇ *vt sep* telefonare a, chiamare ◇ *vi* telefonare.
phone book *n* elenco *m* telefonico.
phone booth *n* cabina *f* telefonica.
phone box *n* *(Br)* cabina *f* telefonica.
phone call *n* telefonata *f*.
phonecard [ˈfəʊnkɑːd] *n* scheda *f* telefonica.

phone number *n* numero *m* di telefono.

photo ['fəutəu] (*pl* **-s**) *n* foto *f inv*; **to take a ~ of** fare una foto a.

photo album *n* album *m inv* portafotografie.

photocopier [ˌfəutəu'kɒpɪəʳ] *n* fotocopiatrice *f*.

photocopy ['fəutəuˌkɒpɪ] ◇ *n* fotocopia *f* ◇ *vt* fotocopiare.

photograph ['fəutəgrɑːf] ◇ *n* fotografia *f* ◇ *vt* fotografare.

photographer [fə'tɒgrəfəʳ] *n* fotografo *m* (-a *f*).

photography [fə'tɒgrəfɪ] *n* fotografia *f*.

phrase [freɪz] *n* espressione *f*.

phrasebook ['freɪzbuk] *n* vocabolarietto *m* con frasi tipiche.

physical ['fɪzɪkl] ◇ *adj* fisico(-a) ◇ *n* visita *f* medica.

physical education *n* educazione *f* fisica.

physically handicapped ['fɪzɪklɪ-] *adj* handicappato fisico (handicappata fisica).

physics ['fɪzɪks] *n* fisica *f*.

physiotherapy [ˌfɪzɪəu'θerəpɪ] *n* fisioterapia *f*.

pianist ['pɪənɪst] *n* pianista *mf*.

piano [pɪ'ænəu] (*pl* **-s**) *n* pianoforte *m*.

pick [pɪk] ◇ *vt (select)* scegliere; *(fruit, flowers)* cogliere ◇ *n (pickaxe)* piccone *m*; **to ~ a fight** attaccar briga; **to ~ one's nose** mettersi le dita nel naso; **to take one's ~** scegliere.

◆ **pick on** *vt fus* prendersela con, prendere di mira.

◆ **pick out** *vt sep (select)* scegliere; *(see)* individuare, riconoscere.

◆ **pick up** ◇ *vt sep (lift up)* raccogliere; *(collect)* passare a prendere; *(learn)* imparare; *(habit)* prendere; *(bargain)* trovare; *(hitchhiker)* far salire; *(inf: woman, man)* rimorchiare ◇ *vi (improve)* riprendersi; **to ~ up the phone** *(answer)* rispondere al telefono.

pickaxe ['pɪkæks] *n* piccone *m*.

pickle ['pɪkl] *n (Br: food)* sottaceti *mpl*; *(Am: pickled cucumber)* cetriolo *m* sottaceto.

pickled onion ['pɪkld-] *n* cipollina *f* sottaceto.

pickpocket ['pɪkˌpɒkɪt] *n* borsaiolo *m*.

pick-up (truck) *n* camioncino *m*.

picnic ['pɪknɪk] *n* picnic *m inv*.

picnic area *n area per picnic*.

picture ['pɪktʃəʳ] *n (painting)* quadro *m*; *(drawing)* disegno *m*; *(photograph)* fotografia *f*; *(on TV)* immagine *f*; *(film)* film *m inv*.

◆ **pictures** *npl*: **the ~s** *(Br)* il cinema.

picture frame *n* cornice *f*.

picturesque [ˌpɪktʃə'resk] *adj* pittoresco(-a).

pie [paɪ] *n (savoury)* pasticcio *m*; *(sweet)* torta *f*.

piece [piːs] *n* pezzo *m*; **a 20p ~** un pezzo da 20 penny; **a ~ of advice** un consiglio; **a ~ of clothing** un capo di vestiario; **a ~ of furniture** un mobile; **to fall to ~s** andare in pezzi; **in one ~** tutto intero.

pier [pɪəʳ] *n* molo *m*.

pierce [pɪəs] *vt* forare, perforare; **to have one's ears ~d** farsi i buchi alle orecchie.

pig [pɪg] *n* maiale *m*, porco *m*.

pigeon ['pɪdʒɪn] *n* piccione *m*.

pigeonhole ['pɪdʒɪnhəul] *n* casella *f*.

pigskin ['pɪgskɪn] *adj* di cinghiale.

pigtails ['pɪgteɪlz] *npl* trecce *fpl*.

pike [paɪk] *n (fish)* luccio *m*.

pilau rice ['pɪlau-] *n* riso *m* pilaf.

pilchard ['pɪltʃəd] *n* sardina *f*.

pile [paɪl] ◇ *n (heap)* mucchio *m*; *(neat stack)* pila *f* ◇ *vt* ammucchiare; ~s of *(inf: a lot)* mucchi di.

◆ **pile up** ◇ *vt sep* ammucchiare ◇ *vi (accumulate)* ammucchiarsi.

piles [paɪlz] *npl* (MED) emorroidi *fpl*.

pileup ['paɪlʌp] *n* tamponamento *m* a catena.

pill [pɪl] *n* pillola *f*.

pillar ['pɪləʳ] *n* colonna *f*.

pillar box *n (Br)* cassetta *f* delle lettere.

pillion ['pɪljən] *n*: **to ride ~** viaggiare sul sellino posteriore.

pillow ['pɪləʊ] *n* cuscino *m*.

pillowcase ['pɪləʊkeɪs] *n* federa *f*.

pilot ['paɪlət] *n* pilota *mf*.

pilot light *n* fiamma *f* pilota.

pimple ['pɪmpl] *n* foruncolo *m*.

pin [pɪn] ◇ *n (for sewing, safety pin)* spillo *m*; *(drawing pin)* puntina *f*; *(Am: brooch, badge)* spilla *f* ◇ *vt (fasten)* attaccare con uno spillo; **a two-~ plug** una spina bipolare; **~s and needles** formicolio *m*.

pinafore ['pɪnəfɔːʳ] *n (apron)* grembiule *m*; *(Br: dress)* scamiciato *m*.

pinball ['pɪnbɔːl] *n* flipper *m inv*.

pincers ['pɪnsəz] *npl (tool)* tenaglie *fpl*.

pinch [pɪntʃ] ◇ *vt (squeeze)* pizzicare, dare un pizzicotto a; *(Br: inf: steal)* fregare ◇ *n (of salt)* pizzico *m*.

pine [paɪn] ◇ *n* pino *m* ◇ *adj* di pino.

pineapple ['paɪnæpl] *n* ananas *m inv*.

pink [pɪŋk] ◇ *adj* rosa *(inv)* ◇ *n (colour)* rosa *m inv*.

pinkie ['pɪŋkɪ] *n (Am)* mignolo *m*.

PIN number *n* numero *m* di codice segreto.

pint [paɪnt] *n (in UK)* = 0,568 l, pinta *f*; *(in US)* = 0,473 l, pinta; **a ~ (of beer)** *(Br)* ≃ una birra grande.

pip [pɪp] *n (of fruit)* seme *m*.

pipe [paɪp] *n (for smoking)* pipa *f*; *(for gas, water)* tubo *m*.

pipe cleaner *n* scovolino *m*.

pipeline ['paɪplaɪn] *n* conduttura *f*; *(for oil)* oleodotto *m*.

pipe tobacco *n* tabacco *m* da pipa.

pirate ['paɪrət] *n* pirata *m*.

Pisces ['paɪsiːz] *n* Pesci *mpl*.

piss [pɪs] ◇ *vi (vulg)* pisciare ◇ *n*: **to have a ~** *(vulg)* pisciare; **it's ~ing down** *(vulg)* piove a dirotto.

pissed [pɪst] *adj (Br: vulg: drunk)* sbronzo(-a); *(Am: vulg: angry)* incazzato(-a).

pissed off *adj (vulg)* incazzato(-a).

pistachio [pɪ'stɑːʃɪəʊ] (*pl* **-s**) ◇ *n* pistacchio *m* ◇ *adj* al pistacchio.

pistol ['pɪstl] *n* pistola *f*.

piston ['pɪstən] *n* pistone *m*.

pit [pɪt] *n (hole)* buca *f*, fossa *f*; *(coalmine)* miniera *f* (di carbone); *(for orchestra)* fossa dell'orchestra; *(Am: in fruit)* nocciolo *m*.

pitch [pɪtʃ] ◇ *n (Br:* SPORT*)* campo *m* ◇ *vt (throw)* lanciare; **to ~ a tent** piantare una tenda.

pitcher ['pɪtʃəʳ] *n* brocca *f*.

pitfall ['pɪtfɔːl] *n* insidia *f*, pericolo *m*.

pith [pɪθ] *n (of orange)* parte *f* interna della scorza.

pitta (bread) ['pɪtə-] *n tipo di schiacciatina di origine mediorientale.*

pitted ['pɪtɪd] *adj (olives)* snocciolato(-a).

pity ['pɪtɪ] *n (compassion)* pietà *f*; **to have ~ on sb** avere pietà di qn; **it's a ~ that ...** è un peccato che ...; **what a ~!** che peccato!

pivot ['pɪvət] *n* perno *m*.

pizza ['piːtsə] *n* pizza *f*.

pizzeria [ˌpiːtsə'riːə] *n* pizzeria *f*.

Pl. *(abbr of Place) abbreviazione di strada in alcuni indirizzi.*

placard ['plækɑːd] *n* cartello *m*.

place [pleɪs] ◇ *n (location)* posto *m*, luogo *m*; *(house, flat)* casa *f*; *(seat, proper position, in race, list)* posto ◇ *vt (put)* collocare, mettere; *(an order, bet)* fare; **in the first ~** *(firstly)* in primo luogo; **to take ~** avere luogo, avvenire; **to take sb's ~** *(replace)* prendere il posto di qn; **all over the ~** dappertutto; **in ~ of** al posto di.

place mat *n (heat-resistant)* sottopiatto *m*; *(linen)* tovaglietta *f*.

placement ['pleɪsmənt] *n (work experience)* stage *m inv*.

place of birth *n* luogo *m* di nascita.

plague [pleɪg] *n* peste *f*.

plaice [pleɪs] *(pl inv) n* platessa *f*.

plain [pleɪn] ◇ *adj (simple)* semplice; *(in one colour)* in tinta unita; *(clear)* chiaro(-a); *(paper)* non rigato(-a); *(pej: not attractive)* scialbo(-a) ◇ *n* pianura *f*.

plain chocolate *n* cioccolato *m* fondente.

plainly ['pleɪnlɪ] *adv* chiaramente.

plait [plæt] ◇ *n* treccia *f* ◇ *vt* intrecciare.

plan [plæn] ◇ *n (scheme, project)* piano *m*, progetto *m*; *(drawing)* pianta *f* ◇ *vt (organize)* programmare, progettare; **have you any ~s for tonight?** hai qualche programma per stasera?; **according to ~** secondo i piani; **to ~ to do sthg, to ~ on doing sthg** progettare di fare qc.

plane [pleɪn] *n (aeroplane)* aereo *m*; *(tool)* pialla *f*.

planet ['plænɪt] *n* pianeta *m*.

plank [plæŋk] *n* asse *f*, tavola *f*.

plant [plɑːnt] ◇ *n* pianta *f*; *(factory)* stabilimento *m*, fabbrica *f* ◇ *vt* piantare; **'heavy ~ crossing'** 'uscita mezzi pesanti'.

plantation [plæn'teɪʃn] *n* piantagione *f*.

plaque [plɑːk] *n* placca *f*.

plaster ['plɑːstə^r] *n (Br: for cut)* cerotto *m*; *(for walls)* intonaco *m*; **in ~** *(arm, leg)* ingessato.

plaster cast *n (for broken bones)* ingessatura *f*.

plastic ['plæstɪk] ◇ *n* plastica *f* ◇ *adj* di plastica.

plastic bag *n* sacchetto *m* di plastica.

Plasticine® ['plæstɪsiːn] *n (Br)* plastilina® *f*.

plate [pleɪt] *n (for food)* piatto *m*; *(of metal, glass)* piastra *f*.

plateau ['plætəʊ] *n* altopiano *m*.

plate-glass *adj* di vetro piano.

platform ['plætfɔːm] *n (at railway station)* marciapiede *m* (di binario); *(raised structure)* piattaforma *f*; *(stage)* palco *m*; **~ 12** binario 12.

platinum ['plætɪnəm] *n* platino *m*.

platter ['plætə^r] *n* (CULIN) piatto *m* *(di affettati, frutti di mare assortiti ecc.)*.

play [pleɪ] ◇ *vt (sport, game)* giocare a; *(musical instrument, music)* suonare; *(opponent)* giocare contro; *(CD, tape, record)* mettere (su); *(role, character)* interpretare ◇ *vi* giocare; *(musician)* suonare ◇ *n (in theatre, on TV)* dramma *m*, commedia *f*; *(button on CD, tape recorder)* play *m inv*.

◆ **play back** *vt sep (tape)* riascoltare; *(video)* rivedere.

◆ **play up** *vi (machine, car)* fare i capricci.

player ['pleɪə^r] *n (of sport, game)* giocatore *m* (-trice *f*); *(of musical instrument)* suonatore *m* (-trice *f*).

playful ['pleɪfʊl] *adj* scherzoso(-a), giocoso(-a).

playground ['pleɪgraʊnd] *n (in school)* cortile *m* per la ricreazione; *(in park etc)* parco *m* giochi.

playgroup ['pleɪgruːp] *n* asilo *m* infantile.

playing card ['pleɪɪŋ-] *n* carta *f* da gioco.

playing field ['pleɪɪŋ-] *n* campo *m* sportivo.
playroom ['pleɪrʊm] *n* stanza *f* dei giochi.
playschool ['pleɪsku:l] = **playgroup**.
playtime ['pleɪtaɪm] *n* ricreazione *f*.
playwright ['pleɪraɪt] *n* drammaturgo *m* (-a *f*).
plc *(Br: abbr of public limited company)* = S.r.l. *(quotata in borsa)*.
pleasant ['pleznt] *adj* piacevole, gradevole; *(person)* simpatico(-a).
please [pli:z] ◇ *adv* per favore, per piacere ◇ *vt* far piacere a; ~ **take a seat** prego, si sieda; **yes ~!** si, grazie!; **whatever you ~** quello che ti pare.
pleased [pli:zd] *adj* contento(-a); **to be ~ with** essere contento di; ~ **to meet you!** piacere!
pleasure ['pleʒəʳ] *n* piacere *m*; **with ~** con piacere; **it's a ~!** non c'è di che!, prego!
pleat [pli:t] *n* piega *f*.
pleated ['pli:tɪd] *adj* pieghettato(-a).
plentiful ['plentɪfʊl] *adj* abbondante.
plenty ['plentɪ] *pron*: **there's ~** ce n'è in abbondanza; ~ **of** un sacco di.
pliers ['plaɪəz] *npl* pinze *fpl*.
plimsoll ['plɪmsəl] *n (Br)* scarpa *f* da tennis.
plonk [plɒŋk] *n (Br: inf: wine)* vino *m* da poco.
plot [plɒt] *n (scheme)* complotto *m*; *(of story, film, play)* trama *f*; *(of land)* appezzamento *m*.
plough [plaʊ] ◇ *n (Br)* aratro *m* ◇ *vt (Br)* arare.
ploughman's (lunch) ['plaʊmənz-] *n (Br) piatto a base di formaggi, sottaceti e pane, spesso servito nei pub*.
plow [plaʊ] *(Am)* = **plough**.
ploy [plɔɪ] *n* tattica *f*.
pluck [plʌk] *vt (eyebrows)* depilare; *(chicken)* spennare.
plug [plʌg] *n (electrical)* spina *f*; *(for bath, sink)* tappo *m*.
◆ **plug in** *vt sep* attaccare (a una presa).
plughole ['plʌghəʊl] *n* buco *m (della vasca, ecc.)*.
plum [plʌm] *n* susina *f*, prugna *f*.
plumber ['plʌməʳ] *n* idraulico *m*.
plumbing ['plʌmɪŋ] *n (pipes)* tubature *fpl*.
plump [plʌmp] *adj* grassoccio(-a).
plunge [plʌndʒ] *vi (fall)* precipitare, cadere; *(dive)* tuffarsi; *(decrease)* precipitare.
plunge pool *n* piscina *f* piccola.
plunger ['plʌndʒəʳ] *n (for unblocking pipe)* sturalavandini *m inv*.
pluperfect (tense) [,plu:'pɜ:fɪkt] *n*: **the ~** il piucchepperfetto.
plural ['plʊərəl] *n* plurale *m*; **in the ~** al plurale.
plus [plʌs] ◇ *prep* più ◇ *adj*: **30 ~** più di 30.
plush [plʌʃ] *adj* lussuoso(-a).
plywood ['plaɪwʊd] *n* compensato *m*.
p.m. *(abbr of post meridiem)*: **at 3 ~** alle 3 del pomeriggio; **at 10 ~** alle 10 di sera.
PMT *n (abbr of premenstrual tension)* sindrome *f* premestruale.
pneumatic drill [nju:'mætɪk-] *n* martello *m* pneumatico.
pneumonia [nju:'məʊnjə] *n* polmonite *f*.
poached egg [pəʊtʃt-] *n* uovo *m* in camicia.
poached salmon [pəʊtʃt-] *n* salmone *m* bollito.
poacher ['pəʊtʃəʳ] *n* bracconiere *m*.
PO Box *n (abbr of Post Office Box)* C.P.
pocket ['pɒkɪt] ◇ *n* tasca *f* ◇

adj tascabile.

pocketbook ['pɒkɪtbʊk] *n (notebook)* taccuino *m*; *(Am: handbag)* borsetta *f*.

pocket money *n (Br)* paghetta *f*, settimana *f*.

podiatrist [pə'daɪətrɪst] *n (Am)* pedicure *mf*, callista *mf*.

poem ['pəʊɪm] *n* poesia *f*.

poet ['pəʊɪt] *n* poeta *m* (-essa *f*).

poetry ['pəʊɪtrɪ] *n* poesia *f*.

point [pɔɪnt] ◇ *n* punto *m*; *(tip)* punta *f*; *(Br: electric socket)* presa *f* ◇ *vi*: **to ~ to** indicare; **five ~ seven** cinque virgola sette; **what's the ~?** a che serve?; **there's no ~** è inutile; **to be on the ~ of doing sthg** essere sul punto di fare qc.

◆ **points** *npl (Br: on railway)* scambio *m*.

◆ **point out** *vt sep (object, person)* indicare; *(fact, mistake)* far notare.

pointed ['pɔɪntɪd] *adj (in shape)* appuntito(-a).

pointless ['pɔɪntlɪs] *adj* inutile.

point of view *n* punto *m* di vista.

poison ['pɔɪzn] ◇ *n* veleno *m* ◇ *vt* avvelenare.

poisoning ['pɔɪznɪŋ] *n* avvelenamento *m*, intossicazione *f*.

poisonous ['pɔɪznəs] *adj* velenoso(-a).

poke [pəʊk] *vt (with finger, stick, elbow)* dare un colpetto a.

poker ['pəʊkə^r] *n (card game)* poker *m*.

Poland ['pəʊlənd] *n* la Polonia.

polar bear ['pəʊlə-] *n* orso *m* bianco.

Polaroid® ['pəʊlərɔɪd] *n (photograph)* foto *f inv* polaroid®; *(camera)* polaroid® *f inv*.

pole [pəʊl] *n (of wood)* palo *m*.

Pole [pəʊl] *n (person)* polacco *m* (-a *f*).

police [pə'li:s] *npl*: **the ~** la polizia.

police car *n* auto *f inv* della polizia.

police force *n* forze *fpl* di polizia OR dell'ordine.

policeman [pə'li:smən] (*pl* **-men** [-mən]) *n* poliziotto *m*.

police officer *n* agente *m* di polizia.

police station *n* posto *m* di polizia.

policewoman [pə'li:s,wʊmən] (*pl* **-women** [-,wɪmɪn]) *n* donna *f* poliziotto.

policy ['pɒləsɪ] *n (approach, attitude)* politica *f*; *(for insurance)* polizza *f*.

policy-holder *n* assicurato *m* (-a *f*).

polio ['pəʊlɪəʊ] *n* polio *f*.

polish ['pɒlɪʃ] ◇ *n (for cleaning)* lucido *m*, cera *f* ◇ *vt* lucidare.

Polish ['pəʊlɪʃ] ◇ *adj* polacco(-a) ◇ *n (language)* polacco *m* ◇ *npl*: **the ~** i polacchi.

polite [pə'laɪt] *adj* cortese, gentile.

political [pə'lɪtɪkl] *adj* politico(-a).

politician [,pɒlɪ'tɪʃn] *n* politico *m*.

politics ['pɒlətɪks] *n* politica *f*.

poll [pəʊl] *n (survey)* sondaggio *m* (d'opinioni); **the ~s** *(election)* le elezioni.

pollen ['pɒlən] *n* polline *m*.

Poll Tax *n (Br) tassa comunale pro capite.*

pollute [pə'lu:t] *vt* inquinare.

pollution [pə'lu:ʃn] *n* inquinamento *m*.

polo neck ['pəʊləʊ-] *n (Br: jumper)* maglione *m* a collo alto.

polyester [,pɒlɪ'estə^r] *n* poliestere *m*.

polystyrene [,pɒlɪ'staɪri:n] *n* polistirolo *m*.

polytechnic [,pɒlɪ'teknɪk] *n* = politecnico *m*.

polythene bag ['pɒlɪθi:n-] *n* sacchetto *m* di plastica.

pomegranate [ˈpɒmɪˌgrænɪt] *n* melagrana *f*.

pompous [ˈpɒmpəs] *adj* pomposo(-a).

pond [pɒnd] *n* stagno *m*.

pontoon [pɒnˈtuːn] *n (Br: card game)* ventuno *m*.

pony [ˈpəʊnɪ] *n* pony *m inv*.

ponytail [ˈpəʊnɪteɪl] *n* coda *f* di cavallo.

pony-trekking [-ˌtrekɪŋ] *n (Br)* escursione *f* a dorso di pony.

poodle [ˈpuːdl] *n* barboncino *m*.

pool [puːl] *n* pozza *f*; *(for swimming)* piscina *f*; *(game)* biliardo *m* a buca.

◆ **pools** *npl (Br)*: **the ~s** = il totocalcio.

poor [pɔːʳ] ◇ *adj* povero(-a); *(bad)* mediocre, scadente ◇ *npl*: **the ~** i poveri.

poorly [ˈpɔːlɪ] ◇ *adv* malamente, male ◇ *adj (Br: ill)*: **to be ~** stare poco bene.

pop [pɒp] ◇ *n (music)* musica *f* pop ◇ *vt (inf: put)* mettere ◇ *vi (balloon)* scoppiare; **my ears popped** mi si sono stappate le orecchie.

◆ **pop in** *vi (Br: visit)* fare un salto.

popcorn [ˈpɒpkɔːn] *n* popcorn *m*.

Pope [pəʊp] *n*: **the ~** il papa.

pop group *n* gruppo *m* pop.

poplar (tree) [ˈpɒpləʳ-] *n* pioppo *m*.

pop music *n* musica *f* pop.

poppadom [ˈpɒpədəm] *n pane indiano molto sottile e croccante*.

popper [ˈpɒpəʳ] *n (Br)* bottone *m* a pressione.

poppy [ˈpɒpɪ] *n* papavero *m*.

Popsicle® [ˈpɒpsɪkl] *n (Am)* ghiacciolo *m*.

pop socks *npl* gambaletti *mpl*.

pop star *n* pop star *f inv*.

popular [ˈpɒpjʊləʳ] *adj* popolare; *(fashionable)* in voga.

popularity [ˌpɒpjʊˈlærətɪ] *n* popolarità *f*.

populated [ˈpɒpjʊleɪtɪd] *adj* popolato(-a).

population [ˌpɒpjʊˈleɪʃn] *n* popolazione *f*.

porcelain [ˈpɔːsəlɪn] *n* porcellana *f*.

porch [pɔːtʃ] *n (entrance)* portico *m*; *(Am: outside house)* veranda *f*.

pork [pɔːk] *n* carne *f* di maiale.

pork chop *n* braciola *f* OR costoletta *f* di maiale.

pork pie *n* pasticcio *m* di maiale.

pornographic [ˌpɔːnəˈgræfɪk] *adj* pornografico(-a).

porridge [ˈpɒrɪdʒ] *n* porridge *m*, farinata *f* d'avena.

port [pɔːt] *n* porto *m*.

portable [ˈpɔːtəbl] *adj* portatile.

porter [ˈpɔːtəʳ] *n (at hotel, museum)* portiere *m*; *(at station, airport)* facchino *m*.

porthole [ˈpɔːthəʊl] *n* oblò *m inv*.

portion [ˈpɔːʃn] *n* porzione *f*.

portrait [ˈpɔːtreɪt] *n* ritratto *m*.

Portugal [ˈpɔːtʃʊgl] *n* il Portogallo.

Portuguese [ˌpɔːtʃʊˈgiːz] ◇ *adj* portoghese ◇ *n (language)* portoghese *m* ◇ *npl*: **the ~** i portoghesi.

pose [pəʊz] ◇ *vt (problem, threat)* porre ◇ *vi (for photo)* posare.

posh [pɒʃ] *adj (inf) (person, accent)* snob *inv*, raffinato(-a); *(hotel, restaurant)* elegante, di lusso.

position [pəˈzɪʃn] *n* posizione *f*; *(fml: job)* posto *m*; **'~ closed'** *(in bank, post office etc)* 'sportello chiuso'.

positive [ˈpɒzətɪv] *adj* positivo(-a); *(certain, sure)* sicuro(-a), certo(-a).

possess [pəˈzes] *vt* possedere.

possession [pəˈzeʃn] *n (thing owned)* bene *m*.

possessive [pəˈzesɪv] *adj* possessivo(-a).

possibility [ˌpɒsəˈbɪlətɪ] *n* possibilità *f inv*.

possible [ˈpɒsəbl] *adj* possibile; **it's ~ that we may be late** può darsi che facciamo tardi; **would it be ~ ...?** sarebbe possibile ...?; **as much as ~** il più possibile; **if ~** se possibile.

possibly [ˈpɒsəblɪ] *adv (perhaps)* forse.

post [pəʊst] ◇ *n (system, letters, delivery)* posta *f*; *(pole)* palo *m*; *(fml: job)* posto *m* ◇ *vt (letter, parcel)* spedire (per posta); **by ~** per posta.

postage [ˈpəʊstɪdʒ] *n* affrancatura *f*, spese *fpl* postali; **~ and packing** spese di spedizione (postale); **~ paid** franco di porto, affrancatura pagata.

postage stamp *n (fml)* francobollo *m*.

postal order [ˈpəʊstl-] *n* vaglia *m inv* postale.

postbox [ˈpəʊstbɒks] *n (Br)* cassetta *f* delle lettere.

postcard [ˈpəʊstkɑːd] *n* cartolina *f*.

postcode [ˈpəʊstkəʊd] *n (Br)* codice *m* (di avviamento) postale.

poster [ˈpəʊstəʳ] *n* manifesto *m*, poster *m inv*.

poste restante [ˌpəʊstresˈtɑːnt] *n (Br)* fermo posta *m*.

post-free *adv* in franchigia postale, con affrancatura pagata.

postgraduate [ˌpəʊstˈgrædʒʊət] *n laureato(-a) che frequenta un corso di specializzazione*.

postman [ˈpəʊstmən] (*pl* **-men** [-mən]) *n* postino *m*.

postmark [ˈpəʊstmɑːk] *n* timbro *m* postale.

postmen *pl* → **postman**.

post office *n (building)* ufficio *m* postale; **the Post Office** = le Poste e Telecomunicazioni.

postpone [ˌpəʊstˈpəʊn] *vt* rinviare, rimandare.

posture [ˈpɒstʃəʳ] *n* postura *f*.

postwoman [ˈpəʊstˌwʊmən] (*pl* **-women** [-ˌwɪmɪn]) *n* postina *f*.

pot [pɒt] *n (for cooking)* pentola *f*; *(for jam, paint)* vasetto *m*, barattolo *m*; *(for coffee)* caffettiera *f*; *(for tea)* teiera *f*; *(inf: cannabis)* erba *f*; **a ~ of tea** un tè *(servito in una teiera)*.

potato [pəˈteɪtəʊ] (*pl* **-es**) *n* patata *f*.

potato salad *n* patate *fpl* in insalata.

potential [pəˈtenʃl] ◇ *adj* potenziale ◇ *n* potenziale *m*.

pothole [ˈpɒthəʊl] *n (in road)* buca *f*.

pot plant *n* pianta *f* da vaso.

pot scrubber [-ˈskrʌbəʳ] *n* paglietta *f*.

potted [ˈpɒtɪd] *adj (meat, fish)* in vasetto, in scatola; *(plant)* in vaso.

pottery [ˈpɒtərɪ] *n (clay objects)* ceramiche *fpl*; *(craft)* ceramica *f*.

potty [ˈpɒtɪ] *n (inf)* vasino *m*.

pouch [paʊtʃ] *n (for money, tobacco)* borsellino *f*.

poultry [ˈpəʊltrɪ] *n & npl* pollame *m*.

pound [paʊnd] ◇ *n (unit of money)* sterlina *f*; *(unit of weight)* = 453,6 g, libbra *f* ◇ *vi (heart)* battere forte; *(head)* martellare.

pour [pɔːʳ] ◇ *vt* versare ◇ *vi (flow)* riversarsi; **it's ~ing (with rain)** sta piovendo a dirotto.

♦ **pour out** *vt sep (drink)* versare.

poverty [ˈpɒvətɪ] *n* povertà *f*, miseria *f*.

powder [ˈpaʊdəʳ] *n* polvere *f*; *(cosmetic)* cipria *f*.

power [ˈpaʊəʳ] ◇ *n (control, authority)* potere *m*; *(ability)* capacità *f inv*; *(strength, force)* potenza *f*; *(energy)* energia *f*; *(electricity)* corrente *f* ◇ *vt* azionare; **to be in ~** essere al potere.

power cut *n* interruzione *f* di corrente.

power failure *n* interruzione *f* di corrente.
powerful ['paʊəfʊl] *adj* potente.
power point *n (Br)* presa *f* di corrente.
power station *n* centrale *f* elettrica.
power steering *n* servosterzo *m*.
practical ['præktɪkl] *adj* pratico(-a).
practically ['præktɪklɪ] *adv (almost)* praticamente.
practice ['præktɪs] ◇ *n (training)* pratica *f*; *(training session)* allenamento *m*, esercizio *m*; *(of doctor, lawyer)* studio *m*; *(regular activity, custom)* consuetudine *f* ◇ *vt (Am)* = **practise**; **out of ~** fuori allenamento.
practise ['præktɪs] ◇ *vt (sport, music, technique)* allenarsi a, esercitarsi a OR in ◇ *vi (train)* allenarsi, esercitarsi; *(doctor, lawyer)* esercitare ◇ *n (Am)* = **practice**.
praise [preɪz] ◇ *n* elogio *m*, lode *f* ◇ *vt* elogiare, lodare.
pram [præm] *n (Br)* carrozzina *f*.
prank [præŋk] *n* burla *f*.
prawn [prɔːn] *n* gamberetto *m*.
prawn cocktail *n* cocktail *m inv* di gamberetti.
prawn crackers *npl* nuvolette *fpl* di drago.
pray [preɪ] *vi* pregare; **to ~ for sthg** *(fig)* pregare per qc, invocare qc.
prayer [preəʳ] *n* preghiera *f*.
precarious [prɪ'keərɪəs] *adj* precario(-a).
precaution [prɪ'kɔːʃn] *n* precauzione *f*.
precede [prɪ'siːd] *vt (fml)* precedere.
preceding [prɪ'siːdɪŋ] *adj* precedente.
precinct ['priːsɪŋkt] *n (Br: for shopping)* centro *m* commerciale *(chiuso al traffico)*; *(Am: area of town)* circoscrizione *f*.
precious ['preʃəs] *adj* prezioso(-a).
precious stone *n* pietra *f* preziosa.
precipice ['presɪpɪs] *n* precipizio *m*.
precise [prɪ'saɪs] *adj* preciso(-a).
precisely [prɪ'saɪslɪ] *adv* precisamente.
predecessor ['priːdɪsesəʳ] *n* predecessore *m*.
predicament [prɪ'dɪkəmənt] *n* situazione *f* difficile.
predict [prɪ'dɪkt] *vt* predire.
predictable [prɪ'dɪktəbl] *adj* prevedibile.
prediction [prɪ'dɪkʃn] *n* predizione *f*.
preface ['prefɪs] *n* prefazione *f*.
prefect ['priːfekt] *n (Br: at school)* studente *m* (-essa *f*) con funzioni disciplinari.
prefer [prɪ'fɜːʳ] *vt*: **to ~ sthg (to)** preferire qc (a); **to ~ to do sthg** preferire fare qc.
preferable ['prefrəbl] *adj* preferibile.
preferably ['prefrəblɪ] *adv* preferibilmente.
preference ['prefərəns] *n* preferenza *f*.
prefix ['priːfɪks] *n* prefisso *m*.
pregnancy ['pregnənsɪ] *n* gravidanza *f*.
pregnant ['pregnənt] *adj* incinta.
prejudice ['predʒʊdɪs] *n* pregiudizio *m*.
prejudiced ['predʒʊdɪst] *adj*: **~ (against)** prevenuto(-a) (contro); **~ (in favour of)** bendisposto(-a) (verso).
preliminary [prɪ'lɪmɪnərɪ] *adj* preliminare.
premature ['premə,tjʊəʳ] *adj* prematuro(-a).

premier ['premjəʳ] ◇ *adj* primo(-a) ◇ *n* primo ministro *m*.

premiere ['premɪeəʳ] *n* prima *f*.

premises ['premɪsɪz] *npl* locali *mpl*; **on the ~** sul posto.

premium ['pri:mjəm] *n (for insurance)* premio *m*.

premium-quality *adj (meat)* di prima qualità.

preoccupied [pri:'ɒkjʊpaɪd] *adj* preoccupato(-a).

prepacked [ˌpri:'pækt] *adj* preconfezionato(-a).

prepaid ['pri:peɪd] *adj (envelope)* con affrancatura pagata.

preparation [ˌprepə'reɪʃn] *n* preparazione *f*.

◆ **preparations** *npl (arrangements)* preparativi *mpl*.

preparatory school [prɪ'pærətrɪ-] *n (in UK)* scuola *f* elementare privata; *(in US)* scuola *f* secondaria privata *(che prepara agli studi universitari)*.

prepare [prɪ'peəʳ] ◇ *vt* preparare ◇ *vi* prepararsi.

prepared [prɪ'peəd] *adj (ready)* preparato(-a), pronto(-a); **to be ~ to do sthg** essere disposto(-a) a fare qc.

preposition [ˌprepə'zɪʃn] *n* preposizione *f*.

prep school [prep-] = **preparatory school**.

prescribe [prɪ'skraɪb] *vt* prescrivere.

prescription [prɪ'skrɪpʃn] *n (paper)* ricetta *f*; *(medicine)* medicine *fpl*.

presence ['prezns] *n* presenza *f*; **in sb's ~** in presenza di qn.

present [*adj & n* 'preznt, *vb* prɪ'zent] ◇ *adj (in attendance)* presente; *(current)* attuale ◇ *n (gift)* regalo *m* ◇ *vt* presentare; *(offer)* offrire; **the ~ (tense)** il (tempo) presente; **at ~** al momento, attualmente; **the ~** il presente; **to ~ sb to sb** presentare qn a qn.

presentable [prɪ'zentəbl] *adj* presentabile.

presentation [ˌprezn'teɪʃn] *n (way of presenting)* presentazione *f*; *(ceremony)* consegna *f* (ufficiale).

presenter [prɪ'zentəʳ] *n (of TV, radio programme)* presentatore *m* (-trice *f*).

presently ['prezəntlɪ] *adv (soon)* fra poco, a momenti; *(now)* attualmente.

preservation [ˌprezə'veɪʃn] *n* tutela *f*, protezione *f*.

preservative [prɪ'zɜ:vətɪv] *n* conservante *m*.

preserve [prɪ'zɜ:v] ◇ *n (jam)* marmellata *f* ◇ *vt (conserve)* mantenere; *(keep)* preservare, proteggere; *(food)* conservare.

president ['prezɪdənt] *n* presidente *mf*.

press [pres] ◇ *vt (push)* premere, pigiare; *(iron)* stirare ◇ *n*: **the ~** la stampa; **to ~ sb to do sthg** insistere perché qn faccia qc.

press conference *n* conferenza *f* stampa.

press-stud *n* bottone *m* a pressione, automatico *m*.

press-ups *npl* flessioni *fpl* (sulle braccia).

pressure ['preʃəʳ] *n* pressione *f*.

pressure cooker *n* pentola *f* a pressione.

prestigious [pre'stɪdʒəs] *adj* prestigioso(-a).

presumably [prɪ'zju:məblɪ] *adv* presumibilmente.

presume [prɪ'zju:m] *vt (assume)* presumere, supporre.

pretend [prɪ'tend] *vt*: **to ~ to do sthg** far finta di fare qc.

pretentious [prɪ'tenʃəs] *adj* pretenzioso(-a).

pretty ['prɪtɪ] ◇ *adj* grazioso(-a), carino(-a) ◇ *adv (inf) (quite)* piuttosto, abbastanza; *(very)* assai.

prevent [prɪ'vent] *vt* evitare; **to ~ sb/sthg from doing sthg** impedire a qn/qc di fare qc.

prevention [prɪ'venʃn] *n* prevenzione *f*.

preview ['pri:vju:] *n* anteprima *f*.

previous ['pri:vjəs] *adj* precedente.

previously ['pri:vjəslɪ] *adv (formerly)* precedentemente, in precedenza; *(earlier, before)* prima.

price [praɪs] ◇ *n* prezzo *m* ◇ *vt* fissare il prezzo di.

priceless ['praɪslɪs] *adj* inestimabile, senza prezzo.

price list *n* listino *m* prezzi.

pricey ['praɪsɪ] *adj (inf)* costoso(-a).

prick [prɪk] *vt* pungere.

prickly ['prɪklɪ] *adj (plant, bush)* spinoso(-a).

prickly heat *n* sudamina *f*.

pride [praɪd] ◇ *n (satisfaction, self-respect)* orgoglio *m*; *(arrogance)* superbia *f* ◇ *vt*: **to ~ o.s. on sthg** vantarsi di qc.

priest [pri:st] *n* prete *m*, sacerdote *m*.

primarily ['praɪmərɪlɪ] *adv* principalmente.

primary school ['praɪmərɪ-] *n* scuola *f* elementare.

prime [praɪm] *adj (chief)* fondamentale; *(beef, cut)* di prima qualità.

prime minister *n* primo ministro *m*.

primitive ['prɪmɪtɪv] *adj* primitivo(-a).

primrose ['prɪmrəʊz] *n* primula *f*.

prince [prɪns] *n* principe *m*.

Prince of Wales *n* Principe *m* di Galles.

princess [prɪn'ses] *n* principessa *f*.

principal ['prɪnsəpl] ◇ *adj* principale ◇ *n (of school)* direttore *m* (-trice *f*); *(of university)* rettore *m* (-trice *f*).

principle ['prɪnsəpl] *n* principio *m*; **in ~** in linea di principio.

print [prɪnt] ◇ *n (words)* caratteri *mpl*; *(photo, of painting)* stampa *f*; *(mark)* impronta *f* ◇ *vt (book, newspaper, photo)* stampare; *(publish)* pubblicare; *(write)* scrivere a stampatello; **out of ~** esaurito.

◆ **print out** *vt sep* stampare.

printed matter ['prɪntɪd-] *n* stampe *fpl*.

printer ['prɪntəʳ] *n (machine)* stampante *f*; *(person)* tipografo *m* (-a *f*).

printout ['prɪntaʊt] *n* stampato *m*.

prior ['praɪəʳ] *adj (previous)* precedente; **~ to** *(fml)* precedente.

priority [praɪ'ɒrətɪ] *n (important thing)* elemento *m* prioritario; **to have ~ over** avere la priorità rispetto a.

prison ['prɪzn] *n* prigione *f*.

prisoner ['prɪznəʳ] *n* prigioniero *m* (-a *f*).

prisoner of war *n* prigioniero *m* (-a *f*) di guerra.

prison officer *n* guardia *f* carceraria.

privacy ['prɪvəsɪ, *Am* 'praɪvəsɪ] *n* privacy *f*.

private ['praɪvɪt] ◇ *adj* privato(-a); *(confidential)* confidenziale; *(place)* appartato(-a); *(bathroom)* in camera ◇ *n* (MIL) soldato *m* semplice; **in ~** in privato.

private health care *n* assistenza *f* medica privata.

private property *n* proprietà *f* privata.

private school *n* scuola *f* privata.

privilege ['prɪvɪlɪdʒ] *n* privilegio *m*; **it's a ~!** è un onore!

prize [praɪz] *n* premio *m*.

prize-giving [-,gɪvɪŋ] *n* premiazione *f*.

pro [prəʊ] (*pl* **-s**) *n (inf: profession-

al) professionista *mf*.
♦ **pros** *npl*: **the ~s and cons** i pro e i contro.
probability [,prɒbə'bɪlətɪ] *n* probabilità *f*.
probable ['prɒbəbl] *adj* probabile.
probably ['prɒbəblɪ] *adv* probabilmente.
probation officer [prə'beɪʃn-] *n* *persona incaricata di seguire i criminali in libertà vigilata*.
problem ['prɒbləm] *n* problema *m*; **no ~!** *(inf)* non c'è problema!
procedure [prə'siːdʒə^r] *n* procedura *f*.
proceed [prə'siːd] *vi (fml)* procedere; '**~ with caution**' 'procedere con cautela'.
proceeds ['prəʊsiːdz] *npl* ricavato *m*.
process ['prəʊses] *n* processo *m*; **to be in the ~ of doing sthg** star facendo qc.
processed cheese ['prəʊsest-] *n* formaggio *m* fuso.
procession [prə'seʃn] *n* processione *f*.
prod [prɒd] *vt (poke)* pungolare.
produce [prə'djuːs] ◇ *vt* produrre; *(cause)* creare ◇ *n* prodotti *mpl* agricoli.
producer [prə'djuːsə^r] *n* produttore *m* (-trice *f*).
product ['prɒdʌkt] *n* prodotto *m*.
production [prə'dʌkʃn] *n* produzione *f*.
productivity [,prɒdʌk'tɪvətɪ] *n* produttività *f*.
profession [prə'feʃn] *n* professione *f*.
professional [prə'feʃənl] ◇ *adj (relating to work)* professionale; *(not amateur)* professionista ◇ *n* professionista *mf*.
professor [prə'fesə^r] *n* professore *m* (-essa *f*).
profile ['prəʊfaɪl] *n* profilo *m*.
profit ['prɒfɪt] ◇ *n* profitto *m* ◇ *vi*: **to ~ (from)** trarre profitto (da).
profitable ['prɒfɪtəbl] *adj (financially)* rimunerativo(-a); *(useful)* vantaggioso(-a).
profiteroles [prə'fɪtərəʊlz] *npl* profiterole *m inv*.
profound [prə'faʊnd] *adj* profondo(-a).
program ['prəʊgræm] ◇ *n* (COMPUT) programma *m*; *(Am)* = **programme** ◇ *vt* (COMPUT) programmare.
programme ['prəʊgræm] *n (Br)* programma *m*.
progress [*n* 'prəʊgres, *vb* prə'gres] ◇ *n (improvement)* progresso *m*; *(forward movement)* moto *m* ◇ *vi (work, talks, student)* progredire; *(day, meeting)* andare avanti; **to make ~** *(improve)* fare progressi; *(in journey)* avanzare; **in ~** in corso.
progressive [prə'gresɪv] *adj (forward-looking)* progressista.
prohibit [prə'hɪbɪt] *vt* proibire; '**smoking strictly ~ed**' 'è severamente vietato fumare'.
project ['prɒdʒekt] *n* progetto *m*; *(at school)* ricerca *f*.
projector [prə'dʒektə^r] *n* proiettore *m*.
prolong [prə'lɒŋ] *vt* prolungare.
prom [prɒm] *n (Am: dance)* ballo *m (per studenti)*.
promenade [,prɒmə'nɑːd] *n (Br: by the sea)* lungomare *m inv*.
prominent ['prɒmɪnənt] *adj (person)* importante; *(noticeable)* evidente.
promise ['prɒmɪs] ◇ *n* promessa *f* ◇ *vt & vi* promettere; **to show ~** promettere (bene); **I ~!** te lo prometto; **I ~ (that) I'll come** prometto che verrò; **to ~ sb sthg** promettere qc a qn; **to ~ to do sthg** promettere di fare qc.
promising ['prɒmɪsɪŋ] *adj* promettente.

promote [prəˈməʊt] *vt (in job)* promuovere.

promotion [prəˈməʊʃn] *n* promozione *f*.

prompt [prɒmpt] ◇ *adj (quick)* pronto(-a) ◇ *adv*: **at six o'clock ~** alle sei in punto.

prone [prəʊn] *adj*: **to be ~ to sthg** essere incline a qc; **to be ~ to do sthg** essere incline a fare qc.

prong [prɒŋ] *n (of fork)* dente *m*.

pronoun [ˈprəʊnaʊn] *n* pronome *m*.

pronounce [prəˈnaʊns] *vt (word)* pronunciare.

pronunciation [prəˌnʌnsɪˈeɪʃn] *n* pronuncia *f*.

proof [pruːf] *n (evidence)* prova *f*; **to be 12% ~** *(alcohol)* avere 12 gradi.

prop [prɒp]: **prop up** *vt sep (support)* sostenere.

propeller [prəˈpelə^{r}] *n* elica *f*.

proper [ˈprɒpə^{r}] *adj (suitable)* adatto(-a); *(correct)* giusto(-a); *(socially acceptable)* decoroso(-a).

properly [ˈprɒpəlɪ] *adv (suitably)* adeguatamente; *(correctly)* correttamente.

property [ˈprɒpətɪ] *n* proprietà *f inv*.

proportion [prəˈpɔːʃn] *n* proporzione *f*; *(in art)* proporzioni *fpl*.

proposal [prəˈpəʊzl] *n (suggestion)* proposta *f*.

propose [prəˈpəʊz] ◇ *vt (suggest)* proporre ◇ *vi*: **to ~ (to sb)** fare una proposta di matrimonio (a qn).

proposition [ˌprɒpəˈzɪʃn] *n (offer)* proposta *f*.

proprietor [prəˈpraɪətə^{r}] *n (fml)* proprietario *m* (-a *f*).

prose [prəʊz] *n (not poetry)* prosa *f*; (SCH) traduzione *f (dalla madrelingua)*.

prosecution [ˌprɒsɪˈkjuːʃn] *n* (JUR: *charge*) azione *f* giudiziaria.

prospect [ˈprɒspekt] *n (possibility)* prospettiva *f*; **I don't relish the ~** non mi attira la prospettiva.

◆ **prospects** *npl (for the future)* prospettive *fpl*.

prospectus [prəˈspektəs] (*pl* **-es**) *n* prospetto *m*.

prosperous [ˈprɒspərəs] *adj* prospero(-a).

prostitute [ˈprɒstɪtjuːt] *n* prostituta *f*.

protect [prəˈtekt] *vt* proteggere; **to ~ sb/sthg from** proteggere qn/qc da; **to ~ sb/sthg against** proteggere qn/qc da.

protection [prəˈtekʃn] *n* protezione *f*.

protection factor *n* fattore *m* di protezione.

protective [prəˈtektɪv] *adj (person)* protettivo(-a); *(clothes)* di protezione.

protein [ˈprəʊtiːn] *n* proteina *f*.

protest [*n* ˈprəʊtest, *vb* prəˈtest] ◇ *n* protesta *f* ◇ *vt (Am: protest against)* protestare contro ◇ *vi*: **to ~ (against)** protestare (contro).

Protestant [ˈprɒtɪstənt] *n* protestante *mf*.

protester [prəˈtestə^{r}] *n* dimostrante *mf*.

protractor [prəˈtræktə^{r}] *n* goniometro *m*.

protrude [prəˈtruːd] *vi* sporgere.

proud [praʊd] *adj (pleased)* orgoglioso(-a); *(pej: arrogant)* superbo(-a); **to be ~ of** essere orgoglioso di.

prove [pruːv] (*pp* **-d** OR **proven** [pruːvn]) *vt (show to be true)* dimostrare; *(turn out to be)* dimostrarsi.

proverb [ˈprɒvɜːb] *n* proverbio *m*.

provide [prəˈvaɪd] *vt* fornire; **to ~ sb with sthg** fornire qc a qn.

◆ **provide for** *vt fus (person)* provvedere a.

provided (that) [prəˈvaɪdɪd-] *conj* purché.

providing (that) [prəˈvaɪdɪŋ-] =

provided (that).
province ['prɒvɪns] *n* regione *f*.
provisional [prə'vɪʒənl] *adj* provvisorio(-a).
provisions [prə'vɪʒnz] *npl* provviste *fpl*.
provocative [prə'vɒkətɪv] *adj* provocatorio(-a).
provoke [prə'vəʊk] *vt* provocare.
prowl [praʊl] *vi* muoversi furtivamente.
prune [pru:n] ◇ *n* prugna *f* secca ◇ *vt (tree, bush)* potare.
PS *(abbr of postscript)* P.S.
psychiatrist [saɪ'kaɪətrɪst] *n* psichiatra *mf*.
psychic ['saɪkɪk] *adj* dotato(-a) di poteri paranormali.
psychological [,saɪkə'lɒdʒɪkl] *adj* psicologico(-a).
psychologist [saɪ'kɒlədʒɪst] *n* psicologo *m* (-a *f*).
psychology [saɪ'kɒlədʒɪ] *n* psicologia *f*.
psychotherapist [,saɪkəʊ'θerəpɪst] *n* psicoterapeuta *mf*.
pt *(abbr of pint)* pt.
PTO *(abbr of please turn over)* v.r.
pub [pʌb] *n* pub *m inv*.
puberty ['pju:bətɪ] *n* pubertà *f*.
public ['pʌblɪk] ◇ *adj* pubblico(-a) ◇ *n*: **the ~** il pubblico; **in ~** in pubblico.
publican ['pʌblɪkən] *n (Br)* gestore *m* (-trice *f*) di un pub.
publication [,pʌblɪ'keɪʃn] *n* pubblicazione *f*.
public bar *n (Br) sala di un pub, in cui le bevande costano meno.*
public convenience *n (Br)* gabinetti *mpl* pubblici.
public footpath *n (Br)* sentiero *m*.
public holiday *n* giorno *m* festivo.
public house *n (Br: fml)* pub *m inv*.
publicity [pʌb'lɪsɪtɪ] *n* pubblicità *f*.
public school *n (in UK)* scuola *f* privata; *(in US)* scuola statale.
public telephone *n* telefono *m* pubblico.
public transport *n* trasporti *mpl* pubblici.
publish ['pʌblɪʃ] *vt* pubblicare.
publisher ['pʌblɪʃə^r] *n (person)* editore *m* (-trice *f*); *(company)* casa *f* editrice.
publishing ['pʌblɪʃɪŋ] *n (industry)* editoria *f*.
pub lunch *n pranzo semplice e a basso costo servito in un pub.*
pudding ['pʊdɪŋ] *n (sweet dish)* budino *m*; *(Br: course)* dessert *m inv*.
puddle ['pʌdl] *n* pozzanghera *f*.
puff [pʌf] ◇ *vi (breathe heavily)* ansare ◇ *n (of air, smoke)* sbuffo *m*; **to ~ at** tirare una boccata di.
puff pastry *n* pasta *f* sfoglia.
pull [pʊl] ◇ *vt* tirare; *(trigger)* premere ◇ *vi* tirare ◇ *n*: **to give sthg a ~** dare una tirata a qc; **to ~ a face** fare una smorfia; **to ~ a muscle** farsi uno strappo muscolare; **'pull'** *(on door)* 'tirare'.
◆ **pull apart** *vt sep (machine, book)* fare a pezzi.
◆ **pull down** *vt sep (lower)* abbassare; *(demolish)* demolire.
◆ **pull in** *vi (train)* arrivare; *(car)* accostare.
◆ **pull out** ◇ *vt sep (tooth, cork, plug)* estrarre ◇ *vi (train)* partire; *(car)* entrare in corsia; *(withdraw)* ritirarsi.
◆ **pull over** *vi (car)* accostare.
◆ **pull up** ◇ *vt sep (socks, trousers, sleeve)* tirare su ◇ *vi (stop)* fermarsi.
pulley ['pʊlɪ] (*pl* **pulleys**) *n* carrucola *f*.
pull-out *n (Am: beside road)* piazzola *f* (di sosta).

pullover ['pʊl,əʊvə^r] *n* pullover *m inv*.
pulpit ['pʊlpɪt] *n* pulpito *m*.
pulse [pʌls] *n* (MED) polso *m*.
pump [pʌmp] *n* pompa *f*.
◆ **pumps** *npl (sports shoes)* scarpe *fpl* da ginnastica.
◆ **pump up** *vt sep* gonfiare.
pumpkin ['pʌmpkɪn] *n* zucca *f*.
pun [pʌn] *n* gioco *m* di parole.
punch [pʌntʃ] ◇ *n (blow)* pugno *m*; *(drink)* punch *m inv* ◇ *vt (hit)* sferrare un pugno a; *(ticket)* forare.
Punch and Judy show [-'dʒuːdɪ-] *n spettacolo di burattini*.
punctual ['pʌŋktʃʊəl] *adj* puntuale.
punctuation [,pʌŋktʃʊ'eɪʃn] *n* punteggiatura *f*.
puncture ['pʌŋktʃə^r] ◇ *vt* forare ◇ *n*: **to get a ~** forare (una gomma).
punish ['pʌnɪʃ] *vt*: **to ~ sb (for sthg)** punire qn (per qc).
punishment ['pʌnɪʃmənt] *n* punizione *f*.
punk [pʌŋk] *n (person)* punk *mf inv*; *(music)* musica *f* punk.
punnet ['pʌnɪt] *n (Br)* cestino *m*.
pupil ['pjuːpl] *n (student)* alunno *m* (-a *f*); *(of eye)* pupilla *f*.
puppet ['pʌpɪt] *n* burattino *m*.
puppy ['pʌpɪ] *n* cucciolo *m*.
purchase ['pɜːtʃəs] ◇ *vt (fml)* acquistare ◇ *n (fml)* acquisto *m*.
pure [pjʊə^r] *adj* puro(-a).
puree ['pjʊəreɪ] *n* purè *m inv*.
purely ['pjʊəlɪ] *adv (only)* soltanto.
purity ['pjʊərətɪ] *n* purezza *f*.
purple ['pɜːpl] *adj* viola *(inv)*.
purpose ['pɜːpəs] *n* scopo *m*; **on ~** apposta.
purr [pɜː^r] *vi (cat)* fare le fusa.
purse [pɜːs] *n (Br: for money)* portamonete *m inv*; *(Am: handbag)* borsa *f*.
pursue [pə'sjuː] *vt (follow)* inseguire; *(study)* continuare; *(matter, inquiry)* approfondire.
pus [pʌs] *n* pus *m*.
push [pʊʃ] ◇ *vt* spingere; *(button, doorbell)* premere; *(product)* pubblicizzare ◇ *vi* spingere ◇ *n*: **to give sb/sthg a ~** dare una spinta a qn/qc; **to ~ sb into doing sthg** spingere qn a fare qc; **'push'** *(on door)* 'spingere'.
◆ **push in** *vi (in queue)* passare avanti.
◆ **push off** *vi (inf: go away)* andarsene.
push-button telephone *n* telefono *m* a tastiera.
pushchair ['pʊʃtʃeə^r] *n (Br)* passeggino *m*.
pushed [pʊʃt] *adj (inf)*: **to be ~ (for time)** essere a corto di tempo.
push-ups *npl* flessioni *fpl* (sulle braccia).
put [pʊt] (*pt & pp* **put**) *vt* mettere; *(responsibility)* dare; *(pressure)* esercitare; *(express)* esprimere; *(a question)* porre; *(estimate)* stimare; **to ~ a child to bed** mettere a letto un bambino; **to ~ money into sthg** investire soldi in qc.
◆ **put aside** *vt sep (money)* mettere da parte.
◆ **put away** *vt sep (tidy up)* mettere via.
◆ **put back** *vt sep (replace)* mettere a posto; *(postpone)* posporre; *(clock, watch)* mettere indietro.
◆ **put down** *vt sep (on floor, table)* posare; *(passenger)* far scendere; *(Br: animal)* abbattere; *(deposit)* dare in acconto.
◆ **put forward** *vt sep (clock, watch)* mettere avanti; *(suggest)* suggerire.
◆ **put in** *vt sep (insert)* inserire; *(install)* installare.
◆ **put off** *vt sep (postpone)* rimandare; *(distract)* distrarre; *(repel)* disgustare; *(passenger)* far scendere.

◆ **put on** *vt sep (clothes, glasses, make-up)* mettersi; *(weight)* mettere su; *(television, light, radio)* accendere; *(CD, tape, record)* mettere; *(play, show)* mettere in scena.

◆ **put out** *vt sep (cigarette, fire, light)* spegnere; *(publish)* pubblicare; *(hand, arm, leg)* stendere; *(inconvenience)* disturbare; **to ~ one's back out** farsi male alla schiena.

◆ **put together** *vt sep (assemble)* montare; *(combine)* mettere insieme.

◆ **put up** ◇ *vt sep (tent, statue, building)* erigere; *(umbrella)* aprire; *(a notice, sign)* mettere; *(price, rate)* aumentare; *(provide with accommodation)* ospitare ◇ *vi (Br: in hotel)* alloggiare.

◆ **put up with** *vt fus* sopportare.

putter ['pʌtəʳ] *n (club)* putter *m inv.*

putting green ['pʌtɪŋ-] *n* campo *m* da minigolf.

putty ['pʌtɪ] *n* stucco *m.*

puzzle ['pʌzl] ◇ *n (game)* rompicapo *m*; *(jigsaw)* puzzle *m inv*; *(mystery)* enigma *m* ◇ *vt* confondere.

puzzling ['pʌzlɪŋ] *adj* sconcertante.

pyjamas [pə'dʒɑːməz] *npl (Br)* pigiama *m.*

pylon ['paɪlən] *n* traliccio *m.*

pyramid ['pɪrəmɪd] *n* piramide *f.*

Pyrenees [ˌpɪrə'niːz] *npl*: **the ~** i Pirenei.

Pyrex® ['paɪreks] *n* pyrex® *m.*

Q

quail [kweɪl] *n* quaglia *f*.

quail's eggs *npl* uova *fpl* di quaglia.

quaint [kweɪnt] *adj* pittoresco(-a).

qualification [ˌkwɒlɪfɪˈkeɪʃn] *n* *(diploma)* qualifica *f*; *(ability)* qualità *f inv*.

qualified [ˈkwɒlɪfaɪd] *adj* *(having qualifications)* qualificato(-a).

qualify [ˈkwɒlɪfaɪ] *vi* *(for competition)* qualificarsi; *(pass exam)* abilitarsi.

quality [ˈkwɒlətɪ] ◇ *n* qualità *f inv* ◇ *adj* di qualità.

quarantine [ˈkwɒrəntiːn] *n* quarantena *f*.

quarrel [ˈkwɒrəl] ◇ *n* lite *f* ◇ *vi* litigare.

quarry [ˈkwɒrɪ] *n* *(for stone, sand)* cava *f*.

quart [kwɔːt] *n* *(in UK)* = 1,136 l, ≃ litro *m*; *(in US)* = 0,946 l, ≃ litro.

quarter [ˈkwɔːtəʳ] *n* *(fraction)* quarto *m*; *(Am: coin)* quarto di dollaro; *(4 ounces)* quarto di libbra; *(three months)* trimestre *m*; *(part of town)* quartiere *m*; **(a) ~ to five** *(Br)* le cinque meno un quarto; **(a) ~ of five** *(Am)* le cinque meno un quarto; **(a) ~ past five** *(Br)* le cinque e un quarto; **(a) ~ after five** *(Am)* le cinque e un quarto; **(a) ~ of an hour** un quarto d'ora.

quarterpounder [ˌkwɔːtəˈpaʊndəʳ] *n* grosso hamburger *m inv*.

quartet [kwɔːˈtet] *n* quartetto *m*.

quartz [kwɔːts] *adj* *(watch)* al quarzo.

quay [kiː] *n* banchina *f*.

queasy [ˈkwiːzɪ] *adj* *(inf)*: **to feel ~** avere la nausea.

queen [kwiːn] *n* regina *f*.

queer [kwɪəʳ] *adj* *(strange)* strano(-a); *(inf: homosexual)* omosessuale; **to feel ~** *(ill)* sentirsi male.

quench [kwentʃ] *vt*: **to ~ one's thirst** dissetarsi.

query [ˈkwɪərɪ] *n* quesito *m*.

question [ˈkwestʃn] ◇ *n* *(query, in exam, on questionnaire)* domanda *f*; *(issue)* questione *f* ◇ *vt* *(person)* interrogare; **it's out of the ~** è fuori discussione.

question mark *n* punto *m* interrogativo.

questionnaire [ˌkwestʃəˈneəʳ] *n* questionario *m*.

queue [kjuː] ◇ *n* *(Br)* coda *f* ◇ *vi* *(Br)* fare la coda.

◆ **queue up** *vi* *(Br)* fare la coda.

quiche [kiːʃ] *n* torta *f* salata.

quick [kwɪk] ◇ *adj* rapido(-a) ◇ *adv* rapidamente.

quickly [ˈkwɪklɪ] *adv* rapidamente.

quid [kwɪd] *(pl inv)* *n* *(Br: inf)* sterlina *f*.

quiet ['kwaɪət] ◇ *adj* silenzioso(-a); *(calm, peaceful)* tranquillo(-a) ◇ *n* quiete *f*; **in a ~ voice** a bassa voce; **keep ~!** silenzio!; **to keep ~** *(not say anything)* tacere; **to keep ~ about sthg** tenere segreto qc.

quieten ['kwaɪətn]: **quieten down** *vi* calmarsi.

quietly ['kwaɪətlɪ] *adv* silenziosamente; *(calmly)* tranquillamente.

quilt [kwɪlt] *n (duvet)* piumino *m*; *(eiderdown)* trapunta *f*.

quince [kwɪns] *n* mela *f* cotogna.

quirk [kwɜːk] *n* stranezza *f*.

quit [kwɪt] (*pt & pp* **quit**) ◇ *vi (resign)* dimettersi; *(give up)* smettere ◇ *vt (Am: school, job)* lasciare; **to ~ doing sthg** smettere di fare qc.

quite [kwaɪt] *adv (fairly)* abbastanza; *(completely)* proprio; **not ~** non proprio; **~ a lot (of)** un bel po' (di).

quiz [kwɪz] (*pl* **-zes**) *n* quiz *m inv*.

quota ['kwəʊtə] *n* quota *f*.

quotation [kwəʊ'teɪʃn] *n (phrase)* citazione *f*; *(estimate)* preventivo *m*.

quotation marks *npl* virgolette *fpl*.

quote [kwəʊt] ◇ *vt (phrase, writer)* citare ◇ *n (phrase)* citazione *f*; *(estimate)* preventivo *m*; **he ~d me a price of £50** mi ha dato un prezzo indicativo di 50 sterline.

R

rabbit [ˈræbɪt] *n* coniglio *m*.
rabies [ˈreɪbiːz] *n* rabbia *f*.
RAC *n* = ACI *m*.
race [reɪs] ◇ *n (competition)* gara *f*; *(ethnic group)* razza *f* ◇ *vi (compete)* gareggiare; *(go fast)* correre; *(engine)* imballarsi ◇ *vt (compete against)* gareggiare con.
racecourse [ˈreɪskɔːs] *n* ippodromo *m*.
racehorse [ˈreɪshɔːs] *n* cavallo *m* da corsa.
racetrack [ˈreɪstræk] *n (for horses)* ippodromo *m*.
racial [ˈreɪʃl] *adj* razziale.
racing [ˈreɪsɪŋ] *n*: **(horse) ~** corse *fpl* (di cavalli).
racing car *n* automobile *f* da corsa.
racism [ˈreɪsɪzm] *n* razzismo *m*.
racist [ˈreɪsɪst] *n* razzista *mf*.
rack [ræk] *n (for coats)* attaccapanni *m inv*; *(for plates)* scolapiatti *m inv*; *(for bottles)* portabottiglie *m inv*; **(luggage) ~** portabagagli *m inv*; **~ of lamb** carrè *m inv* di agnello.
racket [ˈrækɪt] *n (for tennis, badminton, squash)* racchetta *f*; *(noise)* baccano *m*.
racquet [ˈrækɪt] *n* racchetta *f*.
radar [ˈreɪdɑːʳ] *n* radar *m inv*.
radiation [ˌreɪdɪˈeɪʃn] *n (nuclear)* radiazione *f*.
radiator [ˈreɪdɪeɪtəʳ] *n* radiatore *m*.
radical [ˈrædɪkl] *adj* radicale.
radii [ˈreɪdɪaɪ] *pl* → **radius**.
radio [ˈreɪdɪəʊ] (*pl* **-s**) ◇ *n* radio *f inv* ◇ *vt (person)* chiamare via radio; **on the ~** alla radio.
radioactive [ˌreɪdɪəʊˈæktɪv] *adj* radioattivo(-a).
radio alarm *n* radiosveglia *f*.
radish [ˈrædɪʃ] *n* ravanello *m*.
radius [ˈreɪdɪəs] (*pl* **radii**) *n* raggio *m*.
raffle [ˈræfl] *n* lotteria *f*.
raft [rɑːft] *n (of wood)* zattera *f*; *(inflatable)* materassino *m* (gonfiabile).
rafter [ˈrɑːftəʳ] *n* travicello *m*.
rag [ræg] *n (old cloth)* straccio *m*.
rage [reɪdʒ] *n* rabbia *f*.
raid [reɪd] ◇ *n* raid *m inv*; *(robbery)* scorreria *f* ◇ *vt (subj: police)* fare irruzione in; *(subj: thieves)* fare razzia in.
rail [reɪl] ◇ *n (bar)* sbarra *f*; *(for curtain)* asta *f*; *(on stairs)* corrimano *m inv*; *(for train, tram)* rotaia *f* ◇ *adj* ferroviario(-a); **by ~** in treno.
railcard [ˈreɪlkɑːd] *n (Br) (for young people) tessera per riduzione ferroviaria*; *(for pensioners)* = carta d'argento.
railings [ˈreɪlɪŋz] *npl* ringhiera *f*.
railroad [ˈreɪlrəʊd] *(Am)* = **railway**.

railway [ˈreɪlweɪ] *n* ferrovia *f*.

railway line *n (route)* linea *f* ferroviaria; *(track)* binario *m*.

railway station *n* stazione *f* ferroviaria.

rain [reɪn] ◇ *n* pioggia *f* ◇ *v impers* piovere; **it's ~ing** sta piovendo.

rainbow [ˈreɪnbəʊ] *n* arcobaleno *m*.

raincoat [ˈreɪnkəʊt] *n* impermeabile *m*.

raindrop [ˈreɪndrɒp] *n* goccia *f* di pioggia.

rainfall [ˈreɪnfɔːl] *n* precipitazione *f*.

rainy [ˈreɪnɪ] *adj* piovoso(-a).

raise [reɪz] ◇ *vt* sollevare; *(increase)* aumentare; *(money)* raccogliere; *(child, animals)* allevare ◇ *n (Am: pay increase)* aumento *m*.

raisin [ˈreɪzn] *n* uva *f* passa.

rake [reɪk] *n (gardening tool)* rastrello *m*.

rally [ˈrælɪ] *n (public meeting)* comizio *m*; *(motor race)* rally *m inv*; *(in tennis, badminton, squash) serie di scambi della palla*.

ram [ræm] ◇ *n* montone *m* ◇ *vt (bang into)* speronare.

Ramadan [ˌræməˈdæn] *n* Ramadan *m inv*.

ramble [ˈræmbl] *n* camminata *f*.

ramp [ræmp] *n (slope)* rampa *f*; *(in roadworks)* dislivello *m*; *(Am: to freeway)* rampa *f* d'accesso; **'ramp'** *(Br: bump)* 'fondo dissestato'.

ramparts [ˈræmpɑːts] *npl* bastioni *mpl*.

ran [ræn] *pt* → **run**.

ranch [rɑːntʃ] *n* ranch *m inv*.

ranch dressing *n (Am) maionese piuttosto liquida e piccante*.

rancid [ˈrænsɪd] *adj* rancido(-a).

random [ˈrændəm] ◇ *adj* a caso ◇ *n*: **at ~** a caso.

rang [ræŋ] *pt* → **ring**.

range [reɪndʒ] ◇ *n (of radio, telescope)* portata *f*; *(of aircraft)* raggio *m*; *(for shooting)* campo *m* di tiro; *(of prices, temperatures, goods)* gamma *f*; *(of hills, mountains)* catena *f*; *(cooker)* cucina *f* economica ◇ *vi (vary)* variare.

ranger [ˈreɪndʒə^r] *n (of park, forest)* guardia *f* forestale.

rank [ræŋk] ◇ *n (in armed forces, police)* rango *m* ◇ *adj (smell, taste)* rancido(-a).

ransom [ˈrænsəm] *n* riscatto *m*.

rap [ræp] *n (music)* rap *m inv*.

rape [reɪp] ◇ *n* stupro *m* ◇ *vt* stuprare.

rapid [ˈræpɪd] *adj* rapido(-a).

◆ **rapids** *npl* rapide *fpl*.

rapidly [ˈræpɪdlɪ] *adv* rapidamente.

rapist [ˈreɪpɪst] *n* stupratore *m*.

rare [reə^r] *adj (not common)* raro(-a); *(meat)* al sangue.

rarely [ˈreəlɪ] *adv* raramente.

rash [ræʃ] ◇ *n* eruzione *f* cutanea ◇ *adj* impulsivo(-a).

rasher [ˈræʃə^r] *n* fettina *f* di pancetta.

raspberry [ˈrɑːzbərɪ] *n* lampone *m*.

rat [ræt] *n* ratto *m*.

ratatouille [rætəˈtuːɪ] *n* ratatouille *f inv*.

rate [reɪt] ◇ *n (level)* tasso *m*; *(charge)* tariffa *f*; *(speed)* ritmo *m* ◇ *vt (consider)* reputare; *(deserve)* meritare; **~ of exchange** tasso di cambio; **at any ~** in ogni caso; **at this ~** di questo passo.

rather [ˈrɑːðə^r] *adv (quite)* piuttosto; **I'd ~ not** preferirei di no; **would you ~ ...?** preferisci ...?; **~ than** piuttosto che; **~ a lot** molto.

ratio [ˈreɪʃɪəʊ] (*pl* **-s**) *n* rapporto *m*.

ration [ˈræʃn] *n (share)* razione *f*.

◆ **rations** *npl (food)* razioni *fpl*.

rational [ˈræʃnl] *adj* razionale.

rattle ['rætl] ◇ *n (of baby)* sonaglio *m* ◇ *vi* sbatacchiare.
rave [reɪv] *n (party)* rave *m inv*.
raven ['reɪvn] *n* corvo *m*.
ravioli [ˌrævɪ'əʊlɪ] *n* ravioli *mpl*.
raw [rɔː] *adj (uncooked)* crudo(-a); *(unprocessed)* grezzo(-a).
raw material *n* materia *f* prima.
ray [reɪ] *n* raggio *m*.
razor ['reɪzəʳ] *n* rasoio *m*.
razor blade *n* lametta *f* (da barba).
Rd *abbr* = **Road**.
re [riː] *prep* in merito a.
RE *n (abbr of religious education)* religione *f (materia)*.
reach [riːtʃ] ◇ *vt* raggiungere ◇ *n*: **out of ~** lontano; **within ~ of the beach** a poca distanza dalla spiaggia.
◆ **reach out** *vi*: **to ~ out (for)** allungarsi (per raggiungere).
react [rɪ'ækt] *vi* reagire.
reaction [rɪ'ækʃn] *n* reazione *f*.
read [riːd] (*pt & pp* **read** [red]) ◇ *vt* leggere; *(subj: sign, note)* dire; *(subj: meter, gauge)* segnare ◇ *vi* leggere; **to ~ about sthg** leggere di qc.
◆ **read out** *vt sep* leggere ad alta voce.
reader ['riːdəʳ] *n (of newspaper, book)* lettore *m* (-trice *f*).
readily ['redɪlɪ] *adv (willingly)* prontamente; *(easily)* facilmente.
reading ['riːdɪŋ] *n (of books, papers)* lettura *f*; *(of meter, gauge)* valore *m* indicato.
reading matter *n* qualcosa da leggere.
ready ['redɪ] *adj* pronto(-a); **to be ~ for sthg** *(prepared)* essere preparato(-a) per qc; **to be ~ to do sthg** *(willing)* essere pronto a fare qc; *(likely)* essere sul punto di fare qc; **to get ~** prepararsi; **to get sthg ~** preparare qc.
ready cash *n* contante *m*.
ready-cooked [-kʊkt] *adj* precotto(-a).
ready-to-wear *adj* confezionato(-a).
real ['rɪəl] ◇ *adj* vero(-a); *(world)* reale ◇ *adv (Am)* davvero.
real ale *n (Br) birra rossa prodotta secondo metodi tradizionali.*
real estate *n* proprietà *fpl* immobiliari.
realistic [ˌrɪə'lɪstɪk] *adj* realistico(-a).
reality [rɪ'ælətɪ] *n* realtà *f inv*; **in ~** in realtà.
realize ['rɪəlaɪz] *vt* rendersi conto di; *(ambition, goal)* realizzare; **to ~ (that)** ... rendersi conto che OR di ...
really ['rɪəlɪ] *adv* veramente; *(in reality)* realmente; **do you like it? – no, not ~** ti piace? – veramente no; **~?** *(expressing surprise)* davvero?
realtor ['rɪəltər] *n (Am)* agente *mf* immobiliare.
rear [rɪəʳ] ◇ *adj* posteriore ◇ *n (back)* retro *m inv*.
rearrange [ˌriːə'reɪndʒ] *vt* spostare.
rearview mirror ['rɪəvjuː-] *n* specchietto *m* retrovisore.
rear-wheel drive *n* trazione *f* posteriore.
reason ['riːzn] *n* motivo *m*; **for some ~** per qualche motivo.
reasonable ['riːznəbl] *adj* ragionevole; *(quite big)* buono(-a).
reasonably ['riːznəblɪ] *adv (quite)* piuttosto.
reasoning ['riːznɪŋ] *n* ragionamento *m*.
reassure [ˌriːə'ʃɔːʳ] *vt* rassicurare.
reassuring [ˌriːə'ʃɔːrɪŋ] *adj* rassicurante.
rebate ['riːbeɪt] *n* rimborso *m*.
rebel [*n* 'rebl, *vb* rɪ'bel] ◇ *n* ribelle *mf* ◇ *vi* ribellarsi.

rebound [rɪ'baʊnd] *vi (ball)* rimbalzare.

rebuild [ˌriː'bɪld] (*pt & pp* **rebuilt** [ˌriː'bɪlt]) *vt* ricostruire.

rebuke [rɪ'bjuːk] *vt* rimproverare.

recall [rɪ'kɔːl] *vt (remember)* ricordare.

receipt [rɪ'siːt] *n (for goods, money)* ricevuta *f*; **on ~ of** al ricevimento di.

receive [rɪ'siːv] *vt* ricevere.

receiver [rɪ'siːvəʳ] *n (of phone)* ricevitore *m*.

recent ['riːsnt] *adj* recente.

recently ['riːsntlɪ] *adv* recentemente.

receptacle [rɪ'septəkl] *n (fml)* ricettacolo *m*.

reception [rɪ'sepʃn] *n (in hotel)* reception *f inv*; *(at hospital)* accettazione *f*; *(party)* ricevimento *m*; *(welcome)* accoglienza *f*; *(of TV, radio)* ricezione *f*.

reception desk *n* banco *m* della reception.

receptionist [rɪ'sepʃənɪst] *n* receptionist *mf inv*.

recess ['riːses] *n (in wall)* nicchia *f*; (*Am:* SCH) intervallo *m*.

recession [rɪ'seʃn] *n* recessione *f*.

recipe ['resɪpɪ] *n* ricetta *f*.

recite [rɪ'saɪt] *vt (poem)* recitare; *(list)* elencare.

reckless ['reklɪs] *adj* avventato(-a).

reckon ['rekn] *vt (inf: think)* pensare.

◆ **reckon on** *vt fus* aspettarsi.

◆ **reckon with** *vt fus (expect)* aspettarsi.

reclaim [rɪ'kleɪm] *vt (baggage)* ritirare.

reclining seat [rɪ'klaɪnɪŋ-] *n* sedile *m* reclinabile.

recognition [ˌrekəg'nɪʃn] *n* riconoscimento *m*.

recognize ['rekəgnaɪz] *vt* riconoscere.

recollect [ˌrekə'lekt] *vt* ricordare.

recommend [ˌrekə'mend] *vt* raccomandare; **to ~ sb to do sthg** consigliare a qn di fare qc.

recommendation [ˌrekəmen'deɪʃn] *n (suggestion)* indicazione *f*.

reconsider [ˌriːkən'sɪdəʳ] *vt* riconsiderare.

reconstruct [ˌriːkən'strʌkt] *vt* ricostruire.

record [*n* 'rekɔːd, *vb* rɪ'kɔːd] ◇ *n* (MUS) disco *m*; *(best performance, highest level)* record *m inv*; *(account)* nota *f* ◇ *vt (keep account of)* annotare; *(on tape)* registrare.

recorded delivery [rɪ'kɔːdɪd-] *n* *(Br)* = raccomandata *f*.

recorder [rɪ'kɔːdəʳ] *n (tape recorder)* registratore *m*; *(instrument)* flauto *m* diritto.

recording [rɪ'kɔːdɪŋ] *n* registrazione *f*.

record player *n* giradischi *m inv*.

record shop *n* negozio *m* di dischi.

recover [rɪ'kʌvəʳ] ◇ *vt (stolen goods, lost property)* recuperare ◇ *vi* riprendersi.

recovery [rɪ'kʌvərɪ] *n (from illness)* guarigione *f*.

recovery vehicle *n (Br)* carro *m* attrezzi.

recreation [ˌrekrɪ'eɪʃn] *n* divertimento *m*.

recreation ground *n* parco *m* (giochi).

recruit [rɪ'kruːt] ◇ *n* recluta *mf* ◇ *vt (staff)* assumere.

rectangle ['rekˌtæŋgl] *n* rettangolo *m*.

rectangular [rek'tæŋgjʊləʳ] *adj* rettangolare.

recycle [ˌriː'saɪkl] *vt* riciclare.

red [red] ◇ *adj* rosso(-a) ◇ *n* *(colour)* rosso *m*; **in the ~** in rosso.

red cabbage *n* cavolo *m* rosso.
Red Cross *n* Croce *f* Rossa.
redcurrant ['redkʌrənt] *n* ribes *m inv*.
redecorate [ˌriːˈdekəreɪt] *vt* rimbiancare.
redhead ['redhed] *n* rosso *m* (-a *f*).
red-hot *adj (metal)* rovente.
redial [riːˈdaɪəl] *vi* rifare il numero.
redirect [ˌriːdɪˈrekt] *vt (letter)* spedire a un nuovo indirizzo; *(traffic, plane)* dirottare.
red pepper *n* peperone *m* rosso.
reduce [rɪˈdjuːs] ◇ *vt* ridurre ◇ *vi (Am: slim)* dimagrire.
reduced price [rɪˈdjuːst-] *n* prezzo *m* ridotto.
reduction [rɪˈdʌkʃn] *n* riduzione *f*.
redundancy [rɪˈdʌndənsɪ] *n (Br)* licenziamento *m (per esubero)*.
redundant [rɪˈdʌndənt] *adj (Br)*: **to be made ~** essere licenziato(-a).
red wine *n* vino *m* rosso.
reed [riːd] *n* canna *f*.
reef [riːf] *n* scogliera *f*.
reek [riːk] *vi* puzzare.
reel [riːl] *n (of thread)* rocchetto *m*; *(on fishing rod)* mulinello *m*.
refectory [rɪˈfektərɪ] *n* refettorio *m*.
refer [rɪˈfɜːʳ]: **refer to** *vt fus (speak about)* fare riferimento a; *(relate to)* riferirsi a; *(consult)* consultare.
referee [ˌrefəˈriː] *n* (SPORT) arbitro *m* (-a *f*).
reference ['refrəns] ◇ *n (mention)* riferimento *m*; *(letter for job)* lettera *f* di referenze ◇ *adj (book, library)* di consultazione; **with ~ to** con riferimento a.
referendum [ˌrefəˈrendəm] *n* referendum *m inv*.
refill [*n* ˈriːfɪl, *vb* ˌriːˈfɪl] ◇ *n (for pen)* ricambio *m*; *(inf: drink)* rifornimento *m* ◇ *vt* riempire.
refinery [rɪˈfaɪnərɪ] *n* raffineria *f*.
reflect [rɪˈflekt] *vt & vi* riflettere.
reflection [rɪˈflekʃn] *n (image)* riflesso *m*.
reflector [rɪˈflektəʳ] *n* catarifrangente *m*.
reflex ['riːfleks] *n* riflesso *m*.
reflexive [rɪˈfleksɪv] *adj* riflessivo(-a).
reform [rɪˈfɔːm] ◇ *n* riforma *f* ◇ *vt* riformare.
refresh [rɪˈfreʃ] *vt* rinfrescare.
refreshing [rɪˈfreʃɪŋ] *adj (drink, breeze, sleep)* rinfrescante; *(change)* piacevole.
refreshments [rɪˈfreʃmənts] *npl* rinfreschi *mpl*.
refrigerator [rɪˈfrɪdʒəreɪtəʳ] *n* frigorifero *m*.
refugee [ˌrefjʊˈdʒiː] *n* rifugiato *m* (-a *f*).
refund [*n* ˈriːfʌnd, *vb* rɪˈfʌnd] ◇ *n* rimborso *m* ◇ *vt* rimborsare.
refundable [rɪˈfʌndəbl] *adj* rimborsabile.
refusal [rɪˈfjuːzl] *n* rifiuto *m*.
refuse[1] [rɪˈfjuːz] ◇ *vt (not accept)* rifiutare; *(not allow)* negare ◇ *vi* rifiutare; **to ~ to do sthg** rifiutare di fare qc.
refuse[2] ['refjuːs] *n (fml)* rifiuti *mpl*.
refuse collection ['refjuːs-] *n (fml)* raccolta *f* dei rifiuti.
regard [rɪˈgɑːd] ◇ *vt (consider)* considerare ◇ *n*: **with ~ to** riguardo a; **as ~s** per quanto riguarda.
◆ **regards** *npl (in greetings)* saluti *mpl*; **give them my ~s** li saluti da parte mia.
regarding [rɪˈgɑːdɪŋ] *prep* riguardo a.
regardless [rɪˈgɑːdlɪs] *adv* lo stesso; **~ of** senza tener conto di.
reggae ['regeɪ] *n* reggae *m inv*.
regiment ['redʒɪmənt] *n* reggimento *m*.

region ['ri:dʒən] *n* regione *f*; **in the ~ of** circa.

regional ['ri:dʒənl] *adj* regionale.

register ['redʒɪstəʳ] ◇ *n* registro *m* ◇ *vt* registrare; *(subj: machine, gauge)* segnare ◇ *vi (put one's name down)* iscriversi; *(at hotel)* firmare il registro.

registered ['redʒɪstəd] *adj (letter, parcel)* assicurato(-a).

registration [,redʒɪ'streɪʃn] *n (for course, at conference)* iscrizione *f*.

registration (number) *n (of car)* numero *m* di targa.

registry office ['redʒɪstrɪ-] *n* anagrafe *f*.

regret [rɪ'gret] ◇ *n (thing regretted)* rimpianto *m* ◇ *vt* rimpiangere; **I ~ telling her** mi dispiace (di) averglielo detto; **we ~ any inconvenience caused** ci scusiamo per il disagio causato.

regrettable [rɪ'gretəbl] *adj* spiacevole.

regular ['regjʊləʳ] ◇ *adj* regolare; *(normal, in size)* normale; *(customer, reader)* abituale ◇ *n (customer)* cliente *mf* abituale.

regularly ['regjʊləlɪ] *adv* regolarmente.

regulate ['regjʊleɪt] *vt* regolare.

regulation [,regjʊ'leɪʃn] *n (rule)* norma *f*.

rehearsal [rɪ'hɜ:sl] *n* prova *f*.

rehearse [rɪ'hɜ:s] *vt* provare.

reign [reɪn] ◇ *n* regno *m* ◇ *vi* regnare.

reimburse [,ri:ɪm'bɜ:s] *vt (fml)* rimborsare.

reindeer ['reɪn,dɪəʳ] *(pl inv) n* renna *f*.

reinforce [,ri:ɪn'fɔ:s] *vt (wall, handle)* rinforzare; *(argument, opinion)* rafforzare.

reinforcements [,ri:ɪn'fɔ:smənts] *npl* rinforzi *mpl*.

reins [reɪnz] *npl* redini *fpl*.

reject [rɪ'dʒekt] *vt (proposal, request, coin)* respingere; *(applicant, plan)* scartare.

rejection [rɪ'dʒekʃn] *n* rifiuto *m*.

rejoin [,ri:'dʒɔɪn] *vt (motorway)* riprendere.

relapse [rɪ'læps] *n* ricaduta *f*.

relate [rɪ'leɪt] ◇ *vt (connect)* collegare ◇ *vi*: **to ~ to** *(be connected with)* essere collegato a; *(concern)* riguardare.

related [rɪ'leɪtɪd] *adj (of same family)* imparentato(-a); *(connected)* collegato(-a).

relation [rɪ'leɪʃn] *n (member of family)* parente *mf*; *(connection)* rapporto *m*; **in ~ to** in rapporto a.
♦ **relations** *npl* parenti *mpl*.

relationship [rɪ'leɪʃnʃɪp] *n* rapporto *m*, relazione *f*.

relative ['relətɪv] ◇ *adj* relativo(-a) ◇ *n* parente *mf*.

relatively ['relətɪvlɪ] *adv* relativamente.

relax [rɪ'læks] *vi (person)* rilassarsi.

relaxation [,ri:læk'seɪʃn] *n (of person)* relax *m*.

relaxed [rɪ'lækst] *adj* rilassato(-a).

relaxing [rɪ'læksɪŋ] *adj* rilassante.

relay ['ri:leɪ] *n (race)* staffetta *f*.

release [rɪ'li:s] ◇ *vt (set free)* liberare; *(let go of)* mollare; *(record, film)* far uscire; *(handbrake, catch)* togliere ◇ *n (record, film)* uscita *f*.

relegate ['relɪgeɪt] *vt*: **to be ~d** (SPORT) essere retrocesso.

relevant ['reləvənt] *adj (connected)* pertinente; *(important)* importante; *(appropriate)* appropriato(-a).

reliable [rɪ'laɪəbl] *adj (person, machine)* affidabile.

relic ['relɪk] *n (object)* reperto *m* (archeologico).

relief [rɪ'li:f] *n (gladness)* sollievo *m*; *(aid)* aiuto *m*.

relief road *n* strada *f* di smaltimento.

relieve [rɪ'li:v] *vt (pain, headache)* alleviare.
relieved [rɪ'li:vd] *adj* sollevato(-a).
religion [rɪ'lɪdʒn] *n* religione *f*.
religious [rɪ'lɪdʒəs] *adj* religioso(-a).
relish ['relɪʃ] *n (sauce)* salsa *f*.
reluctant [rɪ'lʌktənt] *adj* riluttante.
rely [rɪ'laɪ] **: rely on** *vt fus (trust)* contare su; *(depend on)* dipendere da.
remain [rɪ'meɪn] *vi* rimanere.
◆ **remains** *npl* resti *mpl*.
remainder [rɪ'meɪndə^r] *n* resto *m*.
remaining [rɪ'meɪnɪŋ] *adj* restante.
remark [rɪ'mɑ:k] ◇ *n* commento *m* ◇ *vt* commentare.
remarkable [rɪ'mɑ:kəbl] *adj* notevole.
remedy ['remədɪ] *n* rimedio *m*.
remember [rɪ'membə^r] ◇ *vt (recall)* ricordare; *(not forget)* ricordarsi (di) ◇ *vi (recall)* ricordarsi; **to ~ doing sthg** ricordarsi di aver fatto qc; **to ~ to do sthg** ricordarsi di fare qc.
remind [rɪ'maɪnd] *vt*: **to ~ sb of sthg** ricordare qc a qn; **to ~ sb to do sthg** ricordare a qn di fare qc.
reminder [rɪ'maɪndə^r] *n (for bill, library book)* sollecito *m*.
remittance [rɪ'mɪtns] *n* rimessa *f*.
remnant ['remnənt] *n* resto *m*.
remote [rɪ'məʊt] *adj* remoto(-a).
remote control *n* telecomando *m*.
removal [rɪ'mu:vl] *n (taking away)* rimozione *f*.
removal van *n* camion *m inv* dei traslochi.
remove [rɪ'mu:v] *vt* togliere; *(clothes)* togliersi.
renew [rɪ'nju:] *vt* rinnovare.
renovate ['renəveɪt] *vt* rinnovare.
renowned [rɪ'naʊnd] *adj* rinomato(-a).
rent [rent] ◇ *n* affitto *m* ◇ *vt (flat)* affittare; *(car, TV)* noleggiare.
rental ['rentl] *n (fee)* affitto *m*.
repaid [ri:'peɪd] *pt & pp* → **repay**.
repair [rɪ'peə^r] ◇ *vt* riparare ◇ *n*: **in good ~** in buone condizioni.
◆ **repairs** *npl* riparazioni *fpl*.
repair kit *n (for bicycle)* borsetta *f* degli attrezzi.
repay [ri:'peɪ] (*pt & pp* **repaid**) *vt* restituire.
repayment [ri:'peɪmənt] *n (of loan)* rimborso *m*.
repeat [rɪ'pi:t] ◇ *vt* ripetere; *(gossip, news)* riferire ◇ *n (on TV, radio)* replica *f*.
repetition [ˌrepɪ'tɪʃn] *n* ripetizione *f*.
repetitive [rɪ'petɪtɪv] *adj* ripetitivo(-a).
replace [rɪ'pleɪs] *vt* rimpiazzare; *(put back)* mettere a posto.
replacement [rɪ'pleɪsmənt] *n (substitute)* sostituto *m* (-a *f*).
replay ['ri:pleɪ] *n (rematch)* partita *f* ripetuta; *(on TV)* replay *m inv*.
reply [rɪ'plaɪ] ◇ *n* risposta *f* ◇ *vt & vi* rispondere.
report [rɪ'pɔ:t] ◇ *n (account)* relazione *f*; *(in newspaper, on TV, radio)* servizio *m*; (*Br:* SCH) = scheda *f* ◇ *vt (announce)* riportare; *(theft, disappearance, person)* denunciare ◇ *vi (give account)* riferire; *(for newspaper, TV, radio)* fare un servizio; **to ~ to sb** *(go to)* presentarsi a qn.
report card *n* = scheda *f (scolastica)*.
reporter [rɪ'pɔ:tə^r] *n* reporter *mf inv*.
represent [ˌreprɪ'zent] *vt* rappresentare.
representative [ˌreprɪ'zentətɪv] *n* rappresentante *mf*.
repress [rɪ'pres] *vt (feelings)* reprimere; *(people)* opprimere.

reprieve [rɪ'pri:v] *n (delay)* sospensione *f*.

reprimand ['reprɪmɑ:nd] *vt* rimproverare.

reproach [rɪ'prəʊtʃ] *vt* rimproverare.

reproduction [,ri:prə'dʌkʃn] *n* riproduzione *f*.

reptile ['reptaɪl] *n* rettile *m*.

republic [rɪ'pʌblɪk] *n* repubblica *f*.

Republican [rɪ'pʌblɪkən] ◇ *n* repubblicano *m* (-a *f*) ◇ *adj* repubblicano(-a).

repulsive [rɪ'pʌlsɪv] *adj* repellente.

reputable ['repjʊtəbl] *adj* di buona reputazione.

reputation [,repjʊ'teɪʃn] *n* reputazione *f*.

reputedly [rɪ'pju:tɪdlɪ] *adv* per quanto si dice.

request [rɪ'kwest] ◇ *n* richiesta *f* ◇ *vt* chiedere; **to ~ sb to do sthg** chiedere a qn di fare qc; **available on ~** (disponibile) su richiesta.

request stop *n (Br)* fermata *f* a richiesta.

require [rɪ'kwaɪə^r] *vt (subj: person)* avere bisogno di; *(subj: situation)* richiedere; **passengers are ~d to show their tickets** i passeggeri sono pregati di presentare i biglietti.

requirement [rɪ'kwaɪəmənt] *n (condition)* requisito *m*; *(need)* esigenza *f*.

resat [,ri:'sæt] *pt & pp* → **resit**.

rescue ['reskju:] *vt* salvare.

research [,rɪ'sɜ:tʃ] *n* ricerca *f*.

resemblance [rɪ'zembləns] *n* somiglianza *f*.

resemble [rɪ'zembl] *vt* somigliare a.

resent [rɪ'zent] *vt* risentirsi per.

reservation [,rezə'veɪʃn] *n (booking)* prenotazione *f*; *(doubt)* riserva *f*; **to make a ~** fare una prenotazione.

reserve [rɪ'zɜ:v] ◇ *n* riserva *f* ◇ *vt (book)* prenotare; *(save)* riservare.

reserved [rɪ'zɜ:vd] *adj* riservato(-a).

reservoir ['rezəvwɑ:^r] *n* bacino *m* (idrico).

reset [,ri:'set] (*pt & pp* **reset**) *vt (watch, device)* rimettere; *(meter)* azzerare.

reside [rɪ'zaɪd] *vi (fml)* risiedere.

residence ['rezɪdəns] *n (fml)* residenza *f*; **place of ~** *(fml)* luogo *m* di residenza.

residence permit *n* permesso *m* di soggiorno.

resident ['rezɪdənt] *n (of country)* residente *mf*; *(of hotel)* cliente *mf*; *(of area, house)* abitante *mf*; **'~s only'** *(for parking)* 'parcheggio riservato ai residenti'.

residential [,rezɪ'denʃl] *adj (area)* residenziale.

residue ['rezɪdju:] *n* residuo *m*.

resign [rɪ'zaɪn] ◇ *vi* dare le dimissioni ◇ *vt*: **to ~ o.s. to sthg** rassegnarsi a qc.

resignation [,rezɪg'neɪʃn] *n (from job)* dimissioni *fpl*.

resilient [rɪ'zɪlɪənt] *adj (person)* che ha buone capacità di ripresa.

resist [rɪ'zɪst] *vt (fight against)* opporre resistenza a; *(temptation)* resistere a; **I can't ~ chocolate** non so resistere al cioccolato; **to ~ doing sthg** trattenersi dal fare qc.

resistance [rɪ'zɪstəns] *n (refusal to accept)* opposizione *f*; *(fighting)* resistenza *f*.

resit [,ri:'sɪt] (*pt & pp* **resat**) *vt* ridare.

resolution [,rezə'lu:ʃn] *n (promise)* proposito *m*.

resolve [rɪ'zɒlv] *vt (solve)* risolvere.

resort [rɪ'zɔ:t] *n (for holidays)* luogo *m* di villeggiatura; **as a last ~** come ultima risorsa.

◆ **resort to** *vt fus* ricorrere a; **to ~ to doing sthg** ricorrere a fare qc.

resource [rɪ'sɔːs] *n* risorsa *f*.
resourceful [rɪ'sɔːsful] *adj* pieno (-a) di risorse.
respect [rɪ'spekt] ◇ *n* rispetto *m* ◇ *vt* rispettare; **in some ~s** sotto certi aspetti; **with ~ to** per quanto riguarda.
respectable [rɪ'spektəbl] *adj (person, job etc)* rispettabile; *(acceptable)* decente.
respective [rɪ'spektɪv] *adj* rispettivo(-a).
respond [rɪ'spɒnd] *vi* rispondere.
response [rɪ'spɒns] *n* risposta *f*.
responsibility [rɪˌspɒnsə'bɪlətɪ] *n* responsabilità *f inv*.
responsible [rɪ'spɒnsəbl] *adj* responsabile; **to be ~ (for)** *(accountable)* essere responsabile (di).
rest [rest] ◇ *n (relaxation)* riposo *m*; *(support)* sostegno *m* ◇ *vi (relax)* riposarsi; **the ~** *(remainder)* il resto; **to have a ~** riposarsi; **to ~ against** appoggiarsi contro.
restaurant ['restərɒnt] *n* ristorante *m*.
restaurant car *n (Br)* carrozza *f* ristorante.
restful ['restful] *adj* riposante.
restless ['restlɪs] *adj (bored, impatient)* insofferente; *(fidgety)* agitato(-a).
restore [rɪ'stɔːʳ] *vt (building, painting)* restaurare; *(order)* ripristinare.
restrain [rɪ'streɪn] *vt* controllare.
restrict [rɪ'strɪkt] *vt* limitare.
restricted [rɪ'strɪktɪd] *adj* limitato(-a).
restriction [rɪ'strɪkʃn] *n* restrizione *f*.
rest room *n (Am)* toilette *f inv*.
result [rɪ'zʌlt] ◇ *n* risultato *m* ◇ *vi*: **to ~ in** avere come conseguenza; **as a ~ of** in seguito a.
resume [rɪ'zjuːm] *vi* riprendere.
résumé ['rezjuːmeɪ] *n (summary)* riassunto *m*; *(Am: curriculum vitae)* curriculum vitae *m inv*.
retail ['riːteɪl] ◇ *n* vendita *f* al dettaglio ◇ *vt (sell)* vendere al dettaglio ◇ *vi*: **to ~ at** essere venduto a.
retailer ['riːteɪləʳ] *n* dettagliante *mf*.
retail price *n* prezzo *m* al dettaglio.
retain [rɪ'teɪn] *vt (fml)* conservare.
retaliate [rɪ'tælɪeɪt] *vi* fare rappresaglie.
retire [rɪ'taɪəʳ] *vi (stop working)* andare in pensione.
retired [rɪ'taɪəd] *adj* in pensione.
retirement [rɪ'taɪəmənt] *n (leaving job)* pensionamento *m*; *(period after retiring)* periodo *m* dopo il pensionamento.
retreat [rɪ'triːt] ◇ *vi (move away)* indietreggiare ◇ *n (place)* rifugio *m*.
retrieve [rɪ'triːv] *vt (get back)* recuperare.
return [rɪ'tɜːn] ◇ *n* ritorno *m*; *(Br: ticket)* biglietto *m* (di) andata e ritorno ◇ *vt (put back)* rimettere; *(give back)* restituire; *(ball, serve)* rimandare ◇ *vi* ritornare; *(happen again)* ricomparire ◇ *adj (journey)* di ritorno; **to ~ sthg (to sb)** *(give back)* restituire qc a qn; **by ~ of post** *(Br)* a giro di posta; **many happy ~s!** cento di questi giorni!; **in ~ (for)** in cambio (di).
return flight *n (journey back)* volo *m* di ritorno.
return ticket *n (Br)* biglietto *m* (di) andata e ritorno.
reunite [ˌriːjuː'naɪt] *vt* riunire.
reveal [rɪ'viːl] *vt* rivelare.
revelation [ˌrevə'leɪʃn] *n* rivelazione *f*.
revenge [rɪ'vendʒ] *n* vendetta *f*.
reverse [rɪ'vɜːs] ◇ *adj* inverso(-a) ◇ *n* (AUT) retromarcia *f*; *(of coin)* rovescio *m*; *(of document)* retro *m* ◇ *vt (decision)* ribaltare ◇ *vi (car, driver)* fare marcia indietro; **in ~ order**

in ordine inverso; **the ~** *(opposite)* l'inverso; **to ~ the car** fare marcia indietro; **to ~ the charges** *(Br)* fare una telefonata a carico del destinatario.

reverse-charge call *n (Br)* telefonata *f* a carico del destinatario.

review [rɪ'vjuː] ◇ *n (of book, record, film)* recensione *f*; *(examination)* esame *m* ◇ *vt (Am: for exam)* ripassare.

revise [rɪ'vaɪz] ◇ *vt* rivedere ◇ *vi (Br: for exam)* ripassare.

revision [rɪ'vɪʒn] *n (Br: for exam)* ripasso *m*.

revive [rɪ'vaɪv] *vt (person)* rianimare; *(economy)* far riprendere; *(custom)* riportare in uso.

revolt [rɪ'vəʊlt] *n* rivolta *f*.

revolting [rɪ'vəʊltɪŋ] *adj* disgustoso(-a).

revolution [ˌrevə'luːʃn] *n* rivoluzione *f*.

revolutionary [revə'luːʃnərɪ] *adj* rivoluzionario(-a).

revolver [rɪ'vɒlvəʳ] *n* revolver *m inv*.

revolving door [rɪ'vɒlvɪŋ-] *n* porta *f* girevole.

revue [rɪ'vjuː] *n* rivista *f (spettacolo)*.

reward [rɪ'wɔːd] ◇ *n* ricompensa *f* ◇ *vt* ricompensare.

rewind [ˌriː'waɪnd] (*pt & pp* **rewound** [ˌriː'waʊnd]) *vt* riavvolgere.

rheumatism ['ruːmətɪzm] *n* reumatismo *m*.

rhinoceros [raɪ'nɒsərəs] (*pl inv* OR **-es**) *n* rinoceronte *m*.

rhubarb ['ruːbɑːb] *n* rabarbaro *m*.

rhyme [raɪm] ◇ *n (poem)* rima *f* ◇ *vi* fare rima.

rhythm ['rɪðm] *n* ritmo *m*.

rib [rɪb] *n (of body)* costola *f*.

ribbon ['rɪbən] *n* nastro *m*.

rice [raɪs] *n* riso *m*.

rice pudding *n* budino *m* di riso *(dolce)*.

rich [rɪtʃ] ◇ *adj* ricco(-a) ◇ *npl*: **the ~** i ricchi; **to be ~ in sthg** essere ricco di qc.

ricotta cheese [rɪ'kɒtə-] *n* ricotta *f*.

rid [rɪd] *vt*: **to get ~ of** sbarazzarsi di.

ridden ['rɪdn] *pp* → **ride**.

riddle ['rɪdl] *n* indovinello *m*.

ride [raɪd] (*pt* **rode**, *pp* **ridden**) ◇ *n (on horse)* cavalcata *f*; *(in vehicle, on bike)* giro *m* ◇ *vi (on horse)* andare a cavallo; *(on bike)* andare in bicicletta; *(in vehicle)* viaggiare ◇ *vt*: **to ~ a horse** andare a cavallo; **to go for a ~** *(in car)* andare a fare un giro.

rider ['raɪdəʳ] *n (on horse)* persona *f* a cavallo; *(on bike)* ciclista *mf*.

ridge [rɪdʒ] *n (of mountain)* cresta *f*; *(raised surface)* increspatura *f*.

ridiculous [rɪ'dɪkjʊləs] *adj* ridicolo(-a).

riding ['raɪdɪŋ] *n* equitazione *f*.

riding school *n* scuola *f* d'equitazione.

rifle ['raɪfl] *n* fucile *m*.

rig [rɪg] ◇ *n (oilrig at sea)* piattaforma *f*; *(on land)* pozzo *m* petrolifero ◇ *vt (fix)* manipolare.

right [raɪt] ◇ *adj* **1.** *(correct)* giusto(-a), corretto(-a); **to be ~** *(person)* avere ragione; **to be ~ to do sthg** fare bene a fare qc; **have you got the ~ time?** ha l'ora esatta?; **that's ~!** esatto!; **is this the ~ way?** è la strada giusta?

2. *(fair)* giusto(-a); **that's not ~!** non è giusto!

3. *(on the right)* destro(-a); **the ~ side of the road** il lato destro della strada.

◇ *n* **1.** *(side)*: **the ~** la destra.

2. *(entitlement)* diritto *m*; **to have the ~ to do sthg** avere il diritto di fare qc.

◇ *adv* **1.** *(towards the right)* a destra;

turn ~ at the post office all'ufficio postale giri a destra.

2\. *(correctly)* bene, correttamente; **am I pronouncing it ~?** lo pronuncio bene?

3\. *(for emphasis)* proprio; **~ here** proprio qui; **I'll be ~ back** torno subito; **~ away** subito.

right angle *n* angolo *m* retto.

right-hand *adj* di destra.

right-hand drive *n* guida *f* a destra.

right-handed [-'hændɪd] *adj (person)* destrimano(-a); *(implement)* per destrimani.

rightly ['raɪtlɪ] *adv (correctly)* correttamente; *(justly)* giustamente.

right of way *n* (AUT) diritto *m* di precedenza; *(path)* sentiero *m*.

right-wing *adj* di destra.

rigid ['rɪdʒɪd] *adj* rigido(-a).

rim [rɪm] *n (of cup)* bordo *m*; *(of glasses)* montatura *f*; *(of wheel)* cerchione *m*.

rind [raɪnd] *n (of fruit)* buccia *f*; *(of bacon)* cotenna *f*; *(of cheese)* crosta *f*.

ring [rɪŋ] (*pt* **rang**, *pp* **rung**) ◇ *n* anello *m*; *(of people)* cerchio *m*; *(sound)* trillo *m*; *(on cooker)* fornello *m*; *(for boxing)* ring *m inv*; *(in circus)* pista *f* ◇ *vt (Br: on phone)* telefonare a; *(bell)* suonare ◇ *vi (bell, telephone)* suonare; *(Br: make phone call)* telefonare; **to give sb a ~** fare una telefonata a qn; **to ~ the bell** suonare il campanello.

◆ **ring back** ◇ *vt sep (Br)* ritelefonare a ◇ *vi (Br)* ritelefonare.

◆ **ring off** *vi (Br)* mettere giù (il telefono).

◆ **ring up** ◇ *vt sep (Br)* telefonare a ◇ *vi (Br)* telefonare.

ringing tone ['rɪŋɪŋ-] *n* segnale *m* di libero.

ring road *n* circonvallazione *f*.

rink [rɪŋk] *n* pista *f* di pattinaggio.

rinse [rɪns] *vt* sciacquare.

◆ **rinse out** *vt sep* sciacquare.

riot ['raɪət] *n* sommossa *f*.

rip [rɪp] ◇ *n* strappo *m* ◇ *vt* strappare ◇ *vi* strapparsi.

◆ **rip up** *vt sep* strappare.

ripe [raɪp] *adj (fruit, vegetable)* maturo(-a); *(cheese)* stagionato(-a).

ripen ['raɪpn] *vi* maturare.

rip-off *n (inf)* fregatura *f*.

rise [raɪz] (*pt* **rose**, *pp* **risen** ['rɪzn]) ◇ *vi* alzarsi; *(sun, moon)* sorgere; *(increase)* aumentare ◇ *n* aumento *m*; *(slope)* salita *f*.

risk [rɪsk] ◇ *n* rischio *m* ◇ *vt* rischiare; **to take a ~** correre un rischio; **at your own ~** a suo rischio (e pericolo); **to ~ doing sthg** rischiare di fare qc; **to ~ it** arrischiarsi.

risky ['rɪskɪ] *adj* rischioso(-a).

risotto [rɪ'zɒtəʊ] (*pl* **-s**) *n* risotto *m*.

ritual ['rɪtʃʊəl] *n* rituale *m*.

rival ['raɪvl] ◇ *adj* rivale ◇ *n* rivale *mf*.

river ['rɪvə^r] *n* fiume *m*.

river bank *n* sponda *f* del fiume.

riverside ['rɪvəsaɪd] *n* riva *f* del fiume.

Riviera [ˌrɪvɪ'eərə] *n*: **the (Italian) ~** la riviera (ligure).

roach [rəʊtʃ] *n (Am: cockroach)* scarafaggio *m*.

road [rəʊd] *n* strada *f*; **by ~** in macchina.

road book *n* atlante *m* stradale.

road map *n* carta *f* stradale.

road safety *n* sicurezza *f* sulle strade.

roadside ['rəʊdsaɪd] *n*: **the ~** il bordo della strada.

road sign *n* segnale *m* stradale.

road tax *n* tassa *f* di circolazione.

roadway ['rəʊdweɪ] *n* carreggiata *f*.

road works *npl* lavori *mpl* stradali.

roam [rəʊm] *vi* vagabondare.
roar [rɔːʳ] ◇ *n (of crowd)* strepito *m*; *(of plane)* rombo *m* ◇ *vi (lion)* ruggire; *(crowd)* strepitare; *(traffic)* rombare.
roast [rəʊst] ◇ *n* arrosto *m* ◇ *vt* arrostire ◇ *adj* arrosto *(inv)*; ~ **beef** roast beef *m*; ~ **chicken** pollo *m* arrosto; ~ **lamb** arrosto di agnello; ~ **pork** arrosto di maiale; ~ **potatoes** patate *fpl* arrosto.
rob [rɒb] *vt (house, bank)* svaligiare; *(person)* derubare; **to ~ sb of sthg** derubare qn di qc.
robber ['rɒbəʳ] *n* rapinatore *m* (-trice *f*).
robbery ['rɒbərɪ] *n* rapina *f*.
robe [rəʊb] *n (Am: bathrobe)* accappatoio *m*.
robin ['rɒbɪn] *n* pettirosso *m*.
robot ['rəʊbɒt] *n* robot *m inv*.
rock [rɒk] ◇ *n* roccia *f*; *(Am: stone)* pietra *f*; *(music)* rock *m*; *(Br: sweet)* bastoncini *mpl* di zucchero ◇ *vt (baby)* cullare; *(boat)* far rollare; **on the ~s** *(drink)* con ghiaccio.
rock climbing *n* roccia *f (sport)*; **to go ~** fare scalate.
rocket ['rɒkɪt] *n (missile)* missile *m*; *(space rocket, firework)* razzo *m*.
rocking chair ['rɒkɪŋ-] *n* sedia *f* a dondolo.
rock 'n' roll [ˌrɒkən'rəʊl] *n* rock and roll *m*.
rocky ['rɒkɪ] *adj* roccioso(-a).
rod [rɒd] *n (pole)* asta *f*; *(for fishing)* canna *f* (da pesca).
rode [rəʊd] *pt* → **ride**.
roe [rəʊ] *n* uova *fpl* di pesce.
role [rəʊl] *n* ruolo *m*.
roll [rəʊl] ◇ *n (of bread)* panino *m*; *(of film)* rullino *m*; *(of paper)* rotolo *m* ◇ *vi (ball, rock)* rotolare; *(ship)* rollare ◇ *vt (ball, rock)* far rotolare; *(cigarette)* arrotolare; *(dice)* tirare.
◆ **roll over** *vi (person, animal)* rivoltarsi; *(car)* ribaltarsi.
◆ **roll up** *vt sep* arrotolare.
roller coaster ['rəʊləˌkəʊstəʳ] *n* otto *m* volante.
roller skate ['rəʊlə-] *n* pattino *m* a rotelle.
roller-skating ['rəʊlə-] *n* pattinaggio *m* a rotelle.
rolling pin ['rəʊlɪŋ-] *n* matterello *m*.
Roman ['rəʊmən] ◇ *adj* romano(-a) ◇ *n* romano *m* (-a *f*).
Roman Catholic *n* cattolico *m* romano (cattolica romana *f*).
romance [rəʊ'mæns] *n (love)* amore *m*; *(love affair)* avventura *f*; *(novel)* romanzo *m* sentimentale.
Romania [ruː'meɪnjə] *n* la Romania.
romantic [rəʊ'mæntɪk] *adj* romantico(-a).
Rome [rəʊm] *n* Roma *f*.
romper suit ['rɒmpə-] *n* pagliaccetto *m*.
roof [ruːf] *n* tetto *m*; *(of cave)* volta *f*.
roof rack *n* portapacchi *m inv*.
room [ruːm, rʊm] *n* stanza *f*, camera *f*; *(space)* spazio *m*.
room number *n* numero *m* di stanza.
room service *n* servizio *m* in camera.
room temperature *n* temperatura *f* ambiente.
roomy ['ruːmɪ] *adj* spazioso(-a).
root [ruːt] *n* radice *f*.
rope [rəʊp] ◇ *n* corda *f* ◇ *vt* legare.
rose [rəʊz] ◇ *pt* → **rise** ◇ *n (flower)* rosa *f*.
rosé ['rəʊzeɪ] *n* vino *m* rosé.
rosemary ['rəʊzmərɪ] *n* rosmarino *m*.
rot [rɒt] *vi* marcire.
rota ['rəʊtə] *n* turni *mpl*.
rotate [rəʊ'teɪt] *vi* ruotare.
rotten ['rɒtn] *adj (food, wood)* marcio(-a); *(inf: not good)* schifoso(-a); **I**

feel ~ *(ill)* mi sento uno schifo.

rouge [ruːʒ] *n* fard *m inv*.

rough [rʌf] ◇ *adj (surface, skin, cloth)* ruvido(-a); *(sea)* burrascoso(-a); *(person)* rude; *(approximate)* approssimativo(-a); *(conditions)* disagiato(-a); *(area, town)* brutto(-a); *(wine)* scadente ◇ *n (on golf course)* rough *m*; **to have a ~ time** passarsela male.

roughly [ˈrʌflɪ] *adv (approximately)* approssimativamente; *(push, handle)* sgarbatamente.

roulade [ruːˈlɑːd] *n* rotolo *m*.

roulette [ruːˈlet] *n* roulette *f*.

round [raʊnd] ◇ *adj* rotondo(-a); *(cheeks)* paffuto(-a).

◇ *n* 1. *(of drinks)* giro *m*; **it's my ~** tocca a me offrire (questo giro).

2. *(of sandwiches)* tramezzini *mpl*.

3. *(of toast)* fetta *f*.

4. *(of competition)* turno *m*.

5. *(in golf)* partita *f*; *(in boxing)* round *m inv*, ripresa *f*.

6. *(of policeman, postman, milkman)* giro *m*.

◇ *adv* 1. *(in a circle)*: **to go ~** girare; **to spin ~** ruotare.

2. *(surrounding)*: **all (the way) ~** tutt'intorno.

3. *(near)*: **~ about** nei dintorni.

4. *(to one's house)*: **to ask some friends ~** invitare (a casa propria) degli amici; **we went ~ to her place** siamo andati da lei OR a casa sua.

5. *(continuously)*: **all year ~** tutto l'anno.

◇ *prep* 1. *(surrounding, circling)* intorno a; **to go ~ the corner** girare l'angolo; **we walked ~ the lake** abbiamo fatto il giro del lago a piedi.

2. *(visiting)*: **to go ~ a museum** visitare un museo; **to show sb ~ sthg** far fare il giro di qc a qn.

3. *(approximately)* circa, pressappoco; **~ (about) 100** circa 100; **~ ten o'clock** verso le dieci.

4. *(near)*: **~ here** da queste parti.

5. *(in phrases)*: **it's just ~ the corner** *(nearby)* è qui vicino; **~ the clock** 24 ore su 24.

◆ **round off** *vt sep (meal, day)* terminare.

roundabout [ˈraʊndəbaʊt] *n (Br) (in road)* isola *f* rotazionale; *(in playground, at fairground)* giostra *f*.

rounders [ˈraʊndəz] *n (Br) gioco a squadre simile al baseball*.

round trip *n* viaggio *m* di andata e ritorno.

route [ruːt] ◇ *n (way)* strada *f*; *(of bus, train)* percorso *m*; *(of plane)* rotta *f* ◇ *vt (change course of)* dirottare.

routine [ruːˈtiːn] ◇ *n* routine *f inv* ◇ *adj* di routine.

row¹ [rəʊ] ◇ *n (line)* fila *f* ◇ *vt & vi* remare; **in a ~** *(in succession)* di fila.

row² [raʊ] *n (argument)* lite *f*; *(inf: noise)* baccano *m*; **to have a ~** litigare.

rowboat [ˈrəʊbəʊt] *(Am)* = **rowing boat**.

rowdy [ˈraʊdɪ] *adj* turbolento(-a).

rowing [ˈrəʊɪŋ] *n* canottaggio *m*.

rowing boat *n (Br)* barca *f* a remi.

royal [ˈrɔɪəl] *adj* reale.

royal family *n* famiglia *f* reale.

royalty [ˈrɔɪəltɪ] *n (royal family)* reali *mpl*.

RRP *(abbr of recommended retail price)* prezzo *m* consigliato.

rub [rʌb] *vt & vi* strofinare; **to ~ sb's back** massaggiare la schiena a qn; **my shoes are rubbing** mi fanno male le scarpe.

◆ **rub in** *vt sep (lotion, oil)* far penetrare sfregando.

◆ **rub out** *vt sep* cancellare.

rubber [ˈrʌbəʳ] ◇ *adj* di gomma ◇ *n* gomma *f*; *(Am: inf: condom)* preservativo *m*.

rubber band *n* elastico *m*.
rubber gloves *npl* guanti *mpl* di gomma.
rubber ring *n* ciambella *f*.
rubbish ['rʌbɪʃ] *n* spazzatura *f*; *(inf: nonsense)* cretinate *fpl*.
rubbish bin *n (Br)* pattumiera *f*.
rubbish dump *n (Br)* discarica *f*.
rubble ['rʌbl] *n* macerie *fpl*.
ruby ['ru:bɪ] *n* rubino *m*.
rucksack ['rʌksæk] *n* zaino *m*.
rudder ['rʌdəʳ] *n* timone *m*.
rude [ru:d] *adj (person)* sgarbato(-a); *(behaviour, joke, picture)* volgare.
rug [rʌg] *n (for floor)* tappeto *m*; *(Br: blanket)* coperta *f*.
rugby ['rʌgbɪ] *n* rugby *m*.
ruin ['ru:ɪn] *vt* rovinare.
◆ **ruins** *npl* rovine *fpl*.
ruined ['ru:ɪnd] *adj (building)* in rovina; *(clothes, meal, holiday)* rovinato(-a).
rule [ru:l] ◇ *n (law)* regola *f* ◇ *vt (country)* governare; **to be the ~** *(normal)* essere la regola; **against the ~s** contro le regole; **as a ~** di regola.
◆ **rule out** *vt sep* escludere.
ruler ['ru:ləʳ] *n (of country)* capo *m* di Stato; *(for measuring)* righello *m*.
rum [rʌm] *n* rum *m inv*.
rumor ['ru:mər] *(Am)* = **rumour**.
rumour ['ru:məʳ] *n (Br)* voce *f*.
rump steak [,rʌmp-] *n* bistecca *f* di girello.
run [rʌn] (*pt* **ran**, *pp* **run**) ◇ *vi* **1.** *(on foot)* correre; **we had to ~ for the bus** abbiamo dovuto fare una corsa per prendere l'autobus.
2. *(train, bus)* fare servizio; **the bus ~s every hour** c'è un autobus ogni ora; **the train is running an hour late** il treno ha un'ora di ritardo.
3. *(operate)* funzionare; **to ~ on sthg** andare a qc.
4. *(tears, liquid, river)* scorrere; **to ~ through** *(river, road)* passare per; **the path ~s along the coast** il sentiero corre lungo la costa; **she left the tap running** ha lasciato il rubinetto aperto.
5. *(play, event)* durare; **'now running at the Palladium'** 'in cartellone al Palladium'.
6. *(nose)* gocciolare, colare; *(eyes)* lacrimare.
7. *(colour, dye, clothes)* stingere.
◇ *vt* **1.** *(on foot)* correre.
2. *(compete in)*: **to ~ a race** partecipare a una corsa.
3. *(business, hotel)* dirigere.
4. *(bus, train)*: **we're running a special bus to the airport** mettiamo a disposizione una navetta per andare all'aeroporto.
5. *(take in car)* dare un passaggio a; **I'll ~ you home** ti do un passaggio (fino) a casa.
6. *(water)* far correre.
◇ *n* **1.** *(on foot)* corsa *f*; **to go for a ~** andare a fare una corsa.
2. *(in car)* giro *m*; **to go for a ~** andare a fare un giro (in macchina).
3. *(for skiing)* pista *f*.
4. *(Am: in tights)* smagliatura *f*.
5. *(in phrases)*: **in the long ~** alla lunga.
◆ **run away** *vi* scappare.
◆ **run down** ◇ *vt sep (run over)* investire; *(criticize)* criticare ◇ *vi (battery)* scaricarsi.
◆ **run into** *vt fus (meet)* incontrare per caso; *(hit)* sbattere contro; *(problem, difficulty)* incontrare.
◆ **run out** *vi (be used up)* esaurirsi.
◆ **run out of** *vt fus* finire, esaurire.
◆ **run over** *vt sep (hit)* investire.
runaway ['rʌnəweɪ] *n* fuggiasco *m* (-a *f*).
rung [rʌŋ] ◇ *pp* → **ring** ◇ *n (of ladder)* piolo *m*.
runner ['rʌnəʳ] *n (person)* corrido-

re *m*; *(for door, drawer)* guida *f*; *(for sledge)* pattino *m*.

runner bean *n* fagiolo *m* rampicante.

runner-up (*pl* **runners-up**) *n* secondo *m* classificato (seconda classificata *f*).

running ['rʌnɪŋ] ◇ *n* (SPORT) corsa *f*; *(management)* amministrazione *f* ◇ *adj*: **three days ~** tre giorni di fila; **to go ~** andare a correre.

running water *n* acqua *f* corrente.

runny ['rʌnɪ] *adj (sauce, egg, omelette)* troppo liquido(-a); *(nose)* che cola; *(eye)* che lacrima.

runway ['rʌnweɪ] *n* pista *f* (di volo).

rural ['rʊərəl] *adj* rurale.

rush [rʌʃ] ◇ *n (hurry)* fretta *f*; *(of crowd)* grosso afflusso *m* ◇ *vi (move quickly)* precipitarsi; *(hurry)* affrettarsi ◇ *vt (work)* fare in fretta; *(food)* mangiare in fretta; *(transport quickly)* portare d'urgenza; **to be in a ~** avere fretta; **there's no ~!** non c'è fretta!; **don't ~ me!** non mettermi fretta!

rush hour *n* ora *f* di punta.

Russia ['rʌʃə] *n* la Russia.

Russian ['rʌʃn] ◇ *adj* russo(-a) ◇ *n (person)* russo *m* (-a *f*); *(language)* russo *m*.

rust [rʌst] ◇ *n* ruggine *f* ◇ *vi* arrugginirsi.

rustic ['rʌstɪk] *adj* rustico(-a).

rustle ['rʌsl] *vi* frusciare.

rustproof ['rʌstpru:f] *adj* inossidabile.

rusty ['rʌstɪ] *adj* arrugginito (-a).

RV *n (Am: abbr of recreational vehicle)* camper *m inv*.

rye [raɪ] *n* segale *f*.

rye bread *n* pane *m* di segale.

S

S *(abbr of south, small)* S.
saccharin ['sækərɪn] *n* saccarina *f*.
sachet ['sæʃeɪ] *n* bustina *f*.
sack [sæk] ◇ *n (bag)* sacco *m* ◇ *vt* licenziare; **to get the ~** essere licenziato.
sacrifice ['sækrɪfaɪs] *n (fig)* sacrificio *m*.
sad [sæd] *adj* triste.
saddle ['sædl] *n* sella *f*.
saddlebag ['sædlbæg] *n* bisaccia *f*.
sadly ['sædlɪ] *adv (unfortunately)* sfortunatamente; *(unhappily)* tristemente.
sadness ['sædnɪs] *n* tristezza *f*.
s.a.e. *n (Br: abbr of stamped addressed envelope) busta affrancata e completa d'indirizzo.*
safari park [sə'fɑːrɪ-] *n* zoosafari *m inv*.
safe [seɪf] ◇ *adj* sicuro(-a); *(out of harm)* salvo(-a); *(valuables)* al sicuro ◇ *n* cassaforte *f*; **a ~ place** un posto sicuro; **(have a) ~ journey!** buon viaggio!; **~ and sound** sano (-a) e salvo(-a).
safe-deposit box *n* cassetta *f* di sicurezza.
safely ['seɪflɪ] *adv (not dangerously)* senza pericolo; *(arrive)* senza problemi; *(out of harm)* al sicuro.
safety ['seɪftɪ] *n* sicurezza *f*.
safety belt *n* cintura *f* di sicurezza.
safety pin *n* spilla *f* da balia.
sag [sæg] *vi* avvallarsi.
sage [seɪdʒ] *n (herb)* salvia *f*.
Sagittarius [ˌsædʒɪ'teərɪəs] *n* Sagittario *m*.
said [sed] *pt & pp* → **say**.
sail [seɪl] ◇ *n* vela *f* ◇ *vi (boat, ship)* navigare; *(person)* andare in barca; *(depart)* salpare ◇ *vt*: **to ~ a boat** condurre una barca; **to set ~** salpare.
sailboat ['seɪlbəʊt] *(Am)* = **sailing boat**.
sailing ['seɪlɪŋ] *n (activity)* vela *f*; *(departure)* partenza *f*; **to go ~** fare della vela.
sailing boat *n* barca *f* a vela.
sailor ['seɪlə[r]] *n* marinaio *m*.
saint [seɪnt] *n* santo *m* (-a *f*).
sake [seɪk] *n*: **for my/their ~** per il mio/il loro bene; **for God's ~!** per l'amor di Dio!
salad ['sæləd] *n* insalata *f*.
salad bar *n (Br: area in restaurant)* tavolo *m* delle insalate; *(restaurant) locale specializzato in insalate.*
salad bowl *n* insalatiera *f*.
salad cream *n (Br) salsa per l'insalata, simile alla maionese.*
salad dressing *n* condimento *m* per l'insalata.
salami [sə'lɑːmɪ] *n* salame *m*.
salary ['sælərɪ] *n* stipendio *m*.
sale [seɪl] *n (selling)* vendita *f*; *(at*

reduced prices) svendita *f*; **'for ~'** 'vendesi'; **on ~** in vendita.
♦ **sales** *npl* (COMM) vendite *fpl*; **the ~s** *(at reduced prices)* i saldi.
sales assistant ['seɪlz-] *n* commesso *m* (-a *f*).
salesclerk ['seɪlzklɜːrk] *(Am)* = **sales assistant**.
salesman ['seɪlzmən] (*pl* **-men** [-mən]) *n (in shop)* commesso *m*; *(rep)* rappresentante *m*.
sales rep(resentative) *n* rappresentante *mf*.
saleswoman ['seɪlz,wʊmən] (*pl* **-women** [-,wɪmɪn]) *n (in shop)* commessa *f*.
saliva [sə'laɪvə] *n* saliva *f*.
salmon ['sæmən] *(pl inv) n* salmone *m*.
salon ['sælɒn] *n (hairdresser's)* salone *m*.
saloon [sə'luːn] *n (Br: car)* berlina *f*; *(Am: bar)* saloon *m inv*; **~ (bar)** *(Br)* sala *f* interna.
salopettes [,sælə'pets] *npl* salopette *f inv*.
salt [sɔːlt, sɒlt] *n* sale *m*.
saltcellar ['sɔːlt,seləʳ] *n (Br)* saliera *f*.
salted peanuts ['sɔːltɪd-] *npl* noccioline *fpl* salate.
salt shaker [-,ʃeɪkəʳ] *(Am)* = **saltcellar**.
salty ['sɔːltɪ] *adj* salato(-a).
salute [sə'luːt] ◇ *n* saluto *m* ◇ *vi* fare il saluto.
same [seɪm] ◇ *adj* stesso(-a) ◇ *pron*: **the ~** lo stesso (la stessa); **they look the ~** sembrano uguali; **I'll have the ~ as her** prendo lo stesso che ha preso lei; **you've got the ~ book as me** hai lo stesso libro che ho io; **it's all the ~ to me** per me è tutto uguale.
samosa [sə'məʊsə] *n fagottino fritto triangolare, ripieno di carne o verdure, tipico della cucina indiana.*
sample ['sɑːmpl] ◇ *n* campione *m* ◇ *vt* assaggiare.
sanctions ['sæŋkʃnz] *npl* sanzioni *fpl*.
sanctuary ['sæŋktʃʊərɪ] *n (for birds, animals)* riserva *f*.
sand [sænd] ◇ *n* sabbia *f* ◇ *vt (wood)* smerigliare.
♦ **sands** *npl* spiaggia *f*.
sandal ['sændl] *n* sandalo *m*.
sandcastle ['sænd,kɑːsl] *n* castello *m* di sabbia.
sandpaper ['sænd,peɪpəʳ] *n* carta *f* vetrata.
sandwich ['sænwɪdʒ] *n* tramezzino *m*.
sandwich bar *n* paninoteca *f*.
sandy ['sændɪ] *adj (beach)* sabbioso(-a); *(hair)* color sabbia *(inv)*.
sang [sæŋ] *pt* → **sing**.
sanitary ['sænɪtrɪ] *adj (conditions, measures)* sanitario(-a); *(hygienic)* igienico(-a).
sanitary napkin *(Am)* = **sanitary towel**.
sanitary towel *n (Br)* assorbente *m* igienico.
sank [sæŋk] *pt* → **sink**.
sapphire ['sæfaɪəʳ] *n* zaffiro *m*.
sarcastic [sɑː'kæstɪk] *adj* sarcastico(-a).
sardine [sɑː'diːn] *n* sardina *f*.
Sardinia [sɑː'dɪnjə] *n* la Sardegna.
SASE *n (Am: abbr of self-addressed stamped envelope) busta affrancata e completa del proprio indirizzo.*
sat [sæt] *pt & pp* → **sit**.
Sat. *(abbr of Saturday)* sab.
satchel ['sætʃəl] *n* cartella *f*.
satellite ['sætəlaɪt] *n (in space)* satellite *m*; *(at airport)* zona *f* satellite.
satellite dish *n* antenna *f* parabolica.
satellite TV *n* televisione *f* via satellite.
satin ['sætɪn] *n* raso *m*.
satisfaction [,sætɪs'fækʃn] *n*

soddisfazione *f*.
satisfactory [ˌsætɪsˈfæktərɪ] *adj* soddisfacente.
satisfied [ˈsætɪsfaɪd] *adj* soddisfatto(-a).
satisfy [ˈsætɪsfaɪ] *vt* soddisfare.
satsuma [ˌsætˈsuːmə] *n (Br)* mandarino *m*.
saturate [ˈsætʃəreɪt] *vt (with liquid)* impregnare.
Saturday [ˈsætədɪ] *n* sabato *m*; **it's** ~ è sabato; ~ **morning** sabato mattina; **on** ~ sabato; **on ~s** il OR di sabato; **last** ~ sabato scorso; **this** ~ questo sabato; **next** ~ sabato prossimo; ~ **week, a week on** ~ sabato a otto.
sauce [sɔːs] *n* salsa *f*.
saucepan [ˈsɔːspən] *n* casseruola *f*.
saucer [ˈsɔːsəʳ] *n* piattino *m*.
Saudi Arabia [ˌsaʊdɪəˈreɪbjə] *n* l'Arabia *f* Saudita.
sauna [ˈsɔːnə] *n* sauna *f*.
sausage [ˈsɒsɪdʒ] *n* salsiccia *f*.
sausage roll *n* rustico *m* con salsiccia.
sauté [*Br* ˈsəʊteɪ, *Am* səʊˈteɪ] *adj* saltato(-a).
savage [ˈsævɪdʒ] *adj* selvaggio(-a).
save [seɪv] ◇ *vt (rescue,* COMPUT*)* salvare; *(money, time)* risparmiare; *(reserve)* tenere; (SPORT) parare ◇ *n* parata *f*.
◆ **save up** *vi* risparmiare; **to** ~ **up (for sthg)** mettere da parte i soldi (per qc).
saver [ˈseɪvəʳ] *n (Br: ticket)* biglietto *m* ridotto.
savings [ˈseɪvɪŋz] *npl* risparmi *mpl*.
savings and loan association *n (Am)* = istituto *m* di credito fondiario.
savings bank *n* cassa *f* di risparmio.
savory [ˈseɪvərɪ] *(Am)* = **savoury**.
savoury [ˈseɪvərɪ] *adj (Br: not sweet)* salato(-a).
saw [sɔː] (*Br pt* **-ed**, *pp* **sawn**, *Am pt & pp* **-ed**) ◇ *pt* → **see** ◇ *n (tool)* sega *f* ◇ *vt* segare.
sawdust [ˈsɔːdʌst] *n* segatura *f*.
sawn [sɔːn] *pp* → **saw**.
saxophone [ˈsæksəfəʊn] *n* sassofono *m*.
say [seɪ] (*pt & pp* **said**) ◇ *vt* dire; *(subj: clock, meter)* segnare ◇ *n*: **to have a** ~ **in sthg** avere voce in capitolo riguardo a qc; **could you** ~ **that again?** può ripetere, per favore?; ~ **we met at nine?** diciamo che ci vediamo alle nove?; **what did you** ~? che cosa hai detto?
saying [ˈseɪɪŋ] *n* detto *m*.
scab [skæb] *n (on skin)* crosta *f*.
scaffolding [ˈskæfəldɪŋ] *n* impalcatura *f*.
scald [skɔːld] *vt* scottare.
scale [skeɪl] *n* scala *f*; *(of fish, snake)* squama *f*; *(in kettle)* incrostazione *f*.
◆ **scales** *npl (for weighing)* bilancia *f*.
scallion [ˈskæljən] *n (Am)* cipollina *f*.
scallop [ˈskɒləp] *n* pettine *m (mollusco)*.
scalp [skælp] *n* cuoio *m* capelluto.
scampi [ˈskæmpɪ] *n* gamberoni *mpl* impanati e fritti.
scan [skæn] ◇ *vt (consult quickly)* scorrere ◇ *n* (MED) esame *m* eseguito con scanner.
scandal [ˈskændl] *n* scandalo *m*.
Scandinavia [ˌskændɪˈneɪvjə] *n* la Scandinavia.
scar [skɑːʳ] *n* cicatrice *f*.
scarce [ˈskeəs] *adj* scarso(-a).
scarcely [ˈskeəslɪ] *adv (hardly)* a malapena.
scare [skeəʳ] *vt* spaventare.
scarecrow [ˈskeəkrəʊ] *n* spaventapasseri *m inv*.

scared ['skeəd] *adj* spaventato(-a).
scarf ['skɑːf] (*pl* **scarves**) *n (woollen)* sciarpa *f*; *(for women)* foulard *m inv*.
scarlet ['skɑːlət] *adj* scarlatto(-a).
scarves [skɑːvz] *pl* → **scarf**.
scary ['skeərɪ] *adj (inf)* terrificante.
scatter ['skætəʳ] ◇ *vt* spargere ◇ *vi* sparpagliarsi.
scene [siːn] *n* scena *f*; *(view)* vista *f*; **the music ~** il mondo della musica; **to make a ~** fare una scenata.
scenery ['siːnərɪ] *n (countryside)* paesaggio *m*; *(in theatre)* scenario *m*.
scenic ['siːnɪk] *adj* pittoresco(-a).
scent [sent] *n* odore *m*; *(perfume)* profumo *m*.
sceptical ['skeptɪkl] *adj (Br)* scettico(-a).
schedule [*Br* 'ʃedjuːl, *Am* 'skedʒʊl] ◇ *n (of work, things to do)* tabella *f* di marcia; *(timetable)* orario *m*; *(list)* tabella ◇ *vt* programmare; **according to ~** secondo la tabella di marcia; **behind ~** in ritardo sulla tabella di marcia; **on ~** puntualmente.
scheduled flight [*Br* 'ʃedjuːld-, *Am* 'skedʒʊld-] *n* volo *m* di linea.
scheme [skiːm] *n (plan)* piano *m*; *(pej: dishonest plan)* intrigo *m*.
scholarship ['skɒləʃɪp] *n (award)* borsa *f* di studio.
school [skuːl] ◇ *n* scuola *f*; *(university department)* facoltà *f inv*; *(Am: university)* università *f inv* ◇ *adj* scolastico(-a); **at ~** a scuola.
schoolbag ['skuːlbæg] *n* cartella *f*.
schoolbook ['skuːlbʊk] *n* libro *m* di testo.
schoolboy ['skuːlbɔɪ] *n* scolaro *m*.
school bus *n* scuolabus *m inv*.
schoolchild ['skuːltʃaɪld] (*pl* **-children** [-tʃɪldrən]) *n* scolaro *m* (-a *f*).
schoolgirl ['skuːlgɜːl] *n* scolara *f*.
schoolmaster ['skuːlˌmɑːstəʳ] *n (Br)* maestro *m*.
schoolmistress ['skuːlˌmɪstrɪs] *n (Br)* maestra *f*.
schoolteacher ['skuːlˌtiːtʃəʳ] *n* insegnante *mf*.
school uniform *n* divisa *f*.
science ['saɪəns] *n* scienza *f*; (SCH) scienze *fpl*.
science fiction *n* fantascienza *f*.
scientific [ˌsaɪən'tɪfɪk] *adj* scientifico(-a).
scientist ['saɪəntɪst] *n* scienziato *m* (-a *f*).
scissors ['sɪzəz] *npl*: **(a pair of) ~** (un paio di) forbici *fpl*.
scold [skəʊld] *vt* sgridare.
scone [skɒn] *n pasta rotonda con uvette che si mangia con burro e marmellata durante il tè*.
scoop [skuːp] *n (for ice cream, flour)* paletta *f*; *(of ice cream)* pallina *f*; *(in media)* scoop *m inv*.
scooter ['skuːtəʳ] *n (motor vehicle)* scooter *m inv*.
scope [skəʊp] *n (possibility)* opportunità *fpl*; *(range)* portata *f*.
scorch [skɔːtʃ] *vt* bruciare.
score [skɔːʳ] ◇ *n (total, final result)* punteggio *m*; *(current position)* situazione *f* ◇ *vt* (SPORT) segnare; *(in test)* totalizzare ◇ *vi* (SPORT) segnare.
scorn [skɔːn] *n* disprezzo *m*.
Scorpio ['skɔːpɪəʊ] *n* Scorpione *m*.
scorpion ['skɔːpjən] *n* scorpione *m*.
Scot [skɒt] *n* scozzese *mf*.
scotch [skɒtʃ] *n* scotch *m inv (whisky)*.
Scotch broth *n minestra a base di brodo di carne, verdure e orzo perlato*.
Scotch tape® *n (Am)* scotch® *m*.
Scotland ['skɒtlənd] *n* la Scozia.
Scotsman ['skɒtsmən] (*pl* **-men**

[-mən]) *n* scozzese *m.*

Scotswoman ['skɒtswʊmən] (*pl* **-women** [-ˌwɪmɪn]) *n* scozzese *f.*

Scottish ['skɒtɪʃ] *adj* scozzese.

scout [skaʊt] *n (child)* scout *mf inv.*

scowl [skaʊl] *vi* aggrottare le ciglia.

scrambled eggs [ˌskræmbld-] *npl* uova *fpl* strapazzate.

scrap [skræp] *n (of paper, cloth)* pezzo *m*; *(old metal)* rottami *mpl* (di metallo).

scrapbook ['skræpbʊk] *n* album *m inv.*

scrape [skreɪp] *vt (rub)* raschiare; *(scratch)* graffiare.

scrap paper *n (Br)* carta *f* da brutta copia.

scratch [skrætʃ] ◇ *n* graffio *m* ◇ *vt (cut, mark)* graffiare; *(rub)* grattare; **to be up to ~** essere all'altezza della situazione; **to start from ~** cominciare da zero.

scratch paper *(Am)* = **scrap paper**.

scream [skri:m] ◇ *n* strillo *m* ◇ *vi* strillare.

screen [skri:n] ◇ *n* schermo *m*; *(hall in cinema)* sala *f*; *(panel)* paravento *m* ◇ *vt (film)* proiettare; *(TV programme)* trasmettere.

screening ['skri:nɪŋ] *n (of film)* proiezione *f.*

screen wash *n* detergente *m* per il parabrezza.

screw [skru:] ◇ *n* vite *f* ◇ *vt (fasten)* avvitare; *(twist)* torcere.

screwdriver ['skru:ˌdraɪvə^r] *n* cacciavite *m inv.*

scribble ['skrɪbl] *vi* scarabocchiare.

script [skrɪpt] *n (of play, film)* copione *m.*

scrub [skrʌb] *vt* strofinare.

scruffy ['skrʌfɪ] *adj* trasandato(-a).

scrumpy ['skrʌmpɪ] *n sidro ad alta gradazione alcolica tipico del sudovest dell'Inghilterra.*

scuba diving ['sku:bə-] *n* immersioni *fpl* (con autorespiratore).

sculptor ['skʌlptə^r] *n* scultore *m.*

sculpture ['skʌlptʃə^r] *n* scultura *f.*

sea [si:] *n* mare *m*; **by ~** via mare; **by the ~** sul mare.

seafood ['si:fu:d] *n* frutti *mpl* di mare.

seafront ['si:frʌnt] *n* lungomare *m.*

seagull ['si:gʌl] *n* gabbiano *m.*

seal [si:l] ◇ *n (animal)* foca *f*; *(on bottle, container, official mark)* sigillo *m* ◇ *vt (envelope, container)* sigillare.

seam [si:m] *n (in clothes)* cucitura *f.*

search [sɜ:tʃ] ◇ *n* ricerca *f* ◇ *vt* perquisire ◇ *vi*: **to ~ for** cercare.

seashell ['si:ʃel] *n* conchiglia *f.*

seashore ['si:ʃɔ:^r] *n* riva *f* del mare.

seasick ['si:sɪk] *adj*: **to be ~** avere il mal di mare.

seaside ['si:saɪd] *n*: **the ~** il mare.

seaside resort *n* località *f inv* balneare.

season ['si:zn] ◇ *n* stagione *f* ◇ *vt* condire; **in ~** *(fruit, vegetables)* di stagione; *(holiday)* in alta stagione; **out of ~** *(fruit, vegetables)* fuori stagione; *(holiday)* in bassa stagione.

seasoning ['si:znɪŋ] *n* condimento *m.*

season ticket *n* abbonamento *m.*

seat [si:t] ◇ *n (place, chair)* posto *m*; *(in parliament)* seggio *m* ◇ *vt*: **the minibus ~s 12** il minibus ha 12 posti a sedere; **'please wait to be ~ed'** *cartello che avvisa i clienti di un ristorante di attendere il cameriere per essere condotti al tavolo.*

seat belt *n* cintura *f* di sicurezza.

seaweed ['si:wi:d] *n* alghe *fpl.*

secluded [sɪ'klu:dɪd] *adj* appartato(-a).

second ['sekənd] ◇ *n* secondo *m* ◇ *num* secondo(-a); ~ **gear** seconda *f*, → **sixth.**

◆ **seconds** *npl (goods)* merce *f* di seconda scelta; *(inf: of food)* bis *m inv*.

secondary school ['sekəndrı-] *n* = scuola *f* media inferiore e superiore.

second-class *adj (ticket)* di seconda classe; *(stamp) per posta ordinaria sul territorio nazionale*; *(inferior)* di seconda categoria.

second-hand *adj* di seconda mano.

Second World War *n*: **the** ~ la seconda guerra mondiale.

secret ['si:krıt] ◇ *adj* segreto(-a) ◇ *n* segreto *m*.

secretary [*Br* 'sekrətrı, *Am* 'sekrə,terı] *n* segretario *m* (-a *f*).

Secretary of State *n (Am: foreign minister)* segretario *m* di Stato, = ministro *m* degli Esteri; *(Br: government minister)* ministro.

section ['sekʃn] *n* sezione *f*.

sector ['sektəʳ] *n* settore *m*.

secure [sı'kjʊəʳ] ◇ *adj (safe, protected)* sicuro(-a); *(firmly fixed)* saldamente assicurato(-a); *(free from worry)* tranquillo(-a) ◇ *vt (fix)* assicurare; *(fml: obtain)* assicurarsi.

security [sı'kjʊərətı] *n (protection)* sicurezza *f*; *(freedom from worry)* tranquillità *f*.

security guard *n* guardia *f* giurata.

sedative ['sedətıv] *n* sedativo *m*.

seduce [sı'dju:s] *vt* sedurre.

see [si:] (*pt* **saw**, *pp* **seen**) ◇ *vt* vedere; *(accompany)* accompagnare ◇ *vi* vedere; **I** ~ *(understand)* capisco; **to** ~ **if one can do sthg** vedere se si può fare qc; **to** ~ **to sthg** *(deal with)* occuparsi di qc; *(repair)* riparare qc; ~ **you!** arrivederci!; ~ **you later!** a più tardi!; ~ **you soon!** a presto!; ~ **p 14** vedi pag. 14.

◆ **see off** *vt sep (say goodbye to)* (andare a) salutare.

seed [si:d] *n* seme *m*.

seedy ['si:dı] *adj* squallido(-a).

seeing (as) ['si:ıŋ-] *conj* visto che.

seek [si:k] (*pt & pp* **sought**) *vt (fml) (look for)* cercare; *(request)* chiedere.

seem [si:m] ◇ *vi* sembrare ◇ *v impers*: **it ~s (that)** ... sembra (che) ...

seen [si:n] *pp* → **see**.

seesaw ['si:sɔ:] *n* altalena *f*.

segment ['segmənt] *n (of fruit)* spicchio *m*.

seize [si:z] *vt (grab)* afferrare; *(drugs, arms)* sequestrare.

◆ **seize up** *vi* bloccarsi.

seldom ['seldəm] *adv* raramente.

select [sı'lekt] ◇ *vt* scegliere ◇ *adj* selezionato(-a).

selection [sı'lekʃn] *n* selezione *f*.

self-assured [,selfə'ʃʊəd] *adj* sicuro(-a) di sé.

self-catering [,self'keıtərıŋ] *adj (flat)* con uso di cucina.

self-confident [,self-] *adj* sicuro(-a) di sé.

self-conscious [,self-] *adj* timido(-a).

self-contained [,selfkən'teınd] *adj (flat)* autosufficiente.

self-defence [,self-] *n* autodifesa *f*.

self-employed [,self-] *adj* che lavora in proprio.

selfish ['selfıʃ] *adj* egoista.

self-raising flour [,self'reızıŋ-] *n (Br)* farina *f* con lievito.

self-rising flour [,self'raızıŋ-] *(Am)* = **self-raising flour**.

self-service [,self-] *adj* self-service *(inv)*.

sell [sel] (*pt & pp* **sold**) *vt & vi* vendere; **to** ~ **for** essere venduto per; **to** ~ **sb sthg** vendere qc a qn.

sell-by date *n* data *f* di scadenza.

seller ['selər] *n (person)* venditore *m* (-trice *f*).

Sellotape® ['selәteɪp] *n (Br)* nastro *m* adesivo.

semester [sɪ'mestər] *n* semestre *m*.

semicircle ['semɪˌsɜːkl] *n* semicerchio *m*.

semicolon [ˌsemɪ'kəʊlən] *n* punto *m* e virgola.

semidetached [ˌsemɪdɪ'tætʃt] *adj* bifamiliare.

semifinal [ˌsemɪ'faɪnl] *n* semifinale *f*.

seminar ['semɪnɑːr] *n* seminario *m*.

semolina [ˌsemə'liːnə] *n* semolino *m*.

send [send] (*pt & pp* **sent**) *vt (letter, parcel, goods)* spedire, mandare; *(person)* mandare; *(TV or radio signal)* trasmettere; **to ~ sthg to sb** mandare qc a qn.

◆ **send back** *vt sep (faulty goods)* rimandare.

◆ **send off** ◇ *vt sep (letter, parcel)* spedire; (SPORT) espellere ◇ *vi*: **to ~ off (for sthg)** ordinare (qc) per corrispondenza.

sender ['sendər] *n* mittente *mf*.

senile ['siːnaɪl] *adj* senile.

senior ['siːnjər] ◇ *adj* di grado superiore ◇ *n (Br:* SCH*)* studente *m* più grande; *(Am:* SCH*) studente dell'ultimo anno di scuola superiore o università.*

senior citizen *n* anziano *m* (-a *f*).

sensation [sen'seɪʃn] *n* sensazione *f*; **to cause a ~** fare colpo.

sensational [sen'seɪʃənl] *adj (very good)* fantastico(-a).

sense [sens] ◇ *n* senso *m*; *(common sense)* buonsenso *m*; *(of word, expression)* senso, significato *m* ◇ *vt* sentire, percepire; **to make ~** avere senso; **~ of direction** senso dell'orientamento; **~ of humour** senso dell'umorismo.

sensible ['sensəbl] *adj (person)* ragionevole, assennato(-a); *(clothes, shoes)* pratico(-a).

sensitive ['sensɪtɪv] *adj* sensibile; *(subject, issue)* delicato(-a).

sent [sent] *pt & pp* → **send**.

sentence ['sentəns] ◇ *n* (GRAMM) proposizione *f*; *(for crime)* sentenza *f*, condanna *f* ◇ *vt* condannare.

sentimental [ˌsentɪ'mentl] *adj (pej)* sentimentale.

Sep. *(abbr of September)* set.

separate [*adj* 'seprət, *vb* 'sepəreɪt] ◇ *adj* separato(-a); *(different)* diverso(-a) ◇ *vt* separare ◇ *vi* separarsi.

◆ **separates** *npl (Br)* coordinati *mpl*.

separately ['seprətlɪ] *adv* separatamente.

separation [ˌsepə'reɪʃn] *n* separazione *f*.

September [sep'tembər] *n* settembre *m*; **at the beginning of ~** all'inizio di settembre; **at the end of ~** alla fine di settembre; **during ~** durante il mese di settembre; **every ~** ogni anno a settembre; **in ~** a settembre; **last ~** lo scorso settembre; **next ~** il prossimo settembre; **this ~** a settembre (di quest'anno); **2 ~ 1995** *(in letters etc)* 2 settembre 1995.

septic ['septɪk] *adj* infetto(-a).

septic tank *n* fossa *f* settica.

sequel ['siːkwəl] *n (to book, film)* seguito *m*.

sequence ['siːkwəns] *n (series)* serie *f inv*; *(order)* ordine *m*.

sequin ['siːkwɪn] *n* lustrino *m*, paillette *f inv*.

sergeant ['sɑːdʒənt] *n (in police force)* = brigadiere *m*; *(in army)* sergente *m*.

serial ['sɪərɪəl] *n (on TV, radio)* sceneggiato *m*, serial *m inv*; *(in maga-*

zine) romanzo *m* a puntate.

series ['sɪəriːz] *(pl inv) n* serie *f inv*.

serious ['sɪərɪəs] *adj* serio(-a); *(illness, problem)* grave, serio; **are you ~?** dici sul serio?

seriously ['sɪərɪəslɪ] *adv (really)* seriamente; *(badly)* gravemente.

sermon ['sɜːmən] *n* sermone *m*.

servant ['sɜːvənt] *n* domestico *m* (-a *f*).

serve [sɜːv] ◇ *vt* servire ◇ *vi* (SPORT) servire; *(work)* prestare servizio ◇ *n* (SPORT) servizio *m*; **to ~ as** *(be used for)* servire da; **the town is ~d by two airports** la città è servita da due aeroporti; **'~s two'** *(on packaging, menu)* 'per due persone'; **it ~s you right!** ben ti sta!

service ['sɜːvɪs] ◇ *n* servizio *m*; *(at church)* rito *m*; *(of car)* revisione *f* ◇ *vt (car)* revisionare; **'out of ~'** 'fuori servizio'; **'~ included'** 'servizio incluso'; **'~ not included'** 'servizio escluso'; **to be of ~ to sb** *(fml)* essere d'aiuto a qn.

◆ **services** *npl (on motorway)* stazione *f* di servizio; *(of person)* servigi *mpl*.

service area *n* area *f* di servizio.

service charge *n* servizio *m*.

service department *n* servizio *m* clienti.

service station *n* stazione *f* di servizio.

serviette [ˌsɜːvɪ'et] *n* tovagliolo *m*.

serving ['sɜːvɪŋ] *n (helping)* porzione *f*.

serving spoon *n* cucchiaio *m* da portata.

sesame seeds ['sesəmɪ-] *npl* semi *mpl* di sesamo.

session ['seʃn] *n* seduta *f*; **a drinking ~** una bevuta.

set [set] (*pt & pp* **set**) ◇ *adj* **1.** *(price, time)* fisso(-a); **a ~ lunch** un menu fisso.

2. *(text, book)* assegnato(-a).

3. *(situated)* situato(-a).

◇ *n* **1.** *(of tools etc)* serie *f inv*; *(of cutlery, dishes)* servizio *m*; **chess ~** gioco *m* degli scacchi.

2. (TV): **a (TV) ~** un apparecchio televisivo, un televisore.

3. *(in tennis)* set *m inv*.

4. *(of play)* scenario *m*.

5. *(at hairdresser's)*: **a shampoo and ~** uno shampoo e messa in piega.

◇ *vt* **1.** *(put)* mettere, posare; **to ~ the table** apparecchiare.

2. *(cause to be)*: **to ~ a machine going** avviare una macchina; **to ~ fire to sthg** dar fuoco a qc.

3. *(clock, alarm, controls)* regolare; **~ the alarm for 7 a.m.** metti la sveglia alle 7.

4. *(price, time)* fissare.

5. *(a record)* stabilire.

6. *(homework, essay)* dare.

7. *(play, film, story)*: **to be ~** essere ambientato(-a).

◇ *vi* **1.** *(sun)* tramontare.

2. *(glue)* fare presa; *(jelly)* rapprendersi.

◆ **set down** *vt sep (Br: passengers)* far scendere.

◆ **set off** ◇ *vt sep (alarm)* far scattare ◇ *vi (on journey)* mettersi in viaggio.

◆ **set out** ◇ *vt sep (arrange)* disporre ◇ *vi (on journey)* mettersi in viaggio.

◆ **set up** *vt sep (barrier)* erigere; *(equipment)* installare.

set meal *n* menu *m inv* fisso.

set menu *n* menu *m inv* fisso.

settee [se'tiː] *n* divano *m*.

setting ['setɪŋ] *n (on machine)* posizione *f*; *(physical surroundings)* scenario *m*; *(atmosphere)* ambiente *m*.

settle ['setl] ◇ *vt (argument)* sistemare, appianare; *(bill)* saldare, regolare; *(stomach, nerves)* calmare;

(arrange, decide on) stabilire, decidere ◇ *vi (start to live)* stabilirsi; *(come to rest)* posarsi; *(sediment, dust)* depositarsi.

◆ **settle down** *vi (calm down)* calmarsi; *(sit comfortably)* accomodarsi.

◆ **settle up** *vi (pay bill)* saldare il conto.

settlement ['setlmənt] *n (agreement)* accordo *m*; *(place)* insediamento *m*.

seven ['sevn] *num* sette, → **six**.

seventeen [ˌsevn'tiːn] *num* diciassette, → **six**.

seventeenth [ˌsevn'tiːnθ] *num* diciassettesimo(-a), → **sixth**.

seventh ['sevnθ] *num* settimo(-a), → **sixth**.

seventieth ['sevntjəθ] *num* settantesimo(-a), → **sixth**.

seventy ['sevntɪ] *num* settanta, → **six**.

several ['sevrəl] *adj & pron* parecchi(-chie), diversi(-e).

severe [sɪ'vɪəʳ] *adj (conditions, damage, illness)* grave; *(criticism, person, punishment)* severo(-a); *(pain)* violento(-a), forte.

sew [səʊ] *(pp* **sewn***) vt & vi* cucire.

sewage ['suːɪdʒ] *n* acque *fpl* di scarico.

sewing ['səʊɪŋ] *n (activity)* cucito *m*; *(things sewn)* lavoro *m*.

sewing machine *n* macchina *f* da cucire.

sewn [səʊn] *pp* → **sew**.

sex [seks] *n (gender)* sesso *m*; *(sexual intercourse)* rapporto *m* sessuale; **to have ~ (with)** avere rapporti sessuali (con).

sexist ['seksɪst] *n* sessista *mf*.

sexual ['sekʃʊəl] *adj* sessuale.

sexy ['seksɪ] *adj* sexy *(inv)*.

shabby ['ʃæbɪ] *adj* trasandato(-a).

shade [ʃeɪd] ◇ *n (shadow)* ombra *f*; *(lampshade)* paralume *m*; *(of colour)* sfumatura *f*, tonalità *f inv* ◇ *vt (protect)* fare ombra a.

◆ **shades** *npl (inf: sunglasses)* occhiali *mpl* da sole.

shadow ['ʃædəʊ] *n* ombra *f*.

shady ['ʃeɪdɪ] *adj (place)* ombroso(-a); *(inf: person, deal)* losco(-a).

shaft [ʃɑːft] *n (of machine)* albero *m*; *(of lift)* pozzo *m*.

shake [ʃeɪk] *(pt* **shook**, *pp* **shaken** ['ʃeɪkn]) ◇ *vt (tree, rug, person)* scuotere; *(bottle, dice)* agitare; *(shock)* scuotere, turbare ◇ *vi* tremare; **to ~ hands (with sb)** dare OR stringere la mano (a qn); **to ~ one's head** *(saying no)* scuotere la testa.

shall [*weak form* ʃəl, *strong form* ʃæl] *aux vb* **1.** *(expressing future)*: **I ~ be ready soon** sarò pronto tra poco.

2. *(in questions)*: **~ I buy some wine?** devo comprare del vino?; **~ we listen to the radio?** vogliamo ascoltare la radio?; **where ~ we go?** dove andiamo?, dove vogliamo andare?

3. *(fml: expressing order)*: **payment ~ be made within a week** il pagamento dovrà essere effettuato entro una settimana.

shallot [ʃə'lɒt] *n* scalogno *m*.

shallow ['ʃæləʊ] *adj* poco profondo(-a).

shallow end *n (of swimming pool)* lato *m* meno profondo.

shambles ['ʃæmblz] *n* macello *m*, casino *m*.

shame [ʃeɪm] *n* vergogna *f*; **it's a ~** è un peccato; **what a ~!** che peccato!

shampoo [ʃæm'puː] *(pl* **-s***) n* shampoo *m inv*.

shandy ['ʃændɪ] *n bevanda a base di birra e limonata.*

shape [ʃeɪp] *n* forma *f*; **to be in good/bad ~** essere in/fuori forma.

share [ʃeəʳ] ◇ *n (part)* parte *f*; *(in*

company) azione *f* ◇ *vt* dividere.
◆ **share out** *vt sep* dividere.
shark [ʃɑ:k] *n* squalo *m*, pescecane *m*.
sharp [ʃɑ:p] ◇ *adj (knife, razor)* affilato(-a); *(pin, nails)* appuntito(-a); *(teeth)* aguzzo(-a); *(clear)* nitido(-a); *(quick, intelligent)* acuto(-a), scaltro (-a); *(rise, change, bend)* brusco(-a); *(painful)* acuto, lancinante; *(food, taste)* aspro(-a) ◇ *adv (exactly)* in punto.
sharpen ['ʃɑ:pn] *vt (pencil)* temperare; *(knife)* affilare.
shatter ['ʃætəʳ] ◇ *vt (break)* frantumare ◇ *vi* frantumarsi.
shattered ['ʃætəd] *adj (Br: inf: tired)* distrutto(-a).
shave [ʃeɪv] ◇ *vt* radere, rasare ◇ *vi* radersi, rasarsi ◇ *n*: **to have a ~** farsi la barba.
shaver ['ʃeɪvəʳ] *n* rasoio *m* elettrico.
shaver point *n* presa *f* per rasoio elettrico.
shaving brush ['ʃeɪvɪŋ-] *n* pennello *m* da barba.
shaving cream ['ʃeɪvɪŋ-] *n* crema *f* da barba.
shaving foam ['ʃeɪvɪŋ-] *n* schiuma *f* da barba.
shawl [ʃɔ:l] *n* scialle *m*.
she [ʃi:] *pron* lei; **~'s tall** è alta.
sheaf [ʃi:f] (*pl* **sheaves**) *n (of paper, notes)* fascio *m*.
shears [ʃɪəz] *npl* cesoie *fpl*.
sheaves [ʃi:vz] *pl* → **sheaf**.
shed [ʃed] (*pt & pp* **shed**) ◇ *n* capanno *m* ◇ *vt (tears, blood)* versare.
she'd [*weak form* ʃɪd, *strong form* ʃi:d] = **she had, she would**.
sheep [ʃi:p] *(pl inv) n* pecora *f*.
sheepdog ['ʃi:pdɒg] *n* cane *m* pastore.
sheepskin ['ʃi:pskɪn] *adj* di pelle di pecora.
sheer [ʃɪəʳ] *adj (pure, utter)* puro(-a); *(cliff)* a picco, a strapiombo; *(stockings)* velato(-a).
sheet [ʃi:t] *n (for bed)* lenzuolo *m*; *(of paper)* foglio *m*; *(of glass, metal)* lastra *f*; *(of wood)* pannello *m*.
shelf [ʃelf] (*pl* **shelves**) *n* scaffale *m*.
shell [ʃel] *n (of egg, nut, animal)* guscio *m*; *(on beach)* conchiglia *f*; *(bomb)* granata *f*.
she'll [ʃi:l] = **she will, she shall**.
shellfish ['ʃelfɪʃ] *n (food)* frutti *mpl* di mare.
shell suit *n (Br)* tuta *f* in acetato.
shelter ['ʃeltəʳ] ◇ *n* riparo *m*, rifugio *m*; *(at bus stop)* pensilina *f* ◇ *vt (protect)* proteggere, riparare ◇ *vi* proteggersi, ripararsi; **to take ~** mettersi al riparo.
sheltered ['ʃeltəd] *adj (place)* riparato(-a).
shelves [ʃelvz] *pl* → **shelf**.
shepherd ['ʃepəd] *n* pastore *m*.
shepherd's pie ['ʃepədz-] *n tortino a base di carne macinata coperta da uno spesso strato di purè di patate*.
sheriff ['ʃerɪf] *n (in US)* sceriffo *m*.
sherry ['ʃerɪ] *n* sherry *m inv*.
she's [ʃi:z] = **she is, she has**.
shield [ʃi:ld] ◇ *n* scudo *m* ◇ *vt* proteggere.
shift [ʃɪft] ◇ *n (change)* cambiamento *m*; *(period of work)* turno *m* ◇ *vt* spostare ◇ *vi (move)* spostarsi; *(change)* mutare, cambiare.
shin [ʃɪn] *n* stinco *m*.
shine [ʃaɪn] (*pt & pp* **shone**) ◇ *vi* brillare, splendere ◇ *vt (shoes)* lucidare, lustrare; *(torch)* puntare.
shiny ['ʃaɪnɪ] *adj* scintillante, lucido(-a).
ship [ʃɪp] *n* nave *f*; **by ~** *(travel)* con la nave; *(send, transport)* via mare.
shipwreck ['ʃɪprek] *n (accident)* naufragio *m*; *(wrecked ship)* relitto *m*.

shirt [ʃɜːt] *n* camicia *f*.
shit [ʃɪt] ◇ *n (vulg)* merda *f* ◇ *excl (vulg)* merda!
shiver [ˈʃɪvəʳ] *vi* rabbrividire.
shock [ʃɒk] ◇ *n (surprise)* shock *m inv*; *(force)* urto *m*, scossa *f* ◇ *vt (surprise)* colpire, scioccare; *(horrify)* scioccare; **to be in ~** (MED) essere sotto shock.
shock absorber [-əbˌzɔːbəʳ] *n* ammortizzatore *m*.
shocking [ˈʃɒkɪŋ] *adj (very bad)* terribile.
shoe [ʃuː] *n* scarpa *f*.
shoelace [ˈʃuːleɪs] *n* stringa *f*.
shoe polish *n* lucido *m* da scarpe.
shoe repairer's [-rɪˌpeərəz] *n* calzolaio *m*.
shoe shop *n* negozio *m* di calzature.
shone [ʃɒn] *pt & pp* → **shine**.
shook [ʃʊk] *pt* → **shake**.
shoot [ʃuːt] (*pt & pp* **shot**) ◇ *vt (kill, injure)* sparare a; *(gun)* sparare; *(arrow)* tirare, scoccare; *(film)* girare ◇ *vi (with gun)* sparare; *(move quickly)* sfrecciare; (SPORT) tirare ◇ *n (of plant)* germoglio *m*.
shop [ʃɒp] ◇ *n* negozio *m* ◇ *vi* fare acquisti.
shop assistant *n (Br)* commesso *m* (-a *f*).
shop floor *n (place) area di una fabbrica dove lavorano gli operai.*
shopkeeper [ˈʃɒpˌkiːpəʳ] *n* negoziante *mf*.
shoplifter [ˈʃɒpˌlɪftəʳ] *n* taccheggiatore *m* (-trice *f*).
shopper [ˈʃɒpəʳ] *n* cliente *mf*, acquirente *mf*.
shopping [ˈʃɒpɪŋ] *n* spesa *f*; **to do the ~** fare la spesa; **to go ~** andare a fare spese.
shopping bag *n* borsa *f* per la spesa.
shopping basket *n* sporta *f* per la spesa.
shopping centre *n* centro *m* commerciale.
shopping list *n* lista *f* della spesa.
shopping mall *n* centro *m* commerciale.
shop steward *n* rappresentante *mf* sindacale.
shop window *n* vetrina *f*.
shore [ʃɔːʳ] *n* riva *f*; **on ~** a terra.
short [ʃɔːt] ◇ *adj (not tall)* basso(-a); *(letter, speech)* corto(-a), breve; *(hair, skirt)* corto; *(in time, distance)* breve ◇ *adv (cut hair)* corti ◇ *n (Br: drink)* bicchierino *m*; *(film)* cortometraggio *m*; **to be ~ of sthg** *(time, money)* essere a corto di qc; **to be ~ for sthg** *(be abbreviation of)* essere l'abbreviazione di qc; **to be ~ of breath** essere senza fiato; **in ~** in breve.
◆ **shorts** *npl (short trousers)* calzoncini *mpl*, pantaloncini *mpl*; *(Am: underpants)* boxer *mpl*.
shortage [ˈʃɔːtɪdʒ] *n* carenza *f*.
shortbread [ˈʃɔːtbred] *n* biscotto *m* di pasta frolla.
short-circuit *vi* fare cortocircuito.
shortcrust pastry [ˈʃɔːtkrʌst-] *n* pasta *f* frolla.
short cut *n* scorciatoia *f*.
shorten [ˈʃɔːtn] *vt* accorciare.
shorthand [ˈʃɔːthænd] *n* stenografia *f*.
shortly [ˈʃɔːtlɪ] *adv (soon)* presto, fra poco; **~ before** poco prima di.
shortsighted [ˌʃɔːtˈsaɪtɪd] *adj* miope.
short-sleeved [-ˌsliːvd] *adj* a maniche corte.
short-stay car park *n* parcheggio *m* a tempo limitato.
short story *n* racconto *m*, novella *f*.
short wave *n* onde *fpl* corte.
shot [ʃɒt] ◇ *pt & pp* → **shoot** ◇ *n (of gun)* sparo *m*; *(in football, tennis,*

golf etc) tiro *m*; *(photo)* foto *f inv*; *(in film)* ripresa *f*; *(inf: attempt)* prova *f*, tentativo *m*; *(drink)* bicchierino *m*.

shotgun ['ʃɒtgʌn] *n* fucile *m* da caccia.

should [ʃʊd] *aux vb* **1.** *(expressing desirability)*: **we ~ leave now** ora dovremmo OR sarebbe meglio andare.

2. *(asking for advice)*: **~ I go too?** devo andarci anch'io?

3. *(expressing probability)*: **she ~ be home soon** dovrebbe arrivare a momenti.

4. *(ought to)*: **they ~ have won the match** avrebbero dovuto vincere la partita.

5. *(fml: in conditionals)*: **~ you need anything, call reception** se dovesse aver bisogno di qualcosa, chiami la reception.

6. *(fml: expressing wish)*: **I ~ like to come with you** mi piacerebbe venire con voi.

shoulder ['ʃəʊldə^r] *n* spalla *f*; *(Am: of road)* corsia *f* d'emergenza.

shoulder pad *n* spallina *f*.

shouldn't ['ʃʊdnt] = **should not**.

should've ['ʃʊdəv] = **should have**.

shout [ʃaʊt] ◇ *n* grido *m*, urlo *m* ◇ *vt & vi* gridare, urlare.

◆ **shout out** *vt sep* gridare.

shove [ʃʌv] *vt (push)* spingere; *(put carelessly)* ficcare, cacciare.

shovel ['ʃʌvl] *n* pala *f*.

show [ʃəʊ] (*pp* **-ed** OR **shown**) ◇ *n (at theatre, on TV)* spettacolo *m*; *(on radio)* programma *m*; *(exhibition)* mostra *f* ◇ *vt* mostrare; *(represent, depict)* raffigurare; *(accompany)* accompagnare; *(film, TV programme)* dare ◇ *vi (be visible)* vedersi, essere visibile; *(film)* essere in programmazione; **to ~ sthg to sb** mostrare qc a qn; **to ~ sb how to do sthg** mostrare a qn come fare qc.

◆ **show off** *vi* mettersi in mostra.

◆ **show up** *vi (come along)* farsi vivo, arrivare; *(be visible)* risaltare.

shower ['ʃaʊə^r] ◇ *n (for washing)* doccia *f*; *(of rain)* acquazzone *m* ◇ *vi* fare la doccia; **to have a ~** fare la doccia.

shower gel *n* gel *m inv* per la doccia.

shower unit *n* blocco *m* doccia.

showing ['ʃəʊɪŋ] *n (of film)* proiezione *f*.

shown [ʃəʊn] *pp* → **show**.

showroom ['ʃəʊrʊm] *n* salone *m* d'esposizione.

shrank [ʃræŋk] *pt* → **shrink**.

shrimp [ʃrɪmp] *n* gamberetto *m*.

shrine [ʃraɪn] *n* santuario *m*.

shrink [ʃrɪŋk] (*pt* **shrank**, *pp* **shrunk**) ◇ *n (inf: psychoanalyst)* strizzacervelli *mf inv* ◇ *vi (clothes)* restringersi; *(number, amount)* ridursi, diminuire.

shrub [ʃrʌb] *n* arbusto *m*.

shrug [ʃrʌg] ◇ *n* scrollata *f* di spalle ◇ *vi* scrollare le spalle.

shrunk [ʃrʌŋk] *pp* → **shrink**.

shuffle ['ʃʌfl] ◇ *vt (cards)* mischiare ◇ *vi (walk)* camminare strascicando i piedi.

shut [ʃʌt] (*pt & pp* **shut**) ◇ *adj* chiuso(-a) ◇ *vt* chiudere ◇ *vi (door, mouth, eyes)* chiudersi; *(shop, restaurant)* chiudere.

◆ **shut down** *vt sep* chiudere i battenti.

◆ **shut up** *vi (inf: stop talking)* tacere, stare zitto; **~ up!** chiudi il becco!

shutter ['ʃʌtə^r] *n (on window)* imposta *f*; *(on camera)* otturatore *m*.

shuttle ['ʃʌtl] *n (plane, bus etc)* navetta *f*.

shuttlecock ['ʃʌtlkɒk] *n* volano *m*.

shy [ʃaɪ] *adj* timido(-a).

Sicily ['sɪsɪlɪ] *n* la Sicilia.
sick [sɪk] *adj (ill)* malato(-a); **to be ~** *(vomit)* vomitare; **to feel ~** *(nauseous)* avere la nausea; **to be ~ of** *(fed up with)* essere stufo(-a) di.
sick bag *n sacchetto di emergenza per viaggiatori che soffrono di nausea e vomito.*
sickness ['sɪknɪs] *n (illness)* malattia *f*.
sick pay *n* indennità *f* per malattia.
side [saɪd] ◇ *n* lato *m*; *(of road, pitch)* margine *m*; *(of river)* sponda *f*; *(team)* squadra *f*; *(in argument)* parte *f*; *(Br: TV channel)* canale *m* ◇ *adj (door, pocket)* laterale; **at the ~ of** a fianco di; *(road)* al margine di; *(river)* sulla riva di; **on the other ~** dall'altra parte; **on this ~** da questo lato; **~ by ~** fianco a fianco.
sideboard ['saɪdbɔːd] *n* credenza *f*.
sidecar ['saɪdkɑːʳ] *n* sidecar *m inv*.
side dish *n* contorno *m*.
side effect *n* effetto *m* collaterale.
sidelight ['saɪdlaɪt] *n (Br: of car)* luce *f* di posizione.
side order *n* contorno *m*.
side salad *n* insalata *f* di contorno.
side street *n* traversa *f*.
sidewalk ['saɪdwɔːk] *n (Am)* marciapiede *m*.
sideways ['saɪdweɪz] *adv (move)* di lato, di fianco; *(look)* di traverso.
sieve [sɪv] *n* setaccio *m*.
sigh [saɪ] ◇ *n* sospiro *m* ◇ *vi* sospirare.
sight [saɪt] *n (eyesight)* vista *f*; *(thing seen)* spettacolo *m*; **at first ~** a prima vista; **to catch ~ of** intravedere; **in ~** in vista; **to lose ~ of** perdere di vista; **to be out of ~** non essere visibile.
◆ **sights** *npl (of city, country)* luoghi *mpl* di maggiore interesse.
sightseeing ['saɪtˌsiːɪŋ] *n*: **to go ~** fare un giro turistico.
sign [saɪn] ◇ *n (in shop, station)* insegna *f*; *(next to road)* segnale *m*, cartello *m*; *(symbol, indication)* segno *m*; *(signal)* segnale ◇ *vt & vi* firmare; **there's no ~ of her** non c'è traccia di lei.
◆ **sign in** *vi (at hotel, club)* firmare il registro (all'arrivo).
signal ['sɪgnl] ◇ *n* segnale *m*; *(Am: traffic lights)* semaforo *m* ◇ *vi (in car, on bike)* segnalare.
signature ['sɪgnətʃəʳ] *n* firma *f*.
significant [sɪg'nɪfɪkənt] *adj (large)* considerevole; *(important)* importante.
signpost ['saɪnpəʊst] *n* cartello *m* stradale.
sikh [siːk] *n* Sikh *mf inv*.
silence ['saɪləns] *n* silenzio *m*.
silencer ['saɪlənsəʳ] *n (Br:* AUT*)* marmitta *f*.
silent ['saɪlənt] *adj* silenzioso(-a).
silk [sɪlk] *n* seta *f*.
sill [sɪl] *n* davanzale *m*.
silly ['sɪlɪ] *adj* sciocco(-a), stupido(-a).
silver ['sɪlvəʳ] ◇ *n (substance)* argento *m*; *(coins)* monete *fpl* d'argento ◇ *adj* d'argento.
silver foil *n* stagnola *f*, carta *f* argentata.
silver-plated [-'pleɪtɪd] *adj* placcato(-a) d'argento.
similar ['sɪmɪləʳ] *adj* simile; **to be ~ to** essere simile a.
similarity [ˌsɪmɪ'lærətɪ] *n (resemblance)* somiglianza *f*; *(similar point)* affinità *f inv*.
simmer ['sɪməʳ] *vi* cuocere a fuoco lento.
simple ['sɪmpl] *adj* semplice.
simplify ['sɪmplɪfaɪ] *vt* semplificare.
simply ['sɪmplɪ] *adv* semplicemente.

simulate ['sımjʊleıt] *vt* simulare.

simultaneous [*Br* ˌsıməl'teınjəs, *Am* ˌsaıməl'teınjəs] *adj* simultaneo(-a).

simultaneously [*Br* ˌsıməl'teınjəslı, *Am* ˌsaıməl'teınjəslı] *adv* simultaneamente.

sin [sın] ◇ *n* peccato *m* ◇ *vi* peccare.

since [sıns] ◇ *adv* da allora ◇ *prep* da ◇ *conj (in time)* da quando, da che; *(as)* dato che, poiché; **ever ~** *prep* fin da ◇ *conj* da che, fin da quando.

sincere [sın'sıəʳ] *adj* sincero(-a).

sincerely [sın'sıəlı] *adv* sinceramente; **Yours ~** Distinti saluti.

sing [sıŋ] (*pt* sang, *pp* **sung**) *vt & vi* cantare.

singer ['sıŋəʳ] *n* cantante *mf*.

single ['sıŋgl] ◇ *adj* solo(-a); *(man)* celibe; *(woman)* nubile ◇ *n* *(Br: ticket)* biglietto *m* di sola andata; *(record)* 45 giri *m inv*; **every ~** ogni.

◆ **singles** ◇ *n* (SPORT) singolo *m* ◇ *adj (bar, club)* per single.

single bed *n* letto *m* a una piazza.

single cream *n (Br)* panna *f* liquida.

single parent *n* genitore *m* single.

single room *n* camera *f* singola.

single track road *n* strada *f* a una carreggiata.

singular ['sıŋgjʊləʳ] *n* singolare *m*; **in the ~** al singolare.

sinister ['sınıstəʳ] *adj* sinistro(-a).

sink [sıŋk] (*pt* **sank**, *pp* **sunk**) ◇ *n* lavandino *m* ◇ *vi (in water, mud)* affondare; *(decrease)* calare, diminuire.

sink unit *n* blocco *m* lavello.

sinuses ['saınəsız] *npl* seni *mpl* paranasali.

sip [sıp] ◇ *n* sorso *m* ◇ *vt* sorseggiare.

siphon ['saıfn] ◇ *n* sifone *m* ◇ *vt* travasare.

sir [sɜːʳ] *n* signore *m*; **Dear Sir** Egregio Signore; **Sir Richard Blair** Sir Richard Blair.

siren ['saıərən] *n* sirena *f*.

sirloin steak [ˌsɜːlɔın-] *n* bistecca *f* di lombo.

sister ['sıstəʳ] *n* sorella *f*; *(Br: nurse)* caposala *f*.

sister-in-law *n* cognata *f*.

sit [sıt] (*pt & pp* **sat**) ◇ *vi* sedere; *(be situated)* trovarsi ◇ *vt (to place)* far sedere; *(Br: exam)* sostenere, dare; **to be sitting** essere seduto.

◆ **sit down** *vi* sedersi; **to be sitting down** essere seduto.

◆ **sit up** *vi (after lying down)* tirarsi su a sedere; *(stay up late)* stare in piedi fino a tardi.

site [saıt] *n* luogo *m*; *(building site)* cantiere *m*.

sitting room ['sıtıŋ-] *n* salotto *m*.

situated ['sıtjʊeıtıd] *adj*: **to be ~** essere situato(-a).

situation [ˌsıtjʊ'eıʃn] *n (state of affairs)* situazione *f*; *(fml: location)* ubicazione *f*; **'~s vacant'** 'offerte di lavoro'.

six [sıks] *num adj & n* sei; **to be ~ (years old)** avere sei anni; **it's ~ (o'clock)** sono le sei; **a hundred and ~** centosei; **~ Hill Street** Hill Street (numero) sei; **it's minus ~ (degrees)** è meno sei.

sixteen [sıks'tiːn] *num* sedici, → **six**.

sixteenth [sıks'tiːnθ] *num* sedicesimo(-a), → **sixth**.

sixth [sıksθ] ◇ *num adj, adv & pron* sesto(-a) ◇ *num n* sesto *m*; **the ~ (of September)** il sei (di settembre).

sixth form *n (Br) ultimi due anni facoltativi della scuola superiore.*

sixth-form college *n (Br) istituto che prepara agli esami dell'ultimo anno di scuola superiore.*

sixtieth ['sıkstıəθ] *num* sessantesimo(-a), → **sixth**.

sixty ['sɪkstɪ] *num* sessanta, → **six**.

size [saɪz] *n* dimensioni *fpl*; *(of clothes, hats)* taglia *f*, misura *f*; *(of shoes)* numero *m*; **what ~ do you take?** che taglia porta?; **what ~ is this?** che taglia è?

sizeable ['saɪzəbl] *adj* notevole.

skate [skeɪt] ◇ *n (ice skate, roller skate)* pattino *m*; *(fish: pl inv)* razza *f* ◇ *vi* pattinare.

skateboard ['skeɪtbɔːd] *n* skateboard *m inv*.

skater ['skeɪtəʳ] *n* pattinatore *m* (-trice *f*).

skating ['skeɪtɪŋ] *n*: **to go ~** andare a pattinare.

skeleton ['skelɪtn] *n* scheletro *m*.

skeptical ['skeptɪkl] *(Am)* = **sceptical**.

sketch [sketʃ] ◇ *n (drawing)* schizzo *m*; *(humorous)* sketch *m inv*, scenetta *f* ◇ *vt* schizzare.

skewer ['skjʊəʳ] *n* spiedo *m*.

ski [skiː] (*pt & pp* **skied**, *cont* **skiing**) ◇ *n* sci *m inv* ◇ *vi* sciare.

ski boots *npl* scarponi *mpl* da sci.

skid [skɪd] ◇ *n* slittamento *m*, sbandamento *m* ◇ *vi* slittare, sbandare.

skier ['skiːəʳ] *n* sciatore *m* (-trice *f*).

skiing ['skiːɪŋ] *n* sci *m*; **to go ~** andare a sciare; **a ~ holiday** una vacanza sulla neve.

skilful ['skɪlfʊl] *adj (Br)* abile.

ski lift *n* sciovia *f*.

skill [skɪl] *n (ability)* abilità *f inv*; *(technique)* tecnica *f*.

skilled [skɪld] *adj (worker, job)* qualificato(-a); *(driver, chef)* provetto(-a).

skillful ['skɪlfʊl] *(Am)* = **skilful**.

skimmed milk ['skɪmd-] *n* latte *m* scremato.

skin [skɪn] *n* pelle *f*; *(on fruit, vegetable)* buccia *f*; *(on milk)* pellicola *f*.

skin freshener [-ˌfreʃnəʳ] *n* tonico *m*.

skinny ['skɪnɪ] *adj* magrissimo(-a).

skip [skɪp] ◇ *vi (with rope)* saltare la corda; *(jump)* saltellare ◇ *vt (omit)* saltare ◇ *n (container)* cassonetto *m*.

ski pants *npl* pantaloni *mpl* da sci.

ski pass *n* ski-pass *m inv*.

ski pole *n* racchetta *f* da sci.

skipping rope ['skɪpɪŋ-] *n* corda *f* per saltare.

skirt [skɜːt] *n* gonna *f*.

ski slope *n* pista *f* da sci.

ski tow *n* ski-lift *m inv*.

skittles ['skɪtlz] *n* birilli *mpl*.

skull [skʌl] *n* cranio *m*.

sky [skaɪ] *n* cielo *m*.

skylight ['skaɪlaɪt] *n* lucernario *m*.

skyscraper ['skaɪˌskreɪpəʳ] *n* grattacielo *m*.

slab [slæb] *n (of stone, concrete)* lastra *f*.

slack [slæk] *adj (rope)* non tirato(-a); *(careless)* negligente; *(not busy)* calmo(-a); *(period)* morto(-a).

slacks [slæks] *npl* pantaloni *mpl*.

slam [slæm] *vt & vi* sbattere.

slander ['slɑːndəʳ] *n* calunnia *f*; *(in law)* diffamazione *f*.

slang [slæŋ] *n* slang *m*, gergo *m*.

slant [slɑːnt] ◇ *n (slope)* pendenza *f* ◇ *vi* pendere.

slap [slæp] ◇ *n (smack)* schiaffo *m* ◇ *vt* schiaffeggiare.

slash [slæʃ] ◇ *vt (cut)* tagliare; *(face)* sfregiare; *(fig: prices)* ridurre ◇ *n (written symbol)* barra *f*.

slate [sleɪt] *n (rock)* ardesia *f*; *(on roof)* tegola *f* di ardesia.

slaughter ['slɔːtəʳ] *vt (people, team)* massacrare; *(animal)* macellare.

slave [sleɪv] *n* schiavo *m* (-a *f*).

sled [sled] = **sledge**.

sledge [sledʒ] *n* slitta *f*.

sleep [sli:p] (*pt & pp* **slept**) ◇ *n* sonno *m* ◇ *vi* dormire ◇ *vt*: **the house ~s six** la casa ha sei posti letto; **did you ~ well?** hai dormito bene?; **I couldn't get to ~** non riuscivo a prender sonno; **to go to ~** addormentarsi; **to ~ with sb** andare a letto con qn.

sleeper ['sli:pəʳ] *n (train)* treno *m* con vagoni letto; *(sleeping car)* vagone *m* letto; *(Br: on railway track)* traversina *f*; *(Br: earring)* campanella *f*.

sleeping bag ['sli:pɪŋ-] *n* sacco *m* a pelo.

sleeping car ['sli:pɪŋ-] *n* vagone *m* letto.

sleeping pill ['sli:pɪŋ-] *n* sonnifero *m*.

sleeping policeman ['sli:pɪŋ-] *n (Br) piccolo dosso stradale che ha la funzione di rallentare il traffico.*

sleepy ['sli:pɪ] *adj* insonnolito(-a); **I'm ~** ho sonno.

sleet [sli:t] ◇ *n* nevischio *m* ◇ *v impers*: **it's ~ing** sta nevischiando.

sleeve [sli:v] *n (of garment)* manica *f*; *(of record)* copertina *f*.

sleeveless ['sli:vlɪs] *adj* senza maniche.

slept [slept] *pt & pp* → **sleep**.

slice [slaɪs] ◇ *n* fetta *f* ◇ *vt* affettare, tagliare a fette.

sliced bread [ˌslaɪst-] *n* pane *m* a cassetta.

slide [slaɪd] (*pt & pp* **slid** [slɪd]) ◇ *n (in playground)* scivolo *m*; *(of photograph)* diapositiva *f*; *(Br: hair slide)* fermacapelli *m inv* ◇ *vi (slip)* scivolare.

sliding door [ˌslaɪdɪŋ-] *n* porta *f* scorrevole.

slight [slaɪt] *adj (minor)* lieve; **the ~est** il minimo (la minima); **not in the ~est** niente affatto.

slightly ['slaɪtlɪ] *adv (a bit)* leggermente; **I know him ~** lo conosco appena.

slim [slɪm] ◇ *adj (person, waist)* snello(-a) ◇ *vi* dimagrire.

slimming ['slɪmɪŋ] *n* dimagrimento *m*.

sling [slɪŋ] (*pt & pp* **slung**) ◇ *vt (inf: throw)* buttare ◇ *n*: **to have one's arm in a ~** portare il braccio al collo.

slip [slɪp] ◇ *vi* scivolare ◇ *n (mistake)* errore *m*; *(of paper)* foglietto *m*; *(petticoat)* sottoveste *f*.

◆ **slip up** *vi (make a mistake)* fare un errore.

slipper ['slɪpəʳ] *n* pantofola *f*.

slippery ['slɪpərɪ] *adj* scivoloso(-a).

slip road *n (Br)* raccordo *m* autostradale.

slit [slɪt] *n* fessura *f*.

slob [slɒb] *n (inf)* sciattone *m* (-a *f*).

slogan ['sləʊgən] *n* slogan *m inv*.

slope [sləʊp] ◇ *n (incline)* pendio *m*; *(hill)* fianco *m*; *(for skiing)* pista *f* da sci ◇ *vi (hill, path)* scendere; *(floor, roof, shelf)* essere inclinato.

sloping ['sləʊpɪŋ] *adj (floor, roof, shelf)* inclinato(-a); *(hill)* degradante.

slot [slɒt] *n (for coin)* fessura *f*; *(groove)* scanalatura *f*.

slot machine *n (vending machine)* distributore *m* automatico; *(for gambling)* slot-machine *f inv*.

Slovakia [slə'vækɪə] *n* la Slovacchia.

slow [sləʊ] ◇ *adj* lento(-a); *(business)* fiacco(-a) ◇ *adv* lentamente; **'slow'** *(sign on road)* 'rallentare'; **a ~ train** un accelerato; **to be ~** *(clock)* essere indietro.

◆ **slow down** *vt sep & vi* rallentare.

slowly ['sləʊlɪ] *adv* lentamente.

slug [slʌg] *n (animal)* lumacone *m*.

slum [slʌm] *n (building)* baracca *f*.

◆ **slums** *npl (district)* bassifondi *mpl*.

slung [slʌŋ] *pt & pp* → **sling**.

slush [slʌʃ] *n* neve *f* in parte sciolta.

sly [slaɪ] *adj (cunning)* astuto(-a); *(deceitful)* scaltro(-a).

smack [smæk] ◇ *n (slap)* schiaffo *m* ◇ *vt* schiaffeggiare.

small [smɔːl] *adj* piccolo(-a); *(in height)* basso(-a).

small change *n* spiccioli *mpl*.

smallpox [ˈsmɔːlpɒks] *n* vaiolo *m*.

smart [smɑːt] *adj (elegant, posh)* elegante; *(clever)* intelligente.

smart card *n* carta *f* intelligente.

smash [smæʃ] ◇ *n* (SPORT) smash *m inv*, schiacciata *f*; *(inf: car crash)* scontro *m* ◇ *vt (plate, window)* frantumare ◇ *vi (plate, vase etc)* frantumarsi.

smashing [ˈsmæʃɪŋ] *adj (Br: inf)* fantastico(-a).

smear test [ˈsmɪə-] *n* striscio *m*, pap-test *m inv*.

smell [smel] (*pt & pp* **-ed** OR **smelt**) ◇ *n* odore *m*; *(bad odour)* puzza *f* ◇ *vt (sniff at)* annusare; *(detect)* sentire odore di ◇ *vi* avere un odore; *(have bad odour)* puzzare; **to ~ of sthg** *(pleasant)* profumare di qc; *(unpleasant)* puzzare di qc.

smelly [ˈsmelɪ] *adj* puzzolente.

smelt [smelt] *pt & pp* → **smell**.

smile [smaɪl] ◇ *n* sorriso *m* ◇ *vi* sorridere.

smoke [sməʊk] ◇ *n* fumo *m* ◇ *vt & vi* fumare; **to have a ~** fumare una sigaretta.

smoked [sməʊkt] *adj* affumicato(-a).

smoked salmon *n* salmone *m* affumicato.

smoker [ˈsməʊkəʳ] *n (person)* fumatore *m* (-trice *f*).

smoking [ˈsməʊkɪŋ] *n* fumo *m*; **'no ~'** 'vietato fumare'.

smoking area *n* area *f* per fumatori.

smoking compartment *n* scompartimento *m* per fumatori.

smoky [ˈsməʊkɪ] *adj (room)* fumoso(-a).

smooth [smuːð] *adj (surface, skin, road)* liscio(-a); *(takeoff, landing)* dolce, morbido(-a); *(flight, journey, life)* tranquillo(-a); *(mixture, liquid)* vellutato(-a), omogeneo(-a); *(wine, beer)* amabile; *(pej: suave)* mellifluo(-a).

◆ **smooth down** *vt sep* lisciare.

smother [ˈsmʌðəʳ] *vt (cover)* coprire.

smudge [smʌdʒ] *n* sbavatura *f*.

smuggle [ˈsmʌgl] *vt* contrabbandare.

snack [snæk] *n* spuntino *m*, snack *m inv*.

snack bar *n* snack-bar *m inv*, tavola *f* calda.

snail [sneɪl] *n* chiocciola *f*.

snake [sneɪk] *n (animal)* serpente *m*.

snap [snæp] ◇ *vt (break)* spezzare ◇ *vi (break)* spezzarsi ◇ *n (inf: photo)* foto *f inv*; *(Br: card game)* rubamazzo *m*.

snare [sneəʳ] *n (trap)* trappola *f*.

snatch [snætʃ] *vt* strappare.

sneakers [ˈsniːkəz] *npl (Am)* scarpe *fpl* da ginnastica.

sneeze [sniːz] ◇ *n* starnuto *m* ◇ *vi* starnutire.

sniff [snɪf] ◇ *vi* tirar su col naso ◇ *vt (smell)* annusare.

snip [snɪp] *vt* tagliare.

snob [snɒb] *n* snob *mf inv*.

snog [snɒg] *vi (Br: inf)* pomiciare.

snooker [ˈsnuːkəʳ] *n* snooker *m (specie di biliardo giocato con 22 palle)*.

snooze [snuːz] *n* pisolino *m*.

snore [snɔːʳ] *vi* russare.

snorkel [ˈsnɔːkl] *n* respiratore *m* (subacqueo).

snout [snaʊt] *n* muso *m*, grugno *m*.

snow [snəʊ] ◇ *n* neve *f* ◇ *v impers*: **it's ~ing** sta nevicando.
snowball ['snəʊbɔːl] *n* palla *f* di neve.
snowdrift ['snəʊdrɪft] *n* cumulo *m* di neve.
snowflake ['snəʊfleɪk] *n* fiocco *m* di neve.
snowman ['snəʊmæn] (*pl* **-men** [-men]) *n* pupazzo *m* di neve.
snowplough ['snəʊplaʊ] *n* spazzaneve *m inv*.
snowstorm ['snəʊstɔːm] *n* bufera *f* di neve.
snug [snʌg] *adj (person)* comodo(-a); *(place)* accogliente.
so [səʊ] ◇ *adv* 1. *(emphasizing degree)* così, talmente; **it's ~ difficult (that ...)** è così difficile (che ...).
2. *(referring back)*: **I don't think ~** credo di no; **I'm afraid ~** temo proprio di sì; **if ~** se è così, in tal caso.
3. *(also)*: **~ do I** anch'io.
4. *(in this way)* così, in questo modo.
5. *(expressing agreement)*: **~ there is** proprio così, già.
6. *(in phrases)*: **or ~** all'incirca; **~ as** per, così da; **~ that** affinché, perché.
◇ *conj* 1. *(therefore)* quindi, perciò; **nobody answered ~ we went away** non rispondeva nessuno perciò ce ne siamo andati.
2. *(summarizing)* allora; **~ what have you been up to?** allora come vanno le cose?
3. *(in phrases)*: **~ what?** *(inf)* e allora?; **~ there!** *(inf)* ecco!
soak [səʊk] ◇ *vt (leave in water)* mettere a bagno OR a mollo; *(make very wet)* impregnare, infradiciare ◇ *vi*: **to ~ through sthg** infiltrarsi in qc.
◆ **soak up** *vt sep* assorbire.
soaked [səʊkt] *adj* fradicio(-a).
soaking ['səʊkɪŋ] *adj* fradicio(-a).
soap [səʊp] *n* sapone *m*.
soap opera *n* soap opera *f inv*, telenovela *f*.
soap powder *n* detersivo *m* in polvere.
sob [sɒb] ◇ *n* singhiozzo *m* ◇ *vi* singhiozzare.
sober ['səʊbə[r]] *adj (not drunk)* sobrio(-a).
soccer ['sɒkə[r]] *n* calcio *m*.
sociable ['səʊʃəbl] *adj* socievole.
social ['səʊʃl] *adj (problem, conditions, class)* sociale.
social club *n* circolo *m* sociale.
socialist ['səʊʃəlɪst] ◇ *adj* socialista ◇ *n* socialista *mf*.
social life *n* vita *f* sociale.
social security *n* previdenza *f* sociale.
social worker *n* assistente *mf* sociale.
society [sə'saɪətɪ] *n* società *f inv*; *(organization, club)* associazione *f*, società.
sociology [ˌsəʊsɪ'ɒlədʒɪ] *n* sociologia *f*.
sock [sɒk] *n* calzino *m*.
socket ['sɒkɪt] *n (for plug)* presa *f*; *(for light bulb)* portalampada *m inv*.
sod [sɒd] *n (Br: vulg: nasty person)* stronzo *m* (-a *f*).
soda ['səʊdə] *n (soda water)* seltz *m inv*; *(Am: fizzy drink)* spuma *f*.
soda water *n* acqua *f* di seltz.
sofa ['səʊfə] *n* divano *m*, sofà *m inv*.
sofa bed *n* divano *m* letto.
soft [sɒft] *adj (bed, ground, skin)* soffice, morbido(-a); *(breeze, tap, sound)* leggero(-a).
soft cheese *n* formaggio *m* molle.
soft drink *n* analcolico *m*.
software ['sɒftweə[r]] *n* software *m inv*.
soil [sɔɪl] *n (earth)* suolo *m*.
solarium [sə'leərɪəm] *n* solarium *m inv*.

solar panel ['səʊlə-] *n* pannello *m* solare.
sold [səʊld] *pt & pp* → **sell**.
soldier ['səʊldʒə^{r}] *n* soldato *m*, militare *m*.
sold out *adj* esaurito(-a).
sole [səʊl] ◇ *adj (only)* solo(-a), unico(-a); *(exclusive)* esclusivo(-a) ◇ *n (of shoe)* suola *f*; *(of foot)* pianta *f*; *(fish: pl inv)* sogliola *f*.
solemn ['sɒləm] *adj (person)* serio(-a); *(occasion)* solenne.
solicitor [sə'lɪsɪtə^{r}] *n (Br)* = notaio *m*.
solid ['sɒlɪd] *adj* solido(-a); *(not hollow)* pieno(-a); *(gold, silver, oak)* massiccio(-a); *(uninterrupted)* ininterrotto(-a); **three hours ~** tre ore intere.
solo ['səʊləʊ] (*pl* **-s**) *n* assolo *m*; **'~ m/cs'** *(traffic sign)* 'riservato ai motocicli'.
soluble ['sɒljʊbl] *adj* solubile.
solution [sə'lu:ʃn] *n* soluzione *f*.
solve [sɒlv] *vt* risolvere.
some [sʌm] ◇ *adj* 1. *(certain amount of)*: **~ meat** della carne; **~ money** del denaro; **I had ~ difficulty getting here** ho avuto qualche difficoltà ad arrivare qui.
2. *(certain number of)*: **~ sweets** delle caramelle; **~ boys** dei ragazzi; **~ people** della gente; **I've known him for ~ years** lo conosco da anni.
3. *(not all)* certi(-e); **~ jobs are better paid than others** certi lavori sono pagati meglio di altri.
4. *(in imprecise statements)*: **she married ~ writer (or other)** ha sposato un certo scrittore; **they're staying in ~ posh hotel** stanno in un albergo di lusso.
◇ *pron* 1. *(certain amount)* un po'; **can I have ~?** me ne dai un po'?; **~ of the money** una parte dei soldi.
2. *(certain number)* alcuni(-e), certi(-e); **can I have ~?** me ne dai qualcuno?; **~ (of them) left early** alcuni (di loro) sono andati via presto.
◇ *adv (approximately)* circa; **there were ~ 7,000 people there** c'erano circa 7 000 persone.
somebody ['sʌmbədɪ] = **someone**.
somehow ['sʌmhaʊ] *adv (some way or other)* in qualche modo, in un modo o nell'altro; *(for some reason)* per qualche motivo.
someone ['sʌmwʌn] *pron* qualcuno.
someplace ['sʌmpleɪs] *(Am)* = **somewhere**.
somersault ['sʌməsɔ:lt] *n* capriola *f*, salto *m* mortale.
something ['sʌmθɪŋ] *pron* qualcosa; **it's really ~** è veramente eccezionale; **or ~** *(inf)* o qualcosa del genere; **~ like** all'incirca, pressappoco.
sometime ['sʌmtaɪm] *adv*: **~ in May** in maggio.
sometimes ['sʌmtaɪmz] *adv* a volte.
somewhere ['sʌmweə^{r}] *adv (in or to unspecified place)* da qualche parte, in qualche posto; *(approximately)* all'incirca.
son [sʌn] *n* figlio *m*.
song [sɒŋ] *n* canzone *f*.
son-in-law *n* genero *m*.
soon [su:n] *adv* presto; **how ~ can you do it?** fra quanto può farlo?; **~ as** (non) appena; **as ~ as possible** al più presto possibile; **~ after** poco dopo; **~er or later** prima o poi.
soot [sʊt] *n* fuliggine *f*.
soothe [su:ð] *vt* calmare; *(pain)* alleviare.
sophisticated [sə'fɪstɪkeɪtɪd] *adj (refined, chic)* sofisticato(-a), raffinato(-a); *(complex)* sofisticato, complesso(-a).
sorbet ['sɔ:beɪ] *n* sorbetto *m*.
sore [sɔ:^{r}] ◇ *adj (painful)* doloran-

te; *(Am: inf: angry)* incavolato(-a) ◇ *n* piaga *f*; **to have a ~ throat** avere mal di gola.

sorry ['sɒrɪ] *adj*: **I'm ~!** scusa!; **I'm ~ I'm late** scusa il ritardo; **~?** *(asking for repetition)* scusa?; **to feel ~ for sb** dispiacersi per qn; **I'm ~ you can't come** mi dispiace che tu non venga; **I'm ~ about the mess** scusa il disordine.

sort [sɔ:t] ◇ *n* tipo *m* ◇ *vt* ordinare; **~ of** *(more or less)* più o meno; **it's ~ of difficult** è piuttosto difficile.

◆ **sort out** *vt sep (classify)* ordinare; *(resolve)* chiarire.

so-so *adj & adv (inf)* così così.

soufflé ['su:fleɪ] *n* soufflé *m inv*.

sought [sɔ:t] *pt & pp* → **seek**.

soul [səʊl] *n (spirit)* anima *f*; *(soul music)* musica *f* soul.

sound [saʊnd] ◇ *n* suono *m*; *(noise)* rumore *m*; *(volume)* volume *m* ◇ *vt (horn, bell)* suonare ◇ *vi (alarm, bell, voice)* suonare; *(seem to be)* sembrare ◇ *adj (building, structure)* solido(-a); *(heart)* sano(-a); *(advice, idea)* valido(-a); **to ~ like** sembrare; *(seem to be)* sembrare, avere l'aria di.

soundproof ['saʊndpru:f] *adj* insonorizzato(-a).

soup [su:p] *n* zuppa *f*, minestra *f*.

soup spoon *n* cucchiaio *m* da minestra.

sour ['saʊə^r] *adj (taste)* aspro(-a); *(milk)* acido(-a); **to go ~** inacidire.

source [sɔ:s] *n (supply, origin)* fonte *f*; *(cause)* causa *f*; *(of river)* sorgente *f*.

sour cream *n* panna *f* acida.

south [saʊθ] ◇ *n* sud *m*, meridione *m* ◇ *adj* del sud ◇ *adv (fly, walk)* verso sud; *(be situated)* a sud; **in the ~ of England** nel sud dell'Inghilterra.

South Africa *n* il Sudafrica.

South America *n* l'America *f* del sud, il Sudamerica.

southbound ['saʊθbaʊnd] *adj* diretto(-a) a sud.

southeast [,saʊθ'i:st] *n* sud-est *m*.

southern ['sʌðən] *adj* meridionale, del sud.

South Pole *n* Polo *m* Sud.

southwards ['saʊθwədz] *adv* verso sud.

southwest [,saʊθ'west] *n* sud-ovest *m*.

souvenir [,su:və'nɪə^r] *n* souvenir *m inv*, ricordo *m*.

Soviet Union [,səʊvɪət-] *n*: **the ~** l'Unione *f* Sovietica.

sow[1] [səʊ] (*pp* **sown** [səʊn]) *vt (seeds)* seminare.

sow[2] [saʊ] *n (pig)* scrofa *f*.

soya ['sɔɪə] *n* soia *f*.

soya bean *n* seme *m* di soia.

soy sauce [,sɔɪ-] *n* salsa *f* di soia.

spa [spɑ:] *n* terme *fpl*.

space [speɪs] ◇ *n* spazio *m*; *(empty place)* posto *m*; *(room)* spazio, posto; *(period)* periodo *m* ◇ *vt* distanziare.

spaceship ['speɪsʃɪp] *n* astronave *f*.

space shuttle *n* shuttle *m inv*.

spacious ['speɪʃəs] *adj* spazioso(-a).

spade [speɪd] *n (tool)* vanga *f*, badile *m*.

◆ **spades** *npl (in cards)* picche *fpl*.

spaghetti [spə'getɪ] *n* spaghetti *mpl*.

Spain [speɪn] *n* la Spagna.

span [spæn] ◇ *pt* → **spin** ◇ *n (of time)* periodo *m*, arco *m* di tempo.

Spaniard ['spænjəd] *n* spagnolo *m* (-a *f*).

spaniel ['spænjəl] *n* spaniel *m inv*.

Spanish ['spænɪʃ] *adj* spagnolo(-a); *(language)* spagnolo *m*.

spank [spæŋk] *vt* sculacciare.

spanner ['spænə^r] *n* chiave *f (arnese)*.

spare [speə^r] ◇ *adj (kept in reserve)* di riserva; *(not in use)* in più ◇ *n* *(spare part)* ricambio *m*; *(spare wheel)* ruota *f* di scorta ◇ *vt*: **to ~ sb sthg** *(money)* dare qc a qn; **can you ~ me ten minutes?** hai dieci minuti?; **with ten minutes to ~** con dieci minuti di anticipo.

spare part *n* pezzo *m* di ricambio.

spare ribs *npl* costine *fpl* di maiale.

spare room *n* camera *f* degli ospiti.

spare time *n* tempo *m* libero.

spare wheel *n* ruota *f* di scorta.

spark [spɑːk] *n* scintilla *f*.

sparkling [ˈspɑːklɪŋ-] *adj (mineral water, soft drink)* frizzante.

sparkling wine *n* vino *m* frizzante.

spark plug *n* candela *f*.

sparrow [ˈspærəʊ] *n* passero *m*.

spat [spæt] *pt & pp* → **spit**.

speak [spiːk] (*pt* **spoke**, *pp* **spoken**) ◇ *vt (language)* parlare; *(say)* dire ◇ *vi* parlare; **who's ~ing?** *(on phone)* chi parla?; **can I ~ to Sarah? – ~ing!** *(on phone)* posso parlare con Sarah? – sono io!; **to ~ to sb about sthg** parlare a qn di qc.

◆ **speak up** *vi (more loudly)* parlare più forte.

speaker [ˈspiːkəʳ] *n (at conference)* oratore *m* (-trice *f*); *(loudspeaker, of stereo)* altoparlante *m*; **an English ~** una persona che parla inglese.

spear [spɪəʳ] *n* lancia *f*.

special [ˈspeʃl] ◇ *adj* speciale ◇ *n*: **'today's ~'** 'piatto del giorno'.

special delivery *n (Br)* = espresso *m*.

special effects *npl* effetti *mpl* speciali.

specialist [ˈspeʃəlɪst] *n (doctor)* specialista *mf*.

speciality [ˌspeʃɪˈælətɪ] *n* specialità *f inv*.

specialize [ˈspeʃəlaɪz] *vi*: **to ~ (in)** specializzarsi (in).

specially [ˈspeʃəlɪ] *adv (specifically)* specialmente; *(on purpose)* appositamente; *(particularly)* particolarmente.

special offer *n* offerta *f* speciale.

special school *n (Br)* = scuola *f* speciale.

specialty [ˈspeʃltɪ] *(Am)* = **speciality**.

species [ˈspiːʃiːz] *n* specie *f inv*.

specific [spəˈsɪfɪk] *adj (particular)* specifico(-a).

specification [ˌspesɪfɪˈkeɪʃn] *n (of machine, car)* caratteristiche *fpl* tecniche.

specimen [ˈspesɪmən] *n* (MED) campione *m*; *(example)* esemplare *m*.

specs [speks] *npl (inf)* occhiali *mpl*.

spectacle [ˈspektəkl] *n (sight)* scena *f*.

spectacles [ˈspektəklz] *npl* occhiali *mpl*.

spectacular [spekˈtækjʊləʳ] *adj* spettacolare.

spectator [spekˈteɪtəʳ] *n* spettatore *m* (-trice *f*).

sped [sped] *pt & pp* → **speed**.

speech [spiːtʃ] *n (ability to speak)* parola *f*; *(manner of speaking)* modo *m* di parlare; *(talk)* discorso *m*.

speech impediment [-ɪmˌpedɪmənt] *n* difetto *m* di pronuncia.

speed [spiːd] (*pt & pp* **-ed** OR **sped**) ◇ *n* velocità *f inv*; *(fast rate)* alta velocità; *(of film)* sensibilità *f inv*; *(bicycle gear)* marcia *f* ◇ *vi (move quickly)* andare velocemente; *(drive too fast)* andare a velocità eccessiva; **'reduce ~ now'** 'rallentare'.

◆ **speed up** *vi* accelerare.

speedboat [ˈspiːdbəʊt] *n* fuoribordo *m inv*.

speeding [ˈspiːdɪŋ] *n* eccesso *m* di velocità.

speed limit *n* limite *m* di velocità.

speedometer [spɪ'dɒmɪtəʳ] *n* tachimetro *m*.

spell [spel] (*Br pt & pp* **-ed** OR **spelt**, *Am pt & pp* **-ed**) ◇ *vt (word, name)* scrivere; *(subj: letters)* formare la parola ◇ *n (period)* periodo *m*; *(magic)* incantesimo *m*.

spelling ['spelɪŋ] *n (correct order)* ortografia *f*.

spelt [spelt] *pt & pp (Br)* → **spell**.

spend [spend] (*pt & pp* **spent** [spent]) *vt (money)* spendere; *(time)* passare.

sphere [sfɪəʳ] *n* sfera *f*.

spice [spaɪs] ◇ *n* spezia *f* ◇ *vt* condire con delle spezie.

spicy ['spaɪsɪ] *adj* piccante.

spider ['spaɪdəʳ] *n* ragno *m*.

spider's web *n* ragnatela *f*.

spike [spaɪk] *n (metal)* punta *f*.

spill [spɪl] (*Br pt & pp* **-ed** OR **spilt**, *Am pt & pp* **-ed**) ◇ *vt* versare ◇ *vi* versarsi.

spin [spɪn] (*pt* **span** OR **spun**, *pp* **spun**) ◇ *vt (wheel)* far girare; *(washing)* centrifugare ◇ *n (on ball)* effetto *m*; **to go for a ~** *(inf)* andare a fare un giro in macchina.

spinach ['spɪnɪdʒ] *n* spinaci *mpl*.

spine [spaɪn] *n* spina *f* dorsale; *(of book)* costa *f*.

spinster ['spɪnstəʳ] *n* zitella *f*.

spiral ['spaɪərəl] *n* spirale *f*.

spiral staircase *n* scala *f* a chiocciola.

spire ['spaɪəʳ] *n* guglia *f*.

spirit ['spɪrɪt] *n* spirito *m*; *(mood)* umore *m*.

◆ **spirits** *npl (Br: alcohol)* superalcolici *mpl*.

spit [spɪt] (*Br pt & pp* **spat**, *Am pt & pp* **spit**) ◇ *vi (person)* sputare; *(fire, food)* scoppiettare ◇ *n (saliva)* saliva *f*; *(for cooking)* spiedo *m* ◇ *v impers*: **it's spitting** pioviggina.

spite [spaɪt] : **in spite of** *prep* nonostante.

spiteful ['spaɪtfʊl] *adj* malevolo(-a).

splash [splæʃ] ◇ *n (sound)* tonfo *m* ◇ *vt* schizzare.

splendid ['splendɪd] *adj* splendido(-a).

splint [splɪnt] *n* stecca *f*.

splinter ['splɪntəʳ] *n* scheggia *f*.

split [splɪt] (*pt & pp* **split**) ◇ *n (tear)* strappo *m*; *(crack, in skirt)* spacco *m* ◇ *vt (wood, stone)* spaccare; *(tear)* strappare; *(bill, cost, profits, work)* dividere ◇ *vi (wood, stone)* spaccarsi; *(tear)* strapparsi.

◆ **split up** *vi (couple)* lasciarsi; *(group)* dividersi.

spoil [spɔɪl] (*pt & pp* **-ed** OR **spoilt**) *vt (ruin)* rovinare; *(child)* viziare.

spoke [spəʊk] ◇ *pt* → **speak** ◇ *n* raggio *m*.

spoken ['spəʊkn] *pp* → **speak**.

spokesman ['spəʊksmən] (*pl* **-men** [-mən]) *n* portavoce *m inv*.

spokeswoman ['spəʊks,wʊmən] (*pl* **-women** [-,wɪmɪn]) *n* portavoce *f inv*.

sponge [spʌndʒ] *n (for cleaning, washing)* spugna *f*.

sponge bag *n (Br)* nécessaire *m inv* (da viaggio).

sponge cake *n* pan *m* di Spagna.

sponsor ['spɒnsəʳ] *n (of event, TV programme)* sponsor *m inv*.

sponsored walk [,spɒnsəd-] *n* marcia *f* di beneficenza.

spontaneous [spɒn'teɪnjəs] *adj* spontaneo(-a).

spoon [spu:n] *n* cucchiaio *m*.

spoonful ['spu:nfʊl] *n* cucchiaiata *f*.

sport [spɔ:t] *n* sport *m inv*.

sports car [spɔ:ts-] *n* automobile *f* sportiva.

sports centre [spɔ:ts-] *n* centro *m* sportivo.

sports jacket [spɔ:ts-] *n* giacca *f* sportiva.

sportsman ['spɔːtsmən] (*pl* **-men** [-mən]) *n* sportivo *m*.
sports shop [spɔːts-] *n* negozio *m* di articoli sportivi.
sportswoman ['spɔːts,wʊmən] (*pl* **-women** [-,wɪmɪn]) *n* sportiva *f*.
spot [spɒt] ◇ *n (of paint, rain)* goccia *f*; *(on clothes)* macchia *f*; *(on skin)* brufolo *m*; *(place)* posto *m* ◇ *vt* notare; **on the ~** *(at once)* immediatamente; *(at the scene)* sul posto.
spotless ['spɒtlɪs] *adj* pulitissimo(-a).
spotlight ['spɒtlaɪt] *n* riflettore *m*.
spotty ['spɒtɪ] *adj* brufoloso(-a).
spouse [spaʊs] *n (fml)* coniuge *mf*.
spout [spaʊt] *n* beccuccio *m*.
sprain [spreɪn] *vt (ankle, wrist)* slogarsi.
sprang [spræŋ] *pt* → **spring**.
spray [spreɪ] ◇ *n (aerosol)* spray *m inv*; *(for perfume)* vaporizzatore *m*; *(droplets)* spruzzi *mpl* ◇ *vt* spruzzare.
spread [spred] (*pt & pp* **spread**) ◇ *vt (butter, jam, glue)* spalmare; *(map, tablecloth, blanket)* stendere; *(legs, fingers, arms)* distendere; *(disease, news, rumour)* diffondere ◇ *vi* diffondersi ◇ *n (food)* crema *f* da spalmare.
◆ **spread out** *vi (disperse)* disperdersi.
spring [sprɪŋ] (*pt* **sprang**, *pp* **sprung**) ◇ *n (season)* primavera *f*; *(coil)* molla *f*; *(in ground)* sorgente *f* ◇ *vi (leap)* balzare; **in (the) ~** in primavera.
springboard ['sprɪŋbɔːd] *n* trampolino *m*.
spring-cleaning [-'kliːnɪŋ] *n* pulizie *fpl* di Pasqua.
spring onion *n* cipollina *f*.
spring roll *n* involtino *m* primavera.
sprinkle ['sprɪŋkl] *vt*: **to ~ sthg with sugar** spolverizzare qc di zucchero; **to ~ sthg with water** spruzzare dell'acqua su qc.
sprinkler ['sprɪŋkləʳ] *n (for fire)* sprinkler *m inv*; *(for grass)* irrigatore *m*.
sprint [sprɪnt] ◇ *vi (run fast)* scattare ◇ *n (race)*: **the 100-metres ~** i 100 metri piani.
Sprinter® ['sprɪntəʳ] *n (Br: train) treno usato su brevi distanze.*
sprout [spraʊt] *n (vegetable)* cavoletto *m* di Bruxelles.
spruce [spruːs] *n* abete *m*.
sprung [sprʌŋ] ◇ *pp* → **spring** ◇ *adj (mattress)* a molle.
spud [spʌd] *n (inf)* patata *f*.
spun [spʌn] *pt & pp* → **spin**.
spur [spɜːʳ] *n (for horse rider)* sperone *m*; **on the ~ of the moment** d'impulso.
spurt [spɜːt] *vi* sprizzare.
spy [spaɪ] *n* spia *f*.
squall [skwɔːl] *n* burrasca *f*.
squalor ['skwɒləʳ] *n* squallore *m*.
square [skweəʳ] ◇ *adj (in shape)* quadrato(-a) ◇ *n (shape)* quadrato *m*; *(in town)* piazza *f*; *(on chessboard)* scacco *m*; **2 ~ metres** 2 metri quadrati; **it's 2 metres ~** misura 2 metri per 2; **we're (all) ~ now** *(not owing money)* adesso siamo pari.
squash [skwɒʃ] ◇ *n (game)* squash *m*; *(Am: vegetable)* zucca *f*; *(Br: drink)*: **orange/lemon ~** sciroppo *m* di arancia/limone ◇ *vt* schiacciare.
squat [skwɒt] ◇ *adj* tozzo(-a) ◇ *vi (crouch)* accovacciarsi.
squeak [skwiːk] *vi (door, wheel)* cigolare; *(mouse)* squittire.
squeeze [skwiːz] ◇ *vt (tube, orange)* spremere; *(hand)* stringere ◇ *vi*: **to ~ in** infilarsi.
squid [skwɪd] *n* calamaro *m*.
squint [skwɪnt] ◇ *n* strabismo *m* ◇ *vi*: **to ~ at** guardare con gli occhi socchiusi.

squirrel [*Br* 'skwɪrəl, *Am* 'skwɜː-rəl] *n* scoiattolo *m*.

squirt [skwɜːt] *vi* schizzare.

St *(abbr of Street)* V.; *(abbr of Saint)* S.

stab [stæb] *vt (with knife)* pugnalare.

stable ['steɪbl] ◇ *adj* stabile ◇ *n* stalla *f*.

stack [stæk] *n (pile)* pila *f*; **~s of** *(inf: lots)* un mucchio di.

stadium ['steɪdjəm] *n* stadio *m*.

staff [stɑːf] *n (workers)* personale *m*.

stage [steɪdʒ] *n (phase)* stadio *m*; *(in theatre)* palcoscenico *m*.

stagger ['stægəʳ] ◇ *vt (arrange in stages)* scaglionare ◇ *vi* barcollare.

stagnant ['stægnənt] *adj* stagnante.

stain [steɪn] ◇ *n* macchia *f* ◇ *vt* macchiare.

stained glass [ˌsteɪnd-] *n* vetro *m* colorato.

stainless steel ['steɪnlɪs-] *n* acciaio *m* inossidabile.

staircase ['steəkeɪs] *n* scala *f*.

stairs [steəz] *npl* scale *fpl*.

stairwell ['steəwel] *n* tromba *f* delle scale.

stake [steɪk] *n (share)* quota *f*; *(in gambling)* posta *f*; *(post)* palo *m*; **at ~** in gioco.

stale [steɪl] *adj (food)* stantio(-a).

stalk [stɔːk] *n* gambo *m*.

stall [stɔːl] ◇ *n (in market, at exhibition)* banco *m* ◇ *vi (car, engine)* spegnersi.

◆ **stalls** *npl (Br: in theatre)* platea *f*.

stamina ['stæmɪnə] *n* resistenza *f*.

stammer ['stæməʳ] *vi* balbettare.

stamp [stæmp] ◇ *n (for letter)* francobollo *m*; *(in passport, on document)* timbro *m* ◇ *vt (passport, document)* timbrare ◇ *vi*: **to ~ on sthg** pestare qc.

stamp-collecting [-kəˌlektɪŋ] *n* filatelia *f*.

stamp machine *n* distributore *m* di francobolli.

stand [stænd] (*pt & pp* **stood**) ◇ *vi (be on feet)* stare in piedi; *(be situated)* trovarsi; *(get to one's feet)* alzarsi ◇ *vt (place)* mettere; *(bear)* sopportare; *(withstand)* tollerare ◇ *n (stall)* banco *m*; *(for umbrellas)* portaombrelli *m inv*; *(for coats)* attaccapanni *m inv*; *(on bike, motorbike)* cavalletto *m*; *(at sports stadium)* tribuna *f*; **newspaper ~** edicola *f*; **to be ~ing** stare in piedi; **to ~ sb a drink** offrire da bere a qn; **'no ~ing'** *(Am:* AUT*)* 'divieto di sosta'.

◆ **stand back** *vi* tirarsi indietro.

◆ **stand for** *vt fus (mean)* stare per; *(tolerate)* tollerare.

◆ **stand in** *vi*: **to ~ in for sb** sostituire qn.

◆ **stand out** *vi* spiccare.

◆ **stand up** ◇ *vi (be on feet)* stare in piedi; *(get to one's feet)* alzarsi ◇ *vt sep (inf: boyfriend, girlfriend etc)* tirare un bidone a.

◆ **stand up for** *vt fus* difendere.

standard ['stændəd] ◇ *adj (normal)* standard *(inv)* ◇ *n (level)* livello *m*; *(norm)* standard *m inv*; **up to ~** (di livello) soddisfacente.

◆ **standards** *npl (principles)* principi *mpl*.

standard-class *adj (Br: on train)* di seconda classe.

standby ['stændbaɪ] *adj (ticket)* stand-by *(inv)*.

stank [stæŋk] *pt* → **stink**.

staple ['steɪpl] *n (for paper)* punto *m* metallico.

stapler ['steɪpləʳ] *n* cucitrice *f*.

star [stɑːʳ] ◇ *n* stella *f* ◇ *vt (subj: film, play etc)* avere come protagonista.

◆ **stars** *npl (horoscope)* oroscopo *m*.

starboard ['stɑːbəd] *adj* di tribordo.

starch ['stɑːtʃ] *n* amido *m*.

stare [steə^r] *vi*: **to ~ at** fissare.
starfish ['stɑːfɪʃ] *(pl inv) n* stella *f* marina.
starling ['stɑːlɪŋ] *n* storno *m*.
Stars and Stripes *n*: **the ~** la bandiera a stelle e strisce.
start [stɑːt] ◇ *n (beginning)* inizio *m*; *(starting place)* partenza *f* ◇ *vt* cominciare, iniziare; *(car, engine)* mettere in moto; *(company, club)* fondare ◇ *vi* cominciare; *(car, engine, on journey)* partire; **prices ~ at** OR **from £5** i prezzi partono da 5 sterline; **to ~ doing sthg** OR **to do sthg** cominciare a fare qc; **to ~ with** ... per cominciare ....
◆ **start out** *vi (on journey)* partire; *(be originally)* cominciare.
◆ **start up** *vt sep (car, engine)* mettere in moto; *(business)* intraprendere; *(shop)* aprire.
starter ['stɑːtə^r] *n (Br: of meal)* antipasto *m*; *(of car)* starter *m inv*; **for ~s** *(in meal)* per antipasto.
starter motor *n* motorino *m* di avviamento.
starting point ['stɑːtɪŋ-] *n* punto *m* di partenza.
startle ['stɑːtl] *vt* far trasalire.
starvation [stɑː'veɪʃn] *n* fame *f*.
starve [stɑːv] *vi (have no food)* morire di fame; **I'm starving!** muoio di fame!
state [steɪt] ◇ *n* stato *m* ◇ *vt (declare)* dichiarare; *(specify)* specificare; **the State** lo Stato; **the States** gli Stati Uniti.
statement ['steɪtmənt] *n (declaration)* dichiarazione *f*; *(from bank)* estratto *m* conto.
state school *n* scuola *f* statale.
statesman ['steɪtsmən] (*pl* **-men** [-mən]) *n* statista *m*.
static ['stætɪk] *n (on radio, TV)* scarica *f* (elettrostatica).
station ['steɪʃn] *n* stazione *f*.
stationary ['steɪʃnərɪ] *adj* stazionario(-a).
stationer's ['steɪʃnəz] *n (shop)* cartoleria *f*.
stationery ['steɪʃnərɪ] *n* cancelleria *f*.
station wagon *n (Am)* station wagon *f inv*.
statistics [stə'tɪstɪks] *npl (facts)* statistiche *fpl*.
statue ['stætʃuː] *n* statua *f*.
Statue of Liberty *n*: **the ~** la Statua della Libertà.
status ['steɪtəs] *n (legal position)* stato *m*; *(social position)* condizione *f* sociale; *(prestige)* prestigio *m*.
stay [steɪ] ◇ *n (time spent)* soggiorno *m* ◇ *vi (remain)* rimanere; *(as guest)* alloggiare; *(Scot: reside)* abitare; **to ~ the night** passare la notte.
◆ **stay away** *vi*: **to ~ away (from)** *(not attend)* non andare (a); *(not go near)* stare lontano (da).
◆ **stay in** *vi* rimanere a casa.
◆ **stay out** *vi (from home)* rimanere fuori.
◆ **stay up** *vi* rimanere alzato.
STD code *n* prefisso *m*.
steady ['stedɪ] ◇ *adj (not shaking, firm)* stabile; *(gradual, stable)* costante; *(job)* fisso(-a) ◇ *vt (stop from shaking)* tenere fermo.
steak [steɪk] *n (type of meat)* carne *f* di manzo; *(piece of meat)* bistecca *f*; *(piece of fish)* trancia *f*.
steak and kidney pie *n pasticcio di carne di manzo e rognone*.
steakhouse ['steɪkhaʊs, *pl* -haʊzɪz] *n* ristorante *m* specializzato in bistecche.
steal [stiːl] (*pt* **stole**, *pp* **stolen**) *vt* rubare; **to ~ sthg from sb** rubare qc a qn.
steam [stiːm] ◇ *n* vapore *m* ◇ *vt (food)* cuocere a vapore.
steamboat ['stiːmbəʊt] *n* battello *m* a vapore.
steam engine *n* locomotiva *f* a vapore.

steam iron *n* ferro *m* a vapore.
steel [sti:l] ◇ *n* acciaio *m* ◇ *adj* di acciaio.
steep [sti:p] *adj (hill, path)* ripido(-a); *(increase, drop)* notevole.
steeple ['sti:pl] *n* campanile *m*.
steer ['stɪəʳ] *vt (car, boat, plane)* condurre.
steering ['stɪərɪŋ] *n* sterzo *m*.
steering wheel *n* volante *m*.
stem [stem] *n* stelo *m*.
step [step] ◇ *n (stair)* gradino *m*; *(rung)* piolo *m*; *(pace)* passo *m*; *(measure)* misura *f*; *(stage)* mossa *f* ◇ *vi*: **to ~ on sthg** calpestare qc; **'mind the ~'** 'attenti al gradino'.
◆ **steps** *npl (stairs)* scala *f*.
◆ **step aside** *vi (move aside)* farsi da parte.
◆ **step back** *vi (move back)* tirarsi indietro.
step aerobics *n* step *m*.
stepbrother ['step,brʌðəʳ] *n* fratellastro *m*.
stepdaughter ['step,dɔ:təʳ] *n* figliastra *f*.
stepfather ['step,fɑ:ðəʳ] *n* patrigno *m*.
stepladder ['step,lædəʳ] *n* scala *f* (a pioli).
stepmother ['step,mʌðəʳ] *n* matrigna *f*.
stepsister ['step,sɪstəʳ] *n* sorellastra *f*.
stepson ['stepsʌn] *n* figliastro *m*.
stereo ['sterɪəʊ] (*pl* **-s**) ◇ *adj* stereofonico(-a) ◇ *n (hi-fi)* stereo *m inv*; *(stereo sound)* stereofonia *f*.
sterile ['steraɪl] *adj* sterile.
sterilize ['sterəlaɪz] *vt* sterilizzare.
sterling ['stɜ:lɪŋ] ◇ *adj (pound)* sterlina ◇ *n* sterlina *f*.
sterling silver *n* argento *m* di buona lega.
stern [stɜ:n] ◇ *adj* severo(-a) ◇ *n* poppa *f*.
stew [stju:] *n* stufato *m*.
steward ['stjʊəd] *n (on plane, ship)* steward *m inv*; *(at public event)* membro *m* del servizio d'ordine.
stewardess ['stjʊədɪs] *n* hostess *f inv*.
stewed [stju:d] *adj (fruit)* cotto(-a).
stick [stɪk] (*pt & pp* **stuck**) ◇ *n (of wood)* bastone *m*; *(of chalk)* pezzetto *m*; *(of celery)* costa *f* ◇ *vt (glue)* attaccare; *(push, insert)* ficcare; *(inf: put)* ficcare ◇ *vi (become attached)* attaccarsi; *(jam)* incastrarsi.
◆ **stick out** *vi (protrude)* sporgere; *(be noticeable)* saltare agli occhi.
◆ **stick to** *vt fus (decision, promise)* mantenere; *(principles)* tener fede a.
◆ **stick up** ◇ *vt sep (poster, notice)* attaccare ◇ *vi* sporgere.
◆ **stick up for** *vt fus* difendere.
sticker ['stɪkəʳ] *n* adesivo *m*.
sticking plaster ['stɪkɪŋ-] *n* cerotto *m*.
stick shift *n (Am: car)* auto *f* con cambio manuale.
sticky ['stɪkɪ] *adj (substance, hands, weather)* appiccicoso(-a); *(label, tape)* adesivo(-a).
stiff [stɪf] ◇ *adj* duro(-a); *(back, neck, person)* rigido(-a) ◇ *adv*: **to be bored ~** *(inf)* essere annoiato a morte.
stile [staɪl] *n gradini per scavalcare un recinto*.
stiletto heels [stɪ'letəʊ-] *npl* tacchi *mpl* a spillo.
still [stɪl] ◇ *adv* ancora; *(despite that)* comunque ◇ *adj (motionless)* immobile; *(quiet, calm)* calmo(-a); *(not fizzy)* non gassato(-a); **we've ~ got ten minutes** abbiamo ancora dieci minuti; **~ more** ancora di più; **to stand ~** stare fermo.
Stilton ['stɪltn] *n* stilton *m (formaggio simile al gorgonzola)*.
stimulate ['stɪmjʊleɪt] *vt (encourage)* stimolare.

sting [stɪŋ] (*pt & pp* **stung**) ◇ *vt* pungere ◇ *vi (skin, eyes)* pizzicare.
stingy [ˈstɪndʒɪ] *adj (inf)* tirchio(-a).
stink [stɪŋk] (*pt* **stank** OR **stunk**, *pp* **stunk**) *vi (smell bad)* puzzare.
stipulate [ˈstɪpjʊleɪt] *vt* stipulare.
stir [stɜːʳ] *vt* mescolare.
stir-fry ◇ *n* piatto *m* saltato ◇ *vt* saltare *(in padella)*.
stirrup [ˈstɪrəp] *n* staffa *f*.
stitch [stɪtʃ] *n (in sewing, knitting)* punto *m*; **to have a ~** *(stomach pain)* avere una fitta.
◆ **stitches** *npl (for wound)* punti *mpl*.
stock [stɒk] ◇ *n (of shop, business)* stock *m inv*; *(supply)* scorta *f*; (FIN) azioni *fpl*; *(in cooking)* brodo *m* ◇ *vt (have in stock)* avere in magazzino; **in ~** in magazzino; **out of ~** esaurito.
stock cube *n* dado *m* (per il brodo).
Stock Exchange *n* Borsa *f* valori.
stocking [ˈstɒkɪŋ] *n* calza *f*.
stock market *n* borsa *f* valori.
stodgy [ˈstɒdʒɪ] *adj (food)* pesante.
stole [stəʊl] *pt* → **steal**.
stolen [ˈstəʊln] *pp* → **steal**.
stomach [ˈstʌmək] *n (organ)* stomaco *m*; *(belly)* pancia *f*.
stomachache [ˈstʌməkeɪk] *n* mal *m* di stomaco.
stomach upset [-ˈʌpset] *n* disturbo *m* di stomaco.
stone [stəʊn] ◇ *n (substance)* pietra *f*; *(in fruit)* nocciolo *m*; *(measurement: pl inv)* = 6,35 kg; *(gem)* pietra preziosa ◇ *adj* di pietra.
stonewashed [ˈstəʊnwɒʃt] *adj* délavé *(inv)*.
stood [stʊd] *pt & pp* → **stand**.
stool [stuːl] *n (for sitting on)* sgabello *m*.
stop [stɒp] ◇ *n (for bus, train)* fermata *f*; *(in journey)* tappa *f* ◇ *vt (cause to cease)* porre fine a; *(car, machine)* fermare; *(prevent)* impedire ◇ *vi* fermarsi; **to ~ sb/sthg from doing sthg** impedire a qn/qc di fare qc; **to ~ doing sthg** smettere di fare qc; **to put a ~ to sthg** porre fine a qc; **'stop'** *(road sign)* 'stop'; **'stopping at ...'** *(train, bus)* 'ferma a ...'.
◆ **stop off** *vi* fare una sosta.
stopover [ˈstɒpˌəʊvəʳ] *n* sosta *f*.
stopper [ˈstɒpəʳ] *n* tappo *m*.
stopwatch [ˈstɒpwɒtʃ] *n* cronografo *m*.
storage [ˈstɔːrɪdʒ] *n* immagazzinaggio *m*.
store [stɔːʳ] ◇ *n (shop)* negozio *m*; *(supply)* scorta *f* ◇ *vt* immagazzinare.
storehouse [ˈstɔːhaʊs, *pl* -haʊzɪz] *n* magazzino *m*.
storeroom [ˈstɔːrʊm] *n* stanzino *m*.
storey [ˈstɔːrɪ] (*pl* **-s**) *n (Br)* piano *m*.
stork [stɔːk] *n* cicogna *f*.
storm [stɔːm] *n* tempesta *f*.
stormy [ˈstɔːmɪ] *adj (weather)* burrascoso(-a).
story [ˈstɔːrɪ] *n (account, tale)* storia *f*; *(news item)* notizia *f*; *(Am)* = **storey**.
stout [staʊt] ◇ *adj (fat)* corpulento(-a) ◇ *n (drink)* birra *f* scura.
stove [stəʊv] *n (for cooking)* cucina *f*; *(for heating)* stufa *f*.
straight [streɪt] ◇ *adj (not curved)* diritto(-a); *(hair, drink)* liscio(-a); *(consecutive)* di seguito ◇ *adv (in a straight line)* dritto; *(upright)* in posizione eretta; *(directly, without delay)* direttamente; **~ ahead** sempre diritto; **~ away** subito.
straightforward [ˌstreɪtˈfɔːwəd] *adj (easy)* semplice.
strain [streɪn] ◇ *n (force)* sforzo *m*; *(tension, nervous stress)* tensione *f*;

(injury) distorsione *f* ◇ *vt (muscle, eyes)* sforzare; *(food)* scolare; *(tea)* filtrare.

strainer [ˈstreɪnəʳ] *n* colino *m*.

strait [streɪt] *n* stretto *m*.

strange [streɪndʒ] *adj (unusual)* strano(-a); *(unfamiliar)* sconosciuto(-a).

stranger [ˈstreɪndʒəʳ] *n (unfamiliar person)* sconosciuto *m* (-a *f*); *(person from different place)* forestiero *m* (-a *f*).

strangle [ˈstræŋgl] *vt* strangolare.

strap [stræp] *n (of bag, camera)* tracolla *f*; *(of watch, shoe)* cinturino *m*; *(of dress)* bretella *f*.

strapless [ˈstræplɪs] *adj* senza spalline.

strategy [ˈstrætɪdʒɪ] *n (plan)* strategia *f*.

Stratford-upon-Avon [ˌstrætfədəpɒnˈeɪvn] *n* Stratford-upon-Avon.

straw [strɔː] *n* paglia *f*; *(for drinking)* cannuccia *f*.

strawberry [ˈstrɔːbərɪ] *n* fragola *f*.

stray [streɪ] ◇ *adj (animal)* randagio(-a) ◇ *vi* vagare.

streak [striːk] *n (stripe, mark)* striscia *f*; *(period)* periodo *m*.

stream [striːm] *n (river)* ruscello *m*; *(of traffic, people, blood)* flusso *m*.

street [striːt] *n* via *f*, strada *f*.

streetcar [ˈstriːtkɑːʳ] *n (Am)* tram *m inv*.

street light *n* lampione *m*.

street plan *n* piantina *f*.

strength [streŋθ] *n* forza *f*; *(of structure)* robustezza *f*; *(influence)* potere *m*; *(strong point)* punto *m* di forza; *(of feeling, smell)* intensità *f*; *(of drink)* gradazione *f* alcolica.

strengthen [ˈstreŋθn] *vt (structure)* rafforzare.

stress [stres] ◇ *n (tension)* stress *m inv*; *(on word, syllable)* accento *m* ◇ *vt (emphasize)* sottolineare; *(word, syllable)* accentare.

stretch [stretʃ] ◇ *n (of land, water)* distesa *f*; *(of time)* periodo *m* ◇ *vt* tendere; *(body)* stirare ◇ *vi (land, sea)* estendersi; *(person, animal)* stirarsi; **to ~ one's legs** *(fig)* sgranchirsi le gambe.

◆ **stretch out** ◇ *vt sep (hand)* tendere ◇ *vi (lie down)* distendersi.

stretcher [ˈstretʃəʳ] *n* barella *f*.

strict [strɪkt] *adj (person)* severo(-a); *(rule, instructions)* rigido(-a); *(exact)* stretto(-a).

strictly [ˈstrɪktlɪ] *adv* strettamente; **~ speaking** per essere precisi.

stride [straɪd] *n* falcata *f*.

strike [straɪk] (*pt & pp* **struck**) ◇ *n (of employees)* sciopero *m* ◇ *vt (fml: hit)* colpire; *(fml: collide with)* urtare; *(a match)* accendere ◇ *vi (refuse to work)* scioperare; *(happen suddenly)* colpire; **the clock struck eight** l'orologio ha battuto le otto.

striking [ˈstraɪkɪŋ] *adj (noticeable)* impressionante; *(attractive)* appariscente.

string [strɪŋ] *n* spago *m*; *(of pearls, beads)* filo *m*; *(of musical instrument, tennis racket)* corda *f*; *(series)* serie *f inv*; **a piece of ~** un pezzo di spago.

strip [strɪp] ◇ *n* striscia *f* ◇ *vt (paint, wallpaper)* togliere ◇ *vi (undress)* spogliarsi.

stripe [straɪp] *n* striscia *f*.

striped [straɪpt] *adj* a strisce.

strip-search *vt* perquisire (facendo spogliare).

strip show *n* spogliarello *m*.

stroke [strəʊk] ◇ *n* (MED) colpo *m*; *(in tennis)* battuta *f*; *(in golf)* tiro *m*; *(swimming style)* stile *m* ◇ *vt* accarezzare; **a ~ of luck** un colpo di fortuna.

stroll [strəʊl] *n* passeggiata *f*.

stroller [ˈstrəʊlər] *n (Am: pushchair)* passeggino *m*.

strong [strɒŋ] *adj* forte; *(structure, bridge, chair)* robusto(-a); *(feeling,* *smell)* intenso(-a).

struck [strʌk] *pt & pp* → **strike**.

structure [ˈstrʌktʃəʳ] *n* struttura *f*.

struggle [ˈstrʌgl] ◇ *n (great effort)* sforzo *m* ◇ *vi (fight)* lottare; *(in order to get free)* divincolarsi; **to ~ to do sthg** sforzarsi di fare qc.

stub [stʌb] *n (of cigarette)* mozzicone *m*; *(of cheque, ticket)* matrice *f*.

stubble [ˈstʌbl] *n (on face)* barba *f* ispida.

stubborn [ˈstʌbən] *adj (person)* ostinato(-a).

stuck [stʌk] ◇ *pt & pp* → **stick** ◇ *adj (jammed)* incastrato(-a); *(unable to continue, stranded)* bloccato(-a).

stud [stʌd] *n (on boots)* borchia *f*; *(fastener)* bottone *m* automatico; *(earring)* miniorecchino *m*.

student [ˈstjuːdnt] *n* studente *m* (-essa *f*).

student card *n* carta *f* dello studente.

students' union [ˌstjuːdnts-] *n (place)* circolo *m* studentesco.

studio [ˈstjuːdɪəʊ] (*pl* **-s**) *n* studio *m*.

studio apartment *(Am)* = **studio flat**.

studio flat *n (Br)* monolocale *m*.

study [ˈstʌdɪ] ◇ *n (learning)* studio *m* ◇ *vt & vi* studiare.

stuff [stʌf] ◇ *n (inf)* roba *f* ◇ *vt (put roughly)* ficcare; *(fill)* riempire.

stuffed [stʌft] *adj (food)* ripieno(-a); *(inf: full up)* pieno(-a); *(dead animal)* imbalsamato(-a).

stuffing [ˈstʌfɪŋ] *n (food)* ripieno *m*; *(of pillow, cushion)* imbottitura *f*.

stuffy [ˈstʌfɪ] *adj (room, atmosphere)* che sa di chiuso.

stumble [ˈstʌmbl] *vi (when walking)* inciampare.

stump [stʌmp] *n (of tree)* ceppo *m*.

stun [stʌn] *vt (shock)* sbalordire.

stung [stʌŋ] *pt & pp* → **sting**.

stunk [stʌŋk] *pt & pp* → **stink**.

stunning [ˈstʌnɪŋ] *adj (very beautiful)* favoloso(-a); *(very surprising)* sbalorditivo(-a).

stupid [ˈstjuːpɪd] *adj* stupido(-a).

sturdy [ˈstɜːdɪ] *adj* robusto(-a).

stutter [ˈstʌtəʳ] *vi* balbettare.

sty [staɪ] *n (pigsty)* porcile *m*; *(on eye)* orzaiolo *m*.

style [staɪl] ◇ *n* stile *m* ◇ *vt (hair)* acconciare.

stylish [ˈstaɪlɪʃ] *adj* elegante.

stylist [ˈstaɪlɪst] *n (hairdresser)* acconciatore *m* (-trice *f*).

sub [sʌb] *n (inf) (substitute)* riserva *f*; *(Br: subscription)* quota *f* (d'iscrizione).

subdued [səbˈdjuːd] *adj (person)* abbacchiato(-a); *(lighting, colour)* smorzato(-a).

subject [*n* ˈsʌbdʒekt, *vb* səbˈdʒekt] ◇ *n (topic)* argomento *m*; *(at school, university)* materia *f*; (GRAMM) soggetto *m*; *(fml: of country)* cittadino *m* (-a *f*) ◇ *vt*: **to ~ sb to sthg** sottoporre qn a qc; **'~ to availability'** 'fino ad esaurimento'; **they are ~ to an additional charge** sono suscettibili di soprapprezzo.

subjunctive [səbˈdʒʌŋktɪv] *n* congiuntivo *m*.

submarine [ˌsʌbməˈriːn] *n* sottomarino *m*.

submit [səbˈmɪt] ◇ *vt* presentare ◇ *vi* sottomettersi.

subordinate [səˈbɔːdɪnət] *adj* subordinato(-a).

subscribe [səbˈskraɪb] *vi (to magazine, newspaper)* abbonarsi.

subscription [səbˈskrɪpʃn] *n* abbonamento *m*.

subsequent [ˈsʌbsɪkwənt] *adj* successivo(-a).

subside [səbˈsaɪd] *vi (ground)* cedere; *(noise, feeling)* smorzarsi.

substance [ˈsʌbstəns] *n* sostanza *f*.

substantial [səbˈstænʃl] *adj (large)* sostanziale.

substitute ['sʌbstɪtju:t] *n (person)* sostituto *m* (-a *f*); *(thing)* surrogato *m*; (SPORT) riserva *f*.
subtitles ['sʌb,taɪtlz] *npl* sottotitoli *mpl*.
subtle ['sʌtl] *adj (difference, change)* sottile; *(person, plan)* astuto(-a).
subtract [səb'trækt] *vt* sottrarre.
subtraction [səb'trækʃn] *n* sottrazione *f*.
suburb ['sʌbɜ:b] *n* sobborgo *m*; **the ~s** la periferia.
subway ['sʌbweɪ] *n (Br: for pedestrians)* sottopassaggio *m*; *(Am: underground railway)* metropolitana *f*.
succeed [sək'si:d] ◇ *vi (be successful)* avere successo ◇ *vt (fml: follow)* succedere a; **to ~ in doing sthg** riuscire a fare qc.
success [sək'ses] *n* successo *m*.
successful [sək'sesfʊl] *adj (plan, attempt)* riuscito(-a); *(film, book, politician)* di successo; **to be ~** *(person)* riuscire.
succulent ['sʌkjʊlənt] *adj* succulento(-a).
such [sʌtʃ] ◇ *adj* tale ◇ *adv*: **~ a lot** così tanto; **it's ~ a lovely day** è una giornata così bella; **~ good luck** una tale fortuna; **~ a thing should never have happened** una cosa simile non sarebbe mai dovuta accadere; **~ as** come.
suck [sʌk] *vt* succhiare.
sudden ['sʌdn] *adj* improvviso(-a); **all of a ~** all'improvviso.
suddenly ['sʌdnlɪ] *adv* improvvisamente.
sue [su:] *vt* citare in giudizio.
suede [sweɪd] *n* pelle *f* scamosciata.
suffer ['sʌfə^r] ◇ *vt (defeat, injury)* subire ◇ *vi* soffrire; **to ~ from** *(illness)* soffrire di.
suffering ['sʌfrɪŋ] *n* sofferenza *f*.
sufficient [sə'fɪʃnt] *adj (fml)* sufficiente.
sufficiently [sə'fɪʃntlɪ] *adv (fml)* sufficientemente.
suffix ['sʌfɪks] *n* suffisso *m*.
suffocate ['sʌfəkeɪt] *vi* soffocare.
sugar ['ʃʊgə^r] *n* zucchero *m*.
suggest [sə'dʒest] *vt* suggerire; **to ~ doing sthg** suggerire di fare qc.
suggestion [sə'dʒestʃn] *n (proposal)* suggerimento *m*; *(hint)* accenno *m*.
suicide ['sʊɪsaɪd] *n* suicidio *m*; **to commit ~** suicidarsi.
suit [su:t] ◇ *n (for man)* vestito *m*; *(for woman)* tailleur *m inv*; *(in cards)* seme *m*; (JUR) causa *f* ◇ *vt (subj: clothes, colour, shoes)* star bene a; *(be convenient for)* andare bene a; *(be appropriate for)* addirsi a; **to be ~ed to** essere adatto a.
suitable ['su:təbl] *adj* adatto(-a); **to be ~ for** essere adatto a.
suitcase ['su:tkeɪs] *n* valigia *f*.
suite [swi:t] *n (set of rooms)* suite *f inv*; *(furniture)*: **a three-piece ~** un divano e due poltrone (coordinati).
sulk [sʌlk] *vi* mettere il broncio.
sultana [səl'tɑ:nə] *n (Br)* uva *f* sultanina.
sultry ['sʌltrɪ] *adj (weather, climate)* caldo umido (caldo umida).
sum [sʌm] *n* somma *f*.
◆ **sum up** *vt sep* riassumere.
summarize ['sʌməraɪz] *vt* riassumere.
summary ['sʌmərɪ] *n* riassunto *m*.
summer ['sʌmə^r] *n* estate *f*; **in (the) ~** d'estate; **~ holidays** vacanze *fpl* estive.
summertime ['sʌmətaɪm] *n* estate *f*.
summit ['sʌmɪt] *n (of mountain)* cima *f*; *(meeting)* summit *m inv*.
summon ['sʌmən] *vt (send for)* convocare; (JUR) citare.
sumptuous ['sʌmptʃʊəs] *adj* sontuoso(-a).
sun [sʌn] ◇ *n* sole *m* ◇ *vt*: **to ~ o.s.**

prendere il sole; **to catch the ~** prendere il sole; **in the ~** al sole; **out of the ~** al riparo dal sole.
Sun. *(abbr of Sunday)* dom.
sunbathe ['sʌnbeɪð] *vi* prendere il sole.
sunbed ['sʌnbed] *n* lettino *m*.
sun block *n* crema *f* solare a protezione totale.
sunburn ['sʌnbɜːn] *n* scottatura *f*.
sunburnt ['sʌnbɜːnt] *adj* scottato(-a).
sundae ['sʌndeɪ] *n gelato guarnito con frutta o cioccolato, nocciole e panna montata.*
Sunday ['sʌndɪ] *n* domenica *f*, → **Saturday**.
Sunday school *n* = scuola *f* di catechismo.
sundress ['sʌndres] *n* prendisole *m inv*.
sundries ['sʌndrɪz] *npl (on bill)* varie *fpl*.
sunflower ['sʌnˌflaʊəʳ] *n* girasole *m*.
sunflower oil *n* olio *m* di semi di girasole.
sung [sʌŋ] *pt* → **sing**.
sunglasses ['sʌnˌglɑːsɪz] *npl* occhiali *mpl* da sole.
sunhat ['sʌnhæt] *n* cappello *m (per il sole)*.
sunk [sʌŋk] *pp* → **sink**.
sunlight ['sʌnlaɪt] *n* luce *f* del sole.
sun lounger [-ˌlaʊndʒəʳ] *n (chair)* lettino *m*.
sunny ['sʌnɪ] *adj (day)* di sole; *(weather)* bello(-a); *(room, place)* soleggiato(-a); **it's ~** c'è il sole.
sunrise ['sʌnraɪz] *n* alba *f*.
sunroof ['sʌnruːf] *n* tettuccio *m* apribile.
sunset ['sʌnset] *n* tramonto *m*.
sunshine ['sʌnʃaɪn] *n* luce *f* del sole; **in the ~** al sole.
sunstroke ['sʌnstrəʊk] *n* insolazione *f*.
suntan ['sʌntæn] *n* abbronzatura *f*.
suntan cream *n* crema *f* abbronzante.
suntan lotion *n* lozione *f* abbronzante.
super ['suːpəʳ] ◇ *adj* fantastico(-a) ◇ *n (petrol)* super *f inv*.
superb [suː'pɜːb] *adj* splendido(-a).
superficial [ˌsuːpə'fɪʃl] *adj* superficiale.
superfluous [suː'pɜːflʊəs] *adj* superfluo(-a).
Superglue® ['suːpəgluː] *n* colla *f* a presa rapida.
superior [suː'pɪərɪəʳ] ◇ *adj* superiore ◇ *n* superiore *mf*.
supermarket ['suːpəˌmɑːkɪt] *n* supermercato *m*.
supernatural [ˌsuːpə'nætʃrəl] *adj* soprannaturale.
Super Saver® *n (Br: rail ticket) biglietto ferroviario a tariffa ridotta, con condizioni particolari.*
superstitious [ˌsuːpə'stɪʃəs] *adj* superstizioso(-a).
superstore ['suːpəstɔːʳ] *n* grande supermercato *m*.
supervise ['suːpəvaɪz] *vt* sorvegliare.
supervisor ['suːpəvaɪzəʳ] *n (of workers)* sovrintendente *mf*.
supper ['sʌpəʳ] *n (evening meal)* cena *f*; *(before bed)* spuntino *m*.
supple ['sʌpl] *adj* agile.
supplement [*n* 'sʌplɪmənt, *vb* 'sʌplɪment] ◇ *n* supplemento *m*; *(of diet)* integratore *m* alimentare ◇ *vt* integrare.
supplementary [ˌsʌplɪ'mentərɪ] *adj* supplementare.
supply [sə'plaɪ] ◇ *n (store)* scorta *f*; *(providing)* approvvigionamento *m*; *(of electricity, gas etc)* erogazione *f* ◇ *vt* fornire; **to ~ sb with sthg** fornire qc a qn.
◆ **supplies** *npl* scorte *fpl*.
support [sə'pɔːt] ◇ *n (for cause,*

candidate) appoggio *m*; *(object, encouragement)* sostegno *m* ◇ *vt (cause, campaign, person)* appoggiare; (SPORT) tifare per; *(hold up)* sostenere; *(financially)* mantenere.
supporter [sə'pɔ:tə^r] *n* (SPORT) tifoso *m* (-a *f*); *(of cause, political party)* sostenitore *m* (-trice *f*).
suppose [sə'pəʊz] ◇ *vt (assume)* immaginare; *(think)* credere ◇ *conj* = **supposing**; **I ~ so** penso di sì; **you were ~d to be home at six o'clock** dovevate essere a casa alle sei; **it's ~d to be the best** è ritenuto il migliore.
supposing [sə'pəʊzɪŋ] *conj* supponendo che.
supreme [sʊ'pri:m] *adj* eccezionale.
surcharge ['sɜ:tʃɑ:dʒ] *n* sovrapprezzo *m*.
sure [ʃʊə^r] ◇ *adj* sicuro(-a) ◇ *adv (inf: yes)* certo!; *(Am: inf: certainly)* certamente; **to be ~ of o.s.** essere sicuro di sé; **to make ~ that** ... assicurarsi che ...; **for ~** di sicuro.
surely ['ʃʊəlɪ] *adv* sicuramente.
surf [sɜ:f] ◇ *n (foam)* spuma *f* ◇ *vi* fare surf.
surface ['sɜ:fɪs] *n* superficie *f*.
surface area *n* superficie *f* (esterna).
surface mail *n* posta *f* ordinaria.
surfboard ['sɜ:fbɔ:d] *n* tavola *f* da surf.
surfing ['sɜ:fɪŋ] *n* surf *m*; **to go ~** andare a fare surf.
surgeon ['sɜ:dʒən] *n* chirurgo *m*.
surgery ['sɜ:dʒərɪ] *n (treatment)* chirurgia *f*; *(Br: building)* ambulatorio *m*; *(Br: period)* orario *m* d'ambulatorio.
surname ['sɜ:neɪm] *n* cognome *m*.
surplus ['sɜ:pləs] *n* eccedenza *f*.
surprise [sə'praɪz] ◇ *n* sorpresa *f* ◇ *vt* sorprendere.
surprised [sə'praɪzd] *adj* sorpreso(-a).
surprising [sə'praɪzɪŋ] *adj* sorprendente.
surrender [sə'rendə^r] ◇ *vi* arrendersi ◇ *vt (fml: hand over)* consegnare.
surround [sə'raʊnd] *vt* circondare.
surrounding [sə'raʊndɪŋ] *adj* circostante.
◆ **surroundings** *npl* dintorni *mpl*.
survey ['sɜ:veɪ] *n (investigation)* studio *m*; *(poll)* sondaggio *m*; *(of land)* rilevamento *m* (topografico); *(Br: of house)* sopralluogo *m*.
surveyor [sə'veɪə^r] *n (Br: of houses)* perito *m*; *(of land)* agrimensore *m*.
survival [sə'vaɪvl] *n* sopravvivenza *f*.
survive [sə'vaɪv] ◇ *vi* sopravvivere ◇ *vt* sopravvivere a.
survivor [sə'vaɪvə^r] *n* sopravvissuto *m* (-a *f*).
suspect [*vb* sə'spekt, *n & adj* 'sʌspekt] ◇ *vt* sospettare ◇ *n* sospetto *m* ◇ *adj* sospetto(-a); **to ~ sb of sthg** sospettare qn di qc.
suspend [sə'spend] *vt* sospendere.
suspender belt [sə'spendə-] *n* reggicalze *m inv*.
suspenders [sə'spendəz] *npl (Br: for stockings)* giarrettiere *fpl*; *(Am: for trousers)* bretelle *fpl*.
suspense [sə'spens] *n* suspense *f*.
suspension [sə'spenʃn] *n* sospensione *f*.
suspicion [sə'spɪʃn] *n (mistrust, idea)* sospetto *m*; *(trace)* accenno *m*.
suspicious [sə'spɪʃəs] *adj (behaviour, situation)* sospetto(-a); **to be ~ of** *(distrustful)* sospettare di.
swallow ['swɒləʊ] ◇ *n (bird)* rondine *f* ◇ *vt & vi* ingoiare.
swam [swæm] *pt* → **swim**.
swamp [swɒmp] *n* palude *f*.
swan [swɒn] *n* cigno *m*.
swap [swɒp] *vt (possessions,*

places) scambiare; *(ideas, stories)* scambiarsi; **to ~ sthg for sthg** scambiare qc con qc.

swarm [swɔːm] *n (of bees)* sciame *m*.

swear [sweəʳ] (*pt* **swore**, *pp* **sworn**) ◇ *vi (use rude language)* imprecare; *(promise)* giurare ◇ *vt*: **to ~ to do sthg** promettere di fare qc.

swearword [ˈsweəwɜːd] *n* parolaccia *f*.

sweat [swet] ◇ *n* sudore *m* ◇ *vi* sudare.

sweater [ˈswetəʳ] *n* maglione *m*.

sweatshirt [ˈswetʃɜːt] *n* felpa *f*.

swede [swiːd] *n (Br)* rapa *f* svedese.

Swede [swiːd] *n* svedese *mf*.

Sweden [ˈswiːdn] *n* la Svezia.

Swedish [ˈswiːdɪʃ] ◇ *adj* svedese ◇ *n (language)* svedese *m* ◇ *npl*: **the ~** gli svedesi.

sweep [swiːp] (*pt & pp* **swept**) *vt (with brush, broom)* scopare.

sweet [swiːt] ◇ *adj* dolce; *(kind)* gentile, carino(-a) ◇ *n (Br) (candy)* caramella *f*; *(dessert)* dolce *m*.

sweet-and-sour *adj (pork)* in agrodolce; *(sauce)* agrodolce.

sweet corn *n* granturco *m*.

sweetener [ˈswiːtnəʳ] *n (for drink)* dolcificante *m*.

sweet potato *n* patata *f* americana.

sweet shop *n (Br)* negozio *m* di dolciumi.

swell [swel] (*pp* **swollen**) *vi (ankle, arm etc)* gonfiarsi.

swelling [ˈswelɪŋ] *n* gonfiore *m*.

swept [swept] *pt & pp* → **sweep**.

swerve [swɜːv] *vi (vehicle)* sterzare.

swig [swɪg] *n (inf)* sorsata *f*.

swim [swɪm] (*pt* **swam**, *pp* **swum**) ◇ *n* nuotata *f*, bagno *m* ◇ *vi (in water)* nuotare; **to go for a ~** andare a fare il bagno.

swimmer [ˈswɪməʳ] *n* nuotatore *m* (-trice *f*).

swimming [ˈswɪmɪŋ] *n* nuoto *m*; **to go ~** andare in piscina.

swimming baths *npl (Br)* piscina *f* coperta.

swimming cap *n* cuffia *f*.

swimming costume *n (Br)* costume *m* da bagno.

swimming pool *n* piscina *f*.

swimming trunks *npl* costume *m* da bagno *(da uomo)*.

swimsuit [ˈswɪmsuːt] *n* costume *m* da bagno.

swindle [ˈswɪndl] *n* truffa *f*.

swing [swɪŋ] (*pt & pp* **swung**) ◇ *n (for children)* altalena *f* ◇ *vt & vi (from side to side)* dondolare.

swipe [swaɪp] *vt (credit card etc)* far passare nel lettore magnetico.

Swiss [swɪs] ◇ *adj* svizzero(-a) ◇ *n (person)* svizzero *m* (-a *f*) ◇ *npl*: **the ~** gli svizzeri.

Swiss cheese *n* formaggio *m* svizzero.

swiss roll *n rotolo di pan di Spagna farcito di marmellata.*

switch [swɪtʃ] ◇ *n (for light, power, television set)* interruttore *m* ◇ *vt (change)* cambiare; *(exchange)* scambiare ◇ *vi* cambiare.

◆ **switch off** *vt sep* spegnere.

◆ **switch on** *vt sep* accendere.

switchboard [ˈswɪtʃbɔːd] *n* centralino *m*.

Switzerland [ˈswɪtsələnd] *n* la Svizzera.

swivel [ˈswɪvl] *vi* girarsi.

swollen [ˈswəʊln] ◇ *pp* → **swell** ◇ *adj (ankle, arm etc)* gonfio(-a).

swop [swɒp] = **swap**.

sword [sɔːd] *n* spada *f*.

swordfish [ˈsɔːdfɪʃ] *(pl inv) n* pesce *m* spada.

swore [swɔːʳ] *pt* → **swear**.

sworn [swɔːn] *pp* → **swear**.

swum [swʌm] *pp* → **swim**.

swung [swʌŋ] *pt & pp* → **swing**.
syllable ['sɪləbl] *n* sillaba *f*.
syllabus ['sɪləbəs] *n* programma *m*.
symbol ['sɪmbl] *n* simbolo *m*.
sympathetic [ˌsɪmpə'θetɪk] *adj (understanding)* comprensivo(-a).
sympathize ['sɪmpəθaɪz] *vi*: **to ~ (with)** *(feel sorry)* provare compassione (per); *(understand)* capire.
sympathy ['sɪmpəθɪ] *n (understanding)* comprensione *f*.
symphony ['simfənɪ] *n* sinfonia *f*.
symptom ['sɪmptəm] *n* sintomo *m*.
synagogue ['sɪnəgɒg] *n* sinagoga *f*.
synthesizer ['sɪnθəsaɪzə[r]] *n* sintetizzatore *m*.
synthetic [sɪn'θetɪk] *adj* sintetico(-a).
syringe [sɪ'rɪndʒ] *n* siringa *f*.
syrup ['sɪrəp] *n (for fruit etc)* sciroppo *m*.
system ['sɪstəm] *n* sistema *m*; *(hi-fi, computer, for heating etc)* impianto *m*.

T

ta [tɑː] *excl (Br: inf)* grazie!
tab [tæb] *n (of cloth, paper etc)* etichetta *f*; *(bill)* conto *m*; **put it on my ~** lo metta sul mio conto.
table ['teɪbl] *n (piece of furniture)* tavolo *m*; *(of figures etc)* tavola *f*.
tablecloth ['teɪblklɒθ] *n* tovaglia *f*.
tablemat ['teɪblmæt] *n* sottopiatto *m*.
tablespoon ['teɪblspuːn] *n* cucchiaio *m* da tavola.
tablet ['tæblɪt] *n (pill)* compressa *f*; *(of chocolate)* tavoletta *f*; **~ of soap** saponetta *f*.
table tennis *n* ping-pong® *m*.
table wine *n* vino *m* da tavola.
tabloid ['tæblɔɪd] *n* tabloid *m inv*.
tack [tæk] *n (nail)* puntina *f*.
tackle ['tækl] ◇ *n (in football)* tackle *m*; *(in rugby)* placcaggio *m*; *(for fishing)* attrezzatura *f* ◇ *vt (in football)* contrastare; *(in rugby)* placcare; *(deal with)* affrontare.
tacky ['tækɪ] *adj (inf: jewellery, design etc)* pacchiano(-a).
taco ['tækəʊ] (*pl* **-s**) *n* taco *m* *(schiacciatina a base di farina di granturco farcita di carne o fagioli, tipica della cucina messicana)*.
tact [tækt] *n* tatto *m*.
tactful ['tæktfʊl] *adj* discreto(-a).
tactics ['tæktɪks] *npl* tattica *f*.
tag [tæg] *n (label)* etichetta *f*.
tagliatelle [ˌtægljə'telɪ] *n* tagliatelle *fpl*.
tail [teɪl] *n* coda *f*.
◆ **tails** ◇ *n (of coin)* croce *f* ◇ *npl (formal dress)* frac *m inv*.
tailgate ['teɪlgeɪt] *n (of car)* portellone *m*.
tailor ['teɪlə^r] *n* sarto *m*.
Taiwan [ˌtaɪ'wɑːn] *n* Taiwan *f*.
take [teɪk] (*pt* **took**, *pp* **taken**) *vt*
1. *(gen)* prendere.
2. *(carry, drive)* portare.
3. *(do, make)* fare; **to ~ a bath/shower** fare un bagno/una doccia; **to ~ an exam** fare OR dare un esame; **to ~ a decision** prendere una decisione.
4. *(time, effort)* volerci, richiedere; **how long will it ~?** quanto ci vorrà?; **it won't ~ long** non ci vorrà molto tempo.
5. *(size in clothes, shoes)* portare, avere; **what size do you ~?** *(clothes)* che taglia porta?; *(shoes)* che misura porta?
6. *(subtract)* sottrarre, togliere.
7. *(accept)* accettare; **do you ~ traveller's cheques?** accettate traveller's cheques?; **to ~ sb's advice** seguire il consiglio di qn.
8. *(contain)* contenere.
9. *(control, power)* assumere; **to ~ charge of** assumere la direzione di.

10. *(tolerate)* sopportare.
11. *(assume)*: **I ~ it that ...** suppongo che ...
12. *(rent)* prendere in affitto.
◆ **take apart** *vt sep (dismantle)* smontare.
◆ **take away** *vt sep (remove)* portare via; *(subtract)* togliere.
◆ **take back** *vt sep (return)* riportare; *(statement)* ritrattare.
◆ **take down** *vt sep (picture, decorations)* togliere.
◆ **take in** *vt sep (include)* includere; *(understand)* capire; *(deceive)* abbindolare; *(clothes)* restringere.
◆ **take off** ◇ *vi (plane)* decollare ◇ *vt sep (remove)* togliere; *(as holiday)*: **to ~ a week off** prendere una settimana di ferie.
◆ **take out** *vt sep (from container, pocket)* tirare fuori; *(loan, insurance policy)* ottenere; *(go out with)* portare fuori.
◆ **take over** *vi* assumere il comando; **to ~ over from sb** prendere le consegne da qn.
◆ **take up** *vt sep (begin)* dedicarsi a; *(use up)* prendere; *(trousers, dress)* accorciare.

takeaway ['teɪkə,weɪ] *n (Br) (shop) locale che prepara piatti pronti da asporto*; *(food)* cibo *m* da asporto.
taken ['teɪkn] *pp* → **take**.
takeoff ['teɪkɒf] *n (of plane)* decollo *m*.
takeout ['teɪkaʊt] *(Am)* = **takeaway**.
takings ['teɪkɪŋz] *npl* incasso *m*
talcum powder ['tælkəm-] *n* borotalco® *m*.
tale [teɪl] *n (story)* storia *f*; *(account)* racconto *m*.
talent ['tælənt] *n* talento *m*.
talk [tɔ:k] ◇ *n (conversation)* conversazione *f*; *(speech)* discorso *m* ◇ *vi* parlare; **to ~ to sb (about sthg)** parlare con qn (di qc); **to ~ with sb** parlare con qn.
◆ **talks** *npl* negoziati *mpl*.
talkative ['tɔ:kətɪv] *adj* loquace.
tall [tɔ:l] *adj* alto(-a); **how ~ are you?** quanto sei alto?; **I'm five and a half feet ~** sono alto un metro e 65.
tame [teɪm] *adj (animal)* addomesticato(-a).
tampon ['tæmpɒn] *n* tampone *m*.
tan [tæn] ◇ *n (suntan)* abbronzatura *f* ◇ *vi* abbronzarsi ◇ *adj (colour)* marrone chiaro *(inv)*.
tangerine [,tændʒə'ri:n] *n (fruit)* mandarino *m*.
tank [tæŋk] *n (container)* serbatoio *m*; *(vehicle)* carro *m* armato.
tanker ['tæŋkə^r] *n (truck)* autocisterna *f*.
tanned [tænd] *adj (suntanned)* abbronzato(-a).
tap [tæp] ◇ *n (for water)* rubinetto *m* ◇ *vt (hit)* dare un colpetto a.
tape [teɪp] ◇ *n (cassette, video)* cassetta *f*; *(in cassette)* nastro *m*; *(adhesive material)* nastro *m* adesivo; *(strip of material)* fettuccia *f* ◇ *vt (record)* registrare; *(stick)* attaccare con nastro adesivo.
tape measure *n* metro *m*.
tape recorder *n* registratore *m*.
tapestry ['tæpɪstrɪ] *n* arazzo *m*.
tap water *n* acqua *f* di rubinetto.
tar [tɑ:^r] *n (for roads)* catrame *m*; *(in cigarettes)* condensato *m*.
target ['tɑ:gɪt] *n* bersaglio *m*.
tariff ['tærɪf] *n (price list)* tariffario *m*; *(Br: menu)* listino *m* prezzi; *(at customs)* tariffa *f* doganale.
tarmac ['tɑ:mæk] *n (at airport)* pista *f*.
◆ **Tarmac®** *n (on road)* asfalto *m*.
tarpaulin [tɑ:'pɔ:lɪn] *n* telone *m*.
tart [tɑ:t] *n (sweet)* crostata *f*.
tartan ['tɑ:tn] *n (design)* scozzese *m*; *(cloth)* tartan *m*.
tartare sauce [,tɑ:tə-] *n* salsa *f* tartara.

task [tɑːsk] *n* compito *m*.

taste [teɪst] ◇ *n* gusto *m*; *(flavour)* gusto, sapore *m* ◇ *vt (sample)* assaggiare; *(detect)* sentire il gusto di ◇ *vi*: **to ~ of sthg** sapere di qc; **it ~s bad** ha un cattivo sapore; **it ~s good** ha un buon sapore; **to have a ~ of sthg** *(food, drink)* assaggiare qc; *(fig: experience)* provare qc; **bad ~** cattivo gusto; **good ~** buon gusto.

tasteful ['teɪstfʊl] *adj* di buon gusto.

tasteless ['teɪstlɪs] *adj (food)* insipido(-a); *(comment, decoration)* di cattivo gusto.

tasty ['teɪstɪ] *adj* gustoso(-a).

tattoo [tə'tuː] (*pl* **-s**) *n (on skin)* tatuaggio *m*; *(military display)* parata *f*.

taught [tɔːt] *pt & pp* → **teach**.

Taurus ['tɔːrəs] *n* Toro *m*.

taut [tɔːt] *adj* teso(-a).

tax [tæks] ◇ *n (on income)* imposta *f*, tasse *fpl*; *(on import, goods)* tassa *f* ◇ *vt (goods, person)* tassare.

tax disc *n (Br)* = bollo *m*.

tax-free *adj* esentasse *(inv)*.

taxi ['tæksɪ] ◇ *n* taxi *m inv* ◇ *vi (plane)* rullare.

taxi driver *n* tassista *mf*.

taxi rank *n (Br)* posteggio *m* dei taxi.

taxi stand *(Am)* = **taxi rank**.

T-bone steak *n* costata *f* alla fiorentina.

tea [tiː] *n* tè *m inv*; *(evening meal)* cena *f*.

tea bag *n* bustina *f* di tè.

teacake ['tiːkeɪk] *n panino dolce all'uvetta*.

teach [tiːtʃ] (*pt & pp* **taught**) ◇ *vt (subject)* insegnare; *(person)* insegnare a ◇ *vi* insegnare; **to ~ sb sthg, to ~ sthg to sb** insegnare qc a qn; **to ~ sb (how) to do sthg** insegnare a qn a fare qc.

teacher ['tiːtʃə^r] *n* insegnante *mf*; *(in primary school)* maestro *m* (-a *f*); *(in secondary school)* professore *m* (-essa *f*).

teaching ['tiːtʃɪŋ] *n* insegnamento *m*.

tea cloth = **tea towel**.

teacup ['tiːkʌp] *n* tazza *f* da tè.

team [tiːm] *n* squadra *f*.

teapot ['tiːpɒt] *n* teiera *f*.

tear¹ [teə^r] (*pt* **tore**, *pp* **torn**) ◇ *vt (rip)* strappare ◇ *vi (rip)* strapparsi; *(move quickly)* precipitarsi ◇ *n (rip)* strappo *m*.

◆ **tear up** *vt sep* strappare.

tear² [tɪə^r] *n* lacrima *f*.

tearoom ['tiːrʊm] *n* sala *f* da tè.

tease [tiːz] *vt* prendere in giro.

tea set *n* servizio *m* da tè.

teaspoon ['tiːspuːn] *n* cucchiaino *m*.

teaspoonful ['tiːspuːnˌfʊl] *n* cucchiaino *m*.

teat [tiːt] *n (of animal)* capezzolo *m*; *(Br: of bottle)* tettarella *f*.

teatime ['tiːtaɪm] *n* ora *f* del tè.

tea towel *n* strofinaccio *m*.

technical ['teknɪkl] *adj* tecnico(-a).

technical drawing *n* disegno *m* tecnico.

technicality [ˌteknɪ'kælətɪ] *n (detail)* dettaglio *m* tecnico.

technician [tek'nɪʃn] *n* tecnico *m* (-a *f*).

technique [tek'niːk] *n* tecnica *f*.

technological [ˌteknə'lɒdʒɪkl] *adj* tecnologico(-a).

technology [tek'nɒlədʒɪ] *n* tecnologia *f*.

teddy (bear) ['tedɪ-] *n* orsacchiotto *m*.

tedious ['tiːdjəs] *adj* noioso(-a).

tee [tiː] *n* tee *m inv*.

teenager ['tiːnˌeɪdʒə^r] *n* adolescente *mf*.

teeth [tiːθ] *pl* → **tooth**.

teethe [tiːð] *vi*: **to be teething** mettere i denti.

teetotal [tiːˈtəʊtl] *adj* astemio(-a).
telegram [ˈtelɪgræm] *n* telegramma *m*.
telegraph [ˈtelɪgrɑːf] ◇ *n* telegrafo *m* ◇ *vt* telegrafare.
telegraph pole *n* palo *m* del telegrafo.
telephone [ˈtelɪfəʊn] ◇ *n* telefono *m* ◇ *vt (person)* telefonare a ◇ *vi* telefonare; **to be on the ~** *(talking)* essere al telefono; *(connected)* avere il telefono.
telephone booth *n* cabina *f* telefonica.
telephone box *n* cabina *f* telefonica.
telephone call *n* telefonata *f*.
telephone directory *n* elenco *m* telefonico.
telephone number *n* numero *m* di telefono.
telephonist [tɪˈlefənɪst] *n (Br)* centralinista *mf*.
telephoto lens [ˌtelɪˈfəʊtəʊ-] *n* teleobiettivo *m*.
telescope [ˈtelɪskəʊp] *n* telescopio *m*.
television [ˈtelɪˌvɪʒn] *n* televisione *f*; *(set)* televisore *m*; **on (the) ~** *(broadcast)* alla televisione.
telex [ˈteleks] *n* telex *m inv*.
tell [tel] (*pt & pp* **told**) ◇ *vt* dire; *(story, joke)* raccontare; *(distinguish)* distinguere ◇ *vi*: **I can ~** si vede; **can you ~ me the time?** sa dirmi l'ora?; **to ~ sb sthg** dire qc a qn; **to ~ sb about sthg** raccontare qc a qn; **to ~ sb how to do sthg** dire a qn come fare qc; **to ~ sb to do sthg** dire a qn di fare qc.
◆ **tell off** *vt sep* rimproverare.
teller [ˈteləʳ] *n (in bank)* cassiere *m* (-a *f*).
telly [ˈtelɪ] *n (Br: inf)* tele *f*.
temp [temp] ◇ *n* impiegato *m* straordinario (impiegata *f* straordinaria) ◇ *vi* avere un impiego temporaneo.
temper [ˈtempəʳ] *n (character)* carattere *m*; **to be in a ~** essere in collera; **to lose one's ~** andare in collera.
temperature [ˈtemprətʃəʳ] *n* temperatura *f*; **to have a ~** avere la febbre.
temple [ˈtempl] *n (building)* tempio *m*; *(of forehead)* tempia *f*.
temporary [ˈtempərərɪ] *adj* temporaneo(-a).
tempt [tempt] *vt* tentare; **to be ~ed to do sthg** essere tentato di fare qc.
temptation [tempˈteɪʃn] *n* tentazione *f*.
tempting [ˈtemptɪŋ] *adj* allettante.
ten [ten] *num* dieci, → **six**.
tenant [ˈtenənt] *n* inquilino *m* (-a *f*).
tend [tend] *vi*: **to ~ to do sthg** tendere a fare qc.
tendency [ˈtendənsɪ] *n* tendenza *f*.
tender [ˈtendəʳ] ◇ *adj* tenero(-a); *(sore)* dolorante ◇ *vt (fml: pay)* presentare.
tendon [ˈtendən] *n* tendine *m*.
tenement [ˈtenəmənt] *n* caseggiato *m*.
tennis [ˈtenɪs] *n* tennis *m*.
tennis ball *n* palla *f* da tennis.
tennis court *n* campo *m* da tennis.
tennis racket *n* racchetta *f* da tennis.
tenpin bowling [ˈtenpɪn-] *n (Br)* bowling *m*.
tenpins [ˈtenpɪnz] *(Am)* = **tenpin bowling**.
tense [tens] ◇ *adj* teso(-a) ◇ *n* (GRAMM) tempo *m*.
tension [ˈtenʃn] *n* tensione *f*.
tent [tent] *n* tenda *f*.
tenth [tenθ] *num* decimo(-a), → **sixth**.

tent peg *n* picchetto *m* da tenda.

tepid ['tepɪd] *adj (water)* tiepido(-a).

tequila [tɪ'kiːlə] *n* tequila *f*.

term [tɜːm] *n (word, expression)* termine *m*; *(at school, university)* trimestre *m*; **in the long ~** a lungo andare; **in the short ~** a breve scadenza; **in ~s of** per quanto riguarda; **in business ~s** dal punto di vista commerciale.

◆ **terms** *npl (price, of contract)* condizioni *fpl*.

terminal ['tɜːmɪnl] ◇ *adj (illness)* terminale ◇ *n (for buses)* capolinea *m*; *(at airport)* terminal *m inv*; (COMPUT) terminale *m*.

terminate ['tɜːmɪneɪt] *vi (train, bus)* fare capolinea.

terminus ['tɜːmɪnəs] *n (of buses)* capolinea *m*; *(of trains)* stazione *f* terminale.

terrace ['terəs] *n (patio)* terrazza *f*; **the ~s** *(at football ground)* le gradinate.

terraced house ['terəst-] *n (Br)* casa *f* a schiera.

terrible ['terəbl] *adj* terribile; *(very ill)*: **to feel ~** stare malissimo.

terribly ['terəblɪ] *adv (extremely)* terribilmente; *(very badly)* malissimo.

terrier ['terɪə^r] *n* terrier *m inv*.

terrific [tə'rɪfɪk] *adj (inf) (very good)* fantastico(-a); *(very great)* grande.

terrified ['terɪfaɪd] *adj* terrorizzato(-a).

territory ['terətrɪ] *n (political area)* territorio *m*; *(terrain)* terreno *m*.

terror ['terə^r] *n* terrore *m*.

terrorism ['terərɪzm] *n* terrorismo *m*.

terrorist ['terərɪst] *n* terrorista *mf*.

terrorize ['terəraɪz] *vt* terrorizzare.

test [test] ◇ *n (at school)* prova *f*; *(check)* controllo *m*; (MED) esame *m* ◇ *vt (check)* controllare; *(give exam to)* esaminare; *(try)* provare; **driving ~** esame di guida.

testicles ['testɪklz] *npl* testicoli *mpl*.

tetanus ['tetənəs] *n* tetano *m*.

text [tekst] *n* testo *m*.

textbook ['tekstbʊk] *n* libro *m* di testo.

textile ['tekstaɪl] *n* tessuto *m*.

texture ['tekstʃə^r] *n* consistenza *f*; *(of fabric)* trama *f*.

Thai [taɪ] *adj* tailandese.

Thailand ['taɪlænd] *n* la Tailandia.

Thames [temz] *n*: **the ~** il Tamigi.

than [*weak form* ðən, *strong form* ðæn] ◇ *prep* di ◇ *conj* che; **you're better ~ me** sei più bravo di me; **I'd rather stay in ~ go out** preferisco restare a casa piuttosto che uscire; **more ~ six** più di sei.

thank [θæŋk] *vt*: **to ~ sb (for sthg)** ringraziare qn (per qc).

◆ **thanks** ◇ *npl* ringraziamenti *mpl* ◇ *excl* grazie!; **~s to** grazie a; **many ~s** grazie infinite.

Thanksgiving ['θæŋks,gɪvɪŋ] *n* festa *f* del Ringraziamento *(festa nazionale americana)*.

thank you *excl* grazie!; **~ very much!** tante OR mille grazie!; **no ~!** no, grazie!

that [ðæt, *weak form of pron senses 3, 4 & conj* ðət] (*pl* **those**) ◇ *adj* **1.** *(referring to thing, person mentioned)* quel/quello (quella/quell'), quegli/quei (quelle) *(pl)*; **~ book** quel libro; **who's ~ man?** chi è quell'uomo?; **those chocolates are delicious** quei cioccolatini sono buonissimi.

2. *(referring to thing, person further away)* quello(-a) là; **I prefer ~ book** preferisco quel libro; **I'll have ~ one** prendo quello là.

◇ *pron* **1.** *(referring to thing mentioned)* ciò; **what's ~?** che cos'è (quello)?; **I can't do ~** non posso farlo; **who's ~?** chi è quello?; **is ~ Lucy?** è Lucy?

2. *(referring to thing, person further away)* quello(-a), quelli(-e) *(pl)*.

3. *(introducing relative clause)* che; **a shop ~ sells antiques** un negozio che vende oggetti d'antiquariato; **the film ~ I saw** il film che ho visto.

4. *(introducing relative clause: after prep)* cui; **the person ~ I was telling you about** la persona di cui ti stavo parlando; **the place ~ I'm looking for** il posto che sto cercando.

◇ *adv* tanto, così; **it wasn't ~ bad/good** non era così cattivo/buono.

◇ *conj* che; **tell him ~ I'm going to be late** digli che farò tardi.

thatched [θætʃt] *adj (roof)* di paglia.

that's [ðæts] = **that is**.

thaw [θɔː] ◇ *vi (snow, ice)* sciogliersi ◇ *vt (frozen food)* scongelare.

the [*weak form* ðə, *before vowel* ðɪ, *strong form* ðiː] *definite article* **1.** *(gen)* il/lo (la), i/gli (le); **~ book** il libro; **~ man** l'uomo; **~ mirror** lo specchio; **~ woman** la donna; **~ island** l'isola; **~ men** gli uomini; **~ girls** le ragazze; **~ Wilsons** i Wilsons.

2. *(with an adjective to form a noun)*: **~ British** i britannici; **~ young** i giovani.

3. *(in dates)*: **Friday ~ nineteenth of May** venerdì diciannove maggio; **~ twelfth** il dodici; **~ forties** gli anni quaranta.

4. *(in titles)*: **Elizabeth ~ Second** Elisabetta Seconda.

theater ['θɪətə^r] *n (Am) (for plays, drama)* = **theatre**; *(for films)* cinema *m inv*.

theatre ['θɪətə^r] *n (Br) (for plays)* teatro *m*.

theft [θeft] *n* furto *m*.

their [ðeə^r] *adj* il loro (la loro), i loro (le loro) *(pl)*.

theirs [ðeəz] *pron* il loro (la loro), i loro (le loro) *(pl)*; **a friend of ~** un loro amico.

them [*weak form* ðəm, *strong form* ðem] *pron (direct)* li (le); *(indirect)* gli; *(after prep with people)* loro; *(after prep with things)* essi(-e); **I know ~** li conosco; **it's ~** sono loro; **send it to ~** mandaglielo; **tell ~** diglielo; **he's worse than ~** è peggio di loro.

theme [θiːm] *n* tema *m*.

theme park *n* parco *m* di divertimenti.

themselves [ðəm'selvz] *pron (reflexive)* si; *(after prep)* se stessi (se stesse), sé; **they did it ~** l'hanno fatto da soli.

then [ðen] *adv* allora; *(next, afterwards)* dopo, poi; **from ~ on** da allora in poi; **until ~** fino ad allora.

theory ['θɪərɪ] *n* teoria *f*; **in ~** in teoria.

therapist ['θerəpɪst] *n* terapeuta *mf*.

therapy ['θerəpɪ] *n* terapia *f*.

there [ðeə^r] ◇ *adv (at, in, to that place)* lì, là ◇ *pron*: **~ is** c'è; **~ are** ci sono; **is anyone ~?** c'è nessuno?; **is Bob ~, please?** *(on phone)* c'è Bob, per cortesia?; **we're going ~ tomorrow** ci andiamo domani; **over ~** laggiù; **~ you are** *(when giving)* ecco a lei.

thereabouts [,ðeərə'baʊts] *adv*: **or ~** o giù di lì.

therefore ['ðeəfɔː^r] *adv* perciò.

there's [ðeəz] = **there is**.

thermal underwear [,θɜːml-] *n* biancheria *f* termica.

thermometer [θə'mɒmɪtə^r] *n* termometro *m*.

Thermos (flask)® ['θɜːməs-] *n* thermos® *m inv*.

thermostat ['θɜːməstæt] *n*

termostato *m*.

these [ðiːz] *pl* → **this**.

they [ðeɪ] *pron* essi (esse); *(referring to people)* loro; **~'re tall** sono alti.

thick [θɪk] *adj (in size)* spesso(-a); *(hair)* folto(-a); *(sauce, smoke)* denso(-a); *(fog)* fitto(-a); *(inf: stupid)* tonto(-a); **it's one metre ~** ha uno spessore di un metro.

thicken [ˈθɪkn] ◇ *vt (sauce, soup)* rendere più denso ◇ *vi (mist, fog)* infittirsi.

thickness [ˈθɪknɪs] *n* spessore *m*.

thief [θiːf] (*pl* **thieves** [θiːvz]) *n* ladro *m* (-a *f*).

thigh [θaɪ] *n* coscia *f*.

thimble [ˈθɪmbl] *n* ditale *m*.

thin [θɪn] *adj* sottile; *(person, animal)* magro(-a); *(soup, sauce)* liquido(-a).

thing [θɪŋ] *n* cosa *f*; **the ~ is** il fatto è.

◆ **things** *npl (clothes, possessions)* cose *fpl*; **how are ~s?** *(inf)* come vanno le cose?

thingummyjig [ˈθɪŋəmɪdʒɪg] *n (inf)* coso *m*.

think [θɪŋk] (*pt & pp* **thought**) ◇ *vt* pensare ◇ *vi* pensare; **to ~ that** pensare che; **to ~ about** pensare a; **to ~ of** pensare a; **to ~ of doing sthg** pensare di fare qc; **I ~ so** penso di sì; **I don't ~ so** penso di no; **do you ~ you could ...?** potrebbe ...?; **I'll think about it** ci penserò; **I can't ~ of his address** non mi viene in mente il suo indirizzo; **to ~ highly of sb** avere una buona opinione di qn.

◆ **think over** *vt sep* riflettere su.

◆ **think up** *vt sep* escogitare.

third [θɜːd] *num* terzo(-a), → **sixth**.

third party insurance *n* assicurazione *f* contro terzi.

Third World *n*: **the ~** il Terzo Mondo.

thirst [θɜːst] *n* sete *f*.

thirsty [ˈθɜːstɪ] *adj*: **to be ~** avere sete.

thirteen [ˌθɜːˈtiːn] *num* tredici, → **six**.

thirteenth [ˌθɜːˈtiːnθ] *num* tredicesimo(-a), → **sixth**.

thirtieth [ˈθɜːtɪəθ] *num* trentesimo(-a), → **sixth**.

thirty [ˈθɜːtɪ] *num* trenta, → **six**.

this [ðɪs] (*pl* **these**) ◇ *adj* **1.** *(referring to thing, person mentioned)* questo(-a); **these chocolates are delicious** questi cioccolatini sono buonissimi; **~ morning** stamattina; **~ week** questa settimana.

2. *(referring to thing, person nearer)* questo(-a); **I prefer ~ book** preferisco questo libro; **I'll have ~ one** prendo questo.

3. *(inf: when telling a story)*: **there was ~ man ...** c'era un tizio ...

◇ *pron* **1.** *(referring to thing, person mentioned)* questo(-a); **~ is for you** questo è per te; **what are these?** che cosa sono questi?; **~ is David Gregory** *(introducing someone)* questo è David Gregory; *(on telephone)* sono David Gregory.

2. *(referring to thing, person nearer)* questo(-a).

◇ *adv*: **it was ~ big** era grande così.

thistle [ˈθɪsl] *n* cardo *m*.

thorn [θɔːn] *n* spina *f*.

thorough [ˈθʌrə] *adj (check, search)* accurato(-a); *(person)* preciso(-a).

thoroughly [ˈθʌrəlɪ] *adv (completely)* a fondo.

those [ðəʊz] *pl* → **that**.

though [ðəʊ] ◇ *conj* benché, sebbene ◇ *adv* tuttavia; **even ~** anche se.

thought [θɔːt] ◇ *pt & pp* → **think** ◇ *n* pensiero *m*; *(idea)* idea *f*.

thoughtful [ˈθɔːtfʊl] *adj (quiet and serious)* pensieroso(-a); *(considerate)* premuroso(-a).

thoughtless ['θɔːtlɪs] *adj* sconsiderato(-a).
thousand ['θaʊznd] *num* mille; **a** OR **one ~** mille; **~s of** migliaia di, → **six**.
thrash [θræʃ] *vt (inf: defeat heavily)* battere.
thread [θred] ◇ *n (of cotton etc)* filo *m* ◇ *vt (needle)* infilare.
threadbare ['θredbeəʳ] *adj* logoro(-a).
threat [θret] *n* minaccia *f*.
threaten ['θretn] *vt* minacciare; **to ~ to do sthg** minacciare di fare qc.
threatening ['θretnɪŋ] *adj* minaccioso(-a).
three [θriː] *num* tre, → **six**.
three-D *n*: **in ~** tridimensionale.
three-piece suite *n* divano *m* e due poltrone coordinati.
three-quarters ['-kwɔːtəz] *n* tre quarti *mpl*; **~ of an hour** tre quarti d'ora.
threshold ['θreʃhəʊld] *n (fml)* soglia *f*.
threw [θruː] *pt* → **throw**.
thrifty ['θrɪftɪ] *adj* parsimonioso(-a).
thrilled [θrɪld] *adj* contentissimo(-a).
thriller ['θrɪləʳ] *n* thriller *m inv*.
thrive [θraɪv] *vi (plant, animal, person)* crescere bene; *(business, tourism, place)* prosperare.
throat [θrəʊt] *n* gola *f*.
throb [θrɒb] *vi (noise, engine)* vibrare; **my head is throbbing** ho un mal di testa lancinante.
throne [θrəʊn] *n* trono *m*.
throttle ['θrɒtl] *n (of motorbike)* valvola *f* a farfalla.
through [θruː] ◇ *prep* attraverso; *(because of)* grazie a; *(from beginning to end of)* per tutta la durata di; *(across all of)* per tutto(-a) ◇ *adv (to other side)* attraverso; *(from beginning to end)* dall'inizio alla fine ◇ *adj*: **to be ~ (with sthg)** *(finished)* avere finito (con qc); **you're ~** *(on phone)* è in linea; **Monday ~ Thursday** *(Am)* dal lunedì al giovedì; **to go ~** *(to somewhere else)* passare; **to let sb ~** far passare qn; **I slept ~ the entire film** ho dormito per tutto il film; **~ traffic** traffico *m* di attraversamento; **a ~ train** un treno diretto; **'no ~ road'** *(Br)* 'strada senza uscita'.
throughout [θruː'aʊt] ◇ *prep (day, morning, year)* per tutto(-a); *(place, country, building)* in tutto(-a) ◇ *adv (all the time)* per tutto il tempo; *(everywhere)* dappertutto.
throw [θrəʊ] (*pt* **threw**, *pp* **thrown** [θrəʊn]) *vt* gettare; *(ball, javelin)* lanciare; *(dice)* tirare; **to ~ sthg in the bin** gettare qc nel cestino.
◆ **throw away** *vt sep (get rid of)* buttare OR gettare via.
◆ **throw out** *vt sep (get rid of)* buttare OR gettare via; *(person)* buttare fuori.
◆ **throw up** *vi (inf: vomit)* rimettere.
thru [θruː] *(Am)* = **through**.
thrush [θrʌʃ] *n (bird)* tordo *m*.
thud [θʌd] *n* tonfo *m*.
thug [θʌg] *n* delinquente *mf*.
thumb [θʌm] ◇ *n* pollice *m* ◇ *vt*: **to ~ a lift** fare l'autostop.
thumbtack ['θʌmtæk] *n (Am)* puntina *f* da disegno.
thump [θʌmp] ◇ *n (punch)* pugno *m*; *(sound)* tonfo *m* ◇ *vt* picchiare.
thunder ['θʌndəʳ] *n* tuono *m*.
thunderstorm ['θʌndəstɔːm] *n* temporale *m*.
Thurs. *(abbr of Thursday)* gio.
Thursday ['θɜːzdɪ] *n* giovedì *m inv*, → **Saturday**.
thyme [taɪm] *n* timo *m*.
Tiber ['taɪbəʳ] *n*: **the ~** il Tevere.
tick [tɪk] ◇ *n (written mark)* segno *m*; *(insect)* zecca *f* ◇ *vt* spuntare ◇

vi (clock, watch) fare tic tac.

◆ **tick off** *vt sep (mark off)* spuntare.

ticket ['tɪkɪt] *n (for travel, cinema, theatre, match)* biglietto *m*; *(label)* etichetta *f*; *(speeding ticket, parking ticket)* multa *f*.

ticket collector *n* controllore *m*.

ticket inspector *n* controllore *m*.

ticket machine *n* distributore *m* automatico di biglietti.

ticket office *n* biglietteria *f*.

tickle ['tɪkl] *vt* fare il solletico a.

ticklish ['tɪklɪʃ] *adj*: **to be ~** soffrire il solletico.

tick-tack-toe *n (Am)* tris *m (gioco)*.

tide [taɪd] *n (of sea)* marea *f*.

tidy ['taɪdɪ] *adj (room, desk, person)* ordinato(-a); *(hair, clothes)* in ordine.

◆ **tidy up** *vt sep* riordinare, mettere in ordine.

tie [taɪ] (*pt & pp* **tied**, *cont* **tying**) ◇ *n (around neck)* cravatta *f*; *(draw)* pareggio *m*; *(Am: on railway track)* traversa *f* ◇ *vt (fasten)* legare; *(laces)* allacciare; *(knot)* fare ◇ *vi (draw)* pareggiare.

◆ **tie up** *vt sep (fasten)* legare; *(laces)* annodare.

tied up ['taɪd-] *adj* occupato(-a).

tiepin ['taɪpɪn] *n* fermacravatta *m inv*.

tier [tɪəʳ] *n (of seats)* fila *f*.

tiger ['taɪgəʳ] *n* tigre *f*.

tight [taɪt] ◇ *adj* stretto(-a); *(rope)* teso(-a); *(chest)* chiuso(-a); *(inf: drunk)* sbronzo(-a) ◇ *adv (hold)* stretto(-a).

tighten ['taɪtn] *vt* stringere.

tightrope ['taɪtrəʊp] *n* corda *f (sulla quale si esibiscono i funamboli)*.

tights [taɪts] *npl* collant *m inv*; **a pair of ~** un paio di collant.

tile ['taɪl] *n (for roof)* tegola *f*; *(for floor, wall)* mattonella *f*, piastrella *f*.

till [tɪl] ◇ *n (for money)* cassa *f* ◇ *prep* fino a ◇ *conj* finché non.

tiller ['tɪləʳ] *n* barra *f* del timone.

tilt [tɪlt] ◇ *vt* inclinare ◇ *vi* inclinarsi.

timber ['tɪmbəʳ] *n (wood)* legname *m*; *(of roof)* trave *f*.

time [taɪm] ◇ *n* tempo *m*; *(measured by clock)* ora *f*; *(of train, flight, bus)* orario *m*; *(moment)* momento *m*; *(occasion)* volta *f* ◇ *vt (measure)* cronometrare; *(arrange)* programmare; **to ~ sthg well** fare qc al momento giusto; **I haven't got the ~** non ho tempo; **it's ~ to go** è ora di andare; **what's the ~?** che ore sono?; **two ~s two** due per due; **two at a ~** due per volta; **five ~s as much** cinque volte tanto; **in a month's ~** fra un mese; **to have a good ~** divertirsi; **all the ~** sempre; **every ~** ogni volta; **from ~ to ~** di tanto in tanto; **for the ~ being** per il momento; **in ~** *(arrive)* in tempo; **in good ~** per tempo; **last ~** l'ultima volta; **most of the ~** la maggior parte del tempo; **on ~** puntuale; **some of the ~** parte del tempo; **this ~** questa volta.

time difference *n* differenza *f* di fuso orario.

time limit *n* termine *m* massimo.

timer ['taɪməʳ] *n* timer *m inv*.

time share *n* multiproprietà *f inv*.

timetable ['taɪm,teɪbl] *n* orario *m*; *(of events)* calendario *m*.

time zone *n* fuso *m* orario.

timid ['tɪmɪd] *adj (shy)* timido(-a); *(easily frightened)* pauroso(-a).

tin [tɪn] ◇ *n (metal)* stagno *m*; *(container)* scatola *f* ◇ *adj* di latta.

tinfoil ['tɪnfɔɪl] *n* stagnola *f*.

tinned food [tɪnd-] *n (Br)* cibo *m* in scatola.

tin opener [-ˌəʊpnəʳ] *n (Br)* apriscatole *m inv*.

tinsel [ˈtɪnsl] *n* fili *mpl* argentati *(per decorare l'albero di Natale)*.

tint [tɪnt] *n* tinta *f*.

tinted glass [ˌtɪntɪd-] *n* vetro *m* colorato.

tiny [ˈtaɪnɪ] *adj* molto piccolo(-a).

tip [tɪp] ◇ *n (point, end)* punta *f*; *(to waiter, taxi driver etc)* mancia *f*; *(piece of advice)* suggerimento *m*; *(rubbish dump)* discarica *f* ◇ *vt (waiter, taxi driver etc)* dare la mancia a; *(tilt)* inclinare; *(pour)* versare.
◆ **tip over** ◇ *vt sep* rovesciare ◇ *vi* rovesciarsi.

tire [ˈtaɪəʳ] ◇ *vi* stancarsi ◇ *n (Am)* = **tyre**.

tired [ˈtaɪəd] *adj* stanco(-a); **to be ~ of** *(fed up with)* essere stanco di.

tired out *adj* esausto(-a).

tiring [ˈtaɪərɪŋ] *adj* faticoso(-a).

tissue [ˈtɪʃuː] *n (handkerchief)* fazzolettino *m* di carta.

tissue paper *n* carta *f* velina.

tit [tɪt] *n (vulg: breast)* tetta *f*.

title [ˈtaɪtl] *n* titolo *m*.

T-junction *n* incrocio *m* a T.

to [*unstressed before consonant* tə, *unstressed before vowel* tʊ, *stressed* tuː] ◇ *prep* **1.** *(indicating direction)* a; **to go ~ Milan** andare a Milano; **to go ~ France** andare in Francia; **to go ~ school** andare a scuola; **to go ~ the office** andare in ufficio.
2. *(indicating position)* a; **~ the left/right** a sinistra/destra.
3. *(expressing indirect object)* a; **to give sthg ~ sb** dare qc a qn; **to listen ~ the radio** ascoltare la radio.
4. *(indicating reaction, effect)* a; **to be favourable ~ sthg** essere favorevole a qc; **~ my surprise** con mia grande sorpresa.
5. *(until)* fino a; **to count ~ ten** contare fino a dieci; **we work from nine ~ five** lavoriamo dalle nove alle cinque.
6. *(indicating change of state)*: **to turn ~ sthg** trasformarsi in qc; **it could lead ~ trouble** potrebbe causare problemi.
7. *(Br: in expressions of time)*: **it's ten ~ three** sono le tre meno dieci; **at quarter ~ seven** alle sette meno un quarto.
8. *(in ratios, rates)*: **40 miles ~ the gallon** = 100 chilometri con 7 litri; **there are sixteen ounces ~ the pound** sedici once fanno una libbra.
9. *(of, for)*: **the keys ~ the car** le chiavi dell'automobile; **a letter ~ my daughter** una lettera a mia figlia.
10. *(indicating attitude)* con, verso; **to be rude ~ sb** essere scortese con qn.
◇ *with infinitive* **1.** *(forming simple infinitive)*: **~ walk** camminare; **~ laugh** ridere.
2. *(following another verb)*: **to begin ~ do sthg** cominciare a fare qc; **to try ~ do sthg** cercare di fare qc.
3. *(following an adjective)*: **difficult ~ do** difficile da fare; **ready ~ go** pronto a partire.
4. *(indicating purpose)* per; **we came here ~ look at the castle** siamo venuti qui per visitare il castello.

toad [təʊd] *n* rospo *m*.

toadstool [ˈtəʊdstuːl] *n* fungo *m* velenoso.

toast [təʊst] ◇ *n (bread)* pane *m* tostato; *(when drinking)* brindisi *m inv* ◇ *vt (bread)* tostare; **a piece** OR **slice of ~** una fetta di pane tostato.

toasted sandwich [ˈtəʊstɪd-] *n* toast *m inv*.

toaster [ˈtəʊstəʳ] *n* tostapane *m inv*.

toastie [ˈtəʊstɪ] = **toasted sandwich**.

tobacco [təˈbækəʊ] *n* tabacco *m*.

tobacconist's [təˈbækənɪsts] *n (shop)* tabaccaio *m*.

toboggan [tə'bɒgən] *n* toboga *m inv*.

today [tə'deɪ] ◇ *n* oggi *m* ◇ *adv* oggi.

toddler ['tɒdlə^r] *n* bambino *m* (-a *f*) *(che muove i primi passi)*.

toe [təʊ] *n (of person)* dito *m* del piede.

toe clip *n* puntapiedi *m inv*.

toenail ['təʊneɪl] *n* unghia *f* del piede.

toffee ['tɒfɪ] *n (sweet)* caramella *f* mou *(inv)*.

together [tə'geðə^r] *adv* insieme; ~ **with** insieme a.

toilet ['tɔɪlɪt] *n (room)* gabinetto *m*; *(bowl)* water *m inv*; **to go to the** ~ andare al gabinetto; **where's the** ~? dov'è il gabinetto?

toilet bag *n* nécessaire *m inv* da toilette.

toilet paper *n* carta *f* igienica.

toiletries ['tɔɪlɪtrɪz] *npl* prodotti *mpl* cosmetici.

toilet roll *n* rotolo *m* di carta igienica.

toilet water *n* acqua *f* di colonia.

token ['təʊkn] *n (metal disc)* gettone *m*.

told [təʊld] *pt & pp* → **tell**.

tolerable ['tɒlərəbl] *adj (fairly good)* passabile; *(bearable)* sopportabile.

tolerant ['tɒlərənt] *adj* tollerante.

tolerate ['tɒləreɪt] *vt* tollerare.

toll [təʊl] *n (for road, bridge)* pedaggio *m*.

tollbooth ['təʊlbu:θ] *n* casello *m*.

toll-free *adj (Am)*: ~ **number** ≃ numero *m* verde.

tomato [*Br* tə'mɑ:təʊ, *Am* tə'meɪtəʊ] (*pl* **-es**) *n* pomodoro *m*.

tomato juice *n* succo *m* di pomodoro.

tomato ketchup *n* ketchup *m*.

tomato puree *n* conserva *f* di pomodoro.

tomato sauce *n* sugo *m* di pomodoro.

tomb [tu:m] *n* tomba *f*.

tomorrow [tə'mɒrəʊ] ◇ *n* domani *m* ◇ *adv* domani; **the day after** ~ dopodomani; ~ **afternoon** domani pomeriggio; ~ **morning** domani mattina; ~ **night** domani sera.

ton [tʌn] *n (in Britain)* = 1016 kg; *(in U.S.)* = 907 kg; *(metric tonne)* tonnellata *f*; **~s of** *(inf)* un sacco di.

tone [təʊn] *n (of voice)* tono *m*; *(on phone)* segnale *m*; *(of colour)* tonalità *f inv*.

tongs [tɒŋz] *npl (for hair)* arricciacapelli *m inv*; *(for sugar)* mollette *fpl*.

tongue [tʌŋ] *n* lingua *f*.

tonic ['tɒnɪk] *n (tonic water)* acqua *f* tonica; *(medicine)* ricostituente *m*.

tonic water *n* acqua *f* tonica.

tonight [tə'naɪt] ◇ *n (night)* questa notte *f*; *(evening)* questa sera *f* ◇ *adv (night)* stanotte, questa notte; *(evening)* stasera, questa sera.

tonne [tʌn] *n* tonnellata *f*.

tonsillitis [,tɒnsɪ'laɪtɪs] *n* tonsillite *f*.

too [tu:] *adv (excessively)* troppo; *(also)* anche; **it's ~ late to go out** è troppo tardi per uscire; ~ **many** troppi(-e); ~ **much** troppo(-a).

took [tʊk] *pt* → **take**.

tool [tu:l] *n* attrezzo *m*.

tool kit *n* attrezzi *mpl*.

tooth [tu:θ] (*pl* **teeth**) *n* dente *m*.

toothache ['tu:θeɪk] *n* mal *m* di denti.

toothbrush ['tu:θbrʌʃ] *n* spazzolino *m* da denti.

toothpaste ['tu:θpeɪst] *n* dentifricio *m*.

toothpick ['tu:θpɪk] *n* stuzzicadenti *m*.

top [tɒp] ◇ *adj (highest)* più alto(-a); *(step, stair)* ultimo(-a); *(best)* migliore; *(most important)* più importante ◇ *n (of stairs, hill, page)* cima *f*; *(of table)* piano *m*; *(of class,* *league)* primo *m* (-a *f*); *(for bottle, tube, pen)* tappo *m*; *(for jar, box)* coperchio *m*; *(of pyjamas, bikini)* sopra *m inv*; *(blouse)* camicetta *f*; *(T-shirt)* maglietta *f*; **at the ~ (of)** *(stairs, list, mountain)* in cima (a); **on ~ of** *(table etc)* sopra, su; *(in addition to)* oltre a; **at ~ speed** a tutta velocità; **~ gear** = quinta *f*.

◆ **top up** ◇ *vt sep (glass, drink)* riempire ◇ *vi (with petrol)* fare il pieno.

top floor *n* ultimo piano *m*.

topic ['tɒpɪk] *n* argomento *m*.

topical ['tɒpɪkl] *adj* d'attualità.

topless ['tɒplɪs] *adj*: **to go ~** mettersi in topless.

topped [tɒpt] *adj*: **~ with** *(cream etc)* ricoperto(-a) di.

topping ['tɒpɪŋ] *n* guarnizione *f (su pizza ecc.)*.

torch [tɔːtʃ] *n (Br: electric light)* torcia *f* elettrica.

tore [tɔːʳ] *pt* → **tear**[1].

torment [tɔː'ment] *vt (annoy)* tormentare.

torn [tɔːn] ◇ *pp* → **tear**[1] ◇ *adj (ripped)* strappato(-a).

tornado [tɔː'neɪdəʊ] (*pl* **-es** OR **-s**) *n* tornado *m*.

torrential rain [tə,renʃl-] *n* pioggia *f* torrenziale.

tortoise ['tɔːtəs] *n* tartaruga *f*.

tortoiseshell ['tɔːtəʃel] *n* tartaruga *f*.

torture ['tɔːtʃəʳ] ◇ *n* tortura *f* ◇ *vt* torturare.

Tory ['tɔːrɪ] *n membro del partito conservatore britannico*.

toss [tɒs] *vt (throw)* lanciare; *(salad, vegetables)* mescolare; **to ~ a coin** fare testa o croce.

total ['təʊtl] ◇ *adj* totale ◇ *n* totale *m*; **in ~** in totale.

touch [tʌtʃ] ◇ *n (sense)* tatto *m*; *(small amount)* tantino *m*; *(detail)* tocco *m* ◇ *vt* toccare ◇ *vi* toccarsi; **to get in ~ (with sb)** mettersi in contatto (con qn); **to keep in ~ (with sb)** tenersi in contatto (con qn).

◆ **touch down** *vi (plane)* atterrare.

touching ['tʌtʃɪŋ] *adj* toccante.

tough [tʌf] *adj* duro(-a); *(resilient)* tenace; *(hard, strong)* resistente.

tour [tʊəʳ] ◇ *n (journey)* viaggio *m*; *(of city, castle etc)* visita *f*; *(of pop group, theatre company)* tournée *f inv* ◇ *vt* visitare; **on ~** in tournée.

tourism ['tʊərɪzm] *n* turismo *m*.

tourist ['tʊərɪst] *n* turista *mf*.

tourist class *n* classe *f* turistica.

tourist information office *n* ufficio *m* d'informazione turistica.

tournament ['tɔːnəmənt] *n* torneo *m*.

tour operator *n* operatore *m* turistico (operatrice turistica *f*).

tout [taʊt] *n* bagarino *m*.

tow [təʊ] *vt* rimorchiare.

toward [tə'wɔːd] *(Am)* = **towards**.

towards [tə'wɔːdz] *prep (Br)* verso; *(with regard to)* nei confronti di; *(to help pay for)* per.

towaway zone ['təʊəweɪ-] *n (Am)* zona *f* rimozione forzata.

towel ['taʊəl] *n* asciugamano *m*.

toweling ['taʊəlɪŋ] *(Am)* = **towelling**.

towelling ['taʊəlɪŋ] *n (Br)* spugna *f*.

towel rail *n* portasciugamano *m*.

tower ['taʊəʳ] *n* torre *f*.

tower block *n (Br)* grattacielo *m*.

Tower Bridge *n* Tower Bridge *(famoso ponte levatoio di Londra)*.

Tower of London *n*: **the ~** la Torre di Londra.

town [taʊn] *n* città *f*; *(town centre)* centro *m* (città).

town centre *n* centro *m* (città).

town hall *n* comune *m*.

towpath ['təʊpɑːθ, *pl* -pɑːðz] *n* alzaia *f*.

towrope ['təʊrəʊp] *n* cavo *m* di rimorchio.

tow truck *n (Am)* carro *m* attrezzi.

toxic ['tɒksɪk] *adj* tossico(-a).

toy [tɔɪ] *n* giocattolo *m*.

toy shop *n* negozio *m* di giocattoli.

trace [treɪs] ◇ *n* traccia *f* ◇ *vt (find)* rintracciare.

tracing paper ['treɪsɪŋ-] *n* carta *f* da ricalco.

track [træk] *n (path)* sentiero *m*; *(of railway)* binario *m*, rotaie *fpl*; (SPORT) pista *f*; *(song)* pezzo *m*.

◆ **track down** *vt sep* trovare.

tracksuit ['træksu:t] *n* tuta *f* da ginnastica.

tractor ['træktə^r] *n* trattore *m*.

trade [treɪd] ◇ *n* (COMM) commercio *m*; *(job)* mestiere *m* ◇ *vt* scambiare ◇ *vi* commerciare.

trade-in *n* permuta *f*.

trademark ['treɪdmɑ:k] *n* marchio *m* di fabbrica.

trader ['treɪdə^r] *n* commerciante *mf*.

tradesman ['treɪdzmən] (*pl* **-men** [-mən]) *n (deliveryman)* addetto *m* alle consegne; *(shopkeeper)* commerciante *mf*.

trade union *n* sindacato *m*.

tradition [trə'dɪʃn] *n* tradizione *f*.

traditional [trə'dɪʃənl] *adj* tradizionale.

traffic ['træfɪk] (*pt & pp* **-ked**) ◇ *n (cars etc)* traffico *m* ◇ *vi*: **to ~ in** trafficare in.

traffic circle *n (Am)* rotatoria *f*.

traffic island *n* salvagente *m*.

traffic jam *n* ingorgo *m*.

traffic lights *npl* semaforo *m*.

traffic warden *n (Br)* = vigile *m* urbano *(addetto al controllo dei divieti e limiti di sosta)*.

tragedy ['trædʒədɪ] *n* tragedia *f*.

tragic ['trædʒɪk] *adj* tragico(-a).

trail [treɪl] ◇ *n (path)* sentiero *m*; *(marks)* tracce *fpl* ◇ *vi (be losing)* essere in svantaggio.

trailer ['treɪlə^r] *n (for boat, luggage)* rimorchio *m*; *(Am: caravan)* roulotte *f inv*; *(for film, programme)* trailer *m inv*.

train [treɪn] ◇ *n (on railway)* treno *m* ◇ *vt (teach)* formare; *(animal)* addestrare ◇ *vi* (SPORT) allenarsi; **by ~** in treno.

train driver *n* macchinista *m*.

trainee [treɪ'ni:] *n (for profession)* tirocinante *mf*; *(for trade)* apprendista *mf*.

trainer ['treɪnə^r] *n (of athlete etc)* allenatore *m* (-trice *f*).

◆ **trainers** *npl (Br: shoes)* scarpe *fpl* da ginnastica.

training ['treɪnɪŋ] *n (instruction)* formazione *f*, addestramento *m*; *(exercises)* allenamento *m*.

training shoes *npl (Br)* scarpe *fpl* da ginnastica.

tram [træm] *n (Br)* tram *m inv*.

tramp [træmp] *n* vagabondo *m* (-a *f*).

trampoline ['træmpəli:n] *n* trampolino *m*.

trance [trɑ:ns] *n* trance *f*.

tranquilizer ['træŋkwɪlaɪzər] *(Am)* = **tranquillizer**.

tranquillizer ['træŋkwɪlaɪzə^r] *n (Br)* tranquillante *m*.

transaction [træn'zækʃn] *n* transazione *f*.

transatlantic [,trænzət'læntɪk] *adj* transatlantico(-a).

transfer [*n* 'trænsfɜ:^r, *vb* træns'fɜ:^r] ◇ *n* trasferimento *m*; *(of power, property)* passaggio *m*; *(picture)* decalcomania *f*; *(Am: ticket) biglietto che dà la possibilità di cambiare autobus, treno ecc. senza pagare alcun supplemento* ◇ *vt* trasferire ◇ *vi (change bus, plane etc)* cambiare; **'~s'** *(in airport)* 'transiti'.

transfer desk *n* banco *m* transiti.

transform [træns'fɔːm] *vt* trasformare.

transfusion [træns'fjuːʒn] *n* trasfusione *f*.

transistor radio [træn'zɪstəʳ-] *n* transistor *m inv*.

transit ['trænzɪt] : **in transit** *adv* in transito.

transitive ['trænzɪtɪv] *adj* transitivo(-a).

transit lounge *n* sala *f* transiti.

translate [træns'leɪt] *vt* tradurre.

translation [træns'leɪʃn] *n* traduzione *f*.

translator [træns'leɪtəʳ] *n* traduttore *m* (-trice *f*).

transmission [trænz'mɪʃn] *n* trasmissione *f*.

transmit [trænz'mɪt] *vt* trasmettere.

transparent [træns'pærənt] *adj* trasparente.

transplant ['trænsplɑːnt] *n* trapianto *m*.

transport [*n* 'trænspɔːt, *vb* træn'spɔːt] ◇ *n (cars, trains, planes etc)* trasporti *mpl*; *(moving)* trasporto *m* ◇ *vt* trasportare.

transportation [ˌtrænspɔː'teɪʃn] *n (Am) (cars, trains, planes etc)* trasporti *mpl*; *(moving)* trasporto *m*.

trap [træp] ◇ *n* trappola *f* ◇ *vt*: **to be trapped** *(stuck)* essere intrappolato.

trapdoor [ˌtræp'dɔːʳ] *n* botola *f*.

trash [træʃ] *n (Am: waste material)* spazzatura *f*.

trashcan ['træʃkæn] *n (Am)* pattumiera *f*.

trauma ['trɔːmə] *n (bad experience)* trauma *m*.

traumatic [trɔː'mætɪk] *adj* traumatico(-a).

travel ['trævl] ◇ *n* viaggi *mpl* ◇ *vt (distance)* percorrere ◇ *vi* viaggiare.

travel agency *n* agenzia *f* di viaggi.

travel agent *n* agente *mf* di viaggi; **~'s** *(shop)* agenzia *f* di viaggi.

Travelcard ['trævlkɑːd] *n biglietto che dà accesso ai mezzi pubblici di Londra per un'intera giornata.*

travel centre *n (in railway, bus station) ufficio informazioni e biglietteria.*

traveler ['trævlər] *(Am)* = **traveller**.

travel insurance *n* assicurazione *f* viaggio.

traveller ['trævləʳ] *n (Br)* viaggiatore *m* (-trice *f*).

traveller's cheque *n* traveller's cheque *m inv*.

travelsick ['trævəlsɪk] *adj*: **to be ~** *(in car)* soffrire il mal d'auto; *(on boat)* soffrire il mal di mare; *(on plane)* soffrire il mal d'aria.

trawler ['trɔːləʳ] *n* peschereccio *m*.

tray [treɪ] *n* vassoio *m*.

treacherous ['tretʃərəs] *adj (person)* infido(-a); *(roads, conditions)* insidioso(-a).

treacle ['triːkl] *n (Br)* melassa *f*.

tread [tred] (*pt* **trod**, *pp* **trodden**) ◇ *n (of tyre)* battistrada *m inv* ◇ *vi*: **to ~ on sthg** calpestare qc.

treasure ['treʒəʳ] *n* tesoro *m*.

treat [triːt] ◇ *vt* trattare; *(patient, illness)* curare ◇ *n* regalo *m*; **to ~ sb to sthg** offrire qc a qn.

treatment ['triːtmənt] *n* (MED) cure *fpl*; *(of person)* trattamento *m*; *(of subject)* trattazione *f*.

treble ['trebl] *adj* triplo(-a).

tree [triː] *n* albero *m*.

trek [trek] *n* escursione *f*.

tremble ['trembl] *vi* tremare.

tremendous [trɪ'mendəs] *adj (very large)* enorme; *(inf: very good)* formidabile.

trench [trentʃ] *n* fosso *m*.

trend [trend] *n (tendency)* tendenza *f*; *(fashion)* moda *f*.

trendy ['trendɪ] *adj (inf)* alla moda.

trespasser ['trespəsəʳ] *n*: **'~s will be prosecuted'** 'vietato l'accesso; i trasgressori saranno puniti ai termini di legge'.
trial ['traɪəl] *n* (JUR) processo *m*; *(test)* prova *f*; **a ~ period** un periodo di prova.
triangle ['traɪæŋgl] *n* triangolo *m*.
triangular [traɪ'æŋgjʊləʳ] *adj* triangolare.
tribe [traɪb] *n* tribù *f inv*.
tributary ['trɪbjʊtrɪ] *n* tributario *m*, affluente *m*.
trick [trɪk] ◇ *n* trucco *m*; *(conjuring trick)* gioco *m* di prestigio ◇ *vt* imbrogliare, ingannare; **to play a ~ on sb** giocare un brutto tiro a qn.
trickle ['trɪkl] *vi (liquid)* gocciolare, colare.
tricky ['trɪkɪ] *adj* difficile.
tricycle ['traɪsɪkl] *n* triciclo *m*.
trifle ['traɪfl] *n (dessert)* zuppa *f* inglese.
trigger ['trɪgəʳ] *n* grilletto *m*.
trim [trɪm] ◇ *n (haircut)* spuntata *f* ◇ *vt (hair, beard)* spuntare; *(hedge)* regolare.
trinket ['trɪŋkɪt] *n* ciondolo *m*, gingillo *m*.
trio ['tri:əʊ] (*pl* **-s**) *n* trio *m*.
trip [trɪp] ◇ *n (journey)* viaggio *m*; *(short)* gita *f*, escursione *f* ◇ *vi* inciampare.
◆ **trip up** *vi* inciampare.
triple ['trɪpl] *adj* triplo(-a).
tripod ['traɪpɒd] *n* treppiedi *m inv*.
triumph ['traɪəmf] *n* trionfo *m*.
trivial ['trɪvɪəl] *adj (pej)* insignificante, banale.
trod [trɒd] *pt* → **tread**.
trodden ['trɒdn] *pp* → **tread**.
trolley ['trɒlɪ] (*pl* **-s**) *n (Br: in supermarket, at airport, for food etc)* carrello *m*; *(Am: tram)* tram *m inv*.
trombone [trɒm'bəʊn] *n* trombone *m*.
troops [tru:ps] *npl* truppe *fpl*.
trophy ['trəʊfɪ] *n* trofeo *m*.
tropical ['trɒpɪkl] *adj* tropicale.
trot [trɒt] ◇ *vi (horse)* trottare ◇ *n*: **on the ~** *(inf)* di fila.
trouble ['trʌbl] ◇ *n* problemi *mpl* ◇ *vt (worry)* preoccupare; *(bother)* disturbare; **to be in ~** essere nei guai; **to get into ~** mettersi nei guai; **to take the ~ to do sthg** darsi la pena di fare qc; **it's no ~** non si preoccupi; *(in reply to thanks)* di niente.
trough [trɒf] *n (for drinking)* abbeveratoio *m*.
trouser press ['traʊzəʳ-] *n* stiracalzoni *m inv*.
trousers ['traʊzəz] *npl* pantaloni *mpl*; **a pair of ~** un paio di pantaloni.
trout [traʊt] *(pl inv) n* trota *f*.
trowel ['traʊəl] *n (for gardening)* paletta *f*.
truant ['tru:ənt] *n*: **to play ~** marinare la scuola.
truce [tru:s] *n* tregua *f*.
truck [trʌk] *n (lorry)* camion *m inv*, autocarro *m*.
true [tru:] *adj* vero(-a).
truly ['tru:lɪ] *adv*: **yours ~** distinti saluti.
trumpet ['trʌmpɪt] *n* tromba *f*.
trumps [trʌmps] *npl* atout *m inv*.
truncheon ['trʌntʃən] *n* sfollagente *m inv*.
trunk [trʌŋk] *n (of tree)* tronco *m*; *(Am: of car)* bagagliaio *m*; *(case, box)* baule *m*; *(of elephant)* proboscide *f*.
trunk call *n (Br)* interurbana *f*.
trunk road *n (Br)* strada *f* statale.
trunks [trʌŋks] *npl* costume *m* da bagno da uomo.
trust [trʌst] ◇ *n (confidence)* fiducia *f* ◇ *vt (believe, have confidence in)* fidarsi di, aver fiducia in; *(fml: hope)* sperare.
trustworthy ['trʌst,wɜ:ðɪ] *adj*

degno(-a) di fiducia.

truth [tru:θ] *n (true facts)* verità *f*; *(quality of being true)* veridicità *f*.

truthful ['tru:θfʊl] *adj (statement, account)* veritiero(-a); *(person)* sincero(-a).

try [traɪ] ◇ *n (attempt)* tentativo *m*, prova *f* ◇ *vt* provare; (JUR) giudicare ◇ *vi* provare; **to ~ to do sthg** provare a fare qc.

◆ **try on** *vt sep (clothes)* provare, provarsi.

◆ **try out** *vt sep* provare.

T-shirt *n* maglietta *f*.

tub [tʌb] *n (of margarine etc)* vaschetta *f*; *(inf: bath)* vasca *f* (da bagno).

tube [tju:b] *n (container)* tubetto *m*; *(Br: inf: underground)* metropolitana *f*; *(pipe)* tubo *m*; **by ~** in metropolitana.

tube station *n (Br: inf)* stazione *f* della metropolitana.

tuck [tʌk] **: tuck in** ◇ *vt sep (shirt)* mettersi dentro; *(child, person)* rimboccare le coperte a ◇ *vi (inf)* mangiare di buon appetito.

tuck shop *n (Br) piccolo negozio di merendine, caramelle ecc., presso una scuola.*

Tudor ['tju:dəʳ] *adj* Tudor *(inv) (sedicesimo secolo).*

Tues. *(abbr of Tuesday)* mar.

Tuesday ['tju:zdɪ] *n* martedì *m inv*, → **Saturday**.

tuft [tʌft] *n* ciuffo *m*.

tug [tʌg] ◇ *vt* tirare ◇ *n (boat)* rimorchiatore *m*.

tuition [tju:'ɪʃn] *n* lezioni *fpl*.

tulip ['tju:lɪp] *n* tulipano *m*.

tumble-dryer ['tʌmbldraɪəʳ] *n* asciugabiancheria *m inv*.

tumbler ['tʌmbləʳ] *n (glass)* bicchiere *m (senza stelo)*.

tummy ['tʌmɪ] *n (inf)* pancia *f*.

tummy upset *n (inf)* disturbi *mpl* di pancia.

tumor ['tu:mər] *(Am)* = **tumour**.

tumour ['tju:məʳ] *n (Br)* tumore *m*.

tuna (fish) [*Br* 'tju:nə, *Am* 'tu:nə] *n (food)* tonno *m*.

tuna melt *n (Am) crostino di tonno e formaggio fuso.*

tune [tju:n] ◇ *n (melody)* melodia *f* ◇ *vt (radio, TV)* sintonizzare; *(engine)* mettere a punto; *(instrument)* accordare; **in ~** *(person)* intonato; *(instrument)* accordato; **out of ~** *(person)* stonato; *(instrument)* scordato.

tunic ['tju:nɪk] *n* tunica *f*.

Tunisia [tju:'nɪzɪə] *n* la Tunisia.

tunnel ['tʌnl] *n* tunnel *m inv*, galleria *f*.

turban ['tɜ:bən] *n* turbante *m*.

turbo ['tɜ:bəʊ] (*pl* **-s**) *n (car)* turbo *m inv*.

turbulence ['tɜ:bjʊləns] *n (when flying)* turbolenza *f*.

turf [tɜ:f] *n (grass)* tappeto *m* erboso.

Turin [tjʊ'rɪn] *n* Torino *f*.

Turk [tɜ:k] *n* turco *m* (-a *f*).

turkey ['tɜ:kɪ] (*pl* **-s**) *n* tacchino *m*.

Turkey *n* la Turchia.

Turkish ['tɜ:kɪʃ] ◇ *adj* turco(-a) ◇ *n (language)* turco *m* ◇ *npl*: **the ~** i turchi.

Turkish delight *n dolciume fatto di gelatina e ricoperto di zucchero a velo.*

turn [tɜ:n] ◇ *n (in road)* curva *f*; *(of knob, key, switch)* giro *m*; *(go, chance)* turno *m* ◇ *vt* girare; *(a bend)* prendere; *(become)* diventare; *(cause to become)* far diventare ◇ *vi* girare; *(person)* girarsi; *(milk)* andare a male; **to ~ into sthg** *(become)* diventare qc; **to ~ sthg into sthg** trasformare qc in qc; **to ~ left/right** girare a sinistra/a destra; **it's your ~** tocca a te; **at the ~ of the century** all'inizio del secolo; **to take it in ~s to do sthg** fare qc a turno; **to ~ sthg inside out** rigirare qc.

◆ **turn back** ◇ *vt sep (person, car)* mandare indietro ◇ *vi* tornare indietro.

◆ **turn down** *vt sep (radio, volume, heating)* abbassare; *(offer, request)* rifiutare.

◆ **turn off** ◇ *vt sep (light, TV, engine)* spegnere; *(water, gas, tap)* chiudere ◇ *vi (leave road)* girare, svoltare.

◆ **turn on** *vt sep (light, TV, engine)* accendere; *(water, gas, tap)* aprire.

◆ **turn out** ◇ *vt fus (be in the end)* rivelarsi ◇ *vt sep (light, fire)* spegnere ◇ *vi (come, attend)* affluire; **to ~ out to be sthg** risultare essere qc.

◆ **turn over** ◇ *vi (in bed)* girarsi, rigirarsi; *(Br: change channels)* cambiare canale ◇ *vt sep* girare.

◆ **turn round** ◇ *vt sep (car, table etc)* girare ◇ *vi (person)* girarsi, voltarsi.

◆ **turn up** ◇ *vt sep (radio, volume, heating)* alzare ◇ *vi (come)* venire.

turning ['tɜːnɪŋ] *n (off road)* svolta *f*.

turnip ['tɜːnɪp] *n* rapa *f*.

turn-up *n (Br: on trousers)* risvolto *m*.

turps [tɜːps] *n (Br: inf)* trementina *f*.

turquoise ['tɜːkwɔɪz] *adj* turchese.

turtle ['tɜːtl] *n* tartaruga *f* (acquatica).

turtleneck ['tɜːtlnek] *n* maglia *f* lupetto.

Tuscany ['tʌskənɪ] *n* la Toscana.

tutor ['tjuːtə^r] *n (private teacher)* insegnante *m* privato (insegnante *f* privata).

tuxedo [tʌk'siːdəʊ] (*pl* **-s**) *n (Am)* smoking *m inv*.

TV *n* tivù *f inv*, TV *f inv*; **on ~** alla tivù.

tweed [twiːd] *n* tweed *m*.

tweezers ['twiːzəz] *npl* pinzette *fpl*.

twelfth [twelfθ] *num* dodicesimo(-a), → **sixth**.

twelve [twelv] *num* dodici, → **six**.

twentieth ['twentɪəθ] *num* ventesimo(-a); **the ~ century** il ventesimo secolo, → **sixth**.

twenty ['twentɪ] *num* venti, → **six**.

twice [twaɪs] *adv* due volte; **it's ~ as good** è due volte meglio; **~ as much** il doppio.

twig [twɪg] *n* ramoscello *m*.

twilight ['twaɪlaɪt] *n* crepuscolo *m*.

twin [twɪn] *n* gemello *m* (-a *f*).

twin beds *npl* letti *mpl* gemelli.

twine [twaɪn] *n* spago *m*.

twin room *n* stanza *f* a due letti.

twist [twɪst] *vt (wire)* torcere, piegare; *(rope, hair)* attorcigliare; *(bottle top, lid, knob)* girare; **to ~ one's ankle** slogarsi la caviglia.

twisting ['twɪstɪŋ] *adj (road, river)* tortuoso(-a).

two [tuː] *num* due, → **six**.

two-piece *adj (swimsuit, suit)* a due pezzi *(inv)*.

type [taɪp] ◇ *n (kind)* tipo *m* ◇ *vt & vi* battere a macchina.

typewriter ['taɪpˌraɪtə^r] *n* macchina *f* da scrivere.

typhoid ['taɪfɔɪd] *n* tifoidea *f*.

typical ['tɪpɪkl] *adj* tipico(-a).

typist ['taɪpɪst] *n* dattilografo *m* (-a *f*).

tyre ['taɪə^r] *n (Br)* gomma *f*, pneumatico *m*.

U

U *adj (Br: film)* per tutti.
UFO *n (abbr of unidentified flying object)* UFO *m inv*.
ugly ['ʌglɪ] *adj* brutto(-a).
UHT *adj (abbr of ultra heat treated)* UHT.
UK *n*: **the ~** il Regno Unito.
ulcer ['ʌlsəʳ] *n* ulcera *f*.
Ulster ['ʌlstəʳ] *n* l'Ulster *m*.
ultimate ['ʌltɪmət] *adj (final)* finale; *(best, greatest)* ideale.
ultraviolet [ˌʌltrə'vaɪələt] *adj* ultravioletto(-a).
umbrella [ʌm'brelə] *n* ombrello *m*.
umpire ['ʌmpaɪəʳ] *n* arbitro *m*.
UN *n (abbr of United Nations)*: **the ~** l'ONU *f*.
unable [ʌn'eɪbl] *adj*: **to be ~ to do sthg** non poter fare qc.
unacceptable [ˌʌnək'septəbl] *adj* inaccettabile.
unaccustomed [ˌʌnə'kʌstəmd] *adj*: **to be ~ to sthg** non essere abituato(-a) a qc.
unanimous [juː'nænɪməs] *adj* unanime.
unattended [ˌʌnə'tendɪd] *adj (baggage)* incustodito(-a).
unattractive [ˌʌnə'træktɪv] *adj (person, idea)* poco attraente; *(place)* privo(-a) di attrattiva.
unauthorized [ˌʌn'ɔːθəraɪzd] *adj* non autorizzato(-a).
unavailable [ˌʌnə'veɪləbl] *adj* non disponibile.
unavoidable [ˌʌnə'vɔɪdəbl] *adj* inevitabile.
unaware [ˌʌnə'weəʳ] *adj*: **to be ~ of sthg/that** ignorare qc/che.
unbearable [ʌn'beərəbl] *adj* insopportabile.
unbelievable [ˌʌnbɪ'liːvəbl] *adj* incredibile.
unbutton [ˌʌn'bʌtn] *vt* sbottonare.
uncertain [ʌn'sɜːtn] *adj* incerto(-a).
uncertainty [ˌʌn'sɜːtntɪ] *n* incertezza *f*.
uncle ['ʌŋkl] *n* zio *m*.
unclean [ˌʌn'kliːn] *adj* sporco(-a).
unclear [ˌʌn'klɪəʳ] *adj* non chiaro(-a).
uncomfortable [ˌʌn'kʌmftəbl] *adj (person, chair)* scomodo(-a); *(fig: awkward)* a disagio.
uncommon [ʌn'kɒmən] *adj (rare)* raro(-a).
unconscious [ʌn'kɒnʃəs] *adj (after accident)* privo(-a) di sensi; *(unaware)* inconsapevole.
unconvincing [ˌʌnkən'vɪnsɪŋ] *adj* poco convincente.
uncooperative [ˌʌnkəʊ'ɒpərətɪv] *adj* poco disposto(-a) a collaborare.
uncork [ˌʌn'kɔːk] *vt* stappare.
uncouth [ʌn'kuːθ] *adj* villano(-a),

grossolano(-a).
uncover [ʌn'kʌvəʳ] *vt* scoprire.
under ['ʌndəʳ] *prep* sotto; *(less than)* meno di, al di sotto di; *(according to)* secondo; **children ~ ten** bambini sotto i dieci anni; **~ the circumstances** date le circostanze; **to be ~ pressure** essere sotto pressione.
underage [ʌndər'eɪdʒ] *adj* minorenne.
undercarriage ['ʌndəˌkærɪdʒ] *n* carrello *m*.
underdone [ˌʌndə'dʌn] *adj* poco cotto(-a).
underestimate [ˌʌndər'estɪmeɪt] *vt* sottovalutare.
underexposed [ˌʌndərɪk'spəʊzd] *adj (photograph)* sottoesposto(-a).
undergo [ˌʌndə'gəʊ] (*pt* **-went**, *pp* **-gone**) *vt* subire.
undergraduate [ˌʌndə'grædjʊət] *n* studente *m* universitario (studentessa *f* universitaria).
underground ['ʌndəgraʊnd] ◇ *adj (below earth's surface)* sotterraneo(-a); *(secret)* clandestino(-a) ◇ *n (Br: railway)* metropolitana *f*.
undergrowth ['ʌndəgrəʊθ] *n* sottobosco *m*.
underline [ˌʌndə'laɪn] *vt* sottolineare.
underneath [ˌʌndə'niːθ] ◇ *prep & adv* sotto ◇ *n* sotto *m*.
underpants ['ʌndəpænts] *npl* mutande *fpl*, slip *m inv*.
underpass ['ʌndəpɑːs] *n* sottopassaggio *m*.
undershirt ['ʌndəʃɜːt] *n (Am)* maglietta *f*.
underskirt ['ʌndəskɜːt] *n* sottoveste *f*.
understand [ˌʌndə'stænd] (*pt & pp* **-stood**) ◇ *vt* capire; *(believe)* credere ◇ *vi* capire; **I don't ~** non capisco; **to make o.s. understood** farsi capire.
understanding [ˌʌndə'stændɪŋ] ◇ *adj* comprensivo(-a) ◇ *n (agreement)* accordo *m*; *(knowledge)* conoscenza *f*; *(interpretation)* interpretazione *f*; *(sympathy)* comprensione *f*.
understatement [ˌʌndə'steɪtmənt] *n*: **that's an ~!** a dir poco!
understood [ˌʌndə'stʊd] *pt & pp* → **understand**.
undertake [ˌʌndə'teɪk] (*pt* **-took**, *pp* **-taken**) *vt* intraprendere; **to ~ to do sthg** impegnarsi a fare qc.
undertaker ['ʌndəˌteɪkəʳ] *n* impresario di pompe funebri.
undertaking [ˌʌndə'teɪkɪŋ] *n (promise)* promessa *f*; *(task)* impresa *f*.
undertook [ˌʌndə'tʊk] *pt* → **undertake**.
underwater [ˌʌndə'wɔːtəʳ] ◇ *adj* subacqueo(-a) ◇ *adv* sott'acqua.
underwear ['ʌndəweəʳ] *n* biancheria *f* intima.
underwent [ˌʌndə'went] *pt* → **undergo**.
undesirable [ˌʌndɪ'zaɪərəbl] *adj* indesiderato(-a).
undo [ˌʌn'duː] (*pt* **-did**, *pp* **-done**) *vt (coat, shirt)* sbottonare; *(shoelaces)* slacciare; *(tie)* sciogliere il nodo di; *(parcel)* sfare.
undone [ˌʌn'dʌn] *adj (coat, shirt)* sbottonato(-a); *(shoelaces)* slacciato(-a).
undress [ˌʌn'dres] ◇ *vi* spogliarsi ◇ *vt* spogliare.
undressed [ˌʌn'drest] *adj* spogliato(-a); **to get ~** spogliarsi.
uneasy [ʌn'iːzɪ] *adj* a disagio.
uneducated [ˌʌn'edjʊkeɪtɪd] *adj* non istruito(-a).
unemployed [ˌʌnɪm'plɔɪd] ◇ *adj* disoccupato(-a) ◇ *npl*: **the ~** i disoccupati.
unemployment [ˌʌnɪm'plɔɪmənt] *n* disoccupazione *f*.
unemployment benefit *n* sussidio *m* di disoccupazione.

unequal [ˌʌn'iːkwəl] *adj (not the same)* disuguale; *(not fair)* iniquo(-a).

uneven [ˌʌn'iːvn] *adj (surface, speed, beat)* irregolare; *(share, distribution)* ineguale.

uneventful [ˌʌnɪ'ventful] *adj* tranquillo(-a).

unexpected [ˌʌnɪk'spektɪd] *adj* inaspettato(-a).

unexpectedly [ˌʌnɪk'spektɪdlɪ] *adv* inaspettatamente.

unfair [ˌʌn'feəʳ] *adj* ingiusto(-a).

unfairly [ˌʌn'feəlɪ] *adv* ingiustamente.

unfaithful [ˌʌn'feɪθful] *adj* infedele.

unfamiliar [ˌʌnfə'mɪljəʳ] *adj* sconosciuto(-a); **to be ~ with** non conoscere bene.

unfashionable [ˌʌn'fæʃnəbl] *adj* fuori moda.

unfasten [ˌʌn'fɑːsn] *vt (seatbelt, belt, laces)* slacciare; *(knot)* sfare, sciogliere.

unfavourable [ˌʌn'feɪvrəbl] *adj* sfavorevole.

unfinished [ˌʌn'fɪnɪʃt] *adj* incompiuto(-a).

unfit [ˌʌn'fɪt] *adj (not healthy)* non in forma; **to be ~ for sthg** *(not suitable)* essere inadatto(-a) a qc.

unfold [ʌn'fəuld] *vt* spiegare *(tovaglia, cartina)*.

unforgettable [ˌʌnfə'getəbl] *adj* indimenticabile.

unforgivable [ˌʌnfə'gɪvəbl] *adj* imperdonabile.

unfortunate [ʌn'fɔːtʃnət] *adj (unlucky)* sfortunato(-a); *(regrettable)* infelice; **it is ~ that** è un peccato che.

unfortunately [ʌn'fɔːtʃnətlɪ] *adv* sfortunatamente.

unfriendly [ˌʌn'frendlɪ] *adj* poco amichevole.

unfurnished [ˌʌn'fɜːnɪʃt] *adj* non ammobiliato(-a).

ungrateful [ʌn'greɪtful] *adj* ingrato(-a).

unhappy [ʌn'hæpɪ] *adj (sad)* infelice; *(not pleased)* insoddisfatto(-a); **to be ~ about sthg** essere insoddisfatto di qc.

unharmed [ˌʌn'hɑːmd] *adj* indenne.

unhealthy [ʌn'helθɪ] *adj (person)* malaticcio(-a); *(food, smoking)* dannoso(-a) per la salute; *(place)* malsano(-a).

unhelpful [ˌʌn'helpful] *adj (person)* poco disponibile; *(advice, instructions)* inutile.

unhurt [ˌʌn'hɜːt] *adj* indenne.

unhygienic [ˌʌnhaɪ'dʒiːnɪk] *adj* non igienico(-a).

unification [ˌjuːnɪfɪ'keɪʃn] *n* unificazione *f*.

uniform ['junɪfɔːm] *n* uniforme *f*.

unimportant [ˌʌnɪm'pɔːtənt] *adj* senza importanza.

unintelligent [ˌʌnɪn'telɪdʒənt] *adj* poco intelligente.

unintentional [ˌʌnɪn'tenʃənl] *adj* involontario(-a).

uninterested [ˌʌn'ɪntrəstɪd] *adj* indifferente.

uninteresting [ˌʌn'ɪntrestɪŋ] *adj* poco interessante, noioso(-a).

union ['juːnjən] *n (of workers)* sindacato *m*.

Union Jack *n*: **the ~** *la bandiera nazionale del Regno Unito.*

unique [juː'niːk] *adj* unico(-a); **to be ~ to** essere proprio(-a) di.

unisex ['juːnɪseks] *adj* unisex *(inv)*.

unit ['juːnɪt] *n* unità *f inv*; *(department, building)* reparto *m*; *(piece of furniture)* elemento *m*; *(machine)* apparecchio *m*.

unite [juː'naɪt] ◇ *vt* unire ◇ *vi* unirsi.

United Kingdom [juː'naɪtɪd-] *n*: **the ~** il Regno Unito.

United Nations [juː'naɪtɪd-] *npl*: **the ~** le Nazioni Unite.

United States (of America) [juːˈnaɪtɪd-] *npl*: **the** ~ gli Stati Uniti (d'America).

unity [ˈjuːnətɪ] *n* unità *f*.

universal [ˌjuːnɪˈvɜːsl] *adj* universale.

universe [ˈjuːnɪvɜːs] *n* universo *m*.

university [ˌjuːnɪˈvɜːsətɪ] *n* università *f inv*.

unjust [ˌʌnˈdʒʌst] *adj* ingiusto(-a).

unkind [ʌnˈkaɪnd] *adj* scortese.

unknown [ˌʌnˈnəʊn] *adj* sconosciuto(-a).

unleaded (petrol) [ˌʌnˈledɪd-] *n* benzina *f* senza piombo.

unless [ənˈles] *conj* a meno che non; ~ **it rains** a meno che non piova.

unlike [ˌʌnˈlaɪk] *prep* a differenza di; **that's ~ her** non è da lei.

unlikely [ʌnˈlaɪklɪ] *adj* improbabile; **he is ~ to arrive before six** è improbabile che arrivi prima delle sei.

unlimited [ʌnˈlɪmɪtɪd] *adj* illimitato(-a); ~ **mileage** = chilometraggio illimitato.

unlisted [ʌnˈlɪstɪd] *adj (Am: phone number)*: **to be** ~ non essere sull'elenco telefonico.

unload [ˌʌnˈləʊd] *vt* scaricare.

unlock [ˌʌnˈlɒk] *vt* aprire.

unlucky [ʌnˈlʌkɪ] *adj (unfortunate)* sfortunato(-a); *(bringing bad luck)* che porta sfortuna.

unmarried [ˌʌnˈmærɪd] *adj* non sposato(-a).

unnatural [ʌnˈnætʃrəl] *adj (unusual)* inconsueto(-a); *(behaviour, person)* poco naturale.

unnecessary [ʌnˈnesəsərɪ] *adj* inutile.

unobtainable [ˌʌnəbˈteɪnəbl] *adj (product)* non disponibile; *(phone number)* non ottenibile.

unoccupied [ˌʌnˈɒkjʊpaɪd] *adj (place, seat)* libero(-a).

unofficial [ˌʌnəˈfɪʃl] *adj* non ufficiale; *(strike)* non autorizzato(-a).

unpack [ˌʌnˈpæk] ◇ *vt (bags, suitcase)* disfare ◇ *vi* disfare le valigie.

unpleasant [ʌnˈpleznt] *adj (smell, weather, etc)* sgradevole; *(person)* spiacevole, antipatico(-a).

unplug [ʌnˈplʌg] *vt* staccare.

unpopular [ˌʌnˈpɒpjʊləʳ] *adj* impopolare.

unpredictable [ˌʌnprɪˈdɪktəbl] *adj* imprevedibile.

unprepared [ˌʌnprɪˈpeəd] *adj* impreparato(-a).

unprotected [ˌʌnprəˈtektɪd] *adj* senza protezione.

unqualified [ˌʌnˈkwɒlɪfaɪd] *adj (person)* non qualificato(-a).

unreal [ˌʌnˈrɪəl] *adj* irreale.

unreasonable [ʌnˈriːznəbl] *adj* irragionevole.

unrecognizable [ˌʌnrekəgˈnaɪzəbl] *adj* irriconoscibile.

unreliable [ˌʌnrɪˈlaɪəbl] *adj* inaffidabile.

unrest [ˌʌnˈrest] *n* agitazione *f*.

unroll [ˌʌnˈrəʊl] *vt* srotolare.

unsafe [ˌʌnˈseɪf] *adj (dangerous)* pericoloso(-a); *(in danger)* in pericolo.

unsatisfactory [ˌʌnsætɪsˈfæktərɪ] *adj* insoddisfacente.

unscrew [ˌʌnˈskruː] *vt (lid, top)* svitare.

unsightly [ʌnˈsaɪtlɪ] *adj* brutto(-a).

unskilled [ˌʌnˈskɪld] *adj (worker)* non qualificato(-a).

unsociable [ʌnˈsəʊʃəbl] *adj* poco socievole.

unsound [ˌʌnˈsaʊnd] *adj (building, structure)* poco saldo(-a); *(argument)* che non regge.

unspoiled [ˌʌnˈspɔɪlt] *adj (place, beach)* incontaminato(-a).

unsteady [ˌʌnˈstedɪ] *adj* instabile; *(hand)* malfermo(-a).

unstuck [ˌʌnˈstʌk] *adj*: **to come** ~

(label, poster etc) staccarsi.
unsuccessful [ˌʌnsək'sesful] *adj* che non ha successo.
unsuitable [ˌʌn'su:təbl] *adj* inadatto(-a), inadeguato(-a); *(moment)* inopportuno(-a).
unsure [ˌʌn'ʃɔ:ʳ] *adj*: **to be ~ (about)** non essere sicuro(-a) (di).
unsweetened [ˌʌn'swi:tnd] *adj* senza zucchero.
untidy [ʌn'taɪdɪ] *adj (person)* disordinato(-a); *(room, desk)* in disordine.
untie [ˌʌn'taɪ] (*cont* **untying** [ˌʌn'taɪɪŋ]) *vt (person)* slegare; *(knot)* sciogliere, sfare.
until [ən'tɪl] ◇ *prep* fino a ◇ *conj* finché; *(after negative, in past)* prima che, prima di; **it won't be ready ~ Thursday** non sarà pronto prima di giovedì.
untrue [ˌʌn'tru:] *adj* falso(-a).
untrustworthy [ˌʌn'trʌstˌwɜ:ðɪ] *adj* che non è degno(-a) di fiducia.
untying *cont* → **untie**.
unusual [ʌn'ju:ʒl] *adj* insolito(-a).
unusually [ʌn'ju:ʒəlɪ] *adv (more than usual)* insolitamente.
unwell [ˌʌn'wel] *adj* indisposto(-a); **to feel ~** non sentirsi bene.
unwilling [ˌʌn'wɪlɪŋ] *adj*: **to be ~ to do sthg** non voler fare qc.
unwind [ˌʌn'waɪnd] (*pt & pp* **unwound** [ˌʌn'waʊnd]) ◇ *vt* svolgere ◇ *vi (relax)* rilassarsi, distendersi.
unwrap [ˌʌn'ræp] *vt* aprire.
unzip [ˌʌn'zɪp] *vt* aprire (la cerniera di).
up [ʌp] ◇ *adv* **1.** *(towards higher position)* su, in alto; **to go ~** salire; **we walked ~ to the top** siamo saliti fino in cima; **to pick sthg ~** raccogliere qc.
2. *(in higher position)* su, in alto; **she's ~ in her bedroom** è su nella sua stanza; **~ there** lassù.
3. *(into upright position)*: **to stand ~** alzarsi; **to sit ~** *(from lying position)* tirarsi su a sedere; *(sit straight)* stare seduto diritto.
4. *(to increased level)*: **prices are going ~** i prezzi stanno salendo.
5. *(northwards)*: **~ in Scotland** in Scozia.
6. *(in phrases)*: **to walk ~ and down** andare su e giù; **~ to ten people** fino a dieci persone; **are you ~ to travelling?** te la senti di viaggiare?; **what are you ~ to?** cosa stai combinando?; **it's ~ to you** sta a te decidere; **~ until ten o'clock** fino alle dieci.
◇ *prep* **1.** *(towards higher position)*: **to walk ~ a hill** salire su per una collina; **I went ~ the stairs** sono salito per le scale.
2. *(in higher position)* in cima a; **~ a hill** in cima ad una collina; **~ a ladder** in cima ad una scala.
3. *(at end of)*: **they live ~ the road from us** abitano un po' più su di noi.
◇ *adj* **1.** *(out of bed)* alzato(-a); **I was ~ at six today** mi sono alzato alle sei oggi.
2. *(at an end)*: **time's ~** tempo scaduto.
3. *(rising)*: **the ~ escalator** la scala mobile per salire.
◇ *n*: **~s and downs** alti e bassi *mpl*.
update [ˌʌp'deɪt] *vt* aggiornare.
uphill [ˌʌp'hɪl] *adv* in salita.
upholstery [ʌp'həʊlstərɪ] *n* tappezzeria *f*.
upkeep ['ʌpki:p] *n* manutenzione *f*.
up-market *adj* rivolto(-a) alla fascia alta del mercato.
upon [ə'pɒn] *prep (fml: on)* su; **~ hearing the news** ... dopo aver appreso la notizia ...
upper ['ʌpəʳ] ◇ *adj* superiore ◇ *n (of shoe)* tomaia *f*.
upper class *n*: **the ~** i ceti alti.
uppermost ['ʌpəməʊst] *adj*

(highest) il più alto (la più alta).

upper sixth *n (Br:* SCH*) secondo anno del corso biennale che prepara agli 'A levels'.*

upright ['ʌpraɪt] ◇ *adj (person)* diritto(-a); *(object)* verticale ◇ *adv* diritto.

upset [ʌp'set] (*pt & pp* **upset**) ◇ *adj (distressed)* addolorato(-a) ◇ *vt (distress)* addolorare, sconvolgere; *(cause to go wrong)* scombussolare; *(knock over)* rovesciare; **to have an ~ stomach** avere disturbi intestinali.

upside down [ˌʌpsaɪd-] ◇ *adj* capovolto(-a); *(person)* a testa in giù ◇ *adv* sottosopra.

upstairs [ˌʌp'steəz] ◇ *adj* di sopra ◇ *adv (on a higher floor)* di sopra, al piano superiore; **to go ~** andare di sopra.

up-to-date *adj (modern)* moderno(-a); *(well-informed)* aggiornato(-a).

upwards ['ʌpwədz] *adv (to a higher place)* verso l'alto, in su; *(to a higher level)* verso l'alto; **~ of 100 people** più di 100 persone.

urban ['ɜːbən] *adj* urbano(-a).

urban clearway [-'klɪəweɪ] *n (Br) strada con divieto di sosta.*

Urdu ['ʊəduː] *n* urdu *m.*

urge [ɜːdʒ] *vt*: **to ~ sb to do sthg** esortare qn a fare qc.

urgent ['ɜːdʒənt] *adj* urgente.

urgently ['ɜːdʒəntlɪ] *adv (immediately)* d'urgenza, urgentemente.

urinal [ˌjʊə'raɪnl] *n (fml) (bowl)* orinale *m*; *(place)* vespasiano *m.*

urinate ['jʊərɪneɪt] *vi (fml)* urinare.

urine ['jʊərɪn] *n* urina *f.*

us [ʌs] *pron* ci; *(after prep)* noi; **they know ~** ci conoscono; **it's ~** siamo noi; **send it to ~** mandacelo; **tell ~** dicci; **they're worse than ~** sono peggio di noi.

US *n (abbr of United States)*: **the ~** gli USA.

USA *n (abbr of United States of America)*: **the ~** gli USA.

usable ['juːzəbl] *adj* utilizzabile.

use [*n* juːs, *vb* juːz] ◇ *n* uso *m* ◇ *vt* usare; *(run on)* andare a; **to be of ~** essere utile, servire; **to have the ~ of sthg** avere accesso a qc; **to make ~ of sthg** sfruttare qc; **'out of ~'** 'guasto'; **to be in ~** essere in uso; **it's no ~** non serve a niente; **what's the ~?** a che scopo?; **to ~ sthg as sthg** usare qc come qc; **'~ before …'** *(food, drink)* 'da consumarsi preferibilmente entro …'.

◆ **use up** *vt sep* consumare.

used [*adj* juːzd, *aux vb* juːst] ◇ *adj (towel, glass etc)* sporco(-a); *(car)* usato(-a) ◇ *aux vb*: **I ~ to live near here** una volta abitavo qui vicino; **I ~ to go there every day** una volta ci andavo tutti i giorni; **to be ~ to sthg** essere abituato(-a) a qc; **to get ~ to sthg** abituarsi a qc.

useful ['juːsfʊl] *adj* utile.

useless ['juːslɪs] *adj* inutile; *(inf: very bad)*: **he's ~** non è buono a nulla.

user ['juːzəʳ] *n* utente *mf.*

usher ['ʌʃəʳ] *n (at cinema, theatre)* maschera *f.*

usherette [ˌʌʃə'ret] *n* maschera *f.*

USSR *n*: **the (former) ~** l'(ex) URSS *f.*

usual ['juːʒəl] *adj* solito(-a); **as ~** *(in the normal way)* come al solito.

usually ['juːʒəlɪ] *adv* di solito.

utensil [juː'tensl] *n* utensile *m.*

utilize ['juːtəlaɪz] *vt (fml)* utilizzare.

utmost ['ʌtməʊst] ◇ *adj* estremo(-a) ◇ *n*: **to do one's ~** fare tutto il possibile.

utter ['ʌtəʳ] ◇ *adj* totale ◇ *vt (word)* proferire, pronunciare; *(cry)* emettere.

utterly ['ʌtəlɪ] *adv* completamente, del tutto.

U-turn *n (in vehicle)* inversione *f* a U.

vacancy ['veɪkənsɪ] *n (job)* posto *m* vacante; **'vacancies'** 'si affittano camere'; **'no vacancies'** 'completo'.

vacant ['veɪkənt] *adj* libero(-a).

vacate [və'keɪt] *vt (fml: room, house)* lasciare libero.

vacation [və'keɪʃn] ◇ *n (Am) (period of time)* vacanze *fpl*; *(time off work)* ferie *fpl* ◇ *vi (Am)* passare le vacanze; **to go on ~** andare in vacanza.

vacationer [və'keɪʃənər] *n (Am)* villeggiante *mf*.

vaccination [,væksɪ'neɪʃn] *n* vaccinazione *f*.

vaccine [*Br* 'væksi:n, *Am* væk'si:n] *n* vaccino *m*.

vacuum ['vækjʊəm] *vt* pulire con l'aspirapolvere.

vacuum cleaner *n* aspirapolvere *m inv*.

vague [veɪg] *adj* vago(-a); *(shape, outline)* indistinto(-a).

vain [veɪn] *adj (pej: conceited)* vanitoso(-a); **in ~** invano.

Valentine card ['væləntaɪn-] *n biglietto che si manda per San Valentino alla persona che si ama o di cui si è innamorati.*

Valentine's Day ['væləntaɪnz-] *n* San Valentino.

valet ['væleɪ, 'vælɪt] *n (in hotel) chi si occupa del servizio lavanderia e stiratura.*

valet service *n (in hotel)* servizio *m* di lavanderia; *(for car)* servizio di lavaggio.

valid ['vælɪd] *adj (ticket, passport)* valido(-a).

validate ['vælɪdeɪt] *vt (ticket)* convalidare.

Valium® ['vælɪəm] *n* valium® *m*.

valley ['vælɪ] *n* valle *f*.

valuable ['væljʊəbl] *adj (jewellery, object)* di valore; *(advice, help)* prezioso(-a).

◆ **valuables** *npl* oggetti *mpl* di valore.

value ['vælju:] *n (financial)* valore *m*; *(usefulness)* utilità *f*; **a ~ pack** una confezione formato famiglia; **to be good ~ (for money)** essere conveniente.

◆ **values** *npl (principles)* valori *mpl*.

valve [vælv] *n* valvola *f*.

van [væn] *n* furgone *m*.

vandal ['vændl] *n* vandalo *m* (-a *f*).

vandalize ['vændəlaɪz] *vt* vandalizzare.

vanilla [və'nɪlə] *n* vaniglia *f*.

vanish ['vænɪʃ] *vi* svanire, scomparire.

vapor ['veɪpər] *(Am)* = **vapour**.

vapour ['veɪpər] *n (Br)* vapore *m*.

variable ['veərɪəbl] *adj* variabile.

varicose veins ['værɪkəʊs-] *npl* vene *fpl* varicose.

varied ['veərɪd] *adj* vario(-a).
variety [və'raɪətɪ] *n* varietà *f inv.*
various ['veərɪəs] *adj* vari(-e).
varnish ['vɑːnɪʃ] ◇ *n* vernice *f* ◇ *vt* verniciare.
vary ['veərɪ] *vi & vt* variare.
vase [*Br* vɑːz, *Am* veɪz] *n* vaso *m.*
Vaseline® ['væsəliːn] *n* vaselina *f.*
vast [vɑːst] *adj* vasto(-a).
vat [væt] *n* tino *m.*
VAT [væt, viːeɪ'tiː] *n (abbr of value added tax)* IVA *f.*
vault [vɔːlt] *n (in bank)* camera *f* blindata; *(in church)* cripta *f.*
VCR *n (abbr of video cassette recorder)* videoregistratore *m.*
VDU *n (abbr of visual display unit)* monitor *m inv.*
veal [viːl] *n* vitello *m.*
veg [vedʒ] *abbr* = **vegetable**.
vegan ['viːgən] ◇ *adj* vegetaliano(-a) ◇ *n* vegetaliano *m* (-a *f*).
vegetable ['vedʒtəbl] *n* verdura *f.*
vegetable oil *n* olio *m* vegetale.
vegetarian [ˌvedʒɪ'teərɪən] ◇ *adj* vegetariano(-a) ◇ *n* vegetariano *m* (-a *f*).
vegetation [ˌvedʒɪ'teɪʃn] *n* vegetazione *f.*
vehicle ['viːəkl] *n* veicolo *m.*
veil [veɪl] *n* velo *m.*
vein [veɪn] *n* vena *f.*
Velcro® ['velkrəʊ] *n* velcro® *m.*
velvet ['velvɪt] *n* velluto *m.*
vending machine ['vendɪŋ-] *n* distributore *m* automatico.
venetian blind [vɪˌniːʃn-] *n* veneziana *f.*
Venice ['venɪs] *n* Venezia *f.*
venison ['venɪzn] *n* carne *m* di cervo.
vent [vent] *n (for air, smoke etc)* presa *f* d'aria.
ventilation [ˌventɪ'leɪʃn] *n* ventilazione *f.*
ventilator ['ventɪleɪtəʳ] *n* ventilatore *m.*
venture ['ventʃəʳ] ◇ *n* impresa *f* ◇ *vi (go)* avventurarsi.
venue ['venjuː] *n* luogo *m (di partita, concerto ecc.).*
veranda [və'rændə] *n* veranda *f.*
verb [vɜːb] *n* verbo *m.*
verdict ['vɜːdɪkt] *n* verdetto *m.*
verge [vɜːdʒ] *n (of road, lawn, path)* bordo *m*; **'soft ~s'** 'banchina non transitabile'.
verify ['verɪfaɪ] *vt* verificare.
vermin ['vɜːmɪn] *n roditori che portano malattie e distruggono raccolti.*
vermouth ['vɜːməθ] *n* vermut *m inv.*
versa → **vice versa**.
versatile ['vɜːsətaɪl] *adj* versatile.
verse [vɜːs] *n (of song, poem)* strofa *f*; *(poetry)* versi *mpl.*
version ['vɜːʃn] *n* versione *f.*
versus ['vɜːsəs] *prep* contro.
vertical ['vɜːtɪkl] *adj* verticale.
vertigo ['vɜːtɪgəʊ] *n*: **to suffer from ~** soffrire di vertigini.
very ['verɪ] ◇ *adv* molto ◇ *adj*: **at the ~ bottom** proprio in fondo; **~ much** molto; **not ~ big** non molto grande; **my ~ own room** una stanza tutta per me; **~ rich** ricchissimo, molto ricco; **it's the ~ thing I need** è proprio quello di cui avevo bisogno.
vessel ['vesl] *n (fml: ship)* vascello *m.*
vest [vest] *n (Br: underwear)* maglietta *f*; *(sleeveless)* canottiera *f*; *(Am: waistcoat)* gilè *m inv.*
Vesuvius [vɪ'suːvjəs] *n* Vesuvio *m.*
vet [vet] *n (Br)* veterinario *m* (-a *f*).
veteran ['vetrən] *n (of war)* vecchio combattente *m.*
veterinarian [ˌvetərɪ'neərɪən] *(Am)* = **vet**.
veterinary surgeon ['vetərɪnrɪ-] *(Br: fml)* = **vet**.
VHF *n (abbr of very high frequency)* VHF *f.*

VHS *n (abbr of video home system)* VHS *m*.
via ['vaɪə] *prep (place)* via; *(by means of)* tramite.
viaduct ['vaɪədʌkt] *n* viadotto *m*.
vibrate [vaɪ'breɪt] *vi* vibrare.
vibration [vaɪ'breɪʃn] *n* vibrazione *f*.
vicar ['vɪkəʳ] *n* pastore *m*.
vicarage ['vɪkərɪdʒ] *n* presbiterio *m*.
vice [vaɪs] *n (moral fault)* vizio *m*; *(crime)* crimine *m*; *(Br: tool)* morsa *f*.
vice-president *n* vice-presidente *mf*.
vice versa [,vaɪsɪ'vɜːsə] *adv* viceversa.
vicinity [vɪ'sɪnətɪ] *n*: **in the ~** nelle vicinanze.
vicious ['vɪʃəs] *adj (attack)* violento(-a); *(animal)* feroce; *(comment)* cattivo(-a), maligno(-a).
victim ['vɪktɪm] *n* vittima *f*.
Victorian [vɪk'tɔːrɪən] *adj* vittoriano(-a).
victory ['vɪktərɪ] *n* vittoria *f*.
video ['vɪdɪəʊ] (*pl* **-s**) ◇ *n (video recording)* video *m inv*; *(videotape)* videocassetta *f*; *(video recorder)* videoregistratore *m* ◇ *vt (using video recorder)* videoregistrare; *(using camera)* filmare; **on ~** su videocassetta.
video camera *n* videocamera *f*.
video game *n* videogioco *m*.
video recorder *n* videoregistratore *m*.
video shop *n* videoteca *f*.
videotape ['vɪdɪəʊteɪp] *n* videocassetta *f*.
Vietnam [*Br* ,vjet'næm, *Am* ,vjet'nɑːm] *n* il Vietnam.
view [vjuː] ◇ *n* vista *f*; *(opinion)* opinione *f* ◇ *vt (house)* vedere; *(situation)* considerare; **in my ~** secondo me; **in ~ of** *(considering)* considerato; **to come into ~** apparire.
viewer ['vjuːəʳ] *n (of TV)* telespettatore *m* (-trice *f*).
viewfinder ['vjuː,faɪndəʳ] *n* mirino *m*.
viewpoint ['vjuːpɔɪnt] *n (opinion)* punto *m* di vista; *(place)* punto d'osservazione.
vigilant ['vɪdʒɪlənt] *adj (fml)* vigile.
villa ['vɪlə] *n* villa *f*.
village ['vɪlɪdʒ] *n* paese *m*.
villager ['vɪlɪdʒəʳ] *n* abitante *mf* di paese.
villain ['vɪlən] *n (of book, film)* cattivo *m*; *(criminal)* malvivente *mf*.
vinaigrette [,vɪnɪ'gret] *n condimento per insalata a base di olio, aceto, sale, pepe ed erbe aromatiche.*
vine [vaɪn] *n (grapevine)* vite *f*; *(climbing plant)* rampicante *m*.
vinegar ['vɪnɪgəʳ] *n* aceto *m*.
vineyard ['vɪnjəd] *n* vigna *f*.
vintage ['vɪntɪdʒ] ◇ *adj (wine)* d'annata ◇ *n (year)* annata *f*.
vinyl ['vaɪnɪl] *n* vinile *m*.
viola [vɪ'əʊlə] *n* viola *f*.
violence ['vaɪələns] *n* violenza *f*.
violent ['vaɪələnt] *adj* violento(-a).
violet ['vaɪələt] ◇ *adj* viola *(inv)* ◇ *n (flower)* viola *f*.
violin [,vaɪə'lɪn] *n* violino *m*.
VIP *n (abbr of very important person)* vip *mf inv*.
virgin ['vɜːdʒɪn] *n* vergine *f*.
Virgo ['vɜːgəʊ] (*pl* **-s**) *n* Vergine *f*.
virtually ['vɜːtʃʊəlɪ] *adv* praticamente.
virtual reality ['vɜːtʃʊəl-] *n* realtà *f* virtuale.
virus ['vaɪrəs] *n* virus *m inv*.
visa ['viːzə] *n* visto *m*.
viscose ['vɪskəʊs] *n* viscosa *f*.
visibility [,vɪzɪ'bɪlətɪ] *n* visibilità *f*.
visible ['vɪzəbl] *adj* visibile.
visit ['vɪzɪt] ◇ *vt (person)* andare a trovare; *(place)* visitare ◇ *n* visita *f*.
visiting hours ['vɪzɪtɪŋ-] *npl* ora-

rio *m* delle visite.

visitor ['vɪzɪtəʳ] *n (to person)* visita *f*; *(to place)* visitatore *m* (-trice *f*).

visitor centre *n (at tourist attraction) punto accoglienza per i visitatori di musei ecc.*

visitors' book *n* registro *m* dei visitatori.

visitor's passport *n (Br)* passaporto *m* provvisorio.

visor ['vaɪzəʳ] *n* visiera *f*.

vital ['vaɪtl] *adj* vitale.

vitamin [*Br* 'vɪtəmɪn, *Am* 'vaɪtəmɪn] *n* vitamina *f*.

vivid ['vɪvɪd] *adj* vivido(-a).

V-neck *n (design)* scollo *m* a V.

vocabulary [və'kæbjʊlərɪ] *n* vocabolario *m*.

vodka ['vɒdkə] *n* vodka *f*.

voice [vɔɪs] *n* voce *f*.

voice mail *n* messaggeria *f* vocale.

volcano [vɒl'keɪnəʊ] (*pl* **-es** OR **-s**) *n* vulcano *m*.

volleyball ['vɒlɪbɔːl] *n* pallavolo *f*.

volt [vəʊlt] *n* volt *m inv*.

voltage ['vəʊltɪdʒ] *n* voltaggio *m*.

volume ['vɒljuːm] *n* volume *m*.

voluntary ['vɒləntrɪ] *adj* volontario(-a).

volunteer [ˌvɒlən'tɪəʳ] ◇ *n* volontario *m* (-a *f*) ◇ *vt*: **to ~ to do sthg** offrirsi di fare qc.

vomit ['vɒmɪt] ◇ *n* vomito *m* ◇ *vi* vomitare.

vote [vəʊt] ◇ *n* voto *m*; *(number of votes)* voti *mpl* ◇ *vi*: **to ~ (for)** votare (per).

voter ['vəʊtəʳ] *n* elettore *m* (-trice *f*).

voucher ['vaʊtʃəʳ] *n* buono *m*.

vowel ['vaʊəl] *n* vocale *f*.

voyage ['vɔɪɪdʒ] *n* viaggio *m (per mare)*.

vulgar ['vʌlgəʳ] *adj* volgare.

vulture ['vʌltʃəʳ] *n* avvoltoio *m*.

W *(abbr of west)* O.
wad [wɒd] *n (of paper, banknotes)* fascio *m*; *(of cotton)* batuffolo *m*.
waddle ['wɒdl] *vi* camminare come una papera.
wade [weɪd] *vi* camminare *(a fatica)*.
wading pool ['weɪdɪŋ-] *n (Am)* piscina *f* per bambini.
wafer ['weɪfəʳ] *n (biscuit)* cialda *f*.
waffle ['wɒfl] ◇ *n (pancake) cialda dalla caratteristica superficie a quadretti che si mangia con sciroppo d'acero, panna o frutta* ◇ *vi (inf)* parlare molto e dire poco.
wag [wæg] *vt* agitare.
wage [weɪdʒ] *n* salario *m*.
◆ **wages** *npl* salario *m*.
wagon ['wægən] *n (vehicle)* carro *m*; *(Br: of train)* vagone *m*.
waist [weɪst] *n* vita *f*.
waistcoat ['weɪskəʊt] *n* gilè *m inv*.
wait [weɪt] ◇ *n* attesa *f* ◇ *vi* aspettare; **to ~ for sb to do sthg** aspettare che qn faccia qc; **I can't ~!** non vedo l'ora!
◆ **wait for** *vt fus* aspettare.
waiter ['weɪtəʳ] *n* cameriere *m*.
waiting room ['weɪtɪŋ-] *n* sala *f* d'attesa OR d'aspetto.
waitress ['weɪtrɪs] *n* cameriera *f*.
wake [weɪk] (*pt* **woke**, *pp* **woken**) ◇ *vt* svegliare ◇ *vi* svegliarsi.
◆ **wake up** ◇ *vt sep* svegliare ◇ *vi* svegliarsi.
Waldorf salad ['wɔːldɔːf-] *n insalata a base di mele, sedano e noci, condita con maionese*.
Wales [weɪlz] *n* il Galles.
walk [wɔːk] ◇ *n (journey, path)* passeggiata *f* ◇ *vi* camminare ◇ *vt (distance)* percorrere a piedi; *(dog)* portare a spasso; **to go for a ~** andare a fare una passeggiata; **it's a short ~** a piedi è vicino; **to take the dog for a ~** portare a spasso il cane; **'walk'** *(Am)* 'avanti'; **'don't ~'** *(Am)* 'alt'.
◆ **walk away** *vi* andarsene.
◆ **walk in** *vi* entrare.
◆ **walk out** *vi (leave angrily)* andarsene.
walker ['wɔːkəʳ] *n* camminatore *m* (-trice *f*).
walking boots ['wɔːkɪŋ-] *npl* scarponcini *mpl*.
walking stick ['wɔːkɪŋ-] *n* bastone *m*.
Walkman® ['wɔːkmən] *n* walkman® *m*.
wall [wɔːl] *n* muro *m*; *(internal)* parete *f*, muro.
wallet ['wɒlɪt] *n (for money)* portafoglio *m*.
wallpaper ['wɔːl,peɪpəʳ] *n* carta *f* da parati.

wally ['wɒlɪ] *n (Br: inf)* cretino *m* (-a *f*).
walnut ['wɔːlnʌt] *n (nut)* noce *f*.
waltz [wɔːls] *n* valzer *m inv*.
wander ['wɒndəʳ] *vi* vagare.
want [wɒnt] *vt* volere; *(need)* aver bisogno di; **to ~ to do sthg** voler fare qc; **to ~ sb to do sthg** volere che qn faccia qc.
war [wɔːʳ] *n* guerra *f*.
ward [wɔːd] *n (in hospital)* reparto *m*.
warden ['wɔːdn] *n (of park)* guardiano *m*; *(of youth hostel)* custode *mf*.
wardrobe ['wɔːdrəʊb] *n (cupboard)* armadio *m*; *(clothes)* guardaroba *m inv*.
warehouse ['weəhaʊs, *pl* -haʊzɪz] *n* magazzino *m*.
warm [wɔːm] ◇ *adj* caldo (-a); *(person, smile)* cordiale; *(welcome)* caloroso(-a) ◇ *vt* scaldare, riscaldare; **to be ~** *(person)* avere caldo; **it's ~** *(weather)* è OR fa caldo.
◆ **warm up** ◇ *vt sep* scaldare, riscaldare ◇ *vi (get warmer)* scaldarsi, riscaldarsi; *(do exercises)* riscaldarsi; *(machine, engine)* scaldare.
war memorial *n* monumento *m* ai caduti.
warmth [wɔːmθ] *n* calore *m*.
warn [wɔːn] *vt* avvertire, avvisare; **to ~ sb about sthg** avvisare qn di qc; **to ~ sb not to do sthg** avvertire qn di non fare qc.
warning ['wɔːnɪŋ] *n (of danger)* avvertimento *m*; *(advance notice)* preavviso *m*.
warranty ['wɒrəntɪ] *n (fml)* garanzia *f*.
warship ['wɔːʃɪp] *n* nave *f* da guerra.
wart [wɔːt] *n* verruca *f*.
was [wɒz] *pt* → **be**.
wash [wɒʃ] ◇ *vt* lavare ◇ *vi* lavarsi ◇ *n*: **to give sthg a ~** dare una lavata a qc; **to have a ~** lavarsi; **to ~ one's hands/face** lavarsi le mani/il viso.
◆ **wash up** *vi (Br: do washing-up)* lavare i piatti; *(Am: clean o.s.)* lavarsi.
washable ['wɒʃəbl] *adj* lavabile.
washbasin ['wɒʃˌbeɪsn] *n* lavabo *m*.
washbowl ['wɒʃbəʊl] *n (Am)* lavabo *m*.
washer ['wɒʃəʳ] *n (ring)* rondella *f*.
washing ['wɒʃɪŋ] *n* bucato *m*.
washing line *n* corda *f* del bucato.
washing machine *n* lavatrice *f*.
washing powder *n* detersivo *m* in polvere.
washing-up *n (Br)*: **to do the ~** fare i piatti.
washing-up bowl *n (Br)* bacinella *f*.
washing-up liquid *n (Br)* detersivo *m* liquido per piatti.
washroom ['wɒʃrʊm] *n (Am)* bagno *m*, gabinetto *m*.
wasn't [wɒznt] = **was not**.
wasp [wɒsp] *n* vespa *f*.
waste [weɪst] ◇ *n (rubbish)* rifiuti *mpl* ◇ *vt* sprecare; **a ~ of money** uno spreco di denaro; **a ~ of time** una perdita di tempo.
wastebin ['weɪstbɪn] *n* cestino *m* (dei rifiuti).
waste ground *n* terreno *m* abbandonato.
wastepaper basket [ˌweɪst'peɪpəʳ-] *n* cestino *m* (per la carta straccia).
watch [wɒtʃ] ◇ *n (wristwatch)* orologio *m* ◇ *vt (observe)* guardare; *(spy on)* sorvegliare; *(be careful with)* fare attenzione a.
◆ **watch out** *vi (be careful)* stare attento, fare attenzione; **to ~ out for** *(look for)* cercare.

watchstrap [ˈwɒtʃstræp] *n* cinturino *m* dell'orologio.

water [ˈwɔːtəʳ] ◇ *n* acqua *f* ◇ *vt (plants, garden)* annaffiare ◇ *vi (eyes)* lacrimare; **it makes my mouth ~** mi fa venire l'acquolina in bocca.

water bottle *n* borraccia *f*.

watercolour [ˈwɔːtəˌkʌləʳ] *n* acquerello *m*.

watercress [ˈwɔːtəkres] *n* crescione *m*.

waterfall [ˈwɔːtəfɔːl] *n* cascata *f*.

watering can [ˈwɔːtərɪŋ-] *n* annaffiatoio *m*.

watermelon [ˈwɔːtəˌmelən] *n* cocomero *m*, anguria *f*.

waterproof [ˈwɔːtəpruːf] *adj* impermeabile.

water purification tablets [-pjʊərɪfɪˈkeɪʃn-] *npl* compresse *fpl* per la disinfezione dell'acqua.

water skiing *n* sci *m* nautico.

watersports [ˈwɔːtəspɔːts] *npl* sport *mpl* acquatici.

water tank *n* cisterna *f*.

watertight [ˈwɔːtətaɪt] *adj* stagno(-a).

watt [wɒt] *n* watt *m inv*; **a 60-~ bulb** una lampadina da 60 watt.

wave [weɪv] ◇ *n* onda *f*; *(of crime, violence)* ondata *f* ◇ *vt (hand)* agitare; *(flag)* sventolare ◇ *vi (to attract attention)* fare un cenno (con la mano); *(when greeting, saying goodbye)* salutare con la mano.

wavelength [ˈweɪvleŋθ] *n* lunghezza *f* d'onda.

wavy [ˈweɪvɪ] *adj (hair)* ondulato(-a).

wax [wæks] *n (for candles)* cera *f*; *(in ears)* cerume *m*.

way [weɪ] *n (manner, means)* modo *m*; *(route)* strada *f*; *(direction)* parte *f*, direzione *f*; *(distance travelled)* tragitto *m*; **which ~ is the station?** da che parte è la stazione?; **the town is out of our ~** la città non è sulla nostra strada; **to be in the ~** essere d'intralcio; **to be on the ~** *(person)* stare arrivando; *(meal)* essere in arrivo; **to get out of sb's ~** lasciar passare qn; **to get under ~** cominciare; **a long ~ away** lontano; **to lose one's ~** smarrirsi; **on the ~ back** al ritorno; **on the ~ there** all'andata; **that ~** *(like that)* in quel modo; *(in that direction)* da quella parte; **this ~** *(like this)* in questo modo; *(in this direction)* da questa parte; **'give ~'** 'dare la precedenza'; **'~ in'** 'entrata'; **'~ out'** 'uscita'; **no ~!** *(inf)* neanche per sogno!

WC *n (abbr of water closet)* W.C. *m inv*.

we [wiː] *pron* noi; **~'re fine** stiamo bene.

weak [wiːk] *adj* debole; *(drink)* leggero(-a); *(soup)* liquido(-a).

weaken [ˈwiːkn] *vt* indebolire.

weakness [ˈwiːknɪs] *n* debolezza *f*.

wealth [welθ] *n* ricchezza *f*.

wealthy [ˈwelθɪ] *adj* ricco(-a).

weapon [ˈwepən] *n* arma *f*.

wear [weəʳ] (*pt* **wore**, *pp* **worn**) ◇ *vt* portare, indossare ◇ *n (clothes)* abbigliamento *m*; **~ and tear** usura *f*.

◆ **wear off** *vi* passare.

◆ **wear out** *vi* consumarsi.

weary [ˈwɪərɪ] *adj* stanco(-a).

weasel [ˈwiːzl] *n* donnola *f*.

weather [ˈweðəʳ] *n* tempo *m*; **what's the ~ like?** che tempo fa?; **to be under the ~** *(inf)* sentirsi poco bene.

weather forecast *n* previsioni *fpl* del tempo.

weather forecaster [-fɔːkɑːstəʳ] *n* meteorologo *m* (-a *f*).

weather report *n* bollettino *m* meteorologico.

weather vane [-veɪn] *n* banderuola *f*.

weave [wiːv] (*pt* **wove**, *pp*

woven) *vt* tessere.

web [web] *n (of spider)* ragnatela *f*.

Web site *n* (COMPUT) sito *m* Web.

Wed. *(abbr of Wednesday)* mer.

wedding ['wedɪŋ] *n* matrimonio *m*.

wedding anniversary *n* anniversario *m* di matrimonio.

wedding dress *n* abito *m* da sposa.

wedding ring *n* fede *f*.

wedge [wedʒ] *n (of cake)* fetta *f*; *(of wood etc)* cuneo *m*.

Wednesday ['wenzdɪ] *n* mercoledì *m inv*, → **Saturday**.

wee [wiː] ◇ *adj (Scot)* piccolo(-a) ◇ *n (inf)* pipì *f*.

weed [wiːd] *n* erbaccia *f*.

week [wiːk] *n* settimana *f*; **a ~ today** oggi a otto; **in a ~'s time** fra una settimana.

weekday ['wiːkdeɪ] *n* giorno *m* feriale.

weekend [ˌwiːk'end] *n* fine settimana *m inv*.

weekly ['wiːklɪ] ◇ *adj* settimanale ◇ *adv* ogni settimana ◇ *n* settimanale *m*.

weep [wiːp] (*pt & pp* **wept**) *vi* piangere.

weigh [weɪ] *vt* pesare; **how much does it ~?** quanto pesa?

weight [weɪt] *n* peso *m*; **to lose ~** dimagrire; **to put on ~** ingrassare. ♦ **weights** *npl (for weight training)* pesi *mpl*.

weightlifting ['weɪtˌlɪftɪŋ] *n* sollevamento *m* pesi.

weight training *n* allenamento *m* ai pesi.

weir [wɪəʳ] *n* chiusa *f*.

weird [wɪəd] *adj* strano(-a).

welcome ['welkəm] ◇ *adj (guest)* benvenuto(-a); *(appreciated)* gradito(-a) ◇ *n* accoglienza *f* ◇ *vt (greet)* dare il benvenuto a; *(be grateful for)* gradire ◇ *excl* benvenuto!; **you're ~ to help yourself** si serva pure; **to make sb feel ~** far sentire qn benaccetto; **you're ~!** prego!

weld [weld] *vt* saldare.

welfare ['welfeəʳ] *n (happiness, comfort)* benessere *m*; *(Am: money)* sussidio *m*.

well [wel] (*compar* **better**, *superl* **best**) ◇ *adj* bene ◇ *adv* bene; *(a lot)* molto ◇ *n* pozzo *m*; **to get ~** guarire; **to go ~** andar bene; **~ done!** bravo!; **it may ~ happen** è assai probabile che accada; **it's ~ worth it** ne vale ben la pena; **as ~** *(in addition)* anche; **as ~ as** *(in addition to)* oltre a.

we'll [wiːl] = **we shall, we will**.

well-behaved [-bɪ'heɪvd] *adj* educato(-a).

well-built *adj* aitante.

well-done *adj (meat)* ben cotto (-a).

well-dressed [-'drest] *adj* vestito(-a) bene.

wellington (boot) ['welɪŋtən-] *n* stivale *m* di gomma.

well-known *adj* noto(-a).

well-off *adj (rich)* ricco(-a).

well-paid *adj* ben pagato(-a).

welly ['welɪ] *n (Br: inf)* stivale *m* di gomma.

Welsh [welʃ] ◇ *adj* gallese ◇ *n (language)* gallese *m* ◇ *npl*: **the ~** i gallesi.

Welshman ['welʃmən] (*pl* **-men** [-mən]) *n* gallese *m*.

Welsh rarebit [-'reəbɪt] *n crostino di formaggio fuso.*

Welshwoman ['welʃˌwʊmən] (*pl* **-women** [-ˌwɪmɪn]) *n* gallese *f*.

went [went] *pt* → **go**.

wept [wept] *pt & pp* → **weep**.

were [wɜːʳ] *pt* → **be**.

we're [wɪəʳ] = **we are**.

weren't [wɜːnt] = **were not**.

west [west] ◇ *n* ovest *m*, occidente *m* ◇ *adj* dell'ovest ◇ *adv (fly, walk)* verso ovest; *(be situated)* a ovest; **in the ~ of England**

nell'Inghilterra occidentale.

westbound ['westbaʊnd] *adj* diretto(-a) a ovest.

West Country *n*: **the ~** l'Inghilterra *f* sud-occidentale.

West End *n*: **the ~** *(of London) zona occidentale del centro di Londra, celebre per i suoi negozi, cinema e teatri.*

western ['westən] ◇ *adj* occidentale ◇ *n (film)* western *m inv*.

West Indies [-'ɪndiːz] *npl* le Indie Occidentali.

Westminster ['westmɪnstəʳ] *n quartiere nel centro di Londra.*

Westminster Abbey *n* l'abbazia *f* di Westminster.

westwards ['westwədz] *adv* verso ovest.

wet [wet] (*pt & pp* **wet** OR **-ted**) ◇ *adj (soaked, damp)* bagnato(-a); *(rainy)* piovoso(-a) ◇ *vt* bagnare; **to get ~** bagnarsi; **'~ paint'** 'vernice fresca'.

wet suit *n* muta *f*.

we've [wiːv] = **we have**.

whale [weɪl] *n* balena *f*.

wharf [wɔːf] (*pl* **-s** OR **wharves** [wɔːvz]) *n* banchina *f*.

what [wɒt] ◇ *adj* **1.** *(in questions)* che, quale; **~ colour is it?** di che colore è?; **he asked me ~ colour it was** mi ha chiesto di che colore era. **2.** *(in exclamations)*: **~ a surprise!** che sorpresa!; **~ a beautiful day!** che bella giornata!

◇ *pron* **1.** *(in direct questions)* (che) cosa; **~ is going on?** (che) cosa succede?; **~ are they doing?** (che) cosa fanno?; **~ is that?** (che) cos'è?; **~ is it called?** come si chiama?; **~ are they talking about?** di (che) cosa parlano?; **~ is it for?** a (che) cosa serve?

2. *(in indirect questions, relative clauses)* cosa; **she asked me ~ had happened** m'ha chiesto cos'era successo; **she asked me ~ I had seen** mi ha chiesto cosa avevo visto; **she asked me ~ I was thinking about** m'ha chiesto a cosa pensavo; **~ worries me is ...** ciò che OR quello che mi preoccupa ...; **I didn't see ~ happened** non ho visto cos'è successo; **you can't have ~ you want** non puoi avere quello che vuoi.

3. *(in phrases)*: **~ for?** a che scopo?, perché?; **~ about going out for a meal?** cosa ne diresti di mangiare fuori?

◇ *excl* come?

whatever [wɒt'evəʳ] *pron*: **take ~ you want** prendi quello che vuoi; **~ I do, I'll lose** qualsiasi cosa faccia, perderò; **~ that may be** quale che sia.

wheat [wiːt] *n* grano *m*, frumento *m*.

wheel [wiːl] *n* ruota *f*; *(steering wheel)* volante *m*.

wheelbarrow ['wiːl,bærəʊ] *n* carriola *f*.

wheelchair ['wiːl,tʃeəʳ] *n* sedia *f* a rotelle.

wheelclamp [,wiːl'klæmp] *n* bloccaruota *m inv*.

wheezy ['wiːzɪ] *adj* ansante.

when [wen] ◇ *adv* quando ◇ *conj* quando; *(although, seeing as)* sebbene, mentre; **~ it's ready** quando è pronto; **~ I've finished** quando avrò finito.

whenever [wen'evəʳ] *conj* ogni volta che; **~ you like** quando vuoi.

where [weəʳ] *adv & conj* dove; **this is ~ you'll be sleeping** è qui che dormirà.

whereabouts ['weərəbaʊts] ◇ *adv* dove ◇ *npl*: **his ~ are unknown** nessuno sa dove si trovi.

whereas [weər'æz] *conj* mentre.

wherever [weər'evəʳ] *conj* dovunque; **~ you like** dove vuoi; **~ that may be** dove che sia.

whether ['weðəʳ] *conj* se; **~ you like it or not** ti piaccia o no.

which [wɪtʃ] ◇ *adj (in questions)* quale; ~ **room do you want?** quale stanza vuole?; ~ **one?** quale?; **she asked me ~ room I wanted** mi ha chiesto quale stanza volevo.
◇ *pron* **1.** *(in questions)* quale; ~ **is the cheapest?** qual è il più economico?; ~ **do you prefer?** quale preferisci?; **he asked me ~ was the best** mi ha chiesto quale era il migliore; **he asked me ~ I preferred** mi ha chiesto quale preferivo.
2. *(introducing relative clause)* che; **the house ~ is on the corner** la casa che è all'angolo; **the television ~ I bought** il televisore che ho comprato.
3. *(introducing relative clause: after prep)* il quale (la quale); **the settee on ~ I'm sitting** il divano su cui siedo; **the book about ~ we were talking** il libro di cui stavamo parlando.
4. *(referring back)* il che, cosa che; **he's late, ~ annoys me** è in ritardo, il che mi secca molto.

whichever [wɪtʃ'evəʳ] ◇ *pron* quello(-a), quelli(-e) *(pl)* che ◇ *adj*: **take ~ chocolate you like best** prendi il cioccolatino che preferisci; ~ **chocolate you take** qualsiasi cioccolatino tu prenda.

while [waɪl] ◇ *conj* mentre; *(although)* sebbene ◇ *n*: **a ~** un po' (di tempo); **for a ~** per un po'; **in a ~** fra un po'.

whim [wɪm] *n* capriccio *m*.

whine [waɪn] *vi* gemere; *(complain)* frignare.

whip [wɪp] ◇ *n* frusta *f* ◇ *vt (with whip)* frustare.

whipped cream [wɪpt-] *n* panna *f* montata.

whirlpool ['wɜːlpuːl] *n (Jacuzzi)* vasca *f* per idromassaggi.

whisk [wɪsk] ◇ *n (utensil)* frusta *f*, frullino *m* ◇ *vt (eggs, cream)* sbattere.

whiskers ['wɪskəz] *npl (of person)* favoriti *m*; *(of animal)* baffi *m*.

whiskey ['wɪskɪ] (*pl* **-s**) *n* whisky *m inv (irlandese o americano)*.

whisky ['wɪskɪ] *n* whisky *m inv (scozzese)*.

whisper ['wɪspəʳ] *vt & vi* sussurrare.

whistle ['wɪsl] ◇ *n (instrument)* fischietto *m*; *(sound)* fischio *m* ◇ *vi* fischiare.

white [waɪt] ◇ *adj* bianco(-a); *(tea)* con latte ◇ *n* bianco *m*; *(person)* bianco *m* (-a *f*); ~ **coffee** caffè *m inv* con latte.

white bread *n* pane *m* bianco.

White House *n*: **the ~** la Casa Bianca.

white sauce *n* besciamella *f*.

white spirit *n* acquaragia *f*.

whitewash ['waɪtwɒʃ] *vt* imbiancare.

white wine *n* vino *m* bianco.

whiting ['waɪtɪŋ] *(pl inv) n* merlango *m*.

Whitsun ['wɪtsn] *n* Pentecoste *f*.

who [huː] *pron (in questions)* chi; *(in relative clauses)* che.

whoever [huː'evəʳ] *pron* chiunque; ~ **it is** chiunque sia.

whole [həʊl] ◇ *adj* intero(-a) ◇ *n*: **the ~ of the journey** tutto il viaggio; **on the ~** nel complesso; **the ~ time** tutto il tempo.

wholefoods ['həʊlfuːdz] *npl* prodotti *mpl* integrali.

wholemeal bread ['həʊlmiːl-] *n (Br)* pane *m* integrale.

wholesale ['həʊlseɪl] *adv* (COMM) all'ingrosso.

wholewheat bread ['həʊlˌwiːt-] *n (Am)* = **wholemeal bread**.

whom [huːm] *pron (fml: in questions)* chi; *(in relative clauses)* che; **to ~?** a chi?; **the person to ~ I wrote** la persona alla quale ho scritto.

whooping cough ['huːpɪŋ-] *n* pertosse *f*.

whose [huːz] *adj & pron*: ~ **jumper is this?** di chi è questo maglione?; **she asked ~ jumper it was** ha chiesto di chi era il maglione; **this is the woman ~ son is a priest** questa è la donna il cui figlio è un prete; ~ **is this?** di chi è questo?

why [waɪ] *adv & conj* perché; ~ **not?** perché no?; ~ **not do it tomorrow?** perché non farlo domani?

wick [wɪk] *n (of candle, lighter)* stoppino *m*.

wicked ['wɪkɪd] *adj (evil)* malvagio(-a); *(mischievous)* malizioso(-a).

wicker ['wɪkəʳ] *adj* di vimini.

wide [waɪd] ◇ *adj* largo(-a); *(opening)* ampio(-a); *(range, variety)* vasto(-a); *(difference, gap)* grande ◇ *adv*: **to open sthg ~** spalancare qc; **how ~ is the road?** quanto è larga la strada?; **it's 12 metres ~** è largo 12 metri; ~ **open** spalancato.

widely ['waɪdlɪ] *adv (known)* generalmente; *(travel)* molto.

widen ['waɪdn] ◇ *vt (make broader)* allargare ◇ *vi (gap, difference)* aumentare.

widespread ['waɪdspred] *adj* molto diffuso(-a).

widow ['wɪdəʊ] *n* vedova *f*.

widower ['wɪdəʊəʳ] *n* vedovo *m*.

width [wɪdθ] *n* larghezza *f*.

wife [waɪf] (*pl* **wives**) *n* moglie *f*.

wig [wɪg] *n* parrucca *f*.

wild [waɪld] *adj (animal, plant)* selvatico(-a); *(land, area)* selvaggio(-a); *(uncontrolled)* sfrenato(-a); *(crazy)* folle; **to be ~ about** *(inf)* andare pazzo(-a) per.

wild flower *n* fiore *m* di campo.

wildlife ['waɪldlaɪf] *n* flora e fauna *f*.

will¹ [wɪl] *aux vb* **1.** *(expressing future tense)*: **I ~ see you next week** ci vediamo la settimana prossima; ~ **you be here next Friday?** sarai qui venerdì prossimo?; **yes I ~** sì; **no I won't** no.

2. *(expressing willingness)*: **I won't do it** mi rifiuto di farlo.

3. *(expressing polite question)*: ~ **you have some more tea?** vuole ancora un po' di tè?

4. *(in commands, requests)*: ~ **you please be quiet!** volete tacere!; **close that window, ~ you?** chiudi la finestra, per favore.

will² [wɪl] *n (document)* testamento *m*; **against one's ~** contro la propria volontà.

willing ['wɪlɪŋ] *adj*: **to be ~ to do sthg** essere disposto(-a) a fare qc.

willingly ['wɪlɪŋlɪ] *adv* volentieri.

willow ['wɪləʊ] *n* salice *m*.

win [wɪn] (*pt & pp* **won**) ◇ *n* vittoria *f* ◇ *vt* vincere; *(support, approval, friends)* guadagnarsi ◇ *vi* vincere.

wind¹ [wɪnd] *n* vento *m*; *(in stomach)* aria *f*.

wind² [waɪnd] (*pt & pp* **wound**) ◇ *vi (road, river)* snodarsi ◇ *vt*: **to ~ sthg round sthg** avvolgere qc intorno a qc.

◆ **wind up** *vt sep (Br: inf: annoy)* dare sui nervi a; *(car window)* tirare su, chiudere; *(clock, watch)* caricare.

windbreak ['wɪndbreɪk] *n* frangivento *m*.

windmill ['wɪndmɪl] *n* mulino *m* a vento.

window ['wɪndəʊ] *n (of house)* finestra *f*; *(of shop)* vetrina *f*; *(of car)* finestrino *m*.

window box *n* cassetta *f* per fiori.

window cleaner *n* lavavetri *mf*.

windowpane ['wɪndəʊˌpeɪn] *n* vetro *m*.

window seat *n (on plane)* posto *m* finestrino.

window-shopping *n*: **to go ~** andare a guardare le vetrine.

windowsill ['wɪndəʊsɪl] *n* davanzale *m*.

windscreen ['wɪndskriːn] *n (Br)*

parabrezza *m inv*.
windscreen wipers *npl (Br)* tergicristalli *mpl*.
windshield ['wɪndʃi:ld] *n (Am)* parabrezza *m inv*.
Windsor Castle ['wɪnzə-] *n* il castello di Windsor.
windsurfing ['wɪnd,sɜ:fɪŋ] *n* windsurf *m*; **to go ~** fare del windsurf.
windy ['wɪndɪ] *adj* ventoso(-a); **it's ~** c'è vento.
wine [waɪn] *n* vino *m*.
wine bar *n (Br)* = enoteca *f*.
wineglass ['waɪnglɑ:s] *n* bicchiere *m* da vino.
wine list *n* lista *f* dei vini.
wine tasting [-'teɪstɪŋ] *n* degustazione *f* dei vini.
wine waiter *n* sommelier *mf inv*.
wing [wɪŋ] *n* ala *f*; *(Br: of car)* fiancata *f*.
◆ **wings** *npl*: **the ~s** *(in theatre)* le quinte.
wink [wɪŋk] *vi* strizzare l'occhio.
winner ['wɪnəʳ] *n* vincitore *m* (-trice *f*).
winning ['wɪnɪŋ] *adj* vincente.
winter ['wɪntəʳ] *n* inverno; **in (the) ~** d'inverno.
wintertime ['wɪntətaɪm] *n* inverno *m*.
wipe [waɪp] *vt* pulire; **to ~ one's hands/feet** pulirsi le mani/le scarpe.
◆ **wipe up** ◇ *vt sep (liquid)* asciugare; *(dirt)* pulire ◇ *vi (dry the dishes)* asciugare i piatti.
wiper ['waɪpəʳ] *n (windscreen wiper)* tergicristallo *m*.
wire ['waɪəʳ] ◇ *n* filo *m* di ferro; *(electrical)* filo (elettrico) ◇ *vt (plug)* collegare.
wireless ['waɪəlɪs] *n* radio *f inv*.
wiring ['waɪərɪŋ] *n* impianto *m* elettrico.
wisdom tooth ['wɪzdəm-] *n* dente *m* del giudizio.
wise [waɪz] *adj* saggio(-a).
wish [wɪʃ] ◇ *n (desire)* desiderio *m* ◇ *vt (desire)* desiderare; **best ~es** *(for birthday, recovery)* auguri; *(at end of letter)* cordiali saluti; **I ~ you'd told me earlier!** perché non me l'hai detto prima!; **I ~ I was younger** vorrei tanto essere più giovane; **to ~ for sthg** desiderare qc; **to ~ to do sthg** *(fml)* desiderare fare qc; **to ~ sb luck/happy birthday** augurare buona fortuna/buon compleanno a qn; **if you ~** *(fml)* se vuole.
witch [wɪtʃ] *n* strega *f*.
with [wɪð] *prep* **1.** *(gen)* con; **come ~ me** vieni con me; **a man ~ a beard** un uomo con la barba; **a room ~ a bathroom** una camera con bagno.
2. *(at house of)* da, a casa di; **we stayed ~ friends** siamo stati da amici.
3. *(indicating emotion)* di, per; **to tremble ~ fear** tremare di paura.
4. *(indicating opposition)*: **to argue ~ sb** litigare con qn; **to fight ~ sb** combattere contro qn.
5. *(indicating covering, contents)* di; **to fill sthg ~ sthg** riempire qc di qc; **topped ~ cream** ricoperto di panna.
withdraw [wɪð'drɔ:] (*pt* **-drew**, *pp* **-drawn**) ◇ *vt (take out)* ritirare; *(money)* prelevare ◇ *vi (from race, contest)* ritirarsi.
withdrawal [wɪð'drɔ:əl] *n (from bank account)* prelievo *m*.
withdrawn [wɪð'drɔ:n] *pp* → **withdraw**.
withdrew [wɪð'dru:] *pt* → **withdraw**.
wither ['wɪðəʳ] *vi* appassire.
within [wɪ'ðɪn] ◇ *prep (inside)* all'interno di; *(not exceeding)* entro ◇ *adv* all'interno, dentro; **~ walking distance** raggiungibile a piedi; **~ 10 miles of ...** a non più di 10

miglia da ...; **it arrived ~ a week** è arrivato nel giro di una settimana; **~ the next week** entro la prossima settimana.

without [wɪð'aʊt] *prep* senza; **~ doing sthg** senza fare qc.

withstand [wɪð'stænd] (*pt & pp* **-stood**) *vt* resistere a.

witness ['wɪtnɪs] ◇ *n* testimone *mf* ◇ *vt (see)* assistere a.

witty ['wɪtɪ] *adj* arguto(-a).

wives [waɪvz] *pl* → **wife**.

wobbly ['wɒblɪ] *adj (table, chair)* traballante.

wok [wɒk] *n padella larga e profonda usata nella cucina cinese.*

woke [wəʊk] *pt* → **wake**.

woken ['wəʊkn] *pp* → **wake**.

wolf [wʊlf] (*pl* **wolves** [wʊlvz]) *n* lupo *m*.

woman ['wʊmən] (*pl* **women**) *n* donna *f*.

womb [wu:m] *n* utero *m*.

women ['wɪmɪn] *pl* → **woman**.

won [wʌn] *pt & pp* → **win**.

wonder ['wʌndə^r] ◇ *vi (ask o.s.)* chiedersi, domandarsi ◇ *n (amazement)* meraviglia *f*; **to ~ if** domandarsi se; **I ~ if I could ask you a favour?** potrei chiederle un favore?

wonderful ['wʌndəfʊl] *adj* meraviglioso(-a).

won't [wəʊnt] = **will not**.

wood [wʊd] *n (substance)* legno *m*; *(small forest)* bosco *m*; *(golf club)* mazza *f* di legno.

wooden ['wʊdn] *adj* di legno.

woodland ['wʊdlənd] *n* terreno *m* boschivo.

woodpecker ['wʊd,pekə^r] *n* picchio *m*.

woodwork ['wʊdwɜ:k] *n* (SCH) falegnameria *f*.

wool [wʊl] *n* lana *f*.

woolen ['wʊlən] *(Am)* = **woollen**.

woollen ['wʊlən] *adj (Br)* di lana.

woolly ['wʊlɪ] *adj* di lana.

wooly ['wʊlɪ] *(Am)* = **woolly**.

Worcester sauce ['wʊstə^r-] *n* salsa *f* Worcester.

word [wɜ:d] *n* parola *f*; **in other ~s** in altre parole; **to have a ~ with sb** parlare con qn.

wording ['wɜ:dɪŋ] *n* formulazione *f*.

word processing [-'prəʊsesɪŋ] *n* videoscrittura *f*.

word processor [-'prəʊsesə^r] *n* sistema *m* di videoscrittura.

wore [wɔ:^r] *pt* → **wear**.

work [wɜ:k] ◇ *n* lavoro *m*; *(painting, novel etc)* opera *f* ◇ *vi* lavorare; *(operate, have desired effect)* funzionare; *(take effect)* fare effetto ◇ *vt (machine, controls)* far funzionare; **out of ~** senza lavoro; **to be at ~** *(at workplace)* essere al lavoro; *(working)* lavorare; **to be off ~** *(on holiday)* essere in ferie; *(ill)* essere in malattia; **the ~s** *(inf: everything)* tutto quanto; **how does it ~?** come funziona?; **it's not ~ing** non funziona.

◆ **work out** ◇ *vt sep (price, total)* calcolare; *(understand)* capire; *(solution)* trovare; *(method, plan)* mettere a punto ◇ *vi (result, be successful)* funzionare; *(do exercise)* fare ginnastica; **it ~s out at £20 each** *(bill, total)* fa 20 sterline a testa.

worker ['wɜ:kə^r] *n* lavoratore *m* (-trice *f*).

working class ['wɜ:kɪŋ-] *n*: **the ~** la classe operaia.

working hours ['wɜ:kɪŋ-] *npl* orario *m* di lavoro.

workman ['wɜ:kmən] (*pl* **-men** [-mən]) *n* operaio *m*.

work of art *n* opera *f* d'arte.

workout ['wɜ:kaʊt] *n* allenamento *m*.

work permit *n* permesso *m* di lavoro.

workplace ['wɜ:kpleɪs] *n* posto *m* di lavoro.

workshop [ˈwɜːkʃɒp] *n (for repairs)* officina *f*.

work surface *n* piano *m* di lavoro.

world [wɜːld] ◇ *n* mondo *m* ◇ *adj* mondiale; **the best in the ~** il migliore del mondo.

worldwide [ˌwɜːldˈwaɪd] *adv* in tutto il mondo.

World Wide Web *n*: **the ~** il World Wide Web.

worm [wɜːm] *n* verme *m*.

worn [wɔːn] ◇ *pp* → **wear** ◇ *adj (clothes, carpet)* consumato(-a).

worn-out *adj (clothes, shoes etc)* consumato(-a); *(tired)* esausto(-a).

worried [ˈwʌrɪd] *adj* preoccupato(-a).

worry [ˈwʌrɪ] ◇ *n* preoccupazione *f* ◇ *vt* preoccupare ◇ *vi*: **to ~ (about)** preoccuparsi (per).

worrying [ˈwʌrɪɪŋ] *adj* preoccupante.

worse [wɜːs] ◇ *adj* peggiore ◇ *adv* peggio; **to get ~** peggiorare; **~ off** *(in worse position)* in una situazione peggiore; *(poorer)* più povero.

worsen [ˈwɜːsn] *vi* peggiorare.

worship [ˈwɜːʃɪp] ◇ *n* culto *m* ◇ *vt* adorare.

worst [wɜːst] ◇ *adj* peggiore ◇ *adv* peggio ◇ *n*: **the ~** il peggiore (la peggiore).

worth [wɜːθ] *prep*: **how much is it ~?** quanto vale?; **it's ~ £50** vale 50 sterline; **it's ~ seeing** vale la pena vederlo; **it's not ~ it** non ne vale la pena; **£50 ~ of traveller's cheques** traveller's cheques per un valore di 50 sterline.

worthless [ˈwɜːθlɪs] *adj* di nessun valore.

worthwhile [ˌwɜːθˈwaɪl] *adj*: **to be ~** valere la pena.

worthy [ˈwɜːðɪ] *adj (winner, cause)* degno(-a); **to be ~ of sthg** essere degno di qc.

would [wʊd] *aux vb* **1.** *(in reported speech)*: **she said she ~ come** ha detto che sarebbe venuta.
2. *(indicating condition)*: **what ~ you do?** tu cosa faresti?; **what ~ you have done?** tu cosa avresti fatto?; **I ~ be most grateful** le sarei molto grato.
3. *(indicating willingness)*: **she ~n't go** non ci è voluta andare; **he ~ do anything for her** farebbe qualsiasi cosa per lei.
4. *(in polite questions)*: **~ you like a drink?** vuole qualcosa da bere?; **~ you mind closing the window?** le spiacerebbe chiudere la finestra?
5. *(indicating inevitability)*: **he ~ say that** era ovvio che dicesse così.
6. *(giving advice)*: **I ~ report it if I were you** se fossi in voi lo riferirei.
7. *(expressing opinions)*: **I ~ prefer ...** preferirei ...; **I ~ have thought (that) ...** avrei pensato che ...

wound[1] [wuːnd] *n* ferita *f* ◇ *vt* ferire.

wound[2] [waʊnd] *pt & pp* → **wind**[2].

wove [wəʊv] *pt* → **weave**.

woven [ˈwəʊvn] *pp* → **weave**.

wrap [ræp] *vt (package)* incartare; **to ~ sthg round sthg** avvolgere qc intorno a qc.

♦ **wrap up** ◇ *vt sep (package)* incartare ◇ *vi (dress warmly)* coprirsi bene.

wrapper [ˈræpəʳ] *n (for sweets)* carta *f*.

wrapping [ˈræpɪŋ] *n* involucro *m*.

wrapping paper *n (for present)* carta *f* da regalo; *(for parcel)* carta da pacchi.

wreath [riːθ] *n* corona *f*.

wreck [rek] ◇ *n (of plane, car)* rottame *m*; *(of ship)* relitto *m* ◇ *vt (destroy)* distruggere; *(spoil)* rovinare; **to be ~ed** *(ship)* fare naufragio.

wreckage [ˈrekɪdʒ] *n (of plane,*

car) rottami *mpl*; *(of building)* macerie *fpl*.

wrench [rentʃ] *n (Br: monkey wrench)* chiave *f* inglese; *(Am: spanner)* chiave.

wrestler [ˈreslə^r] *n* lottatore *m* (-trice *f*).

wrestling [ˈreslɪŋ] *n* lotta *f* libera.

wretched [ˈretʃɪd] *adj (miserable)* infelice; *(very bad)* orribile.

wring [rɪŋ] (*pt & pp* **wrung**) *vt (clothes, cloth)* strizzare.

wrinkle [ˈrɪŋkl] *n* ruga *f*.

wrist [rɪst] *n* polso *m*.

wristwatch [ˈrɪstwɒtʃ] *n* orologio *m* da polso.

write [raɪt] (*pt* **wrote**, *pp* **written**) ◇ *vt* scrivere; *(cheque, prescription)* fare; *(Am: send letter to)* scrivere a ◇ *vi* scrivere; **to ~ to sb** *(Br)* scrivere a qn.

◆ **write back** *vi* rispondere.

◆ **write down** *vt sep* scrivere.

◆ **write off** ◇ *vt sep (Br: inf: car)* distruggere ◇ *vi*: **to ~ off for sthg** richiedere qc per posta.

◆ **write out** *vt sep (list, essay)* scrivere; *(cheque, receipt)* fare.

write-off *n (vehicle)* rottame *m*.

writer [ˈraɪtə^r] *n (author)* scrittore *m* (-trice *f*).

writing [ˈraɪtɪŋ] *n (handwriting)* scrittura *f*; *(written words)* scritto *m*; *(activity)* scrivere *m*.

writing desk *n* scrivania *f*.

writing pad *n* blocchetto *m* per appunti.

writing paper *n* carta *f* da lettere.

written [ˈrɪtn] ◇ *pp* → **write** ◇ *adj (exam, notice, confirmation)* scritto(-a).

wrong [rɒŋ] ◇ *adv* male ◇ *adj (incorrect, unsuitable)* sbagliato(-a); *(bad, immoral)*: **it's ~ to steal** non si deve rubare; **what's ~?** cosa c'è che non va?; **what's ~ with her?** cos'ha?; **something's ~ with the car** la macchina ha qualcosa che non va; **to be ~** *(person)* sbagliarsi; **to be in the ~** essere in torto; **to get sthg ~** sbagliare qc; **to go ~** *(machine)* non funzionare più; **'~ way'** *(Am) cartello che segnala agli automobilisti il senso vietato*.

wrongly [ˈrɒŋlɪ] *adv (accused)* ingiustamente; *(informed)* male.

wrong number *n*: **to get the ~** sbagliare numero.

wrote [rəʊt] *pt* → **write**.

wrought iron [rɔːt] *n* ferro *m* battuto.

wrung [rʌŋ] *pt & pp* → **wring**.

XYZ

xing *(Am: abbr of crossing)*: **'ped ~'** 'passaggio pedonale'.
XL *(abbr of extra-large)* XL.
Xmas ['eksməs] *n (inf)* Natale *m*.
X-ray ◇ *n (picture)* radiografia *f* ◇ *vt* fare una radiografia a; **to have an ~** farsi una radiografia.

yacht [jɒt] *n* yacht *m inv*.
yard [jɑːd] *n (unit of measurement)* = 91,44 cm, iarda *f*; *(enclosed area)* cortile *m*; *(Am: behind house)* giardino *m*.
yard sale *n (Am) vendita di oggetti di seconda mano organizzata da un privato nel giardino di casa*.
yarn [jɑːn] *n (thread)* filato *m*.
yawn [jɔːn] *vi (person)* sbadigliare.
yd *abbr* = **yard**.
yeah [jeə] *adv (inf)* sì.
year [jɪə^r] *n* anno *m*; **next ~** l'anno prossimo; **this ~** quest'anno; **I'm 15 ~s old** ho 15 anni; **I haven't seen her for ~s** *(inf)* sono anni che non la vedo.
yearly ['jɪəlɪ] *adj* annuale, annuo(-a).
yeast [jiːst] *n* lievito *m*.
yell [jel] *vi* urlare.
yellow ['jeləʊ] ◇ *adj* giallo(-a) ◇ *n* giallo *m*.
yellow lines *npl* strisce *fpl* gialle *(che regolano la sosta dei veicoli)*.
Yellow Pages® *n*: **the ~** le Pagine gialle.
yes [jes] *adv* sì; **to say ~** dire di sì.
yesterday ['jestədɪ] ◇ *n* ieri *m* ◇ *adv* ieri; **the day before ~** l'altro ieri; **~ afternoon** ieri pomeriggio; **~ morning** ieri mattina.
yet [jet] ◇ *adv* ancora ◇ *conj* ma; **have they arrived ~?** sono già arrivati?; **the best one ~** il migliore fino a questo momento; **not ~** non ancora; **I've ~ to do it** devo ancora farlo; **~ again** ancora una volta; **~ another delay** ancora un altro ritardo.
yew [juː] *n* tasso *m (pianta)*.
yield [jiːld] ◇ *vt* dare, rendere ◇ *vi (break, give way)* cedere; **'yield'** *(Am:* AUT*)* 'dare la precedenza'.
YMCA *n associazione cristiana dei giovani che offre alloggi a buon prezzo*.
yob [jɒb] *n (Br: inf)* teppista *mf*.
yoga ['jəʊgə] *n* yoga *m*.
yoghurt ['jɒgət] *n* yogurt *m inv*.
yolk [jəʊk] *n* tuorlo *m*, rosso *m* d'uovo.
York Minster [jɔːk'mɪnstə^r] *n* la cattedrale di York.
Yorkshire pudding ['jɔːkʃə-] *n focaccina soffice servita tradizionalmente con arrosti di manzo*.
you [juː] *pron* **1.** *(subject: singular)* tu; *(subject: polite form)* lei; *(subject: plural)* voi; **~ Italians** voi italiani.

2. *(direct object: singular)* ti; *(direct object: polite form)* la; *(direct object: plural)* vi; **I called ~, not him** ho chiamato te, non lui.
3. *(indirect object: singular)* ti; *(indirect object: polite form)* le; *(indirect object: plural)* vi.
4. *(after prep: singular)* te; *(after prep: polite form)* lei; *(after prep: plural)* voi; **I'm shorter than ~** sono più basso di te/lei/voi.
5. *(indefinite use)* si; **~ never know** non si sa mai; **swimming is good for ~** nuotare fa bene.

young [jʌŋ] ◇ *adj* giovane ◇ *npl*: **the ~** i giovani.

younger [ˈjʌŋgəʳ] *adj (brother, sister)* minore, più giovane.

youngest [ˈjʌŋgəst] *adj (brother, sister)* minore, più giovane.

youngster [ˈjʌŋstəʳ] *n* giovane *mf*.

your [jɔːʳ] *adj* **1.** *(singular subject)* il tuo (la tua), i tuoi (le tue) *(pl)*; *(singular subject: polite form)* il suo (la sua), i suoi (le sue) *(pl)*; *(plural subject)* il vostro (la vostra), i vostri (le vostre) *(pl)*; **~ dog** il tuo/suo/vostro cane; **~ house** la tua/sua/vostra casa; **~ children** i tuoi/suoi/vostri bambini; **~ mother** tua/sua/vostra madre.
2. *(indefinite subject)*: **it's good for ~ health** fa bene alla salute.

yours [jɔːz] *pron (referring to singular subject)* il tuo (la tua), i tuoi (le tue) *(pl)*; *(polite form)* il suo (la sua), i suoi (le sue) *(pl)*; *(referring to plural subject)* il vostro (la vostra), i vostri (le vostre) *(pl)*; **a friend of ~** un tuo/suo/vostro amico; **are these shoes ~?** queste scarpe sono tue/sue/vostre?

yourself [jɔːˈself] (*pl* **-selves**) *pron* **1.** *(reflexive: singular)* ti; *(reflexive: polite form)* si; *(reflexive: plural)* vi.
2. *(after prep: singular)* te; *(after prep: polite form)* sé; *(after prep: plural)* voi.
3. *(emphatic use: singular)* tu stesso(-a); *(emphatic use: polite form)* lei stesso(-a); *(emphatic use: plural)* voi stessi(-e); **did you do it ~?** *(singular)* l'hai fatto da solo?

youth [juːθ] *n (period of life)* gioventù *f*; *(quality)* giovinezza *f*; *(young man)* giovane *m*.

youth club *n* circolo *m* giovanile.

youth hostel *n* ostello *m* della gioventù.

Yugoslavia [ˌjuːgəˈslɑːvɪə] *n* la Jugoslavia.

yuppie [ˈjʌpɪ] *n* yuppie *mf inv*.

YWCA *n associazione cristiana delle giovani che offre alloggi a buon prezzo.*

zebra [*Br* ˈzebrə, *Am* ˈziːbrə] *n* zebra *f*.

zebra crossing *n (Br)* strisce *fpl* pedonali.

zero [ˈzɪərəʊ] (*pl* **-es**) *n* zero *m*; **five degrees below ~** cinque gradi sotto zero.

zest [zest] *n (of lemon, orange)* scorza *f*.

zigzag [ˈzɪgzæg] *vi* procedere a zigzag.

zinc [zɪŋk] *n* zinco *m*.

zip [zɪp] ◇ *n (Br)* cerniera *f* OR chiusura *f* lampo *(inv)* ◇ *vt* chiudere la cerniera di.

◆ **zip up** *vt sep* chiudere la cerniera di.

zip code *n (Am)* codice *m* di avviamento postale.

zipper [ˈzɪpəʳ] *n (Am)* cerniera *f* OR chiusura *f* lampo *(inv)*.

zit [zɪt] *n (inf)* brufolo *m*.

zodiac [ˈzəʊdɪæk] *n* zodiaco *m*.

zone [zəʊn] *n* zona *f*.

zoo [zuː] (*pl* **-s**) *n* zoo *m inv*.

zoom (lens) [zuːm-] *n* zoom *m inv*.

zucchini [zuːˈkiːnɪ] *(pl inv) n (Am)* zucchine *fpl*.

Achevé d'imprimer par l'Imprimerie
Maury-Eurolivres à Manchecourt
N° de projet 10096640 - OTB 52° - 7500
Dépôt légal : juin 2002 - N° d'imprimeur : 95174

Imprimé en France - (Printed in France)